ENCYCLOPEDIA OF APPLIED
ETHICS

VOLUME 3

J–R

ENCYCLOPEDIA OF APPLIED ETHICS

VOLUME 3

J–R

ACADEMIC PRESS

SAN DIEGO   LONDON   BOSTON   NEW YORK   SYDNEY   TOKYO   TORONTO

Academic Press
a division of Harcourt Brace & Company
525 B Street, Suite 1900, San Diego, California 92101-4495, USA
http://www.apnet.com

Academic Press Limited
24-28 Oval Road, London NW1 7DX, UK
http://www.hbuk.co.uk/ap/

Library of Congress Card Catalog Number: 97-074395

International Standard Book Number: 0-12-227065-7 (set)
International Standard Book Number: 0-12-227066-5 (v. 1)
International Standard Book Number: 0-12-227067-3 (v. 2)
International Standard Book Number: 0-12-227068-1 (v. 3)
International Standard Book Number: 0-12-227069-X (v. 4)

PRINTED IN THE UNITED STATES OF AMERICA
97 98 99 00 01 02 MM 9 8 7 6 5 4 3 2 1

CONTENTS

CONTENTS OF OTHER VOLUMES

CONTENTS OF VOLUME 2

CONTENTS OF VOLUME 4

CONTENTS BY SUBJECT AREA

LEGAL ETHICS

ETHICS IN EDUCATION

ETHICS AND POLITICS

CONTRIBUTORS

G. JOHN M. ABBARNO
HOMELESSNESS
D'Youville College
Buffalo, New York

FRANCIS J. AGUILAR
CORPORATIONS, ETHICS IN
Harvard University
Cambridge, Massachusetts

WILLIAM AIKEN
CHILDREN'S RIGHTS
Chatham College
Chatham, New York

TIMO AIRAKSINEN
PROFESSIONAL ETHICS
University of Helsinki
Helsinki, Finland

LARRY ALEXANDER
FREEDOM OF SPEECH
University of San Diego
San Diego, California

ANDREW ALEXANDRA
EXECUTIVE COMPENSATION
Charles Sturt University
Bathurst, New South Wales, Australia

GARLAND E. ALLEN
GENETICS AND BEHAVIOR
NATURE VERSUS NURTURE
Washington University
St. Louis, Missouri

JONATHAN ALDRED
WILDLIFE CONSERVATION
Cambridge University
Cambridge, England, UK

DAVID ARCHARD
CHILD ABUSE
University of St. Andrews
Fife, Scotland, UK

MARY BETH ARMSTRONG
CONFIDENTIALITY, GENERAL ISSUES OF
California Polytechnic Institute
San Luis Obispo, California

RICHARD J. ARNESON
EQUALITY AND EGALITARIANISM
University of California, San Diego
San Diego, California

ROBERT L. ARRINGTON
ADVERTISING
Georgia State University
Atlanta, Georgia

RICHARD ASHCROFT
HUMAN RESEARCH SUBJECTS, SELECTION OF
University of Bristol
Bristol, England, UK

SUE ASHFORD
TERRORISM
University of Western Australia and Murdoch
University
Medina, Western Australia

ROBIN ATTFIELD
ENVIRONMENTAL ETHICS, OVERVIEW
University of Wales, Cardiff
Cardiff, Wales, UK

ROBERT D. BAIRD
HINDUISM
School of Religion, University of Iowa
Iowa City, Iowa

DOUGLAS BAKER
LAND USE ISSUES
University of Northern British Columbia
Prince George, British Columbia

NORMAN BARRY
WELFARE POLICIES
University of Buckingham
Buckingham, England, UK

BERNARD H. BAUMRIN
DIVORCE
    City University of New York
    New York, New York

JOHN D. BECKER
NATIONAL SECURITY ISSUES
WARFARE, STRATEGIES AND TACTICS
    United States Air Force Academy
    Colorado Springs, Colorado

HUGO ADAM BEDAU
CAPITAL PUNISHMENT
CIVIL DISOBEDIENCE
    Tufts University
    Medford, Massachusetts

RON L. P. BERGHMANS
COERCIVE TREATMENT IN PSYCHIATRY
    Institute for Bioethics
    Maastricht, The Netherlands

ROBERT H. BLANK
FETAL RESEARCH
    University of Canterbury
    Canterbury, England, UK

PAULA BODDINGTON
SELF-DECEPTION
    Australian National University
    Canberra, Australia

ANNIE BOOTH
LAND USE ISSUES
    University of Northern British Columbia
    Prince George, British Columbia

STEPHEN BOSTOCK
ZOOS AND ZOOLOGICAL PARKS
    Glasgow Zoo and University of Glasgow
    Glasgow, Scotland, UK

ANDREW BRENNAN
GAIA HYPOTHESIS
    The University of Western Australia
    Nedlands, Western Australia

ANDREW BRIEN
JURY CONDUCT
MERCY AND FORGIVENESS
    Australian National University
    Canberra, Australia

ROGER L. BURRITT
ENVIRONMENTAL COMPLIANCE BY INDUSTRY
    Australian National University
    Canberra, Australia

EDMUND F. BYRNE
PRIVACY
    Indiana University
    Indianapolis, Indiana

JOAN C. CALLAHAN
BIRTH-CONTROL ETHICS
    University of Kentucky
    Lexington, Kentucky

EAMONN CALLAN
PLURALISM IN EDUCATION
    University of Alberta
    Edmonton, Alberta

ARTHUR L. CAPLAN
INFORMED CONSENT
    University of Pennsylvania
    Philadelphia, Pennsylvania

ALEXANDER MORGAN CAPRON
DEATH, DEFINITION OF
    University of Southern California
    Los Angeles, California

ALAN CARLING
EXPLOITATION
    University of Bradford
    Bradford, England, UK

STANLEY R. CARPENTER
SUSTAINABILITY
    Georgia Institute of Technology
    Atlanta, Georgia

RUTH CHADWICK
GENETIC SCREENING
ORGAN TRANSPLANTS AND DONORS
    Centre for Professional Ethics
    University of Central Lancashire
    Preston, England, UK

TIMOTHY CHAPPELL
PLATONISM
THEORIES OF ETHICS, OVERVIEW
    University of Manchester
    Manchester, England, UK

VICHAI CHOKEVIVAT
AIDS IN THE DEVELOPING WORLD
    Thai Department of Health and Human Welfare

JOHN CHRISTMAN
PROPERTY RIGHTS
    Virginia Polytechnic Institute and State University
    Blacksburg, Virginia

JOHN P. CLARK
POLITICAL ECOLOGY
    Loyola University
    New Orleans, Louisiana

ANGUS CLARKE
GENETIC COUNSELING
    University of Wales College of Medicine
    Cardiff, Wales, UK

MARGARET COFFEY
BROADCAST JOURNALISM
    Australian Broadcasting Corporation
    Malvern, Australia

DAVID CONWAY
LIBERALISM
    Middlesex University
    London, England, UK

LINDSEY COOMBES
MENTAL HEALTH
Oxford Brookes University
Oxford, England, UK

WILLIAM COONEY
RIGHTS THEORY
Briar Cliff College
Sioux City, Iowa

PRESTON K. COVEY
GUN CONTROL
Center for the Advancement of Applied Ethics
Carnegie Mellon University
Pittsburgh, Pennsylvania

CHRISTOPHER J. COWTON
SOCIALLY RESPONSIBLE INVESTMENT
University of Huddersfield
Queensgate, Huddersfield, England, UK

CHARLES CRITCHER
MEDIA DEPICTION OF ETHNIC MINORITIES
Sheffield Hallam University
Sheffield, England, UK

THOMAS CLOUGH DAFFERN
NATIVE AMERICAN CULTURES
University of London
London, England, UK

TIM DARE
APPLIED ETHICS, CHALLENGES TO
The University of Auckland
Auckland, New Zealand

MICHAEL DAVIS
CONFLICT OF INTEREST
Illinois Institute of Technology
Chicago, Illinois

ANGUS DAWSON
PSYCHOPHARMACOLOGY
University of Liverpool
Liverpool, England, UK

JUDITH WAGNER DECEW
WARFARE, CODES OF
Clark University
West Newton, Massachusetts

C. A. DEFANTI
BRAIN DEATH
United Hospitals of Bergamo
Bergamo, Italy

CARLOS DEL RIO
AIDS IN THE DEVELOPING WORLD
Emory University

PHILIP E. DEVINE
HOMICIDE, CRIMINAL VERSUS JUSTIFIABLE
PUBLISH-OR-PERISH SYNDROME
Providence College
Providence, Rhode Island

BERNARD DICKENS
PATIENTS' RIGHTS
University of Toronto Law School
Toronto, Ontario

SUSAN DIMOCK
CRIME AND SOCIETY
JUVENILE CRIME
York University
North York, Ontario

SUSAN DODDS
SEX EQUALITY
University of Wollongong
Wollongong, Australia

STRACHAN DONNELLEY
HUMAN NATURE, VIEWS OF
The Hastings Center
Briarcliff Manor, New York

JUDE P. DOUGHERTY
THOMISM
Catholic University of America
Washington, DC

NIGEL DOWER
DEVELOPMENT ETHICS
DEVELOPMENT ISSUES, ENVIRONMENTAL
WORLD ETHICS
University of Aberdeen
Aberdeen, Scotland, UK

HEATHER DRAPER
EUTHANASIA
University of Birmingham
Birmingham, England, UK

DENIS DUTTON
PLAGIARISM AND FORGERY
University of Canterbury
Christchurch, New Zealand

SUSAN EASTON
PORNOGRAPHY
Brunel University
Uxbridge, England, UK

ANDREW EDGAR
QUALITY OF LIFE INDICATORS
SPORTS, ETHICS OF
University of Wales
Cardiff, Wales, UK

BENGT ERIK ERIKSSON
PREVENTIVE MEDICINE
University of Linköping
Linköping, Sweden

GAVIN FAIRBAIRN
SUICIDE
North East Wales Institute of Higher Education
Wrexham, Wales, UK

JOHN FENDER
ALTRUISM AND ECONOMICS
University of Birmingham
Birmingham, England, UK

DAVID E. W. FENNER
ARTS, THE
University of North Florida
Jacksonville, Florida

J. CARL FICARROTTA
MORAL RELATIVISM
United States Air Force Academy
Colorado Springs, Colorado

BETH A. FISCHER
SCIENTIFIC PUBLISHING
University of Pittsburgh
Pittsburgh, Pennsylvania

ANTHONY FISHER
CHRISTIAN ETHICS, ROMAN CATHOLIC
Australian Catholic University
Ascot Vale, Australia

CHARLES J. FOMBRUN
REPUTATION MANAGEMENT BY CORPORATIONS
New York University
New York, New York

NORMAN FORD
FETUS
Caroline Chisholm Centre for Health Ethics
East Melbourne, Australia

CLAIRE FOSTER
RESEARCH ETHICS COMMITTEES
King's College
London, England, UK

LESLIE PICKERING FRANCIS
RAPE
University of Utah
Salt Lake City, Utah

LUCY FRITH
REPRODUCTIVE TECHNOLOGIES
University of Liverpool and University of Oxford
England, UK

K. W. M. FULFORD
MENTAL ILLNESS, CONCEPT OF
University of Warwick
Coventry, England, UK

SUSANNE GIBSON
ABORTION
ACTS AND OMISSIONS
University College of St. Martin
Lancaster, England, UK

CHRISTOPHER GILL
GREEK ETHICS, OVERVIEW
University of Exeter
Exeter, England, UK

RAANAN GILLON
BIOETHICS, OVERVIEW
Imperial College
London University
London, England, UK

ANDREW GILMAN
PERSONAL RELATIONSHIPS
Andover Newton Theological School
Stratham, New Hampshire

DONALD A. GRAFT
SPECIESISM
Software Engineer Manager
Pondicherry, India

WILLIAM GREY
PLAYING GOD
University of Queensland
Queensland, Australia

MATTHEW W. HALLGARTH
CONSEQUENTIALISM AND DEONTOLOGY
United States Air Force Academy
Colorado Springs, Colorado

JOCELYN Y. HATTAB
PSYCHIATRIC ETHICS
Talbia Mental Health Center
Hebrew University
Jerusalem, Israel

HETA HÄYRY
GENETIC ENGINEERING
PATERNALISM
University of Helsinki
Helsinki, Finland

MATTI HÄYRY
GENETIC ENGINEERING
University of Helsinki
Helsinki, Finland

TIM HAYWARD
ANTHROPOCENTRISM
University of Edinburgh
Edinburgh, Scotland, UK

ADAM M. HEDGECOE
GENE THERAPY
GENOME ANALYSIS
Centre for Professional Ethics
University of Central Lancashire
Preston, England, UK

ERIC HEINZE
VICTIMLESS CRIMES
University of London
London, England, UK

SIRKKU HELLSTEN
DISTRIBUTIVE JUSTICE, THEORIES OF
University of Helsinki
Helsinki, Finland

ALAN HOLLAND
ECOLOGICAL BALANCE
Lancaster University
Lancaster, England, UK

SØREN HOLM
AUTONOMY
EMBRYOLOGY, ETHICS OF
University of Copenhagen
Copenhagen, Denmark

TERRY HOPTON
POLITICAL OBLIGATION
University of Central Lancashire
Preston, England, UK

J. STUART HORNER
MEDICAL ETHICS, HISTORY OF
University of Central Lancashire
Preston, England, UK

GILLIAN HOWIE
GENDER ROLES
University of Liverpool
Liverpool, England, UK

RICHARD HUGMAN
ETHICS AND SOCIAL SERVICES, OVERVIEW
Curtin University of Technology
Perth, Australia

GEOFFREY HUNT
WHISTLE-BLOWING
European Centre for Professional Ethics
University of London
London, England, UK

DOUGLAS N. HUSAK
DRUGS: MORAL AND LEGAL ISSUES
Rutgers University
New Brunswick, New Jersey

JENNIFER JACKSON
BUSINESS ETHICS, OVERVIEW
University of Leeds
Leeds, England, UK

MARJA JÄRVELÄ
ENVIRONMENTAL IMPACT ASSESSMENT
The University of Jyväskylä
Jyväskylä, Finland

MARGOT JEFFREYS
AGED PEOPLE, SOCIETAL ATTITUDES TOWARD
Centre of Medical Law and Ethics
King's College
London, England, UK

MARIANNE M. JENNINGS
ELECTION STRATEGIES
Arizona State University
Tempe, Arizona

EDWARD JOHNSON
INTELLIGENCE TESTING
MEDIA OWNERSHIP
POLITICAL CORRECTNESS
University of New Orleans
New Orleans, Louisiana

JEFFERY L. JOHNSON
NUCLEAR DETERRENCE
Eastern Oregon State College
LaGrande, Oregon

PAULINE JOHNSON
SEXISM
Macquarie University
Sydney, Australia

TREVOR JONES
POLICE AND RACE RELATIONS
Policy Studies Institute
London, England, UK

RABINDRA N. KANUNGO
LEADERSHIP, ETHICS OF
McGill University
Montreal, Quebec

HELMUT F. KAPLAN
VEGETARIANISM
University of Salzburg
Salzburg, Austria

PAUL KELLY
CONTRACTARIAN ETHICS
London School of Economics
London, England, UK

DAMIEN KEOWN
BUDDHISM
Goldsmiths College, University of London
London, England, UK

JACINTA KERIN
SEXUAL ORIENTATION
Monash University
Toronto, Ontario

EDWARD W. KEYSERLINGK
MEDICAL CODES AND OATHS
McGill University
Montreal, Quebec

JUKKA KILPI
MERGERS AND ACQUISITIONS
University of Helsinki
Helsinki, Finland and Monash University
Clayton, Victoria, Australia

DAHLIAN KIRBY
TRANSSEXUALISM
University of Wales
Cardiff, Wales, UK

STEPHEN KLAIDMAN
FREEDOM OF THE PRESS IN THE USA
   Georgetown University
   Washington, DC

JAMES W. KNIGHT
BIRTH-CONTROL TECHNOLOGY
   Virginia Polytechnic Institute and State University
   Blacksburg, Virginia

LORETTA M. KOPELMAN
FEMALE CIRCUMCISION AND GENITAL MUTILATION
MEDICAL FUTILITY
   East Carolina University School of Medicine
   Greenville, North Carolina

MARK KUCZEWSKI
CASUISTRY
   Medical College of Wisconsin

PAUL ALFRED KURZMAN
WORKPLACE ETHICS: ISSUES FOR HUMAN SERVICE
  PROFESSIONALS
   Hunter College, City University of New York
   New York, New York

KRISTIINA KUVAJA-PUUMALAINEN
ENVIRONMENTAL IMPACT ASSESSMENT
   Jyvaskyla University
   Jyvaskyla, Finland

WILL KYMLICKA
ETHNOCULTURAL MINORITY GROUPS, STATUS AND TREATMENT OF
   University of Ottawa
   Ottawa, Ontario

OLLI LAGERSPETZ
TRUST
   Abo Academy
   Abo, Finland
   and The University of Wales at Swansea

DAVID LAMB
DEATH, MEDICAL ASPECTS OF
   University of Birmingham
   Birmingham, England, UK

HAROLD Q. LANGENDERFER
ACCOUNTING AND BUSINESS ETHICS
   University of North Carolina
   Chapel Hill, North Carolina

DUNCAN LANGFORD
INTERNET PROTOCOL
   University of Kent
   Canterbury, England, UK

ROBERT LARMER
IMPROPER PAYMENTS AND GIFTS
   University of New Brunswick
   Fredericton, New Brunswick

OLIVER LEAMAN
JUDAISM
   Liverpool John Moores University
   Liverpool, England, UK

GRANT S. LEE
TAOISM
   Colorado State University
   Fort Collins, Colorado

KEEKOK LEE
BIODIVERSITY
   The University of Manchester
   Manchester, England, UK

STEVEN LEE
NUCLEAR TESTING
   Hobart and William Smith Colleges
   Geneva, New York

BURTON M. LEISER
CORPORAL PUNISHMENT
SLAVERY
   Pace University
   Briarcliff Manor, New York

A. CARL LEOPOLD
STEWARDSHIP
   Boyce Thompson Institute for Plant Research
   Cornell University
   Ithaca, New York

HARRY LESSER
AGEISM
   University of Manchester
   Manchester, England, UK

CAROL LEVINE
CUSTODY OF CHILDREN
   The Orphan Project
   New York, New York

MAIRI LEVITT
RELIGION IN SCHOOLS
   University of Central Lancashire
   Preston, England, UK

XIAORONG LI
WOMEN'S RIGHTS
   University of Maryland
   College Park, Maryland

JUDITH LICHTENBERG
OBJECTIVITY IN REPORTING
   University of Maryland
   College Park, Maryland

C. DAVID LISMAN
ETHICS EDUCATION IN SCHOOLS
   Community College of Aurora
   Aurora, Colorado

ANDROS LOIZOU
THEORIES OF JUSTICE: RAWLS
   University of Central Lancashire
   Preston, England, UK

VALERIE C. LORENZ
GAMBLING
   Compulsive Gambling Center, Inc.
   Baltimore, Maryland

ROBERT B. LOUDEN
VIRTUE ETHICS
   Westfalische WIlhelms-Universitat
   Munster, Germany

JOHN LYDEN
CHRISTIAN ETHICS, PROTESTANT
   Dana College
   Omaha, Nebraska

CHRIS MACDONALD
EVOLUTIONARY PERSPECTIVES ON ETHICS
   University of British Columbia
   Vancouver, British Columbia

CARLOS MAGIS
AIDS IN THE DEVELOPING WORLD
   Conasida, Mexico

THOMAS MAGNELL
EPICUREANISM
   Drew University
   Madison, New Jersey

RUDOLPH J. MARCUS
GOVERNMENT FUNDING OF RESEARCH
   Ethics Consultant
   Sonoma, California

IAN MARKHAM
RELIGION AND ETHICS
   Liverpool Hope University College
   Liverpool, England, UK

GARY T. MARX
ELECTRONIC SURVEILLANCE
UNDERCOVER INVESTIGATIONS, ETHICS OF
   Center for Advanced Study in the Behavioral
   Sciences
   Stanford, California

RICHARD O. MASON
GENETIC RESEARCH
INFORMATION MANAGEMENT
   Southern Methodist University
   Dallas, Texas

TODD MAY
POSTSTRUCTURALISM
   Clemson University
   Clemson, South Carolina

MARY ANN MCCLURE
INFERTILITY
   John Jay College of Criminal Justice
   New York, New York

PATRICIA E. MCCREIGHT
ENVIRONMENTAL COMPLIANCE BY INDUSTRY
   Australian National University
   Canberra, Australia

TONY MCGLEENAN
GENETIC TECHNOLOGY, LEGAL REGULATION OF
   The Queen's University of Belfast
   Belfast, Northern Ireland, UK

C. B. MEGONE
ARISTOTELIAN ETHICS
   University of Leeds
   Leeds, England, UK

GREGORY MELLEMA
COLLECTIVE GUILT
   Calvin College
   Grand Rapids, Michigan

MANUEL MENDONCA
LEADERSHIP, ETHICS OF
   McGill University
   Montreal, Quebec

MICHAEL A. MENLOWE
SAFETY LAWS
   University of Edinburgh
   Edinburgh, Scotland, UK

BEN MEPHAM
AGRICULTURAL ETHICS
   University of Nottingham
   Loughborough, England, UK

SEUMAS MILLER
TABLOID JOURNALISM
   Charles Sturt University
   Wagga Wagga, Australia

JEAN-NOËL MISSA
PSYCHOSURGERY AND PHYSICAL BRAIN MANIPULATION
   Free University of Brussels
   Brussels, Belgium

DARRELL MOELLENDORF
IMPERIALISM
   University of Witwatersrand
   Johannesburg, South Africa

PETER MOIZER
AUDITING PRACTICES
   University of Leeds
   Leeds, England, UK

DAVID WENDELL MOLLER
DEATH, SOCIETAL ATTITUDES TOWARD
   Indiana University
   Indianapolis, Indiana

J. DONALD MOON
COMMUNITARIANISM
   Wesleyan University
   Middletown, Connecticut

EMILIO MORDINI
SUGGESTION, ETHICS OF
Psychoanalytic Institute for Social Research
Rome, Italy

JONATHAN D. MORENO
INFORMED CONSENT
SUNY Health Science Center at Brooklyn
Brooklyn, New York

MAURIZIO MORI
LIFE, CONCEPT OF
Center for Research in Politics and Ethics
Milan, Italy

STEPHEN J. MORSE
INSANITY, LEGAL CONCEPT OF
University of Pennsylvania Law School
Philadelphia, Pennsylvania

PETER MUNZ
DARWINISM
Victoria University of Wellington
Wellington, New Zealand

TIMOTHY F. MURPHY
AIDS
University of Illinois College of Medicine
Chicago, Illinois

CHARLES R. MYERS
MILITARY CODES OF BEHAVIOR
United States Air Force Academy
Colorado Springs, Colorado

JAN NARVESON
CONSUMER RIGHTS
EGOISM AND ALTRUISM
STOICISM
University of Waterloo
Waterloo, Ontario

DEMETRIO NERI
EUGENICS
University of Messina
Messina, Italy

NINA NIKKU
PREVENTIVE MEDICINE
University of Linköping
Linköping, Sweden

RICHARD NORMAN
PACIFISM
University of Kent
Canterbury, England, UK

DAVID NOVITZ
LITERATURE AND ETHICS
University of Canterbury, New Zealand
Christchurch, New Zealand

KATHERINE O'DONOVAN
FEMINIST JURISPRUDENCE
Queen Mary's Westfield College
University of London
London, England, UK

JOHN O'NEILL
TRUTH TELLING AS CONSTITUTIVE OF JOURNALISM
Lancaster University
Lancaster, England, UK

GERALD M. OPPENHEIMER
HEALTH CARE FINANCING
Brooklyn College, City University of New York
Brooklyn, New York

R. WILLIAM OUTHWAITE
DISCOURSE ETHICS
University of Sussex
Sussex, England, UK

GUILLERMO OWEN
GAME THEORY
Naval Postgraduate School
Monterey, California

ROBERT A. PADGUG
HEALTH CARE FINANCING
Brooklyn College, City University of New York
Brooklyn, New York

GABRIEL PALMER-FERNÁNDEZ
CIVILIAN POPULATIONS IN WAR, TARGETING OF
Youngstown State University
Youngstown, Ohio

MARK PARASCANDOLA
ANIMAL RESEARCH
Smithsonian Fellow
Washington, D.C.

JENNETH PARKER
PRECAUTIONARY PRINCIPLE
Lecturer
Hastings, England, UK

MICHAEL PARKER
MORAL DEVELOPMENT
The Open University
Milton Keynes, England, UK

ELLEN FRANKEL PAUL
AFFIRMATIVE ACTION
SEXUAL HARASSMENT
Bowling Green State University
Bowling Green, Ohio

MICHEL PETHERAM
CONFIDENTIALITY OF SOURCES
The Open University
Milton Keynes, England, UK

JON PIKE
STRIKES
Glasgow University
Glasgow, Scotland, UK

EVELYN PLUHAR
ANIMAL RIGHTS
The Pennsylvania State University, Fayette Campus
Uniontown, Pennsylvania

GAYNOR POLLARD
RELIGION IN SCHOOLS
University College Chester
Chester, England, UK

NELSON POTTER
KANTIANISM
University of Nebraska-Lincoln
Lincoln, Nebraska

IGOR PRIMORATZ
PROSTITUTION
Hebrew University
Jerusalem, Israel

JANE PRITCHARD
CODES OF ETHICS
Centre for Professional Ethics
University of Central Lancashire
Preston, England, UK

ROBERT PROSSER
TOURISM
University of Birmingham
Birmingham, England, UK

LAURA M. PURDY
CHILDREN'S RIGHTS
Wells College
Aurora, New York

K. ANNE PYBURN
ARCHAEOLOGICAL ETHICS
Indiana University
Indianapolis, Indiana

MAUREEN RAMSAY
MACHIAVELLIANISM
University of Leeds
Leeds, England, UK

DOUGLAS B. RASMUSSEN
PERFECTIONISM
St. John's University
Jamaica, Queens, New York

KATE RAWLES
BIOCENTRISM
Lancaster University
Lancaster, England, UK

RUPERT READ
COURTROOM PROCEEDINGS, REPORTING OF
University of Manchester
Manchester, England, UK

FREDERIC G. REAMER
SOCIAL WORK
Rhode Island College
Providence, Rhode Island

MICHAEL REISS
BIOTECHNOLOGY
Homerton College, Cambridge
Cambridge, England, UK

TONY RILEY
HOMOSEXUALITY, SOCIETAL ATTITUDES TOWARD
Yale University School of Medicine
New Haven, Connecticut

SIMON ROGERSON
COMPUTER AND INFORMATION ETHICS
De Montfort University
Leicester, England, UK

BERNARD E. ROLLIN
VETERINARY ETHICS
Colorado State University
Fort Collins, Colorado

RICHARD D. RYDER
PAINISM
Tulane University
New Orleans, Louisiana

MARK SAGOFF
ENVIRONMENTAL ECONOMICS
University of Maryland
College Park, Maryland

HANS-MARTIN SASS
ADVANCE DIRECTIVES
Kennedy Institute of Ethics
Georgetown University
Washington, DC

GEOFFREY SCARRE
UTILITARIANISM
University of Durham
Durham, England, UK

UDO SCHÜKLENK
AIDS IN THE DEVELOPING WORLD
HOMOSEXUALITY, SOCIETAL ATTITUDES TOWARD
ORGAN TRANSPLANTS AND DONORS
SEXUAL ORIENTATION
Centre for Professional Ethics
University of Central Lancashire
Preston, England, UK

ADINA SCHWARTZ
PUBLIC DEFENDERS
John Jay College of Criminal Justice
City University of New York
New York, New York

ANNE SELLER
PACIFISM
University of Kent
Canterbury, England, UK

JOHN J. SHEPHERD
ISLAM
University College of St. Martin
Lancaster, England, UK

RUBEN SHER
AIDS TREATMENT AND BIOETHICS IN SOUTH AFRICA
National AIDS Training and Outreach Program
Johannesburg, South Africa

DARREN SHICKLE
PRIVACY VERSUS PUBLIC RIGHT TO KNOW
RESOURCE ALLOCATION
    University of Sheffield
    Sheffield, England, UK

KRISTIN SHRADER-FRECHETTE
HAZARDOUS AND TOXIC SUBSTANCES
NUCLEAR POWER
    University of South Florida
    Tampa, Florida

DEBORAH H. SIEGEL
ADOPTION
    School of Social Work
    Rhode Island College
    Providence, Rhode Island

ANITA SILVERS
DISABILITY RIGHTS
    San Francisco State University
    San Francisco, California

NIKKY-GUNINDER KAUR SINGH
SIKHISM
    Colby College
    Waterville, Maine

ANTHONY J. SKILLEN
RACISM
    University of Kent
    Canterbury, England, UK

JOHN SNAPPER
TRADE SECRETS AND PROPRIETARY INFORMATION
    Illinois Institute of Technology
    Chicago, Illinois

EUGENE SPAFFORD
COMPUTER SECURITY
    Purdue University
    West Lafayette, Indiana

CLIVE L. SPASH
WILDLIFE CONSERVATION
    Cambridge University
    Cambridge, England, UK

PAUL SPICKER
POVERTY
SOCIAL SECURITY
SOCIAL WELFARE: PROVISION AND FINANCE
    University of Dundee
    Dundee, Scotland, UK

R. E. SPIER
SCIENCE AND ENGINEERING ETHICS, OVERVIEW
    University of Surrey
    Guildford, England, UK

DEAN A. STEELE
HONOR CODES
    United States Air Force Academy
    Colorado Springs, Colorado

ELIZA STEELWATER
HUMANISM
    University of Illinois
    Champaign, Illinois

EDWARD STEIN
SEXUAL ORIENTATION
    Yale University
    New Haven, Connecticut

JON STEWART
EXISTENTIALISM
    Søren Kierkegaard Research Center
    University of Copenhagen
    Copenhagen, Denmark

TADEUSZ SZUBKA
FREUDIANISM
    University of Queensland
    Brisbane, Australia

WIN TADD
NURSES' ETHICS
    University of Wales
    Cardiff, Wales, UK

CARL TALBOT
DEEP ECOLOGY
ENVIRONMENTAL JUSTICE
    University of Wales, Cardiff
    Cardiff, Wales, UK

JULIA PO-WAH LAI TAO
CONFUCIANISM
    City University of Hong Kong
    Kowloon, Hong Kong

LAURENCE THOMAS
FRIENDSHIP
    Syracuse University
    Syracuse, New York

JOHN J. TILLEY
HEDONISM
    Indiana University/Purdue University
    Indianapolis, Indiana

G. E. TOMLINSON
GENETIC RESEARCH
    University of Texas
    Dallas, Texas

ROSEMARIE TONG
FEMINIST ETHICS
    Davidson College
    Davidson, North Carolina

MAX TRAVERS
COURTROOM PROCEEDINGS, REPORTING OF
    Buckinghamshire College

JOHN C. TULLOCH
VIOLENCE IN FILMS AND TELEVISION
    Charles Sturt University
    Bathurst, Australia

MARIAN I. TULLOCH
VIOLENCE IN FILMS AND TELEVISION
Charles Sturt University
Bathurst, Australia

RICHARD H. S. TUR
LEGAL ETHICS, OVERVIEW
Oriel College
Oxford, England, UK

ROBERT TWYCROSS
PALLIATIVE CARE
Oxford University and Churchill Hospital
Oxford, England, UK

CAROLE ULANOWSKY
FAMILY, THE
The Open University
Milton Keynes, England, UK

GREGORY UNGAR
ELECTRONIC SURVEILLANCE
University of Colorado
Boulder, Colorado

JORGE M. VALADEZ
INDIGENOUS RIGHTS
Marquette University
Milwaukee, Wisconsin

JOHANNES J. M. VAN DELDEN
DO-NOT-RESUSCITATE DECISIONS
Center for Bioethics and Health Law
Utrecht University
Utrecht, The Netherlands

WIBREN VAN DER BURG
SLIPPERY SLOPE ARGUMENTS
Tilburg University
Tilburg, The Netherlands

PAUL VIMINITZ
NUCLEAR WARFARE
University of Waterloo
Waterloo, Ontario

ANDREW VINCENT
MARX AND ETHICS
University of Wales, Cardiff
Cardiff, Wales, UK

ROBERT WACHBROIT
HEALTH AND DISEASE, CONCEPTS OF
Institute for Philosophy and Public Policy
University of Maryland
College Park, Maryland

NEIL WALKER
POLICE ACCOUNTABILITY
University of Aberdeen
Aberdeen, Scotland, UK

DANIEL WARNER
CITIZENSHIP
Graduate Institute of International Studies
Geneva, Switzerland

DAVID WASSERMAN
DISCRIMINATION, CONCEPT OF
Institute for Philosophy and Public Policy
University of Maryland
College Park, Maryland

JOHN WECKERT
SEXUAL CONTENT IN FILMS AND TELEVISION
Charles Sturt University
Bathurst, New South Wales, Australia

CHARLES WEIJER
RESEARCH METHODS AND POLICIES
Joint Centre for Bioethics
University of Toronto/Mount Sinai Hospital
Toronto, Ontario

D. DON WELCH
SOCIAL ETHICS, OVERVIEW
Vanderbilt University School of Law
Nashville, Tennessee

JOS V. M. WELIE
PLACEBO TREATMENT
Creighton University
Omaha, Nebraska

CELIA WELLS
CORPORATE RESPONSIBILITY
Cardiff Law School
University of Wales
Cardiff, Wales, UK

CAROLINE WHITBECK
RESEARCH ETHICS
Massachusetts Institute of Technology
Cambridge, Massachusetts

MARGARET WHITELEGG
ALTERNATIVE MEDICINE
University of Central Lancashire
Preston, England, UK

URBAN WIESING
MEDICAL ETHICS, USE OF HISTORICAL EVIDENCE IN
University of Münster
Münster, Germany

JOHN R. WILCOX
HIGHER EDUCATION, ETHICS OF
Manhattan College
Riverdale, Bronx, New York

RICHARD R. WILK
ARCHAEOLOGICAL ETHICS
Indiana University
Indianapolis, Indiana

BERNARD WILLIAMS
CENSORSHIP
University of California, Berkeley

CHRISTOPHER WINCH
AUTHORITY IN EDUCATION
   Nene College
   Northhampton, England, UK

EARL R. WINKLER
APPLIED ETHICS, OVERVIEW
   University of British Columbia
   Vancouver, British Columbia

CLARK WOLF
THEORIES OF JUSTICE: HUMAN NEEDS
   University of Colorado
   Boulder, Colorado

PAUL ROOT WOLPE
INFORMED CONSENT
   University of Pennsylvania
   Philadelphia, Pennsylvania

MICHAEL WREEN
PATENTS
   Marquette University
   Milwaukee, Wisconsin

MICHAEL J. ZIGMOND
SCIENTIFIC PUBLISHING
   University of Pittsburgh
   Pittsburgh, Pennsylvania

A GUIDE TO THE ENCYCLOPEDIA

The *Encyclopedia of Applied Ethics* is a complete source of information contained within the covers of a single unified work. It is the first reference book that addresses the relatively new discipline of applied ethics in a comprehensive manner; thus in effect it will provide the first general description of the components and boundaries of this challenging field.

The Encyclopedia consists of four volumes and includes 281 separate full-length articles on the whole range of applied ethics. It includes not only entries on the leading theories and concepts of ethics, but also a vast selection of entries on practical issues ranging from medical, scientific, and environmental ethics to the ethics of social relationships and social services. Each article provides a detailed overview of the selected topic to inform a broad spectrum of readers, from research professionals to students to the interested general public.

In order that you, the reader, will derive maximum benefit from your use of the *Encyclopedia of Applied Ethics,* we have provided this Guide. It explains how the Encyclopedia is organized and how the information within it can be located.

ORGANIZATION

The *Encyclopedia of Applied Ethics* is organized to provide the maximum ease of use for its readers. All of the articles are arranged in a single alphabetical sequence by title. Articles whose titles begin with the letters A to D are in Volume 1, articles with titles from E to I are in Volume 2, and those from J to R are in Volume 3. Volume 4 contains the articles from S to Z and also the Index.

So that they can be easily located, article titles generally begin with the key word or phrase indicating the topic, with any descriptive terms following. For example, "Distributive Justice, Theories of" is the article title rather than "Theories of Distributive Justice" because the specific phrase *distributive justice* is the key term rather than the more general term *theories*. Similarly "Sports, Ethics of" is the article title rather than "Ethics of Sports" and "Human Nature, Views of" is the title rather than "Views of Human Nature."

TABLE OF CONTENTS

A complete alphabetical table of contents for the *Encyclopedia of Applied Ethics* appears at the front of each volume of the set, beginning on page *v* of the Introduction. This list includes not only the articles that appear in that particular volume but also those in the other three volumes.

The list of article titles represents topics that have been carefully selected by the Editor-in-Chief, Prof. Ruth Chadwick, Head of the Centre for Professional Ethics, University of Central Lancashire, UK, in collaboration with the members of the Editorial Board.

In addition to the alphabetical table of contents, the Encyclopedia also provides a second table of contents at the front of each volume, one that lists all the articles according to their subject area. The Encyclopedia provides coverage of 12 specific subject areas within the overall field of applied ethics, as indicated below:

- **Theories of Ethics**
- **Ethical Concepts**
- **Medical Ethics**
- **Scientific Ethics**
- **Environmental Ethics**
- **Legal Ethics**
- **Ethics in Education**
- **Ethics and Politics**
- **Business and Economic Ethics**
- **Media Ethics**
- **Ethics and Social Services**
- **Social Ethics**

ARTICLE FORMAT

Articles in the *Encyclopedia of Applied Ethics* are arranged in a single alphabetical list by title. Each new article begins at the top of a right-hand page, so that it may be quickly located. The author's name and affiliation are displayed at the beginning of the article. The article is organized according to a standard format, as follows:

- Title and Author
- Outline
- Glossary
- Defining Statement
- Main Body of the Article
- Cross-References
- Bibliography

OUTLINE

Each article in the Encyclopedia begins with an Outline that indicates the general content of the article. This outline serves two functions. First, it provides a brief preview of the article, so that the reader can get a sense of what is contained there without having to leaf through the pages. Second, it serves to highlight important subtopics that are discussed within the article. For example, the article "Genome Analysis" includes the subtopic "The Human Genome Project."

The Outline is intended as an overview and thus it lists only the major headings of the article. In addition, extensive second-level and third-level headings will be found within the article.

GLOSSARY

The Glossary contains terms that are important to an understanding of the article and that may be unfamiliar to the reader. Each term is defined in the context of the particular article in which it is used. Thus the same term may appear as a Glossary entry in two or more articles, with the details of the definition varying slightly from one article to another. The Encyclopedia includes more than 1,000 glossary entries.

The following example is a glossary entry that appears with the article "Precautionary Principle."

indicator species A particular species whose presence (or absence) is regarded as characteristic of a given environment, and whose ability or failure to thrive there is thus thought to be indicative of the overall ecological status of this environment.

DEFINING STATEMENT

The text of each article in the Encyclopedia begins with a single introductory paragraph that defines the topic under discussion and summarizes the content of the article. For example, the article "Biotechnology" begins with the following statement:

BIOTECHNOLOGY is the application of biology for human ends. It involves using organisms to provide humans with food, clothes, medicines, and other products.

CROSS-REFERENCES

Nearly all of the articles in the Encyclopedia have cross-references to other articles. These cross-references appear at the end of the article, following the conclusion of the text. They indicate related articles that can be consulted for further information on the same topic, or for other information on a related topic. For example, the article "Biotechnology" contains cross-references to the articles "Agricultural Ethics," "Animal Research," "Eugenics," "Genetic Counseling," and "Genetic Engineering."

BIBLIOGRAPHY

The Bibliography appears as the last element in an article. It lists recent secondary sources to aid the reader in locating more detailed or technical information. Review articles and research papers that are important to an understanding of the topic are also listed.

The bibliographies in this Encyclopedia are for the benefit of the reader, to provide references for further reading or research on the given topic. Thus they typically consist of no more than ten to twelve entries. They are not intended to represent a complete listing of all the materials consulted by the author in preparing the article, as would be the case, for example, with a journal article.

INDEX

The Subject Index in Volume 4 contains more than 5000 entries. The entries are listed alphabetically and indicate the volume and page number where information on this topic will be found. Within the entry for a given topic, references to the coverage of the topic also appear alphabetically. The Index serves, along with the alphabetical Table of Contents, as the starting point for information on a subject of interest.

PREFACE

Applied Ethics has come to prominence as a field of study in the last 25 to 30 years, after a period in which the prevailing view among philosophers, at least, was that Philosophy could not usefully be applied to practical problems. The importance of Applied Ethics became obvious first in the medical context, where in the aftermath of World War II and the expanding interest in human rights, developments in technology gave rise to challenging ethical issues such as the use of transplant technology and the allocation of scarce resources such as kidney dialysis. Questions such as the extent to which health care professionals should intervene to extend life became extensively debated. Medical Ethics as a defined area became established, with principles such as autonomy being given central importance. In more recent times contested topics have included assisted reproduction and the advances in and implications of human genome analysis. The latter have led to controversy not only about the options concerning the applications of the technology in medical practice, but also about their wider social uses and even their implications for the meaning of what it is to be human.

Applied Ethics is, however, by no means confined to the medical context and to the social implications of technologies that have been developed for medical purposes or have clear medical applications. Ethical issues arise in any area of life where the interests of individuals or groups conflict, including the interests of different species. In compiling the Encyclopedia we became increasingly aware of the enormity of the task—the list of topics covered could have been expanded indefinitely. We chose to concentrate, however, on areas we regarded as central in contemporary society such as issues concerning the environment, law, politics, the media, science and engineering, education, economics, the family and personal relationships, mental health, social work, policing and punishment, minority rights.

In addition to these areas in which particular issues arise, it is essential for those engaged in Applied Ethics to reflect on what, if anything, is being applied. We therefore included a number of entries on ethical and philosophical approaches, both historical and contemporary, religious and secular. There are different models concerning what is involved in Applied Ethics—for example, whether it is a matter of "applying" a particular theory to a specific ethical dilemma; or whether phenomena, specific developments, particular cases, can affect the development of appropriate theory; whether there is room for a ëbottom-upí rather than a ëtop-downí approach. Some would argue that a central task of Applied Ethics, and one that is prior to the application of theory, is the very identification of the moral dimensions of a situation. Thus we have also included entries on Applied Ethics itself and on challenges to it.

Several disciplines may be involved in Applied Ethics; one branch of Applied Ethics, for example, Bioethics, is commonly explicated in terms of ethical, legal and social issues. In this Encyclopedia by no means all the entries are written by philosophers: some are written by practitioners in the particular field in question; other disciplines represented include law and economics. The Encyclopedia will be a reference work for use by a number of readerships, working in a variety of specialisms; but particularly for students in higher education studying on Applied Ethics courses, for which there is increasing demand. It also has much to offer the general reader interested in the ethical issues arising in contemporary social life.

The number of people who have enabled this enterprise to come to fruition is very large. I should like to thank, first, the members of the Editorial Board and Advisory Council, for participating in the project and for their expert advice on and help with the selection and reviewing of material; the reviewers of the articles, for their time in making the assessments of individual submissions; the University of Central Lancashire, for providing research assistance in the Centre for Professional Ethics—first Jane Pritchard and then Adam Hedgecoe, without whom I cannot imagine how the task would have been completed; and of course Academic Press, especially Scott Bentley and Naomi Henning, for their unfailing support throughout, but also their colleagues in the San Diego office who looked after me extremely well on my visit in 1996. All of my colleagues in the Centre for Professional Ethics have given their support to the project—some by writing entries themselves. Finally, the authors of the articles deserve a very large thank you, for contributing their expertise in their field and for working to very tight deadlines to produce the 281 entries in this Encyclopedia.

RUTH CHADWICK

JUDAISM

Oliver Leaman
Liverpool John Moores University

Talmud Discussions of the sages, of great importance in defining the nature of Jewish law.
Torah God's teaching to the Jews, often identified with the whole of doctrinal Judaism.
yetzer ha-ra Evil inclination, which leads human beings to bring about evil.
yetzer ha-tov Good inclination, which makes it possible for human beings to do good.

GLOSSARY

aggadah Stories, legends, and historical accounts of early Judaism.
Conservative A Jewish religious movement in the United States that accepts the modification of some parts of halakhah, but also believes in the validity of much of traditional Judaism.
goses A dying person.
halakhah Jewish law, a combination of oral and written law.
Noachide law Law that applies to the whole of humanity.
Orthodox A Jewish religious movement that adheres to a traditional interpretation of Jewish law.
Reform A Jewish religious movement designed to adapt Judaism and its customs to modern conditions.
rodef An aggressor.

JUDAISM is a religion that lays down for its followers rules dealing with conduct—rules which are based both on interpretations of scripture and on general moral principles. As society has changed, so too have the older rules had to be adapted to contemporary problems and new technologies, and this has led to a range of positions on ethical problems. The 20th century has led to novel problems, in particular through the creation of the State of Israel, the Holocaust, and developments in medicine. In addition, widespread changes to the status of women and concerns for the environment have involved a questioning of previous interpretations of Jewish ethics. As with all major religions, no consensus has arisen that encapsulates all possible Jewish responses to ethical issues, but a range of answers have been developed, a range which is linked both to traditional religious understandings and to the contingencies of modern ethical life.

I. HISTORY OF JEWISH ETHICS

A. The Nature of Judaism

Judaism is the religion of the Jewish people. Before the destruction of the Second Temple in 70 C.E. the religious practices of the Jews were centered on the sacrificial cult and the Bible.

The destruction of the Second Temple led to the construction of new religious institutions that shifted the emphasis from the temple cult to the home and the synagogue. The role of the priest became largely irrelevant, to be replaced by the rabbi, primarily a teacher with specialized knowledge of halakhah, Jewish law and ritual. The traditional Jew is bound by the system of halakhic rules, while the gentile is commanded by God only to keep the seven Noachide laws. Judaism is based on the Torah, which can have a narrower or a wider sense. According to the former, it consists of the five books of Moses, the first five books of the Bible, but it is also used to refer to the whole of the Hebrew Bible, or even the whole of traditional Jewish law and practice. It is a product of the covenant of God with Israel, revealed to Moses during the wanderings of the Israelites in the desert after the escape from Egypt.

In different times and places the Torah has been reinterpreted by religious authorities to show the relevance of past insights to current issues, but according to the traditionalists the basic meaning of the text is unchanging and cannot be altered to take account of different circumstances. Jews who are not traditionalists are prepared to accept that quite radical changes in Jewish practice are appropriate in certain circumstances, and they would regard human reason itself as an important criterion of which changes are permissible and which are not to the understanding of the implications of Torah.

B. Ethical Texts and Authors

Although there are few discussions that are specifically of ethics in early Judaism, the Bible and the Talmud are replete with material of ethical relevance. The latter is a compilation of halakhah and aggadah, of legal and ritual issues together with theological and ethical discussions. As one might expect in any religious text, there are a large number of ethical discussions, and these tend to be oriented to helping Jews determine their practice. In the medieval period there appeared a wide range of ethical literature, and the most important moral thinkers then were Bahya ibn Paquda (11th cen-

tury C.E.) and Moses Maimonides (12th century C.E.). Bahya sought to counter the emphasis in Jewish ethics on halakhah by insisting on the importance of inner obligations and emphasizing character and personal virtues.

Maimonides had an immense influence on ethical discussions through his *Mishneh Torah* and other legal and philosophical works in which he tried to codify halakhah and produce a fairly Aristotelian account of how we ought to behave. This concentrated on the scope for developing appropriate moral dispositions by avoiding extremes, and argued that halakhah was an appropriate mechanism to this end. The opinions of Maimonides continue to be highly influential today in the Jewish world.

C. Modern Jewish Ethics

The greatest change in Jewish ethics occurred at the time of the European Enlightenment in the 18th century. This saw the emancipation of the Jewish population in Europe, albeit in a piecemeal manner, and forced Jews to confront secular ethics in ways that proved very threatening to their identity as Jews. The central problem was, and remains, how Jews can preserve their distinctiveness from the gentile population while at the same time participating fully in the gentile world. From an ethical point of view, this can be formulated in terms of the relationship between Jewish ethics and general ethics. How far should Jews restrict their ethical practice to what has come to them through their religion, and how far should their behavior be affected by ethical sources that are not specifically Jewish? These central questions led to the creation of roughly three broad categories of religious allegiance.

Orthodoxy or traditional Judaism accepts that the Torah is the direct revelation of the divine will, and halakhah stems directly from his will. Any Jew at any place and any time is obliged to obey it. Of course, there can be developments in halakhah, yet these are only acceptable if they go through the appropriate mechanisms of rabbinic authority. Directly opposed to this approach is what is called in the United States and Europe "Reform." The Reform movement regards divine revelation as changing and progressive, and not as something that can be captured perfectly within the bounds of halakhah. On the whole the Reform movement tends to link Jewish ethics with the teachings of the prophets, which they see as coming close to modern forms of liberalism. In between these two positions comes the Conservative movement, which respects halakhah as a route to understanding God's purposes, but which does not regard it as normative for all Jews at all times. It is important to appreciate that these distinctions between different approaches to the nature of Judaism have significant effects on attitudes to applied and theoretical ethics.

II. MEDICAL ETHICS

A. Definition of Death

The procedure in medical ethics is often to identify precedents in rabbinic Judaism that incorporate principles which can produce Jewish norms on specific issues; for example, the problem of determining when someone is dead. According to modern medicine, brain death is the criterion of death, but in the traditional Jewish writings we have criteria based on respiratory and cardiac failure. Some contemporary rabbis would not accept that brain death and irreversible coma constitute death in Jewish law. Others, however, would argue that since the brain and the brain stem control breathing and the heart, if there is irreversible failure in the brain area, then the person is dead, even though there may be some cardiac activity. For them, changing scientific knowledge can be used to guide Jewish interpretation, so that today we can appreciate that the notion of respiratory and circulatory death is really brain death. Since we are now able to keep many physical systems operating even without the activity of the brain, clearly such a discussion could have important practical consequences. It could mean that someone who was brain dead would have to be kept "alive" on a ventilator even though there was no prospect of any mental functioning ever resuming.

B. Euthanasia and Birth Control

Euthanasia is a good example of a situation in which the different types of rabbis have rather similar views. There is a lot of evidence from the Talmud that the *goses,* the dying individual, is not to have his end hastened even when this would prevent pain. The point which is frequently made is that the dying person is in every way a living person, and must be treated with the same consideration as every other living person. Even if a patient is terminally ill, in a lot of pain, and requests to be dispatched, this cannot be allowed under Judaism. Any physician who acts in such a way as to cause such a patient to die is guilty of murder. On the other hand, if there is some action that prevents an easy death, then it should be avoided.

Of course, eliminating pain is an important value, but when it comes into conflict with the preservation of life it has to be recognized as of lesser value. That does not mean that in every case the physician has to do all she can to prolong life, and some treatment may relieve pain at the expense of length of life. Some rabbis would accept here that there is nothing wrong with such treatment, especially as pain itself may shorten life, and certainly would degrade its quality. The important point to grasp here is that, except for the Reform movement, the correct decision is not up to the individual. It is for the appropriate rabbinic authorities to use their skill at interpreting the Torah and relating it to everyday life to come to a decision.

Some rabbis do want to emphasize the role of the individual agent in coming to an appropriate decision in cases of apparent moral conflict. They would argue that the rate of progress and change in medical technology has outstripped the capacity of halakhah to produce relevant precedents on the basis of which ethical decisions can be taken. This leads to a different approach to the relationship between humanity and God, according to which there has to be a balance between trust in God on the one hand and the affirmation of human autonomy on the other. God has given his creatures the ability to make free decisions, and they have to use that ability to work out how to act in difficult cases, where the traditional answer seems to be out of step with present medical realities. On this approach the issue is no longer that of the quantity of life only, but its quality also, since we have the right as free agents to decide on what notion of quality of life best represents the sort of humanity which God has created. This is particularly relevant in cases such as that of contraception. To interfere with natural processes and limit children accordingly is to deny God his power to decide issues of who is to live. Yet if a family cannot flourish with yet more children, it is sensible to seek to preserve the quality of family life by restricting births. The important point to make about this approach is that it no longer attributes final authority to the rabbinate to make appropriate decisions. It is up to each individual to work out for himself or herself what the nature of the covenantal relationship they have with the deity is, and what implications that has for their practice.

A danger in this sort of approach is that it threatens to break the links with judicial ways of deciding such issues. It turns every agent into his or her own guide, and as a result may diminish the significance of Judaism on the character of their decisions. Also, it severs the links between the present and the past, and it is surely on such links that religion itself rests. It is not as though the precedents and examples that exist in halakhah can only be interpreted in just one way. They themselves embody the flexibility to respond to modern circumstances, since we can use analogy to link present problems to older principles and accounts. Legal texts have to be interpreted and made relevant to particular cases, and they are based on a sufficiently rich and complex tradition for this to be possible. If one uses the feelings one has in a particular situation as the guide to deciding the moral issue, one's decision will be arbitrary and only loosely based on Judaism. If, on the other hand, one takes these feelings into account and uses them to help interpret the traditional law, one can arrive at a far more appropriate way of solving issues in medical ethics from a Jewish perspective. Traditionalists would argue that there is sufficient flexibility within halakhah for changes in technology to be dealt with acceptably under existing rules and religious principles.

III. ABORTION

Killing a fetus is not equivalent to murder in Jewish ethics, since the fetus is regarded as part of the mother. When the choice is between the life of the mother and the birth of the child, the decision has to be made in favor of the mother. The fetus has the status of a *rodef*, an aggressor against the life of the mother, and one has the right of self-defense to kill the aggressor. Once the child is born, and the head emerges, then the situation is different, since there are now two lives in existence, and one is not permitted to prefer one above the other. But there is no absolute right to be born, nor to be conceived. The fetus is always secondary to the welfare of the mother. On the other hand, abortion should not be brought about just because a birth would be inconvenient to the mother. There have to be solid medical reasons for believing that the fetus would, if permitted to be born, seriously affect the well-being of the mother either physically or mentally. This has led some rabbis to permit abortion in the case of seriously malformed fetuses. Indeed, if a fetus is a medical danger to the mother, then its destruction is required, not just permitted.

The only grounds for abortion according to halakhah are medical, and economic, social, or other reasons are not justified. Some have argued that this is unsatisfactory as the final word on the Jewish position, since what makes a mother more important morally than her fetus is the fact that she has a much better defined series of experiences and ideas, so that in a sense she is much more of a person than the fetus. It follows that it is unreasonable to limit abortion to cases where the mother's medical welfare is in question. It might be helpful to preserving her intellectual, spiritual, ethical, and emotional health, and thus should be permitted. Why should her mental life not be considered as of equal importance to her physical life, the objection goes? Some authorities do permit abortion when this might prevent mental illness, but this might be felt to be too restrictive. If a woman sincerely believes that the birth of a child would be a serious blow to her sense of who she is, and in that sense constitute serious harm, then it might be possible to argue from a Jewish basis that abortion in such cases is justified. In no case could it be argued that abortion is justified merely because the birth would be inconvenient, but if it would seriously affect the projects of the mother, where this is taken in its widest personal sense, some would suggest that there are reasonable Jewish grounds for abortion for nonmedical reasons.

IV. PUNISHMENT

The normal ways of analyzing punishment is in terms of deterrence or retribution. The references in the Bible to punishment makes it clear that God regards it as a reassertion of the moral order which is brought into the world with the creation. Punishment brings the world back nearer to its original state. The references to "eye for eye, tooth for tooth" (Lev. 24:20; Exod. 21:23–5) were not interpreted rigidly by the commentators, since it is difficult to be precise about how to compensate for injuries.

On the other hand, there was less argument about the appropriate penalty for murder, which really did call for execution. One reason for this is to acknowledge the significance of murder as an act, and also to prevent the rich from using their wealth to avoid the full implications of their actions, which would be possible if they could use financial compensation as a means of avoiding the ultimate penalty. Yet it was difficult to establish that a murder took place, since the legal requirements for proof were set very high. It seems that when Jewish judges in the distant past had the power to sanction executions, they were very loathe to do so, a tradition that persists today in modern Israel. There the death penalty is only available for treason or genocide, crimes which are directed at the whole of the community. Only the Nazi concentration camp transport director Adolf Eichmann has been executed in Israel.

Of course, one of the major differences between the modern state and ancient times is that now there is a prison system. The Bible does not refer to imprisonment as a sanction, although the Talmud does, and prison sentences do make possible the assertion of divine justice through restriction on liberty. It also serves to deter others from committing a crime, and is directed at the criminal and no one else. The objectionable nature of capital punishment is worth preserving, in the view of many rabbis, by the ability to punish adequately without taking this final step.

V. SEXUALITY

On the halakhic version of Jewish ethics, sex as an activity is a natural right and a reflection of the biblical injunction, "Be fruitful and multiply" (Gen. 1:28; 9:1). This is not a specific instruction to Jews, but to humanity as a whole, and reflects the essential nature of human life. Sexuality is based on the natural order which originates with God, and society should follow natural needs instead of seeking to oppose them. The family is the appropriate context for sexuality, and incestuous, homosexual, and nonhuman sexual relationships are thus inappropriate. Homosexuality is wrong because it involves the participants taking on female and male roles that are out of line with their natural sexual constitutions. Formalizing homosexual relationships as legitimate is to be opposed, since it results in a deformed version of heterosexual family life.

Although men rather than women seem to be the initiators of marriage, the development of Jewish matrimonial law represents the gradual emancipation of women from relationships that resemble slavery. For example, there was a gradual historic move away from polygamy and concubinage to monogamy, something on which Maimonides took a leading position. Only in monogamy can there be true mutuality in sexual and personal relationships, and women can be seen as more than a mere sexual object. Since women have to consent to marriage, it has to be a mutual arrangement in order to be valid. Marriage cannot only be a civil contract, but is a covenant based on the covenant between God and Israel. The idea of marriage as a holy covenant is rooted in the idea of the human being as the image of God. Perhaps the best example of this in the Bible is the way in which the Song of Songs uses the allegory of male–female love to express God's love for the people of Israel. Although sexual love does involve pleasure, it involves more than this. True sexuality means going beyond the body but through the body, and within the covenant of marriage it becomes the way two moral beings mutually acknowledge God's love, which unlike human love is unending.

These halakhic requirements are probably little practiced among the modern Jewish community, which is just as liable to be involved in premarital sex or homosexuality as any other group in society. The idea that the only acceptable expression of sexuality is within the traditional heterosexual family sanctified through religious marriage is very alien to the experience of most Jews in modern society. This has led some to argue that since family structures are changing, the traditional criteria of valid Jewish relationships are no longer appropriate.

A truly egalitarian approach to the family will give women far more power than under halakhic Judaism, and will respect the whole gamut of family structures that different people have created. Many may find satisfying personal relationships out of marriage—in heterosexual relationships without marriage, in gay and lesbian relationships, in collectives, or even in isolation. The argument would go that this is not contrary to the values of the traditional family, but an extension of those values to include a far wider social constituency. Those involved in alternative family structures should be made part of the community and not treated as irremediably marginal. There is scope for finding arguments for diverse lifestyles from the basic principles of Jewish ethics, especially if we pay appropriate respect to passages requiring sympathy and acceptance of the stranger in the community.

Feminism has led to a thorough reappraisal of the role of women in Judaism. Traditional Judaism tends to regard women as inferior, in the sense that they have fewer rights and limited roles in the religion as compared with men. Of course, the argument by the traditionalists would be that women are not inferior to men, but just different, and halakhic Judaism respects women in respecting this difference. Yet there is no question that over a whole range of Jewish religious and ceremonial duties, women have less status than do their male peers. Does it appear likely that God wishes the hierarchy between male and female in Jewish ritual to exist?

We could certainly find such arguments for differentiation of role, but surely not for the superiority of one group of his creatures over another just by virtue of their gender. Perhaps it would be better to interpret this hierarchy in terms of an ancient division of power and society rather than any purpose of the deity. If the inequality between the sexes has no positive religious function, if equality is a positive value in Judaism, and if it is possible to reinterpret halakhah in more progressive ways to take account of changing circumstances, then there could be a change in the halakhic rules to help modern Jews make sense of the present in terms of the past.

VI. POWER, THE HOLOCAUST, AND THE STATE OF ISRAEL

The Holocaust had an enormous effect on the intellectual life of Jews, since its dimension led to a serious questioning of many of the principles of Judaism. Some thinkers argued that it called for an entirely new way of thinking, while others categorized it as one among a long line of catastrophes which does not essentially require special conceptual treatment. It did raise as an important fact the way in which the relative impotence of Jews had made their destruction possible, and indeed easy, and supported the Zionist contention that only in a Jewish state would the Jewish people have the opportunity to take control of their lives and organize an effective defense against their enemies. The religious idea of such a state is that it would be built on justice and be an example to the world of how to shape a society that is instrumental in finally redeeming the whole of humanity. The secular view is that the Jews should be like any other ethnic group and have their own state in which they can pursue ordinary and safe lives, free from interference from those who would otherwise be antagonistic toward them.

Before the creation of the State of Israel, Jewish ethics had tended to be critical of the exercise of power of one group of people over others, and especially of violence. Even anger was regarded as a heinous crime by many leading rabbis. With the founding of the State out of conflict with its neighbors and Palestinian inhabitants, and the continuing wars ever since, the question has arisen of how power should be exercised.

Some thinkers who argue that the Holocaust should be the principle behind present policy advocate a very tough attitude to potentially hostile internal and external forces, and seek to justify the severity of that response in terms of the disaster experienced during the Holocaust. In the Holocaust God did not intervene to save six million Jews from destruction, and today it is incumbent upon Jews to take on themselves the responsibility for their own survival. This will sometimes involve killing innocent people, if they are close to the enemy, or acting disproportionately when retaliating for some injury done to the State of Israel. This is justified in terms of the necessity to avoid innocent Jews being killed as occurred on such a large scale in the Holocaust.

Others would argue that Israel is a state just like other states, and it should be governed by exactly the same principles which represent the ethically acceptable rules of government. Sometimes this will involve the use of violence and injury to the innocent, but Israel has no greater moral standing for its actions just because of the link between its Jewish inhabitants and the Holocaust. Some thinkers would argue against this, suggesting that Israel cannot just be an ordinary state, since it has the role of being a light to the nations, in the sense that it is supposed to show the rest of the world how humanity can be perfected and redeemed. It follows that the moral standards which Israel applies should be higher than those current elsewhere, and self-consciously so. If they are not, then Israel is just a country like any other country, and has denied its special and distinctive status.

VII. ECONOMIC JUSTICE

Judaism puts great emphasis on work and on the human effort that is a vital part of continuing the creation of the world after God started it off. There seems to be general acceptance of the division between the rich and the poor, with an emphasis on the importance of the need for charity, fairness, justice, and compassion in the interrelationships of people. The world is not a place to be shunned—material products can be beneficial and should be used to yield increasing amounts of welfare for humanity.

Human beings are driven by two sorts of urges, a good urge (*yetzer ha-tov*) and an evil inclination (*yetzer ha-ra*). The former enables human beings to transcend their own narrow selfishness and to obey God's law. The evil inclination directs us toward ourselves instead of toward God and others, and we have the duty to try to control it and limit its power over us. One might think that the rabbis would argue that we would be better off without the evil inclination, but they do not do so. Instead, they point out that without selfish impulses we should be unable to set about accumulating wealth or creating anything at all, so in fact this inclination is a motive that can lead to a lot of good. It needs to be controlled and limited by the desire to be good, but it is an essential part of our lives as human beings.

Some people prosper in a society with inequality, and some suffer, and it does not seem that in this world the level of welfare matches ethical worth. This is to be mitigated by a system of charity and philanthropy, and the economic system should be run with honesty and justice. There is nothing other-worldly about Jewish thought here. Although it is certainly true that the world was created by a just and good God, he did not create a world which does not require any further human effort to bring it to perfection. On the contrary, he wants his creatures to imitate his performance of the creation by giving us the ability to use the material world to improve life generally for the community and specifically for ourselves. He could have instantly created a utopia, which indeed did exist before the expulsion of Adam and Eve from the Garden of Eden, yet in a utopia there would be no scope for human beings to acquire merit through their own actions and struggles. Jewish tradition calls for the limitation of the free market, however, in order to balance out the welfare of different groups in society, and for the active participation of wealthier citizens in the support and encouragement of the less fortunate.

VIII. THE ENVIRONMENT

Is there a specifically Jewish approach to ecology and the human relationship to the resources of the world? Some have seen Genesis 1:28 as allowing human beings to do exactly as they wish in the natural world, since it states that "God blessed them; and God said to them: Be fruitful and multiply, and replenish the earth, and subdue it; and have dominion over the fish of the sea, and over the fowl of the air, and over every living thing that moves on the earth." This verse could be taken to show that God gives everything in the world to human beings to use as they wish, but it could also be understood as referring to the role of human beings as the dominant species in the world, able to change the environment and exercise power in ways not available to other creatures. It does not follow from this that there is any special license to do as one wishes.

In support of this more restricted version of acceptable human behavior is the rabbinic principle of avoiding at all costs pain to living creatures. In support of this principle one notes that the laws of the Sabbath command rest for animals on that day (Exod. 20:11; Deut. 5:14) and the particular rules of slaughter are directed to preserving the sense of reverence for life by proscribing the eating of blood (the seat of life) and going to lengths to avoid suffering in the animal which is to be killed in order to sustain human life.

Human beings take their place in the universe with other creatures, and they are all the creation of God. We have no right to exploit our fellow creatures, nor the natural resources of our world, since these were not created for our exclusive use, and we live in an environment which was not made by us. Jewish law places strong restrictions on the sorts of damage which can be done to the environment even within the context of war, and the limitations on what can be done with property extend even to one's own private property. After all, our property is really God's property, and we have no right to do anything we like with it.

This is well represented in the laws of the Sabbatical and Jubilee years. The former regulates how every seventh year the fields should be allowed to lie fallow and the produce made available to the poor. The Jubilee year occurs every 50 years, and all property that was sold in the previous 50 years is supposed to be returned to its original owner without compensation. This represents graphically the principle that God owns the earth and everything in it, and so any act of wanton destruction or careless environmental damage is an abuse against God. The natural order of the world is a reflection of the creative power of the deity, and as such should be dealt with sympathetically and humbly. It follows that Judaism implies a careful treatment of the environment, with due consideration to all the other natural creatures existing in it.

IX. TRADITIONALISM AND ITS ENEMIES

The traditionalist line of interpretation might appear rigid and uncompromising, but this is far from the case. Traditionalist also have to use the corpus of commentary to make sense of modern problems, and the nature of that tradition of commentary is that it is often quite open-ended. That is, it consists of different rabbis debating over the correct Jewish position. The orthodox rabbi will have to make a decision as to which authority to accept as the best, and this will clearly involve not only a sifting through the traditional texts, but also of reason itself. This is even more the case with nontraditionalists, who will seek to think about particular Jewish texts which might be selected in accordance with the interests and ideas of the particular thinker, and which will then be subjected to the application of reason. This may seem a rather arbitrary process, but really it is not. Both types of thinkers will be trying to construct from what they take to be authoritative texts a solution, a "Jewish solution." Of course, in reality there are great difficulties in talking about a "Jewish" applied ethics as though this could only be one set of principles. Given the ambiguous nature of religious texts, and the changing nature of the ethical environment, Jewish thinkers will always use their creativity to try to find satisfying Jewish answers to ethical questions.

Most Jews today live as full citizens in liberal democracies, and for them the issue of how they are to relate to the secular world is a vitally important one. How far are they to act as ordinary citizens, and how far are they to act as Jews? Assimilation has become a threatening demographic factor in modern Jewish life, in a world which is still recovering from the devastation of the Jewish population in the Holocaust, and the attractions of the modern world have led many Jewish thinkers to emphasize the compatibility between Jewish ethics and the ethics of the general community.

On the other hand, many orthodox thinkers would wish to preserve the distinctions between Jewish ethics and those of the secular world, and they would argue that in any case the rationale for Jewish ethics lies within revelation and nothing else. Nonetheless, there is little problem in finding a variety of appropriate Jewish answers to the issues which arise in applied ethics, and although these answers may not all be compatible, they will all be based on the notion of the nature of divine revelation and the principles first embodied in the covenant between God and the Jews.

Also See the Following Article

RELIGION AND ETHICS

Bibliography

Borowitz, E. (1990). "Exploring Jewish Ethics." Wayne State Univ. Press, Detroit.

Cohn-Sherbok, D. (1996). A new agenda for society. In "The Liberation Debate: Rights at Issue" (Leahy M. and Cohn-Sherbok D., pp. 213–216. Routledge, London.

Dorff, E. (1996). "This is my Lover, This is my Friend": A Rabbinic Letter on Intimate Relations." Rabbinical Assembly, New York. [the Conservative Movement's official document on issues of sex and marriage]

Dorff, E., and Newman, L. (Eds.) (1995). "Contemporary Jewish Ethics and Morality: A Reader." Oxford Univ. Press, New York.

Feldman, D. (1968). "Marital Relations, Birth Control, and Abortion in Jewish Law." New York Univ. Press, New York; reprinted Schocken (1975).

Frank, D., and Leaman, O. (Eds.) (1996). "History of Jewish Philosophy." Routledge, London.

Kogan, B. (Ed.) (1990). "A Time to Be Born and a Time to Die." De Gruyter, New York.

Leaman, O. (1995). "Evil and Suffering in Jewish Philosophy." Cambridge Univ. Press, Cambridge.

Novak, D. (1992). "Jewish Social Ethics." Oxford Univ. Press, New York.

Plaskow, J. (1991). "Standing Again at Sinai." Harper Collins, San Francisco.

Sinclair, D. (1989). "Tradition and the Biological Revolution." Edinburgh Univ. Press, Edinburgh.

JURY CONDUCT

Andrew Brien
Massey University

I. The Purpose and Nature of the Jury
II. Ethical Issues in Jury Conduct: The Jury as an Institution
III. Ethical Issues in Jury Conduct: The Operation of Juries
IV. Conclusion

GLOSSARY

jury The contemporary jury is a committee of men and women selected from the general community who take an oath to decide, fairly and without prejudice and on the evidence presented to them, disputed matters of fact and, having done that, render a verdict accordingly.

jury nullification A decision by a jury not to uphold or apply the law in a certain case, on the grounds that to do so would be an injustice to the defendant.

shared deliberation The practice of participating in a group discussion, contributing to it, and responding to the contributions of others, so as to test explanations, justifications, interpretations, evaluations, and analyses of evidence with the aim of reaching a collective decision.

TRIAL BEFORE A JURY of one's peers, or more generally, placing a question before a jury for it to answer, is a defining feature of English law and many of those legal systems that count the English legal model as their ancestor. In such systems, which include those of the United States, Canada, Australia, New Zealand, Scotland, and Wales, the jury is found in criminal and civil trials, which are conducted on an adversarial basis, as well as in inquests, such as coronial enquiries, which are conducted on an inquisitorial basis.

The use of the jury is atypical: in many of the sophisticated legal systems of the world the jury has a very limited role or is completely unknown. Attempts to graft the jury onto systems in which it is not used or expand its use in systems where its use is limited, have been unsuccessful. It remains predominantly and Anglo-American institution.

Despite arguments that the conduct of juries render them an imperfect body to use in the administration of justice—claims that we shall consider in this article—it remains an institution that draws overwhelming support from legal practitioners and the general public in those jurisdictions in which it operates.

I. THE PURPOSE AND NATURE OF THE JURY

Jurors are the sole determiners of fact: they find the facts on the testimony given. Judges state the law. Using the facts as determined and the law as expounded to them by the judge, juries render a verdict. As well, in certain civil actions in which a person is alleged to have harmed another (such as defamation), juries may also assess the degree of harm and recommend the level of compensation. Although required to follow the directions of the presiding judge, when they deliberate juries are effectively and legally autonomous from the legislature, the executive, and the judiciary.

Juries reach their decisions by practicing "shared deliberation," a practice that rests upon each juror's responsible self-government, autonomy, impartiality, and common sense. It assumes that each juror will bring to the deliberations his or her own analysis and interpretation and that this will be tested by the other jurors, and that this will yield to a more reliable, collective decision.

Juries are lay bodies; it is assumed that jurors have no expert or intimate prior knowledge of the law or the legal system. In most jurisdictions people who have such knowledge, such as judges, lawyers, prison officers, police officers, or even their immediate families, are excluded from jury service. The aim is to empanel a body of ordinary community members—amateurs—who will bring to the consideration of the evidence not only the values and mores of the society, but also the common sense, fairmindedness, and experience of the ordinary "person in the street." This is a stance that someone enmeshed and in the machinations of the legal system is apt to lose, and that would prevent such people from engaging in the practice of shared deliberation and reaching a fair and right verdict.

Juries are usually selected from those members of a community who are enrolled to vote and who have been resident in a community for some period of time. In many jurisdictions noncitizens who meet a residence requirement are entitled to vote; consequently, juries in these jurisdictions consist not only of citizens but noncitizens who are registered voters. It is not, therefore, citizenship per se that qualifies a person for jury service, but *membership* of a community. This holds true also of those juries that are not created from lists of registered voters but that are still representative of the community. The reason is that in being a juror a person is expected to bring to the court and jury room the stance of the average community member. Such a stance can be obtained only through *membership* of the community and this can be attained only through being resident in a community and part of its life for an extended period of time. Juries then, are not committees of one's fellow *citizens* but fellow community members—or as was said in olden times, one's "country." This also signifies that the questions sent to a jury are matters of concern for the entire community. They are not issues important only to the governors of the com-

munity or to the victims of a crime. The jury then is an institution of civic engagement. It represents the interconnected welfare of all community members and the fact that all community members are individuals embedded in a social network characterized by mutual concern and protection.

The value of juries has been the subject of a long debate that has recruited some of the foremost minds in legal and political philosophy, including Montesquieu, William Blackstone, Thomas Jefferson, Jeremy Bentham, and de Tocqueville. The debate falls into two broad areas each focused on jury conduct: ethical considerations about the value of institution itself, based on the way that juries in general do and can conduct themselves; and considerations about the way that juries ought to behave and ought to be induced to behave.

II. ETHICAL ISSUES IN JURY CONDUCT: THE JURY AS AN INSTITUTION

A. Advantages of the Jury to the Administration of Justice

Jury conduct—the way juries reach a verdict—is by the practice of shared deliberation. Within the legal system this makes them unique as an institution. In fact, a properly functioning jury can operate in no other way, because it is, by its nature, a committee of amateurs who all freely discuss the evidence and reach a collective decision. Shared deliberation is superior to other types of deliberative practice. As we shall see, it is more likely to produce a decision that is superior in a number of different ways to decisions produced through other deliberative processes, such as through the deliberation of legal professionals alone or bodies led by them. Now, the outcome of any court action is a decision: a defendant may be found guilty or not guilty; a fact proved or not; a finding returned. Leading to that decision evidence is heard, tested in court, and then deliberated upon. Juries are superior to other deliberative bodies because through their conduct, through, that is, shared deliberation, juries fortify the deliberative process and most importantly, the decisions that result, the very object of court action.

Juries fortify the deliberative process and the results of it in a number of distinct ways. For example, laws are framed in general terms: they define general classes. As a result they are blind to the individualizing features of each particular case. Such individualizing features are important in accurate deliberation, because they may provide good reasons for exempting a person from the application of that law.

Through the practice of shared deliberation juries are capable of seeing and taking into account the individualizing features of particular cases far better than actors enmeshed in the culture of the legal system. Such actors may find it easier and more convenient to apply the law strictly, whereas jurors are more likely to be unconstrained by legal precedent: they will, typically, have no knowledge of any precedents nor will they possess the various preconceptions that legal practitioners are apt to develop through familiarity with the legal system. In general, jurors bring to their deliberations the common sense and decency of disinterested members of the community who are not caught up in the prevailing legal culture. Juries are then better placed to deliberate fairly over the evidence presented and produce verdicts that are fair, reasonable, and warranted by the case.

Moreover, juries can, better than other deliberative bodies, take account of salient moral considerations that rest upon the features of individual cases. In that way juries are better able to inject into the administration of justice considerations such as equity, right, humanity, compression, and mercy that apply to individual cases rather than general classes of cases. Each case will be decided on its merits. (For these reasons, the fact that jurors are amateurs is not regarded as a deficiency of the institution, but rather, one of its great strengths!) Thus, by engaging in shared deliberation juries act as counterweights to not only the blindness to individual circumstances of general laws but also the tendency to ignore salient moral values. In these ways, jury conduct fortifies the deliberative process, because they make it more likely that the decision attained will be based both on a fair consideration of the evidence and salient moral values and that it will be, therefore, appropriate to the case at hand.

Further, jurors bring to their deliberations collective recall. While each juror will remember only some aspects of the case, together they will recall it all, much more so than a judge sitting alone or with a few colleagues. Consequently, each salient aspect of the case can be explored and subjected to scrutiny from many different angles. Prejudice, neglect of salient details, or preconceptions that may taint a decision are more likely to be revealed in the course of the deliberations; decisions, evaluations, and interpretations are more likely to be thoroughly scrutinized, and in this way biases and omissions are more likely to be excluded. For these reasons, it is believed that jurors stand in a better posi-

tion to deliberate wisely and decide a case on its merits than a judge sitting alone, or with lay assessors who may be tempted to follow the presiding judge's lead.

The thought behind all this is that 12 heads are better than one. If ordinary, reasonable people enter into the practice of shared deliberation in good faith, willing to listen and discuss the issues, then the plurality of values, views, experiences, and analyses they bring to the evidence will contribute to the practice of deliberation. It will yield a richer and deeper understanding of the case and an outcome that is more likely to be right in terms of the evidence and the community sentiments concerning what is fair and reasonable.

Finally, courts are often called upon to make difficult decisions. Placing the responsibility for such decisions on the shoulders of one person may expose that person to all kinds of intimidation and hostility. Dividing the responsibility for a decision between actors tends to blur the focus for any grievance and consequently, protects the judge (to some extent, at least) from the wrath of disgruntled litigants or defendants.

B. Credibility of the Justice System

In the Anglo-American legal tradition, the party bringing an allegation (the Crown, the people, the plaintiff) bears the burden of proof. In trials before a jury they must convince a panel of disinterested amateurs who are independent of all those in the proceedings. Independence provides greater likelihood of impartiality and a fair decision. The assumption is that if a group of reasonable people, after having heard the evidence and deliberated over it are convinced that something is the case, then it probably is. Establishing legal liability in this way fosters trust in the administration of justice and adds to the credibility of individual decisions.

As well, it is far more difficult to corrupt 12 community members, who have been selected from a larger body itself chosen at random from the general community, and who have no shared history prior to the case, than it is to corrupt a stable body of judges and assessors. Juries then are believed to be more likely to be free from corruption than a permanent or semipermanent body. For this reason juries are believed to be more likely to deliver fair verdicts.

Moreover, it is unlikely that a group of citizens would condemn one of their own unless the evidence truly supported that conclusion. The verdict is more likely to be reliable. This adds still more credibility to a verdict than a decision reached by a judge who, received belief has it, may well be out of touch with community values and sentiments or who may have been subverted by endemic corruption in the judicial system or by outside pressures.

The effect of this is that involving lay people in the administration of justice—as occurs with jury service—fosters trust, a sense of ownership, and the faith of the community toward not only the process and its results, but the entire system of justice. The reason is that community members need to be assured on an ongoing basis that the system is working well, and the jury is part of this assurance process. As a result, the courts are believed to do, not the government's bidding, or that of powerful interests, but to serve the community, impartially. Community members will be less likely to believe that the system is corrupt or a verdict unreliable or against the community interest, if a jury has had a hand in it. Confidence in the system leads to easy, voluntary compliance. This is essential to a system of law that relies largely upon the voluntary obedience of those governed by it—as is the case in the Anglo-American tradition.

C. Social and Political Justifications

The jury is not merely a legal institution, considered essential to the effective administration of justice in the Anglo-American legal tradition. It is also a social and political institution that is considered one of the essential components of the system of checks and balances that characterize the Anglo-American system of government. The jury has this role through its conduct. It is, as the great eighteenth-century jurist William Blackstone eulogized, one guarantor of civil liberties. The thought is this: no jury can be focused to convict nor will it suffer any penalty for delivering a verdict against the evidence or against the wishes of the powers that be. So, the jury can protect ordinary citizens from harsh and repressive laws, politically or vindictively motivated prosecutions, and biased judges.

The reason the jury can do this is that judges state the law to the jury, but they do not determine the facts or guilt; those are the tasks of the jury alone. This prevents control over the judicial process—and outcome—falling into the hands of one actor in the system. (It is analogous to the separation of powers in political society.) Such a practice reduces the possibility of corruption and better ensures the proper administration of justice. In this way, juries restrict the power of judges, the executive, and the legislature over the judicial process, and in that way it fortifies the liberties of community members. The presence of the jury and the way it conducts itself increases the likelihood that the public interest will be served. A collateral justification is that

citizens, knowing that there is a mechanism that protects their liberties and promotes the public interest, will come to trust the system of justice more.

Juries are selected from a wide cross-section of society; they are democratic institutions. The institution of the jury embodies democratic values, such as that those in positions of power must be accountable to the people, and that the authority of the legal process comes ultimately from the consent of the people themselves. Behind this is the thought that in democratic societies, the people or their representatives, must sit in all the institutions of state, to ensure accountability, to maintain the focus of the institution toward the community, to inject shared deliberation into decision-making, and to remind all those in the community that the source of continuing legitimacy of those institutions is the will of the people. On this view, the institution of the jury and jury conduct (involving shared deliberation, one of the hallmarks of the democratic process) are justified on the ground that this institution is part of the framework that goes to make and maintain a democratic society.

Further, jury conduct, involving as already noted, shared deliberation, is essentially democratic. Each juror, like each elector, has a say in the discussion leading to the collective decision. Jury conduct is not, however, a "free-for-all" argument. Juries are self-correcting and self-moderating ensuring that shared deliberation is practiced. The biases and unconscientiousness of one juror will be counterbalanced by the conscientiousness, fairness, and diligence of others. Such is the general attachment to these values—the level of civic virtue—that the failure on the part of one will be rectified by the civic virtue of the others on an impartially selected jury that represents a cross section of the community. As a result, in reaching their individual points of view, jurors listen to the evidence, assess it, evaluate and judge it, and develop a point of view, not as isolated individuals but as members of a committee. They expound the reasons for their point of view, thus exposing it to examination by others with different views, and as well, they test the views of others through critical analysis. The same conduct is at work in a well-functioning and thriving democracy. This has led the jury to be described as a "miniature parliament." Juries are then, by their conduct, an embodiment of the ideals of a deliberative democratic state, only operating on a smaller scale.

Moreover, juries are one of the natural institutions of a deliberative democracy. Juries, like deliberative democracies, are inclusive of all community members; like deliberative democracies they are drawn from the fundamental democratic category: community membership. Jury conduct rests on the practice of shared deliberation, as do deliberative democracies. Deliberative democracies operate upon the principle that the continuing legitimacy of institutions is dependent upon the participation in the deliberative process and consent of the community. This principle receives concrete expression in a number of different ways, the most familiar of which is that the hands of powerful actors in the society should be constrained and monitored by ordinary community members, selected through a process that minimizes the possibility of corruption, and who have the responsibility of auditing the behavior of the powerful so as to protect the interests of individuals and the community. The jury, given its conduct, is an institution that embodies this ideal, as we have seen. Arguably then, no deliberative democracy—which is the model for the Anglo-American political tradition—could fail to accord the jury a place in its institutional arrangements.

D. The Paradox of the Jury

Apart from the advantages conferred upon the administration of justice through shared deliberation, all the other justifications for the jury rest upon it *failing* to act as a fact finding body—the only role in law that it is supposed to have. To be sure, juries possess a discretion to do justice or mercy, in their own right, because they can prevent the rigid application of a law, or they may ignore a law altogether. This is called "returning a mercy verdict," "acquitting in the teeth of the evidence," "jury nullification," or "delivering a perverse verdict." To do this and ignore or dilute the law is not merely to judge the facts but judge the law itself. While the capacity to judge the law provides a number of justifications for this institution it does so at the cost of effectively undermining the jury's alleged function in the law. The jury then rests upon two mutually incompatible bases: it can live up to its justifications only at the cost of abjuring its reputed function. This is paradoxical.

The solution is to reject the doctrine that juries ought only to find the facts, and agree that they can also judge the law. Must juries have this power? They must, because the only way to deprive juries of the power to judge the law would involve destroying the institution itself. The argument is this. In order to deprive a jury of this power its verdict must be evaluated by some other body to determine whether the jury reached its verdict only on the facts. Such a body would then be doing the same job as the jury, as it would need to

determine whether the jury's verdict was warranted by the facts alone or incuded some consideration of the merit of the law. Such second guessing of the jury's verdict would deprive the jury of any purpose in the legal system, as the other body, charged with evaluating the jury's decision, could do the initial assessment itself. It would also diminish the credibility of the system, as the feeling would arise that a jury's decision would be allowed to stand only if it "got it right" by the lights of some other body not directly in touch with the views of the community. Under such circumstances, there seems no reason to persist with the jury at all. This was clearly set out in 1670 in *Bushell's Case* [Vaughn 135]: "For if the Judge, from the evidence, shall by his own judgment first resolve upon any tryal what the fact is, and so knowing the fact shall then resolve what the law is, and order the jury penally to find accordingly, what either necessary or convenient use can be fancied of juries, or to continue tryals by them at all?" Therefore, in a legal system that persists with the institution of the jury that institution will be independent and the way a jury makes its decision—that is, the contents of its deliberations—will not be open to review by some other body. Consequently, juries have the power—albeit de facto—to try the law in order that they can fulfill the role that they are supposed to have within the legal system: that of being at trial the sole determiner of legal liability.

(This, of course, needs a little qualification. Juries may be directed to acquit by a judge when it becomes clear that *in law* the accused has no case to answer. Juries can never be directed to convict. After a trial, a guilty verdict may be appealed to a higher court, on a matter of law, or more rarely, fact. For example, a judge may have given a wrong ruling on the admissibility of some evidence or new information may have emerged that, had the jury considered it, a different verdict may have been reached. For these sorts of reasons new trials may be ordered. Should a person be acquitted, that is the end of the matter: the decision cannot be reviewed. The reasoning behind this asymmetry is that the system should respect individuals and protect their liberty. Thus, it must be designed to protect the innocent while preventing abuse by its governors. Respect for individuals and their liberties, on the one hand, is embodied in the moral principles that only the guilty should suffer and that it is morally worse to punish the innocent than let the guilty go free; and on the practical observation that mistakes do happen. Consequently, some mechanism is required to review guilty verdicts to ensure that they are right. On the other hand, respect for individuals and their liberties are protected by prohibiting the review of acquittals. This prevents persistent prosecutions for the same offense and so eliminates one avenue for maliciously motivated trials. The aim is to maximize the benefits to the community of jury conduct while minimizing the risks to the community of investing actors, in this case, prosecutors, with enormous power.)

Ought juries to retain the power to nullify the law? No legislator can ever frame a law to take account of all possible circumstances; and no bill of rights can ever guarantee that a government, a legislator, or a prosecutor will always act fairly or in the public interest. Cases will inevitably arise that clearly fall under a law as it is framed but for which, for a variety of reasons, it will be morally desirable make an exception. This is the application of equity and moral right in judgment, leading to the tailoring of the response of the legal system to the specific case. Juries therefore need the power to nullify the law when the law, as framed, would hold a person liable and when it would be morally wrong to do so.

Juries, moreover, have political purposes and justifications: they are, as we saw, part of the system of checks and balances; they are one guarantor of a community's liberties. In addition, they have a duty to do equity and right. Juries can do these things only if they can judge the law as well as the facts and nullify the law when they see fit. Therefore, juries ought to be empowered to judge the law so that it is possible for them to fulfill their justifications.

Moreover, it is a well-attested phenomenon in legal systems that when the courts come to apply considerations of equity and right they experience—for a variety of reasons—considerable inertia in deviating from a strict application of the law. Juries, in contrast, can take a lead. Being drawn from the community they are less likely to experience such inertia or to be swayed by powerful interests; and, when allowed to think things through without interference or heavy hints as to the verdict, usually do not find it as difficult to do equity and right, as courts on occasion can. Juries require the power to nullify the law, therefore, as a counterweight to the conservatism of the courts or the machinations of judicial and political officeholders. In this way they are likely to increase the likelihood that the outcome of the administration of justice will be fair, equitable, right, and humane.

Through having the power to nullify the law, juries have the capacity to tailor the law to the individual case. Not only is this morally desirable, but it promotes confidence and trust by the citizenry in the system of law and government. Citizens then have good grounds to think that odious laws that attack the liberties of the community will be struck down by the jury and that the arbitrary use of power by government, judge, or other agent of the state, will be similarly constrained—should it come before a jury. For these reasons, juries need the power to nullify the law.

E. Disadvantages of the Jury

The arguments against the jury focus on its conduct and fall under four headings: it is incompetent, it is prejudiced, it wages war on the law, and its alleged advantages do not exist.

F. Incompetence

Juries are often called upon to apply complex laws that may be difficult to understand; they may have to assess complex scientific evidence, or as in white-collar fraud cases, evaluate intricate financial testimony. Yet juries, drawn as they are from a cross-section of the community and possessing no especial talents, may be unable to do any of these things, either through lack of expertise, ignorance, or even stupidity. Moreover, jurors are not experienced in the assessment of different sorts of testimony. For example, they may regard eyewitness testimony more highly than is warranted, or prefer it to scientific evidence because the eyewitness testimony is easier to understand. Or a jury may be so impressed with scientific evidence that they exclude all argument to the contrary and fail to evaluate it, instead blindly relying on the experts. Even if they can assess testimony, in a long and complex trial they may not be able to recall salient pieces of evidence or do so accurately, or be able to follow the judge's summing up or the directions given to them. Juries make mistakes. Consequently, trials before a jury involve a greater risk of error and mistrial, or defendants being acquitted on purely technical grounds.

These problems are compounded by the fact that juries do not usually ask questions, may not be permitted to, or may be actively discouraged from doing so. They may not be fully aware of their powers—for example, they may be unaware that they can return a conviction of a lesser crime (manslaughter rather than murder), or acquit in the teeth of the evidence. Moreover, evidence is presented to them in an unstructured, fragmentary form and in a way—by examination and cross-examination—with which they may be unfamiliar, and which is highly unusual in everyday life. In any case, it is not the best way to impart information. As well, they may not have access to important documents or exhibits, transcripts of evidence, or the crime scene.

The very process of trial by jury seems designed to encourage juries to behave in irrational and incompetent ways.

In addition, jury trials are more expensive, take longer, and occupy the time of a far greater number of people than trials before a judge alone or a bench of judges, or a bench including lay assessors. Juries seem then incapable of expeditiously administering justice.

Further, skillful counsel can manipulate a jury through eloquence or the artful presentation of evidence; and judges can guide a jury to a decision by suggesting to them the appropriate verdict, perhaps not in so many words, but through a summing up slanted one way rather than another, or even a strategically raised eyebrow.

Finally, the court environment and its process can be intimidating. Jurors are usually unaware of the way the courts operate, unfamiliar with legal language and behavior, their duties as a juror, and what they can and cannot do. Consequently, they do what they believe is expected of them, rather than what they think is right, given the evidence.

G. Prejudice

Juries seem more ready to acquit and to reject police evidence, indicating a bias toward defendants in some cases. Moreover, juries can be tampered with. Jury lists can be manipulated to exclude certain classes of people, for example, the poor or racial minorities. When a particular jury is empanelled, counsel can exercise influence by way of their challenges, so that the resulting jury is biased toward one side rather than another. Or a jury simply may be bigoted, either because the jurors themselves are bigots or because they have been tainted by pretrial publicity, publicity in the course of a trial, or through encountering other prejudicial material during a trial. It seems difficult, then, to empanel and maintain an impartial jury.

H. At War with the Law

Juries bend the law or ignore it altogether. In doing this they usurp the role of the legislature and inject into the legal system uncertainty and the rule of individuals rather than the rule of laws. Juries then are at odds with fundamental elements of the Anglo-American political tradition.

As well, such is the mystique surrounding the jury and the reluctance of appeal courts to interfere with a jury's decision, that when a jury does make a mistake it may well be difficult to reverse it. Jury decisions seem

almost unassailable. This is compounded by the fact that juries deliberate in secret, and they do not have to give, and routinely do not provide, reasons for their decisions. It is difficult to see where they may have gone wrong. As well, the membership of the jury is determined by lot, informed guesswork, and the self-interest of defense or prosecution rather than objectively assessed merit. For these reasons, juries are not competent, accountable, and open institutions. This runs against democratic principles, not notably that the best should hold offices of responsibility by common consent and do their work as far as possible in the sunshine.

I. Alleged Advantages

Community involvement is considered a major advantage of the jury. Yet, juries are ineffective when a section of a community, such as a racial and social group, is estranged from the body politic. Juries including or dominated by such groups may be biased, deliver wrong verdicts, or be unable to reach a decision while juries drawn from the dominant culture may deliver verdicts that fail to attract the confidence of the estranged group. Thus, community involvement in the administration of justice may actually prevent justice being done.

This is really part of a more general problem. Juries evolved within racial and normatively homogenous societies. Contemporary societies are no longer racially or culturally homogenous and now contain a plethora of values. How then can a jury represent community values? It cannot. How, if jurors' values are so different, can they engage in the shared deliberation that is necessary in order to reach a verdict? They cannot. How, if there is such a diversity of values, can jurors bring to their deliberations the common sense and knowledge of the customs and values of a neighborhood—the very things that affect a person's agency, and in virtue of which an action will be judged reasonable or not? They cannot.

Far from being the great palladium of individual liberties, as advocates maintain, the record of the jury tells a different story. There are many cases in which jurors have convicted in cases in which the prosecution was vindictive, politically motivated, or motivated by a desire to repress dissent. Further, repressive laws will simply not be put to the test before a jury, thus depriving the jury system of an opportunity to exercise its power to nullify odious laws.

In the jury room, jurors may be subjected to domination or bullying by other jurors. This subverts the deliberative process, the very justification for the jury. The solution often advocated is to abolish the jury and replace it with a body of people not so easily intimidated.

Finally, through strategic challenges to types of juror (Blacks, Whites, women, men, wealthy, or poor, depending on the case and defendant) or through the selection of a venue with a particular demographic profile, it is possible to "stack" the jury; that is, manipulate the composition of a jury to such an extent that it will favor the defense or the prosecution. If it is so easy to subvert a jury, so the argument goes, then juries ought to be abolished and a more reliable body created to carry out its functions.

No doubt individual juries at various times have warranted these criticisms. The issue, however, is whether these criticisms are generally sound. The criticisms are of two sorts: those resolved through empirical study and those resolved through philosophical argument.

J. The Empirical Arguments

The results of a number of detailed empirical studies, conducted over the past half century, have shown that in four cases out of five the jury and the judge reach the same conclusion. In the fifth case the differences in verdict are largely due to the jury and the judge sharing a different sense of justice, right, or equity. Problems in interpreting and understanding the evidence appear to be negligible; the strangeness of the court proceedings and surroundings, and intimidation by them or counsel, also seem to have little effect. As well, while in some very small number of cases sympathy may play a part in a decision, in general, juries seem fairly immune to it. In cases where sympathy has been at work, it is not at all clear that this should be problematic. To argue that is to assume that sympathy, mercy, and compassion are not morally appropriate responses for a jury. This is a mistake. It is true that there are occasions in ordinary life when it is morally right to make these responses. As well, one role of the jury is to do equity and right, by the lights of common sense morality. Therefore, on morally appropriate occasions, the juries ought to allow mercy, compassion, and sympathy to guide their deliberations. The fact that a jury does so is not a sign of incompetence but rather that it may in fact be doing its job.

As well, domination or bullying of a jury by fellow jurors is not problematic. It is a rare occurrence, usually corrected by the other jurors. In those rare cases when it is not, a mechanism could be provided whereby it is brought to light. For example, in some jurisdictions, after they deliver their verdict, jurors may be asked

individually whether they voted for the verdict; and after a verdict is delivered jurors often talk to the media. When such irregularities do appear they could provide a good grounds for a new trial, on the basis that the jury's deliberations had failed.

Jury selection is not problematic. Stacked juries, for example by race, gender, or ethnicity, can be eliminated by requiring juries to be broadly representative of the community, thus preventing juries being dominated by one single group. As well, choosing a venue advantageous to one side can be prohibited. More subtle attempts at injury tampering, through the use of "scientific" juror profiles and market research techniques to select the ideal juror and eliminate the least desirable ones, have been shown to be ineffective in general: with few exceptions, studies have shown that verdicts are much more likely to be influenced by the evidence and argument than the jurors' personal characteristics. Even so, in order to maintain community confidence in this institution, it may be prudent to prohibit the use of "scientific" juror profiles and market research techniques when selecting jurors.

Nor is it problematic that juries make mistakes. Judges make mistakes, too. Unlike an incompetent judge, who may make many mitakes over the course of a judicial career, a jury can do so only once, because a new jury is empanelled for each case. Further, in the very small number of cases in which a biased jury reaches a wrong verdict against a defendant, such miscarriages of justice easily can be remedied by appeal courts being more willing to overturn such verdicts. The initial criticism was that juries are more *systematically* incompetent than other possible ways of determining legal liability. The conclusion, on the evidence, is that in the vast majority of cases juries are competent. Therefore, these criticisms provide no reason to do away with the jury.

If juries and judges do agree so often, and the outcomes of the two types of trial are likely to be fairly similar, why persist with the jury when trials could be cheaper and quicker without them? It is the collateral advantages of jury conduct that maintain the justification for this institution. First, there are those cases when a jury acquits and a judge would convict. In such cases, when corruption has been excluded, the jury exercises one of its essential functions: the tailoring of a general law to the individual case, so as to avoid moral mischief. Second, the jury fosters community involvement, participation, and ownership in the administration of justice, and all that goes with it: accountability of the judiciary and the legislature to the people, trust and confidence in the administration of justice, and confidence in the verdict. Third, the jury is part of the system of checks and balances that go to preserve the liberties of citizens.

K. Reform and Democratization

While in the past juries may have been corrupt, the democratization of the jury has lessened this. Further protecting the juries from undue influence and developing better selection methods, such as requiring a minimum level of education and telling jurors what they can and cannot do, will enhance the performance of the jury still further. Ensuring that juries reflect the groups within a community will increase the credibility of their decisions and decrease the alienation of minority groups from the justice system. The solution then is not to abolish the jury but reform it.

Reforming the jury in these ways will remove that objection which says that juries are empanelled without reference to their merit—something which is opposed to the Anglo-American political tradition in which merit for public office is the basis of public service. The thought is that the skills that are required of a juror are the same required of any member of a community who interacts effectively with others. No especial expertise is needed, apart from a capacity to apprehend information, reason about it critically, and engage in shared deliberation. This can be tested well enough through requiring a certain minimum level of education and by pretrial examination by counsel. So, the traditional test for public service in the Anglo-American political tradition (namely, appointment on merit) would be met.

Reform, however, has not focused on measures that would assist the jury in deliberating better, but on the very areas where most caution needs to be exercised: jury size and majority verdicts. Smaller juries, which are used in some civil trials and occasionally in criminal trials, produce variations in verdict when tested against larger groups, typically of 12. The reason is that smaller juries are less representative of the variety of views found within the community. This, the evidence suggests, diminishes the capacity of a jury to deliberate effectively and so perform properly.

Majority verdicts are similarly problematic. A majority need not listen to the minority; it can be ignored, a verdict returned nevertheless, and in this way rigorous deliberation may be avoided. Unanimous verdicts, in contrast, require the majority to listen to the dissenters, in order to deal with their concerns and persuade them. All members of the jury must test and defend their interpretations of the evidence and their judgments. This is shared deliberation and it can only lead to a clearer understanding of the issues. Unanimous verdicts, therefore, promote the practice of shared deliberation that is the very heart of jury conduct. Moreover, it seems true that if 1 percent in 12 genuinely and sincerely doubts that a case has been made, then there may be a reasonable doubt as to the guilt of the accused. For this reason, unanimous verdicts provide a credibility to a conviction that majority verdicts cannot attain.

In order to ensure that jury conduct is such as to increase the quality of deliberation and accuracy of the verdict, in addition to the reforms mentioned already, it may well be prudent to ensure that no jury, criminal or civil, (a) falls below 10 people and then to that level only in relatively minor civil and criminal cases, and (b) to require unanimity at first and allow, reluctantly, a majority verdict only after some days of deliberation.

The democratization of the jury has had an important effect on jury conduct. In the past juries may not have been as staunch defenders of the community's liberties as proponents of this institution have suggested. Part of the reason was that juries were composed of men from propertied classes while the defendants were from various underclasses: the poor, the colored, or women. However, as democratization of the jury advanced, the likelihood increased that juries would return verdicts in favor of defendants who faced morally unjustifiable prosecutions. For example, in nineteenth-century Britain more than 20 offenses were punishable by death. Juries regularly convicted of lesser, noncapital offenses; or they refused to convict at all. More recently, the English civil servant Clive Ponting was acquitted by a jury when he was prosecuted by the British government for providing a member of Parliament with classified information about the controversial sinking of the Argentine cruiser *General Belgrano* during the Falklands conflict. As well, in trials involving mercy killers, victims of domestic violence and draft evaders, to name just some examples, juries frequently acquit or return guilty verdicts for lesser offenses.

L. The Philosophical Arguments

Juries face two major philosophical objections. First, jury conduct presumes that society is normatively homogenous. Modern society is not. Thus, juries lack a cultural basis upon which any justification must rest. The heart of this objection is that only a community that possesses common values—is normatively homogenous—can engage in the practice of shared deliberation, which is at the heart of jury conduct.

This is mistaken. No jury has ever had complete normative homogeneity: there has always been a plurality of values represented on juries. Nevertheless, amidst such diversity of values, jurors have, much more often than not, deliberated and reached decisions. The reason is that complete normative homogeneity is not required for shared deliberation. All that is required is that the deliberators have enough values in common so that deliberation can occur. In contemporary society, although there is a diversity of values there is also a common core of values held by the vast majority of society members and so shared deliberation is in general possible. Typically, these values concern what is reasonable, given the circumstances, and what sorts of actions are wrong and which ought to be punished. In any case, jurors who possess extreme or unconventional views are usually detected in the selection process and excluded from service. (Hung juries—juries that are incapable of reaching a shared decision—may be evidence of too much normative diversity. Hung juries, however, are relatively rare). That this is so easy to see: contemporary members of society identify and pursue many common goals. They do so without too much trouble: we do not see chaos about us everywhere, for example. Such deliberation over the goals to be pursued, collective action to attain them and coordination of individual action, would all be impossible unless there were some shared values that grounded the deliberation over the goals to be pursued, the proper means of attaining those goals, and the sorts of actions to be performed and those to be avoided. The conclusion is that the lack of complete normative homogeneity is not important: it does not prevent shared deliberation because the society shares enough values in common to make deliberation possible.

Nor does the level of normative diversity that happens to exist impede jury functioning. Jurors generally share enough core values in common to seed the deliberative process. Once seeded, shared deliberation will involve the jurors considering the evidence before them from a variety of views; that is, using the plurality of values found on the jury. This will yield a richer analysis of the case. So, far from undermining collective deliberation, a plurality of values can ground more effective shared deliberation. The fact that juries contain a plurality of values is not a weakness of juries, but a great strength of that institution and long thought to be so. Effective jury conduct is then a balancing act: ensuring a sufficient number of shared values to seed shared deliberation while also allowing sufficient diversity of other, noncore values, to promote this practice.

The arguments against the jury, based upon normative diversity ignore a fundamental democratic truth. It is one that juries through their conduct constantly

demonstrate: that a good sized committee of fair-minded people of diverse backgrounds is capable of deliberating and reaching a good and fair decision together that is unmatched in wisdom and quality by one person deliberating alone.

Second, jury conduct usurps the legislature. Their conduct puts them at war with the law. These objections misconceive the political status of the jury and its actions. Each jury is a small parliament that operates with the consent of the people, in the knowledge that, in appropriate cases the jury will bend the law and nullify its letter while maintaining the spirit of the legal tradition. The thought is that the law as framed may be too general and therefore apt to cause moral mischief if thoughtlessly and rigorously applied. It is a waste of legislative time to try to fashion specific laws: the process would be too time consuming, the result would be complex and difficult to implement; and in any case, no legislator and anticipate in advance all the nuances of human behavior that will affect the treatment that a person is justified in receiving. A specific response— rather like a decree—can be entrusted to a body with clear knowledge of the case and imbued with the mores of the community. In this view, the jury and the legislature have different functions: the legislature to form general laws; the jury to tailor the law to specific cases. Such activity does not then usurp the legislature, because laws are framed with the power of the jury in mind.

Moreover, the jury is part of the system of checks and balances that work together to make the system of government. As a totality this ensures that those with power over others, such as the judiciary, the legislature, the executive, exercise their power responsibly, accountably, and in the public interest. In such a system, the jury usurps the role of the legislature no more than the constitution or the common law; for these too have the capacity to declare any act of the legislature, executive, or judiciary to be contrary to the public interest, however that is embodied. In this analysis, the jury is simply an element in the system that ensures that the community is governed well without being governed tyrannically; it in no way usurps the *role* of the legislature but rather is one of the mechanisms that ensures that the legislature fulfills its allocated *function* in the system of government.

Nor is the power of the jury at war with the law. The jury exists within the system of laws as a mechanism empowered to identify appropriate exceptions to general laws and do equity and right by them. The jury can, then, administer any law not by its letter, but according to the spirit of the entire system. Moreover, when a jury nullifies a law it does so only in a specific case, while leaving the system intact, and the law, although nullified in this case, is still capable of being used on other appropriate occasions. Far from being at war with the law, the jury bolsters the administration of justice, by refusing to apply the law to inappropriate cases or an inappropriate law to a case that merits some sort of legal response.

What of the charge that the jury is opposed to the Anglo-American political tradition of openness and accountability? As we know, jury decisions are discussed after they have been delivered and in many cases jurors discuss publicly the process of deliberation within the jury room after the verdict has been given. It is true that to promote free and shared deliberation public opinion is not allowed to influence the deliberative process, hence the necessity to deliberate in secret. Nevertheless, public opinion after the verdict does operate as a check on jury conduct: all jurors know that their verdict will be scrutinized by their fellow community members. Moreover, while community members may disagree over the verdict, and this is to be expected in an open society, jurors will know that what will not be tolerated by the public is corrupt deliberation and that it is highly likely that such corruption will eventually emerge into the light of day. The facts that juries are subject to the gaze of the public, that their verdicts are open to discussion after the event, and that both the community and the juries know this, makes juries accountable and open and generates public trust and confidence in the institution. In this respect, jury conduct is similar to the conduct of a nation's cabinet. Ideally, that institution operates on the basis of shared deliberation; and the historical record shows that in democracies this is usually the case. Discussions are held in private. All members of the cabinet, like all jurors, are bound to keep the discussions confidential at the time. Eventually, the nature of the discussion makes it into the public domain and the community can judge. For this reason, jury conduct is not at all opposed to the Anglo-American political tradition of openness and accountability as practiced in the tradition of cabinet government.

This analogy should not be pushed too far and the major difference between juries and cabinets is to be found in the way in which the conduct of each is motivated. In democracies governments must maintain the confidence and trust of the electorate to remain in power. Threats of community sanction, through the withdrawal of confidence and trust, do have an effect upon policy formulation and implementation. It is unclear, however, whether it is the threats of community

sanction (or the threats of sanction from other jurors serving on a particular jury) that motivates a jurors' conscientiousness, diligence, and jury conduct in general. It is just as feasible and more likely that jury conduct is motivated by each juror's civic virtue and by the fact that they have promised to render a fair and true verdict. Community sanctions, to be sure, are always in the background, as a last resort, to motivate honest jury conduct. However, in sensational cases juries frequently provide verdicts that are opposed to public opinion. When questioned it becomes clear that the jurors were motivated to render a fair and true verdict rather than an expedient one. It is likely that juries in less sensational cases are similarly motivated. So, as they participate in the practice of shared deliberation it is unlikely that it is fear of community sanction or the sanction of their colleagues, that motivates a jury but rather each individual juror's desire to do what is right.

III. ETHICAL ISSUES IN JURY CONDUCT: THE OPERATION OF JURIES

The major ethical issue facing an individual jury concerns the basis upon which it makes its decision. This resolves into three questions: What ought a jury to be told about its powers? What ought a jury to consider? and Would jury conduct be enhanced if "professional" jurors were empanelled?

What ought a jury to be told about its powers? Overwhelmingly, judges believe that juries should not be told that they can convict on lesser offenses or decline to convict altogether. They fear that if juries know their powers the result will be chaos: juries will do what they want without reference to the evidence or the law. Jurors, when polled after they have served, overwhelmingly believe that they should be told.

The view of the judges is unsustainable. First, studies indicate that when juries are informed in general terms about their power to nullify the law there is little or no appreciable difference in their behavior. There is no rash of failures to convict in justifiable cases, as the judges fear; rather, cases that are the fitting object of jury mercy are more likely to receive it.

Second, given the role of jury is to do equity and right, and more generally to serve as guarantors of community liberties, then the jury must be aware that it can respond to the individual case and evaluate law as well as fact. To withhold this information is to deprive the jury of this power by preventing the jury from considering whether it ought to exercise some of the very functions that justify the institution.

What ought a jury to consider? The standard answer is only the evidence with which it has been provided. However, one justification for the jury is that it can bring to its deliberations 12 points of view from varying backgrounds, thus better ensuring the equitable and right decision. So, it is assumed in the very justification for the jury that the jurors will take into their deliberations various pieces of information about what is reasonable and what is not, and all this will assist them in their understanding. Should a jury consider the merits of the law too? Again, the answer is clear: given the fact that the jury must do equity and right and that it has a social and political function, it must at least consider whether this type of case is the sort that merits the full force of the law.

Ought a jury to seek further information? Certainly, if this will aid it in is determination of the facts. Such information may be additional testimony or it may be evidence as to the habitual nature of an offender. Such matters are best left to the discretion of the trial judge and cannot be subsumed under a general rule; although the presumption must be in favor of a jury knowing if it is likely that the information sought is going to assist the jury in its deliberations, without unduly prejudicing the defendant's right to a fair hearing.

Ought there to be "professional" jurors: members of the community who have been specially trained in the assessment of certain sorts of evidence and who may, on this basis, be selected for jury service repeatedly? The suggestion is that such jurors will enhance jury conduct by bolstering the practice of shared deliberation. The problem with professional jurors is that over time they would develop a familiarity with the court system. Far from being an advantage, such familiarity may retard shared deliberation. For example, a person with specialized knowledge may constrain the discussion—the other jurors may be lazy and simply accept the expert's opinion—and thereby prevent important avenues of deliberation from being fully explored. Moreover, such jurors would no longer be a "person in the street" but rather run the risk of being captured by the culture of the legal system and its biases—as lawyers are—such as dispositions to follow precedent or regard certain sorts of defendant as being more likely to have offended. Decisions may then be made not on the evidence and common sense, but on the basis of bias, preconceptions, and laziness. Thus, one of the motivations for the jury—shared deliberation by an impartial cross-section of the community, who have no

special axes to grind—would be defeated and there would be no point in having the jury.

Nevertheless, owing to the advances of science and the creativity of criminals, forensic testimony—such as DNA evidence—is being used more and is becoming more complex. Assessing such evidence is becoming harder, and the ordinary "person in the street" may well know little or nothing of such complex evidence. To this challenge several responses appear attractive. First, it may be worthwhile to brief jurors before a trial on the salient aspects of forensic science likely to be encountered. Second, jurors may be invited to ask questions about the nature of the tests, so as to bolster their understanding of the science and the evidence. Third, it may be necessary in some cases to require of jurors a higher level of education in order that they be eligible for jury service. In the end, however, the policies adopted to facilitate deliberation over complex testimony must be based upon empirical evidence of the effect of those policies on jury conduct. That the conduct of the jury must be enhanced by such changes, most particularly, that they can better engage in accurate shared deliberation, is the sole criterion by which the usefulness of such policies must be measured. Much work in this area needs to be done.

IV. CONCLUSION

While the right to a trial by jury has been retained for the most serious criminal cases, overall the use of the jury has been steadily declining. Many defendants who could elect to go before a jury decide to have their case heard by a judge: the likely penalty is usually lower, a decision is quicker. Further, as a result of legislative changes and the development of case law, many allegations, whether criminal or civil, can now only be heard before a judge or panel of judges. Given this drift away from the use of juries, does the jury have a future?

Juries, it has been suggested here, do serve important functions in the administration of justice, as well as socially and politically. Their importance will become all the greater as the power of governments increases, through the growth in their capacity to collect, collate, and share information on citizens—and to abuse that power. It seems worthwhile then, to reserve, at a minimum, all serious cases for consideration by a jury. Such cases would be those involving homicide, governmental corruption, treason, large-scale fraud, or any trial in which a person faces imprisonment for more than 12 months. It may be useful also to remit to juries other matters of public interest, such as allegations of abuse of administrative, legislative, and police powers and questions in coronial inquests. In such cases the jury serves not only as a regulatory mechanism on the activities of government but also as a test of credibility of the system of justice, as well as of individual decisions.

Moreover, the jury fosters a sense of community. It promotes a sense of ownership of the social infrastructure and engenders trust in, and compliance with, the social and political system. This is especially important in a world in which there is increasing alienation from the fabric of civil society, and a weakening of individuals' sense of membership and citizenship, what might be called civic engagement. Alexis de Tocqueville made this point well when he wrote, "Juries ... make all ... feel that they have duties toward society and that they take a share in its government. By making men pay attention to things other than their own affairs, they combat that individual selfishness which is like rust in society" (*Democracy in America*).

Finally, jury conduct is an element in that patchwork of protections that make up the system of checks and balances. As the capacity to abuse governmental power increases juries protect ordinary citizens from that power. It is, then, a palladium of community and individual liberty in an uncertain world. The conclusion to be drawn is that far from decreasing the use of the jury—as seems to be the trend—its unique nature, the way juries conduct their activities and the collateral advantages that flow from this institution and its conduct, speak instead to its more widespread use.

Acknowledgments

Jane Willmott, Peter Schouls, and Sir Hugh Williams discussed jury conduct with me. Their comments were very valuable and to them I am deeply appreciative.

Bibliography

The best recent discussions of the jury are:
Abramson, J. (1994). *We, the jury*. New York: Basic Books.
Hans, V. P., & Vidmar, N. (1986). *Judging the jury*. New York: Plenum Press.
Other discussions worth consulting are:
Cornish, W. R. (1968). *The Jury*. London: Allen Lane.
Devlin, P. (1956). *Trial by jury*. London: Stevens & Sons.
Forsyth, W. (1994). *History of Trial by Jury*. Law Book Exchange.
Kalven, H., & Zeisel, H. (1966). *The American jury*. Boston: Little Brown.
Williams, G. (1955). *The proof of guilt*. London: Stevens & Sons.

JUVENILE CRIME

Susan Dimock
York University

GLOSSARY

closed custody Incarceration in a locked institution, such as a juvenile penitentiary.

deterrence A purpose commonly attributed to punishment, whereby the threat of punishment prevents persons who would otherwise commit a crime from doing so.

juvenile crime Any unlawful criminal act committed by a person designated as a youthful, juvenile, or young offender under the criminal code of a legal jurisdiction.

open custody Incarceration in a nonlocked institution, such as a halfway house.

sentence The penalty imposed upon an offender after a verdict of guilty to a criminal charge has been rendered by a court of law.

JUVENILE CRIME is a topic that has come to increasing prominence in recent years throughout North America and parts of Europe. In the news media (both legitimate and tabloid varieties), in documentaries, in movies, and on television programs we are inundated with a vision of an increasingly violent youth population. Gang violence, murder, rape, organized theft, drive-by shootings, serious drug abuse, and more acts of criminal wrongdoing by young people, we are told, are on the rise at alarming rates. This mood of almost panic concerning youth crime has, not surprisingly, been met by demands from citizens' groups, victims' rights groups, and law enforcement agencies upon politicians to get tougher with young offenders. And these interest groups have been sufficiently effective both in producing near hysteria in the general population and in convincing the members of society that the cause of increased youth crime is the lenient laws governing the treatment of young offenders, that politicians in Canada, the United States, the United Kingdom, and many European jurisdictions have recently begun to make a get-tough policy on youth crime important parts of their national election platforms. This article questions the wisdom of that approach.

I. DEFINITION OF JUVENILE CRIME

For the purposes of this discussion we shall consider crime to be any act that contravenes the provisions found within the criminal law of a recognized jurisdiction. In confining our attention to breaches of a particular criminal code, we are focusing on those actions that a society deems most intolerable and for which it is willing to impose significant penalties. We also thereby rule out of our analysis any specifically "youth crimes," such as truancy; we are concerned with the question of how we should respond to serious crime committed by children.

The definition of a juvenile of the purposes of this study is more difficult to articulate, because different jurisdictions employ different classificatory schemes. A juvenile offender is defined by age, however, and not by the seriousness of his or her crime. Generally, the definition of a juvenile or young offender includes a minimum age, before which a child cannot be considered an offender and cannot be charged with a criminal offense. The age ranges between 10 in the United Kingdom and in some American states, to 12 in many other states and in Canada, to 15 in Sweden and Finland. The juvenile classification is also upper bounded, after which age a person accused of a crime is tried as an adult. Again, there is considerable variety in specifying the upper age of youth: from 16 or 17 in some jurisdictions, or in some places for the most serious of crimes, to the most standard age of 18 in many American states and in Canada, to 21 in some European countries.

Although there is considerable variation in the age during which time a person is considered a juvenile for the purposes of criminal law liability, the idea behind these classificatory schema is that very young children cannot properly be held legally accountable for actions that contravene the law, because they lack the intellectual and emotional maturity needed to form the requisite intent to violate the law and to know the nature and consequences of their actions.

As they approach adolescence, however, youths can be expected to gain sufficient emotional and cognitive capacities to exercise limited responsibility for their own actions; they acquire in this time the abilities both to appreciate the nature of what they do and the consequences of their actions, as well as the self-control needed to conform to the law. We do not assume, however, that these capacities are fully developed, and so we limit both the rights of adolescents and their responsibility under the law. We limit the legal rights and privileges of children because they lack the emotional and mental capacities to exercise them responsibly. In doing so, we also protect them from undertaking responsibilities that are beyond their capacities to fully understand or execute. Likewise, we recognize that their limited capacities also limit their culpability for wrongdoing. This fact is recognized in our making special provision for the treatment of juveniles who come into conflict with the criminal law. Unlike very young children, who are treated as wholly lacking responsibility for wrongdoing, juveniles are treated as having diminished responsibility, due to their intellectual and emotional immaturity.

II. IS JUVENILE CRIME REACHING CRISIS PROPORTIONS?

It order to assess the claims of those who advocate a tougher approach to juvenile crime, it is necessary to ask whether youth crime is, as they claim, rising at alarming rates. Clearly the level of youth crime varies significantly from jurisdiction to jurisdiction, as does its rate of increase or decrease. Thus, it is very difficult to answer general questions of the type posed in this section heading. It is certain, for example, that violent crimes committed by juveniles increased dramatically in some American states between 1985 and 1994, and have declined since 1995. This points to an important fact that must be kept in mind: trends in the volume of crime tend not to be steadily unidirectional, but to vary over time. By contrast with the U.S. experience, there is little evidence of an actual rise in violent crime among Canadian youths during the same time period.

The difficulty of assessing juvenile crime rates is exacerbated even within a given jurisdiction, however, because the principal indicators of crime—the number of crimes reported to police, the number of persons charged with crimes, and the number of persons sentenced at trial—may all rise or fall independently of actual crime rates. Thus, crime statistics can often be misleading if not analyzed in a way that is sensitive to extraneous changes. For example, crime may appear to be rising because there is less social tolerance of crime committed by youths. What would once have been treated as a schoolyard tussle and dealt with by school officials and parents may now be reported to police as an assault, thus increasing the level of reported crime. While such changes in social reporting practices have no doubt influenced the reported level of some less serious offenses, it seems unlikely to have influenced the reporting of violent offenses. The level of crime reported to police and resulting in the laying of charges has no doubt also increased over the past 15 years as our notion of crime has expanded; our perceptions of sexual assault, date rape, and domestic violence as crimes has increased the number of harms that are thought worthy of reporting to police and worthy of prosecution by law enforcement agencies; such changes would increase the indicators of crime although they may not reflect any actual change in the number of incidents being performed. Crime rates may also reflect a change in police charging practices. Activities that would once have received an informal reprimand and resulted in being driven home in a police cruiser may now result in charges being laid, in part in response to demands for tougher treatment of juvenile offenders. Thus, the very statistics that are used to demonstrate an increase in juvenile crime and upon which cries for tougher laws are based may themselves reflect that social pressure via police practices in charging youths. All of this is meant only to give those who demand harsher laws for the treatment of juvenile offenders pause in considering the severity of the problem for which they demand action.

It is also important to keep in mind that most juvenile offenders commit nonviolent crimes. By far the greatest percentage of young offenders who come to the attention of juvenile courts are charged with theft, breaking and entering, common assault (which results in no bodily harm to the victim), and violating prior court orders. The number of violent crimes committed by young persons is still relatively small.

This is not to deny that youth crime is a serious social problem, nor that it is a problem which is growing at alarming rates in some jurisdictions, especially in the United States. Nonetheless, it is clear that the fear of youth violence greatly exceeds its actual proportions, and any practicable proposals for dealing with juvenile crime must begin with facts, not fantasy.

III. LEGAL RESPONSES TO JUVENILE CRIME

Although different legal jurisdictions have developed different policies for the treatment of young offenders, I shall concentrate in what follows on general features that are for the most part shared across North American and European jurisdictions. It is widely recognized that, because of their youth, juvenile offenders ought to be treated differently than adult offenders. This is so not only because they have diminished capacities for conforming to the law, and so are thought to be less culpable for their wrongdoing, but also because they have special needs, again based on their immaturity. Furthermore, there is a reluctance to treat youthful transgressions of the law in such a way as to negatively impact the life-prospects of young offenders; a youthful mistake, even if serious, should not ruin a person's life. Accordingly, most European and common-law jurisdictions have established special provisions for the han-

dling of young offenders. These typically include a system of separate and specialized youth courts and correctional systems, a wide array of sentencing options—from closed or open custody to probation, compensation, restitution, community service, voluntary or involuntary treatment—as well as restrictions on the maximum penalties to which young offenders can be liable. The penalties to which young offenders are liable, except for perhaps the most serious violent crimes, which may be transferred to adult court, are substantially less than those to which adults who have been found guilty of committing the same offense are liable.

The specific systems that are in place for dealing with juvenile offenders are typically dominated by one of three models of criminal justice, or, as is often confusingly the case, by a combination thereof. These typically are referred to as the justice, welfare, or crime control models.

A. The Justice Model

Responses to crime that are dominated by the justice model emphasize the responsibility, accountability, and culpability of offenders. This view is associated with the traditional conception of punishment as "retributive," which holds that punishment is deserved by offenders just in virtue of their criminal wrongdoing. Sentencing in this view is to reflect a commitment to "just deserts," that is, to ensuring that sentences are proportional to the seriousness of the current offense and nothing else. Seriousness, in turn, is a function of two factors: the harmfulness/wrongfulness of the offense together with the culpability of the offender. The correct interpretation of both factors in determining the seriousness of offenses is a matter of dispute. What is clear in this view, however, is that sentencing should be based on the offense, rather than on the particular characteristics of the offender, except insofar as offender characteristics affect culpability. The special needs or difficult circumstances of any individual offender are considered irrelevant for the purposes of sentencing on the justice model. Likewise, this model treats as irrelevant the past criminal record of an offender, because it too is a characteristic of a particular offender and so is irrelevant to determining the offender's just deserts for the current offense.

While the justice model may seem out of place in dealing with juvenile offenders, given their diminished capacities and reduced culpability, the inclusion of considerations of justice in youth corrections has beneficial effects. In particular, it emphasizes protection of the rights of the individual, insists on due process, and restrains such arbitrary practices as indeterminate sentencing or the imposition of excessively harsh or punitive sentences for a relatively minor offense based upon the past behavior of the individual and for which the offender may already have been punished. It introduces a certain measure of uniformity and fairness into the trial and sentencing processes.

Notwithstanding these important benefits, the justice model as applied to juvenile crime has serious problems as well. In emphasizing the accountability and responsibility of offenders, it may simply be inapplicable to young offenders who lack the capacities for full responsibility. Furthermore, in treating as irrelevant the characteristics of particular offenders, it fails to tailor its response to the specific needs of any offender and so will find its recommendation at odds with those that are aimed at assisting young persons to conform to the law in the future through rehabilitation and training and counseling, which must be individualized.

B. The Child Welfare Model

The child welfare approach to youth crime prioritizes the needs and welfare of young persons above other considerations (such as desert, punishment, deterrence, and societal protection). In this model the corrections service ought not to treat the child as a criminal, but as misdirected and in need of aid and assistance. The pretrial and trial processes are designed to discover the particular causes of the offender's difficulties, be they cognitive or emotional problems of the youth or environmental factors, and to diagnose the offender's needs. Any sentence imposed is to be based on this diagnosis and aimed at rehabilitating the offender, and will be individualized to meet his or her specific needs and circumstances. Given the emphasis on rehabilitation, the specific offender characteristics are by far the most important element in determining the proper sentence, and outweigh even such considerations as the seriousness of the current offense. This allows a consideration of the offender's past criminal record.

While the welfare model of juvenile justice seems on the face of it humane and oriented toward the right goal—helping young persons live within the law—it faces serious theoretical and practical difficulties. In the first place, in eschewing punishment as a goal of corrections, it ignores the deterrent value of punishment. More importantly, it ignores society's right to be protected from crime. It also ignores the seriousness of the crime committed. Furthermore, the welfare model depends for its success upon the availability and success of various treatment and training programs. The record

of most rehabilitative programs is not encouraging. And in an age of increasingly diminished treatment programs and rehabilitative projects for young offenders, we cannot assume the availability of adequate resources to make this model workable in practice. Such an approach also leads to questionable legal practices: a lack of uniformity in dispositions or sentences, a trampling of due process rights, too much power being granted to social welfare authorities, indeterminate sentences, and enforced treatment.

In spite of these difficulties, it becomes clear when we examine the causes of youth crime and our response to it that we must keep the welfare of young offenders firmly in view and that rehabilitation must remain the central *raison d'etre* of our juvenile justice systems.

C. The Crime Control Model

In this model of juvenile justice the purpose of punishment is the protection of society, which is accomplished through deterrence and incapacitation. This model allows consideration of both the current offense and the characteristics of the offender to be used in determining sentence: the seriousness of the offense must be considered because more serious crimes must be deterred more vigorously than less serious ones and so require more frightful penalties, and those who commit more serious crimes need to be incapacitated more fully than those who commit less serious crimes; the court must also consider those offender characteristics that influence the likelihood that the offender will engage in future criminal activity and the seriousness of future offenses. Thus, the prior criminal record of the offender is relevant in considering the degree of incapacitation that is required for individual offenders.

In many ways the problem with this model of crime control parallels those that plague the deterrence model of punishment more generally. Most importantly, we know that punishment is not an effective deterrent of crime when the risk of being apprehended and punished is low; the best guess is that punishment is ineffective as a deterrent if the likelihood of being punished is below 30%. The reality is that most crimes, even the most serious, are not punished at this rate. This undercuts the effectiveness of punishments as a means of protecting society against crime. This problem is exacerbated at the level of juvenile justice, moreover, because of the wide range of sentencing discretion that judges enjoy in juvenile court systems, and because of the public perception, inflamed by those who want politicians to take a tougher stance on youth crime, that juveniles who commit even serious crimes often receive only negligible penalties. It might also be that the deterrent model is itself out of place when dealing with young offenders. For the deterrent model of punishment depends upon a potential offender calculating the benefits of crime weighed against the risk of punishment. Such calculations may exceed the deliberative and imaginative capacities of many adolescents. Even if punishment was an effective deterrent, however, this would not support what most advocates of the get-tough approach want, which is increasingly severe penalties. In principle the deterrent value of any penalty depends upon two factors: the severity of the penalty and the likelihood that it will be imposed. In reality we know that the severity of the penalty is significantly less important than the likelihood of being punished. This has been made painfully obvious in the United States, where recent increases in the severity of juvenile sentences, increases in the transfer of juvenile cases to adult court, and even the use of capital punishment against adolescent offenders has had no appreciable deterrent effect on the rising level of violent youth crime.

The model is not much more promising if one concentrates on the role of incapacitation rather than deterrence. Even if society is protected by the incapacitation of offenders, which need not be effected by closed custody, under the provisions of most juvenile justice systems the maximum sentence that an offender might serve is limited and so these offenders will be released back into society in relatively short order. Unless incapacitation has been supplemented with rehabilitation programs that can address the specific needs of the offender, society is not protected by the temporary incapacitation of dangerous youths. In the case of those who commit relatively minor and nonviolent offenses, there is evidence that strongly suggests that they will emerge from incapacitating custody with a higher likelihood of recidivism than they would if they have received adequate noncustodial attention in the first place. It would seem from all we know, in fact, that punishment alone does not protect society from crime; if that is our goal, then punishment must be combined with rehabilitation.

IV. THE LIMITS OF LAW

All of the foregoing has spoken to the role of law in responding to youth crime. This is a very limited picture, however, for the law is not the principal determinant of criminal behavior. Indeed, the law steps in only when children are already in trouble, when they have failed to live within the law. Such a reactive approach to the problem of juvenile crime must be seen as a second-best approach. If society is truly concerned about youth crime, then an analysis of the causes of crime must be the beginning of our search for solutions, rather than a reliance on law after all else has failed. Those on the political "right," who advocate the abolishment or severe restriction of special criminal provisions for youthful offenders, and an increase in the penalties to which youthful offenders can be liable, must come to recognize that it is not flexible, lenient, or even lax laws that produce child crime. Children do not engage in acts of violence because they know they will only receive a sentence of 3 years, rather than 15, if caught. On the other hand, those on the political "left," who insist that all children are victims and must be cared for and rehabilitated rather than punished must also attend to realities, both concerning the resources that are available for such humane purposes as well as their limited effectiveness, and not insist on the implementation of policies that deny adolescents all responsibility for themselves, as well as the rights that accompany such responsibility, and produce adults who never learn how to cease being children.

A. The Causes of Juvenile Crime

The sad fact is that we do not know what drives juveniles to crime. Or, rather, we know too much about what contributes to youth crime. Less paradoxically, there is no one single determinant of criminality among juveniles, and suggestions that *the* cause of escalating juvenile crime is separate criminal provisions for young offenders is as unrealistic as the claim that divorce is *the* cause of youth crime. In fact, the latter at least is a determinate, while the former is not. While we cannot identify any one factor as the cause of rising youth crime rates, we do however know much about the conditions that influence an adolescent's propensity to commit crime. The following factors are all, uncontroversially I believe, recognized as being positively correlated with juvenile crime: chronic familial difficulties, including spousal abuse among parents, parental separation and divorce, child abuse and neglect, family poverty, criminality of parents, parental or sibling substance abuse; personal substance abuse; multiple placements outside of the familial home; conduct, neurophysiological and cognitive disorders, especially those that interfere with success at school and peer relations; school dropout; low employment prospects; reductions in social services for children with special needs; lax gun control laws.

With the exception of the last item on this list, concerning gun control laws, the causes of juvenile crime cannot be addressed through legislative changes to criminal codes. They are social problems, and the rise of youth crime must be traced to the familial breakdown, familial abuse, poverty, inadequate life-prospects due to high unemployment (which is often made worse for members of marginalized groups in society), crime and substance abuse, which are increasingly characteristic of modern industrial society. These difficulties cannot be solved by putting our children into prisons. Rather, they require a substantial redirection of efforts and funds away from the corrections system toward the provision of adequate social, health, and educational services for all children in society, for counseling services for challenged youths and for their families, and for proactive interventions into the lives of high-risk youths. We need as societies to take collective responsibility for the growth and development of our children and adolescents.

V. CONCLUSION

Those who advocate stiffer penalties and tougher laws for dealing with the problem of youth crime will no doubt want to dismiss the suggestion made just above as unrealistic utopian claptrap. Yet we should not be so quick to dismiss this suggestion, for it is neither unrealistic nor utopian. We know that the earlier intervention into the lives of high-risk children occurs the greater is the chance of successfully directing them away from crime. We also know from the few successful rehabilitation programs that have been implemented that they depend upon taking a comprehensive approach to the factors that contribute to a particular individual's propensity to commit crime.

This suggestion may seem particularly unrealistic in a time of government cutbacks in virtually all social programs, including family support, education, health care, counseling services, special-needs services for children, unemployment insurance, and so on. In those cost-cutting measures, however, the costs of our correctional services virtually never get considered. The fact is that our criminal justice systems are very expensive. Police, courts, custodial, and noncustodial corrections services do not come cheaply. In 1992 and 1993, the Canadian criminal justice system cost $9.57 billion; youth corrections accounted for $488 million of that. It cost $237 per day to keep a young offender aged 16 or 17 in a secure custody facility; the cost for housing an offender in an open custody facility for the same age group was $167 per day. The annual costs in 1992 and 1993 were $86,505 for secure custody and $60,955 for open custody. The cost for those under the age of 16 is even higher (Canada, Ministry of Correctional Services).

Now it might be thought that this is the price we have to pay to contain violence and maintain an acceptable level of safety in our communities. But the fact is that more than three quarters of the young persons who are in custody in Canada have been sentenced for nonviolent offenses. It costs between $240 million and $267 million per year to keep those nonviolent offenders in custody in Canada (John Howard Society of Ontario Fact Sheet #6: Crime Control and Public Expenditure, September 1995). This situation is reproduced throughout North America and Europe.

It is neither unrealistic nor utopian to believe that public revenues can be better spent by providing the education, counseling, and social services needed to prevent crime in the first place. To effect the changes that would be required to significantly reduce juvenile crime would require a recommitment to children at all levels of society, however, and to providing the services that will enable them to lead productive and fulfilling lives within the limits of the law. While we cannot abolish the use of custody as a means of incapacitating dangerous members of society, young or not, our emphasis must shift away from the use of custody to the community-based, noncustodial programs that provide long-term support to children at risk and their families. We must tackle the causes of youth crime, rather than holding children responsible for actions performed under desperate circumstances and subjecting them to penal institutions and practices that we know produce greater criminality.

Also See the Following Articles

CHILDREN'S RIGHTS • CRIME AND SOCIETY

Bibliography

Allen, R. (1993). Responding to youth crime in Norway: Suggestions for England and Wales. *Howard Journal of Criminal Justice,* 32(3), 99–114.

American Psychological Association. (1993). *Report of the commission on youth and violence.* Washington DC: APA.

Bernard, T. (1992). *The cycle of juvenile justice.* New York: Oxford University Press.

Corrado, R. R., Bala, N., Linden, R., & LeBlanc, M. (Eds.). (1992). *Juvenile justice in Canada: A theoretical and analytical assessment.* Toronto: Butterworths.

Gendreau, P., et al. (1995). Does "punishing smarter" work? An assessment of the new generation of alternative sanctions in probation. *Forum on Corrections Research, 5,* 31–34.

Greenwood, P. W., Model, K. E., Rydell, C. P., & Chiesa, J. (1996). *Diverting children from a life of crime: Measuring costs and benefits.* Santa Monica, CA: The Rand Corporation.

Hyton, J. H. (Ed.). (1994, July). *Canadian Journal of Criminology: Special Edition on "The Young Offenders Act."* This edition contains many valuable articles; I am especially indebted to those by Peter J. Carrington and Sharon Moyer, and Nicholas Bala.

Krisberg, B., & Austin, J. F. (1993). *Reinventing juvenile justice.* Newbury Park, CA, London, and New Delhi: Sage Publications.

Palmer, T. (1992). *The re-emergence of correctional intervention.* Newbury Park, CA, London, and New Delhi: Sage Publications.

Thornton, W., & Voight, D. (1992). *Delinquency and justice.* New York: McGraw Hill.

Wiebush, R. E. (1993). Juvenile intensive supervision: The impact of felony offenders diverted from institutional placement. *Crime and Delinquency, 39,* 68–89.

KANTIANISM

Nelson Potter
University of Nebraska-Lincoln

GLOSSARY

autonomy Self-determination for individual moral agents. In Kant "autonomy" includes (a) the power to make one's own decisions; (b) the power for one's action to be motivated free of determination by alien desires, including those of the agent; (c) equality of rights in relation to others; contrasted with **heteronomy.**

categorical imperative A statement expressing a moral demand, either the most general moral demand of the "supreme principle of morality," or a specific demand, such as "Do not make lying promises." These moral demands are called "categorical" because the demands they express are not conditional upon any of the agent's personal wishes or desires. They are contrasted with nonmoral demands, called "hypothetical imperatives" (q.v.).

deontological vs. teleological ethics Two contrasting families or sorts of ethical theories. Deontological theories take as basic moral terms "ought," "duty," "right," "wrong," "forbidden," "required," and so on. Teleological theories take as basic another group of moral terms, including "good," "desirable," "end or goal."

duties to oneself Extrasocial duties that relate to one's self-respect, and to the maintenance and development of one's powers as a moral agent. Kant, unlike many other moral theorists, emphasizes the importance of such duties.

hypothetical imperative Hypothetical imperatives are nonmoral demands that express means–end relationships, such as "If you want to avoid an infection, then apply an antiseptic to all cuts." The if clause refers to a desire or wish that, if one had it, would motivate one to act on the "then" clause. Because hypothetical imperatives are only "valid" for individuals who are motivated by the desire mentioned in the if clause, they do not express moral demands, which are, in contrast, not conditional in this way, and are hence expressed by "categorical imperatives" (q.v.).

maxim For an agent to make a decision to act is for her to adopt a "maxim," in Kant's terminology, which gives a general description of the proposed action, as a means to the agent's goal.

respect for persons A basic idea of Kantian ethics; the requirement that we regard each person, including oneself (see "duties to oneself," above), as possessing inherent dignity and infinite worth, and concludes that we must limit the pursuit of our own goals when such pursuit would violate these rights.

universalization According to Kant, to test our actions morally, we should perform the thought experiment of "willing the maxim of our action as a universal law." To do this is to imagine that *everyone* chooses to perform the same action we are considering, when they were in similar circumstances. When we "could not will" the results of such universalizing, the proposed actions must be rejected as contrary to morality. See the discussion of the lying promise and the duty of aiding others (under "positive duties to others"), below.

KANTIANISM is an approach to moral questions that finds actions to be right or wrong, because (1) they respect or fail to respect the inherent dignity of (human) persons, including the agent, who are affected by the action, or because (2) of formal considerations such as an action's being unfair because we could not allow everyone the same authorization to perform it. Both kinds of considerations, neither of which directly relate to either beneficial or harmful consequences of the action, are thought by Kant to be equivalent and coextensive rationales.

I. THE HISTORICAL KANT

Kantianism is an approach to moral questions that has its origin in the writings on moral philosophy by the German philosopher Immanuel Kant (1724–1804). Kant's ideas about morality have been immensely influential since he published them, chiefly in his works *Groundwork of the Metaphysics of Morals* (1785), *Critique of Practical Reason* (1787), and *Metaphysics of Morals* (1797–1798).

A. The Categorical Imperative and the Hypothetical Imperative

One of the leading ideas of Kant's moral philosophy is that moral demands are expressed as *categorical imperatives,* such as "Do not tell lies," or "Develop your talents." These are contrasted with nonmoral (e.g., merely prudential) demands, such as, "If you wish not to gain weight, eat only low-fat foods," or "If you wish to read a good detective story, you ought to read one by Conan Doyle." Such nonmoral demands are called "hypothetical imperatives," because the "if" clause in each one mentions a condition, which is a desire one might or might not have, and the other part of the imperative mentions a means for satisfying this desire. We would be moved to act on such hypothetical imperatives only if we had the desire mentioned in the "if" clause. These hypothetical imperatives, because they merely inform us how to satisfy desires we already have, are nonmoral in character.

In contrast, categorical imperatives are *unconditional* in their demands: "No matter what your personal desires or preferences, you are morally obliged to refrain from lying." This unconditional character is an aspect of both the rationale for claiming that we have a moral duty, and of the moral motive that ought to move the agent to perform the duty. The only morally good actions are actions motivated by the only moral motive, the motive of duty; such a motive is a motivational source of actions that is distinct from any merely personal desire or preference. We all have the power to act from such a purely moral motive, Kant believes, and we must both determine what our obligations are and then act to fulfill them independently of any concern for merely personal desire fulfillment. To do one's duty from such a moral motivation is to act "from duty" rather than merely "in accord with duty."

B. Teleological versus Deontological Moral Theories

When we act for the sake of accomplishing some personal goal, our actions are chosen for teleological reasons, that is, because of the ends or goals that such actions would help to bring about. For example, when one is thirsty, she may seek out a water fountain to obtain a thirst-quenching drink. A teleological moral theory chooses actions based on the ends or goals that the acts can help bring about; in such a theory terms such as "good," "end or goal," and "desirable" are the primary conceptions. A deontological moral theory, in contrast, determines moral obligations without reference to any such personal ends: "Lying is wrong, regardless of how personally advantageous, or even beneficial to others it may be to lie." In such a theory terms such as "duty," "forbidden," "obligatory," said of actions, are the primary conceptions. Kant's moral theory is usually seen as a clearly deontological moral theory.

C. Different Formulations of the Categorical Imperative

Kant presents several different formulations of what he calls *the* categorical imperative, the "supreme principle of morality," and describes these different formulations as equivalent. We will here mention the three formulations that are most important for deriving particular duties. We will not be able to discuss the complex scholarly topic of how these formulations are related, and whether Kant's claim of equivalence can be defended. The different ideas mentioned in each formulation are identified with Kant and his moral tradition.

1. The First Formulation

(1) What is often called "the first formulation of the categorical imperative" is: "Act only on that maxim that you can will at the same time as a universal law" (G. IV, 421). Maxims are statements of personal intentions; to formulate an agent's maxim, we thus describe a (proposed) action as the agent herself thinks of it, for example, in relation to the agent's intentions and goals.

2. The Lying Promise Example

To give one of Kant's own examples, "When I believe myself to be in need of money, I will borrow money and promise to pay it back, although I know that I can never do so" (G, IV, 422). Can such a maxim of making a lying promise be "willed as a universal law"? Kant says that it cannot because if everyone in similar circumstances made such lying promises, it would become known that such promises were unreliable, and then such promises would no longer be effective in getting one the money one wishes for. Lying promises succeed in getting money only because others are being honest; the liar's actions are thus parasitic upon those of honest people. If everyone lied, no one could successfully accomplish the goal of getting the money he needed *through* such a lie.

Here, the universal practice of making lying promises defeats the aim of the individual lying promisor; hence, Kant says, such a maxim produces a "contradiction in conception," which means that the agent's end is inevitably defeated. This contrasts with the "contradiction in the will" that is illustrated by our failure to render assistance to others, an example discussed below, under "Positive Duties to Others."

3. A Principle of Justice or Fairness

Thus we see that this "universal law" version of the categorical imperative is a moral principle of justice or fairness. It tells us that we may not do things that we could not allow everyone else similarly situated also to do. We may not permit ourselves special moral privileges, or make ourselves arbitrary exceptions to general moral rules.

4. Theft

Another important application of this "universal law" principle concerns theft. One may steal a television receiver from its rightful owner in order to have the use of it, or to have the benefit of the cash obtained from selling it. But if such an action were right, it would also be right to steal from the stealer; but such theft would defeat the purpose of the stealer, which is to have the benefits of possession for himself. Thus, if we imagine theft being practiced universally, it would tend to be a self-defeating activity, and hence it is an action that "could not be willed as a universal law." (Sometimes such points are put as follows: Theft undermines the institution of property; lying undermines the institution of truth-telling. The difficulty with this way of putting the point, aside from the fact that Kant makes no mention of "institutions," is that actions *intended* to undermine such institutions may be morally unobjectionable, because such actions would not be self-defeating.)

5. The Second Formulation

(2) The "second formulation" of the categorical imperative is one that requires respect for persons, or, as Kant puts it, treating all persons, including ourselves, as "ends-in-themselves." As he also puts the point, to violate this principle is to treat the person in question "merely as a means." For example, any act of intentional deception (including the lying promise discussed above) entails a disregard for the person deceived, whose personhood is not being respected because he is being left out of consideration by the deception. The deceived one cannot possibly share the deceiver's motive; in contrast, a benevolent person can sympathetically share the goal of the person he is assisting. Similarly, Kant urges, if someone neglects to develop his own talents, because he prefers to live at ease rather than engaging in the strenuous work needed for such self-development, then he is "using" his own self, his personhood, simply as a means to his personal end of relaxing and enjoying life. This means that such a person is disregarding the higher moral purposes that, in virtue of his personhood, are appropriate for his life, including having the capability of acting to benefit others. For example, medical training is strenuous, complicated, and demanding, but an agent who has such training will be a better position to be helpful to those around her. Hence, after leaving aside the expected benefits to oneself of being able to expect to receive a higher income as a medical doctor than as an unskilled laborer, there are also moral reasons for undertaking such a strenuous training, namely, that after such training one would be able to benefit others to a greater degree.

6. The Third Formulation: Two Versions

(3) A third version of the categorical imperative is variously stated by Kant to be a principle of *autonomy* or to be the idea of being simultaneously a legislator and a subject in an abstract ideal society, the "kingdom of ends." Some interpreters regard these as two distinct formulations. Autonomy or self-determination has both

internal and external (social, interpersonal) aspects; it also can be regarded as (intellectual) self-determination in making one's own judgments and decisions, or as motivational self-determination, which in Kant's view means allowing reasons instead of emotions or desires to become the motives of one's actions. Many other writers make important use of the idea of autonomy; sometimes these uses refer to Kant, and sometimes they do not. One needs to be alert to different meanings of this term as used by different writers. The "kingdom of ends" is an abstract ideal of a society in which each member makes universal laws for all subjects to follow, and in which each member is also a subject, constrained to obey such laws. This idea of the kingdom of ends thus combines elements of Kant's first two formulations of the categorical imperative—the idea of each rational will making universal (moral) legislation, and the idea of individual members as ends-in-themselves. It is also a sort of abstract model of the form of state Kant preferred: a republican government, with each individual functioning variously as citizen, sovereign, and subject, and equal to every other individual.

D. Good Motives for Action

There are also other aspects of Kant's ethics that are influential, but that relate less directly to applied ethics. Kant insists that the morally good person would not merely do what is right, but would do what is right from the proper motive. This proper motive is called by Kant the motive of duty, which means that the reasons that justify the action as morally required are also the motivating reasons for doing the action. This rules out as lacking in moral goodness extraneous motives, as when one publicly gives to charity for the sole aim of achieving a favorable reputation as a generous person. Kant also has a complex metaphysical theory of freedom, and is well known for his "moral proofs" of immortality of the soul and of the existence of God.

E. Political/Social Applications

The social and political ideals of universal political equality and self-determination and human rights are central to Kant's political and social philosophy. This makes him a central figure of the eighteenth-century movement called "the Enlightenment." Kant, whose views were very much influenced by Rousseau, was also close to the republican political ideals of the French revolution, namely, the equal rights to participation in the state of all citizens, and the rejection of heritary class privileges.

F. The Rationale for Punishment

Among other influential aspects of Kant's moral philosophy is his discussion of punishment. He has seemed to most readers to be a paradigm of a harsh retributivist, and he explicitly defended the *lex talionis* (law of retaliation). The retributivist says that punishment is to be justified not by the future benefits that result from the punishment, such as deterrence of others from committing similar crimes, or by the reform of the person punished, or even by the pleasure of those who see the punishment as a vindication of the law and an authoritative condemnation of the wrongful act. It is rather to be justified simply as an appropriate response to wrongdoing, a response in kind, a retaliation, as in the Biblical statement of "an eye for an eye, a tooth for a tooth, a life for a life." Based on this approach, for example, Kant favored capital punishment for the crime of murder. Such an approach to the justification of punishment seems natural for a deontologist such as Kant, who refuses to measure beneficial and harmful consequences in determining right or wrong, but who rather looks to inherent characteristics of actions. Such a retributive justification for punishment is entirely backward looking to the nature of the action whose commission is to be punished, rather than forward looking to the beneficial consequences that may be thought to result from the punishment, in particular the deterring of others from similar antisocial actions, because of their fear of similar punishment.

G. Punishment and Deterrence

In spite of this portrayal of Kant as a pure retributivist, he was concerned with the role of deterrence produced by punishment in assuring order and hence the guarantee of personal and property rights within the state. And he is in addition clearly concerned that the person punished not be abused in such a way as to cause his humanity to be held in contempt; for this reason he was opposed to torture executions.

H. A Gross Misinterpretation

Sometimes Kant's ethics is grossly misinterpreted as a theory that requires unconditional and unquestioning obedience of political authority. Such an interpretation regards the "categorical imperative" as an order from a political authority. Such an interpretation is sometimes presented as a part of German cultural history that helped prepare the way for the unquestioning obedience to all orders that was required by the Nazi regime (1933–1945) in Germany.

I. Kant's True Ideals: Autonomy

But Kant clearly believes in the self-determination of all individuals, and favors republicanism in politics—the fundamental equality of all citizens. And the categorical imperative refers not to external orders from a military or police commander, but to the inner demands that morality makes upon each of us as moral persons. Kant urges that it is only when we act upon the moral demands that we subject ourselves to that we are truly self-determining or "autonomous." In contrast, to act for the sake of desire fulfillment, is to be merely reacting to alien forces impinging upon us (viz., our desires), and hence such actions are described by Kant as "heteronomous." (Note, however, that actions in pursuit of such personal ends are not wrong, unless they have us acting against a competing moral imperative.) It has even been urged by one recent writer writing in a Kantian spirit (Robert Paul Wolff) that the most natural political philosophy for a Kantian ethical theory, with its emphasis on autonomy, is anarchism—the denial of the moral authority of any political orders that could be imposed from outside the agent.

J. Positive Duties to Others

Kant believed that our duties to others included not just negative duties of abstaining from deception, and, in many cases, coercion, but also positive duties to promote the welfare of others, and to seek to benefit their lives. Thus actions of mutual aid, of good samaritanism, and, more broadly, of beneficence, are part of our duties of respect for the persons of others. In Kant's late work on moral philosophy, he makes a distinction among duties to others, between duties of love and duties of respect. The former, more positive duties, when carried out, create an obligation of gratitude, while the latter, by which we recognize the respect we owe another, do not (MS, VI, 448–450). The rationale presented for such duties in the discussion of the fourth example in the *Groundwork* was that although there is no contradiction involved in one person willing that she never undertake to render assistance to another, we would find it impossible to accept the implications of such a universal practice, i.e., we "could not will" the universalization of such a maxim of nonassistance. This is because we are limited, finite beings, and it is always possible that we might be in need of such assistance ourselves. To will a universal maxim of nonassis-

tance would be to deny ourselves such assistance should such a need arise, and given the demanding nature of our needs, we could not accept such an outcome; that is, we could not help but want help.

Notice that such a rationale for being a Good Samaritan is different from a similar sounding prudential argument that seeks to show that it is to our advantage to render aid to other. This argument claims that if we do not help others when they are in need, they will be unwilling to help us when we are the ones in need. The moral argument in contrast makes no such estimate of likelihood of receiving help; it rather urges that if we could not help but want help when in need ourselves, then in fairness we must take a similar attitude toward similar needs in others, and render assistance.

K. Duties to Oneself

Another special feature of Kantian ethics was his emphasis on extrasocial moral duties, called duties to oneself. These include the duty to abstain from suicide, from gluttony and drunkeness, and avarice, and servility, and to develop one's talents. Interestingly, lying is sometimes treated by Kant as fundamentally a violation of a duty *to oneself,* rather than as a violation of a duty to others. Violations of duties to oneself are all treated as violations of the inner moral self-respect or integrity without which morality has no firm hold on any moral agent.

L. Can There Be Exceptions?

Kant seems to have thought that at least some moral rules, such as "Do not lie" are completely without exceptions. Thus he argued that if a demented person comes to your door asking after a person you know to be hiding in your house, with the intention of murdering him, it would be wrong to lie to this person. This position has seemed to many to be wrong, and not to be required by the logic of the general Kantian position. It is sometimes urged that such "exceptions" to the general rule against lying mark off a *class* of cases that could be described in an agent's moral maxim. If this is right, then lying in such cases need not be a mere arbitrary exception in the name of self-interest, which is how Kant generally thinks of wrongful action.

II. THE GENERAL CHARACTER OF KANTIAN ETHICS

The Kantian approach to answering questions of moral right and wrong today is most often contrasted with the alternative approach of utilitarianism, or more broadly, consequentialism, which assesses actions based on their beneficial and/or harmful consequences for all affected by the action. The characteristics of the Kantian approach include not attending to beneficial or harmful consequences, hence a nonteleological approach. Kantianism is strongly opposed to deception as incompatible with respect for persons, even if it should be on balance the most beneficial action possible in the circumstances. Coercion is limited to those cases that are compatible with respect for persons, such as emergency aid to crime victims, penal punishment, and so on. Coercion must be limited to that which helps to protect the rightful freedom of others.

A. The Role of Consequences

The common mark of Kantian thinking in applied ethics is the omission of the consideration of consequences, whether they affect oneself or others, and the attention to the inherent character of moral actions, including formal considerations of fairness. (Because of this emphasis, Kant's ethical theory is sometimes described as "formalistic.") For example, the Kantian rationale against lying would not mention that if you lie, people will come to mistrust you (a bad consequence), nor that you will spread abroad in the society such mistrust as would be harmful to the continued smooth functioning of the society (another bad consequence), nor that you will suffer if your lie is discovered, nor that others (e.g., who are expecting the repayment of a loan) may be harmed (also bad consequences); the Kantian rationale rather mentions the wrongness of lying apart from its consequences, and its essential unfairness, because the liar's success in achieving his aim is parasitic on the trust that has been produced by the truthful behavior of others. The retributive justification of punishment is responsive only to the character of the act being punished, rather than to the beneficial deterrent effects or lack thereof from engaging in such punishing. The Kantian moral stance against lying or for punishment in a given case may seem more "absolutist" or moralistic because it is less responsive to particular circumstances. Certain cases of lying may seem to be *on the whole, and all things considered,* beneficial, and therefore are to be recommended according to a consequentialist theory, as an exception to the general moral rule against lying, whereas a Kantian approach to the issue may not permit such exceptions. Notoriously, it has seemed to some that consequentialists could justify punishing an innocent person (because beneficial deterrent effects would be equally great so long as it was generally *believed*

that the person punished was guilty), but the Kantian approach would presumably reject such an action, regardless of beneficial consequences. For these reasons Kantian ethics is sometimes contrasted with "situation ethics."

On the other hand, Kantian respect for persons would often require us to consider how actions are likely to affect individuals. Actions harmful to persons, whether oneself or others, and particularly actions lowering one's rational powers would likely be wrong on Kantian grounds for those reasons.

B. Respect for Persons

The Kantian commitment to respect for persons makes it a good and helpful framework for understanding the ethics of various professional relations, such as attorney/client, and doctor/patient. For example, sometimes it may seem beneficial on the whole to withhold the dire truth from patients about their terminal illnesses, but such denial of the truth would be a failure to respect the patient as a person, and therefore would most likely be argued against from a Kantian approach. Such a withholding of information would deny the patient the right to make his own decisions in full knowledge of his situation, and hence would be a denial of Kantian autonomy. Respect for persons also requires a proper self-respect, and would be critical of the moral and self-regarding fault of servility, which is a failure to stand up for one's rights and prerogatives as a human being (see Thomas Hill's well-known "Servility and Self-Respect").

C. A Hard Case

Kant himself took the position (in a late paper) that even when a demented person asks you where his intended murder victim is, you should not lie to such a person, an example that is often updated to claim that one should not lie even to a member of the Gestapo when he asks where certain Jews (whose location you know) are to be found. To many this seems an extreme and indefensible position, and it has been maintained that such an extreme position is not a necessary outcome of the Kantian approach, which arguably allows of certain classes of exceptions to general moral rules, especially when the goal is as urgent as the protection of a human life, and the person who might be lied to or misled clearly has no right to know the whereabouts of his intended victim. The status of such exceptions remains a difficult and controversial issue of Kant interpretation.

D. Opposed Theories May Lead to Same Conclusion

Sometimes the consequentialist and the Kantian may argue for the same moral conclusion, but arrive at such a conclusion by a somewhat different route. For example, both theoretical approaches conclude that urgent attention needs to be given to human suffering, such as that involved in famines and wars. But the central point in reaching such a conclusion for the Kantian is respect for the persons adversely affected, whereas the central point in reaching such a conclusion for the consequentialist is the minimization of pain and the maximization of pleasure or happiness.

E. Hare and Singer: Describing Actions

Kant has been an explicit influence on a number of writers in ethical theory in the second half of the twentieth century. R. M. Hare and Marcus Singer have developed versions of generalized or universalized utilitarianism that were influenced by Kant. For both an action is right or wrong depending on whether the consequences of all instances of the action as described are better or worse than alternative actions (and action descriptions) open to the agent. Both of these theories may have a problem with finding a unique correct description of an action for the purposes of moral evaluation, and sometimes this is also said to be a problem for Kant's ethics as well. The same action (e.g., "telling a lie about intentions to repay a loan, in order to get the money one needs") may be described overly broadly ("making a statement"), or in too detailed a way ("a lie told by a 34-year-old left-handed, red-haired women on a Tuesday afternoon at 2 p.m. in order to obtain loan proceeds of exactly $873"). Such an action may be wrong according to the first description, but not wrong according to the other two descriptions, because, depending on the description, the class of actions whose consequences are considered will be different in each case.

Kant himself has no explicit discussion of this problem, probably because in his view the agent's original choice is expressed in what he calls a *maxim,* which describes the agent's chosen action as if it were the adoption of a general policy of action. In the maxim the intended action is described as a means to the agent's goal, and this constraint on the description of the action is arguably sufficient to determine how the action should be described for the purposes of moral evaluation.

Gewirth and Donegan present more formalistic, rationalistic theories of ethics, which may also be described as "Kantian."

F. Rawls on Justice

John Rawls, in his well-known book *A Theory of Justice* (1971), develops a theory that corresponds mainly to that part of Kant's moral philosophy described as *Recht* (right, law), in presenting a theory of social justice. The first principle of justice for Rawls, although it has relations to Kant's universal law formulation of the categorical imperative, is even closer to Kant's description of the first principle of *Recht*: "[E]ach person is to have an equal right to the most extensive basic liberty compatible with a similar liberty for all" (TJ, p. 60; cf. Kant, MS, VI, 231). As stated this is a principle of basic social equality of rights, although how it is to be interpreted with respect to economic equality, and whether it extends beyond what may be called equality of opportunity, are matters of debate.

G. Respect for Persons

The Kantian idea of respect for persons is widely influential as a framework to use for understanding the ethical dimensions of professional relationships, such as doctor–patient, attorney–client, police–citizen, or social worker–citizen. Because it embodies the idea of a plurality of self-determining individuals in relations that presuppose certain inviolable rights, it is likely to provide a reliable understanding of relevant frameworks of rights within which important social transactions can occur.

Also See the Following Articles

Bibliography

Kant, I. *Gesammelte schriften.* Edited by the Prussian Academy of Sciences. This now standard edition of Kant's works includes his published work in the first nine volumes, in the original German (or in a few cases Latin). The standard practice for giving references is to give the Akademie pagination (except for the *Critique of pure reason,* where pagination from the first or second editions is used). Most English translations also include the Akademie pagination. Among excellent translations of major works are those by H. J. Paton of the *Groundwork of the metaphysics of morals,* and by Mary Gregor of the *Metaphysics of morals.*

Herman, B. (1992). *The practice of moral judgment.* Cambridge: Harvard University Press.

Hill, T., Servility and Self-Respect. much reprinted.

O'Neill, O. (1985). *Faces of hunger.* London: George Allen and Unwin.

Rawls, J. (1971). *A theory of justice.* Cambridge: Harvard University Press.

Singer, M. (1961). *Generalization in ethics.* New York: Alfred A. Knopf.

LAND USE ISSUES

Douglas Baker and Annie Booth
University of Northern British Columbia

GLOSSARY

bioregionalism Human interaction with a landscape that observes the physical, biological, and cultural characteristics that define specific landscapes.

ecology The study of the relationships among organisms and between organisms and their environment.

paradigm A system of beliefs and observations that characterize a particular theory or social movement.

property rights The fact of having an enforceable claim to the use or benefit of something. Property rights specify both the proper relationships among people with respect to the use of things and the penalties for violating those relationships.

sustainable development Development that meets the needs of the present without compromising the ability of future generations to meet their own needs.

LAND USE ETHICS are derived from people's and cultures' perceptions of land, land use, land as property, and property rights. Land use ethics, then, are embedded within socially defined cultural and geographical landscapes, both historically and currently, but these are constantly changing landscapes that are defined by new ways and changing values. Different claims to land and the "proper" use of land are often based in different philosophical justifications of the rights to property. Land use ethics are founded in these justifications. Often, how we define our right to a resource will affect the structure of property rights that is put in place. Thus, the way in which a right is justified can affect the way in which it is articulated and defended. Different normative approaches that define the right to property also form the basis of land use ethics. What is deemed ethical with respect to how the land is used is justified according to the individual's or society's perceived right to property.

Land use ethics can be viewed in the context of property rights and how individuals justify their right to property. The dominant property rights paradigms that form the bases of land use ethics in Western societies provide an overview of different ethical foundations. The land use ethic that people subscribe to (or not) is inherently tied to how they justify their right to property.

I. LAND USE ETHICS AND PROPERTY RIGHTS

The most basic definition of a land ethic is an individual's or a society's personal relationship with the land. In this definition, the ethic is value-neutral; it can range across a spectrum of "good" to "bad" according to individual judgment. It also may vary depending on time and circumstances. Large-scale deforestation, for example, might be acceptable if you know that on the other side of the mountain and onto the next mountain the forest is ecologically intact. If you know that the other side of the mountain and the mountain after have also been subject to massive logging, your decision to log might now be ethically wrong if you, or your society, value ecological soundness. Thus any number of ethical approaches to the land can be described by the term "land ethics."

However, for many people the term "land ethics" implies a positive relationship with the land, positive in the sense that the land is neither ecologically or aesthetically injured by human activity. Again this is a very general definition, but most resource managers or environmentalists use the definition drawn up by one the first writers to specifically address the concept of land ethics, Aldo Leopold. A forester and wildlife biologist as well as a fine writer, Aldo Leopold's essay, "The Land Ethic," received relatively little attention upon its posthumous publication in 1949. Since the 1960s and 1970s, however, "The Land Ethic" has been recognized as a vital vehicle for increasing our understanding of more appropriate human–land relations. "The Land Ethic" remains today a key definition of an applied ethic that suggests how the policy makers and ordinary land owners and managers must change to take into account different values, "ethics" if you will, of the land and its human and nonhuman elements. How individuals evaluate whether an action on the landscape is "good" or "bad" varies considerably. There is no standard ethic that dictates a set of suitable actions to all people.

Shrader-Frechette suggests that there are four different land ethics that have emerged as proposed solutions to environmental crises (1987. *Environment Professional*, 9, 121–132). The generic categories she uses are:

1. Land reform ethics that have evolved as a result of inequitable distributions of property
2. Land use ethics that define a moral code to control spillover impacts of air and water pollution
3. Land community ethics that respond to environmental degradation by enlarging the moral community to include plants, animals, and all the components of the biosphere
4. Land rights ethics which question the traditional legal standing of land and propose to extend it beyond an anthropocentric realm to extending rights to all members of the biotic community, such as trees and soil

What these land ethics have in common is the concept of property rights. One of the primary foundations of people's ethical behavior with respect to the environment is derived from the individual's perception of his or her right to resources. How people articulate their rights to resources and how they respond to their right is based upon different philosophical justifications. The justification of the right to property forms the foundation of the ethical relationship that the individual has with that resource base. Thus, different justifications of property have different ethical relationships with respect to the use of the property. A person's relationship with their environment is dependent on how they perceive their rights to property and how anyone or thing may be affected by that right.

A. What Are Property Rights?

Property rights are commonly identified as a right to own or possess something, such as land or an automobile, and to be able to dispose of it as one chooses. However, this is only one aspect of property rights that focuses on the exclusive right to ownership. To have a right to property is also to have an enforceable claim to the use or benefit of something; the concept of a property right distinguishes between momentary use or possession of something and a claim to the thing which will be enforced by society or the state. For example, the claim can be in the form of a license or lease to common property that gives the individual exclusive rights to secure a portion of that property, such as a through a fishing license. So, property rights distinguish not only exclusive ownership of private property, but also rights shared and observed with others in common property. Property rights specify both the proper relationships among people with respect to the use of things and the penalties for violating those relationships. Property rights are often referred to in the literature as a bundle of rights, in which ownership is distributed in a variety of ways.

Bundles of rights confer certain opportunity sets for the individual. The opportunity set defines the various lines of action open to the holder of the bundle. As well, the relative capacity of the individual to make use of the rights is important in defining their opportunity set. The available resources, technology, and knowledge determine the extent to which a person can exercise his or her property rights.

Both property rights and the opportunity provided by those rights are conditional to a time and place. Every society describes a unique relationship with its people to the available resource base, and thereby formulates a system of property rules, which become a cultural artifact.

Systems of rights may be diverse. One example is the Songlines of the Aboriginals of Australia, which define territory according to ancestral songs that defined a stretch of country according to verses in the song. A man's verses were his title deeds to territory. Another model is found among the Gitksan, an indigenous band in northern British Columbia. They use Hereditary Chiefdoms to ensure that someone has the responsibility to maintain a piece of property and to decide who governs resource gathering. Someone harvesting without permission of the Hereditary Chief traditionally risked execution. Today provincial forestry staff use the chiefdoms to provide a method for ensuring sustainable timber management without risk of execution. However, the meaning of property is not constant and changes over time, across societies, and within societies.

Property rights require a recognition by others of one's claim to resources through relationships of power, kinship, or convention. Levels of recognition within a society may range from a formal declaration recognized by legislation to an informal custom. Thus, depending upon the shifting sands of recognition, property "rights" could come and go. Of course this is what happens in practice, with emergent claims being placed on the agenda of current politics. At any time, however, there are degrees of recognition of rights claims. Some are backed fully by law, others by administrative custom, and others only by assertions about morality. Even the most formally recognized rights may clash, for legal frameworks are rarely fixed or absolutely clear.

Property rights form a complex set of social relationships that require recognition and enforcement by the collectivity. Bromley has defined property rights as a triadic relationship that depends upon three sets of variables: (a) the nature and kinds of rights that are exercised and their correlative duties and obligations; (b) the individuals or groups in whom these rights and duties are vested; and (c) the objects of social value over which these property relations pertain (D. W. Bromley, 1991. *Environment and Economy: Property Rights and Public Policy.* Basil Blackwell, Oxford). Thus, the property rights structure that is put in place by a society is dependent on the interaction of the rights holder and that society.

Different justifications of the rights to property have a significant effect on the way in which we structure our access to resources. Land use ethics are rooted in the justification of the right to property because the justification defines the parameters of whether an action

on the land is appropriate. How individuals define their rights to resources ultimately determines the ethical basis for utilizing those resources. Modern "Western" property rights are founded on certain philosophies which represent the foundation of modern economic and political theory in North America today. These philosophic bases for property rights contribute to the "Dominant Social Paradigm," which is formed by a collection of values, attitudes, and beliefs through which individuals or a society interpret the meaning of the world. The theories that will be examined in this assessment can be divided into three general categories: instrumental, self-developmental, and environmental.

B. Instrumental Views of Property

The instrumental view of labor and property is based essentially on the utility of both labor and property to the individual. Labor is a cost incurred by people who want to consume the goods made available by the earth. It is necessary because nature will not satisfy human needs without the expending of labor. Similarly, property rights are only justified using the same type of instrumental rationalization.

Within the context of the instrumental view of property, there exist several subtheories that contribute to this paradigm. However, we will discuss only labor theory, utilitarian theory, and political liberty as means for describing an instrumental view of property rights.

1. Labor and Property Rights

John Locke, in his *Two Treatises of Government* (1690), provides a justification of property rights by virtue of the labor invested in property. Locke's contention is that God has given the world to all men in common, the "fruits it naturally produces" and "the beasts it feeds."

Locke derives the right of ownership from the prior property rights invested in the body. Each person's body is one's property and its produce (labor) is also one's property. Property rights then are derived from nature by virtue of the labor invested, and the product of that labor becomes the individual's property.

It is worthwhile to note that Locke places a limit to what people can extract by virtue of their labor—nature is not a boundless resource. The ethical basis for acquiring property comes from the labor of the individual, but not to the point of spoiling the natural world for others to enjoy. The ethic associated with the Labor theory is strictly anthropocentric, but it is guided by Christian constraint as to what is proper with respect to land use.

2. Utilitarian Philosophy and Property Rights

There are two general theories outlining the utilitarian approach to property rights. The first is the classical or traditional argument derived from Jeremy Bentham and John Stuart Mill. The second approach has been referred to by scholars as the neoclassical or economic theory of property rights. The classical utilitarian justification of property rights provides a normative theory which holds that moral and legal rules are acceptable to the extent that they promote happiness. Individual or collective actions are to be directed in such a manner as to maximize the good of the whole society and thereby increase the level of happiness. Property rights become a means to promote the level of happiness and build up a concept of ownership from other rights not essentially connected with property.

The justification of property rights hinges on the need for security to allow the natural incentive to labor to succeed; in order to achieve this, institutions are necessary (some), as well as a system of property rights to secure the interaction of those institutions. Traditional criticism of the classical utilitarian model is centered on the difficulty of measuring human happiness and the difficulty of interpersonal comparisons. How does one determine whether people or society is happier? As well, what constitutes a moral basis for property is also a problem for "modern" Western societies.

The difficulties associated with the normative aspects of utility have led economists to favor a neoclassical model. The qualitative characteristics of utility were rejected by economists because they were nonobservable. Within the neoclassical context, property rights become justified as a means to increase economic efficiency; when the cost of "disutilities" to individuals becomes greater than the cost of maintaining a system of property rights, then a system of rights becomes justified by considerations of economic utility. Welfare and institutional economics have devoted a considerable amount of energy defining property rights for efficient resource allocation, externalities, and common property resources. Market logic is applied to institutional and resource problems to define efficient and socially optimal solutions according to the theory of individual utility maximization.

A common criticism of this approach to property rights is that economic efficiency may not be an overriding moral value. The notion of utility maximization as a social goal has little to do with principles of altruism, personal values, or community concerns. Optimum efficiency is presented as a value-free welfare criterion and does nothing to provide a recognition of social values. A second argument deals with the premise that any change in the allocation or distribution of property rights which does not move things toward an economic ideal is an unjustified allocation of property rights. It seems that if people do not meet the efficiency criterion, their rights to property are not justified. The neoclassical economic model does not deal with an array of issues such as nonmarket values, future generations, or, simply, personal preferences to be inefficient.

3. Liberty and Property Rights

The political liberty or modern liberty justification of property rights is based in the moral justification of political liberty for the individual: it is wrong for one person to interfere with what another is doing; liberty is an individual possession and a person's freedom is analogous to what he or she may do without fear of reprisal. However, a regulation of acquisitive activities by individuals is required to keep people from infringing on each other's rights. Thus, a system of property rights is required to preserve liberties to which people are entitled.

Property rights are a derivative rather than a fundamental right; the justification of property rights assumes the prior justification of an extensive system of political liberty. Property rights provide a means to preserve the individual's liberty. Ownership ensures that an individual has rights over resources to prevent interference. A society dedicated to liberty achieves it by respecting an individual's property.

Macpherson notes that nothing has given more trouble in liberal democratic theory than the liberal property right (C. B. Macpherson, 1978. *Property: Mainstream and Critical Positions*. Univ. of Toronto Press, Toronto). The inherent conflict that occurs is reconciling a property right system with the liberal ethical right of all individuals to use and develop their individual capacity.

C. Self-Developmental View of Property

The self-developmental view of property and labor is based on two propositions. The first is that there should be something intrinsically satisfying about labor that helps develop the human character. The process of work, in itself as well as its results, is a rewarding experience. Secondly, the relationship between people and what they own is intrinsically significant; there is a bond between people and their property. The role of property is to allow society the opportunity to work at tasks which will develop people as distinct individuals and a social order to allow this. The self-developmental view of property places an emphasis on the explanation of social institutions in a historical process, where the educational and cultural impact on individuals justifies or condemns the institutions. This view of property focuses on the role of individuals and their environment. Thus, not only is the individual considered, but also the abiotic and biotic communities of which that individual is comprised. The ethical basis for land use decision must tie in the community as well as individual actions.

D. Environmentalism and Property Rights

The third type of justification for property rights is based in the environment. The "New Environmental Paradigm" provides an alternative means from the previous justifications for understanding property rights. The environmental movement has posed a challenge to the Dominant Social Paradigm for land use and resource management practices.

No single set of theories characterize an environmental justification of property rights. Rather, the spectrum of theories range from principles of deep ecology to guidelines for the environmental professional. The concept of environmental property rights is increasingly important to understand because much of the resource use conflict that has "sprung up" over the last decades involves an environmental stand by the public and lobby groups.

A general understanding of the positions in environmental ethics can be provided with the following overview categories:

1. Instrumental Views

This range of views presents nature as instrumental—as "stockpile and sewer" or "sanctuary and library." The environment is valued insofar as it is useful to humankind and helps us to achieve other things we value. Humans are the sole measure of value.

2. Environmental Values

The environment is valued intrinsically, as something valuable in itself. Nash notes, "nature has intrinsic value and consequently possesses at least the right to exist" (R. F. Nash, 1989. *The Rights of Nature*, pp. 9–10. Univ. of Wisconsin Press, Madison). This position is sometimes called "biocentrism," "ecological egalitarianism," or "deep ecology," and it accords nature an ethical status at least equal to that of humans. Such a conception of rights means that humans have duties or obligations toward nature, including, presumably, consideration within property rights. Thus, we return to Leopold's Land Ethic (or perhaps that of indigenous peoples') for

criteria upon which to build a different set of property rights which include the rights of nonhumans.

3. Environmental Morality

This perspective(s) of nature incorporates the view that we owe certain duties toward nature and the idea that some aspects of the nonhuman world have rights against humankind. This school of thought is distinctly different from environmental values because a person that intrinsically values nature does not necessarily believe that duties are owed nature or that the environment has rights.

If, as Leopold and others argue, we owe certain duties toward nature and some aspects of the nonhuman world have rights against mankind, we must construct a new system of morality which will quite likely hold consequences for Western property rights theory. With regard to property rights, then, environmental morality acts as an addendum to, say, libertarian or utilitarian values. Nash (1989) suggests that, in fact, environmental ethics can be viewed as a new application of the libertarian ethic.

For example, in our pursuit of a libertarian ethic, we ensure the individual's continued right to liberty by adopting environmental constraints on the market system. By doing so, we adopt a solution to the historical contradiction in the libertarian justification of property rights: a new paradigm requires that property be defined as an individual right, including the natural world as a somewhat largish "individual," not to be excluded from the use or benefit of the achievements of society. A classic example of this is found in Aldo Leopold's Land Ethic, where the rights of the landscape and natural world are integrated into individual human rights.

II. LEOPOLD'S LAND ETHIC

A. Defining the Land Ethic

Leopold, of course, did not write in a vacuum, and he was certainly not the first to argue that humans needed to reconsider their treatment of the land, nor was he the first practitioner. Leopold himself recognized older views of appropriate land–human interactions to be found in historical and contemporary native American/ First Nation communities and cultures throughout North America (and indeed South and Central America), the indigenous peoples. The "ethics" contained in traditional social prescriptions, actions, stories, spirituality, ways of making a living, and other cultural constructs might be construed as leading to similar ends as Leopold might have imagined. Indigenous land ethics are too complex to be discussed adequately in this entry, so we will therefore focus on Leopold's land ethics.

Although observations on the detrimental impact of human activities on the land go back at least to the time of Plato, Leopold's writings were a mirror of both changing knowledge (the growth of ecology as a science) and newly changing values. In his 1949 Preface to the manuscript that became *A Sand County Almanac*, Leopold offers some explanation as to his motivation in formulating his Land Ethic. He writes,

> Conservation is getting nowhere because it is incompatible with our Abrahamic concept of land. We abuse land because we regard it as a commodity belonging to us. When we see land as a community to which we belong, we may begin to use it with love and respect. There is no other way for land to survive the impact of mechanized man. … (A. Leopold, 1949. *A Sand County Almanac*, pp. xviii–xix. Ballantine, New York)

Leopold began his "Land Ethic" with a bare-bones description of what an ethic was, a socially constructed measure of a good–bad action or belief: "An ethic, ecologically, is a limitation on freedom of action in the struggle for existence. An ethic, philosophically, is a differentiation of social from anti-social conduct. These are two definitions of one thing" (Leopold, 1949, 238).

Ethics were dependent upon individuals being willing to give up some of their own interests in recognition that there were advantages to be had in existing in an interactive community, Leopold's "community of interdependent parts." A land ethic simply involved extending consideration of good–bad behavior from human–human interactions to human–nonhuman interactions by redefining the composition of a community in which such ethically based interactions occurred. Rather than limiting ethical consideration to the community of humans, the land ethic was extended to the entire abiotic and biotic community. It is, essentially, an extension of consideration of ethical regard in a linear fashion, from man to man, then to men of different races, then to women and children, then to animals, and then to the land collectively: the shorthand history of environmental ethics in general. Such a linear discussion hides the fact that in many Western cultures this evolution has jumped around in a nonlinear fashion, retrogressed, and leaped forward again. For example, at the same time that Leopold was arguing for the extension of ethics from human–human to human–

land, Germany's Nazis were demonstrating that the extension of ethics from man to men of other races and women, in some circumstances, had failed. However, to Leopold, the time seemed right for a human–land extension to lessen the threat of human activities.

B. Linking Ethics and Ecology

The genuis of Leopold's Land Ethic was his linkage of ethics to ecology. He changed the basis for arguing something was ethically good from human and individually based attributes, the infliction of pain on a pet dog, for example, to an assessment of ethical good based on ecological good. Thus Leopold's change in the definition of community is key; what was right for the ecological community, as a whole, became also ethically right: "A thing is right when it tends to preserve the integrity, stability, and beauty of the biotic community. It is wrong when it tends otherwise" (Leopold, 1949, 262).

At the heart of Leopold's ethic was an understanding of land as something far more complex than a set of resources, or even a collection of individual plants and animals. Rather it was a set of ecological interactions and relationships, interactions and relationships that could be disrupted only at great risk to the health and integrity of the land. Resource managers, and others who might be involved with a piece of land, who adopted this Ethic absorbed what Leopold termed an "ecological consciousness," "and this in turn reflects a conviction of individual responsibility for the health of the land. Health is the capacity for self-renewal" (Leopold, 1949, 258). Interestingly, while the target of the Land Ethic was North American society, the application of the Ethic relied upon individuals to take up their responsibility for the land. While society might come to be involved as more individuals adopted this sense of ethical goodness, it would still appear to be a community of individuals individually accepting their land responsibility. The appeal of such a construct for resource managers seems apparent.

Recently, J. B. Callicott (1996. *Environmental Ethics, 18*, 353–372) has questioned the foundation of Leopold's Land Ethic in his exploration of deconstructive ecology and sociobiology. Changes in the theory of how ecosystems function within these disciplines challenge the basis of Leopold's ideas of community-based ecosystems. Developments in deconstructive ecology and sociobiology suggest that organisms are "selfish" and that communities may live in a state of chaos rather than harmony. But Callicott suggests that even though the dynamics of the ecosystem may be different from Leopold's definition, the application of the Land Ethic remains valid (if updated) within the context of the new theories.

C. Aesthetics and Love

Leopold's Ethic also incorporated two, possibly more challenging ideas: aesthetics and love. His statement of ethical assessment included beauty within ecological criteria. In part this is a more difficult concept to incorporate because beauty is often in the eye of the beholder: one person's paradise is another's howling wilderness. Beauty changes across cultures and across time. For who's sense of beauty do you work toward? Further, what might be "popularly" beautiful might not be ecologically healthy. Given time Leopold might have changed his definition, which was, what is ecologically healthy is by definition beautiful. Leopold's sense of the beautiful in nature is certainly evident in his writing, and remains what draws many people into reading his work. And it might well remain necessary as the mechanism for drawing people beyond appreciating nature writing to appreciating nature in and of itself. The ability to perceive beauty in nature may be what leads people to develop that next element in the Ethic: love.

> We can be ethical only in relation to something we can see, feel, understand, love, or otherwise have faith in. (Leopold, 1949, 251)

> It is inconceivable to me that an ethical relation to land can exist without love, respect, and admiration for land, and a high regard for its value. (Leopold, 1949, 261)

Love is perhaps the most difficult element to incorporate into resource management plans. However, it remains an important part of the Land Ethic for it injects into an otherwise scientific assessment of ecological soundness that element of caring that forces an acceptance and willingness to sacrifice for the sake of perhaps long-term, distant ecological needs. Mandating love, of course, as with most ethical precepts, is impossible, at which point the scientific assessment becomes a moral fail-safe system.

Lastly, the Land Ethic involves changing "the role of *Homo sapiens* from conqueror of the land-community to plain member and citizen of it. It implies respect for his fellow-members, and also respect for the community as such" (Leopold, 1966, 240). It made humans ethically and ecologically part of the natural community—no better and no worse than any other member. The key,

of course, was the definition of community, which for Leopold seems to have been a community of ecological definition. The whole point was to enlarge the moral community to include the land. Community then became subject to ecological definition, with humans part of the ecological circle.

There are, of course, far more subtleties in Leopold's writing than can be summarized here. For the purposes of this discussion, the key point in a land ethic is that its central framework is ecological. Love, respect, beauty, and community health all grow out of the community's ecological wholeness.

III. BIOREGIONALISM: THE APPLICATION OF A LAND ETHIC

One example of an intersection between land use planning and ethics can be found in the idea of "bioregionalism." Bioregionalism comes out of the environmental movement of 1960s, and in its ideals, there is a lingering taste of the counterculture "back-to-the-land" movement of that era. However, the idea of bioregionalism has gone further than either the original counterculture movement or the "environmental movement." Bioregionalism is a critique of modern social initiatives, such as uncontrolled and ill-considered development projects, which would include everything from the process of industrialization, to hydroelectric dams, and to the Green Revolution as the source of much of the environmental degradation found on the planet.

The developers of the idea drew upon a term, "bioregion," under which they could assemble a theory of effective conservation: one had to work with the boundary lines drawn by nature rather than politicians. "Natural resources" and ecological problems ignored national and political boundaries, and therefore so should appropriate development strategies.

Bioregionalism drew upon a number of previously existing ideas. The most interesting of these roots, for the purposes of this discussion, are the roots grounded in the theory and science of regional planning going back to end of the World War II. The influence of planners and thinkers such as Lewis Mumford, Jane Jacobs, Leopold Kohr, Ian McHarg, and E. F. Schumacher are apparent. Artur Glikson, a colleague of Lewis Mumford's, for example, argued that the traditional "rural region" was a combination of a human environment, in which people lived, worked, played, celebrated, and participated in social networks, and of a healthy physical landscape, with functioning hydrological and soil systems. The similarities to bioregional-ist thought of the 1970s and 1980s are inescapable.

Part of the focus of bioregional research of key inter-est to planners involves the explication of how people take a living from the land. Thus, bioregionalism centers around the identification of, and with, a bioregion. A bioregion is a piece of land that is defined by physical, biological, and cultural characteristics. This suggests that a bioregion is as much a human creation as it is a biological reality.

Bioregionalism, however, implies more than merely identifying units of distinctive cultural/biological char-acteristics. It means discovering and living within the constraints and possibilities imposed by the character of the bioregion. It means living in a manner that is, to use a modern buzzword, "sustainable" over a long time period. Thus, the bioregionalist does not attempt to grow citrus fruits and grass lawns in the desert. Instead the bioregionalist looks at what *can* grow natu-rally in the region, what native resources can be devel-oped, and what lifestyles can be sustained within the dictates of the region's characteristics.

Bioregionalism means not only living with a region's limitations, it means using the region's resources for the benefit of the region. This implies a different sort of economy, an economy under the control of the region. Under typical polarized development, removing territo-rial economic control only exacerbates the inequities of such a system. One need only look at "developing" countries who are trapped in transnational trade net-works to understand the consequences of wealth being directed outward.

Bioregionalists argue that community, human and natural, is the level at which living should be done. Implicit in bioregionalism is the idea of decentraliza-tion, in both political and economic spheres. People who live-in-place are those who, logically, have the best sense of what is right for that region, and who, therefore, should make the decisions affecting the region. However, an interest and devotion to the community and region does not imply willful blind-ness and disinterest in the world outside. Lewis Mum-ford argued that regionalism and universalism are united. If people cannot bond with the smaller com-munity, then they will be unable to relate to the larger world community. If, however, there is no interest in the larger world then the individual is doomed to isolation.

Bioregionalists, then, work toward a goal of sustain-able development. They focus on key ecological com-ponents which require protection, including water supplies, forests, and indigenous cultures. And they recommend that steps be taken to change conventional development projects into projects that would have fewer ecological consequences and would be "sustain-able." In other words, projects should be designed so that they do not destroy natural resources but use them in a manner that will allow them to also be used long into the future. What is implied by the idea of sustainable development is clearly similar to what bioregionalists are working toward: a way of living with the land which supports human needs, both physical and psychological, but which does not result in the irreversible degradation or destruction of the natural communities which are the basis of human support.

IV. CONCLUSION

Land ethics are ethical systems that govern human use of land and all of its components (e.g., plants, animals, and subsistence-based human societies). Philosophi-cally speaking, "ethics" are value neutral; they are sys-tems that define the spectrum of bad–good, which var-ies through time and space. So owning slaves might be ethical in one century, but not in another. "Land ethics" differ because there is an "absolute bad," past which we cannot go: ecological extinction. There is, within some philosophical circles, an "absolute good," which is increasing ecological enhancement of an ecosystem, although at this end it is moving toward the good rather than absolute attainment which is important, given de facto "natural" evolution and change.

Within the definition of "land ethics," there are infi-nite human systems designed to govern human relation-ships with land. These systems include the models that we discussed in this article, property rights, Leopoldian land ethics, and bioregionalism. These are of increasing significance as the world populations attempt to move toward "sustainable" practices, which is why we have chosen to discuss them. There are other models out there. One could argue that the most useful approach to assessing and implementing such models is to start from what we (or others) have presented and then moving outward. As in ecosystems, flexibility and adap-tion are crucial.

Also See the Following Articles

BIODIVERSITY • DEVELOPMENT ETHICS • ECOLOGICAL BALANCE • ENVIRONMENTAL JUSTICE • INDIGENOUS RIGHTS

Bibliography

Berg, P. (1995). "Discover Your Life Place: A Bioregional Workbook." Planet Drum Foundation, San Francisco.

Bromley, D. W. (1991). "Environment and Economy: Property Rights and Public Policy." Basil Blackwell, Oxford.

Callicott, J. B. (1996). Do deconstructive ecology and sociobiology undermine Leopold's Land Ethic? In *Environ. Ethics* **18**, 353–372.

Callicott, J. B. (1994). "Earth's Insights: A Survey of Ecological Ethics from Mediterranean Basin to the Australian Outback." Univ. of California Press, Berkeley.

Callicott, J. B. (1989). "In Defense of the Land Ethic: Essays on Environmental Philosophy." Univ. of New York Press, Albany.

Devall, W., and Sessions, G. (1985). "Deep Ecology." Peregrine Smith, Layton.

Leopold, A. (1949). "A Sand County Almanac." Ballantine, New York.

Macpherson, C. B. (1978). "Property: Mainstream and Critical Positions." Univ. of Toronto Press, Toronto.

Meine, C. (1988). "Aldo Leopold: His Life and Work." Univ. of Wisconsin Press, Madison.

Nash, R. F. (1989). "The Rights of Nature." Univ. of Wisconsin Press, Madison.

Shrader-Frechette, K. (1987). Four land ethics: An overview. *Environ. Professional* **9**, 121–132.

LEADERSHIP, ETHICS OF

Rabindra N. Kanungo and Manuel Mendonca
McGill University

I. The Need for Ethical Leadership
II. The Three Dimensions of Ethical Leadership
III. Conclusion

Glossary

affiliative assurance A manifestation of the need for affiliation in a manner that interpersonal relations are intended to serve one's own interests rather than those of the other, or of the organization.

affiliative interest A manifestation of the need for affiliation in a manner that interpersonal relations are intended to serve the interests of others and of the organization.

control strategy The leader's use of power or influence derived from the leader's position, and rewards and sanctions to ensure followers' commitment and loyalty, and compliance with the leader's directives.

economic imperialism A belief that material possessions are the measure of one's success; and, therefore, ought to be the principal guide for one's actions.

empowering strategy Acts of the leader to increase the followers' self-efficacy belief and their capacity for self-determination in the realization of the leader's vision.

institutional power The exercise of power prompted by the motive to serve others or the organization.

moral altruism A regard for others even when it involves considerable harm to one's self.

mutual altruism A regard for others with the expectation of benefit for self.

transactional influence A leadership influence process that relies on control strategies in order to elicit followers' compliance with leader's directives without any intention of promoting their personal growth and development.

transformational influence A leadership influence process that relies on empowerment strategy intended to enhance the followers' personal growth and development as they work towards the realization of the leader's vision.

ETHICAL LEADERSHIP is vital in an organization. Leadership provides direction and it enables the organization to achieve its objectives. True leadership behavior is more than the routine maintenance activities of procuring and allocating resources, monitoring and directing followers, and building group cohesion. It assesses the followers' needs and expectations, and it influences them to work toward realizing the leader's vision for the benefit of the followers and the organization. The leader's vision inspires and articulates the organization's mission, which provides the basis for the organization's objectives and goals, communicates the beliefs and values that influence and shape the organization's culture and behavioral norms, and its strategies, policies, and procedures.

However, it is the leader's ethical conduct guided by

moral principles and integrity that gives legitimacy and credibility to the vision and sustains it. Without ethical leadership, the organization is a soulless structure. When the leader's moral integrity is in doubt, then the leader's vision—however noble, well-crafted, and articulated, is viewed with scepticism by the followers, loses its vigor, and is incapable of moving them to work toward its realization.

Ethical leadership can be said to exist when moral intent and principles inform and guide the leader's actions in achieving the vision.

I. THE NEED FOR ETHICAL LEADERSHIP

A. Effects of Unethical Practices

Impressive breakthroughs in technology are providing new and better products and services . . . improved communications are transforming the world into a global village . . . democracies are sprouting in former communist lands. These changes are viewed as signs of progress in modern society. However, in the wake of such progress, there are reports of widespread bribery by Italian and Japanese government officials, exorbitant executive salaries in North America in the midst of employee layoffs in their organizations, extensive environmental pollution in eastern Europe, and other instances of immoral or morally questionable conduct in organizations. In many otherwise prosperous and affluent cities, there has been an increase in the number of homeless people. Even those who are fortunate enough to have a job find that work is *not* an opportunity for growth, but a source of anxiety and insecurity.

Such observations point to the need for ethical leadership in organizations. Organizational leaders need to be more sensitive to their moral obligations to the larger society, which includes all their stakeholders—consumers, employees, suppliers, governments, local communities, and so on. A long time ago, Aristotle's "Politics" suggested that the state comes into being to provide law and order but continues for the sake of good law, good order, and noble actions. In a similar vein, the raison d'etre of leadership in organizations is to support some "good" and be in accord with the "highest excellence." Therefore, leaders have the responsibility to ensure that organizational policies and actions ". . . promote the public good . . . advance the basic beliefs of our society . . . contribute to its stability, strength and harmony" (Drucker P. (1968) *The Practice of Management,* p. 461. London: Pan Books, Ltd.). It is the

recognition of this responsibility that has led several large corporations to formulate Codes of Ethics for their organizations.

B. Need for Ethical Leaders and Ethical Environment

1. Need for Ethical Leaders

An organization's code of ethics establishes principles that should govern the leader's behavior, and the leader's mission of uplifting the moral climate of the organization. The efficacy of an organization's code of ethics depends upon the extent to which its spirit and principles permeate the thinking and decision-making at all levels of the organization. To ensure the acceptance of, commitment to, and compliance with the code of ethics, the leader must develop morally as a person and also assist in the moral development of the followers. As Andrews observed: ". . . the problem of corporate ethics has three aspects: the development of the executive as a moral person; the influence of the corporation as moral environment; and the actions needed to map a high road to economic and ethical performance—and to mount guard-rails to keep corporate wayfarers on track."

It is not enough that leaders are intelligent, industrious, and competent in their technical speciality because studies have shown that, despite these desirable qualities, they might be ineffective because they lack ethical qualities and are perceived as "arrogant, vindictive, untrustworthy, selfish, emotional compulsive, over-controlling, insensitive, abrasive . . ." (Hogan, R., Curphy, G. J., & Hogan, J. (1994). What we know about leadership effectiveness and personality. *American Psychologist,* 49(6), 493–504).

2. Need for Ethical Environment

The nature of the moral environment of an organization depends on the moral caliber of its members. However, the moral caliber of members is largely determined by people in leadership positions. The manner in which leaders function in these positions of influence can directly contribute to the strengthening or the deterioration of the moral fiber of society. The lives of a Socrates, Buddha, Mohammed, Lao Tse, Gandhi—to name a few—attests to their salutary influence in their own day, as well as for all time. On the other hand, the case of senior government officials in France, who knowingly permitted the use of contaminated blood resulting in the deaths of several hundred hemophiliacs, strikingly illustrates the harm that a few can inflict upon individuals and society. When people in leadership positions compromise their moral values, they do more than physical harm. Their callous neglect or compromise of moral values also contributes to creating an atmosphere of moral cynicism that, like a cancer, corrodes the moral health of society.

C. Challenges to Ethical Leadership

The role of a leader has always carried with it grave and onerous responsibilities. The burden of this role poses rather unique and formidable challenges because of the fundamental shift in societal norms and values. People are increasingly influenced by the norms of "economic imperialism" and the cult of "self-worship."

1. "Economic Imperialism"

Economic imperialism demands that money and material possession be the primary yardstick to measure success and failure in every sphere of human life, and therefore be valued more than everything else in society. In a free and competitive economic environment, to be selfish is regarded as a virtuous act. The concept of "enlightened self-interest," which underlies Jeremy Bentham's utilitarian moral philosophy, provides the ideological justification for the notion of economic imperialism. The acceptance of economic imperialism as a societal norm has encouraged the cult of self-worship.

2. Cult of Self-Worship

The cult of self-worship is based on the assumption that ". . . reward for the self (i.e., egoism) is the only functional ethical principle" (Vitz, P. C. (1994). *Psychology as Religion: The Cult of Self-Worship* (2nd Ed.), p. xi. Grand Rapids, MI: W. B. Eerdmans Publishing Co.). Underlying these approaches is the emphasis on the rights of the individual to fulfil their life ambitions in any form or manner they choose without much regard or concern for one's duties and obligations to others. This focus on self is an ". . . extreme expression of individualistic psychology first created by a frontier society and now supported and corrupted by consumerism" (Vitz, 1994, p. 21).

On the issue of self-love, the observation of Campbell more than two decades ago, is most pertinent: ". . . there is in psychology today a general background assumption that the human impulses provided by biological evolution are right and optimal, both individually and socially, and that repressive or inhibitory moral traditions are wrong. This assumption may now be regarded as scientifically wrong. Psychology, in propagating this background perspective in its teaching . . . helps to un-

dermine the retention of what may be extremely valuable social-evolutionary systems which we do not fully understand." These remarks highlight the absolute need for moral leadership in organizations and in society in order to achieve the common goal of human welfare at personal, organizational, and societal levels.

II. THE THREE DIMENSIONS OF ETHICAL LEADERSHIP

A. The Meaning of "Leadership" and "Ethical"

How can we judge leadership in an organization to be ethical or unethical? In order to answer this question, we must first understand what we mean by the terms "leadership" and "ethical."

1. The Meaning of "Leadership"

The term "leadership" refers to a set of *role behavior or actions* on the part of a person who assumes the leadership role in an organization either through formal appointment or through informal choice of organizational members. The term also implies that the leader *influences* the followers' values, beliefs, and behavior through his/her actions. Leadership therefore can be viewed from two vantage points: (i) as a set of role behavior directly contributing to the formulation and achievement of organizational objectives, and to the development of cohesive organizational environments; or (ii) as a set of strategies and tactics to influence the followers' values, beliefs, and behavior so that organizational objectives can be achieved through them.

2. The Meaning of "Ethical"

The term "ethical" means that which is morally good, that which is considered morally right (as opposed to legally or procedurally right). According to Thomas Aquinas, the ethical motive of an action should be judged on the basis of three factors: the objective *act itself*, the subjective *motive of the actor*, and the *context* in which the act is performed.

The actor, in order to be ethical, must engage in objectively good or virtuous acts instead of evil acts or vices. The actor must also have good intentions without which an objectively good act cannot be considered ethical. For instance, an act of charitable donation to avoid income tax vitiates the moral goodness of the act. Furthermore, the context or the situation in which the act is performed must also be considered . A charitable donation to defend one's country in the face of foreign aggression may be ethically justified but a similar act to support terrorist organizations in peacetime is morally wrong.

Hence, if leadership acts are to be ethically justified, they must be right in respect of all three factors: the objective act, the motive and the context.

B. Manifestations of Ethical Leadership

Leaders are responsible for the development of moral organizational climate. In this respect, leaders have to act for both their own moral self-development and the moral development of the followers. Moral self-development requires building the leader's personal character through cultivating virtues. Moral development of followers can be facilitated by the leader through the use of morally appropriate influence strategies and tactics. All these leadership acts, however, have to be guided by moral intent. Ethical leadership therefore manifests itself in three ways or has three dimensions: leadership *motives*, leadership *influence strategies*, and leadership *preparation* or *character formation*. Ethical leaders always operate with an altruistic intent; they utilize empowering strategies to influence followers and they cultivate virtues and abstain from vices for building their own inner strength. These three dimensions are discussed separately in the following sections.

1. Leadership Motives: Altruistic or Egotistic

The overarching motive for ethical leadership is the leader's altruistic intent as opposed to egotistic intent. Leaders are truly effective only when they are motivated by a concern for others, when their actions are invariably guided primarily by the criteria of *the benefit to others even if it results in some cost to self*. The underlying rationale or purpose for having a leader in a group or an organization is to move it toward the pursuit of objectives that, when attained, would produce benefits to the organization, its members, and to society at large. The leader's efforts and strategies in the areas of planning for the organization, and controlling and coordination of follower activities are justified and assume meaning and significance only to the extent that these are intended to serve the interests of the organization, its members, and the larger society. Because the "other"— that is, the organization members and society at large, is the raison d'etre of the leader's efforts then the altruistic motive becomes the only consistent motive for the leader role. Therefore, leadership effectiveness is assured only by altruistic acts that reflect the leader's

incessant desire and concern to benefit others despite the risk of personal cost inherent in such acts.

The altruistic motive of helping others is an acquired motive that develops through early training and socialization. Influences of family and educational and religious institutions lead to the formation of internal moral codes of reciprocity and social responsibility. The reciprocity norm dictates that individuals should help those who have helped them. This norm generally applies when people are interacting with their equals or with those who possess greater resources. However, when individuals deal with their dependants who are unable to reciprocate, such as in the case of leaders, then the inner moral code of social responsibility may be evoked. The norm of social responsibility refers to an internalized belief that to help others without any consideration, such as an expected future personal benefit, in return, is a moral imperative. Such internalized beliefs regarding social and moral obligations constitute the basis of an altruistic motive of leaders that, in turn, energizes their altruistic behavior.

a. Mutual Altruism and Moral Altruism

When leaders' altruistic concern is combined with a concern for their own self-interest, the resulting behavior can be called *utilitarian* or *mutual altruism*. The motivational basis of utilitarian altruism is the expectations about the mutually beneficial consequences of the obligatory behavior. But leaders also reflect a helping concern for others without any regard for self-interest and even when such concern involves considerable personal sacrifice or inconvenience—that is, harming self-interest. This behavior can be categorized as *genuine* or *moral altruism*. The primary motivational force behind moral altruism is the internalized social responsibility norms or moral imperatives. Moral philosophers may argue about different normative theories of ethics or morality, but the values inherent in the choice of "others before myself" or "moral altruism" are universal and form part of the heritage of all cultures.

In spite of the high value attached to moral altruism as a motive for effective leadership around the world, its critical role is often ignored to avoid any discussion of moral and ethical issues in leadership. Instead, it has been suggested that effective leadership is motivated by other needs such as the needs for affiliation, power, and achievement. But a closer look at the leadership phenomena reveals that these needs explain the basis of effective leadership only to the extent that they are a manifestation of the overarching altruistic need. Stated differently, leader behaviors are ineffective when guided solely by one or more of these needs with a total disregard for altruism. On the other hand, leader behaviors are effective when motivated by these needs as an *operative manifestation* or expression of altruism.

b. Altruism and Affiliation Motive

Leaders who are high on affiliation motivation, regard warm and friendly relationships with their followers as extremely important and, therefore, make considerable effort to be sensitive to followers' feelings and to conform to their wishes. These characteristics of the need for affiliation would suggest a concern for others and, hence, compatible with the characteristics of the altruistic motive. However, Boyatzis posited two manifestations of the need for affiliation: "affiliative assurance" and "affiliative interest." Leaders high on "affiliative assurance" emphasize relationships to protect them from a deep sense of insecurity, and therefore behave in a noninterfering manner even when the situation demands otherwise. They are reluctant to give negative feedback to their subordinates and yield to requests from others for the sole reason of not wanting to incur their displeasure. Leaders motivated by affiliative assurance produce low morale among followers. According to McClelland and Burnham, followers feel "weak, irresponsible, and without a sense of what might happen next, or even of what they ought to be doing."

On the other hand, individuals high on "affiliative interest" emphasize relationships in a manner that is consistent with the demands of the organization. It has its origin in the individual's recognition that uncertainty while facing problems needs to be reduced by information sharing. A leader's affiliative interest manifests itself in helpful but task-oriented interventions, which demonstrates a high degree of "interpersonal competence." Such leaders relate to others with the full recognition that they are individual persons with ideas and resources and that they are partners in the problem-solving and related activities necessary for attaining task objectives. Consequently, supportive feelings permeate the interpersonal relations motivated by affiliative interest. Thus, it is clear that the leaders who are high on affiliative assurance behave in self-serving ways that are incompatible with moral altruism. On the other hand, the motivation of organizational leaders who are high on affiliative interest is consistent with and conducive to underlying moral altruism.

c. Altruism and Power Motive

When one thinks of a leader, the notion that immediately comes to mind is "power." Undeniably, the power motivation or a high need for power has driven many a leader. Power, particularly in a democracy, has a very unfavorable press, but the leader has to have power to influence others. Similar to the affiliation motivation, there are two types of power motivations. In one case, the leader is motivated by power for personal aggrandizement; in the other case, the leader is motivated by the power to serve the purpose of the institution. McClelland and Burnham term the former as the personal power need and the latter as the institutional power need.

Leaders high on personal power need are preoccupied with their self-interests and concerns even at the cost of the organization's welfare and effectiveness. When power is exercised in this manner, the leaders demand and expect followers' loyalty and efforts to be directed toward the achievement of the leader's personal goals. For this purpose, the leaders tend to exercise their formal authority or position power. They use the carrot-and-stick approach to induce follower compliance. The personal power need of the leader would seem to be rooted in a deep-seated sense of personal insecurity that manifests itself in dictatorial forms of behavior and defensive feelings in relation to the followers. These leaders, insensitive to the needs of their followers, expect the followers' unquestioning obedience to and compliance with their authority and decisions.

On the other hand, the dominant preoccupation of leaders high on institutional power need is the interests of the organization and its members. Such leaders subordinate their personal or self-interest to that of the organization, which then becomes the sole reason for their desire to influence and control others. Leaders who are high on institutional power motivation emphasize orderliness, discipline, and task structure primarily to ensure the accomplishment of the organization's objectives. For this purpose, they draw primarily on the resources of their personal power base or their inner strength—that is, expertise or attractiveness as perceived by the followers. When they are required to use rewards and sanctions as means of control and influence, they do so impartially and equitably.

Contrary to the personal power need, the institutional power need is derived from the leader's identification with and commitment to the organization's objectives and interests. For this reason power becomes the vehicle to serve the needs of the organization and its members. It is manifested in behaviors and feelings that serve to help and support the followers in accomplishing their tasks. Furthermore, being aware of their need to remedy the inadequacies in their competencies and abilities, the institutional power need makes leaders not only establish open communication with their followers, but it also makes them create a climate in which followers are encouraged to provide suggestions and criticisms of the leaders' decisions and actions. The discussion of the personal power need relative to the institutional power need suggests that personal power need clearly places the interests of self before that of others, and might even be at considerable cost to others; personal power need is the antithesis of altruism. On the other hand, the institutional power need is a form of moral altruism as it places the interest of others before and might even be at the cost to self.

d. Altruism and Achievement Motive

Leaders high on the achievement motive derive satisfaction from achieving their goals, as well as from their relentless efforts in pursuit of achievement almost as an end in itself. They assume a high degree of personal responsibility but also tend to be self-oriented in that they view organizational resources and support primarily in terms of their own objectives. However, similar to the affiliation and power needs, the need for achievement may take two forms: according to Mehta, a leader may be motivated either by "personal achievement" or by "social achievement." McClelland and Burnham note that leaders driven by personal achievement motives are more likely to engage in behaviors that benefit self rather than others "... because they focus on personal improvement and doing things better by themselves, achievement-motivated people want to do things themselves."

On the other hand, leaders driven by the social achievement motive show a concern for others and initiate efforts "... in terms of articulation of individual and collective capability, concern for a better quality of life and need to engage in meaningful organizational and social action in order to influence the environment," according to Mehta. Thus, leaders motivated by social achievement would generally tend toward efforts that primarily benefited others and therefore reflect altruism. However, leaders motivated by personal achievement could also engage in efforts that benefit others when the objective of their efforts also included the interests of others. For example, when leaders engage in self-development the objective might be viewed as "personal achievement." However, if the ultimate objective of the leader is to prepare himself or herself to better serve the followers, then such achievement motivation would be congruent with the altruistic motive.

TABLE I

Two Contrasting Leadership Motive Patterns

Underlying motive	Altruistic (Intent to) (benefit) (others)	Egotistic (Intent to) (benefit) (self)
Operative needs	Affiliative interest Institutional power Social achievement Self-discipline/self-development	Affiliative assurance Personal power Personal achievement Self-aggrandizement
Moral intent	Ethical	Unethical
Leadership effectiveness	High	Low

e. Differences Between Altruistic and Egotistic Motivation

The motivation underlying leader behaviors can be characterized either as altruistic or egotistic. The altruistic motivation of a leader manifests itself at the operative level in terms of affiliative interest, institutional power need, self-discipline or self-development, and social achievement needs. The egotistic motivation of a leader, on the other hand, expresses itself in affiliative assurance, personal power need, and personal achievement chiefly in terms of self-aggrandizement. These differences are summarized in Table 1.

f. Extent of Altruism Practiced by Corporate Leaders

A recent survey indicated that the extent of altruism in corporate America is on the increase. In the survey, 52.5% of corporate executives stated that, in the last 20 years, acts of corporate altruism have increased; whereas, 31.7% believe that these have stayed the same, and 15.8% believe that it has decreased (Viega, J. F., & Dechant, K. (1993). Fax Poll: Altruism in corporate America. *Academy of Management Executive,* 7(3), pp. 89–91). The survey also found that the corporate leaders' altruistic acts were motivated, to a large extent, by "utilitarian altruism" rather than by "genuine altruism."

2. Leadership Influence Strategy: Transactional or Transformational

There are two basic approaches available to a leader who wants to influence followers' beliefs, attitudes and behaviors: transactional and transformational modes of influence.

a. The Transactional Influence Mode

In the transactional mode, the leader uses the power of her position, and rewards and sanctions under her control to ensure that followers perform the required behavior and demonstrate the desired commitment and loyalty. The followers exhibit such compliance behaviors and attitudes in order to gain valued rewards and to avoid possible sanctions under the control of the leaders. Clearly, the leaders who adopt the transactional influence mode use control strategies to elicit follower compliance and do not intend to promote the growth and development of followers. The transactional influence process, therefore, has serious ethical and moral implications. This approach to exercising influence by controlling and exchanging valued resources tends to regard followers, at best, as providers of knowledge, abilities, skills, and efforts that the leaders need to accomplish their own objectives. At worst, it views followers as mere instruments or appendages of machines that can be traded so long as the price is right. Consequently, it offends against the dignity of the human person; it also frustrates the basic human need to maintain self-worth and, as a result, causes much psychological and, sometimes physical, harm to employees.

This approach is not conducive to the development of the organization's moral environment, which is a crucial responsibility of organizational leaders. When leaders use control strategies as in a transactional mode, followers cease to experience dignity, meaning, and community so essential for the growth of both the organization and its members. Control strategies could create a climate that breeds dysfunctional norms and values that lead to conflict rather than cooperation among followers who will place their own interests before those of others without any regard for the superordinate interests of the organization, and to the organization's responsibilities and obligations to its external stakeholders.

b. The Transformational Influence Mode

In the transformational influence mode, the leader uses empowerment instead of control strategy to bring about a change in the followers' core beliefs and values as he moves the organization toward its future goals. It is the leader who formulates the future goal or vision for the organization. In order to move the organization toward its goals, the leader uses his personal expertise and goodwill primarily to transform followers' beliefs and values to be congruent with the vision, rather than just to elicit their overt compliance behavior. Use of empowerment strategy achieves two objectives: (a) followers internalize the beliefs and

values inherent in the vision formulated by the leader and (b) followers change their self-efficacy beliefs by feeling more empowered or competent in handling the required tasks for the realization of the vision. What does empowerment strategy involve? Conger and Kanungo identified several steps a leader takes while using this strategy.

First, a leader must identify the contextual conditions responsible for the feelings of powerlessness among followers and attempt to reduce or eliminate them. Second, the leader must develop followers to feel more competent by using a number of leadership practices such as encouraging followers' participation in decision-making and in task-goal setting, providing helpful feedback on task accomplishment, providing exemplary behavior worthy of imitation, expressing confidence in followers' capability, and so on. Followers' participation in decision-making, goal setting, and so on provides opportunity to test their own efficacy. Sashkin considers such participation as an ethical imperative because it leads to followers' self-development. Exemplary behavior of the leaders empowers followers to believe that they too can behave in a like manner. When such beliefs are widespread in an organization, the overall effectiveness of the organization increases, and the moral environment is restored. When a leader uses empowerment strategy to transform followers, the latter clearly understand the thrust of the leader's message and intent: "I will attend to your personal growth and competence regardless of the personal cost and sacrifice to me."

c. Differences between Transactional and Transformational Influence Modes

In the preceding discussion on modes of influence processes, several significant contrasts between the two influence processes can be identified. These are presented in Table 2.

In the transactional mode the leader induces followers' compliance through the control strategy, which involves the social exchange of valued resources available to the leader. These resources are the ability to reward, punish, or use legal authority to enforce compliance by the followers. However, such compliance by followers often leads to self-denial and the loss of self-worth, with the result that they might not function much differently from programmed robots. The near destruction of the follower's self-esteem for the benefit of the leader makes the transactional influence process highly offensive to the dignity of the human person and, therefore, it cannot be considered to be an ethical social influence process.

TABLE II

A Comparison of the Transactional and Transformational Leadership Influence Processes

Leadership influence process	Transactional leadership	Transformational leadership
Strategies	Control	Empowerment
Leader objective in terms behavioral outcomes	Emphasis on compliance behavior	Changing followers' core attitudes, beliefs and values
Underlying psychological mechanism	Social exchange of valued resources	Increasing self-efficacy belief, and self-determination
Power base	Coercive, legal, and reward resources under leader's control	Leader's expertise and attractiveness
Attitude change process and effects	Compliance, which under excessive control, often leads to demolishing followers' self-worth, and to their functioning as programmed robots.	Identification and internalization leading to followers' self-growth and to their functioning as autonomous persons
Moral nature of influence	Unethical	Ethical
Long-term effectiveness	Low	High

On the other hand, in the transformational mode, the leader's objective is to change the followers' core attitude and values through empowerment strategies. The followers' empowering experience increases their self-efficacy belief and their capacity for self-determination. The leader's transformational influence comes from two sources: (i) the leader's expertise; and (ii) the leader's selfless efforts and altruistic intent. The power or influence derived from expertise makes the leader credible and trustworthy to the followers; the leader's selfless efforts and altruistic intent in the realization of the vision enhances the leader's attractiveness to the followers. The empowerment strategy also brings about an attitude change in the followers through the identification and internalization. When followers find their leader to be knowledgeable and attractive, in the sense just described, they tend to imitate the leader's behavior and to internalize the leader's beliefs, attitudes, and values.

However, unlike the transactional mode, the processes in the transformational mode are designed by the leader to increase the followers' self-growth, enhance their self-worth, and enable them to function as autonomous persons. These effects reflect the leader's altruistic value and orientation and promote the dignity of the human person. Therefore, when leaders adopt the transformational influence process mode, their leadership is more likely to be ethical, more effective, and more enduring.

3. Leadership Preparation: Sources of Ethical Power

The preceding discussion pointed out the need for altruistic intent and transformational mode of influences in ethical leadership. What can leaders do to prepare themselves and their organizations to meet the challenging demands of such ethical imperatives? It is not enough for the leader to distinguish between morally good or evil motives or acts. The leader must make an effort to habitually incorporate moral principles in her beliefs, values, and behavior. If ethical leadership is essentially transformational in nature, then it involves both the self-transformation of the leaders and of the followers.

Ethical leaders readily recognize that the self-transformation ought to begin with one's self. In the context of ethical management, Blanchard and Peale offer inspiring and practical principles of ethical power. These are purpose, pride, patience, persistence, and perspective. Leaders can tap these sources of ethical power as they go about their task of self-transformation.

a. Purpose

The critical set of behaviors of the leader are to evaluate the status quo, to formulate and articulate a vision that is discrepant from the status quo, and to take the means. These are personal sacrifice, building trust among followers, and using unconventional behavior to achieve the vision. The leader often exercises her ethical power by subjecting the vision as well as the means to achieve it to the rigorous scrutiny of the purpose that is intended to be served. What higher purpose does the vision serve? In the context of the business organization, it is universally admitted that the business must be profitable. But, the ethical leader stops to ask: Are profits a means or an end in itself? Corporations committed to a higher purpose "... exist to provide society with the goods and services it needs, to provide employment, and to create a surplus of wealth (profit) with which to improve the general standard of living and quality of life" (O'Toole, S. (1985). Vanguard Management: Redesigning the Corporate Future. Garden City, NY: Doubleday). The scrutiny of the vision in the perspective of its higher purpose will cause the leader to practice primarily the virtues of prudence and justice. Furthermore, the habit of questioning the purpose of one's actions in the light of ethical principles demonstrates the strength of the leader's character that enhances the followers' perception of the trustworthiness of the leader.

b. Pride

The leader obviously needs to have high self-esteem. This self-esteem originates from a healthy pride in one's accomplishments as well as the esteem of one's followers. However, the leader's behaviors are not designed to merely gain the acceptance of the followers. For example, in formulating the vision the leader ought to take into account the needs and aspirations of the followers, but the leader ought not to allow the desire to be accepted by the followers to compromise the vision, when such compromise will jeopardize the higher purpose. In other words, the leader does not look to the followers for affiliative assurance to reinforce her self-love, but rather for transforming the followers to accept and realize the vision. Ethical leaders exhibit healthy pride, not vanity. The dividing line between healthy pride and vanity is unbelievably thin because of the strong egotistic tendency in human beings, but ethical leaders recognize that inordinate self-love is a human vice and not a virtue.

c. Patience

As the leader works toward the realization of the vision, she is certain to come across obstacles from the environment (internal or external) or from the reluctance of the followers to accept and be committed to the vision. It takes time and effort to overcome such obstacles that are inevitable in a worthy and noble endeavor. Hence, the need for patience. A leader bears the present difficulties with calm and serenity because of her faith in the vision. The leader develops an inner realization that "in good time" the difficulties will be resolved. The faith referred to here is not fatalism that inevitably paralyzes action. Rather, it is the vision and the leader's conviction that the vision will be achieved that contribute to the leader's constancy of purpose, and leads the leader to continue undaunted with what needs to be done.

This will particularly be the case with a leader who strives to exercise prudence and fortitude. The practice of prudence enables the leader to properly assess all facts and circumstances surrounding one's decisions, and the practice of fortitude develops the capacity to act positively in the midst of difficulties. The relevance of prudence for leadership is reflected in the leader's need to be sensitive to the environment; the relevance of fortitude is demonstrated by the fact that the leader is called upon to perform behaviors that involve great personal risks and sacrifices. As a result, the patient leader who is in the habit of practicing prudence and fortitude will not be inclined to resort to unethical practices when things do not go as planned.

d. Persistence

The power of persistence is best captured in Winston Churchill's bulldog-like perseverance—that is, to Never! Never! Never! Never! Give Up! Persistence does not mean a stubborn obstinacy. Rather, the leader will not allow difficulties to weaken her resolve to "stay the course"; instead, the leader continues to take the steps necessary, even those involving personal risk and sacrifice, in order to achieve the vision. It is perfectly human to justify unethical practices when one feels overwhelmed by insurmountable internal or external difficulties. The practice of fortitude allows one to strive to overcome difficulties not because it is convenient or pleasant to do so, but because one's duty requires that it be done. This idea is forcefully expressed by John Boyt Stookey of National Distillers (now Quantum Chemical) when he declared: "One of the things ... that we mean by ethical behavior is that we will forego profit in order to adhere to a standard of conduct. I believe that's a message a CEO needs to convey loud and clear to an organization and I find myself doing that" (Watson, C. E. (1991). *Managing with Integrity: Insights from America's C.E.O.s*, p. 186. New York: Praeger).

e. Perspective

As Blanchard and Peale note, "Perspective is the capacity to see what is *really* important in any given situation." The habit of reflection is critical to acquiring a sense of perspective. And reflection is simply not possible unless one devotes some time each day to silence—a resource that has been recommended by wise men of all time and from all cultures, and yet the one resource that remains most untapped. Silence is more than refraining from noise; it is the inner silence that allows one to reflect on the higher purpose, to question one's decisions in the light of that purpose, and to seek the strength not to betray it. Silence allows one to listen to the inner stirrings of the spirit. It is needed to make distinctions between right and wrong, and to discern what one ought to do.

The preceding discussion has touched on several suggestions available to leaders in their efforts to develop the inner strength they need to function as ethical, moral persons. The ascetical literature, however, emphasizes that the enduring effectiveness of these suggestions very much depends upon their habitual practice and, more importantly, on a specific time the leader sets aside for the ascetical practice of "examination of conscience."

III. CONCLUSION

Ethical leadership enables organizational leaders to be sensitive to their moral obligations to the organization's stakeholders and to society at large. The overarching motive for ethical leadership is the leader's altruistic intent, which is expressed in the transformational mode of influencing the followers. For this purpose, the leader needs to develop as a moral person and she needs to create the moral environment in the organization that is conducive for ethical behavior. The leader's effort to apply the principles of ethical power is a practical first step toward ethical leadership.

Also See the Following Articles

ALTRUISM AND ECONOMICS • CORPORATIONS, ETHICS IN • EGOISM AND ALTRUISM • MACHIAVELLIANISM • UTILITARIANISM

Bibliography

Andrews, K. R. (1989, Sept.–Oct.). Ethics in practice. *Harvard Business Review,* 99–104.

Berenbeim, R. E. (1987). *Corporate ethics.* New York: Conference Board, Inc.

Blanchard, K., & Peale, N. V. (1988). *The power of ethical management.* New York: Fawcett Crest.

Boyatzis, R. E. (1982). *The competent manager: A model for effective performance.* New York: Wiley.

Campbell, D. (1975, December). On the conflicts between biological and social evolution and between psychology and moral tradition. *American Psychologist,* 30, pp. 1103–1126.

Conger, J. A., & Associates (1994). *Spirit at work: Discovering the spirituality in leadership.* San Francisco, CA: Jossey-Bass.

Conger, J. A., & Kanungo, R. N. (1988). The empowerment process: Integrating theory and practice. *Academy of Management Review,* 13(3), 471–482.

Howell, J. M., & Avolio, B. J. (1992). The ethics of charismatic leadership: Submission or liberation. *Academy of Management Executive,* 6(2), 43–54.

Kanungo, R. N. (1992). Alienation and empowerment: Some ethical imperatives in business. *Journal of Business Ethics,* 11, pp. 413–422.

Kanungo, R. N., & Conger, J. (1993) Promoting altruism as a corporate goal. *Academy of Management Executive,* 7(3), 37–48.

Kanungo, R. N., & Mendonca, M. (1996). *Ethical dimensions of leadership.* Thousand Oaks, CA: Sage Publications.

McClelland, D. C., & Burnham, D. H. (1995, January–February). *Harvard Business Review,* pp. 126–139.

Sashkin, M. (1984, Spring). Participative management is an ethical imperative. *Organizational Dynamics,* 5–22.

Srivastva, S., Cooperrider and Associates. (1990). *Appreciative management and leadership: The power of positive thought and action in organizations.* San Francisco, CA: Jossey-Bass.

LEGAL ETHICS, OVERVIEW

Richard H. S. Tur
Oriel College, Oxford

GLOSSARY

act utilitarianism The view that the goodness of any act depends solely on the overall state of affairs consequent upon it. Some utilitarians reject such direct consequentialism in favor of rule utilitarianism according to which the rightness of any act depends not upon the act itself or its direct consequences but upon its conformity with a set of rules, themselves justified by their overall consequences.

Chinese wall A term of uncertain provenance to describe arrangements within a commercial enterprise or a law firm to screen information from those who are ethically or legally unentitled to that information. Some judges have seen the nomenclature as an attempt to clothe with the respectability of antiquity a practice that they consider both disreputable and ineffective. It may involve an allusion to attempts by President Nixon's government to establish contact that apparently met with "a Chinese wall of silence." Polite usage favors the alternative expression "cone of silence."

compleat An archaic variant of "complete"; the allusion is to Izaak Walton's *The Compleat Angler* (1653 & 1655), which contains much more than practical hints on angling with quotations for Pliny, pastoral songs and ballads, and glimpses of an idyllic rural life of well-kept inns and tuneful milkmaids. Accordingly, to be "compleat" is to be complete in a very special way.

ethical drift The author's term for the process whereby past departures from an ethical standard harden into a less-demanding standard for the future, and so on.

irrebuttable presumption In the law of evidence, a presumption is an inference or conclusion of fact that may or must be drawn from other established facts. Presumptions are irrebuttable or conclusive where a conclusion must be drawn by law from certain facts and they cannot be disproved by any contrary evidence however strong. In reality, an irrebuttable presumption is not a rule of evidence at all but a fixed rule of law. Rebuttable presumptions are conclusions that, by law, are required to be drawn on the absence of evidence to the contrary.

natural person A human being, as distinguished from an artificial person or corporation recognized by the law as having legal personality, for example, a company.

role morality The idea, associated with the philosopher Bradley, that the demands of morality are not those of a remote logical abstraction but those of a role in a concrete historical community.

Watergate A complex of apartments, offices, and a hotel beside the Potomac river in Washington that was the headquarters of the Democratic Party during the 1972 U.S. presidential election. On June 17, five men were caught in these headquarters with electronic eavesdropping equipment and, with two accomplices later arrested, were all found to have been paid by the Republican Committee for the Re-Election of the President. Their trial and the subsequent disclosures led to a political crisis and the eventual resignation of President Nixon. The relevance for legal ethics is the number of lawyers involved in the wider conspiracy.

LEGAL ETHICS, at the most general level of discourse, is the philosophical study of the moral values inherent in legal practice and of the rules and principles that ought to govern the conduct of individual lawyers. More narrowly, "legal ethics" often refers to a written code of conduct for lawyers usually promulgated, administered, and enforced by a national or regional governing body of the profession such as the Law Society (England), the American Bar Association, the Queensland Law Society, or the California Bar Association. An understanding of legal ethics, in both senses, requires an appreciation of the nature of a "profession," of "professional ethics," of "role morality," and of "ethics" in general. There is a debate in the literature as to whether the term "ethics" is appropriate at all in this universe of discourse on the basis that what lawyers and law teachers call legal ethics is not *ethics* at all, but merely regulations made by administrative agencies based upon command and sanction rather than on conscience and insight. On the other hand, there are writers who argue that general ethics should be modeled on legal ethics and that a life in the law is an adventure in applied ethics. Thus, as befits a philosophical topic, there are arguments about the status of the subject. A respectable case can be made either way and legal ethics can be taught merely as just another set of "black letter rules" to be mastered and manipulated by legal practitioners. However, critical reflection on the values inherent in legal practice and reflective engagement with the moral mission of lawyering certainly contributes to our understanding of the lawyer's predicament, and may improve the ethical quality of the legal profession.

I. INTRODUCTION

Historically, legal ethics was taught, if at all, by the legal profession rather than in universities. This has

now changed or is changing throughout the common law world, not least because of the initiative of the American Bar Association in 1986, following on the embarrassments of Watergate, requiring that "Law schools should give continuing attention to the form and content of their courses in ethics and professionalism. They should weave ethical and professional issues into courses in both substantive and procedural fields." This development gradually attracted the interest of legal philosophers and of philosophers of education and, in consequence or otherwise, legal ethics has increasingly attracted the attention of moral philosophers where debate has been joined on the side of Kantian universalism against sociological arguments that a profession entails a special role morality. Traditional moral philosophy treats moral reasoning from the moral point of view, that is to say, from the point of view of the universal agent. This perspective reinforces the view that professional duties are so different from moral duties that the very idea of professional *ethics*, including legal *ethics,* is misconceived. Some traditional moral philosophers, applying abstract universal principles, and crisp utilitarian calculations, have condemned legal practice as an institutional exemption from moral conscience and have criticized lawyers' codes of professional ethics as permitting or even requiring conduct by lawyers on behalf of clients that harms identifiable third parties or society in general and that even lawyers themselves would accept as being morally wrong if done other than in the course of legal practice. As Macaulay put it, "with a wig on his head and a band round his neck a lawyer will do for a guinea what, without these appendages, he would think it wicked and infamous to do for an empire." Accordingly, these philosophers have urged radical revision of legal practice and lawyers' professional codes.

Legal ethicists have countered this with the view that traditional moral philosophers themselves misconceive the nature of ethics and miss an important opportunity to glean something of general value from the way lawyers handle the ethical problems of legal practice. The insistence of traditional moral philosophers on a core set of critical substantive values applicable to all, irrespective of social role and circumstance, unfortunately diverts attention from the interesting possibility that not only are there competing ethical values but also there are structurally different theories of the nature of ethics. Perhaps a sensitive appreciation of legal ethics would contribute to a better understanding of a different theoretical approach to moral philosophy. The traditional approach to moral philosophy may be too logical, too abstract, and too rational, and it may be that professional ethics in general and legal ethics in particular support and reinforce *applied* rather than theoretical moral philosophizing. The suggestion, then, is that legal ethics, with its emphasis on roles and relationships, might have as much to contribute to moral philosophy as moral philosophy has to teach legal ethics. This suggestion is all the more apt at a time when there has been a revivification of virtue ethics and an increased focus on the concrete.

This general point has been well made by Alasdair MacIntyre, author of *After Virtue: A Study in Moral Theory* (1981), a seminal work in the field of virtue ethics, in an earlier article entitled "What Has Ethics to Learn from Medical Ethics?" (1978). Here, he criticizes moral philosophers as "a kind of intellectual peace corps, treating the medical profession as a morally underdeveloped country." Similarly, legal ethicists, such as Schneyer, have criticized moral philosophers for their missionary zeal, seeking to change legal practice, perhaps out of all recognition, rather than understand and nurture it. MacIntyre is highly critical of privileging the abstract agent. He claims that "any rational moral evaluation requires seeing an actor in some role ... no one is ever an abstract moral agent ... moral agency is embodied in roles such as that of the physician, the patient or the nurse." He then seems to suggest that traditional moral philosophizing may have matters upside down: "If moral agency is exercised through roles, then the questions that ought to be addressed are much more specific than those with which moral philosophy is conventionally concerned ... The moral agent turns out to be no more and no less than both the sum and the unity of his roles embodied in a single person. The abstract ghost of conventional ethics, man as such ... has to be replaced by this much more interesting figure."

This is a promising inversion from the perspective of legal ethics. Schneyer observes that "... it often seems difficult to discern the principles that would or should govern one's behaviour in a given situation without imagining oneself in some social role, relationship or practice tradition." It follows that role and situation—context—is important in answering a whole host of ethical questions such as whether one can act in a manner that will cause harm to an identifiable third party. What is intellectually exciting about this is the invitation to reconstruct ethics from the bottom up, as it were, rather than from the top down. None of us experiences ethical problems in the abstract, universalistic realm of the pure moral agent. We, all of us, experience moral problems in context, usually that of a rela-

tionship, or a role, such as spouse, parent, friend, lover, doctor, teacher, lawyer, police officer, journalist, soldier, or executioner.

It is of more than passing interest that this reconstructed approach to moral philosophy is similar in its concerns to some aspects of feminist ethical debate. What is at issue is whether legal ethics is contained within or is distinct from ethics in general. Moral philosophers critical of lawyers have argued that lawyers should take ethical responsibility for their clients' ends and assess these according either to current morality or to some privileged critical substantive theory, such as utilitarianism, rights, or universal categorical imperatives. Moral philosophy in that tradition is a highly rational and deductive business. Criticisms in a different voice, and here one thinks of Held, Menkel-Meadow, Minow, and Smart, among others, repudiate this rationalist, deductive, computational approach to ethics and they privilege, instead, intuition, emotion, caring, connectedness, and context. On this second approach, ethical thinking is a very intuitive business, devoid of hierarchical principles, and seeing the ethical point is rather like seeing the point of a joke. Ethical thinking, on this view is, like the common law, a wilderness of single instances and not a matter of deduction from given principles. Thus, in opposition to a rationalist "ethics of justice" an "ethics of care," perhaps drawing on Aristotle and Hume, is advocated and developed into an ethics of feeling, of intuition, even of love, sometimes meaning Christian love, with an emphasis on the concrete as in Fletcher's *Situation Ethics* (1966). The ethical thrust of both *Orley Farm* (1862) by Trollope and *Mitigating Circumstances* by Rosenberg (1993) turn in part upon the legitimacy of role morality and, in particular, upon the ideas that a mother's role, or a lawyer's, may involve dispensation from the prompting of universalistic moral conscience, or of community morality and that, in matters of existential ethical choice, the concrete and specific may trump the abstract and general.

That abstract, general principles may be trumped in practice gives rise to two questions about the professional conduct of lawyers. First, should lawyers go beyond current professional standards, rejecting neutrality, and seek to impose their own personal morality on clients, withdrawing from acting if needs be? An unqualified "yes" to this question seems to call into question the very existence of client autonomy, and the established role of the legal profession in an adversary system but an unqualified "no" exposes the legal profession to legitimate criticism for facilitating morally unconsionable or undesirable ends, to the detriment of identifiable third parties or to society as a whole. The second question is should lawyers pursue objectives for clients where the lawyer disapproves of the client's ends or where clients' projects involve or might involve law-breaking? Those who say "yes" seek to hear a multiplicity of voices within the legal system. Those who say "no" are conscious of the lawyer's duty to uphold the law. In answering either question we encounter moral dilemmas which cannot be solved without the exercise of personal judgment.

Traditional moral philosophy appears to exclude or minimize the possibility of genuine moral conflict. Such conflict as there may be is that between the agent's desires and the requirements of the rational and universal moral code, but there can be no conflicts within such a system. Genuine moral conflict is constituted by conflicting moral duties and that entails conflicting moral imperatives. Such conflicting imperatives may be best explained as features of two incompatible roles such that, for example, one may fight as a patriot and nationalist for the liberation of one's country or remain at home as a caring spouse and parent. Moral conflict arises from one person having more than one role and recognizing the moral pull of each while conscious of the impossibility of satisfying both in the particular circumstances that give rise to the conflict. The suggestion is that, properly understood, the lawyer's role-differentiated morality justifies a negative answer to the first and a positive answer to the second question. It seems that those philosophers who answer the two questions stated above otherwise, whatever their intentions, imply the submerging of the lawyer's role into that of the ordinary moral agent and seek to substitute the content of their privileged moral philosophy for the content of the law and of the specialist role, morality of lawyering. Thus, even though both law and professional ethics impose a duty of confidentiality on the lawyer in respect of anything learned within the lawyer–client relationship, these philosophers would require disclosure or whistle-blowing by the lawyer if universalistic or community morality called for it. A preferable alternative to the imposition of external values is to attempt to construct a coherent view of the lawyer's role and ethical mission, from the perspective of the practice of law even though that requires some departure from prevailing moral theories and an acceptance that in legal practice, as in life, one is bound to encounter conflicting values and moral dilemmas, to which there may be no easy, or uniquely right, answer.

II. THE LAWYER'S ROLE

Lawyers are in both a privileged position and in a predicament. They are privileged by reason of their close involvement in the law-making and law-applying enterprise that converts social situations into legal categories, and offers legal remedies in a wide range of circumstances. This is a power. Lawyers operate mysterious levers whereby the hopes of clients may be realized, and fears allayed. The lawyer's power is considerable because every concrete social situation is unique and there is nearly always some room for choice in the application of general, abstract rules to particular facts. There is always a range of legal strategies available in any situation. Lawyers, alone or negotiating with a professional colleague representing a contrary interest, are frequently the first, only, and last decision makers in a wide range of circumstances calling for interpretation and application of statutes, common law principles, and administrative regulations. And even where a dispute ends up in a court or tribunal, lawyers frequently were involved in the earlier stages, framing the terms of the dispute for further processing by judges.

Lawyers function as gatekeepers between citizens and officials, as mediators between individuals and the state, and as filters between individuals and remedies. On one side there are individual values and aspirations and on the other, there are opposing and constraining collective values and norms. Ideally, the lawyer seeks to reconcile so far as possible the interests of clients and the demands of the community and of the state. At its best, lawyering is about sensitive judgment and contested claims. It is about self and others and it involves striking a balance between the demands made upon the citizen to conform as a team player and the individual's need for freedom and self-expression. How lawyers view the law and how far they recognize the ethical discretion inherent in law making and law applying shapes their perception of their role; and consciously or not, their perception of the worth of clients' aspirations may shape the strategy and determine the ingenuity and energy deployed in acting. A "compleat" legal practitioner enjoys the great power of using all the legal resources of the system to further the client's interests.

This power and privilege brings with it responsibility and therein lies the predicament. The central questions remain: How damaging in social terms may be the consequences of vigorous lawyering? How far, if at all, may a lawyer assist a client against the law? And how far, if at all, may a lawyer seek to insinuate or impose moral views on a client? The literature of lawyers' ethics reveals a debate between revisionist moral activism and the passivity borne of the standard conception of the lawyer's role. But even a passive lawyer cannot escape moral conflict. The matter was very well put by Frideman and Zile in 1964: "The lawyer ... is assumed to serve two masters, his client on the one hand, and society on the other ... Since the state's control [over the lawyer in the United States] is so weak, one danger is that the lawyer will tend to neglect the interests of society in favour of the exclusive interests of his client—he may be tempted to pervert the course of justice because his economic advantage depends exclusively, if he is a private practitioner, on his ability to satisfy his clients ... Thus in the United States the urge to professionalise, to increase standards, to inculcate morality on the part of the lawyer, is necessary precisely because state control is so weak that internal (psychological, social, and professional) controls are of grave importance. In a totalitarian society, the need for professionalism arises out of precisely the opposite phenomenon. Here state control is so unlimited and (at least potentially) so unrestrained that the lawyer is gravely tempted to neglect the interests of his clients in order to advance the interests of society (that is, of the state, since totalitarian states define the social interest as identical with state interests). Particularly since lawyers are not directly compensated by their clients, since they are in some sense employees of the state, since advancement and success depends on satisfying the state rather than particular clients—during the darkest days, even personal freedom or life itself depended upon satisfying the state—the lawyer needs professionalisation as a bulwark against interference with what he considers proper application of his skills in a professional manner. Freedom to act as a lawyer means, in such a society, freedom from excessive dependence on the state; in a democratic society, freedom to act as a lawyer means freedom from excessive dependence on the client."

The lawyer's predicament, then, is to be eternally ground between the nether wheel of the client's aspirations, reasonable or not, and the upper wheel of the state's constraints, just or unjust. Given these conflicting pressures, it is unsurprising that the standard conception of the lawyer's role emphasizes neutrality and nonaccountability. On this view lawyers are morally responsible neither for the state of the law nor for clients' ends but may commit themselves wholly to either as a partisan, doing everything for clients that clients would themselves do, if they had the lawyer's knowledge. It does not follow from this that lawyers are indifferent to the moral dimension and lawyers may

be deeply troubled by what their calling requires of them. For example, not everyone is cut out to be a criminal defense lawyer as Dershowitz vividly illustrates in *The Advocate's Devil* (1994), where one consequence of the central and morally disturbing case in the novel is that the defense lawyer's daughter decides not to become a lawyer because she wants a career in which doing the right thing always helps people and not one where she would have to make tragic choices between people.

The moral dilemma in the novel is a carefully crafted version of a standard ethical problem for lawyers, namely, whether to blow the whistle on a client although the case does not fall within any of the recognized exceptions to the clear and binding professional duty of confidentiality. The dilemma is exacerbated by the lawyer's daughter being placed at risk: "Abe [Ringel, the central character and a criminal defense lawyer] had stopped being a lawyer. Now he was a father determined to save his little girl's life. Maybe it was better for ten guilty men to go free than for one innocent to be wrongly convicted—but not if one of those guilty men was going after your own daughter! Abe [previously characterized as a stickler] was now willing to disobey any rule, violate any law, break any commandment, to stop his diabolical former client from hurting his daughter." Clearly, circumstances can be imagined and even occur where a criminal defense lawyer will feel irresistible moral pressure to breach a rule of professional conduct. Sometimes, of course, the lawyer will be able to stretch the rule but sometimes, and this was the case crafted in the novel, whistle-blowing would be in direct breach of the relevant code of professional responsibility and there is simply no good-faith way to wriggle out of the rule. In such circumstances, and this was the situation in the novel, the lawyer is in a horrible moral dilemma and crisis because the tension between the general moral duty to prevent avoidable serious harm to another and the professional duty to preserve confidentially can tear a person apart, particularly where personal identity is closely bound up with professional persona, which it is likely to be if character and personality is related to what we do daily for many years.

It is perhaps a sad irony that the rules of professional conduct by which some lawyers set such great store cannot be so perfectly drafted as to eliminate tragic choices. Dershowitz fully understands this point and put the following words into the mouth of his principal character at the close of the book: "Some existential moral issues are so complex that they are not amenable to simple solution by the adoption of a blanket rule. Every lawyer will have to continue to struggle with the dilemma of whether or when to blow the whistle on a client."

III. CONFIDENTIALITY

Turning from confidentiality and crime to civil process, the following is a brief summary of *Spaulding v. Zimmerman* 116 NW 2d 704 (1962). A motorist negligently collides with and injures a pedestrian. Both parties consult lawyers. Both lawyers obtain medical reports. The medical report obtained by the motorist's lawyer indicates an aortic aneurism, caused by the collision, which is life threatening although safely operable whereas the medical report obtained by the pedestrian's lawyer makes no mention of any such condition. In the course of negotiations it soon becomes apparent to the motorist's lawyer that the pedestrian's lawyer is wholly unaware of the existence of the aortic aneurism and is willing to accept on behalf of the injured client a sum considerably lower than appropriate to the actual circumstances. In that state of knowledge, does the motorist' lawyer do anything improper in concluding a binding settlement at the lower figure? Is it ethical for a lawyer to take advantage of the other side's ignorance of crucial facts?

Professionally, lawyers are obligated to live by a code of silence—their duty of confidentiality—that prohibits disclosure of information concerning their clients' affairs. Although this duty is subject to exceptions and qualifications, the general understanding is that lawyers simply cannot talk about their clients' affairs, no matter how beneficial disclosure might be in terms of the common good. From an act–utilitarian perspective there is something quite mad about thus deliberately sealing the lips of those particularly well placed to encounter fraud and corrupt practices and blow the whistle. Consider, for example, widespread loss and distress associated with massive banking, insurance, and pension frauds. These simply could not occur without the services of accountants and lawyers who, as professionals, must have at least an inkling of the true nature of their principals' activities and, given the social cost, a powerful justification is surely required for trumping social welfare with the lawyer's right (and duty) of silence. The duty of confidentiality is obviously open to abuse and exploitation by unscrupulous clients and unethical lawyers alike secure in the knowledge that they are unlikely to be called to account for activities that by their very nature must be kept secret. Confidentiality, it seems, may erode responsibility. And clients' interests in secrecy may erode ethical standards where,

for example, lawyers assist corporate clients so to structure the minutes of their internal proceedings and other documents in order to attract protection from discovery under the doctrine in legal professional privilege, which immunizes relevant information even from discovery by order of a court. Many professions share with lawyers a duty of confidentiality but a court may order disclosure; for example, journalists have been ordered to disclose sources. That creates an ethical dilemma for the journalist in that obedience to the court order entails breach of a professional duty and adherence to the standards of the profession entails punishment for contempt of court. Lawyers, however, are in an exceptional situation in that some confidential information is privileged at common law and even a court cannot order disclosure. Although in strict law the privilege is that of the client and may be waived, the consequence is that vital information is unavailable to the court. The justification for all this is that no one would be free to consult a lawyer if the lawyer were a listening post for the state, but this obviously handicaps the adversary system of justice in pursuit of truth. The powerful case that can be assembled in defense of legal professional privilege in the case of the criminal defense lawyer where the liberties of the client are at risk and a privilege against self-incrimination is recognized, does not entail that similar constraints should apply in civil litigation and one possible reform is the abolition of legal professional privilege in civil litigation, at least where the client is other than a natural person.

Because much of a lawyer's conduct is secret it is vital to the general good of society that lawyers, individually and collectively, maintain high ethical standards. Where lawyers, individually or collectively, set their own standards, there is a standing risk that client service considerations will outweigh considerations of social utility and that the pursuit of private interests will outweigh and obscure social responsibility. Moreover, lawyers may be pressured by influential and wealthy clients into activities that are seriously detrimental to society. Lawyers face great temptations in circumstances in which detection is highly unlikely and economic considerations may overwhelm ethical scruples. The lawyer's role thus calls for considerable moral insight, a high degree of integrity, and even courage.

The doctrines of client confidentiality and legal professional privilege are taken by many lawyers to be absolute, but that may be misconceived both as a matter of general principle, and of practice. Confidentiality does not necessarily mandate nondisclosure. It merely provides a reason for nondisclosure that may or may not be outweighed by other considerations. Privilege, however, prevents communications between a client and a solicitor from being disclosed, even in a court of law. Privilege is an impediment, not an inducement, to frank testimony, and it detracts from the fairness of the trial by denying a party access to relevant documents or at least subjecting him to surprise. It follows that in principle privilege should be kept within very narrow limits and granted only where there are compelling reasons and indeed there are several important limitations.

First, where the client is seeking legal services for the purposes of fraud, privilege is lost because whether the lawyer is an innocent dupe or a knowing accomplice, the lawyer does not act "in the ordinary scope of professional employment." Second, privilege is lost where a lawyer seeks to defend a charge of professional misconduct brought by the client. The supportive reasoning here is that by bringing the complaint the client has implicitly waived privilege. However professional bodies and the common law have not adequately addressed the problem where allegation of misconduct are made by a third party, including the professional body, in circumstances where the client is content with the fruits of the lawyer's alleged misconduct and refuses to waive privilege. In the remote jurisdiction of the Northern Territory of Australia, however, there has been a court ruling to the effect that the public interest in high ethical standards in the legal profession trumps the public interest, which underpins the doctrine of legal professional privilege. Third, many jurisdictions have passed statutes expressly or impliedly overriding legal professional privilege.

In the United Kingdom three statutory provisions bear directly upon the scope of confidentiality and legal professional privilege. Under section 24 of the Drug Trafficking Offences Act, 1986 "a person"—which includes "a lawyer"—concerned in the retention or control of the proceeds of drug trafficking is required to report the matter and is expressly immunized from any contractual liability for breach of any restriction upon the disclosure of information. Next, under section 12 of the Prevention of Terrorism (Temporary Provisions) Act, 1989, "A person [including a lawyer] may notwithstanding any restriction on the disclosure of information imposed by contract disclose to a constable a suspicion or belief that any money or property is or is derived from terrorist funds." Lastly, section 18 of the Prevention of Terrorism (Temporary Provisions) Act, 1989 requires a person to disclose information about acts of terrorism. This requirement is subject to a defence of "reasonable excuse" which, in the opinion of the (English) Law Society might be satisfied by a claim that

the information was received by a lawyer within the scope of professional employment and is therefore confidential and privileged, although that interpretation does not appear consistent with the other sections or with the general purpose of the legislation. It is, however, consistent with the readiness of professional bodies to regard with jealous anxiety any erosion of confidentiality and privilege, which are widely regarded by lawyers as absolute values.

In Australia, there are wide-ranging statutory duties under the Financial Transactions Reports Acts 1988–1991 to report certain cash and financial transactions, but lawyers are not included. Accordingly, a suspicion or belief that monies are derived from or used in connection with drug trafficking or other serious crime imposes no legal duty on Australian lawyers to report and confidentiality would appear to impose an ethical duty of silence unless the lawyer concluded that these activities are likely to result in serious bodily harm. The National Crimes Authority reported that money from crime had been laundered through the Queensland real estate industry. It was alleged that lawyers faked documents, including mortgage loans and tenancy agreements, to facilitate the investment of the proceeds of crime in real estate and have passed money through their trust accounts to avoid detection. The National Crimes Authority therefore advocated a change in the law. In America, the Inland Revenue Code compels those engaged in trade or business who receive more that $10,000 in cash in one transaction to report that fact. American lawyers fiercely resisted this legislation as damaging to the lawyer–client relationship but it passed into law and has been upheld as constitutional.

At times, government policy will be inconsistent with the lawyer's traditional role as partisan advocate, zealously pursuing the client's interests independently of the general ethics of the matter or the impact upon the wider community. Full implementation of government policy may be prejudiced by the lawyer's traditional commitment to secrecy and client service and lawyers will necessarily encounter pressures to reconsider their role and social responsibilities. This is well caught by the following judicial observation: "The right of one party to have discovery and inspection and the right of the other, within certain areas, to be protected from inspection are parallel rights; in itself neither is paramount over the other." A recognition that confidentiality and disclosure are of equal status, in litigation and beyond, leads to serious questions about limiting client confidentiality and privilege in the interests of disclosure for the public good. Reflective legal practitioners and engaged ethics teachers are therefore drawn increasingly into a sensitive balancing exercise calling for fine judgment, rather than the automatic application of an absolute rule in all cases, whatever the wider consequences. Here, too, a life in the law is an adventure in applied ethics.

IV. CONFLICT OF INTEREST

In *Australian Commercial Research and Development Ltd v. Hampson* [(1991) 1 Qd R 508] where, remarkably, the plaintiff had briefed 15 Queen's Counsel to give an opinion on the same matter, and subsequently sought to have one of them, the defendant barrister, restrained from acting on the other side, the judge summarized the applicable *legal* principles as follows:

1. That a legal practitioner has acted previously for a client does not, of itself, preclude that practitioner from acting for another person in the same proceedings; BUT
2. A legal practitioner will be restrained from acting for the new client where confidential information has been obtained from the former client, AND
3. It is probable that real prejudice and real mischief will result; THEREFORE
4. Courts should take a cautious approach to allowing a lawyer to act against a former client where (a) confidential information was communicated; (b) that information is relevant to present litigation; and (c) the information is still available to the lawyer, NOT LEAST BECAUSE
5. A lawyer changing sides during a case conflicts with justice being seen to be done.

These principles entail that a lawyer cannot readily act against a former client and that the courts will grant injunctions where there is a probability of prejudice. However, the historical *ethical* standard seems to have been more demanding in that a possibility of prejudice rather than a probability sufficed. One would certainly have reservations about a criminal trial where the prosecuting lawyer formerly acted for the defendant even without a probability that real prejudice and real mischief would result. This concern is reinforced by the consideration that a lawyer must use all relevant knowledge as well as skill on behalf of the client. Ordinarily, all members of the firm have (imputed) knowledge of the affairs of the former client and all are subject to the ethical requirement of confidentiality in respect of that information. In taking on a new client with an interest opposed to that of the former client, the lawyer falls under a duty of loyalty to the new client, which is sometimes put in terms of "zealous advocacy" but might be better put as a general duty faithfully to use best endeavors to further the client's interests. And at that point a conflict of duties emerges in that the lawyer has a duty of confidentiality in respect of information acquired from one client and a duty to use that knowledge to the advantage of the new client. It is difficult to see how anyone can fully discharge these two conflicting duties—confidentiality to one, and loyalty to another, although some lawyers reconcile the two on the basis that it is only their *legal* knowledge and not their knowledge of fact that they are bound to use for the benefit of clients.

However, established ethical imperatives appear to have been eroded, especially by megafirms anxious to retain clients despite the exponential tendency of conflicts as firms merge or expand by recruiting from other firms. The likelihood is that the legal standard (probability) will simply have to be altered to match the ethical standard (possibility) in order to avoid "ethical drift" and further erosion of public confidence in the administration of justice. In this respect, at least, self-regulation does not appear to be working, and ethical imperatives seem likely to be converted (by the courts) into legal standards. This is well illustrated by a decision of the Canadian Supreme Court. In *Martin v. MacDonald Estate* [1991] 1 W W R 705 the plaintiff brought an action for an accounting. The defendant's solicitor was assisted by a junior member of the firm who was actively engaged in the file and privy to many confidences disclosed by the defendant. Later this junior joined the firm representing the plaintiff. The plaintiff had been represented by that firm for years and was understandably reluctant to change solicitors. Affidavits were sworn that the case had not been and would not be discussed with the new recruit. She also swore that she had not and would not betray confidences.

The sole issue was the appropriate standard to be applied in determining whether the plaintiff's firm was disqualified from continuing to act by reason of conflict of interest. A four-judge majority held even the "probability of mischief" test insufficient. The test actually adopted is that a reasonably informed person would be satisfied that no use of confidential information would occur. Such matters are not usually susceptible of proof and the majority therefore adopted two presumptions. First, given a lawyer–client relationship the court should infer that confidential information had passed unless the solicitor could satisfy the court of the contrary. Obviously, this will be a difficult burden to discharge. Second, the court should assume that lawyers who work together share confidences, unless satisfied on the basis of clear and convincing evidence that all reasonable measures had been taken to prevent information seeping from the "tainted" lawyer to others. Mere undertakings and affidavits would never be enough and a court would be unlikely to accept "Chinese walls" or "cones of silence" as effective screening other than in very exceptional circumstances.

Far reaching as this is, and sufficient though it was on the facts to disqualify the plaintiff's solicitors from acting, it did not go far enough for the concurring three-judge minority. The majority had attempted to balance three competing values—the maintenance of the high standards of the legal profession and the integrity of the judicial system; the right of litigants not to be deprived of their counsel without good cause; and reasonable mobility in the legal profession. The three-judge minority thought it less a balancing exercise and more a matter of priority: "Neither the merger of law firms nor the mobility of lawyers can be permitted to adversely affect the public's confidence in the judicial system ... it is fundamentally important that justice not only be done but appear to be done in the eyes of the public." Accordingly, this three-judge group adopted irrebuttable presumptions, thereby imposing an even stricter duty upon lawyers.

So-called "Chinese walls" have come in for widespread judicial criticism in England and in Australia as well as in Canada, and even those judges who would allow a lawyer to rebut the presumption of seepage of information take the view that Chinese walls would be effective only in the most exceptional circumstances. It has been denounced judicially as a device to justify large firms of lawyers representing conflicting interests at the same time.

Some lawyers have remained anxious to service corporate clients with potentially conflicting interests and have attempted to restructure a large firm into several separate sections so that each is in effect a separate and independent firm. But such restructing itself raises serious questions. Genuine severance would actually resconstitute the large firm as several smaller firms.

Anything short of that would still leave the large firm open to ethical criticism and legal action given, first, that the knowledge of any one partner is the imputed knowledge of all, and secondly, that a solicitor is duty bound faithfully to use best endeavors in the interest of the client. Furthermore, unless the discrete sections are not only separate but equal, the large firm of solicitors is choosing, through its management partners, to allocate a poorer quality service to some clients. In England *The Law Society's Guide to the Professional Conduct of Solicitors* deals very plainly with the matter: "If a solicitor ... has acquired relevant knowledge concerning a former client during the course of acting for him, he ... must not accept instructions to act against him". The [English] Law Society does not, however, regard its own rule as absolute and, in further guidance, it allows that "in certain exceptional circumstances, however—and it is to be emphasized that the circumstances will indeed be rare—the best interests of the client(s) may permit the firm to continue acting for one or, just possibly, both clients." The mechanism that might permit such acting is the Chinese wall but such information barriers are only appropriate where there is "an overriding and compelling need."

The whole tenor of the judgments suggest that establishing such a need will be no easy matter. A judge in New South Wales observed, "Here in Sydney and now there is a thriving diverse and talented legal profession and the court need not fear that a litigant who is deprived of the services of one firm will not be able to retain adequate representation." Similarly, the Canadian Supreme Court observed that "... the legal profession has many able counsel" and a guidebook for Scottish solicitors acknowledge that "in a city such as Edinburgh or Glasgow there is no reason why, if there is any question of conflict, a client should not be sent elsewhere."

V. FAMILY LAWYERING

The relaxed attitude of practitioners to conflicts in the commercial sphere contrasts sharply with the position in matrimonial causes. It is, perhaps, too readily assumed that parties' *interests* are necessarily opposed in divorce. Emotional conflict, of course, is common but in many, perhaps most, cases the parties do have a common interest in the expeditious and economical resolution of their dispute and in the welfare of their children, if any. Yet the conflicts are emphasized and the common interests are marginalized in traditional family lawyering and standard legal ethics. It follows that legal advice comes in adversarial idiom, failing therefore to meet the needs of couples who *can* agree.

Some legal ethicists have proposed that the law and legal ethics should be adjusted to permit one lawyer to act for a divorcing couple, where appropriate, and always with the informed consent of the parties. Family lawyers should be encouraged to assist divorcing couples reach legally binding arrangements for the termination of their relationship as a married couple; for the distribution of their property; and for the welfare of their children, if any. Although potentially very attractive to consumers of legal services, this proposal is resisted by lawyers because radical individualism and separate representation are very deeply embedded in the common law, however inefficient or ethically questionable.

Consider the following case: You are a sole practitioner in a general practice and have acted for many years for a husband and wife. In fact, you went to school with them both and you have been friends for many years. You have acted for them in their business dealings and in various conveyances. One day you are approached in your office by the wife who is clearly upset. She tells you that she has decided to separate from her husband and she wants you to act for her in the divorce. There are substantial assets that will have to be divided up and there are also two young children of the marriage. The wife is distraught and insists that you are the only lawyer whom she knows and she will feel very uncomfortable if she has to go to anyone else.

Even if the husband agrees that you can act, the current rules are unhelpful in that the practitioner shall not represent conflicting interests in litigation and while a practitioner may act for conflicting interests in other matters with informed consent, the practitioner who has ceased to act for one party should not continue to act for the other. It might just be possible, given informed consent, for a lawyer to assist a divorcing couple in preparing an agreement that could form the basis of a consent order but it seems that the couple would each have to be passed over to separate lawyers for the ensuing court applications. Some adjustment in these rules is clearly necessary if an ethically sensitive and caring family lawyer is to act for the couple on the basis that this will produce by far the best outcome for the parties.

American ethicists have addressed the problem faced by lawyers dealing with the special needs of elderly clients and their families. One has written: "Lawyers are dissatisfied with current ethical guidelines because they do not adequately address their role in advising families with whom they have had a long-standing professional relationship. In particular, elder lawyers worry about the conflict of interest rules. They fear that if literally applied, the rules will disqualify multiple representation of family members with whom the elder lawyer has had a continuing professional relationship." Similar ethical dilemmas exist in family law generally, such as estate planning and domestic relations. The central question is the identity of the client. Can a family lawyer act for a family unit or must there be separate representation for each family member?

Batt illustrates the difficulties with a hypothetical case from an *ABA Legal Awareness Project:* A lawyer has a long-standing professional relationship with the elder family—spouses Mr. and Mrs. A. Being a trusted family legal adviser he has, in recent years, provided legal advice to their daughters C and C. Mrs. A, the increasingly disoriented Mr. A, and the two middle-aged daughters now seek legal advice. It seems that Mrs. A can no longer care for her aged spouse and is considering long-term institutional care. The daughters (and heirs) have concurrent, potentially conflicting, worries regarding their mother's financial well-being and what they perceive as their father's inevitable need for institutional care. The daughters do not want to jeopardize their mother's financial stability by incurring the costs associated with long-term convalescent care of their father, but they also understand that he is becoming hard to handle. Mr. A does not want to be placed in a nursing home, but he trusts the family as well as the elder lawyer's judgment. Independent as ever, Mr. A insists on assuming responsibility for the fee. Batt proposes that elder lawyers should treat the family entity as the client. In America, this "entity theory of representation" is found in *Model Rule* 1.13 in respect of corporations. Representing the family would allow the lawyer "to harmonize potential differences so as to devise a legally sound solution to family problems" and to maintain a degree of independence from individual family members. When acting for the family, the lawyer would have "a mandate to address family interests even to the potential detriment of individual members." Individual members could withdraw at any time and obtain separate legal representation but contrary to current legal ethics, the family lawyer could continue to represent the family unit until dismissed. Apart from the initial implausibility of regarding the "organization" language of *Model Rule* 1.13 as apt to include families, there is much morally to be gained for family lawyers in such an approach.

Schaffer is another American commentator who has argued compellingly for family representation. Just as Batt understands that "the elderly person may be more concerned with his relationships with others than with his finances or place a higher value on tranquility within his family than upon asserting his individual right," so Schaffer emphasizes the special nature of family relationships, citing the words of Anne Tyler's kidnapped housewife, Charlotte in the novel *Earthly Possessions,* "I saw that all of us lived a sort of a web, criss-crossed by strings of love and need and worry … It appeared that we were all taking care of each other, in ways an outsider might not notice."

Shaffer illustrates the problem with the case of the unwanted will: John and Mary, a middle-aged couple with adult children want their will drafted before beginning a vacation trip abroad. Based on John's instructions, the lawyer prepares a pair of parallel wills, each leaving all property to the surviving spouse, or, if both are dead, to their children in equal shares. On a second visit to the office, the lawyer presented the prepared wills to the couple, and John executes his. The lawyer then suggests to John that he would like to be alone with Mary before she signs. The lawyer asks Mary if the will is as she would have made it had her husband not been present at the conference and if the will were to be secret from her husband. She says no, that the will as drawn contains several provisions that are contrary to her wishes, and that she would change if her husband were not to know the ultimate disposition of her estate. However, she says that she would not be willing to precipitate the domestic discord and confrontation that would occur if her husband were to learn that she had drawn a will contrary to his wishes and in accordance with her own desires.

Shaffer puts Mary's concern into context by supposing some further facts, namely that one of the couple's children, Henry, was married for 10 years to Susan but is now divorced and the grandchildren live with Susan. At the conference, John said that "Henry's share" should go to Henry if alive and if dead, to Henry's children, and Mary sat silent. On her own, however, Mary says that she wants some of her family's property to go to Susan.

Shaffer is highly critical of "the legal ethics of radical individualism"; he thinks that "families are prior to individuals" and he is convinced "that a family is something worth representing." He emphasizes that "what is present in the law office is a family" and rejects the one-lawyer-for-each-person way of approaching the problem then resolving it with the ethics of autonomy as leaving "the family out of account." Shaffer's treatment of the case of the unwanted will is, ultimately, inconclusive and not everyone would accept as well-founded his perception of a "religious tradition in ordinary Wednesday-afternoon law practice," but there is an obviously challenging ethical dimension to his view that in the case of the unwanted will "the most *irresponsible* thing a lawyer could do is to send either of these people to another lawyer, or both of them to two other lawyers." The family lawyer is involved in "deep … family things" and should attempt to *mediate* as "lawyer for the family." Clearly, the life of the family lawyer, as contemplated by Batt and by Schaffer is an adventure in applied ethics.

VI. CONCLUSION

Kronman brilliantly develops the idea that any instrumental justification for the life of a lawyer whether couched in terms of income to be earned or in terms of social good to be done misses the point and presses on to offer an intrinsic justification. The life of the lawyer, he suggests, is is to be justified not by what it brings but by what it is. It is the life of the good judge. Judgment, for Kronman, is "non-deductive and non-intuitive" in that it has an argumentative dimension. Furthermore, judgment is constitutive in that the important life decisions one makes constitutes, at least in part, the self that one becomes. Good judgment is concomitant with good character. The better the judgment the greater the chances that individuals can live amicably with themselves. One develops self-knowledge and character through the exercise of judgment.

Kronman clinches his argument with an account of the good lawyer whose work is marked by subtlety and imagination and, above all, wisdom. The characteristic virtue of the lawyer is, indeed, judgment. There is intrinsic worth in the life of the lawyer who lives up to the high ideals of the profession. The intrinsically good person is the person of developed and sound practical wisdom and a life in the law is conducive to such character. In short, to be a lawyer is a better way to be. Kronman is well aware of the modern tendencies, economic and educational, that threaten the realization of this ideal. Indeed, much depends upon the economic, educational, and professional culture surrounding the individual lawyer. That may be as destructive of the virtue that Kronman extols as supportive of it.

Much depends upon the ethos of lawyering in a community. Standards can decline as well as improve and there is a considerable body of evidence throughout the common law world that lawyers' standards are unacceptably low. If, over time, the moral edge is eroded and the moral boundaries pushed out, without adverse critical reaction, the new boundaries become the accepted standard. That the ethical standards of the legal profession have fallen seems to be widely accepted and effort is directed less toward denying it than explaining it, usually by way of some version of economic determinism. The official reaction to the drop in standards has been an attempt to raise the level of performance by implementing codes of conduct, increasing (self-) regulation and concentrating on education—the residual legatee of all social problems—but, sensibly, not only for those intending one day, perhaps, to practice law but also, by way of continuing legal education, for those already in practice.

Lawyers' ethics matter; not simply to lawyers, but to everyone because erosion of lawyers' ethical standards redounds upon the quality of the criminal and civil justice systems and ultimately upon the quality of life. Lawyers' ethics matter too, not only to practicing lawyers but also, and importantly, to law teachers who must convey some sense of the process values of the law and of the ethical standards essential to good lawyering. There is more to law than the letter, or the reasoning, however sophisticated. There is also ethical sensitivity and judgment and if a life in the law is an adventure in applied ethics, a legal education that rests content with doctrinal expertise is radically incomplete.

Also See the Following Articles

BUSINESS ETHICS, OVERVIEW • MEDICAL CODES AND OATHS • SOCIAL ETHICS, OVERVIEW

Bibliography

Batt (1992). The family unit as client: A means to address the ethical dilemmas confronting elder law attorneys. 6 *Georgetown Journal of Legal Ethics* 319.

Freedman (1990). *Understanding lawyers' ethics.* Matthew Bender.

Freedman (1966). Professional responsibility of the criminal defense lawyer: The three hardest questions. 64 *Michigan Law Review* 1469.

Frideman & Zile (1964). Soviet legal profession: Recent developments in law and practice. *Wisconsin Law Rev* 32.

Fried (1976). The lawyer as friend: The moral foundations of the lawyer client relation. 85 *Yale Law Journal* 1060.

Hazard (1990). Ethical opportunity in the practice of law. *San Diego Law Rev* 127.

Held (1987). Feminism and moral theory. In Meyers & Kittay, *Women and moral theory,* 111.

Held (1983). The division of moral labor and the role of the lawyer. In Luban, *The good lawyer,* 60.

Kronman (1987). A life in the law. 54 *University of Chicago Law Review* 835.

Luban (1988). *Lawyers and justice.* Princeton: Princeton University Press.

Luizzi (1993). *A Case for legal ethics: Legal ethics as a source for a universal ethic.* State University of New York.

Menkel-Meadow (1995). Portia redux: Another look at gender, feminism and legal ethics. In Sampford & Parker (Eds.)., *Legal ethics and legal practice.* Oxford: Oxford University Press, 25.

MacIntyre (1981). *After virtues: A study in moral theory.* Notre Dame, IN: University of Notre Dame Press.

MacIntyre (1978). What has ethics to learn from medical ethics? 2 *Phil Exchange* 37.

Probert & Brown (1966–67). Theories and practices in the legal profession. XIX *University of Florida Law Rev* 447–485.

Simon (1988). Ethical discretion in lawyering. 101 *Harvard Law Review* 1083.

Shaffer (1987). The legal ethics of radical individualism. 65 *Texas Law Review* 963.

Schneyer (1984). Moral philosophy's standard misconception of legal ethics. *Wisconsin Law Review* 1529.

Tur (1995). Lawyers' ethics and criminal justice. Attwool & Goldberg (Eds.)., In Criminal Justice. Franz Steiner.

Tur (1995). Family lawyering and legal ethics In Sampford & Parker (Eds.), *Legal ethics and legal practice,* p. 145. Oxford: Oxford University Press.

Tur (1994). Accountability and lawyers. In Chadwick (Ed.) *Ethics and the professions,* p. 58. Avebury.

Tur (1992). An introduction to lawyers' ethics. 10 *Journal of Professional Legal Education* 217.

LIBERALISM

David Conway
Middlesex University

GLOSSARY

classical liberalism That form of liberalism that favors minimal government, and that rejects both the equalization of life prospects and improvement of positive liberty as legitimate objects of governmental activity.

collectivism The assignment of greater value to specific forms of social life or collectivity than to individuals and the attainment of their goals and objectives.

equality A social ideal equated by classical liberals with the possession of the same basic rights, and by modern liberals with the possession of the same life prospects.

individualism The assignment of greater value to individuals and the attainment of their personal goals and objectives than to specific forms of social life or collectivity.

individuality The respects in which each human being differs in taste, personality, and capacity from every other.

liberalism The political philosophy championing liberty on the grounds that the function of government is to promote the good of the governed, not that of the governors, and that individuals, not their governments, are (normally) the best judges of what is good for them.

liberty The condition enjoyed by one or more persons in the absence of barriers to action.

life prospects The expectations of life that a person enjoys in virtue of his or her natural endowment and social circumstance, including the basic socioeconomic structure of his or her society.

modern liberalism That form of liberalism that favors more-than-minimal government in order to maximize positive liberty and/or to equalize life prospects.

negative liberty The condition enjoyed by one or more persons in the absence of barriers to action imposed by other people.

perfectionism The view that individuals have a good that consists of something other than the attainment of whatever is the object of their own fully informed reflective preferences.

positive liberty The condition enjoyed by one or more persons in the absence of all barriers to action, both artificial and natural; hence, equivalent to the power or ability to act.

rights Entitlements belonging to those who possess them against others to certain positive acts or to certain acts of forbearance.

rule of law The limiting of all state officials in all public activities within the compass of fixed known laws that accord all citizens equal civil and political rights.

separation of powers Constitutional provision expressly forbidding lawmakers from being able either to execute and enforce the law or to decide who has broken it.

LIBERALISM is a political philosophy that is principally distinguished from its rivals by advocating a comparatively much more restricted role for government in organizing and directing the lives of individuals. All, and only, liberals favor so large a legally defined and protected sphere within which members of society are to be at perfect liberty from the state and from other forms of coercive interference to determine for themselves their own life plans and activities, including the terms and conditions of their association with others.

Traditionally, liberals have delineated their favored sphere by identifying rights that they claim, should be legally accorded and upheld by the state. Through advocating the appropriate set of related legal rights, all liberals have, with only minor exceptions and qualifications, supported the following liberties: freedom of religious worship, freedom of thought and expression, liberty of association and contract, freedom to acquire and hold private property, (including the right to private property in the means of production), plus a certain set of political liberties associated with the functioning of representative democracy, such as the right to vote and stand for political office. For the liberal, the reason why people should enjoy the liberty to engage in these activities is not that they constitute a particular special class or set of activities, but that people should be entitled to do *whatever* they want, provided that in doing so they impose no "barriers" to others being able to act similarly.

Liberals maintain that human beings are unable to enjoy such individual spheres of liberty in the absence of governments promulgating and enforcing laws designed to delineate and protect such spheres. By maintaining this, liberalism distinguishes itself from anarchism, a political philosophy that supposes that individuals are capable of simultaneously enjoying such spheres of liberty without need of the institution of government.

Among liberals, considerable diversity of opinion remains on two closely connected issues. The first is whether, or what, additional legal rights, besides the most obvious ones connected with favored liberties, the state must uphold so that everyone can enjoy all the liberties favored by liberals, or else so that other more contentious goals can be reached, most notably, (greater) equality. The second is whether, or how far, any or all of the liberties favored by all liberals may

or must be curtailed in order to accommodate these additional legal rights. On this pair of issues, a notable faultline occurs within liberalism. It divides those liberals who do from those who do not see the need for rights in addition to the most obvious ones on whose need all liberals agree, and, hence, between those liberals who do and those who do not see need for any curtailments to any of the liberties favored by all liberals. Historically speaking, liberals tended for a long time to deny the need for any legal rights other than a commonly favored core set, and, hence, for any curtailments to the liberties favored by all liberals. Only in the twentieth century has it become customary for self-styled liberals to do otherwise. For this reason, liberalism of the former type has often been called *classical liberalism*, and of the latter, *revisionary* or *modern liberalism*.

I. PRINCIPAL ADVERSARIES OF LIBERALISM

Apart from the previously prevailing systems of hierarchical absolutism that liberalism came into being to overthrow, liberalism has, historically, had to contend with three principal adversaries. The first is socialism or communism, especially, of the Marxist variety. The second is Nazism and, to a lesser degree, Fascism. The third is conservatism. The first two adversaries, but far less so the third, favor a more collectivist approach to economic organization and activity than is favored by any variety of liberalism. Socialism does so through favoring public ownership and control of the principal means of production and central state economic planning. Fascism and Nazism do so, through favoring a more veiled form of economic collectivism known as *corporatism.* This involves nominally privately owned companies operating under strict state supervision and direction. The principal difference between these two systems is that, whereas, like liberalism, socialism postulates a fundamental moral equality between all human beings, and, hence, is universalist in scope and moral orientation. Fascism and Nazism both combine corporatism with an ardent and chauvinistic form of nationalism that holds one national or ethnic group superior to all others.

All three adversaries of liberalism assign for the state a much greater and more active role than does even the most interventionist form of modern liberalism. Socialism does so primarily in the economic sphere for the sake of achieving (greater) equality of life prospects.

The remaining two adversaries of liberalism do so primarily in the political and personal spheres. In the case of Fascism and Nazism, this is ostensibly for the sake of advancing the strength of some privileged national or racial group. Conservatism endorses restrictions on personal freedom for the sake of the good of society's members, construed in some perfectionist way. In the case of liberalism, supreme ethical value is attached to individual human beings and to the satisfaction of their individual reflective preferences, with collectivities and social institutions being viewed as possessed of no more than instrumental value in achieving this end. By contrast, liberalism's three prinicipal adversaries attach supreme value to something else. Either, as in the case of socialism and Nazism, supreme value is attached to some form of collectivity, with individuals and their ends being subordinated to it, or else, as with conservatism, it is attached to certain established forms of life to which not all societal members might themselves attach value. Accordingly, while liberalism is individualistic in both an ethical and a economic sense, its principal adversaries are either collectivist or perfectionist in various ways.

II. HISTORY OF LIBERALISM

A. Seventeenth Century

Liberalism acquired its main contours in England during the 17th century. This was a period of profound and tumultuous constitutional upheaval. It witnessed, in turn and in close succession, the forcible deposition and execution of one monarch, civil war, the creation of a short-lived republic, the restoration of monarchy, and, finally, in 1688, the replacement of one line of hereditary monarchs by another more prepared to accept the ultimate sovereignty of parliament.

   This decisive shift in power from a hereditary monarch, claiming to rule by divine right, to a partially elected parliament is known as the "Glorious Revolution." Although this revolution was not self-consciously undertaken in the name of liberty, the ensuing constitutional settlement involved the enshrining in law, albeit in germinal form, of many of the political institutions integral to liberalism. These included regular and frequent parliaments, parliamentary control of the executive through making the latter financially dependent on the former, independence of the judiciary, freedom of speech in political debate, and (limited) religious toleration. At a time when, throughout most of continental Europe political absolutism was gaining ever greater ascendancy, England made a decisive break with this tendency and initiated a new form of constitutional limited parliamentary government that was to become the envy of and model for later generations of liberals elsewhere.

   Arguably, the earliest and historically most influential written formulation of liberalism was that of John Locke. Composed towards the end of the 17th century to support parliament in its struggle against the monarchy, Locke's writings introduce many key liberal notions which, during the succeeding century and a half, were to spread their influence across both sides of the Atlantic. These include, principally, the idea of the fundamental moral equality of all human beings in respect of basic rights, the notions of rule of law and separation of powers, but, also, above all, the idea of their being strict moral limits to political authority.

B. Eighteenth Century

Arguably, the supreme historical achievement of liberalism has been less the development and refinement of a distinctive set of liberal notions and doctrines than their partial and still incomplete realization in practice. So far as this is concerned, the most significant episodes in the history of liberalism have been a pair of political revolutions that have jointly determined the political landscape of modernity. The first is the American Revolution of 1776, the second the French Revolution of 1789. The former led to the creation of the United States of America, the written constitution of which was self-consciously drafted in accord with Locke's principles and tenets. The latter forever destroyed the elaborate French system of absolute monarchy and landed aristocracy known as the *ancien régime*. In so doing, it initiated in Europe a prolonged period of similar profound political change, culminating in the adoption throughout of broadly liberal tenets by the end of the first half of the nineteenth century.

C. Nineteenth Century

In many ways, the nineteenth century represents the high watermark of liberalism. In England and the United States, it was a period of minimum state interference and maximum negative liberty. Elsewhere, after suffering an initial setback, following the defeat of Napoleon and the restoration of monarchy at the Congress of Vienna in 1815, liberalism made steady inroads throughout Europe. However, as liberal ideals spread eastward, so they led to an awakening of nationalist aspiration and sentiment that, in time, was to result in some distinctly illiberal consequences.

In the second half of the nineteenth century, liberalism started to undergo, a metamorphosis wherein it lost much of its original classical form and acquired much of its distinctly modern character. From the beginning of the 19th century until 1870, political and economic reform in Europe seemed definitely to be moving in the direction of reducing governmental interference in the realms of economic activity and personal association and life-style. After 1870, however, the rise of nationalism in Germany led to a reversal of these trends. The introduction of tariff barriers by Germany was accompanied by its buildup of military might as well as by its introducing a system of state welfare. Other countries, most notably England, were obliged to follow Germany's example in order to preserve their own national security in the face of the unmistakeably mounting German threat.

Some liberals, notably Herbert Spencer, took cautionary note of this growth in governmental regulation and activity, and heralded it as marking the imminent demise of liberalism. Other liberals, however, such as Thomas Henry Green and Leonard Hobhouse, reinterpreted liberalism so that these trends became viewed less as a departures from than as the means to the realization of its ultimate objectives. This revision was largely accomplished by means of a corresponding revision in the notion of liberty itself. Within classical liberalism, liberty had always been construed in a negative fashion as the absence of deliberately imposed constraints and compulsion designed to prevent someone from doing what they would otherwise do, or compelling them to do that which they would otherwise not choose to do. The new revisionary liberalism found such a form of liberty an uninspiring political ideal. For them, liberty became equated with the removal of all impediments to worthwhile action, not just those deliberately imposed by human beings. Thus, liberty became transmuted into a positive notion in which it is equated with the power or ability to engage in worthwhile forms of action. In contrast with classical liberalism, therefore, the new revisionary liberalism started to construe as restrictions to liberty impediments to worthwhile action that had never been deliberately imposed by anyone upon those who suffered from them, such as poverty and disease. In the name of liberty itself, therefore, modern liberals were wont to call for state action to remove these barriers to worthwhile activity. In this fashion, the new revisionary form of liberalism developed, advocating in the name of positive freedom a more active and extensive role for the state than classical liberals had ever previously thought necessary or desirable.

D. Twentieth Century

Whether through having become convinced by the theorizing of such revisionary liberals as Thomas Green and Leonard Hobhouse, or whether from more pragmatic concerns connected with the need to match the economic protectionism and increasing threatening military posture of Germany, or whether it was competition with parties that had begun to court the newly enfranchised working classes through appealing to their short-term economic interests, the English Liberal Party underwent a profound sea change. It introduced compulsory social security and pensions, and, at the same time, it gave trades unions certain legal immunities that vastly increased their economic and subsequently their political power. By the outbreak of the First World War, much of the original classical liberal agenda seemed to have been abandoned and many of its earlier accomplishments reversed.

To say that, by the start of World War I, liberalism had been supplanted from its former position of preeminence would be an exaggeration. In Britain and in the United States, many of its fundamental objectives had been more or less achieved. Setting aside the brief interlude of Nazism during the 1930s, liberalism has succeeded this century in becoming and remaining the dominant political ideology in Europe and North America, albeit in a much more attenuated form than previously. This is so much so today that, throughout this region, all the main political parties subscribe to broadly liberal values and tenets. This remains so, even when the official names of these parties include the appellations "conservative" and even latterly "communist." To this extent, liberalism has become the dominant political orthodoxy of the Western world today. This is not to say that no major ideological issues continue to divide the major political parties of Western liberal democracies. These controversies, however, tend to be concerned with how best to realize what their protagonists take to be authentically liberal ideals and values, or at least how to realize other values without compromising liberal ones, rather than whether to. In sum, the main political issue today is that between classical liberalism and its modern, revisionary counterpart.

The twentieth century has seen liberalism triumph against both its principal sets of adversaries, socialism and Nazism. Socialism originated in the first half of the 19th century as a reaction to the harsh economic and social conditions that followed industrialization in the early part of that century. However, it only acquired its main theoretical and practical influence after the

Russian Revolution of 1917 made it the official ideology of the Union of Soviet Socialist Republics. During the succeeding 70 years, the Soviet Union attempted to put into effect a socialist agenda. Its collapse at the end of the 1980s signaled the end of that experiment. Ever since, socialism would appear to have lost whatever allure and ideological influence it enjoyed during the heyday of Soviet power.

The other principal adversaries of liberalism. Nazism and Fascism, are essentially 20th century phenomena. They developed in the 1930s, again ostensibly to remedy the allegedly grave social and economic deficiencies of economic liberalism, but without succumbing to the equally spurious and utopian egalitarian promises of communism. The impetus to their development was the same aggressive nationalism that had first surfaced in Germany at the end of the nineteenth century and that led to the First World War. Its reemergence there in the 1930s led directly to the conflagration of the Second. With the allied victory in 1945, both Nazism and Fascism appeared to have been decisively and permanently laid to rest, at least at the level of practical politics.

The end of the Second World War, therefore, saw the Western liberal democracies emerge triumphant over one of its principal adversaries. However, their liberal character had been seriously compromised and weakened by their having had to place themselves on a wartime footing during the immediately preceding period. This had involved their having had to start to engage in unprecedentedly large amounts of central economic planning and direction, as well as in increased state provision of welfare services. After 1945, the liberal democracies also found themselves challenged by a militarily more powerful Soviet Union, which had been allowed to extend its influence to the whole of Eastern Europe as the price of having helped defeat Nazism.

For a long time after 1945, it was almost *de rigueur* to accept the need for massive state intervention in the economy and for state provision of welfare and other social services. This social-democratic consensus, however, was to receive an abrupt and increasingly powerful challenge from the 1970s onward. At the theoretical level, the challenge was led by a growing band of political theorists and economists, among them, most notably, Milton Friedman and Friedrich Hayek. They sought a return to a more classically liberal economic policy agenda to counteract the growing ravages of inflation, which, so they argued, had been brought on by excessive government spending and unduly pro-union employment policies. Their theoretical challenge received

profound practical reinforcement at the end of the decade when "conservative" administrations were elected to office in both Britain and the United States, ostensibly set upon cutting back the size of the state. Simultaneously, the Cold War was stepped up through intensifying the arms race whose wildly escalating costs, towards the end of the 1980s, undoubtedly helped to hasten the demise of the Soviet Union.

Since the defeat of Nazism in 1945, and, more especially, since the collapse of Soviet Communism at the end of the 1980s, the main ideological debates in the West have been conducted largely within the parameters of broadly liberal assumptions. They have centered primarily on how best to interpret and realize liberal political ideals and values. By far the most important issue has been how far, if at all, economic liberty needs to be curtailed on behalf of a greater equality of life prospects than would otherwise be obtained. Only slightly less important has been the question of how far, if at all, the state may or must remain neutral in matters of personal morality and life-style. Preoccupation with these issues in recent times has led to a significant revival of interest in liberal theory.

III. THE EVOLUTION OF LIBERAL THEORY

A. Locke

Although some modern scholars would contest the view, 17th-century England may justly be regarded as the birthplace of liberalism, and John Locke its first systematic exponent. This exposition is contained in the second of his *Two Treatises of Government,* entitled "An Essay Concerning the True Original, Extent, and End of Civil Government." First published in 1690, this work represents the fruits of many previous years of intellectual labor on Locke's part. Here, in a timeless prose of almost magisterial clarity, are to be found many of the central tenets and notions of liberalism, including an immensely influential account and defense of the institution of private property, including property in land.

To appreciate the immense and seminal importance of Locke's political writings in the evolution of liberal theory, it is necessary to set his views besides those of another somewhat earlier, but no less great, 17th-century thinker, Thomas Hobbes. Both employ a common vocabulary and methodology to arrive at conclusions about the nature and the function of government. Both started by acknowledging the reality of a *law of nature,* the specific injunctions of which were supposedly both discoverable by reason and of binding moral force in the prepolitical condition called by both the *state of nature*. This law was said to confer on all human beings certain *natural rights*. Among these, for both thinkers, was a natural right to liberty. Both regard the state of nature as unattractive and unstable, because it is ineluctably bound to issue in a "war of each against all." From these mutual hostilities, individuals can escape only by entering with each other into some form of *social contract*. In entering into it, they agree to relinquish their natural right to liberty and place themselves under the authority of a common sovereign, be it a monarch or an elected parliament, in return for receiving from it protection against those who have not done likewise.

Despite the vast measure of agreement between them, however, the specific political conclusions at which Hobbes and Locke respectively arrive are decidedly different. So different are the political conclusions drawn by Hobbes and Locke from an essentially common stock of assumptions that, despite Hobbes having the better claim to being considered progenitor of the individualism underlying liberalism, it is Locke who must be credited with having been the first to enunciate a distinctively liberal account of the scope and function of government. For Hobbes, exit from the state of nature requires that individuals engage in an act of *unconditional* surrender of natural liberty, and hence their acquiring an *unconditional* obligation to obey the sovereign. From it, individuals are to be considered released only when such obedience would frustrate the original purpose with which they had put themselves under this authority. This occurs if the sovereign ceases to offer them effective protection, as a result, for example, of being overwhelmed by a foreign power or as a result of civil war. This also occurs if their sovereign orders some act that would directly imperil their lives, for example to commit suicide or to submit themselves to judicial execution. Because, for Hobbes, the principal function of a sovereign is to maintain peace, the sovereign is required by Hobbes to act as sole authoritative interpreter of the law of nature, a task that demands him to become the head of a national church to which all citizens must belong.

By contrast, in Locke's view, individuals may and should be thought of as having surrendered to the sovereign only so much of their natural liberty as is required for the peaceful and impartial resolution of conflicts between themselves and others. From this, Locke derives a number of important classical liberal inferences. First, *government must be limited* in scope and function. It must be strictly confined only to such tasks as it was

expressly created to fulfill and no others. This implies that government has no legitimate authority to engage in any activity not strictly necessary for the public or common good. Second, in the manner in which government goes about fulfilling its strictly limited set of legitimate functions, it must at all times be bound by *the rule of law*. That is, at all times, in all dealings with individual citizens, government must act in accord with known published laws and due process. For any of its officers to act otherwise is for them to vitiate the central purpose for which the state was created: that there should be "a known authority, to which every one of the society may appeal upon . . . any controversy that may arise, and which every one of the society ought to obey." Only where the rule of law obtains, so that everyone, including government officials, acts in accord with known standing laws, can individuals enjoy a greater, rather than a lesser, security than they would know in the state of nature. Unless the rule of law prevails vis-a-vis government, argues Locke, less security will be enjoyed. For government concentrates power in such a way that, relative to each individual, an arbitrary government not bound by law poses a greater threat than is constituted in the state of nature by the combined sum of all the separate threats posed by all the separate individuals. Third, in order for a state to be bound by the rule of law, there must be a *separation of powers*. That is, those who make and execute the laws must be numerically different from one another as well as from the people who decide what the law is at any given time and whether it has been broken by anyone on any particular occasion. There thus has to be a clear separation of powers between the three distinct branches of government: the legislature, which makes new laws and decides taxes, the executive, which collects revenue and deals with day-to-day matters, including the arrest of those accused of breaking the law, and the judiciary, which determines whether the law has been broken in any instance. Without such a separation, it will be impossible for either the executive or the legislature to be confined within the law, or for the executive to resist the temptation to abuse its power for the sake of personal advantage. From these premises and inferences, Locke draws out two further important inferences. The first is that individuals retain a *right of revolution* if, through replacing the rule of law by rule through arbitrary personal decree, the sovereign should have abused its position of trust in which it has been placed. The second is that there is no need for the state to demand uniformity in the matter of religious belief and practice, and, hence, there can and should be *religious toleration*.

B. The American Revolution

Locke's ideas and nostrums were to be taken up by the American revolutionaries and find reflection in their Declaration of Independence issued in 1776 to justify their action of that year. It famously begins:

> We hold these truths to be self-evident, that all men are created equal, that they are endowed by their Creator with certain unalienable Rights, that among these are Life, Liberty, and the pursuit of Happiness. That to secure these rights, Governments are instituted among men, deriving their just powers from the consent of the governed. That whenever any form of Government becomes destructive of these ends, it is the right of the People to alter or to abolish it, and to institute new government, laying its foundation on such principles and organizing its powers in such form, as to them shall seem most likely to effect their Safety and happiness.

C. The French Revolution

The American Declaration inspired the French revolutionaries to compose their Declaration of the Rights of Man and of Citizens in 1789. It prefixed the French constitution of 1791. Consisting of 17 short paragraphs listing the main "sacred" inalienable natural rights, a brief illustrative quotation reveals how greatly the French revolutionaries were influenced by Locke.

> I. Men are born, and always continue, free and equal in respect of their rights. Civil distinctions, therefore, can be founded only on public utility.
>
> II. The end of all political associations, is the preservation of the natural and imprescriptible rights of man; and these rights are liberty, property, security, and resistance of oppression.
>
> IV. Political liberty consists in the power of doing whatever does not injure another. The exercise of the natural rights of every man, has no other limits than those which are necessary to secure to every *other* man the free exercise of the same rights; and these limits are determinable only by the law.
>
> V. The law ought to prohibit only actions hurtful to society. What is not prohibited by the law, should not be hindered; nor should anyone be compelled to do what the law does not require.

> X. No man ought to be molested on account of his opinions, not even on account of his *religious* opinions, provided his avowal of them does not disturb the public order established by the law.
>
> XVI. Every community in which a separation of powers and a security of rights is not provided for, wants a constitution.
>
> XVII. The right to property being inviolable and sacred, no one ought to be deprived of it, except in cases of evident public necessity, legally ascertained and on condition of a previous just indemnity.

Although unmistakeably classical liberal in tone, it proved far easier for the French revolutionaries to do away with the *ancien régime* than to create a form of polity that instantiated their ideals. Such, sadly, has proved the typical fate of all violent political revolutions, with the arguable exception of the American Revolution. This, however, stopped well short of accomplishing all that liberal ideals demanded as far as Black slavery in the South was concerned.

D. Adam Smith

It is, however, in a region of human endeavor far removed from the febrile world of the political revolutionary that liberalism was to receive its greatest theoretical advance in the eighteenth century. Undoubtedly, this occurred in a field of scholarship where it assumed the form of a single text. More than any other, this one can be regarded as providing the theory of society upon which liberalism has ever since principally relied. The work is Adam Smith's *Wealth of Nations*, published in 1776. To the liberal political principles set out by Locke, Smith appended a detailed theory about the workings of society. Without recourse to any questionable or, at least, indemonstrable postulates, such as those of natural law, Smith purports to demonstrate why economic liberty best advances material prosperity. So convincing was this demonstration widely taken to be that, until challenged by Marx's *Capital* in the mid-19th century, the only remaining question for political economists appeared to be how this wealth should be distributed.

By means of a famous example of a pin factory, Smith exhibits wealth to be a function of the productivity of labor that, in turn, is presented as a function of the degree to which a division of labor has brought about specialization. Smith's key contention was that economic liberty maximizes the rate at which the division of labor develops and, hence, the rate at which national wealth increases. Economic liberty does so, argues Smith, by providing maximum personal incentive and opportunity for individuals to introduce new forms of division of labor and other innovations of productive technique that increase the productivity of labor.

Smith calls his optimal economic system, *the system of natural liberty,* implying that it would spontaneously emerge in the absence of artificial barriers to it. It is described by Smith in words that have ever since proved as adequate a summary statement as has ever before or since been given of the classical liberal ideal of minimal government. "Every man, as long as he does not violate the laws of justice, is left perfectly free to pursue his own interest his own way. ... The sovereign has only three duties ... : first, the duty of protecting the society from ... violence and invasion ... ; secondly, the duty of protecting ... every member ... from the injustice or oppression of every other member ... ; and, thirdly, the duty of erecting and maintaining certain public works."

E. John Stuart Mill

If Adam Smith may be regarded as having supplied the canonical vindication of liberalism on economic grounds, it was left to one of his fellow Scots a century later to provide what has become the canonical vindication of liberty on ethical grounds. The writer in question is John Stuart Mill, and the work of vindication, his essay, "On Liberty," published in 1859. Here, Mill sought to defend, as he puts it, "one very simple principle, as entitled to govern absolutely the dealings of society with the individual in the way of compulsion and control." That principle is that "the only purpose for which power can be rightfully exercised over any member of a civilized community, against his will, is to prevent harm to others. His own good, either physical or moral, is not a sufficient warrant."

Drawing heavily on the writings of an earlier nineteenth-century German liberal, Wilhelm van Humboldt, Mill defended his principle by arguing that such a measure of liberty as it prescribes is necessary for the maximum possible human self-expression and development. In their turn, these are presented as needed for maximum possible human fulfilment and happiness. Self-expression is needed to enable each to realize his or her *individuality.* Individuals must be free to choose their own life plan. This is partly because everyone is different and only their being able to choose for themselves is likely to result in their finding the plan most suited to their own unique personality. It is also partly because it is only by choosing his or her own life plan that a person calls into play and employs their distinctively human intellectual and moral faculties. The precise details of Mill's argument matter less than the fact that, unlike Adam Smith, Mill argues on behalf of liberty by appealing to its ostensible ethical as opposed to its economic benefits.

F. Twentieth-Century Developments

In the 20th century, liberal theory has undergone two successive major developments. The first has been the development during the earlier two-thirds of this century of various forms of revisionary liberalism. These have sought to argue to be consistent with or required by liberalism a far greater degree of state intervention than traditionally has been associated with it. The second has been the revival of classical liberalism during the last third of the century that has sought to recover many of the insights of the earlier liberalism that the development of revisionary liberalism had tended to obscure or overlook.

Accepting the need for religious liberty, political liberty, and liberty of association, modern liberalism has sought primarily to provide moral legitimation for various curtailments of economic liberty. Such curtailments include various forms of constraint on freedom of contract between employers and employees, such as minimum wage laws, antidiscrimination laws, and compulsory health insurance and pensions, plus redistributive state welfare programs financed by means of steeply progressive taxation. The rationale for these policy prescriptions have been several. Some have argued them necessary to realize the original objective of liberty. For example, Hobhouse argued that some form of protection was necessary so far as the labor market is concerned in order that the terms of association between employers and employees are not so heavily weighted in favor of the former as for the latter to be effectively subjected to an insidious form of compulsion.

1. John Rawls

By far the most important rationale for the more interventionist policy agenda they favor has been an appeal to moral requirements supposedly deriving from the fundamental moral equality of human beings. While eschewing out-and-out equality of income, modern liberals have invariably maintained that, to do justice to this fundamental moral equality, the state must do much more than was favored by classical liberalism.

In relation to justifying greater state intervention through appeal to the moral demands made by the ideal of equality, the writings of one twentieth-century modern liberal stand out above all others. This is John Rawls. His *Theory of Justice,* published in 1971, makes a central appeal to this moral equality to provide moral legitimation for, if not itself explicitly to endorse, the fully fledged welfare states that had become very much the Western orthodoxy after the Second World War.

Rawls contends that the system of natural liberty, as enunciated by Adam Smith and other classical liberals, is unjust because it is unfair. It is said to be unfair on the grounds of its underservedly offering an advantage to those born into more affluent income groups or with superior natural endowments without their having done anything to deserve these advantages. Within the system of natural liberty, such individuals are liable to enjoy better life prospects than others. To eliminate these unfair inequalities, argues Rawls, justice requires that all individual natural endowments and other material assets be treated as a common stock. The benefits of this common stock are to be distributed equally, unless an unequal distribution is likely to be of benefit to all, and most notably to the least well-endowed.

Rawls argues for his proposed egalitarian modification of the system of natural liberty by stating that people would opt for it whenever they are unable to gain unequal benefit from any undeserved superior endowment they might happen to possess. He illustrates this claim by proposing a variant of social-contract theory. In it, contractors are invited to select principles for distributing the benefits of social cooperation without knowing their own identities. In this *original position,* as he calls it, the identities of the contracting parties remain hidden from them by a "veil of ignorance." In such circumstances, argues Rawls, they will opt for what he calls the *difference principle.* This states that "social and economic inequalities are to be arranged so that they are both: (a) to the greatest benefit of the least advantaged; and (b) attached to offices and positions open to all." Any other option is liable to expose them to worse life prospects, and, in circumstances of such uncertainty, argues Rawls, it is rational to be risk averse. Although Rawls never attempted to spell out in any detail the policy implications of his so-called "difference principle," it has been widely taken to provide an endorsement for extensive egalitarian state redistribution.

2. The Revival of Classical Liberalism

The other notable major 20th-century development in liberal theory has been the revival of classical liberalism. This his been led by a spate of thinkers, such as Milton Friedman, Friedrich Hayek, and Robert Nozick. Together, they have sought to recover many of the original insights and arguments in favor of more nearly minimal government. In part, they have attempted to redraw attention to the benefits to the least well-endowed of the invisible hand of the market. In part, they have drawn attention to the indissoluble connections between economic liberties on the one hand and political and civil liberties on the other. They have argued the latter require the former, so that curtailments of the former implicitly threaten the latter.

IV. CURRENT CONTROVERSIES

In the twilight years of the 20th century, liberalism appears to have emerged unscathed from the assaults made against it by its earlier rivals, and it appears to have acquired within the West at least a position of unrivalled supremacy as a political philosophy. However, although seemingly unthreatened by any rival, a number of highly pertinent questions concerning both its interpretation and its adequacy remain unresolved. Above all, four issues continue to remain the focus of intense speculation.

A. Liberty and Equality

The first issue concerns the moral demands that flow from the moral equality of all human beings. Does such equality demand, as classical liberals maintain, no more than that the state accord its members equal civil and political rights, and equal treatment before the law? Or does it demand of the state that it equalize the life prospects of citizens, a task that might well require it treat members unequally, for example, by taxing some more than others, and by giving more to others than to some?

How much equalizing of life prospects should or may the state go in for, beyond enforcing the life, liberty, and property of its citizens? This remains the big unresolved question dividing liberals today. Those who argue in favor of the state going beyond the classical liberal minimal agenda, typically, do so by appealing to equality.

Classical liberals maintain that all such attempts by the state to go in for such equalizing of life prospects involve unjustifiable departures by the state from the strict moral inpartiality between citizens that their moral equality demands. Respect for their equal moral status demands from the state only that it affords equal protection of its citizens' lives, liberties, and property. That, due to morally fortuitous differences between them, they are liable to prosper differently from one another when it does, should not be the business of the state. In the view of classical liberals, the state uses some as means and thereby denies them equal status, when for the sake of others, it makes demands of them that it does not impose on others, whether by taxation or by setting limits to the terms of their association. As well as confiscatory taxation for redistributive purposes, the same fundamental injustice is claimed by classical liberals to be done, when the state forbids some (employers) to discriminate against others (their choice of potential employees) on grounds of race and sex, but permits employees to choose prospective employers on such grounds.

It is clear that if classical liberalism wins this debate, much more than the welfare state will have to be dismantled. The entire edifice of state regulation in the sphere of employment will need radical revision, and many agencies set up in the name of this or that form of equality will have to be dismantled, too.

B. State Neutrality and Personal Life-Style

A second issue that is the focus of intense concern today concerns the moral adequacy of something equally favored by both classical and modern liberals alike. This is state neutrality in relation to matters of personal morality and life-style. Doubts about the wisdom of such neutrality have surfaced from conservatives who have questioned the wisdom or need for this degree of moral latitude.

Common ground among both classical and modern liberals is support for the state remaining neutral in matters of personal morality and life-style. What is done behind the closed doors of informed consenting adults is their own matter alone in which the state has no business to interfere, no matter how imprudent or morally repugnant such conduct might generally be felt to be. Conservatives who otherwise tend to favor economic liberty will often object to such neutrality on the grounds that nothing good is served by it and that it undoes socially beneficial habits of probity and restraint whose formation and maintenance require state support in the shape of an enforced public morality. One extreme example of this is the question whether adults should be legally permitted to take addictive drugs, but the same question can also be extended to matters of sexual morality.

C. Community and Liberty

A third issue that has risen to the top of the political agenda of late concerns how conducive or subversive

liberalism is of the various forms of communal association within which, traditionally, most human beings have found meaning and moral purpose. Is liberalism, no matter whether it be of the modern of the classical variety, inherently antagonistic to traditional forms of communal association and ethical life? Do the latter require from their participants a form of whole-hearted identification and from the state a degree of public reenforcement that are precluded by liberalism?

It is often argued that the relentless forces of economic and moral individualism unleashed by liberalism are subversive of all those traditional forms of communal association, such as family, neighborhood, and nation, without which a society becomes a mass of deracinated and anomic individuals, prone to all manner of social maladies. The escalating recent figures of violent crime and family breakdown are sometimes cited as evidence of liberalism's deleterious effects upon valuable forms of community.

To this charge, liberals of different shades of opinion are prone to respond in different ways. Some modern and classical libertarian liberals seemingly welcome the breakdown of these traditional forms, claiming no value in them. The traditional nuclear family, for example, is sometimes viewed by both sets of liberals as having no especial positive value, and arguably, some negative value. Accordingly, such liberals express no regret at its apparent demise and do not consider liberalism at fault if it has contributed to it. The same goes for national allegiance and patriotic sentiment. However, those liberals who do value these traditional forms of communal association can remain very exercised by this problem. Modern liberals tend to attribute the fault to the economic individualism that their brand of interventionist liberalism would counter. Classical liberals maintain it has been the very state interventionist measures that modern liberals have championed that have led to family breakdown, and through that to the rise of delinquency and violent crime. In their view, worthwhile forms of community are not only not undermined, but are positively bolstered by the minimal government they favor. For them, it is the overextended welfare state that modern liberalism has helped spawn that must be regarded as the prime culprit in the decline of community.

D. Liberalism and Democracy

The fourth and final issue continuing to divide classical and modern liberals concerns the status and value of democratic political institutions in relation to liberal aspirations and ideals. Classical liberals regard democracy as, at best, no more than a means—albeit an indispensable one—through which to ensure that those who govern do not abuse their positions of power and overstep their legitimate functions. For classical liberals, there is no guarantee that democracy will not itself become illiberal or result in illiberal outcomes. For them democratic institutions and procedures neither have any special moral value of their own, nor do they confer any such value upon the legislative outcomes arrived at by means of them.

By contrast, modern liberals tend to regard the democratic process as an indispensable means and medium through which members of society attain and exercise their positive liberty. Furthermore, such liberals tend to believe that the democratic process confers moral authority and legitimacy upon practically whatever legislative measures are its products. The prevalence of such a view in the 20th century has allowed modern democracies to become a competition between contending parties, each of which seeks votes by offering electorates a more enticing political agenda, regardless of whether or how far its enactment would encroach on fundamental economic and other liberties. Whereas modern liberals seek to extend democratic participation, classical liberals are more concerned with seeking to ensure adequate constitutional safeguards and checks against the ever-present threat of tyranny of the majority.

V. CONCLUSIONS

Liberalism appears to have emerged triumphant from the trials and tribulations to which it was exposed earlier in the 20th century. Yet its very essence has by no means been conclusively settled, nor has its moral robustness been decisively established.

Traditionally, liberals have found in liberalism a moral vision of an ideal form of society suitable for all humanity. Their hope and aspiration has been that, eventually, liberal political institutions and values will gradually extend themselves to all parts of the world,

which in time will acquire a liberal complexion. For them, liberal values are coextensive with those of civilization itself.

Others of a more post-modern persuasion have seen in liberalism, at best, only a solution for one particular range of peoples: those who harbor within their midst a plurality of conflicting conceptions of the good life but who must live and cooperate together in one political society. For those who hold such a view, there is no reason to think liberalism has much, if anything, to offer the residents of more traditional societies that harbor only one form of social life.

Whether, or how far, liberalism will extend itself beyond the frontiers of Western Europe and North America to eventually embrace the entire world, and whether, if it does, the world will be better or worse for such a development, are questions that will undoubtedly continue to exercise thinkers well into the third millennium, if not beyond. At a more parochial and practical level, so far as the Western liberal democracies are concerned, so too will the question whether the traditional liberal goals of liberty, equality, and fraternity are better promoted through greater or lesser government. As a political philosophy, liberalism might well be going into the third millennium with no real competitors on the horizon, but its future shape and destiny remain profoundly uncertain.

Also See the Following Articles

EQUALITY AND EGALITARIANISM • MARX AND ETHICS • PERFECTIONISM • THEORIES OF JUSTICE: RAWLS

Bibliography

Conway, D. (1995). *Classical liberalism: The unvanquished ideal.* London and New York: Macmillan and St. Martin's Press.

Galston, W. A. (1991). *Liberal purposes: Goods, virtues, and diversity in the liberal state.* Cambridge and New York: Cambridge University Press.

Gray, J. (1993). *Post-liberalism* London and New York: Routledge.

Mulhall, S. & Swift, A. (1992). *Liberals and communitarians.* Oxford and Cambridge, MA: Blackwell.

Paul, E. F., Paul, J., & Miller F. (Eds.). (1996). *The communitarian challenge to liberalism.* Cambridge: Cambridge University Press.

LIFE, CONCEPT OF

Maurizio Mori
Center for Research in Politics and Ethics, Milan

GLOSSARY

efficient causality An Aristotelian concept indicating the relation in which an event is brought about by another one occurring earlier (or in some case at the same time), as is usual in physical sciences.

holistic causality A relationship in which an event is brought about not by an earlier event but by its position in a complex whole. In this sense some events depend on the action of an organism as a whole, and this fact is not reducible to any sort of efficient causality.

iatromechanics A school of biology and medicine which flourished in the 17th and 18th centuries and according to which biological phenomena should be explained on the basis of mechanical principles.

reism (or "thing-ism") A commonsensical view according to which reality is made up of mere "things", i.e., spatiotemporal entities delimited by sharp boundaries, and "things" are derived by fusion with other "things."

teleology A basic property typical of living processes, which show a peculiarly goal-directed tendency, so that it appears as if some former events are "pulled" from events occurring later. Also the philosophical study of manifestations of design or purpose in living phenomena.

LIFE is a very varied phenomenon, so instead of speaking of *the* concept of life, it would be more adequate to speak of various concepts of life. In order to make clear such concepts we need to contrast life and nonliving matter, and capture some basic empirical properties which are typical of life in itself. These are commonly recognized to include spontaneity, self-regulation, reproduction, and reactivity and adaptability (within some limits). Since all these properties are present in protoplasmatic activity, life is defined as protoplasmatic activity. There are different theories trying to account for living phenomena. Vitalism and mechanism are two opposing ones, but both in some sense are inadequate. Organicism seems to be more adequate because it can account for the typical teleology manifested by living processes and for different levels of life depending on different degrees of organizational complexity. From an organicismic conception follow some practical implications, such as the distinction between biological life and biographical life, and furthermore some issues concerning the "beginning of life" are clarified.

I. INTRODUCTORY GENERAL DISTINCTIONS

When a person with ethical interests speaks of "life," very likely such a term is used to mean "human life," i.e., the sort of life that you, the reader, have while reading this entry. In this sense, "life" usually refers mainly to mental or intellectual states that a person has simply by existing, and for this reason when we say, "that person is very lively," we mean he or she is witty and has many ideas; similar expressions are used for groups of people. In common usage, "life" mostly indicates a peculiar property which is typical of human persons, and this use is justified by the fact that in our Western culture there is a strong tendency to believe that humans are at the top of the world and radically different from the rest of nature, so that we distinguish between "us" (human persons) and the remaining part of the world, living and nonliving alike. Even if we share with other living beings many characteristics, we tend to assume that our life is so special and peculiar that we forget our common organic basis, and other living beings appear to us mostly as nonliving entities. We assume that our life transcends that of other living entities, and this makes a crucial difference. In fact, from a normative viewpoint our treatment of living beings is similar to that of inorganic entities, since both are at our disposal and we can do with them what we wish. On the other hand, we think that human persons deserve strong protection and that their lives have very high value.

In the last three decades or so, the common meaning of the term has been blurred under the influence of new practical controversies such as those over abortion and brain death, and more recently *in vitro* fertilization. A "pro-*life* movement" has spread throughout the world, and "life" nowadays assumes in some contexts a more biological connotation. Often discussions are focused on the question of when life begins or when life ends, or similar ones that assume "life" to be equivalent to *human* life, and expressions such as "sanctity of life" or "sacredness of life" have become common.

It is not clear what the precise meaning of the term "life" is in such contexts, but it is clear that these controversies compel us to develop a more rigorous and precise concept of life. In the past this problem was merely theoretical and speculative, but nowadays recent scientific and technological advancements require a clearer view on the subject: science and technology work as a sort of magnifying glass which show that such a problem is more complex than we thought, so that a more adequate concept is needed.

When we attempt to carry out this task, the first problem we have to face is whether (human) "life" is a *descriptive* or an *evaluative* notion, i.e., whether we can get a clear idea of life merely by looking at some phenomena, or whether our perspective of these phenomena depends ultimately on our previous values—or thirdly, whether in this case facts and values are inextricably bound so that it is almost impossible to distinguish between them clearly. Much of contemporary debate on the concept of (human) life concerns this controversy, and it is not certain that it can be definitely solved. But certainly the controversy can be dealt with in a better way once we have a clearer concept of what life is and of its peculiar characteristics. For this reason it is useful to start from scratch, and this procedure seems useful since when we depart from the top of the scale of living beings (i.e., from the life of "persons"), the evaluative controversies are less prominent and therefore it is easier to reach a clearer view of the whole subject.

II. EMPIRICAL CHARACTERISTICS OF LIFE

The general concept of "life" has a crucial role in our thinking since it sets the distinction between the living and the nonliving, which is a crucial category of our worldview. In order to make clear the concept it is useful to start with a simple empirical remark: life *in general* (in a strict sense of the term) does not exist since we always see specific pieces of *living matter*. "Life" is a term denoting an abstract entity which, as such, does not exist because in reality there are only concrete and specific living entities. Therefore we must be aware that the term "life" indicates a characteristic or a set of characteristics which are typical of living bodies or organisms. Life is always *individual* in the sense that it occurs in a strictly delimited spatiotemporal place and with a specific form, deriving from another entity by means of specific generation. Life is always *specific* and *particular* since there is no undifferentiated "general living plasm," but always a specific form of life. It has been estimated that on Earth there are about 3,000,000,000 species, of which only a third are known, showing the great variety of living beings in the world. However, we should not forget that the amount of living material is but a fraction of that of inorganic matter—a thin pellicle about 1/1,000,000,000 of the planet's weight.

Looking at living things, we can detect some general features which certainly are constituents of our common concept of "life." The first visible characteristic is that living matter is in a state of constant change which is directed from within: new matter is assimilated and other matter is excreted in a process called "metabolism," so that a sort of internal equilibrium is maintained. This is what is referred to by the latin expression, *vita in motu* (life consists of movement). Some authors point out that such constant change has a peculiar character since it is spontaneous, and that spontaneity of continuous change is a basic property of life. According to other latin dicta, *vita in motu spontaneo* or *vita in motu ab intrinseco* (life consists of spontaneous movement or of movement from within). In this sense, the entire essence of life consists of being a sort of self-starting process.

There is a second visible aspect of life to be considered: living matter is not only self-starting, but it is also able to maintain an *internal equilibrium* by means of a self-regulating process so that the equilibrium depends on self-regulation produced by the whole entity. It is as if the whole living matter controls its own internal equilibrium, which is a function of the whole. In this case a special sort of causality seems to be at work, since it is the whole that determines the effects of the part and its working. For this reason, sometimes we speak of a holistic causality in which the behavior of a part is controlled by the whole and its nature (and not by antecedent conditions of parts as in the *linear* causality typical of physical sciences).

Holistic causality appears clearly in the normal working of self-regulation of a living organism, but it is even clearer in the process of growth. Consider a simple example such as a watermelon growing on a vine: if such a growth consisted only of a number of cell divisions, then the watermelon would turn out to be more or less spherical. But at a certain point, the watermelon "stops" cell division in some parts in order to reach its correct shape. Moreover, at some other point the cells differentiate in function, so that those that are in the center become seeds and those at the border become the rind: apparently this process of differentiation depends on the position occupied by the cell and not on something internal to the cell. Finally, after a period of constant growth the watermelon concludes its growing and after some time decay takes place. So we have a simple case illustrating self-regulation depending on holistic causality, which seems to be typical of living phenomena.

The third visible aspect is that living entities at some time may give origins to another living being similar to them: we say that living things reproduce, while inorganic matter does not. There are several modes of reproduction, and some seem quite peculiar, but reproduction is another basic characteristic of life. Any living entity comes from another, and grows for a certain period and then dies out, completing its life cycle. Not only is any single individual in constant change, but its group is as well since it is possible that some variation occurs through reproduction, resulting in a change in the life of the group.

The fourth (and last) visible aspect of life is the ability of react and adapt to the environment, at least up to a point. Life presents a peculiar inner capacity to react to external stimuli. This characteristic is quite remarkable in animal life, where such a response is different not only from the predictable way in which certain chemicals react with other chemicals, but also because, especially in higher organisms, such reactions may be learned.

When all of the four preceding characteristics are present, we are sure that there is a living thing. But each property may be present in different degrees, and in some cases one may be absent or manifest only at a certain time. Thus it may become problematic to decide whether a given entity is living or not. Let us consider, for instance, a piece of matter presenting only one, two, or three of the four listed characteristics: is it alive or not? Do we need all four characteristics together or only some of them? And if only some, then how many?

III. PROBLEMS OF A PLAUSIBLE DEFINITION OF "LIFE"

The answers to the previous questions are interesting for a number of reasons, the first of which is their relevance for a possible solution to the biological controversy about whether viruses are living entities. A virus is a collective term denoting entities with quite different natures ranging from giant protein molecules, such as the tobacco-mosaic virus, to sets of molecules approaching a bacterial structure, such as the agent causing spotted fever. However, viruses have the property of multiplying by division: for instance, if a plant is inoculated with a few hundred molecules of crystallized tobacco-mosaic virus, we observe an enormous increase of the virus substance throughout the plant. Since viruses are capable of reproducing (covariant reduplication), we may ask whether they are alive or not.

Whichever the answer, this shows that the line between the living and the nonliving is not always as sharp and clear as sometimes we commonly think: we have to realize that between the most complex phenomena of inorganic matter and the simplest ones of organic matter there is no clear-cut boundary. Does this mean that such a distinction is nonexistent and that it is simply an illusion? Certainly not, at least so far as we think that there is a distinction between black and white, even if in certain occasions they merge into gray and it is difficult to draw a clear distinction and say when black ends and white begins. In one sense, it is impossible to discover such a line, because it is somewhat "arbitrary" depending on a decision: we decide that up to a certain point it is "black," and after that it is "gray" and then "white." Something similar happens in the case of "life": it is clear that a piece of iron is different from a cat, but at a certain point the living merges into the nonliving and here we need a definition which is not "arbitrary" and is supported by good reasons showing its alleged adequateness to our task.

For our biological knowledge, an adequate definition of life seems to require more than mere covariant reduplication and to include the ability to carry out primary syntheses typical of protoplasm, which is a feature peculiar to a cell as a whole. In fact, one dictionary of biology says that life is "the sum of the properties of protoplasm, namely metabolism, growth, irritability, movement and reproduction as manifested by a cell or a group of cells or an organism by which is distinguished from inorganic or nonliving matter" (E. B. Steen, 1971. *Dictionary of Biology.* p. 278 New York: Barnes & Noble).

I think that there are good reasons to accept this definition, which is adequate as far as we consider life present on our planet, but do we really want to accept it as *the* definition of "life" as such? Let's grant that we limit the word "life" to the sum of the properties of protoplasm and to protoplasmatic activity: what to say then of the possibility of extraterrestrial life? Should we think that varieties of protoplasm are widespread over the universe or can we think of different forms of life in which some combinations of carbon are unecessary? Moreover, what to say of disembodied life? If life is by definition protoplasmatic activity, should we say that a "disembodied life" (i.e., not connected with protoplasm) is simply a self-contradiction? How can we think of a life that is not connected with protoplasm if we assume that it is a property of protoplasm?

A precise and definite answer to such questions is beyond the scope of this entry, but they are important for anyone thinking on various concepts of "life." However, in the rest of this entry we will accept the biological definition of life as protoplasmatic activity, which seems

quite uncontroversial among scholars. However, at this point new problems come in if we want to deepen our concept of life. We may ask, "what makes protoplasmatic activity so special and peculiar?" According to one respected biologist, "protoplasm is a bridge anchored at one end in the simple stuff of chemistry and physics, but at the other reaching far across into the mysterious dominions of the human spirit" (E. W. Sinnott, 1950. *Cell and Psyche* (p. 19). New York: Harpor Torchbooks), and we may ask whether it is possible to explain protoplasmatic activity. Or should we take it as something unexplicable? N. Bohr seemed to hold such a view, writing that

the existence of life must be considered as an elementary fact that cannot be explained, but must be taken as a starting point in biology, in a similar way as the quantum of action, which appears as an irrational element from the point of view of classical mechanical physics, taken together with the existence of elementary particles, forms the foundation of atomic physics. (N. Bohr, 1993. "Light and Life", *Nature,* 131 p. 421)

On the other hand, many biologists think that life can (at least in principle) be explained according to the laws of physical nature, and therefore life is nothing so special, being nothing else but a more complicated form of inorganic matter.

IV. ALTERNATIVE THEORIES OF LIFE: VITALISM VS. MECHANISM

Here we face an important philosophical issue which is crucial for different concepts of life and also for the place that we assign to humankind, since we ourselves are living organisms. Such a controversy, which is often labeled as *mechanism* vs. *vitalism,* was already known in ancient Greek where atomists held a form of mechanism according to which life is a kind of self-moving matter, while Platonists defended a sort of vitalism posing a sharp distinction between matter and life. Aristotle tried, in a sense, to reconcile the opposition, observing that any object is constituted by "matter" and "form," and living entities are alive because they have a special form. Therefore, life is not sharply distinguished from matter, since there is a continuous improvement before that matter is prepared to accept its proper form. This holds for the distinction between inorganic matter and life, as well as for various kinds of life.

The Aristotelian view was forcefully challenged in the 17th century by founders of the new science and modern philosophy. Descartes was one of those critics and formulated the theory of the *béte machine* (beast-machine), according to which animals (as well as any form of life) were interpreted as machines of a very complicated kind. Living organisms are certainly more complex than anything else, but in principle they are comparable with man-made machines whose actions are governed by the laws of physics. This is a basic tenet of mechanism: the same laws of physics govern the inorganic world and living entities.

The application of methods of physical sciences to life led to enormous successes, and Descartes initiated the so-called *iatromechanic* school of biology and medicine, which tried to explain the function of muscles and bones, the movement of blood, and other phenomena on the basis of mechanical principles. Harvey's discovery of the circulation of blood looked as a first strong confirmation of iatromechanical views, marking the beginning of modern physiology. According to Descartes, however, man was the only living entity not submitted to the laws of nature, since he assumed (indeed he claimed to have proved) that men are endowed with a spiritual soul capable of free will, a feature sufficient to distinguish human beings from the rest of nature.

Vitalists retorted that apart from man (a unique and very special case in the whole creation), the activity of living things could not be explained by means of the laws of physics simply because organic structures and functions are purposeful and life is clearly a purposeful activity. In other words, life is radically different from nonliving matter because living processes are goal-directed or teleological (from *telos,* goal). In order to make clear this concept, we may consider the following figure:

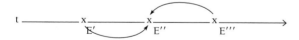

The arrow t indicates a sequence of time in which event E″ is to be explained. According to our physical model this can be done only by means of "efficient causality," i.e., showing that there is a temporally antecedent event E′ that is causing E″ ("efficient causality" being a sort of "linear causality"). However, in teleological explanation the situation seems to be reversed, since it is the subsequent event E‴ which appears to be "causing" the antecedent event E″, as if E‴ would be "pulling from the future." In biology such teleological explanations are rather common, as when we explain that the heart pulses in order to circulate the blood: in this case the heart's beating seems to be caused by an event

(circulation of the blood) which temporally comes after the fact to be explained. In this sense, living processes seem to show a sort of "intention" similar to our conscious intentions, and this fact was interpreted as a confirmation that life is not a mere product of a blind chance (but had to be produced by a supernatural mind). This view stressing that purposeful activity typical of living beings makes them radically different from nonliving matter seemed to find strong support from the fact that organic compounds, which are characteristic of living entities, in nature are found exclusively in living beings and could be produced only in life processes.

This controversy was ongoing when in 1828 Woehler produced urea in the laboratory, the first organic compound ever synthesized, issuing a stroke to vitalism and an important point in support of mechanism. Since then organic chemistry and biochemistry have become prominent fields in modern science and many organic compounds are nowadays synthesized regularly and rather easily. A further point in favor of mechanism came from Darwin's theory of evolution, according to which the origin of purposiveness in the living world can be explained on the basis of chance variations and natural selection, so that the analogy with conscious intentions becomes senseless, as well as the idea of a purposive supernatural agent. For these reasons, in the second half of the 19th century mechanism was triumphant and gained credibility.

Mechanistic biology was at its highest point at the close of the century when Hans Driesch performed his classical experiment which led him to reject the physicochemical theory of life (even if he was one of the founders of developmental mechanics, the science devoted to experimental investigation of embryonic development). Driesch divided into two halves a sea urchin's fertilized egg at the beginning of its development, and he realized that each half gave origin to a full organism. This fact was flatly contrary to physical laws, from which one should expect that from half an embryo only half an animal would develop. But these physical laws had been violated not only in the indicated sense, but also in the reverse sense, since under certain conditions two different germs could unify themselves into one organism and produce a unitary giant larva. Therefore, Driesch drew the conclusion that "in the embryo, and similarly in other vital phenomena, a factor is active which is fundamentally different from all physicochemical forces, and which directs events in anticipation of the goal" (L. von Bertalanffy, 1952. *Problems of life* (p. 6). New York: Harper Torchbooks), and Driesch called this special factor, which "carries the goal within itself" so to produce a typical organism in normal as well as in experimentally disturbed situations, entelechy.

Once again we see that it was teleology that distinguished the living from the nonliving, even if it is important to remember that starting from such a remark vitalists concluded that (being goal directed) life has a special creativity and spontaneity which places it outside the realm of any natural science. For this reason life is a sort of peculiar élan vital (or will to live) which cannot be captured by science but only by a special intuition: science looks for regularity and universal laws while life is creative and always changing, and therefore it is unexplicable in scientific terms.

Here we individuate two very different and opposite concepts of life: for mechanism life is nothing else than more complicated inorganic matter, while for vitalism life is a unique phenomenon which can never be generalized because of its spontaneity. However, it is useful to reflect a bit deeper on the vitalist claim in light of an example. If you tap your cat with a stick, you have a range of possible responses: sometimes the cat runs away, other times it is pleased and plays with the stick, and sometimes it responds aggressively. Many more reactions are possible, but for our task those listed are enough to show that there is a variability of response, and our first problem is to know whether such responses are lawful or not. Vitalists deny that there is any lawfulness and regularity, claiming that living organisms have a typical spontaneity that creates novelties violating any law. One can agree that the cat's reaction is hardly explicable with a physical law, but it is difficult to deny that the cat's behavior is not lawful. We can admit that living organisms have a greater range of variability in their responses that exceed our present ability to grasp them, but it is difficult to claim that they cannot be studied scientifically: if such a scientific study was possible, then it would show new regularities and laws which are different from current physical laws, but which are still interesting and significant. This view holds that we have to realize that biology has its own laws, which for the time being are different from those of other natural sciences (mainly physics and chemistry).

This view is compatible with that version of mechanism which is ready to recognize that up to now biology has not been reduced to physical sciences, even if it is *in principle* reducible to it: a first step toward reaching a better unifying theory is to start with a rigorous inquiry of different specific laws in various fields. If this were the core of the controversy, we could obtain a peaceful agreement, but unfortunately it is a stronger view which is held, pointing out that not only are bio-

logical laws empirically different from physical laws, but that they are intrinsically different and irreducible to them. In other words, biology is a science which is different from physics.

V. A THIRD THEORY OF LIFE: ORGANICISM

This view is usually supported by holders of the *organismic conception* who want to suggest a third way between the Scylla of vitalism (which is against any scientific inquiry of life which is per se resistent to science) and the Cariddis of mechanism (which has a unique and too narrow view of science, assuming that physics is the model of scientific thinking). According to organicism we must abandom the analytical and summative conception typical of physics, according to which any phenomenon can be explained by splitting it into its elementary units and then recombining these units into the original unit. This method cannot work in biology because organisms are whole in themselves and cannot be split into parts (because they die). As Bertalanffy says,

it is impossible to resolve the phenomena of life completely into elementary units; for each individual part and each individual event depends not only on condition within itself, but also to a greater or lesser extent on the conditions within the *whole,* or within superordinate units of which it is a part. (1952, 12)

Moreover, the whole presents properties which are absent from its isolated parts, and this fact shows that what is crucial in life is organization. As Bertalanffy again points out,

the problem of life is that of *organization*. As long as we single out individual phenomena we do not discover any fundamental difference between the living and the non-living.... There is no "living substance".... Rather life is bound to individualized and organized systems, the destruction of which puts an end to it. (1952, 12–13)

Having stressed the relevance of organization for life, the organicismic view changes quite significantly our common sense concept of life itself because we now have to realize that "life" is a general term indicating a great variety of living matter which may be very different according to various kinds of organization. Apart from those authors who assume that "organization" is a primitive term incapable of any further analysis (probably collapsing in a version of vitalism), usually organization has to do with *relations* between the constituents of a living entity, and it becomes immediately clear that more complex organization will give rise to higher forms of life. Therefore, organicism holds that there are different *levels* of life, corresponding to different complexities of organization, and that higher levels are irreducible to lower levels, just as living phenomena are irreducible to mere inorganic matter. Moreover, any level presents properties typical of the kind of organization involved, and in higher levels there is an *emergence* of new properties. In a sense, here the concept of "organization" seems to substitute for the older Aristotelian concept of "form": for Aristotle any entity was identified by its form, while now different kinds of life are identified by their proper "organization."

In any case, organicism gives an important contribution to our analysis of the concept of life, since in this view life is irreducible to mere inorganic matter and is an organized process pursuing self-maintenance according to the devices proper to the level of complexity manifested by the system. Therefore, life indicates a quite complex and variegated set of phenomena deserving more specific attention, and at this point we have to specify other properties in order to reach the precision needed by the subject.

VI. BASIC THEORETICAL PROPERTIES OF LIFE

When we consider "life" in a more accurate way (as we need to), we have to realize that living processes show the following basic properties: teleology, organization, and various levels of existence corresponding to degrees of organizational complexity.

While both mechanism and vitalism are monochromatic, or "flat," in the sense that both see life as a single phenomenon with only one dimension, even if in opposite directions (respectively reduced to matter and to spirit), organicism is polychromatic and more varied, allowing a more subtle analysis of concepts of life. Particularly interesting for our purposes is the doctrine of various levels of life, comprising three basic levels: (1) the level of the cell, which is the simple system capable of autonomous life; (2) the level of multicellular organizations forming living individuals; and (3) the level of communities consisting of many multicellular individual organisms.

Let us examine each level separately, since the higher presuppose the lower, but present some properties that are irreducible to the lower. In this sense, we can individuate various concepts of life, so that on the one hand we can easily explain the great multiplicity of the living forms we see over the Earth, and on the other we can hope to better understand the problem I pointed out at the opening, concerning whether the concept of (human) life is descriptive or normative (or inextricably both).

The cellular level is certainly the fundamental unit of life since all living beings are constituted by some combination of cells. From a biological viewpoint, characteristic of this level is the fact that

> the organization of the protoplasm is not static but dynamic. The primary orderliness of processes cannot be attributed to pre-established structural conditions. Rather the process as a whole carries its order in itself, representing a self-regulating steady state. Therefore, the system appears to be widely tolerant of disturbances, so long as fixed structural conditions are scarce. (Bertalanffy, 1952, 34)

From our viewpoint, which is more interested in conceptual analysis, it may be remarked that typical of the cellular level is the fact that life is characterized by spatiotemporal contiguity limited by sharp borders. This is clear when we consider a colony of several single cells or an agglomeration of cells: in these cases the entity looks like an individual because its shape is spatiotemporally limited, but in reality there are several individuals, each performing the whole of its functions. If the larger shape is split, no death occurs but a simple scission of different individuals: a worm is a good example, since we all know that if a worm is split it continues to live.

The situation changes significantly at the next level, because the life of multicellular organisms is characterized not only by spatiotemporal contiguity, but also by a *relation* of strict subordination of the parts to the whole, so that a part cannot live detached from the whole. For this reason, multicellular organisms show a *hierarchical order* according to which the different parts of the individual differentiate themselves in order to perform special functions. There is a strong specialization of cells to form different organs, so that a multicellular organism maintains its general goal (self-preservation) by a cooperation of different subsystems, each having a more limited and specific teleology.

This remark is important because the death of a multicellular organism occurs when such a relation breaks down, so that the whole individual falls apart, even if some part may continue to have residual life: for a certain time there are metabolic activities in the parts even if the whole teleological process has already vanished. On the other hand, the life of a multicellular organism depends on the presence of this relation of strict subordination of the parts to the whole, where such a subordination can be of different kinds according to the degree of complexity of the organism. In this sense, since Aristotle's time it has been common to distinguish three great genera (or reigns) of being, i.e., the vegetal, the animal, and the human (in the strict sense of being capable of intellectual activity). Needless to say that the dividing line between each class is not sharp and linear, but in general the vegetal level is typical of plant life, which is characterized by relatively little specialization, as shown by the fact that we can take a part of smaller branch of a tree and get from it a new sample of the tree. Vegetal life presents only few functions beside metabolism, namely, growth and reproduction. When we pass to the second level, we find animal life, which is much more complex and specialized, at least in higher species such as mammals, which have a central nervous system and sexual reproduction. In this case there is movement and sentience (i.e., the capacity to feel pain and pleasure), and a capacity for learning special responses to stimuli. At the top of this scale there is intellectual life, which according to the Western tradition is reserved only for human persons who are able not only to move rapidly and to feel pain and pleasure, but also to have symbolic activity, abstract thinking, and a complex language in order to communicate efficiently.

VII. PRACTICAL IMPLICATIONS

Having distinguished three differnt levels of life (and their corresponding concepts) of multicellular organisms, we can approach our original question concerning the nature of the concept of "human life" (whether it is a descriptive or a normative concept). First of all, it is of interest to point out that in Western traditions it is usual to invest great value only in *intellectual life,* and attribute little or no value to other forms of life (vegetal and even animal). This is clear if we consider that according to most legislations living organisms of lower kinds are considered as mere "things," i.e., something at disposal of the human person so that any behavior toward it need not be justified. Moreover, it

is important to keep in mind that human life includes all the lower levels of organization, and it is important to state the relations among them. This is a source of problems, mainly because technological advancements can keep alive some lower subsystems of the human multicellular organism while the highest are already destroyed or dead. In this case we may ask whether the relation of strict subordination of the parts to the whole is still present or has already disappeared, and if the answer is in the second sense, there is problem with our right conduct. Similar problems arise at the other end of the spectrum, since *in vitro* fertilization allows us to create new human fertilized cells, so making practically relevant (and not only a mere abstract speculation) the question of whether in the very first cells, the relation of strict subordination is required. Apparently the answer seems to be in the negative, since there is no adequate organization, but certainly there is quite a controversy on the issue.

For these reasons, many contemporary authors draw a sharp distinction between *biological life* and *biographical life,* where the latter is equivalent to intellectual life since it presupposes mental states, memories, etc. On the other hand, mere "biological life" is metabolic activity occurring in a human organism which has lost or not yet acquired higher functions because of the absence of the whole brain or significant parts of it. Once accepting such a distinction, its practical consequences depend on whether or not one accepts the already mentioned assumption typical of Western societies that tends to not attribute value to lower levels of life. Those favoring it are inclined to say that mere biological life in itself has little value, even if this does not mean that such a life is valuable because it matters to other people or because (as in the case of the embryo) it matters to a future person.

Others strongly criticize the distinction between biological and biographical life, holding that human life must be always protected in itself, because it is always a great gift. However, this view either introduces a version of vitalism, by saying that "human life" has a special value only because of its intrinsic constitution (independent of its actual organization), or such a view uses the expression "human life" in a wider sense which includes in its meaning also the transmission of life. These two different aspects are of course strongly connected, since if human life had an intrinsic value, then it is plausible to think that also its transmission should deserve a very special care. Since for centuries reproduction and sexuality were considered a sort of sacred field, this distinction did not emerge; but after the "sexual revolution" of the 1960s, diffusion of contraception, and a sort of "secularization" of sexuality (seen as a normal function of the person), no special value seems to be conferred upon transmission of life by most people, and the idea of an intrinsic value of human life as such appears to be outmoded.

However, this general thesis has been reworded, saying that from conception human life ought to be endowed with peculiar value because either the zygote is already a person or conception is the only "nonarbitrary" point concerning the beginning of "human life." There is not enough space for a detailed examination of these arguments here, but from our viewpoint both these positions seem to presuppose an unstated assumption which can conveniently be called "reism" (or "thing-ism"), i.e., the view that reality is made up of "things" which come into being by fusion with other "things" (spatiotemporal entities delimited by sharp borders). So, for instance, when some flour (a "thing") is mixed with some milk and eggs (another "thing"), we have a new compound (a new "thing") which can assume various shapes without any significant (substantial) change. This frame of reasoning is typical of common sense, and for this reason it is familiar: when such a frame is applied to reproduction we are led to think that fertilization is the crucial event. At conception (or fertilization) two separate "things" (the gametes) fuse themselves together, giving origin to a new "thing" (the zygote), and this event seems to point to a "natural" and "nonarbitrary" watershed within a more complex process.

Assuming the reistic viewpoint we can easily understand the attractiveness of the idea that human life begins at conception, but also we understand its basic fault: reism is a commonsensical way of thinking and cannot be used in an alleged scientific explanation of a sophisticated biological process such as reproduction. In other words, reism is wrong and misleading because it introduces without any ado or qualifications a mere commonsensical assumption within a biological theoretical context. Since biology is nowadays a mature science with its own theory, when we face reproduction and we want to explain it, we have to abandon mere common sense (and its reistic assumptions), operate a sort of new "Copernican revolution," and accept a more adequate biological way of thinking. It then becomes clear that in biology there are no "things," but rather processes which are goal-directed and more or less complex. Therefore the question of when life begins is clearly misleading, and a more appropriate one is, "when does the reproductive process begin?"

Once we assume such a biological way of thinking, it is clear on the one hand that conception is just *one* stage (and not the crucial one) within the more complex process of reproduction, which has its own teleology starting with the formation of the gametes and ending at birth, and on the other hand that throughout reproduction the human living process becomes more and more complex, passing various stages before reaching human intellectual life, so that we have to recognize that such a concept is a descriptive one. At the beginning of this entry, I pointed out that many authors hold that such a concept is an inextricable mixture of descriptions and evaluations, and now I have pointed out the reasons for which I think it is a descriptive concept, even if we can confer evaluative meaning on the whole reproductive process or to some special stage.

A good reason to attribute a special value to the transmission of human life can be found in the fact that reproduction is basic for the continuation of life and maintainance of societies and social life. In this sense, we reach the last level of biological organizations, that of superindividual organizations, i.e., societies. This level is crucial since every organism is begotten by its like, and many organisms beget new organisms themselves. In this sense, each living being is part of a larger stream of life, and the hierarchical structure of life does not end up with the organism itself, but may concern various organisms and a part of society. Looking at societies, we have to understand the specific role of each individual. There are many sorts of societies in which each individual has a specific role, as happens in societies of insects, ants, and bees, where animals of different castes (workers, soldiers, reproductors, etc.) appear to be subordinate "organs" working for the whole society.

In higher organisms, however, individuals assume a stronger position and we might have conflicts between the claims of the group and the claims of single individuals. In human society social life receives special attention, and there are opposite theories explaining the nature of social life. There are two major schools: communitarians seem to think that social life has its own criteria, and that single individuals should see themselves as part of the whole instead of social atoms detached from the vital rest. On the other end, individualists deny most of what communitarians believe, holding that human societies are the result of single individuals, and that individual claims come first. However, the concept of *social life* is quite different compared to the others examined in this entry, and must be postponed to another occasion.

Also See the Following Articles

ABORTION • ANIMAL RIGHTS • BRAIN DEATH • DEATH, DEFINITION OF • EUTHANASIA • GENE THERAPY • HOMICIDE, CRIMINAL VERSUS JUSTIFIABLE • REPRODUCTIVE TECHNOLOGIES

Bibliography

Allen, G. (1978). *Life science in the twentieth century.* Cambridge: Cambridge Univ. Press.

Beckner, M. (1959). *The biological way of thinking.* New York: Columbia, Univ. Press.

Coleman, W. (1977). *Biology in the nineteenth century.* Cambridge: Cambridge Univ. Press.

Dobzhansky, T. (1969). *The biology of ultimate concern.* London: Rapp and Whiting.

Matthen, M. & Linsky, B. (Eds.) (1988). *Philosophy and biology. Canadian Journal of Philosophy,* **14** (Suppl.).

Mori, M. (1996). *Aborto e morale.* Milano: le Saggiatore.

Sober, E. (1993). *Philosophy of biology.* London: Oxford Univ. Press.

Waddington, C. H. (1962). *The nature of life.* New York: Atheneum.

LITERATURE AND ETHICS

David Novitz
University of Canterbury, New Zealand

I. Traditional Connections between Literature and Ethics
II. Literature as a Source of Moral Understanding
III. Conclusion

GLOSSARY

Aesthetic Movement An artistic movement of the late 19th and early 20th centuries that espoused the view that art ought to be produced only for its own sake, and appreciated only in terms of its formal features, never its message or its intended function.

Enlightenment, the An 18th century philosophical movement that stressed the importance of reason, sense experience, and the autonomy of individuals. It marks the beginning of modern philosophy.

eudaimonia The state of flourishing achieved, according to Aristotle, through a life well lived.

New Criticism A literary movement of the mid-20th century that was greatly influenced by the principles of the Aesthetic Movement.

postmodernism The view that the Enlightenment emphasis on rationality, truth, sense experience, and the moral autonomy of individuals is mistaken—that there is no such thing as truth, reason, morality, or genuine personal autonomy.

LITERATURE AND ETHICS are connected by the widely held belief that literary works of art enlarge our moral sympathies and guide us in matters of value in ways that are at once to be welcomed and feared. This article explores this connection between literature and ethics from both a historical and a contemporary perspective.

I. TRADITIONAL CONNECTIONS BETWEEN LITERATURE AND ETHICS

A. The Greek View

The ethical dimension of literature was first remarked in the works of Plato and Aristotle. The Homeric poems were a core element of Greek education, and it was through them that children were introduced to the rudiments of theology and ethical behavior. Plato, however, believed that literature was not well-placed to achieve these ends. His criticisms were expressed through the voice of Socrates, who (especially in the *Republic*) maintained that since art merely imitates appearances and plays on the emotions, it is bound to mislead the intellect—not just by imparting false views of the gods but also, and more particularly, by playing on our emotions and corrupting our character. And so, in the *Republic*, Book 2, Socrates contends that in the ideal republic "the first thing will be to establish a censorship of the writers of fiction, and let the censors receive any tale of fiction which is good, and reject the bad; and we will desire mothers and nurses to tell their children the authorised ones only." Given this view, it is not surprising that Socrates seeks (in Book 3) to remove from literature anything at all that can lead to mistaken beliefs and misguided values. Emotions that are often part of poetry—grief, love, and fear—are considered dangerous, partly because it is not appropriate for a hero to grieve deeply or to experience excessive emotions. Literature should provide a moral ideal for ordinary people, and insofar as poetry and drama about the gods and the heroes play on and encourage base emotion, they fail to provide the proper moral example.

On Plato's view, therefore, literature must not be considered for its own sake. Implicitly, the early 20th century idea of art for art's sake is considered by him and rejected. What is attractive to the senses, emotionally stimulating, and seemingly beautiful may have dreadful moral effects, and may instill false beliefs, values, and ideals, and so should be viewed with the caution and respect due to any dangerous instrument.

It is in Book 10 of the *Republic* that Socrates launches his famous attack on all representative or imitative arts insofar as they are valued as representations of reality. Because the poet and the dramatist only imitate the appearances of human virtue, they may be technically brilliant imitators without knowing anything at all about that which is imitated. So it does not follow from the fact that Homer gives such a convincing portrayal of human nature and godly behavior that he knows very much about either. Like painting, literary imitation is considered by Plato to be little more than a form of amusement and entertainment that cannot tell us anything about the nature of virtue. It cannot provide us with genuine insight and understanding, and the amusement that it offers is likely to be harmful since so many people are beguiled by literature into adopting false opinions and misleading ideas of virtue. People, Plato thinks, will expect of literature the sorts of truths about reality and virtue that only philosophers are competent to offer.

By contrast, Aristotle in the *Poetics* has a very high regard for the ethical value of tragedy, and the feelings or emotions that it occasions. For, on his view, the tragic action of drama always results from a character flaw of the tragic hero or heroine. Whatever else it does, a tragedy makes manifest the fact that a person with a flawed character cannot flourish; indeed, such a person must be wretched and cause wretchedness in the lives of others. *Eudaimonia* (happiness or flourishing) is the ultimate aim of a life well lived. The good (or ethical) life, for Aristotle, is a life that achieves *eudaimonia*. Part

of what tragedy does is bring us to dwell on and consider the sorts of character deficiencies that prevent flourishing in the course of a lifetime. What a tragedy represents, Aristotle tells us, is not human beings but the actions of human beings in the development and course of a particular life. It is by showing how human beings of a certain character live, and what sorts of lives they live, that the ethical value of this literary form emerges. According to Aristotle in the *Poetics* and the *Politics*, tragedy has both cognitive and motivational value, and it teaches us something about human character and the emotions. The pity and fear that the play arouses in its viewers indirectly motivate us to avoid certain forms of behavior and ways of living, and to embrace others (M. C. Nussbaum, 1986. *The Fragility of Goodness: Luck and Ethics in Greek Philosophy,* pp. 378–394). Cambridge Univ. Press, Cambridge).

B. The Modern View

Enlightenment philosophers were uniformly skeptical of the creative imaginings of poets and novelists. On their view, the fanciful or creative imagination could never be a secure basis for knowledge about the world or for moral understanding. Descartes was flatly dismissive of the literary or poetic imagination and denied that it could have any role at all to play in the acquisition of genuine knowledge or understanding. The imagination, on his view, "inasmuch as it differs from the power of understanding, is in nowise a necessary element in my nature or in my essence" (quoted in D. Novitz, 1986. *Knowledge, Fiction, and Imagination,* chap. 2. Temple Univ. Press, Philadelphia). And, in the same vein, Malebranche devoted the whole of the second book of his *Recherche de la Vérité* to establishing that the imagination is the source of all sorts of deceptions and must be severely constrained.

Francis Bacon was not much kinder. Although he allowed the imagination a role in poetry, he denied that it could have any part to play in the acquisition of knowledge. The imagination, on his view, may "sever that which nature hath joined, and so make unlawful matches and divorces of things." It "hardly produces sciences" but only poetry which is "to be accounted rather as a pleasure or play of wit than a science." Likewise, Thomas Hobbes maintained that "Fancy without the help of Judgement is not commended as a Vertue," and where it does so function, "Fancy is one kind of Madnesse." It was this that led John Locke to maintain that "if the fancy be allowed the place of judgement at first in sport, it afterwards comes to usurp it. ... There are so many ways of fallacy, such arts of giving colours, appearances, and resemblances by this court dresser, the fancy, that he who is not wary to admit nothing but truth itself . . ." cannot but be caught. The products of fancy are epistemically and morally suspect, and this is why metaphors, allusions, and figures of speech generally are described as "perfect cheats" when "we would speak of things as they are."

Similar views are found in Hume and Kant. Hume regards fancy as a possible source of the destruction of human nature. It is the origin of "the loose and indolent reveries of a castle builder" and the inventions of poets, each of which is "to be regarded as an idle fiction." However, the fanciful imagination is "neither unavoidable to mankind, nor necessary, or so much as useful in the conduct of life. . . ."

Like Hume, Kant has harsh things to say about the fanciful imagination. In *Anthropologie* (31, VII, 174) he tells us that "phantasy" is nothing other than the uncontrolled spatial imagination which runs riot in daydreams or nightmares. However, it can be controlled, and when it is, we speak of composition. The most obvious example of this is to be found in artistic composition, but even so, whether controlled or uncontrolled, the imagination thus conceived is altogether incapable of enhancing either our moral or our epistemic understanding. Fancy, in Kant's words, is "the mere play of the imagination": it is an "unruly" imagination, an imagination ungoverned by rules, which can help us to make sense of our experience (Novitz, 1986, 22–27).

The sole aim of the fanciful or creative imagination, according to the modernism that began at the time of the Enlightenment, is to afford pleasure and delight. Given the role of fancy in artistic creation, this too is conceived of as the aim of art. It is a view that we find in Hume's famous essay, "Of the Standard of Taste," and in Kant's *Critique of Judgment;* a view that came to dominate the Aesthetic Movement of the late 19th century, and the New Criticism of the mid-20th century.

Nonetheless, Kant did not think of beauty in art as wholly unrelated to morality. On his view, beauty is the symbol of the morally good, and he believes that we cannot explain aesthetic experience unless we relate it to our moral natures as human beings. Still more, the genius of some artists allows them, through the free (or imaginative) use of their cognitive powers, to express what Kant calls "aesthetical ideas": ideas, that is, that are the product of a creative or fanciful imagination but which nonetheless move beyond the limits of the artist's and our own experience to express ideas that are rich in moral understanding and that elude the constraints of our conceptual comprehension (*Critique of Judgment,* sect. 49).

Taking his cue from Kant, Friedrich Schiller argued that it "is only through beauty that man makes his way to freedom" (1795. *On the Aesthetic Education of Man,* Letter 2, par. 5). Only beauty, he thought, has the power to change the will of human beings in ways that can cure their savagery, liberate them from cruel orthodoxies, and make them beautiful (Letter 15, par. 3) What we find, then, is that even though Enlightenment thought is suspicious of the powers of the creative imagination, Kant, and the romantics who followed him, argues that the free play of the creative imagination is linked to moral understanding. Through the work of these philosophers, Enlightenment theories of art and literature eventually caught up with the literature of the day, which was widely perceived as morally instructive—sometimes, too, as morally enlightening.

C. The Postmodern View

The Romantics—most especially Johann Fichte, Friedrich Schelling, and Samuel Taylor Coleridge—took from Kant the idea that our concepts and ideas help fix the nature of reality. Unlike Kant, though, they argued in a variety of ways that there were no fixed structures of the human mind that were productive of human experience, so that, in their view, the productive acts of the imagination actually determine our experience of the world. Still more, since they could find no basis for the Kantian distinction between the world as experienced by us (the phenomenal world) and the world as it is in itself (the noumenal world), these same acts of the imagination were thought to help shape the world itself.

Although not often seen as such, this move in romantic epistemology and metaphysics heralded the onset of postmodernism. The first genuinely postmodern thinker was Friedrich Nietzsche, who can also usefully be thought of as a romantic. Not only does he regard all of what we call knowledge as the product of fancy, but in his famous essay, "On Truth and Falsity in Their Ultramoral Sense," he denies that there is any room for the notion of truth. Our primal acts of fancy, if found to be useful, are designated as true, but truth itself, he contended, is no more than a "mobile army of metaphors." It is an honorific term, applied to our favored metaphors because they afford us control and power, not because they correspond to how things are. On his view, when we "talk about trees, . . . we believe we know something about the things themselves, and yet we only possess metaphors of the things, and these metaphors do not in the least correspond to the original essentials." "On Truth and Falsity in their Ultramoral Sense." In Oscar Levy, Ed., Maximilian A. Mügge, trans. *The Complete Works of Friedrich Nietzsche* (18 Vols. Allen & Unwin, London, 1911) Vol. 2, p 178.

On the postmodern view, therefore, it is not just art and literature that involve imaginative play; indeed, since the use of all language is wholly unconstrained by any extralinguistic, extratextual reality, all language is a form of play. Because of this, the distinction that we like to draw between fictional literature on the one hand and histories or factual reports on the other is thought to collapse. In a typically paradoxical way, fiction becomes primary; factual reports become a mere fiction.

This view of literature has clear moral implications, for according to it, since there is no extratextual reality, the way in which we talk and write, the texts we create, are themselves constitutive of reality, of the way things are. Dominant narratives do not just shape our view of ourselves and the world around us; they are either partly or wholly constitutive of ourselves and our world. This is why Nietzsche could say that we construct ourselves in the way that an artist constructs a work of art, and why Richard Rorty could defend the view that "language goes all the way down"—that there is no way that things are independent of our descriptions of it (R. Rorty, 1982. *The Consequences of Pragmatism*. Univ. of Minnesota Press, Minneapolis). On this view, literature offers us a way not just of construing, but of constructing the world; it offers us a "vocabulary" that cannot be dislodged by appeal to reasons or the facts of the matter because it, and it alone, determines what will count as reasons and as facts of the matter. Plainly, then, if a literary work comes to dominate, it will decisively influence not just how people think of themselves, but the sorts of people that they are. Vicious narratives will make people vicious; kind and compassionate ones will have the opposite effect.

What is interesting about this view, is the formative power that it affords to literature and the cinema. In this postmodernists are right. They correctly gauge the power of dominant narratives and cinematic and television images to shape and mold lives and worlds (D. Novitz, 1992. *The Boundaries of Art*. Temple Univ. Press, Philadelphia). But since they cannot anchor descriptions or narratives in any extralinguistic reality, it seems as if anything goes: that the most attractive narratives or literary works must win—just in virtue of their seductive power (R. Rorty, 1989. *Contingency, Irony, and Solidarity*. Cambridge Univ. Press, Cambridge). And this has frightening moral consequences, for on one interpretation of a postmodern view, the narratives that are found to be attractive by a majority of people, even

when they are viciously racist, cruel, and unjust, become cognitively unassailable yardsticks of normality and of acceptable behavior.

But postmodernists like Derrida and Rorty are wrong to suppose that language goes all the way down—that there is no independent way of assessing the accuracy and rationality of the narratives that we tell about our countries and ourselves. There are facts of the matter, and by appealing to them dominant narratives (derived, perhaps, from literature, television, or the cinema) may be shown to fit or to misrepresent the way the world is. It is particularly important to see that the facts in terms of which we assess a given narrative or "vocabulary" may be known independently of any specific history or story. It seems plain, for instance, that I can learn that people desire and need food, or that there was an earthquake yesterday or a power cut today without believing or inventing a specific story that somehow informs my experience. There simply is no good reason for denying (as some postmodernists do) the existence of prenarrative facts, or for insisting that all experience and knowledge must be mediated by, or derived from, narrative. Not all explanations are narratives, nor are all theories, descriptions, lists, annals, or chronicles. To suppose that they are, or to suppose that all experience is bred of narrative, is to so stretch the meaning of this word as to render it blunt and all but useless. To inform someone that food nourishes or that people deprived of water must die of dehydration is not to tell a *story* in anything but the most extended sense of this word. Narratives involve stories in a much fuller, more literary sense, and can be assessed by appeal to nonnarrative facts.

So although the narratives that we inherit from good literature, the cinema, the theater, or television may greatly influence our lives and our thinking, there really is no reason to suppose that we cannot assess them for their adequacy and their accuracy. This is important, because it allows us to assess their moral value independently of the narratives and artistic construals themselves.

II. LITERATURE AS A SOURCE OF MORAL UNDERSTANDING

A. The Acquisition of Moral Beliefs and Values

The Greek, modernist, and postmodernist views of literature and ethics all allow that, in one way or another, literature can affect our moral values and our moral understanding. The question is how? After all, a good deal of fictional literature does not describe actual people and their behavior, and so is neither true nor false of the world that we inhabit. How can such literature nonetheless impart moral values that regulate actual lives?

People who have been initiated into the practice of fiction, who know the appropriate stance to take toward it (P. Lamarque and S. H. Olsen, 1994. *Truth, Fiction, and Literature: A Philosophical Perspective,* chap. 2. Clarendon Press, Oxford), will imagine the lives of fictional characters and engage emotionally with them, either by sharing their fears or elation or else by feeling a certain degree of concern for them. Attentive readers who are properly engaged in the fiction, and who identify in this way with the characters of fiction, will inevitably find themselves confronted by a range of demanding ethical questions—questions that are pertinent not just to the lives of fictional characters but to their own lives as well (Novitz, 1986, chap. 6). Should Dorothea Brooke (in George Eliot's *Middlemarch*) be the dutiful wife that she is to Casaubon? How should Rosamund deal with Lydgate's impending bankruptcy and disgrace? Is Caleb Garth's highly principled behavior justified, or is it a kind of bigotry—an attempt to ignore the complexities of the world by appeal to principles that overlook the nuances and unspoken demands of particular situations? How ought Will Ladislaw to respond to Dorothea in view of Casaubon's deeply insulting will? And so on, almost without end.

It is impossible to read a good deal of fictional literature without being confronted with questions of this sort, and without being made to think deeply and imaginatively about the ethical problems that they address. This is true not only of the literary classics—the novels of Jane Austen, Emily Brontë, George Eliot, and Henry James, or the plays of Shakespeare, Marlowe, and Webster—but is true as well of contemporary novels like those of Iris Murdoch, Antonia Byatt, Margaret Attwood, Chaim Potok, Carol Shields, Joanna Trollope, and Roddy Doyle. All deal extensively with ethical problems—with problems, as Hilary Putnam put it, about how people ought to live.

A good author will often sketch such problems in consummate and highly convincing detail, so that the situations that the reader is invited to imagine and to consider from a moral point of view have all the complexity and distinctiveness of the moral quandaries that confront us in our everyday lives. The advantage of literary fiction, of course, is that readers can consider such problems and learn from them without the enormous emotional and social upheavals that frequently accompany ethical problems and dilemmas in everyday

life. It is in the process of doing this that the reader is brought to assess the adequacy of his or her own moral understandings. When, for instance, one is confronted through literary fiction with the emotionally and intellectually barren life that Dorothea endures while married to Mr. Casaubon, one is forced to return, time and again, to one's notions about the moral desirability of unqualified fidelity in marriage. Ought Dorothea to remain devoted to a man whom she has discovered to be so cold, remote, and intellectually unstimulating? And if not, what ought she to do to alleviate her situation? The options are limited; the stresses are real and deeply impoverishing.

Reflection on situations like these does not straightforwardly impart new moral values. What it does, however, is test and tease one's moral beliefs and understanding—beliefs, say, about the devotion and sacrifice that marriage ought properly to require. It is not as if George Eliot tells us what would be morally correct, or how Dorothea ought to behave with respect to Mr. Casaubon. But, when once initiated into the practice of fiction, we cannot help thinking about these and related questions, and in the process we may discover that some of our moral views about marriage are wanting or deficient—that they need to be reconsidered, broadened, or narrowed.

Unlike philosophy, fictional literature deals in the concrete and the particular, not the abstractions of ethical theory. As a result, it introduces into our moral thinking all the special and peculiar demands of circumstance, and all the complexities that test or challenge the broad ethical principles and theories that traditional philosophical approaches to ethics encourage. It is in this way that literature inclines its readers to test their moral understanding by bringing them to apply it to complex and demanding imaginary situations that have been imagined in fine and nuanced detail by their authors. At times one will come to see that one's moral beliefs do not cater in any adequate way for the complex situations in which they are asked to do service. As a result, the reader knows that they are not entirely satisfactory, and there may be a shift of values consequent upon this.

Narratives may, of course, be more or less subtle, and their moral subtlety is given considerable prominence by Martha Nussbaum in explaining the moral influence of literature (M. Nussbaum, 1992. *Love's Knowledge: Essays on Philosophy and Literature.* Oxford Univ. Press, Oxford). But it is interesting to note that narratives may also undermine subtlety in ways that enhance our moral vision (E. John, 1995. *Philos. Lit.* **19**, 308–319). On this view subtlety sometimes needs to be subverted, for, if we (as members, say, of the white middle-classes) regard Toni Morrison's account of the impoverished lives of black schoolgirls in *The Bluest Eye* as "subtle," then this can only be because we normally confine black schoolgirls to the fringes of our moral awareness, and do not think of them as full persons with ordinary moral claims. Morrison's story convinces us that they are indeed full persons, so that at the very point that we are most inclined to see her narrative as subtle, we also recognize how inappropriate it is—morally speaking—to think of it in this way. Herein resides the subversion of subtlety, and the use of the narrative to bring the reader to see black children as full persons who bear more than their fair share of the world's problems.

Notice that in order for John's account of the subversion of subtlety to work in a way that is fully convincing, there has to be life beyond the narrative: a way in which the world is, which dominant narratives encourage us to ignore or else to confine to the periphery. One reason why people tend to overlook the lot of black schoolgirls is because our interest is not urged in that direction; the dominant narratives in our society—narratives about heroes and saints, political figures, and successful lives that are derived from novels, plays, and the movies—do not have much to say about black schoolgirls. They direct our attention elsewhere, and Morrison's text can correctly be seen as drawing our attention to what was previously there to be noticed, but which an institutionalized insensitivity, directed perhaps by the literary canon, had to some extent prevented us from noticing.

So it seems wrong to argue, as Rorty and other postmodernists do, that Morrison just offers a narrative redescription of the world but that there is no world "out there," no nonnarrative facts in terms of which to check her redescription. The way things *are* sometimes shocks and surprises, and sometimes intrudes upon and subverts existing views of the world. The feelings of girls like Pecola and Claudia (in *The Bluest Eye*)—their naked, raw experience of the world and its indifference—are sharply, and nonnarratorially, painful to them. They feel, perhaps without being able to articulate it, that the way in which society construes their lives is inadequate to the brute realities that they face, and does no justice to their needs and their desires. But they have only the dominant narratives or (to use Rorty's term) "vocabulary" in terms of which to describe their lives, and they know at some deep level of feeling and hurt that it is not true to their experience, and that it perpetuates their disadvantage.

In this sense, our experience of the world comes well before narrative and the dominant "vocabularies,"

and it is part of the merit of *The Bluest Eye* that it draws our attention to, and enables us to articulate, prenarrative experiences in ways that draw attention to the moral inadequacies both of the narratives that rule our lives and of our responses to those narratives. Of course, it is true that narratives may help us to construe our experiences, and (as in the present case) may help us to recognize and accept the claims—the preexisting claims—of those who are ignored and relegated to the margins. But from time to time, the way things are just does not fit the categories and pigeonholes carved out by our inherited narratives, forms of life, and Rortian "vocabularies," and we are awakened to their inadequacies (Novitz, 1986, 66–71; 1992, chap. 10).

B. Empathy and Compassion

We cannot read fictional literature *as fiction* without imagining the various scenarios sketched by an author, and without a mind to what it is like to be in those situations. We sometimes sympathize with heroes or heroines and feel concern for them on account of what they confront in their lives. At least as often, we feel with them and share their joy, elation, and grief, and so develop a range of empathic beliefs about what it feels like to be in precisely those situations. Such affective and emotional responses to fiction form an integral part of appreciating fiction and develop our capacity to empathize and feel compassion for others (S. Feagin, 1996. *Reading with Feeling,* chaps. 1 and 11. Cornell Univ. Press, Ithaca, NY/London).

Because of this, some literature has done an enormous amount to allow people to escape the narrow, sometimes sectarian points of view encouraged by an awareness of their own interests, or by religious and political ideologies. Literary fiction brings readers to grasp the points of view of fictional characters in ways that particular interests, politics, or religions sometimes expressly forbid. In the process, novels and dramas arguably alter the understanding (and the values) of countless individuals—and they do so, for the most part, without the pain and upheaval that often accompany such changes in real life. Our identification with Emma Bovary, Stephen Dedalus, or Frederica West enlarges our sympathies and makes us susceptible to new ways of thinking and feeling. In bringing us, in this way, to identify imaginatively with fictional creatures, novels (like television and the cinema) have given us a way of thinking about actual people; a way that helps us not just to understand their actions from their point of view but also, on occasions, to abandon some or all of the feelings of resentment and hostility that might previously have been occasioned by their actions. In other words, literary fiction itself provides us with a model of thinking that encourages certain moral virtues—the virtues of compassion and forgiveness.

We can see now why it is sometimes argued that the knowledge and understanding afforded by literature is "dangerous," for it requires "personal change as a condition of coming to possess it" (B. Harrison, 1991. *Inconvenient Fictions: Literature and the Limits of Theory*, chap. 1. Yale Univ. Press, New Haven, CT). It is dangerous, too, because such knowledge gives us an internal perspective on the issues that confront characters of fiction. We are brought to share their perceptions and understanding as well as their emotional turmoil; because of this we come to understand differently—in ways that are not available to an "external," wholly passionless, perspective.

In arguing along these lines, Harrison explicitly rejects the paradigm of knowledge handed down to us by John Locke and other Enlightenment philosophers, "which includes the ideal of a unified science whose basic deliverances would be expressed in an austere, pre-theoretical language of bare empirical description." According to Harrison, what fictional literature does is destabilize our received ways of making sense of the world: it possesses the power "to administer shocks to the systems of categories and assumptions which we inhabit." In so doing, of course, it may bring us to see that "the language we ordinarily speak, the scuffed, second-hand and limited range of conceptual options … fail seriously to be adequate to the full range of natural possibility." It is not, Harrison thinks, that literature ought to convey "Great Truths"; what it should and often does do is "reveal to us the limitations of a commonplace language" (Harrison, 1991, 9–17).

C. Literature as Moral Philosophy

If Harrison is right, fictional literature does not only inform us about moral issues and change us as moral agents, it also affects the way in which we conceptualize, and, because of this, may also on occasions help "show the fly the way out of the fly bottle." It may, in other words, do some of the work of philosophy.

Various claims have been made about the relation of moral philosophy to literature. Some argue that the connection is intimate and necessary, and others that it is merely contingent. According to Martha Nussbaum, in *Love's Knowledge* (1992), since moral reasoning requires attention to the fine detail of the situations in which human beings find themselves, we cannot develop an adequate moral philosophy that is inattentive

to such detail. Without it, moral philosophy can deal only in the sorts of generalities that lack all awareness of the incommensurable goods that people have to decide between in the course of a life. This, on her view, is the kind of detail that is "rarely" found in philosophical texts; the entire style of philosophy, which deals in abstractions and generalities, is antithetical to the detail required for adequate moral theorizing. However, good literature does furnish this sort of detail, and allows us a delicately nuanced awareness in terms of which to test and formulate moral theory.

And so, in the opening paragraphs of *Love's Knowledge*, Nussbaum asks,

> How should one write, what words should one select, what forms and structures and organization, if one is pursuing understanding? (Which is to say, if one is, in that sense, a philosopher?) Sometimes this is taken to be a trivial and uninteresting question. I shall claim that it is not. Style itself makes its claims, expresses its own sense of what matters. Literary form is not separable from philosophical content, but is, itself, a part of content—an integral part, then, of the search for and the statement of truth. (Nussbaum, 1992, 3)

The claim, of course, is not that we cannot develop moral theories, and so practice moral philosophy, without the benefit of literature—it is that if we think of philosophy as textually based, then in order to practice moral philosophy properly, we will need texts that introduce us to the fine and demanding, the subtle, detail of everyday life. It is this that good literature provides more readily than philosophical tracts; this simply because while philosophy is very general or abstract, literature is much more concerned with the particular (albeit imaginary) details of human lives. Still more, literature often requires us to consider, and perhaps resolve, certain moral quandaries, and in the process presents to us, feelingly, "the riskiness of the lived deliberative situation" (Nussbaum, 1992, 142); something that moral philosophy needs to take into account if it is to develop adequate decision procedures and action-guiding theories. In this way, literature becomes a useful, and a readily available, component of good moral theorizing. The claim is not that it is essential, only that it can generally improve our moral reasoning.

Lamarque and Olsen argue against this thesis. On their view, the thesis is ambiguous as between the claim that literature is necessary for moral philosophy and the claim that it can improve or heighten our moral sensitivity. But the first view, they argue, is logically independent of the second (Lamarque and Olsen, 1994, 388). In this they are doubtless correct, but this claim does not establish that certain literary works—those that sketch human life in credible detail and that give rise, in the process, to credible moral problems—cannot play the useful role of helping philosophers to determine the adequacy of existing normative ethical theories, and to help them formulate more adequate theories. So far as I can tell, this is all that Nussbaum claims when she speaks of the role that literature can play in moral theorizing. The thesis does not amount to the claim that every literary work invariably serves moral philosophy, only that some works do, and that they need not always do so very well.

Harrison's view, we have seen, is somewhat stronger than this. He believes that literature contributes to the philosophical enterprise generally since it brings us to recognize and sometimes acknowledge the inadequacy of our inherited ways of thinking, and to adopt different ways of construing and understanding. And this, of course, is intrinsic to the philosophical enterprise. Even so, there is no suggestion that literature always does this, or that moral philosophy somehow requires attention to literary works.

Richard Eldridge's thesis is stronger yet (R. Eldridge, 1989. *On Moral Personhood: Philosophy, Literature, Criticism, and Self-Understanding.* The Univ. of Chicago Press, Chicago). On his view, philosophy forms part of a quest for self-understanding, but often offers "theoretical characterizations . . . that we cannot wholly live." In order to avoid this, he thinks that we need to understand ourselves through the particular cases depicted in narratives. We will "show ourselves to ourselves through the work of reading" (Eldridge, 1989, 20). Such literary representations of what it is to be a person are always, so Eldridge contends, a "moral enterprise." We discover ourselves through our acquaintance with literature, so that literature bears importantly on the sort of people that we become; it "supports a general characterization" of our own nature, and with it our "moral personhood." At this point, Eldridge tells us, the distinction between literature and philosophy begins to dissolve, for narratives that deal with particular circumstances always assume general propositions about persons and about "what makes sense," while our more general presuppositions, he thinks, only gain what sense they have from "the particular narratives that draw on them." Here narrative, in the form of literature, is considered to be deeply implicated in moral and all other philosophy. On Eldridge's view, then, there is no sustainable distinction between philosophy and literature—a view that he can reach only by extending the scope of the terms "narrative" and "literature" in ways that make them less than useful.

III. CONCLUSION

Whatever their views of the connection of literature to moral philosophy, those who participate in the current debate concerning literature and ethics are all convinced that literature is capable of a profound impact not only on the moral theories but also on the moral values to which readers subscribe. Literature, they believe, can and does impact on the sense that we have of ourselves as persons—on our capacity to empathize and project ourselves imaginatively into the situations of other moral subjects—and so on our behavior as moral agents.

But many questions remain unanswered. What is it that convinces us that a particular literary fiction has justly undermined our moral beliefs? Why should literature be allowed to hold the trump cards in this matter? Is literature no more than an "intuition pump" in terms of which to develop and judge our moral theories and insights? What, then, validates the intuitions that literature appeals to? Is it, at root, the case that the appeal to literature in ethics is no more than an appeal to moral intuitionism?

These and other questions have yet to receive the close attention that they deserve. What is clear, though, is that good literature furnishes us with a situation in which to apply and test the adequacy of our moral beliefs and theories, and so furnishes us with a means of refining and sharpening them by making them more adequate to the world in which we live.

Also See the Following Articles

ARISTOTELIAN ETHICS • ARTS, THE • PLATONISM

Bibliography

Eldridge, R. (1989). "On Moral Personhood: Philosophy, Literature, Criticism, and Self-Understanding." The Univ. of Chicago Press, Chicago.

Feagin, S. (1996). "Reading with Feeling." Cornell Univ. Press, Ithaca, NY/London.

Harrison, B. (1991). "Inconvenient Fictions: Literature and the Limits of Theory." Yale Univ. Press, New Haven, CT.

John, E. (1995). Subtlety and moral vision in fiction. *Philos. Lit.* **19**, 308–319.

Lamarque, P., and Haugom, S. H. (1994). "Truth, Fiction, and Literature: A Philosophical Perspective." Clarendon Press, Oxford.

Novitz, D. (1986). "Knowledge, Fiction and Imagination." Temple Univ. Press, Philadelphia.

Novitz, D. (1992). "The Boundaries of Art." Temple Univ. Press, Philadelphia.

Nussbaum, M. C. (1986). "The Fragility of Goodness: Luck and Ethics in Greek Philosophy." Cambridge Univ. Press, Cambridge.

Nussbaum, M. C. (1992). "Love's Knowledge: Essays on Philosophy and Literature." Oxford Univ. Press, Oxford.

Rorty, R. (1982). "The Consequences of Pragmatism." Univ. of Minnesota Press, Minneapolis.

Rorty, R. (1989). "Contingency, Irony, and Solidarity." Cambridge Univ. Press, Cambridge.

MACHIAVELLIANISM

Maureen Ramsay
University of Leeds

GLOSSARY

acts and omissions doctrine A doctrine stating that the failure to perform an act with foreseen consequences is morally less bad than to perform the same act with the same consequences.

autonomy of politics The view that moral considerations are irrelevant to political affairs.

consequentialism A group of theories holding that the rightness or wrongness of an action depends entirely on the effects which the action has. Utilitarianism is a classic example of consequentialism.

deontological theories Theories claiming that the rightness or wrongness of an action depends solely on what kind of act it was. These theories stress that certain moral obligations and duties are absolutely binding irrespective of the consequences.

political realism Theories that claim to study the realities of the world as it is, as opposed to idealism.

raison d'état The justification of political action on grounds of reasons or interests of states.

rule-utilitarianism A theory holding that an action is right if it conforms to a rule the general following of which could have good consequences.

MACHIAVELLIANISM is associated with the doctrine of moral expediency and deviousness in political actions; the divorce of politics from private morality; the justification of all political means, even the most unscrupulous on grounds of reasons of state and the use of fraud, force, coercion, and deceit for political ends.

What is understood by the term Machiavellianism is almost exclusively derived from different interpretations of Machiavelli's teachings in *The Prince*. Machiavellianism is generally interpreted as an immoral doctrine, and so is a term of reproach and dishonor. But, it has also been seen as a recognition of the necessities and realities of political life and so as amoral, objective, or descriptive, rather than immoral. Contemporary writers grappling with the problem of the need for "dirty hands" in politics, see in Machiavellianism a justification for moral principles and practices appropriate to political actions, different from those which govern private life.

I. MACHIAVELLI AND MACHIAVELLIANISM IN *THE PRINCE*

Niccolo Machiavelli (1469–1527) was a Florentine secretary and political writer. He wrote *The Prince* in order to win favor and gain employment with the Medici. The book was intended as a practical advice document in the genre of treatises dealing with the problems of princely rule. Since ancient times political writers had been concerned with princes and princedoms. In the princely literature from the Middle Ages to the Renaissance, political moralists had compiled a list of cardinal and princely virtues that it was the duty of a good ruler to acquire. The prince, like his subjects was advised to be liberal, generous, merciful, truthful, kind, chaste, reliable, tolerant, and devout. It was assumed that it was rational to act morally, that public virtue was identical to private virtue, that ethics and politics were inseparable.

Machiavelli complained that such advice could only apply to perfect princes living in perfect states, neither of which actually exist. Machiavelli's unique contribution to princely literature was his discussion of actual political situations with the aim of formulating rules for political conduct useful for those who govern the state. In Chapter 15, he announces that he is departing from the methods of his idealistic predecessors in order to "write something useful to him who comprehends it." The novelty of Machiavelli's new political method lay in his claim to be concerned with the "truth of the matter as facts show" rather than with ideal or imaginary situations. He aimed to examine human nature and the state as they exist in reality in order to bring out what was typical and general in political conduct and so to establish rules and define maxims for political behavior and successful political action. Machiavelli claimed that his conclusions were based on facts drawn from history and his own observations and practical experience.

The application of this new historical and practical method yielded the conclusion that the goals of politics were the acquiring and holding down of power, the stability of the state, and the preservation of order. Therefore, in order to provide useful advice, Machiavelli was concerned to establish from historical example and factual evidence the kinds of qualities rulers must have and the actions they must take in order to establish, maintain, or restore order and stability. These qualities were psychological and social rather than moral; these actions were governed by prudential technical rules about means to ends, rather than moral rules. Machiavelli, though, does not completely disregard conventional morality. He admits that it is praiseworthy for a prince to embody the qualities of liberality, mercy, honesty, kindness, chastity, and tolerance, which are normally considered good. He exhorts his prince to act according to the accepted virtues of truth, charity, humanity, and religion when he can. However, the prince must be adaptable and "have a mind ready to turn in any direction as Fortune's winds and the variety of affairs require ... he holds to what is right when

he can and knows how to do wrong when he must" (Chapter 18).

The prince must cultivate not conventional virtue, but Machiavellian virtù. The prince must display those qualities, capacities, and dispositions necessary to establish, restore, and maintain the stability of the state, to win honor and glory for himself and to overcome the blows of Fortune. He must be bold, resolute, and flexible, prepared to break promises and act against charity, humanity, and religion. The prince must combine the cunning of the fox with the strength of the lion, devious, ruthless, violent, or cruel as the necessities of the situation dictate. To achieve political goals, the prince must be unconstrained by normal ethical ideals and adopt methods, which although contrary to these ideals, will lead to beneficial political consequences. Political necessity frequently demands that the prince learn to act immorally, that he learns how not to be good. The political situation is such that if the prince practices traditional virtues, they will be his destruction, if his practices are vicious they will result in safety or well-being.

Machiavelli draws on historical examples to illustrate that morally good actions can lead to evil results and that immoral actions may have beneficial consequences. Cesare Borgia's cruelty united the Romagna and brought it peace and loyalty. The mercy of the Florentine people led to the ruin of Pistoia. Well-intentioned moral actions or refusals to act immorally can have far worse consequences than timely, bold, and resolute action. In this manner he argues that meanness, cruelty, the breaking of promises, and deceit are more politically efficacious than the practice of the conventional virtues of mercy, faith, integrity, and religion. The prince need only to appear to have these virtues. In practice, he must adopt the necessary immoral means because "as to the actions of all men and especially those of princes ... everyone looks to their result" (Chapter 18).

Machiavelli argues his case against a backdrop of assumptions about the timeless and unchanging nature of human motives and aspirations. Machiavelli's view of human beings as natural egoists with a lust for domination, glory, and power led him to see history as an arena of conflict involving deceit, treachery, and violence. The result was interstate aggression and domestic turmoil. The causes of this conflict were psychological, located in the nature of human beings, but the solution was social and political. Conventional morality is ineffective and inappropriate to establishing and maintaining order and stability. At certain political conjunctures, it is necessary to employ evil means to achieve the desired result.

II. CONFLICTING INTERPRETATIONS OF MACHIAVELLI AND MACHIAVELLIANISM

A. An Immoral Doctrine

Machiavelli's claim that actions are judged by their consequences and that political success is incompatible with moral means, has led to the conclusion in popular imagination that Machiavelli was the author of the dictum, "the end justifies the means." Machiavelli did not actually express his ideas in this formula, nor was he the first writer to recognize the element of expediency involved in successful political action. This had been acknowledged at least since the time of Aristotle and was raised in the princely literature of the fifteenth century Italian humanists. These were, according to Gilbert, forerunners to the more explicit ideas of Machiavelli in their halting suggestions that beneficial consequences might necessitate or even excuse immoral means (Gilbert., A. (1938). *Machiavelli's prince and its forerunners*. Durham, NC: Duke University Press). But, it is generally acknowledged that Machiavelli was unique in taking the suggestions of other political thinkers to their most extreme conclusion by forcefully attempting to demonstrate the incompatibility between the demands of traditional morality and the requirements of power politics. And it is this crucial and perennial problem of the relationship between means and ends, ethics and politics, that have inspired most interest in and interpretations of his philosophy and subsequent condemnations of or justifications for Machiavellianism.

If Machiavelli's writings are interpreted as advocating the achievement of political ends by any means, then it is not difficult to see why Machiavellianism is associated with the principles of expediency rather than morality and with reprehensible, unscrupulous, scheming, duplicitous, and cunning political practice. That Machiavelli advocated Machiavellianism of this kind was the view of many writers from his own time to the present. Machiavelli has been castigated as a man inspired by the devil, an immoral writer, and a deliberate teacher of evil. This was the view of the Renaissance dramatists and was shared by Cardinal Pole, Bodin, and Frederick the Great. In recent times it has been restated by Jacques Maritain (Maritain., J. (1942). The end of machiavellianism. *Review of Politics* 4, 1–33) and Leo Strauss (Strauss., L. (1958). *Thoughts on Machiavelli*. Glencoe, IL: The Free Press).

It is in this sense that popular culture uses the term Machiavellianism, understanding it as an immoral doctrine that licenses the abandoning of any and all moral scruples in the quest for political power. Contemporary tyranny is believed to have its roots in the Machiavellian principle that any end justifies any means.

B. An Amoral Doctrine

1. Raison d'état

Other interpreters of Machiavelli find the association of Machiavellianism with immorality inappropriate. Following Croce, they argue that Machiavelli recognized the "autonomy of politics." (Croce., B. (1925). *Elementi di politica*. Bari: Laterza). In this view, the realm of politics has its own logic and laws, it is "beyond good and evil." In politics, evaluations of actions are made without reference to extrapolitical or moral factors. End–means calculations are relevant and appropriate in politics, because politics is primarily and rightly concerned with preserving and furthering the interests of the state. Chabod argued that Machiavelli "swept aside every criterion of action not suggested by the concept of raison d'état." (Chabod., F. (1958). *Machiavelli and the renaissance*. Cambridge, MA: Harvard University Press.

The concept of raison d'état was familiar in the late Middle Ages and inherent in the practice of fifteenth-century politics. But, Meinecke claims that Machiavelli was the first person to recognize the true nature of raison d'état, that is the element of necessity in political conduct. (Meinecke., F. (1957). *Machiavellianism*. (D. Scott, Trans.). London: Routledge). According to raison d'état, the striving for security and self-preservation at any price is behind all state action, it is its "first law of motion." The state is impelled by egoism for its own survival and advantage. It follows that raison d'état refers to what the statesman must do, what it is logical and rational to do in order to preserve the health and strength of the state. Meinecke calls Machiavelli the forefather of modern Machiavellianism—the pursuit of power political ends by all necessary means unimpeded by irrelevant moral considerations. The end dictates the rationality of the necessary means.

From the embryo of Machiavelli's writing grew a developing and changing Machiavellianism. This is seen in seventeenth- and eighteenth-century doctrines of the best interests of states, theories of sovereignty, and raison d'état that reach their supreme climax in Hobbes' *Leviathan*. Though the term raison d'état was seldom used in the nineteenth century, its spirit continues into the present in the terminology of the problem of power, power politics and the power state. It is seen in utilitarian calculations regarding the best interest of states, in the idea of the rationality of the politics of interest and in its most modern form in the political realism and realpolitik that is the dominant school of thought in international relations theory.

2. Political Realism

Political realists, like apologists for raison d'état, assume that the struggle for survival and security, power, and dominance by sovereign and self-seeking states characterizes and propels international politics. World politics is inherently conflictual. Statesmen think and act in the national interests defined in terms of security or power. In their relationships with other states, they must at times pursue courses of action that would be legally or morally wrong if applied to domestic politics or to individuals within states.

Machiavellianism understood as political realism is supposedly an amoral doctrine. It locates political activity in an autonomous realm, free from the constraints and limitations of moral judgments. Political judgment is reduced to what is rationally required given the realities of political power. It implies that moral considerations, impulses and principles have no place in politics, precisely because politics is concerned with preserving and furthering interests. Like Machiavelli, political realists claim to be studying the world as it is, rather than how we would like it to be.

C. An Objective Science of Politics

The problem of the relationship between necessary means and political ends has led others to see in Machiavelli and Machiavellianism, not an immoral or amoral doctrine but an ethically neutral technical imperative of the form "if you want to achieve *x*, do *y*." The ends themselves are not justified as rational or good, the means to achieve them neither praised nor blamed. They are advocated only as what is necessary to achieve the end in question. Thus, Machiavelli was and Machiavellianism is both ethically neutral and politically uncommitted. Because this technical imperative can apply to a variety of political actors, princes, tyrants, republicans, or democrats, Machiavillianism can be described as an applied science that informs political actors about what they must do, if they want to achieve their ends, whether these be liberatory, revolutionary, democratic, nationalistic, or despotic.

Others, too, regard Machiavellianism as an objective, value-free political science. Burnham for instance claims that Machiavelli applied the methods of science to politics. (Burnham., J. (1943). *The Machiavellians*. New York: The John Day Co.). This method consists of describing and correlating observable social facts in

order to discover constant patterns in history, and on the basis of these formulating hypotheses about the nature of power and testing them against publicly available facts. Machiavellianism is thus a distinctive tradition of political thought that regards the primary subject matter for political science as the struggle for social power. Burnham located the elite theorists Mosca, Michels, and Pareto as well as Sorel in this tradition. Machiavellianism is not an immoral doctrine. It simply tells us the truth about the nature of politics, power relations, and the strategies of fraud and force that are used to maintain and legitimize elite domination.

Others doubt that Machiavellianism as a method tells us the whole truth about the nature of politics. It is generally agreed that Machiavelli himself was not a systematic, analytic, political thinker (see Anglo., S. (1969). *Machiavelli, a dissection*. London: Victor Gollancz). His methodology was consistent only insofar as it yielded a number of artistic, intuitive generalizations made by reflection on personal experience and observation, supplemented by the inaccurate and selective use of historical evidence. Modern Machiavellianism, too, is thought to be an inadequate account of the nature of politics. Relying on oversimple generalizations, it fails to explain opposition and conflict in political power relations and reduces the science of politics to the science of control and coercion, fraud and force. In doing so, it obscures the differences and complexities in social and historical experience.

Whether or not Machiavellianism is a valid method for discovering the truth about politics, it is impossible to deny that political practice is littered with countless examples that testify to the widespread use of Machiavellian techniques. Politicians follow in Machiavelli's footsteps when they sanction violence to defend their power positions, when they resort to fraud and force to eliminate opposition, when they break their promises, when they manipulate the sentiments of their subjects, when they deceive them through propaganda, lies, and silence, when they justify these methods in the name of the national interest or the public good. Machiavellianism is descriptive if not explanatory. We can agree that the methods advocated by Machiavelli are depressingly familiar in the conduct of political affairs, without agreeing that they are rationally required or that they are inevitable, or part of the human condition or that they are justified.

D. A Consequentialist Morality

Machiavellianism has been justified as a specific morality appropriate to political activity that differs from and outweighs considerations that are appropriate in the sphere of ordinary private morality. The contrast between the public and private spheres is not a contrast between expediency in one and principle in the other, or immorality versus morality, but a contrast between one type of morality and another. One, is appropriate to public political life, the other to private life. The morality appropriate to political life is a utilitarian or consequentialist morality whereby actions are judged to be morally right according to the good consequences they promote. In this view, Machiavelli did not divorce politics from ethics, but implied that morality in politics must be consequentialist.

Machiavelli vividly illustrated the incompatibility between consequentialist ethics and all other forms. Consequentialist ethics clash with Christian, traditional, and Kantian ethics; any kind of moral absolutism or idealism; any ethics that has as its source and criterion of value the word of God, eternal reason, or the dictates of conscience; ethics that stress intention, personal integrity, or that embody abstract conceptions of justice, fairness, or individual rights. In short, consequentialist ethics conflict with any ethic that places restrictions on the means no amount of good consequences would sanction or permit.

The case for consequentialism in political life rests on the claim that it would sometimes be morally wrong for politicians to refuse on moral grounds to override standards that are adhered to outside politics. It would be irresponsible to act out of pure motives of individual conscience or in accordance with absolute principles or ideals without measuring the consequences of such actions. In practical politics there has always been the problem of adopting other than a consequentialist ethic when ends that are judged to be good cannot be achieved without recourse to means, which if judged according to the principles of alternative moral traditions would be impermissible, but which if adhered to, would make the end unrealizable.

The case against moral purism as argued for in contemporary literature and found in embryonic form in Machiavelli depends on the rejection of the Acts and Omissions doctrine. The Acts and Omissions doctrine states that failure to perform an act with certain foreseen consequences is morally less bad than to perform an act with the same foreseen consequences. Machiavelli shows, like others who reject this doctrine, that certain omissions are as blameworthy as certain acts and sometimes more so because those who fail to act, whatever their good intentions are causally responsible for the harm they could have prevented. If any action that employs violent, cruel, or otherwise immoral means is

the only way to achieve a good end, then those who fail to act will be responsible for maintaining the status quo and for allowing worse consequences to result. As Machiavelli noted, it is not the most moderate and morally pure who have provided the fewest victims in history (Chapter 16 and 17).

At certain political conjunctures there can be no moral purity in decision making. It is illusory to think that good ends can always be achieved by adhering to absolute moral principles. Utilitarian justifications for war or revolutionary violence are often underpinned by these kinds of arguments. Idealism and moral absolutism are not only incompatible with achieving the common good, preserving freedom, ending institutional violence, or liberating humanity but can in themselves be immoral. Failure to resist force with force, violence with violence will involve allowing the evils of the status quo to continue or to lead to worse consequences, increasing human suffering. In these circumstances abstaining from so-called immoral means is self-deceiving, self-indulgent, and morally wrong.

The idea that it is impossible to apply in politics the same moral standards that are appropriate in the private sphere is the Machiavellian heritage. If there are two moralities, one suited for public life and another for private life, then Machiavellianism in politics is not an immoral nor an amoral doctrine, but a different moral practice. If, in the political sphere actions are rightly judged by their consequences, it follows that the morally right thing to do in politics is unproblematically whatever leads to good consequences. There is no conflict with or between other moral principles when calculating the best means to achieve political goals. Political consequentialism justifies the apparent immorality of the means to secure these, as it is not only different from ordinary or private morality, but in the political sphere completely replaces it.

III. THE DILEMMA OF DIRTY HANDS IN POLITICS

A. The Moral Problem

The condemnations and justifications for Machiavellianism considered so far tend to ignore the moral problems in political action. Those who condemn Machiavellianism as an immoral doctrine, suggest that it is possible in politics to keep to moral principles that set constraints on the ways in which people can be treated, and that if this is done, no moral problems arise. Those who see Machiavellianism as an amoral doctrine simply dismiss morality as an irrelevancy. Straightforward consequentialism dissolves the moral problems by theoretical fiat. But others who justify consequentialism in politics recognize that there is a conflict between this and other ethical standpoints that gives rise to complex moral dilemmas. Like Machiavelli, they recognize that keeping to moral principles can in itself be morally problematic and that consequentialist morality is appropriate to the political sphere. However, they do not fully endorse the utilitarian view that there is no moral problem as long as good ends are achieved. They acknowledge that competing moral principles are not so easily jettisoned and that the conflict between consequentialist and conventional ethics is not so easily smoothed away. This was implicitly recognized by Machiavelli himself. Although Machiavelli endorsed a consequentialist ethic and justified this public morality on grounds of reasons of state, he also stated that it cannot be good to lie, cheat, murder, to be cruel and faithless. This is why Machiavelli urges the prince to learn how not to be good.

Machiavelli, like many Marxist and revolutionary thinkers following him thought such actions were necessary to achieve a better, more humane future, but he did not deny the contradiction of achieving moral ends through immoral means. Trotsky confirms this view.

> Nevertheless do lying and violence in themselves warrant condemnation? Of course as does the class society which generates them. A society without contradictions will naturally be a society without lies and violence. However, there is no bridge to that society save by revolutionary, that is, violent means.... From the point of view of "eternal truths" revolution is of course anti-moral. But this means idealist morality is counter revolutionary, that is in the service of the exploiters. (Trotsky., L. (1973). *Their morals and ours*, p. 46. New York: Pathfinder).

Consequentialism in politics is both right and wrong. This apparent contradiction implicit in Machiavelli and in revolutionary thinkers is explicit in the modern discussion of the dilemma of dirty hands, which highlights the paradox of actions that are morally justifiable, even obligatory, but despite this morally wrong. Walzer, in his discussion of this paradox argues that "a particular act of government may be exactly the right thing to do in utilitarian terms and yet leave the man who does it guilty of a moral wrong" (Walzer., M. (1973). Political action: The problem of dirty hands. *Philosophy and Public Affairs*. 2, No. 2.161).

From a consequentialist perspective that evaluates actions from an impersonal point of view in terms of outcomes, particular acts of torture, deception, and killing may be justified. At the same time, though, they may be condemned from a deontological or absolutist ethical stance that justifies actions from the perspective of the moral agent.

Walzer argues against the possibility and desirability of a morality of absolute principle in politics. If a politician never violated moral rules and kept his hands clean, he would fail to do the right thing in utilitarian terms and he would also fail to live up to the responsibilities and duties of his office. Walzer argues that consequentialism is necessary in politics, but insists that the politician is nevertheless guilty if he breaks moral rules in order to achieve good ends. The moral politician is one who knows he has done something wrong and who is prepared to get his hands dirty to do the right thing. Bernard Williams takes a similar line, arguing for the necessity of consequentialism in politics and at the same time acknowledging the wrongness of the actions involved. He writes:

> [I]t is a predictable and probable hazard of public life that there will be these situations in which something morally disagreeable is clearly required. To refuse on moral grounds ever to do anything of that sort is more than likely to mean that we cannot even pursue the moral ends of politics. (Williams., B. (1978). Politics and Moral Character. In S. Hampshire (Ed.), *Public and private morality.*, p. 62. Cambridge: Cambridge University Press).

However, Williams also argues that the moral disagreeableness of the act is not thereby cancelled out or annulled. Although the moral justification for a political act is consequentialist, there is a moral remainder, an "uncancelled moral disagreeableness," a moral cost involved. In these views, judgments we make about political actions are both consequentialist, that is, end-orientated and action- or agent-orientated. What, though, is the significance of this agent orientation and these moral costs if consequentialist morality predominates in politics? The problem for Williams and Walzer is to show how to pursue political ends using consequentialist calculation without endorsing Machiavellianism in its worst sense.

B. Moral Costs

Walzer tries to answer this by discussing three views of moral costs, Machiavellian, Weberian, and those of

Camus in *Just Assassins*. According to Walzer, the Machiavellian view is that the political actor who must do terrible things, simply throws away morality for the good results that will thereby be achieved. Moral costs and immoral means are subject only to prudential control. For Weber, the good man with dirty hands is a tragic hero who is horribly aware that he is doing bad in order to achieve good and that in doing so he surrenders his soul. The moral costs here are measured by the tragic hero's capacity for suffering. In these two traditions the moral costs are simply set aside or acknowledged within the confines of the individual's conscience.

In *Just Assassins*, Camus' good men with dirty hands are innocent criminals, just assassins who, having killed, are prepared to die and will die by execution. Execution is self-punishment and expiation of moral costs. Hands are washed clean on the scaffold. For Walzer, this is the most attractive view of the moral costs involved in consequentialist action. Although there is no executioner waiting in the wings to administer punishment, it requires us to imagine a punishment that fits the crime and to examine the nature of the crime. This refers us back to the moral code that has been violated. If we could enforce moral sanctions against the politician, then we could "honour that man who did bad in order to do good, and at the same time we could punish him. We could honour him for the good he has done, and we could punish him for the bad he has done" (p. 179).

Walzer is right in finding the first two views inadequate in that they simply set aside moral standards and moral costs. But, surely the third view too is an inadequate acknowledgment of moral costs. Walzer writes as if the problem of dirty hands was simply a matter of trying to discover some form of social acknowledgment and public sanction for the necessary wrong politicians do when they act to achieve good results. Now, even if this were practically possible, the notion of punishing the politician for the immoral means he inevitably uses, like the other two views, focuses too much on the man with dirty hands. It seems to sanction his actions as long as he is punished for them after the event. All three views overlook the significance of the moral wrong done to the victims of the immoral means and do nothing to limit them. The bad may be acknowledged, but it is not compensated for or annulled by punishing the perpetrator of the crimes. It is not as if the wrong had never been done. If moral costs are only counted after the event in the private or public guilt or suffering of the politician, then it is difficult to see how this acknowledgment alone can give

grounds for any constraints on the means to achieve desirable political goals. It could license the use of immoral means as long as they were acknowledged as being immoral. Acknowledgment of moral costs has no practical purchase in limiting them.

The only way in which recognition of moral costs could provide restrictions on immoral means here is if the guilt of the politician prevented him from using them in the future. Williams argues that if politicians find certain actions morally disagreeable, then this is not only a correct reaction, but a socially useful habit. Only those who are reluctant to break moral codes and who are sensitive to the moral costs involved will have a chance of not doing so and abiding by the rules on other occasions when the consequences do not justify breaking them. This conclusion, though, does not give any criteria for judging what are permissible means to justified ends. In these circumstances it seems that recognition of moral costs does nothing to prevent their sacrifice.

Other writers on the problem of dirty hands too, are vague about the limits on permissible means. Nagel (Nagel., T. (1978). Ruthlessness in public life. In S. Hampshire. op.cit.) claims that some agent-centered restrictions apply to public as well as private life, but some are weaker, permitting coercive, manipulative, and obstructive methods not allowable for individuals. Again, greater lassitude about means is allowable given the good consequences that result. For Nagel, agent-centered restrictions in public life seem to come only from the requirement of impartiality. Nagel argues that in public life there is no right to self-indulgence or favoritism for public officials. Politicians are required to treat people equally. They must be impartial and leave no room for the personal attachments that shape individual lives. Means that involve partiality, nepotism and patronage are thereby ruled out in political life. This balance of outcome- and action-orientated morality justifies the design of public institutions whose offices can do what would be unsuitable in private life. Attempts to limit incidences of dirty hands are to be achieved by a tighter specification of the moral rules that govern institutions and offices, some in terms of consequences and some in terms of impartiality. On Nagel's argument then, the only restrictions on means is the requirement that they be impartial.

It seems then that those who want to argue that Machiavellianism in politics is both right and wrong, right because of the end result the action produces, and wrong from the perspective of the moral agent, end up endorsing a Machiavellianian political morality where moral rules and principles give way to consequentialist morality. Acknowledging and recognizing the wrong that is done cannot have any moral significance if this moral sense is ultimately overridden by utility considerations. One of the reasons for the difficulty of finding a significant place for ordinary morality in politics is the general belief that consequentialism is appropriate to the public realm. If this is so, then ordinary moral principles are bound to play a subsidiary role.

C. The Distinction between Public and Private Morality

To show that consequentialism is appropriate to the public realm, these writers have to make a sharp distinction between the public and the private sphere and show that there is something special and different about politics and public life that separates them from personal life. Although they recognize that dirty hands are a general and familiar feature of both public and private life, the following considerations are said to magnify the problem in politics. (1) The moral problems associated with violence, the threat of violence or of force occur more frequently in public life and in the execution of public policies than they do in private life. They are always a prospect in politics and in the normal run of things do not occur in private life. (2) Political actors are responsible for policies that have greater and more enduring consequences that change or effect the lives of a greater number of people than the actions of private individuals. (3) In modern democratic politics, actors in political life are representatives of and accountable to the people. They have obligations and duties attached to their representative roles that require them to serve the interests of and explain and justify their policies to those they represent. (4) The impersonality required for public life implies a heightened concern with results and a stricter requirement of impartiality in the morality appropriate to it.

What is morally special about the political realm then, is the extent and frequency of moral dilemmas, the number of people affected, the far-reaching consequences of political decisions, the assumption of a political role that carries added responsibilities, and the requirement of impartiality. These are said to lead to a bias toward consequentialist morality in politics and the justifiable employment of means that in private life would be prohibited.

It could be argued though that some of these considerations that mark out politics as a special realm could just as easily prohibit consequentialism as endorse it. Consequentialism in politics is not obviously justified by reference to the frequency of moral dilemmas or to the possibility of the use or threat of violence or force that is constantly present in political life. If it is true that danger is ever present and that conflict is more frequent than in personal relations, this could be all the more reason for adhering to moral principles rather than a justification for overriding them . The frequency of moral conflict and the greater possibility of violence and force does not automatically license fewer moral restraints or legitimize methods excluded for private individuals. The mere existence of violence and force cannot justify the general habit of performing such deeds or even for thinking that they are always necessary. Similarly, although some political decisions can have far-reaching consequences that affect large numbers of people, this might lead us to suppose that political actors and policy makers should be more cautious and more reluctant to employ Machiavellian methods or to depart from moral standards than actors in political life. This is so, especially given fallibility in calculating consequences and the unpredictable nature of the consequences of political choices.

The argument that representation and impartiality justify a bias towards consequentialism does not necessarily follow. If the morality of roles requires politicians to act in the interests of those they represent, and if impartiality requires that each person is treated equally, then it is not obvious that public action and policies should be governed by a consequentialist ethic. In fact, it is these very considerations that have led other theorists to argue for a political morality of basic rights and liberties that are not subject to political bargaining or the calculation of social interests, which cannot be overridden by policies aimed at the overall social good. This is because choosing on the basis of overall social goals, where the good to be achieved is calculated according to the general interests, gives insufficient attention to the distribution of the good. It results in unjust allocation of benefits and burdens, and people are not treated impartially or with equal concern and respect. Aggregate benefits can only be achieved at the expense of overriding the interests of some individuals for the good of others, and this violates their moral claim to be treated equally.

Rights-based theories respond to a defect in consequentialist thinking that allows the use of means that sacrifice some individuals for the sake of others. They claim that this is not consistent with the basic right to equal concern and respect or a commitment to the equal worth of each individual. It is precisely this that places limits on the way people can be treated to benefit others or to benefit society generally. All agree that a society that protects the interests of each individual will be one that secures some basic rights and liberties that cannot be subject to utilitarian calculation. Rights reflect the fact that no moral balancing act can take place between individuals if the interests of each are to be protected.

D. Democratic Dirty Hands

The claim that in a modern democratic society, public officials are representatives of the people and accountable to them and it is this that justifies consequentialism raises special problems for the use of democratic dirty hands. In this respect, the most problematic means are those that involve concealment, deceit, secrecy, and manipulation. Public officials could justify these means as necessary for the good of those they represent. They could claim that they cannot announce decisions for planning or escalating war, for the employment of intelligence agents or undercover surveillance because prior knowledge of these would defeat the purposes for which they are employed. Similarly, public knowledge about economic decisions or policies such as plans for devaluation or information about the extent of debt, about unemployment or crime figures, about trading arms to hostile governments, about the causes of and policies to deal with disease or epidemics could seriously sabotage important and worthy political projects. Secrecy and deception are justified in order to secure vital objectives that are in the national interest. They are thought to be justified because it is assumed that politicians are acting in our name and in our interests, and because of this, in a hypothetical situation of foreknowledge we would endorse or consent to the deception in advance. However, actual instances of government lying are not so easily justifiably in this way.

It cannot be assumed that citizens would have consented to or approved of either the deception or the end to be achieved if they had known about them in advance in some counterfactual situation. If politicians deceive citizens, these acts by virtue of their secrecy and public ignorance of them cannot meet the criteria of accountability because they cannot be made public. Citizens cannot collectively decide whether politicians ought to use immoral means to achieve a moral end. Concealment, deceit, secrecy, and manipulation prevent citizens from making judgments about the acceptability of moral costs or the wrongness of government actions and decisions. They contradict the basic principles of democratic society based on consent, and politicians fail to discharge their obligations to explain and justify their policies to those they represent.

Those who argue that politicians are justified in the use of these means seem to take it for granted that politicians represent the general interests and that they act with good judgment. In this case justification for lying and secrecy and indeed any other immoral means must, to some extent, depend on whether in fact the ends to be achieved do represent the general interest and on whether judgments about the necessity and efficacy of the means to meet them are sound and likely to be shared. If justification for the use of immoral means depends on judgments about the value or worth of the ends they achieve, then it is clear that some political ends are too contestable for their pursuit to be justified by reference to universally shared ends. Given diverse conceptions of the good and the plurality of values in liberal democratic society, every political decision will be only partially representative.

In theory, there may not be a difficulty in justifying the pursuit of ends that are in everyone's interests such as the preservation of law and order, national security, freedom, peace, and economic prosperity. In practice, though, the scope of these ends is so wide that almost any policy can come within their boundaries and be said to serve them. Politicians use deceit for private gain, to stay in power, or to cover up their mistakes. They advocate and implement policies advance class or business interests. They appeal to and rationalize these as necessary for the common good in order to justify them. Their self-seeking and particular ends masquerade as the public interest.

Even when politicians genuinely believe that their decisions are necessary to secure a universally shared end, they can make distorted judgments about what is in the general interests. This can be the result of an ideological perspective that conflates particular and different interests with dominant interests, of a misplaced paternalism, or it can simply be the result of error or self-deception. In addition, politicians may make mistakes about the necessity and appropriateness of the means to achieve the general interest. They may overestimate the benefits to be achieved and underestimate the moral costs involved. They may overlook the possibilities of alternative solutions to the problem that do not involve immoral means.

Consequentialism is difficult to justify in political practice. This is because the ends pursued might not be representative or universally desirable and because mistakes can be made about the necessity, appropriateness, and efficacy of the means. Genuine utilitarian calculations are not discredited simply because politicians manipulate them to further their own or ideological interests or because they make incompetent decisions and dubious predictions about the good to be achieved. But, once the end–means calculation is defended as the proper way to think in politics, it is open to corruption and distortion.

Even if politicians calculate impartially and rationally to achieve universal ends, the use of deceit or immoral means can have bad long term consequences. One—because the habitual use of these means can corrupt and spread, leading to a decline in the standards of public life. Politicians can become so used to making "moral" excuses that they become insensitive to the truth and to their obligations to explain and justify their policies to those they represent. Deceit and manipulation may be the first resort of politicians whenever they decide that a particular case requires it and whenever they can convince themselves that as a result people will be better off. Two—because if lies and deceit are used these can have detrimental effects once they are discovered and brought to light. They can lead to cynicism, disrespect, and distrust of politicians, and undermine confidence in the political system generally. Three—related to this, the use of exceptional or immoral means can logically contradict and be incompatible with moral notions embodied in the end being pursued. This was the basis of some anarchists' objections to the instrumental violence advocated by revolutionaries to achieve liberatory ends. The ends and means should be integrally related, that is, the means should stand in logical relation to the ends they serve. The character of the revolutionary movement and the means it employs should reflect the character of the society it wants to build. Conversely, the character of that society should determine the character of the struggle of which it is the outcome. If revolutionaries resort to force and violence this will inevitably effect and contradict the possibility of achieving a society without lies or violence.

Of course, if the use of immoral means has bad or counterproductive effects, then political consequentialism would not endorse them. Utilitarian considerations themselves can provide restrictions on immoral means when there are strong utilitarian reasons for adhering to moral rules. Exceptional measures that seem to be justified by their results may create a precedence with disastrous long-term consequences. It is for this reason that rule-utilitarians claim that utilitarianism does not license actions that would normally be classed as immoral. Moral principles, rules and practices are protected precisely because their protection brings about the best overall consequences.

Those who justify consequentialism in politics, though, assume that it is not generally the case that acting in accordance with moral rules will have good consequences. At least they assume that there are occa-

sions and political conjunctures when it is simply not possible to achieve the desired end without dirty hands. Some political ends and some political situations are such that they cannot be achieved without recourse to immoral means.

IV. RESOLVING THE DILEMMA

A. Feminist Challenges to the Public/Private Distinction

The notion that it is impossible to apply in politics the same standards that are appropriate to the private sphere has in recent times been criticized by radical feminists. They question the very legitimacy of the distinction between the private and public spheres of action and so the belief that there are different standards of morality appropriate to each. The radical feminists slogan that "the personal is political" is associated with the claim that male power is not confined to the public world of politics but also extends to areas of personal life, such as the family, domestic labor, and sexuality, which are normally seen as private and nonpolitical. But, for many radical feminists, the personal is political also means that women's traditional nurturing role and experience of intimate relations provides a fund of values that should inform, inspire, and regulate political life. These values are variously expressed as "maternal virtues" and as "ethic of care." They arise from female practices associated with their mothering and caring roles (see Gilligan., G. (1982). *In a different voice*. Cambridge: Harvard University Press, and Ruddick., S. (1990). *Maternal thinking*. London: Women's Press). They express connectedness and responsiveness to the needs of others informed by love, empathy, compassion, and responsibility.

For Tronto, care is both a moral virtue and the basis for political action. Political morality and private morality should not be separate, but connected through the concept of care, which can describe both a moral and political version of the good life. (Tronto., J. (1993). *Moral boundaries*. London: Routledge).

B. The Male Bias in Machiavellianism

Feminists argue that the divorce of political from private morality that defines Machiavellianism is inextricably linked to male values, assumptions, and modes of reasoning. Moreover, the picture political realists give of human nature and politics that supposedly describes the world as it is, is informed by assumptions that are stereotypically male. Like Machiavelli, subsequent realists suppose that politics is concerned with gaining and maintaining power through force and strength. They emphasize the violence and force that are ever-present possibilities in public life, and they reduce what it is rational to do in politics to impersonal ends–means calculation. This male ethos pervades the discourse of action, conflict, confrontation, conquest, and domination in *The Prince*, and is seen in Machiavelli's admiration for and prioritization of the masculine qualities displayed in bold, belligerent, resolute, and effective actions.

Elshtain argues that Machiavelli, theorist of sovereignty, apologists for raison d'état and that modern forms of political realism presume

a world of sovereign states each seeking to enhance or secure its own power. Sovereignty is the motor that moves the realist system as well as its (nearly) immutable object. Struggle is endemic to that system and force is the court of last resort.

In a world of sovereign and suspicious states conflict is inevitable. This presumption excludes the possibility of "a politics not reducible to who controls or coerces whom" (Elshtain., J. (1985). Reflections on war and political discourses, pp. 40, 42. *Political theory* (Vol 14., No. 1).

This dominance/submission narrative characteristic of realpolitik texts is the foundation for justifying political strategies based on assumptions about the human condition and oversimple generalization about human nature. Machiavelli thought that human beings in general were fickle, ungrateful, and untrustworthy, eager for gain, domination, and power, who always judge actions by their results. For Machiavelli, the need for dirty hands was part of the human as well as the political condition. Political realism is underpinned by a conception of human beings as competing individuals concerned with furthering their own interests. The relations with others in the political sphere are characterized by suspicion, anticipation of the threat of force or violence, and instrumental calculation.

According to feminists, these generalizations and assumptions about human beings obscure their differences and complexities. In particular, they do not take account of female concerns and values derived from their experience of altruism, nurturing, empathy, and mutual support. The discourse of conflict, conquest, and prudential calculation denies the reality of human interdependence and the importance of care, reciprocity, and cooperation in human relationships. Emphasis

on the rationality and necessity of end–means calculations and evaluating actions from an impersonal point of view devalues female ways of thinking and reasoning, which are intuitive and empathetic, attentive and responsive to particular needs in particular situations. The consequence of these denials is the subordination of female values, the exclusion of alternative solutions to conflict, and the elimination of space for a noninstrumental political morality.

Feminists suggest how female values, imperatives, and modes of reasoning associated with mothering and care could be translated into political values and extended to the public sphere. Ruddick links maternal thinking, the life-preserving values implicit in the practice of mothering, to peace politics and nonviolent conflict resolution. Bubeck (Bubeck., D. (1995). *Care, gender and justice*. Oxford: Oxford University Press) lists how private values can become public ones. The value of meeting needs may become a citizen obligation and inform the values of the welfare state because the providing and receiving of care is important to the flourishing and welfare of political society. Attention and responsiveness to other people's needs and interests is also crucial in modern democratic society characterized by a plurality of different needs and interests. Values associated with caring may enrich and improve political discussion. From carers' knowledge of human need and interdependency, from their ability to respond creatively and imaginatively to political problems, solutions may be derived that are different from those of strategic political realists.

C. Conclusion

Feminist discussion does not explicitly show how such a unified morality of the public and the private spheres could solve the moral problems associated with Machiavellianism. But they do show that the Machiavellian problem occurs within a theoretical framework and a political context that presupposes and endorses male characteristics, values, and norms. Because these are not universal, feminist analysis casts doubt on whether the proper ends of politics are power, control, and the protection of individual interests. They challenge the view that conflict is endemic and the appropriateness of a political morality that embodies male views of human nature and rationality. In doing so, they challenge the assumption that violence, fraud, and force are necessary in politics, and that the end–means calculation is the rational and realistic response to political problems.

Implicitly they draw attention away from the problems connected with justifying actions that require dirty hands that those who have condemned and defended Machiavellianism have grappled with for so long. Instead, they draw attention to the circumstances in which the problems of Machiavellianism arise and that cause dirty hands to be necessary. Perhaps it is these circumstances rather than the acts necessitated by them that warrant moral evaluation and criticism.

Machiavellian realists claim that in the world as it is, with men as they are, a consequentialist approach and the dilemmas it brings are unavoidable if political goals are to be achieved. If this is so, it would be more realistic to concentrate on transforming these contingent aspects of political life to see how far change might eliminate the need for dirty hands and for condemning, justifying, or defending Machiavellianism in practice.

Also See the Following Articles

ACTS AND OMISSIONS • CONSEQUENTIALISM AND DEONTOLOGY • FEMINIST ETHICS • UTILITARIANISM

Bibliography

Coady., C. (1991). Politics and the problem of dirty hands. In P. Singer (Ed.), *A comparison to ethics.* Oxford: Blackwell.

Coady., C. & O'Neill., O. (1990). Messy morality and the art of the possible. *Proceeding of the Aristotelian Society*, Sup. Vol. 64.

Günsberg, M. (1995). *The end justifies the means*: End-orientation and the discourses of power. In M. Coyle (Ed.), *Niccolo Machiavelli's The Prince: New interdisciplinary essays.* Manchester: Manchester University Press.

Ramsay., M. (1995). Machiavelli's political philosophy in *The Prince.* In M. Coyle (Ed.), Niccolo Machiavelli's *The Prince:* New interdisciplinary essays. Manchester: Manchester University Press.

Stocken., M. (1990). *Plurality and conflicting values.* Oxford: Oxford University Press.

MARX AND ETHICS

Andrew Vincent
University of Wales, Cardiff

Glossary

alienation The key idea is that humans have forfeited something that is crucial to their nature and development—most significantly, the ability to determine their own lives—to some other person or group. However, in Marx, the idea is complex and it implies alienation from one's fellow workers, from the product of one's labor, and from one's own self.

capitalism For Marx, this is a historically specific mode of production and a distinct form of social and economic organization, based upon commodity production, in which there is a characteristic system of private property ownership, particularly in the means of production. Capitalism is characterized by the ownership of a particular class (the bourgeoisie), who subsist by the extraction of surplus value from the actual producers—the proletariat.

class In Marx, this term refers to large social groups linked together in certain social relations, within a mode of production. Each class receives differential rewards, power, and status. Historical development takes place through the economic and political struggle between classes.

dialectical materialism A philosophical doctrine that holds that matter and material interests are primary to human life and that there are inherent laws of motion implicit within material concerns, which progress by a process of contradiction and conflict. Thus, the motion of any given society is determined by the patterns of conflict and contradiction implicit within the constituent social and political elements.

ideology In Marxism, this term generally indicates the world view or key ideas of the dominant class; often this implies a false or distorted view of the world.

transformative criticism A process of philosophical criticism, initiated by the German philosopher Ludwig Feuerbach, whereby the subject and object of a proposition are reversed or transformed.

MARX neither wrote any systematic works on ethics nor saw himself as a moral philosopher. For posterity, he has had a reputation for an antimorality stance. However, there are profound ambiguities on this issue and many Marxist scholars and practitioners have, nonetheless, wanted to see an ethical component in his theories. Regardless of whether or not there is such a thing as Marxist ethics, Marx's observations on ethics are both immensely penetrating and they contain an extremely subtle interweaving of philosophical, political, economic, anthropological, and sociological strands. Marx was at the center of many crucial late nineteenth-century intellectual and political debates, and what he has to say about ethics is still critically relevant today, if only to act as a critical counterweight to some of the current perceptions of what constitutes ethical discourse.

I. THE PROBLEM OF MARX AND ETHICS

There are a number of problems for anyone trying to grasp Marx's view of ethics. First, neither Marx nor Engels developed an overt ethical theory, nor wrote a systematic treatise on ethics. In fact, much of the time, Marx was predisposed to simply ignore the question of ethics (and law, for that matter) as peripheral to his theoretical and practical concerns. Marx's ethical thought is, in fact, often overwhelmingly negative in character. This is fine if one's purpose is solely "critique," but it is a definite handicap if one wishes to say something more positive about the nature of ethical activity under socialism. Marx offers fairly sparse fare for ethically motivated socialists.

A second problem relates to the sources of Marx's observations on ethics. It has already been noted that Marx did not have a positive normative theory of ethics. It is also clear that what he does say about ethics, by way of negative critique, does not appear in any systematic format. There are early works that begin to say something more systematic; however, such writings have often been dismissed—although not by all writers by any means—as either immature juvenilia or early philosophical polemic that lack the systematic and scientific standards of the mature writings like *Capital*. In consequence, the observations on ethics that we do have are fragmentary and must be picked out from a diverse body of writings.

Marx's writings are, in fact, markedly eclectic, and they can be roughly divided into four, often overlapping, types: first, the early more philosophically inclined pieces, clearly more critically inspired by the German philosopher G. W. F. Hegel. Under this rubric would be included the *Economic and Philosophic Manuscripts* (1844), *The Holy Family* (1844), *The German Ideology* (1845/1846), and *The Poverty of Philosophy* (1847). The second type of writing is the polemical pieces written for particular political objectives. The most famous of these is *The Communist Manifesto* (1847/1848). The overt character of these polemical writings—despite their wide dissemination, immense in-

fluence and popularity—is their simplification of issues and doctrines. This can be a problem in assessing what Marx actually believed, rather than what he needed to put forward for polemical thrust. This is a particular problem in the sphere of morality where Marx does clearly make moral claims, in some more polemical pieces, but then, in private correspondence, disavows them to friends on the grounds that such claims are expected by his audience. He noted to Engels that, with regard to the Rules of the First International, he felt "obliged to insert phrases about 'duty' and 'right' … ditto about 'truth, morality and justice,' but these are placed in such a way that they can do no harm" (quoted in Wood, 1994, p. 511) The third group of writings relates to Marx's observations on particular historical events. Probably the most famous of these, and the most convoluted and ambiguous, is the *Eighteenth Brumaire of Louis Bonaparte* (1852). The writings in this context employ Marx's immensely sophisticated method of close historical/economic analysis, although the final upshot of such pieces has given rise to many hostages to fortune—especially over the general theories of ethics, law, and the state. The final group of writings settle upon his systematic economic theories. The most famous of these are the earlier *Grundrisse* (1857/1858) and the later *Capital* (1867–1885), which remained incomplete at Marx's death. In sum, Marx's observations on ethics must be, and usually are, picked out from these diverse writings. It is hardly surprising that there should be oddities, fierce contestation, and discrepancies over such fragments.

A related point to the diversity of these writings is the fact that many commentators on Marx argue that there is a marked shift or break in his overall perspective. The shift is usually seen to occur between the "younger" and the "older" Marx. The character of the shift—which was called the "epistemological break" by the French Marxist Louis Althusser—is between an earlier philosophically and morally inclined Marx, clearly critically inspired by Hegel, and the mature Marx, focused on political economy and intent upon constructing a positivist empirically based social and economic science of history and society. This judgment, on the distinction between the late and the early Marx, is often supposed to direct our attention to the late Marx and a consequent dismissal of the early, philosophical Marx. In this reading, Marx's early interest in *alienation* (which has a strongly moral edge to it) is superseded by a superior social scientific theory of economic *exploitation*. The development of a clearer vision of the early Marx was partially hampered by the fact that the key early writings—*The Economic and Philosophic Manu-*

scripts—were not actually discovered and published until the 1920s, and their full effect was not really felt until the 1950s and 1960s. Marx never contemplated their publication during his lifetime. Whether one takes the epistemological break seriously or not, there are undoubtedly subtle changes in Marx's perspective on many issues, including ethics. The more positivist inclinations are certainly more apparent in the older Marx. These cannot be ignored by the student of Marx, although what one reads into these changes remains contestable.

Another problem concerns Marx's intellectual relation with Friedrich Engels. There has been a tendency in Marxist writings and in early Soviet and Chinese dogmatics to closely associate the two men with one pristine doctrine. Marx's definite turn to economics (political economy) was confirmed through his initial contact with Engels' writings. As editor of the *Deutsch-Französische Jahrbücher* in Paris, in November 1843, Marx had received an article from Engels entitled "Outline of a Critique of Political Economy," which stimulated the economic turn in his own work. Their working relation began a year later in 1844. However, despite their collaboration on works like *The German Ideology* and *The Communist Manifesto,* it is far from clear that we should associate them, especially on questions of their philosophical and ethical beliefs. This point has been made by a number of scholars, although it is still far from resolved. It is clear, for example, that Marx did not try to formulate a doctrine of naturalistic materialism, whereas Engels clearly lays out such a doctrine, particularly in popularizing works like *The Dialectics of Nature* (1878), *Socialism: Utopian and Scientific* (1880), and the *Anti-Dühring* (1885). Marx did not use terms like "dialectical materialism" or "historical materialism." Marx certainly was interested in social determinism and a humanistic materialism, yet he did not apply the notion of dialectics to nature. His beliefs remained firmly fixed in the social sphere of human emancipation. Engels was far more ambitious—some would say foolhardy—extending dialectics to the natural world. The ultimate consequence of Engels' doctrines was a virtual reenactment of an older form of mechanistic materialism, resonant of the French Enlightenment, which Marx had attacked in his early unpublished work, the *Theses on Feuerbach.* Engels' doctrines later became established in the writings of Lenin, particularly in Lenin's philosophical work *Materialism and Empirio-Criticism* and Plekhanov's *Materialism Militant,* and subsequently it dominated much of the theoretical output of the Second International and the leading Marxist party of the time in Germany—the *Sozialdemokratische Partei Deutsch-*lands (SPD). However, Marx's epistemology, if it can be summarized, hung uneasily between a classical materialism and an idiosyncratic use of left Hegelian idealism. One can overemphasize the differences between Engels and Marx; however, we ignore them at our costs. If we are trying to understand Marx, it is not wise to place too much reliance on Engels' own personal output.

One final problem concerns Marx's terminology. This concerns an ambiguity over the German word *Recht.* It is virtually equivalent to the terms *jus, droit,* or *diritto,* as distinct from *lex, loi,* or *legge.* This distinction does not really work so well in English. *Recht* can imply law in a more conventional English reading and, thus, can be regarded as distinct from morals. Yet, *Recht* is not limited to law, but can encompass the issues of justice, rights, and ethics. In Hegel, for example, the initial focus of Marx's interest, *Recht* embodied these themes, but also, what he called the "ethical life" (*Sittlichkeit*), the state and aspects of world history. In fact, the work on which Marx spent so much time in the early 1840s, Hegel's *Grundlinien der Philosophie des Rechts,* is sometimes translated as the philosophy of law, the philosophy of the state, and, more usually, the philosophy of right. It is important to bear in mind this ambiguity when considering Marx's observations on *Recht;* much of what Marx has to say about law also bears upon ethics. In this sense, in Marx, the clear separation between ethics, politics, and law is somewhat artificial.

Finally, despite the work of the Soviet jurist Evgeny Pashunakis in the 1920s and 1930s, and also that of Karl Renner in Austria, the interest in Marx on law and ethics was not really a subject of wide-ranging debate until the 1960s and 1970s. What was discovered in the 1970s, presumably under the impact of the Italian Marxist Antonio Gramsci, was the conception of law and ethics as a crucial part of the intellectual hegemony of capitalist societies. In this sense, the more wide-ranging and popular interest in Marx on ethics and law is a relatively recent development. A related point to this is that since the inception of this debate there has been vigorous opposition to the idea that Marx has any moral concerns. (Tony Skillen, 1974; Kai Nielsen, 1980).

II. PHILOSOPHICAL BACKGROUND

It is important not to separate Marx's writings into discrete elements. Marx's reflections on ethics, law, political economy, and politics are not isolated components. They fit together in systematic ways. The underpinning for this systematic linkage lies in Marx's early philosophical interests, which are crucial for grasping his views on ethics.

There are three points to note concerning Marx's philosophical background that are relevant for his later project and his overall understanding of ethics. First, the premises for his critique of ethics (and law) are derived from his initial philosophical criticism of religion. Second, his analysis of ideology and the "illusory" character of bourgeois thought in general lie in early essays like "On the Jewish Question." Finally, his first inkling of the economic roots to ethical, social, and political thought can also be found in his early essays— particularly, the *Economic and Philosophic Manuscripts*. I take the first two issues as most significant. The last point, to a large degree, follows from the first two.

First, from the late 1830s Marx had determined to get to know Hegel "from beginning to end." Together with Bruno and Edgar Bauer, Arnold Ruge, Max Stirner, and Ludwig Feuerbach (the so-called young Hegelians), Marx studied Hegel's works assiduously over the late 1830s and early 1840s. Feuerbach was the most influential figure in the group. He had started initially as a disciple of Hegel, and in some ways he never gave this up. Feuerbach, however, did engage in a *dialectical* critique of Hegel—using Hegel's own method to criticize him. Hegel's definition of humanity through its reflective abilities, specifically through the notion of Spirit (*Geist*), is, for Feuerbach, inverted reality. Hegel explained humanity through consciousness (or mind); however, for Feuerbach, it is sensuous and materially rooted humans who think, not abstract consciousness or mind. The transcendental ego of Kant, the absolute ego of Fichte, or Hegel's notion of Spirit (the great themes of classical German Idealist philosophy) were all seen by Feuerbach as sensuous human creations. Thus, the basis of Feuerbach's critique of Hegel is that the latter was offering, unwittingly, an "esoteric theology." Humans are not vehicles for Spirit (*Geist*); rather, humans create the notion of Spirit. In fact, for Feuerbach, humans create God in their own image. Philosophy reflects human needs.

The above critique of Hegel's epistemology was directly related to Feuerbach's equally important examination of religion in *The Essence of Christianity* (1841). For Feuerbach Hegel's philosophy is the last speculative outpost of God. Both speculative philosophy and religion have to be led from the realm of mental abstractions into the realm of sensuous, materially based humanity. For Feuerbach, in essence, all "theology is anthropology." The true object of religion is not God, but idealized humanity. Religion is the alienated form

of the individual's recognition of his own nature. God is the creation of the human imagination, unknowingly idealizing itself. Thus, Feuerbach claimed that some radical demythologizing was needed. Love of God is really love of humanity in symbolic, inverted form. The separation between God and humanity is really a separation within humanity itself. Religion is a form of alienation from our essential sensuous natures. This demythologizing was to be accomplished by the technique Feuerbach called "transformative criticism," namely, the subject and predicate of propositions are interchanged. For example, an understanding of God is not crucial for understanding humanity, conversely an understanding of humanity is crucial for understanding the idea of God. The real subject is humanity, the predicate is God.

The above argument affected profoundly the thinking of the young Hegelians and is crucial for grasping Marx's conception of ethics. Marx, particularly, was initially enthralled with Feuerbach, but soon turned to his own critique of the young Hegelians, especially Feuerbach. In his *Theses of Feuerbach* he argued that Feuerbach's great achievement had been to bring holy ideas down to earth; however, he had remained with an abstract materialism and theoretical humanism. What was needed was a practical humanism and a new understanding of materialism that took account of the social and economic reality. Philosophy must be moved away from mental abstractions and contemplation into the realm of social, political, and economic realities. Feuerbach was thus also subject to the demystification of transformative criticism. Practical and sensuous humanity, embroiled in economic and social realities, is the real subject, not theoretical humanity. As Marx noted, "Feuerbach resolves the religious essence into the human essence. But the human essence is no abstraction … In its reality it is the ensemble of the social relations" (Karl Marx, 1970, p. 122). This critique of Feuerbach also forms the basis to Marx's critique of Hegel, religion, and, ultimately, ethics. It also led him to his crucial life project—the study of political economy.

Marx accepts, implicitly, one theme from both Hegel and Feuerbach. Philosophy is about emancipating human beings. History is imbued with teleological significance as the growing possibility for and the realization of freedom, although this theme becomes shrouded in his later writings. Religion also purports to be about emancipation; however, for Marx, again, the reality is inverted. As he states: "The criticism of religion ends with the doctrine that man is the highest being for man" (Marx, 1971, p. 123). Religion, per se, could not be overcome by simply drawing people's attention to its inverted logic (pace Feuerbach). For Marx, one has to grasp, critically, the social, political, and economic roots as to why people sought consolation in religion. A criticism of religion was in essence social and economic criticism. This exactly paralleled his criticisms of Hegel's notion of the state.

For Hegel, humans are partly self-interpreting creatures. There is no sense in which we are simply the passive products of historical forces. For Marx, Hegel's view is correct, but again the reality had been inverted. Hegel, for Marx, made the "exoteric esoteric" (Marx, 1974, p. 47). Hegel grasped the centrality of labor (self-production), but only in its mental form (in consciousness). Thus, Marx refers to Hegel's philosophy as "concealed criticism that is still obscure to itself" (Marx, 1971, p. 163). For Marx, humans produce themselves by actual labor and through the ensuing social relations in the world. Thus, Marx moved from regarding Hegel's philosophy as an esoteric psychology, to regarding it as an esoteric economic thesis. Hegel's philosophy had a correct content but in an inverted and mystified form. Marx, in fact, treats Hegel's *Rechtsphilosophie* as summing up German reality at that time (in its mystified form). As Marx put it: "The criticism of German philosophy of the state and of law which was given its most consistent, richest and final version by Hegel, is ... the critical analysis of the modern state and the reality that depends upon it" (Marx, 1971, p. 122). Hegel had argued that humanity and civil society were in large part the product of the state. The state is seen to stand above the conflicts of society. However, for Marx, again the reverse is true. Individuals in civil society, embroiled in economic forces and classes, and hedged about by private property rights, with particular notions of morality, produce the state, which, of necessity, reflects differential and unequal property relations and powers. Property rights and moral beliefs are embedded in the state. The state exists to maintain these interests. The modern state gives people legal rights and ethical freedoms, premised on the idea of humans possessing property. However, such property is of necessity premised upon the alienation and denial of such freedom to a large proportion of the population. As Marx observed, the critic must now grasp "the essential connection of private property, selfishness, the separation of labour, capital and landed property, of exchange and competition, of the value and degradation of man" (Marx, 1971, p. 134). The logic of private property is the same as that logic of religion. As human beings alienate their essence into God, so workers alienate their essence into the production of goods. Workers, in receipt of wages, only secure a small proportion of what they produce.

Thus, they alienate their essence into goods that others consume, use, or embody in their private property—a property upheld by the state, morality, and the legal system.

Moving now to the second point of this section: Marx's early essay, "On the Jewish Question," deals, on the surface, with question of the repeal of legal disabilities for Jews in Germany. The essay is interesting on a number of counts; however, one point will suffice for the present discussion. Marx indicates that the illusions that were to be found in the religious consciousness could also be found in rights, ethics, and law. The basic point was that humans turned to religion in particular historical circumstances. Young Hegelians, like Bruno Bauer, had argued that the demands for Jewish emancipation precluded genuine emancipation, because the demand was formulated in religious terms—namely—Jews. The state, for Bauer, must abolish all religious categories. The secular state provided the real solution for Bauer. Marx responded to this by arguing that religion per se was not the problem, but rather the state and legal system itself. Religion is an illusory (if crucially important) pathology, but it is a reflection of a broader "illusion" pathology within the secular state. A secular state does not free human beings. Rather, the state embodies as many, if not more, illusions than religion—in fact illusions of secular states are structurally similar, and in fact, related to religion. Underpinning the modern state are the illusions about private property and commerce, and the legal and moral structures that uphold them.

The final theme to mention, with regard to his early writing, concerns his essay on the "Debates on the Law on Theft of Wood" in the *Rheinische Zeitung* in late 1842. This essay, as Marx later observed, was the first time that he saw clearly the socioeconomic issues that underpinned law and ethics—viewed through the lens of the transition from feudalism to capitalism. The common, feudal, and customary right of gathering wood was effectively being "privatized" by commercial society. Rural poverty was itself the product of the redefinition of property as "private property." In this sense modern ethics and law were facilitating capitalism. Oddly, in this essay, Marx's solution was a restoration of older customary rights (although a slightly odd use of it) against the new right of private property. As he put it: "We reclaim for poverty the right of custom which is not a local one but which is that of poverty in all lands" (Marx, 1971, pp. 49–50). It is worth noting, however, that many of Marx's early writings do not envisage the abandonment of ethics, law, or the state. He adopts, in fact, a quasi-natural ethics and customary law position (from a strictly secularist standpoint), arguing, in essence, that certain newer laws are not really valid or real in the context of what real law "ought" to be like—namely, law ought to be (as Marx put it) "the positive existence of freedom" (Marx, 1971, p. 36). It is also clear that he was not envisaging the abolition of the state; conversely, he anticipated a more radical democratic state upholding the fundamental rights and freedoms of the masses. In many ways these quasi-natural law themes and concerns with democratization of the state do not disappear in his later writings; rather, they submerge below the surface. The surface, in many later writings, is more positivist and economic in character; however, the underlying themes of human emancipation as a genuine need of human nature, the correct ways in which humans "ought" to act toward each other, and the future structural character of society still subsist, but certainly not in any easy or comfortable relation with political economy.

III. MATERIALISM AND ANTIMORALISM

From this philosophical background there were two very broad avenues that Marx's theory of morality could take. He could push the argument of political economy and go farther down the positivistic road of determinism. The end result, qua ethics, would be, at most, a sophisticated sociology of ethics that would deny its autonomy or usefulness to socialists. The other broad direction would be to retain some of the early beliefs in emancipation of human nature and the teleological destiny of humans to determine their own destinies in a free society.

By the 1840s Marx had fully adopted a version of materialism. There are various senses that can be attached to the term materialism. Marx had little interest in mechanistic Enlightenment materialism, seeking to explain humanity via certain mechanistic analogies. Strict physical or naturalistic materialism and behaviorism were also of little interest. Marx's materialism is premised on his turn to political economy and must also be set against his reaction to Hegel's idealism, mentioned in the previous section. Put at its simplest, Marx insisted that human beings must physically subsist and labor to subsist before they speculate or think about their condition. Admittedly, production for existence requires detailed thought; however, it is important to grasp the nisus of human thought. The basic components of his materialism can thus be stated as follows:

in laboring for subsistence, humans use certain technologies or modes of production. In working within a mode of production (whether in a medieval rural context with a plow or within a nineteenth-century factory with a machine) humans come into social relations of production, that is, relations with other humans beings within the productive process. Social relations of production crystallize into groups called classes, whose characters are determined by the particular form and patterns of ownership of a mode of production. As modes of production change, so do social relations of production. In capitalism, for example, there are two fundamental classes. Proletarian workers sell their labor for a wage. Workers embody value in objects through their labor, yet they produce more than they receive. The wage only provides subsistence. The capitalist class sells the products of the workers (their extracted labor value) to gain profit. Capitalism thus subsists by extracting labor value from its workforce. In consequence the interests of the capitalist class necessarily conflict with those of the proletariat. Thus, material conditions of economic life form the real basis of social existence. Cultural and political structures can only be understood via these material conditions and the ensuing class struggles. Marx, in one of his more synoptic semiautobiographical pieces of writing, *Preface to the Critique of Political Economy,* called this process the "leading thread" of his studies (Marx and Engels, 1968, p. 182). Thus, social and economic being form the basis to cultural and political endeavors. We can observe here the "transformative criticism" at work again in the basic rudiments of Marx's thought. Put crudely, the "subject" of reality is not self-conscious thought and material life the "predicate"; the converse is true. It is important to bear this method in mind, namely, that Marx comes to his basic materialist conclusions from a philosophical direction.

The basic idea of "base" and "superstructure" follows neatly from the materialist thesis. As Marx put it unequivocally in his *Preface to a Critique of Political Economy:*

> With the change of the economic foundation the entire immense superstructure is more or less rapidly transformed. In considering such transformations a distinction should always be made between the material transformation of the economic conditions of production, which can be determined with the precision of natural science, and the legal, political, religious, aesthetic or philosophic—in short, ideological forms in which men become conscious of this conflict . . . Just as

our opinion of an individual is not based on what he thinks of himself, so we can not judge of such a period of transformation by its own consciousness; on the contrary, this consciousness must be explained rather from the contradictions of material life (Marx and Engels, 1968, pp. 182–183).

This quotation clearly takes a "reductionist" or "instrumental" view of the superstructure. One important facet of that superstructure is ideology—as mentioned in the above quote. Because the material basis is primary, ideas have to be explained via their connection to the material base. Moral ideas, as part of that efflux, cannot be explained in themselves. They are part of the ideology of bourgeois society and must be grasped through the economic interests of the bourgeoisie. Thus, moral ideas tell us virtually nothing substantive. As Marx states in *The Communist Manifesto,* "Does it require deep intuition to comprehend that man's ideas, views and conceptions, in one word, man's consciousness, changes with every change in the conditions of his material existence"; on the next page he continues, "Communism abolishes eternal truths, it abolishes religion and all morality, instead of constituting them on a new basis" (Marx and Engels, 1967, pp. 102–103). The point could hardly be clearer.

It is understandable, in this reductionist reading, that Engels and others should thus have referred to ideology as the "false-consciousness." Morality as ideology is therefore always a form of illusion. Its chief illusion is its general inability to see its own class basis. This does not mean that individuals are not really motivated by such beliefs. It is concerned rather with the crucial question: What is the real meaning of bourgeois morality? The real meaning lies, for Marx, in the relation between class, ownership, and material interest. Morals are, in effect, a condensation of the economic interests of the dominant class that controls the state apparatus. The state is viewed as the "executive committee to manage the affairs of the bourgeoisie," and it acts as the oppressive agent for bourgeois interests in civil society, suppressing proletarian demands in favor of capital accumulation. The personnel of the state owe allegiance to one particular class—the bourgeoisie. Morality is part of this oppressive mechanism and embodies the ideological mystifications of bourgeois intellectualism. Moral beliefs are thus class-based phenomena. Class, in Marx, refers to large social groups linked together in certain social relations within a mode of production. Each class receives differential rewards, power, and status. Relations between classes tend to be conflicting and often exploitative. Morality is therefore not a representation of any overarching good. It is rather integral to certain specific class, economic-based interests in society. The history of morality is therefore subsumable under a history of class interests. Moral philosophers might thus be regarded, quite legitimately, as professional ideologists or "waged hacks" for the bourgeoisie.

From the same perspective, the justice that we observe in liberal societies is another aspect of bourgeois ideology. It concentrates, minimally, on how goods might be distributed (if it gets as far as distributive justice) and it ignores the massive inequalities implicit in the production process itself. In other words, it shuts the stable door after the capitalist horse has bolted. For Marx, the equal rights of liberal states have grossly unequal effects. The rights of human beings are in reality the rights of bourgeois men in civil society. Such rights protect individual capitalists in their exploitative practices and in the unequal economic results of such practices. Rights are thus associated with individuals who "own" them in order to protect private interests. They, unwittingly, shield the basic inequalities and exploitative practices of bourgeois culture, although, this, in itself, is not grounds for moral outrage. Such inequality and exploitation is simply what one would expect from such a society.

Marx found this whole moral and justice scenario irksome. In fact, he considered the moral ideas of fellow socialists repellent, pouring scorn on Saint Simon, Fourier, Proudhon, Owenites, and Christian Socialists. He regarded such moralizing as one of the endemic faults of utopian socialism. Thus, Marx quite explicitly takes an antijustice, antirights, and antimorality stance. As he stated in the *German Ideology:* "communists do not preach *morality* at all" (Marx and Engels, 1970, p. 104). With genuine communism there would be no classes, no coercion, no conflict, and no private ownership; in consequence, there would be no need for justice or rights. If there is abundance and communal ownership, then there is no reason for principles of allocation, or any allocating or adjudication mechanisms. If the material conditions of life are transformed then the need for the moral "ought" becomes redundant verbiage. Class conflict is the prerequisite of the state and morality. This view was later crystallized in Lenin's work, *The State and Revolution.* This idea, in turn, gave rise to the idea—initiated by Engels and carried on by Lenin—that the state (and presumably morality) will "wither away."

Thus—given Marx's antiutopianism, his stress on materialism and determinism, his conception of ideology as superstructural, his implicit sociological relativism—the idea of Marxist ethics looks a remote option. For Marx, there is no impartial benevolence, no detached reason, no universal neutrality, no universal human rights, and no disinterested moral rules. Morality simply glides over the surface of the brute material realities. The most that can be said about it, in Marx, is that it serves the functions of mystificatory (if still effective) social integration and cohesion and helps regulate economic exchange in civil society. It is, presumably, partly in this spirit that Allen Wood has commented that justice exists as a *function* of a mode of production. Justice is not "independent" of material interests. It is not an abstract impartial rule; rather, it is an intrinsic functional aspect of modes of production and their social relations (Wood, 1981 and 1994). Thus, it follows that justice or injustice discourse have little efficacy. The working class needs to shed the illusions of morality to make progress. Another way of putting this is to say that if capitalist relations are just, then whatever serves the material interests of the proletariat, in its historical trajectory, is also just. Ethics is subordinated to historical causality. This thesis sacralizes any and every act as potentially moral—including what might, in other circumstances, be considered heinous acts—as long as they are functional for the material interests of a class. This dilemma—the so-called "dirty hands" problem in ethics, or in some readings, the "means–end" problem—pervades the history of Marxism in the twentieth century in both theory and practice. This is, roughly, the general position of Lenin, Plekhanov, and Trotsky (see particularly Trotsky, 1973).

IV. MARX AND MORALS

Notwithstanding the above arguments, it is clear that there is one insuperable problem—or paradox as Steven Lukes calls it—in reading Marx. As Lukes notes, in spite of the strong antimoralistic image of Marx, nonetheless, "open practically any Marxist text . . . and you will find condemnation, exhortation, and the vision of a better world" (Lukes, 1985, p. 3). Even in late works, like *Capital,* Marx uses unmistakable evaluative language. Terms like "robbery," "booty," "embezzlement," "torture," and "brutality," and phrases like, "naked self-interest and callous cash payment," "degradation of personal dignity," "shameless, direct and brutal exploitation," are used to describe capitalist practices. In addition, there is an implicit moral teleology in Marx, namely, a sense of purpose in historical development, a deep-rooted but pervasive assumption of the rightful

historical triumph of working class and the inevitable, but also highly desirable, collapse of capitalism. Further, there is a strong sense of the moral superiority of socialism to other forms of life and an ingrained assumption concerning the cooperative instincts of humans when they are not distorted by classes and exploitation. To be truly human is to exercise untrammeled rationality and self-determination. Marx's whole notion of communism is premised on this moral point about human nature. Some of these moral themes can be (and have been) picked out by commentators, some making a case for "Marxist ethics."

Before examining some of these more substantive themes, certain ambiguities in Marx's materialist views (outlined in the previous section) have to be analyzed, partly because many of the arguments for Marxist morality find their leverage in these ambiguities. There are a number of such ambiguities; however, only five will be reviewed briefly here to illustrate the point: materialism, class, the state, ideology, and the base and superstructure relation.

The first ambiguity concerns the doctrine of materialism itself. There are competing versions of it within Marx's oeuvres. Although it is a rough and ready distinction, we can call these the stricter and looser versions. There are parallels to this distinction in other areas of Marx's thought and there remains considerable debate as to where Marx's sympathies lay. The stricter materialism might also be called "unidirectional determinism." Material conditions causally determine thought and political and social structures. This is the dimension that Engels, Lenin, Plekhanov, and Kautsky picked up on, and it reappears in structuralist Marxism, among other varieties, in the later twentieth century. This materialism looks, and occasionally tries to act more like a natural science. In some analyses of Marx it is connected the idea of the "epistemological break," namely, the mature Marx is the "natural scientist" and "unidirectional determinist." The alternative "looser" materialism can be observed in the elusive Marxist doctrine of "praxis" (where "theory" and "practice" have a symbiotic relation). The basic logic of a praxis argument denies the basic premise of the unidirectionality claim; namely, it asserts that reflective thought and consciousness (as embodied in philosophical, moral, or legal thought) can actually affect our material conditions. We can accommodate our theory to our practice, and vice versa. Put simply, reflective thought has definite efficacy, it is not just an epiphenomenon of the material conditions of life. This form of looser materialism can be observed in some of Marx's writings and in the subsequent Marxist tradition in writers such as Antonio Gramsci, Georg Lukács, Walter Benjamin, and Karl Korsch. Such a looser materialism is also more aware of the high contestable nature of economic and social categories (for a summary of later twentieth-century developments in Marxism, see Hindess, 1995).

The second ambiguity concerns the concept of class. In the stricter materialist view—which can be called "class reductionism"—classes are relatively simply delineated. Under capitalism, one class (the bourgeoisie) is associated particularly with economic ownership and state power. It is this class that shapes ideology. However, in other writings, Marx sees classes as more complex, fragmented, often containing fractions with no overt connection to political power or ideological domination. The state and its cultural systems, in this reading, clearly do not embody the interests of a ruling class. In addition, there can be, as Marx demonstrated with great verve in the *18th Brumaire,* intraclass conflict between fractions. Marx mentions four fractions within the bourgeoisie that often conflict: landed property, the financial aristocracy, the industrial bourgeoisie, and the commercial bourgeoisie. Further, the lumpenproletariat are kept separate from the proletariat, and the petty bourgeoisie from the peasantry. Morality, in this fraction perspective, can actually become a site of class struggle. Morals are therefore not always necessarily in the interest of one class. In fact, many moral beliefs could theoretically benefit the working class. In addition, the notion of class remains deeply ambiguous, because nowhere does Marx explain its precise relation to property ownership.

The third ambiguity concerns the nature of the state. The doubts over the relation between class and state, outlined in the *18th Brumaire,* led Marx to suggest that in the conditions that pertained in France in the period 1848–1850, the state did not represent *any* bourgeois fractions, or even the bourgeoisie in general. In fact, Marx contends that the state may work against the interests of the bourgeoisie. This effectively undermined both the idea of the direct synonymity of class to law, morals, and the state, and also the necessity of class for even analyzing the state (both these views are, though, strongly maintained by Marx and Engels in *The Communist Manifesto,* among other writings). It is these qualifying arguments of Marx that enabled the development of what is now called "state autonomy theory," which has powerfully shaped late twentieth-century Marxist studies. The theory, in varying degrees, sees the state and ideology as factors of cohesion, sites of struggle between fractions of classes, and processes that

may even regulate class conflict. The basic point is that legal and moral reasoning takes on a relative autonomy from the economic base of society.

A fourth ambiguity concerns Marx's use of ideology. In his early writings Marx appeared to be contrasting "ideology" to "reality as practice"—a form of materialist philosophical ontology. Liberal capitalism was in an equivalent position to religion as a distortion of the human essence. Later this contrast became ideology (as distortion or simple belief) as against natural science (as truth or knowledge). In both these views, it remained unclear as to what to include under the term ideology. In some writings, it appeared to be all-inclusive—consciousness in general. In other writings, he appeared to limit himself to economic, moral, and political ideas. The question (which is still unresolved) arose at the time as to whether natural science was part of ideology or was wholly distinct. Marx also did not explain the precise mechanisms of determinism. For example, it is not clear (taking A as the economic base and B as moral ideology), whether "determine" means that A causes B, tends to affect B, or sets parameters to B, or, alternatively, whether there is a symbiotic relation of A to B.

Marxists have gone on struggling with the concept of ideology to the present day. Some, like Gramsci, found inspiration in ideas of "relative autonomy," which allows some leeway for discrete modes of reasoning. In Gramsci's thesis (which for some is present in Marx's writings, such as the *18th Brumaire*), domination under capitalism is not simply achieved by coercion, but, subtly, through the hegemony of ideas. The ideology of the ruling class becomes vulgarized into the common sense of the average citizen. Power is not just crude legal force, but conversely domination of language and culture. Morals, for example, become internalized within the consciousness of each citizen. The masses are quelled and coopted through this internalization of ideas. The hegemonic ideas become the actual experiences of the subordinate classes. Bourgeois hegemony molds the personal convictions and norms of the proletariat. Gramsci thus called for a struggle at the level of ideology. Organic proletarian intellectuals should combat this by developing a counterhegemony to traditional intellectuals upholding bourgeois hegemony. In sum, this perspective does not consider morality as just instrumental. Morality does not necessarily uphold the interests of the ruling class and it is not simply determined by the economic base; in fact it may have some counterdetermining role on the base itself. It also implies that there can be a socialist morality.

A fifth ambiguity concerns the relationship between base and superstructure. There are both interactive and passive notions of this relationship. The passive notion sees a precise causal relationship. The interactive idea sees a looser, symbiotic relationship between base and superstructure. This latter notion leads some critics to bewail even the use of terms like "base" and "superstructure." It is argued that it would be far better if we treated these terms as more or less useful metaphors, not referring to any empirical reality. As in many of Marx's writings, half the problem here might simply be because Marx never really addresses the problem head on. The terms occur in certain writings, but Marx did not appear to have any inkling of how much significance was going to be placed on them by subsequent generations.

However, many Marxists writers find themselves uniformly uneasy with passive reductionism. In this more sceptical reading, Marx's famous *Preface* (mentioned above) is not regarded as an adequate representation of Marx's views. Gramsci, for example, regularly dismissed this more passive view in the curt phrase "economism." For such critics, passive reductionism contains an impoverished and simplistic conception of ethics, it does not grasp the more interactive quality of our moral beliefs, and it ignores the conflicts between classes over moral authority. It also does not explain how the economic base actually "determines" morality. Marx's texts, it is argued, are rife with potential for more interactive readings. However, the Marx of the *Preface*, could reply to this criticism by arguing that such a view is in imminent danger of "fetishism," namely, where ethics is seen as autonomous from economic or class factors. However, most exponents of interactionism would not want to argue that morality has *total* autonomy, rather than moral (and political) beliefs can, in certain circumstances, act upon material life and can either facilitate or work against a particular structure of domination.

V. MARX'S MORALITY

The above ambiguities loosened the hold of the stricter materialist interpretation of Marxism. This hold was further weakened by the consideration of substantive ethical elements within Marx. Shortly after Marx's death, one of the more important theoretical movements to develop in Germany was one concerned with adapting Kantian moral philosophy to Marxist socialism. The so-called Marburg school of Kantians (figures like F. A. Lange and Karl Vorländer) and also, to a much lesser extent, some of the Austro-Marxists (like Max Adler and Otto Bauer), developed Kantian perspec-

tives, much to the ire of writers like Rosa Luxemburg, Plekhanov, Lenin, and Trotsky. The more famous, if not particularly well-developed account of the Kantian/Marxist moral theory, is the conclusion to E. Bernstein's *Evolutionary Socialism,* entitled "Kant not Cant"; the cant in this case being the stricter materialism.

As a number of writers have argued, underlying Marx's whole enterprise is a deep ethical impulse focusing on emancipation. Marx, even in his later writings, appeared to believe that there is a condition of freedom and wholeness for human beings (communism), where their *real natures* will flourish. This forms the crucial motif to Steven Lukes' work on Marx and morality. Emancipation, to Lukes, concerns "free time." Emancipation is freedom from "extraneous purposes" (Lukes, 1985, p. 89). For Kamenka, this underlying commitment to emancipation in Marx is a continuation of themes from classical German Idealist thought. It is the self-realizing, self-determining, autonomous self that forms the underlying motif. The true ethical end is the truly free human being, free from class, ideological superstition, and exploitation—"extraneous purposes." The human being is viewed as an "unconditional" subject. Anything that turns humans into objects is immoral. This notion of positive freedom, wholeness, and perfectibilism behind the veil, is implicit in both the discussion of alienation (in the earlier writings), and is restlessly present just under the surface of the later discussions of exploitation and communism. This vision of freedom is subtly linked to Marx's strong communitarianism, namely, his deeply rooted belief that humans are social creatures and can only really develop freely within a particular type of community (communism). This is the community that is distorted and lost and will be eventually recovered. It is the telos of humans to develop historically toward such a society. Marx did not like to be associated with such a view, because it smacked of romantic utopianism; however, it is undeniably there throughout the corpus of his writings.

Alienation is a prime example of such millennial perfectibilism lost and regained. The idea developed initially in a theological context. Humans were alienated from God through their sin. In Hegel, the alienation is philosophical: Spirit (or mind) externalizes itself in the world. It becomes alien to itself. The task of thought is to overcome the self-alienation of spirit, to perceive itself at home in the world. Overcoming alienation is realizing that the world is not alien to our thought. For Feuerbach, however, the real alienation is that human beings have placed their essence into either God or the Hegelian Spirit. To overcome alienation is to transform the subject and object—to realize that God is idealized humanity. For Marx, on the other hand, alienation takes on a number of subtle forms. The basic idea is that human alienation is more immediate and practical. In discussing the topic, Marx speaks, initially, of alienation through labor. Labor creates capital, and capital escapes the control of labor and takes on a supposedly independent existence (commodity fetishism), which in turn dominates the original producer. Workers thus find they are alienated from the product of their labor. Labor, in this capitalist context, is no longer free and creative. It is necessary for subsistence and thus exercises alien compulsion over the worker. In consequence, workers are alienated from free creativity (which is the true nature of human beings), and they are thus also alienated from their fellow human beings. Overcoming alienation implies ultimately overthrowing the economic and social forms that generate the loss of reality and the self. The solution to the riddle of history and human alienation is communism. There is strong sense here of a definite underlying human nature, with specifiable needs, that can flourish under a specific type of community, which recognizes certain "natural laws," not necessarily as overt imperatives from some external authority, but more as natural, noncoercive norms derived from practical reason.

Some writers have also claimed that it is possible to identify a communist theory of justice. In certain writings, particularly *The Critique of the Gotha Programme*, Marx does indicate that there would be a principle of justice under communism—"from each according to his abilities, to each according it his needs." (Marx and Engels, 1968, pp. 324–325) Such a notion of justice would presumably prevent unequal access to the means of production, and it would prohibit alienation and exploitation. It would also respond distributively to human needs—although Marx leaves the concept of "need" fairly open. Needs for social relations, satisfying labor, and the like, move well beyond physical subsistence. It is difficult not to consider some of Marx's needs as "wants" or "interests," which are surely markedly different notions.

Tom Campbell, among a number of recent theorists, believes that we can reconcile Marx's historicism, and aspects of a looser materialism, with a belief in communist justice and the moral superiority of such a society. He distinguishes a formal from a material notion of justice. The former is understood as procedural adherence to rules, the latter concerns the justice of the rules themselves. Campbell suggests that Marx moves between these two senses. If justice is simply about formal procedures, then it is internal to law and the state. Therefore, the abolition of the state will mean the abolition of law and justice. However, if justice concerns the content of the rules, then it is concerned with social norms that validate rules and will not necessarily disappear with the abolition of the state. Justice, for Campbell, can therefore be said to be about the content of noncoercive social norms. This claim frees justice from coercive force—although it is not clear in this argument whether social norms are the same as laws. It is also not at all clear what noncoercive rules would look like in practice or whether they could function at all. However, the upshot of this argument, for Campbell, is that socialist legality is possible. He suggests that a similar argument can be made out for socialist rights and for morality in general. The binding quality of rights will be dependent on willing acceptance rather than coercion. Thus, "If part of formal justice involves treating individuals according to their rights, then we have a working tie-up between quasi-juridicial conceptions of rights and justice which have potential application to socialist societies" (Campbell, 1988, p. 186).

However, Campbell's thesis overlooks Marx's scepticism concerning the *conditions* of any justice (formal or material), as usually analyzed in liberal theory, namely, scarcity, human egoism, limited altruism, self-interest, conflicting claims, and lack of perfect information. Marx denies that these *conditions* are fixed aspects of any society. They are rather features of a particular society at a particular historical moment in its development. *Conditions* change with modes of production and patterns of class ownership. This opens up the question again of the necessity of even speaking of justice or morality under socialism. As Marx and Engels noted in *The Holy Family*.

> If enlightened self-interest is the principle of all morality, man's private interest must be made to coincide with the interest of humanity ... If man is shaped by the environment, his environment must be made human.

VI. WHAT KIND OF MORALITY?

In sum, therefore, for some scholars, Marx was committed to a richly textured set of normative ideas (Little, 1989; Brenkert, 1984). In this view, there are clear resources for constructing a socialist morality. Ideas like emancipation, self-determination, self-realization, the dignity of humanity, and the centrality of certain needs provide a framework of goods. Theories of alienation, exploitation, and the division of labor furnish critical tools for analyzing society. Ideas of radical democracy, popular rights, and communist justice provide tools for addressing political theory.

However, even if one acknowledges a moral content to Marx's views, the issue still remains, for contemporary commentators, concerning the type of morality in Marx. The first point to note, again, is that Marx was not a moral philosopher. He had little interest in the topic, and he wrote in a philosophical milieu that did not have the kinds of sensitivities markedly present in late twentieth-century thought. There is, indeed, a certain "academic artifice" in isolating something called moral philosophy in Marx. However, in the search for moral identification, some have found elements of an Aristotelian naturalism in Marx (Campbell, 1988, p. 199; Wood, 1994, p. 521; MacIntyre, 1974, p. 206). Alternatively, it is clear that many of the Marburg Kantians of the 1890s (mentioned earlier) found a deontological element in Marx. Certainly, the separation between empirical facts and moral values, in Marx, and the concentration on the autonomy, self-determination, and the freedom of the subject (and the resolve that humans should not be treated as commodified objects), could be seen to have a Kantian ring. For Marx, as for most German Idealist philosophers, Kant was the philosopher of the French Revolution, although, as Kamenka adds, this is a "Prometheanised Kant . . . without the conflict between duty and inclination, without . . . the noumenal . . . without Kant's recognition of the independent requirements of logic and 'reason'" (Kamenka, 1969, p. 12). Yet Marx, in *The German Ideology,* is also adamant in his dismissal of Kant as the wrong-headed apologist of the German bourgeoisie. Thus, Lukes notes that Marx was unremittingly antideontological. Lukes suggests that Marx was a consequentialist moral thinker. Consequentialism is seen to have a specific "utilitarian accent" (Lukes, 1985, pp. 142–144). However, once again, what has to born in mind is Marx's disdain for utilitarianism in, for example, *The German Ideology.* Utility, for Marx, is a false metaphysical abstraction. As Kamenka remarks, the relation of utilitarianism to Marxism is merely "superficial." (Kamenka, 1969, p. 3) Utility only made headway, for Marx, within classical political economy, both constituting an ideological apologia for rapacious capitalism. Kamenka, conversely, sees Marx's moral thought as an "uncritical conflation" of a host of different moral theories jumbled together (Kamenka, 1969, p. 1ff).

The real problem with trying to assimilate Marxism to universalist, ahistorical, and inertial moral doctrines like Aristotelianism, naturalism, Kantianism, utilitari-

anism, or consequentialism is that Marx conceives of human consciousness changing according to its object—an object that is itself mutating with material conditions. Even in the more interactive, looser perception of materialism, human thought is still decisively related to material conditions of life, which alter over time. This doctrine might be seen as a form of sociological and evolutionary naturalism, although another way of seeing this is as a version of Hegelian ethics. In this latter perspective, moral ideas are not a universal schema, consulted by abstract impartial reason; conversely, morality is rooted in particular societies and in forms of life. Morality always has a history and communal context. This, of course, gives rise to the specter of anthropological and historical relativism. In one sense, what we have in Marx is a Hegelian ethics without Spirit, without the Hegelian state, and without the focus on Reason (*Vernunft*). Nonetheless, there is still an underlying objectivist teleology and belief in the destiny of humanity to acquire freedom. This is a secularized, but still optimistic, messianism. The underlying belief in the telos of emancipation and untrammeled self-determination is *not* relativistic. Societies are on *one* particular track. Thus, because Marx repudiated bourgeois morality does not mean he was not concerned about value judgments and human welfare. To reject bourgeois morality is not to reject the behavior enjoined by morality. One can do what is right without invoking a moral code enjoining one to do what is right. Marx is advocating, what now might look like a very Enlightenment idea, namely, rational self-transparency and demystification. This is what Lukes hints at in his resolution to the paradox of morality. *Emancipation* is freedom from the bondage of bourgeois morality (*Recht*). The withering of *Recht* is a withering of abstract bourgeois morality. In rational transparency the individual becomes truly ethical and leaves morality (*Recht*) behind. However, what that communist morality or rational self-transparency actually looks like in practice remains obscure in Marx, and we certainly would not want to consult actual Marxist societies in the twentieth century to find out.

VII. CONCLUSION

Marx's conception of ethics is not easy to summarize for reasons that have been spelled out in this essay. One major difficulty is the fragmentary nature of his writings and the fact that we do not have a systematic treatise to refer to. In addition, there are often subtle changes in perspective that mark out stages in his intellectual career. There *are* ethical themes that run through his work, which can be observed in his ideas on alienation and communism. His sporadic normative reflections appear to reflect these themes. As such, there are aspects of an historical, evolutionary, naturalistic, and quasi-Hegelian ethics present in Marx. Partly because of the subtle changes in perspective, there are also a considerable number of unresolved tensions in his work. For example, Marx's attraction to determinism and materialism does not rest easily with underlying themes of ethics, praxis, and positive freedom. This tension will remain unresolved because there are unequivocal examples of Marx's adherence to a much more committed determinism and materialism, as much as there are also clear examples of his ethical interests. This tension affects the whole manner in which we can approach Marx over the question of ethics.

However, even if it is agreed that Marx did have a theory of ethics, there still remain a number of related difficulties. Many writers might now content that his analysis of class exploitation misses the fact that many groups in society—women, racial minorities, the handicapped, the old, and the now growing underclass—do not fit into any conventional class analysis. They are exploited and they have moral and physical needs, but they do not fit into the Marxian framework of the exploited (namely, proletarian male workers). In this sense, it might be contended that Marx's theories on society have a somewhat dated character. They relate closely to the cultural structures of late nineteenth- and early twentieth-century industrial societies. Marx's ethical ideas are also hampered to a large degree by some of the materialistic aspirations of nineteenth-century science and social theory, as well as the millennial yearnings of sections of the late nineteenth-century industrial working class. Nonetheless, Marx's theories are both fecund and rife with potential, and the future may see an efflorescence of ethical interests.

Bibliography

Brenkert, G. (1984). *Marx's ethics of freedom.* London: Routledge and Kegan Paul.

Campbell, T. (1988). *Justice.* London: Macmillan.

Hindess, B. (1995). Marxism. In R. E. Goodin and P. Pettit (Eds.), *A companion to contemporary political philosophy* (pp. 312–332). Oxford: Blackwell.

Kamenka, E. (1969). *Marxism and ethics.* London: Macmillan.

Little, D. (1989). Socialist morality: Towards a political philosophy for democratic socialism. In E. F. Paul, F. D. Miller, J. Paul, & D. Greenberg (Eds.), *Socialism* (pp. 1–24). Oxford: Blackwell.

Lukes, S. (1985). *Marxism and morality.* Oxford: Clarendon Press.

MacIntyre, A. (1974). *A short history of ethics.* London: Routledge and Kegan Paul.

Marx, K. (1974). *Hegel's philosophy of right and Marx's commentary.* The Hague: Martinus Nijhoff.

Marx, K. (1970). *The German ideology: With additional writings.* (C. J. Arthur, Ed.). London: Lawrence and Wishart.

Marx, K. (1971). *Early writings.* (David McLellan, Ed.). Oxford: Blackwell.

Marx, K., & Engels, F. (1968). *Selected writings.* London: Lawrence and Wishart.

Marx, K., & Engels, F. (1967). *The communist manifesto.* Middlesex: Penguin Books.

Nielsen, K. (1980). Marxism, ideology and moral philosophy, *Social Theory and Practice* 6, 53–68.

Skillen, T. (1974). Marxism and morality. *Radical Philosophy* 8, 11–15.

Trotsky, L. (1973). *Their morals and ours* (with John Dewey and George Novack). New York: Pathfinder Press.

Wood, A. (1981). *Karl Marx.* London: Routledge and Kegan Paul.

Wood, A. (1994). Marx against morality. In Peter Singer (Ed.). *A Companion to ethics* (pp. 511–533). Oxford: Blackwell.

MEDIA DEPICTION OF ETHNIC MINORITIES

Charles Critcher
Sheffield Hallam University

GLOSSARY

assimilation The view or assumption that ethnic minorities should adopt the culture of the ethnic majority.

ethnocentricity A view of the world in which other groups are judged according to the cultural values and ideals of one's own ethnic group.

genre A particular type or format of media output, e.g., soap opera, situation comedy, or news.

multiculturalism The view or assumption that ethnic minority and majority cultures should coexist on equal terms.

news values A working set of criteria that govern how the newsworthiness of a story is assessed by journalists.

stereotype The attribution of a set of fixed characteristics to all members of a particular social group, usually of a negative kind.

THE MEDIA DEPICTION OF ETHNIC MINORITIES is an ethical issue for media practitioners, media regulators, and media publics. The ethics of professionalism and the ethics of media policy are intimately related to the ethics of public life. Ultimately at stake is the cultural right of any group to an accurate media representation of its way of life, part of a general claim to equal citizenship. Our discussion of the issue begins with a clarification of key concepts.

The conventional definition of *mass media* is that they are communicative forms involving the simultaneous transmission of noninteractive messages to large, heterogeneous audiences. They are also normally operated for commercial profit and subject to some form of government regulation. Such a definition encompasses what we commonly think of as the major mass media: television and radio, and newspapers and magazines. Film is a mass medium in definitional terms, though traditionally film scholars have studied it separately. It will be included here. More ambiguously placed are what are more often termed products of mass culture such as popular literature and music. As a consequence, they will occupy a tangential place in this discussion.

The term "mass" has become more problematic since it is an inheritance from a time when media outlets, especially in broadcasting, were restricted by the availability of wavelengths. When only a few television or radio stations are available, they will divide the large audience up between them. However, the use of FM bands on radio and the multiplicity of channels made available by cable and satellite (likely to expand further via digital technology) have rapidly increased the number of outlets. The result has been to begin to fragment the audience and reduce the extent to which it follows the same programs.

There is no simple way of objectively defining the existence of an *ethnic minority*. In any society there will exist groups who in some way are regarded or regard themselves as different from the rest of the population, but there is no simple threshold beyond which they qualify as an "ethnic group." Ethnic minorities are distinguished from the rest of the population by a range of attributes, the most important of which include religion, language, kinship, dress, diet, music, cultural heritage, and even body language. A group exhibiting just one of these characteristics, such as religion or language, will not necessarily be an ethnic group, though their combination is likely to provide a foundation for ethnic identity.

"Race" is a further complication. Though few now claim biological differences between "races," skin color remains a powerful signifier of difference. It may serve to define an ethnic minority even in the absence of many of the other characteristics so far considered. Over generations the constituent elements of ethnicity may change, as children lead a bilingual and bicultural experience. Ethnic intermarriage may blur the boundaries of the group.

Any attempt to arrive at a consistent definition of ethnic minorities must also recognize the enormous variety of experience among such groups which may belie any attempt to cateogrize them together. What all ethnicities share is a dependence for their existence on members' sense of belonging. People belong to ethnic groups when they subjectively identify with them. Ethnic membership is a result of choice; people can opt to move out of or, more rarely, into an ethnic group, whereas they can never leave or join a racial grouping. Overall, ethnic groups may be seen to exist to the extent that groups see themselves as ethnically distinct.

The term "minority" implies that ethnic groups do not constitute the numerical majority. There is, however, a linguistic sleight of hand here. It appears that minorities possess ethnicity while majorities do not. One rarely hears the term "ethnic majority," but that is the logical corollary of "ethnic minority" and is the term that will be used here. Sometimes implicit in the political use of the term "minority" is emphasis on ethnic minorities' subordination to the majority group. This may vary across political, economic, and cultural dimensions but is rarely totally absent. This structured inequality built into majority–minority relations will be a consistent aspect of our discussion.

The messages of the media are complex. Some, such as radio, are exclusively oral. Newspapers rely heavily on language but their use of typography and photographs means they also depend upon the impact of visual messages. Television uses speech, written language, and still and moving pictures. The manipulation of such techniques in film is more self-conscious and resource-intensive than in any other medium. This is also the only mass medium to be almost entirely fictional, all the others containing both factual and fictional material. In looking at media representations of ethnic minorities, we are concerned with what is said, what is written, what is shown in still photographs and in film, and sometimes with all these simultaneously. What the media say cannot easily be divorced from how they say it.

I. THE CONTEMPORARY CONTEXT

A. The Ubiquity of Ethnic Minorities

The presence of ethnic minority groups is now the rule rather than the exception in most nations of the world. Many societies comprise several ethnic groups, with considerable variation in the extent to which any one group is dominant.

While the terms ethnic minority and ethnic majority may be universally applicable, there are very great differences between the groups who may be similarly categorized. Important are differences in size, geography, and history. Ethnic minorities may severally or together be a small or a large proportion of a given country's population. They may be geographically concentrated in one area or type of area, such as urban conurbations, or they may be dispersed in small clusters throughout the country. History provides some of the greatest differences because it is there we find the reasons why such minorities have come to be where they are.

There are at least six historical categories to which any ethnic minority can belong:

1. Indigenous peoples where the majority are settlers (e.g., American Indians or Australian aborigines)
2. Indigenous peoples who have been incorporated into a new society by the formation of a nation-state, often as a result of colonial conquest (e.g., Africa, Asia)
3. Peoples forcibly transported as labor through systems of slavery or indentured labor (e.g., peoples from Africa, the Indian subcontinent, and China)
4. Peoples who are economic migrant settlers (e.g., from Europe in previous times to Europe today)

5. Peoples who are temporary economic migrants or "guest workers" (e.g., Turks in Western Europe)
6. Peoples who are political refugees from persecution (e.g., Jews who fled fascism)

Ethnic minorities may have resided in their current location from time immemorial, for the past 150 years, for the last 30 years, or only for the last decade. This is bound to affect minorities' perceptions of their old and new homelands and the majority's acceptance of the legitimacy of their presence.

B. The Economic and Political Disadvantages of Ethnic Minorities

Whether newcomers or old-timers, ethnic minorities appear to experience difficulty in achieving significant access to the commanding heights of political and economic power. They may find a niche in the middle ranges of powerful institutions, in the polity as government administrators, and in the economy as small-scale entrepreneurs. However, in any society where ethnicity is a significant way of differentiating between groups, the majority group is likely to resist any minority attempt to compete for political and economic power. This invariably extends to a cultural struggle over the right to be heard, in which the media are crucial.

C. Media Representations as Status Indicators

Since the media tend to be produced and consumed by the majority ethnic group, representations of ethnic minorities are an important indicator of how majorities view minorities. At one extreme, ethnic minorities might be accepted as an integral part of the society (part of us) and its self-image; at the other extreme, they may be represented as permanent outsiders who are unable to fulfil the conditions necessary for full membership of society (the category of them). One way of conceptualizing this insider or outsider status is in terms of citizenship.

D. Ethnic Minorities, the Media, and Citizenship

Ethnic minorities are frequently denied, and thus attempt to claim, civil rights, either at basic levels of rights to permanent settlement and to vote or at more advanced levels of rights to equal opportunities in education and employment. In this apparently inevitable conflict, the media occupy a strategic role as reporters and commentators. A frequent point of evaluation of their performance is the extent to which they give a fair hearing to the minority's claim to rights. They may act as referees to the conflict or they may favor one side. The media themselves may operate to exclude minorities from their production staff or output. The media thus perform this dual role: they are the forum where the arguments should be heard and are themselves implicated in the power structures which the minorities may wish to reform.

E. Variations in Media Systems

Across the world, media systems vary in their state of development, the extent of government control, and the degree of commercialization. In democracies, the press acts as a commercial enterprise free from direct government control, so that ethical standards cannot easily be enforced. Television and radio systems normally operate under licence, to which there may be attached some obligations to serve the whole community. This is a usual requirement of public service broadcasting systems. Advertisements in the press and broadcasting are subject to general laws, but otherwise tend to be self-regulated by the industry itself. There is a global tendency to deregulate media systems which causes problems for the enforcement of basic ethical standards. How sensitive the media are to serving ethnic minorities and to granting them equal representation may depend in part on the extent and kind of the ethical standards required by regulatory systems.

II. KEY QUESTIONS

A. Inclusion versus Exclusion

An initial question about media representation might be, to what extent is the presence of ethnic minorities acknowledged or ignored? In an ideal situation, the media would acknowledge ethnic diversity within a framework of common citizenship. Then we might expect ethnic minority members to appear in the media in the same proportional frequency and on essentially the same terms as members of the ethnic majority. This would apply to appearances as members of the public, reporters, artistic performers, and spokespersons, across the full range of the media: in newspapers and magazines, on radio and television, and in film and popular culture. Alternatively ethnic minorities might appear in the media more unevenly, for example, in sport and entertainment rather than in news and current affairs. And when they do appear in the latter, it may be mainly when they represent a "problem" to the dominant group. In the most extreme case, the media may simply act as if ethnic minorities do not exist.

B. Accuracy versus Distortion

The second question is, how far are media accounts of ethnic minorities accurate or distorted? There is clearly some difficulty defining what an "accurate" portrayal of an ethnic minority might be. Nevertheless there are some areas of "fact" where such accuracy can be defined and, if necessary, measured. These include: (i) historical facts about minorities—how they came to be part of the society, and how they were treated in the past by dominant groups; (ii) demographic facts about minorities—their size, age distribution, birth and marriage rates, etc.; (iii) cultural facts about minorities—languages spoken, religious practices, kinship networks, dietary and dress customs, and the like; and (iv) social facts about minorities–their proportional membership of the workforce or the unemployed, educational attainment, involvement in the welfare system, and role as perpetrators and victims of crime.

Extensive data of this kind about ethnic minorities are known, at least in advanced democratic societies, because they are routinely collected by government and related agencies. These can then be compared with media portrayals to assess their degree of accuracy and the nature of any systematic distortions. It is also possible to check the accuracy of specific news stories, especially where subsequently there are official investigations, the results of which can be compared with the way the media represented the event.

C. Sensitive Understanding versus Rigid Stereotyping

This question is, to what extent do media representations contribute to sensitive understanding or to rigid stereotyping of ethnic minorities? This discussion frequently hinges around accusations that the media tend to indulge in stereotypes of ethnic minorities. Perceived characteristics of an ethnic minority—how they look, speak, or behave—are exaggerated and rigidified so that all members of the group are assumed to conform to the stereotype. This may prevent ethnic minorities being presented as both sharing cultural affiliations and being individually unique—much like the dominant majority.

D. Multiculturalism versus Assimilation

This last question is, do the media support multiculturalist or assimilationist ideals of ethnic relations? Multi-culturalism accepts that society will be enriched by the equal coexistence of many cultures whose varying customs and institutions can be accommodated within a society based upon principles of common humanity. Assimilation assumes that the ultimate goal is for all members of society to share one culture and become similar to one another. That culture is, unsurprisingly, the culture of the ethnic majority, with some minimal adjustments to incorporate its new recruits. Evidence for the kinds of view adopted by the media are most often to be found when the media are in a editorializing or a didactic mode—when they directly address the "problem" of ethnic minorities.

III. EVIDENCE ABOUT MEDIA REPRESENTATIONS

A. News Coverage

Analysis of the ways ethnic minorities are depicted in the news media has proceeded by identifying the themes and issues with which ethnic minorities tend to be associated and those which are ignored (see Tables I and II). It thus deals with sins of commission and sins of omission. Despite the differences in media systems and ethnic minority populations, there is a remarkable degree of unanimity among researchers in the USA, Western Euorpe, and Australia about which issues and themes emerge most consistently in news coverage of ethnic minorities.

I. Immigration

Most ethnic minority groups are immigrants of one kind or another. The question of immigration policy, how many should be allowed in and from where and under what conditions, looms large in news coverage. It is generally triggered by a news event, such as the actual or imminent arrival of refugees, or by a news issue, such as recurrent concerns with the problem of illegal immigrants. Immigration is generally perceived as a threat. Its desirability is calculated in terms of the costs to the ethnic majority of accepting people who are economically destitute and culturally different. Where the causes of refugee status are political, there is a constant preoccupation with the possibility that asylum seekers are bogus, since their motivations are actually economic. It appears difficult to find in the news media any view of immigration as natural or desirable, rather than an unwelcome imposition. These trends have been found in relation to migrant Mexican workers in the USA, African-Asians and Hong Kong

TABLE I

Frequencies of General Subjects in the Dutch
Press, August 1985–January 1986

Subject	% all subjects
Immigration	20.8
Discrimination	16.7
Crime	9.1
Social affairs	5.7
Research	5.7
Work, unemployment	5.1
Politics	4.6
Race relations	4.2
Housing	3.9
Education	3.7
Culture	3.5
Religion	2.5
Health	2.3
Other	10.7
Total	100

Source: Van Dijk, T. A. (1991). *Racism and the Press*,
table 4.4, p. 111. Routledge, London/New York.
Reproduced by permission.

Chinese in the United Kingdom, Sri Lankan Tamils in
the Netherlands, and Boat People in Australia.

2. Law and Order

Ethnic minorities frequently appear in the media as
perpetrators of crime, either individually in relation to
specific incidents or generally as part of crime waves

TABLE II

Frequencies of General Subjects in Stories about Black
Americans during Three Local Television Newscasts in Chicago
on December 1–7, 1989

Category	% all categories
Violent crime	41
Intraparty political conflict	19
Candidacy of black judge for county board	15
Nonviolent crime	1
Other	24
Total	100

Source: Entman, R. (1990). Modern racism and images of blacks
in local television news. *Crit. Studies Mass Commun.* 7(4), 332–345.
Reproduced by permission.

or trends. In both the USA and the United Kingdom,
controversies have arisen over the media's tendency to
reproduce uncritically police statistics which claim a
disproportionate involvement of ethnic minorities in
street crime. Hence the term "mugging," which has no
legal standing, has become synonymous with gratu-
itously violent crime committed by young black men
on the streets. In fact, ethnic minority crime is rarely
disproportionately high and most violent crime is in-
traethnic, but this does not dissuade the news media
from contributing to the belief that young men from
ethnic minorities constitute a physical threat to members of ethnic majorities, to whom they are represented
as a symbol of fear.

Next to street crime in importance is drug taking,
especially associated with African-Americans in the
USA and Afro-Caribbeans in the United Kingdom. The
emphasis is on any violent event which can be related
to drug gangs. Individual drug takers are less likely to
be seen as victims of their habit than as resorting to
crime in order to support it. That members of ethnic
majorities may take and deal in drugs as frequently as
ethnic majorities is largely ignored in favor of depicting
drugs as an ethnic minority issue.

Violent crime and the drug problem are only two
manifestations of the general problem of law and order
associated with ethnic minorities. Coverage of political
demonstrations by ethnic minorities is generally com-
mensurate with the level of conflict and violence, especially with the police. Such demonstrations are ignored
when they are peaceful and reported solely in terms of
violence when they are not. Often there is an implication that political activity is only a cover for the real
objectives, to attack people, property, and the police.

Coverage of urban unrest in the USA and the United
Kingdom demonstrates most of these characteristics.
The immediate trigger for such disturbances or their
long-term economic and social causes are generally
marginalized in order to emphasize damage to property,
injuries to police, and the helplessness of innocent victims, all of which are more newsworthy and photogenic
than long-standing grievances over equal opportunities
or relations with the police, as the following attests to:

The media report and write from the standpoint of a white man's world. The ills of the ghetto,
the difficulties of life there, the Negro's burning
sense of grievance, are seldom conveyed. Slights
and indignities are part of the Negro's daily life,
and many of them come from what he now calls
"the white man's press"—a press that repeatedly,
if unconsciously, reflects the biases, the paternal-

ism, the indifference of white America. (National Advisory Commission on Civil Disorders, 1968. *Report of the National Advisory Commission on Civil Disorders,* p. 366. U.S. Government, Washington, DC)

Attributions of motive are simplified into mob mentalities, criminal tendencies, and opportunistic vandalism. Rather than as a desperate form of social protest, urban unrest is seen as primarily a problem of law and order, the solution to which is to restore order on the streets and apprehend as many of the culprits as possible.

More than any other of the major news issues in relation to ethnic minorities, that of law and order seems to be racialized. It is black youth, rather than those from Asian or other ethnic minority groups, who are associated with crime and disorder. The victims of such crime are presented as members of the ethnic majority or other law-abiding ethnic minorities. This has been found to be so of African-Americans in the USA, Afro-Caribbeans in the United Kingdom, Surinamese in the Netherlands, and aborigines in Australia.

3. Welfare and Social Problems

Ethnic minorities are generally portrayed less in terms of what they put into society than what they are seen to be taking out. Ethnic minorities are seen as troublesome, causing or exacerbating social problems which require public expenditure in such areas as social security, housing, and education. Whether or why their needs might be greater than those of the majority population are rarely considered. The implication, sometimes made explicit in media editorials, is that ethnic minorities are being accorded special privileges not available to the majority population who nevertheless have to pay for them through taxation. These trends appear regardless of the type of welfare system.

4. Politics

All the issues reviewed so far have direct implications for political leaders. The media are therefore likely to reproduce the pronouncements of ethnic majority leaders who, almost inevitably, call for measures to control immigration, crime, and welfare expenditure. Crucial for any kind of balance is the extent to which such views are challenged by other political views, especially those of ethnic minority leaders. Evidence suggests that ethnic minority interests are more likely to be represented by "liberal" members and groups from within the majority community than by their own leaders. Even when represented, such leaders are likely to be the subject of hostile questioning or investigation into their alleged links with "extremist" groups or statements.

Thus ethnic minority leaders' experience of the mass media is that they are likely to be marginalized, required to respond to an agenda set by the ethnic majority or liable to be dismissed as extremists. This pattern is reproduced in all democratic societies so far studied.

5. Ethnic Minorities as Victims

It has thus been demonstrated that ethnic minorities appear in the news as and when their existence and presence is seen to create a problem for the ethnic majority. The question then arises as to how the media cover those issues where the ethnic majority constitutes a problem for the ethnic minority. About these the media are reticent. Discrimination receives some minimal coverage but is regarded as caused by a few prejudiced individuals. The possibility that discrimination is a pervasive and persistent ethnic minority experience is rarely addressed by the news agenda. Even its most extreme manifestation, violence against ethnic minorities by members of the ethnic majority, is habitually underrepresented. Ethnic majority members are much more likely than ethnic minority members to commit acts of racial violence, but only rarely are such events recognized as news. The prevailing image is one of the ethnic majority as the victims of ethnic minorities; the reverse is rarely considered.

The general pattern of social disadvantage experienced by ethnic minorities is not a central news issue. That such groups live in the worst housing, go to the worst schools, and receive the worst treatment by the police and other public services remain peripheral. Even the attempts to remedy this situation, known variously as equal opportunity policies or affirmative action programs, are now regarded by the media with suspicion. A news story is more likely to occur when a member of the ethnic majority is denied access to a resource as a result of such programs than when an ethnic minority member demonstrates their benefit.

6. Summary

Wilson and Guttierez hypothesized five stages in the press representation of ethnic minorities: excluded, threatening, confrontational, stereotyped, and accepted (C. C. Wilson and F. Gutierrez, 1995. *Race, Multiculturalism and the Media.* Sage, London and Thousand Oaks, CA). Evidence supports the pervasive presence of the first four, and a general absence of the fifth, in contemporary news media coverage.

B. Media Entertainment: Television

Television entertainment is more complex to analyze than news. We are dealing here with programs which set out to entertain rather than inform, with no obligation to be balanced or impartial, and which incorporate a whole range of genres: situation comedies, soaps and drama, and game and chat shows. It is less easy to ask straightforward questions about the content or meaning of such entertainment forms.

With the exception of some Australian work, almost all the evidence about the representation of ethnic minorities in media entertainment comes from the USA. The generalizability of its findings cannot therefore be guaranteed, though the export of American programs across the world means they are a universal source of ethnic minority imagery.

1. African-Americans on U.S. Television

Greenberg and Brand have summarized quantitative research findings about ethnic minorities in U.S. prime-time television in the 1980s (B. S. Greenberg and J. E. Brand, 1994. In *Media Effects* (J. Bryant and D. Zillmann, Eds.), pp. 273–314. Erlbaum, Hillsdale, NJ). Of every 100 prime-time characters, African-Americans constituted no more than 8 and other minorities together 4. African-American females were much less prominent than males, and females from other ethnic minorities were virtually absent. Analysis of the roles they played or performed indicated that they were nearly always peripheral or subordinate to ethnic majority performers and in positions of low social status. Interethnic relations were generally formal and work-related rather than informal or sociable. The overall conclusion was that ethnic minority members on television appeared to be apart or separate from ethnic majority members, even when they appeared together.

There is some agreement that African-Americans now appear more frequently in television entertainment but that this quantitative gain does necessarily imply qualitative improvement. Game and talk shows that involve the audience appear to be the only genres where ethnic minorities appear on television as frequently as they do in the population at large. They are rarely central in soap opera and drama serials, except those located in a work setting, such as hospitals and police stations, where ethnic presence seems to be more easily accommodated.

2. African-Americans in Situation Comedies

The genre in which African-Americans appear to have achieved the most prominence is situation comedy, even though some of the most popular and frequently exported situation comedies of the mid-1990s largely exclude an ethnic minority presence. Prominence in situation comedies is double-edged: though it invites identification with black characters, it may also draw on established stereotypes of African-Americans as comic figures. Further complexity arises from the fact that situation comedies stand or fall by their ability to make the (largely ethnic majority) audience laugh. Accurate representation of ethnic identity is secondary to this overriding objective.

The debate about the terms on which African-Americans can succeed in U.S. prime-time television is encapsulated in the arguments about the phenomenal success—not least with minority audiences—of the all-black situation comedy "The Cosby Show." On no other program has the "burden of representation" fallen so heavily.

On the one hand, critics of the show argue that it is a misrepresentation of African-American experience. In their professional jobs and affluent lifestyle, the Huxtables are atypical. Despite its internal conflicts, the Huxtable family is basically harmonious, its teenagers immune to the temptations of sex or drugs. Though there is a positive identification with black culture, the Huxtables never experience personal or institutional racism. This is a black family sanitized for the consumption of a white audience.

On the other hand, the show is viewed as positive in several senses. First, it demonstrates, not least to a white audience, that African-Americans are not necessarily welfare dependents or living in dysfunctional families. Second, it normalizes blackness, since the audience is invited to laugh at recognizable universal human situations. Third, and as a consequence, it demonstrates that African-Americans can appear on prime-time television without inhabiting the stereotypical roles to which they might otherwise be allocated.

These two views are not wholly incompatible. It is possible to argue that the show simultaneously reveals the extent to which African-Americans can penetrate entertainment television and the conditions which have to be met for that incursion to be acceptable. Similar arguments can be applied to the most prominent Afro-Caribbean star on British television, Lenny Henry, who has an unrivaled capacity to raise questions of ethnic difference while ridiculing them through laughter.

3. Ethnic Minorities on Australian and British Television

Evidence from Australia suggests that entertainment forms tend to exclude ethnic minority performers. Successfully exported soap operas deny or marginalize the existence of aborigines. Asians and Pacific peoples appear to occupy the same position as Hispanics in the USA, being largely absent from entertainment television. Other than the occasional situation comedy, European ethnic minorities, such as Greeks or Italians, appear infrequently. Their only contribution to the Australian way of life seems to be culinary.

In the United Kingdom, Afro-Caribbeans have appeared as hosts of game and entertainment programs, though systematic evidence is lacking. Some of the most popular soaps habitually feature ethnic minority characters, issues of racism being neither exaggerated nor ignored. However, the Asian ethnic minority appears much less frequently, and other groups, such as Africans, hardly at all.

4. Summary

Television entertainment features ethnic minorities even less than the news. Only African-Americans in the USA and Afro-Caribbeans in the United Kingdom appear with any frequency. Even then, they are restricted to particular genres, such as occupational soaps or situation comedies. It would appear that ethnic majorities wish to be entertained largely by members of their own group and will tolerate ethnic minorities only under very restrictive conditions.

C. Media Entertainment: Films

Analysis of the representation of ethnic minorities in film has largely concentrated on Hollywood, given its domination of the international market. The recycling of films on television means that past representations are still readily available in the present and cannot simply be consigned to history. Findings are complex to summarize since research tends, in the tradition of film criticism, to involve very detailed textual analysis of films taken to be exemplars of particular traditions or viewpoints.

1. The Native American Indian

The ethnic minority to have been most misrepresented by Hollywood is the Native American Indian. There has been a move away from the stereotypes of Indians as ignoble savages which disfigured the Western genre in the past. Yet, even as Hollywood has apparently moved to a more sympathetic view, there are still evident tendencies toward historical and cultural inaccuracies, a preference for white stars to play Indian heroes, or for the whole issue to be seen from a white point of view. For example, the film *Dances with Wolves* self-consciously sets out to tell the story of the West from the Indian point of view, inviting the audience to invert its usual ethnic sympathies. The Indian way of life is represented as palpably more civilized than that of the white invaders. Yet the whole narrative is structured around the dilemmas of the white hero, Kevin Costner,

with whom we are asked to identify. Thus, even where white people rather than Indians are portrayed as destructive, intrusive, and uncivilized, it is a white point of view on which the film hinges.

2. African-Americans

In Hollywood's portrayal of African-Americans, there are still traces of what have been identified as the five main stereotypes of the African-American, all of which ensured African-Americans a manageable and predictable place in the white world of Hollywood.

In *Toms, Coons, Mulattoes, Mammies and Bucks* (1989, New York, Continuum) Donald Bogle surveys representations of Blacks in Hollywood cinema, especially emphasizing the unequal struggle between Black performers and the stereotypical roles offered them by Hollywood. Bogle's very title announces the five major stereotypes:

1. the servile "Tom" (going back to Uncle Tom in *Uncle Tom's Cabin*);
2. the "Coon" (Step'n Fetchit is the archetypal example), a type itself subdivided into the "pickanniny" (the harmless eye-popping clown figure) and the Uncle Remus (naive, congenial folk philosopher);
3. the "Tragic Mulatto," usually a woman, victim of dual racial inheritance, who tries to "pass for White" in films such as *Pinky* and *Imitation of Life;* or else the demonized mulatto man, devious and ambitious, like Silas Lynch in *Birth of a Nation;*
4. the "Mammy," the fat, cantankerous but ultimately sympathetic female servant who provides the glue that keeps households together (the Aunt Jemima "handkerchief head" in one variant) such as Hattie McDaniel in *Gone With the Wind;* and
5. the "Buck," the brutal hypersexualized Black man, a figure of menace, inherited from the stage, whose most famous filmic incarnation is perhaps Gus in *Birth of a Nation.*

(E. Shohat and R. Stam, 1994. *Unthinking Eurocentrism: Multiculturalism and the Mass Media,* p. 195. Routledge, London/ New York.

As in television, African-Americans appear to have moved from the periphery to the center of the action, with some commercially successful films featuring black heroes and even predominantly black casts. Some black directors, such as Spike Lee, have even managed to produce successful films which address in popular form the experiences and dilemmas of the black community.

However, it has been argued that more typically black characters achieve filmic prominence in roles which are assigned to blackness. They are subordinate to narratives and situations defined by the majority culture. The association of African-Americans with crime, for example, is given a new twist but not ruptured if an African-American is not the criminal but the cop, especially if he operates in an uneasy alliance with a white partner. Such black characters, it is argued, live on the edge, always on the verge of transgressing the rules they are supposed to uphold. Thus even where the ethnic blackness of the character is emphasized–in language, bodily posture, dress, and cultural affiliation—his presence in the white world is conditional upon acceptance of the white terms in which the film world is cast. Even such minimal gains have not been enjoyed by female black stars and roles. The most prominent female actors are those who have already achieved prominence as comics, singers, or even models, thus ensuring their acceptability to the largely white audience.

3. Appropriating Ethnic Minority Cultures

While black characters remain peripheral, Hollywood has appropriated aspects of ethnic minority cultures and histories in order to reproduce them through white eyes. Musicals invariably pull on African-American and Hispanic traditions but their stars and settings are invariably white. Black historical struggles, such as the 1960s civil rights movement, are seen through the eyes of white liberals struggling with their consciences with mass black activism as a backcloth. The multiethnic tradition of American culture and history is distorted so that the prime movers are portrayed to be white.

4. Other Ethnic Minorities

Other ethnic minorities fare no better. Latino peoples are represented through another series of stereotypes: bandido, greaser, revolutionary, or bullfighter. Almost all appear in films set in the past; the contemporary experience of this group remains unrepresented. Of Koreans, Chinese, and Japanese, there is no sign, except in the displaced form of the enemy in films about the Vietnam war. The one exception appears to be the Jewish minority, where representation by Hollywood has been at once low-key and careful, attributed to the considerable Jewish influence over development of the film industry.

5. Summary

The evidence to support any generalizations about Hollywood's representation of ethnic minorities is necessarily soft and interpretative rather than hard and factual. Yet the weight of evidence suggests that, as in other media, the film industry finds it difficult to represent ethnic minorities in terms other than those derived from the ethnic majority. It would appear that Hollywood has largely failed to acknowledge the multiethnic nature of the society in which it operates or even of the audiences to which it appeals. The experience of ethnicity is refracted through the lens of the white ethnic majority.

D. Other Media Content

1. Advertising

The purpose of television advertising is to market goods and services to a mass consumer market. Where, as is often the case, ethnic minorities lack significant spending power, we might expect commercials to be directed at the ethnic majority and consequently use the images they find most salient. Greenberg and Brand (1994) have summarized relevant research, mainly on U.S. television commercials in the mid-1980s. African-Americans appeared in less than 20% of commercials, and only 2% featured blacks alone. Though recent data are lacking, the suggestion is that African-Americans appear more as background than foreground and rarely interact with whites. Also remaining to be updated are data from the 1970s suggesting that African-Americans in commercials were more passive than whites, were less likely to initiate activity, and lacked command over space or technology.

The increasing consumer power of African-Americans and their prominence as sports and music stars with marketing potential may have recently increased their visibility and status in U.S. television commercials but we cannot be sure. Other ethnic minorities, especially Hispanics, are largely absent from television commercials, outside their own cable and satellite stations.

Australian television commercials appear to be even less likely than their U.S. counterparts to reflect multiculturalist ideals, with the exception that the art and music of aborigines may be used in a mythologized form to evoke the spiritual inheritance of Australia. Much of prime-time television advertising is more concerned with conveying an idealized image of the white Australian family with a blonde mother as the key figure. Little research has been conducted in the United Kingdom, but a useful hypothesis would be the replication of the U.S. case, with the slow emergence of Afro-

Caribbeans in largely minor roles outside sport and music but the almost total absence of any Asian or other ethnic minorities.

Overall, in their general exclusion or marginalization of ethnic minorities, television commercials would appear to offer images of ethnic minorities even less developed than those in the news and entertainment programs in which they are inserted, certainly in the United States and Australia, probably in the United Kingdom and possibly elsewhere.

2. Children's Television

Demographic trends, educational objectives, and ethnic minority children as a commercial market might be thought to encourage greater ethnic diversity on children's television. Evidence suggests that this is generally not the case. Greenberg and Brand's 1994 summary of relevant U.S. research suggests that only African-American males are marginally more evident on children's than adult television. African-American females, Hispanics, Asians, and other ethnic minorities are virtually absent. Black characters are peripheral rather than central and segregated from white characters so that there is little interethnic interaction. The staple diet of U.S. children's television, cartoons, are considered to be less representative than other types of programs and more likely to contain ethnic minority stereotypes. Advertisements showed more evidence of ethnic diversity, especially in homilies from large food corporations, but girls, Hispanics, and Asians remained underrepresented. The most consistently high-profile and positive images of ethnic minorities occurred in public service programs, where as many as a quarter of all characters were from ethnic minorities.

The importation from the United States of children's programs has led to an increase in the portrayal of ethnic minorities on Australilian children's television, but its own ethnic minorities. Asians, aborigines, and Pacific children, remain largely invisible. There is little systematic evidence from the United Kingdom, but Asians are again conspicuous by their absence, despite the prominence of Afro-Caribbeans as children's television presenters.

In an extensive analysis of mainly U.S. imported cartoons, Jakubowicz *et al.* traced a greater diversity of ethnic minority characters who nevertheless occupied marginal roles (1994. *Racism, Ethnicity and the Media.* Allen & Unwin, New South Wales, Australia). Heroic figures were mainly white or occasionally African-American; other ethnic minorities were hardly represented at all, and stereotypes of other cultures appeared in portrayals of foreign lands.

The increasingly global dependence on U.S. children's programs, especially on cable and satellite channels, and the weakness of public service broadcasting cancel out demographic trends so that children's television reproduces the same bias toward ethnic majorities to be found in adult television.

3. Sports

For complex reasons, African-Americans in the United States and Afro-Caribbeans in the United Kingdom are significantly overrepresented as top-level performers in major spectator and televised sports: track and field in both countries, football and basketball in the United States, and soccer in the United Kingdom. Any definition of news or entertainment that excludes sports will thus omit an arena where the achievements of at least one ethnic minority would ensure their prominence in media coverage. This would be no guarantee against stereotyping, since natural athleticism is established as a white view of the black "race." Sport constitutes a useful case study of whether evidence of ethnic minority achievement challenges media stereotypes.

Studies in the 1970s and 1980s, mainly of football and basketball television coverage in the USA, suggested that positive images of African-Americans as athletes were heavily qualified by the white structures of authority, promotion, and audiences into which they were inserted. It was also suggested that mainly white commentators tended to be more disparaging of black than white athletes. The more recent introduction of black coaches and commentators may have modified this bias, though evidence to test this assumption appears to be lacking. Nor are there any substantial studies of the way ethnic minorities in sports are represented in the press or specialized sports magazines. Also unanswered are questions about female ethnic minority sports stars, whose representation may well be doubly skewed by both ethnicity and gender.

Often qualified and subject to stereotyping, the continuing achievements of black people in sports, and their consequent marketing potential, seem likely to act as a positive counterbalance to negative stereotyping elsewhere in the media. It may be of marginal economic and political significance, but its symbolic impact, for both majority and minority communities, may be substantial.

4. Popular Music

Popular music is another area where academic categories may exclude an important sphere of ethnic minority achievement. Music channels, background music on television advertisements, and the music press may include potentially positive representations. There may still be tendencies toward exclusion, such as MTV's initial resistance to black performers or hostility toward the ethnic assertiveness of "gangsta" rap. The stereotype that African peoples are naturally rhythmic may also be drawn upon.

Yet popular music provides evidence of ethnic minority success and even of control, since, almost uniquely, pop videos are a media form where black performers are in charge of their own projected images. The ubiquitous presence in popular music of African-Americans in the United States and Afro-Caribbeans in the United Kingdom has not been adequately studied. This is ironic, since along with sports, music may be the source of much imagery of ethnic minorities among both majority and minority populations, especially the young.

IV. KEY ANSWERS

We can now consider the answers provided by the evidence to the questions posed in Section II.

A. Inclusion versus Exclusion

Many ethnic minorities—Hispanics in the USA, Asians in the United Kingdom, aborigines in Australia—are largely excluded from media representation. The main exception is where they appear in the news as troublesome. Othewise—in television entertainment, in films, in adverts, and even on children's television—they appear hardly at all. African-Americans are more likely to appear in media entertainment but only in the restricted roles of comedians or marginal characters. It is unclear how far this is counterbalanced by their prominence in the sports and music programs. Overall we find, dependent on the ethnic minority, the medium, and the country, a range of representations, from outright exclusion to minimal and conditional inclusion. What we do not find is any evidence of inclusion which is quantitatively and qualitatively equal to that of the ethnic majority.

B. Accuracy versus Distortion

In the news, it has been found that basic facts about ethnic minorities, such as immigration or crime figures, are distorted or glossed over. News events are constructed through the views of white authority while there is little attempt to portray the daily experience of ethnic minorities, especially of discrimination. In the entertainment media, their cultural heritage is inaccurately portrayed and history rewritten to favor the ethnic majority. Whether focusing on an individual event,

a social trend, or an historical image, the media generally appear unable to represent the presence of ethnic minorities with any degree of accuracy.

C. Sensitive Understanding versus Rigid Stereotyping

As a compressed form of communication, the media are apt to resort to stereotypes. Media news coverage of ethnic minorities is replete with such images: the illegal immigrant, the street criminal, and the welfare scrounger. Slightly different stereotypes appear in the entertainment media, where differences of accent and lifestyle are the sources of comedy or tension. Where desirable images of social life are being conveyed, as in advertising, ethnic minorities are never central. Even children's television, with the exception of public service broadcasting, fails to reflect the realities of multiethnic communities. Those members of ethnic minorities who achieve public prominence as politicians, broadcasters, athletes, or musicians may escape the stereotypes, but they can also be used to perpetuate them. What seems difficult is for the media to accept ethnicity as one of many diversities of identity which can be recognized without resorting to stereotypical images.

D. Multiculturalism versus Assimilation

There seems little doubt that the media do acknowledge the cultural variety produced by the presence of ethnic minorities but do not appear to value it. The ultimate test comes when the media represent "The Nation" and its way of life. Whether such national images appear in feature films, soaps, or advertisements, ethnic minorities are invariably marginalized or excluded. The least-included groups are those whose way of life cannot easily be assimilated by that of the ethnic majority. It is no accident that Asians are frequently the most excluded group. Adherence to their own languages, religions, food, dress, and kinship systems daily present their otherness to the ethnic majority. Where such variety cannot be accommodated in the representation of "The Nation," then we may conclude that multiculturalist ideals are absent and that assimilation is the implicit model of the integration of ethnic minorities into society.

E. Summary

The evidence suggests that there is an overall pattern to media representations of ethnic minorities. It is one which tends toward their outright exclusion or highly conditional inclusion, to distorted rather than accurate depiction of their lives, to interpretations in terms of rigid stereotypes rather than sensitive understanding, and to underlying ideals which are assimilationist rather than multiculturalist. Some news or entertainment programs, some films or advertisements, and some music or sports channels may be partly exempt from such a judgment. (For a review of some examples from European television see C. Frachon and M. Vargaftig, Eds., 1995. *European Television: Immigrants and Ethnic Minorities*. Libbey, London). However, for the vast majority of media output in all the nations where there has been systematic study, these tendencies have been found to be consistent. We now consider why these have come to be the predominant patterns of media representation of ethnic minorities.

V. EXPLAINING MEDIA REPRESENTATIONS

There is substantial agreement about the main explanations for the nature of ethnic minority representation in the media, though scholars differ about which explanations should be given most weight. Here we look at five possible explanations, working from the most concrete to the most abstract kind of explanation.

A. Media Ownership

The media are major economic institutions, the source of much commercial profit and cultural power. It is thus not surprising that they tend to be owned and controlled by members of majority ethnic groups, who directly or indirectly decide the view of the world which the media convey. This is argued to lead to negative views of ethnic minority groups for two reasons. Firstly, the owners share the cultural perspective of the majority group, which is likely to be hostile or indifferent to the presence and needs of ethnic minority groups. Secondly, such owners are likely to have a heavy investment in society as it is, so are unsympathetic to the reforms which ethnic minorities and their allies may be demanding.

Paper pays for racial bias
Martin Wainwright

A newspaper group is to apologise and pay £13,000 to a black woman who was warned in an interview that she would need to accept phrases like "black bastard" as typical office banter if she was given a job.

Claudia Baptiste, aged 28, who was described as an excellent candidate by the Telegraph and Argus in Bradford, failed to get either of two advertising jobs after saying that she found such language offensive and unacceptable.

A three-man industrial tribunal in Leeds ruled unanimously that the evening newspaper, which last year won a Race in the Media award for its coverage of the city's riots, had discriminated racially against Ms Baptiste. The chairman, John Prophet, said that the episode had been "totally unacceptable". Although the interviewer, advertising manager Jane Holt, has subsequently been promoted, Bradford and District newspapers managing director Tim Blott said she had been disciplined.

The Telegraph and Argus, which serves an area with a large ethnic population, also agreed to give all staff a written warning within two weeks that racially offensive comments would result in disciplinary action, including dismissal.

Ms Baptiste said after the ruling: "Anyone who has suffered from racial discrimination should come forward and protest. No one should accept it." (The Guardian, London and Manchester, UK, October 10, 1996.)

B. Media Staffing

Surveys confirm the impression that ethnic minorities are underrepresented in media personnel. They are particularly excluded from higher levels of management. Apart from their functions in sports and entertainment, they are also conspicuous by their absence as media performers. The media appear to reproduce the patterns of exclusion and discrimination which ethnic minorities experience in other areas of employment.

As in other institutions such as the police, staff drawn almost wholly from the ethnic majority are likely to reinforce each others' prejudices and misconceptions about ethnic minorities. They neither encounter nor have to allow for the views of those from other groups. Even where ethnic minority members do join media staff, they often find themselves regarded as accountable for and experts on the activities of ethnic minorities, and are expected to cover or produce any story or program with an ethnic minority slant. This restricts the scope of their activity and career advancement. They are effectively treated first and foremost as members or representatives of their ethnic group, rather than as media staff on an equal footing with their ethnic majority counterparts.

By excluding, marginalizing, and occupationally stereotyping their ethnic minority staff, media institutions often reproduce the same patterns of discrimination in employment to be found in society at large. It may not be surprising if they find it difficult to admit to the pervasiveness of discrimination when they themselves practice it.

C. Professional Practices

This explanation looks at how the media operate, regardless of the ethnic composition of its personnel or ownership. The emphasis is on occupational routines and practices regarded as professionally acceptable which nevertheless militate against adequate representations of ethnic minorities. Such professional practices are to be found across the range of media. In television, the expected formula for a situation comedy may imply that any tensions between characters, such as those arising from ethnicity, should be defused rather than left unresolved. In popular cinema, the expectation that the major protagonists should be male, preferably white, and certainly an adherent of dominant cultural values may implicitly marginalize ethnic minority characters.

The most documented example of professional practices having an observable effect on the representation of ethnic minorities is news coverage on any medium. A set of expectations about what the news is or should be like have been identified: the kinds of people and events who make the news. Less formal prescriptions than a working set of assumptions common among media professionals, such news values contain a set of attributes which any event must possess in order for it to become headline news.

A simple example is that a major news value is negativity. The more negative an event is, the more likely it is, all other things being equal, to become news. Studies consistently find that the news conveys a negative portrait of ethnic minorities, emphasizing their involvement in or presentation of problems, especially around urban unrest, crime, and welfare issues. A conspiracy against ethnic minorities need not be posited to explain this tendency. It is simply how all news works. There is always more bad than good news. To that extent, media representations of ethnic minorities in the news may only be following the implicit rules they follow for all news selection and presentation.

Once selected, news events have to be constructed into a story. They have to be assembled in terms which make sense to the audience: a sequence of events, some notion of cause and effect, and commentary from eyewitnesses and responsible authorities. Here the media tend to rely on official sources of evidence or to give more authority to their views, regardless of the kind of event. When the event relates to ethnic minorities, for example any event involving relations between the police and ethnic minorities, then we may find an in-built bias toward the police version of events. This is the normal procedure of news making: the police belong to that category of official institutions who are perceived as the source of knowledgeable and authoritative statements. Any group which is critical of the police will find itself disadvantaged whenever it seeks to challenge the police version of an event or an issue. This is an integral part of news making; it is not specific to ethnic minorities and reflects the general distribution of power in society.

There are many other aspects of the news-making process which operate in this way. They affect such media practices as headlines, photographs, and who gets quoted in what order. They are not designed to disadvantage ethnic minorities in particular, and it may not be necessary to attribute them to ethnic bias. They are simply the outcome of the application of established routines of news making.

D. Audience Maximization

All media are involved in a constant effort to maximize their audience because their major sources of profit are advertising, sponsorship, and consumer subscriptions. The bigger (or sometimes more affluent) the audience, the greater the profits. The equation is simple. Maximization of audiences requires reaching as many consumers as possible. Since the ethnic majority is by definition the largest and generally the most affluent group, the media will initially look to them for its source of custom. Penetration of the ethnic minority audience may be a bonus but is not a necessity.

The media are thus driven to present the kinds of factual and fictional material they believe will appeal to the majority of their potential audience. This requires news coverage of the kinds of events and people the audience recognize and fictions which speak to their experience. Their view of what is expected and unexpected, normal and deviant, and who are "us" and who are "them" becomes part of the routine of making sense of factual and fictional material. Without it, media output would not make sense to its audience. Hence the media are drawn to the view of the majority group because they constitute most of the audience. It may also be assumed that the majority group expects to be addressed in the media, especially on the television screen, by members of their own group, from whom they also expect their fictional heroes to be recruited.

The media's orientation to their audiences, advertisers, and sponsors tends to make them reluctant to try anything or anyone which would breech the audience's expectations. They perceive the audience to want what it already knows and likes. Ethnic minority members may be acceptable in particular niches, such as comedy, sport, music, or even cookery, but otherwise they are not expected to feature prominently in the media. The few exceptions—ethnic minority performers whose success attracts attention—prove the rule.

All these commercial imperatives impel the media to reproduce the ideas and prejudices of the ethnic majority. As long as ethnic minorities remain an insignificant proportion of viewers, listeners, or readers they will not be seen as a viable media market.

E. Ideologies and Belief Systems

The final explanation moves into a different terrain of argument, moving beyond the detail of media institutions. It argues that the media, whether factual or fictional, are engaged in a process of sense making. In order to understand the news story, situation comedy, or Hollywood feature film, the audience must be presented with a framework of reference which it understands.

Any representation of ethnic minorities will therefore be located in the common understandings of producers and audiences about the nature of ethnic relations. This is indivisible from what is regarded as a crucial ideological function of the media, to demarcate the boundaries of society—to specify "us," who belong to the society and identify with its values and respect its institutions, as compared with "them," who do not really belong, since they seek to undermine society's values and institutions. This makes it difficult for ethnic minorities to avoid being defined as "them." If they demand change, or if they want their values, such as religion, to be enshrined in institutions such as the education system, then they may be seen as trying to redraw the boundaries of membership in society.

Moreover, in its sense of who belongs and who does not, the media will draw on a set of sedimented ideas about groups derived from selective views of history and geography. Ethnic minorities in the West, for example, may be seen as belonging to groups or hailing from parts of the world which have yet to reach the "civilized" level of the West. Their strangeness of religion, language, dress, etc., are regarded as markers of their being both different and inferior. They will become accepted

only insofar as they abandon the markers of their ethnicity and adopt the ways of ethnic majority. Even then, they may not be fully accepted if they remain visibly different in terms of "race."

The media's treatment of ethnic minorities cannot, in this view, be divorced from their ideological presuppositions about ethnicity and race which invariably cast the ethnic majority as possessing the most advanced culture to which others are by definition inferior. To an extent, such tendencies work independently of, though they may be reinforced by, other forms of explanation. Changes in media ownership, staffing, professional practices, or audience maximization would not necessarily alter the ideological function of the media. From this point of view, the debate over media representations of ethnic minorities is only part of a wider struggle over ideological domination, which is regarded as in its own way as important as political and economic inequalities.

VI. PROSPECTS FOR REFORM

Each of the explanations of the way the media represent ethnic minorities points to possible remedies for the situation.

A. Media Ownership

The need here is for greater diversity in the ownership of the media to include ethnic minority members or at least those sympathetic to their cause. This is very difficult, since there is a global trend toward the domination of media ownership by large corporations. Governments are generally and increasingly resistant to the regulation of media ownership, other than preventing extreme monopolies. There is thus little prospect for change in the ownership of the press or mainstream television stations, though there is some room for maneuvering on the margins. The franchising of local radio stations may involve a commitment to community broadcasting and a persuasive case can be made for the appropriateness of ethnic minority ownership. New television stations can be designed to represent minority interests not catered for by the mainstream media and ethnic minorities are one such interest. The remit of the Special Broadcasting Service in Australia is one example.

The Special Broadcasting Service's mission is to contribute to a more cohesive, equitable and harmonious Australian society by providing an innovative and quality multilingual radio and television service which depicts the diverse reality of

Australia's multicultural society and meets the needs of Australians of all origins and backgrounds. (Jakubowicz, 1994, 144)

A more enduring one, if only because of its profitability, is Channel Four in the United Kingdom, whose commitment to experimental and minority broadcasting has given airtime to new kinds of perspectives, including those from within the minority communities.

B. Media Staffing

Prospects for reform here are potentially greater, provided an ethical commitment is forthcoming from media owners and management. The clear underrepresentation of ethnic minorities in virtually all parts of the media industry can be remedied by the application of equal opportunity policies and even some positive discrimination. The BBC in the United Kingdom, for example, has a specialist training program for ethnic minority recruits, and some college training courses openly or tacitly seek to attract ethnic minority students. As important is the need to raise awareness of the issues amongst ethnic majority staff. Journalistic and broadcasting training would benefit from consideration of ethical issues of reporting in a multiethnic society. The current backlash against equal opportunity policies does not give rise to optimism, but it is still possible to question the extent and causes of the apparent lack of ethnic representativeness among media employees.

C. Professional Practices

This area is very resistant to change, since the demand seems to be to reform the very nature of media practices governing the production of news reports, advertising messages, television series, or feature films. The most to be hoped for is the institution of codes of practice to govern professional conduct, such as that of the National Union of Journalists in the United Kingdom. In theory it ought to be possible to extend codes which currently govern the representation of violence and sex to that of ethnicity. The signs are not particularly encouraging, since there is much resistance on the grounds of media freedom. Where there has been change, as in Hollywood's representation of native American Indians, the main cause has been a shift in cultural attitudes outside the media. All that can be done is to draw attention to the worst kinds of abuse in media representation and their relationship to professional practices.

D. Audience Maximization

There are some positive trends here, rooted in the changing economics of the media industries. Especially in broadcasting, the multiplicity of channels means that a viable audience is now much smaller, a trend reinforced by some advertisers' preference for niche rather than mass marketing. Combined with any minimal improvement in the consumer power of one or more ethnic minorities, it means that they can emerge as viable audiences, an example being the proliferation of Spanish stations on cable television in the United States. Paradoxically, the competition for audiences can equally produce a lesser willingness to depart from established formats for fear of losing the audience. While media outlets may emerge which address ethnic minorities as consumers and thus avoid ethnic stereotypes, such representations may not reach the ethnic majority who watch or listen to their own stations. Talk radio in the USA and Australia has a tarnished reputation for giving vent to virulent prejudice against ethnic minorities, often endorsed by host broadcasters. What is known as the fragmentation of the media broadcasting audience may simply mean an increase in the ethnic exclusivity of individual outlets.

E. Ideologies and Belief Systems

These are quite clearly the most resistant to change, though this is not to say that they remain static. In the USA, the United Kingdom, and Australia biologically based theories of racial superiority have become less and less tenable and have been displaced by ideas which stress cultural difference rather than biological inferiority as the basis for ethnic incompatibility. The media are quite clearly one of the important articulators of changes in perceptions of ethnic minorities. There is always room to reveal the inconsistencies within the media, where news coverage or entertainment material is at variance with a media organization's avowed commitment to interethnic harmony. Yet in other ways the media may be seen as a symptom rather than a cause of ethnic ideologies and their reform only one aspect of a wider ideological struggle.

F. Social Change

It has been argued that trends outside the media will bring about change in media representations of ethnic minorities. In discussing the situation in the USA, for example, various commentators have stressed the importance of demographic and economic change. It is possible that early in the 21st century, ethnic minorities may constitute a majority of the U.S. population. In such a context, it may no longer be viable to assume that the media should continue to largely address what was the ethnic majority. At the same time, the emergence of a middle class, especially among African-Americans, will provide an economic incentive to address this audience in terms it appreciates. The fragmentation of the media audience into segments induced by the expansion of channels will further enhance the viability of ethnic minority niche markets.

It remains to be seen whether these changes, still at an embryonic stage, will bring in their wake radical changes in the ways the media represent ethnic minorities. Evidence about local media in U.S. cities where ethnic minorities are already numerically significant does not suggest that such changes will necessarily be rapid or far-reaching. It may be significant that some of the most often cited harbingers of change come from outside the media and are expected to induce reforms by the media following their own established commercial logic rather than from any changes in that logic itself.

VII. CONCLUSION: THE ETHICS OF ETHNICITY

Media representation of ethnic minorities is an ethical issue with public, political, and professional dimensions. For the public, it is an issue of what kind of society we believe we are or wish to be members of. Is it a society which seeks to convert its ethnic minorities to the ways of the ethnic majority, to assimilate them? Or is it one which can tolerate and even welcome a diversity of skin colors, languages, religious practices, kinship structures, dress, and diet, the position of multiculturalism? This issue is directly connected to our conception of citizenship: who is regarded as a member of society and what rights, including the right to accurate media representation, such membership entails.

The second dimension is political, especially the formulation of media policy. There appears to be a reluctance to require the mass media to give equality of representation to ethnic minorities or even to provide an effective means of redress where members of ethnic minorities feel they have been misrepresented. The issue is largely left to the consciences and professional codes of media communicators.

In the third dimension, professional ethics, the issue of representing ethnic minorities does not seem a pressing one. With a few honorable exceptions, media owners, managers, and practitioners have not seen the treatment of ethnic minorities as central to their codes of professional ethics. Such strategically placed individuals have somehow suppressed their professional responsibility for the quality of relationships between ethnic groups. While they may as individuals be genuinely appalled at the ethnic hatreds which cause so much violence around the world, they make no connection to their own failure to contribute to interethnic understanding.

The media may be only one influence, but it is an important one, on the state of interethnic relations in any context. Media personnel may only reflect the unthinking attitudes prevalent in their own ethnic group, but their role in society requires them to do more. Media regulators may fear a backlash from the ethnic majority but have responsibilities to the wider multiethnic community. We, as citizens, need to do more to ensure that the media equally represent humankind in all its welcome diversity. The alternative is the perpetuation of the mutual incomprehension of ethnic groups, from which conflict of many different kinds seems bound to follow.

Also See the Following Articles

DISCRIMINATION, CONCEPT Of • ETHNOCULTURAL MINORITY GROUPS, STATUS AND TREATMENT OF • MEDIA OWNERSHIP • OBJECTIVITY IN REPORTING • POLICE AND RACE RELATIONS • RACISM

Bibliography

Cottle, S. (1992). Race, racialization and the media. *Sage Race Relations Abstr.* **17**(2), 3–57.

Downing, J., and Husband, C. (1995). Media flows, ethnicity, racism and xenophobia. *Electronic J. Commun.* **5**, 2/3.

Greenberg, B. S., and Brand, J. E. (1994). Minorities and the mass media: 1970s to 1990s. In "Media Effects: Advances in Theory and Research" (J. Bryant and D. Zillman, Eds.), pp. 273–314. Erlbaum, Hillsdale, NJ.

Jakubowicz, A., Goodall, H., Martin, J., Mitchell, T., Randall, L., and Seneviratne, S. (1994). "Racism, Ethnicity, and the Media." Allen & Unwin, New South Wales, Australia.

MacDonald, J. F. (1992). "Blacks and White TV: African Americans in Television Since 1948," 2nd ed. Hall, Chicago.

Shah, E. (1995). Race, nation and news in the United States. *Electronic J. Commun.* **5**, 2/3.

Shohat, E., and Stam, R. (1994). "Unthinking Eurocentrism: Multiculturalism and the Media." Routledge, London/New York.

Van Dijk, T. A. (1991). "Racism and the Press." Routledge, London/New York.

Wilson, C. W., and Gutierrez, F. (1985). "Minorities and Media: Diversity and the End of Mass Communication." Sage, Newbury Park, CA.

MEDIA OWNERSHIP

Edward Johnson
University of New Orleans

GLOSSARY

cyberspace The representational "place" defined by computerized interactions, named by William Gibson in the 1984 science-fiction novel *Neuromancer*.

factoid A piece of unimportant information whose very existence is an artifact of the power to report it (such as some of the excessively arcane statistics sports commentators like to inject into their coverage); a pseudo-fact; meaningless information masquerading as a fact; presumptuous trivia.

media event An event that exists, or has significance, only for the purpose of being represented or reported in the media.

panopticism Life under conditions of absolute subjection to surveillance.

simulacrum A sign that presents itself *as* a sign, while in fact representing nothing (or, sometimes, representing the fact that it represents nothing).

MEDIA OWNERSHIP is shorthand for a number of interconnected problems concerning access to, and con-

trol of, communications media. Briefly, critics assert (or deny) the existence of inequality in people's access to mass communications, and discuss how this is (or is not) connected with inequalities of wealth and power.

I. BAGDIKIAN'S RECKONING

About communications media, at the end of the 20th century, three facts are beyond dispute: more media outlets exist, telecommunications is more important, and media ownership is more concentrated than ever before.

These facts are tied to three important changes during the course of the century. The first change has been *technical*. New forms of communication have been developed—telephone, radio, television, photocopy, fax, computer, the Internet, etc.—and have been repeatedly refined. The second change has been *social*. Each new form of communication has defined a new dimension for human interaction and created new possibilities for social relations and novel categories of human interaction. The third change has been *economic*. Because these technical changes involve the transformation of materials, they define new kinds of property. Because these social changes open up avenues of influence, they define new sorts of social control. Who will own this property? How will this control be exercised? When Ben Bagdikian published the first edition of *The Media Monopoly* in 1983, he pointed out that ownership of most of the major media was consolidated in only about 50 corporations. By the time he published the fourth edition in 1992, the number had dropped to 20.

There are more media outlets and fewer media owners, but what impact (if any) does this have on the content or the effects of the media? The Swedish anthropologist Ulf Hannerz, in *Cultural Complexity* (1992), notes that the issue is typically framed along the following lines:

> Will more media power bring us closer to Orwell's 1984 . . . if media power keeps cumulatively concentrating in the same hands? Or will a computer literate society make totalitarianism and its knowledge hoarding impossible, as more people can answer back, and as the hackers will always get the secrets in the end?

Howard Rheingold, in *The Virtual Community: Homesteading on the Electronic Frontier* (1993), formulates the issue in terms of similar poles of opposition: the reinvigorated democracy of a kind of "electronic agora" (the ancient Greek marketplace) versus an electronic Panopticon.

The Panopticon, a design by English philosopher Jeremy Bentham (1748–1832) for a building that would permit absolute and unobserved observation of its inmates, was introduced into current discussion by French social theorist Michel Foucault (1926–1984), in *Surveiller et punir* (1975; translated as *Discipline and Punish* in 1977). This book, along with Foucault's other work, has exercised considerable influence on the radical reconceptualization of modern life. According to its subtitle, it is a study of "the birth of the prison," but it is in fact an examination of the formation of the "disciplinary society." A general theme running through Foucault's several studies—of asylum, clinic, prison, language, knowledge, and sexuality—is the ever increasing imposition of socially defined order on the life of the individual. Foucault explored the emergence of discourses which exercised power through their definition of knowledge, and attempted to excavate the suppressed facts about the struggles that had taken place over the imposition of these disciplinary discourses.

The "panopticism" which characterizes modern life establishes a structure of power that is indifferent as to who exercises it. Foucault asked, "Do you think it would be much better to have the prisoners operating the Panoptic apparatus and sitting in the central tower, instead of the guards?" It also makes those who are supervised themselves part of the mechanism, in two senses. They are part of the mechanism, in the first place, because part of the effectiveness of supervision derives from one's awareness of being supervised; one thus becomes the principle of one's own subjection. One is part of the mechanism also in the sense that one can take part in the supervision of others. The Panopticon even "enables everyone to come and observe any of the observers." The Panopticon thus provides a model for the functioning of a society in which "disciplinary mechanisms" have become ubiquitous.

If there is a central political problem about the prison, in Foucault's view, it involves the fact that the "mechanisms of normalization," for which the prison served as incubator, exercise a widespread and increasing influence throughout society. "Is it surprising that prisons resemble factories, schools, barracks, hospitals, which all resemble prisons?" The extension of this framework to electronic media is obvious. Rheingold sees himself as following Foucault in worrying about whether "the machinery of the worldwide communications network constitutes a kind of camouflaged Panopticon (1993)". Similarly, Mark Taylor and Esa Saarinen see the "media philosophy" they propose in *Imagologies* (1994) as an extension of Foucault's "microphysics of power to the world of media."

A less dramatic picture of the issues of media ownership can be drawn in terms of the handy formula—offered by Werner Severin and James Tankard in *Communication Theories* (1991)—that "media ownership determines media control, which, in turn, determines media content, which is probably the major cause of media effects". Each link in this chain raises questions.

II. MEDIA OWNERSHIP AND MEDIA CONTROL

Ownership and control are not the same thing. People's use of their property operates within the parameters of certain social determinations; the use of an automobile or a gun, for example, is plainly subject to sensible restrictions. Furthermore, if what one owns is some kind of public treasure, then the public can specify limits that define the owner's responsibilities. Some possessions, in other words, involve a public trust.

These points, however, presuppose that the law functions to enforce the limitations in question. To the extent that it fails to do so (whether through incompetence, oversight, or corruption), the power of ownership will not be restrained. A standard argument from anticorporate critics is that the economic power of the corporation is such as to allow it to override legal limits through the exercise of political influence.

William Greider, in *Who Will Tell the People: The Betrayal of American Democracy* (1992), provides a detailed argument that social control (government) fails because those who know the system realize that their goals can be achieved through intervention, licit or illicit, at many points in the path from law to enforcement. The interpretations of administrators can function effectively to reverse the intention of a statute. Indeed, politicians often legislate merely symbolic gestures whose actual effect in practice they know will be (in fact, they *count* on its being) quite different. As politico Stuart Eizenstat instructed Greider, "The law's always up for grabs. That's why you win elections and appoint judges." Greider himself endorses Bagdikian's suggestion that limits be placed on cross ownership of media, noting,

Media owners usually hide behind the First Amendment when such questions are raised, but the practical effect of media concentration is actually to restrict the "free speech" of everyone else, the voiceless citizenry. Who gets to enter the debate? The choice belongs to reporters and editors and producers and, really, to the companies they work for.

Lawrence Grossman also argues that First Amendment considerations should not be an obstacle to enforcing antitrust laws against media conglomerates. We must distinguish, he says in *The Electronic Republic* (1995), "between the *medium*, on which reasonable limits of ownership can and must be imposed, and the *message*, which must be kept entirely free from government interference, regulation, and restriction."

Those who are not alarmed by Bagdikian's dwindling list of media owners can insist that ownership is not the same as control for another reason. Operating a media enterprise is a large and complex business, in which many individuals leave (albeit to varying degrees) their personal mark on what happens. Does the corporation's ownership "really" determine the choices of its many agents, the reporters, editors, producers, etc.? An example of a negative answer is given by Martin Seiden in *Access to the American Mind: The Impact of the New Mass Media* (1991). He dismisses Bagdikian's worries and sees the real problem with the media as being the power of journalists, rather than the power of their corporate owners:

The real corporate conspiracy would appear to be the corporations' bond of uncritical silence regarding the operation of their media. Corporate executives appear to be paralyzed by the fear of being devoured by the mindless swarm if they interfere. What sensible executive would jeopardize his company's profit-and-loss statement by triggering a strike because he took issue with one of the journalists' sacred causes?

Analyses of this kind can also point to pollsters, lawyers, or other minions of corporate power—indeed, even to corporate executives *qua* individual decision makers—as those in whose hands media control actually resides. From this perspective, media ownership does not necessarily determine media control, because those who actually exercise the control, who make the relevant decisions, must be understood as having a culture and an agenda of their own, one not necessarily consonant with the interests of the owners.

Many studies of the actual functioning of complex, and especially bureaucratic, organizations suggest that the processes of evasion and circumvention that characterize the government can be expected to compromise any simple account of the exercise of corporate power. As Len Masterman points out in *Teaching the Media* (1985),

... we have to revise any simplistic notion we may have that commercial ownership of the media inevitably involves the cynical manipulation of audiences, that public service broadcasting is untainted by commercial considerations, or that media institutions necessarily exercise tight control over every aspect of their corporate enterprises. We have to recognise, as always, that the media are sites for struggle between conflicting interests, and that ownership/management power is not absolute, monolithic or uncontested.

Of course, the fact that the behavior of individuals is shaped by factors other than the announced (or, even, real) goals of the organizations of which they are members should not lead us to belittle the shaping influence exerted by economic power and vested, to some degree, in ownership. As Greider observes, "the politicians dare not challenge the structure of media ownership, for that would provoke severe retribution from press and television and their corporate owners.... If the people do not raise these questions, they will not be raised at all."

III. MEDIA CONTROL AND MEDIA CONTENT

Whether owner or manager, *somebody* makes decisions, and those decisions determine what is in fact transmitted through media. At least, this seems true for those media that involve broadcast programming. Not every medium does this. The telephone, for example, largely separates issues of ownership and control from questions of content, at least in principle. The content of conversations is not dictated, and within broad limits not much regulated, by the medium itself. (Though, even here, computerized commercial calling and aggressive telephone marketing have tended to introduce an asymmetric intrusiveness into phone use.)

With regard to broadcast media, however, it can be argued that media control determines media content, and that concentration of control leads to both narrowing and degradation of content. Bagdikian puts the case bluntly: "The greater the dominance of a few firms, the more uniformity in what each of them produces." Changes may sometimes involve an ideological concern, or a desire to manipulate public opinion to advantage, but often they reflect simple adherence to narrow economic interests with little regard to larger social effects. Bagdikian argues that

> ... there is no reason to expect that a person skilled at building a corporate empire is a good judge of what the generality of citizens in a community need and want to know. Today, news is increasingly a monopoly medium in its locality, its entrepreneurs are increasingly absent ones who know little about and have no commitment to the social and political knowledge of a community's citizens.

Local media coverage may be simply reduced or replaced with less expensive syndicated, or already-owned, material. Lawrence Grossman, a former president of NBC news recalls,

> It did not take long, however, before the press of daily deadlines, budget constraints, and the need to cover the same major unfolding stories as everyone else took us back to the practice of reacting to the themes and priorities of others—mostly what the president, the Congress, and top government departments and agencies decided to announce as the news of that day.

Edward Herman and Noam Chomsky, authors (separately and together) of many books critical of the media as government propaganda, remark in *Manufacturing Consent: The Political Economy of the Mass Media* (1988),

> Partly to maintain the image of objectivity, but also to protect themselves from criticisms of bias and the threat of libel suits, they need material that can be portrayed as presumptively accurate. This is also partly a matter of cost: taking information from sources that may be presumed credible, or that will elicit criticism and threats, requires careful checking and costly research.

Ostensibly "technical" decisions may effectively determine both access and content. Thus, Bagdikian argues that a question such as that of the

> "... allocation of the electromagnetic spectrum" tends to be handled in seclusion as an engineering task, but in reality, once in place the technical decision determines who will be given exclusive rights to broadcast to the public.... [For] by the time the systems are committed to certain kinds of equipment and practices, they effectively exclude the public from access to their media.

Such technical issues may not only determine who is able to afford to operate a broadcast medium, but may also affect the character and persuasiveness of the content. Robert Ray, in *A Certain Tendency of the Hollywood Cinema, 1930–1980* (1985), observes that

> ... technological improvements in photography, film, and television have always carried concealed political implications. Each improvement, in effect, has redefined what counts as an acceptable (and therefore "realistic" and "unbiased") picture of the world, escalating the standard so as to keep it always just out of reach of all but the most powerful. Those images that fall short of the accepted norm appear not only as amateurish, but more importantly, as less "real". While the images produced by those in power seem to be merely an "objective" record of the way things are, less-than-standard images always appear as the products of special interests.

Evidently, there is a good deal of ground for concern about the ways in which, in both news and entertainment, more power in fewer hands affects media content. Some analysts, however, continue to see content as ultimately answerable to the audience. According to some, the media give people what they want, because otherwise people will pick something else they like better. This analysis puts emphasis on the increasing number and variety of options. Critics concede the increase in quantity, but dispute the claim of quality or real diversity, seeing the competition as largely among small variants of more-of-the-same—in Bruce Springsteen's phrase, "67 channels and nothing on."

A defender of the status quo may reply that the better alternatives the critic calls for are spurious because, when given a choice, people mostly do not select them. The critic insists that the choice has not been real, etc., etc. And so the largely unedifying debate proceeds. One side insists on what people in fact choose and ignores the shaping effects of the status quo. The other side insists on what people would (or, perhaps, should) choose and ignores the implicit appeal to paternalism. It is not that people are not free to purchase, say, *Mother Jones* instead of (or in addition to) *TV Guide*. If the audience prefers looking at "Baywatch" reruns to watching city council meetings, is that evidence of manipulation, or rather an expression of the very autonomy and diversity democracy aspires to celebrate and protect?

To the critic, of course, there is something doubtful about the idea of mass consumerism of any kind as an expression of individuality, but the relevant notions are difficult to get into focus. A century of debate about highbrow, middlebrow, and lowbrow has settled little, and yet it has been, as Robert Ray puts it, "an age that has seen popular culture become, for most people, the *only* culture." The triumph of popular culture, though still lamented by many, is tied to the capitalistic exploitation of mass media in complex ways that defy easy analysis.

Michael Parenti, a left/progressive thinker who has published a number of books critical of the media, laments in *Inventing Reality: The Politics of News Media* (2nd. ed., 1992) the fate of radical newspapers: "Skyrocketing postage rates effect a real hardship on small dissident publications. While defending such increases as economy measures, the government continues to subsidize billions of pieces of junk mail sent out every year by business and advertising firms." One need not dismiss claims about hostility on the part of the government to observe that, for the typical consumer, the catalog from Sears may in fact be of greater interest than, say, the latest issue of *Lies of Our Times*. How much of the "ideological monopoly" lamented by critics like Parenti is in fact a reflection of the actual shared values of the masses?

Like all chicken-or-egg questions, this one is unanswerable without an appeal to some normative theory about human nature, the good life, the just society, etc. How such an appeal is to be negotiated without begging the question remains a puzzlement. We can appeal, like the influential German philosopher Jürgen Habermas, to the idea of "undistorted communication," but such a notion resolves nothing; it merely provides terminology for further debate.

For some, the very fact that we have become consumers of the "spectacle" provided by society is the fundamental problem. But any gesture to reject the spectacle immediately is co-opted and becomes a part of it. As the Situationist International movement—articulated in such works as Guy Debord's *Society of the Spectacle* (1967) and *Comments on the Society of the Spectacle* (1988)—saw it, "There is no gesture so radical that ideology will not try to recover it." And yet, as Sadie Plant says, in *The Most Radical Gesture* (1992), her valuable study of the movement, "the awareness that even the most radical of gestures can be disarmed continues to encourage a search for irrecuperable forms of expression and communication."

For others, the pervasiveness and intrusiveness of the increasingly inescapable symbolic environment must be accepted as the new reality—indeed, *hyper*reality—of human existence. As Rheingold puts it, "Hyper-reality is what you get when a Panopticon evolves to the point where it can convince everyone that it doesn't exist." It is the age of what French philosopher Jean Baudrillard, in *Simulacra and Simulation* (1981, trans. 1994), calls the "simulacrum." It is the age of the "factoid." It is the age of the celebrity, who is "famous for being famous." It is, in sum, a world in which media (collectively out of control in the sense of producing cumulatively unwanted effects) increasingly take each other and themselves as their content.

IV. MEDIA CONTENT AND MEDIA EFFECTS

If even the seemingly short step from control to content is uncertain, it should be no surprise that the relation between content and effects has been much disputed. Communication theorists have disagreed vociferously over the course of the century, some arguing that media have only "limited effects" on people's attitudes and behavior, with others insisting that they are "powerful agents of social change." The fact that, as Christopher Simpson documents in *Science of Coercion* (1994), communication research had its roots in the government's development of psychological warfare techniques—along with the extensive and expensive use of media for purposes of advertising—make it surprising that so many communications theorists have argued for limited effects. (Or, perhaps, not surprising at all.)

Herbert Schiller, the author of many critiques of media imperialism, from *Mass Communications and American Empire* (1969) to *Culture, Inc.: The Corporate Takeover of Public Expression* (1989), expresses astonishment at the limited-effects theory: "... the power of the Western cultural industries is more concentrated and formidable than ever; their outputs are more voluminous and widely circulated; and the transnational corporate system is totally dependent on information flows." How is it possible to suppose the effects of all this to be limited? The answer for recent critics is that media power is balanced by *audience* power. "First, it is claimed, the new information technologies afford greater choice. The second support factor derives from an appraisal of the audience, which finds it heterogeneous, comprised of a large number of social subgroups, each with its own history, experience, and interests." Schiller disputes each of these arguments.

The first argument, essentially that put forward by Ithiel de Sola Pool in *Technologies of Freedom* (1983), points to the increase in viewing choice made possible by cable TV and VCRs. At its crudest, the argument amounts to seeing media freedom as "channel surfing," the power to put together one's own viewing experience out of fragments of public meaning. Against this argument, Schiller contends that the actual diversity is spurious, because the power remains in the same place. "Has the sponsor disappeared from cable television? Is commercialism and consumerism absent? Where are the sharply drawn social dramas?" Furthermore, the media are still owned, and the infrequent participation of the community through public-access channels reflects the struggle with "cable owners who find it outrageous to be compelled to yield the tiniest fraction of their revenue- producing facilities for community use."

The second argument is analogous to reader-response criticism and other literary theories emphasizing the priority of how a text is received and interpreted by its audience over whatever its author may have intended: "Diversity, ... in this way of looking at television, does not require a variety of programmatic material. It is provided by the viewers in their capability to produce a diversity of readings or meanings in the single program." Schiller devotes extensive discussion to this second argument, but his basic response boils down to the observation that, as a passsage he quotes puts it, "television—along with most other commercial enterprises—exploits the competitive fragmentation among people who belong to what is objectively, the same, subordinate class." Or, to put the point the other way, "The ultimate message in TV ... is that the dominating class has the same basic problems as the dominated and is itself not in control of its destiny." What is wrong with this message? "Theories that ignore the structure and locus of representational and definitional power and emphasize instead the individual's message transformational capability present little threat to the maintenance of the established order."

Put in other words, Schiller's message, like that of many radical media critics, is that to locate freedom in marginal differentials of response to the mass-mediated environment is counterrevolutionary because it leads one to define one's situation not in (objective?) terms of the interests of one's class but rather in (subjective?) terms of one's creation of an individual style or response to reality. In terms popularized by Richard Rorty, it is to be paying attention to private "irony" rather than public "solidarity." Rorty's (liberal) view is that one needs both, and that there is no way to adjudicate their competing claims.

For the radical critic, the fact that individual styles have themselves become commodities—buy Michael Jordan's basketball shoe and "be like Mike"—only emphasizes the primacy of the need to see who is really doing the defining. But from another perspective, even commodified individualities can to some extent be viewed as grist for the mill of self-creation. They are what John Milton said a good book was, "the precious life-blood of a master-spirit." (Collect the whole set.)

Some writers hold out the hope that the new technologies of communication may yet enable us to reconcile self-creation and solidarity. Russell Neuman, in *The Future of the Mass Audience* (1991), suggests that "narrowcasting" (as opposed to broadcasting) may help us rediscover "virtual communities of like-minded individuals ... who will band together and speak out spontaneously in response to a public concern or event," thereby recreating "the essence of the vigorous citizen-based democracy." Against this optimism must be set journalist Georgie Anne Geyer's warning:

In some ways, the Internet does give demonstrators across the globe the technological means to bypass national boundaries and to appeal vaguely to 'solidarity'. On the other hand, it tends to weaken and destroy the kind of discipline, organized, across-class-lines appeals that always underlie every real revolution.

Still, Taylor and Saarinen are no doubt right to insist: "Where would Socrates hold his dialogues today? In the media and on the net."

Not only private life and civic life may come together in "cyberspace," but work life is being altered as well. Some have seen electronic communication as enhancing the speed and efficiency of networked knowledge, allowing people to work together from various locations and increasing scheduling autonomy, though not without some important dislocations as individual identity metamorphoses into universal product code. Joshua Meyrowitz explored the impact of electronic media on social behavior in *No Sense of Place* (1985). Barbara Garson foresaw computers turning the office of the future into the factory of the past in *The Electronic Sweatshop* (1988). Shoshana Zuboff provided an insightful study of the future of work and power with *In the Age of the Smart Machine* (1988). Stanley Deetz analyzed developments in communication and the politics of everyday life in *Democracy in an Age of Corporate Colonization* (1992).

The business world has also been transformed by economic changes made possible by the new media. In his valuable study of the film industry, *American Film Now* (Rev. ed., 1984), James Monaco notes

> ... a kind of Gresham's law of culture. As the craft becomes able to accomplish more with less, to realize record-setting profits with the flimsiest of raw materials, bad product drives out good.... The definitive irony of film culture in the seventies (as in all contemporary media culture from television to records to books) is that the refinement of the craft results in less freedom rather than more for the "artists"....

The criterion of the media of the 1970s, he observed, was "form follows finances." The age of the blockbuster was born.

By 1980, the destructive effects of "the big-time, big-money, winner-take-all system" had spread from television, movies, and records to the book trade, as Thomas Whiteside documented in *The Blockbuster Complex: Conglomerates, Show Business, and Book Publishing* (1981):

> The kind of emotional remoteness from "the product" which one senses in the conglomerates' central-management people now seems to be communicating itself to the people who are di-

rectly in charge of the publishing houses owned by the conglomerates, and more and more it seems that books are being regarded as interchangeable products.

Wall Street merger guru Felix Rohatyn summed it up succinctly: "Everything in this world has turned into show business."

Robert Frank and Philip Cook argue, in *The Winner-Take-All Society* (1995), that a similar process has spread to many areas of society: "In effect, the reward structure common in entertainment and sports—where thousands compete for a handful of big prizes at the top—has now permeated many other sectors of the economy." The growth of winner-take-all markets, they argue, is due to "the rapid erosion of the barriers that once prevented the top performers from serving broader markets." This erosion is due to a number of factors, but especially to changes in the media. "Perhaps the most profound changes in the underlying forces that give rise to winner-take-all effects have stemmed from technological developments in two areas—telecommunications and electronic computing." They argue that the winner-take-all system is costly and unproductive, and conclude that "rising inequality is more likely to curtail than to stimulate economic growth." The good news is that this would mean that there is no necessary opposition between economic growth and the curtailment of extreme inequality. The bad news is that, as they concede, most economists disagree with them.

V. AGAMEMNON'S SCEPTER

In Book II of the *Iliad*, the founding work of the long cultural tradition that stretches from the poet Homer down to Homer Simpson, Agamemnon's golden scepter functions as a symbol for the divine right of the king. When the troops are in turmoil, Odysseus borrows the scepter and goes to rally them, urging that "we cannot all be kings." Odysseus is soon successful and everyone keeps to his place, except for Thersites, whom Homer describes (in Samuel Butler's translation) as "a man of many words, and those unseemly; a monger of sedition, a railer against all who were in authority, who cared not what he said, so that he might set the Achaeans in a laugh." Thersites is ugly— itself an objection in ancient Greek culture, as Nietzsche liked to emphasize—and he has "a shrill squeaky voice." Thersites complains about Agamemnon's greed and proposes that the armies go home. Odysseus tells him to shut up, and threatens him, and finally beats him with the scepter until he is silent. This provides a fitting emblem of the way in which wealth and violence constrain participation in the debate over public policy. To be sure, a right to speak is not the same as a right to a megaphone. But what if some of the others have megaphones?

In his discussion of impairments in thinking and communication in *Inquiry and Change: The Troubled Attempt to Understand and Shape Society* (1990), Charles Lindblom says: "Among the defects of the existing competition of ideas, none seems more impairing or more easily remedied, given the will, than that well-financed communications, whether well-financed by the state, by private organizations, or by wealthy elites, overpower poorly financed ones." His suggestions for possible reforms include constraints on corporate spending on mass communications (and not just in electioneering) and perhaps limits on advertising and sales-promotion communications. He also calls into question "corporate influence on education and research ... indeed, the whole scope of corporate philanthropy."

Lindblom even goes so far as to broach the issue of the harmful effects on inquiry of inequality of wealth. He holds that genuine competition of ideas

> ... has to go further than [merely] to permit people to listen and read as they wish. If impairing influences have narrowed the range of ideas to which people choose to attend, then their freedom, however prized, to listen and read as they wish will not open them to a competition of ideas, but will leave them impaired.

Underlying Lindblom's project is the desire to distinguish inequalities necessary to the efficient operation of socially desirable mechanisms (functional inequalities) from inequalities that have illegitimately "attached" themselves to the functional inequalities. As we all know, "these 'attached' inequalities are often energetically rationalized, justified, defended, and enlarged when possible by the advantaged. Hence, sorting out useful from attached inequalities in control becomes subordinated to the struggle of the advantaged to maintain their advantages." Such illegitimate inequalities can be criticized not only from an egalitarian point of view (which sees equality as valuable in and of itself, other beings being equal), but also because they impair clear thinking, plain speaking, and the efficient operation of social mechanisms. Their criticism thus is part of the project of increasing the "rationality" of society. This project is, as Lindblom recognizes, a legacy of the En-

lightenment. Accordingly, it rouses the enthusiasm and the worries common to such attempts to rationalize life.

Whether one is more enthusiastic or more worried will depend on whether one thinks that what afflicts human life is too much irrationality or too narrow a view of rationality. The former (pro-Enlightenment) attitude characterizes thinkers from Plato to Carl Sagan. The latter view, suspicious of the claim of rationality to be comprehensive, stretches a zigzag course from Aristophanes to Euripides to Edmund Burke to Nietzsche to Foucault. Liberal reformers criticize conservatives for wanting to preserve the status quo, with its ignorance and inequities. Conservatives criticize liberals for being naive about human nature, and for being willing to impose their ideas of the human good on others. Radicals insist that the status quo already imposes on people a particular idea of the human good, a strikingly one-sided idea which is maintained by violence (or the threat of violence) and, thanks to the media, by distraction and illusion—bread and circuses at Eleven.

These views disagree about how values such as freedom and equality are to be understood in the actual conditions of social life. Nowhere is this disagreement more perplexing than in the question of control of media in an increasingly media-dependent world. As anthropologist Ulf Hannerz suggests,

> The problem of the asymmetry of input mode in the cultural apparatus, especially as constituted by the media, then, is that it allows little active participation in the production of certain kinds of symbolic form. At the same time, the presence of the cultural apparatus may allow people to cultivate a sensibility to symbolic forms which, without it, would not have been available at the same level of development at all.

The standard defense of corporate cultural "development" is that it makes life better. Though this is not always true, the interesting questions arise in those cases where it arguably is true, for the standard radical criticism of corporate cultural "imperialism" is that, whatever its superficial benefits, it supplants indigenous cultural systems and substitutes structural inequalities of power. What critics worry about is not so much Orwell's *1984*, as Huxley's *Brave New World*—less the jackboot in the face than designer boots in the window.

Whatever our ultimate destination, there is no doubt that the journey is a short one over the "information superhighway" to the "global village." En route, many now suggest, we are likely to see the end of the nation-state as the dominant force in world politics. James

Martin, who in 1978 presciently described *The Wired Society*, observed that

> patriotism is declining and may decline more with decades of advanced global communications. Some people will feel more loyalty to their global cultural thread than to their country.... The shape of cultural patterns is often determined more by money than by aesthetic or abstract values. The imperative to maximize profits will increasingly be an imperative to market internationally and hence design products for international markets.

Theodore Zeldin, in *An Intimate History of Humanity* (1994), has described the change in more personal terms:

> ... the earth is in the early stages of being crisscrossed afresh by invisible threads uniting individuals who differ by all conventional criteria, but who are finding that they have aspirations in common. When nations were formed, all the threads were designed to meet at a central point; now there is no centre any more; people are free to meet whomever they wish.

With the end of the nation-state may come as well the end of the kind of literacy that has been part of nationalism. With this literacy may go, as Bill Readings suggested in *The University in Ruins* (1996), both the book and the university as we have known them. What cultural forms might replace their claim on our attention, or their effect in our lives, remains to be seen. Stay tuned.

Also See the Following Articles

BROADCAST JOURNALISM • FREEDOM OF THE PRESS IN THE USA • INFORMATION MANAGEMENT • INTERNET PROTOCOL • OBJECTIVITY IN REPORTING • POLITICAL CORRECTNESS • TABLOID JOURNALISM

Bibliography

Ansolabehere, S., et al. (1993). *The media game: American politics in the television age.* New York: Macmillan.

Bagdikian, B. H. (1992). *The media monopoly* (4th ed.). Boston: Beacon.

Branscomb, A. W. (1994). *Who owns information?* New York: Basic Books.

Ewen, S. (1996). *PR! A social history of spin.* New York: Basic Books.

Frank, R. H., & Cook, P. J. (1995). *The winner-take-all society: Why the few at the top get so much more than the rest of us.* New York: Free Press.

Grossman, L. K. (1995). *The electronic republic: Reshaping democracy in the information age.* New York: Viking Penguin.

Herman, E. S. (1995). *Triumph of the market: Essays on economics, politics, and the media.* Boston: South End.

Poster, M. (1990). *The mode of information: Poststructuralism and social context.* Chicago: Univ. of Chicago Press.

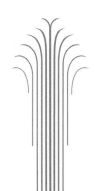

MEDICAL CODES AND OATHS

Edward W. Keyserlingk
McGill University

GLOSSARY

medical code An organized summary of the general moral standards, responsibilities, and rules of practice for medical clinicians and researchers generally, and/or a particular specialty, usually formulated exclusively by an authoritative body of medical peers and intended to provide guidance to the physicians in question, patients, the public, and other professionals about conduct which the formulating body considers to be acceptable and unacceptable.

medical oath A vow formulated by an authoritative religious or professional body which is sometimes taken by persons entering the medical profession and by which they promise to adhere to the ethical obligations of the profession as specified in the oath.

MEDICAL CODES AND OATHS are as diverse as the bodies that have formulated them. An examination of their history, evolution, and contemporary role indicates that there remain areas of uncertainty about their origins. There is considerable variation in the nature of the bodies which formulated them and in their intended function and their wording. In the differing moral values and assumptions expressed, they are products of their contemporary and evolving cultural, social, and professional contexts. There remain divergent views about their usefulness, their function, and who should formulate them. All of these factors will be briefly addressed in this article.

I. FROM RELIGIOUS TO SECULAR OATHS AND CODES

In view of space limitations and the ready availability of detailed historical analyses and full texts of medical codes and oaths from ancient times to the present (R. Veatch, 1995. In *Encyclopedia of Bioethics* (W. T. Reich, Ed.), rev. ed., pp. 1419–1435. Simon and Schuster–Macmillan, New York; C. M. Spicer, ibid., pp. 2599–2842), this section will be brief and selective.

A. Religious Oaths and Codes—From a Greek to a Christian Hippocrates

The earliest known medical oaths, prayers, and codes were essentially religious in their sources and orientation. While religiously inspired medical oaths and codes did not disappear and still persist, modern times witnessed the gradual emergence of secular codes devoid of any overt religious affiliation or influence. Nevertheless, the latter recast and promulgate many of the moral principles inherited from those earlier, more religiously inspired documents.

The earliest, most influential and enduring example is the Oath of Hippocrates, generally conceded to have originated in the 4th century B.C.E., or at least to have been influenced mainly by the teachings of the 4th century B.C.E. Greek philosopher and religious leader Pythagoras (L. Edelstein, 1943. *Bull. History Med.* 5(1), 1–64). The first statement of the oath reads, "I swear by Apollo, Physician and Asclepius and Panaceia and all the gods and goddesses, making them my witnesses, that I will fulfill according to my ability and judgment this oath and this covenant." In the oath the physician is required to benefit the sick, maintain confidentiality, keep medical knowledge secret except from others who swore this oath, and avoid sexual relations with those in the houses visited, intentional injustice, and the administration of deadly poisons and abortive remedies. The provisions of the Hippocratic oath were, and remained for centuries, in sharp contrast with much practice in Hellenistic medicine, where, for instance, suicide and infanticide were permitted. Indicative of its endurance is the fact that it continues to be administered to graduating students in many medical schools. For instance, a 1991 study reported that this was the case in 60 of the 141 American medical schools (E. Dickstein, J. Erlen, and J. A. Erlen, 1991. *Acad. Med.* **66**(10), 622–624).

A number of other early medical prayers and oaths clearly reflect the belief that succesful healing and adherence to moral responsibilities required submission to and assistance from the deity. The oldest known Hebrew medical text (300–700 C.E.) is the *Oath of Asaph*. It is replete with references to God. One of the professions the medical student makes is that "He causeth healing plants to grow and doth implant in the hearts of sages skill to heal by His manifold mercies. . . ." Like the Hippocratic oath, and perhaps influenced by it, the *Oath of Asaph* prohibited the provision of deadly poisons and abortive remedies and the betrayal of confidences. But reflecting Talmudic ethics it obliges physicians to "not harden your hearts against the poor and the needy, but heal them. . . ."

Another example from Jewish sources is the familiar and influential Daily Prayer of a Physician, once thought to be the work of the Jewish philosopher and physician Moses Maimonides (1135–1204), though now ascribed by many to Marcus Herz, an 18th century German physician. Those professing it proclaim, in part, "Thou hast endowed man with the wisdom to relieve the suffering of his brother, to recognize his disorders, to extract the healing substances, to discover their powers and to prepare and to apply them to suit every ill." It highlights the duty to make patient concerns primary and underlines the essential link between the possession of virtues such as courage, humility, gentleness, and wisdom, and the practice of healing.

Less overtly religious but still religiously inspired are two additional oaths. One is the 1st century C.E. Indian Oath of Initiation (Caraka Samhita), which calls on the student to adopt what is in effect a Hindu style of life including asceticism, celibacy, and the rejection of meat. It requires that the needs of patients be the first consideration and calls for devotion to both one's mentors and one's duty. Another is the Chinese Five Commandments and Ten Requirements, dating from the 17th century C.E., the most detailed account available of Chinese medical ethics. It is clearly inspired by Confucianism in that the primary virtues promoted are compassion and humaneness. It is notable for the injunctions to treat all patients equally, to provide medicine freely to the poor, and to provide needy patients with financial assistance since "without food, medicine alone can not relieve the distress of a patient."

The earliest known Christian medical oath dates from the 10th or 11th century, "From the Oath According to Hippocrates Insofar as a Christian May Swear It." As the title suggests, it is an adaptation of the Hippocratic oath which substitutes Christian submission to God for that of the Greek gods and makes Christian brotherhood the basis of medical teaching. A number of other such Christian adaptations of the Hippocratic oath exist (C. D. Leake, 1927. *Percival's Medical Ethics*. Williams and Wilkins, Baltimore).

B. The Shift to Secular Codes—From Percival to Helsinki

The appearance of medical codes in the West and the shift to secular versions were typified and strongly influenced by the 1803 treatise by the eminent Manchester, England, physician Thomas Percival entitled, *Medical Ethics; or, A Code of Institutes and Precepts Adapted to the Professional Conduct of Physicians and Surgeons*. The Percival code does make an eloquent plea for tenderness toward patients, though "condescension and authority" are featured as well. However, in large part the focus is on the relationships between medical professionals. Both the original and the shorter 1794 version as well as the expanded 1803 version were intended mainly to address and resolve the serious disputes between British medical practitioners of that time—surgeons, physicians, and apothecaries. This "professional etiquette" element and the concern to distinguish between "orthodox" and "unorthodox" medicine continued and continues to be a feature to varying degrees in subsequent medical codes of most countries. For example, the absence of state medical licensure laws and the resulting arrival on the medical practice scene of those with varying degrees of training and competing approaches largely explain the 1874 code of ethics of the American Medical Association. It was in large part a partisan attack by allopathic practitioners against those in the homeopathic and other schools of medical science, and insisted on the rejection and refusal of professional relationships with those considered to be charlatans because they lacked "orthodox" training (Veatch, 1995).

The adoption and promulgation of the Declaration of Geneva in 1948 (amended in 1968 and 1983) by the newly established World Medical Association and that association's 1949 International Code of Medical Ethics represent a notable further stage in the evolution of medical oaths and codes, namely the trend to establish international ethical standards of medical practice. The Declaration was meant to modernize and secularize the Oath of Hippocrates, and (like the International Code of Medical Ethics) to in effect take a strong stance against the recent medical atrocities in Nazi Germany. In brief, very general and largely uncontroversial statements it lists the humanitarian goals of medicine, including the rejection of discrimination on grounds of religion, nationality, race, party politics, or social standing. The impact, or at least the formal use, of the Declaration has been considerable. For example, a 1991 study reported that graduating medical students recited it in 47 of the 141 medical schools in the United States. The World Medical Association continued to concern itself with the application of international medical ethics standards and codes by going beyond medical practice and into the area of medical research.

In 1954 it produced the Principles for Those in Research and Experimentation, which led to the Declaration of Helsinki in 1964, which was subsequently revised in 1975, 1983, and 1989.

The 1947 Nuremberg Code on the subject of medical research on human subjects, responding to research atrocities in Nazi Germany and research horror stories in some other countries, represents yet another stage and source of medical codes. Not only is it secular and international, but also governmental in origin, a product of international law. It influenced the above-mentioned codes of the World Medical Association and led to the formulation of national research ethics codes in many countries, some of which, such as those in the United States, take the form of government regulations. In a number of other countries, for instance, Canada, the medical research ethics codes are promulgated by government agencies, and medical researchers must demonstrate adherence to those guidelines as one of the conditions for government agency funding. In some cases countries, or one or more legal jurisdictions within them, have translated medical codes of ethics into legal regulations which govern the medical profession or specialty and the medical peer review bodies which rule on the misconduct of members.

C. Codes from Nonmedical Sources—From the UN to Nurses

Worthy of attention in any account of medical codes and oaths are a number of medically related codes and declarations from non-medical sources, especially patients rights documents from the United Nations and international associations, and codes of ethics by other nonmedical health care professions. In the former category are notably the following United Nations documents: the 1948 Universal Declaration of Human Rights, the 1959 Declaration of the Rights of the Child, and the 1971 Declaration on the Rights of Mentally Retarded Persons. In this same patient's rights category is the World Medical Association's 1981 Declaration of Lisbon on the Rights of the Patient.

In the latter category, that of nonmedical health care professions, are the ethics codes of hospital associations, the earliest and most influential of which was the 1973 (revised 1992) A Patient's Bill of Rights by the American Hospital Association. Given the close working relations between physicians and nurses, nursing codes of ethics not surprisingly impact upon the ethics of medical practice and the formulation of medical codes of ethics. Hospital administrators and nurses have proven to be particularly responsive to patient rights claims and pressures. Hospital and nursing codes of ethics have generally taken the lead in focusing on patient's rights.

Despite the now long-established secular codes of ethics, and perhaps at least partly in response to them, religiously inspired codes and oaths persist. Those who base their medical ethics upon particular religious beliefs and morality find the provisions of secular professional codes too general in nature and in some respects offensive to their beliefs. The codes of Catholic hospital associations, for example, take exception to the generally permissive stance regarding abortions in contemporary secular medical codes. Some medical schools administer the Prayer of Maimonides rather than recent medical oaths or the Oath of Hippocrates.

II. BALANCING BENEFICENCE AND INDIVIDUALISM WITH AUTONOMY, RIGHTS, AND SOCIETY

A. For the Benefit of the Patient

It is possible to read too much into too little in an attempt to discern patterns and stages in the historical evolution and content of medical oaths and codes. Given their brief, summary, and stark nature, the documents in question generally provide little or no argumentation, explanation, development, or context by which to evaluate and compare them. They are not except in the most skeletal sense instances of applied or normative ethics, the considered application of moral principles to concrete situations. The most one can reliably discern is an evolution from the physician's obligation of beneficence toward individuals, that is, the physician as the interpreter and provider of benefit to the individual patient, to the added and sometimes conflicting duties of respecting patients' rights and promoting the well-being of the community.

The Hippocratic oath typifies the earliest focus, one which persisted until recent medical codes. The physician taking the Hippocratic oath promises to act "for the benefit of the patient, according to my ability and judgment." Specific references to additional and balancing considerations such as patient choice, patient values, patient autonomy, patient rights, informed consent, or truth telling do not appear in medical oaths and codes until very recent times. The claim made by some (Veatch, 1995; Edelstein, 1943) that the Hippocratic qualifier "according to my ability and judgment" is in itself clear evidence that this oath and tradition is "paternalistic," may be too strong. Even modern codes and treatises on medical ethics emphasize the centrality of medical ability and judgment in contributing to patient benefit. The paternalism label is more accurately based on the lack of reference to what present-day standards consider to be the final arbiter of medical recommendations about patient benefit, namely the values and choice of that patient.

Even in the Hippocratic oath and tradition, benefit to the individual patient may not have been the only norm to be observed. The provision of both deadly drugs and abortive remedies were prohibited. Whether that tradition considered them instances of nonbeneficial care or inherently wrong or dangerous to the larger community is unknown. It may well be that these prohibitions constitute a very early instance of a medical oath considering the interests of society or community to be higher than those of the individual patient.

B. Obligations to Community

The physician's obligation to the broader community only becomes explicit in recent oaths and codes. The first provision of the 1948 Declaration of Geneva states, "I solemnly pledge myself to consecrate my life to the service of humanity." The 1957 code of the American Medical Association, Principles of Medical Ethics, includes a similar principle. The latter makes it clear that benefit to the individual patient and that to the community are not always seen as distinct or competing, but can be closely related as well. The physician should participate "in activities which have the purpose of improving both the health and well-being of the individual and the community." On the other hand most contemporary medical codes acknowledge that in some cases a physician will be faced with a choice between an obligation to an individual patient and one to society. Confidentiality is an example. Whereas both the Declaration of Geneva and the International Code of Ethics insist upon absolute secrecy regarding patient information, codes such as those of the American Medical Association, the Canadian Medical Association, and the British Medical Association recognize exceptions in the interests of protecting others or society. It is worth noting, however, that the conflicts, exceptions, and justifications are typically not characterized as "ethical" but as legal. For example, the American Medical Association affirms in the Principles of Medical Ethics that "a physician ... shall safeguard patient confidences within the constraints of the law." In that Association's 1994 revision of the Current Opinions of the Council on Ethical and Judicial Affairs it clarifies that the relevant exceptions are, for example, notifying law enforcement authorities when a patient threatens serious bodily harm to another person, or reporting communicable diseases as required by applicable statutes or ordinances.

C. The Adoption of Rights Language

Consideration for patient's "rights" in medical codes and oaths, and the use of rights language, is relatively recent. As already noted, the earliest focus on rights in health care codes emerged from nursing and hospital associations. It is now commonplace for medical codes and oaths to refer to the rights of patients, typically including under that heading the choice of physician, informed consent, treatment refusal, and confidentiality. The shift to a rights approach represented a significant move away from paternalism, an acknowledgment that in part because health and health care is only one element in a patient's well-being, informed and competent patients are in a better position than physicians to decide what is not to their benefit according to their own individual needs and values.

However, given the summary nature of medical codes and oaths, they do not address complex and clinically practical moral issues such as how to resolve potential conflicts of rights or the limitations of a rights approach. An acknowledgment of the latter is suggested in the Canadian Nursing Association's 1991 Code of Ethics for Nursing. After affirming that clients possess both legal and moral rights, the code warns that "emphasizing the rights of clients may also seem unduly legalistic and restrictive, ignoring the fact that sometimes ethics require nurses to go beyond the letter of the law."

III. THE FUNCTIONS OF MEDICAL CODES IN THE CONTEXT OF PROFESSIONAL ETHICS

A. Standards, Principles, and Rules

Contemporary medical codes are intended to be in effect codifications of the professional ethics of physicians. As such they are subject to description, analysis, and evaluation from the perspective of that subset of ethics. They illustrate many of the limits, strengths, and debates about professional ethics generally.

One finds in contemporary medical codes at least elements of three kinds of professional norms: standards (or virtues), principles (or responsibilities), and rules (M. D. Bayles, 1981. *Professional Ethics*. Wadsworth, Belmont, CA). Standards in medical codes are in effect about the prescribed virtues, dispositions, and character traits a physician should have and the vices a physician should avoid. Those typically promoted are truthfulness, honesty, diligence, discretion, compassion, and competence. Medical codes do not argue the case for virtues or defend a theory as to whether or how a virtuous character influences or leads to moral conduct. The cause–effect link is simply assumed. At the same time and in varying degrees medical codes also state or imply that the perceived moral character

of the physician is a basis for a trusting relationship between patient and physician (Spicer, 1995).

Responsibilities (or principles) specify general obligations but leave space for the physician's judgment and discretion in specific cases. Examples are the responsibility to respect patient choices, to respect life, and to provide only appropriate diagnostic procedures. How these responsibilities are to be carried out in different cases is not predetermined and specified.

As for another feature of professional ethics, namely rules, medical codes contain them as well. Rules prescribe specific conduct about which there will normally be no place for physician discretion. In medical codes, as in professional ethics generally, the activities prescribed or prohibited are those about which there is the most unanimity or consensus in the profession. The obligation to obtain informed consent before treating, the duty to maintain confidentiality, and the duty to treat one's patient are examples. Contemporary medical codes insist upon all of these and other rules. When one or another applies, it decides the issue and must be respected.

The reality is, of course, that there can be exceptions and rules can conflict. A family physician wishing to test the spouse of an HIV-positive patient who refuses permission to reveal his or her HIV status is faced with a conflict between treating the spouse and maintaining confidentiality. Only one rule can prevail, not both, but which one? Codes will typically provide only general guidance about exceptions and ways to resolve the competing rules. For example, the Code of the Professional Corporation of Physicians of Quebec has a rule insisting upon confidentiality of medical information about a patient, but adds in part that the doctor may reveal such facts "where the patient or the law authorizes him or if there should be a just and imperative motive related to the health of the patient or the welfare of others." The physician's question will of course be whether the threat to the spouse if not tested would ground a sufficiently "just and imperative" motive to justify breaking confidentiality. In some jurisdictions the ruling of a court may be relevant and even decisive, but generally speaking, in deciding which rule should apply in this case there will be no escape from at least a degree of physician judgment and discretion.

B. Protecting the Profession or Protecting the Patient

As expressions of the ethics of the medical profession, codes formulated by medical associations are similarly focused more or less exclusively on the values and goals of that profession. The most prominent and influential such value is variously expressed as healing, promoting the best interests of the patient, or doing no harm to patients. Some do not feel that the focus on a single predominant professional goal or value is sufficient justification for professional norms. That would, they claim, unduly segregate the norms and the professionals from other societal values. Deriving all the norms of a professional ethic and code from the primary professional value risks segregating it and members of that profession from other societal values. A preferable justification and evaluation of professional norms, it is claimed, is the extent to which they also reflect, or at least do not do not endanger or disregard, the values of patients and the public.

Applying that standard, it is not clear that basing a medical code on the ideal of the profession necessarily in itself endangers other societal values or promotes the exemption of physicians from ordinary norms. That danger would be a real one to the extent that self-interest, cohesion, and etiquette of the profession were to take precedence in the codes over the values of patients and others. That tendency is now less prevalent in medical codes than was once the case. Secondly, that danger would be greater were it not that the professional ideal of healing or benefiting the patient is increasingly balanced in contemporary medical codes with the ideals of respecting patient wishes and the physician's duties to society. Thirdly, because physicians have a unique and societally accepted role, it should not surprise or be seen as unacceptable that they emphasize a value or values reflecting that role. Commentators generally insist, however, that physicians are not thereby released from adherence to ordinary norms of morality. Like ordinary citizens they are, for instance, subject to the ordinary norms prohibiting fraud, assault, and homicide. Precisely because of their professional role and responsibilities, some of their professional norms are more stringent than those applying to ordinary citizens. Examples are the rules about maintaining patient confidentiality already referred to and the professional norms and code provisions about maintaining physical and emotional boundaries between physician and patient. Consider the matter of sexual relations. According to ordinary norms of morality they are permitted if both parties freely consent. However, because free consent in a professional–client relationship is open to question, professional norms prohibit sexual relations between physicians and patients. As has been noted, this and similar professional norms are not contrary to or independent of what is morally acceptable for other citizens—it is more precisely a specification of the ordinary

norm, the moral continuity between them being the requirement of free consent (Bayles, 1981).

IV. THE LIMITATIONS OF MEDICAL CODES AND OATHS

As already indicated, medical codes and oaths have a variety of functions. They also have a number of limitations. Their limitations are for the most part imposed by the nature and goals of professional codes and oaths and the fact that most are formulated and revised exclusively by medical associations and on the basis of professional consensus. Within those terms of reference it would probably be accurate to claim that they are more "limited" than "defective." Codes and oaths are not, after all, especially in these times, the only or primary expression of medical ethics by physicians. They are not designed or suited to carry all the freight their critics sometimes expect. It is of course also the case that their terms of reference are themselves the object of some debate and criticism, for instance, the legitimacy of codes of ethics promulgated and policed exclusively by physicians themselves. Some of the limitations merit more detailed attention.

A. General and Uncontentious

The fact that secular medical codes and oaths are generally formulated by a process of consensus within the profession and are meant to be acceptable to all or most members necessarily imposes several constraints. That is particularly the case in liberal, democratic, and pluralist societies in which it can be expected that physicians will have widely divergent views on a number of morally contentious contemporary issues, are culturally and religiously diverse, and are reluctant to surrender or have curtailed their personal views or professional independence.

The consensus factor largely explains why the codes of standards, principles, and rules intended to guide physicians are correspondingly general, uncontentious, and devoid of elaborated moral theory defending and ranking the enunciated standards, principles, or rules and applying them to complex moral dilemmas. The positions adopted have already been agreed upon and widely practiced before the code was written. They are of little help regarding new, troubling, and complex ethical problems. This should not be surprising given the mechanics involved in consensus seeking—consultation, negotiation, trade-offs, and compromise.

It should be noted that physicians need not and do not rely for help in resolving troublesome ethical dilemmas exclusively on medical codes. In some cases medical associations provide more detailed and defended positions in other forms and forums. For example, in the American Medical Association the Council on Ethical and Judicial Affairs issues as a part of the code of ethics, and regularly revises, the "Current Opinions with Annotations," including a long series of relatively elaborate comments on current ethical problems, including, for instance, parental consent, child abuse, allocation of resources, and gene therapy. There is as well growing attention to ethical issues in the medical literature. Physicians increasingly consult bioethical literature featuring philosophical and religious analyses of ethical problems.

Despite the generality of medical codes and oaths they can nevertheless serve a useful purpose. Insofar as the codes focus on moral principles, these codes can at least serve in the same role as moral principles do. Ethical principles such as respect for life and respect for patient autonomy are too general and indeterminate to carry the whole load in resolving ethical problems. Nevertheless, they can set the moral tone, establish moral parameters, and serve as tests of the more specific rules (H. D. Aiken, 1962. *Reason and Conduct.* Knopf, New York).

B. Reflections of Positive Morality of Physicians

By general consensus medical codes are for the most part mirrors of the positive morality and interests of the members of the profession rather than accounts of the profession's moral aspirations or challenges to reform and improve conduct (A. L. Caplan, 1978. *Hastings Center Rep.* 8(4), 18). In large part they reflect and reenforce current practice and the moral status quo rather than question it or propose new directions. That too may be at least in part a result of the reductionist impact of consensus seeking. An additional factor may be that because most medical codes are formulated exclusively by physicians, they are only marginally influenced by the evolving values and viewpoints of the public, related professions, and patients. When they have been revised to include, for instance, provisions about patient autonomy and informed consent, the impulse to do so appears to have come more from external legal and consumer pressure than from within the profession.

In varying degrees medical codes and oaths are less and less reflections of even the positive morality of the profession. Attempts to revise the codes on some matters to bring them into line with present medical thinking and practice are increasingly hindered by the growing divergence of views among physicians. An example is the issue of (active) medical euthanasia. At one time in the not so distant past there was seemingly near unanimity that medical euthanasia should be prohibited, and the medical codes reflected and continue to reflect that view. However, contemporary surveys in a number of countries now indicate that physicians may be more or less equally divided about whether, in varying circumstances, active medical euthanasia should be decriminalized and allowed. That being so, current codes are clearly out of step with the views of a large proportion of physicians. But since codes are typically revised only in the event of the consensual agreement of the physicians they cover, it becomes increasingly unlikely that there will be code revisions on such matters, and therefore increasingly likely that medical codes will be seen as irrelevant by a large proportion of physicians.

There are, on the other hand, examples of medical codes and oaths which appear to do more than merely reflect the positive morality and interests of the profession—which do emphatically insist that physicians strive to be ever more virtuous and to improve and change their conduct from that which prevails (E. W. Keyserlingk, 1993. In *Applied Ethics* (E.R. Winkler and J. R. Coombs, Eds.), pp. 390–415. Blackwell, Oxford, UK). The most obvious examples, however, tend to be either religious in origin and content, or formulated by international medical organizations or by nonmedical associations and organizations, in some cases to confront instances of medical atrocities or horror stories. What enabled these codes to go beyond merely reflecting current morality may be that those who wrote them did not do so on the basis of medical consensus alone. As well, their values, sources and contributors went beyond those of physicians alone.

One example is the already discussed Oath of Hippocrates. It required a morality stricter than that prevailing in contemporary Greek society and ethics, and rejected conduct widely practiced by physicians at the time, such as dispensing poisons or abortive remedies. Given that it appears to have had no impact on medical practice by Greek physicians at the time or for centuries afterward, it could be considered the first example of the ineffectiveness of a medical oath or code which challenges, rather than reflects, current practice.

Another example is the Prayer of Maimonides, also already mentioned. It is patently Jewish in inspiration and content. It calls upon the physician to submit to divine authority and dedicate himself to a life of faith and increasing virtue.

In more recent times perhaps the best example of a secular medical code which is more than a reflection of current medical practice is the Nuremberg Code. It was formulated from outside the profession and in the context of international law. The protections it promulgated for subjects of medical research were occasioned by medical atrocities in the Nazi era and by the worldwide lack of such clear and defensible guidelines in existing medical codes. In effect the Nuremberg Code reflected, adapted, and imposed upon medical research many of the principles and moral perceptions evolving in contemporary society at that time.

C. Western Medical Codes for a Multicultural World

International medical codes and oaths such as the Declaration of Geneva, the International Code of Medical Ethics, the Nuremberg Code, the Declaration of Helsinki, and a number of other codes formulated by international medical and governmental bodies reflect what many claim is an almost exclusively Western, and even North American, ethical perspective although they are intended for application on a worldwide basis. For example, they almost uniformly require respect for autonomy and adopt a largely rights-based approach. For many the export of such medical codes to non-Western cultures constitutes a violation of those cultures and indicates a serious limitation if not defect of medical codes of ethics outside their Western habitat. Others are of the view that medical codes highlighting respect for persons and autonomy can be educational and can contribute to the correction of abuses everywhere, and that in any case respect for persons may not be an exclusively Western ideal.

Some are of the view that respect for persons may already be, in varying degrees and expressions, an indigenous principle in all societies, and that where it is invisible and at risk the reasons may have more to do with economic, social, and political circumstances than that people care about radically different things (J. Rachels, 1980. *Hastings Center Rep.* **10**(3), 32–38). The major limitation in international medical codes may not be their focus on respect for persons, respect for autonomy, and patient/subject rights, but that there is insufficient attention, in both national and international codes, to issues of distributive and social justice (Keyserlingk, 1993). Medical codes, national and international, generally focus on the duties of individual physicians, not on the responsibilities of the profession itself

to society, by for example, in various settings and cultures contributing to and advocating for the availability of adequate health care. Admonishments in international medical codes to respect patient autonomy would arguably have more impact, relevance, and credibility in countries with high poverty, inadequate and poorly distributed health services, low employment, widespread sexual discrimination, few opportunities, and constant political unrest if they were accompanied by corresponding obligations of physicians and others to contribute to the amelioration of those social conditions.

V. CONCLUSION

Medical codes and oaths have a long and important history reflecting the evolving self-perception of medicine through the centuries, from paternalist beginnings toward a growing acknowledgment of patient autonomy. They continue to serve as one means of expressing the moral aspirations of physicians, but are more typically vehicles to promote the cohesion and interests of the profession. The standards, principles, and rules contained in secular medical codes and oaths are, and will remain, necessarily general and uncontentious in nature given that these documents reflect the consensus of the profession. They do nevertheless establish important moral parameters for the practice of ethical medicine. Those oaths and codes based on religious values and those which are nonmedical or international in origin do sometimes challenge contemporary practice, respond to instances of medical abuse, and urge physicians to be more virtuous. Beyond their inclusion in formal occasions such as graduation ceremonies, their practical usefulness and relevance have been decreasing for some time given that physicians with increasingly divergent values and views are faced with moral issues of growing complexity and contentiousness, issues not for the most part foreseen or analyzed in medical codes.

Also See the Following Articles

AIDS TREATMENT AND BIOETHICS IN SOUTH AFRICA • CODES OF ETHICS • MEDICAL ETHICS, HISTORY OF • PROFESSIONAL ETHICS • RELIGION AND ETHICS

Bibliography

Aiken, H. D. (1962). "Reason and Conduct." Knopf, New York.
Bayles, M. D. (1981). "Professional Ethics." Wadsworth, Belmont, CA.

Caplan, A. L. (1978). Cracking codes. *Hastings Center Rep.* **8**(4), 18.

Dickstein, E., Erlen, J., and Erlen, J. A. (1991). Ethical principles contained in currently professed medical codes. *Acad. Med.* **66**(10), 622–624.

Edelstein, L. (1943). The Hippocratic Oath: Text, translation, and interpretation. *Bull. History Med.* **5**(1), 1–64.

Keyserlingk, E. W. (1993). Ethics codes and guidelines for health care and research: Can respect for autonomy be a multicultural principle? In "Applied Ethics" (E. R. Winkler and J. R. Coombs, Eds.), pp. 390–415. Blackwell, Oxford, UK.

Leake, C. D. (1927). "Percival's Medical Ethics." Williams and Wilkins, Baltimore.

Rachels, J. (1980). Can ethics provide answers? *Hastings Center Rep.* **10**(3), 32–38.

Spicer, C. M. (Ed.) (1995). Appendix: Codes, oaths and directives related to bioethics. In "Encyclopedia of Bioethics" (W. T. Reich, Ed.), rev. ed., pp. 2599–2842. Simon and Schuster–Macmillan, New York.

Veatch, R. (1995). Medical codes and oaths: I. History; II. Ethical analysis. In "Encyclopedia of Bioethics (W. T. Reich, ed.), rev. ed., pp. 1419–1435. Simon and Schuster–Macmillan, New York.

MEDICAL ETHICS, HISTORY OF

J. Stuart Horner
University of Central Lancashire

GLOSSARY

empiric One who practices medicine or surgery without scientific knowledge.

Enlightenment A movement of social change which began in France in the 18th century.

ethics The science of human duty in its widest sense.

etiquette The conventional rules of behavior in polite society.

gynecology The study of diseases in women, especially the female reproductive system.

medicine The practice of allopathic healing, i.e., the administration of drugs in sufficient dosage to change the body's natural physiological mechanisms.

obstetrics The practice of special skills among women before, during, and after childbirth, usually when some abnormality exists.

regulars Those physicians who were mostly university trained and who followed a "scientific approach" to the practice of medicine

regulation A system of control designed to enforce general rules of behavior.

rules of consultation A code of behavior when more than one doctor is involved in the care of a patient.

MEDICAL ETHICS is not a static term. Its meaning and its principal concerns have changed over time in response to the way that medicine has been regulated as a profession, to the way medical care has been provided and financed, and principally to cultural changes taking place outside medicine in society as a whole.

An historical review must therefore be firmly anchored in a particular period of time and usually a geographical location. The development of medical ethics in Europe has been used to illustrate the principles concerned since, while American medicine has developed in a very different cultural and financial context, there have traditionally been close links between the United States and the United Kingdom. Particularly in the 19th century there appears to have been considerable cross-fertilization of ideas and concepts between the two, although the solutions reached were fundamentally different. Medical ethics is sometimes confused with bioethics, which is one facet of the subject, but which has dominated the agenda for the last 30 years. Since this aspect of medical ethics is particularly influenced by philosophy, legal concepts, and cultural factors, it should surprise no one that different approaches are adopted, both within America and within Europe. Other reference works should be consulted to trace the history of medical ethics in other cultures, such as Africa and Asia.

The practice of medicine has always had a unique capacity for both benefit and harm. Its practitioners would not find it difficult to conceal the death of a patient whether accidentally caused or deliberately induced. They are likely to be privy to information which could seriously prejudice the status of leaders in society. Their skills could be used to conceal an unwelcome pregnancy. For these, and many other reasons, the practice of medicine has usually been associated in most cultures with some form of regulation. This may be either external, usually by the priesthood or by the state, or it may be internal by the profession itself. Essentially medical ethics, or a "code of conduct" for doctors, depends upon the system of regulation which is adopted.

I. THE REGULATION OF MEDICINE

The early history of medical ethics was studied by McIlrath, who concluded that primitive man had a very rigid code of ethics and followed it with great care and fear. The moral basis seemed to be environmental and social factors. In more organized cultures, however, external regulation of medicine was exercised either by the priesthood or by the state.

A. Religious Control in the Ancient World

In ancient Persia a high code of professional behavior was demanded of physicians, but the Zoroastrian religion tied the concept of disease so closely to sin that it was impossible to look elsewhere for causes and cures. Similarly, religion had a stultifying effect on the development of medicine in India.

In some cultures religious control was exercised in conjunction (and possibly in competition) with state control. In central America, for example, religion made a powerful impression on medicine. However, ethics did not depend on religion and the law demanded cruel punishments for the use of black magic by specialists in medical sorcery. Indeed, there were attempts to develop a school of medicine apart from the priesthood,

but the power of the priests prevented this right up to the Spanish Conquest. In Mesopotamia, the physicians were trained in schools attached to the chief temples, yet in Assyria a particularly comprehensive system of state control was established. Similarly McIlrath found that Chinese medicine attempted to do away with magic and irrational methods of treatment. The doctors evolved rules and advice to help the younger men approach their patients and colleagues in as ethical a manneer as possible. He concluded, however, that Confucianism strangled the development of Chinese medicine, surgery, gynecology, and obstetrics. At the same time the state itself had a great interest in medicine. A concept of confidentiality did not exist, since in China physicians were required to report cases of illness to the state.

The pattern, therefore, seems to be an attempt, sometimes with state encouragement, for the profession to try and escape from magical methods but to fall increasingly under the control of state religion. Ancient Egypt is, however, a good example of a system where such a process went into reverse.

Control by the priesthood was not always malign. During the dark ages Jewish doctors were widely praised both ethically and clinically. They were always in demand for the treatment of the most serious cases despite a prohibition by the Christian church. Similarly, the followers of Islam were encouraged to search the past. Arabic doctors successfully transferred Greek thought to the western world, even though Islamic medicine itself declined.

B. State Control in the Ancient World

In Babylonia and Egypt medicine was practiced subject to strict state regulation. The Code of Hammurabi, which dates from about 1727 B.C., is the first attempt by any culture to protect patients from incompetent doctors. It was largely concerned with surgical procedures with very detailed rules and major punishments. Abortion was a very serious matter and the Assyrian laws were particularly strict but probably based on the laws of property. The Incas passed laws requiring that medical practitioners should be properly qualified as both surgeons and physicians. As long ago as the 10th century B.C. all doctors in China were required to pass state examinations before they could practice.

In Egypt there appear to have been specialists who were providing free treatment by 56 B.C. They worked to ancient rules and if they failed to do so and the patient died, the doctor would be tried by law with death as the penalty. Doctors were, nevertheless, treated with great respect and appear to have treated their patients kindly as well as developing a system of ethics on which modern ethical codes continue to be based. This advance seems to have declined under the influence of the priesthood. McIlrath asserts that in Coan times, between the sixth and the fourth century B.C., a diploma was needed before a doctor could take up the position of state physician, and women and slaves were forbidden to practice. This limited form of state regulation obviously did not extend to the actual practice of medicine since most writers quote Athens as the antithesis of Babylonian and Egyptian state regulation. Rome was plagued by slave doctors and quacks, and, despite the existence of a state medical service, no attempt was made even to standardize medical training.

C. Self-Regulation— The Greco-Roman School

Asklepios was a physician hero born in the Thessalian city of Trikka, a descendant of Paeon, the ancient physician of the Gods. Mythology, however, takes the history back much further to 1400 B.C. In these stories Asklepios was born to Koronis, snatched from her funeral pyre by his father Apollo, and given to Chiron to be educated. From this source he learned about the medicinal plants which formed the healer's arts. He also learned about the secret powers of the snake, which was to form the central feature of the Asklepian cult.

The first cult center, or Asklepion, was established at Epidauros, where magical practices involved the induction of sleep in special chambers and the use of the healing snake.

II. THE HIPPOCRATIC TRADITION

Hippocrates, who was born on the island of Kos and died at the age of 93 years in 377 B.C., represents not only a direct descendant from the Asklepian tradition but the first major departure from it. He introduced scientific observation and recording followed by deductive reasoning in medicine. His emphasis that the physician's great duty is to do no harm has remained the cornerstone of medical ethics down the centuries. McIlrath sees in him the physician who demands the right to view disease dispassionately and calmly, free from both religious beliefs and philosophical speculations.

It is a sad irony of history that about the time of the death of Hippocrates an Asklepion was established on Kos surrounded by a sacred forest of cypress trees so

that local guide books confused the two. Hippocrates almost certainly disapproved of the mystical religious cult of Asklepios. He saw medicine as a technical art, learned by careful observation and thought, rather than a religious rite. It was the practitioner's duty to develop, by practice, his competence in these technical skills. He almost certainly disapproved of the priestly mysteries which the Asklepion practiced.

It was precisely because of Hippocrates' objections to these mystical practices that most scholars now accept that he could not have formulated the ethical code which bears his name. That code invokes the sacred names of Apollo and Askelepios, the very mysteries which Hippocrates rejected in the writings that can safely be attributed to him. Carrick notes that the oath was also written in the wrong dialect. Moreover, the ethical values it contains were not those of contemporary practice. Some authors suggest a later Pythagorean origin.

In the time of Hippocrates there seems to have been little regulation of medicine. The Hippocratic writings forthrightly state that

> although the art of healing is the most noble of all the arts, yet, because of the ignorance both of its profession and of their rash critics, it has at this time fallen into the least repute of them all. The chief cause for this seems to me to be that it is the only science for which states have laid down no penalties for malpractice. Ill repute is the only punishment and this does little harm to the quacks who are compounded of nothing else. Such men resemble dumb characters on the stage who, bearing the dress and appearance of actors, yet are not so. It is the same with the physicians; there are many in name, few in fact. (Chadwick, J., & Mann, C. W. (1978), p. 68. Harmondsworth, UK: Penguin Books)

The lack of regulation and the consequent freedom enjoyed by Greek physicians brought with it the opportunity for medical experimentation and the chance for progressive advances in patient care. Nutton believes that it would be wrong to conclude that a professional and philosophical ethic displaced entirely a religious sanction for medical practice. There was, however, no state or professional examination before practice.

The Hippocratic School was probably the first to attempt to establish a code of behavior for the medical profession and to define the doctor's obligations. These were to ensure that medical knowledge was used for good and not for ill, and secondly not to exploit the doctor's privileged relationship with his patients in any way. Hippocrates began to be idealized after the second century A.D. both as a skillful, dedicated, and upright medical practitioner and as one with views on pathology, physiology, anatomy, and physics. Although Galen (born A.D. 129) later became the chief authority on anatomy, physiology, and pathology, Hippocrates remained preeminent in medical ethics.

III. EARLY CHRISTIANITY AND HIPPOCRATIC MEDICINE

The early Christian church had an ambivalent attitude toward the practice of medicine. The feeling seems to have been mutual. Temkin notes that Galen had praised the Christians for their morality but censured Christianity for its emphasis on faith rather than reason. Resort to medicine was seen by many Christians as demonstrating a lack of faith. Jesus, after all, had spent part of his ministry healing the sick, and the early Christians had done the same. Philo was the first Christian to condemn the use of medicine, but Tatian (A.D. 155) believed that even taking medicine was wrong since it put trust in matter. This restriction did not, however, apply to diet or surgery. Christians gradually began to associate the Greek pantheon, including Asklepios, with demons, although Christian doctors retained their ethical allegiance to Hippocratic foundations.

Temkin believes that what distinguished the sincere Christian doctor from the pagan was a new relationship to his faith and its church. There was no fundamental change in his professional ethics. It is often supposed, for example, that selfless devotion without consideration of personal danger was a peculiar contribution which Christianity made to medicine. But this is not so. Doctors were not held in high regard in the ancient world and were expected to take on medicine's risks and unpleasantness long before philosophical notions of philanthropy made an impact. Hippocratic writings were gradually absorbed by Christian writers, e.g., St. Augustine. Throughout the world of pagans and Christians, Hippocrates represented the autonomy of medicine as a sphere of life. Even though many Hippocratic practices have been discarded, the principles associated with his name have stood the test of time and remain as relevant today.

IV. APPARENT STAGNATION

The thousand years between the fall of Rome and the European Renaissance have been difficult ones for med-

ical historians to document, particularly for those whose primary interest is medical ethics. Recent scholarship has cast some light into otherwise dark and shadowy corners. Knowledge of Hippocrates and Galen continued in the eastern Roman Empire until the seventh century and beyond. Saint Jerome (late in the fourth century) wrote a letter of advice to a priest in northern Italy in which he reveals a general familiarity with some Hippocratic teachings. The regulation of physicians in the early Middle Ages seems to have borrowed much more from Hippocrates than from biblical or clerical authorities. There were some efforts to regulate medicine by the state. The Germanic law codes of the Visigoths insisted that a freeborn woman should only be treated in the presence of one or more of her relatives. Similarly, the Ostrogothic kingdom of Italy may have had a state code. Generally, however, in the rest of Europe scientific medicine sank to a low ebb.

After the fall of Alexandria in 642 A.D., Greek learning began to spread rapidly among the Arabs. High ideals were the code of the whole profession. Often, but not always, they held no legal sanction but were passed on by teaching or guilds. Nevertheless, a series of manuscripts show that the classical ideology of Hippocrates was preserved in the monasteries. Many writers trace a revived interest in Hippocrates to Salerno presumably because Emperor Frederick II required its medical students in 1231 to attend lectures on Galen and Hippocrates. Paraphrases of some Hippocratic works reappeared at Salerno in the 11th century and at Toledo where Gerard of Cremona made translations a century later. Between 1280 and 1300 A.D. in the Universities of Montpelier, Bologna, and Paris the original works of Galen and some Arabic texts were translated. This led to greater intellectual rigor which distinguished physicians and surgeons as university educated from the *empirics* who learned largely "on the job." As a result there was a far more technical approach to the patient involving history, examination, and diagnosis. What later became known as medical ethics probably had this technical, intellectual origin.

An example of this process may be found in the work of Gabriele de Zerbi. Many great figures in medical ethics wrote at a time of great institutional or political change and Gabriele de Zerbi was no exception. The growth of university-based medicine was being resisted by the Venetian College of Physicians, which was seeking to wrest power from the Universities of Padua and Venice in licensing medical practice. Zerbi was a philosophy teacher at Padua from about 1467. In 1495 he published his little book, *De Cautelis Medicorum*, which set out to define a sound ethical doctor. He believed that the learned medicine in the universities was the best form of practice and all the others were therefore unethical. Zerbi's "advice to medical men" was designed to benefit the individual but also to enhance the status of the group. Doctors were to be solemn and sober, to have a large prominent house, and to mix with the common people only professionally (and as briefly as possible). They were to mix with the social elite, not to accept hopeless cases, and to take their fees early but not be greedy. A second opinion should be sought if the patient was likely to die. If called in by another doctor one should "close ranks" and support him. Zerbi was critical of the empirics who have "no knowledge of universals." Inevitably it was considered ethical to practice only the "proper" kind of medicine (one's own!) and unethical to do otherwise.

Hippocratic works began to figure prominently in European universities in the 14th century in Latin, and the aphorisms of Hippocrates were available in the vernacular by the 16th century. Forgeries were, however, a problem. The medieval Hippocratic writings revered by physician and layman alike exercised an almost continuous influence on medical theory and practice for nearly a thousand years. In contrast later monastic manuscripts reveal an increasing preoccupation with practical matters of dress, etiquette, and fees.

V. MEDICAL ETHICS IN EARLY MODERN ENGLAND

The controversy between Zerbi's university-trained physicians and the Colleges reappeared in London in 1518. Those physicians who had invested time and money in learning about the medicine of Hippocrates and Galen naturally saw the Royal College in London, which was created in that year, as their institutional home. However it held no monopoly in the practice of healing. Even royalty consulted the empirics. Mothers and wives cured and cared for the most serious of illnesses and many wise women were consulted by the poor. Indeed an act of 1542/1543 (sometimes referred to as the "Quack's Charter") did permit other forms of healing to be practised by empirics.

Christianity provided medicine with a different set of ethical values to those of classically trained physicians, and this difference was to create regular conflicts. Christians recognized a charitable duty to the poor as part of the Christian religious ministry. Many wives of the clergy ministered to the sick and it was a minister who organized the celebrated

quarantine of the plague village of Eyam in Derbyshire in 1665. In contrast learned physicians were seen to be greedy and money grabbing. Nicholas Culpeper in 1659 complained that physicians would not come to a poor man's house who is not able to give them their fee, and the London College felt obliged to set up charitable dispensaries.

In 1585 Richard Bostocke emphasized the heathen and unchristian origins of classical learned medicine. Unorthodox practitioners, often using Christian values, advertised that their remedies were milder and less dangerous than those of the faculty. William Walwyn, the Leveler, in his *Physick for Families* (1669), described his medicines and their cures as "Kindly and Powerful" rather than being "hazardous, painful and dangerous." Thomas O'Dowde used the Christian model of the good physician and even cited Mark 5:26—"she had suffered a great deal under the care of many doctors and had spent all she had, yet instead of getting better she grew worse" (New International Version)—on the title page of his book, *The Poor Man's Physition or the True Act of Medicine*, published in 1665. Both the Christian and the Hippocratic doctor agreed that the patient should not be harmed. The disagreement lay in what was good for the patient and what constituted harm. Thus, not only was the type of training and practice of medicine an ethical issue, but the types of remedies—both medical and surgical—were also the subject of vigorous ethical debate.

In the 17th century patients moved easily between different types of practitioners and ignored the rhetoric that sought to demonstrate that the members of a particular group were the sole practitioners of "proper medicine." Indeed how could anyone make a judgment? There were no statistically based clinical trials and, in retrospect, it can be seen that most of the treatments used by orthodox practitioners were either useless or downright dangerous. Blood letting, for example, was almost a standard procedure whatever the illness. Benjamin Rush (1746–1813), the so-called "American Hippocrates," had exorbitant faith in blood letting. American *regulars* followed his example and bled copiously. The practice of the empirics made sense to the average layperson. It was analogous to the centuries-old practice of offering remedies to family and friends; indeed it is worth remembering that family remedies were sometimes equated with empirical medicine. Physicians were seen as attacking both.

However, empirics and physicians were not clearly and sharply defined. Some empirics were learned men and used that learning for publicity purposes. Equally some physicians, such as Thomas Sydenham (the "English Hippocrates"), used empirical methods while others such as Boyle were not averse to publicity.

Within the classical tradition the situation was also changing in the light of new found scientific discoveries in anatomy and other basic sciences. In the 16th and 17th centuries Galen's theories began to be dismissed, while Hippocrates' reputation began to grow. Sydenham, born in 1624, described Hippocrates as an "unrivalled historian of disease" who had founded the art of medicine on a solid and unshakeable basis. Yet the admiration for Hippocrates was not so much for the anatomy and the physiology of the treatises, as for the detailed and meticulous clinical observations, and the example he set of the doctor's devotion and concern for his patients, together with his uprightness and discretion in his dealings with them.

These disputes in medicine were taking place against the enormous social upheaval of the English Civil War, and the profession could not expect to continue quietly with its own ethical squabbles. Various attempts appear to have been made to create a universal medical care service. This national health service, conceived three whole centuries before its actuality, was clearly motivated by the charitable Christian ideas of the time. Even the practitioners were to be embued with charity rather than profit! Changes in the health care system always have an effect upon medical ethics.

One such reformer was Peter Chamberlen, a Baptist and Fifth Monarchist and Fellow of the Royal College of Physicians, from which he was expelled in 1649. He attributed this expulsion to his practice of administering free medical aid to the poor of London. Another radical, Noah Biggs, believed that orthodox medicine was guilty of malpractice and urged Parliament to consider reform. He used religion as part of his condemnation of the cruelty of learned medicine and argued that orthodox Galenic medicine was itself responsible for disease.

Indeed three distinct strands may be discerned during this period of religious ferment (1640–1660): (1) a rejection of Galen and his medical theories as being of heathen origin; (2) those who doubted whether medicine had any contribution to make at all and who saw healing as a direct spiritual manifestation of God; and (3) those who believed that medicine had a contribution to make but believed that urgent medical reform was necessary to broaden access to its services by including those healers who were not university trained.

Thomas Sydenham saw it as a Christian duty to "improve medicine" by basing it on "research" at the bedside. Sydenham's methods were more like those of the empirics than university-trained doctors and he was criticized for this. Following the restoration of King Charles II, Sydenham (a parliamentarian) was obliged to work with the poor because his political views prevented the usual custom of working with a small group of high-class patients. In consequence he saw large numbers of patients with the same disease and had more opportunity to experiment with treatment. By studying diseases rather than individual patients and noting by trial and error what worked and what did not, Thomas Sydenham was returning beyond Galen and the university tradition to Hippocratic methods.

Legal control of medical excesses was limited. Medical ethics were not codified law and the English legal system was (and perhaps still is) hostile to the codifying tendencies of the continental Roman law tradition.

VI. THE MANNERS OF MEDICAL ETHICS IN 18th-CENTURY ENGLAND

By the beginning of the 18th century there was little or no reference to Hippocrates or to a specific ethical code for doctors in England. Medical ethics concentrated on manners, including dress, deportment, etc. These were the days when one had to look like a doctor. It was an age where fashion reigned preeminent. Both quack cures (which were widely advertised by both regular medical practitioners and others alike) and the treatments of medical men themselves inclined to the exotic. Medicine was based on the master–apprentice model and codes of conduct were inculcated through this relationship.

The new learning heralded by the Renaissance had marked the reemergence of the scientific study of disease which Hippocrates had pioneered. There was a similar renaissance in Hippocratic ideals and of ethics. Nevertheless, the Enlightenment failed to deliver the great expectations for "the relief of man's estate" which the triumphs of the new philosophy and the scientific revolution had promised. Such a judgment seems harsh when the *Philosophical Transactions* of the Royal Society record no less than 220 reports of surgical conditions between 1727 and 1778. Clearly these surgeons were seeking to report their experimentation and experiences to a wide audience of intellectuals in order to broaden the base of general knowledge. Medicine did not, however, wholeheartedly embrace Enlightenment thinkers in the early 18th century. Many eminent physicians explicitly criticized Locke's secularized understanding of the mind and used a model of the human mind which was quite different from, and even diametrically opposed to, Locke's formulation. They did so largely because they wanted to refute monistic materialism and defend the Christian religion.

Disputes between doctors could be conducted in a very public manner. Henry Bracken of Lancaster, a man-midwife, entered into a very public and ultimately unsuccessful dispute with Dr. Christopherson involving the treatment of four patients. He was quite ready to criticize both trained practitioners and boastful quacks and was himself openly criticized for his vanity to patients. This very public dispute may indicate why interest in medical ethics was renewed at the end of the 18th century. It was a time of rapid change in the practice of medicine. There were a number of related factors which are highly relevant in Western Europe, and perhaps America, today:

1. Rapid commercialization was destabilizing the traditional professional hierarchy
2. New medical institutions (the hospitals) were posing fresh problems regarding professional power, collective responsibility, and the division of labor
3. Gentlemanly codes of conduct were proving insufficient for doctors
4. The state, the administration, and the law courts offered few leads and little guidance

By 1770 an ethic based on manners was dead partly because it was seen to be insincere, partly because it was criticized by Scottish Enlightenment thinkers, and partly because of the changing context of medical practice. One interesting example of this is the development of "man-midwifery." The 18th century witnessed a revolution in childbirth practices following, it is believed, the (secret) development of the obstetrical forceps. Previously a women-only ritual, childbirth became—at least among the well to do—the exclusive preserve of male practitioners. Roy Porter comments that

> in America, medical midwifery developed under the influence of William Shippen (1736–1808) who had studied in London with William and John Hunter and under Cullen and Alexander Monro II (1733–1817) in Edinburgh. Shippen taught anatomy and midwifery in Philadelphia from 1763, helping to establish the domination of male operators that became so conspicuous in the USA. (Porter, R., 1995, pp. 430–431. *The Western Medical Tradition* Conrad, L. I., Neve, M., Nutton, V., Porter, R., Wear A., (Eds.) Cambridge/New York, Cambridge University Press)

Four powerful advocates in 18-century England profoundly influenced the ethical response to these wider changes which were taking place.

A. John Gregory

Born in 1724 in Aberdeen and educated in Edinburgh and Leyden, John Gregory has been described as the first modern figure in Anglo-American medical ethics. He became professor of philosophy at Aberdeen between 1747 and 1749 and moved briefly to London before returning to establish a Philosophical Society in Aberdeen. He published his *Lectures on the Duties and Qualifications of a Physician* in 1772, a year before his death. This work considers confidentiality; taking seriously suggestions by the patient; truthfulness, especially if the prognosis is doubtful; and not abandoning dying or hopeless cases. He encouraged students to put patients first during consultations and to dress and behave as a physician. He believed that the chief moral quality of a physician is humanity and that a gentleness of manners and a compassionate heart are needed. His emphasis upon sympathy with the patient was based on the work of David Hume who believed that "sympathy generates within us the very same feeling that another person has." By sympathizing with a patient we share his desire to be relieved of his suffering. Gregory knew both Hume and Adam Smith, who developed the major alternative variant of the concept. Gregory's unique contribution was to apply these philosophical concepts to medicine as a counterbalance to the skepticism of the Scottish Enlightenment.

B. Thomas Gisborne

Thomas Gisborne was born in 1758 and became a leading Church of England writer on ecclesiastical topics. He was vigorously opposed to the utilitarian philosophies of his contemporary, Jeremy Bentham (1748–1832), and of John Stuart Mill, who formed the Utilitarian Society. But Gisborne died in 1846, 15 years before Mill published *Utilitarianism*.

In 1794, while Thomas Percival was working on his *Medical Ethics*, Gisborne produced his major and highly influential work, *An Enquiry into the Duties of Men in the Higher and Middle Classes of Society in Great Britain, Resulting from Their Respective Stations, Professions and Employments*. It passed through six editions over the following 17 years. Gisborne gave much attention to ethical behavior and medical practice. It is no surprise to learn that he was a close friend of Thomas Percival although not perhaps sharing his political philosophies. Gisborne was particularly concerned that medical professionalism should not subvert common fellowship and Christian charity. While recognizing that physicians must build their careers in a competitive market, he believed that it was vital that ambition should always be governed by strict propriety.

Gisborne's text revealed much that was unethical about contemporary medical practice. His criticism of the "sick trade" was very similar to the almost contemporary and far more radical analysis of Thomas Beddoes.

C. Thomas Beddoes

Born in 1760, Thomas Beddoes worked in Bristol and was particularly concerned about ethical standards in medicine. He proposed that quackery should be outlawed and standards for basic medicines established, almost a century before a reluctant parliament accepted their necessity. He also believed that doctors were encouraging consumption of their services and pursuing wealth at the expense of their patients. Such practices are a feature of market-led health care services in our own day. Beddoes also criticized "the patient knows best" philosophy and "demand-led" medicine. He concluded that informed choice is a myth and therefore a true market in health care cannot exist.

D. Thomas Percival

These contributions to medical ethics are largely overshadowed by the later work of Thomas Percival. Born in Warrington in 1740, Percival was part of a wider Whig reform movement of dissenters which eventually won control of Manchester from the Tory Anglican clique which had controlled it. In the 1790s reformist power began to wane and Percival's rules were probably designed more to defend and perhaps preserve a passing order (a not uncommon feature of "medical ethics"). Percival was in the tradition of "virtue ethics." He was interested in how the virtuous physician should behave in private practice and in public politics. Percival acknowledges four sources for his own work:

1. An advisory committee which assembled rules of conduct used by hospitals in England and Scotland
2. Dr. John Gregory
3. The Reverend Thomas Gisborne
4. Comments by 25 people of different disciplines to whom he sent his earlier work, "Medical Jurisprudence"

Percival saw the physician as a quasi-public servant; hence his prohibition on attending duels (which were illegal) and the physician's duty to help the court by giving full and honest evidence. It may also be seen in his perceived duty to provide free medical certificates for civic obligations but to be paid for private certificates. He believed that doctors alone should judge ethical issues and based his code on consideration of actual cases considered by the advisory committee. In a century of manners, criticism of patient care was considered to reflect upon the care of the caregiver. If treatment was changed the first doctor had effectively been slandered for giving "wrong treatment." This inevitably led to personal acrimony between individual practitioners. Percival's response was to submit the dispute to collective decision making by requiring complainants first to submit their grievances to the "faculty." This was Percival's unique contribution since "the ethics of personal honour and virtue had dominated secular ethics for centuries." (Baker, R., 1993, p. 208. *The codification of medical morality.* Dordrecht/Boston/London: Kluwer Academic Publications) In effect he anticipated the process of medical audit by almost 200 years.

Chauncey-Leake was largely responsible for the myth that Percival was only concerned with professional etiquette. In fact Percival distinguished the two very clearly and explicitly states that ethical duties take precedence. Although he did not write rules for regulating formal associations of professionals, the Boston Medical Society used Percival's language to draft their own rules in 1808. Percival's text was widely (but selectively) used in the United States between 1808 and 1846 when the American Medical Association began to draft its ethical code based on Percival's work. As Pickstone aptly comments, "had Percival not existed . . . the Americans would have had to invent him." (Pickstone, J. V., 1993, pp. 162–163. *The codification of medical morality.* Dordrecht/Boston/ London: Kluwer Academic Publications) The case is much less clear for British medicine, although by 1849 British practitioners were well aware of developments in the United States. Indeed there was considerable interchange in Anglo-American ethics between 1765 and 1865. Burns comments that "in fashioning their ideals American physicians borrowed many but not all of the values offered by the British doctors." (Burns, C. R., 1977, p. 303. *Legacies in Ethics and Medicine.* New York: Science History Publications) They also added Benjamin Rush's ideas on the responsibilities of patients! Moreover, Worthington Hooker published a book in Connecticut in 1849 which had a significant influence on British medical ethics.

VII. THE MEDICAL PROFESSION AND THE FIGHT AGAINST QUACKERY

Medical ethics during the 19th century in the United Kingdom and, to a lesser extent, in the United States was dominated by a relentless battle against quackery. Quack medicine grew in the capitalist individualistic culture which the 18th century readily provided. Whether or not quack medicines did much good, they showed sensitivity to customer demand, a demand which they were partly responsible for creating. It was sometimes difficult to distinguish quacks from trained medical practitioners. Both often used similar methods and neither was averse to advertising. Some, like the Quaker practitioner Thomas Hodgkin, or Thomas Beddoes, or James Adair, urged their colleagues to adopt higher ethical standards.

By the late 18th century ordinary regular practitioners, both provincial apothecaries and small town surgeons, began to mount an agitation for the reform of medicine which would effectively outlaw quackery. By the early 19th century this movement had become a determined attack. The medical profession was exhorted to put itself in order by refusing to endorse patent medicines and advertising. Early records of the British Medical Association show that it was virulently opposed to any hint of connivance with those who practiced "peculiar forms of healing." Individual members were punished for giving the remotest comfort to those not practicing allopathic medicine. These other forms of healing were regularly criticized at the Association's annual meetings. Gradually quackery changed from providing a counterfeit service to a series of fringe movements, offering other explanations for disease and providing alternative forms of healing, such as homeopathy and herbalism.

The passage of the Medical Act in 1858 in the United Kingdom might be assumed to mark the end of this process. In fact the battle continued, at least until 1886 when the General Medical Council at least acquired real powers to control admission to the profession, the training of its practitioners, and the supervision of its conduct. It was, however, almost another century before the Council acquired a specific remit to advise on ethical matters.

Yet despite this impressive success in the fight against quackery, the first ethical section held by the British Medical Association at its annual meeting in 1895 could still find matters of concern. It proposed that quackery should be the subject of detailed supervision. It even proposed that the Association should become the controlling body! It further deplored the lack of 'esprit de corps,' a frequently repeated complaint for over 100 years. It recommended that the employment of unqualified assistants in visiting was against the public interest and it urged that all forms of advertising should be prohibited. Indeed the battle to eliminate quackery was not finally abandoned until 1930, when the British Medical Association reluctantly agreed that the regula-

tion of unqualified practice in the United Kingdom was simply not acceptable to Parliament.

VIII. DOCTORS' RELATIONSHIPS WITH EACH OTHER AND WITH THE STATE

Throughout the 18th and 19th centuries medical writers bemoaned the fact that doctors were likely to criticize one another, often in very public ways, apparently in an attempt to gain commercial advantage. Thomas Percival had urged an alternative approach, with all the doctors in a particular locality or an institution working together to promote the interest of medicine as a whole. These arrangements included fee cartels. By the beginning of the 20th century the British Medical Association had recognized that formal methods were required to resolve disputes between individual doctors and to seek to regulate the conduct of doctors in particular situations. An extensive network of ethical committees was therefore created throughout the country to adjudicate on such disputes, following a complaint by a medical practitioner. Such efforts occupied a great deal of the time of the new Central Ethical Committee, established by the Association in 1902.

In 1908, after 3 years of debate and discussion, the Association published its "Rules of Consultation." These sought to regulate the circumstances in which a second opinion was sought. Most medical practitioners at that time carried out a complete spectrum of medical care, from general medicine, through general surgery, to practical obstetrics. Some worked as full-time specialists in the hospitals, but an important section combined the two. A member of the latter group might be called in by a practitioner for a second opinion, only for the patient to desert him (they were usually "him") for the general medical practice undertaken by the specialist practitioner. The rules can be dismissed as a minor matter of medical etiquette. More correctly, they created an ethical model which has become the dominant one in British medicine.

Various forms of medical services were beginning to develop, which disrupted the agreements reached by the profession itself. The state began to provide free health services for school children, expectant mothers, and young babies. Various forms of occupational medicine were developed in some of the larger factories.

A. General Practitioners and the Public Health Service

These relationships were a constant source of friction and a frequent area for ethical debate from the inception of the school health service in 1908 to as recently as 1983. Clearly the problems changed after the creation of the National Health Service in 1948, but were no less persistent, despite the removal of commercial competition. A frequent source of complaint was referral by a school medical officer to a hospital-based consultant, some of whom were themselves initially employed by the school health service itself. They undertook a wide variety of investigations and procedures, including surgery. Clearly the general practitioner had to be informed in order to provide continuing care, while the school medical officer was responsible for the educational implications of any abnormalities found or treatment undertaken.

B. Occupational Medicine

Similarly the occupational health services provided a total range of care for employees. The general practitioner could discover that his patient had had an operation without him being aware of it, although he was usually asked to provide follow up care. Over time a more restricted role for occupational medicine has evolved, in which industrial medical officers provide only emergency prehospital care for conditions occurring on site.

C. Advertisement

The medical profession in the United Kingdom has always vigorously opposed any form of advertising by its practitioners. This probably emanates from its rejection of quackery, which thrived on advertising. Right up to the present day complaints occur about alleged excesses, even though the profession has gradually taken a more relaxed attitude to its initial total prohibition. In the 1990s the government insisted that the profession allow advertising to take place, although most practitioners remain reluctant to use their newfound freedoms.

D. Local Insurance Committees

An Act of Parliament passed in 1911 created the "panel doctor" system for general practitioner care. The latter formed contractual relationships with local insurance committees and the contract was interpreted by local medical committees set up under the Act. Nevertheless, ethical problems continued to be reported to the Central Ethical Committee. Some insurance committees offered unattractive contracts, which were boycotted by the local doctors. Occasionally an outsider would enter into such a contract, whereupon the local medical practitioners would usually take out an ethical dispute against the newcomer. These were either resolved through the profession's local machinery or, in exceptionally difficult cases, referred to central headquarters in London.

E. The National Health Service

When the state finally took responsibility for health care and became in effect a monopoly employer for all medical care staff, the character of the ethical problems once again changed.

No longer was the problem a matter for doctors alone. Most disputes did not in fact arise from contractual problems, although there were a number of bitter struggles earlier in the Service's history. Increasingly the major ethical problem was concerned with the level of funding for the Health Service itself and the legitimate actions which doctors could take to influence the position. Was industrial action acceptable and, if so, of what type? In 1977 a report was issued clarifying the ethical responsibilities of doctors when rationing decisions affected their personal care of individual patients.

IX. THE EMERGENCE OF BIOETHICS

The emergence of bioethics is usually associated with the successful kidney dialysis in 1960 of Clyde Shields by Dr. Belding Scribner in Seattle. From this point onward moral philosophers began to find the moral dilemmas faced by doctors to be a fertile area for study. Such problems had occurred previously. In 1937 the Matrimonial Causes Act in England and Wales required the doctor to choose between a husband and wife, both of whom might be his patients. Similar problems occurred in the early 1960s, when child abuse began to be recognized and effectively diagnosed.

The medical profession seemed surprised by this emerging interest in bioethics, since these dilemmas did not figure prominently in its own ethical debates. Passage of the Abortion Act in 1967, for example, occurred with almost no serious ethical debate within the profession itself, in spite of the fact that the Act directly challenged a prohibition cherished since Hippocratic times. For a time moral philosophers seemed to have these discussions to themselves, with doctors only marginally involved.

As the arguments were dissected in finer and finer detail, the profession began to recognize that some of the conclusions reached were simply incompatible with clinical realities. It was by no means clear when philosophers were merely developing a hypothesis and when their deliberations were actually intended to create ethical rules which doctors could follow. In America institutional ethics committees have been developed on which a wide spectrum of interests may recommend, or even decide, how the responsible doctor should proceed in a particular ethical dilemma. These developments were taking place in a climate of renewed emphasis on the patient's autonomy.

Lawyers were increasingly emphasizing that patients must be fully informed of the decisions they are being asked to make, and this challenged the doctor's traditional task of acting in the patient's best interests. Moreover, bioethicists appeared to be adopting an increasingly amoral position, which doctors found neither helpful nor useful. Gradually quiet acquiescence with legal and philosophical concepts has given way to active antagonism. Doctors do recognize a difference between killing patients and allowing them to die. Even if the law does allow organs to be removed without it, doctors still prefer to enlist the support of relatives. Clinical choices offered to patients or their relatives still tend to err on the side of caution to a greater extent than would be usual in philosophical debate.

X. CONCLUSION

History shows that medical ethics is a constantly evolving process. Different aspects of the subject come into greater prominence at different times in response to the organization of health care, philosophical and legal debate, and advances in medical technology. Despite the present ascendancy of bioethics, the stage is already set for the wheel to turn again at the beginning of the new millenium.

Also See the Following Articles

BIOETHICS, OVERVIEW • MEDICAL CODES AND OATHS • MEDICAL ETHICS, USE OF HISTORICAL EVIDENCE IN • NURSES' ETHICS

Bibliography

Baker, R., Porter, D., & Porter, R. (Eds.) (1993). *The codification of medical morality* (Vol. 1). Dordrecht/Boston/London: Kluwer Academic.

Carrick, P. (1985). *Medical ethics in antiquity.* Dordrecht/Holland: Reidel.

Conrad, L. I., Neve, M., Nutton, V., Porter, R., & Wear, A. (1995). *The western medical tradition 800 BC to AD 1800.* Cambridge: Cambridge Univ. Press.

French, R., & Wear, A. (Eds.) (1989). *The medical revolution of the seventeenth century.* Cambridge: Cambridge Univ. Press.

Porter, R. (1989). *Health for sale—Quackery in England 1660–1850.* Manchester: Manchester Univ. Press.

Porter, R. (Ed.) (1995). *Medicine in the Enlightenment.* Amsterdam/Atlanta, GA: Rodopi.

Temkin, O. (1991). *Hippocrates in a world of pagans and Christians.* Baltimore/London: The Johns Hopkins Univ. Press.

Wear, A., Geyer-Kordesch, J., & French, R. (Eds.) (1993). *Doctors and ethics: The earlier historical setting of professional ethics.* Amsterdam/Atlanta, GA: Rodopi.

Wilson, A. (1995). *The making of man midwifery—Childbirth in England 1660–1770.* London: UCL Press Limited.

MEDICAL ETHICS, USE OF HISTORICAL EVIDENCE IN

Urban Wiesing
University of Münster

I. From the Development of Events to Morality
II. From Morality to the "Stories"
III. Of the Benefit and the Disadvantage of Medical History

GLOSSARY

antibioethics movement A movement that rejects all types of bioethical debates, mainly located in Germany.

Hippocratic oath The promise made by doctors, part of the antique Corpus Hippocraticum.

history (The study of) Events or developments in the past.

philosophy of history Philosophy of the developments of events and the writing of histories.

principlism The area of ethics relating to principles such as beneficience, autonomy, nonmaleficence, and justice.

FOR VARIOUS REASONS the relationship between the history of medicine and medical ethics should be illuminated. On the one hand, affirmative historical references cannot be eliminated from the medical–ethical discussion: no other academic discipline refers to such a long-lasting ethical tradition as medicine with its Hippocratic oath. On the other hand, the medical–ethical discussion, especially the German-speaking one, feeds on the references to historical misdeeds of medicine in a critical manner. The confusion and turmoil in the "Antibioethics Movement" cannot be understood without knowledge of the crimes of the physicians during the Nazi era.

Both examples confirm that history serves as an argument throughout the medical–ethical discussion. To act in medical ethics unhistorically would "require at least a linguistic restraint, for we would be committed to get on with a fragment of our vocabulary and grammar" (A. C. Danto, 1965, *Analytical Philosophy of History*, pp. 7–8. Cambridge Univ. Press, Cambridge).

First, the typical double meaning of the German-speaking term *Geschichte* should be considered. *Geschichte* means the "development of events" as well as their description—events as well as their stories. Each of the two different meanings has a different relationship to medical ethics. Hence, what roles the historical development of events and the historical descriptions have to play in medical ethics must be examined separately. If at all possible, how can medical ethics profit from history in its double sense? This can only be answered against the background of a broader theoretical context.

If history were understood as the product of historians, namely, the description of former events, the question could not be answered without knowing how stories are reasonably written and with the help of which criteria they value. If history were understood as the development of events, the question could not be answered without a materialistic philosophy of history. One would have to know the development "history as such" takes and the consequences for moral decision-making that can be drawn from it.

At first, three propositions that concern the relationship between the history of medicine and medical ethics, and that consider history in the sense of the "development of events," will be discussed. All three theses try to combine history and ethics systematically. But convincing arguments will show them to be untenable. Nevertheless, they are used frequently although implicitly in reasoning, as well as in medicine.

I. FROM THE DEVELOPMENT OF EVENTS TO MORALITY

A. First Thesis

As far as the first thesis orients itself toward the natural sciences, it seems to represent—at least for its scientific part—the way modern medicine sees itself: "Mankind develops continuously from a lower to a higher level in sciences as well as in morality over time"; this development has operated throughout history, which "as a universal history turns all histories into one, into a single history of progress and perfection of mankind" (O. Marquard, *Apologie des Zufälligen*, 1987. p. 56. Stuttgart: Reclam). Under these philosophical premises the apparent deviations from continuing progress cause special difficulties, which, however, can be made to fit with the help of ingenious tricks, such as historical dialectics.

Insofar as the development of history has been realized and described correctly under these premises, the business of ethics is eased enormously concerning its questions of foundation. The value of a norm can be determined by its historical provenance. A norm is a good one when it can be assigned to a higher level in the determined development of history or when it accelerates this course. A norm is to be considered immoral when it hinders the development of history or is assigned to a lower level.

The person who acts in a morally sound manner surely would be in a correct position as regards the inevitable progress of history. More than this, progress determines the morally sound action. And because under these premises mankind becomes more and more civilized—although occasional relapses are taken into account—this understanding of history ennobles the present in principle—especially the avant-garde, as well as the sciences.

But the positivist understanding of history can be criticized by convincing arguments in science as well as in morality. It is very doubtful whether the history of all human beings can be interpreted under only one aspect. Even if things—especially in medicine—only seem to be getting better in view of technological development, the continuing scientific progress can be doubted, as voiced by Ludwig Fleck (1896–1961) and Thomas Kuhn (1922–1996). According to Kuhn science develops itself with the help of changing paradigms that do not always proceed as rationally and positively as many scientists and physicians would like to believe. A postpositivist philosophy of history calls into question a linear progress of knowledge.

If even science advanced continuously it would not be possible to draw a parallel to morality. In addition, believing in the moral history of the perfection of mankind, one pays for the security of morality with an unworthy and therefore immoral relationship to the past. Hence, the past must be assigned to a lower level of morality than the present because morality is continually getting better.

With this understanding of history, it can be explained, for example, why Friedrich Schiller (1759–1805), in his inaugural lecture, talks about "children of different ages, ... which stand around one adult." Their only historical purpose consists of serving as a preparation for the present: "All the preceeding ages have made efforts to bring about our human century—without knowing it or aiming at it" (F. Schiller, 1789. In *Sämtliche Werke* (G. Fricke and H. G. Göpfert, Eds.), p. 754. Wiss. Buchgesellschaft, Darmstadt).

Schiller's statement refers the past and its human beings to a determinated relationship that serves only as a purpose for the present, and it instrumentalizes and incapacitates them. It does not grant the past and the person who thinks differently an intrinsic value; it evaluates and judges them from the perspective of the present only. This is inadmissable, and such a debasement is out of the question.

An evolutionary approach to ethics is inevitably confronted with the same difficulties, as Marquard emphazises:

The universal history—as a theory of the emancipatory revolutionary avant-garde and as a theory of the social evolution—declares the human being to be a triumphant living thing: to be a glorious protagonist of the land of freedom or, at least, to be the current carrier of the yellow trikot of the tour de l'évolution, the world's championship of the art to be left over. But this leads to the fact that the human being rejoices while triumphing over other human beings at the same time. (Marquard, 1987, 64)

Besides the difficulties of a philosophy of history, the belief in continual moral progress can be weakened by citing historical examples. The "dialectics of the enlightenment" can be easily supported with the names of a few cities—the twentieth century is by no means immune to atrocities. In addition, it would be absurd to talk about continual moral progress in medicine: the Hippocratic oath is more than 2000 years old, while the latest version of the Declaration of Helsinki is only a few years old. However, no one will judge the oath because of its age to be inappropriate and the declaration because of its youth to be appropriate.

In short, the thesis of continual scientific and moral progress is not tenable, and the historical origin of a norm as well as its relationship to the admitted development of history does not say anything about its validity.

B. Second Thesis

A second thesis concerning the relationship between history and morality could be the following: There exist timeless, or, to say it in more detail, timelessly valid, moral norms in medicine. In this context the Hippocratic oath is mentioned most often, or more restrictedly the Hippocratic ethos, because single passages of the oath thwart this argument.

This thesis does not argue only with historically constant norms, but also with norms from beyond history—history can develop as it will, but certain norms remain valid. And if the timelessly valid norms were recognized, the business of foundation in medical ethics would be released somewhat from its difficulties. The question of how well founded a norm is equals the question of how exactly the timelessly valid norm is recognized: the moral judgment is transformed into a historical–epistemological one. Reflection upon whether the recognized norms are still up-to-date would be unnecessary, because they are—if recognized correctly—timelessly valid and require an exclusive claim for their truth. Certain discussions that are considered annoying because of their obtrusive recurrence would be brought to an end once and for all.

But exactly this strategy of circumvention should be avoided because moral judgments cannot be substituted by others because of their peculiarities. Even if there are enticing alleviations for ethics under these premises, the thesis of timelessly valid norms should be rejected

for methodological reasons, for how is an observer of the past, and therefore an observer of past *time*, able to recognize something *timelessly* valid? This is impossible—every philosophy of history with this claim will be confronted by the convincing criticism of a theory of knowledge.

Within medicine the citing of supposedly timeless norms only glorifies the medical profession and medicine: "the eternal law," "the holy medical ethos," "the timeless figure of the physician itself"—all these conceptions contribute more to a dogmatic darkening. They oppose a relevant deepening by presenting themselves as unimpeachable and by stylizing their being doubted as a sacrilege from the beginning. These phrasings tend to prevent inquiries, and inquiries especially seem to be a virtue in the ethical discussion—and in view of new challenges they seem to be necessary. In short, one should not talk about timeless or timelessly valid norms.

C. Third Thesis

As a third thesis regarding the relationship between history and morality, a weakened version of the second thesis, is of interest: There have always been certain historical norms in medicine that will also be valid in the future.

The first part of this statement can be supported empirically, but with reservation—certain medical norms in the European tradition have been widely held. After an extensive examination of medical vows, Roth found that certain constant obligations recurred even in different political systems: fundamental helpfulness, *primum nil nocere,* protection of human life, respect for the patient, medical confidentiality and virtuous behavior, faithfulness toward the medical school, cooperation, and an obligation to further education. The fact that medical practice as regards morality has developed quite differently can be traced back to the clear difference between the mere establishing of norms and their efficiency in practice, but this is not the problem discussed here. Despite all the differences within medical practice, Roth talks about a *deontologia medici perennis*.

What can be gained from this empirical knowledge? Is the statement, "There have always been certain norms in medicine over the time known to us, which will also be valid in the future," verified by this? Despite the historical insistency of certain medical norms, the second part, the conclusion, can only be considered with caution; one has to distinguish precisely in this case. Is the second statement justified by historical laws—the norms will be accepted furthermore because of laws—or is it not justified at all; i.e., should the existing norms simply be accepted in the future because they always have been accepted in the past?

The first case—the continued existence of traditional norms because of historical laws—promises enormous alleviations in ethics and a high degree of ethical security, because the person acting in accordance with the norms would become a knowing executor of secure historical laws. But the moral question, once again, would be turned into a historical-epistemological one, which, as mentioned before, is improper. Moreover, historical laws have to be explained before they can be used, and this hardly seems possible.

However, in view of the skeptical objections against the great outlines of systems in the history of philosophy, such as the teleology of the spirit in German Idealism or the teleology of history in Marxism, it is highly questionable, and can hardly be maintained, that history in its totality proceeds in accordance with laws that we know and from which we can infer the future.

History proceeds, to express it fashionably, more chaotically, and cannot be grasped by a theory. Only short- or middle-term reactions can be reconstructed with reservation. If laws in the universal development of history exist, we do not know them. Practical experience supports this insight into the history of philosophy: social-scientific prognostication from historical knowledge is always vague. Hence the statement, "There have always been valid norms in medicine that will be accepted in the future as well as because of historical laws," is untenable in many regards.

In the second case—"in the future the norms that were acknowledged until now should be valid, because it was always like this"—one does not use history as an argument without providing another argument; this is a classic case of traditionalism and can be translated roughly as, It has always been like this and therefore it should remain like this.

In some cases this attitude may lead to quite intelligent results; in view of an increasing "speed of aging" (Lübbe) a certain dullness or even narrow-mindedness toward short-lived trends may be reasonable. But despite a possible situative adequacy, traditionalism as a moral-philosophical maxim is not sufficient, especially in times when, because of technological developments, new questions are always appearing. To declare historically given norms to be valid unreflectedly offends the basic self-esteem of the human being at latest since the enlightenment and proves to be improper in view of new challenges.

Hence, we hold the following for the third thesis: even though for the European tradition an extensive insistence of certain medical norms can be shown de-

scriptively, one still has to examine their validity for the present. And this is what cannot be done by the supposed development of history.

Nevertheless, many authors try to establish a compelling relationship between history and morally sound behavior. The occurence of that simple and false conclusion in large numbers indicates a high interest and an equivalent high degree of uncertainty. "A *horro vacui* drives them to fill with theorems also those fields on the intellectual globe of our knowledge that would be kept blank by those persons who certainly know that there is nothing certain to know" (H. Lübbe, 1973, *Geschichtsphilosophie und politische Praxis*. In R. Kosellek & W.-D. Stemple (Eds.), *Geschichte—Ereignis und Erzählung*, pp. 224. Munich: Fink). In view of the need of regulation and the differentiation of basic convictions—in view of the "moral stress"—it is understandable but still illegitimate to try to achieve moral stability by simple false conclusions. And the enticing alleviations in ethics certainly will not appear. The development of history—this has to be kept in mind—provides no direct solutions for ethical questions. Moral decisions apparently are not connected systematically with the development of history, or such a context cannot be shown philosophically.

This insight corresponds to the historically provable disappearance of the topos *Historia magistra vitae*. On the one hand Koselleck could use the fundamental comparability of the past with the present as an explanation for the long presence of this topos until the eighteenth century. This comparability has not been postulated exactly since the French Revolution promised to introduce an uncomparable new age. In addition, according to Koselleck, the disappearance of the topos can be observed at the moment that history in the singular—thinking of the development of events—replaced history in the plural—thinking of the description of the events; in a moment when history meant both "development" and "story." History itself, "in a meaningful singular without attributed subject or object," without any repeatable exemplarity could not serve as a teacher. It pushed—determining and being determined at the same time—everything forward in accordance with a plan that was yet to be discovered, and it became a legislator. One could not learn from this kind of history, but could only act in its name. The narrated, exemplary past lost its plausibility as a teacher through the laws of the development of history. "History as a single occurence or as a universal context of events was not able to teach the same way as a history that is considered to be an exemplary report" (Koselleck, 1989. Historia Magistra Vitae, Über die Auflösung des Topos im Horizont neuzeitlich bewegter Geschichte. In R. Kosellek (Ed.), *Vergangene Zukunft,* p. 48. Frankfurt: Suhrkamp.

But exactly the alleged laws of history are called into question in the recent philosophy of history. "The substantial [*materialen*] philosophers of history from all directions—whether idealistic or materialistic, naturalistic or cultural—all retreated in favor of a scientific historiography" (Schnädelbach, 1987. Vernunft und Geschichte. Vorträge und Abhandlungen, p. 15. Frankfurt: Suhrkamp). The philosophy of history restricts itself to clarifying the reasonable writing of "histories" as such—the plural cannot be avoided here. "Its capacity for rationalizing does not refer directly to history any more, but to the rational instructions of the science of historiography" (Schnädelbach 1987, p. 16). Therefore it does not seem to be hopeless to reexamine and question the topos *Historia magistra vitae* regarding its credibility under these conditions.

II. FROM MORALITY TO THE "STORIES"

In order to have some positive answers to the question of the beginning—the relationship between history and morality—we can now consider the second meaning of history: the linguistic description of the past in the sense of "stories," the products of historians. Furthermore, it seems proper to reduce the expectations toward a possible interconnection between morality and history right from the beginning: when moral decisions do not result directly from the development of events for principal reasons, it is impossible to deduce them directly from historical knowledge. But with these reduced expectations the question remains whether historical knowledge can contribute indirectly to moral decisions. In order to answer that question, a change of perspective would be useful. Under the changed concept of history in the sense of "story," the relationship between history and ethics in medicine is illuminated from the perspective of ethics.

First, the tasks of ethics should be explained. Birnbacher (1993. Welche Ethik ist als Bioethik tauglich? In J. S. Ach & A. Gaidt (Eds.), *Herausforderung der Bioethik*, pp. 45–67. Stuttgart Bad Canstatt: Frommann-Holzboog) ascribes four closely related tasks to ethics: analysis, criticism, construction, and moral pragmatics. This should be explained:

1. "Analysis means the clarification and reconstruction of moral concepts, arguments, and procedures of foundation, and the revealing of implicit premises and components of meaning with the aim to produce transparency, comprehensibility, and self-understanding" (Birnbacher, 1993, p. 45). This task serves as a starting point for the second task:

2. To criticize "moral concepts, foundations, viewpoints and requirements for truth regarding general cognitive standards such as clarity, unambiguity, explicity, consistency, and plausibility" (Birnbacher, 1993, p. 45).

3. Construction is considered to be the main task and is at the center of attention most of the time: ethics must construct moral norms; it must formulate and justify normative approaches and it must develop possible solutions for certain moral problems.

4. The last task, moral pragmatics, is generally neglected. Ethics must consider moral pragmatical questions: it has to endeavor the conveying, the practical conversion, the motivation, the sanctioning, and the institutional embedding of these questions.

From this perspective one can ask which achievements concerning single tasks can be made by historical knowledge.

A. Analysis

An analysis of given conditions without historical knowledge prevents profound insight into the constellation of problems. One could be tempted to consider ethical problems as unhistorical events. In this case, historical knowledge is almost imperative in order to sharpen the consciousness that ethical problems have a historical genesis and in order to reconstruct discovered conditions in their genesis. The first task of medical ethics cannot be completed with an ahistorical proceeding.

B. Criticism

Concerning the criticism of existing conditions one has to keep in mind that moral criticism is only possible with moral arguments: "A moral judgment can only be criticized normatively by another moral judgment" (p. 17, E. Tugendhat 1993. Vorlesungen über Ethik. Frankfurt: Suhrkamp). In this sense historical knowledge provides only little support: the perspective of the criticism can be raised to a higher viewpoint, it can be put into a broader context, and it can be removed from the direct consternation. Now justifiable, even urgently required criticism as well as unjustifiable, "steril excitement" can be identified. Historical knowledge can warn and sensitize for threatening or imperceptible developments. In addition, it can reduce the deceitful hope for a simple moral solution by historical references.

C. Construction

Which function can history take on concerning the central task of medical ethics—the construction of moral norms? As mentioned before, it is obvious that a moral norm cannot be constructed only on the basis of historical knowledge. However, without historical knowledge—and this is the antithesis—no intelligent construction of moral norms can succeed. This is supported by at least three arguments, although they are weak:

1. Even if one refuses to admit the laws of history in the development of morality or denies the possibility of recognizing them, the fact remains that there is a partial and exemplary wisdom in the past that can be recognized and mediated. Single answers developed in the past can turn out to be appropriate, intelligent, plausible, and morally acceptable under circumstances of the present. Under this precondition one has to ask which structures have remained in relationship to actual problems, which have changed, and which answers of history can serve a practical and reasonable shaping of contemporary medicine. With this kind of proceeding reservations have to be kept in mind: for historical answers can be adopted for the present only if the basic conditions are comparable. The exemplary wisdom of the past has to be considered with skepticism in that moment when the context cannot be compared. At this point it must be mentioned that the principle *Historia magistra vitae* persisted as long as the comparability of the circumstances, the "potential similarity of earthly events" (Koselleck, 1989, p. 40) was given. Moreover, no further fundamental argument can be made, in accordance with which it would be impossible to be more intelligent in the present than in the past and to find a morally better solution. Hence, the partial intelligence, the historical example, is to be transfered to the present only with reservation and only in an examined individual case.

2. As a second argument for the use of historical knowledge in the construction of moral norms, those developments should be considered that we do not want to give up and that we call—somewhat pathetically—"historical achievements"; we possess certain norms that people during earlier times did not possess, that should by no means be given up, and that should be further realized in future. The best example is that of human rights. Even though human rights are still violated everywhere, they are a normative standard that should be maintained. Historical achievements are contingent products of history, which somehow came into being and which we do not want to give up.

But in the moral–philosophical debate historical achievements can only be used as a restricted argument. For as far as they cannot be derived with certainty from the course of the historical development—and just this possibility has been denied from the beginning—their validity can only be justified by a moral decision, and this decision is always made in the present. This means that historical achievements unfortunately are always built of sand: what happens when the majority of people—no matter why—thinks differently about these achievements and wants to do without them?

3. As a third argument for the consideration of historical knowledge in the construction of moral norms we should keep in mind the approach of several medical–ethical theories toward this task. They often start out from present intuitive convictions and plausibilities, they try to clear them up, to systematize them, and to build an ethical system on them; they work in accordance with the "reconstructive model" of ethics, as it came to be called (Birnbacher, 1993). Even though it is controversial whether a "reconstructive model" is suitable for medical ethics or—as Birnbacher requires—whether different models have to be adopted, some theories of medical ethics do in fact follow the reconstructive approach, such as the ethics of principles, which is widespread and extensively worked out in the Anglo-Saxon language area (Beauchamp, T. L., & Childress, J. F. 1994. *Principles of Biomedical Ethics* (4th ed.). New York and Oxford: Oxford University Press.). This way an ethics of principles avoids the difficulties of the final foundation offering principles of the medium level that are acceptable and are widely accepted—mainly the principles of autonomy, beneficence, nonmaleficence, and justice.

This approach is useful because as a practical science medicine has an ambivalent relationship to the final foundation of moral norms. Admittedly, norms that are justified this way—as far as they can exist at all—would strengthen the moral basis of medicine. But in view of the notorious disagreement of moral philosophy, medicine should not wait until undeniable norms with the highest quality of foundation are delivered from there—contrary to expectation—because until now no one has been able to name undeniable norms that are convincing to all. However, medicine is not able to do without norms; it seems to be pragmatic and useful to begin with principles of the middle level and range, which can be considered plausible and acceptable.

Wolfgang Wieland's theory of medical ethics follows a reconstructive approach as well. He begins with the traditional role of the physician and he examines the changes and the challenges of this role. The reconstructive approach is supported by his conviction that every moral regulation is confronted with institutions, which already exist and which do not permit the transposition of moral norms in a trivial manner. Wieland calls it an *Institutionsaporie* (aporia of institutions). An absolute new beginning is not possible because of given historical structures, and therefore ethics is always confronted with historically grown institutions.

What can historical knowledge contribute to a reconstructive approach? First of all, one should clearly keep in mind that a reconstructive way of proceeding in ethics is not based only on historical knowledge, because otherwise it would restrict itself to historical–empirical psychology or the sociology of morality. Ethics wants to do more: it wants to declare norms valid, which is not possible with an exclusive reference to the past. With a reconstructive approach, however, historical knowledge gains special importance. This approach states more precisely the facts given while discussing its genesis, thus illuminating the indispensable starting point.

D. Moral Pragmatics

We consider only very briefly the question of which achievements can be made by historical knowledge for the fourth, mostly neglected task of ethics, namely moral pragmatics. Most of this can be deduced from what has been said before.

Historical knowledge can indicate that in history nothing has changed yet where the difficulties of mediation between ethical theory and medical practice are concerned and that most probably nothing will change (Wieland, 1989). Concerning morally pragmatical questions one could turn—with advisable caution—to the examplary prudence of the past, which can at least be assumed to be useful. The main question would be which pragmatic rules in history have proved to be practical and appropriate? A historical-pragmatical basis of medicine does not offer evidence for certain norms, but it expresses a certain attitude toward the problem of how a moral basis can be achieved (Wiesing, 1995. Zur Verantwortung des Arztes. Stuttgart Bad Cannstatt: Frommann-Holzboog). Searching through history to support ethics is already a preliminary decision for a certain attitude toward history that excludes a completely ahistorical one.

Insofar as morality cannot be deduced systematically from the development of events or historical knowledge, a historical-pragmatical basis stands between dogma and arbitrariness and it necessarily implies some degree of a decision (*Restdezisionismus*). Because this *Restdezisionismus* is formally inevitable it has to be justified as to its contents. Consequently, we identify ourselves in a normative intention with a particular tradition of our own culture (Schnädelbach, 1987, p. 61), which we assume to have a certain degree of practical intelligence and appropriateness. The function of the historical knowledge for ethics—as described before—would be similar to the function of an interesting and very informative text. In this case history is a readable text that can be decoded and can stimulate, as F. Fellmann (1991. Geschichte als Text. Plädoyer für die Geschichtsphilosophie. *Information Philosophie* Heft 4, 91, pp. 5–14.) puts it. Even without systematic development the narrated past is still capable of exemplary intelligence and can illuminate the given convictions in its genesis with the help of the reconstructive approach. Hence, the current moral decision cannot be directly deduced from historical knowledge. History cannot provide solutions for moral questions, but a solid solution without historical knowledge is hardly imaginable. Therefore, the history of medicine is not only a readable text, but also a text that is worth reading for its medical-ethical discourse.

III. OF THE BENEFIT AND THE DISADVANTAGE OF MEDICAL HISTORY

Even though the relationship of history and ethics can be explained in this sense on a theoretical level, it does not provide protection from the dangers of concrete application. One should be warned of the illusion that one can learn from history with certainty and without damage; for historical knowledge in medical ethics is a double-edged sword: it can be used appropriately and at the same time it can cause damage. This becomes obvious when the characteristics of "stories" and their useful criteria are considered more closely.

Whereas one can use the term "correct" in reference to the technical level of historic research, history as a readable text makes different ways of reading a text possible without regarding one way or the other as the correct one. If we want history to contribute to ethics in the way described before, the main problem will be the lack of knowledge of history. Ignorance of the historical facts or knowledge gained by standards other than the common methodological ones are the best precondition in order to coerce history and to abuse it for any possible argumentation. Therefore, a reference to historical knowledge should be adequately profound. The level of historical interpretation, however, is always afflicted with the difficulty that a definite interpretation cannot be found. One need consider the plausibility of interpretation. Hence, using historical knowledge in medical ethics remains a moment of incalculability that challenges the power of judgment. Siefert's 1973 appell has not lost its meaningfulness: The historian is "responsible for the proper use, but also for the abuse of historical sources in the discussion of his age. He fails when he is silent in a critical moment" (Siefert, H. 1973. *Der hippocratische Eid—und wir? Plädoyer für eine zeitgemässe ärztliche Ethik: Ein Auftrag an den Medizinhistoriker,* pp. 7–8. Frankfurt: Carl-Ernst Kohlhauer).

As far as historical knowledge is considered a readable text, it underlies the same danger as other texts that are both readable and worth reading—they can be used in a proper or an improper manner, and they can be beneficial or they can cause damage. Profound historical knowledge, precise following of the historical method, sensitivity for the difficulties of historical interpretation, and clarity about the relationship of ethics and history should make it possible to avoid damage and to use the advantages. The scientific professionalism of the medical historian is demanded.

Also See the Following Article

MEDICAL CODES AND OATHS

Acknowledgment

Revised translation by Eva Maria Laurenz of Zum Verhältnis von Geschichte und Ethik in der Medizin. *Internationalen Zeitschrift für Geschichte und Ethik der Naturwissenschaft, Technik und Medizin* 3 (1995), pp. 129–144, with kind permission of Birkhäuser Verlag, Basel.

Bibliography

Beauchamp, T. L., & Childress, J. F. (1994). *Principles of biomedical ethics,* (4th ed.). New York and Oxford: Oxford Univ. Press.

Birnbacher, D. (1993). Welche Ethik ist als Bioethik tauglich? In J. S. Ach & A. Gaidt (Eds.), Herausforderung der Bioethik pp. 45–67. Stuttgart Bad Cannstatt: Frommann-Holzboog.

Fellmann, F. (1991). Geschichte als Text. Ein Plädoyer für die Geschichtsphilosophie. *Information Philosophie,* Heft 4, 5–14.

Kosellek, R. (1989). Historia Magistra Vitae. Über die Auflösung des Topos im Horizont neuzeitlich bewegter Geschichte. In R. Kosellek (Ed.), *Vergangene Zukunft,* pp. 38–66. Frankfurt: Suhrkamp.

Lübbe, H. (1973). Geschichtsphilosophie und politische Praxis. In R. Kosellek & W.-D. Stempel (Eds.), Geschichte—Ereignis und Erzählung, pp. 223–241. München: Fink.

Roth, G. (1977). Die ärztlichen Eide und Gelöbnisse seit 1918. Eine Typologie des Nachwirkens des Hippokratischen Eides. *Arzt und Christ* 23, 163–178.

Schnädelbach, H. (1987). *Vernunft und Geschichte. Vorträge und Abhandlungen.* Frankfurt: Suhrkamp.

Siefert, H. (1973). *Der hippokratische Eid—Und wir? Plädoyer für eine zeitgemässe ärztliche Ethik: Ein Auftrag an den Medizinhistoriker.* Frankfurt: Carl-Ernst Kohlhauer.

Wieland, W. (1986). *Strukturwandel der Medizin und ärztliche Ethik. Philosophische Überlegungen zu Grundfragen einer praktischen Wissenschaft.* Heidelberg: Carl Winter Universitätsverlag.

Wieland, W. (1989). *Aporien der praktischen Vernunft.* Frankfurt: Vittorio Klostermann.

Wiesing, U. (1995). *Zur Verantwortung des Arztes.* Stuttgart Bad Cannstatt: Frommann-Holzboog.

MEDICAL FUTILITY

Loretta M. Kopelman
East Carolina University School of Medicine

GLOSSARY

absolutely futile Something lacking any instrumental value for achieving some goal or purpose, or as a means to some end.

Best-Interests Standard The standard that, all other things being equal, directs us to select from among options what most informed, rational people of good would regard as maximizing net benefits and minimizing net harms.

contested cases of futile or useful treatments These are (a) grounded in medical science, (b) value laden, (c) at or near the threshold of utility, and (d) burdensome.

instrumental value Something useful or important for achieving some goal or purpose, or as a means to some end.

intrinsic value Something esteemed or important in and of itself.

major medical goals Traditional medical purposes include enhancing people's well-being through opportunities of prevention, diagnosis, or treatment of disease, pain, death, or disability, or by restoration of function.

presumably or virtually futile Something almost certainly lacking instrumental value for achieving some goal or purpose, or as a means to some end, because of its extreme implausibility or repeated failure.

qualitatively futile Something that may achieve some goal or purpose, but one that is unimportant, being neither instrumentally nor intrinsically good.

MEDICAL FUTILITY is a topic that involves judgments about the futility or utility of medical care. These assessments influence whether people can obtain interventions allowing them to live, die, or flourish. Consequently, deeply felt views may surface among patient, doctors, nurses, and family members about what treatments are useful or futile. These disputes raise issues about the clinician–patient relationship, resource allocation, informed consent, communication, empathy, relief of suffering, autonomy, compassionate care, and our duties to people with a very poor quality of life.

After examining what is meant by medical futility in the contested cases, we consider four important ways for resolving these disputes. As we shall see, some favor giving authority in the contested cases (a) to doctors (the physician autonomy model); (b) to patients or their representatives (the patient or surrogate autonomy model); or (c) to what most people in a society approve (the social approval model). Still others reject giving final authority to any one group, favoring (d) a consensus forged from many sources including consideration of clinicians' views, established liberties, social needs, and how most people want to be treated (the overlapping consensus model). In the last section, we consider how our disagreement about what is medically useful or futile may result from incommensurate moral convictions about our duties to incompetent people who have a very poor quality of life. The Best-Interests Standard has been used to resolve disputes over medical futility when the patient is incompetent. Critics charge, however, that the Best-Interests Standard should be abandoned because it: (a) is not objective, (b) may be abused, (c) denies hope, (d) violates the duty to respect the sanctity of life, (e) is unknowable, or (f) is too individualistic. Each of these objections seems problematic, and asking what is best for the incompetent person remains a valuable way to help resolve some disputes about medical futility.

I. THE MEANING OF MEDICAL FUTILITY

If we ask if something is futile, we need to inquire, "Futile for what?" Things can be useful or futile as means to different ends. To be in one's home during the last days of life may be futile from the perspective of prolonging life, yet useful for giving comfort. Thus, depending upon one's goal, something's utility or futility may change. Medicine has various important goals, such as preserving life and relieving suffering. Our disputes may arise from how we rank these values when they conflict. Some hold that prolonging biological life, even permanently unconscious life, is intrinsically valuable and always the most important goal in medicine. Most physicians disagree, maintaining that this stance tends to give too little attention to people's autonomy, suffering, or quality of a life (K. Payne *et al.*, 1996. *Ann. Internal Med.* **125**, 104–110; L. M. Kopelman, A. Kopelman, and T. Irons, 1992. In *Compelled Compassion* (A. L. Caplan, R. H. Blank, and J. C. Merrick, Eds.), pp. 237–266. The Humana Press, Totowa, NJ).

A series of court cases revealed sharp controversies among clinicians, patients, or families about what is medically useful or futile (L. M. Kopelman, 1995. *J. Med. Philos.* **20**, 109–121). These disputed cases include that of Nancy Cruzan, a woman in a coma or persistent vegetative state (PVS) whose family wanted her feeding

tube removed; Baby Doe, an infant with Down's Syndrome whose parents did not want surgery to correct anomalies incompatible with life (Kopelman *et al.*, 1992); Baby L, with multiple disabilities including blindness, deafness, quadriplegia, and arrested development at the 3-month-old level whose mother insisted on maximal treatments; Helga Wanglie, a woman in a PVS whose family said she wanted maximal treatment; and Baby K, an infant with anencephaly (lacking a higher brain) whose mother insisted on maximal treatments; and Baby J, a severely mentally and physically disabled infant whose doctors refused treatments the parents wanted for their infant (F. H. Miller, 1994. *Lancet* **343**, 1584–1585). Examining these contested cases shows that disputes about medical futility are characterized by four features (Kopelman, 1995).

A. Grounded in Medical Science

The first feature these and other contested cases have in common is that they are *grounded in medical science*. These court cases about medically futile treatments arise in the context of standard medical care, so stable scientific information must justify claims about patients' diagnoses, treatments, or prognoses. Reliable information, for example, must support assertions that procedures will fulfill established medical goals such as prolonging life, restoring sentience, or relieving pain. Research and evidence helps distinguish which treatments are useful and which are futile in treating certain conditions. Clinicians should use the best available information to determine when treatments are ideal, standard, innovative, experimental, unverified, or utterly futile. As more information becomes available, our views sometimes change. Earlier disputes about the use of frontal lobotomies to treat severe psychiatric disorders, for example, were resolved with greater information that this procedure caused far more harm than good. Judgments about the utility or futility of medical therapies in the contested cases, then, must be supported by evidence and modified as the relevant evidence changes.

B. Value Laden

Judgments of medical futility, as used in these contested cases, are value-laden judgments incorporating estimates about something's utility relative to some goal, or whether the achievable goal is worth the effort. One person may value life at any price and want maximal therapy, while another believes there are worse things than death. In addition, both professionals and surrogates have many duties to patients, and these express values of respect, fairness, and beneficence (to do good deeds or prevent harm). Yet patients, surrogates, and clinicians may disagree about when therapies are useful or what quality of life should be supported. Disputed cases usually raise troubling questions about how to understand our duties or values, including what constitutes a benefit, and thus whether something is a genuine therapy for a certain condition. These contested cases also arise from concerns about how to fulfill traditional and sometimes conflicting medical goals such as relieving suffering, honoring patients' requests, prolonging life, and being compassionate.

C. At or Near the Threshold

Third, the disputed court cases are *near the borderline between what is considered useless and what is considered beneficial.* Treatments in the contested cases are neither absolutely nor presumably futile (like orthopedic shoes to treat PVS), or those requesting them would not be taken seriously. The dispute is often a matter of whether proposed interventions are qualitatively futile, or whether they achieve an important goal. For example, Baby L's mother understood her daughter would be blind, deaf, quadriplegic, and developmentally arrested at several months of age, but believed that it was paramount to keep her baby alive. In contrast, Baby L's doctors and nurses objected that these painful, life-saving treatments were futile, given her poor prognosis, as well as causing her suffering. Some also mentioned the costs of providing treatments with such dubious, or marginal, benefits.

The problem of distinguishing between the useful and the futile cannot be solved by a different cutoff, since no matter what threshold is selected, there will always be borderline cases. Moreover, the judgment that a treatment is useful or futile is often an amalgam of assessments of different burdens and benefits as measured on different parameters. For example, what is useful to relieve suffering may compromise respiratory function, and what is futile to prolong life for more than a few days may be useful so a family may gather for a death. Consequently, to say that there is no duty to provide futile treatments is an unhelpful guide in the borderline cases because what is contested is whether they are futile.

D. Burdensome

Fourth, these contested cases typically involve *physically, psychologically, or financially burdensome treatments.* If the treatment were merely futile, but not painful or costly, it might simply be provided. Suppose a patient mistakenly believes that he will be cured by getting a daily multivitamin pill. Honoring such simple requests might be very useful, but not because the vitamin itself is considered beneficial by clinicians. Rather, its utility might consist of respecting the patient's desires and lifting his spirits. In contrast, in the contested cases, treatments are generally painful, costly, or rare. Maximal treatment for someone in a persistent vegetative state, such as the previously mentioned cases of Nancy Cruzan and Helga Wanglie, are expensive. In the Cruzan case, the family thought maintaining someone in such a state was wrong, but the doctors insisted upon it. In the Wanglie case, however, the family demanded maximal treatment, and the doctors objected. Some not only opposed the expense of such treatments, but also believed that requiring such support imposed unreasonable suffering, costs, or emotional burden on caregivers or families.

Having clarified what we mean by medical futility, we can see why disputes about medical futility will continue as long as people disagree about patient's needs, resource allocation, how to rank values, or what to do in the borderline cases. Consequently, we turn now to consider alternative proposals for resolving these disputes fairly.

II. PROPOSALS FOR RESOLVING DISPUTES OVER MEDICAL FUTILITY

Ideally, health care choices should represent a socially acceptable consensus among doctors, nurses, and patients or their surrogates about what treatments are reasonable and best suited to the patient. This ideal cannot be fulfilled when, as in the contested cases, people cannot agree about the relevant facts, resource allocation, how to rank values, or what to do in the borderline cases. Several important proposals offer alternative ways of balancing professional norms and social needs with people's rights of self-determination. They give authority in the contested cases (a) to doctors (the physician authority model), (b) to patients or their representatives (the patient or surrogate autonomy model), (c) to what most people in a society approve (the social approval model), or (d) to an overlapping consensus forged from many sources including clinician views, liberties, social needs, and how most people want to be treated (the overlapping consensus model).

A. The Physician Autonomy Model

According to the physician autonomy model, physicians should have unilateral authority to judge what treatments are futile in the contested cases. For example, if a therapy is deemed *qualitatively futile,* or has failed consistently in analogous circumstances, doctors should decide unilaterally not to recommend it as an option and refuse the treatment if requested. There are, however, two very different versions of this view.

A *reductionist version* of the physician autonomy model holds that doctors should have unilateral control of decisions in the contested cases because these disputes over futility are reducible to factual claims in their area of expertise. Decisions about what ought to be done in the contested cases, on the reductionist version of the physician autonomy model, are definable by information about probabilities. If clinicians are experts about when something is quantitatively or absolutely futile, they reason, they should have unilateral authority to resolve disputes in the contested cases.

One difficulty for the reductionist model is that some cases are contested *because* there have been few cases reported from which to draw conclusions. A more fundamental logical problem concerns the difficulty of getting a conclusion about what *ought* to be done from premises stating what *is* the case. The reductionist model suggests that we can draw a moral conclusion about what we ought to do when treatments are minimally beneficial, from probability claims. This is very questionable. The next version of the physician autonomy model avoids the reductionist presuppositions that decisions about what ought to be done in the contested cases can be reduced to factual claims alone.

A professional equipoise version of the physician autonomy model also favors unilateral decision making by physicians but does not claim to eliminate values. Rather it relies upon established values within the medical profession. It acknowledges that some physicians make bad decisions about what is useful or futile, but focuses upon the recommendations of the community of physicians. Clinicians generally agree about what information is relevant and the proper goals of medicine, and this equipoise can offer a stable base for judgments about which treatments are useful or futile. The professional equipoise version of the physician autonomy model avoids the problem we encountered with the reductionist version of this model since it does not attempt to reduce moral decisions to probability claims. It employs values, namely the time-tested traditional goals of medicine to decide how clinicians ought to act. For example, most physicians do not regard main-taining someone in a PVS to be a goal of medicine (Payne *et al.,* 1996). According to the professional equipoise version of the physician autonomy model, doctors should have socially granted authority to refuse unilaterally to do what they consider futile.

This approach to decision-making authority has received social support in countries such as the United Kingdom. For example, *In re J,* the Court of Appeals in London supported the doctors' refusal to treat an infant who was mentally and physically disabled. Lord Balcombe wrote,

> I find it difficult to conceive of a situation where it would be a proper exercise of jurisdiction to make an order positively requiring a doctor to adopt a particular course of treatment unless the doctor himself or herself were asking the court to make such an order. (Miller, 1994, 1585)

The case of Baby K was treated very differently by a Federal Court of Appeals in Virginia. This court rules that doctors had a duty to provide respiratory support to an infant with anencephaly who came to the emergency department despite an explicit Virginia law giving physicians the ability "to refuse to provide treatment that the physician considers medically or ethically inappropriate." The ruling states,

> We recognize the dilemma facing physicians who are requested to provide treatment they consider morally and ethically inappropriate, but we cannot ignore the plain language of the statute [the Emergency Medical Treatment and Active Labor Act] because to do so would transcend our judicial function. (*In re Baby K* 16 F.3d 590 (4th Cir. 1994))

Critics argue that the physician autonomy model, in either form, promotes unjustified paternalism by allowing doctors to control information a reasonable person might want to make treatment decisions (D. Callahan, 1991. *Hastings Center Rep.* **21,** 30–35; R. M. Veatch and C. M. Spicer, 1992. *Am. J. Law Med.* **18,** 15–36). Medical paternalism may threaten the rights of people who, without pertinent information, have no means to exercise self-determination or to protect themselves, or their loved ones, from controversial or unjustified views. The doctrine of informed consent was developed because many people sought more information about their choices and wanted to participate in decisions about their treatments. Defenders of the physician autonomy model point out, however, that society relies upon doctors to make many unilateral decisions, including about which options should be presented to patients. Doctors must use discretion about who gains admission to the hospital, or to treatments, or what treatment options to discuss. Consequently, the charges that the physician autonomy model promotes undue paternalism seems to defenders to be misguided. The doctor's duty is to present the information that a reasonable person would consider material to his or her decision, and if the treatments are genuinely futile, these options should not be presented as options.

This defense by those favoring the physician autonomy model, however, is weakest precisely where there is greatest conflict: in the borderline cases. First, critics argue that the nature and scope of the moral and other values used in these contested cases raise doubts about physicians' claims of expertise to make unilateral decisions (Veatch and Spicer, 1992).

Second, the physician autonomy model presupposes that doctors generally agree about how to resolve contested cases, but this may be untrue. Baruch A. Brody and Amir Halevy examined the statements drafted by a variety of medical professional societies and found that major medical organizations express very different views and values (1995. *J. Med. Philos.* **20**, 123–144). Thus, they questioned whether a sufficient consensus exists about when treatments are medically futile to resolve properly most of the contested cases with unilateral decisions by physicians. Moreover, how would one identify the relevant doctors or community of experts in using the professional equipoise version of the physician authority model? Should the final authority be acclaimed investigators, hardworking clinicians, lay advocates, professional societies, or all of them? As we saw, the professional societies disagree about what constitutes medical futility. Moreover, if the information is so convincing that the treatment is futile, it is likely that administrators will limit physicians discretion; physicians may have very little opportunity to exercise unilateral decision making in such non-borderline cases, their role being supplanted by the administrative decision makers.

Third, agreement among physicians does not guarantee its moral justification. Physicians should agree because their position is worthy; it is not worthy simply because they agree about it. Their agreements might, for example, be wrong because they result from self-interest, bias, or ignorance. Agreement among some groups, then, cannot constitute the final moral appeal about what ought to be done. Despite these criticisms, the professional autonomy model captures the insight that doctors should play a central role in determining which treatments are medically futile.

B. Patient or Surrogate Autonomy Model

Another recommendation is that of the patient or surrogate model which favors giving patients or their representatives authority to decide what ought to be done in the contested cases. Contested cases frequently involve different ways of evaluating and weighing benefits and burdens that are often very personal. Physicians may be medical experts, but they are not experts about people's personal values about what makes life worth living or what constitutes their best interests. It is widely recognized, moreover, that competent patients have moral and legal rights to refuse treatment. When patients are incompetent to express those wishes, their surrogates often have authority to refuse treatments for them.

Patients, or their representatives, however, cannot justifiably interpret the right to refuse treatments as the right to *demand* interventions doctors regard to be futile. Yet, this is what appears to happen in the cases of Baby L and Helga Wanglie. Why do doctors provide futile therapies "on demand"? After all, patients and their representatives cannot usually demand and get such simple things as prompt service or food they like in hospitals; so how can they demand maximal, costly, and scarce treatments and get them? The answer again lies in the nature of the disputes about medical futility. In the contested cases, what patients or surrogates demand is usually close enough to the borderline of what is considered useful that their claims have force. For example, Baby L was extremely disabled, and her mother insisted upon continuing maximal life-saving treatments. The interventions were beneficial in the sense they were keeping her alive. According to the patient or surrogate autonomy model, in the absence of a social policy about what will or will not be provided to extremely disabled infants, these choices should depend upon the patient's or family's personal values (Callahan, 1991; Veatch and Spicer, 1992).

There are problems with this view. While self-determination is an important value, it does not necessarily result in a morally defensible choice in the disputed cases. Neither scientific nor moral reasoning is just a matter of opinion. Patients and surrogates sometimes express indefensible preferences. If adopted, reliance solely on patient and surrogate direction could (1) make patients suffer needlessly; (2) make professionals act in a way they consider against their conscience and harmful to patients; (3) drive up health care costs; (4) thwart efforts to enact justifiable rationing policies; and (5) hamper triage decisions. Thus, patient and family preference cannot be the final appeal in determining the most morally justifiable position since personal opinion alone does not establish a moral, or scientific, justification.

While it seems problematic to give families, or their surrogates, total authority in these contested cases, this model captures the insight that they should have a central role in shaping these decisions. Patients and surrogates generally bear the consequences of medical decisions, and some options suit certain people better than others. Often the surrogate or family sees itself as defender of the patient in an impersonal institution. Nancy S. Jecker and Lawrence J. Schneiderman (1995) argue that people who want "everything done" rarely desire unlimited or inappropriate technical treatment (1995. *J. Med. Philos.* **20**, 145–163). More likely, they fear abandonment for themselves, or their relatives, or grieve about the anticipated loss of identity through their own death, or that of someone they love. Typically, they want to understand what is happening, and be treated with compassion and respect. We need to minimize conflicts that generate the contested cases and emphasize good communication and compassionate care for patients and families.

C. Social Approval Model

Another proposal of the social approval model is that a social agreement is a morally defensible way to settle what ought to be done in the contested cases. The will of the majority could settle which treatments will be regarded as futile or useful in a certain society or community, thus deciding for themselves how to use their own resources, given their values and priorities. Based upon what most people approve when using public funds for health care within their communities, they generate priorities and recommendations that social agreement should be the basis for resolving disputes. This model, however, would result in the loss of autonomy for both patients and doctors. Either doctors or patients may find something to be useful when the community finds it futile. For example, patients and doctors may view expensive treatments to gain another year of life for a cancer patient to be of great value, while the community using other criteria may decide it is not.

The general problem with the social approval model is that people's agreement may reflect the society's inherent prejudices, mistakes, or unjustifiable biases. A socially approved model could unfairly deny goods, benefits, or services for certain racial or religious groups, or neglect gender-specific illnesses. People might also use democratic means to decide that costly interventions should not be used to treat people with drug addictions, sports-related spinal injuries, or psychotic disorders. Disabled people also experience a great deal of unreasonable prejudice and often need special protections. The *majority,* in short, may overestimate the pain of living with disabilities, use poor information, be unjustifiably biased, or simply gamble that they will never need certain costly services. The goal in moral decision making is to establish and carry out a morally defensible policy or action, not perform the statistically most popular act.

Because social agreements can be wrong, they cannot be the final arbiter of moral disputes. Wide social agreements about policy, however, are important if one hopes to gain public support for them. So while they are not the final appeal, social agreements should play an important role in finding good solutions about how to decide contested cases of medical futility. To resolve these issues, we must also consider people's moral duties and rights, and how to allocate resources fairly.

D. The Overlapping Consensus Model

According to the overlapping consensus model, each of these three previous solutions about how to resolve disagreements over medical futility in the borderline cases contains important insights but fails as a final appeal (Kopelman, 1995). Certainly doctors have been given authority by society to make many decisions about health care, resource allocation, and what constitutes useful and futile treatments. Even if they cannot, in the end, be unilateral decision makers in the contested cases, or claim immunity from review, their importance in finding solutions is indisputable. Moreover, the roles of the patients, families, or their representatives are also central. Competent patients, or their surrogates, have the right to refuse treatments. While they may not have the moral or legal right to demand costly treatments (or even demand better food or prompt service), they do have some rights to select between reasonable options, even in the borderline cases. Social agreement about policy is also an indispensable ingredient if one seeks public cooperation, even if it must be balanced by basic rights protecting exploited, vulnerable, or other people whom the majority might disvalue. Society must clarify guidelines for the use of public resources, as well as guard the rights and well-being of people. It also has a legitimate role in setting limits to patients' demands as well as physicians' authority.

Moral justification about what ought to be done cannot be guaranteed by giving unilateral authority to doctors, patients or their surrogates, or the majority in a society. None of these groups should be the final appeal about how we ought to guide our action because their views might result from self-interest, bias, or ignorance. Consequently, models for assessing what ought to be done based upon physician autonomy, patient or surrogate autonomy, and social approval fail as final moral appeals about what ought to be done.

Moral decision making represents an ideal which is easier to articulate than to fulfill. It requires gathering the best available and relevant information, as well as taking account of people's salient interests or welfare. This goal also requires giving and defending justifiable reasons for preferences, such as those about our duties, values, or moral principles, and using methodological ideals of clarity, impartiality, and consistency to reach conclusions. Other important, albeit fallible, considerations in making moral decisions include legal, social, and religious traditions, stable views about how to understand and rank important values, and a willingness to be sensitive to the feelings, preferences, perceptions, and rights of others.

While there are many controversies in the sciences, it is generally assumed that they can, in principle, be resolved by better methodologies, studies, data, hypotheses, or theories. In contrast, there may be a diversity of opinion in moral life that cannot be entirely resolved by these means. This does not mean rational discourse is any less important in morality than it is in science, or that science is value-free or theory-neutral. Rather, it means that reasoned differences of opinion in moral life can occur, and they may result in differences in the balance given to conflicting goods, rights, duties, goals, principles, virtues, or values. Insofar as more than one ranking of them can be justified, different views about what counts as useful or futile in these contested cases may be vindicated, or at least understandable. Even when we do not agree in our moral judgments about these contested cases, we can sometimes recognize that alternative views have merit and tolerance of diverse opinions may be appropriate. Thus, the goal in decision making and policy is to have a special kind of agreement. It is one that is morally justifiable. Agreements tend to be morally worthy when born out of a consensus among reasonable and informed people of good will about what ought to be done.

This model presupposes relatively stable agreements of a complex nature. It relies upon general understanding about when to be tolerant of diverse views and procedures for resolving disputes. It presupposes that informed people of good will want to seek morally justified judgments and actions on these matters. Rather than assigning unilateral authority to someone or some group, this view recommends consensus arising from diverse perspectives and informed by procedures and laws to protect people. This view fails if no such areas of general agreement can be reached and coercion rather than cooperation is needed to set limits. For example, a community consisting of religious fundamentalists and secular humanists might have difficulty clarifying the limits of tolerance, or how to proceed when encountering disagreement. Of course, we might equally question if they really form a community when they are unable to reach accommodations to each others important beliefs.

III. UNDERLYING MORAL DEBATES ABOUT PEOPLE'S QUALITY OF LIFE, SUFFERING, AND THE BEST-INTERESTS STANDARD

In the last sections we saw that disputes about the utility or futility of medical treatment cannot be resolved without establishing the goals for judging utility and futility and procedures for conflict resolution. The goals of medicine offer important guidance in assessing what is medically useful or futile, especially if all could agree about their relative importance. These traditional medical aims include enhancing people's well-being and opportunities through prevention, diagnosis, or treatment of disease, pain, death, or disability, or by restoration of function. One uncontroversial ranking of them, however, seems unlikely. At the heart of the futility debate are disputes about what ought to be done when important goals of medicine seem to conflict. For example, what should be done when our duties to relieve suffering and maintain life seem to conflict?

Our disagreements about which treatments are futile sometimes rest upon deeply held views about when a life is worth living and what is best for people. Consequently, they may persist despite good communication and careful policies. As we saw, in the cases of Helga Wanglie and Baby K, the families insisted, while doctors disagreed, that permanently unconscious life was worth supporting maximally. In contrast, in the case of Nancy Cruzan, the doctors held this view, while the family disagreed. Disputes about the intrinsic value of someone's quality of life, then, may underlie subsequent judgments about that person's best interest, and when treatment is futile.

Typically, competent adults can decide what treatments are in their best interest, and what quality of life they wish to support. This is called the self-determination standard. When people are faced with a choice between prolonging life and preventing great suffering, they sometimes believe there are worse things than dying. Most of us would not want to endure a mindless existence of intense and chronic pain with no prospect of improvement. Some people leave advance directives about their desires in such circumstances or designate surrogates to make decisions for them if they become incompetent. Friends and family can help inform these decisions even when no advance directive has been left and no surrogate appointed. They can have a role in determining what they believe the person would have wanted given his or her values, thereby using the substituted judgment standard.

Incompetent people, such as infants and cognitively impaired persons, who have left no directives cannot make decisions for themselves, so it is up to others to decide for them. The contested cases often arise when people are trying to make decisions for incompetent people. A long-standing and well-accepted medical and legal policy is known as the Best-Interests Standard. It relies on picking from among the options most informed and reasonable people of good will would regard as maximizing the person's overall well-being, all other things being equal. It holds that when children, or other people, cannot make choices for themselves, decision makers should try to select the action that is best, or among the best options, for that individual. Initially, surrogates should concentrate upon what is best for the individual, attempting to identify the person's immediate and long-term interests.

The Best-Interests Standard permits complex judgment about what, all other things being equal, is likely to be best for that individual. For example, the benefit of obtaining a long and healthy life would outweigh the burden of enduring intense pain for a short time. The Best-Interests Standard, however, might also be used to justify withholding or withdrawing maximal life-support treatment from an incompetent person when life has no other prospects but severe and chronic pain. The *all other things being equal* clause in the Best-Interests Standard is important because what is absolutely best for someone may not be the right thing to do. It may be best for someone to have a heart transplant, yet wrong because others have a higher claim to this scarce resource.

The Best-Interests Standard is often an important starting point for dispute resolution about medical futility for incompetent people, because most people regard it as an important guide even if they may disagree about how to apply this norm. For example, we agree that suffering is an important consideration in making treatment decisions, because we believe that we should prevent unnecessary pain. We also generally agree that, in deciding how to assess people's best interests when judging what treatments are useful or futile, we should consider how we would wish to be treated in similar circumstances. If we think it would be terrible to be maintained in certain states such as a PVS, we should not inflict this upon others. Arguably, then, we should not have a policy more burdensome for incompetent people than we would want for ourselves.

The Best-Interests Standard has been attacked. If critics succeed in discrediting this norm, we lose an important way to help resolve disputes over medical futility. It is important, then, to consider the weightiness of these objections. Critics charge that the Best-Interests Standard: (a) is not objective, (b) may be abused, (c) denies hope, (d) violates the duty to respect the sanctity of life, (e) is unknowable, or (f) is too individualistic.

A. The Standard Is Not Objective

Some object that an incompetent person's suffering or quality of life should not play a role in establishing what is best for the patient, or in decisions to withhold or withdraw care. These critics worry that families and doctors may misjudge the nature, or length, of someone's suffering, or quality of life, because they are ignorant or fearful. Moreover, decision makers, typically families and doctors, may imagine that they are considering the person's suffering and best interests when they are really worried about their own emotional, social, or financial burdens. Such considerations may not even be conscious, critics hold, but are still dangerous and misguided. These critics typically maintain that dying is a better criteria for withdrawing or withholding maximal treatment because it is an objective, factual decision based on probabilities concerning survival or physiological effects.

In evaluating this objection, we first need to distinguish among several meanings of the words "subjective" and "objective." Let us do so with reference to pain. First, when subjective means having some relation to the experiences of subjects, and objective means relating to objects, then pain is subjective. But this does not make it either inappropriate or unreliable as a criterion to use in judgments about someone's quality of life. We try to reduce unnecessary suffering because we believe that people's suffering is important and should be part of our deliberations about what we ought to do. In addition, we would not want to rule out subjective considerations generally. Pleasure and happiness are also subjective in the sense of being experiences of subjects, rather than properties of objects, yet we judge whether treatments should be continued when someone experiences a life with pleasure or happiness.

Thus, the subjectivity of the condition, in the sense of its being an experience of subjects, does not rule it out as an important factor in making treatment decisions for others. Competent adults regard the quality of their lives and the avoidance of suffering as appropriate components in making treatment decisions for themselves. People lacking the capacity to decide for themselves deserve equal consideration or protection.

Second, objective and subjective can be understood differently. What is objective can mean what is intersubjectively confirmable, and what is subjective is not. So understood, some statements about quality of life such as pain are objective. Most people who have been on a ventilator say that it is very unpleasant and being unable to move or speak would be a further burden. The fact that most people would not want for themselves a life of chronic pain and immobility, with no hope of improvement or personal interactions, gives objective confirmation to a judgment that some kinds of lives and experiences would be very painful. If most of us agree that something is painful, we have an objective ground for claiming that something is painful.

Third, objective can also refer to something that is factual, and subjectivity to what is not. Critics use this meaning of objective when arguing that the criterion of biological survival is "more objective" than the Best-Interests Standard in selecting treatments because it is a factual standard. These critics, however, are mistaken about the kind of judgment that they make; they are not offering factual claims, but moral judgments. They are advancing what they believe to be an appropriate goal one ought to use in making decisions about when to withhold or withdraw life-supporting treatments. This is a moral claim about how we ought to act, therefore, not a factual claim about the probability of survival or the physiological effects of procedures. As such, it is not different in kind from other judgments about what ought to be done.

B. The Standard May Be Abused

Critics like former president Ronald Reagan (1986. In *Abortion, Medicine and the Law* (J. D. Butler and D. F. Walbert, Eds.), 3rd ed., pp. 352–358. Facts on File, New York) and his surgeon general, C. Everett Koop (1989. *Hastings Center Rep.* **19**(1), 2–3), believe that the Best-Interest Standard, with its incorporation of

quality-of-life considerations, is likely to be abused. For this reason, they sponsored the U.S. federal policy which has come to be called the "Baby Doe Regulations" (Kopelman *et al.*, 1992). Many physicians and others argue these regulations give insufficient recognition to suffering, thereby promoting futile and painful interventions (Kopelman, *et al.*, 1992). Are these judgments, allegedly about when it is in someone's best interest to discontinue or withhold life-sustaining treatments, more likely to be abused than other judgments of comparable complexity?

A. E. Buchanan and D. W. Brock criticize the view that quality-of-life assessments will be routinely abused (1989. *Deciding for Others*. Cambridge Univ. Press, New York). They argue that the courts and others who reject quality-of-life judgments in making decisions for incompetent people have failed to note that there are two ways in which we can understand quality-of-life judgments. Comparative quality-of-life judgments are interpersonal and based on considerations of social worth or the value of a person's life in relation to other people's lives. In contrast, noncomparative quality-of-life judgments try to consider the value of the life to the person, comparing the value of living the individual's life to having no life at all. Both kinds of judgments are important, but fundamentally different, and should be made *separately*. We should separately evaluate noncomparative judgments about whether most people would want to live a certain sort of a life. We should also consider separately such matters as comparative quality of life judgments about such matters as if we approve of everyone obtaining a resource in similar circumstances.

Unfortunately, authors often fail to distinguish between these two kinds of quality-of-life judgments when they discuss criteria for withholding or withdrawing care. In failing to separate and justify these radically different considerations, critics' concerns are fueled that the Best-Interests Standard is really a subterfuge for appraisals of the emotional, financial, or social interests of others; it strengthens their convictions that quality-of-life considerations have no place in decisions to withhold or withdraw care from incompetent persons. Critics, then, have some basis for concern about the possible abuse of so-called futility judgments based upon the Best-Interests Standard and quality-of-life considerations if people do not state clearly whose quality of life they have in mind in deciding whether they should withhold or withdraw treatments. Critics are also correct that some people do not justify their claims that others will really suffer chronic pain without compensatory benefits. To determine if noncomparative quality-of-life judgments are especially open to abuse, they should be compared with other kinds of judgments of similar complexity. Critics show why these different kinds of quality-of-life judgments must be kept distinct, and that a good deal of abuse may come from failing to do this. Resource allocation issues are important, but they should not be snuck into noncomparative quality-of-life considerations.

C. The Standard Denies Hope

Critics, such as Ronald Reagan (1986), object to using the Best-Interests Standard and quality-of-life considerations to assess futility or justify withholding or withdrawing treatment because so doing inappropriately denies hope the patient may recover. On this view, unless one can be certain that a biological life cannot be prolonged, there is always a hope of recovery. Physicians have, of course, been mistaken in the past, and some charge that physicians tend to be too gloomy when making predictions. For example, we cannot be *certain* that someone will not improve or some new treatments will not come along to help.

Medicine deals with probabilities, not certainties, so it is true that one cannot be certain about any patient's prognosis. But certainty is an impractical and immoral standard to use. It is impractical because one can never be absolutely certain, short of death, that a patient will not improve; this standard would never let us stop maximal therapy until the person died. Thousands of unconscious or marginally conscious people would have to be supported, perhaps for many years, if we adopted this rule for making decisions. It is an immoral standard if it causes a great deal of unnecessary suffering.

Competent adults would balk at a rule that they were required to suffer with maximal treatment for many months because someone might possibly survive or improve. Adults consider avoiding pain and suffering relevant to their decisions when they have a very small chance for biological survival. Arguably, incompetent people also deserve protection from the kind of burdensome treatments that few adults would want.

If critics respond that they do not mean one must be *absolutely* certain before it is appropriate to make decisions to withhold or withdraw life-support treatments, they have the problem of fairness and deciding where to draw the line. Suppose, for example, that only 1% of infants in some groups would live after spending 20 very painful months in the neonatal intensive care unit. Is it fair to *require* the 99 to suffer for the sake of the 1?

How we assess hope depends upon our goals. Most adults hope to live, but they also hope to live meaningful and conscious lives without severe and intractable pain. When these goals conflict, competent adults sometimes refuse lengthening their lives by aggressive medical treatments. If justifiable, we should treat people lacking decision-making capacity as we would want to be treated, and so give protection and consideration about pain in making choices for them.

D. The Standard Is Opposed to the Duty to Respect the Sanctity of Life

Some critics, such as Koop (1989), object that respect for the sanctity of life demands that biological life must be fully supported unless people are dying and the quality of someone's life is not relevant—only then can treatments be judged futile. Problems of pain and suffering should be addressed, on this view, but not by means of withholding or withdrawing life-support treatments. Some defend this position on religious grounds, arguing that we have a God-given duty to preserve all human life when we can do so, or that God judges us by how we treat the most helpless people under our care (R. Doerflinger, 1998. *Hastings Center Rep.* **19**(1), 16–19). The sanctity-of-life argument is not always grounded in assumptions about God's will or intentions, however. Some defend it on moral grounds alone, arguing that as a community we need to preserve all human life whenever possible in order to teach and show respect for each human life (Koop, 1989; Reagan, 1986; J. Bopp, Jr., 1990. *Hastings Center Rep.* **20**(1), 42–44). "Sanctity of life" is a complex concept whose meaning and use are difficult to clarify, and there are difficulties with appealing to it as a means to fully support people unless they are dying (Clouser, 1973).

First, some use the sanctity-of-life arguments to appeal to a God-given duty to preserve human life when we can do so. But appealing to such an obligation does not tell us how to fulfill that duty. If a life is filled with pain and suffering, and the person can survive only with maximal treatment, is struggling to preserve that life with the full arsenal of medical technology fulfilling or thwarting a God-given duty? Appeals to what people think is a God-given obligation still requires reason and justification because they do not tell us what God actually thinks, but only their views about God's position. People have appealed to God's position to be for and against wars, abortion, euthanasia, and most other controversial stands. If such appeals do not give compelling reasons, they do not help us settle our disagreements about what we ought to do in cases where we disagree. Such opinions may only harden in people's hearts the belief that they are correct, while failing to give and defend reasons for their correctness.

Second, some assume that we have a duty to save every life we can out of respect for the sanctity of life (Bopp, 1990; Doerflinger, 1989). Yet defenders of the sanctity-of-life position have to give and defend their reasons for believing that maximal care is always the appropriate care for those we are charged to help. Many people sincerely believe that a merciful God would not want someone to be forced to endure medical treatment producing only a life of suffering or minimal consciousness; they do not view death as an evil always to be opposed. Defenders of the sanctity-of-life view thus cannot assume that the appeal to sanctity of life will result in a conclusion supporting their intuitions.

Third, even if we grant that it is of great importance to us as a community to acknowledge the duty to preserve and protect human life from avoidable death, defenders of the sanctity of life need to give and defend their reasons for believing that keeping all people alive is preserving and protecting a human life from an untimely death. Many physicians and others would argue that preserving certain lives is cruel or inappropriate (Payne *et al.*, 1996; Kopelman *et al.*, 1992). Moreover, a community has important responsibilities in addition to those of mutually prolonging each other's biological life. Other important moral goals include preventing unnecessary suffering, promoting empathy, and doing to others what we would have done to us. If we do not acknowledge the suffering that others have to endure, we may lessen our empathy for others and our need to respond to it.

E. Is It Unknowable?

Robert M. Veatch has attacked the Best-Interests Standard, arguing that neither surrogates nor clinicians can be expected to select the option that will be literally best in "promoting the total well-being of the individual" (1994. *Hastings Center Rep.* 25, 5–12). Certainly none of us know what choices are absolutely in the best interests of ourselves or others, given our biases, ignorance, and the uncertainties of life. It is unclear, however, whether the Best-Interests Standard is used in this way. Even Veatch admits that parents and other surrogates are not held "to a literal best interest standard when they make decisions for their wards" (Veatch, 1994, p. 6), but to a standard of reasonableness. For similar reasons, clinicians cannot be expected to know what is literally the total best for their patients when they make recommendations. If the standard is never meant to require acting in the absolutely best interest

of someone, then his criticism does not apply to the standard *as used*. Veatch is correct that clinicians and surrogates may not know the literally best choice for someone, but is that really needed in many cases? A clinician or surrogate may not know what is in someone's total best interest, but still know it is best to tie off someone's spouting artery. Veatch has not shown that our communication, value differences, or uncertainties are so bad that his skepticism is warranted here but not in other matters such as in judging what is best for the environment, public health, schools, etc.

F. Is It Too Individualistic?

Critics argue that the Best-Interests Standard gives us an inappropriate guideline because what is in someone's best interest may be the wrong thing to do (Veatch, 1994). It cannot be right to ignore everyone else's needs and interests in allocating goals, services, or benefits. Many patients may need the same scarce resource, for example, so they all cannot get what is absolutely best. What is marginally beneficial for one individual may not make any sense from the vantage of reasonable allocation decisions. It may be best for the individual to obtain a scarce and expensive resource to extend life for a week; yet it might not be reasonable if, as a result, another whose life which could be extended for many years will be denied access to this treatment. Similarly the family may not be able to set aside every other consideration to do what is best for the sick family member. An elderly, beloved relative might live a few weeks longer if he bankrupted the family, but the family might reasonably consider their own needs and interests.

Since it would be impossible to employ this individualistic interpretation of the Best-Interests Standard, this cannot reflect how it is used. Such a standard could not guide clinical practice as long as patients have conflicting interests, and clinicians and families have other duties. Yet it is useful to assess, *all things being equal,* what is in each patient's best interest, even when there are often other things to consider in deciding what ought to be done. We cannot ignore that patients' needs may conflict, and some comparative and interpersonal judgments or assessments about discontinuing or withholding marginal benefit treatments may have to be made. This standard is used to set goals and assess means that are reasonable and to serve as a threshold of acceptable behavior by surrogates.

Certain social structures, however, may increasingly pit doctors and families as advocates for their patients' needs and interests against health care systems that do not want to pay for treatments. Governmental agencies, third-party payers, and insurance companies interested in cost savings may set thresholds for what is futile based on what they are willing to fund, and leave doctors uncertain about how to deal with too little money for what they believe to be needed care for their patients.

IV. CONCLUSION

Disputes about medical futility may raise substantive moral questions about the meaning and value of human life. They may also demonstrate the pitfalls of poor communication and failure to take the time to clarify people's concerns, problems, feelings, beliefs, and deeply felt needs. Disagreements about which treatments are futile are likely to continue not only because resources are limited, but because informed people of good will disagree about what constitutes a genuine benefit, what ought to be done in the borderline cases, and what role people's quality of life should play in treatment decisions. When dealing with people lacking decision-making capacity, the Best-Interests Standard has been an important guide for helping people decide when treatments are futile or useful. It helps us understand the threshold of acceptable surrogate choice and to balance people's interest and needs when allocating health care benefits. Judgments about medical futility and utility often represent complex assessments of different burdens and benefits, seen and measured by people with differing interests and convictions about when a life is worth living and how they would want to be treated in similar circumstances. The decisions will continue to be momentous because overtreatment may be burdensome to patients and costly to society, yet undertreatment can compromise the rights and dignity of people seeking help.

Also See the Following Articles

ADVANCE DIRECTIVES • BRAIN DEATH • DISABILITY RIGHTS • EUTHANASIA • INFORMED CONSENT • PATIENTS' RIGHTS

Bibliography

Bopp, J. Jr. (1990). Choosing death for Nancy Cruzan. *Hastings Center Rep.* **20**(1), 42–44.

Brody, B. A., and Halevy, A. (1995). Is futility a futile concept? *J. Med. Philos.* **20**, 123–144.

Buchanan, A. E., and Brock, D. W. (1989). "Deciding for Others: The Ethics of Surrogate Decisionmaking." Cambridge Univ. Press, New York.

Callahan, D. (1991). Medical futility, medical necessity: The problem without a name. *Hastings Center Rep.* **21**, 30–35.

Clouser, K. D. (1973). The sanctity of life: An analysis of a concept. *Ann. Internal Med.* **78**, 119–125.

Doerflinger, R. (1989). Assisted suicide: Pro-choice or anti-life? *Hastings Center Rep.* **19**(1), 16–19.

Engelhardt, H. T., Jr. (1996). "The Foundations of Bioethics," 2nd ed. Oxford Univ. Press, New York.

Jecker, N. S., and Schneiderman, L. J. (1995). When families request that "everything possible" be done. *J. Med. Philos.* **20**, 145–163.

Koop, C. E. (1989). The challenge of definition. *Hastings Center Rep.* **19**(1), 2–3.

Kopelman, L. M. (1995). Conceptual and moral disputes about futile and useful treatments. *J. Med. Philos.* **20**, 109–121.

Kopelman, L. M., Kopelman, A., and Irons, T. (1992). Neonatologists, pediatricians and the supreme court criticize the "Baby Doe" regulations. In "Compelled Compassion" (A. L. Caplan, R. H. Blank, and J. C. Merrick, Eds.), pp. 237–266. The Humana Press, Totowa, NJ.

Miller, F. H. (1994). "Infant resuscitation, a US/UK divide. *Lancet* **343**, 1584–1585.

Payne, K., Taylor, R. M., Stocking, C., and Sachs, G. A. (1996). Physicians' attitudes about the care of patients in the persistent vegetative state: National survey. *Ann. Internal Med.* **125**, 104–110.

Reagan, R. (1986). Abortion and the conscience of the nation. In "Abortion, Medicine and the Law" (J. D. Butler and D. F. Walbert, Eds.), 3rd ed., pp. 352–358.

Schneiderman, L. J., Jecker, N. S., and Jonson, A. R. (1990). Medical Futility: Its meaning and ethical implications. *Ann. Internal Med.* **112**(123), 949–954.

Schneiderman, L. J., and Jecker, N. (1993). Futility in practice. *Issues Law Med.* **9**, 101–102.

Veatch, R. M. (1994). Abandoning informed consent. *Hastings Center Rep.* **25**, 5–12.

Veatch, R. M., and Spicer, C. M. (1992). "Medically futile care: The role of physicians in setting limits. *Am. J. Law Med.* **18**, 15–36.

MENTAL HEALTH

Lindsey Coombes
Oxford Brookes University

GLOSSARY

autonomy The capacity for making choices about one's own life

community care An approach to the treatment of people with mental health problems in their own localities.

heteronomy Not being in control of one's life

negative definition of mental health The concept that mental health is the absence of mental illness or disease.

positive definition of mental health The concept that mental health is a state of psychological well-being.

psychotherapy A psychological treatment using the relationship between the therapist and the client to produce changes in cognition, feelings, and behavior.

MENTAL HEALTH is what many people in the caring professions at the present time claim to be working for. The term is used everyday—particularly in the professions—as if it is fully understood. We have mental health services, mental health hospitals, mental health workers, and academic departments of mental health studies. With the increasing practice of community care in mental health work there are expanding groups working for mental health education and mental health promotion who devote their careers to increasing mental health. In spite of the widespread occurrence of the term, it is in fact not clear what is being talked about when it is used.

The first section of this article seeks to provide an overview of the concept of mental health. On the one hand, negative definitions of mental health as the absence of mental illness or disease tend to lead to impoverished conceptions of the term. On the other hand, attempts to provide a positive definition of mental health founder over generalization and vagueness. In the light of these conceptual problems, Section II examines mental health as a possible goal of mental health care. The negative definition of mental health implies a goal of mental health care as the prevention of illness and disease. The positive definition of mental health as well-being has two important versions: well-being as maximal pleasure and well-being as autonomy. Sections III and IV explore a number of ethical issues relating to two important contemporary means of promoting mental health: psychotherapy and community care.

I. CONCEPTUALIZING MENTAL HEALTH

Given the frequent use of the term, it might seem a little strange to begin by asking, "What exactly is mental health?" The term "mental health" is used to mean many things. Much depends upon the particular profession or interest of whoever is seeking mental health. Different professions work with different theories of mental health, and in turn these theories may not be the same as those of the laypeople they are trying to serve. Furthermore, there is evidence that a person's mental health depends on where he or she lives, the sort of society he or she lives in, and his or her gender, race, and age. These issues need to be examined so that the confusion about mental health that has resulted from ambiguity can be clarified.

According to M. Jahoda, "There is hardly a term in current psychological thought as vague, elusive, and ambiguous as the term 'mental health'" (1958, 3. *Current Concepts of Positive Mental Health.* Basic Books, New York). Why this might be so becomes apparent when we reflect on the words that make up the term. "Mental" straightforwardly refers to the mind. However, what mind is, how it works, how it interacts with the body, and what the unity of a mind at any one time consists of are enduring problems of philosophical and scientific discourse. A thorough examination of these problems is beyond the scope of this article, but it is sufficient to note that perspectives of the mind vary from those that deny that conscious experience is relevant at all to those that consider conscious experience the key to understanding human behavior. The salient point is that such diverse perspectives are likely to formulate very different ideas of what a well-functioning mind is, and there is thus a broad scope of conceptions concerning what is to count as healthy or sick behavior.

There are further difficulties when we consider the word "health." Etymologically, the English word health means "wholeness" and carries connotations of self-sufficiency and independence. Ancient Greek has two etymologically distinct words for health: *hygeia* and *euexia*. Hygeia, the source of the modern word hygiene, means living well or, more precisely, a "well way of living"; *euexia* means "good habit." The Greek terms stress the functioning and activity of the whole and suggest that mental health is connected to the way we live. The activities that in the English usage might be seen as signs or effects of mental health—psychological wholeness—might in the Greek sense appear as the essence of mental health. The Greek seems to suggest that to achieve and maintain mental health requires effort and care.

Mental health is neither given nor usually taken away from the outside, nor is it an expected state of affairs. Furthermore, mental health is a matter of degree, and standards of mental health seem to be relative to persons and relative to the time of life for each person. Almost everyone's state of health could be better. Yet as Aristotle pointed out, "health admits of degrees without being indeterminate."

A. Defining Mental Health, Disease, Illness, and Ill Health

1. Negative Definition of Mental Health

One observation regarding the etymological origins of mental health is that both Greek and English words for health are unrelated to words for disease, illness, or sickness. As we will see though, the meaning of health within the Western scientific model of medicine is most often expressed in terms of a negative definition: the absence of disease. Another observation is that that the Greek words for health are completely unrelated to all of the verbs of healing. Yet, in modern Western societies, it is the dominant professional view of health which is perhaps most influential. Indeed, it has been claimed by some that health has been subverted by the medicalization of life.

2. Disease

"Disease," "illness," and "ill health" are often used interchangeably. Disease is the objective state of illness and is verified through the existence of some pathology or abnormality which is capable of detection. The contemporary model of disease is associated with the germ theory of Pasteur and Koch which identified different germs as the specific, distinctive, and necessary causes of different illnesses. For example, the changes in bodily function that occur with the illness tuberculosis can be shown to be caused by the tubercle bacillus. The disease model has a number of important features. First, it assumes that there are discrete, distinct illnesses, involving qualitative breaks in functioning between health and the pathological. Second, it assumes that each illness has its own unique cause, which is the specific cause of the particular illness. This presumption of a specific etiology for each illness then serves as a basis for the differentiation and classification of illnesses.

While the model may be the most appropriate for many infectious diseases, it is arguably of less value in other areas of medicine, including mental health care. As regards mental illnesses, the idea of etiological specificity is problematic because the causes of many conditions are unknown, or a matter of dispute. Not only this, the specificity of many syndromes is problematic as has been demonstrated in several studies of psychiatric diagnosis which suggest that psychiatrists are predisposed to diagnose mental illness as opposed to mental health; are unable to distinguish mental health from mental illness; and are prone to apply different standards according to the gender, social class, and race of presenting individuals. For a more detailed discussion of the concept of disease in mental health care see K. W. M. Fulford's *Moral Theory and Medical Practice* (1990. Cambridge Univ. Press, Cambridge).

3. Illness

Illness is the subjective experience of loss of health. Normally, it is couched in terms of symptoms or loss of function. Illness and disease are not the same, although there is a large degree of coexistence. For example, someone may be diagnosed as having a disease although they have not reported any illness. When someone reports symptoms and shows signs and further investigations such as blood tests demonstrate a disease process, the two concepts of disease and illness coincide. However, this model provides a poor conceptualization of many illnesses, particularly mental illnesses. As has already been noted, the idea of etiological specificity is problematic for mental illness. In practice, therefore, mental illnesses are largely distinguished descriptively in terms of symptom syndromes, although etiological assumptions may be involved in making certain distinctions.

Since mental health workers differ in their theoretical approaches and their ideas about the causes of mental illnesses, and since they do not agree about the precise value and desirable characteristics of classification schemes, it is not surprising to find that there is no single universally agreed upon list of mental illnesses. Most lists include many of the same illnesses but they do not always give the same names or group them in the same manner. Most typological classifications—for example, the *International Classification of Disease-10* and the *Diagnostic and Statistical Manual of Mental Disorders IV*—mention schizophrenia and anxiety states, but the precise delineation of these conditions in the glossary may differ, as may the number and types of illness recognized and their location within the overall classification scheme.

Medical and psychiatric practitioners rarely attempt any formal definition of illness, and mental health legislation in the United Kingdom has followed medical convention in not providing any general definition of mental illness. Mental illness is usually given meaning, though, through the specification of a list of particular illnesses with their own characteristics: it is given an extensive rather than an intensive definition.

B. Mental Health, Illness, and Disease as Social Constructs

1. Critique of Scientific Medicine

The view that health is the absence of disease and illness and that medical treatment can restore the body and mind to good health has been increasingly criticized. The distribution of health and ill health has been analyzed from a historical and social scientific perspective and it has been argued that medicine is not as effective as is often claimed. The contribution of medicine to reduced mortality has been minor when compared with the major impact of improved environmental conditions such as improved sanitation and nutrition. Moreover, most medical interventions have not been proved effective prior to their widespread adoption. Social scientists view health and disease as socially constructed entities: they are produced and negotiated by ordinary people.

2. Mental Illness as Deviancy

Sociologists have put forward the view that any illness can be viewed as a form of deviant behavior. This is because illness is also a social role that provides a way of departing from normal social obligations and is itself governed by its own specific social expectations. These include:

a. That sickness provides an exemption from normal social responsibilities relative to the nature and severity of the illness, this exemption requires legitimization, and it is the doctor who is the legitimizing agent
b. That the sick person cannot be expected, by pulling himself together, to get well by an act of will
c. That there is a definition of the state of being ill as undesirable with its obligation to want to get well
d. That there is an obligation, in proportion to the severity of the condition, to seek technically competent help, namely, that of a doctor, and to cooperate with him or her in the process of trying to get well

Applied to mental illness, psychiatric symptoms are defined as violations of social norms and mental illness can be viewed as a social role. The norms in question are taken for granted and it is societal reaction which transforms the common occurrence of a norm violation into the social role of the mentally ill person. The process is legitimated by the psychiatrist.

3. Medicine and Social Control

Social scientists argue that medicine is a social enterprise closely linked with exercise of professional power. Medicine is not a value-free activity. Rather, it is a powerful means of social control whereby the categories of disease, illness, madness, and deviancy are used to maintain the status quo in society. Doctors who make diagnoses are in a powerful position—they control access to such a power through professional associations with their own vested interests to protect. A stronger form of this argument says that medicine upholds a specific form of economy and/or institutionalized power of men over women.

4. Positive Definition of Health

Another problem with the dominance of scientific medicine in the context of health is the neglect of health as a positive concept. It will be recalled from the etymological discussion of health that the English origins emphasized wholeness and carried connotations of self-sufficiency and independence; both Greek terms stressed the activity and well-functioning of the whole. However, both characterizations imply what is referred to in the literature as a positive definition of health: health is a state of well-being. Perhaps the best known example of a positive conception of health is the World Health Organization's (WHO) definition: "Health is a state of complete physical, mental and social well-being, not merely the absence of disease or infirmity" (WHO, 1946. *Constitution,* WHO, Geneva).

Theorists such as Jahoda are concerned with providing a workable *positive* conception of mental health and explicitly reject attempts to define mental health as the absence of mental illness. She notes that at present "knowledge about deviations, illnesses and malfunctioning far exceeds knowledge about healthy functioning" (1958, 6). The emphasis in this area has been on the study of disease and malfunctioning with the result that the health–disease model has prevailed, influencing theoretical developments and providing a framework according to which treatment and therapy can proceed.

Jahoda is a proponent of the view that mental health and mental illness are not correlative terms, each denoting a state of the organism to be understood in terms of the absence of the other. She claims that a definition of psychological health as the absence of mental disease assumes that health and illness are different only in degrees and that this assumption is not justified. For example, it is possible that the potential for health of two equally sick people might be quite different. Jahoda

believes that this issue deserves further research and that it would be more fruitful to concentrate on "the concept of mental health in its more positive connotation, noting, however, that the absence of disease may constitute a necessary, but not a sufficient condition for mental health" (Jahoda, 1958, 15).

5. Lay Conceptions of Health

The neglect of positive health because of the focus on illness and disease in Western medicine has meant that there has been little interest in how other groups within society conceive health. However, several researchers have studied the general public's beliefs about health, and the findings present an interesting picture. On the one hand, it is apparent that there is overlap with the professional conceptions of health already discussed. But, on the other, it is clear that there are differences as well which can be attributed to age, sex, and class.

There is then a difference between lay and professional concepts of health. Sociologists have described how people operate with both official and lay beliefs about health. Public accounts are couched in terms of scientific medicine and reflect these dominant beliefs. Health and illness are related to medical diagnosis and treatment, and medical terms and events are used to explain health status. Private accounts reflect lay views of health, which typically use more holistic and social concepts to explain health and illness. For example, private accounts relate life to general life experiences, such as employment, housing, and stress. In encounters with strangers who are perceived as professionals, people use public accounts. However, in more informal settings, people use private accounts. The gap between private and public accounts has been identified by some health workers as a problem. The concern centers around two issues, the perceived lack of communication between health worker and client and the client's lack of compliance with prescribed treatment regimes.

6. Cultural Views of Health

Other societies and cultures have their own ways of talking about health which are very different from our own. Jahoda (1958, 15) notes that there is sufficient evidence from anthropology to demonstrate the vast range of what can be considered normal. Cultural anthropologists have convincingly demonstrated a great variety of social norms and institutions in different parts of the world. What one culture considers a disease another may consider a sin, crime, or sign of poverty. Among the dozens of conditions with an emotional or behavioral component that have been described are *amok,* a spree of sudden violent attacks on people, animals, and inanimate objects which afflicts men in Malaysia; *hsieh-ping,* a trance state occurring among Chinese where patients believe themselves to be possessed by dead relatives or friends whom they have offended; *koro,* a delusion found among Chinese men that the penis will retract into the abdomen and ultimately cause death; *mal ojo* or *evil eye* among Latin Americans where the illness is blamed on the "strong glance" of an envious person; *latah,* a syndrome of hypersuggestibility and imitative behavior found in Southeast Asia; and *susto,* a belief in "loss of soul" found in most of Latin America. In any multicultural society a variety of cultural views coexist at any one time, and interpersonal and cross-cultural variations in the referents of health and disease pose serious conceptual problems for those concerned with defining health. Is it possible to arrive at universal concepts of health and disease?

C. Objectivity of Concepts of Mental Health and Illness

1. Concepts of Health and Illness Refer to Physiological and Psychological Functioning, Not Social Behavior

There have been a number of attempts to defend the objectivity of concepts of mental health and illness framed in terms of whether conceptions of health and illness have a social content, that is, whether they depend on the social approval of the behavior in question. The social realm, it is argued, provides an essential context to our judgments of mental health and illness, but does not define their content. Concepts of mental health and illness are often, admittedly, ambiguous, and some, like the notion of a psychopathic personality, raise special problems. Nevertheless, if we concentrate on the disturbance of "part functions" as well as general efficiency we can distinguish mental illness from social deviation.

But what does this argument amount to? The most important claim is the obvious point that concepts of health and illness refer to aspects of physiological and psychological functioning and not to social behavior. This suggests a distinction between mental illness and deviance, the former involving a pathology of mental processes that underlie behavior whereas the latter is defined in terms of the breaking of social rules governing behavior. Physical illness, mental illness, and deviance then differ in their referents: body, mind, and behavior, respectively. This is an important analytical point, though it is not without its problems as far as the group of personality or behavior disorders is concerned,

and, more generally, since assessments of mental processes depend on assessments of behavior. Moreover, it does not establish that the criteria whereby we judge psychological processes to be pathological are any less value laden or any less social in origin. That is, the referent may not be social behavior but the evaluative criteria may be social. The argument is that we can potentially assess the normality of separate psychological functions on a factual, statistical basis in the way that we do for physiological functioning, although it must be recognized that our knowledge of psychological functioning is far more limited.

2. Mental Health and Illness Are Value Free

Boorse exemplifies the attempt, implicit in the preceding argument, to root the objectivity of all notions of health and illness in biology. He admits that the concepts of health and illness, especially in the mental sphere, are usually vague, and he admits that in practice they often incorporate value judgments. Nevertheless, he contends that this is not inevitable. His argument is based on the following notions of health and illness:

> An organism is *healthy* at any moment in proportion as it is not diseased; and a disease is a type of internal state of the organism which: *i* interferes with the performance of some natural function— i.e. some species-typical contribution to survival and reproduction—characteristic of the organism's age; and *ii* is not simply in the nature of the species, i.e. is either atypical of the species or, if typical, mainly due to environmental causes. (C. Boorse, 1976. *Journal for the Theory of Social Behavior* 6, 62–63)

It follows from this, he argues, that concepts of illness are value free since disease is defined as an interference with natural functions, and the functional organization typical of a species is a biological fact. Hence, "whether or not an organism is diseased can be settled in principle by the methods of natural science" (p. 63). And this applies to mental as well as bodily functioning.

Boorse's faith in the possibility of factual definitions of mental health and illness raises a number of problems. Central to them is not so much his particular delineation of the notions of health and illness in general terms—though it could be questioned—as his belief that this delineation extracts the criteria of mental health from the realm of values and puts them squarely into the domain of pure description. First, there is the problem of identifying "natural" psychological functions and interferences with them. Even if we concern ourselves only with what people do and can do rather than what they should do (with statistical norms and capacities rather than ideal norms), it is difficult to see how value judgments can be avoided in making decisions about what constitutes a natural function or an interference with it. The most obvious difficulty is that a majority of people may do many things that we hesitate to call mentally healthy. Thus, mental health may, but need not, be the status of the majority of people (Jahoda, 1958, 16). Consider the case of physical illness and health. No one would be likely to consider a definition of "physical health" based on statistical considerations, for it might turn out that a majority of the population is suffering from some sort of physical disease.

There is yet a further difficulty with the statistical approach to defining "mental health" in terms of the need to assess the relevance of various sorts of behavioral data involved. This is the selection of a reference population—a problem that involves nonstatistical considerations, a factor which indicates the inadequacy of an attempt to define "mental health" on the basis of a purely statistical concept of normality. Moreover, even when the relevant reference population has been delineated, equal weight would not be given to all measurable psychological functions in developing a set of norms against which to evaluate the mental status of individuals. In the domain of mental health, the most that a statistical approach can achieve is a specification of which behaviors and traits are "abnormal" in the general population. But we still require some nonstatistical parameters for deciding which "abnormalities" are to count as illnesses and which "normalities" should be construed as healthy.

Is it reasonable to identify as natural functions, as Boorse suggests, those functions that contribute to survival and reproduction of the species? Moreover, how do we decide what contributes to an interference with a particular function? And even if we can assess the contribution of the particular processes to the survival and the reproduction of the species, are we to be forced to define decisions such as those to remain childless as pathological? The problem is not that there can be no facts, but that when it comes to questions of "how we are constituted" psychologically there can be no merely descriptive, statistical answers. Human psychological functioning is too responsive to the social and cultural context to decide what is "normal" or "natural" without making some value judgments.

It should be apparent by now that there is little agreement on what is meant by mental health. Mental health is used in many different contexts to refer to many different aspects of life. Where people are located socially, in terms of social class, gender, and occupation, will affect their concept of mental health. Disagreement also exists as to the role values play in ascribing and explaining mental health and disease. Social science's perspectives on mental health provide a powerful critique of scientific medicine and point to the importance of social factors in the construction and meaning of mental health. Lay concepts of health derived from different cultures coexist alongside scientific medicine. Attempts to produce a unified concept of mental health appear to founder through overgeneralization and vagueness. If the concept of mental health (and mental illness) is a value-laden social construct, then mental health professions need to ensure that everyone's values are given fair consideration and that basic rights and privileges are not abused.

II. PROMOTING MENTAL HEALTH

A. The End(s) of Mental Health Care

It is perhaps a truism to suggest that the end of mental health care is a mentally healthy human being. As Kass points out, "[mental] health is *a* goal ... few would deny" (L. R. Kass, 1981. In *Concepts of Health and Disease* (A. L. Caplan and H. T. Engelhardt, Eds.), Addison–Wesley, Reading, MA). The question of whether it is *the* only possible goal is debatable as there are many other things which might be thought of as alternative goals for mental health care, e.g., education, social change, behavior change, or less mental illness. It would thus appear that there are perhaps competing ends for health care in general and health promotion in particular.

The medical approach to mental health promotion focuses on activity which aims to reduce morbidity and premature mortality. Activity is targeted toward whole populations or high-risk groups. This kind of health promotion seeks to increase interventions which will prevent ill health and premature death. As we saw in Section I, the medical approach is conceptualized around the absence of disease and can be criticized for ignoring nonmedical factors in health.

The positive definition of mental health focuses on well-being, and thus mental health promotion based on this conception would be about promoting well-being. It might be argued though that the only progress achieved in defining mental health in this way is to shift the vagueness and ambiguity about the concept "mental health" to that relating to "well-being." Nonetheless, there are several important ways in which well-being is conceived that may help to clarify what might be promoted in terms of mental health.

B. Mental Health and Well-Being

1. Well-Being as Pleasure

The first approach to well-being is associated with Bentham (1784–1832), who argued that as human beings are sentient, the only nonderivative goods for people are pleasant experiences and the absence of painful ones. For persons to flourish is simply to have lives filled with the greatest possible amount of pleasure. According to the Benthamite view, the aim of society in general, and mental health care in particular, should be to maximize pleasure. Pleasure and pain are regarded as psychological states which are comparable and measurable according to their duration and intensity. No person's pleasure is in itself more significant than anyone else's. Nobody is to count for anymore than anyone else.

However, Bentham's conception of well-being, by treating all pleasures and pains as strictly commensurable, does allow the possibility of sacrificing some people's welfare in order to promote the more peripheral interests of a large number of others. On this view the only way of improving a person's well-being is to increase his or her pleasure. It does not matter how the pleasure is distributed, although in principle it would require a move toward a more equal distribution of goods and burdens, since, with a few exceptions, the worse off someone is the greater increase in pleasure he or she will recieve from a given size of material benefit. There is, however, no limit to a person's pleasure, and no matter how well off someone is, a further gain in pleasure is no more nor less significant than a gain of similar magnitude for someone far worse off.

Perhaps a close approximation of the ideal Benthamite society is described by Aldous Huxley in *Brave New World*. A policy of well-planned positive eugenics, combined with comprehensive behavior modification and subliminal learning programs throughout childhood, ensures that the whole population is well suited to whatever role is regarded by the rulers as socially desirable for it to fill. There is material abundance, wars are obsolete, personal antagonisms are at a minimum, and people are able to enjoy, through developments in advanced technology, a wide range of thrilling experiences. Anger, anxiety, depression, and other psycholog-

ical states which are either painful or might lead a person who has them to act in an antisocial way are kept firmly under control through the free use of *soma*, a powerful mind-altering drug which replaces unpleasant thoughts and feelings with an overwhelming euphoria.

Huxley's world is an exceedingly pleasurable place. Yet is it a society we should seek to emulate? Many would argue no for the reason that the quality of the inhabitants' lives is seriously impoverished: they are childishly naive, emotionally shallow, and have superficial relationships. Their pleasure is largely an illusion; they are, by design, highly conventional. There is hardly any scope for the development and expression of individuality. The Benthamite vision of well-being is unlikely to be a suitable end for mental health promotion.

Perhaps we do not need to look to fiction for arguments against moving toward a *Brave New World*. Indeed, Huxley stated in the Foreword to the 1950 edition of his novel that he had written it as a warning of the horror that might befall the Western world if urgent steps are not taken to resist it. The fear that mental health care might, directly or indirectly, be an instrument of social conformity, threatening to suppress individuality and social dissent, is taken up by a number of so-called antipsychiatrists such as Szasz. He mounts probably the most famous assault on state-organized pyschiatry, arguing that the psychiatric profession and the institutions of psychiatry have been used, wittingly or unwittingly, as mechanisms for enforcing certain moral standards. He compares psychiatry to the Spanish Inquisition, and the treatment of mental patients to the persecution of witches and heretics. Szasz cites numerous historical examples of psychiatry, backed by the coercive powers of the state, being used to persecute "deviants": masturbators, homosexuals, and unmarried mothers among others.

It is also a concern that governments may choose to abuse mental health care in such a way as to punish various types of nonconformity and to stifle the fundamental freedom of dissent. Bloch graphically describes the plight of a small group of pre-*perestroika* Soviet Union dissenters who

> have been diagnosed, although mentally well, as suffering from such serious psychiatric conditions as schizophrenia and paranoid personality disorder. As a result of their "illness", they have been detained involuntarily in ordinary or prison psychiatric hospitals for periods ranging from weeks to many years. While in hospital some have been given tranquilizing and other drugs for which they have no need; the purpose rather has been

to use medication as a form of social control. (S. Bloch, 1991. In *Psychiatric Ethics* (S. Bloch and P. Chodoff, Eds.), 2nd ed., p. 494. Oxford Univ. Press, Oxford)

2. Well-Being as Autonomy

The second approach to well-being is most closely associated with John Stuart Mill (1806–1873), who, while acknowledging the unique value of pleasure, distinguished between qualities of pleasure and includes the notion of autonomy as necessary for well-being. Mill believed that not only is autonomy a nonderivative good, but that people who have a high degree of autonomy actually do better than those who are deficient in autonomy. He argued that those who have attained a high level of autonomy would prefer to retain it, even if to do so is on balance painful.

What is autonomy? Autonomy literally means "self-rule." The term was first applied in a political sense to Greek city-states. A city had "autonomia" when its citizens made their own laws, as opposed to being under the control of some conquering power. Eventually, autonomy came to be applied to individuals when their decisions and actions were their own—when they were self-determining. Berlin posits a distinction between an agent striving for autonomy and external forces which may control or thwart this wish. The opposite of autonomy is heteronomy, which roughly means not being in control of one's life. These ideas will be expanded upon in Section III.

An "occurrent" sense of autonomy has been distinguished in the literature that refers to people acting autonomously in particular situations. This can be contrasted with dispositional autonomy, which is a claim about the overall course of a person's life. In the second sense, autonomy is exemplified by the notion that one's life, in the main, is ordered according to a plan which expresses one's will. It is this dispositional autonomy that enables the individual to enjoy a life free from self-defeating conflict and attain a state of mental well-being. The distinction is important as Jahoda (1958) has pointed out, because much of the confusion in the area of mental health stems from the failure to establish whether one is talking about mental health as an enduring attribute of a person or a situational attribute of functioning. One area in which the relevance and importance of the distinction is crucial is that of the legal defense of persons charged with a criminal offense on grounds of insanity. Still further implications exist for the selection of criteria according to which persons are committed to and released from mental hospitals.

For Mill, the ultimate test of what constitutes human flourishing is appeal to people's preferences as expressed by the choices they make. Pleasant experiences are intrinsically good, since people choose them for their own sake. However, there are other things beside pleasant experiences that people want for no ulterior reason. It is not plausible to claim (as Mill did not) that the good for individuals is fixed *simply* by consulting their actual choices or preferences, for they may be impaired. Someone who has lived for a very long time in an institution might prefer to remain there, cut off from the outside world. On Mill's view this would not show that staying in the institution was the best thing for that person. What would be good for him or her is fixed by what he or she would choose, were he or she properly informed about the nature of the choice and the other options available. Similarly, it cannot be inferred from his or her extreme reluctance to leave that it is in the best interests of someone who is institutionalized to remain in the institution. Ignorance and irrationality can deny people the chance even to be aware of opportunities which, were they aware of them, they would very much want to pursue.

For Mill our capacity for rational choice is perhaps the most important feature of human nature, being the sine qua non of freedom. We have the capacity to act in pursuit of our own self-chosen—or if not self-chosen, at least self-scrutinized and endorsed—projects. We potentially have the capacity to use our rationality to resist the immediate will to act. For Mill the ultimate criterion of what constitutes human well-being is whatever would be preferred by people whose choices were not constrained by ignorance and irrationality. On this view, in order to decide what it would be for people to flourish, we must address ourselves to what they would choose if their choices were not constrained by heteronomy. These might be accomplishment, choosing one's own life plan, being in touch with reality, enjoyment, and meaningful personal relationships.

For Mill, society's goal should not be simply to produce the greatest balance of pleasures over pains, or even the greatest number of pleasant autonomous experiences. As well as speaking of the greatest happiness, Mill frequently wrote about the "general happiness" as being the goal at which society should aim. On this analysis, the general happiness is a goal which could be attained, were society only organized properly. The Millian conception has a built-in respect for the individual. The general happiness is a state where happiness is general; that is, a state where as many people as possible have attained the state previously described. There is a level of well-being which is such that, beyond it, further gains in welfare are morally insignificant compared with the moral importance of attaining it. The chief responsibility of a society should be to ensure that everyone, or at least as large a proportion of the population as possible, has reached this state.

C. Mental Health Promotion

1. Goal of Mental Health Care

If we take the preceding discussion seriously, then we can see that approaches to promoting mental health based on a Benthamite-like conception of well-being are unlikely to be acceptable to people living in liberal democracies that place great value on autonomy. Being free from mental illness is an important part of being mentally healthy and is a valuable goal of mental health promotion. Public health medicine aimed at prevention of morbidity and premature mortality is an important component of mental health promotion. However, the negative conception of mental health is a narrow one and tends to ignore social and environmental dimensions of health. Additionally, the medical approach encourages dependency on medical knowledge and removes mental health decisions from the people concerned.

It has been suggested above that the most appropriate goal for mental health promotion is positive mental health. One way of conceiving of this is in terms of a Millian well-being based on an appeal to preferences expressed by rational choices with plausible assumptions about what people would choose were their choice unconstrained by irrationality and ignorance. There is an attainable level of well-being which society ought to help as many people as possible to attain.

2. Principles of Mental Health Promotion

These points have been recognized in the health promotion field in recent times: the major causes of death and disease lay not in biomedical factors but the in the environment, individual behaviors, and lifestyles. The World Health Organization (WHO) has built on this and played a key part in shifting the emphasis from medical care to primary *health* care. In 1977 the World Health Assembly at Alma Ata committed all member countries to the principles of Health for All 2000 (HFA 2000) that there "should be the attainment by all the people of the world by the year 2000 of a level of health that will permit them to lead socially and economically productive life." The WHO made explicit five key principles for health promotion:

a. It involves the population as a whole in the context of their everyday life, rather than focusing on people at risk for specific diseases
b. It is directed toward action on the causes or determinants of health to ensure that the total environment which is beyond the control of individuals is conducive to health
c. It combines diverse, but complementary, methods or approaches including communication, education, legislation, fiscal measures, organizational change, community development, and spontaneous local activities against health hazards
d. It aims particularly at effective public participation supporting the principle of self-help movements and encouraging people to find their own ways of managing the health of their community
e. While health promotion is basically an activity in the health and social fields and not a medical service, health professionals—particularly in primary health care—have an important role in nurturing and enabling health promotion

The context for the development of broad-based health strategies will thus need to be based on equity, community participation, and collaboration. The WHO has also identified that improvements in lifestyles, environmental conditions, and health care will have little effect if certain fundamental conditions are not met. These include peace and freedom that the fear of war; equal opportunity for all and social justice; satisfaction of basic needs; and political commitment and public support (WHO, 1985). *Targets for Health for All*. WHO, Geneva).

The WHO also included three ways in which health could be promoted. The first is through *advocacy*: mental health evidence on individual and community mental health needs should be collected which show the implications for mental health of social and political issues. People's knowledge and understanding of the factors which affect mental health should be increased and health promoters of mental health should work to empower people so they may argue and negotiate changes in their personal environment. Second, is *enablement*: mental health promotion should aim to reduce differences in current mental health status and ensure equal opportunities to enable all people to achieve their full mental health potential. Mental health promoters should work to increase knowledge and understanding and individual coping strategies. In an attempt to improve access to health, mental health promoters should work with individuals and communities to identify needs and help to develop support networks in the neighborhood. The third is *mediation:* mental health promotion requires coordination and cooperation by many agencies and sectors. Mental health promoters have a major role to mediate between different interests by providing evidence and advice to local groups and by influencing local and national policy through lobbying, media campaigns, and participation in working groups.

In these declarations by the WHO it is possible to see how the emphasis has moved away from prevention of specific diseases or the detection of risk groups toward the health and well-being of whole populations. Mental well-being in terms of autonomy is a possible goal of mental health promotion. Also, instead of experts and professionals diagnosing problems, the people themselves are helped to define mental health issues of relevance to them in their local community. Instead of mental health being seen as the responsibility of individuals alone, the social factors determining mental health are taken into account and mental health is viewed as the collective responsibility of society.

III. PSYCHOTHERAPY AND MENTAL HEALTH

A. The Goal of Psychotherapy: Autonomy

So far it has been shown that it is very difficult to define mental health in a clear and universal way. Mental health is not synonymous with pleasure, knowledge, absence of illness, or disease, though it includes the capacity for all of these. Of the possible goals of mental health care, it has been suggested that the closest approximation to mental well-being is autonomy. To be autonomous is to be able to determine one's life largely free from external constraints. But, by what means can individual autonomy be brought about? Many proponents of psychotherapy have claimed that autonomy is precisely the aim of psychotherapy.

The account of autonomy given in Section II is important because it can be argued that many people with mental health problems seeking psychotherapy do so because they are mentally heteronomous: they have severe problems in mastering their internal impulses and feelings. These internal experiences may well be perceived as external by the individual—as alien and unwanted intrusions in their life that adversely affect their autonomy. This can occur in three important ways. Firstly, individuals' rationality may be affected so that they are unable to exercise the judgment, calculation, and planning needed to order life in a manner which

is not self-defeating. Secondly, failures in what might be termed strength of will—the courage, perseverance, and preparedness to carry through one's life plans—may bring some diminution of autonomy. Thirdly, lack of self-awareness may result in the individual becoming anomic and unable to carry out his or her life plan. Any or all of these factors result in heteronomy for the individual. Psychotherapy, it is argued, enhances autonomy by increasing the awareness and understanding of the individual as to the true nature of his or her experience. As Freud expressed the idea, "where id is, there ego shall be" (S. Freud (1923). New Introductory Lectures Standard Edition, London, Hogarth 1953–73 vol. 19, p. 105).

But before considering the issues connected with the goals and practice of psychotherapy, it is worth noting that the concept of autonomy (as discussed in Section II) is not free from problems. The difficulty centers around a philosophical problem dating back to Aristotle. What the theories of autonomy have in common is their emphasis on man's inner nature, which he seeks to fulfill; his potentiality, which he needs to actualize, and the inner-self, which develops successfully through self-realization. As a characterization of positive mental health, these notions are problematic since assumptions of man's nature or essence cannot be accepted uncritically. There is no single conception of autonomy; rather, there is one concept, but many conceptions. Autonomy is an abstract notion that specifies in very general terms the role the concept plays. Thus the idea of persons as self-determining is shared by people of very different philosophical positions. But when it comes to specifying more concretely what is the notion of the self or what principles justify interference with autonomy, there will be conflicting views.

B. The Nature of Psychotherapy

Turning now to psychotherapy, the first observation that can be made concerns its enormous diversity: one textbook lists over 300 types. Mercifully, they can be grouped together into a fairly small number of categories according to their theoretical orientation and founders. These include the analytic therapies derived from Freud and Jung; client-centered therapies derived from Rogers; humanistic or active therapies such as Gestalt therapy and psychodrama, started respectively by Perls and Moreno; family therapies derived from the ideas of Bateson and others; and cognitive behavioral therapies associated with Beck. The different orientations can be further classified according to what happens in a therapy session. Directive therapies (cognitive behavior therapy and some types of family therapy) emphasize overt behavior and therapists often issue precise instructions to their clients. Expressive therapies aim to help with emotional expression by evoking feelings within sessions.

Despite the diversity of psychotherapies, Holmes has identified three basic elements which can be found in all forms of psychotherapy: structure, space, and relationship (J. Holmes, 1986. *British Journal of Medical Psychology,* 59, 113–121). A minimum structure for psychotherapy is an agreed and preferably regular time and place within which therapist and client can meet. However, the specific structure of a session varies greatly from the highly structured treatments of cognitive behavior therapy to the relatively unstructured situations of Gestalt Therapy, for example. The therapeutic space of psychotherapy refers to the creation of an opportunity for the client to discover new feelings, possibilities, strengths, actions, and attitudes. The therapeutic relationship is perhaps the most fundamental element in psychotherapy and is the main instrument of treatment to produce change. In cognitive behavior therapy the therapist usually adopts the role of teacher, motivator, and director; in analytic therapy the therapist's job is to help clients discover their own feelings and solutions.

C. Ethical Issues in Psychotherapy

1. The Therapist–Client Relationship

A central ethical issue for psychotherapy concerns the imbalance of power between the therapist and the client. On the one hand, the client's power is the important factor in enabling positive change in the client. On the other hand, there is a risk that the therapist's power may create dependence in clients or lead to financial or sexual exploitation. Lakin has reported that approximately 5% of psychiatrists and psychologists admit to having sexual contact with their clients. Critics of psychotherapy have asserted that the therapist's social and moral values are communicated through the therapist's selective focus in therapy. This selectivity conveys judgments about how to view oneself and implies preferences and directions about how one should live. Worrying accounts of abuse of power in terms of sexual and financial exploitation are provided by J. Masson (1992). *Against Therapy.* Fontana, London). Defenders of psychotherapy argue that the vigilance and restraint needed by therapists to counter these problems are among the foremost duties of the therapist and are the main focus of training and, in particular, supervision.

2. Confidentiality

Confidentiality refers to the boundaries surrounding shared secrets and to the process of guarding these boundaries. The focal point of "confiding," "confidence," and "confidential" is trust, and in terms of ethical principles is based on: (1) respect for persons—a promise given should be kept; (2) nonmaleficence—persons are entitled to be protected from any harm which might come from disclosure; and (3) justice—a person disclosing information should be treated fairly. Breach of confidence under the law remains uncertain, but courts intervene to restrain disclosure of information where: (a) the information is confidential in nature and not a matter of public knowledge; (b) the information was entrusted to another person in circumstances imposing an obligation not to use or disclose that information without the consent of the giver of the information; and (c) protecting confidentiality of that information is in the public interest. Only in exceptional circumstances can breach of confidence be justified. Firstly, disclosure will always be justified legally when the practitioner is compelled by law to give the confidential information to a third party. Secondly, disclosure may be made in the public interest.

Confidentiality in psychotherapy is special because of the nature of the therapeutic relationship. Many of these issues were raised in *Tarosoff v. Regents of the University of California* (1976) (*California Reports,* 3rd ser., p. 425). On 27 October 1969, Prosenjit Poddar killed his girlfriend Tatiana Tarasoff. Two months earlier Poddar had confided to his therapist that he wanted to kill Tarasoff. At his therapist's request the police detained Poddar for questioning, but released him after he appeared rational and denied any intention to kill Tarasoff. Poddar did not return to therapy, apparently because his therapist had breached confidentiality by informing the police. Two months later he shot and stabbed her to death. Tarasoff's parents sued the therapist and his supervisor for negligence in failing to warn Tarasoff or them of the danger she was in. The Supreme Court of California rules that the therapists were at fault, putting forward the maxim that "protective privilege ends where public safety begins." They held that psychotherapists have a legal duty of care to members of the public who are threatened by possible acts of violence of their patients.

The Tarasoff judgment has been criticized by psychotherapists on several grounds. They have held that it places them in an impossible legal position. Therapists are in danger of facing legal proceedings for breach of confidence on the one hand, and on the other they face legal proceedings if they do not break confidence.

3. Informed Consent

If a doctor performs an operation on a patient without their consent the doctor is liable for the tort of battery. Arguably, the same applies to psychotherapy: the therapist is intervening psychologically, potentially invading a person's autonomy. Hence, informed consent is required in psychotherapy, but there are some unique problems that face the therapist in doing so.

The first difficulty is that it may not be desirable to discuss psychotherapeutic techniques in detail with clients. To do so would render the technique ineffective. For example, some therapists use the technique of paradoxical intention, which involves apparently absurd, incongruous, countertherapeutic, or even blatantly false statements aimed at producing a therapeutic response. "Prescribing the symptom" involves the therapist warning the client about the dangers of abandoning the pattern of behavior which led them into therapy. The ultimate aim of the prescription is to jolt the client into changing in the way the prescription warns against. To explain this to the client at the outset of the treatment would be self-defeating. Additionally, it is difficult to explain how psychotherapy works, unless it is experienced—the risk here is that the client may be misled by prior description.

4. Scientific Status of Psychotherapy

A further ethical problem of psychotherapy concerns its scientific status and efficacy. There are three main challenges mounted by critics of psychotherapy regarding its scientific status:

a. The sheer variety of psychotherapies, which makes it exceedingly difficult to investigate scientifically.

b. The standard by which scientific theories are evaluated is according to their "falsifiability," their amenability to empirical testing. Critics argue that the theories of psychotherapy fall short of this fundamental standard, being "unfalsifiable." For example, the theory of the unconscious hypothesizes that the conscious component of human motivation is but a small part of mental life and that most human behavior rests on the basis of unconscious thoughts. But what would count as evidence against such a claim? One would need to produce cases of conscious behavior in which no unconscious forces played a part. But no case could ever be produced and so the theory of the unconscious is unfalsifiable.

c. Other critics have argued that psychotherapy is pseudoscientific, being more like astrology than astronomy. The thrust of his attack can best be grasped through an example. Adlerian psychology posits that human action is motivated by feelings of inferiority of some kind. A man standing on the edge of a treacherous river at the instant that a child falls into the river nearby will either leap into the river or will not. If he does leap into the river, the Adlerian responds by indicating how this supports his theory—the man obviously needed to overcome his feelings of inferiority by demonstrating that he was brave enough to jump into the river. On the other hand, if the man does not jump into the river, the Adlerian can again claim support for his theory—the man has overcome his feelings of inferiority by demonstrating that he has the strength of will to remain on the bank.

5. Efficacy of Psychotherapy

There has been a long-running dispute regarding the efficacy of psychotherapy. Eysenck published a paper which claimed that psychotherapy of neurotic patients was not any more effective than no treatment at all: about two-thirds of both treated and untreated patients showed improvement with time (H. J. Eysenck, 1952. *Journal of Consulting Psychology* **16**, 319–324). By extrapolating from 24 selected studies about psychotherapy that had been carried out before his review, Eysenck concluded that 72% of patients given general psychological care only, and involving no specific psychotherapy, improved, whereas only 44% of patients in psychoanalysis improved. In Eysenck's view psychotherapy is ineffective.

Defenders of psychotherapy argue that Eysenck's findings rest on three crucial errors. First, his choice of evidence was highly selective and ignored those studies which suggested that neurotic symptoms can be persistent and often do not resolve spontaneously without therapy. Second, he failed to distinguish between psychoanalysis proper, which often lasts for several years, and psychoanalytic psychotherapy which, although usually much briefer, can lead to significant symptom reduction sustained over time. Third, he misrepresented the aims of psychotherapy, which are not, as Eysenck suggests, solely concerned with the relief of presenting symptoms.

The difference of opinion between critics and supporters of psychotherapy is characterized by arguments about research methodology. Opponents of psychotherapy point to the poor quality of outcome research and list faults such as contamination, nonrandom allocation, absence of control, and lack of testable theories and hypotheses. Defenders accuse the critics of biased appraisal of the evidence and claim that more recent, better designed studies have consistently shown that psychotherapy is effective both in removing symptoms and in achieving some long-term goals, and produces much more improvement than results from spontaneous remission. Moreover, they argue that the narrow focus on symptom removal disqualifies an important part of what psychotherapy aims to achieve. An individual might emerge from therapy with symptoms controlled rather than eliminated, but feeling more autonomous and understanding some of the causes of his or her problems.

The dispute over "whether psychotherapy works" illustrates how difficult it is to conduct psychotherapy research. Kline has listed many methodological issues in conducting outcome studies, and some commentators have concluded that a strict experimental design for psychotherapy studies is probably impossible (P. Kline, 1992. In *Psychotherapy and Its Discontents* (W. Dryden and C. Feltham, Eds.). Open Univ. Press, Milton Keynes). This does not mean, however, that attempts to evaluate psychotherapy should be abandoned.

Is psychotherapy a means for achieving the goal of mental health? Several writers have answered yes to this question and have argued that the power of psychotherapy to promote emotional and intellectual well-being is a justification of psychotherapy. But reservations about psychotherapy are expressed by some: it is well documented that the power to bring about mental well-being can also cause harm and is therefore dangerous and best avoided. The power differential between therapist and client means that ethical issues such as confidentiality and informed consent must be handled carefully. Additionally, there is an unresolved debate about whether psychotherapy is effective in addressing mental health problems. One thing is clear—it is difficult to devise a therapy that can bring improved mental health to another person.

IV. COMMUNITY CARE AND MENTAL HEALTH

A. Community Care and Mental Health

Community care looks set to become the major form of health and welfare delivery for the mentally ill in Western health care by the year 2000. A broad consensus has developed among consumers, families, and mental health workers that community, rather than institutional, treatment is more consistent with the values of autonomy and choice that underlie contemporary mental health care policies. Indeed it almost appears

that the notion of community has become synonymous with mental health and that community care is—like psychotherapy—a means of promoting it.

1. Defining Community

Community care of the mentally ill is not a new idea and has been debated by those concerned with mental health care for at least the last 200 years. We typically treat it as an objective reality which can be pinned down, but when we question the precise meaning of the term we find that there is little agreement about the term. For example, G. A. Hillery has identified 94 definitions of community in the sociological literature and observed that the only common factor was that they dealt with people.

Despite the different views on the meaning of community it is possible to group together different interpretations as follows:

a. Those that refer to community as a locality, a geographical description of human settlement within a fixed and bounded local territory.

b. Those that refer to community as a local social system, as a set of relationships which take place wholly, or mostly, within a locality. Under this meaning, nothing is implied about the content of these relationships—harmonious relationships are not suggested.

c. Those that refer to community as a type of relationship, more particularly, as a sense of shared identity. This corresponds most closely with the colloquial use of the term as a community "feeling" or "spirit." In this sense, community needs no local basis at all: those that share a common identity may be very widely separated and may never have met, e.g., "the scientific community."

However, whatever view one takes about community, the following assumptions seem to hold: first, community exists; second, the community "cares"; and third, community is a good thing.

2. Community: A Value-Laden Concept

Most writing on community tends to run all of the preceding definitions together. However, one influential assumption has been that life in particular locality promotes a certain relationship structure which results in the presence or absence of community spirit. More often, though, this assumption reflects little more than the prevailing cultural myths and/or the values of the author. Because community tends to symbolize a desire for personal and social fulfillment, community signifies the good life, or utopia. What utopia actually consists of will vary from one person to another, and the concept of community will always be value laden.

Historically, the idea of community emerged as a distinctive concept during the first half of the 19th century out of a fear that contemporary Western society was experiencing a loss of community and that unfortunate social consequences were bound to ensue. The concept of community was used as a means of expressing deeply felt antiurbanism and anti-industrialism in the industrializing nations of northern Europe and North America. A wide spectrum of opinion regarded this new form of society as the very antithesis of community—as impersonal and dehumanizing. In his extraordinary essay of 1911, Simmel contemplated how we respond to and internalize, psychologically and intellectually, the incredible diversity of experiences and stimuli to which modern urban life exposed us. We were, on the one hand, liberated from the chains of subjective dependence and therefore allowed a much greater degree of individual autonomy. But this was at the expense of treating others in objective and instrumental terms. We had no choice except to relate to faceless others via the cold and heartless calculus of necessary money exchanges. Urbanization produces what he called a "blasé attitude." The strong implication is that urbanization and the urban way of life is mentally unhealthy. By way of contrast, community is the epitome of mental health.

3. The Ideology of Community

The characteristics of an ideology are, first, that it is not supported by empirical evidence. The groupings of urban–loss of community–unhealthy versus rural–community–healthy do not hold empirically. Community studies undertaken during the last four decades have established the existence of some remarkably community-like localities in the midst of large cities. Moreover, studies of rural communities have revealed surprising degrees of poverty, unemployment, and multiple deprivation. The second characteristic of an ideology is that it is a distortion of reality: as we have seen, the concept of community was used as a means of expressing deeply felt concerns about a certain kind of social change. These sentiments grew out of the 18th century mood of Romanticism, which stressed the unity of the human and natural world. Writers in this mold were apt to summon up an image of a past Golden Age in which inhabitants of Arcadian "organic communities" lived in happy harmony until they were destroyed by industrialization and urbanization. Third, ideology reflects the interests of dominant groups in society: in his provocative *Fall of Public Man*, Sennett queries our preoccupation with community and argues that our attempt to establish "real communities" is destructive, resulting in a "tyranny of intimacy." A universal human desire is to avoid having to deal with the unknown, particularly outside of the parochial scale. Community feeling has the special role of reinforcing the fear of the unknown and of converting the immediate experience of sharing with others into a social principle. Our concern for community, therefore, actually prevents us from developing a better understanding of the forces which shape our lives. We need to become more aware of the ways that our apparently "private" lives within the small circle of the family and the locality in which we live are themselves shaped by wider structural forces which derive from the public spheres of society.

B. "Community Care"

1. Philosophical Underpinnings

In what sense can the community be said to care? Skidmore, in *The Ideology of Community Care*, draws on the existentialist doctrines of Sartre and Heidegger to provide a rationale for the existence of community (D. Skidmore, 1994. Chapman & Hall, London). Man first exists, encounters himself in the world, and then defines himself. Man is nothing more than what he makes himself, and as such would be condemned to freedom if he had not constructed his social meaning with such vigor. On this view "community spirit" offers a meaning to existence and liberates us from being condemned to freedom.

Skidmore uses the language of geography and families to develop a meaning of community care. Being in one's community offers the individual security, a sense of connection with others, and an identity that is mutually recognized. Each community has a network of caring relationships that evolve naturally. The basic caring unit is that of the family, and it is the aspect of the family which is projected onto the community, but because there are no blood ties involved, relationships develop from attraction. Networked relationships formed in this way have the purpose of mutual care because members project the care they have experienced in the family onto others and believe that they are receiving similar care in return. A person's community is composed of a network of natural carers, and it is in this sense that the community can be said "to care."

2. Exiles from the Community

Developing the geographical theme, Skidmore (1994) suggests that each country has its natives—those who belong and share the same language, customs, and norms. They form networks and share a sense of belonging and security, as previously discussed. However, membership of the network is conditional. Those not able or willing to conform to the norms will be removed from their network, or will remove themselves. In short they will become exiles from their community. The extreme examples of exiles are the so-called mentally ill, who, in the past, have been exiled into special holding institutions ("asylums," "mental hospitals").

3. Failure of Institutional Care

It is now recognized that institutional care of the mentally ill has been spectacularly ineffective. Studies of institutionalization have exposed the antitherapeutic nature of segregative forms of control of the mentally ill. These authors analyzed the ways in which the mentally ill are controlled and manipulated within mental hospitals in the interests of the maintenance of staff power and convenience, and patient compliance and conformity, by use of techniques of degradation and discreditation. This coupled with increasing costs of institutional care have created a strong anti-institutional ideology.

4. Failure of Community Care

Despite the apparent advantages of community-based treatment for the mentally ill, the model has experienced major difficulties regarding implementation: biased funding and ineffective administrative structures have precluded its widespread development. The majority of funding still goes to hospitals which serve only a minority of the mentally ill. In the USA, one study estimated that 60% of state funding goes to hospitals that serve only 7% of the seriously mentally ill (S. S. Sharfstein, A. M. Stoldine, and H. H. Goldman, 1993. *American Journal of Psychiatry, 150*, 1–30). Similar figures exist in Europe and the United Kingdom. Opposition from health care workers employed in hospitals and local communities either dependent on the hospitals or anxious about the thought of seriously mentally ill people being forced upon them have also prevented the development of community treatment programs.

Baldwin has argued that the community care model was useful in the transition from hospital-based health, but that it has been disastrous in providing adequate services to people with mental health problems (S.

Baldwin, 1993. *The Myth of Community Care*. Chapman & Hall, London). In the 1960s and 1970s deinstitutionalization initiatives were based on an economic motive to rationalize services, not on benevolent principles of rights for disadvantaged people. In Europe and North America the policy shift to community care has resulted in tens of thousands of people being discharged from mental health hospitals into the community without adequate provision for support or maintenance. As a consequence, many of these people either died, were reinstitutionalized in prisons, or became homeless and destitute. Moreover, although overall numbers of people permanently institutionalized have fallen since the 1960s, the number of people who received intermittent or short-term hospital services has increased in the same period.

C. Care in the Community vs. Care by the Community

Care *in* the community implies that the client should take an active part in treatment. This requires a major shift of thinking and action on the part of mental health care professionals. Given that most professionals receive their professional education in an institution, this change is likely to be difficult. Many professionals believe that the problems of institutionalization were created by institutions and that the solution is to transfer people into community settings. Institutionalization is the consequence of disempowering people and this can happen in any setting. There is some evidence that primary health care services—for example, small health care centers—are being turned into mini-institutions because the dependence of clients is exchanged from dependence on a large hospital to dependence on a small one.

Care *by* the community recognizes that the responsibility for care is transferred to the client: this may mean using the client's network of relationships, or self-care by the client. It involves empowerment and almost total withdrawal by the professional. It is a moot point as to whether the natural caring relationships described above can be artificially produced in professional relationships. A caring role, such as parent, is full time; the professional career role can only ever be part time and periodic. Additionally, caring is person centered and the participants are self-selected. Professional carers have people referred to them, and because choice is eliminated, the process of caring has been mechanized. Natural caring relationships are not formalized and it is for this reason that they flourish.

Care in the community is not a cheap option in terms of resources, and care by the community is more than the simple transfer of responsibility. If these two points are ignored the danger is that, as Skidmore suggests, a "kingdom or orphans" is created consisting of those evicted from mental hospitals.

In conclusion, community care has become almost synonymous with mental health. As an alternative to the dehumanizing effects of institutionalization experienced by those confined to mental hospital for many years, this is not surprising. The naturally occurring caring relationships within community seem like an obvious way of dealing with mental health problems. However, it has become apparent that what is meant by "community" and "community care" is not a straightforward matter. Community is all too often taken to be a good thing to have. Yet, as we have seen, a multitude of value judgments are implied in the use of the term by different writers. For many people with mental health problems at the present time, community means being forced into an uncaring, unfeeling society. Community care outside of families (and sometimes even where family structures do exist) cannot be guaranteed to occur. Community care is not equivalent to mental health.

Also See the Following Articles

AUTONOMY • COERCIVE TREATMENT IN PSYCHIATRY • HEALTH CARE FINANCING • INSANITY, LEGAL CONCEPT OF • PSYCHIATRIC ETHICS

Bibliography

Baldwin, S. (1993). "The Myth of Community Care." Chapman & Hall, London.

Boorse, C. (1976). What a theory of mental health should be. *Journal for the Theory of Social Behaviour,* 6, 61–84.

Busfield, J. (1986). "Managing Madness." Hutchinson, London.

Dryden, W., and Feltham, C. (Eds.) (1992). "Psychotherapy and Its Discontents." Open Univ. Press, Milton Keynes.

Griffin, J. (1986). "Well-Being." Oxford Univ. Press, Oxford.

Jahoda, M. (1958). "Current Concepts of Positive Mental Health." Basic Books, New York.

Kass, L. R. (1981). Regarding the end of medicine and the pursuit of health. In "Concepts of Health and Disease" (A. L. Caplan, H. T. Engelhardt, Jr., and J. J. McCartney, Eds.). Addison–Wesley, Reading, MA.

Lakin, M. (1988). "Ethical Issues in the Psychotherapies." Oxford Univ. Press, Oxford.

Masson, J. (1992). "Against Therapy." Fontana, London.

Sennett, R. (1977). "The Fall of Public Man." Cambridge Univ. Press, Cambridge.

Skidmore, D. (1994). "The Ideology of Community Care." Chapman & Hall, London.

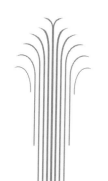

MENTAL ILLNESS, CONCEPT OF

K. W. M. Fulford
Universities of Oxford and Warwick

GLOSSARY

disease and illness Disease refers to specialist (especially medical) knowledge of specific illnesses and their underlying causes; illness refers to patients' actual experiences, in particular the symptoms of disease (the terms are often used interchangeably).

dysfunction and incapacity Dysfunction (in biological contexts) is disturbance of a bodily or mental functional part or system of an organism. Incapacity, in so far as it is distinct from dysfunction, is a disturbance of an agent's power of normal action.

fact and value/description and evaluation These and related distinctions, which are central to our understanding of the concept of mental illness, are the subject of considerable philosophical debate. As commonly understood, facts about, or descriptions of, things are broadly speaking the proper concerns of an objective world of science (including the sci-

ences of the functioning of bodies and minds); values and evaluations (in the sense of judgments of good versus bad) are broadly speaking the proper concerns of ethics and of other aspects of a subjective world of human agents.

insanity Similar in meaning to "madness," but in some contexts with more specific technical uses, especially administrative and legal.

madness A term, nowadays mainly colloquial, used of behavior or experience that is bizarre, extreme, or in other ways unusual, especially where it is or seems to be irrational.

mental disorder A generic term for any defect state or ongoing disturbance of experience or behavior arising in or from the mind. It thus includes (for example, in many legal contexts) mental illness, mental defect, and personality disorder.

mental health This term is used (1) to mean a positive state of mind, one that is more than merely free of mental disorder (this was the platform for the Mental Health Movement, for example), and (2) as a generic term for conceptions of the requirements for good mental health that are not tied, closely or exclusively, to medical psychiatry. The different professional groups involved in multidisciplinary teams—nurses, psychologists, etc.—are usually referred to as mental health professionals.

mental illness The most widely used term for those mental disorders nowadays widely assumed to be generically linked with physical illness. *Severe men-*

tal illnesses, such as schizophrenia and manic-depressive psychosis, broadly correspond with the colloquial "madness" and the legal "insanity."

MENTAL ILLNESS is the most widely used term for those mental disorders, including the traditional "madness" or "insanity," which are nowadays widely regarded as being generically linked with bodily illness. Mental illness and bodily illness are not sharply distinct. Broadly speaking, mental illness involves disturbances of higher mental functions, such as thought, belief, perception, volition, and emotion, either arising in their own right (e.g., respectively, obsessional disorder, delusion, hallucination, addiction, and depression) or operating as the causes of bodily signs and symptoms (e.g., hysterical paralysis).

Whether mental illness is indeed linked generically with bodily illness is a contentious issue. The "medical model," working within a scientific paradigm, has produced dramatic improvements in drug treatments for major disorders such as schizophrenia, but on the other hand, the diagnosis of mental illness, unlike bodily illness, often involves value judgments which may seem to identify it with moral rather than scientific problems. The ambiguous nature of mental illness, as between fact and value, has been at the heart of the long-running debate between medical psychiatry and various forms of antipsychiatry. Recent work on the concept of mental illness has produced a more complete picture in which the two sides of the concept—its factual/scientific and evaluative/human sides—are, in effect, reconciled. This has important implications for practice, underscoring in particular the central place of science in psychiatry while at the same time recognizing the ineliminable role of values not only in treatment choice but also in psychopathology and diagnosis. Although neglected until recently by bioethics, in favor of problems arising in "high-tech" medicine, the value-laden nature of mental illness makes mental health practice more problematic ethically than any other area of health care. It also brings mental health closer than any other area of health care to many of the deepest problems in general philosophy. In mental health practice there is no gap between theoretical and applied ethics.

I. INTRODUCTION

Scratch an ethical problem in clinical work or research in mental health and you will find a deep philosophical difficulty: personal identity (e.g., responsibility in dissociative states, such as multiple personality disorder), the self (e.g., the ethics of psychoanalysis, which in effect reconstructs the self), akratic acts (e.g., the status of compulsive behaviors such as addictions, obsessions, and kleptomania as legal excuses), meanings and causes (e.g., the place of brain scan images as evidence in court), and, more abstract still, issues such as free will (e.g., the age of "criminal responsibility") and the justification of true belief (e.g., the significance of delusions as a ground for involuntary psychiatric treatment).

The shared agenda of philosophy and mental health greatly expands the difficulties of applied ethics in this area. In general surgery, for example, issues of consent to treatment, tricky enough to be sure, can (standardly) assume autonomous agents capable (to the normal extent) of rational choice. In mental health, by contrast, it is these very assumptions that are problematic ethically. Again, in surgery patients may sometimes make irrational, or otherwise apparently nonautonomous, choices *about* their disorder, and this can lead to ethical difficulties. But in mental health it is the *disorder itself* by which rational, and hence autonomous, choice is prejudiced.

Understood in this way, the concept of mental illness (or, more generally, mental disorder) stands as a conduit, or cipher, between the sharp end of practice in mental health and the sharp end of philosophical theory. Small wonder, then, that it has been and remains the subject of a long-running debate. It is the main moves in this debate, the main interpretations or models of mental illness that have been advanced, which are the focus of this article. I will not be considering, directly, the many ethical problems raised by practice and research in mental health (these are comprehensively covered elsewhere). My aim, rather, will be to outline the key logical features of the concept of mental illness and thus to provide an (enlarged) framework for ethical analysis in this most difficult area.

II. TERMINOLOGY AND THE VARIETY OF MENTAL ILLNESS

Much discussion of the concept of mental illness, whether in ethics, law, or philosophy, is flawed by (1) terminological inconsistencies and (2) a failure to recognize the widely diverse conditions which the concept embraces.

A. Terminology: Mental Illness and Mental Disorder

In this article the term "mental illness" covers those mental disorders that are nowadays widely assumed to be generically linked with physical, or bodily, illness. As such, mental illness is a subcategory of mental disorder; other subcategories include mental handicap, personality disorder and reactions to stressors (e.g., postraumatic stress disorder, or PTSD). This is broadly consistent with both medical and legal usage. Modern psychiatric classifications, for example, take themselves to be not just of mental illnesses but of mental *disorders* Similarly, in much mental health legislation (e.g., in the United Kingdom's Mental Health Act, 1983), mental *disorder* is defined as "mental illness, mental handicap, or any other disability or disorder of mind."

B. The Varieties of Mental Illness

Mental illness, although a narrower concept than mental disorder, still covers a wide range of very different conditions. It is important to recognize this. In much of the ethical and philosophical literature on the concept of mental illness it is assumed either that a given disorder (such as hysteria or schizophrenia) is paradigmatic of mental illness in general or that the meaning of mental illness can be adequately captured by a nonspecific and generic notion of irrationality. It is, however, in the *heterogeneity* of the concept that the key to its practical, ethical, and indeed philosophical significance is to be found.

In this section, therefore, the variety of mental illnesses, and of related mental disorders, will be described. Definitions of all the conditions referred to, together with case vignette examples, are given in Box 1, Glossary of Mental Disorders. As this list shows, any aspect of the mind—emotion, belief, volition, etc.— may be "disordered": and psychiatrists, in assessing a patient, run through these aspects in what is called a "mental state examination" (the mental equivalent of a "physical examination"). A traditional and still important subdivision of mental disorders, especially for ethical and legal purposes, is into psychotic and nonpsychotic varieties.

1. Psychotic Disorders

Psychotic disorders are those severe forms of mental illness which, colloquially, and in some legal contexts, would be called madness or insanity. They are characterized by delusions (pathological false beliefs, e.g., believing falsely that you are Mary Magdalene [Case 1b]

or are guilty of some crime [Case 1a]), hallucinations (pathological false perceptions, i.e., not just "hearing voices" but believing them to be real [Case 1b] or seeing things that are not there [Case 4]), and certain disorders of the possession of thought (e.g., thought insertion— the experience of having other people's thoughts inserted into your mind [Case 2]).

The common feature of these symptoms, and the feature that gives them their particular ethical and legal significance, is that the patient characteristically "lacks insight" into their nature as symptoms of mental illness. In Case 1a, for example, the patient did not go to his doctor complaining of "guilty feelings"; he believed he really was guilty of causing the war in the former Yugoslavia. In Case 1b, similarly, the patient did not complain of "hearing voices"; she actually heard people telling her she was Mary Magdalene. And in Case 2, the patient complained that people were using his mind to carry their thoughts. This was not an "as if" experience; far from wanting treatment, he wanted someone to stop the people concerned from abusing him in this way.

2. Nonpsychotic Disorders

Nonpsychotic disorders are usually, though not necessarily, less severe than psychotic disorders. They are characterized by disturbances of emotion (e.g., anxiety [Cases 5 and 6]), depression (Case 7), volition (e.g., obsessive–compulsive disorders, such as compulsive checking as in Case 9), motivation (e.g., hysterical paralysis (Case 8), appetite (e.g., anorexia [Case 12]), sexual function (Case 13), and other drives (e.g., addictions [Case 14]). In all these disorders insight is, characteristically, preserved. Thus a patient with *delusions* of guilt (in which insight is lacking, as in Case 1b) may go to a priest or the police. But a patient with *obsessions* of guilt (in which insight is preserved, as in Case 9) will complain of these as "unwanted thoughts" and may well seek medical help.

Until about ten years ago, most classifications of mental disorders made a primary distinction between psychotic and nonpsychotic forms of mental illness, the term "neurotic" often being used for the latter. In the two most widely used modern classifications, the WHO's *International Classification of Diseases* (or ICD), and the American Psychiatric Association's *Diagnostic and Statistical Manual* (or DSM), this distinction has been replaced by a primary subdivision according to the main symptom groups. Psychiatric classifications remain primarily symptom based, however, in contrast to physical medicine, in which the classification of diseases is nowadays mainly by reference to *causes* (e.g.,

Box 1

Glossary of Mental Disorders[a]

(1a) Manic-depressive illness: Depressed type

Psychotic disorder with depressed mood. The psychoses are severe disorders with loss of insight shown characteristically by delusions, hallucinations, and certain forms of thought disorder (e.g., thought insertion—see Schizophrenia, below).

> Mr. S. D., Age 50, Shop Keeper: Presented in casualty (with his wife) with a 3-week history of "biological" symptoms of depression (early waking, weight loss, fixed diurnal variation of mood) and delusions of guilt (believed he caused the war in former Yugoslavia). History of attempted suicide during previous similar episode. Denied that he was depressed but said he needed something to help him sleep.

(1b) Manic-depressive illness: Manic type

Psychotic disorder with elevated mood. The following case would be one of hypomania, i.e., somewhat less severe than mania. The advent of modern antipsychotic drugs has meant that patients rarely reach the (life threatening) stage of full mania.

> Miss H. M., Age 25, Novice Nun: Brought by superiors for urgent out-patient appointment as they were unable to contain her bizarre and sexually disinhibited behavior (running away from the convent and soliciting "for the Lord"). Showed pressure of speech (continuous talking), grandiose delusions (that her minor charities are saintly acts of "great and enduring moral worth"), and auditory hallucinations (female voices telling her she is Mary Magdalene).

(2) Schizophrenia

Psychotic disorder with specific delusions, hallucinations, and disorders of thought ("first-rank" symptoms) together with a large number of other disturbances, especially of affect and volition.

> Mr. S., Age 18, Student: Emergency psychiatric admission from his college. Behaving oddly (found wandering in bemused and agitated state). Complained that people were talking about him. Showed throught insertion (John Major "using my brain for his thoughts") but no cognitive impairment (see Dementia, below).

(3) Paranoid disorders (e.g., Othello syndrome)

Psychotic disorders with well-developed delusional symptoms (not necessarily of persecution) and little other pathology. In the Othello syndrome the paranoid system is built around delusions of infidelity.

> Mr. A., Age 47, Publican: Seen by general practitioner initially because his wife was depressed. However, Mr. A. complained of anxiety and impotence. GP suspected alcohol abuse. After some discussion, Mr. A. suddenly announced that "the problem" was that his wife was "a tart." Once started, he went on at length about her infidelity, drawing on a wide range of evidence, some of it bizzare (that she washed their towels on a different day; that the pattern of cars parked in the street had changed).

(4) Dementia

Psychotic disorder with progressive impairment of "cognitive" functions—memory, attention, orientation (time, place, person), and general IQ. Due to gross brain pathology, hence sometimes called "organic psychosis." Acute (and usually reversible) disturbances of cognitive functions occur in confusional states (e.g., after a blow to the head or with intoxication). Visual hallucinations are common.

> Mrs. G. M., Age 65, Shopkeeper: Referred by general practitioner when her customers complained that she had started to forget their orders. Family confirmed she had become forgetful and at times seemed confused. She had been complaining of seeing rats in her storeroom but there was no evidence of these. Initially denied problem but on cognitive function testing unable, e.g., to recall a simple name and address after a gap of 5 minutes.

(5) Anxiety disorder: Generalized

Sustained periods of anxiety with associated bodily symptoms in absence of appropriate cause.

> Mrs. B., Age 35, Teacher: Presented to general practitioner complaining of a constant sense of anxiety for which she could give no reason, developing over about 3 months. Had always been a worrier but coped well with a stressful job. Had difficulty getting to sleep and bodily symptoms (palpitation and difficulty swallowing).

(6) Anxiety disorder: Phobic

Pathological anxiety related to a specific object (e.g., thunder phobia, as in the vignette) or situation (e.g., social phobia and agoraphobia) and leading to avoidance of the feared situation.

> Mrs. R. D., Age 23, Housewife: Visited by district nurse at home as she had failed to attend for postnatal follow-up. She explained that she had become afraid to go out because of a fear of thunder. This had been a lifelong fear but had become worse since she gave up work to have her baby. Even approaching the front door produced feelings of panic with bodily symptoms (palpitation, hyperventilation, tingling in her fingers).

(7) Depression: Nonpsychotic

Pathological depression of mood without psychotic features.

> Mr. R. J., Age 32, Bricklayer: Presented to general practitioner complaining of feeling miserable and having difficulty getting to sleep. For some months he had lost his enjoyment of life and tended to lie awake at night worrying about the future, even though he had no particular problems at present. Physical examination was normal and he had not lost weight.

(8) Hysterical disorders

Physical symptoms (e.g., paralysis, blindness, memory loss) due primarily to psychological rather than bodily causes.

> Miss H. P., Age 30, Secretary: Admitted to neurology ward and transferred to psychiatry under protest. Unable to move right hand. No evidence of physical lesion. History of depression and self-injury.

(9) Obsessive–compulsive disorder

Recurrent mental content (obsession) or behavior (compulsion) typically recognized by patient to be irrational and which they (unsuccessfully) try to resist (like a bad case of getting a tune "stuck in your head").

> Mr. O. C., Age 27, Bank Clerk: Three-year history of progressive slowness. Referred with recent depression and anxiety following suspension from work. Showed severe and progressive compulsive checking together with recurrent guilty feelings, both of which he regarded as "ridiculous" but was unable to stop.

(10) Acute reaction to stress

Marked psychological reaction (which may take many different forms) to sudden stressful stimulus. Adjustment disorders are corresponding reactions to more chronic situations (e.g., a grief reaction which becomes excessively extended). These disorders are in many respects the psychological counterpart of physical trauma or wounds.

> Mr. J. B., Age 55, Doctor: Involved in serious car accident while returning from an emergency call-out late at night. No head injury. Was unable to recall the accident. Felt anxious, distressed, and unable to cope with his work for several days. Then developed a brief, self-limiting hypomanic reaction.

(11) Psychopathic personality disorder

Personality disorders differ from illnesses in being more or less fixed features of the way a person feels, thinks, or behaves. With psychopathy the disorder is manifested mainly in repeated delinquency. The conduct disorders of childhood have similar manifestations but are self-limiting. Hyperkinetic syndrome of childhood is pathologically overactive behavior.

> Mr. P. P., Age 23, Unemployed: Seen in casualty by duty psychiatrist. Brought in by girlfriend because he was threatening to kill a rival. Had been drinking. History of repeated criminal assaults. Promiscuous. Showed little understanding of the feelings of others involved or concern about the results of his behavior.

(12) Anorexia nervosa

Pathological disorder of eating in which the patient (who is usually a woman) refuses to eat, may exercise excessively, and abuse laxatives. Self-induced vomiting is common. Patients with anorexia typically perceive themselves as fat despite extreme emaciation. They may show physiological and other changes of starvation (including amenorrhea, i.e., their menstrual periods stopping).

> Miss A. N., Age 21, Student: Four-year history of intermittent anorexia. Currently seriously underweight, exercising, and using laxatives; amenorrheic. Refusing admission on the grounds that she insists she is "too fat."

(13) Sexual disorders

These may involve (1) pathological changes in sexual drive and/or function or (2) disorders of sexual-object choice (e.g., sadism, pedophilia).

> Mr. R. P., Age 22, Postgraduate Student: Attended student counseling service complaining of difficulty maintaining an erection. Had a steady girlfriend and normal sexual interest and drive. Struggling to finish his doctoral thesis.

(14) Alcoholism and drug addiction

Abuse of alcohol or drugs which is out of the patient's control. There is often denial of the problem.

> Mr. A. R., Age 38, Shopkeeper: Self-referral to general practitioner from Relate (marriage guidance counseling). Over several years had increased his alcohol consumption and was now drinking a bottle of spirits and several pints of beer every day. Without a drink in the morning his hands shook. His wife was threatening to divorce him and he had lost many of his customers. However, he was ambivalent about the referral, arguing that he had the problem "under control."

(15) Mental subnormality and developmental disorders of childhood

With mental subnormality there is pathologically low IQ together with varying degrees of emotional and behavioral abnormality persisting from birth. The developmental disorders of childhood include delays in reaching normal milestones; e.g., persistent urinary incontinence ("bed wetting"), delayed walking, talking, or reading.

> [a] Mental disorders represent a very diverse group of conditions. This glossary gives brief definitions and vignette case examples of some of the more common and important mental disorders. An outline of the standard or basic medical classification of these disorders is given in Box 2. The ethical and conceptual relationships between the main groups of disorder is illustrated in the form of a map of psychiatry in Figure 1 (the numbering in this glossary corresponds with that in the map). All the cases described are composites of real patients but with biographical and other identifying details changed.

"B12 deficiency anemia" is anemia due to the deficiency of the vitamin B12). Psychiatry is thus more like neurology in this respect, neurological disorders also being defined mostly by way of *symptoms* and *symptom clusters*. Thus, even "organic disorders," such as dementia (e.g., Case 4), which stand somewhere between psychiatry and neurology, are defined by the presence of particular symptoms (so-called cognitive symptoms, such as disorientation, falling IQ, and memory loss). These symptoms suggest the presence of underlying major brain pathology, but the disorders as such are defined symptomatically. The only consistent exception to this is the addictions (e.g., Case 14), where the causes of the disorder are part of their definition.

C. Recent Medical Classifications of Mental Disorders

The details of modern classifications differ but most have the same basic form. This is given in Box 2, The Basic Classification. Psychotic disorders are now included mainly in the "Organic Disorders" (e.g., Dementia [Case 4]), the "disorders of mood," (i.e., sadness/happiness, as in Case 1a [depression] and Case 1b [manic-depression], respectively), and "other psychotic disorders" (this includes schizophrenia, of which thought insertion is an important symptom (e.g., Case 2); and the paranoid disorders, characterized by well-developed delusional systems (e.g., the "Othello Syndrome" of delusions of infidelity, [Case 3]). The ICD and DSM (see above) both broadly follow this form.

Box 2

The Basic Classification of Mental Disorders[a]

Adult Categories of Mental Illness

Organic Disorders

- Acute (confusional states)
- Chronic (dementias—primary, secondary)
- Neuropsychiatric syndromes (e.g., personality change due to brain tumor)

Alcohol/drug related conditions

- Addiction states
- Complications of use/abuse
- Withdrawal syndromes

Psychotic disorders other than organic and affective

- Schizophrenia
- Persistent delusional disorder
- Brief psychotic episode

Affective disorders (happiness/sadness)

- Depression

  Major ("psychotic"/"biological")

  Minor ("neurotic")

- Hypomania
- Bipolar (swinging between mania and depression)
- Schizoaffective (features of schizophrenia as well as affective disorder)

Anxiety and related disorders

- Anxiety disorder (generalized, phobic, panic)
- Obsessive-compulsive
- Dissociative (e.g., hysteria)
- Somatoform (e.g., psychogenic pain, hypochondriasis)

Disorders of vegetative function

- Eating (anorexia nervosa, bulimia)
- Sexual function (of drive and performance, or of sexual object choice)
- Sleep (insomnia, hypersomnia, sleep terrors, etc.)

Other Categories of Adult Disorder

Personality disorder (very long-term maladaptive personality traits)

Stress-induced disorders (mental disorders resulting from extreme stress; e.g., psychological trauma

Child/Adolescent Disorders

Mental retardation (mild, moderate, severe, profound)

Specific developmental delays (e.g., speech, reading, spelling, arithmetic)

Pervasive disorders (autism; disintegrative psychosis; schizoid disorder of childhood)

Behavioral disorders (hyperkinetic syndrome; conduct disorders, socialized and unsocialized)

Emotional disorders (e.g., separation anxiety, school phobia)

Disorders of physiological functions (e.g., enuresis)

[a] The details of the medical classification of mental disorders varies to some extent from country to country and from authority to authority. However, most systems nowadays recognize the same broad groups of disorders and a "basic classification" along the lines set out here will be found in many textbooks.

The replacement in modern classifications of the traditional psychotic/nonpsychotic distinction by a series of basic categories, defined by symptom groups, represents an important advance in psychiatric nosology. It reflects a recognition that while the *symptoms* presented by a particular patient may be reliably differentiated into psychotic and nonpsychotic, according to the extent to which "insight' is preserved, this is not the case with the broader categories of *mental disorder*. In anorexia nervosa, for example, traditionally among the nonpsychotic disorders, insight, in the relevant sense, is often lacking (e.g., Case 12). Conversely, patients with long-term psychotic disorders, such as schizophrenia, often develop good insight: over a period of time, they learn to distinguish hallucinatory voices from real voices, for example.

Used of the symptoms presented by particular patients, the term "psychotic," and the loss of insight it implies, remains crucially important (1) in medicolegal and ethical contexts (see below), (2) to the communication aspects of practice, including some forms of psychological treatment, and (3) in research. (The term *neurosis* is nowadays used mainly in psychoanalytic contexts.) Used of mental disorders, on the other hand, as in the ICD and DSM, "psychotic" is nowadays a dispositional term: it implies only that these are disorders in which psychotic symptoms characteristically occur.

III. THE CONTESTED NATURE OF MENTAL ILLNESS

Underlying the heterogeneity of the disorders recognized by present-day psychiatry, there has been a long-running debate about the nature of mental illness itself. Until fairly recently, this debate was polarized between psychiatry, with a "medical" model of mental illness as no different in principle from physical illness, and various forms of antipsychiatry, which reject the medical model altogether. Recent developments in our understanding of the concept of mental illness (described in Section III) are best set in the context of this debate.

A. A Brief History of the Concept of Mental Illness

The idea that certain forms of mental disorder might be generically linked with physical illness is not new: the Greeks, for example, had a concept of mental illness. It is also to be found in many different cultures around the world. Until the nineteenth century, however, the idea that mental disorders might be illnesses had to compete on a more or less equal footing with other theories. Mental disorders might reflect moral or spiritual weakness, for instance, or possession states, sometimes beatific, sometimes demonic.

The rise of the medical model in the nineteenth century has been attributed to both scientific and social factors: to the growing successes of medical science in other areas (the germ theory, for instance); but also to changing social attitudes to mental disorder, arising from the need to sequestrate deviants in the work-oriented culture of the Industrial Revolution. Whatever its origins, the scientific basis of psychiatry at this early stage was highly heterogeneous, each school of thought having its own system of classification. Medical psychiatry in its modern form emerged only toward the end of the nineteenth and in the early twentieth centuries. Two figures of central importance at this time were the German psychiatrist Emil Kraepelin, whose classification of the main categories of mental disorder, set out in the eighth edition of his textbook, remains the basis of those in use today (see below); and the German philosopher–psychiatrist Karl Jaspers, whose *General Psychopathology* laid the foundations of modern descriptive psychopathology, by which the symptoms of mental illness are defined.

From the start, though, the medical model, as an explanatory scientific framework for understanding mental disorders, had two main competitors, psychology and psychoanalysis. There had been psychological models of mental disorder earlier in the nineteenth century, and behavioral models became firmly established with the work of Pavlov in Russia. Sigmund Freud, whose early work in Vienna established the main tenets of psychoanalysis, was a contemporary of Jaspers and Kraepelin.

These three approaches to understanding the causes of mental disorder—medical, psychological, and psychoanalytic—are concerned with different domains. As scientific models of mental disorder, therefore, they are not incompatible in principle. The medical model posits disease entities based on (putative) disturbances of brain functioning: mental disorders are thus taken to be comparable with, say, liver diseases based on disturbances of liver functioning. The psychoanalytic model assumes that the origins of mental disorder are to be found in distorted intrapsychic structures to which the subject generally has little or no conscious access (they are thus in the subject's "unconscious"). The scientific status of psychoanalysis remains a contested area: but Freud, who was trained as a neurophysiologist, believed, at least in his early work, that psychoanalysis could reveal psychological structures which would eventually be reduced to brain mechanisms. Psychological theories, of the Pavlovian type, are overtly behaviorist: they deal with the symptoms of mental disorder direct, as learned abnormalities of experience and behavior, rather than attempting to treat their underlying causes. In one of Pavlov's classic experiments, for example, he showed that dogs could be "taught" neurotic symptoms simply by exposing them to inconsistent conditioning.

If these three models are compatible in principle, however (or, at any rate, complementary) they were certainly conceived competitively; and for the first half of this century they developed to a large extent separately. All three achieved considerable influence but generally in different parts of the world; the medical model in the United Kingdom and Germany, for example; the psychoanalytic in France and the USA; and the psychological model in the USSR.

It was only in the period after World War II that a more eclectic approach began to be taken, at least by many practitioners. There were good pragmatic grounds for this, in that all three models were now beginning to pay off in terms of practically effective treatments. The practitioner, uncommitted to a particular theoretical position, could thus pick and choose. It was over this period, for example, that powerful and specific medical treatments first became available for many of the most severe and intractable mental disorders: lithium for mania (especially to prevent relapse), a range of antidepressants for depression, and the neuroleptics for psychotic disorders such as schizophrenia and acute mania. It was over this period, too, that psychoanalytic ideas began to break free from ideology and dogma and to influence theory and practice in a number of fields, such as child development, family psychiatry, psychotherapy, and counseling, as well as providing one of the foundations for the relatively new discipline of social psychiatry. And it was over this period that the potential of psychological treatments (in particular, for emotional disorders such as anxiety and depression) was becoming firmly established (although it was to be a few years before the precedence of these treatments over medical treatments, such as Valium [diazepam], became widely accepted).

For the ideologically committed, though, this meeting of models, far from being welcome, meant a contest for territory. It was over this same period, then, and continuing into the 1960s and 1970s, that a battle for "market share" developed between the three main explanatory schools. More remarkable, though, given the growing successes of all three, it was over this period, too, that a reaction developed against the whole idea of mental illness. This came from a number of disciplinary

perspectives, but it shared with psychology and psychoanalysis a broad opposition to the medical model.

B. Psychiatry and Antipsychiatry

The debate between psychiatry and antipsychiatry in the 1960s and 1970s produced what at first sight appears to have been a bewildering range of views about the concept of mental illness. For many, the medical model was the common enemy; hence the widely adopted generic term antipsychiatry for all those, including many psychoanalysts and psychologists, with opposing views. But among antipsychiatrists, everyone disagreed with everyone else.

In this section the main features of the most influential of the models developed over this period will be outlined. They are summarized in Table I and additional references are given in the Bibliography. Through all the diversity of models of models of mental disorder, seven main varieties can be distinguished: (1) medical, (2) psychological, (3) psychoanalytic, (4) sane reaction, (5) labeling, (6) political, and (7) problems of living.

1. The Medical Model

As the model implicit in medical psychiatry, this model has been hotly defended by a number of authors in direct response to the challenge of antipsychiatry (e.g., Kendell, 1975). The medical model acknowledges that our understanding of brain functioning is less well developed than in the case of other organs. But it assumes that, ultimately, the causes of mental disorders will be found in disturbances of brain functioning, and that mental illness is therefore in principle no different from physical illness. This model is particularly helpful with severe disorders such as the organic and other psychoses.

2. The Psychological Model

Derived from the work of Pavlov and others in learning theory, this model assumes that mental disorders are learned abnormalities of thought, feeling, and behavior (see above). The model has proved to be particularly effective with anxiety disorders and milder forms of depression. Phobias (see Case 6), for example, are nowadays standardly treated by retraining through progressive exposure to the feared situations combined with psychological techniques for reducing anxiety; and some forms of depression are treated by learning to use positive thoughts to counter negative thoughts. The model has recently shown promise also in relation to psychotic symptoms such as auditory hallucinations.

TABLE I

Models of Mental Disorder[a]

Medical model

Mental disorders strictly equivalent to bodily *diseases* such as heart disease or appendicitis. Disease is defined as "biological dysfunction" by anatomical/physiological norms or by "evolutionary norms" (e.g., reduced life/reproductive potential).

Diagnosis: Descriptive, especially of particular symptoms, which are considered equivalent to bodily symptoms and signs (e.g., angina, abdominal tenderness). Hence, descriptive psychopathology is the key diagnostic tool.

Classification: Syndromal; equivalent to syndromal stage in development of disease classification in physical medicine. Distinct categories of disorder defined by statistically significant associations of symptoms. Assumed to be "theory-free." Assumed to point to underlying disorders of brain functioning.

Practice: Diagnosis and treatment choice led by medically qualified doctors: etiology should be primarily brain based (though, like other diseases, mental disorders are influenced by psychological/social factors): treatments primarily physical (drugs, ECT) where these are available; doctor as leader of multidisciplinary team.

Patient: Not responsible (morally); passive in treatment; values (and other aspects of experience of illness) important only in treatment choice.

Research: Brain sciences; modeled on biology.

Exemplars: Kendell; Boorse.

Psychological

Mental disorders understood as learned abnormalities of behavior (which includes thinking, feeling, believing, etc.).

Diagnosis: Assesses functional deficits in affect, thinking, etc.

Classification: Quantitative/dimensional aspects of behavior.

Practice: Assessment and treatment choice led by clinical psychologist; etiology understood via learning theory; treatments primarily psychological (behavioral, cognitive); psychologist as independent professional.

Patient: Not responsible (morally); active in treatment; values important in process as well as choice of treatment.

Research: Psychological science (positivist; statistical tests, etc.).

Exemplars: Eysenck; Rachman.

Psychoanalytic/psychotherapeutic (talking therapies)

Mental disorders symptomatic of unconicious metnal processes (especially conflicts). Distress due to unresolved unconscious conflicts.

Diagnosis: Often uses psychiatric descriptive psychopathological concepts (e.g., obsession, delusion, etc.).

Classification: Elements of unconscious mental life (e.g., unresolved Oedipal complex).

Practice: Diagnosis and treatment led by trained analyst/therapist (a majority are *not* medically qualified); etiology understood via unconscious equivalents of wishes, desires, beliefs, drives, etc.; treatment by trained psychoanalysts/therapists; analyst/therapist as independent professional.

Patient: Not responsible morally; active in treatment; values important in process as well as choice of treatment; treatment usually by way of two-way, dyadic exchange or small group (including family).

Research: Psychoanalytic (mostly via case observations in therapy).

Exemplars: Freud; Klein.

Sane reaction

Mental disorders (especially schizophrenia) represent a sane reaction to an insane society.

Diagnosis: Condition recognized by same features as in medical psychiatry, but not regarded as an illness.

Classification: Not relevant.

Practice: "Patient" allowed to work through psychiatric experiences on a journey of self-discovery to "recovery."

Patient: A moral agent; patient's perspective is paramount.

Research: Sociological work on role of others, especially family, in general and in the maintenance of psychotic experience.

Exemplar: Laing.

Labeling

Mentally disordered individuals are a product of social processes in society as a whole. Distress/disturbed social functioning defined by social norms.

Diagnosis: Not relevant. Mental "disorder" defined by roles adopted within the social group to which the subject belongs.

Classification: Relational concepts (e.g., scapegoating).

continues

continued

Practice: Assessment of social situation; social worker as mediator/facilitator of social processes/change; other interventions (medical, psychological) necessary only to "patch up" social inequities where direct political action is not possible.

"Patient": A client, not responsible individually; values important in generating social action; abnormality defined by social values.

Research: Social science.

Exemplars: Scheff/Mechanic, Rosenhan (labeling theory); Parsons (deviance theory).

Political/control theories

Disorder is a sham, a product of deliberate and motivated misuse of disease/madness labels in exercise of political/personal power over others.

Diagnosis: Categories imposed by others (e.g., "delusion of reconstruction" used as diagnosis for political dissidence in former USSR).

Classification: Not relevant.

Practice: As medical or other models (but as part of deliberate misuse).

Patient: Victim; relevant values are those of *others* (political [USSR]; individual gain [sporadic]).

"Research": Political action/criminal investigation.

Exemplars: Foucault (re: *all* mental disorders); Bloch/Fulford (re: USSR).

Problems of living

Mental disorder is a product of avoidable personal failure (or deliberate contrivance).

Diagnosis: Lay judgments of categories defined by personal/political value norms.

Classification: Moral categories (e.g., malingering); also, vices (e.g., cowardice, sloth); sins (e.g., drunkenness, theft); failings (e.g., foolishness; etc.).

Practice: Assessment of other people, mostly peers, also (in special circumstances) experts—the law, priests, some kinds of counselors (e.g., career advisers); causes—moral weakness, foolishness, etc.; "treatment"—advice, encouragement, punishment; moral/political leaders; doctors, psychologists, etc., have no special role (may be harmful, e.g., offering false excuses).

"Patient": A person; fully responsible morally; values (personal or social) define problems as well as solutions.

Research: N/A. Education and experience relevant; notion of "wisdom" rather than knowledge.

Exemplar: Szasz.

Recent philosophical theories

Central place of values (alongside facts); mental disorder defined by disturbances of action (as well as of function).

Diagnosis: Descriptive psychopathology extended to include intention (volition, etc.) as elements of action.

Classification: Elements of both medical and psychological approaches.

Practice: Diagnosis and treatment choice by multidisciplinary team; causal and meaningful understanding equally important; eclectic treatment choice.

Patient: Not responsible with some disorders (paradigmatically delusion); treatment empowering; patients' values and experience of illness central to diagnostic assessment as well as treatment.

Research: Brain and psychological sciences together with philosophy of action (i.e., aspects of philosophy of mind and moral philosophy); ethnographic and other qualitative methods in clinical research.

Exemplars: Nordenfelt; Fulford; Rosenberg (and a variety of others, mainly in Scandinavian countries).

---

[a] There is a very wide range of theories of the meanings of mental disorder (and of related notions, e.g., mental illness, mental health, insanity). These vary from exclusively "scientific" models (taking mental disorder to be an essentially factual/scientific notion) to exclusively "moral" models (according to which mental disorder is an essentially evaluative/ethical notion), with all varieties in between. Different theories have different implications for each stage of the clinical process.

3. The Psychoanalytic Model

Although sometimes advocated as a sinecure and certainly influential in literature and art as much as medicine, psychoanalysis is nowadays generally considered most helpful for long-term, deeply ingrained disorders with good preservation of insight, especially where these involve relationship difficulties. The traditional focus on wholly unconscious mental processes is no longer universal; but there is a general recognition that there may be important influences on our conscious feelings and behavior of which we are not fully aware. Besides the many schools of psychoanalysis, psychotherapies of various kinds, and counselling, are all important in the multidisciplinary approach to modern psychiatric practice.

4. The Sane Reaction Model

This was the first of the anti-mental illness models to emerge in the 1950s. Advanced by the Scottish psychiatrist R. D. Laing, this model claims that far from people with schizophrenia being mentally ill, their so-called symptoms are the only possible sane reaction to an insane environment. Laing focused particularly on certain kinds of incompatible messages that an adolescent may receive from his or her family. He showed that many of the details of the symptoms of schizophrenia, including the separation of "me" from the thoughts in my head, as in thought insertion (see above, Case 2), could be understood in this way.

5. The Labeling Model

In its most radical form this model portrays the symptoms of mental disorder as arising not from the disorder, but from the effects on the individual of being labeled as mentally disordered. This is now generally accepted as too extreme. But a dramatic demonstration of the power of labeling was an experiment described by the American psychologist David L. Rosenhan in his classic paper *On Being Sane in Insane Places* (*Science* 179, 250–258). He and a number of colleagues had themselves admitted to various mental hospitals by claiming they could hear voices; once admitted, nothing they could say or do would convince the staff that they were sane—even writing research notes was labeled "obsessive writing behavior."

6. The Political Control Model

An important example of this model was developed by the French philosopher-historian Michel Foucault in his monumental *Madness and Civilisation* (1973, New York: Random House). The model emphasizes the extent to which the rise of the medical model in the nineteenth century reflected the need to sequestrate deviants of the work ethic of the Industrial Revolution, and ignores advances in scientific understanding. According to this model, calling someone mentally ill is in effect a way of removing a potentially dangerous deviant from society rather than a genuine attempt to help them through legitimate medical means. Those involved, of course, are often not aware that this is what they are doing; psychiatrists, no more than patients, are in this respect puppets of the wider society.

7. The Problems of Living Model

The name Thomas Szasz (see above) is inseparably linked with the most coherent version of this model. Although a professor of psychiatry, he argues (for exam-

ple in *Madness and Civilization: A History of Insanity in the Age of Reason*. New York: Random House, 1973) that mental disorders are not really illnesses but everyday problems of living. The importance of recognizing this, according to Szasz, is that it restores the locus of responsibility to the individual concerned. By and large, we are not responsible for being ill. Hence, if mental illness is a myth, then (1) the so-called mentally ill, even those with "delusions," are fully responsible in law, and (2) they should not be subject to the indignity of involuntary treatment, even if they are suicidal.

C. Psychiatry, Antipsychiatry, and the Varieties of Mental Illness

The wide range of views about the concept of mental illness which emerged in the 1960s and 1970s can be understood as reflecting different aspects of the concept itself. Figure 1 makes this point schematically. It shows the main categories of mental disorder described in Section 1 displayed in the form of a conceptual map of mental disorder. (The numbers on the map cross-refer to Box 1, Glossary of Mental Disorders.)

As Figure 1 illustrates, mental disorders can be thought of as standing between physical disorders on the one hand (to the right of the map) and moral problems on the other (to the left of the map). Shown this way, the figure illustrates four important conceptual features of a mental disorder. In the remainder of this section, these features will be described and their significance for the psychiatry/antipsychiatry debate will be indicated. In the next section, these same four features will also figure prominently in relation to recent developments in our understanding of the concept of mental illness. Thus, the four conceptual features are:

(*Feature 1*) *Variable Fact/Value Connotations.* Some mental disorders are more, and others less, obviously value-laden. This is reflected in the map in the spread of mental disorders between medicine (fact) and morals (value): disorders which are conceptually close to physical medicine (e.g., dementia) have, like physical illness, predominantly *factual* connotations; but as we move to the left, *value* connotations become more pronounced. One very tangible indication of this is the way in which some of these disorders are defined in modern psychiatric classifications. These classifications claim to be objective, to be based on scientific data. But the definition of "asocial personality disorder," for example, in the American DSM, is in terms of behavior which "violates social rules and norms."

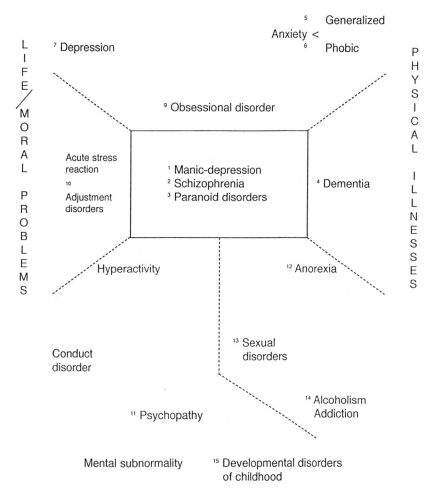

FIGURE 1   A conceptual map of psychiatry. Although not representing an established classification of mental disorders, this map illustrates a number of the features of the conceptual terrain of psychiatry which any theory of the meaning of mental illness must explain. (The numbers cross-refer to the case examples given in Box 1.)

(*Feature 2*) *Variable (Conceptual) Distance from Physical Illness.* The map illustrates the way in which some groups of mental disorders are *prima facie* closer than others to physical illnesses. Thus the organic psychoses, such as the dementias, are so close to physical illness that they are almost universally accepted as part of physical medicine; so much so, indeed, that these disorders are often not thought of as *mental* illnesses at all (they are excluded from mental health legislation covering involuntary treatment in some countries, for example). But the functional psychoses, too, although very much *mental* illnesses, are close to physical illnesses; it is here that medical drug treatments are most

helpful, for example. As we move further to the left across the map, however, the groups of mental disorders shown become less "medical" and more "moral." Alcoholism (medical) is close to drunkenness (moral), for example; personality disorder (medical) is close to delinquency (moral): and hysteria (medical) is close to malingering (moral).

(*Feature 3*) *Distinct Domains.* The major groups of mental disorders form domains that are relatively distinct although generically linked. These domains largely follow the basic classification outlined in Section 1 (see Box 2). A key difference between this conceptual map and standard psychiatric classifications, however, is that the map retains the primary distinction between psychotic and nonpsychotic disorders, the (functional) psychoses being grouped together centrally. As noted earlier, this distinction is important to our understanding especially of the ethical and medicolegal implications of the concept of mental illness.

(*Feature 4*) *Variable Status as Excusing Conditions.* Illness is an excuse; it is something for which, in general, we are not responsible—if I have an off-work certificate from a doctor, I am not malingering. This feature of illness has been emphasized particularly by sociologists, for example in Talcott Parson's now-classic analysis of delinquency (1951, *The Social System*, Glencoe, Illinois: The Free Press). It is a feature of mental disorders, too, but only to the extent that they are conceptually close to physical illnesses. Thus dementia and mental handicap are excuses; functional psychoses (especially where the patient has delusions) are the central case of mental illness as an excuse in law; other mental illnesses may excuse; but the status of disorders to the left of the map—personality disorder, alcoholism, and so forth—as excuses, is at best highly debatable (Aristotle, for example, in the *Nichomachean Ethics*, argued that a crime committed under the influence of alcohol, far from being excused, merited double punishment; our drunken-driving laws are a modern counterpart).

We can now see how the seven main schools of thought about the concept of mental illness, outlined in the previous section, can be understood as focusing (though of course not exclusively) on different aspects of the conceptual map of mental disorder.

Thus, the two most extreme views, the medical model (model 1), with its emphasis on facts and scientific disease theory, and the problems of living model (model 7), with its claim that mental disorders are defined by value norms, are identifiable respectively with the right- and left-hand extremes of the map. The psychological model (model 2) is also a "scientific" model, though with a greater readiness to recognize the importance of individual beliefs and values, at least to treatment. The psychoanalytic model (model 3) is a scientific model in one interpretation (including the early Freud's, see above); but it is also subject to a hermeneutic, or meaning-driven, understanding (as developed, for example, by the French psychoanalyst Paul Ricoeur)—hence its central place between the two extremes in the map. The remaining three models, the sane reaction model (4), the labeling model (5), and the political control model (6), all identify people with mental disorders as being victims (of the family, of false stereotyping, and of society, respectively). Hence they are all to the left (the moral problems) side of the map.

Identifying these models with different parts of the conceptual map of mental disorder makes the point that they are all partial; they all reflect partial, and hence, incomplete, views of mental disorder. We will return to this in the next section. To say that they are partial, however, is not to say that these models are trivial. Far from it. By exploring different aspects of mental disorder, each model has contributed something important to current theory and practice. The medical model (1) has contributed advances in drug treatments and in our understanding of the brain basis of mental disorders. Psychological treatments (model 2), including what are now called cognitive-behavioral therapies, have become the treatments of choice for many forms of anxiety and depressive disorders. Psychoanalysis (model 3), as already noted, has influenced many aspects of practice. Laing's theory of schizophrenia (model 4), although not borne out in detail by subsequent research, inspired careful work on the social and family factors influencing the course of this and other disorders. Labeling theory (model 5) helped to bring about changes in the organization of psychiatric services from institutional to community-based care. The political control model (6) anticipated the institutionalized abuses of psychiatry which occurred in the former USSR and other totalitarian regimes (modern mental health legislation is designed to reduce the risks of such abuses, sporadic or institutionalized—see also below). The radical antipsychiatry of Szasz and others (model 7) helped to found the important and growing user-movement among those with long-term mental disorders.

IV. RECENT MODELS

Important as the models of mental disorder developed in the debate of the 1960s and 1970s have been in shaping theory and practice in mental health, they were, nonetheless, partial. Recent work on the concept of mental illness can be thought of as seeking to move from partial models of this kind to a more complete understanding of the conceptual features of mental disorder. As we will see later, this development in conceptual understanding has run parallel with the shift in the organization of services from doctor-led institutions to community-based multidisciplinary teams, with an increasingly central role for users of services (i.e., patients and informal carers). In terms of our map, the conceptual counterpart of this move is that instead of focusing on one area of the conceptual geography of mental disorder, the aim is to explain the geography of the concept taken as a whole.

Modern work on the concept of mental illness, although detailed and wide-ranging, has produced two main kinds of model, (1) those which attempt to preserve an essentially medical model by making the conceptual connections with physical medicine primary and (2) models emphasizing the two-way connections of mental disorder from medical categories on the one hand to moral on the other. Models of the first kind, which are really a development of the medical model, can be thought of as "fact-*before*-value" models; models of the second kind, which put fact and value on an equal footing, can be thought of as "fact-*plus*-value" models.

A. Fact-before-Value Models

Fact-before-value models can be further subdivided into two main varieties, (a) value excluding and (b) value entailing (or descriptivist).

1. Value Excluding Models

An early exemplar of this approach, which is still among the most persuasive, is a model developed by the American philosopher Christopher Boorse toward the end of the 1970s. Boorse was concerned with the increasing "medicalization" of moral problems: "delinquency, divorce, almost every difficulty" was becoming thought of as an illness (1975, *On the distinction between disease and illness, Philosophy and Public Affairs* 5, 49–68). In terms of the map in Figure 1, then, Boorse's concern was that the scope of the concept of mental illness was being allowed to drift even further to the left, into a part of the logical terrain that, properly speaking, had nothing to do with medicine at all.

To counter this drift, he argued, we need a clearer understanding of the medical concepts. This alone could give us a firm basis for defining the boundary between medicine and morals. The medical concepts, he said, *contra* the traditional medical model, are, indeed, in part evaluative in meaning. However, the evaluative part of the meaning of these concepts is not to be found in the theoretical heart of medicine. Medical theory is *disease* theory. This is scientific; it is "continuous with theory in biology and the other basic sciences" and "it is value-free"; it is defined by biological dysfunction, the criteria for which include the purely factual norms of reduced life and/or reproductive potential. When it comes to the *practice* of medicine, on the other hand, values certainly do come in. Here the relevant concept is illness rather than disease: an illness is a

disease which, directly reflecting value norms, is "serious enough to be incapacitating."

Applying this to mental illness, then, Boorse continued, allows us to mark out the genuinely medical from the moral by the presence or absence of disturbed *mental* functioning, as defined biologically. *Mental* disease theory, it is true, is somewhat behind *bodily* disease theory scientifically. But with future developments in the brain sciences, we can expect the area of genuine mental illness (defined scientifically by reference to factual norms of mental functioning) to become increasingly clearly demarcated from morals.

Boorse's model thus puts facts first: values come in only secondarily to mark out those diseases which are also illnesses. This is why it is a "fact-*before*-value" theory. And in putting facts before values, it also puts medical disease theory, and hence doctors-as-experts, before the patients' actual experiences of illness. In this respect, then (and we will see later that this is crucial to the *ethical* significance of these models) it is consistent with the traditional medical model. It certainly corresponds broadly with the model to which most doctors would subscribe. Whatever their claims to a "bio-psycho-social" model, it is the *biological* model that occupies the largest part of the teaching agenda and attracts most of the research funds. It is this model, too, on which modern classifications of psychiatric disorder, the epitomies of medical theory, are primarily based. The model, moreover, has been highly influential well beyond medicine. Bioethics itself has been shaped by it (see below, Section V).

The model has not gone unchallenged, however. One reason for this is that it is not fully consistent with the conceptual features of mental disorder outlined a moment ago. Thus, it is consistent with features 1–3: feature 1 (variable fact/value connotations) and feature 2 (variable conceptual distance from physical illness) both follow, in Boorse's model, from the relatively underdeveloped state of the mental sciences: feature 3 (different domains) follows, in principle, at least to the extent that mental activity can be broken down into different mental functions (affect, volition, etc.). But the model fails to explain feature 4; it fails to explain why it is that psychotic disorders should be the paradigm case of mental illness as an excuse. On Boorse's model, illness is an excuse to the extent that *dys*functional parts or systems are outside the control of the individual. But as Boorse himself points out, this explanation fits other, *non*psychotic, domains more readily than the psychoses. Obsessive-compulsive disorder, for example, as the Oxford philosopher Jonathan Glover argued in his book on *Responsibility* (1970, London:

Routledge & Kegan Paul), should be paradigmatic if this model were right. Being unable to stop checking things, for example (as in Case 9, Box 1), really does look like a functional *part* or *subsystem* running out of control. Whereas the psychoses seem to involve a disturbance, not of this or that particular function, but, as Boorse puts it, of the individual *as a whole*.

A second and more general line of criticism of fact-before-value models is that they fail in their central claim, namely that disease, even as used in physical medicine, is value free. This point was made as early as the 1960s by the British sociologist Peter Sedgewick. It has been reinforced subsequently by several authors on both sides of the Atlantic. A key observation in this respect is that even those who take the term "disease" to be value free, continue to use it with clear evaluative connotations. This is true in medicine generally: but Boorse himself, having defined disease by reference to value-free statistical norms of "biological functioning," goes on to write of it in value-laden terms as involving, for example, "impaired functional efficiency." It is criticisms of this kind which lead to value-entailing models.

2. Value Entailing (or Descriptivist) Models

The criticism of Boorse's model just outlined connects the debate about mental illness with the long-running debate in theoretical ethics about "is and ought." Much, indeed, of the debate about mental illness, to the extent that it turns on the possibility of value-free definitions of what appear to be value terms (*illness*, *disease*, *dysfunction*, etc.), is no less than a *forme fruste* of the is–ought debate. Certainly, both sides of the is–ought debate, descriptivist and nondescriptivist, have important, if largely unrecognized, contributions to make to our understanding of the concept of mental illness.

The contribution of descriptivism is no less than a better (because a more self-consistent) version of the fact-before-value model. Surprisingly, perhaps, such a model has not been explicitly advanced (I indicate its possibilities in Chapter 3 of my *Moral Theory and Medical Practice*). But such a model could follow, for example, from the work of the Oxford philosopher G. J. Warnock. In his book *The Object of Morals* (1971, *The Object of Morality*, London: Methuen & Co Ltd), Warnock argued that values may, at least in some circumstances, be entailed by facts alone. Where, therefore, Boorse's model seeks to exclude value from the definition of disease, Warnock's descriptivism would, in principle, allow for it to be retained. Descriptivism would allow disease to be both: (1) *defined* by reference to facts alone, while, at the same time (2) capable of carrying *evaluative connotations* (if the facts concerned are of a kind which, according to descriptivism, may entail values). There would then be no inconsistency in defining disease value free, while, at the same time, continuing to use it (as Boorse uses it) with evaluative connotations.

Descriptivism, with its *entailment* of values by facts, thus represents a significant advance over the *exclusion* of values, as advocated by Boorse and others. Whether, though, the facts (in medicine or otherwise) are, or ever could be, of a kind which would allow the descriptivist entailment of values, has been widely disputed by philosophers. Indeed the majority view is nondescriptivist; that however strongly we may feel a particular value judgement is required of a given set of facts, there is no *logical* entailment: there is a strong *psychological* compulsion to condemn, say, vicarious cruelty, but there is no *logical* requirement. Following, then, the eighteenth century empiricist philosopher, David Hume, nondescriptivists such as the Oxford philosopher R. M. Hare (in *The Language of Morals*, Oxford University Press, 1952) have argued that there is "no ought from an is." Nondescriptivism thus puts facts and values on an equal footing, generating fact-plus-value ethical theories against the fact-before-value theories of descriptivism.

B. Fact-plus-Value (Nondescriptivist) Models

Applying nondescriptivist ethical theory to the medical concepts leads to a more radical departure from the medical model. The central claim of the medical model is that at the heart of medicine there is a value-free body of scientific facts. The model thus requires that the *prima facie* evaluative element in the meanings of the core medical terms—*illness*, *disease*, *dysfunction*—is not essential (either by successfully excluding this element, or by showing that it is entailed by the [medical] facts). Nondescriptivism, on the other hand, takes seriously the idea that an evaluative (as well as factual) element is essential to the meanings of the core medical concepts even as they are used in the theoretical heart of the subject.

It should be emphasized right away that nondescriptivism does nothing to undermine the importance of medical *science*. It may help to clarify what is genuinely scientific in medicine; it may also increase our awareness of the extent to which, as many philosophers and sociologists of science have documented, science itself is not "value free." But the positive claim that there is an evaluative element in the meanings of the core medical concepts in no way implies the negative claim that there is no factual element or that the factual element is somehow secondary or unimportant. The model of the medical concepts that is suggested by nondescriptivism is a fact-*plus*-value model, not, as it were, a *value-before-fact* model.

Once the essentially evaluative nature of the core medical concepts is accepted, however, it brings to our understanding of these concepts a whole series of further notions which belong to the moral world of people as distinct from the amoral world of scientific objects. Crucial among these are the notions of agency and action, as distinct from the scientific notions of function and functioning. Again, fact-plus-value theories add to, rather than replace, the scientific medical model. They add to the doctor's knowledge of disease, the patient's experience of illness, and to the analysis of disease in terms of failures of functioning, an analysis of illness in terms of failure of action. As we will see in a moment, "action failure" theories offer a very different slant on the explanation of the distinct domains of mental disorder.

Action failure theories have been developed in two main ways, by relating them to the goals of health and by drawing on the internal structure of action.

1. The Concept of Health

The Swedish philosopher Lennart Nordenfelt, in his *On the Nature of Health: An Action–Theoretic Approach* (Dordrecht, Holland: D. Reidel Publishing Company, 1987), has developed a detailed theory of "vital goals" by which health (as opposed to other positively evaluated notions) may be defined. Illness thus consists in anything that frustrates these goals. This is a rich and detailed theory. Among other results, it links the notions of health and disease firmly not only to the values of the individual patient but also to those implicit in the social context.

2. The Internal Structure of Action

This approach, which is developed in my *Moral Theory and Medical Practice* (CUP, paperback, 1995), is more directly relevant to the concept of *mental* illness. Essentially, it accounts for the rich variety of mental disorders in terms of failures at different parts or stages of the complex "machinery of action."

Function and action are not unconnected, of course, no more indeed than are disease and illness: as I write this, for example, I am writing (this is an action of mine), equally, though, my hand, arm, nerves, etc., are all functioning. Correspondingly, if my arm were to become paralyzed, my *experience* would be of incapacity, of being unable to perform an action (writing) that I can normally perform; but a neurologist, say, would analyze this in terms of disease theory by defining which of the functions underlying my loss of action are impaired. At this level, then, action and function, and with them fact-plus-value and fact-before-value models, are equivalent. With higher and more complex activities, however, it becomes more natural to use action language rather than function language. This is indeed reflected in psychiatric classifications, which, unlike classifications of bodily diseases, are full of terms like volition, motivation, and intention. As we will see, the shift to action language becomes critical when we consider feature 4, the central place of the psychotic disorders in the map of psychiatry.

C. Recent Models and the Map of Mental Disorders

Which of the recent models—value-excluding, descriptivist or nondescriptivist—is right remains an open question. As between descriptivist and nondescriptivist models, the question turns on the relationship between fact and value and hence on all the arguments and counter-arguments in the long-running is–ought debate in ethics. In mental health, though, a nondescriptivist, fact-plus-value model does have the edge in that it explains more effectively than its rivals all four features of the map of mental disorder (Figure 1) and in ways which, as we will see later, point out important lessons for practice.

(*Feature 1*) *Variable Fact/Value Connotations.* In the fact-before-value model, the more value-laden connotations of mental illness compared with physical illness is taken to be a product of the relatively underdeveloped state of psychiatric science. In a fact-plus-value model, this feature of the map of mental disorder follows directly from a general logical property of value terms together with something important about human beings; namely, that we differ over some questions of value more than over others.

Thus, as R. M. Hare, among others, pointed out, *all* value terms, even the most general (such as "good" and "bad") may sometimes have well-marked factual connotations. This happens when the factual *criteria* for the value judgment expressed by a given value term are settled or agreed upon. For example, the use of good in "good eating apple" has, in most everyday domestic contexts, mainly factual connotations: it suggests a clean-skinned, sweet, etc., apple. This is not because "good" in this context is a purely factual term, but because "clean-skinned, sweet, etc." are the factual criteria by which (nearly) everyone, in this context, would judge an apple to be good. These stable or settled factual criteria thus become attached by association to the use of good in this context. By contrast, though, a college committee, say, choosing pictures for their Senior Common Room, will have widely different criteria for "good picture," and the use of "good" in this quite different context will therefore remain clearly value laden.

If this is a property of value terms in general, then, it is in principle sufficient to explain the more value-laden use of illness (as a value term) with respect to mental illness ("mental illness" being like "good picture") and its more fact-laden use in respect of physical illness ("physical illness" being like "good apple"). That is to say, mental illness is more value laden than physical illness because (overall) it is used of behaviors and experiences over which there is *less* agreement, evaluatively speaking. Anxiety, for example, a typical symptom of mental illness, is enjoyed by some (e.g., those who enjoy hang-gliding) but avoided by others. Bodily pain, on the other hand, a typical symptom of physical illness, is, for nearly everyone, at best a necessary evil. To this extent then, mental illness involving anxiety will be a "good picture" case (i.e., relatively value laden) and physical illness involving bodily pain will be a "good apple" case (i.e., relatively fact laden).

(*Feature 2*) *Variable Conceptual Distance from Physical Illness.* In a fact-before-value model this feature, like feature 1, is taken to be a product of psychiatry being underdeveloped scientifically. In a fact-plus-value model it follows from the same basic point about value terms as feature 1, but applied now; not to the difference between mental illness and physical illness, but to the difference between illness (mental or physical) and disease.

Thus, in Boorse's model, illness is defined by reference to disease (illness is a "serious disease," essentially). In a fact-plus-value model this relationship is reversed, disease being defined by reference to illness: a disease is a condition that is *evaluated negatively by most people* as an illness. If disease and illness are both value terms, then disease (in virtue of the property of value terms outlined above under Feature 1) will necessarily have more marked factual connotations than illness. In physical medicine, the causes of disease are better defined than in psychiatry. Hence many disease categories will be causally rather than merely symptomatically defined. This, as in the medical model, will place further conceptual distance between mental and physical disorders. But in a fact-plus-value model, it remains the case that a condition is marked out, ultimately, *as* a disease by the negative value judgement entailed by illness and not vice versa.

(*Feature 3*) *Distinct Domains.* The fact-before-value (medical) model, drawing on concepts from the world of science, analyzes psychopathology by analogy with bodily diseases in terms of disturbances in the functioning of bodily and mental parts and systems. We noted earlier that this fails, in particular, to explain the central place of psychotic disorders. A fact-plus-value model looks rather to the patient's actual experience of illness as an experience of *incapacity*. Drawing on concepts from the world of people, it analyzes different kinds of psychopathology in terms of different kinds of disturbance of agency or failures of action.

(*Feature 4*) *The Central Place of Psychotic Disorders.* This feature of mental disorder, for which the medical model is unable to account (as we saw earlier, it actually gave the wrong result, making psychotic disorders peripheral), falls quite naturally out of a fact-plus-value model.

In a fact-plus-value model the disturbance of rationality involved in psychotic thinking is not (as in the medical model) a disturbance of cognitive functioning, but a disturbance of practical reasoning. This is reasoning of the kind through which we give reasons for our actions. Important evidence for this is the fact that delusions (the central symptom of these disorders) may take the form of value judgements (e.g., as in depressive delusions of guilt) as well as of factual beliefs, since reasons for actions, too, take the form of value judgements or of factual beliefs. Now, reasons of this kind are a central part of what a former Professor of Moral Philosophy at Oxford, J. L. Austin, called the machinery of action. Hence, if illness is to be understood generally, in a fact-plus-value model, in terms of failures of action, then psychotic disorders, as disturbances of reasons for action, necessarily appear at the center of the map as the central species of mental illness.

Modern models of mental disorder thus explain, to different degrees and often in different ways, the major features of the conceptual map of mental disorder. To this extent they represent advances over the more partial models developed in the earlier debate about mental illness. The latter, though, as we saw earlier, although partial, had important implications for practice. In the next section we consider some of the implications of modern models of mental disorder for clinical work in mental health.

V. THE CONCEPT OF MENTAL ILLNESS AND MENTAL HEALTH PRACTICE

How the concept of mental illness is understood, what model of mental illness is adopted, has implications for all aspects of mental health practice. Of particular importance are (1) the relationship between patients and professionals and (2) the relationships among different mental health professionals in the multidisciplinary team. Recognizing these implications is critical to an understanding of the relevance of different models of mental disorder for ethical issues in mental health.

A. The Relationship between Patients (or Users of Health Services) and Professionals

The medical model, through the priority it affords disease theory, subordinates patients to professionals, especially doctors. Modern versions of the medical model, such as Boorse's, recognize the importance of the experience of illness. But whether a particular person's experience is an experience of illness is determined, not directly by the features of their experience as such, but indirectly by the extent to which a professional is able to map the patient's experience on to a recognized disease category. So the patient's experience is subordinate to the professional's specialist knowledge. Essentially the same conclusion follows for a value-entailing (descriptivist) version of the medical model; this, too, being a fact-before-value model.

A fact-plus-value model, by contrast, in recognizing the logical priority of the patient's experience of illness, accommodates specialist knowledge of diseases, but without subordination. Moreover, in identifying the central place of values, it emphasizes the importance of the experiences and perspective of the patient *as an individual*, rather than being concerned (as in a disease-led medical model) with the patient's experience only as it can be mapped on to the general categories of recognized diseases. In both these respects, then, by emphasizing the importance both of the patient's experience and of the patient's values, a fact-plus-value model, in contrast to the medical model, makes the patient rather than the professional central.

B. The Relationships among Professionals

These differences of emphasis between the medical model and a fact-plus-value model are relatively unimportant practically in most areas of physical medicine, at least in hospital practice. This is because in these areas the values by which illness is defined are widely shared and hence are not problematic (appendicitis is a bad condition for anyone). In these areas, that is to say, most illnesses are diseases, so that disease theory approximates to illness experience, and the relevant values, being widely agreed upon, can be ignored.

This is why the medical model, based as it is on technological aspects of medicine, has such wide appeal. Transfer this model to primary care, however, and to mental health in particular, and the simplification upon which it depends (i.e., that the relevant values are widely shared) is no longer available. Indeed mental illness, on a fact-plus-value model, differs from physical illness just in that the values by which *mental* illness is (partly) defined are *not* widely shared. Now, in a liberal society, there is no ready-reckoner mechanism for resolving questions of value. But an important characteristic of a liberal society is that no one perspective, no one professional or personal set of values, is allowed to become dominant. The aim is rather to achieve a balance of values. A headline example of the failure to achieve this balance occurred in the totalitarian regime of the former USSR, where, as is well known, political dissidents were often diagnosed as suffering from mental disorder and "treated" in mental institutions.

What is needed, then, for good clinical care in mental health, is a *balance* of values, and it is this which a well-functioning multidisciplinary team can help to provide. In the medical model, the multidisciplinary team represents a resource of skills for different aspects of management; but the core function of diagnosis is reserved to the doctor as the expert on scientific disease theory. In a fact-plus-value model of mental illness, the multidisciplinary team is crucial to all stages of the clinical process, including assessment and diagnosis.

VI. THE CONCEPT OF MENTAL ILLNESS AND APPLIED ETHICS

The implications of different models of mental disorder for mental health practice clearly have closely related implications for applied ethics. Bioethics, as that part of applied ethics most directly concerned with health care, has traditionally concentrated on ethical problems in high-tech areas of medicine rather than in primary care, including mental health; and on ethical aspects of treatment rather than of diagnosis. This is understandable historically, bioethics having developed as a response to the ethical problems raised by technological advance in medicine. Important work has been done on these problems, much of it indeed relevant to mental health (e.g., the ethical implications of the new technologies for genetic screening). It reflects, though, an essentially medical model in which values are at best peripherally placed, relevant to medical practice but not part of medicine's theoretical core. A fact-plus-value model of mental illness shows, by contrast:

1. That primary care is at least as ethically problematic as high-tech medicine, precisely because this is the area of health care in which values are not widely agreed upon. The problems, it is true, are less high profile. But they are far more pervasive, and hence, at a human level, far more significant. The main complaint patients make against psychiatry is not that they are being diagnosed as mentally ill when they are not (more often, it is the other way around, that they are being denied the services they need on the grounds that they are not ill!); the main complaint is that *their* perspective, *their* values, and *their* beliefs are not being attended to.

2. That assessment and diagnosis, as well as treatment, are critically difficult ethically (as well as scientifically) in primary care and mental health. This follows directly from the key difference between mental illness and physical illness noted earlier; that in respect of mental illness the values by which illness is (partly) defined are less widely agreed upon than in respect of physical illness (mental illness is a "good picture" case, physical illness a "good apple" case, as in the example above). Given the importance of this key difference between them, it is remarkable that the debate about the concept of mental illness in the 1960s and 1970s, despite turning on the significance of its more value-laden nature compared with physical illness and the institutionalized abuse of psychiatry developing over the same period in the USSR, was conducted largely outside the scope of mainline bioethics.

It is important to add that, in addition to these implications for the scope of applied ethics, a fact-plus-value model also gives us a more positive overall picture of mental health. In the medical model, psychiatry inevitably seems second-rate scientifically compared with "high-tech" areas of medicine. Mental health is at the soft end of scientific medicine. A fact-plus-value model repolarizes this view. Technological medicine is seen to be operating in a relatively *simplified* area of practice, one in which questions of value, although arising in principle, can be ignored (i.e., because the relevant values are widely agreed upon). In fact, of course, men-

tal health, to the extent that its "organ" is the brain, is more complex scientifically (empirically and conceptually) than, say, cardiology. A fact-plus-value view shows that it is also more complex ethically.

VII. THE CONCEPT OF MENTAL ILLNESS AND PHILOSOPHY

A fact-before-value model, at least in its value-excluding form, is restricted philosophically. It draws primarily on certain aspects of the philosophy of science; it admits applied ethics (principles, casuistry, and aspects of jurisprudence) to issues of treatment; but it excludes other areas of philosophy altogether by its self-set terms of reference.

A fact-plus-value model, in opening up the field, offers a far richer set of connections with philosophy. In addition to the philosophy of science, the primary place afforded by the theory to the concept of action failure links issues about the nature of mental illness (and hence practical problems of diagnosis) directly to the philosophy of action. Through the philosophy of action, these problems are in turn linked to some of the most difficult questions in the philosophy of mind (about personal identity, agency, intention, and so forth), and through these questions to the deep metaphysical problems of freedom, causality, and, not least, the relationship between mind and body.

The importance of the patient's experience of illness also gives a central place to continental philosophy; there has been a renewal of interest particularly in phenomenology in recent years, driven not so much by ethics as by the needs of the new brain sciences. Developments in dynamic brain imaging and in artificial intelligence models of mental disorder have generated the need for more sophisticated ways of describing the often remarkable disturbances of experience by which such disorders are characterized.

The connections between philosophy and mental health opened up by modern work on the concept of mental illness are not one-way. Philosophy has much to offer mental health. But mental health, as the Oxford philosopher Kathy Wilkes showed in her book *Real People: Personal Identity Without Thought Experiments* (Oxford: Clarendon Press, 1988) has a great deal to offer philosophy. There is indeed, in this area, no real distinction between pure and applied philosophy, pure and applied ethics. As noted at the start of this article, many of the problems with which patients and professionals struggle in day-to-day practice or research in mental health are no less than the flip side of the deep metaphysical problems with which philosophers have been struggling for over 2000 years.

Acknowledgments

Box 1 and Figure 1 are adapted from materials which were first published in Fulford, K. W. M. (1993), "Value, Action, Mental Illness and the Law," in Shute S., Gardner J., and Horder J., Eds. *Action and Value in Criminal Law*. Oxford: Oxford University Press. Box 2 is adapted from Fulford, K. W. M. (1988), "Classification and Diagnosis in Psychiatry," Chapter 1 in Rose N., Ed., *Essential Psychiatry*. Blackwells Scientific Publications.

Also See the Following Articles

FREUDIANISM • INSANITY, LEGAL CONCEPT OF • MENTAL HEALTH • PSYCHOPHARMACOLOGY

Bibliography

Boorse, C. (1976). What a theory of mental health should be. *Journal of Theory Social Behaviour*, **6**, 61–84.

Bolton, D., & Hill, J. (1996). *Mind, meaning and mental disorder: The nature of causal explanation in psychology and psychiatry*. Oxford: Oxford Univ. Press.

Fulford, K. W. M. (1991). The concept of disease. In S. Bloch and P. Chodoff (Eds.), *Psychiatric ethics* (2nd ed., chap. 6). Oxford: Oxford University Press.

Fulford, K. W. M., Smirnoff, A. Y. U., & Snow, E. (1993). Concepts of disease and the abuse of psychiatry in the USSR. *British Journal of Psychiatry*, **162**, 801–810.

Graham, G., & Stephens, G. L. (1994). *Philosophical psychopathology*. Cambridge, MA: The MIT Press.

Kendell, R. E. (1975). The concept of disease and its implications for psychiatry. *British Journal of Psychiatry*, **127**, 305–315.

Kopelman, L. M. (1994.) Normal grief: Good or bad? Health or disease? *Philosophy, Psychiatry, and Psychology*, **1**, 209–220, with Commentaries by Dominian, J., & Wise, T. N., 221–224; response by Kopelman, 226–227.

Littlewood, R., & Lipsedge, M. (1989). *Aliens and alienists: Ethnic minorities and psychiatry* (2nd ed.). London/New York: Routledge.

Sadler, J. S., & Agich, G. J. (1995). Diseases, functions, values, and psychiatric classification. *Philosophy, Psychiatry, and Psychology*, **2**, 219–232.

Szasz, T. S. (1987). *Insanity: The idea and its consequences*. New York: Wiley.

Tyrer, P., & Steinberg, D. (1993). *Models for mental disorder: Conceptual models in psychiatry* (2nd ed.). Chichester, UK: Wiley.

A still valuable review of models of mental disorder is "The Disease Concept in Psychiatry" by Clare, A., Chapter 3 in *Essentials of Postgraduate Psychiatry* (P. Hill, R. Murray, and A. Thorley, Eds.). New York: Academic Press, Grune & Stratton. Representative original articles are to be found in the edited collection, Caplan, A. L., Engelhardt, T., and McCartney, J. J., Eds. (1981). *Concepts of Health and Disease: Interdisciplinary Perspectives*. Reading, Massachusetts: Addison-Wesley Publishing Co.

MERCY AND FORGIVENESS

Andrew Brien
Massey University

GLOSSARY

forgiveness A condition characterized by the dissipation and cessation of a negative attitude or stance (typically, resentment, but also hatred, loathing, or bitterness) that one person, A, feels toward another, B, for actions that B performed, which A found untoward and which generated A's negative attitude.

mercy A condition in which a person who has power over another treats that person, through act or omission, less harshly than, given the circumstances, was likely or for which there was justification or where the mercy giver has strong motivating reasons, either psychological or rational, to allow, permit, or inflict harsh treatment, or ignore the other person's plight. The mercy giver does this by alleviating partially or altogether some threat, burden, suffering, or punishment to which the powerless person is vulnerable or which she is experiencing. Thus, mercy involves a departure from an established course of events through an intervention in them by the mercy giver.

"FORGIVENESS" AND "MERCY" refer to conceptually distinct moral ideals which generate distinctive patterns of ethical behavior in which actors who are vulnerable to some sort of adverse imposition are saved from it through the actions of another. Forgiveness and mercy are, pretheoretically, held to be good since they embody in their practice a number of widely held moral judgments: that where possible it is right and good not to make or allow another to suffer, and that respect for other people is a fundamental moral injunction.

In general the problem for forgiveness and mercy, from the point of view of applied ethics, is that they seemingly conflict with important principles of practical morality, such as reason and justice. Therefore, the problems are (1) can forgiveness and mercy have a place in our practical moral life? (2) what part do forgiveness and mercy have in a moral life? and (3) when is it right to be forgiving or merciful?

I. THE PARADOX OF FORGIVENESS

Forgiveness seems to face a dilemma: either it is immoral or it is pointless. The argument purporting to show the immorality of forgiveness can be set out this way: Forgiveness is characterized by the cessation of a negative stance (such as an attitude of resentment) toward another. This is a stance initially generated by an action that was found in some way untoward or wrong. To forgive without atonement, repentance, or punishment is to overlook and condone the wrong. It is to accept it, even tacitly, and let it stand. The wrong still exists and all that has changed is the forgiver's stance toward the wrongdoer. So, when a person forgives another in the absence of atonement, repentance, or punishment, the wrongdoer escapes any of the deserved consequences of her wrongdoing, including the negative stance of the forgiver. The morally right response to a wrong does not occur. Wilfully failing to respond to a wrong as a person ought is itself morally wrong. Therefore, forgiveness is morally wrong.

The argument purporting to show the pointlessness of forgiveness is this: Forgiveness involves overcoming a negative stance toward a person who has performed some wrong. If a wrongdoer has atoned or annulled her offense through, for example, apology or punishment, then the wrong has disappeared. If the wrong has disappeared then there is no wrong to forgive. Therefore, when a wrongdoer has atoned or suffered punishment, forgiveness is impossible as there is no wrong to forgive. It is pointless.

A. Is Forgiveness Morally Wrong?

The first horn of the dilemma rests upon the claim that forgiveness, in the absence of atonement, repentance, or punishment, necessarily involves some sort of wrong action. Three types of wrongdoing are alleged to be characteristic of forgiveness: (1) a failure to punish; (2) a failure to condemn a wrong and active condoning of it; and (3) a failure to maintain a morally appropriate negative stance toward a wrong action.

B. Does Forgiveness Involve a Failure to Punish Which Is Morally Wrong?

There are two responses. The first is that this criticism rests upon the assumption that all failures to punish wrongdoers are morally wrong. It is far from clear that this is so. To be sure, there are two accounts of the moral status of punishment. One of these, proposed by Kant, says that all wrongs must be punished and that a failure to do so is itself morally wrong. Another account says that all wrongdoing does is make a person liable to punishment; that is, it gives the wronged person (or the state) a right to punish the wrongdoer, but there is no moral obligation on the part of the victim to exercise her right. This is entirely within her discretion. If forgiveness involves a failure to punish and the victims of wrongs have no obligation to punish, then forgiveness is not morally wrong, since a person can decline to punish and do so with moral impunity. In contrast, if forgiveness does involve failing to punish a wrongdoer, and if punishment is morally obligatory, then forgiveness is morally wrong as it would involve a clear breach of a moral duty: the duty to inflict deserved punishment.

This leads to the second response: Does forgiveness necessarily involve a failure to punish? As we saw, forgiveness involves a change in the stance that one person takes toward another. Now, it makes sense to say, "I forgive you, but you must still be punished." This would be meaningless if forgiveness necessarily involved a remission of punishment. Since this locution does make sense, we must conclude that forgiveness does not imply that the forgiver must refrain from punishing the wrongdoer. To be sure, we do talk about forgiving a debt or even forgiving a punishment. To talk this way is to qualify our use of the concept of forgiveness and specify just what we are forgiving: it is no longer the person, but the punishment or the debt. What we mean by this locution is that we are canceling the debt or the punishment—in the same way we cancel our negative attitude toward another when we forgive the person. Such locution cannot be taken to mean that whenever we forgive we cancel a punishment.

Finally, as noted, forgiveness is a certain sort of activity involving a change of stance toward another. The focus of forgiveness is the emotional or attitudinal stance of the victim of a wrong toward the wrongdoer. Punishment, in contrast, is an evaluation of that person's actions and the infliction of suffering upon that person. The focus of punishment is the wrong and the wrongdoer's desert. Thus, forgiveness and punishment are distinct activities that are focused upon different objects. Since all she must do is change her stance toward the other person in order to be said to have forgiven the wrongdoer, it is not a necessary condition of forgiveness that the forgiver remits any or all of the wrongdoer's punishment in order to forgive. Thus, the activity of forgiveness can occur with the activity of punishment. Since forgiveness does not necessarily involve a failure to punish, one of the planks of the argument against the morality of forgiveness is broken, namely, that forgiveness necessarily involves a failure to punish, which is itself morally wrong. The conclusion then is that a person can forgive another, and also inflict a punishment upon that person; thus, forgiveness does not involve a failure to do what one ought. It is not therefore morally wrong.

C. Does Forgiveness Involve a Failure to Condemn a Wrong?

The assumption here is that when a forgiver changes her stance toward the wrongdoer, she ceases to condemn the wrong and begins to condone it. Since wrongs ought to be condemned and ought not to be condoned, forgiveness involves a failure to do what a person ought morally to do. To fail to do what one morally ought is wrong; therefore forgiveness is morally wrong.

Let us suppose that people morally ought to condemn wrongs and that they morally ought not to condone them. Is it true that when Fred forgives Mary he fails to condemn the wrong she has done and in fact comes to condone it? Not at all. At the heart of forgiveness, as already noted, is a change in stance toward the wrongdoer—or as is often said, "a change of heart." Prior to forgiveness, Fred experiences various negative attitudes toward her. He may feel bitter, angry, resentment, and even hatred. These are properties of Fred.

In contrast, condemnation involves necessarily an evaluation of another person or her action and a belief about the moral worth of an action. Typically it involves also a judgment, and a locution signaling the actor's stance, usually of the form, "That action was wrong (or wicked or evil)," or "You are a bad (wicked or evil) person."

Forgiveness and condemnation are distinct activities and are distinct speech acts. In the case of forgiveness a person signals that he no longer has a certain stance toward a wrongdoer. In the case of condemnation a person signals that he believes certain things about another or her action and evaluates that action or that person in a certain way. The two stances are independent: Fred can cease to resent Mary, but still believe that what she did was wrong. Thus, one stance can be held and changed without affecting the other. Forgiveness does not, then, involve any change in the forgiver's evaluation of the act or actor. It does not imply that he ceases to condemn the wrongdoer or the action, and begins to condone her or her action. This can be seen reflected in ordinary language: "What you did was wrong, and you must be punished for it; though I want you to know that I forgive you, and hope that once this is over you will see how wrong it is and why I was so angry."

The error in this argument is to think that when a person changes her negative stance toward another person and forgives him, she also changes her evaluation of the other person or his action. There is, as argued, no logical connection between the two. Given this, we can conclude that forgiveness does not involve

a morally culpable failure to condemn wrongdoing nor lapse into condoning wrong action. Therefore, this argument provides no reason to think that forgiveness is morally wrong.

D. Does Forgiveness Involve a Failure to Maintain a Morally Appropriate Negative Stance?

This version of the argument can be set out this way: Suppose that people are morally obliged to hold certain sorts of stances toward people and actions—negative stances toward wrongdoing and bad actions that are unatoned, unpunished, or unrepented, and positive stances toward right and good actions. Forgiveness in the absence of atonement, punishment, or repentance involves failing to maintain one's negative attitude when one ought to maintain it. Now, failures to do what one morally ought are morally wrong. Therefore, forgiveness is morally wrong.

The crux of this argument is the first premise. Are actors morally obliged to hold certain stances toward people and actions? Consider, first of all, right and good actions and people. People who are moral exemplars are praised and otherwise lauded in the same way that good and right actions often are. They are moral ideals and actors are enjoined to emulate the behavior and characters of such saints and heroes. Praising such exemplars demonstrates our own commitment to the values embodied in their actions and lives.

Moreover, through reflecting on such exemplars and their actions and deeds, praising them, and behaving like them, we not only do right and good things (so the world is a better place, a sound utilitarian reason), we become morally better people. Importantly, we become morally different people, since the attitudes and beliefs we hold about the exemplars become stable features of our dispositional framework and ultimately ground our own moral choices. We cease merely to imitate the exemplars but act autonomously from the same springs. To put this another way, through praising moral exemplars, thinking highly of them, admiring them, and behaving like them, we adopt a certain positive stance toward moral exemplars that in the end leads to the values they embody being engendered in our own moral characters and in the underpinning of our own autonomous decisions. Now, it seems true that not only ought we try to do what is right, but that we ought to ensure that we do what is right. Since positive stances can influence our behavior (by making moral action more likely), they are part of the foundation for right and good action. Therefore, lacking that stance is morally bad. Consequently, actors have a moral obligation to possess certain positive stances toward the world.

Just as positive stances can influence behavior, so too can negative stances: by adopting a negative stance toward some bad person or wrong action, people are more likely to avoid doing that sort of action themselves or seeking to imitate that sort of person. Thus, there are actors and actions toward whom we must have, at least some of the time, negative stances, in order that their wrongdoing does not undermine our own character and actions. Hitler and Stalin are typical gross examples, but the confidence trickster who defrauds a widow of her life's savings or the police officer who victimizes a member of a minority group is also a worthy object of a negative stance. So, any actor concerned to do right and good is morally required to possess certain positive and negative stances toward the world. If this is so, how then can forgiveness be morally right, for it seemingly involves the dissipation of a negative stance that a person morally ought to have?

There is something wrong with this argument. Recall that the purpose of a negative stance was moral improvement and education. While it may be true that actors ought to possess a negative stance (perhaps involving, for example, resentment and anger) toward wrongdoing when there is a lesson to be drawn, it does not show that they ought to maintain such a stance or develop such a stance in the first place if there is no purpose to it. To be sure, given that such stances can be damaging to a person if maintained for a long period of time—for example, they may deform a person into a curmudgeonly, antisocial, suspicious character incapable of living in society with others—it seems reasonable to conclude that once the lesson has been drawn there is no justification for the negative stance to continue. Therefore, forgiveness is in order when there is no further purpose to maintaining the negative stance.

Overall, the conclusion to be drawn is that actors do not have an overarching obligation to cultivate and maintain negative stances toward wrongdoing. They do have an obligation to develop the capacity for appropriate negative stances when such a stance will promote the development in them of an appropriate moral character and encourage them to perform right actions—but then they must forgive the wrongdoer as soon as the moral lesson has been drawn.

E. Is Forgiveness Pointless?

The second horn of the dilemma would seem to show that forgiveness is pointless. This is mistaken. Recall what forgiveness involves: a dissipation of a negative stance that a person has toward another. This is the point of all acts of forgiveness. This stance is generated by the forgiver believing that the person being forgiven performed some untoward action that was directed at the forgiver or someone morally or psychologically proximate, for example, her child.

Whereas appropriate punishment or atonement annuls a wrong, in the sense that it repays the moral debt wrongdoing incurs and so makes further punishment or atonement morally unjustified, appropriate punishment does not erase the memory of the wrong or expunge the fact that the wrong was committed. That will always remain. It is the perceived wrong itself, as we have just seen, rather than the fact that it is unpunished or unatoned, that generates the negative stance, which is what, in turn, forgiveness dissipates. What this shows is that a negative stance toward a person may persist even after she has been punished or she has atoned, because she acted wrongly. For example, a mother may continue to resent a drunk driver who seriously injured her child, even though the driver has been punished, for no other reason than the driver was drunk and injured her child. Punishment, atonement, or any of the other ways in which wrongs are annulled do not, then, eliminate the possibility or the basis of a continuing negative stance and the need for forgiveness. Therefore, punishment or atonement and so on do not deprive forgiveness of a point.

II. FORGIVENESS AND THE MORAL LIFE

The place of forgiveness in the moral life will depend upon the nature of that life. One vision—that of the Stoics—accords emotions, feelings, and attitudes no place at all. The Stoics claim that such stances are free from the influence of reason and so they are uncontrolled by the agent. Moreover, for the Stoics, the moral life is identified with the rational life. Therefore, if human beings are to live a moral life then it must be free from stances that affect behavior but which are not subject to reason. For the Stoics then, the moral life will be one that is free of pity, anger, bitterness, resentment, hatred or love, affection and devotion, and the like, that is, any stance, either positive or negative, that is uncontrolled by reason. Since there is for the Stoic moral agent no negative attitude to overcome, there is no possibility for forgiveness. Thus, in a Stoic moral life, and in fact any moral life which eliminates emotions, feelings, or attitudes, forgiveness has no place.

Such an account of the moral life is highly counter-intuitive. Emotions, feelings, and attitudes, that is to say, stances toward others that are both positive and negative, are natural features of what it is to be human. We cannot entirely avoid them, since we are predisposed by nature to experience them. And in some cases, such as love or friendship, we actively seek them out and believe that we become a complete human being only through experiencing them. Now, not only are such stances natural to us but we can use reason to direct them to a considerable extent. Thus, they are not entirely free from the influence of reason, and cannot for that reason be excluded from the moral life.

Take forgiveness as an example. Acts of forgiveness cannot be commanded: they involve a change of stance, and the adoption of such stances is not under the direct control of the will. For the same reason, Henry cannot command Fred to like his cooking or command that Fred believe him, since attitudes, feelings, and emotions cannot be commanded in the same direct way that a specified bodily movement can. What can be done, however, is that a disposition to forgive can be cultivated and a particular act of forgiveness can be nurtured, through engaging in reasoning processes that will allow the disposition to be realized or which allow forgiveness to occur, even if the actor does not have a settled disposition to forgive. Actors then can work at forgiving another; they can reason it through, analyze the wrong that is causing the negative attitude, and try to understand it. A person may come to see that resentment is pointless, that hatred is a waste of energy, or that the wrong was so insignificant that it does not really matter. Thus, forgiveness is under an actor's indirect control since it can be produced through processes (such as reasoning) that are under an actor's direct command. Consequently, the forgiving stance is not free from the influence of reason. Therefore, it cannot be excluded from the moral life on the Stoics' grounds.

The role that forgiveness plays in the moral life is rather more active than this might suggest. By its nature, forgiveness removes the barriers between people that wrongdoing builds. It encourages wounds to heal, relationships to be restored, and people to interact again. When people forgive they overcome antipathy and come to interact with each other harmoniously, peaceably, and cooperatively. They come to see each other, not through the distorting lens of a negative stance, but in a more life-like manner. In short, forgiveness counteracts the effects of negative stances which tend to fracture social life. It restores both the forgiver and the forgiven to the community. Forgiveness thereby promotes social life itself by removing enmity and promoting harmony and peaceable living.

Now, a moral life is one lived according to certain ideals. Many of the ideals that go to make a moral life can be realized only in harmonious, peaceable society with others. Such a sort of society is itself a moral ideal, as it supports the realization of other ideals and embodies the conception of a morally good life: one free from enmity, hatred, and so on. Since forgiveness, as argued, promotes a harmonious, peaceable social life, it fosters the realization of ideals that are central to the moral life, most particularly, the sort of society that would support the moral life; hence forgiveness forms a central part of any attempt to realize such a life.

A social life fostered by forgiveness, in which people are reinstated to full community membership, is one in which people are in a better position to reach their full potential as people. The thought is that when people live a certain sort of life in society, as they can if they practice forgiveness (and other virtues of course), they come to flourish in ways that are characteristic of human beings. The Ancients called this state and the correlated activity *eudaimonia*. To put this another way, human flourishing (*eudaimonia*) is attained and maintained through certain sorts of activity, one of which is engaging in and maintaining certain sorts of relationships with others that enable people to live a life that is characteristically human, namely, one that is social and directed by reason. Such relationships are, ideally, free from negative stances, since such stances are antisocial: a person who is angry, bitter, resentful, or untrusting is not only alienated from the object of her negative stance, but she is apt also to be suspicious and stunted in her relationships with others. Relationships that promote flourishing will be grounded on positive stances, such as friendship, cooperation, love, care, concern, and respect for others. Such stances tend for the most part to engage actors with each other. Consequently, people who adopt a positive stance toward the world promote human flourishing. Since forgiveness removes negative stances and promotes positive stances, it promotes human flourishing.

Not only does forgiveness promote social life, it embodies it. In overcoming a negative stance and adopting a positive one, a person uses capacities (such as reason) that are characteristic of a person who is flourishing. Moreover, she engages in activities that are characteristically human: social life. In other words, in the very practice of forgiveness not only does forgiveness promote flourishing, it embodies or exemplifies it. Now, one conception of the moral life says that it is one concerned with attaining, practicing, and promoting human flourishing, whether of individuals or of communities. Since forgiveness promotes and exemplifies human flourishing, it is an essential element of the moral life.

Against this it may be argued that flourishing is a false ideal, since there is no single way of life that is characteristically human. If this is so, then the conclusion that forgiveness is an inescapable part of the moral life appears quite uncertain. This is too hasty. At a minimum the moral life is concerned with living a life in which a person does what is right and good and is concerned to do so. Now, it is an uncontroversial judgment that actions, policies, and patterns of behavior that tend to promote individual and communal well-being and welfare are, other things being equal, morally right and good. Thus, a moral life would be one that included such actions when appropriate. Forgiveness, as we have seen, promotes the well-being and welfare of individuals and communities by healing divisions, promoting relationships between people, and fostering community cohesion. For this reason, forgiveness is right (when appropriate) and good. It is, therefore, a part of the moral life.

Forgiveness is rather more prominent in the moral life than this might suggest. Wrongdoing is frequent. Since such wrongdoing generates negative stances, social life is under constant strain. Therefore, the need for forgiveness is constant if social life is to be sustained and be at all tolerable. Forgiveness is not then a moral possibility in a moral life like this—as the dissolution of the paradox shows—but it is, given the way people live, a constant necessity.

So, when is forgiveness right? A person concerned with the fundamental questions of applied ethics—what sort of person do I want to be? what sort of life do I want to lead? how ought I act?—must take into account forgiveness. In this entry there has been no discussion, however, of when forgiveness is morally appropriate, apart from the general observation that forgiveness becomes morally appropriate when the justification for negative stances disappear. What then makes an act of forgiveness morally appropriate will depend upon the circumstances: the nature of the offense, the nature of the offender, and the characteristics of the other people involved. Since life is so complex and allows for many variations that affect the answer, the moral appropriateness of forgiveness cannot be subsumed under a general rule that can be used for clear guidance on all occasions. The best we can do, it seems, is participate in social life and develop a capacity for judgment.

While this will not yield an algorithm that can be used mechanically to determine with precision when forgiveness is morally required, participating in social life and developing a capacity for judgment does encourage actors to develop so-called "rules of thumb." These are rules that do not govern every case and which do not provide in every instance reliable moral advice. They are, however, rules that do tend in many cases to yield the right answer and which are for that reason used as a guide for actors, but to which actors are not committed so strongly that they will fail to deviate from them when the case seems appropriate.

Moreover, actors will develop a collection of paradigm cases of forgiveness and identify other actors who are paradigm exemplars of the virtue of forgiveness. By applying rules of thumb, comparing this case with the paradigm cases, and asking what would this or that exemplar of forgiveness do in this case, decisions may be reached on rational grounds using a morally defensible way of moral thinking.

Forgiveness brings both the forgiver and the forgiven back into human society, reaffirms their worth, and thus encourages human flourishing. It has then positive moral value. As a rule of thumb, then, it ought to be pursued, other things being equal. It would seem that the case must be made against forgiveness, if forgiveness is not to be pursued. In other words, as a rule of thumb forgiveness is always right, unless there are compelling reasons against it, and what actors must do is think through each case using the paradigm cases and exemplars.

III. THE PARADOXES OF MERCY

Mercy appears to be surrounded by a group of interrelated paradoxes. These paradoxes focus on two issues: the moral justification for mercy and the coherence of the concept. The problem concerning mercy's moral justification is well known: when mercy tempers justice, a person is treated less harshly than she would have been in the absence of mercy and in the presence of justice. To be merciful, then, is to fail to do justice. But, to fail to do justice is to act morally wrongly. Therefore, mercy is morally wrong.

This is an important problem. If justice is the foremost virtue of individuals and the first virtue of human institutions, then mercy can seemingly find no place either in our personal moral outlooks or in our institutional arrangements. Yet, we are loath to abandon mercy, fearing that strict adherence to justice would fail to take account of human weakness, moral luck, and susceptibility to temptation.

Thus, our commitment to mercy, in fact its very existence, challenges the primacy of justice in human affairs, and seemingly, a commitment to justice leaves no place for mercy, since mercy apparently involves abandoning a standard to which conventional morality says we ought to remain faithful to.

Not so well known are a number of conceptual problems that, it would appear, dog mercy. For example, one solution to the justification problem is to argue that mercy has moral standing because it is compatible with some richer account of justice. Thus, mercy's moral justification is parasitic upon its relationship with justice. This move will not work. Mercy is supposed to have moral standing grounded upon reasons that have nothing at all to do with justice and which are not morally subordinate to justice. As well, mercy is thought to be conceptually distinct from justice. However, if we use the term "mercy" to refer to specific requirements of justice, for example, the requirement for individuation, then mercy ceases to be distinct from justice; it becomes a part of justice and is in effect redundant. If this is so, then it is not possible to weigh the just course of action against the merciful course of action. In other words, grounding mercy on reasons of justice conflates mercy with justice: it becomes impossible to distinguish the merciful act from the just act. The exhortation to "temper justice with mercy" would become an uninformative tautology. So, if we attempt to solve the moral justification paradox by claiming that the moral acceptability of mercy is parasitic upon it being what justice would license anyway, a conceptual paradox is apparently generated, and all the exhortations to temper justice with mercy degenerate into nonsense. If however, it is maintained that mercy is autonomous from justice, then mercy appears to be immoral.

There are other conceptual problems besides this. For example, if mercy is a rational action, then if it is given once, there is a rational requirement, and not merely the moral requirement to be fair, that mercy be replicated and given to similar cases. This is problematic: a single act of mercy is thought pretheoretically not to generate any rational obligation to replicate that action over similar cases; yet mercy, in virtue of being a rational action, would seem to require just that. Thus, "mercy" is incoherent.

The final paradox is this: Suppose that mercy is morally optional, as is sometimes claimed. How then can we account for the moral criticism and moral condemnation of merciless agents of the sort that rest upon assertions that this or that person deserves mercy and

the merciless actor has failed to give another what she deserves? Such criticism rests upon the assumption that mercy is subject to some sort of moral imperative; that is, it is morally required rather than morally optional. Yet, if mercy is morally optional then there can be no duty to be merciful. Consequently, moral criticism, which is based upon a failure to discharge an alleged duty to be merciful, or the positing upon agents of a duty to act mercifully, is logically impossible. So, logically incompatible properties are predicated of mercy: it must be deserved and required if (certain sorts of) moral criticism of merciless agents is to be possible, and yet supererogatory and optional if mercy is to retain its gift-like nature. Thus, the concept appears incoherent.

Should these moral and conceptual conundrums remain, then it would be impossible to account for mercy in a rationally based moral theory that treats justice as a primary value. Mercy would appear to be an action that agents ought not to perform, a virtue they ought not to cultivate or display, and an ideal that is incoherent and which therefore ought not to be pursued.

A. Is Mercy Immoral?

The conclusion that mercy is immoral is based upon two assumptions: (1) that mercy always involves a failure to do what is just, and (2) that actors must always do what is just. Both assumptions are wrong.

Consider this case: Suppose that Judge Smith despises a particular offender and that he has decided to inflict a very harsh sentence, one that is morally unjust given the seriousness of the crime. Defense counsel makes strenuous appeals, pointing out the offender's deprived childhood, violent upbringing, and so on. Smith relents and imposes a penalty in accord with the offender's deserts. This would be an act of mercy since it involves Smith not treating the offender as harshly as was likely given the circumstances. It is also just. Mercy then does not necessarily conflict with justice in contexts in which justice is the dominant value at work, and it may in fact procure a just outcome.

Consider this case: Suppose that Henry owes Joan $1000, and that repayment has now fallen due. Repaying it now would ruin Henry. Joan becomes aware of this and allows a more lenient repayment schedule. This also is a typical act of mercy, but there is no violation of justice on Joan's part. The conclusion is that mercy does not necessarily conflict with justice, though it does seem confined to cases in which it procures a just outcome or cases where, although justice is not an issue, actors have a right which, if exercised, would cause another to suffer.

Are people morally obliged always to punish wrong-doing? That is, are people morally obliged to do justice? As we saw, one account of punishment says that all wrongs must be punished and that a failure to do so is itself morally wrong. Mercy can involve a failure to punish a person to the extent required by her wrongdoing. That is, mercy can involve not doing justice. Since it is morally wrong, it is claimed, to fail to do justice, and mercy involves failing to do justice, mercy is not, it seems, morally permissible.

Another account of punishment says that all wrong-doing does is make a person liable to punishment and there is no obligation on the part of the victim of the wrong to exercise her right. On this view, mercy (that is, not punishing another who is liable for punishment) is morally permissible since the person who decides whether to punish another is not morally required to punish the wrongdoer. She has a right to punish the wrongdoer—it would be just to do so—and it is a right that she may exercise or not as she pleases. Failure to exercise the right, as occurs when she is merciful, is *not* morally wrong. Therefore, actors need not always do justice, and it is no moral failure to fail to do justice in such cases. They can do much less than justice licenses. That is, they can act mercifully.

Such conclusions, however, rest upon a misconception about the moral nature of mercy. To be sure, it is assumed in both accounts of punishment that the moral standing of mercy is determined by whether an act of mercy violates the requirements of justice. Against this assumption, it is often thought that mercy is morally right for reasons quite distinct from reasons of justice, and these reasons may be so strong that they trump reasons of justice. Suppose that Fred and Katie have both been apprehended for drunk driving. Fred, it turns out, is an habitual offender; he has been convicted five times in the past five years. For Katie, it is her first offense, committed on the way home after an office party. She has also had many years of incident-free driving and it is unlikely that she will reoffend.

Both Katie and Fred committed the same offense. Within standard justice-based systems of punishment a wrongdoer is punished on this occasion *for* a particular wrong action. Consequently, the standard justice-based systems of punishment do not punish according to what a person might do or all the things she may have done or not done in the past, but what she did do on this occasion. In other words, in standard justice-based systems, punishment is not determined by a comprehensive assessment of all a person's actions; rather, it is focused upon an isolated, defined act of wrongdoing. In our example, both Katie and Fred did the same thing.

Given this, justice requires that Katie and Fred receive the same penalty, say, disqualification.

While such a respone may satisfy the demands of justice, in that were both Katie and fred to be punished with the same penalty they would both receive their "just deserts" for their offenses, it appears to be the morally wrong response. We can see moral reasons—though not reasons of justice, but of utility—to distinguish these cases and treat Katie more leniently than Fred. Katie is unlikely to reoffend; Fred may well do so. Katie is not a public menace; Fred is. Deterrence of other would-be offenders is, of course, a consideration, but that may be promoted by a large fine. It would seem, then, that the morally right course of action is to treat Katie more leniently than Fred, that is to say, treat her mercifully. Doing this, however, does involve treating Fred unfairly with respect to Katie. The departure from fairness is licensed, however, by the other non-justice-based moral considerations. These also prevent Fred from claiming that he has a right to mercy because his offense is the same as Katie's. From the point of view of justice his and Katie's offenses are the same; but that does not provide a good reason by itself to treat him to mercy. In other words, treating Katie mercifully does not generate an obligation to treat all cases that are similar to Katie's, from the point of view of justice, with mercy.

What this story shows is that reasons of justice are only one sort of moral reason and that they are not the only sort. There are others besides, such as considerations of utility—as we saw—but also other sorts of reasons that are morally powerful, such as humanity, friendship, familial relationships, and compassion. Sometimes these other reasons will trump the reasons of justice, and other times they will not. Actors then do not always have a duty to do justice. What actors must do—and this is the point of applied ethics—is weigh all the competing morally salient reasons and decide which are the appropriate reasons for this occasion.

Given this, the fact that mercy may conflict with justice, on some occasions, is not morally troubling. If mercy, rather than a just action, is morally right, then mercy is what an actor must do. Thus, departures from justice, as mercy sometimes involves, are not morally wrong. Mercy becomes morally problematic when a person ought to have acted justly but instead acted mercifully. On such occasions, mercy is morally wrong. The conclusion then is that the first paradox is only apparent, since it rests upon two false assumptions.

This analysis of the first paradox reveals much about mercy. First, mercy is a certain sort of action that involves treating a person less harshly than it was likely, given the circumstances, that the person was going to be treated. Second, the reasons that morally justify an act of mercy are not confined to one moral outlook. Mercy may be justified, as we saw, by reasons of justice and utility. Reflection shows that reasons of decency, humanity, compassion, and friendship, and even a conception of human flourishing, among others, are also possible grounds for merciful action. What reasons justify mercy and whether it is justified at all in a particular case will depend upon the features of the case. Finally, given this competition between different moral justifications for action, whether to be merciful or not is a pressing question of applied ethics.

This solution will not find favor with those who believe that justice is the first virtue of human institutions or with those who believe that justice is the whole of morality. For such people, mercy will have only such a place as is consistent with the demands of justice. There are two responses to this.

The first is that it is not clear that justice is necessarily the first virtue of human institutions; that is to say, it is not clear that human institutions ought only to aim for or be guided by the principles of justice—so-called "substantive justice"—or that they ought always to apply established procedures to each and every case—so-called "procedural justice." For example, schools are human institutions. Yet justice is only one value to which schools are committed and which must be taken into account when decisions are made. Of course, schools must ensure fairness, when fairness is appropriate—such as in the marking of assignments. But they must also be concerned with, and be sensitive to, the welfare and well-being of each of their individual pupils and the school community as a whole. So, a pupil who is gifted may require extra resources as may a pupil who is disadvantaged or disruptive. They do not merit such treatment as a matter of justice but because they have a need that it is right to meet, for example, for reasons of humanity or respect. Or it may be right from a utilitarian perspective not to carry out an established procedure and expel a troublesome pupil but to expend further efforts to discover the source of his problems, rather than turn lose on the community a poorly socialized, dangerous individual. Such sorts of decisions involve balancing various moral considerations—for example, needs, welfare, rights, and justice—in order to reach a decision that is morally sound. So, when schools make decisions that favor pupils with special needs they will need to remain mindful of the needs of their ordinary pupils and ensure that their decisions do not make the lot of the worst-off ordinary pupil even worse. (For example, to deprive the worst-off ordinary pupil of a resource in order to feed the intellect of a gifted child would be morally wrong because such an action fails to respect the ordinary child and her needs.) Schools then, are not required to act in a substantively or procedurally just way on every occasion, when there are good clear moral reasons not to.

To be sure, considerations of need, respect, and utility, among others, may be morally salient for institutions, even though they are not considerations of justice, but because they enhance and respect individual well-being and welfare on a particular occasion. On another occasion, the considerations of justice will be most important since on that occasion they enhance and respect individual well-being and welfare. What is clear is that each case will need to be decided on its own merits.

Justice is not, on this view, the first virtue of human institutions; it is one of a number of competing virtues which together realize the purpose of institutions: enhancing and respecting individual human welfare and well-being. This suggests that this, rather than justice, is the first virtue—the most important moral property—of human institutions. Can any justification be given for this view? It does seem intuitively right—after all, it would seem morally perverse to have an institution that did not have as its express purpose the enhancing and respecting of individual welfare and well-being. Nevertheless, this is contested. This problem is one of the central issues in political philosophy and a continuing issue in applied ethics. It is, however, outside the scope of the present entry.

It may be argued that this misses the point. What the claim that "justice is the first virtue of institutions" means is that each person receives equal consideration when decisions come to be made, irrespective of the basis (desert, need, or utility, for example) upon which that decision is made. Institutions morally must consider all individuals and exclude none from consideration if that person is a candidate for institutional attention. What this form of justice requires, in effect, is that all institutions, if they are to be morally well grounded, must give every candidate for institutional attention a hearing (which is normally those people over whom they exercise power).

Now, one of the features of mercy when it is a virtue of persons is that it pays attention to the details of each individual case and does not exclude in advance any person from consideration. It gives every person who is threatened with some burden or suffering some imposition, a hearing. Thus, mercy does not conflict with this sense of justice. Moreover, this form of justice is neutral between the different justifications that may be invoked for a particular act. Acts of mercy are not tied to any one justification. Therefore, no act of mercy will conflict this with form of justice in terms of the sorts of justifications that this form of justice recognizes.

While this demonstrates a compatibility between mercy and justice as the first virtue of institutions, it will not do. On this account, mercy would find its ultimate justification only in a relationship with justice: mercy is permissible because it does not conflict with justice. This runs against the belief that the ultimate moral foundation for mercy has no necessary connection with justice at all.

The solution is to concede that while mercy and this form of justice do share two common features there are important differences. To be sure, both mercy and this form of justice both give people a hearing; secondly, the moral basis of each is grounded upon the moral value that individuals ought to be respected and their well-being and welfare fostered. Nevertheless, they are conceptually distinct in that mercy as a virtue of persons or as a certain sort of morally valuable action is focused upon the plight of the vulnerable and so goes on to treat others gently if the moral reasons exist. In contrast, this form of justice (a virtue of institutions) is neutral between the various principles and values that may ground a decision to act and the sorts of actions that result. What justifies mercy then is not an appeal to a form of justice—the rightness of listening to those within one's power—but the deeper moral values of respect, and individual well-being and welfare.

Given that this form of justice and mercy both appeal to respect for persons and fostering individual well-being and welfare, we must conclude that this form of justice is not the first virtue of institutions, but merely an expression of fundamental moral values which provide a moral foundation to institutions and the actions of institutional actors. As we recall, this is contested. So, the solution to this problem returns us to the dispute in political philosophy and applied ethics that has been mentioned already: whether it is justice or enhancing and respecting individual welfare/well-being that is the most important moral property—the first virtue—of institutions.

The second response is that it is not clear that justice is the whole of morality. There are many actions and relationships that have moral value that is not derived from considerations of justice. For example, it seems right that it is morally right and good for parents to love their children and care for and nurture them, or that friends may be devoted to each other's well-being to the exclusion to some extent of others. Such relationships suspend to a large degree the rules of justice. Yet if justice were the whole of morality then friendship or familial ties—among many other sorts of morally charged relationships—would lack much of the moral standing these relationships have. Since the moral standing of these relationships does not depend on justice but on quite distinct moral values, we must conclude that justice is not the whole of morality.

This is a contentious area, especially in the field of applied ethics. In that field, appeals are often made to considerations of justice to ground a decision. Suddenly abandoning justice as the sole criterion of moral rightness would seem to deprive applied ethics of the certainty that is needed in its practice. Perhaps, however, such certainty is only an illusion, and what thinking about mercy and forgiveness does is show us clearly that applied ethics is likely to be a much more complex matter than would at first sight appear to be the case.

B. Is Mercy Redundant?

Mercy is thought to be conceptually distinct from justice. However, if we use the term "mercy" to refer to, say, the requirement for individuation, then mercy ceases to be distinct from justice; it becomes a part of justice and is in effect, redundant. This conundrum is confused. As we saw, "mercy" is the name of a certain sort of action. It carries no implication concerning the sorts of reasons that provide the moral justification for it. "Justice," in contrast, is used to refer to a certain sort of action that is grounded on certain sorts of reasons, namely, reasons of justice, such as fairness or desert. Thus, an action may be called "mercy" and it may be morally right because it is justified by reasons of justice. Or it may be justified by reasons of humanity, utility, compassion, or decency—in which case it may well be unjust. What mercy does is focus on certain properties of an action: the fact that this action is more lenient than another action which, given the circumstances, was likely. Justice focuses on a different aspect of an action, namely, its justification. Thus, mercy and justice refer to different *aspects* of an action, and even when they are used to refer to the same action they are referring to different aspects of it. For this reason, calling an action "an act of mercy" and describing it as "just" is not redundant: they refer to distinct properties of an action. Since it will be possible to refer to a certain action as "an act of mercy" and the same action as "an act of justice," and be referring to two quite distinct aspects of it, the contrast between acts of mercy and acts of justice can always be drawn. The conclusion, then, is that mercy is not redundant even when it is used to refer actions grounded on considerations of justice. Therefore, this conundrum is only apparent.

C. Mercy and Rationality

If Henry has been merciful to Ralph for a particular reason, call it R, is he required by rationality to be merciful to all other people for whom, if they are like Ralph, R is also a reason? The problem is that it is believed that actors are free to be merciful or not as they please; in other words, mercy is not rationally required. Yet this argument shows that mercy, if given once, apparently constrains merciful actors to be merciful on all other similar occasions; in other words, mercy is rationally constrained. "Mercy" then appears to be incoherent.

The solution is that sometimes mercy is rationally required and sometimes it is not. Suppose that twins, Bill and Ted, rob a bank. Bill and Ted are identical and there are no other reasons that distinguish them rationally and which would show that dissimilar treatment is rationally required. Thus to give mercy to Bill and not to Ted is irrational.

So, where two cases, A and B, are identical and John has a reason, R, to treat A in a certain way, then R will also be a reason to treat case B in the same way. This presumes that other things are equal, however. For example, suppose the context in which this is taking place is one involving great peril and it is the sort of situation in which it would be unreasonable to require a person to act in a certain way. Suppose also that R is a reason with case A for John on this occasion. Now, it is not unreasonable to decline to do something that is beyond the capacities of any reasonable person, even if you have done that sort of action in the past. Thus, John can decline to treat B the same way as A without rational oddity, if the circumstance is extraordinary, say, requiring great courage and John decides that he cannot bring himself to face the same risks twice. The conclusion, then, is that actors are required to act consistently when it is the sort of context where actors can be reasonably expected to act consistently. That is, merciful actors are constrained on some occasions to replicate their acts of mercy.

This conclusion contradicts the belief that merciful actors are always rationally free to act as they please—that a once merciful actor can act differently in similar cases and avoid, nevertheless, accusations of acting inconsistently. The solution to this contradiction is to reject the belief that merciful actors do not have a rational license to act as they please in all cases where mercy is possible. What they do have is a capacity or power

to do what they want, which grounds this, albeit false, belief. Let us put this another way. At the heart of any act of mercy is a power relationship: the mercy giver has, through her actions, the power to harm or benefit others who stand within her power. This is what we mean when we say that Smith is at the mercy of Jones. What having power over another involves is being able to do to that person what one pleases. This is the essence of the belief that mercy givers may do what they please and that acts of mercy are optional and unconstrained. They are, but only in the sense that ultimately the mercy giver must decide to be merciful; the act is up to her and the putative beneficiary stands vulnerable to the mercy giver's power and her decision. Therefore, the belief that merciful actors may act as they please does not show that mercy is rationally unconstrained. It shows only that, by their nature (that is, because they are in a relationship of power), mercy givers have the capacity to act as they please. It does not contradict the conclusion that mercy may on occasion be rationally required. The conclusion, then, is that through analyzing the phenomenon of mercy, this conundrum can be dissolved.

D. Supererogation and Moral Criticism

Supererogatory actions are morally optional and praiseworthy. Actors cannot be criticized, morally at least, for failing to perform such actions. If mercy is supererogatory, how is it possible to criticize merciless people? The conclusion is that mercy is incoherent and can for that reason play no part in ethical thinking. The solution is that mercy is sometimes supererogatory and at other times it is morally mandatory. The conundrum arises by thinking that mercy is always supererogatory. Let us explain this.

When an act of mercy involves sacrifice or risk beyond what it is reasonable to expect, the action is praiseworthy and morally optional. That is to say, it is supererogatory, and moral criticism of actors who decline to be merciful in such cases is logically out of place. For example, when Father Damien goes to live permanently in a leper colony he forsakes a life of his own and exposes himself to the disease. This is an act of mercy (among other sorts of praiseworthy acts); but it is also much more than could be reasonably morally required of any person. It is for this reason supererogatory, and moral criticism of any person who decides not to follow Father Damien is logically out of place.

On other occasions, when it is within the capacities of ordinary people, mercy may be required. For example, suppose a woman is charged with the murder of her pain-stricken and terminally ill husband because, with his consent, she helped him to die. Morally speaking, mercy killers like this are not on a moral par with contract killers. Yet, many legal systems are unable to easily distinguish between these two sorts of case. We depend upon the mercy of judges, juries, and even prosecutors to do so. In such cases, mercy is not supererogatory but obligatory, and actors who fail to be merciful are the worthy objects of moral condemnation. The conclusion then is that this conundrum presents no barrier to mercy finding a place in the moral life.

For some, the solution to this conundrum and the conundrum concerning the rationality of mercy is unacceptable, since it is held that these solutions rest upon a misconception of the nature of mercy. On this view, morally and rationally, mercy is like charity, even in ordinary cases that are well within the capacities of ordinary actors. A person may give to one charitable cause and not another, similar one without doing anything morally wrong or rationally amiss. Mercy, like charity, licenses caprice: it is by its nature essentially rationally and morally discretionary and not subject to specific claims of right, duty, obligation, justice, or desert, so-called "perfect obligations"—though it may be subject to nonspecific duties that allow some latitude in their execution, so-called "imperfect obligations." Thus mercy can be owed to no one in particular and in any particular case it is supererogatory.

There are two responses to this. The first is to argue, much as has been done in the discussion of the last two conundrums, that there is no moral or rational permission to do as one pleases in ordinary cases in which mercy is an option. This is to deny that mercy is morally or rationally capricious in ordinary cases, and this permits the solutions to the conundrums to remain.

Moreover, there is an additional moral argument against the moral capriciousness of mercy. Mercy involves conferring a benefit upon another who is in great need or who is under a great threat, when it is within the mercy giver's direct power to alleviate such needs or threats. The rightness of mercy seems to rest, in part, on the assumption that it is morally wrong to ignore another's plight and allow her suffering to continue when it is within a person's direct power to assist and there are no good moral reasons to allow the suffering or threat to continue. Were mercy capricious, actors would be morally permitted—and it would not be morally wrong—to allow suffering or threats to continue even when it was within their power to alleviate such burdens. This seems morally perverse.

The second response is to argue that the concept of mercy does not necessarily contain a capricious ele-

ment, in which case the solutions to the conundrums can stand. One way to argue against the capricious nature of mercy is to appeal to ordinary language. It is quite coherent to say that "Roberts deserved mercy" or "the judge ought to have been merciful to Smith," both indicating that mercy was not discretionary in these cases. If mercy was essentially morally or rationally discretionary such locutions would be meaningless; yet clearly, they are not. Consequently we must reject the view that mercy is essentially discretionary. It must be noted, however, that these questions are far from settled and are the subject of an ongoing debate.

E. Different Conceptions of Mercy

The discussion in this entry may give the impression that mercy is an uncontested concept. Yet, the contemporary discussion of the paradoxes of mercy takes place against varying conceptions of it. The importance of the conception of mercy in resolving the paradoxes and finding a place for it in applied ethics is now clearly recognized. Consequently, there is debate about the nature of mercy, and it is then a contested concept.

It is worthwhile to quickly look at some of the different conceptions of mercy to see the important points of difference. In this entry a very broad conception of mercy has been used. Mercy can occur in any context in which there is a relationship of power. Mercy does not then involve only the remission of a deserved or merited punishment, but it may also be displayed by a victor to the vanquished, a bandit to a victim, a good samaritan to someone in distress, or a father to a prodigal son. An act of mercy is an action with specific properties, and any action with those properties— typically, treating a person less harshly than there is reason to or a person is motivated to, given the circumstances—will count as an act of mercy. The virtue of mercy is defined by a certain stance that an actor habitually takes toward the world and those in it who are directly vulnerable to that person's power. No particular motivation, such as benevolence, compassion, or love, is considered necessary either for an action to be identified as an act of mercy or for a trait of character to be adjudged the virtue of mercy.

Alwynne Smart, whose paper resurrected this contemporary discussion, held that mercy was confined to contexts of wrongdoing and retributive punishment (1968. *Philosophy, 43,* 345–359). As a result, mercy is unable to find a place within a utilitarian outlook. According to Smart, mercy occurred when a judge—or more generally, a person who had the authority to punish—benevolently decided to impose less than the just penalty. Mercy was justified by the claims that other, non-justice-based obligations have upon us. The reason is that all actions that involve fitting a punishment to the seriousness of a crime in order to ensure that moral justice is done and injustice is avoided—that is, bridging the gap between the justice of a penalty prescribed by law and moral justice—are not genuine acts of mercy. In such cases, according to Smart, it is impossible to maintain the contrast between mercy and justice—which is something that we do in ordinary language.

Jeffrie Murphy shares Smart's view that mercy is found only within the context of retributive punishment and responsibility, and that it is difficult if not impossible for mercy to find a place in a utilitarian outlook. For Murphy, mercy is a distinct moral virtue that springs from certain dispositions and motives—love, benevolence, and compassion—that a judge (or other person who has the duty to inflict punishment upon others) has toward a wrongdoer. According to Murphy, mercy has the deontic status of a free gift, act of love, or compassion. It is beyond the claims of right, duty, obligation, desert, or justice and so cannot be owed to anybody. For Murphy, typically mercy is that action where a judge, out of love or compassion for the plight of a particular offender (who in justice deserves a particular level of punishment), imposes upon that person a penalty less than the offender's just deserts (see J. G. Murphy & J. Hampton, 1990. *Forgiveness and Mercy*. Cambridge: Cambridge Univ. Press).

George Rainbolt takes a broad view of the possible contexts for mercy, and so, in contrast to Smart and Murphy, he rejects their view that mercy is confined only to contexts of retributive punishment (in press. *Nous*, **31**). As well, Rainbolt regards as a necessary feature of all acts of mercy the fact that they occur in contexts in which the putative merciful actors face strong contramotivating reasons—reasons that urge a person not to be merciful—and that all acts of mercy are motivated by compassion. Like Murphy, Rainbolt suggests that mercy is morally and rationally unconstraining; that is, it is a discretionary gift, and it cannot be owed to or claimed by another as a right, duty, or obligation. Thus, any particular instance of mercy is a matter for the mercy giver's caprice. So, for Rainbolt, a person is merciful only when, as a result of her compassion for others, she has the disposition to do merciful acts. An action is merciful only when it is an action in which a person has a fairly strong reason to treat another harshly (or most people in a putative mercy giver's circumstances would have a fairly strong reason to treat

another harshly) and the putative mercy giver intentionally does not do so.

Each of these conceptions of mercy raises problems that must be addressed if mercy is to find a place within moral theory or applied ethics. Moreover, the place that mercy does have will be determined to a large extent by the analysis of the concept. For example, is mercy confined only to contexts of punishment? If it is, then it will have only a limited role in our moral lives and the high moral regard in which this virtue is held is then seemingly unjustified. The task for anyone seeking to place mercy centrally within our moral lives and within the practice of applied ethics will be to develop a conception of mercy that both accords with our intuitions and which can also answer the paradoxes.

IV. MERCY AND THE MORAL LIFE

We have seen that the moral life can be conceived either as an attempt to do what is right—that is, it is a life guided by values, principles, and rules—as a life in which the focus is the ideal of human flourishing and the task of people, their life's work, is to engage in activities that exemplify and promote that ideal. The place of mercy within either of these accounts of the moral life will depend upon the extent to which mercy exemplifies and promotes certain moral principles, rules, or values on the one hand, or human flourishing on the other. Can mercy do this? It seems so.

Although mercy refers to certain sorts of actions, describing an actor as merciful is not merely to say that she performs acts of mercy. It is to say something about her, namely, that when she finds herself with the power in a power relationship she is disposed to interact with other people in certain ways. She approaches them from a particular and unique perspective. The thought is this: mercy is not merely a certain sort of action. It is a way of approaching the world and interacting with other people. It is a stance that a person takes as she moves through the world. For example, she refuses to use the power she possesses merely for the sake of using it. Power will be exercised, but only when there is some point to it, usually that its use will advance human well-being and welfare. For this reason, a person who engages the world through a merciful stance is in control of her own power and uses it according to her own moral judgment.

Further, a person who lives "at the mercy" of another depends upon the assent of the powerful actor for her choices to be realized. Thus, she can never freely exercise important capacities that exemplify human flourishing. Moreover, since she is dependent upon the powerful actor to allow her to live her life, the powerless person lacks autonomy. Therefore, she cannot fully participate in the life of the community—she cannot exercise full community membership. The merciful stance, by its operation, removes the threats facing another person: debts are remitted, punishments reduced or cancelled completely, or threats alleviated. The barriers that prevent participation in community life and the enjoyment of community membership are lessened or removed altogether. In this way the power of the would-be mercy giver is used to dissolve the vulnerability of the powerless person by removing that person from the power of the powerful. The recipient of mercy has been recreated as a social actor, capable of autonomous decision making. Thus, the operation of mercy—through the merciful stance—restores the beneficiary to the life of the community and community membership (or in the case of partial remission of a punishment, puts the wrongdoer on the path to reintegration).

Moreover, the person who has received mercy has been "noticed" by the mercy giver: her individual lot has been examined and used as the basis for her treatment. By seeking the whole story through an examination of a person's lot, the merciful stance respects the intrinsic worth of people: it says that they are so morally important as to warrant such treatment. In this way, a powerless person's individuality is respected and her intrinsic moral value recognized. She has been respected as a person.

Respecting people, considering them to be intrinsically valuable and restoring the beneficiary of mercy to the life of the community and community membership, also lessens the divisions between people. The usual two classes—the powerful and powerless—are to some extent dissolved if those with power move through the community with this stance. In this way, the deleterious effect of power on human relationships is reduced and the damaging stance of an "us and them" mentality cannot so easily grip the community. Thus, the merciful stance respects and promotes individual and social well-being.

The merciful stance leads the merciful actor to not indiscriminately use each right she has, but rather do only what seems to her to be right. She may remit a debt or cancel or reduce a punishment. To operate in this way, that is, operate on the basis of moral decisions, requires that actors be sensitive to others, discern the salient moral properties, evaluate them, and finally reach a judgment. They are disposed to search for the whole story and seek a comprehensive understanding of the lot of others. Consequently, they do not confine

themselves to a consideration of only one type of reason or to looking for one type of reason for action, such as reasons of justice, but look instead at all salient moral reasons. Consequently, the merciful stance enables a person to see into another's lot and reach a better understanding of the moral features of some case, and, ultimately, reach a better decision. Thus, the merciful stance yields better moral outcomes.

Searching for the "full story," seeking understanding of another's lot, is at the heart of the stance that the merciful actor takes toward the world. Through it she will come to know why others are as they are, why they are vulnerable and powerless, and then be in a better position to decide what to do. It may well moderate the anger toward others that leads to negative stances, often prompted by human interaction being dissolved. So, when she has found the "full story" she will be more likely to treat others more leniently than would have been the case had she gone with her initial reactions or perceptions. Thus, seeking the full story exemplifies a merciful approach to the world and leads ultimately to merciful actions.

To sum up, then, the merciful stance produces better moral decisions than decisions based upon a single value; it promotes societal cohesion and membership. It respects the value of individuals. It advances and maintains human welfare and well-being. It subjects power to rational control. Moreover, the merciful stance respects and promotes these concerns. That these things have positive moral value is uncontroversial. They are concerns that have a central place in our moral life, since they speak to our interaction with other people. For these reasons, promoting and respecting them must be part of the moral life, however that is conceived. Consequently, a person who thinks of the moral life as one in which actors are dedicated to living by rules and principles, and ultimately doing what is right, will be committed to developing this stance, as it promotes and exemplifies concerns that are morally desirable.

Similarly, these concerns have a central place in promoting and exemplifying human flourishing. For example, people cannot flourish if their well-being and welfare are threatened; if they are alienated from community membership or if their community is divided; or if their decisions are of poor quality. The merciful stance speaks to all these concerns by its nature, and in that way it promotes human flourishing. Any agent who adopts human flourishing as an ideal would, then, need to cultivate the merciful stance as one means of realizing this ideal.

The merciful stance, however, does not merely promote human flourishing. It also exemplifies it. To be sure, this stance is directed toward other people. By its very operation—for example, being open to the hard lot of others, seeking understanding of it, and seeking to control one's own power and use it for the benefit of others—it involves social engagement, interaction, and participation. Thus, the merciful stance exemplifies social life, an individual's participation in it, and her exercising various human capacities, such as understanding, reason, and choice, that is, activities that exemplify human flourishing. Thus, the merciful stance itself exemplifies human flourishing. Consequently, an actor who has as her ideal human flourishing would necessarily cultivate and realize this stance. The conclusion, then, is that the merciful stance—and the actions that flow from it—is necessary for a flourishing actor's personality and an ineliminable part of her moral life.

The response to these arguments is to argue that morality can do without mercy. It is claimed that one of mercy's chief virtues seems to be that it individuates treatment. Individuation can be attained just as well, so the argument goes, by a sophisticated theory of justice. Mercy, then, is unnecessary. This is mistaken. Justice is myopic: it is sensitive to only some values and as a result, no matter how sophisticated a theory of justice may be, there will always be salient moral considerations that are ignored. Mercy is not morally blind. Consequently, if we seek individuation in our dealings with others, mercy will be necessary. It enables us to see through the power that rights and justice confer and assess cases on all of their moral merits.

Another challenge to mercy comes from the opposite direction. If mercy involves compassion or benevolence, then why not focus on those values? Why introduce the potentially misleading and unnecessary notion of mercy into moral discourse and thereby clutter moral thinking?

This misconceives mercy. The merciful stance is one based upon reason, in which understanding is a central element. Compassion and benevolence, on the other hand, are emotional responses. Reason and understanding are not necessary in generating these responses. Moreover, central to mercy is the awareness on the part of a mercy giver of her power and the plight of the powerless, and a disposition to develop an understanding of it. Compassionate or benevolent people are not so focused. Rather than seeing the plight of others and rationally developing an understanding of it and the right response to it, compassionate or benevolent people actively engaged the other's plight on an emotional level and respond to it on that basis. Therefore, mercy, compassion, and benevolence do different jobs and in different ways. As a result, their moral standing is quite distinct. For these reasons, mercy on the one hand, and

compassion and benevolence on the other, are distinct moral notions and play different roles in our moral thinking and lives. The conclusion, then, is that we cannot do away with mercy either by improving on justice or by abandoning mercy in favor of compassion and benevolence.

When is mercy justified? We saw that mercy was not grounded on one moral outlook. Consequently, no single principle can be developed in order to determine when mercy is justified. Moreover, since life and human action are so varied, and a small alteration in some aspect can have serious moral consequences, it is unlikely that such a principle could ever be developed that would reliably cover all cases.

This is not troubling; since mercy is an essential element in human flourishing, actors will learn to think about the appropriateness of mercy through engaging in social life. Like forgiveness, they may well develop rules of thumb, paradigm cases, and exemplars of the virtue of mercy. By reflecting on each case and applying rules of thumb, paradigm cases, and exemplars, actors will be able to reach a well-grounded decision on grounds that are morally respectable and which can be articulated. Through all this, however, as is the case with forgiveness, since mercy tends to promote and exemplify human flourishing and well-being, as a rule of thumb the presumption is always in favor of mercy: it is always right, unless there are compelling reasons against it. What actors must do is think through each case, using the paradigm cases and exemplars.

What does seem to follow from this discussion is that the merciful stance is of great use in applied ethics. It sensitizes actors to the plight of others and opens the powerful to the salient moral considerations in any person's lot. Importantly, it disposes a person who has power over another to address that person's needs rather than ignore them. Such noticing of others is fundamental in developing cohesive and flourishing communities. So, while the answer to the question of when one ought to be merciful cannot be reached by an appeal to a single principle, what can be said is that actors ought to adopt and cultivate the merciful stance, and the presumption ought always to be in favor of it.

V. CONCLUSION

We have seen that forgiveness and mercy are both essential elements of the moral life. Consequently, in applying ethics to the pressing problems of life—the most significant of which are what sort of person does one want to be and what one ought to do—forgiveness and mercy have central roles to play. Forgiveness ministers to our interpersonal relationships, promotes societal harmony, and allows us to flourish as human beings. Mercy promotes and exemplifies moderation in, and the constructive use of, power. And like forgiveness, mercy promotes and exemplifies human flourishing. However, as is often the case in applied ethics, we cannot adduce a universal principle that can be used to determine those occasions when mercy or forgiveness is morally in order and when it is not. The reason is that mercy and forgiveness pay attention to the particular details of individual cases. Life allows too much variety in its details to be captured in a single timeless, contextless rule or principle. Even if we cannot find a clear injunction for the use of mercy and forgiveness, we can see that these stances have central roles to play in our moral lives. Given that, what it seems we must do, as a matter of applied ethics, is to cultivate forgiving and merciful stances and in that way give ourselves and others the best chance of living together well.

Also See the Following Articles

MORAL DEVELOPMENT • THEORIES OF JUSTICE: HUMAN NEEDS • VIRTUE ETHICS

Acknowledgments

The discussion of the issues in this entry has benefited greatly from comments and discussions from Peter Schouls, George Rainbolt, Jim Battye, and Norvin Richards. To them I am most grateful.

Bibliography

Brien, A. (Ed.) (1997). *The Quality of Mercy: An Anthology of New Articles on Mercy.* Amsterdam/Atlanta: Rodopi.

Brien, A. (in press). Mercy within legal justice. *Social Theory and Practice.*

Calhoun, C. (1992). Changing one's heart. *Ethics,* **103,** 76–96.

Card, C. (1972). On mercy. *Philosophical Review,* **81,** 182–207.

Downie, R. S. (1965). Forgiveness. *Philosophical Quarterly,* **15,** 128–134.

Kolnai, A. (1973–1974). Forgiveness. *Proceedings of the Aristotelian Society,* **74,** 91–106.

Nussbaum, M. (1993). Equity and mercy. *Philosophy and Public Affairs,* **22,** 83–125.

Richards, N. (1992). Forgiveness. In J. Deigh (Ed.), *Ethics and personality: Essays in moral psychology* (pp. 223–243). Chicago: The Univ. of Chicago Press.

Seneca (1985). De Clementia. Trans J. W. Basore. In *Seneca: Moral essays* (Vol. 1). London: Heinemann.

Statman, D. (1994). Doing without mercy. *Southern Journal of Philosophy,* **32,** 331–354.

MERGERS AND ACQUISITIONS

Jukka Kilpi
University of Helsinki and Monash University

I. The Mergers and Acquisitions Phenomenon
II. Mergers and Acquisitions as a Business Activity
III. Social Impacts
IV. Ethical Problems
V. Conclusions

GLOSSARY

acquisition A company's acquiring of a business or other assets from another company.

downsizing The reduction of a company's assets and workforce after a merger or acquisition.

golden handshake or parachute A generous benefits package, normally restricted to top executives, providing them with financial security in the event of a merger and acquisition related dismissal.

greenmail A target company's offer to buy back its shares from a hostile bidder.

investment bank A financial institution specializing in corporate finance and structuring of corporate deals.

junk bond A high-yield, high-risk debt security.

leveraged buyout (LBO) The use of debt to purchase a company.

management buyout (MBO) The purchase by management of the company they work for.

merger Two or more businesses, often of similar size, combining under common ownership.

stakeholder A party who has an interest vested in the company and who is affected by the company's actions.

stockholder An owner of a company's stock.

takeover A bidding company's acquiring control of a target company by purchasing the target's shares. Takeovers of listed, publicly traded companies are the most conspicuous form of M&A activity. **Friendly takeovers** are encouraged and **hostile takeovers** are discouraged by the target company. Whether the takeover is hostile or friendly, the stockholders may decide to sell if the price is right, and if a majority sells, the reluctant ones may be forced to give up their shares anyway.

MERGERS AND ACQUISITIONS (M&A) occur when businesses expand through the purchase of other businesses. They are an alternative to organic growth.

Most spectacular M&A are the multibillion dollar takeovers of public companies. However, corporate deals are made on all levels of business. The bidders are after growth, market share, competitiveness, and financial profit regardless of the value of the transaction. The sellers' motives vary depending on the size and character of their company. Large public companies may sell some of their business in order to improve the focus of their operations. When this occurs they are said to divest. Smaller businesses may also divest, but more often their owners want to cash in and retire or have a change in what they do. Offers to buy listed companies are often hostile, but with unlisted companies friendliness is almost always a precondition of

M&A. It is much harder to proceed in the acquisition without the target's consent if its control is in relatively few hands and there is no public forum facilitating the trading.

On the one hand, M&A activity is said to increase the effectiveness of the companies. It is an engine of the market economy increasing productivity that both improves profits and pushes prices lower. On the other hand, M&A are also said to destroy corporate assets and jobs, which disadvantages and distresses many and is against the ethos of the work ethic. The number of M&A are growing and so is the amount of empirical information of their economic and social impact. Many of the myths and problems associated with corporate deals can be explained or answered in the light of facts. Nevertheless, corporate structuring is not a matter of mere economic and social calculations. Human disadvantages and distress have an ethical dimension that should be accounted for too.

I. THE MERGERS AND ACQUISITIONS PHENOMENON

In the United States the average volume of M&A activity is $50 million per hour. In 1995 this resulted in 5887 deals, valued at $5 million and more, for a total record value of $388 billion. The increase in dealmaking is not limited to the United States. The European Union and other regional alliances integrate the markets for goods and capital. Corporations meet the challenge of cross-border competition by specializing and increasing volumes in their chosen field. M&A are often the most efficient way to implement these goals.

The first wave of corporate mergers and acquisitions took place from 1898 through 1901. Thus, M&A existed long before the 1980s, a decade that made corporate raiders and junk bond whiz kids rich and famous. It did not take long for the kids to grow older and infamous—and maybe less rich too. Penalties for insider trading and other breaches became common in the early 1990s, and the market for corporate control seemed dead in the water.

By the mid-1990s the boom was on again. The difference is that while many of the 1980s acquisitions were financially driven, the 1990s emphasized strategic dealmaking aimed at global competitiveness. Although junk bonds are out, the huge pools of capital raised by acquisition funds may indicate a recovery of financially driven M&A dynamics.

II. MERGERS AND ACQUISITIONS AS A BUSINESS ACTIVITY

The primary economic justification of M&A is better efficiency and valuation. Corporate deals improve the use of inefficient assets and increase the price of undervalued stock. They help companies to achieve geographical reach, brand concentration, and economies of scale. In the end, a better long-term return on assets leads to higher shareholder value.

Financial considerations may also favor M&A. After the transaction, two companies may achieve better interest-tax utilization, debt capacity, or advantages of past tax losses with an immediate positive effect on the bottom line. A company valued by the markets at a discount to the real underlying worth of its assets or business is always a lucrative target.

Sometimes the motives behind an acquisition are more abstract. Companies that are concerned that they are vulnerable to a takeover may seek to defend themselves by taking over other companies, which often leads to an increment in their debt thereby making them both bigger and less appealing as a target. Even top management's ego, desiring more power, prominence, and reward, may sometimes be behind M&A.

III. SOCIAL IMPACTS

The typical economic defense of M&A culminates in the fact that they increase efficiency, which in turn improves shareholder value as well as general welfare. Many critics have pointed out that in the 1980s the outcome was often the opposite: research showed that while the target's shares grew in value shareholders of the acquirer usually gained little and the overall economic strength of firms engaged in mergers actually declined. These results may have been due to the large numbers of financially motivated transactions that were priced and leveraged high and aimed at making a fast buck by asset-stripping. In the more sensible 1990s, studies show that mergers increased both the target's and the bidder's shareholder value and offered genuine cost savings to the companies.

However, the benefits are not distributed equally. In order to make the new corporate entity meaner and leaner, plants and businesses may be closed and employees retrenched. Even if jobs are not threatened, the workers' contracts are often renegotiated after a merger. These measures may have an immediate negative impact upon individuals and communities. Another cause of fear is the fact that the merged company is larger than the two separate companies before the merger. Concentration may decrease competition, push prices up, and reduce the consumer's options. Often in large units the ownership is also more dispersed, which means that the management and executives have a greater say in the firm. This affects the shareholders whose control is diminished.

IV. ETHICAL PROBLEMS

Most of the ethical problems associated with M&A arise from the conflicts of interest between stockholders, management, and other stakeholders. Managers have been shown to use takeovers to prop up their influence and benefits at the expense of the stockholders. Golden handshakes and parachutes may give them advantages that seem unfair when other stakeholders' contracts are terminated without any compensation. Hefty fees for investment bankers who facilitate the deal-making have been seen as unwarranted.

On a more general level, society is seen to suffer from reduced competition and plant closures. In particular, LBOs are claimed to be harmful because greater indebtedness forces companies to downsize. Hostile takeovers have been thought of as unethical because they involve elements of threat. For example, the threat condition in greenmailing consists of the fact that the greenmailer threatens to start a hostile takeover of the raider unless the greenmailer is sold back its own shares.

Takeovers of listed companies have some peculiar causes for ethical concern. M&A usually have both immediate and long-term impacts on the market price of the shares of the companies concerned. The immediate price fluctuations may be especially violent. This sounds the alarm on insider trading. Those who are aware of the coming bid have information that they could use to their own benefit at the cost of the other shareholders. Also, after a public bid has been made, shareholders have to decide whether or not to agree with the bid on the basis of publicly available information, and they may be disadvantaged if that information is wrong or incomplete. Even worse, if there are no rules making it obligatory for bidders to publish their offer the target's shareholders may be led to sell at a price that is clearly undervalued or they may find themselves left stranded as a minority at the mercy of the raider who has secretly bought into the company.

Some of the doubts that business ethicists cast over M&A a decade ago were based on mistaken factual assumptions. For instance, it was claimed that M&A almost always involves junk bond financing. In reality, a majority of takeovers have not been financed through junk bonds. Other facts that have been used to support this criticism, such as the claim that the acquirers' stockholders stand to lose in the long run, may have been correct at the time but are true no more. Market mechanisms do not tolerate continued bad deal-making, and if the shareholders lose in a deal, the deal is a bad one; it is, therefore, no miracle that mischievous corporate structurings are far less common in the 1990s.

Hence, a number of ethical concerns have already been addressed by market forces. The 1990s mergers make both the targets' and the acquirers' shareholders happy, and the corporations report positive news. Recent empirical findings also play down the concerns of decreased competition. There is no evidence that corporate restructuring increased U.S. industrial concentration during the 1980s. M&A can also result in new entities that enhance competition or rescue financially destitute enterprises. There are many examples of successful MBOs.

However, a more sensible market for corporate control has not wiped out all of the problems. Even when the share prices go up and goods cost less, some plants and workers are retrenched. Increasing globalization of business keeps the threat of excessive concentration alive. The tension between management and stockholder interest has not disappeared. Stocks still fluctuate when bids are made.

V. CONCLUSIONS

Do M&A have such harmful consequences that their regulation is warranted? The answer depends on whether one believes that bureaucracy or the judiciary is a better judge of the efficient allocation of economic resources than are the markets. In the United States, a number of federal and state authorities have jurisdiction over M&A, most notably in the areas of antitrust laws, national security, and securities trading. However, no general regulatory framework has emerged in spite of some attempts in Congress. In the United Kingdom, the securities industry has formed a panel for the self-regulation of M&A. It does not have the force of law, but relies on the power of suasion and the withdrawal of the facilities of the markets from offenders. Australia has chosen a black-letter law approach and has extensive M&A rules incorporated in its federal laws. The European Union exercises control over antitrust aspects of mergers, and in many countries labor contracts enjoy much more protection than is the case in the United States.

Many business ethicists have spoken in favor of stricter regulation of M&A. However, most of their arguments rest on negative experiences from the spate of financial raiding during the 1980s. In the light of the empirical facts, M&A in the long run are a useful, rather than harmful, phenomenon and the markets have been capable of rectifying the extravagances without state intervention. We can also ask, who is a better judge of M&A than the markets? Where can we find such infallable authorities who know which mergers are successful and which bring positive results?

What we know about M&A should not shake our confidence in the efficiency of the market. The market has the upper hand in an important sense: its activity is based on voluntary contracts. In the average deal nobody is forced to sell or buy, but the transaction takes place at the discretion of both parties, who receive collateral for what they give up. M&A activity in the marketplace may have some undesirable characteristics, yet these may be a lesser evil than a regulatory straitjacket. It is important, though, that the market is as fully informed as possible and that contractual rights of all stakeholders are respected.

Although M&A contribute to the common good, ethics does not allow us to remain indifferent to the individual suffering that may be caused in particular instances. Challenging and well-paid jobs created in Silicon Valley are meager consolation for redundant steelworkers in the iron belt. The ethical and social implications of M&A call for alertness to curb the excesses and to mitigate the individual and local harms.

Most ethicists share the view that the interests of all stakeholders of the corporation are ethically worth-while. An efficient economy gives us better means to look after those stakeholders who suffer from structural changes. Thus, it would be a disservice for everyone if the drive toward more efficiency were curbed in order to protect the vulnerable victims of that drive. Fairness, understood in terms of John Rawls' theory of justice, requires us to improve the opportunities of those who are hit by M&A, not to make everybody worse off. Education, redundancy packages, relocation assistance, and counseling are examples of measures that soften the corporate restructurings.

Also See the Following Articles

CORPORATIONS, ETHICS OF • EXECUTIVE COMPENSATION • SOCIALLY RESPONSIBLE INVESTMENT

Bibliography

1995 M&A Profile. (1996). *Mergers & Acquisitions*, 30, 5. 37–61.

Achampong, F. K., & Zmedkun, W. (1995). An empirical and ethical analysis of factors motivating managers' merger decisions. *J. Business Ethics*, 14, 855–865.

Carroll, A. B. (1989). Managing public affairs. When business closes down: Social responsibilities and management actions. In E. Iannone (Ed.), *Contemporary Moral Controversies in Business*, pp. 230–240. New York and Oxford: Oxford University Press.

Hanly, K. (1992). Hostile takeovers and methods of defense: A stakeholder analysis. *J. Business Ethics*, 11, 895–913.

Liebeskind, J. P., Opler, T. C., & Hatfield, D. E. (1996). Corporate restructuring and the consolidation of US industry. *J. Industrial Economics*, XLIV, 1, 53–68.

Long-range stock price trends for acquirers in selected acquisitions completed in 1994. (1996). *Mergers & Acquisitions*, 30, 4, 54–55.

Washington's M&A Network (1996). Primary federal regulators of mergers and acquisitions. *Mergers & Acquisitions*, 30, 8, 47–48.

Werhane, P. H. (1990). Mergers, acquisitions and the market for corporate control. *Public Affairs Quarterly*, 4, 1. 81–96.

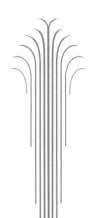

MILITARY CODES OF BEHAVIOR

Charles R. Myers
United States Air Force Academy

GLOSSARY

administrative regulations Regulations governing the behavior of military personnel and describing the conditions under which adverse administrative actions (such as demotion or separation from the service) may be taken against them.

Code of Conduct An executive order first issued in 1955 to describe rules for behavior for United States military personnel who are captured and imprisoned by the enemy.

general articles Provisions of a military justice code describing offenses in general terms; specifically, Articles 133 and 134 of the Uniform Code of Military Justice (which criminalize "conduct unbecoming an officer and a gentleman," "all disorders and neglects to the prejudice of good order and discipline," and

"all conduct of a nature to bring discredit upon the armed forces").

Joint Ethics Regulation The regulation issued by the Secretary of Defense to provide a single source of ethical guidance for United States military personnel and other personnel of the Department of Defense; DoD 5500.7-R, August 1993.

law of war The body of international law, consisting of international agreements and customary law and usually reflected in a nation's military law, governing persons and nations in the conduct of war.

Manual for Courts-Martial An executive order implementing and supplementing the statutory code of military justice.

martial law The government of a civilian population through military institutions.

military justice The body of criminal law and the legal system used to maintain discipline and to administer criminal justice in the military; distinguished from "martial law" and the "law of war."

military offenses Criminal offenses unique to the military, including absence offenses, disrespect and disobedience, and misconduct in wartime.

Uniform Code of Military Justice (UCMJ) The statutory military justice code of the armed forces of the United States; 10 U.S.C. §§ 801–946.

war crimes Violations of the law of war, especially violations of the protections afforded wounded and sick enemy personnel, prisoners of war, and civilian persons and property.

The views presented here are the author's and do not necessarily represent the views of the United States Air Force Academy or any other component of the Department of Defense or the United States government.

MILITARY CODES OF BEHAVIOR, the collections of rules and principles that govern the conduct of members of the armed forces, have a significant part in determining the effectiveness of military forces and so directly affect national security. Military codes are an especially important area of applied ethics because when a nation employs military force or prepares or threatens to do so, more is usually at risk for the nation and individuals than in other activities. This explains why military codes are typically more extensive than civilian codes in their scope and in their demands.

Military codes of behavior reflect the fact that military personnel perform three overlapping roles for society—warrior, public servant, and military professional. First of all, military personnel have extraordinary ethical responsibilities because of their warfighting function. The military is distinguished from the rest of society by its function of preparing for and waging the nation's wars. This function typically demands more order, discipline, and courage than civilian functions. To maintain good order and discipline, the military has codes that impose penalties for certain conduct or otherwise control behavior that civilian society does not regulate as strictly or does not regulate at all. In particular, the military uses the disciplinary and criminal penalties of its "military justice" code to set and enforce standards of behavior, including moral standards, for military personnel. In addition to their warrior role, military personnel are also government officials and have the same ethical responsibilities that other public servants do. "Ethics regulations" prescribe many of these obligations. Finally, as members of the profession of arms, military personnel not only must comply with minimum standards of behavior necessary to maintain good order and discipline, but also must exhibit the character traits and pursue the moral ideals that enable them to make extraordinary personal sacrifices and to inspire others to do so in peacetime operations and in combat. For this, the military has, among other things, written and unwritten "codes of ethics" to set the moral standards and ideals that motivate military personnel to meet the unusually heavy demands of their profession.

I. PURPOSE OF MILITARY CODES OF BEHAVIOR

A. The Military's Function and Purpose

Codes applying ethical rules and principles to particular enterprises are to a large extent shaped by the functions and purposes those enterprises have in society and the conditions under which they are carried out. Thus, the role of military codes of behavior is to enable military personnel to carry out their function and purpose lawfully, ethically, and effectively.

The military function—employing or threatening to employ military force to protect the nation and its interests—differs in significant respects from the civilian professions and other groups in civilian society. Above all, the military function involves life-and-death decisions unlike those in other functions. Other functions—medical practitioners, for example—face decisions of life and death, but they do not involve the application of lethal violence. Other functions—law enforcement personnel, for example—use lethal violence, but not on the scale that the military does. The decisions military personnel make can result in hundreds of deaths or even, in the nuclear age, the destruction of entire cities. Apart from the death and destruction they may be morally obligated to cause in wartime, military personnel in peacetime and wartime make decisions affecting an enormous share of a nation's wealth—expensive weapon systems, extensive real estate, and other valuable resources.

The conditions under which military personnel operate also distinguish them from civilians. In combat and even in peacetime exercises, they must often make terribly momentous decisions in extremely stressful and traumatic situations. They usually make these decision at great risk to themselves and many other persons. Carrying out these decisions typically requires a precision and skill that rivals that needed in any civilian function, and the cost of error is much greater. Moreover, military personnel are morally and legally responsible not only for their own conduct, but also for their subordinates' conduct. Others—physicians, for example—may to some extent be held liable in a civil action for the acts of the personnel they supervise. Military leaders, however, can be held accountable in both criminal and civil proceedings for the functional competence and moral behavior of all persons in their large organizations. Although these subordinates may be very well trained and motivated, usually many of them are also young and inexperienced. In addition, they often serve under difficult conditions in remote locations separated from their families and from the other social constraints that help keep the behavior of most persons within the norms of morality. These features of the military function mark out military society as in many ways separate and distinct from civilian society.

In addition to the distinctive and demanding conditions in which military personnel carry out their function, they have a distinctive and overriding moral purpose. Of course, they share with other government officials the high moral purpose of serving the public—and doing so in a way that earns public confidence. Beyond that, however, they have the moral purpose of preserving the nation. Vital national interests, rights and liberties, and even national survival may depend on how well military leaders organize and train their forces and how well military personnel perform in combat. The military serves as the ultimate defense of the nation, its interests, and its values. Because all of society's other functions depend on the society's survival, there can be no more important moral purpose than the one military personnel serve—at least when the society they serve pursues lawful and moral objectives.

In short, military personnel carry out the function of applying military force to serve the moral purpose of national survival by making life-and-death decisions under conditions that require leadership to an extent no other profession does. It is not surprising, therefore, that military codes tend to go farther than civilian codes in regulating conduct and setting moral ideals.

B. Functional and Professional Justifications for Military Codes

Given the distinctive function and purpose of the military—to employ military force for vital national interests and national survival, military codes of behavior have both a functional and a professional justification.

The functional basis for military codes of behavior is simply that the military function itself defines ethical boundaries for military society. From this perspective, military codes of behavior set out the ethical principles and rules necessary for the successful application of military force. Military personnel have the ethical obligations that other officers and employees of the government do. In addition, however, to succeed in preparing for and waging war and to inspire others to do so, they are morally required to display specific character traits, to perform certain acts, and to achieve particular results. The military function requires military personnel to display character traits like integrity, courage, loyalty, and perseverance. Any suggestion of dishonesty or cowardice can demoralize other military personnel, discredit the armed forces, and so put the military function at risk. In making decisions about acts they are morally obligated to perform, the codes military personnel follow require them to put military duty first. They must subordinate self and all interests to the performance of military duties, and their codes typically require them to avoid even the appearance of a conflict between their official duties and their personal interests. They must understand the military function as too important and too demanding to permit personal interests to interfere with military duties. And when military personnel ask about the consequences they are morally required to achieve, their codes focus on the military mission. The military function demands that military personnel commit themselves to completing all assigned tasks correctly and on time.

The professional justification for military codes of behavior, on the other hand, assumes that the military is not merely a particularly important social function, but is also a particularly important and noble profession. The professional justification determines the ethical domain of military personnel in terms of their moral purpose. From this perspective, it is the purpose of the military as the ultimate safeguard of the nation and its vital interests that defines the military as a profession. Thus, military personnel believe that their many moral responsibilities follow from their morally justified and morally indispensable purpose of preserving the nation and its values. Military personnel strive to develop military virtues, they put duty before self, and they constantly pursue their mission not just because they will thereby better perform the military function, but also because by doing so they protect all other social functions and guard the nation's values. In some contexts, there may be an issue as to exactly who is a military professional. Some would include only military officers in the military profession. Others would include noncommissioned officers (NCOs). This approach reflects the fact that there are good reasons for military codes to hold officers and NCOs to higher standards than junior enlisted persons, but it leaves unclear the status of the young persons who constitute the majority of the armed forces but serve only a few years in the lower enlisted ranks before returning to civilian life. Still, however one resolves this issue, it remains the case that the moral purpose of guarding the nation's values defines the military as a profession.

Military function and purpose are of course inseparably related, and so codes of military behavior typically aim at both. They regulate the military function and also set out moral standards and aspirations that govern the profession of arms. Nevertheless, function or purpose may dominate in any particular code, and there may be some tension between function and profession in designing and interpreting codes. In general, the functional justification underlies a military's code of military justice and its administrative and ethics regulations while a professional justification is sought for its written and unwritten codes of ethics. In any event, the following discussion, taking the codes of the United States armed forces as representative military codes of behavior, indicates how military codes of behavior, unlike most other specialized codes, regulate a separate society in the performance of a social function and also govern a profession.

II. MILITARY JUSTICE

A. Jurisdiction and Procedures

The military needs a separate system of criminal justice to criminalize conduct such as disrespect and cowardice that civilian society has no need to punish and to maintain good order and discipline under conditions where civilian courts are unavailable or inappropriate. This system, known as "military justice," typically provides military forces a separate body of criminal law administered by its own institutions. For the forces of the United States, the principal source of military justice is the statutory Uniform Code of Military Justice (UCMJ), which traces its origin to codes adopted from Great Britain before the American Revolution. A presidential executive order, the Manual for Courts-Martial (MCM), supplements the statute, and a separate system of courts applies and interprets the UCMJ and MCM.

Active-duty military personnel are under the jurisdiction of the UCMJ. The UCMJ also claims jurisdiction over other persons, including former military personnel who committed serious offenses that cannot be tried in civilian courts and persons serving with or accompanying the armed forces either in peacetime outside the United States or in wartime. The Supreme Court has held, however, that courts-martial may not try civilians, at least in peacetime. (United States ex rel. Toth v. Quarles, 350 U.S. 11 (1955); Kinsella v. United States ex rel. Singleton, 361 U.S. 234 (1960)). At one time the United States Supreme Court also limited the subject-matter jurisdiction of courts-martial to offenses that were "service-connected" (O'Callahan v. Parker, 395 U.S. 258 (1969)). The Supreme Court now recognizes, however, that courts-martial have jurisdiction over all offenses under the UCMJ, whether or not they are "service-connected" (United States v. Solorio, 483 U.S. 435 (1987)).

Any person subject to the UCMJ may prefer charges. The accused's commander then decides the disposition of the charges. A commander who receives charges or otherwise has reason to believe that a person under his or her command has committed an offense has several options in addition to taking no action or trial by court-martial. The commander may take administrative action such as a reprimand or otherwise making an unfavorable annotation in the member's service records. In addition, under Article 15 of the UCMJ, the commander may impose certain "disciplinary punishments for minor offenses without the intervention of a court-martial." This nonjudicial punishment may not be imposed if the offender demands a court-martial unless he or she is "attached to or embarked in a vessel."

The UCMJ provides three kinds of courts-martial for the trial of cases—general, special, and summary. The three courts differ as to the level of command at which the courts may be convened, their composition, and the punishment they may adjudge. In any case, a court-martial is an ad hoc tribunal whose members are appointed by a commander authorized to convene courts-martial to try the particular cases that commander (known as the "convening authority") chooses to refer to the court.

Under Article 36 of the UCMJ, the President prescribes rules and "modes of proof" for courts-martial using, "so far as he considers practicable," the principles of law and the rules of evidence used in federal courts. In general, "the Bill of Rights applies with full force to men and women in the military unless any given protection is, expressly or by necessary implication, inapplicable" (United States v. Middleton, 10 M.J. 123, 126 (C.M.A. 1981)). The legal rights of military personnel may be both narrower and broader than those of civilians. For example, rules concerning search and seizure recognize that reasonable expectations of privacy in the military are generally narrower than those in civilian society. Commanders may authorize searches on probable cause, but may also order "inspections" of persons and property to ensure security and military readiness. On the other hand, Article 31 provides military personnel broader protection in confessions than the "Miranda" requirement that civilians in a custodial interrogation be informed of their right to remain silent. Article 31 requires that military suspects be informed of their right to remain silent whether or not the interrogation is custodial and also be informed of the offenses under investigation. The rationale for Article 31 is that military personnel are conditioned to obey and so may believe they have an obligation to make a statement or to say what they believe military superiors want them to say.

Unless an accused elects to be tried by military judge alone, the members of the court-martial (the jurors) make findings as to guilt and also adjudge the sentence. Except in certain capital cases, conviction is by a vote of two-thirds of the members. A vote of less than two-thirds results in an acquittal, not a hung jury. Except for death and lengthy confinement, sentences are also adjudged by a vote of two-thirds of the members. In a trial by military judge alone, the judge enters findings and adjudges the sentence. The punishments courts-martial may adjudge include death, confinement, forfeiture of pay and allowances, fines, demotion (for enlisted persons), and reprimands. A form of punishment unique to the military is the punitive separation. For officers, there is one form of punitive separation, dismissal. For enlisted persons, there are two: the dishonorable discharge and the bad conduct discharge. The dishonorable discharge is the more serious and is reserved for "those who should be separated under conditions of dishonor" after conviction of offenses "requiring severe punishment."

Posttrial review of a court-martial begins with the commander who convened the court-martial. The accused may submit matters for the convening authority's consideration. After considering the advice of his or her staff judge advocate (a military officer who is also an attorney) and the matters submitted by the accused, the convening authority, "in his sole discretion, may approve, disapprove, commute, or suspend the sentence in whole or in part." In every case, there is then some further review of the case. Depending on the approved sentence, the review is either by a judge advocate who has had no prior involvement in the case or by the service's own "court of criminal appeals." After review by the court of criminal appeals, appeals may be heard in the United States Court of Appeals for the Armed Forces (USCAAF), a court of five judges "appointed from civilian life by the President." From USCAAF, an accused may seek review of his or her case by the Supreme Court.

Of all the differences between military justice and civilian criminal law, probably the most important, at least in the United States, is the role of the commander. Until a case reaches USCAAF, military authorities administer the military justice system. Moreover, it is usually commanders who make the critical decisions in investigating and prosecuting a case through the several stages of the military justice process. Commanders of course rely on the advice of judge advocates at every step of the military justice process, but commanders must decide how a case will proceed. Commanders can authorize searches. They usually prefer charges, and they appoint investigating officers. Commanders decide whether to take action under the UCMJ and, if so, whether to impose nonjudicial punishment or to refer the case to a court-martial. They appoint court members, enter into plea bargains, grant immunity to witnesses, and approve or disapprove sentences.

The commander's role in military justice points to the dual function of military justice—justice and discipline. Article 30 provides that when charges are preferred, military officials will then determine "what disposition should be made thereof in the interest of justice and discipline." Thus, the same officer who is responsible for maintaining good order and discipline is also responsible for administering military justice. Some argue the role of commanders in military justice is so extensive and their concern for good order is necessarily so strong that they will too readily promote discipline at the expense of justice. Commanders might, for example, give more weight to the deterrent effect of a conviction and sentence than to fairness to the accused. This, however, is a false dilemma. Effective commanders, as well as the judge advocates who advise them, understand that they can preserve discipline only by administering military justice with fairness and integrity.

B. Offenses

1. Military Crimes

Most offenses punishable under civilian criminal law—murder and larceny, for example—are also punishable under military law. In addition, however, military law also defines a number of offenses that ordinarily are not crimes when committed by civilians. The military offenses defined by the UCMJ generally fall into four classes: absence, disrespect and disobedience, misconduct in combat, and abuse of public trust.

The most serious absence offense is desertion. Desertion is an unauthorized absence with the intent to remain away permanently or to avoid hazardous or important duties. Absence offenses also include other unauthorized absences and missing the movement of a ship, aircraft, or unit.

Punishable acts of disrespect include disrespectful or insubordinate words or behavior toward military superiors, an officer's "contemptuous words" about the President or certain other public officials, and mistreatment of subordinates. A service member who disobeys a lawful order given by a military superior may be punished under the UCMJ. In addition, it is a criminal offense to disobey the punitive (as opposed to merely advisory) provisions of a regulation. The prosecution must prove the accused knew of the regulation unless it is a "lawful general order or regulation," one issued at a fairly high level of command.

There are several offenses that constitute criminal misconduct in combat, many of them punishable by death. "Misbehavior before the enemy," a capital offense, includes: "shamefully" abandoning any place or property one has a duty to defend; "cowardly conduct"; "cast[ing] away . . . arms or ammunition"; and "run[ning] away." Compelling a commander to surrender and improper use of a countersign are also capital offenses, as are aiding the enemy and "forcing a safeguard" (violating a guard posted to protect persons, places, or property of the enemy or a neutral). Misbehavior as a prisoner of war and looting and pillaging are also criminal offenses, although not capital.

Military offenses that can be defined as an abuse of the trust the public places in military personnel include false official statements and allowing military property to be damaged or wrongfully disposed of. Improperly "hazarding" a vessel through collision, stranding, or otherwise is an offense. Malingering and drunkenness on duty also breach the public trust and are punishable under the UCMJ.

Military law thus criminalizes more kinds of conduct than civilian criminal codes do. Military law is also broader in another important way. To a much greater extent than in civilian law, the "mens rea" element of an offense requires only negligence rather than the more purposeful intent required for most crimes in civilian codes. For example, it is an offense for a military member to miss the movement of a ship or aircraft "through neglect or design." The loss or destruction of military property is punishable whether it "was willfully caused by the accused or was the result of neglect by the accused." Criminal dereliction occurs when a person "willfully or negligently fails to perform that person's duties or when that person performs them in a culpably inefficient manner." Punishable conduct "prejudicial to good order and discipline" extends to "all disorders and neglects." Attaching criminal culpability to negligence in handling military matters reflects the moral principle that "the line between incompetence and immorality is a thinner one in the military profession than in almost any other human vocation" (Wakin 1986 xi).

2. General Articles

In addition to the punitive articles identifying specific offenses, the UCMJ has two "general articles": Article 134 that makes punishable offenses "not specifically mentioned" in the UCMJ and Article 133 that denounces "conduct unbecoming an officer and a gentleman."

Article 134 describes three categories of offenses. The first is "all disorders and neglects to the prejudice of good order and discipline." The "prejudice" must be "reasonably direct and palpable." This category also includes breaches of "customs of the service." A "custom" is a long established practice that has attained the force of law. "Fraternization," an officer's improper association with enlisted members, may be punished as a breach of custom—provided the prosecution can prove the existence of a custom against fraternization. The second category is "all conduct of a nature to bring discredit upon the armed forces." The reason for punishing such conduct is that lowering the military in the public esteem affects public confidence in the military's ability to perform its function, makes military service more difficult for others on active duty, and may also affect those considering military service. Article 134's third clause addresses "crimes and offenses not capital." This clause brings under the UCMJ noncapital federal crimes and also state criminal law under the Assimilative Crimes Statute (18 U.S.C. § 13), which federalizes the criminal law of the surrounding state for some military installations. Examples of the many offenses that, according to the MCM, may be prosecuted under Article 134 include: adultery, dishonorable failure to pay a debt, disloyal statements, drinking liquor with a prisoner, altering a public record, breaking a medical quarantine, and wearing unauthorized insignia or decorations.

The relation between law and morality is much closer in military justice than in civilian law, and the relation is nowhere closer than in Article 133's proscription of "conduct unbecoming an officer and a gentleman." "Conduct unbecoming" is defined in terms of the common ethical experience of officers. Article 133's predecessor article under the Articles of War concerned "such a gentleman as an officer of the army is expected to be, *viz.* a man of honor; that is to say, a man of high sense of justice, of an elevated standard of morals and manners." The present MCM points out that Article 133 is based on the fact that "[t]here are certain moral attributes common to the ideal officer and the perfect gentleman, a lack of which is indicated by acts of dishonesty, unfair dealing, indecency, indecorum, lawlessness, injustice, or cruelty." More specifically, Article 133 concerns the officer's standing and character. The officer is not held to unrealistically high standards, but may be punished for acts that seriously compromise his or her standing as an officer or character as a gentleman. It is, for example, conduct unbecoming to cheat on an exam, to using insulting language about an officer to other military personnel, to associate with known prostitutes, or to fail to support one's family.

Although the "general" articles may seem so general as to be unfair, in practice the MCM's explanation of Articles 133 and 134 and the customs of the services do in fact give fair notice to military personnel of what conduct is prohibited. And, in any event, the Supreme Court found that the general articles are not unconstitutionally vague in view of the fact that Congress can "legislate both with greater breadth and with greater flexibility" when making rules for military society than it can for civilian society (Parker v. Levy, 417 U.S. 733, 756 (1974)). The primary reason for the greater breadth and flexibility in military rule-making is the importance of the military function to society and the great extent to which that function depends on moral behavior. The result is that military law speaks more directly of morality and so is more a matter of "applied ethics" than civilian criminal codes.

3. War Crimes

Another class of offenses for which military personnel may be tried by court-martial is "war crimes," violations of the law of war. The "law of war" thus constitutes another code prescribing behavior for military personnel.

The law of war—the recognition by civilized peoples that there are legal and moral restraints on initiating and waging war—originated in the ancient world. Its contemporary development is based on the Lieber Code, a compilation of customary law written by an American law professor and issued by the United States government for its forces during the Civil War. A succession of treaties codified much of the customary law of war before World War II began. Following the war, the Nuremberg Tribunal drew on those treaties and customary international law to define war crimes as "violations of the laws or customs of law," including harm to civilians or prisoners of war or destruction of property "not justified by military necessity." This definition distinguishes war crimes from the other classes of crimes tried at Nuremberg, "crimes against peace" (the unlawful initiation of hostilities) and "crimes against humanity" (the killing or injuring of a nation's own inhabitants). There has been continued codification of the law of war in international agreements since World War II, of which the best known are the four Geneva Conventions concerning the protection required to be given to wounded and sick military personnel, prisoners of war, and civilian populations.

The specific provisions of Geneva Conventions and other laws of war for the most part follow from the general principles of discrimination and proportionality. The principle of discrimination requires military personnel always to discriminate between combatants and noncombatants in the application of military force.

The principle of proportionality requires military personnel to use only that amount of military force that is proportional to achieving a lawful military objective. Complying with these principles at all levels of military operations under the stressful and uncertain circumstances of combat poses tremendous legal and moral obligations on military personnel.

Many violations of the law of war are also offenses under military justice codes and civilian law. The intentional killing of innocent civilians, for example, is both a war crime under international law and murder under military justice codes and civilian law. Military personnel may thus be tried for war crimes in several forums—international tribunals, civilian courts, military commissions, or courts-martial. The Nuremberg trials were before an international tribunal. General Yamashita, who was convicted of and executed for war crimes because of the atrocities soldiers under his command committed in the Philippines, was tried by a United States military commission. Lieutenant Calley was tried by a United States court-martial for murder and manslaughter in the My Lai massacre.

III. ADMINISTRATIVE REGULATIONS

The military regulates the behavior of military personnel not only by means of its criminal code of military justice, but also through administrative regulations. These regulations set standards of various kinds. For example, military personnel are required to meet certain levels of physical fitness and must maintain their weight or body fat within specified limits, and they must responsibly manage their financial affairs and support their dependents. Regulations also prescribe adverse administrative actions commanders may take when a member violates the service's standards or regulations. These adverse actions include: counseling, reprimands, unfavorable notations in the member's records that may affect assignments or promotion, demotion of enlisted persons, removal from a promotion list, or separation from the service.

Separation from the service for cause is perhaps the most serious administrative action that may be taken against a military member. According to the directive governing the separation of enlisted persons from the United States military, the purpose of administrative separation is "to promote the readiness of the Military Services by maintaining high standards of conduct and performance." One effect of continuously evaluating the suitability of military personnel for continued military service on the basis of their duty performance and discipline is, according to this directive, "to strengthen the concept that military service is a calling different from any civilian occupation." For enlisted persons, the reasons for administrative separation include: conscientious objection, fraudulent entry into military service, unsatisfactory performance, failure in alcohol abuse rehabilitation, and misconduct. Misconduct may be a pattern of misconduct consisting solely of minor disciplinary infractions, a pattern of misconduct consisting of discreditable involvement with civil or military authorities or conduct prejudicial to good order and discipline, or the commission of a serious offense. Officers may be separated for substandard performance of duty and also for "acts of misconduct or moral or professional dereliction." Upon separation, the member's service is characterized as "honorable," "general," or "under other than honorable conditions." The characterization of the member's discharge affects government benefits based on the member's military service and also his or her opportunities for civilian education and employment.

For cadets and midshipmen at the service academies, disenrollment is another form of administrative separation. Cadets and midshipmen can be disenrolled for a variety of reasons, including academic deficiency. From the perspective of applied ethics, perhaps the most important reason for disenrollment is violation of the academy's "honor code." Honor codes typically provide that persons subject to the code will not lie, steal, or cheat. Some codes, like that of the United States Air Force Academy, further provide that persons under the code will not "tolerate" in their ranks those who do lie, steal, or cheat. That is, a cadet violates the honor code by failing to report another cadet's lying, stealing, or cheating.

In addition to the administrative measures commanders and supervisors can take to correct behavior, they of course have many ways to recognize, reward, and motivate superior performance by military personnel. These include: awards of various kinds such as recognition as a "distinguished graduate" in a course or as the "outstanding company grade officer" of the unit; decorations for meritorious service, outstanding achievement, and heroism; and, of course, favorable recommendations for promotion and assignment.

IV. ETHICS REGULATIONS

Statutes regulate many aspects of the behavior of government officers and employees, including military personnel. Executive orders implement the statutes and prescribe additional rules, principles, and values for officers and employees. For the United States, the Office of Government Ethics (OGE) prescribed "standards of ethical conduct for the executive branch" (5 CFR 2635), including the military services. The Department of Defense (DOD) republished the OGE regulations and related executive orders and supplemented them with additional rules and guidance in its "Joint Ethics Regulation" (JER) (DoD 5500.7-R, 30 August 1993). The JER is a voluminous publication intended to "provide ... a single source of standards of ethical conduct and ethics guidance" for military personnel, as well as for the services' civilian officers and employees. Although the OGE regulations do not themselves apply to enlisted members (because they are not, strictly speaking, either "officers" or "employees" of the government), the JER makes them applicable to enlisted members in same way they apply to officers. Some provisions of the JER are printed in bold type to indicate that they are "punitive regulations" so that violations are punishable under the UCMJ.

The "standards of ethical conduct" addressed by the JER include rules on gifts from sources outside the government, gifts between military personnel, conflicting financial interests, impartiality in performing official duties, misuse of position, off-duty employment and other outside activities, political activities, and post-service employment. In each of these areas, the rules cover an extended variety of circumstances and implement or supplement a patchwork of statutes and regulations. As a result, the rules are very detailed and complex—so detailed and complex that the JER requires that in almost every case an "ethics counselor" must be an attorney.

The JER's many pages of rules on gifts illustrate its detail and complexity. In general, a military member may not accept gifts from persons seeking action by the service, persons doing business or seeking to do business with the service, or persons who have interests that may be affected by the performance of the member's duties. In addition, military personnel may not accept any gift given because of the member's official position. Neither may they accept gifts from subordinates or make gifts to superiors. Gifts given to family members or even to charities suggested by the military member are imputed to be gifts to the military member. Similarly, gifts from a subordinate's family members are imputed to be gifts from the subordinate. But there are numerous exceptions to the gift rules. The OGE regulations are so detailed as to provide, in a long list of exceptions, that "gift" does not include "greeting cards" or "modest items of food and refreshments, such as soft drinks, coffee and donuts, offered other than as part of a meal." In recognition of the responsibility of military members to maintain good relations with the civilian community, the JER goes on to provide, as another exception, that military members may accept an unsolicited gift of free attendance at an event sponsored by a state or local government or by a civic organization exempt from taxation—subject to certain additional conditions. Rules on such matters as use of one's rank in outside activities and the use of a government telephone for an unofficial call are equally comprehensive.

Some military personnel are in a position to control the expenditure of vast sums in procuring weapon systems, other military supplies and services, and military construction. As a result, the JER also provides extensive rules, many based on statute, concerning integrity in the procurement process and post-service employment with government contractors.

Although its detailed legalistic rules are probably the JER's best-known provisions, the JER does also provide, in its concluding chapter, more general guidance on "ethical conduct." This chapter republishes an executive order on "Principles of Ethical Conduct for Government Officers and Employees" and a statutory "Code of Ethics for Government Service" (5 U.S.C. § 7301) that apply to all government employees. In addition, this chapter of the JER sets out for DOD "primary ethical values" and an "ethical decision-making plan."

In general, DOD's ethical values and decision-making plan, like the rest of the JER, treat the military member more as a public servant than as warrior or military professional. DOD's 10 "primary ethical values" are: honesty, integrity, loyalty, accountability, fairness, caring, respect, promise keeping, responsible citizenship, and pursuit of excellence. The JER defines all of these values in terms of public service and good government with no reference to warfighting. For example, "pursuit of excellence" is defined as "striv[ing] beyond mediocrity," not as military victory. "Loyalty" is not defined as unit cohesiveness, but as "the bond that holds the nation and the Federal Government together and the balm against dissension and conflict." Similarly, DOD's 10-step "ethical decision-making plan" is not tailored to the military function or profession. Instead, it presents a sound process for identifying and selecting ethical options that could be used by any government official or, for that matter, any person.

V. CODES OF MILITARY ETHICS

It is common to speak of the military way of life as a "warrior code" or a "military code." Soon after the United States entered World War II, for example, General MacArthur spoke of "the unbreakable spirit of the free man's military code in support of our just cause." MacArthur said that this ancient code "embraces the things that are right and condemns the things that are wrong" and that it would "stand the test of any ethics or philosophies that the world has ever known" (The Unbreakable Spirit Code, *Vital Speeches of the Day* 1942, 397). Used in this sense, the "military code" is an ethical code, a code of right and wrong. Moreover, it is a ethical code directly bound to the military profession's moral purpose of preserving the nation and its values.

Such a "military code" is, of course, not a written, formal professional code of ethics like those adopted by associations of lawyers, physicians, and other professionals. It is instead a vast assortment of written and unwritten, official and unofficial principles, precepts, and guidelines drawn from a variety of sources. Military personnel of the United States, for example, find elements of their military code in numerous official sources, including the Constitution, the UCMJ, and ethics regulations. Other particularly important official sources are the enlisted and officer oaths of office with their promises of "true faith and allegiance" and the officer's commission with its reference to the president's "special trust and confidence" in the officer's "patriotism, valor, fidelity, and abilities." In addition, there is the "Code of Conduct," an executive order issued after the Korean conflict and revised after Vietnam. This six-paragraph code provides specific standards of behavior for prisoners of war, but opens with a general reference to service "in the forces which guard my country and our way of life" and ends with an affirmation that "I am ... responsible for my actions and dedicated to the principles which made my country free." Other sources of the United States military code include the services' mottoes (of which the best known is "Semper Fidelis" of the Marine Corps), the services' customs and courtesies, their traditions, and their stories of heroism and courage.

For the United States' armed forces, "core values" have recently become yet another means of further elaborating the military code. For members of the Navy and the Marines Corps, the core values are honor, courage, and commitment. At one point the Air Force had a list of seven core values, including courage and tenacity, but then simplified the values to "integrity first, service before self, and excellence in all we do." In many ways, these values directly reflect an older code of "duty, honor, country." At one point the Army's "vision" described the Army as a "values-based organization" with an "ethos" based on the values of duty, integrity, and selfless service; these values were in turn supported by the "professional qualities" of commitment, competence, candor, compassion, and courage. Later the Army identified seven core values: duty, integrity, loyalty, selfless service, honor, courage, and respect. It remains to be seen just how enduring and extensive a role the services' articulations of "core values" will have in the military code. In any event, however, the current interest in core values continues the various formal and informal programs the services have long had to guide their personnel in moral development and decision-making.

There is some question, however, whether these quasi-official and unsystematic "military codes" provide sufficient ethical guidance for armed forces in complex and diverse societies. The complexity of modern warfare and military service, mirroring the complexity of modern society, raises novel and difficult moral and legal issues. In addition, given the diverse backgrounds from which persons enter military society, it is not always clear what ethical values they bring to military service. Under these conditions, many see a need for a detailed, written code clearly defining the ethical obligations and ideals of military service. The proliferation of codes of ethics in the other professions and ethical breakdowns within the military—especially incidents in Vietnam such as the My Lai massacre and the Lavelle case—have generated numerous proposals for an authoritative code of professional military ethics.

Proposals for a formal code come from inside and outside the profession, from military officers and from philosophers. Most of the proposals are for a code for the officers of a particular branch of the armed forces, but some proposals address noncommissioned officers, other enlisted personnel, and civilian employees or discuss the possibility of a single code for all the armed forces. One proposal, for example, sets out six "tenets," including "I shall use the utmost restraint in the use of force, using only as much as necessary to fulfill my mission" and "I shall always remember that those under my command are moral beings worthy of respect and I shall never command them to do what is immoral" (DeGeorge 30). Another proposal calls for four codes, three to regulate behavior (an internal code to govern relationships among military personnel, a fighting code to control behavior toward enemy military personnel and civilians, and a code of rules for prisoners of war) together with a "creedal" code of ethics discussing general concepts of duty and honor or the virtues of the ideal military professional (Fotion and Elfstrom 76–79). Arguments for promulgating a formal code of ethics claim that such a code would not only give clear and specific ethical guidance, but would also serve as the basis for training military personnel, promote discussion of military ethics, and serve as a standard for evaluating and changing elements of the informal military code and the code of military justice.

The armed forces of some nations have adopted formal codes of military ethics. The Israel Defense Forces (IDF), for example, have an ethical code called "The Spirit of the IDF" that codifies values and principles from three traditions: the Jewish people, the democratic State of Israel, and the IDF's "fighting heritage." The 11 "core values" of the IDF code include such things as "purity of arms" ("the IDF soldier shall use force and weapons to subdue the enemy only to the extent required, and shall refrain from causing unnecessary injury to human life—to body, dignity and property") and "discipline" ("the IDF soldier shall act to carry out all that is required of him fully and successfully, according to orders, in letter and in spirit, within the framework of the law"). These core values are then expressed in "principles," including rules for behavior "in the face of the enemy" and rules for military personnel not on active duty.

Most nations, including the United States, have not, however, adopted a formal code of military ethics. Of the several reasons for this, perhaps the most practical is simply that military personnel do not need a "code of ethics" in addition to the many codes of behavior they already have. Military justice codes, administrative regulations, and ethics regulations already thoroughly regulate the behavior of military personnel and have stronger ethical overtones than their civilian counterparts. Military personnel may need ethical guidance in addition to these existing codes, but it seems doubtful they need it in the form of yet another code. In addition, the JER now claims to be the single source of ethical guidance for all DOD personnel and so raises an issue as to the authority for another formal code of ethics for the military personnel of the United States. In addition, because many of the existing codes originate far back in military history, the military does not need a code of professional ethics somehow to legitimate itself as a profession.

Another reason for not promulgating a formal code of professional military ethics has to do with the moral character expected of military personnel. Some have argued that a formal code, especially an ethical code for officers, could actually undermine the profession. The military profession, according to this argument, depends on the moral character of its individual members even more than the other professions do. Military virtues such as courage, loyalty, and obedience matter more in the military than character traits do in civilian society. The importance of moral virtues and character in the military is also reflected in the criminalization of "conduct unbecoming" understood as the betrayal of the moral attributes expected of an officer. Standards of behavior can and must be codified, but it remains doubtful that any code can adequately delineate the standards and ideals of moral character required of military members. A code of military ethics therefore could risk trivializing and distorting the ethical content of the profession, especially the individual moral character required of military personnel.

This argument—that a formal code of professional military ethics could devalue military character—points to a central issue for applied ethics for military personnel. That issue is the scope of the moral character expected of military personnel—whether a good military member needs to develop only military qualities or must be a good person in every respect. At one extreme on this issue is the position taken by General Maxwell Taylor. In Taylor's view, the moral horizon of military personnel *qua* military personnel is limited to accomplishing the military mission effectively. In this account of military ethics, the moral ideal for a military member is simply a person "who can be relied upon to carry out all assigned tasks and missions and, in doing so, get the most from his available resources with minimum loss and waste," and we would have no reason or need to assume that "his private life is above reproach" (Taylor 11, 14). This view sets out a functional basis for military codes of behavior. This moral standard—carrying out all assigned tasks in support of dangerous and complex military missions—is a terrifying responsibility. Yet some demand even more of the military professional, and so at the other extreme is the position taken by Sir John Winthrop Hackett. In Hackett's view, military professionals are expected to be good persons in every way, in their public and private lives, and this expectation in fact distinguishes the military profession from other professions. Thus, a person "can be a superb creative artist, for example, or a scientist in the very top flight, and still be a very bad man," but "[w]hat the bad man cannot be is a good sailor, or soldier, or airman" (Wakin 119). Bad persons cannot be good military professionals because they cannot lead others and inspire them to make the extraordinary sacrifices demanded of military personnel. In this view, which sets out a professional basis for military codes of behavior, the military becomes the nation's greatest moral strength.

The reality, of course, is between these two extremes. These extremes do, however, represent the limiting cases of military codes of behavior—and make it clear that even in a "minimalist" view of military codes, military personnel are held to unusually important and demanding standards. Military codes regulate a separate society of public officers and employees performing a specialized social function. Because of the precision, discipline, and public confidence required to carry out the military function effectively, military codes regulate more kinds of behavior, and regulate behavior more thoroughly, than do civilian codes. But the military is also a profession with a singular moral purpose—preserving the nation and protecting its interests and values. For these reasons, the moral standards and ideals of military codes, especially with respect to moral character, must be more explicit, more intrusive, and more demanding than those of civilian codes.

See Also the Following Article

WARFARE, CODES OF

Bibliography

DeGeorge, R. T. (1984, December). Defining moral obligations: The need for a military code of ethics. *Army*, 22–30.

Edel, A., Flower, E., & O'Connor, F. W. (1994). *Critique of applied ethics: Reflections and recommendations.* Philadelphia: Temple University Press.

Fields, R. (1991). *The code of the warrior: Its history, myth, and everyday life.* New York: Harper Perennial.

Fotion, N., & Elfstrom, G. (1986). *Military ethics: Guidelines for peace and war.* Boston: Routledge & Kegan Paul.

Gaston, J. C., & Hietala, J. B. (Eds.). (1993). *Ethics and national defense: The timeless issues.* Washington, DC: National Defense University Press.

Hartle, A. E. (1989). *Moral issues in military decision making.* Lawrence: University Press of Kansas.

Joint Ethics Regulation, DoD 5500.7-R (1993).

Manual for Courts-Martial, United States (1995 Edition).

Matthews, L. J., & Brown, D. E. (Eds.) (1989). *The parameters of military ethics.* McLean, Virginia: Pergamon-Brassey's International Defense Publishers, Inc.

Myers, C. R. (1995). Officership and a code of ethics. *USAFA Journal of Legal Studies* 5, 9–22.

Military ethics: Reflections on principles—the profession of arms, military leadership, ethical practices, war and morality, educating the citizen-soldier (1987). Washington, DC: National Defense University Press.

Taylor, M. (1980). A do-it-yourself professional code for the military. *Parameters* X, 10–15.

Toner, J. H. (1995). *True faith and allegiance: The burden of military ethics.* Lexington: The University Press of Kentucky.

Wakin, M. M. (Ed.). (1986). *War, morality, and the military profession* (2nd ed.). Boulder: Westview Press.

MORAL DEVELOPMENT

Michael Parker
The Open University

GLOSSARY

autonomy Self-government; individual freedom.
deontology An approach to moral theory which argues that the right course of action ought to be judged according to principles of duty or obligation which are self-evident or self-sustaining and not in need of derivation from other more fundamental moral truths such as those about consequences of actions.
development The process of growing fuller, more mature, or more organized.
heteronomy Government by others.
stage of development Discrete and identifiable periods in development having a certain structural unity.
utilitarianism An approach to moral theory which argues that the right course of action is the one which brings about the greatest happiness to the greatest number of people. No moral principle or rule is absolute. Actions are to be judged in terms of their consequences.

MORAL DEVELOPMENT refers to the growth of moral understanding in individuals. In this respect it concerns a person's progressive ability to understand the difference between right and wrong, to care about the difference between them, and to act on the basis of this understanding.

If a community or social group is to persist, there must exist certain practices and forms of social relationship which facilitate the maintenance and preservation of its ways of life. Some of these practices are likely to be overtly concerned with the transmission of these ways of life to future generations through socialization or education since the possibility of social maintenance is at least to some extent dependent upon the bringing to bear of these ways of life upon individuals in the course of their development.

If a community or social group is to develop or change it must also be possible for individuals to come to have an effect upon the ways of life of the community in which they live, and this means that while on the one hand social stability requires the bringing to bear of practices upon the lives of individuals, it is also important for individuals to enjoy a certain amount of autonomy and independence. Clearly the degree of autonomy communities allow will vary widely. It is possible to imagine a community in which the preservation of tradition is highly valued and deviation from traditional ways of life is considered taboo. But even here the openness of the community to the individual will be important because the possibility of passing on traditions through teaching and other forms of social interaction means that the ways of life of the community have to become part of a dialogue with the individual.

They have to achieve meaning within the life of the individual, and for this to be possible the actions of individuals must themselves achieve meaning within the community. An implication of this is that the development both of communities and of individuals must involve an interweaving of the two complementary themes of autonomy and heteronomy. This inevitably means that there will be tension between the need for autonomy and the need for social responsibility, and this is a tension which will express itself in moral questions about the relation of self and others and in the question of what constitutes a healthy balance between autonomy and heteronomy.

Emile Durkheim argued that there are three basic elements central to the internalization of moral values: "the spirit of authority and discipline," the "attachment to social groups," and "autonomy of self-determination." He argued that each of these is essential and that too much of one can lead to excessive integration, and too much of another to excessive individualism. In this Durkheim identifies an important feature of any workable theory of moral development, for any such theory has to be able to explain not only the importance both of autonomy and of heteronomy, but also how the balance between the two is established and negotiated.

Nevertheless, while these features are important elements of an understanding of social change and social stability, they cannot in themselves provide an explanation of moral "development," for the concept of development implies the existence of changes which are both ongoing and progressive. The claim that our understanding of morality "develops" implies that our understanding is somehow progressively more adequate—that we are increasingly able to distinguish between right and wrong. If an explanation of moral development is to be coherent it must explain how change occurs from an understanding which is philosophically less adequate to one which is more adequate, and this means that a theory of moral development must also be in part a philosophical account of the relative adequacy of various forms of moral understanding and moral theory.

I. PIAGET

A. Piaget's Theory of Moral Development

A question which has arisen fairly naturally out of the idea that moral understanding develops during childhood concerns the extent to which it is possible to identify a universal path of moral development. Is it possible to identify stages of moral development which are characteristic of all people of a similar age? Is there a theoretical perspective from which it is possible to assess the moral development of all human beings? An important and related question concerns the link between a person's moral understanding and their other competencies. What, for example, is the relationship between a person's moral development and their cognitive development? Both Lawrence Kohlberg and Jean Piaget have argued for a systematic link between the two and argue that moral development follows on from cognitive development. It is in this context that Piaget's theory of cognitive development has been extremely influential in theories of moral development.

For Piaget, as a structuralist, understanding and knowledge are to be interpreted in terms of structural wholes. It is possible to conceive of "items of knowledge" only insofar as they are seen as instances. I am able to recognize an object as a tree or perform an addition sum, for example, only insofar as I am able to relate it to a general epistemic structure. Hence the link between moral and cognitive development. Piaget interprets the growth of understanding as the development of cognitive structures and suggests that such development follows a universal path. This does not mean that all people at a similar age will necessarily hold similar beliefs or share the same understanding, but that the developmental form of the cognitive structures of each will be similar in important respects. Piaget argues that cognitive development consists of a hierarchical series of stages, each building upon the foundation of the previous, and that development progresses from the egocentric or subjective toward the decentered or objective, each stage being progressively less egocentric than the preceding.

Piaget identifies three major stages in cognitive development, though there are also several important substages. The important stages and substages are (i) the sensorimotor stage, (ii) the preoperational substage, (iii) the concrete operations substage, and (iv) the final stage of "formal operations." Each of these stages represents a development from the immediate and the concrete toward the formal and the decentered.

B. Piaget's Stages of Moral Development

Most of Piaget's discussion of moral development is contained within *The Moral Judgement of the Child*. The book records how, using empirical research based on the clinical interview, Piaget studied the ways in which children and young people discriminate rules in games and in play. In his research Piaget identified the existence of two major stages of moral development. The first is the stage he identifies as that of "heteronomous morality" or "moral realism" in which the very young child bases moral judgments on unilateral respect for authority figures: "Unilateral respect ... begets in the young child a morality of obedience which is characterised primarily by a heteronomy that declines later to make way, at least partially, for the autonomy characteristic of mutual respect" (J. Piaget, 1982. *The Essential Piaget* (H. Gruber and J. Voneche, Eds.), p. 156. Routledge & Kegan Paul, London).

The second stage Piaget identifies is that of "autonomous morality" or a morality of "mutual respect" in which the young person, by middle childhood to early adolescence, begins to develop a sense of autonomy and reciprocity. In this stage, social experience becomes the motor of increasingly cooperative egalitarian growth. The step from the first stage to the second is enabled by the child's cognitive development from a perspective based on "egocentrism" toward a "decentered" way of thinking. Piaget argues that this shift makes possible the placing oneself in the viewpoint of another person which is the crucial step in moral development. From this point onward Piaget envisages a gradual, natural process of unfolding moral development ending in mature cooperation.

C. Criticism of Piaget

If Piaget's theory of development has been highly influential, it has also been the subject of a great deal of criticism. Perhaps the main criticism has concerned Piaget's claims about the egocentrism of young children. Philosophical argument and empirical research since Piaget wrote *The Moral Judgement of the Child* have tended to suggest that children are not as egocentric as he claimed, and that in fact the very possibility of cognitive development is dependent upon engagement in social interactions from the first moments of life. Margaret Donaldson and others have argued that the difficulties young people face with Piaget's test have to do with features of the tests themselves rather than young people's ability to decenter.

Another important criticism has concerned Piaget's claim that morality and cognitive development are interdependent. To what extent can it be right to say that our morality is tied to our understanding? While it is obviously true that we need to have some understanding of moral concepts if we are to come to grasp the moral implications of our actions, it is surely wrong to suggest that the development of understanding is of itself a necessary and sufficient condition or moral development. Piaget, however, seems to be claiming more than this. He seems to be suggesting that the more cognitively developed we become the more moral we will be. But to what extent is it true to say that cognitive development inevitably leads to moral development in this way? One way of conceptualizing this criticism of Piaget would be to say that his theory of development appears to offer a theory of the development of the form of moral thinking without regard to its content. It focuses on the stucture of our moral thinking while saying little about our actual beliefs. It is not made clear by Piaget how the development of moral form can lead to the development of moral content.

Finally, Piaget's research methodology has also been the subject of criticism. Margaret Donaldson's comments have already been referred to. Carol Gilligan criticizes Piaget's use of a small sample as the basis for his research and argues that this inevitably gives Piaget's theory of development a male bias.

II. KOHLBERG

A. Kohlberg's Theory of Moral Development

If one name is synonymous with the study of moral development it is Lawrence Kohlberg. Kohlberg's theory is heavily indebted to Piaget. Like Piaget, he argues that moral development is made possible by cognitive development, and, like Piaget, he believes it to be possible to identify a universal series of invariant, hierarchical stages in moral development.

Kohlberg argues that the stages he identifies are of a qualitative philosophical character and that movement through these stages is enabled and stimulated both by problem solving and by the fact that each stage is philosophically more adequate than the one which precedes it. Kohlberg's is in many ways a philosophical theory. He is concerned not only with the achievement by young people of certain virtues but with their understanding of certain principles of justice. In addition to providing a theory of moral development, Kohlberg can also be seen as offering a hierarchy of moral theory.

Nevertheless, like Piaget, Kohlberg's account of moral development is founded upon empirical research and the clinical interview. He attempted to overcome some of the weaknesses of Piaget's research, however, by using a larger and socially diverse sample.

B. An Outline of Kohlberg's Stages

The stages of moral development identified by Kohlberg as a result of his research are as follows.

Level I—Preconventional

Stage 1. Avoid breaking rules backed by punishment, obedience for its own sake, and avoiding physical damage to persons and property.

Stage 2. Following rules only when it is to someone's immediate interest; acting to meet one's own interests and needs, and letting others do the same. Right is also what is fair, what's an equal exchange, a deal, an agreement.

Level II—Conventional

Stage 3. Living up to what is expected by people close to you or what people generally expect of people in your role as son, brother, friend, etc. "Being good" is important and means having good motives and showing concern about others. It also means keeping mutual relationships such as trust, loyalty, respect, and gratitude.

Stage 4. Fulfilling the actual duties to which you have agreed. Laws are to be upheld except in extreme cases where they conflict with other fixed social duties. Right is also contributing to society, the group, or the institution.

Level III—Postconventional or Principled

Stage 5. Being aware that people hold a variety of values and opinions, and that most values and rules are relative to your group. These relative values should usually be upheld, however, in the interest of impartiality and because they are the social contract. Some nonrelative values and rights like life and liberty, however, must be upheld in any society and regardless of majority opinion.

Stage 6. Following self-chosen ethical principles. Particular laws or social agreements are usually valid because they rest on such principles. When laws violate these principles, one acts in accordance with the principle. Principles are universal principles of justice: the equality of human rights and respect for the dignity of human beings as individual persons.

The moral stage which someone has reached can be determined, Kohlberg suggests, by the interpretation of their responses to moral dilemmas such as Heinz's Dilemma, in which subjects are told the story of a man called Heinz who learns that his wife has a kind of cancer which is treatable by one drug only. The druggist wants $2000 for a small dose (this is 10 times what the drug costs to produce) but Heinz can only raise $1000, for which the druggist will not sell him the drug. In desperation Heinz breaks into the store and steals the drug for his wife. Subjects are asked what they think of Heinz's actions and their moral stage is assessed by seeing how their response to the dilemma matches those associated with Kohlberg's descriptions of the stages. Kohlberg argues that no more than 25 to 35% of the adult population reaches stage six. Children and young people tend to be at stages one and two, and most adults are at stages three and four.

Interestingly, Kohlberg's stages suggest that he believes the right choice would be for Heinz to steal the drug. This is because "life is more important than property." As a principle Kohlberg argues this is only adequately grasped by those in stage six. This stage is more adequate than earlier stages because it brings the child closer to a grasp of the concept of justice and because it is more closely related to the cognitive capacity for taking the viewpoints of others or "reversibility." At the heart of Kohlberg's approach is the Piagetian view that human beings start out with an egocentric point of view and as a result of their cognitive development gradually come to develop a more decentered, universalizable view which is capable of taking the viewpoints of others into account and which is grasped fully only by the achievement of stage six.

Kohlberg's empirical and psychological ordering of the moral stages clearly has philosophical implications and can be interpreted as a philosophical argument about the adequacy of various moral theories, for in addition to his conceptualization of development as a shift from the egocentric to the decentered, there is a sense in which development is from the philosophically less adequate to the more adequate and can be seen as a hierarchy of moral theories. The philosophical implications of Kohlberg's stages therefore are profound, suggesting, for example, that deontological moral theory (stage six) is more adquate philosophically than utilitarianism (stage five).

C. Some Criticisms of Kohlberg

The dependence of Kohlberg's approach upon that of Piaget means that it suffers from some of the same weaknesses. One of the most serious of these is the tendency to overidentify moral development with the development of the form of cognitive structure. This seems to be contrary to our sense that a person's beliefs are central to whether or not we consider them to be moral. Kohlberg's stages appear to be unable to take this into account. This is a particular problem in relation to Kohlberg's fourth stage. In this stage the right thing to do is identified with fulfilling our obligations to our community, social group, or institution. The problem with this, as I have suggested, is that it makes no reference to content or context, and this means that no moral distinction can be made between the development of a person who abides by the social practices of a modern democratic state and that of one who does so in Nazi Germany. Moral development cannot be explained in terms of the development of form alone.

A further important weakness in Kohlberg's approach is the claim, which is implicit in the hierarchy of his stages, that thought which is based on deontological considerations is more philosophically adequate than that based upon utilitarian principles for that reason alone. But this is not something which can simply be stated. There is a continuing philosophical debate about the relative merits of these approaches which cannot be simply waved away. The idea that utilitarian philosophers are morally underdeveloped simply because they are utilitarians seems absurd. Kohlberg's attachment to deontological moral theory leads him to believe that principles and the grasping of principles are central to moral judgment and suggests that we need to have grasped a moral rule to make a moral judgment. But this again is a moot philosphical point. Is it really the case that we need to be able to identify a rule in order to identify the relevant facts to a moral dilemma?

Kohlberg's theory implies that there is an important distinction to be made between simply doing the right thing and actually grasping the rules or principles underlying such actions. But is this a distinction which has any validity? Surely when we act on moral principles we are in fact being virtuous. Gilligan argues that the elevation of justice to the top of the ethical shopping list is unjustified and leads to a rather hollow view of morality. It is not enough simply to know the difference between right and wrong, one has to care. Kohlberg's emphasis on justice reveals a neglect of the importance of feeling and emotion. He seems to imply that emotions are an irrational or nonrational element in moral thinking. But caring for others is central to such considerations. Gilligan argues that this neglect of the role of care is related to and perpetuates the undervaluing of women's moral development. She argues that both Kohlberg and Piaget based their research findings largely upon work with boys and men and consequently fail to recognize the moral development of girls and women. Gilligan argues that a recognition of the unique moral voice of women would lead to an increase in the value of the ethic of care, which could in turn lead to a model of moral development which would be much more positive about children and also women.

III. GILLIGAN

A. Gilligan's Theory of Moral Development

Carol Gilligan criticizes the model of moral development developed by Kohlberg and Piaget. She argues firstly that it is in fact a model of male development only. Piaget's research was carried out on an all-male sample, as was Kohlberg's original study, and Gilligan argues that this bias inevitably led them to undervalue women's distinctive moral vision and hence to underestimate the moral development of girls and women themselves.

Gilligan also argues that Piaget's and Kohlberg's views of moral development are overly individualistic, overemphasising the value of independence at the expense of interdependence. Gilligan suggests that this is a reductionist view of morality which reveals only half the story of moral development. She argues that in fact morality comprises two complementary aspects and cannot be reduced to rational individualism without an important loss of explanatory power, Kohlberg's recognizably Kantian view of morality in terms of the rights, liberties, and duties of individuals is a form of reductivism. Morality is also concerned with interdependence and can also be expressed in terms of responsibility and care. Whereas the individualistic approach of Kohlberg and Piaget leads to a language of rights, liberties, and duties, the recognition of interdependence produces a language of care and responsibility, and a recognition of the need to avoid hurting others. Both of these elements are essential to any workable theory of morality.

Gilligan argues that the vision of morality as an ethic of care is one more often than not expressed by women. Her empirical claim is that women speak in a different voice than men, a voice that is undervalued by traditional models of moral development. It is for this reason that women tend to score less well on Kohlberg's tests and their moral vision is undervalued.

> ... the world she knows is a different world from that refracted by Kohlberg's construction of Heinz's dilemma. Her world is a world of relationships and psychological truths where an awareness of the connection between people gives rise to a recognition of responsibility for one another, a perception of the need for response. Seen in this light, her understanding of morality as arising from the recognition of relationship, her belief in communication as the mode of conflict resolution, and her conviction that the solution to the

dilemma will follow from its compelling representation seem far from naive or cognitively immature (1993. *In a Different Voice: Psychological Theory and Women's Development, p. 30. Harvard Univ. Press, Cambridge*)

B. Gilligan's Phases of Moral Development

From the perspective of an ethic of care it is possible, Gilligan argues, to identify a developmental path quite different to that described by Kohlberg. She uses empirical research to identify a developmental sequence in the ethic of care made up of three moral perspectives or "phases."

Phase 1. "... an initial focus on caring for the self in order to ensure survival." (1993, p. 74)

Phase 2. "... a transitional phase in which this judgment is seen as selfish. The criticism signals a new understanding of the connection between self and others which is articulated by the concept of responsibility. The elaboration of this concept of responsibility and its fusion with a maternal morality that seeks to ensure care for the dependent and unequal characterises the second perspective. At this point, the good is equated with caring for others." (1993, p. 74)

Phase 3. "The third perspective focuses on the dynamics of relationships and dissipates the tension between selfishness and responsibility through a new understanding of the interconnection between the other and self. Care becomes the self-chosen principle of a judgment that remains psychological in its concern with relationships and response but becomes universal in its condemnation of exploitation and hurt." (1993, p. 74)

For Gilligan, the direction of moral development from the perspective of an ethic of care is not simply a progression from egocentrism to decentrism. The development of an ethic of care is to be understood in terms of a "progressively more adequate understanding of the psychology of human relationships—an increasing differentiation of self and other and a growing comprehension of the dynamics of social interaction" (1993, p. 74).

Gilligan does not argue that Kohlberg's model ought to be abandoned altogether, but that it tells only half the story of moral development. Any workable theory of moral development must incorporate an ethic of care and a recognition of our essential interdependence. And while Gilligan argues that it tends to be the case empirically that women express an ethic of care, she argues

that any full understanding of morality must incorporate both aspects of development.

The different voice I describe is characterised not by gender but theme. Its association with women is an empirical observation, and it is primarily through women's voices that I trace its development. But this association is not absolute, and the contrasts between male and female voices are presented here to highlight a distinction between two modes of thought. (1993, 1–2).

C. Some Criticisms of Gilligan

Interestingly, Gilligan's work has been criticized on similar grounds to those she uses to attack Kohlberg and Piaget. The sample for her research has been criticized for being too small and selective, consisting as it does of mostly upper middle class subjects. Gilligan herself does in fact recognize this and has called for more research in this area.

Gilligan's interpretations of her findings have also been questioned by some researchers. Prakash, for example, has suggested that Gilligan's findings might also be interpreted to suggest that the differences between women and men could be seen as different expressions of love and responsibility rather than as the expression of quite different moral visions.

The idea that there is an ethic of care which is unique to women has also come under attack from some feminists on the grounds that the idea that women's development is essentially different to men's is often used as a tool for discrimination.

Supposedly "female" values are not only the subject of little agreement among women; they are also deeply mired in conceptions of "the feminine" which depend on the sort of polarisation between "masculine" and "feminine" which has itself been so closely related to the subordination of women. There is no autonomous realm of female values, or of female activities which can generate "alternative" values to those in the public sphere; and any conception of a "female ethic" which depends on these ideas cannot, I think, be a viable one. (J. Grimshaw, 1993. In *A Companion to Ethics* (P. Singer, Ed.), p. 498. Blackwell, Oxford)

Nevertheless, Gilligan's work is an important contribution to the debate. It is clear that she is not arguing that the ethic of care is inferior to other ethical visions. Her claim is that any workable theory of moral development must be capable of explaining the importance of the relationships between autonomy and care for others. She argues that theories of moral development have tended to be overly rationalistic.

IV. CONCLUSIONS

The concepts of "moral development" and of a "theory of moral development" imply that it might be possible to conceive of changes in moral understanding as being progressive. This suggests that it might be possible to describe one form of moral thinking as more adequate than another. The concepts of "development" and of this kind of progression in theory have received increasing criticism from postmodernists. However, even if the critique of the concept of progress itself is set aside, there is no evidence from philosophy to suggest that there is any consensus among philosophers about a hierarchy of moral theory. This suggests that the developmentalist project itself may be open to question.

Notwithstanding this criticism, it may well prove possible on empirical grounds to identify a pattern in the growth of understanding in young people of the existence and nature of moral problems. It may well be that as young people get older their understanding of moral dilemmas tends to become more complex and sophisticated. There seems to be no reason to suppose, however, that the growth of understanding need involve general, conceptual shifts or stages rather than the growth of concepts and practices in a more local sense.

Finally, Carol Gilligan is surely right to criticize overly-individualistic approaches to the growth of understanding. Any workable theory of the growth of moral understanding has to be able to explain the fact that such growth leads to an understanding which is largely shared and intersubjectively maintained, and this is only possible within the context of a theoretical approach which take seriously the embeddedness of human beings in social forms of life. It is also important, however, that any such theory is able to recognize the importance of individual autonomy and creativity. But Gilligan is wrong to suggest that a morality of care is a prerequisite of the fulfilment of individual goals. The two aspects of human experience, the social and the individual, are truly interdependent and each make the other possible.

Any workable theory of moral theory has to be able to address the fact that the moral is concerned not only with the eradication of inequality and the protection of freedom, but also with the promotion of moral community and of care for others. It also has to be capable of recognizing that these two tasks are intimately interconnected.

Also See the Following Articles

AUTONOMY • CONSEQUENTALISM AND DEONTOLOGY • MORAL RELATIVISM • UTILITARIANISM

Bibliography

Donaldson, M. (1978). "Children's Minds." Fontana, London.
Kohlberg, L. (1984). "The Psychology of Moral Development: The Nature and Validity of Moral Stages." Harper & Row, New York.
Mischel, T. (Ed.) (1971). "Cognitive Development and Epistemology." Academic Press, New York.
Parker, M. (1995). "The Growth of Understanding." Ashgate, Aldershot.
Rich, M., and DeVitis, J. (1985). "Theories of Moral Development." Thomas, Springfield, IL.
Thomas, L. (1993). Morality and psychological development. In "A Companion to Ethics." (P. Singer, Ed.). Blackwell, Oxford.
Walkderdine, V. (1988). "The Mastery of Reason." Routledge, London.

MORAL RELATIVISM

J. Carl Ficarrotta
United States Air Force Academy

GLOSSARY

absolutism The general idea that whatever moral rules there are apply to everyone. A weaker version allows that at least some moral rules apply to everyone.

cultural relativism The general idea that the moral principles one ought to follow are the principles that just happen to be endorsed in one's own cultural group.

moral theory An attempt to systematize, explain, relate, prioritize, and otherwise make sense of moral experience.

nihilism From the Latin root that means "nothing," the idea that there are no genuine moral prescriptions. Ordinary moral experience is illusory and those who believe there are moral prescriptions are badly mistaken.

objectivism The general idea that what binds people in morality binds them independently of any particular person's or group of persons' belief or opinion.

subjectivism The general idea that the content of morality is completely a function of individual tastes, attitudes, or opinions.

MORAL RELATIVISM is a thesis about the nature of morality. Beyond this true but unhelpful characterization, it is a concept in serious need of clarification. The phrase labels several different even if related claims, and we must take care to sort them out. Perhaps most often it is understood as the thesis that the moral principles one is bound by are just the principles that happen to be endorsed in one's own group. Right and wrong are essentially group or culture-relative concepts. Others believe that the content and normative force of morality are relative not to the group, but rather to the individual. Inside these two broad kinds of relativism (group and individual), there are many different positions that come about as a result of clarifications, refinements, and qualifications of the main ideas. Contrast relativism properly with a family of views that share a commitment, in varying degrees, to moral *absolutism*. Let us call absolutism roughly the idea that the moral rules (and whatever we decide about their content, level of detail, sensitivity to context or circumstance, etc.) bind everyone alike, universally, regardless of who they are or to what group they belong.

So "moral relativism" as it is bandied about in common usage stands for a number of different ideas. This is even more so in the philosophical literature, where we can find many sophisticated attempts to attack, defend, or refine the idea of moral relativism. This essay aims to serve only as an introduction to the issues of moral relativism. We will outline (sometimes in simplified form) some of the various positions that are held. We will try to make clear what they mean, examine some arguments for and against each, establish some of the moral and intellectual consequences of holding them, and see how they can fit into a larger framework for moral thinking. As part of all this, we will also get straight what moral relativism is *not*, sharpening these various positions by contrasting them to nihilism, objectivism, merely descriptive claims, and worries about certainty in moral thinking.

I. RELATIVISM AND MORAL THEORY

Morality, in one form or another, is one of the nearly universal features of human life. We praise and blame certain actions, endorse and pursue values, recommend various character traits, etc. In general, we judge one another and ourselves in moral terms and think these moral judgments carry with them a certain kind of prescriptive authority. Throughout intellectual history, there have been thinkers who have attempted to tell a deeper and more complete story about the nature of morality. These thinkers have often looked for overarching principles of morality that systematize, explain, relate, prioritize, and otherwise make sense of all the moral concepts we use, rules we think ought to be followed, values we endorse, and character traits we recommend. For the purposes of this entry, let us call the results of such an enterprise a *moral theory*.

People often presuppose a moral theory of a sort when they do thinking about morality. Insofar as they are able (if asked) to say what they assume about questions of system, relation, priority, explanation, etc., they reveal to what extent they have begun to use a moral theory. Moral relativism is not necessarily a theory, though in some of its forms it might be. It sometimes is thought to function as a moral theory, since it sometimes is understood as an attempt to explain and make sense of moral experience. Alternatively, we might think that moral relativism is not a full theory itself, but says something about the proper limits on the scope and content of any particular moral theory. That is, relativism may claim that moral theories, whatever else they do, must be less than universal in their development and application. Conversely, the shape of the moral theory to which one is committed will also affect whether and in what way one is committed to relativism. So the enterprise of moral theorizing in general and one's views on relativism can overlap and be intimately related.

On the other hand, relativism may be a stand against theory altogether. In discussions of moral issues, we often hear that of course, when it comes to morality, "it's all relative." The slogan is now part of a "conventional

wisdom" (or lack of it) on these matters. What the expression actually *means* in these contexts is seldom clear to, or appreciated by, those who use it. But in much popular discourse, the assertion often amounts to an attempt to end the very discussion that gave rise to its utterance. That is, it can carry with it an implicit recommendation to refrain from further reflection or argument—when it does, whatever else is meant by mouthing the relativist thesis, it means there can be no rational point to engaging in moral argument or seeking a deeper understanding of moral principles. In cases like these, moral relativism is, in some inchoate way, a stand *contra* to reason giving and moral theorizing.

So far, we have seen two kinds of variation in how we might understand moral relativism. First, we can mean that morality is relative broadly either to groups or to individuals. Second, we can mean for relativism to function as a theory, as a limit on or part of a theory, or as a statement of a case against theory. Having made these distinctions, it should be easy for us to see how the various versions of relativism we examine below will answer them. But before moving to more particular permutations of relativism, we should take note of some things relativism is *not*.

II. WHAT RELATIVISM IS NOT

A. Moral Nihilism

Call moral nihilism the view that, in truth, there just is not anything that we ought or ought not to do, endorse, or be like. For the moral nihilist, moral systems are elaborately worked out mistakes, roughly like astrology or witchcraft, that have nothing real at their foundation. While many people busy themselves with talk about duty, good character, morally permissible actions, etc., the nihilist thinks that prescriptive talk about what one morally ought to do is in fact about nothing. We often assume that there really are such things as genuine moral prescriptions, and that whatever they turn out to be like in more detail, they ought to count with us in our thinking and doing. But the nihilist thinks this is false. There is much more we might say to qualify, explicate, and refine this radical view, but suffice it to say that, excepting perhaps psychopaths, it does not mesh very well with our ordinary moral experience.

Relativism is not nihilism. Relativism in all its forms still retains the central notion that there are things we ought and ought not to do, endorse, or be like. Granted, the relativist may end up saying, for example, that what is right in one culture may not be right in another, or that a certain thing is right for me but not for you. Nevertheless, the moral relativist still holds on to the idea that morality properly prescribes.

B. A Merely Descriptive Thesis

Obviously, there are variations in belief about morality and what it requires. Much overlap notwithstanding, the set of beliefs generally espoused in one group are not often identical to the set of beliefs we find in another. Just as obviously, there are agreements and disagreements (some of them apparently intractable disagreements) between individuals, even among those who belong to the same group. There are several views about the best way ultimately to understand these agreements and disagreements, but the variations in moral opinion are an incontrovertible fact. Some of the variations may reflect different beliefs about nonmoral facts, nonmoral conceptual issues, mistakes in reasoning, etc. But some of the variations have so far defied an easy analysis in such terms. Indeed, any adequate account of morality ought to include some explanation of these many disagreements we appear to have.

Relativism is more than this merely descriptive observation of varying beliefs. The relativist does not just notice that people have different beliefs about what they ought to do, endorse, or be like. The relativist also thinks that each of these different and often conflicting beliefs can be correct, or in some sense true. Of course, there are interesting disagreements in philosophy about "truth" and "correctness" and what it means for something to be true; yet whatever "truth" or "correctness" means, it is not just whatever a person or group happens to assert or believe. Hence the mere fact of disagreement in beliefs about morality is compatible with one party being right and the rest being wrong. But the relativist does not think that only one party can be right when there are different and conflicting beliefs. The relativist thinks it is possible for variations in belief to correspond with variations in what the parties in reality ought to do, endorse, or be like. The prescriptions that truly ought to guide us can, according to the relativist, be different.

Of course, the relativist need not think that because one believes a certain thing about a moral issue that one is automatically correct, simply because one believes it. A relativist can still leave room for the possibility of mistakes. Maybe a person believes a certain action is right for her, but in fact it is not. Maybe most people in a culture believe a certain practice is permissible in their culture, but they are not correct about what is *really* permissible in their culture. Certainly, a still different (and somewhat peculiar) kind of relativist might

think that merely believing a proposition in the moral realm is what makes it turn out to be true or correct. But a relativist need not think this way.

In any case, the main idea here is that all relativists claim more than a merely descriptive thesis about the fact of varying beliefs. The relativist also thinks it possible for all or part of the variations to be legitimate or proper. That is, the different beliefs we have about moral issues all might be true beliefs about what different people actually ought to do.

C. Objectivism and Subjectivism

We often confuse the question of whether morality is relative with the question of whether it is objective or subjective. Though very closely related, these are separable issues. Generally, an objective claim carries with it a special kind of authority, an insistence that the claim is true or correct independent of what any particular person happens to believe or not believe. A claim is relative when it may not be correct or true *of* (or perhaps *for*) all people or things, but it could be objective within its own sphere of application. While we should not draw too close an analogy between relativity in the physical sciences and moral relativity, we can use relativity in physics to illustrate the difference between questions of objectivism and relativism. For instance, just because observations of simultaneity are relative to a frame of reference does not mean they are not objective. Taller than and shorter than relations provide a more mundane instance of context relative judgments that are still objective.

So what is objectivity in morality, and how is it related to moral relativism? David Wong has summarized the features that would make a morality objective. If we claim morality is objective, then we mean most, and perhaps all, of the following things:

1. Moral statements have truth values
2. There are good and bad arguments for the moral positions people take
3. Nonmoral facts (states of affairs that obtain in the world and that can be described without use of moral terms such as "ought," "good," and "right") are relevant to the assessment of the truth value of moral statements
4. There are moral facts (that may or may not be reducible in some way to nonmoral facts)
5. When two moral statements conflict as recommendations to action, only one statement can be true
6. There is a single true morality

Objectivism in morality is more often than not associated with a predilection for some kind of absolutism, but as we shall see, there are some ways of formulating a relativistic view of morality that are compatible with many or most of these six claims. Perhaps it is only number six, the claim about "one true morality," that is incompatible with relativism (and we will examine this more closely below). Maybe, as Wong thinks, this incompatibility with claim number six is what sets relativism apart from absolutism. Importantly, saying that a view is relativistic is not exactly the same thing as saying it is not at all objective. So depending on how we state our relativistic thesis, objectivity of a sort and relativity are not mutually exclusive.

Indeed, in varying degrees these six claims about objectivity capture important features of our common moral understanding and experience, and no sensible and adequate view of morality should go too far afield of that experience. The objective "feel" of much moral discourse is as much a part of moral experience as the disagreements we seem to have, and it cannot be ignored in our moral theorizing. These features of objectivity are part of what we mean when we use moral language, and a good analysis should either incorporate and account for that fact or explain why we were mistaken to so use the words. Thus if a way of understanding moral relativism turns out to be not at all objective in the ways Wong listed, so much the worse for that version of relativism. But different forms of moral relativism can be more or less objective.

Much of what is called subjectivism in morality (and a similar idea called expressivism) is the rough opposite of objectivism. On this view, moral statements are not rational judgments made in light of independently existing moral standards. Rather, they are reports (or expressions) of an attitude on the part of an individual. To the moral subjectivist, moral statements are like statements on other purely subjective matters of tastes, likes, and attitudes. Hence moral statements do not really have truth values (even if we are inclined to think they do). Mounting rational arguments for moral positions does not make sense, any more than it would make sense to argue about the "best" flavor of ice cream. Nor are so-called moral disagreements important, for there is not an interesting disagreement between a person who says "I like vanilla," and one who says, "I don't." Hence, even if differences in morality could properly be called disagreements, there are not any disagreements that could be resolved by rational argument. For the subjectivist (and expressivist) there are no moral facts, past the facts about individual people's attitudes toward things.

Subjectivism and relativism are not identical concepts either. Most subjectivists, since they typically expect great variation in the attitudes of individuals (and hence "their morality"), are likely also to be relativists. So these two views often go hand in hand. But they need not. Many forms of relativism do not include the belief that morality is grounded in the attitudes of individuals. And we might even imagine a possible (even if unlikely) universal agreement in human attitudes about certain things, perhaps based on some psychobiological feature of the human being. The fact that we are able to imagine this nonrelative subjectivism shows that the concepts of subjectivism and relativism are not identical. There are as well more sophisticated forms of subjectivism and expressivism which postulate that moral attitudes, while still subjective, are toward rules or norms (or even whole systems of rules or norms), not just moral issues taken one at a time. These more sophisticated views are also logically compatible with both relativist and nonrelativist leanings.

D. Worries about Certainty

Sometimes moral judgments and decisions are simple, clear, and easy to make. But moral issues can on occasion be very complex. Many things can contribute to uncertainty in moral judgment. We can lack full information. We can be uncertain about the consequences of our actions. We might be confused over what rule applies or takes precedence in a particular situation. Sometimes we are undecided about the nonmoral concepts that are relevant to our decisions. Some people do not believe they are very smart, and do not have confidence in any of their judgments, moral or otherwise. As a result of one or more of these possibilities, we sometimes lack full confidence in our moral judgments. In situations where we have this lack of confidence, we are rightly inclined to be tolerant of a reasonable range of disagreement with our moral judgments and decisions. Such a tolerance in regards to hard cases does not necessarily amount to moral relativism.

There will be easy to decide cases for both the relativist and the nonrelativist. Also, the conditions that result in uncertainties obtain for the relativist and the nonrelativist alike. Even a moral absolutist who also strongly endorses all six of Wong's criteria of moral objectivity will still encounter situations that give rise to uncertainty. And even the most simplistic relativist will be able to identify times when it is easy to see "what's right for him" or "what's right in our culture." So an occasional lack of confidence, and a resulting toleration of some differing opinions, is not the same thing as relativism. Whether a relativist or not, we will sometimes have confidence and sometimes be uncertain. There are hard or borderline cases on both sides of this debate about the nature of morality.

III. CRUDE RELATIVISM: THE GROUP

Having surveyed some of the things that relativism is not, it is now time to examine some of the things it might be. Crude relativism, or what Bernard Williams has called "vulgar" relativism, is a seriously inadequate position. We call a position a "straw man" when it is easy to refute and no one seriously believes it anyway. In one sense crude relativism is a "straw man" because it is so easy to discredit. On the other hand, it must be examined, since many unreflectively believe it to be true. It is very popular with people who have not thought carefully about the nature of morality. Much has been written contra this kind of relativism, and the discussion that follows includes material drawn freely from the literature cited in the Bibliography.

One kind of crude relativism claims that the moral principles one ought to follow are the principles that just happen to be endorsed in one's own group. This position is sometimes referred to as cultural relativism. The moral rules and values as we find them in a group can result from any number of historical and cultural conditions or accidents, but there is no rational justification for the rules and values that would allow us to evaluate their content or construct a robust moral theory. There is, on this crude relativist story, no deeper rationale for moral principles to be had and therefore no rational way to adjudicate conflicts of moral rules between groups.

Because of all this, the crude relativist typically thinks it illegitimate to judge other cultures morally, for this would amount to irrationally imposing on others our contingently arrived at values. Remember that for this kind of relativist, we are bound only by the moral rules and values that are found in our own group. Judging a person by the rules or values of a different group would be to judge inappropriately, trying to use rules or values that do not apply. Hence most crude relativists conclude that we ought to be tolerant of (in the sense of not judging) other groups' moral codes and the behaviors permitted by them. After all, thinks the crude relativist, "who's to say" what's right?

There are internal inconsistencies with this position, as well as problems with the available argumentive support for it. But before addressing those issues, we should review some of the unpalatable consequences that result from taking this version of relativism seriously. While not "knockdown" arguments against the position, these considerations will give many people pause and a desire to formulate a better view. We might say that crude relativism, besides its other problems, gives us some intellectual "heavy baggage" to carry.

A. Some Consequences of Believing This Kind of Relativism

First, when this kind of relativist embraces the toleration thesis, he may not legitimately judge or criticize the moral practices of other groups, no matter how heinous he finds them to be. Human sacrifice, apartheid, slavery, ritual torture, genocide, and the like, any or all of them must be morally tolerated if a group's moral rules permit them. It is hard to imagine, to cite another example, what "human rights" would amount to according to this version of relativism. Of course, if members of a group do things that are not permitted by their own morality, then we may criticize them on that basis (so long as they also happen to endorse consistency), but that is a different matter. If the practices we find objectionable are permitted morally in the group, then we ought to be silent. This most people find difficult to do in all cases—hence the "heavy baggage." This lack of any universally binding and common moral rules also makes intergroup relations hard to evaluate in moral terms. Evidently, when the values and rules of different groups clash, there will be no systematic and rational way to resolve these intergroup clashes. Only bargaining based on fortuitous overlaps of rules, trickery, or violence are available when groups collide, and no one may legitimately judge (in moral terms) how things turn out.

Second, and for similar reasons, this sort of relativist may not legitimately criticize his own group's moral rules. He has already stipulated in his view that there is no basis on which to make such a critique. The rules are proper as we find them, and there is no deeper rationale with which to engage in an evaluation. Now we often do want to criticize the moral rules in our own group, and think we have good reasons for doing it. But this kind of relativist robs us of those reasons or principles since they are not already present in the received view. For example, imagine belonging to a group wherein ritual human sacrifices are permitted by the group's moral rules. How would a moral criticism of that practice, if one was inclined to mount one, ever begin? The existing rules permit it, and the relativist has stipulated there are no other rules that apply to that group. Criticisms would be without a basis and nothing more than pointless grousing. So this is another difficulty.

Third, there is also no way for the crude relativist to make sense of the notion of moral "progress." If a change in the moral rules hapens, then it must be accepted just as it happens. There can be no sense in which one moral rule or system of rules is "better" or "worse" than another, for there are no deeper or constant principles (that transcend a given rule system) by which to make such an assessment. We would be forced to refrain from saying, for instance, that the abolition of slavery in America was an instance of moral progress (except in the sense that slavery and then its abolition followed one after the other).

The previous three unhappy consequences of holding crude relativism all charitably allowed a somewhat dubious assumption. We assumed we could discern what the rules are and the extent of the culture or group to which they apply. But this in fact poses a fourth nasty difficulty for the crude relativist. What sort of nonarbitrary way do we have for these purposes of marking out membership in a group? Is it everyone that lives in a certain geographic region? Who speaks the same language? Who eats the same kind of food? These are all fine for some purposes, but seem unconnected to determining what moral rules ought to govern the group thereby marked out. We could say that being bound by a common set of rules is what makes the group in question. But then we would be saying that one is bound by the rules of the group to which one belongs, and one belongs to a group in virtue of what rules one is bound by. If this is not viciously circular, it plainly is not helpful.

What the rules are is no easier to discern. Are they what the simple majority of the group thinks the rules are? Two-thirds or better? Is it a statistical distillation of what a group actually does? Can there be a difference between what people believe the rules are and what they really are? If so, how could we tell if there was such a difference without a theoretical story that stands in part outside the group's beliefs? None of this strikes me as impossible for the crude relativist to work out, but work these difficult issues he must. Producing some sort of solutions to them is another burden the crude relativist must bear, and is one of the difficulties that comes with the thesis.

B. Possible Motives for Adopting the Position

Given all these difficult consequences of holding the position, why would someone be inclined to believe in crude relativism? Well, in the first place many who initially assert the view as we have couched it might not be aware of these consequences. Also, some may think embracing this view is the only way to avoid another unflattering and untenable position—crude relativists might wrongly be afraid their only alternative is a crude and unsophisticated absolutism. They may believe that if they are not crude relativists, then they must believe there is a simplistic, inflexible, and universal moral rule for every occasion in every time and place. This is not so, as we shall see in more detail below, since there is room for much acceptable variation and "free play" in most otherwise nonrelativist views of morality. We should expect that even if there is a deep, universal moral principle or set of principles (whether it be promoting utility, respecting persons, self-interest, flourishing, loving one's neighbor, etc.), it will be fleshed out with somewhat different particular rules in differing social, historical, and economic circumstances. It is perfectly plausible that there be a rich diversity of sound moral rule systems that are informed by a unity of deep moral principles. But a failure to realize this and a fear of crude absolutism (perhaps thought of as a kind of fanaticism) may explain why many people throw their lot in with crude relativists.

Perhaps the crude relativist falls for a common albeit fallacious argument. James Rachels has called it the "Cultural Differences Argument" (1986. In *The Elements of Moral Philosophy*, p. 15. Random House, New York). It is simple and has only two steps. The first is the premise of the argument, which is a statement of the obvious and observable disagreements in moral belief we previously noticed (Section II.B). The argument then concludes with the claim that there is no "right answer" and that moral relativism in its crude form must be true. To see how defective this reasoning is, imagine analogously that we observe disagreement on the answer to a tough math problem. Such disagreement by itself would not establish that there is no right answer. In addition, the argument moves (very quickly) from a *descriptive* claim about differences in people's moral beliefs to a *prescriptive* claim about what they ought to believe and are morally bound to do. Many believe the move from "is" to "ought" in cases like this also constitutes a fallacy in reasoning.

The argument also seems to make too much of the observed differences in moral belief. Indeed, there are many points of moral agreement between cultures and individuals. There may even be some moral rules all extant groups must observe lest they not survive as groups. A sort of moral Darwinism might guarantee that all surviving groups will have rules concerning the care of children, social cooperation, property, controlling violence, etc. Of course, none of this establishes what rules or deep principles we ought to endorse. It just weakens a bit the premise of the cultural differences argument (namely, that different cultures have different moral codes). The agreement we find between groups is no more significant than the disagreement. Trying to make the simple fact of a certain amount of agreement do more, and establish a transcultural moral system, would make the same mistakes in reasoning we just saw in the cultural differences argument. In any event, if we are to believe crude relativism is correct, we should not (in fact, could not) conclude this on the strength of the cultural differences argument alone. The argument is a dismal failure, and we must have some other (not yet offered) reasons for endorsing crude relativism.

C. Logical Inconsistencies

So there are unattractive consequences of taking this crude view seriously, there appear to be plausible alternatives available for explaining existing variation in moral codes, and relativism has little or no positive argumentive support. But that is not the worst of it for the crude relativist. Maybe worst of all is the fact that the crude relativist position is intrinsically incoherent.

The relativist thinks we ought to follow the moral rules that bind our own group. Presumably this is a rule that applies to everyone. Hence there is at least one rule that applies to all people regardless of the group to which they belong. But this is just what the relativist denies. Likewise, we have seen that part of what follows from what the crude relativist thinks is that we ought to be tolerant of other groups' moral codes. It is somehow not legitimate to "impose" one's moral rules on those of another group. But if this is so, then we have yet another cross-group moral rule, namely, to be tolerant in this sense. Using crude relativism, we contradict again just what crude relativism asserts. Indeed, a general mutual respect and tolerance for other individuals and groups could generate quite a few more specific moral rules, and could serve as the basis for a universal, and hence to some extent absolutist, morality. So the toleration thesis does more than bring "heavy baggage" to the relativist—it also leads her into logical contradiction.

There is no easy way out of this for the crude relativist. Perhaps she will retract part of her claim, and allow that one group, using its own standards, *may* legitimately judge another group and its standards. To what, then, does relativism amount? It would then allow the same kind of cross-group moral judgment and enforcement of which even the crudest absolutist would approve. This dilemma as it stands is intellectually intolerable, and any defensible form of relativism must show how it does not fall victim to it.

Crude relativism may be logically unstable in yet another way. Either we have reasons for endorsing the morality in our group or we do not. If we have no reasons or arguments for what rules we should follow or why we ought to follow those rules in particular, then morality is essentially arbitrary. Then there is no normative bite, for it would be very strange to say we ought to do something yet have no reason to do it. So without some structure of moral reasons, we move to nihilism, not relativism. And we already saw (Section II.A) that these are not the same thing.

On the other hand, if we give noncircular reasons or mount an argument as to why we should do what the particular rules of our culture require, we have the beginnings of a rationale that might be used to evaluate the rules in any culture. When there are reasons that can be given for the rules and values of a group, the argument that supports them would presumably apply to any similarly situated group. Naturally, this approach would allow for some variation of rules as a function of situation, but presumably any comprehensive moral code, even a universally applicable one, would take some account of that sort of variation (see discussion in Section V.A). The fact remains that a reasoned defense of one's own morality at once provides a tool that might be used to undertake an evaluation of any morality.

Admittedly, however, if one has a view that also relativizes what counts as a rationale defense, this argument loses a good bit of its force. But it does not seem desirable to claim that what will count as a reason for us (or even just me) would not count as a reason for a similarly situated them (or you). To make a claim like this convincing, we would need to distort part of what it means to give a reason. Indeed, a view that relativizes what counts as rational could rob us of the resources we need to talk coherently between groups about anything at all. Such are the lengths to which a moral relativist must go to give "reasons" for his moral rules and still remain a relativist. This possibility opens a difficult area in the philosophy of rationality, with issues that are beyond the scope of this entry. In any event, the crude relativist will not want to defend his own moral rules using a universally applicable argument, lest he undermine his own relativist convictions.

As a possible way out of this, the crude relativist might try the following line of thought. We might make the plausible hypothesis, as did Aristotle, that no chain of justification and reason giving can go on indefinitely.

At some point we run up against norms (and/or facts) that primarily do the justifying in our system of belief, and are not justified themselves. And so (on this hypothesis) any moral system at all will eventually "bottom out" in a principle or set of principles that we cannot further justify. Why then is the crude relativist any worse off then anyone else? Is not, "Do what is required in your own culture," a moral principle that we can claim binds everyone, on a par with (even if it competes with) "Love your neighbor" or "Respect persons" or "Maximize happiness"? And does not invoking this relativist principle as an ultimate source of justification avoid the undermining problem that reason giving was supposed to present the relativist?

Well, the relativist principle is not exactly on a par with these other substantive principles. The relativist principle, merely in stating it, does not tell us what we are supposed to do, or to what ultimately, we are actually committed. "Love your neighbor," while abstract, has content to be unpacked just as it sits. In contrast, "Do what is required in your own culture" is more like, "Do what the king says," or, "Endorse the values that correspond to the roll of these dice." These are not properly commitments to values or principles, but are rather placeholders for whatever values or principles that come up. As such, it is hard to see how "placeholder" principles can do any real justifying of other values, rules, principles, etc., in a normative system. Without filling in the content, we cannot possibly make out if they justify anything else. Fill in the content, and the relativist is right back where we started—if the substantive principle provides justification in his own group's moral system, we are left without a story as to why it will not do the same kind of work in another group's system. Notice that this difference between real principles or values and "placeholders" cuts off this escape no matter what sort of justificatory system the relativist chooses. He will have the same problem whether he uses a broadly foundational approach like we just examined, a coherence-style approach to justification, etc.

Hence, we can see the shape of another broad dilemma the crude relativist must negotiate. He can opt to give no ultimate reasons behind his (or any other) moral code, and be pushed to moral nihilism. Or he can try to mount some rational defense of his morality, reveal the structure of his normative justifications, and thereby begin the dismantling of his own crude relativism. These two end points, a rational morality or moral nihilism, are both logically stable positions (that is, not incoherent, self-contradictory, or self-defeating), but crude relativism in relation to a group is not.

D. Summary

Crude relativism that locates morality in the rules of a group, whatever those rules happen to be, has many problems. It does capture some though not all of the features Wong outlined that would make mortality objective, and insofar as it does, reflects some of our common moral experience. It also has a story to tell about moral disagreement. Still, there is just as much about the idea and the consequences of holding it that is strongly counterintuitive ("heavy baggage"). It may look at first like a moral theory, in that it offers an explanation of the nature and source of morality. Indeed, many who assert the thesis seem to think that it functions this way. But it is more a stand against theorizing, in that it cuts off any chance to tell a principled story about how moral rules should be systematized, related, prioritized, and otherwise made sense of. Crude relativism insists on a radically contingent structure in our local moral systems, if we happen to discern any structure at all. Maybe worst of all, this crude version, especially with its toleration thesis, flatly contradicts itself and is self-defeating.

IV. CRUDE RELATIVISM: THE INDIVIDUAL

Before, in Section II.C, we said that relativism was not identical with subjectivism. So not all kinds of relativism are at the same time subjective. However, there is another crude version of relativism that is an immediate consequence of being a certain kind of subjectivist. It is also an inadequate position, a "straw man," because of its many defects, but we must examine it because (like crude cultural relativism) of its popularity. We will consider it next.

This kind of relativism asserts that the moral principles one ought to follow are the principles that one just happens to endorse as an individual. A person who believes this will often say that she must do "what's right for me." No one may legitimately decide this for her, or criticize what she does decide. Moral judgments are immune from third party criticism and are only a matter of individual opinion. We may not legitimately judge the moral views and decisions of others. Moreover, people can come to their moral opinions in any way they think is best. Morality is essentially about individual attitudes and merely a matter of taste. After all (and once again), "who's to say" what is right? Given our earlier characterization of subjectivism, it should be obvious how this particular kind of relativism is also a kind of moral subjectivism.

A. Some Consequences of Believing This Kind of Relativism

Some of the unhappy consequences of believing this kind of relativism parallel very closely the "heavy baggage" of the crude cultural relativist (Section III.A). We may not legitimately criticize a person's moral choices, no matter how heinous we find them. The content of morality for a given individual is a matter only for that individual to decide, and we may not properly impose our morality on anyone else. For example, laws that punish certain kinds of moral choices can have no legitimate moral basis, for laws inevitably do coerce and impose on some people. Conflicts, as we saw with the cultural relativist, can be resolved only via fortuitous common ground, trickery, or violence. But over and against this view, while we can manage to have an attitude of "live and let live" in regard to many choices, it is not easy to regard it as morally "correct" for another to, say, rob us or do violence to our person. So this is a hard consequence to accept.

Also, it is hard to imagine how rational moral reflection or self-evaluation would proceed on this model of morality. With the crude cultural relativist, there was the parallel difficulty of being unable to criticize the moral principles of one's own group. Here, how could we evaluate our own moral principles and values? There is no meaningful way to do this, since all moral principles that apply to a person emanate from the attitudes, feelings, and thoughts of that person. There is no independent standard for deciding whether the morality of any given person is "good" or "bad," "correct" or "incorrect." And as moral progress made no sense for a group of crude relativists, moral growth is a nonsensical concept for the individual—only mere change is possible.

Last, there is a huge gap between how this kind of relativist-subjectivist must interpret moral disagreement and our ordinary understanding of it. When expressing a genuine moral disagreement in a matter of some importance, it is not as if we ordinarily mean something like, "I don't much like what you're doing . . . but I see that you do." Recall the need for any adequate view of morality to have at least some of the features that mark out objectivity (Section II.C). Those features are embedded deeply in our ordinary moral language and concepts, and any way of looking at morality should either incorporate them or at least explain why we should not. This kind of relativism eschews them altogether, and in so doing is very far removed from our common moral experience. The words "right," "wrong," "moral disagreement," etc., do not mean the same things anymore on this way of thinking. Such a radically revisionist approach is hard to take, and this is yet another reason we might be averse to accepting it unless we were presented some very persuasive arguments in its favor.

B. Possible Motives for Adopting This Position

So again, there are difficulties that come with accepting the crude relativist's idea. Why then do some people settle on this position? What convinces or motivates them it is the right way to think about morality, even while it is so difficult to live with what it recommends?

Of course, someone might fall for a suitably adjusted version of the cultural differences argument (Section III.B). But the "individual differences argument" would fare no better than the cultural differences argument as a piece of rational support. It has all the same defects.

Perhaps, again like the person driven to crude cultural relativism, the motive is in part an aversion to something else: we do not want to be (or suffer) the crude absolutist. We know how irritating (even dangerous) some moralists can be. Some people believe they have the "right" answer for everyone and for every occasion, and too often for people like this it is a pretty simplistic answer. But we know there are some sensible variations in what is morally permissible and required, depending on circumstances. The crude absolutist often fails to notice a morally permissible range of choices, and rushes to judge when we choose differently than he. Sometimes the crude absolutist insists that something is a moral matter that just is not. Moreover, special roles (parent, doctor, police officer, etc.) sometimes create special obligations and permissions, but the crude absolutist can be oblivious to the distinctions. We also might disagree with the crude absolutist on the level of urgency appropriate for correcting some misconduct; not all moral transgressions are equally horrible, and a failure to discern this can lead the crude absolutist to harass with zeal and fanaticism some people who are immoral in a relatively innocuous way.

All these kinds of irritating disagreements (and more) do not necessarily imply relativism. But wrangling with the absolutist is hard. Rather than saying or being told we are just wrong, or doing the work of resolving the problems and disagreements through education, reflection, debate, and other kinds of hard thinking, we might want to take what looks at first like the easy way out. We might think too quickly that there is no other alternative. As a result, we might then embrace crude relativism with respect to the individual, and not realize that what we thereby take on is more difficult and less tenable than what we were trying to avoid. But as was the case with the cultural relativist, we should resist giving in to these motives, for there are more adequate ways to respond to moral disagreement that do not require us to be a crude absolutist.

C. Logical Inconsistencies

Just as there were problems in the logic of crude cultural relativism (Section III.C), there are very similar problems in the logic of this kind of relativist. Is each person morally bound to follow the rules he feels apply to himself? Surely he is, or this view is simply a kind of nihilism. Then once again, we have a rule that binds everyone, namely, that every person is bound by their own morality. The relativist must assert what his own view denies. Presumably, whatever reasons that made the relativist averse to any universal rules would make him uncomfortable about this one. But if those reasons are undermined by the assertion of the one rule, then the whole view might be in danger of collapse. If there is one rule, what would be so hard for the relativist to take about more than one?

Also, coupling relativism with a universal rule of tolerance is just as devastating for this kind of crude relativist as it was for the crude cultural relativist. The idea flatly contradicts itself, and cannot be accepted as it is formulated. It also looks susceptible to the same justificatory instability we saw in Section III.C. If people have reasons for what they think is "right for them," then we have a basis for evaluating the moral rules that others follow, and we move away from thoroughgoing relativism. If people have no reasons for what they believe, then from where does the normative force come? So this kind of relativist, just like the cultural relativist, teeters between nihilism and at least some minimal form of universal morality.

D. Summary

The second kind of relativism we surveyed was no better than the first. Crude relativisms (tethered to either the group or the individual) do not work. They each assert complete relativity, which then leads to universal tolerance, hence bringing them both into self-contradiction. There are extremely hard to take intellectual consequences that flow from both types, and the argumentive support for them is weak. Nor does either version take adequate account of the objective features we think

morality has, even though in this regard crude cultural relativism does not fail so badly as relativism to the individual. More defensible forms of relativisms must avoid these problems.

V. MORE DEFENSIBLE FORMS OF RELATIVISM

Crude forms of relativism are not the only kinds. Of course, no defensible version can assert in the same breath radical relativity and universal tolerance. But there may be forms of relativism which do not make this error. Also, to accommodate the apparent objectivity that attends moral judgment and discourse, other versions of relativism might be nonrelative in regard to fundamental principles, but still leave room for relativistic variation at the more detailed levels of implementing the moral system. Still others could accept a more radical relativity, while at the same time putting at least some constraints on what will count as an acceptable moral rule or an adequate moral system. Indeed, there are a number of possibilities besides the crude ones we just examined. In short, there are ways to introduce varying amounts of relativity into morality without falling into the abject foolishness found in crude relativism.

Introducing some kind of relativity into morality seems like something we might want to do. We insisted on some elements of objectivity (Section II.C) in an adequate conception of morality, but we also insisted on some explanation of the disagreements, some of them intractable, that we appear to have (Section II.B). More, we would like to explain the disagreement without being a crude absolutist, wherein we commend one true morality, complete in all its excruciating and simplistic detail, ruling out of court any and all variation from it as plainly immoral and mistaken. In short, we want our explanation of morality to be plausible. But to do this, we must (while avoiding the pitfalls of crude relativism) do as Bernard Williams recommends: Rather than asking if we must think in a relativistic way (which clearly we cannot if we insist on doing it crudely and all the way down), we should ask rather "how much *room* we can coherently find for thinking like this" (1985. In *Ethics and the Limits of Philosophy*, p. 160. Harvard Univ. Press, Cambridge, MA).

A. Adjustments for Roles and Circumstances

Anything short of the crudest absolutism ought to be able to accommodate this next kind of relativism. Imagine there is one true morality, which makes the same basic demands of all people. We should expect that any version of such a morality will create different roles in the human societies it aims to regulate. Perhaps parents will have moral obligations that others do not to care for their children. Children might have fewer obligations than adults. Doctors, lawyers, clergy, military professionals, etc., might have obligations assumed in taking on their professional roles that others do not have, or have to a lesser degree. So even for someone with absolutist tendencies, not everyone must have exactly the same moral obligations, since some moral rules can be relative to roles.

Circumstances, in several ways, could also relativize moral requirements in what is an otherwise absolutist system. Absolute moral requirements are often abstract, "high level," and near the explanatory center of a given moral theory. General and organizing moral precepts like "Love your neighbor as yourself," "Always respect the human person," or "Try to promote human happiness" give rise to more specific rules, but these specific rules can vary somewhat with context and circumstances. For example, consider the moral rules that prohibit lying. Depending on our larger theory, we usually can identify a deeper reason that we should not lie, a larger moral point to the prohibition. And a deeper reason could at once generate some exceptions for things like tact, games where deception is part of the rules, situations wherein horrible consequences would issue from the truth, etc. There are also wide variations in the social, historical, and economic conditions under which people live. These variations too could account for different specific implementations of more or less absolute, universally binding moral rules. As an instance of this kind of variation, a moral rule that requires us to respect our elders might have a very different look in one culture than it does in another. So roles and circumstances make room for a certain kind of moral relativity even within an otherwise objective and absolutist system. This kind of relativity does not appear to be liable to any of the criticisms we leveled at the crude relativist, and may begin to explain at least some of the moral disagreements we seem to have.

Having recognized this, we should notice another interesting possibility. Recall that on Wong's analysis, some people mean, when they claim morality is objective, that there is "one single morality." Objectivists who believe this are also, on Wong's analysis, absolutists. Presumably, even those who believe there is "one single morality" could accept what we have shown here about roles and circumstances. The same morality could have a unity of higher level principles and a plurality of lower level

rules—a relativity that accounts for roles and circumstances. This should make us wonder what makes any "one" morality a single entity. Is there room for even more variation and complexity within what counts as "one" morality? Imagine a more radical relativist who wants to claim that he believes in one single morality too, but what he calls the single true morality is a big conjunction of all the different and relative moralities that bind each culture and individual. So the single true morality for this relativist says "A" to culture "B," says "C" to culture "D," says "E" to Jason, and says "F" to Julie, even at the most general and abstract levels. I imagine most people sympathetic to an absolutist-style approach would not be agreeable to calling this big conjunction a single morality. But it points to the extreme on an interesting continuum, and shows that the idea of "one" morality (which Wong thought was the distinguishing mark of an absolutist way of thinking) is not unambiguous. Having noticed this, we will set it aside.

Now some might doubt that the kind of moral variation we have explored in this section, accounting only for roles and circumstances, is really a "robust" or genuine form of moral relativity at all. In all these cases, the different moral requirements attached to roles and circumstances are explained by another, more general, nonrelative moral principle that binds everyone, and which is hence not relative. Gilbert Harman has suggested that the idea of moral relativism requires rather "that two people can be subject to different moral demands and not be subject to some more basic demand that accounts for this, given their situation" (1978, in *Values and Morals* (A. Goldman and J. Kim, Eds.), p. 145. Reidel, Dordrecht). Let us examine some other forms of relativism that have this more basic variation and see, as Williams recommends, how much room there is to think coherently in this way.

B. Some Sample Versions

A complete survey of the literature on more defensible forms of relativism (or a thorough sifting of even a small part of it) is far beyond the scope of this entry. Instead, in this section we will look briefly at just two examples of how one might form a relativist outlook without succumbing to the errors of the crude relativist. Early on, we established that whether and to what extent someone is willing to accept relativism can in part be a function of the moral theory to which she is committed. Each of the following sample versions of relativism follows a typical pattern. It starts from a certain view about the nature of morality, a theory if you will, and then concludes that there follows from it a certain amount of "robust" relativism (relativism that is more than just a function of roles or circumstances). If one finds the starting theory acceptable, then one may be inclined to give the concomitant relativity a chance. Then we can look into whether those forms of relativism avoid the problems of the crude versions, while still plausibly accounting for both objectivity and disagreement in morality.

1. Gilbert Harman

This sample version of relativism is based on an idea that has been elaborated by Gilbert Harman. His moral theory contains the assumption that no one is truly bound by moral demands he does not himself accept. Starting from this, he then characterizes morality as deriving from an implicit agreement among members of a group. Each member of the group intends to keep the agreement, so long as the other members comply. The agreement is not to be thought of as the completion of an explicit ritual, but rather as an agreement in the intentions of the members—a coinciding of what each intends to do. The rules of morality are to be found in the content of this agreement, which each member of the group obviously accepts in virtue of having already formed the intentions. Moral judgments and evaluations are made using the rules so derived. Relativity follows from this because the moral rules that derive from the agreement bind only the parties to that agreement. There are as many relative moralities as there are separate implicit agreements of this sort.

How does this sort of relativism fare? The morality that gives rise to it is not a form of nihilism. Harman says we ought to do what we have compelling reasons to do, and having an intention to do something provides an immediate and compelling reason to do it. So we ought to do what this morality, based on an implicit agreement of intentions, prescribes. It is objective in some ways, and not objective in others. This kind of relativist can agree in his own way with five of Wong's six criteria. On this view, moral statements have truth values, there are good and bad arguments for moral opinions, nonmoral facts can be relevant to moral judgment, and there are moral facts. All of this makes sense against the backdrop of the agreement. Also, if there are conflicting recommendations for action, only one can be true, since a person presumably is not party to more than one agreement. Still, none of this makes sense outside the agreement, and so the view denies there is "one single morality."

It is required by this version of relativism that we refrain from evaluating morally members of another group that do not share an agreement with us. This is because it makes no sense to criticize someone for failing to live up to an agreement to which they are not a party. So this form of relativism requires a toleration clause, at least when it comes to moral evaluation, but it attempts to explain why this does not involve us in a contradiction. Also, we might be less worried about the "baggage" of having to tolerate something we judge by our own standards to be heinous. This is because presumably people will not be inclined to agree to the worst sorts of things we might imagine (setting aside for the moment concerns over coercion and false consciousness), and this puts a limit on the kinds of morality that are possible or likely. More, notice that this version does not imply a "hands-off" toleration of others. We need not like what the other group does or thinks, nor are we *a priori* constrained from trying to change their agreement. We may even try to come to an implicit agreement across groups. But until there is such an agreement, moral evaluations outside an agreement make no sense.

Along similar lines, critiques and judgments of progress internal to the group cannot be made in strictly moral terms, but might make sense in other terms, such as coherence, desires, what is possible, changing circumstances and attitudes, what is generally rational, and whether there is in fact agreement. So there can be progress of a sort in a group's moral system, but not strictly moral progress. For this version of relativism, it is not as if anything goes, even though there is lots of room for choice and variation. Still, it is not clear whether the revisions to ordinary moral language demanded by this idea are modest enough to be acceptable.

This short exposition explores only a few things we might say for and against this kind of relativism. The main point here is that it does seem to avoid the more egregious errors of the crude versions. And where there is "baggage" that remains, it seems lightened a bit. It is a form of relativism that can sustain a serious debate without immediately falling into contradiction or completely ignoring important features of our common moral experience. It is a defensible, if not yet completely defended, form of relativism. Disagreement with this kind of relativist will turn on more interesting issues.

2. David Wong

This next sample of relativism is a version recommended by Wong. He begins by assuming that morality is a social construction designed both to resolve internal conflicts in our own personal requirements and to resolve interpersonal conflicts of interest. Now these are only "formal" constraints, and while there are some moral systems that will not do the trick here, almost infinite variation is possible. There clearly will be no single best way to balance these competing concerns, and different moral systems will reflect differing historical contingencies, varying social choices for resolution, the plasticity of human desires, and some variations in human nature (without necessarily denying that there are constant features of human nature as well).

Of course, we should immediately wonder what will count as a successful resolution of these inter- and intrapersonal requirements and interests. Wong called the criteria we use to decide success the marks of an "adequate moral system." Now it may be that there is just one set of criteria for what counts as an adequate moral system, with relative moralities ranging within those criteria. Wong thinks we could also entertain different ideas of what counts as a successful resolution, and hence have different ideas of what we will accept as an adequate moral system. This would further multiply the range of acceptable moralities, but still does not require that anything goes.

If we agree with Wong on the purposes of morality, and recognize that different social groups have chosen to fulfill those purposes in different ways, then tolerance in our evaluations of the moral judgments of other groups is required. Especially if there are elements of our own morality that let us recognize the other group as subscribing to an adequate moral system, then we will be obligated to respect the legitimacy of their choices and judgments in moral matters. But not every moral system, however we happen to find it, necessarily qualifies as adequate and immune from criticism. So an unqualified universal tolerance is not required by Wong's view. Also, like the Harman version of moral relativism, Wong's can answer to five of his own six criteria for moral objectivity. The difficult consequences of holding crude relativism, what we called the "heavy baggage," are also at least partially blunted in much the same ways as they are for a Harman-style approach.

So we have another version of relativism that is not badly defective in the ways that plague crude relativism. There are many interesting ways to test, attack, defend, or elaborate this basic idea, which for now we simply gesture toward. Once again, the main idea here is not to provide an outline of the fully worked out and defended thesis, but simply to show that there are such possible versions that avoid the obvious pitfalls of crude, and unfortunately, very popular forms of relativistic thinking.

C. Limits and Possibilities

We have examined only two versions of relativism that may be defensible elaborations of the main idea. There are other defensible elaborations already in the literature (for just one notable example, see H.-N. Castañeda, 1974. *The Structure of Morality*. Thomas, Springfield, IL) and others might be developed in the future. Yet as we explore relativism in its various forms, we should recognize that there will be several limiting pressures on the shape any such theory can reasonably take— boundaries any version of it must respect if it is to be defensible. Put in another way, such limits when we find them begin to answer Williams' question about how much room there is to think in a relativistic way. We will now make explicit two such limits, which we have been negotiating implicitly throughout all the previous discussions of relativism.

The first and most obvious limiting pressure for any relativist thinker is the one imposed by the crude relativist's toleration problem. Let us review the difficulty as it was explained in Section III. If we say that what binds anyone morally is in no way universal, then we must refrain from judging others using moral standards that do not (on the relativist view) actually bind them. This at once requires that we all be tolerant in the moral judgments we make concerning others. Hence the contradiction: universally required tolerance in a system that denied any such universality. Any defensible form of relativism must somehow avoid this difficulty.

The easiest and most straightforward way to respond to this pressure is to give up the relativistic claim that it is *all* relative. Harman's view requires that a moral system be an implicit agreement. This is a substantive and nonrelative demand about the nature of morality, which clearly places at least some limits on the content of every moral system. Of course, Harman tried to defuse our contradiction in another way as well: he tried to show how, on his view, cross-group moral evaluations make no sense, which cuts off the argument before it starts. But an insistence that morality should derive from an implicit agreement is a nonrelative, cross-cultural, and morally loaded requirement, and may carry with it several more suppressed assumptions of a nonrelative, moral nature (nature of the agreement, extent of the group, etc.). So his system avoids the contradiction by introducing a nonrelative claim.

Wong's view has a similar nonrelative element. Morality must adequately resolve inter- and intrapersonal conflicts of interest. When the standard of adequacy is nonrelative, how this would limit the shape and point of morality is obvious. Even when the standard of adequacy is relativized, which Wong is willing to entertain, there is a certain nonrelative, "metarestriction" on what any moral system can look like (namely, that it must meet the relativized standards of adequacy).

Still, that version of Wong's view may press the outer limits of what can count as an acceptable response to the contradiction.

So recall Harman's own very plausible test for a "real" relative morality. It must not recognize some more basic, nonrelative requirement that explains and countenances apparent differences between it and other moral systems. Does Harman's relativism pass his own test? Could any defensible version of relativism that avoids the contradiction pass? When we make nonrelative claims about the nature and point of morality in general, then I suspect we invariably make some basic, nonrelative claims about its content, or at least restrictions on its content. And this would make it difficult for any defensible form of relativism to be what Harman might accept as a completely robust form of it. Perhaps these suggestions begin to gauge how much room there is for the relativist—apparently a good deal of room, so long as the relativism does not go "all the way down."

The second limiting pressure for relativistic thinking is less sharp but just as important. We saw examples of this pressure when we introduced concerns about accounting for the objective qualities of moral experience, the nature of moral language, and worries about the "heavy baggage" that comes with some forms of relativism. Specifically, we will not embrace a form of relativism (or any other moral theory for that matter) that requires us to give up or revise too much in our overall conceptual scheme. To be sure, no single item in what Quine called our "web of belief" is immune from revision or rejection. But there are certain relatively fixed points in moral thinking, ideas Rawls has labeled "considered judgments," that we will not be inclined to tinker with very extensively. Some particular moral prohibitions (e.g., genocide, torturing the innocent, and slavery) and some ideas about moral concepts (e.g., morality is prescriptive or moral discourse has some features of objectivity) must be accounted for or at least persuasively explained away. Failing on this count would be to flirt with giving up the moral enterprise altogether. So while it will be harder to tell exactly whether and when this limit has been exceeded, its pressure is always present for the would-be relativist, as it is for any moral theorist.

A final thought. Even if some form of relativism turns out to be correct, there is embedded within most defensible relativisms an interesting possibility. Williams has observed that relativism is most often tied up with a belief that moral sytems are not literally true, but are rather "things to be true to" (1981. In *Moral Luck,* p. 143. Cambridge Univ. Press, Cambridge). In a world where people are ever more aware of variations in moral belief and commitment, many have come to be sympathetic to some kind of moral relativism. But this very awareness has gone hand in hand with interaction and confrontation. This interaction in turn, coupled with our reflection on these issues, has made it impossible for everything to remain the same. When we examined samples of some more defensible relativist systems, we saw that what we are "true to" responds to interactions: interactions often given rise to agreements (like in Harman's system), or result in problems of interpersonal conflict that need resolution (like in Wong's system). So interaction results in natural tendencies to expand the relevant group and move toward consistency. These are pressures that may well tend to bring varying moral commitments closer together. So even if some relativists are right about the nature of morality, the very global interaction that causes us seriously to entertain relativism in the first place may lead us eventually to a moral system possessed of more universally binding elements.

VI. CONCLUSION

All the various forms of moral relativism may turn out to be just plain wrong. We have examined some very good reasons to think that its crude versions are mistaken. But in its noncrude, more defensible versions, this is not obviously the case. Granted, the defensible versions of relativism may make theoretical assumptions we find disagreeable. Or there may be requirements to rethink some of our moral concepts in ways we find difficult to accept. But these disagreements and others like them are interesting ones, and of the kind that occupy the center stage in any serious thinking about morality.

Bibliography

Cutler, H. M. (1993). Is it all a matter of opinion: Relativism versus objectivism. In "Ethical Argument: Critical Thinking in Ethics," pp. 1–30. Paragon, New York.
Gibbard, A. (1990). Normative objectivity. In "Wise Choices, Apt Feelings," pp. 153–250. Harvard Univ. Press, Cambridge, MA.
Harman, G. (1975). Moral relativism defended. *Philosophical Rev.* 84, 3–22.
Rachels, J. (1986). The challenge of cultural relativism. In "The Elements of Moral Philosophy," pp. 12–24. Random House, New York.
Williams, B. (1972). Interlude: Relativism. In "Morality," pp. 20–25. Cambridge Univ. Press, Cambridge.
Williams, B. (1981). The truth in relativism. In "Moral Luck," pp. 132–143. Cambridge Univ. Press, Cambridge.
Wong, D. B. (1984). "Moral Relativity." Univ. of California Press, Berkeley.

NATIONAL SECURITY ISSUES

John D. Becker
United States Air Force Academy

GLOSSARY

actors Those entities, such as states, alliances, international organizations, and transnational organizations, that play roles in the conduct of national security. Other actors may be selected individuals and groups in a particular state or region.

approaches The methods and manners in which states conduct the business of national security. Approaches derive from national security structures and strategies.

commitments Specific actions at specific times and places. Commitments specify a state's interests and objectives in a given situation.

interests Highly generalized abstractions that reflect a state's basic wants and needs. They are sometimes difficult to identify because they are rarely clean-cut and tend to overlap with other interests.

issues Points of debate or controversy that concern the national security of a state.

objectives The goals or aims of what a country endeavors to do; more tangible and easier to change than interests.

operations other than war (OOTW) Operations that involve the employment of military and nonmilitary resources, but without the intention of using violent force as a primary means to achieve a specific end or set of ends. OOTW include such actions as peacekeeping, counterdrug operations, and disaster relief.

peacetime concerns Those important political and economic concerns that nations normally conduct with each other, when not at war or in hostile conflict.

policies Patterns of actions to attain specific objectives.

power The ability to get others to do things, particularly something they would not do of their own volition. Power is dynamic, subjective, relative, and situational. It is expressed in many ways, such as coercion, persuasion, bargaining, and threats, and through various forms, including the military, political, economic, and sociopsychological.

programs A plan to allocate resources in support of objectives, policies, and commitments.

purpose An expression of an enduring value or values in which a state (or nation) is rooted. A national purpose is more or less permanent, tends to be an end rather than a means, and is desired in and of itself, not simply as a means of attaining something else.

strategy A plan of action, using available resources to obtain certain goals over time. There are national strategies, grand strategies, and military strategies.

structures The organizational arrangement established by a state to allow it to conduct the business of national security.

war A state of open armed conflict between states (or coalitions of states), or between parties in a state, carried on by force of arms for various reasons. There are various types of wars, ranging across the spectrum of conflict, including attack or raids, low-intensity conflicts, limited wars, general wars, and nuclear war.

NATIONAL SECURITY ISSUES are those points of debate or controversy that concern the security of a state. The principal term, national security, has traditionally signified the protection of a state's people and territories against physical assault. Yet, since World War II and the rapid transformation of the international political system, the term has taken on a more comprehensive meaning. National security now includes the protection, through a variety of means, of vital economic and political interests, the loss of which could threaten fundamental values and the life of the state.

National security is conducted in the context of a bifurcated environment, divided into global and domestic parts. The global part of the environment includes factors such as perceived threats of and between states, states' geographic locations and physical conditions, international laws, customs, and agreements, trade relations and other international economic concerns, as well as the flow of strategic information and intelligence. The domestic part of the environment is composed of factors such as states' worldviews, their internal public attitudes, economic conditions including national security budgets, competing political ideologies and elections, bureaucratic agendas and contests, their social and cultural conventions, in addition to respective legal and ethical norms.

The national security environment is, in turn, cast with numerous actors who play various roles. These actors include the states themselves—along with their prominent leaders and private individuals—their corresponding political, military, and economic alliances, international and transnational organizations, and the media and mass communication groups. Additionally, legislative and judicial branches of a state's government play roles in the national security framework, as do other groups, such as prominent minorities and opposing political parties in states' populations.

Within this environment, and among these actors using power, the business of national security is determined and carried out. While there are significant differences in various states as to how those processes are carried out, all states end up with at least three things: a national security structure, a national security strategy, and a national security approach.

Additionally, as part of the process of national security, issues of applied ethics are raised and considered. These issues include traditional just war concerns which are often broken into two types—*jus ad bellum* (justice of war) and *jus in bello* (justice in war). They also include questions about nontraditional issues, such as OOTW and future war concerns, as well as issues like human rights, economic rights, and environmental rights.

I. NATIONAL SECURITY STRUCTURES

A national security structure is the organizational arrangement established by a state to allow it to conduct the business of national security. The national security structure will vary depending upon a number of factors, including the type of government organization and the level of political development. Typically, however, it will be vested in the executive branch of a state and it will include representatives from the state department or diplomatic corps, the armed forces, those involved with foreign trade and commerce, and the intelligence services. It may also include a special coordinator for national security affairs, as in the United States or in Russia. Additionally, it may draw upon other representatives from government or actors from the national security environment, who are concerned or involved with a particular issue or set of issues.

An example of a national security structure can be seen in that of the United States. At the center of the structure is the White House Office—this office houses the staff members of the President, including his personal and political assistants. The specific organization of the White House Office is a reflection of the President's personal style. Another key element is the National Security Council, which serves as the formal coordination and policy planning group. It is composed of the President, the Vice President, the Secretary of Defense, and the Secretary of State. It is supported by a combined military and civilian staff, with the Assistant to the President for National Security Affairs serving as its head. Other key elements include the Department of State, the Department of Defense, the Central Intelligence Agency, and the Office of Management and Budget. And, of course, other agencies, such as the Department of Energy, the Department of Treasury, and the Federal Bureau of Investigation, are involved on an ad hoc basis.

Another dimension of the structure includes the unofficial organization, which may range from a "kitchen cabinet"—personal friends and confidants of the President, to previous Presidents ands former senior officials, key members of Congress, the media, and the business community, to the others like the President's relatives, including spouses and siblings.

The interaction and inputs from all of these actors, in both formal and informal organizations, provide the structure that will shape and develop the strategies and approaches that a state takes to national security issues.

II. NATIONAL SECURITY STRATEGIES

From this structure, the key actors will determine a national security strategy. A strategy is simply a plan of action, using available resources, to obtain certain goals over time. Thus, a national security strategy is a state's plan, which fuses all of its available resources, during peace as well as war, to attain national interests and objectives. A national security strategy will normally include two other strategies—a grand strategy and a military strategy. A grand strategy involves employing national power under all circumstances to exert desired degrees and types of control over a state's enemies or opponents. Threats, force, indirect pressure, diplomacy, subterfuge, and other imaginative means are all employed in grand strategy.

For example, before the Persian Gulf War, the United States developed and employed a grand strategy against Iraq. This strategy included President George Bush's use of media in establishing the "line in the sand"; the use of economic sanctions and ultimately, embargo; the establishment of a political and military coalition to fight Iraq; declarations of support by both the U.S. Congress and the United Nations; and the veiled threats of using nuclear weapons in response to any Iraqi use of chemical or biological weapons. In short, these various tactics were woven together into a single, integrated plan—a grand strategy for going to war with Iraq.

Military strategy, on the other hand, is predicated on physical violence or the threat of violence. It seeks to obtain national security interests and objectives through the use of arms. It involves, as General Karl von Clausewitz noted, the use of engagements to attain the object of war. There are a variety of approaches to military strategy including sequential and cumulative, direct and indirect, deterrent and combative, and counterforce and countervalue.

In the earlier example of the Persian Gulf War, the U.S. military strategy was clearly articulated by Chairman of the Joint Chiefs of Staff, General Colin Powell, who said the military was "Going to cut off it's head, and then kill it." What this meant was that the United States planned first to destroy the command and control structure of the Iraqi's armed forces and second to destroy their fighting forces.

The difference between grand strategy and military strategy is simple then: the first is the purview of statesmen while the latter is the territory of generals. Moreover, military strategy should be understood as a subset of the larger, grand strategy.

III. NATIONAL SECURITY APPROACHES

The intermediate step between national security structure and national security strategy is the national security process. While the exact processes differ as do states' structures and strategies, all follow a similar path. This path starts at a nation's purpose and progresses through interests, objectives, policies, commitments, and programs.

Every state has a national purpose. This national purpose is an expression of the enduring values in which a state is rooted. In the United States, for example, the Declaration of Independence and the Constitution are such expressions. In the first case, "... We hold these truths to be self-evident, that all men are created equal, that they are endowed by their Creator with certain unalienable Rights, that among these are Life, liberty, and the pursuit of Happiness. ...." In the second case, the preamble notes, "We the people of the United States, in order to form a more perfect union, establish justice, insure domestic tranquillity, provide for the common defense, promote the general welfare, and secure the blessings of Liberty ourselves and our Prosperity, do ordain and establish this constitution for the United States of America."

Expressions of national purpose differ depending upon cultural, economic, historical, political, and moral precedents, yet often focus on similar themes including domestic order, the welfare of the nation, and national security. It is important to note that a national purpose is marked by certain characteristics: it is more or less permanent, it tends to be an end rather than a means, and it is desired in and of itself, not simply as a means of attaining something else.

Deriving from a state's national purpose are its national interests. Interests are highly generalized abstractions that reflect a nation state's basic wants and needs.

They include such things as political integrity and territorial integrity. They are sometimes difficult to identify because they are rarely clean-cut and they tend to overlap or interlock with other interests.

An example of national interests can be found in Operation Just Cause, the U.S. military intervention in Panama. One of the reasons the administration gave for intervening was the repeated abuse of U.S. nationals and military personnel by local officials and police. This need to protect U.S. citizens abroad is considered a common national interest. Another example of a threatened national interest was the requirement to protect the Panama Canal, in which the United States has economic, political, and military needs. Economically, the Canal is important to our trade relations. Politically and militarily, it is important both as a symbol and carries treaty obligations for the U.S. defense establishment.

Emerging from national interests are national security objectives. These objectives spell out what a country is trying to do. These objectives might be understood as goals, aims, or purposes. They are similar to interests but more tangible and easier to change. If one of the United States' national interests is to ensure access to oil supplies in the Middle East, then some of its objectives might be maintaining stability in the region, strengthening its allies such as Israel in the region, and constraining "rogue" states like Iraq and Iran.

Interests and objectives require specifics actions, like policies, commitments, and programs, to be translated from abstractions to actual activities. Policies are patterns of actions designed to attain specific objectives. In the previous example of the United States objective to have access to Middle East oil, a supporting policy might include providing financial aid to developing countries in the region, providing military assistance to pro-U.S. countries, and denying technology to anti-U.S. countries. Correspondingly, commitments are specific actions at specific times and places, and programs are resource allocation plans. So military assistance to a pro-U.S. country, like Saudi Arabia, might include shipments of a dozen advanced fighter aircraft in one year, shipments of 50 tanks in the next year, and training aid teams, with repair parts, during both years.

This, then, is an example of how states approach the handling of national security issues, within the context of their organizations and strategies.

IV. NATIONAL SECURITY ISSUES

Examples of specific national security issues include arms control, energy resources, environmental prob-
lems, foreign trade, international terrorism, the uses of outer space, and the war on drugs. These various issues occur along what might be considered a continuum—a continuum of national security. This continuum includes three key concerns: wars, operations other than war, and peacetime concerns. Let us consider each element in turn.

A. War

On one side of the continuum is war, a state of open armed conflict between states, or between parties in a state, carried on by force of arms for various purposes. There are various types of wars, ranging across a spectrum of conflict, including attacks or raids, low-intensity conflicts, limited wars, general wars, and nuclear war. War is a primary national security issue.

An attack or raid is a limited military action, meant to inflict a minimal amount of damage or destruction on an enemy, for a specific reason. The forces employed in an attack or raid vary from air-launched cruise missle strikes to large-scale land assaults by either an army or marine force. For example, in 1986, U.S. warplanes bombed Libya, targeting Mu'ammar Qaddafi's headquarters at Tripoli, leaving 15 civilians dead. This raid was a retaliatory attack for the Libyan bombing of a West Berlin discotheque that killed and injured several hundred people, including American soldiers stationed in Germany.

Low-intensity conflict (LIC) is a limited political-military struggle, meant to achieve political, social, economic, and psychological objectives. It is often protracted and it ranges from various types of pressure (diplomatic, economic, and psychosocial pressures) through terrorism and insurgency. LIC is most often constrained to a geographic area and is characterized by restraint on weaponry, tactics, and level of violence.

Three examples indicate the breadth and diversity of LIC. First, early American involvement in the Vietnam war, with the use of Army Special Forces troops and other military advisors, was an example of a guerrilla war. Using unconventional tactics, these American forces and their South Vietnamese allies fought against communist guerrillas from North Vietnam. This war was indeed a political-military struggle and it was also a protracted conflict.

For a second example, consider the Israeli response to the terrorist seizure of a civilian airliner in June 1976. Palestine Liberation Organization (PLO) terrorists hijacked an Air France jet and diverted it to the Entebbe airport in Urganda. They held 98 Israeli passengers and the plane's crew as hostages, demanding that numerous

PLO prisoners held in various countries be released in exchange. The Ugandan government, then lead by the dictator Idi Amin, cooperated with the terrorists. The Israeli government launched a rescue raid, by commandos, which overcame Ugandan and PLO forces, and liberated the hostages.

Finally, a third example of LIC is psychological warfare. Psychological warfare is really fighting with words, using communications technology to advance both propaganda and psychology. In Haiti, recently, U.S. psychological operations troops sent pamphlets and papers throughout the island, encouraging Haitians to cooperate with American forces as they arrived.

Limited wars or conventional wars are armed conflicts between two or more states. They are most often what we mean by "war." The means and ends are still constrained but are greater than those found in LIC. The resources of all states in a limited war may be fully mobilized and their own survival may be at risk, but it is still limited in that it is not a regional or global conflict. Examples of limited war include the U.S. involvement in Korea, Panama, and the Persian Gulf wars.

Next, there is general war. This is armed conflict between major powers. States such as the United States, Russia, or China employ their total resources—political, economic, military—in the conflict and, in fact, the survival of one or more belligerent may be jeopardized. General wars have included World War I and World War II.

Finally, there is nuclear war. Simply put, this horrific, and so far theoretical notion is that states make use of nuclear weapons in the fighting of a general war. In this type of conflict, nuclear weapons, in various forms—submarine-launched missiles, land-based rocket-launched missiles, and aircraft-launched bombs and/or missiles—attack either countervalue (basically, cities or people) targets or counterforce (military or nuclear weapons) targets. Although nuclear weapons have been used in war, by the United States on Japan in World War II, no nuclear war has ever been waged.

B. Operations Other Than War

Moving toward the middle of the national security spectrum, one finds operations other than war (OOTW). These are concerns that may involve the employment of military and nonmilitary resources, but without the intention of using violent force as a primary means to achieve a specific end or set of ends. OOTW include such actions as peacekeeping, counterdrug operations, and disaster relief.

Recent U.S. national security operations have been almost exclusively OOTW. For example, when the United States and others decided to intervene in the affairs of Somalia, they did so under the rubric of humantiarian intervention. Military forces, in conjunction with diplomatic and relief organizations (both domestic and international) established an infrastructure in 1992 and 1993 that allowed the storage and distribution of food, water, and medical care. Additionally, in the American involvement with Haiti, U.S. Special Forces troops, in conjunction with diplomatic negotiators, worked to achieve a peaceful transition between governments.

Domestically, all national security operations except perhaps civil wars are OOTW, ranging from hurricane relief to assisting firefighters in battling large-scale fires to helping with flooding throughout a country. Combined efforts are also seen in counterdrug operations where U.S. military forces work with intelligence services, satellite support services, and law enforcement agencies, as well as with diplomatic services and other nations, in an effort to stem the flow of drugs into this country.

Although there has been much discussion as to whether operations of this type are ones that our national security resources should be employed on, it is important to recognize that they are not new. For instance, after the American Civil War, national security resources (specifically the Army) were used in suppressing the Pullman riots in Chicago, repressing the various Indian tribes throughout the west, exploring and mapping the Pacific Northwest and Alaska, conducting excursions into Mexico and other Latin American countries, and construction projects, like the Panama Canal.

C. Peacetime Concerns

On the other side of the continuum of national security is peace. Peace is not simply some type of tranquillity, but consists of those important political and economic concerns that nations normally conduct with each other when not at war or in hostile conflict. Common peacetime concerns include diplomacy, trade and economic interactions, and deterrence.

Diplomacy involves the normal, day-to-day, relationships between states and other transnational organizations. There are both formal diplomatic channels, usually represented by a corps of professional diplomats who work in embassies in other states, as well as informal diplomatic channels, represented by other, nonprofessional envoys, who may work directly for a nation's leadership in dealing with other nations. Both representatives deal with a variety of activities including communications between nations, political dealings, economic issues, and military cooperation. They work on issues ranging from nuclear disarmament talks to trade treaties to refugee settlements.

Economic transactions between states include trade, trade balances with corresponding imports and exports levels, economic growth between and in other states, economic assistance programs such as loans and grants, and also tarrifs and other barriers across respective borders.

Deterrence and defense are also peacetime concerns. Deterrence is simply the notion that a state, through the size and power of its military forces, can affect the actions of another state. For example in the Cold War between the United States and the former Soviet Union, both states' military forces with their large and vast nuclear arsenals served to deter nuclear wars.

Defense, too, is a peacetime concern. States constantly struggle, through the development of their understanding of potential and actual threats, their development of strategies to deal with those threats, and the procurement and sustainment of military forces, with the issue of what is an adequate defense. This is, perhaps, the critical issue in national security, because how strong a state is perceived to be affects all of its dealings with other states. It also impacts on the rest of a state's internal governance through the sharing and distribution of fiscal resources for other domestic departments and programs.

In sum, it remains important to note the wide variety of national security issues that states encounter occur across a continuum. This national security continuum includes war, operations other than war (OOTW), and peacetime concerns. It should also be noted that rarely does a state focus on just one part of the continuum. Rather, it faces various issues across the continuum simultaneously with other different states. Accordingly, the management of national security is difficult but critical to a state's life.

V. APPLIED ETHICS ISSUES

As part of the process of national security, issues of applied ethics are raised and considered. These issues include traditional just-war concerns, which are often broken into two types—*jus ad bellum* (justice of war) and *jus in bello* (justice in war). They also include questions about nontraditional issues, such as OOTW

and future war concerns, as well as issues such as human rights, economic rights, and environmental rights.

In the first case, war, including LIC, a great deal of discussion is focused on whether a state is justified in its actions of starting and conducting war. In Western history, the issue has been addressed by just-war tradition or just-war theory. Philosophers ranging from Augustine to Aquinas to Grotius have contributed to this discussion. Considerations include just cause, right authority, right intention, proportionality of ends, last resort, reasonable chance of success, and the aim of peace. The satisfaction of these criteria produces a "just war" versus and "unjust" war.

In the second case, the issues are generally about the conduct of the war itself. The focus is on how soldiers and their commanders conduct the war and whether that conduct is ethical or not. Primary considerations include the proportionality of means and ends, as well as noncombatant protection and immunity.

In the third case, the issues also draw upon ethical principle but in relation to OOTW, including humanitarian intervention and peacekeeping missions. Often efforts are made to balance one ethical principle against another principle—for example, saving the lives of a state's starving people versus violating the political autonomy of that state. Considerations include those found in the earlier cases but with distinctive approach on nonlethal force.

In conclusion, the purpose of applied ethics in national security issues includes justifying the use of force by a political community (or a state), warranting protection of fundamental rights and values, and explaining the relation of ends to means in political life. Ethical issues are addressed in the structure, strategies, and approaches of national security.

Also See the Following Articles

PACIFISM • TERRORISM • WARFARE, CODES OF • WARFARE, STRATEGIES AND TACTICS

Bibliography

Becker, J. D., Gibson, W. H., Hittinger, J. P. (1996). *Moral dimensions of the military profession.* Boulder, CO: American Heritage Custom Publishing.
Hardin, T., & Mapel, D. R. (Eds.) (1992). *Traditions of international ethics.* New York: Cambridge University Press.
Lykke, A. F., Jr. (Ed.) (1989). *Military strategy: Theory and application.* Carlisle Barracks, PA: U.S. Army War College.
Rosenthal, J. H. (Ed.) (1995). *Ethics and international affairs: A reader.* Washington, DC: Georgetown University Press.
Wells, D. R. (Ed.) (1995). *An encyclopedia of war and ethics.* Westport, CT: Greenwood Publishing Group.

NATIVE AMERICAN CULTURES

Thomas Clough Daffern
University of London

GLOSSARY

culture The overall term used here for the Amerindian way of life in all its forms.

ethics The framework of theory and practice concerning the appropriateness or otherwise of given actions and ways of being in the world, in this context according to traditional Amerindian teachings.

Great Mystery/Great Spirit Terms used as translations for numerous Amerindian terms denoting the highest essence of ultimate reality; the guiding, creative, dynamic, compassionate, directive spiritual force underlying all realms of existence, including our own.

Medicine Wheel The systematic cartographic representation of the wheel of existence which defines the cosmological and ethical consciousness of Amerindian culture. Although arising specifically from the plains Indians, the basic ideas found in the Medicine Wheel occur universally in some form in all Amerindian cultures.

mother earth The divine feminine spiritual being which upholds all life and to whom mankind owes great reverence and love.

shaman or medicine man/woman These terms denote those who have developed their spiritual awareness to a high degree, and perform the role of healer, doctor, counselor, priest, magician, psychotherapist, and teacher to the wider tribal community.

teachings/traditions The collective body of knowledge underlying the ethical viewpoint of Amerindian culture.

NATIVE AMERICAN (AMERINDIAN) CULTURE covers a wide range of different tribal traditions. The purpose of this entry is to share in depth something of their ethical teachings and traditions, and to present them both historically and conceptually, asking above all how Amerindian ethical insights are being applied in the contemporary world. The concept of "applied ethics" per se being somewhat alien to Amerindian thinking, for whom all ethical teachings are meant to be applied in all aspects of one's life, our focus has been on the general context of ethical theory and practice in Amerindian culture, drawing out the specificity of "application" as we proceed. Our purpose has been to present a wide overview of the potential and actual contribution of Amerindian ethical thinking to modern debates on comparative global philosophy and ethics, in the belief that although its representatives may be relatively few in number, it is important for the voice of Amerindian ethical teachings to be heard at this point in world history.

I. THE QUESTION OF ORIGINS

One of the most intriguing and heated controversies in contemporary archaeological and anthropological scholarship concerns the chronological and geographical origins of Amerindian culture. There are numerous unresolved questions in contemporary scholarship about the antiquity and origins of Amerindian culture: exactly when did *Homo sapiens sapiens* first arrive in the American continent, and at which entry point or points? Of which ethnic, cultural, and linguistic types were these proto-Amerindian peoples? To all these questions there is as yet no definitive answer, but rather a continuing debate.

In recent years the trend arising from further archaeological discoveries has been to push the "entry point" further and further backward in time, from an earlier generation of scholars who had fixed ideas that man first entered America about 12,000 B.C. via the Bering Straits to a realization that *Homo sapiens sapiens* has been living in the Americas since approximately 60,000 B.C., that is, almost as long as anywhere else on the planet. This debate is important since it parallels certain discussions in philosophical circles as to the inherent value and significance of Amerindian ethical beliefs.

If European or Europeanizing scholars (initially Christian, now largely post-Christian) could dismiss man's presence in the New World as a relatively recent phenomena, this served two useful purposes simultaneously: firstly, it pacified the conscience of European settlers in the Americas since if mankind's presence there was not too primordial, claims to absolute ownership could be disputed. Secondly, if Amerindian cultural systems were not as old as others, say, in the Middle East, it marginalized their significance: they would be at best of interest to specialist anthropologists, rather than to mainstream philosophers and theologians.

The fact that the original chronological certainties are giving way to doubt and considerable questions at the same time as a renaissance of interest in the inherent value and wisdom of native Amerindian spiritual and ethical teachings is therefore hardly coincidental. A postmodernist historiography reconceiving Amerindian history in terms of multiple entry points, numerous overlapping cultural influences, unanswered and perhaps unresolvable questions, and being open to the inevitability of surprise and paradox and grace would surely find itself undergoing some kind of metamorphosis of content and methodology and some breakdown of the barriers of subject and object, or study and student. In the ethical perspective of Amerindian teachings, in asking questions about the ancestors of the Amerindian peoples, we are asking questions also about our own ancestors, for all human and animal life is for them bound up in the great wheel of interconnectedness. Perhaps the true answers to the questions of origin will only come as we reflect deeper on their meaning and purpose, and ask them from deeper and deeper places within ourselves, for ethics and epistemology, and virtue and cognition, conjoin into a greater unity of being, knowing, and doing in the Amerindian way.

II. DIVERSITY AND UNIVERSALITY OF BELIEF

Differences between the ethical beliefs of different Amerindian tribal groups and regions abound more in the details than in the generality. To what extent is it possible to generalize about the ethical beliefs and practices of a whole continent, and to what extent is it necessary to be specific? For the purposes of this entry an attempt will be made both to generalize where possible, extrapolating certain common themes and practices from across the full range of Amerindian ethical beliefs, and to be specific where necessary.

Obviously, ethical teachings differed from tribe to tribe, and from linguistic group to linguistic group in relation to the precise ecological and cultural niche occupied. For forest-based Amerindian cultures in the Amazonian basin, the ethical system revolved around the forest as provider and nourisher, with the animals, trees, and plants of the forest being seen as the supreme gifts of the spiritual world. For the plains Indians of North America, the bison, the local plants and animals of the plains and sacred hills, and the terrain itself were the locus of the sacred teachings of the tribes. Thus the outer details differ according to topography and ecology.

On the other hand, there is enough of a common thread of meaning and content running throughout the various diverse teachings to justify treating Amerindian ethics as a single, albeit complex, field of study.

III. THE SOURCES OF OUR UNDERSTANDING OF AMERINDIAN ETHICS

What are our sources for understanding native Amerindian ethical beliefs? Fortunately there is a rich mine of information and interpretation available to us. One of the key points to be noted is that the ethical teachings of Amerindian cultures were very largely oral in their transmission, with the spoken word being the essential vehicle for the transmission of teachings. While pre-Columbian Aztec and Mayan cultures did have advanced writing systems, as did some tribes in northeastern America, and some texts have come down containing ethical sayings, proverbs, poems of admonition and entreaty etc., it would be true to say that the greatest source of information has come from oral testimony.

In oral societies, the storyteller's role is supreme, a guardian of tradition and myth, and a repository of the ethical teachings of the tribe, cloaked in images, plot, and dénouement. Amerindian culture is particularly rich in such storytelling, and many of the religious and theological beliefs can best be ascertained through attention to the rich mythological worlds of the folktale.

It is not necessarily the case that such stories are self-consciously didactic, but rather that for the Amerindian people life itself is a concatenation of stories within stories, which we weave together, making sense and meaning of our lives. Such stories are peopled with animal deities, the spirits of nature, and the divine intermingling with human affairs. The cosmic and the human stories are interwoven. There is no ethic of arrogance for the "two leggeds" (human beings) given sanction to dominate other life-forms. Animals are crucially important in the role of the Amerindian folktale, as befits a culture still dependent largely on hunting, which certainly seems to be a direct descendent of Palaeolithic hunting cultures, whose religious sensibilities are shamanic in content. Agriculture is also central to the beliefs of many of the more advanced Amerindian cultures, where plant beings are invested with numinous identities, and in effect worshipped as healers, nurturers, and bringers of life.

The contribution of anthropologists and mythographers has been essential in mapping the role of the storyteller in shaping the ethical imagination of Amerindian cultures; from French Jesuit priests, to Spanish missionaries, to Anglo-Saxon Protestants, to contemporary academic anthropologists, the reduction of the corpus of Amerindian myth and story to written form has been a complex process several centuries in the making, and one which is still underway.

As yet, however, there has been no construction of a core "sacred text" from the oral teachings of Amerindian shamans and medicine men; there has rather been a diversity, a plurality, of such teachings, given from different teachers at different times and recorded in different contexts. We have recordings and transcripts of speeches given at different times of contact between Amerindian and Western cultures. Often, since the whites held the upper hand politically, these utterances are of great depth and ethical beauty, representing an archetypal clash between the spiritual innocence of the noble savage and the harsh realities of a developing, scientific and technological society.

Later, we have considered teachings put into print by respected elders of Amerindian spiritual teachings, in a conscious attempt to transmit the heritage and legacy of their values. We also have music and artistic creativity, all of which can tell us a great deal about the ethical beliefs of Amerindian culture, which will be discussed in greater detail in the following sections. Nowadays we have new and imaginative media being utilized to transmit Amerindian ethical beliefs: film, music, books, cards, games, pilgrimages, and sweat lodges. Indeed there is a growing interest in Amerindian values, particularly in certain circles within the "counterculture" which often stands opposed to mainstream Western values and has arisen since the 1960s and 1950s, first in the USA and then in Europe, with various strands of the peace movement and environmental movements being strongly influenced by Amerindian values. From this cultural mixture we have reports of lived experiences, of Westerners who have taken Amerindian shamanic cultural patterns to heart and shaped their lives accordingly. This entry draws on aspects of all these sources in what follows.

IV. RITUAL AS APPLIED ETHICS

The connection of ethics and ritual in all cultures is powerful and self-evident. There is no greater binding thread which links a people into a common ethical vision than the shared experience of sacred rites. For Amerindian peoples, as for all upholders of primal faith traditions, it would be true to say that all of life is seen as taking place within the wider context of lived ritual experience. While the details of rituals varied from tribe to tribe, the common element linking them all was the affirmation of interconnectedness, both horizontal, in the sense of social integrity, and vertical, in the sense of transpersonal linkage between the human world and the world of spirit.

As agents and tools to effect this interconnectedness, the Amerindians used a variety of means: initiation rites (rites of passage) occurred at key moments of the life cycle, celebrating and marking birth, childhood, puberty and adolescence, adulthood, mating and marriage, and the taking on of mature responsibilities within the tribe. While certain ethical teachings were transmitted and cultivated by specialists, so to speak, a key feature of Amerindian culture was the communal nature of their ritual forms: these were ceremonies in which the whole tribe participated, giving Amerindian ritual a participatory quality.

A key word for denoting their essence would be Vision: ritual was used to enhance the perceptive faculties of ordinary consciousness into the greater view that comes with the collective invocation of the spiritual. The Vision Quest is a term of great importance here: all members of the tribe were encouraged and enabled to achieve his or her own personal vision of their place in the natural and supernatural worlds. Fasting and solitude facilitated the Vision Quest, leading to the blending of a new identity in which the lesser sense of self melts into a greater vision of self in relation to other.

Often the successful Vision Quest would lead to the acquisition of a new name, taken from the encounter with spirit helpers, usually in animal form, glimpsed in ecstatic consciousness, and which henceforth were understood to be available as helpers or guardians for the ongoing spiritual unfoldment of the life of each individual in the wider context of the tribal community. Large birds of prey, the eagle or the condor, were seen as the preeminent animals bestowing vision for their faculty of flight and distance viewing. Eagle feathers were worn as sacred objects by plains Indian tribes as a mark of constant remembrance of the necessity to refer even smaller ethical decisions to the wider perspective bestowed by Vision.

The smoking of tobacco, usually in pipes, was also used preeminently in ritual contexts to denote and facilitate the achievement of Vision. Smoke rising was seen as a signifier of prayer, in the way that both smoke and prayers ascend into the air. The sacred peace pipe was also a key part of horizontal ritual in which those ingesting together were henceforth bound in brotherhood and amity, as children of one spirit, offering prayers together toward the unknowable. Ritual dance, music, and chanting were also vital; the Sun Dance ceremonies are one of the best documented examples of the intense self-inflicted pain which Amerindian peoples associated with the pain of achieving completeness. Life for the Amerindian was hard, with ever present concerns over food shortage, dependency on the animals and crops for nourishment, conflict and warfare between tribes, and then the constant pressure of encroaching European civilization.

For males, the path of the warrior was celebrated and affirmed as an example of self-sacrificial giving on behalf of the individual for the sustenance of the community, even to the point of death. In the Sun Dance rituals, the individual braves willingly surrendered themselves to intense pain in order to prove their ability to transcend the normal pain threshold and to rise into a superhuman state of awareness and courage. Even here the underlying ethic was one of interconnectedness: attached to a central tree of life by thongs piercing their breasts, the braves danced around the central tree, acting out dramatically the idea that each individual life is an offering to be given up toward the central axis of being.

More generally, the ritual use of sacred objects figured widely as intrinsic aspects of the Amerindian ethical system. Here the Western mind might be confronted with an intellectual difficulty of appraisal: modernist philosophers tend to see ethics as an abstract, intellectual discipline, in which the cult of the text reigns supreme. Sacred objects and their use in ritual are relegated to a prerational stage of development, belonging to the cult of the Mysteries, which have been largely banished from the groves of Academe (except for graduation ceremonies and the like).

Such objects were drawn almost exclusively from the natural world. Feathers from different birds were highly prized; and sacred stones and rocks were carried for their healing properties. Trees, plants, and herbs; sacred places and sites in nature; and jewelery made of turquoise and coral, or gold and silver, all held a vital place as markers and signs of the greater Medicine Wheel in the context of which Amerindian life was held to have its deepest meanings. Smaller sacred objects were personalized to the owners and carried in medicine bundles which had acquired deep personal meaning over years of use; they were used as adjuncts to meditation and prayer, or for their presumed healing and oracular properties. In this sense, everything could be seen as invested with medicinal properties of psychology value to the well-being of the individual and the tribal community.

V. DRUGS AND THE QUEST FOR VISION

The ritual use of plants raises the important role given to the use of hallucinogenic and consciousness-altering plants and drugs (e.g., peyote) in producing transpersonal or altered-state experiences. The widespread use of mind-altering natural substances as a key part of the Amerindian life cycle is well documented: the peyote cult of North American Indians has continued into modern times as central to their religious rites, and forms the basis of the Native American Church.

Mescalito, the deity presiding over the peyote cactus, is revered as a great spiritual guardian and force of spiritual illumination, accessed through ingesting the buttons of the Mescal cactus (*Lophophora williamsii*), leading to euphoric altered states of consciousness. These experiences lead to an increase of the capacity for Vision, resulting in concomitant emotional states of linkage and connectedness with all aspects of reality. The consciousness of the participant melts into a generalized field of awareness in which distinctions of ego and other blur and fade, instead, what remains is the harmony or pattern running throughout the natural world, with human life being experienced as an integral part of the wider sacred web of existence.

Other drugs are also used among different tribes across the American continent. Psilocybin mushrooms (*Psilocybe mexicana*) were widely used by Central American tribes until being banned by the Spanish conquistadors, and were among the first to be researched and experimented with by Western anthropologists and cross-

cultural explorers and ethnomycologists. Yaghe (ayahuasca, *Bannisteriopsis caapi*) is a vine-derived psychoactive drug used ritually by Colombian Indians which induces intense shamanic visionary experiences under the auspices of its presiding deity, Yaghe. Contemporary experimenters report a flourishing subculture in Colombia using this vine, in which the overarching ethic is one of reverence and love for the female earth deity, creatress and guardian of all life. Cocaine (*Erythroxylon coca*) played a similar role in Inca civilization as a sacred stimulant deified as Mama Coca, being ingested ritually by the Inca royal family until being banned by the Spanish invaders, only to resurface in modern times as a major export crop grown in large parts of South America.

The important point to note about the role all these plants played in Amerindian culture was that their use was tied into a wider web of ethical consciousness, in which the effects of ingesting the sacred plants induced a reorientation of the individual psyche to a wider axis of concern for the web of life in its entirety. The complex ethical and political problems of widespread drug abuse in the contemporary world, and the accompanying blanket condemnation of their use, has to be set against this wider context.

In effect, in the meeting of European and Amerindian cultures, we could be said to have a conflict of different drug cultures, with alcohol being the primary drug ingested by the invaders. In European cultures, alcohol likewise plays a central role in the predominant religious rituals (Christianity), and on the whole its use is managed and controlled by a culture well equipped to handle its excessive use. Likewise Amerindian cultures knew how to use psychoactive drugs and stimulants to achieve positive effects of benefit to the individual and the community.

In recent times, however, both cultural systems have reeled under the forced assimilation of alien drug usage, with the widespread misuse of cocaine and psychedelics by Europeans and of alcohol by Amerindians reaping tragic consequences of psychological damage. Perhaps it is only by sharing cultural values at the deepest possible level, in which drug use would again be placed in a wider ethical and ritual framework as an aid toward transcendent self-discovery, that the solution of this contemporary ethical dilemma can be effected.

VI. ECOETHICS AND AMERINDIAN CULTURE

The significance of ecoethics and attitudes to nature in Amerindian culture is perhaps potentially the most important contribution which Amerindian ethical traditions have to offer to the world's general store of ethical knowledge. As we have seen, the living landscape of the earth is considered holy in and of itself to all Amerindian cultures. Each rock formation, hill, mountain, and river system was experienced as a locus for numinous experience. Such sites were not set apart from the everyday locale of human habitation, but rather human life was seen as played out in the wider environs of sacred landscape.

An ethic of reverence and awe for the beauty of nature runs through all Amerindian ethical teachings, with the result that all the modern conclusions of environmental ethics were already practices observed among Amerindian cultures. Pollution, waste, and environmental damage were seen as religious crimes in which the inherent rights of other living beings were desecrated by human selfishness. The notion that human beings have a sort of divinely sanctioned license to use and abuse natural resources to their own exclusive ends irrespective of their wider environmental effects was completely alien to this indigenous value system based on mutual rights and responsibilities. Rather, all of nature was seen as coparticipating in the continuous creative abundance of natural energies: animals, plants, minerals, and the natural elements were all understood as being part of a greater whole, in which context the human contribution was one of mutual love and harmonious interaction. Such an attitude was not based on sentiment alone, but rather on precise knowledge of the natural world, in all its detail, handed down traditionally from generation to generation, with the result that the ethic of custodianship and conservation was inherent in the general Amerindian ethical framework.

Not surprisingly, then, the influence of Amerindian ideas on contemporary ecophilosophy and conservation movements has been profound, both intellectually and politically. Amerindian spiritual leaders have been outspoken in their calls to the international community to honor and protect the natural resources of both the American continent and globally. The decision by the international community to hold the United Nations Conference on Environment and Development (UNCED) in Brazil in 1992, the then largest ever gathering of world political leaders, to consider the impact of global economic policies on the world's environment was undoubtedly partly inspired by the growing deterioration of the Amazonian rainforest in the face of increasing exploitative development practices.

Amerindian culture does not conceive of the world in conventional economic terms, in which nature's supply of "resources" can be commercially exploited for the benefit of outside interest groups. Far from being a conglomerate of commodities, nature is conceived as a living being with her own inherent value, in which human life is a coparticipant and cobeneficiary. Agricultural practices based on the large-scale monocultural farming of land that have replaced indigenous diversity and small-scale communal husbandry are alien in both thought and application to the ethos underlying the Amerindian relationship to the land. Nutritive crops were deified and respected, being cultivated in cyclical rotation, with accompanying ritual festivals and sacred observances, always with the sense that human beings owed an immense debt of gratitude to the land which sustains us.

Although animals were hunted for food, they were similarly divinized, and our human dependence on the animal world for nourishment and the supply of essential artifacts led to a complex attitude of reverence and respect for each animal species so used. The notion that animals willingly sacrificed themselves for the benefit of humanity was regarded as a teaching for mankind that we should similarly cultivate a willingness to surrender ego and indeed life itself for the benefit of the greater whole.

Widespread and wholesale destruction of animal species, as occurred with the European decimation of the once plentiful bison herds of the North American plains, was literally incomprehensible to the Amerindian mind: it went against every tenet of their indigenous ethical beliefs. The Indians' hunting pattern took pains to preserve the wider species context of the given animal, and permission was always asked of the guiding spirit of the species in question (bison, caribou, seal, etc.), through prayer and invocation, to derive nourishment sufficient to maintain both the human community and the animal species itself.

The Amerindian appreciated the fact that humans have of necessity to uphold an ethic of mutual sustenance, whose main thrust is the continued abundant survival of the entire interconnected web of all living species, rather than the super-dominance of man at the expense of other species. Moving testimonies abound from Amerindian ethical teachers during the 19th century whose voices were raised in prophetic protest against this wanton and needless pattern of slaughter. Such voices undoubtedly influenced many of the forerunners of the conservation movement in modern times, and the whole growing movement worldwide of concern for the environment and the conservation of species derives continuing inspiration from core values which are central to the Amerindian ethical worldview.

The Amerindian nutritive ethic also differed from extreme vegetarianism: the codependent life cycle, in which species sacrifice themselves as food for each other, always maintaining balance and harmony in so doing, was acknowledged as the natural way ordained by the Great Spirit, with an emphasis always on taking the minimum needed for life sustenance, and an attitude of thankfulness.

Another contemporary ethical issue in which an Amerindian voice is being heard concerns the practices of mining corporations throughout the Americas. Uranium mining in the United States and Canada often takes place on Amerindian reservation land. Uranium tailings have created large swathes of desecration over territory which to *homo economicus* is merely waste land awaiting development, but which is sacred to the tribes concerned. High cancer and leukaemia mortality rates among Amerindian peoples due to radioactive pollution released by the uranium industry have been well documented by dissident scientists, and Amerindian spiritual leaders have been outspoken in their attempts to seek legal redress for such injuries, in their attempt to reverse the prevailing practices of the uranium industry.

Disputes over who has the right of access to mine natural resources from the ground is a growing feature of Amerindian concerns, with environmental mediation being developed to seek a middle way of mutual benefit. Likewise, large-scale gold mining, which utilizes cyanide to exact the precious metal from gold-bearing ores, and which leaves in its wake massive lakes of cyanide sludge, doing untold damage to the water table, has also been a matter of great concern.

Again, gold was seen as a sacred metal in Amerindian culture, of largely ritual and ceremonial use, to signify spiritual qualities of benefit to mankind, and it was extracted in nondestructive ways. The idea of gold as a commodity whose value is so great that any environmental damage consequent to its mining is acceptable is a notion alien to the Amerindian ethical system. Gold and all other precious metals and minerals were seen as arising from the ground naturally as offerings from the womb of the earth mother, and their beauty and utility were celebrated as such with thankfulness. But the wider beauty of the tribal community living in harmony with the natural order was more important, and the long-term well-being of its people and their environment were never to be sacrificed to the short-term greed of individuals and enterprises.

VII. ATTITUDES TO THE LAND

At the heart of the Amerindian attitude to nature was a guiding ethic of reverence of the land itself, as a living,

breathing being, on which we move and have our being. The guiding injunction was to "walk lightly on the earth"—to respect and honor the very ground which upholds us all as something sacred in its own right. European notions of exclusive land ownership were therefore something completely alien. The whole idea of the ownership of land did not arise, any more than one can talk of the ownership of wind—the land was the visible body of the divine locus of human existence, and as such inalienable and unownable. Land was owned if at all by the creator of everything, the Great Spirit, and human beings—tribes, communities, and individuals—were merely temporary custodians, placed here to care and love the manifest world.

The gradual process over several hundred years by which native Americans have been marshaled into smaller and smaller strips of territory, cemented by numerous treaties (often broken anyway), has led not only to the material degradation of once proud people, but also to their spiritual alienation and malaise. The essential nomadism of the spirit, in which peoples could wander freely across the land in their hunting cycles, or through their forest terrain, engaging with the ever changing spectacle of the seasons, taking what they needed from each place to sustain them on their cyclical journey, has given way to ever smaller domains to call home, usually on land of the poorest quality, far from their natural habitats.

Not surprisingly, therefore, such alienation has given rise to all kinds of contemporary psychological and social problems on modern Indian reservations, with alcoholism, suicide, and depression being widespread. At the heart of this problem lies a difference of attitudes based in a far-reaching ethical divergence. In one view the land is seen as a common bounty to be shared among all people, in so far as they are able to live in harmony and reverence on it, and the concept of ownership is replaced by that of custodianship. In the second view land is seen merely as a commodity to be bought and sold for personal gain and for commercial exploitation regardless of the wider environmental impact of such practices.

The overall Amerindian ethos could be summed up by the teaching that each generation has responsibility for its actions to the seventh generation; that is, each action that one undertakes should be assessed and weighed for its likely impact and consequences on one's descendants, up to the seventh generation hence. If one seriously reflects on each undertaking in this spirit, it was held that one is less likely to commit mistakes and errors, misguidedly pursing actions which may result in seeming good results for one's own immediate advantage, yet which have long-term detrimental effects. This principle, which in many ways can be seen as a deepening and temporal extension of Kant's basic ethical position, has become well known as a touchstone for environmental ethicists in general and has been widely adopted beyond the bounds of Amerindian culture per se.

VIII. SHAMANISM

A further key question to be considered is the relationship between Amerindian ethical culture and shamanic beliefs in general. Can we categorize Amerindian spirituality as a subcategory of shamanism in general? Originally identified from the scientific study of religious practices among the Ural-Altaic peoples of central Asia, shamanism has come to be used as the generic descriptor of a pattern of spiritual practice widely held by primal peoples in large parts of the world—in Asia, the Pacific Islands, Melanesia, parts of Africa, and indeed throughout the Americas. Mircea Eliade's pioneering study (1951. *Shamanism: Archaic techniques of ecstasy.* Bollingen Foundation, Princeton University Press.) has now been supplemented by a large descriptive and analytic literature detailing the key motifs of shamanic beliefs. The factor that gives a particular importance to the study of shamanism is that we are here confronted with a system of spirituality which in all probability most closely answers to the Ur beliefs of most if not all of humankind, once practiced by all ancestors of modern man throughout the globe.

As might be expected from preliterate cultural patterns, it is difficult to ascribe consistent and comprehensively formulated systems of belief and practice to shamanism, which was rather a pragmatic and experiential attempt by early mankind to respond to the existential condition of life in nature, characterized by its harsh and challenging conditions. It is possible, however, to distinguish certain key characteristics which occur wherever shamanism is operative, including Amerindian practices.

One such characteristic is a focus on healing, for the shaman is preeminently a healer, using magic powers, particularly the spirit flight, to effect healing, both physical and spiritual. Illness is often thought of as a case of "soul loss" in which the integrity of body, mind, and spirit has been damaged, and the living soul of the patient has been captured or alienated by harmful spirits. The healer in this case would undertake an often arduous inner journey in which he or she would, in the spirit world, travel in search of the misplaced soul

in order to restore it to full conscious union with the patient's body. Such healings were often communal ritual affairs, accompanied by singing and drumming, leading to a state of trance in which the shaman would himself willingly undergo an out-of-the-body experience. Shamans were in effect priests and doctors (in Amerindian culture known as medicine men), whose primary ethical concern was caring, working as healers and doctors, and often possessing significant knowledge of healing herbs and other natural remedies in addition to their supernormal abilities.

The path to becoming a shaman in Amerindian traditions, as in other primal cultures, was by way of personal vocation. The apprentice shaman would have himself undergone some kind of death and rebirth experience, which precipitated his desire to help share his knowledge of the supernatural terrain for the benefit of his fellows. Lucid and extraordinary dreams were also seen as containing healing significance but were similarly a spontaneous occurrence which might result in the recipient being projected along the path of becoming a medicine man. Naturally the context in which such experiences were interpreted varied from tribe to tribe, but the overall context was always the same: animal beings were seen as beneficent spirits who would assist the shaman in his work of healing, shaman's being able to summon particular species of helpers according to their own personal histories of encounter and spiritual interaction.

The regalia of the shaman was impressive, using the full panoply of healing accoutrements, sacred objects, stones, feathers, herbs, natural medicinal compounds, prayers, musical instruments, and sometimes psychoactive substances to aid in the achievement of extrasensory perceptive diagnosis and therapy. Interestingly, many of the healing effects achieved by shamans mirror certain practices which modern medical science has also come to value in the form of psychotherapy and analysis. Similarly much of the natural medical wisdom possessed traditionally by Amerindian medicine men has been validated by modern scientific medical pharmacology as constituting a priceless store of intuitive and traditional healing knowledge whose gradual loss over past centuries is only now being repaired through a mutual exchange of methodologies by both practitioner groups.

The experiential study of shamanism has also become of greater interest, with a number of anthropologists and cross-cultural explorers sitting at the feet of traditional shamanic healers to experience from the inside some of the secrets of their craft. A further feature of Amerindian medicine which deserves consideration is the high degree of significance attached to crystals and sacred rocks by Amerindian teachings. Crystals were held to be luminous vehicles for the manifestation of spiritual power by Amerindian shamans and medicine men long before their adoption by the modern "New Age" movement. Mention should also be made in this context of the phenomenal growth of interest in shamanism in general, and Amerindian shamanism in particular, by students and practitioners from non-Amerindian backgrounds, who nevertheless see in these teachings insights of extraordinary ethical value.

IX. THE MEDICINE WHEEL

The importance of the native Indian concept of "medicine" cannot be overemphasized. The "medicine man" was the primary repository for the ethical teachings of each tribe, and was seen as the holder of the wisdom which lay as the guarantor of the continued well-being of the community. What did this wisdom consist of at its root?

The primary architectonic against which illness, healing, and ethical action were measured is what is known in North Amerindian culture as the Medicine Wheel or the Sacred Hoop. This can best be understood as a way of systematizing the balanced and harmonious relationships between all phenomena in nature which were felt to underlie existence, and whose interflowing cycles held the key to the mysteries of change and transformation. As modern science and medicine could be said to rely on the periodic table of the elements for its primary analytic framework, so Amerindian ethics relied on the Medicine Wheel. How exactly did it work? Each direction in space was seen as embodying not simply a geographical space, but also an ideal topography, correlating to certain spiritual and noumenal qualities as follows:

East: illumination, light, fire, eagle, birth, entry, initiation, clarity, spiritual body, wisdom of the spirit, gold color, faculty of vision
South: water, emotional body, heart wisdom, sea green color, faculty of feeling
West: earth, physical body, body wisdom, reddish-black color, faculty of sensing
North: air, mental body, wisdom of the mind, bluish-white color, faculty of thinking

These spatial coordinates correlate with an entire psychic wholeness denoting the full complexity of human experience. They are a way of typologizing the disparateness of life—of synthesizing apparent chaos into an ordered pattern of meanings. Their importance as the bedrock of Amerindian ethical teachings cannot be overemphasized. Every act of ethical decision making and every act of ceremony or ritual observance, from the briefest moment of individual prayer to large-scale communal rites involving entire tribal groupings, were placed within the overall context of this conceptual and spiritual framework.

The ethical importance of the Medicine Wheel could perhaps be best summed up by the idea of achieving wholeness through balance: implicit in the Medicine Wheel is the idea that all reality depends on the complex interaction of a pattern of balancing forces. Out of their creative tension arises all the phenomena of being, inner and outer, and within which field of energies we human beings live out the structures of our lives. Different individuals may be oriented toward different propensities, taking protection from the ruling spirits of different cardinal directions: they would take power and guidance from that source in order to inform and inspire them when confronted by difficult choices.

At different times of life this basic orientation might change; indeed it was expected to do so, for the Wheel was not conceived of as static. Rather, the journey of life was itself a journey of circumambulation from the point of birth in the east, toward the mastery of the emotional body in the south, through the mature familiarity with physical reality achieved in the west, and returning to the north and the way of wisdom in old age. Similarly, the sun's wheel moved from east to west during the course of the day, returning again to the east overnight for rebirth, mirroring the journey of souls from life to life, for metempsychosis (in various forms) was sometimes implicit in the teachings of the Medicine Wheel, and is certainly so today.

It is worth noting here that teachings concerning the Medicine Wheel are regarded as the innermost secrets of Amerindian spiritual culture, and while the basic framework of understanding is readily available to inquirers, there is considerable debate within the contemporary Amerindian community as to the wisdom of sharing too detailed a knowledge of their more esoteric teachings with representatives of other cultures. This debate indicates one thing of primary importance: that Amerindian ethical culture is a living tradition, sustained and revitalized by lineages of spiritual teachers over the several centuries of Western cultural dominance, and which has reemerged in recent years to assert its own unique perspective on matters of spirituality and ethics on equal terms with other such similar systems worldwide.

In fact equivalents of the Medicine Wheel are found in most other ethical systems worldwide, with similar use being made of the cardinal directions as correlates of spiritual principles. In European culture, alchemy and the hermitic tradition, freemasonry, witchcraft, and astrology all make use of a similar spatial correlation, as do their equivalents in Islamic Sufism, Jewish Kabbalah teachings, and Christian esotericism. The basic principles of sacred architecture likewise follow similar ideas, with the primary orientation of temples and churches toward the east, for instance, being true of sacred structures such as Stonehenge, Newgrange, or King Solomon's Temple in Jerusalem. In Chinese traditions, the elements and the directions were similarly organized into an overall pattern of meaning.

Interestingly, the precise correlations seem to differ from culture to culture: the Amerindian correlations given above are different than those of the Chinese, the European, the Asian Indian, etc. Does this mean then that none of them are really "true," that we are dealing here with a set of widespread but irrational beliefs? The point surely is that we are in an area of psychological truth, which serves the given community with a binding structure of meaning, giving harmony and wholeness to the wider network of relationships of which life itself exists. The fact that the precise orientations vary from culture to culture is far less important than the fact that most premodern spiritual traditions seem to have at their heart some sort of system of spatiopsychological orientation. In fact, in a relativistic world, one would surely expect different cultures to view things differently, since their viewing places are different, situated in different geographical regions, with different elemental associations for different directions. Paradoxically, the very diversity of correlations is both evidence of the profound psychological need being addressed here, and the underlying wisdom of the whole idea manifesting as the Medicine Wheel.

Recognizing that without some such system of sacred cartography the individual soul is lost and literally disoriented, knowledge of the Medicine Wheel was traditionally imparted to Amerindians during the course of their own individuation through the cycle of rituals accompanying their growth toward maturity, as it still is, wherever the bonds of their own ethical teachings have held strong. Arguably, Amerindian teachings about the Medicine Wheel hold a key of knowledge of greater service to the contemporary human predicament than other such systems, for whereas in Western culture, for instance, the cosmic mandala has largely deteriorated into popular astrological prognostic systems, and in China into a system of divination and geomancy, Amerindian culture preserves a far greater degree of individual freedom and responsibility.

Each individual is taught the basic correlations as a tool for making sense of events and situations, but there is no sense of inevitability or predestination about the system. One is given the map and then left free to experience, to wander on the pilgrimage of life from place to place, all of them equally sacred although diverse. The spiritual tolerance and maturity evidenced in Amerindian ethical thought at its most mature undoubtedly owes much to the idea of unity-in-diversity implicit in the Medicine Wheel: each quadrant offers vision and learning appropriate to its station, in which the guiding form is the circle rather than a hierarchical orientation as found in many other so-called advanced cosmological patterns. Amerindian ethical thought could indeed be designated as "circle wisdom" in which all points of the compass are equally proximate to the central, ineffable Great Spirit whose domain is the center and the transcendant.

X. COSMOLOGY

As we have seen, then, the cosmological context of Amerindian ethical beliefs was primary in providing an overarching spatiopsychological cartography to enable individual life decisions to be referred to a greater context, both communal and cosmic. Of equal importance was the Amerindian understanding of time, creation, eschatology, and the relationship between different worlds. The understanding of the interrelations of this world to other worlds gave a basic humility and sacredness to the Amerindian worldview.

Most Amerindian traditions speak of a cycle of world creations, in which our existing human world is but one. The Hopi Indians, for example, speak of our world as being the fourth in a cycle of worlds, whose successive creation and destruction is essentially an ethical teaching. The first world (Tokpela), a place of purity and innocence, was eventually destroyed by fire due to the increasing confusion and ignorance among the first peoples: only a chosen, specially instructed remnant of humanity being saved. The second world (Tokpa) was destroyed by water after greed and competition for material goods had overcome human beings—again only a remnant were saved.

The third world (Kuskurza) followed the same pattern, being peopled extensively by cities and people skilled in all manner of crafts and trades, until evil also overcame it and it too was destroyed by a great flood which washed away all trace of its former civilizations.

Emerging again, the survivors peopled the fourth world (Tuwaqachi), which is the one we now inhabit. The ethical import of this drama is self-evident: unless we too maintain harmony and a sense of loyalty to cosmic law, our world also will be subject to destruction as were the previous three.

Recently Hopi teachers have shared further teachings from their vast store of oral culture, urgently advising and admonishing non-Amerindian peoples to return to the observance of cosmic law as the creator intended, to fulfill our part in the grand harmony of creation with humility and reverence, or to suffer the disastrous consequences. There is nothing fixed or inevitable about the ethical deterioration of mankind, however.

The Navaho and Hopi nations among others also predict the possibility of a fifth world of peace arriving if we can learn to master our negative energies and to control our destructive and violent natures. They understand the sacred purpose of their sharing their ethical vision with other peoples at this time to be a way of hastening the arrival of this fifth world of harmony and peace, which has been prophesied by many of their spiritual leaders. Given the suffering experienced by Indian nations at the hands of Western conquerors over generations, it is surely a mark of their spiritual maturity that their eschatological predictions are inclusive, rather than full of revenge. In the fifth world of peace, people of all nations, all cultures, and all religions will learn to live in harmony and fellowship, respecting the ways of nature and living according to the cosmic laws of sufficiency, mutuality, and love.

XI. THE DARKER SIDES OF AMERINDIAN CULTURE

The double record of Amerindian ethical culture in practice is historically well known, particularly from Central America, where the practice of human sacrifice is all too well attested. This presents the student of Amerindian ethics and spirituality with very serious problems of appraisal and analysis, since it is hard to retain conventional academic "epoche," nor indeed is it clear why one should try to do so. Undoubtedly, Aztec culture in particular had succumbed to practices of ritual human sacrifice on a massive scale, which were in turn caught up in warfare and organized violence on a large scale.

Rather than simply condemn, however, our purpose here is to understand, and from an empathic perspective, since it must be remembered that human sacrifice and cannibalism seem to have been part of most if not all primitive cultural traditions at certain stages of their past, including European.

Recent studies have confirmed the widespread prevalence of human sacrifice throughout the Amerindian peoples from prehistoric times onward. Aztec culture was the most notorious and best documented example of such practices on a massive scale. Intimately associated with the pursuit of warfare, human sacrificial victims were usually taken from the large numbers of prisoners taken in battle by the Aztec warriors, who were a fierce warrior class which achieved dominance in what became known as Mexico in the few centuries prior to the arrival of the Spaniards. The Aztec priesthood cloaked these mass sacrificial rites with an aura of sanctity, in which the bleeding hearts of the victims were sundered from the breasts of living victims as an offering to the Sun God. Their understanding was that the deity required such ritual human sacrifices on a regular basis in order to sustain the cosmos as we know it. We are entitled to ask what kind of ethical outlook gave rise to such notions.

Recorded in detail by the Franciscan Friar Bernadino de Sahagun, on the basis of extensive research, interviews, etc., we learn that the cult of human sacrifice was intimately connected to the overall religious atmosphere pervading Aztec culture. Victims were dressed up in complex, multicoloured regalia, and a veritable pageantry of killing accompanied their end. Sometimes the victims were accorded semidivine status, and regarded as if the embodiment of deities themselves, being given pre-execution honors, awarded concubines for their pleasure, etc., before meeting their end in full ritual splendor at the hands of the officiating priests. It could be argued that these displays were an evolved ritual drama teaching certain basic ethical ideas concerning the frailty and evanescence of human life: since life invariably ends in death anyway, why not celebrate death in full glory, making a pageant out of it? People no doubt went away from these spectacles doubly focused on the preciousness of their mortal existence, determined to enjoy life's fleeting pleasures while they may.

A body of poetry has also come down from Aztec culture which maintains this basic ethical attitude, that mankind's wisest stance is a sort of philosophical hedonism in the face of inevitable doom and death. Deeper teachings are also ascertainable, namely, that the Gods themselves, taking on the form of their victims, are offered as a sacrifice by the priests as a lesson of their own beneficence and magnanimity in allowing our lives here to be maintained at the cost of their own spectacular sufferings. Some scholars have also argued that human sacrifice reached such large-scale proportions in ancient Mexico in order to provide a needed dietary supplement, since usually victims were also ingested afterward by those in attendance. While there have been even a few recent instances of cannibalism in extremis for reason of survival (the Donner mission, plane crashes, etc.), the evidence shows that this was not the primary reason for Amerindian practice, which was rather bound up with their ritual practices.

While Aztec culture has had the worst press, it is important to realize that these practices were widespread throughout most Amerindian cultures, albeit on a lesser scale. The Carib Indians indeed gave their name to "cannibalism" per se; the Yamessee Indians on the Savannah River, the Natchez of the Lower Mississippi, The Cherokee, the Hurons, The Iroquois, the Shawnee, the Algonkians, the Hasirai, and the Kwakiutls of the far northwest all provide documentary and witness evidence of atrocities, e.g., slow killing of captives by torture, usually accompanied by ritual glorification. Among the Kwakiutls, a subsect of Hamatsas, a sort of initiatory brotherhood bound by gruesome ties, regularly consumed human flesh.

Among the Incas and their forebears, the Olmecs and Moche Indians, evidence of human sacrificial rites dates back to at least 2000 B.C., while at the height of the Inca Empire in the Peruvian Andes instances of human sacrifice usually accompanied the death of royalty. Other tribes in South America known to practice ritual human sacrifice included the Aucas of Colombia, and the Jivaros of Ecuador, and the Tupinambas of Brazil. Even today in contemporary South America, strange sects seem to flourish from time to time which advocate ritual human sacrifice as somehow required by their understanding of the divine.

While all these actions are a matter of factual record, the interpretations and causal explanations remain a matter of controversy, as do the implications for an overall assessment of Amerindian ethics. Some contemporary apologists for the nobility of Amerindian culture are quick to point out that some of the worst practices of torture were learned from the European conquerors of the Americas. The point has also been well made that at the time of the European conquest the Inquisition and the witchburning craze were in full swing, and it has been estimated that the King of Spain, for example, through the practices of the Spanish Inquisition (which was directly answerable to the monarch rather than to the Pope), managed an annual head count of some 400 souls executed by burning and torture for reasons of suspected heresy. Jews, Moriscos, witches, and assorted dissidents were dispatched in religious executions as gruesome as those of the Amerindian natives.

Likewise Protestant colonial powers, during the period of their expansion in the New World, also engaged in a mass campaign of religious slaughter of suspected witches and other religious deviants (including Catholics, and especially Jesuits) whose total number of victims amounted to some several millions.

Nevertheless, and given the fact that ritual cannibalism was practiced in the Amerindian context, the implications for our understanding of Amerindian ethics of such practices could be summed up by saying that in Amerindian culture we have a living record of some of the darker and more primal instincts and practices, such as human sacrifice and cannibalism, lasting for a longer period than in many other cultures. The tragic implications of this, however, are not confined merely to an assessment of Amerindian ethics, since all the evidence points to the fact that at some stage in their evolution all human societies indulged in ritual human sacrifice and cannibalism, from the earliest Palaeolithic times onward. It could be said that in Amerindian culture we have a dark mirror for the human condition per se, which raises many awkward and still unresolved questions.

What is it about this darker aspect of human beings which causes us to ritually kill one another, even in the belief that such behavior has divine sanction? What social and psychological forces impel human beings to such acts of cruelty and violence? The teachings of Amerindian ethics on these questions would seem congruous with certain gnostic traditions, namely, that there are indeed forces of malevolence and darkness implicit in the very fabric of existence, against whose overwhelming power human beings are frail and weak by comparison, veritable playthings of the Gods. Since death and violence seem implicit in the way creation is organized, the Amerindian response was to act out this violence in a ritualized manner, believing that thereby even worse calamities and destruction were being obviated.

Furthermore, the entire thrust of Amerindian spirituality was to follow a way of humility and balance, attempting to walk the way of life in the light of the Medicine Wheel, or its equivalent, and to achieve some sort of harmony, a balancing of the complex features of the human psyche in the midst of nature and grandeur of the cosmos, embracing head on the danger and challenges involved in human life, and yet doing so with courage and dignity while striving to achieve harmony and full humanhood even in the face of the immense terror at the darker aspects of existence. This is the reason that Amerindian ethical teachings have such poignancy, both such as have come down historically and such as are practiced and disseminated today, for there is nothing in Amerindian tradition that seeks to flee or explain away the darker forces of life and death; rather they are confronted, challenged, and accommodated through ritual and spiritual practice and through the cultivation of an inner attitude of humility and stoicism in the face of the incomprehensible powers of existence, in a way which is of universal significance. Here is the essential struggle of light and dark, or good and evil, working out their drama in the human soul and raising questions which no culture has as yet managed to answer convincingly—while the forms of killing may differ, the mass killing fields of modern warfare, even among so-called civilized nations, hardly indicated much greater success in understanding and taming the more negative regions of the human psyche.

XII. WAR AND PEACE

At this point it is appropriate to turn to a consideration of Amerindian attitudes to war and peace, given that many of the difficult issues already considered also involved warfare and organised tribal violence. Studies of warfare in tribal societies worldwide indicate that while organized violence seems to be a feature of most tribal cultures, in most cases the levels of actual violence and killing are more restricted than in advanced societies.

Instead, warfare among Amerindian tribal peoples was more a ritualistic display of bravery and resourcefulness in which the chief aim was to uphold the honor of one's own tribal grouping against rivals. Practices of mass slaughter or genocide, induced environmental destruction, etc., were unknown, as was the idea of a professional soldiery in a western sense, dedicated to killing. Instead, when warfare broke out between neighboring tribes, all able-bodied males took part, following ritual blessings and invocations of the deities, in campaigns which often involved daring, bravado, and surprise attack.

The practice of "counting coup" was of primary importance here, denoting a way in which individual acts of bravery were accorded greatest significance during warfare, in which tokens showing the successful humiliation of one's opponent were celebrated and given ritual acknowledgment. The ruthless slaughter or violation of one's opponents and their families, on the other hand, would have been taken as showing moral weakness and

imbecility on the part of otherwise honorable braves. Counting coup could be achieved in a number of ways: stealing your enemy's horse, striking him, seizing his medicine bundle, or taking his weapons; only as a last resort did it involve killing him. The practice of scalping was taught to the Amerindians of North America by European trappers who used to sell such scalps to their wealthy fellows as a token of the "savagery" of their enemies.

Nevertheless, one must not over romanticize the point: once galvanized, Amerindian peoples were every bit as warlike as their European enemies, and as capable of committing acts of torture and brutality. It would seem that this propensity exists in all peoples, whether primitive or "civilized," the only difference being the degree of professionalism brought to the task. Where Amerindian culture itself reached degrees of urbanization, as in Central America and among the Incas, warfare also reached a higher degree of sophistication and became something of a regular sport practiced by the nobility at the expense of ordinary people. As we have seen, captives taken in battle were often later ritually sacrificed as offerings to the deities.

However, the overriding desire for peace also was etched into the ethical outlook of Amerindian culture, and a number of moving testimonies remain of Amerindian leaders who appealed for peace and harmony to prevail in relations with the Europeans, and between their own tribes. Over the past centuries of contact, a number of leaders also emerged who advocated a specific vision of brotherhood to replace prevailing armed anarchy. Several tribes also developed advanced political mechanisms for resolving differences without recourse to open warfare. Certainly, whenever disputes did arise, it was always felt to be favorable to try to resolve such matters by open debate in tribal or intertribal council, and the elders were expected to play the role of arbiter and mediator if at all possible. In such cases, recourse was also held to the dimension of the transcendent when particularly difficult quarrels were felt to require considerable meditation and prayer as an aid to seeing a way to solve the problem.

The military history of Amerindian culture has been more or less one of continual defeat, with the gradual encroachment on their tribal territories of European conquerors, and the often cynical abrogation of treaties and agreements which ought to have preserved their rights more securely. There were of course several spectacular military successes achieved, but these individual victories did little to reverse the general trend of overall defeat. Even to this day, however, the problem of whether one should use violence in defense of one's cultural rights has not been fully resolved among Amerindian peoples.

In recent decades, there have been several incidents in which young Amerindian rights activists have taken arms against government agents, in both the USA and Canada. In Latin America, Amerindians constitute a high proportion of the membership of revolutionary groups who have taken to armed struggle against their political overlords. At the same time, many Amerindians have also taken their part in the peace movement, inspired by the transcultural possibilities of nonviolent resistance to oppression and injustice, and contemporary Amerindian ethical teachers and cultural leaders as a whole are sketching out a path of cultural coexistence and convergence at the highest possible levels of mutual understanding and tolerance, drawing on the native Medicine Wheel teachings to teach harmony and balance between all peoples, and to call mankind to the great promise of a new age of multicultural harmony and spiritual unity as prophesied in their most sacred traditions.

In this regard, Amerindian military eschatology seems utterly devoid of the idea of the necessity of final revenge or apocalyptic warfare before the final triumph of "the good" over the "evil others" who can then be scapegoated and destroyed. On the contrary, Amerindian ethics would seem to offer a more inclusive worldview, an understanding that all peoples have committed acts of heroism as well as acts of cruelty, and a teaching that the real victory will come when all peoples rise up to achieve their highest potential and live harmoniously with one another, sharing the fruits of the earth and respecting the sacred ways of all peoples.

In this respect, the voices of contemporary Amerindian ethical leaders are beginning to be heard in international congresses devoted to the search for peace between representatives of all different religions, participating, for example, in the Sixth World Congress of Religion and Peace held in the Vatican and Riva del Garda, Italy, in November 1994, the first ever such major interfaith gathering held in the Vatican (inside the College of Cardinals in the presence of Pope John Paul 2nd), where the author had the privilege of discussing Amerindian spiritual approaches to peace with a number of representatives of Amerindian ethical teachings. In the search for peace, no one religious or ethical tradition has all the answers. Contemporary Amerindian leaders recognize as much as anyone that we all need to sit together to discuss and share our paths and perspectives to effect the healing of the legacy of violence that still threatens us all.

XIII. SPIRITUALITY AND PRAYER

Prayer and meditation were and are an essential aspect of Amerindian ethical culture. The overall ethic of interconnectedness adhered to arose out of lived spiritual experience, rather than being a superimposition derived from intellectual categories. The idea of formal times set aside for prayer in the sense of other religious traditions was somewhat alien to these people. Every moment is seen as holy, every day has the potential of being a sacred or holy day or Sabbath, and within the heart of each moment an attitude of prayerfulness should be cultivated. Such was the overriding attitude of the Amerindian, for whom spiritual practice and everyday life went hand in hand, the sphere of the sacred penetrating the sphere of the mundane without separation.

At the same time, the general attitude of prayerfulness was felt to be heightened by traveling through particular places and times, which were felt to be strongly endowed with numinous power. Special features of the landscape, mesas (rock formations), rivers, waterfalls, oases, particular trees, etc., could generate strong feelings of awe and religious sanctity, and it was felt that prayers offered at these places would have particular power. Tobacco was a ubiquitous symbol of prayer. Smoked symbolically and sparingly in ceremonial pipes, rather than consumed addictively as in the modern world, the ascending blue-gray smoke was felt to symbolize the ascending spiritual intent arising from the depths of the human soul at the moment of prayer.

Prayers could either be spoken aloud, in the form of supplication, or uttered silently in the mind as pure thought. Sometimes they could be sung as chants, often to the accompaniment of rhythmic drumming or dancing and the stamping of feet. The overall attitude expressed was one of spiritual humility and thankfulness in which individuals recognize their loving dependence on the supreme spiritual source of creation as embodied above all in nature. Amerindian prayers praise nature for her gifts and beauties, and give thanks to the Great Spirit for the chance to be a part of creation. They express the feeling that mankind is intimately a part of nature, one aspect of an indivisible whole.

Sometimes there is great poignancy and grief over the destruction, violence, and pain which Amerindian culture has witnessed in the recent past, yet such sorrow always manages to rise above bathos to a call for healing and repair out of faith that the spiritual source is indeed powerful enough to effect such transformation.

Grandfather,
Look at our brokenness.
We know that in all creation
Only the human family
Has strayed from the Sacred Way.
We know that we are the ones
Who are divided
And we are the ones
Who must come back together
To walk in the Sacred Way.
Grandfather,
Sacred One,
Teach us love, compassion and honor
That we may heal the earth
and heal each other.

(OJIBWAY PRAYER)

As we can see, then, Amerindian prayer life belongs to the universal heritage of human spirituality, on an equal footing with any of the other great spiritual traditions of humanity. Recently, spiritual pilgrims from other cultures have been making bridges of transcultural exploration in an effort to understand the dynamics of Amerindian spiritual life from within. A Roman Catholic priest, for example, has been invited to participate in the sacred ceremonies of the sacred pipe, one of the holiest sacred objects of Amerindian culture, a gift to mankind from the White Buffalo Woman.

The importance of prayer as the originating context of Amerindian ethics cannot be overemphasized. Defining prayer as the ritual consecration of consciousness through the use of sacred speech, we can see how the whole orientation of consciousness toward an ethical life evolves out of this consecration, the sense that there is indeed a greater context, a "transcendent holiness" who is the object or recipient of one's prayers.

Similarly, then, there is a transcendent otherness which is the field in which one's individual actions are to be placed and weighed. Neither thoughts, deeds, nor prayers take place in a vacuum, but rather ripple out from soul to soul—such is the basic experience arising from this orientation. Such an attitude, without which prayer is impossible, requires both a spiritual humility and a sense of interconnectedness between one's own interior subjectivity and the cosmic and natural world around us. There is a web of sympathy connecting mind to mind, and spirit to spirit, and this mind and spirit are woven behind the tapestry of nature, which the Amerindian knew so well. Just as the ethical life of Amerindians was a "natural ethics" arising from their observation of and participation in the processes of the world of nature (the seasons, the interplay of the elements and plant life, the practices of the animal

world in all their glorious complexity), so too was their spirituality and prayer life a natural orientation arising from their lived response to the awesome beauty of nature and the vast American continent in all its diversity and grandeur in which they found themselves.

XIV. THE METAPHYSICAL SUBSTRATUM OF AMERINDIAN ETHICS

As we have seen, the practice of prayer depended for Amerindian consciousness on the notion of a "transcendent holiness." We must next ask exactly how this notion, often translated into English as "the Great Spirit," influenced the Amerindian ethical system—what thinking or spiritual experience lay behind the belief in the Great Spirit, and how did such belief differ from the more traditional, Euro-Mediterranean-derived understanding of God?

The Great Spirit had many different names in different tribal languages, e.g., Wakontaka (Oglala, Lakota, Dakota), Wakanda (Sioux, Omaha), Itzmana (Mayan), Mahpiyato (South Dakota), Tungrangayak (Eskimo), Wah-Kon-Tah (Osage), Taiowa (Hopi). There seem to be four interconnected levels of conceptualization among Amerindians concerning the nature of ultimate reality. On the one hand, gods, deities, or spiritual beings of a higher order than humankind were visioned along animal, human, or vegetative lines as superhuman equivalents to their terrestrial counterparts. Thus, the ideal archetype of the spider, eagle, condor, snake, or corn plant figures often in the creation stories of the Amerindians. At a second level, the entire earth itself was often seen as something sacred and divine, an earth mother being, with the divine father symbolized by the sky or the spirit behind the sun.

At a third level, Amerindians conceptualized the Great Spirit, an intangible, numinous, felt presence which though mysterious and awesome, was yet compassionate, wise, all loving, and all creative, containing within itself all the mysterious powers of the creative process as manifesting on every other realm in the cosmos. Beyond even the Great Spirit was the acknowledged, intangible sustaining source of all beings and of all universes, and the source even of the creativity of the Great Spirit. This ultimate level of being could only be expressed as a term, which translates as the Great Mystery. Through prayer and the enactment of sacred rituals, it was felt that human beings were able to enter into participative communion with all these various metaphysical levels of being.

Although certain classes or individuals, medicine men and women or shamans, had a peculiarly intimate knowledge of the inner terrains of spirit, and were able to manipulate and navigate their own psyches along the inner worlds, Amerindian metaphysics did not subscribe to the view that only an esoteric elite could have contact with the spiritual worlds. All humans were born with an innate knowledge of the creative powers which had endowed them with life, and by searching in themselves, in the webs of their own experiences, and above all in the phenomena of the natural world, it was felt possible and appropriate to call on the divine beings who direct our destiny for guidance and illumination.

It is important here to emphasize again that while Amerindian culture did not until recently produce a literate tradition of ethical and metaphysical analysis, it did bring forth a highly evolved hermeneutics of nature in which the texts presented in the natural world, of stones, trees, mountains, rivers, winds, animals, and precious minerals and metals, were interpreted metaphysically as representative signs or manifestations of spiritual and creative power. It was in learning to navigate their lives through the way of everyday nature that Amerindians developed both their ethical and their metaphysical orientation.

Such attitudes fitted congruously with certain motifs prevalent in the deist Enlightenment which developed in both Europe and the Americas simultaneously with the gradual intellectual discovery of Amerindian beliefs and practices, and also later in the Romantic movement which carried forward a similar pantheistic project concerning a reevaluation of the sacredness of nature. Although the full history of the direct and indirect influence of Amerindian ethical beliefs on the history of global ethics has yet to be written, a few pointers need to be mentioned here to indicate fruitful lines of research.

XV. AMERINDIAN AND OTHER WESTERN ETHICAL SYSTEMS

The discovery and evaluation of the significance of Amerindian culture by European intellectuals has a complex history, not without controversy, and the utmost significance for more mainstream intellectual history. The fact that the Americas were "rediscovered" at the time of the Renaissance is the first major fact to note: 1492, the year of Columbus's first voyage to the Americas, coincided with the full flood of Renaissance human-

ist thinking, centered initially in Florence and other Italian mercantile centers, and radiating out across Europe from the Kremlin to St. Andrews.

The "discovery" of Amerindians caused great internal debates in the Catholic church. Did Amerindians have souls? Was their genealogy traced in Genesis? If Christianity was indeed the universal truth intended by God for all mankind, why had it taken the divine planners so long to transmit the "good news" to so large a portion of humanity? The discovery of so vast a continent, complete with advanced urban civilizations with their own inherent spiritual traditions, posed a major challenge to the worldview of medieval Christianity in its rearguard battle against the rising forces of humanism, skepticism, and scientific relativism then gaining ascendancy.

Champions appeared to argue for the legal rights of native Amerindians, questioning from within the teachings of Catholicism the unjust enslavement of native peoples. Bartholomew de Las Casas (1474–1566), at first a wealthy Hispanic landowner in Hispaniola, underwent a conversion and became a Dominican monk, horrified at the excesses he had witnessed, and subsequently devoted his entire life to defending the natural rights of native Americans. His writings, notably, *The History of the Indies,* argued with impassioned and meticulous scholarship against the triumphalist ethic of conquest and slavery that demonized and dehumanized native Americans.

While a host of other unsung Catholic conscience bearers followed Bartholomew in trying to defend the rights of native Americans (such as Thomas of Berlanga, the First Bishop of Panama), the initial revulsion against Amerindian culture occasioned by reports of human sacrifice and cannibalism led to a general ethic of neglect and destruction in which the Catholic mind sought conquest and conversion and even extermination as the carrying out of God's will for the natives.

While interest in the details of Amerindian belief systems was largely restricted to scholars, gradually a slow cultural convergence took place in Latin American countries, in which native customs and spiritual beliefs intermingled colorfully with Catholicism in a creative symbiosis which allowed both European and native elements to coexist side by side. The importance given to the Virgin Mary in Catholicism, for example, married well with the native traditions of divine feminine deities, usually associated with the fruitfulness of the earth and the fertility of nature. The strong aesthetic content of Catholic ritualism also tallied well with the love of pageantry and religious ritual existing in native Amerindian culture.

The Catholic church left a shadow long and deep across Amerindian culture, often through the agency of the religious orders, whose overall effects have yet to be chronicled and assessed comprehensively. One particular Franciscan professor of Lullian Philosophy from the University of Majorca left a particularly prescient mark. From his post in Spain, Fray Junipero Serra was sent to hold the Chair of Philosophy at the University of Mexico for several years before being sent, at the express wish of the king of Spain, to conduct a mission among the native American tribes of California. Although he would have much preferred to remain in his academic studies of Raymond Lull's *Ars Magna,* with its promise of a universal system of spiritual logic to decode the nature of existence, Fray Junipero found himself giving birth to the sequence of mission stations that to this day line the Californian coast, choosing names for them from his religious nomenclature, out of which humble beginnings great cities of global significance have subsequently sprung: Los Angeles, San Diego, San Francisco, which in turn gave birth to the founding of the United Nations.

While scholars still argue over the details, it can be stated confidently that the discovery of the New World gave a decisive impetus to the forces of change working in European culture, eventuating in the Reformation (and Counter-Reformation) and eventually the Enlightenment. The notion of a New World, peopled with "noble savages," a "virgin" land ready and waiting for the outflow of the most creative impulses of an expanding, world-oriented Renaissance culture, provided both a physical and an intellectual stimulus to the inquiring minds of the day.

Francis Bacon, who was active in British colonial ventures in the New World, provided in his *New Atlantis* an idealized response to this stimulus: a Renaissance thinker par excellence, warts and all, Bacon represents the tradition of utopian intellectuals giving birth simultaneously to new intellectual territory, and demanding new territories in which to locate their working out in practice. For the Puritan founding fathers, New England represented a similar adventure into the unknown where they could construct their theocratic utopias based on biblical models of righteousness.

Ironically, these early colonists would have largely perished but for the kindness and hospitality of the native Americans (for whom hospitality is a sacred duty), yet at the same time they generally ignored the existing spiritual and ethical teachings of the native inhabitants, believing their own imported traditions to be "sufficient for godliness." The Quakers represented an honorable exception to the prevailing tradition of treachery which soon became a feature of the Anglo-Saxon colonization. William Penn (1644–1718) and

John Woolman (1720–1772) both pursued a policy of active tolerance and sympathy for Amerindian culture, and found "that of God" equally within the Amerindian soul as any other.

As Deism became fashionable among European intellectuals, greater interest was shown in the traditional teaching of Amerindian culture, and mythographers, naturalists, and explorers began to record Amerindian traditions on their own terms, and with growing fascination. Thomas Jefferson, John Adams, Tom Paine, and George Washington—the founding fathers of American democracy and representatives of enlightened Deism—were all greatly interested in the moral teachings and spiritual traditions of native Americans, with Tom Paine perhaps coming closest to a position approximating that of the Amerindians themselves: "Does not the Creation, the universe we behold, preach to us the existence of an almighty power, that governs and regulates the whole? ... As for morality, the knowledge of it exists in every man's conscience" (1794, The Age of Reason).

Of all later American intellectuals, perhaps Thoreau best carried forward this conviction that the divine is manifest primarily in the natural world: "The charm of the Indian to me is that he stands free and unconstrained in Nature, is her inhabitant and not her guest, and wears her easily and gracefully." (Milton Meltzer and Walter Harding (1962). *A Thoreau Profile.* (p. 274). Concord: Thoreau Foundation). It was always a dream of Thoreau to write a book about Amerindian culture, based initially in the passion he had for collecting Amerindian artifacts in his native fields and woods. In preparation for his task he read some 200 volumes on the subject and wrote 11 manuscripts containing more than half a million words of notes and quotations before illness prevented the achievement of his dream. As well as providing an enduring influence for the liberator of "Indian Indians," Gandhi, Thoreau's other great legacy to intellectual history is the first recorded usage of the word "ecology," a term which in his mind was equivalent to the Amerindian understanding of the interconnectedness of the world of nature and the world of morality.

Meanwhile, in Europe, the continuing resonances of the discovery of the New World continued to reverberate on the pioneers of Romanticism. William Blake's untutored genius represented the radical reaction against "single vision and Newton's sleep" and looked to the Amerindian as an exemplar of indigenous wisdom.

"I then asked Ezekiel, why he eat dung, and lay so
   long on his right and left side? He answered, the
   desire of raising other men into a perception of

the infinite; this the North American tribes practise, and is he honest who resists his genius or conscience, only for the sake of present ease or gratification?"

(*The Mamage of Heaven and Hell*, W. Blake, Plate 12, 1790.)

Following the Deist liberation from textual religion, as the Romantics found a renewed faith in the divine manifested within nature, Rousseau led the way in terms of ethical theory in his attack on the artificiality and corrupting influences of civilization, arguing that morality's most secure location is to be found in the innate natural propensities of human nature left to its own authentic flowering. Rousseau and many other representatives of the French Enlightenment, including Diderot, Raynal, and Bougainville, undertook a reappraisal of the advantages of European civilization as compared with the ancient cultures of colonized territories, particularly the New World, and found the so-called primitive cultures to have a more authentic, and less schooled and artificial, system of morality. The ideal of the "noble savage" crystallized in popular imagination and summed up the ideal which inspired both the French Revolution and the Romantic revolution.

Although paradoxical at first sight, if it is understood that the revolutionaries saw their work as a renovation, a return from later corruption to the pristine condition of unsullied humanity, to which end in the French Revolution they went so far as to resurrect the pagan deities, the paradox dissolves in the circular notion of reasoning implied in the whole idea of "revolution."

The Romantic revolutionary movement of the late 18th and early 19th centuries was more a product of the intellectuals, poets, occultists, and Freemasons of the 18th century searching for their "lost word" of esoteric secrets, listening with awe to the discussion of Benjamin Franklin with Court de Gebelin and their "Philadelphian" vision of a world commonwealth based on brotherly love, freedom, tolerance, and harmony. Primitivism had become the rage as a guarantor of purity in an inversion of traditional Christian thinking about the fall of man, and naturally Amerindian culture was held in high esteem as an example of "noble savagery" at its most excellent.

Unfortunately, just as the darker sides of Amerindian culture were glossed over by such adulation, irrational forces of militarism, nationalism, and totalitarianism overtook the revolutionary movement, leaving the authentic illuminati of Romantic revolutionism (Weishaupt, Bonneville, Nodier, etc.) in a political wilderness from which they have never really recovered. Further paradoxes emerge when one considers the influence of Amerindian culture on the birth of Marxism, which sought to establish itself as the only authentic scientific revolutionary creed, thereby only masking and suppressing the essentially romantic fideism at its core.

The writings of Lewis Henry Morgan gave the first detailed scientific evidence for the existence of a stage of human community which he termed primitive communism, based on his direct experience of Iroquois social arrangements. The Iroquois lived communally, with basic resources being owned collectively, and without a hierarchy of property-owing governance policing the social life of the tribe. Instead, "liberty, equality and fraternity" were truly lived out among the Iroquois, according to Morgan's studies (*Ancient Society*, 1871), in a way that the French Revolutionaries had failed to actualize. Even the structure of Amerindian village architecture reflected the communal nature of their social arrangements, as Morgan outlined in his next work (*House and House-Life of the American Aborigines*, 1881).

These writings inspired Marx and Engels (in his *Origin of the Family*) to argue that this stage of primitive communism was a universal state in all human societies, when first evolving, prior to subsequent stages of growing economic and social sophistication. The Marxist argument, complete with Hegelian inevitability, saw human social evolution as a complicated spiral from primitive communism (as exemplified by the Iroquois) through social stratification, sophistication, class society, and exploitation to, once the political and intellectual victory of the Marxist Communist movement had succeeded worldwide, a reversion to communism, but now at a much higher level of technical and intellectual sophistication, shorn of all irrational trappings, cultural baggage, "rural idiocy," etc.

Given the modern sufferings of the Amerindian peoples due to the Cold War, caused by the immense militarization of the American West and its use for uranium mining, nuclear weapons testing, etc., it is ironic to say the least that the founders of Marxism were so inspired by the primitive harmony of Iroquois life as described by a pioneering 19th century anthropologist.

Further direct influence of Amerindian ethical teachings is evidenced in the later "back-to-nature" movements of the late 19th and 20th centuries, which took a number of forms. The ideas of Baden Powell and the founding of the Boy Scout movement were to a considerable extent inspired by a romanticized view of Amerindian practices. The teachings of Ernest Thompson Seton (1860–1946) laid particular stress on Amerindian examples of woodcraft practice; Seton moved from the United Kingdom to Canada and the USA, and founded the Woodcraft Indians in 1902 on a tract of land in New York State which he had acquired to found a nature reserve. Seton combined a romantic socialism with a reverence for the outdoor lifestyle of the Amerindian, and worked hard to ensure the protection of remaining tribes throughout North America, with the establishment of proper reservations, etc. He remained active also in the Boy Scout movement proper and oversaw the establishment of the American branch of the movement in 1910.

Disappointed with Baden Powell's militarism during World War I, Ernest Westlake (1856–1922) and his son, Aubrey Westlake, Quaker idealists inspired largely by Amerindian models, founded the Order of Woodcraft Chivalry in 1916 with Ernest Thompson Seton as its Grand Chieftain. Another significant British back-to-nature movement which took inspiration from Seton was the "Kindred of the Kibbo Kift" founded in 1920 by another Quaker, John Hargrave, who advocated a universal religion based on the worship of the Great Spirit as the path to world peace and harmony, which inspired many radical proto-Greens and ecologists with a vision of the revival of civilization through renewed experience of life in nature under canvas, and whose legacy lives on to this day in such circles.

Further important influences of Amerindian teachings can be seen in the underground revival of ancient witchcraft, or Wiccan, circles. Gerald Gardner, who was initially instrumental in refounding these traditions in the 1950s, seems to have derived considerable inspiration from contact with the more radical neopagan and pantheistic "back-to-nature circles" of the Order of Woodcraft Chivalry and its offshoots. Contemporary wiccans and neopagans see considerable congruence between their beliefs in a continuous primal nature religion, worshipping both the Earth Mother Goddess and the Male Horned God of fertility in complex and still largely secret rituals, complete with initiation rites, which have managed to survive centuries of persecution in Europe, and the primal religious traditions of Amerindian shamans.

The contemporary flourishing of neopaganism and ecofeminism, with Wicca as its major focus, organized in a decentralized and spontaneous way in covens and groves throughout Britain and the Commonwealth, Europe, North America, and elsewhere, can indirectly if not directly trace considerable influence to the inspiration of Amerindian teachings. A similar sort of ethical outlook characterizes both traditions: a respect and reverence for the earth, for the animal and plant worlds, and for herbs and their powers of healing; a love of ritual and initiation rites; the use of chanting and drumming; even the use of hallucinogenic drugs to induce ecstatic states of consciousness.

Not surprisingly, therefore, some commentators and contemporary scholars have found great parallels between the two traditions and postulate historic linkages dating back to primal shamanic practices, which modern cultural borrowings have only reaffirmed rather than generated ab initio. A similar story could be related of the modern rebirth of Druidry, dating back to the time of William Blake, Tom Paine, Nicholas Bonneville Iolo Morganwyg, and the Deistic enlightenment, when Druidry became fashionable again in radical circles advocating a return to the natural religion of the ancients—inspired in part by the search for Europe's own indigenous "noble savagery."

A further process of cultural fusion has been underway in recent decades, involving dialogues between contemporary Buddhist and Amerindian ethical beliefs. Advocates of Zen and Tibetan Buddhist teachings have found considerable inspiration and congruence with native Amerindian ethical systems. The Medicine Wheel teachings, for example, are echoed in many ways in Buddhist Tantric doctrines, and a lively international counterculture has developed in which Amerindian teachings are given substantial recognition alongside a more Buddhist-influenced cultural milieu. The poetry of Gary Snyder is an artistic example of this synthesis.

XVI. AMERINDIAN ETHICAL BELIEFS AND THE "NEW AGE" MOVEMENT

Similarly, Amerindian ethical teachings have been adopted enthusiastically by the contemporary "New Age" movement—that complex milieu of transformational practices and beliefs with a thousand schools and teachers, yet, purposely perhaps, with little overall coherent central narrative. In certain of its branches, the New Age movement shows decidedly Amerindian influences with a respect for all things shamanic, its love of nature and embracing of ecological and environmental concerns, its reevaluation of the sacredness of the divinity of the feminine and womankind, and its rejection of an absolutist Christianity proclaiming itself as the sole way to salvation.

Other New Age overlaps with Amerindian culture include the modern phenomenon of channeling and the whole notion of spirit guides (often thought of in New Age circles as discarnate souls or extraterrestrial spirit beings). For a technologically advanced society, these are in many ways similar in functional terms to the power animals of Amerindian shamans used in healing, prophecy, clairvoyance, etc. Similarly criticism could also be leveled that their reliance on external spiritual "props," showmanship, and "miracles" detracts from the hard work of ordinary everyday ethical decision making without recourse to the supernatural, since most people do not have the "luxury" of such experiences.

Among spiritualists and theosophists who believe in life after death, and the wisdom of seeking guidance from discarnate entities, Amerindian spirit guides have been very much in vogue for decades. Perhaps the most famous of these was the spirit of White Eagle, who is believed by her followers to have overshadowed the Englishwoman Grace Cooke, leading to the founding of a substantial international religious and ethical organization, the White Eagle Lodge. While suspending judgment on the validity of such practices, the main point to observe here is how strong the influence of the Amerindian presence has been on spiritual movements and countercultures, of a largely unorthodox nature, in past decades, indicating if nothing else the powerful impact of Amerindian beliefs on the imagination and ideals of many sincere spiritual seekers worldwide, far from the shores of the Americas.

Another congruence between New Age and Amerindian beliefs is in the efficacy of crystals for healing purposes. The language of contemporary New Age mystics in describing the intangible healing energies of crystals is quite compatible with the indigenous spiritual value placed on these sacred minerals by native American teachings, which always regarded them as part of their "Medicine."

The final question to pose here is whether, in some ways, the contemporary controversies about New Age teachings, with attacks from fundamentalist Christians exposing it as the "work of the Devil" and from Roman Catholic theologians as "the revival of gnostic heresy," can be seen as reviving earlier spiritual controversies and questions concerning the relationship between the great revealed monotheistic religious systems of European and Middle Eastern derivation and the pagan traditions of native North America. Is it possible to argue that elements of New Age theological profusion, in which pluralism, tolerance, and an orientation toward feelings rather than ideas are the order of the day, combined with a strong sense of inwardness and a love of experiential mysticism and ceremony, are partly the result of the influence of Amerindian ethical and spiritual norms?

Contemporary moves are also being made in Christian theological circles to accommodate afresh certain insights from Amerindian teachings. Within the Anglican and Episcopalian church, the movement of Creation Theology (as it is sometimes known), associated with the work of, for example, Dean Morton Smith of the Cathedral of St. John the Divine, Reverend Donald Reeves, Matthew Fox and Martin Palmer, has proved a fertile field for Amerindian teachings. The ancient Celtic churches, as represented, for example, by the theologian John Scotus Erigena, with their nonhierarchical structures and their love both of the divine found immanent in Nature and also of the feminine principle of nature, are highly compatible with elements of Amerindian spirituality. Likewise panentheism and process theology, as pioneered by Charles Hartshorne and A. N. Whitehead, have opened up a climate of metaphysical dialogue and ethical exchange.

In the Catholic church also, several more adventurous theologians, particularly, of course, American theologians, have tried to incorporate certain of the most creative and life-affirming elements of Amerindian teachings into their theologies, including the Liberation theologians of Latin America, Thomas Merton, and many Jesuits concerned with extending the insights of Ignatian spirituality.

A further aspect of Amerindian spirituality which has found resonances with aspects of New Age and innovative Christian practice concerns a shared love of pilgrimage, arising from the understanding of the holiness of certain sacred places which are endowed with particular numinous power. All Amerindian cultures share a profound love of nature, not in the abstract, but in the actual practice of pilgrimage and sacred journeying, believing that in moving from sacred site to sacred site, with different places being more appropriate at particular times of the calendrical cycle, one is actually moving through the realms of experience appropriate to particular teachings associated with that region. Many contemporary groups and individuals have drawn power and insight from the revival of these traditions, and draw on Amerindian thinking on the subject to inspire and revitalize their love and engagement with the sacred places associated with their own traditions.

XVII. AMERINDIAN ETHICAL BELIEFS AND EROTIC EXPERIENCE

A further aspect of Amerindian ethical culture to consider concerns their attitude to sexuality and the erotic. Generally a freer attitude prevailed in Amerindian culture than in more traditionally conservative societies, with a strong role being held by women in the overall tribal structures. Amerindian art is replete with pictorial and sculptural representation on erotic themes, indicating a high degree of awareness and sensitivity to the power of erotic experience. The arts of lovemaking were understood in Amerindian culture to be sacred in their provenance, and deities of love and the erotic were a feature of all Amerindian pantheons and ethical systems.

Marriage was generally a freer form of relationship based on love and sympathy between couples, with mutual rights and duties being negotiated between the parties and their unions being celebrated with sacred rituals, dancing, feasting, and prayer, as in other primitive societies worldwide. The cult of virginity, and associated themes of antisexuality found in some cultures, was noticeably absent from Amerindian thought and practice. Instead, it was expected that adolescents would explore fully their libidinous natures during their youth, and Amerindian teachings recognized the profound learning and wisdom that can be generated between individuals through intimate contact.

Generally speaking there was respect among Amerindian culture for sexual difference, with men and women having different rituals and sacred initiations at different times of their journey through life, with young men being expected to undertake hazardous and arduous Vision Quests to prove their manhood, and women undertaking sweat lodges and ritual confinement and seclusion at the time of the menarche, for instance, without there being any sense of hierarchical evaluation implied by such practices. Men and women were acknowledged as different, and the difference was celebrated and affirmed as a key aspect of the plan of the Great Spirit to ensure fertility and the ongoing cycle of creation. Homosexuality was also tolerated by Amerindian culture and most tribes had one or two individuals with unusual sexual preferences or an unclear gender orientation. Often they played the role of the Joker or Trickster to the conventional norms and values of the tribe, and their colorful wisdom would be accepted and honored as shedding light on common matters from a different perspective.

The role of children was vital for Amerindian culture, with children occupying an honored and central place in their traditional tribal societies. Open displays of affection and the close proximity of children to the everyday working affairs of the community were encouraged, such that contemporary anthropologists studying the sociological and psychological effects of touch and affection on overall psychical well-being and nonaggression in children have often referred to Amerindian culture as an exemplar of good practice.

XVIII. AMERINDIAN ETHICS AND ARTISTIC CREATIVITY

The close relationship between ethics and aesthetics was a major feature of Amerindian culture. As befits a culture in which literacy developed late and under foreign influences, the principles of ethics were communicated from generation to generation both in oral form and largely in aesthetic expression. Sandpaintings, for example, are an advanced feature of Amerindian creativity in which the complex teachings associated with the Medicine Wheel are expressed in large mandalas of colored sand, produced to traditional designs, in which color, positioning, shape, and line all conveyed spiritual ideas. The production of a sandpainting was itself both an aesthetic and spiritual experience in which the creative artist, often a shaman or medicine woman, would cocreate the painting with others who had sought his or her advice or help. Having created the mandala, the questioners would then be seated in the center of the work and encouraged to reflect and pray on the problem at hand, deriving insight and guidance from the structured representation of visual meanings surrounding them.

Rock paintings were also created at many sacred sites around the countryside, representing power animals and "mythical" and divine figures taken from the rich storehouse of the Amerindian aesthetic repertoire. The primitive and abstract style of Amerindian painting, in which the spiritual idea behind visual forms is represented rather than the photographic likeness, and which often told stories in semicartographic form, can be said to have influenced to a considerable degree certain modernist and abstract trends within modern art during the last 100 years, as classical European art developed a parallel fascination with all things primitive and "untamed" parallel to a similar fascination in certain philosophical circles (a development analyzed in depth by the important but neglected philosopher of modernist aesthetic experience, Jean Gebser).

Music too played a vital role in Amerindian culture, with song being an essential accompaniment to people's lives. Music as a performance art was undeveloped as in Western canons, however. Amerindian music was a lived experience in which the whole community participated, raising their voices in song, and telling stories about the Gods and sacred animals, or about their own lives or the lives of their ancestors, thereby celebrating the moral principles contained therein. Flute music, drums, and above all the human voice were felt sufficient to express the sacred power of music to elevate and sensitize the human soul.

The sacred chant was the preferred form of Amerindian musical expression, with its rhythmic, simple melodies achieving considerable emotional and spiritual impact. There were and are chants for accompanying every stage of life: childbirth, lovemaking, crop planting, hunting, feasting, marriage, healing, times of sacred stillness and meditation, seasonal rituals, and death and burial rites. Always a feature of Amerindian sacred rituals, the shamanic experience was accompanied by chanting, singing, and drumming as an essential part of the visionary healing quest undertaken for and with the community.

Without a system of musical notation, some of these traditions have been lost, but enough survives among skilled upholders of the tradition, or has been recorded by musicologists over past decades, to affirm the power and beauty of Amerindian musical culture and its important role in generating a climate of ethical awareness to the beauty and preciousness of life's patterns of meaning, conveyed through the harmonies and rhythms of songs and chants.

Personal aesthetic taste was also important to Amerindian culture and included colorful ornamentation and jewelery, face painting, and the wearing of sacred objects such as feathers or precious stones sewn into one's dress. Amerindian tribes throughout the continent love colorful displays in their appearance and have a highly developed sense of aesthetic beauty. Their jewelery and dresses have become world famous, and are now exported and emulated internationally.

It is important to remember, however, that for the Amerindian, the cultivation of personal beauty was a far deeper matter than for the votaries of the modern fashion industry. It was a matter of sacred vocation, an ethical duty of the highest order, for the great Spirit has created men and women beautiful, in a beautiful world, in order to celebrate and affirm and sustain the creation.

There is nothing in Amerindian culture of the aesthetic schizophrenia affecting "puritan" societies which deemphasizes personal adornment as a sin, insisting that the only authentic realm of beauty is in the invisible domain of ethical goodness. A commonly used description summing up the entire range of ethical and spiritual beliefs evidenced by Amerindian culture is "the way of beauty"—one practices the Amerindian system of ethics by walking "the beauty way," which is understood as an all-inclusive process affecting both inner and outer aspects of life. It was this all-inclusive aesthetic of appreciation and gratitude that inspired the heart of Amerindian ethical beliefs at their best, and that lives on to this day. As an Amerindian chant puts it,

> I walk in beauty
> Beauty before me
> Beauty behind me
> Beauty all around me.

XIX. AMERINDIAN APPLIED ETHICS AND THEIR IMPLICATIONS FOR POLITICAL PHILOSOPHY

While the American revolution was fought in the name of republican democracy, and religious freedom was enshrined, in the words of Thomas Jefferson, in the American Constitution, the advent of the USA has offered an ambiguous legacy to Amerindian cultures within its borders. The history of the expansion of the original 13 colonies to the present boundaries is a history of encroachment and conquest of Indian lands, accompanied by bloodshed, treachery, and brutality. The full story of the Bureau of Indian Affairs would make a most interesting tale of the working out of internal ethical dilemmas, with the doctrine of Manifest Destiny competing for allegiance with the principles of toleration and respect on which the American Constitution were supposedly founded.

Not surprisingly, perhaps, Amerindian peoples have presented a dilemma to the political processes of modernity, with the major project of nation-state building sitting uncomfortably against the successful, autonomous polities already established in the American continent for thousands of years before the arrival of Europeans. After the initial period of colonialism and conquest ended, with its tragic story of blood and violence having played out to the full, resulting in near genocide in many instances, the difficult task has begun of constructing a model of political coexistence while at the same time affirming cultural autonomy and difference.

While in some American nations Amerindians have been at the forefront of armed revolutionary movements, in the hope that revolutionary change would usher in greater degrees of cultural autonomy, economic security and civil rights, other Amerindian leaders have been at the forefront of what has become known as the "Fourth World movement." Seeking to deconstruct nationalism and to pioneer pluralist models of nationhood based on semiautonomous bioregions, Amerindians have joined their voices to the growing international chorus of disenfranchised "small peoples," whose ethnic, cultural, linguistic, and religious identities grant them a sense of separate vocation as a "people," yet whose political and military power have been too slight for them to qualify for full political nationhood in the cut throat world of international real-politik. One strategy pursued by the Fourth World, or "Peoples' Rights," movement has been to campaign for reform of the United Nations to enable the voice of disenfranchised cultural minorities to be heard on the world stage and to discuss issues of common concern in a revised UN General Assembly structure, or in a parallel second Peoples Assembly.

Given the likelihood that such reforms will take a long time, in the interim Amerindian campaigners have taken full advantage of the growing openness of the United Nations machinery for an increased role for nongovernmental organizations, and have begun to take full advantage of channels of international political networking arising out of the major UN conferences on sustainable development, social development, etc., to present their case for cultural autonomy alongside other similarly disenfranchised peoples. This set of problems, in the post-Cold War world, has become, arguably, the most pressing set of problems affecting the contemporary international arena, generating devastating internal conflict within nation states, and straddling state boundaries in messy and complex ways.

It is highly likely, therefore, that the consistent witness of Amerindian peoples, such as the Hopis, Iroquois, and Hurons, to their need for cultural autonomy within a wider national and international framework of coexistence can serve as useful guidance to other peoples in similar situations. Importantly, Amerindian leaders in this debate continuously stress the importance of their moral, ethical, and spiritual voice on the world stage as being of far greater significance than their small numbers would indicate. The predicament of Amerindian peoples therefore poses a double dilemma to the prevailing international system: firstly, prevailing structures make it difficult for their voices to be heard at all, and secondly, their experiences of what constitutes a "people" do not follow the overriding paradigm of secular nationhood, but rather is based on the sacred web that binds a sustainable community generation after generation, living in harmony with the natural ecology of its own bioregion.

According to the Amerindian perspective, the question of whether or not the international community can find a solution to these problems is also part of the much greater set of questions hanging over the problematique of human survival as a whole. If the traditional Amerindian voice were to be heard effectively on the world stage, what insights and values from their own legal and moral traditions would be most likely offered?

Amerindian legal norms and practices were obviously less highly developed than those in more complex urban, literate civilizations. Their systems of justice were informally structured and the key role was given to problem-solving efforts by the whole tribe thinking through problems together, rather than individuals being given executive and judicial power in a formal way

to impose solutions. When disagreements and conflicts arose in Amerindian culture, full discussion of all sides of the issue was the norm, with the ingenious device of the "talking stick" symbolizing the practice of ensuring that all parties were heard fully and allowed to present their own perspectives in turn. Amerindian political culture was based on unspoken norms, valuing politeness, tolerance, and open-mindedness; anyone holding the talking stick was guaranteed freedom from interruption and rudeness. The basic understanding was that in any given dispute what mattered was to arrive at a common perception of truth that could unite and rebind the wounds of a divided community.

Among the Iroquois Peace Confederacy a specific teaching brings the 12 Cycles of Truth to bear on particularly intractable problems as a means to achieve peace: learning the truth, honoring the truth, accepting the truth, observing the truth, hearing the truth, presenting the truth, loving the truth, serving the truth, living the truth, working the truth, walking the truth, and being grateful for the truth. Not surprisingly, with traditions such as these, some contemporary Amerindians are also at the forefront of conflict resolution work and mediation training, seeking alternatives to violence through the "council model" of dispute resolution.

Most importantly, though, the Amerindian voice on the world stage offers the possibility of a greater role for wisdom and strong ethical vision at the level of spiritual guidance amid the complex thickets of policy dilemmas facing the global political arena. The role of the wise elder, or wisdom keeper, was always honored in Amerindian tribal culture, such that if no clear decision could be agreed collectively, the tribal elders, valued for their vision, experience, and wisdom, would finally be called on to arbitrate. They would only do so after first calling for spiritual guidance from the Great Spirit, and would do their best to achieve solutions which would alienate or offend no one in the community, unless unavoidably so.

While Amerindian societies were not completely free of crime, levels of intratribal violence and crime were minimal and usually policed through social sanctions, except in more developed urban societies where a higher degree of internal militarization existed. In effect, the judges of the tribes were also the shamans, the holders of vision, combining in essence the prophetic and judicial roles on a day-to-day basis, which in Western societies have been kept more distinct. One would have to go back to the time of the Biblical prophets to find a parallel. Yet this is the perhaps the greatest gift contemporary Amerindian culture can offer: to remind the world community, with its overspecialization and obsession with scientific solutions to its pressing problems, that there is still an important role for the voice of simple, integrative wisdom above the clamor from the competing voices of the "experts."

XX. REPRESENTATIONS OF AMERINDIAN CULTURE—PERCEIVING THE "OTHER" IN THE SMOKING MIRROR

Literature has provided an important vehicle for the propagation of Amerindian ethical teachings, paradoxically, largely through the writings of non-Amerindians, for several centuries. From the earliest *History of the Indies* by Bartholomew de Las Casas to the contemporary writings of Carlos Castaneda, most people encounter Amerindian ethical thought in the form of the written word. For this reason it is worth considering briefly whether this outlet has served effectively and accurately to advance understanding about the Amerindian way of life.

Longfellow's (1807–1882) poetic output, particularly the *Song of Hiawatha*, served to bring home to an international audience the profundity and beauty of Amerindian thought for the first time. While critics argue over their evaluations of the poetic rating of Longfellow's work, there can be little doubt that his writings played a major role in advancing sympathy for the plight of the Amerindian and struck a sympathetic chord in the collective imaginations of their audience which reverberates to this day.

Frank Waters' pioneering studies of the Hopi Indians and the other tribes of the American southwest also deserve mention as a nonfictional account which achieves literary stature as an impassioned plea for tolerance and understanding of a people whose myths and belief system have never before or since been so comprehensively presented to the public. *Bury My Heart at Wounded Knee* presented an Amerindian version of the conquest of the American West by Dee Brown for the first time.

Carlos Castaneda's series of books purporting to be his account of an initiatory training over many years under the tutelage of a Yaqui Indian shaman and sorcerer, Don Juan, played an important role in the 1960s and 1970s in bringing to the attention of a disaffected generation the indigenous traditions of Amerindian culture. While controversy still rages over the authenticity or otherwise of these writings, there can be little doubt of the great impact which Castaneda's chronicle had

on a younger generation in search of alternative cultural values than was available to them from their own resources. Castaneda manages to convey something of the immense profundity and beauty about the worldview of Amerindian shamanism in a way which few other writers have done. The very fact that the chronicles present such a strange and extraordinary sequence of events and perceptions only adds to their power to shift assumptions and to bring home the importance of a closer understanding of the significance of Amerindian teachings. To this day, Castaneda's writings have remained one of the primary entry points into an engagement with Amerindian ethical thought for the general reading public.

The writings of Black Elk, the medicine man from the plains Indians, presented detailed knowledge about the Medicine Wheel or Sacred Hoop teachings for the first time to a mass audience, a path later followed by Hyemeyohsts Storm's *Seven Arrows*. Grey Owl achieved a wide popularization of Amerindian ideas for a largely Canadian audience. Even though it turned out that his ancestry was more Scottish and British than Amerindian, he had adopted the lifestyle of the Canadian Indian wholeheartedly and became their most important literary representative north of the border. Farley Mowatt undertook a similar task for the far north caribou hunting tribes of Ihalmiut Eskimos in his classic book, *The People of the Deer*.

The work of a New Englander, Helen Hunt Jackson (1830–1885), a friend of Emily Dickinson, also did much to popularize Amerindian culture, both in her detailed report, "A Century of Dishonour" (1881), and in her novel *Ramona*, set among the Amerindians of southern California. The extraordinary story of the last surviving member of a northern Californian tribe, Ishi, who literally walked out of the woods one day into civilization, having had no previous contact with Europeans, also caused a considerable impact on the reading public when it was first published. D. H. Lawrence's sojourn in Mexico produced his novel, *The Plumed Serpent* (1926), which presented a mixture of Lawrence's own views on life grafted onto a background of a revival of ancient Aztec belief systems.

Many poets have also drawn inspiration from Amerindian culture, particularly modernists such as Charles Olson (1910–1970), who in his *Maximus* poems envisions the resacralization of contemporary American culture by drawing heavily on its Amerindian past. Jerome Rothenberg has perhaps done more than any other contemporary American poet to attempt a fusion between Western and Amerindian cultural values, and he lived for a while as an honorary member of an Indian tribe in New York state, producing *The Seneca Journal* as a result. Rothenburg's work has given birth to a whole new literary field of ethnopoetics, in which he seeks the revitalization of contemporary poetic themes from the fusion with oral and tribal Amerindian cultures.

The role of Amerindian culture in the history of the film industry is of similar significance as a major way in which Amerindian ethical values have been presented to a mass audience. One could almost catalog the gradual ethical maturation of Hollywood from its early representation of the Amerindian in its early cowboys-and-Indians stereotypes of "goodies and baddies," in which the Amerindians were demonstrably "the baddies," to the sophistication of more recent films such as *Little Big Man, Dances with Wolves, The Mission,* and *The Emerald Forest.* In these latter films, the authentic story of Amerindian culture begins to be told effectively, subtly reversing yet capitalizing on earlier genres, with considerable space being devoted to conveying some of the beauty and grandeur of Amerindian ethical teachings. In the contemporary world, where films and television dominate the imaginal content of most people's understanding of history, this reevaluation of the meaning of Amerindian culture is of great significance, as is the fact that their commercial success also indicates the wide popular appeal of this reevaluation.

XXI. CONTEMPORARY INTERFAITH AND GLOBAL ETHICAL DIALOGUE

It is important to consider the contributions being made by Amerindian religious leaders to the growing tradition of interfaith dialogue and the search for a global ethics which is gathering pace as the century draws to an end. The first ever gathering of religious leaders on a global scale to discuss common concerns took place in Chicago in 1893, the occasion of Vivekanada's historic address to the assembled religious leaders representing many diverse viewpoints and philosophies of life. While a few Amerindian spiritual leaders were sometimes involved in such gatherings in the early days, it is not until recent years that the voice of Amerindian spirituality has begun to be heard effectively.

At the 1993 Parliament of World Religions, again held in Chicago in commemoration of the centenary of the previous such meeting, a large number of Amerindian spiritual leaders took part in the proceedings, and their views were to some extent reflected in the final documents, with its call to a global ethics which would enable the best ethical teachings of the world's various spiritual and philosophical systems to come together in a common endeavor to solve the many practical, concrete, and tragic problems facing the international community.

The organizations spearheading this international effort at interfaith collaboration on global ethics include the World Conference on Religion and Peace (WCRP). Founded in Kyoto in 1970 at the first ever global conference of religious representatives, WCRP has continued to hold global gatherings every 5 years since and has established chapters in over 50 countries around the world. The Canadian chapter is particularly active on Amerindian issues, and in 1992 organized a peace bus of interfaith representatives which toured Amerindian reservations.

At WCRP IV in Nairobi in 1984, two Amerindians participated formally, Harold Belmont from the Hopi Tribe and Art Solomon from Canada, and at one point they led the conference of religious delegates in a meditation on ecological themes, saying, "everything that has been created is sacred, including fire, water, air, plants, animals, birds, fish, which were here on the sacred Mother earth before there was human life." It was at WCRP V in Melbourne that questions of the rights of indigenous peoples and their spiritual representatives came to the fore in a major way, with the question of Australian aboriginal rights being strongly represented. Finally, at WCRP VI in Italy, 1994, the Amerindian presence was more strongly felt, with an inspiring blessing ritual conducted by a medicine man from Montana held for the benefit of the assembled religious leaders from all over the world.

In spite of these advances, however, it must be said that generally speaking the organized global structures and institutions dealing with interfaith dialogue continue to marginalize pagan and indigenous religious and spiritual traditions. Tokenism is hardly the same as authentic existential exchange. Too often the major players in the interfaith community (the Vatican, the World Council of Churches, and the official Islamic and Jewish bodies worldwide) continue to regard primal religions as somehow less worthy of serious dialogue than other fellow "monotheistic" traditions. There seems to be an enormous difficulty for the major world religions in acknowledging Amerindian religious traditions on equal terms—which is a problem for primal religions in general in the contemporary world.

There are signs, however, that this spirit is slowly changing, and that leading institutions of responsible interfaith dialogue, such as the World Conference on Religion and Peace, the World Congress of Faiths, the Temple of Understanding, the International Association for Religious Freedom, UNESCO and other UN cultural agencies, and the various theosophically inspired organizations, are beginning to understand that the "peace between religions" which Hans Kung speaks about as a precursor to overall international peace cannot bypass indigenous cultures and religions, but must rather make special efforts to embrace and include them in its overall fields of dialogue, recognizing that the prevailing paradigms of interfaith dialogue may themselves be changed somewhat in the process from an academic-intellectual and pragmatic action-oriented mixture to one which embraces living spiritual experience and the freedom to open up to the spontaneous miracles of the natural order.

XXII. AMERINDIAN EDUCATIONAL DEVELOPMENTS AND ETHICS

One crucial aspect of Amerindian ethical knowledge remains to be discussed, namely, the educational structures and institutions whereby such knowledge is transmitted. Traditionally, the learning process in Amerindian culture was bound up intimately with everyday life pursuits, and there was no rigid segregation between "learning time" (i.e., school), work, and play for Amerindian children and young adults. Formal education as familiar in Western culture took place in the initiatic framework of the ritual ceremonies discussed above, and occurred at key moments of passage in the life of individuals and the community as a whole. The tribal culture itself was the Amerindian school and university combined in one.

With the concentration of Amerindian tribes into reservations in the USA, the Bureau of Indian Affairs imposed schooling systems on young Amerindians according to Western models, but on the whole these attempts have failed to address the special learning needs of the indigenous Amerindian peoples. Similar stories of inadequate provision exist in other countries in the Americas. As a result the drop out and "failure" rates among Amerindian students are proportionately extremely high. Low self-esteem, depression, alcoholism, and high suicide levels are the inevitable result of the imposition of educational patterns which fail to speak creatively to the authentic intellectual and spiritual needs of Amerindian youth. Fortunately, there are at present various moves underway toward developing educational facilities at all levels for Amerindian peoples to take charge of their own learning process, and to take in hand their own higher education and ethical welfare.

The percentage of Amerindian students able to take up university places is woefully inadequate, and few courses and degrees are available in which their own ethical values compose part of the curriculum. Several colleges are in the process of being formed in different tribal areas to provide a mixture of indigenous and Western education, but these remain at the exploratory stage, and more support is needed for these innovative initiatives. As yet, therefore, there is still no fully recognized and accredited university which is dedicated to the teaching and transmission of both the traditional Western curriculum and also Amerindian values and traditional knowledge, and until this takes place it is unlikely that the undoubted ethical and philosophical wisdom inherent in Amerindian culture will be heard effectively in circles of influence and responsibility.

What has happened instead is that Amerindian educationalists and spiritual leaders have pioneered the development of informal education, using workshop structures to convey the content of their ancient ethical visions, both in the American continent and now increasingly worldwide. The importance of the preservation and reempowerment of autonomous Amerindian ethical beliefs and practices to our common world heritage and to contemporary debates in global ethics in general cannot be overemphasized, and in this context it is to be hoped that American educational planners and philosophers of education will give the greatest possible attention to rethinking the overall educational provision available to Amerindian peoples, and to those in the higher education sector in particular.

It is worth remarking in closing that the 18th century Anglo-Irish philosophical idealist, Bishop Berkeley, after whom the University of California at Berkeley, one of the USA's most progressive universities, is named, nursed as a favorite pet project of his the establishment of a university for the education of young Amerindian students, a dream which he was unfortunately unable to fulfill. It is a sad reflection on how slowly the wheels of educational progress turn, that even to this day his project has still not been realized.

XXIII. AMERINDIAN ETHICS IN CONTEMPORARY ACADEMIA

A final question for consideration concerns the relative standing of the study of Amerindian ethical, philosophical, and religious systems in contemporary philosophy and academia in general. What are the possible reasons for its low prioritization? In an increasingly competitive academic climate, serious research into traditional Amerindian ethical knowledge has been hampered both by lack of funding and by the prevailing paradigms of learning present in contemporary academia. Spiritual values by and large only intrude marginally into higher education systems, and then usually only in specific denominational contexts. Some serious research into Amerindian ethical beliefs has of course been underway on an objective basis, and here the importance of the work of anthropologists and other scholars in attracting research interest to Amerindian cultural and ethical matters is great.

Here Levi Strauss's studies of South American cultural patterns have been seminal, as has been Benjamin Lee Whorff's study of Amerindian linguistics and its philosophical implications. Mircea Eliade's pioneering critical studies of comparative shamanism opened up the way for a renaissance of scientific interest in comparative shamanism including Amerindian ethical and spiritual teachings, and a generation of younger scholars of comparative religion have continued to explore this rich seam of studies.

In the field of general cultural and psychological studies, Carl Jung's work has opened up the important project of the analytical study of Amerindian mythological and ethical symbolism, but by and large this work has been pursued outside of academia per se by independent authors and scholars such as Joseph Campbell. Contemporary feminist academics and students of women's studies courses have also given serious attention to Amerindian ethical teachings, as have those working in the fields of peace research, conflict resolution, and cross-cultural communication.

Academics working in interdisciplinary fields to do with oral culture, poetics and performance, theater studies, and the anthropology of ritual and drama have also been involved in Amerindian studies. Natural scientists, naturalists, ecologists, and particularly those involved in the field of medical research have also been concerned with traditional Amerindian ecological and pharmacological knowledge and healing systems.

Among philosophers, interest has been less marked, with mainstream academic philosophy departments by and large neglecting the rich potential of the study of Amerindian ethical and philosophical systems, mainly because traditional philosophical teaching is concerned with texts and textual analysis, and generally speaking lacks the intellectual equipment to encounter living oral philosophical systems as a valid field of study and inquiry. With recent postmodernist developments in contemporary philosophy, however, the study of the living philosophical heritage of Amerindian culture may well become more attractive as a topic. Perhaps not surprisingly it is among contemporary ecophilosophers and academics interested in the philosophy of religion that Amerindian ethics are being studied most seriously. Yet is it possible, finally, to speak of an Amerindian philosophical tradition?

It depends how one defines philosophy, and who has the institutional and economic power to make their definition apply—but in the last analysis the question should only be resolved on a moral and factual basis. Perhaps one should always, in the Socratic tradition, answer one question with another, and confess that a contemporary Amerindian shaman would be equally permitted to ask of European or Western civilization, as did Gandhi in a different context, whether the West itself actually possesses an authentic living philosophical tradition that is not simply a detailed study of texts and their transmission, or an overemphasis on a narrowly defined overintellectualism, developed at the expense of the living human being in the context of the natural and supernatural worlds as a whole.

Also See the Following Articles

BIODIVERSITY • ECOLOGICAL BALANCE • ENVIRONMENTAL JUSTICE • INDIGENOUS RIGHTS • RELIGION AND ETHICS

Bibliography

Campbell, J. (1988). *Historical atlas of world mythology.* Perennial Library, Harper & Row.
Foster, S., & Little, M. (1987). *Sun Bear, the book of the vision quest.* Englewood Cliffs, NJ: Prentice Hall.
Gill, S. D. (1987). *Mother Earth: An American Story.* University of Chicago Press.
Johnson, S. (1994). *The book of the elders: The life stories of great American Indians.* Sante Fe, NM: Harper Collins.
Neidhart, J. (1961). *Black Elk speaks.* Lincoln: Univ. of Nebraska.
Sams, J. (1990). *Sacred path cards.* San Fransisco: Harper Collins.
Steltenkamp, M. (1982). *The sacred vision: Native American Indian religion and its practice today.* NJ: Paulist Press.
Terma Co. (1994). *The box: Remembering the gift.* Santa Fe, NM: Terma Co.
Waters, F. (1963). *Book of the Hopi.* New York: Ballantine Books.

NATURE VERSUS NURTURE

Garland E. Allen
Washington University

GLOSSARY

genotype The genetic endowment that an organism receives from its parent(s); thus a one-celled organism that divides by cell division produces two daughter cells that are identical genotypically (i.e., have identical genotypes); a sexually reproducing organism has a genotype composed of contributions (one-half) from each parent.

heritability The portion of the variability in the phenotypic expression of a trait within a given population that can be ascribed to genetic factors rather than to variability in the environment to which the population is exposed. In the absence of rigorous breeding data, heritability is a statistical tool that provides a means of estimating the extent to which observed differences between individual organisms in a popu-

lation are due to genetic rather than environmental differences.

nature In this context, a general term applied to the claim that much of human personality, mental ability, and behavior is determined by heredity (i.e., in modern terminology, by genes). Those who hold this position generally view human behavior and intellectual capacities as limited by natural endowment, and difficult if not impossible to modify significantly in an individual case.

norm of reaction The relationship between the range of environments in which an organism develops and the expression of a particular genotype under that range of conditions. Thus, gene A may produce phenotype A1 in environment X, but A2 in environment Y. Norm of reaction focuses on the *relationship* between genes and environment as determined by the effect of different environments on phenotypic outcome.

nuture The general view that much of human behavior, including personality traits, mental abilities, and the like, is determined by experience—by contact between the individual and his or her environment—and is thus flexible and modifiable within rather wide limits.

phenotype Traits developed in an organism, or the way the organism appears to an observer. For example, a blue color is one phenotype for eye color in humans, while brown color is another (different) phenotype. Phenotypes result from the interaction of an organism's genetic endowment and its environment.

NATURE AND NURTURE refer to the two factors that contribute to the form and function of organisms. In current discussions this is also referred to as heredity and environment, or biological and cultural determinism. The recognition that both factors are involved in the normal development of any organism, and their juxtaposition as mutually exclusive, has given rise to the nature–nurture (or heredity–environment) debate from classical times to the present.

I. THE NATURE–NURTURE DEBATE

While the nature–nurture debate technically refers to all traits (physical, physiological and behavioral) in all organisms (plants, animals, microorganisms) it is most often, and most heatedly debated when the organism in question is human beings. Proponents of the "naturist" argument claim that for many traits or characteristics of the organism, biological inheritance is the major determiner of how the adult appears or behaves. The implication of the naturist position is that because a trait is biologically determined it cannot be altered much, if at all, by environmental intervention. On the other hand, proponents of the "nurturist" position argue that many traits, especially human personality, mental, and social traits, are not determined in any specific way by biological inheritance, but are developed (i.e., learned or conditioned) from interactions with the outside world. The implication of the nurturist position is that many human mental and personality traits can be modified through exposure to new environments. In the economic and social spheres, naturists maintain that people's social position (job level, income, educational level, and degree of economic responsibility) is far more rigidly determined at the time of conception, while nurturists maintain that social and economic position, along with educational level, are developed through exposure to particular (favorable or unfavorable) environments.

Ethical concerns surrounding the nature–nurture debate derive from the fact that, historically at least, two very different sets of social and economic policies have been associated with each position. Naturist positions have generally been used to justify the status quo and/or support restrictive and conservative social concepts. In the mid-nineteenth century data suggesting that African slaves in the South had smaller brains than whites were used to oppose emancipation. Later claims of the supposed genetic inferiority of Poles, Italians, Irish, and Turks were used to pass compulsory sterilization laws in the United States and in Germany in the 1920s and 1930s, and restrictive immigration laws in the United States in 1924. For example, by 1935 over 21,000 people had been forcibly sterilized in U.S. institutions for the "feebleminded" and insane, on the grounds that their mental or personality deficiencies were genetically determined and thus would be likely to be passed on to their offspring. Virtually all of those sterilized were from economically poor backgrounds and/or ethnic and racial minorities. More recent (1968) claims that African-Americans are genetically inferior in intelligence to whites began with the claim that enrichment programs for disadvantaged children, such as Head Start, probably did little good because native intelligence could not be molded much by educational experience. The implication behind hereditarian arguments has generally been that if it is genetic, it cannot be changed. Thus, hereditarians have generally argued that it is economically wasteful and socially foolish to devote scarce societal resources on those who are constitutionally unable to take advantage of them.

The nurturist position, on the other hand, has generally been associated with a stronger belief in human malleability and with liberal social and economic policies. Abolitionists opposed brain size comparisons of slaves to whites because they believed that blacks had the basic human abilities to function as free and independent people (not all abolitionists thought blacks were equal to whites, however). In the 1920s, Journalist Walter Lippman opposed strong genetic claims about inherited intellectual limitations because he believed that all people, if given a chance, could improve themselves intellectually, socially, and economically; in other words, they were not restricted by the genes inherited from their parents.

Hereditarians often complain that liberals and progressives oppose genetic determinism primarily because they do not like the conclusions—namely, that all people are not created (biologically) equal. Naturists accuse nurturists of failing to look objectively at the research data, thereby allowing political persuasions to affect their judgment of the science. For their part, nurturists argue that naturists also have a political agenda, but that they do not acknowledge it, therefore casting themselves unwittingly in the role of advocates rather than scientists. The debate has endless dimensions.

It should be pointed out that there is nothing inherent in the naturists' position that leads necessarily to conservative social policies, nor anything inherent in the nurturists' position that leads necessarily to liberal social policies. Determining that some behavioral, mental, or emotional problem is genetic could just as well be used to argue for liberal policies that call for allocating more resources to such afflicted individuals, rather than less. Likewise, determining that a given condition such as criminal behavior is largely due to socioeconomic environment could be used easily to justify conservative policies such as harsher penalties, allocation of less resources to such individuals, etc. The social policies that come into play in these issues are based on social and political philosophy, and are not imposed by the science. Even if the hereditarian positions were agreed to be true, the social policies they give rise to are determined by social, not scientific, considerations.

II. THE NATURE–NURTURE CONTROVERSY FROM ANCIENT TIMES TO THE 19TH CENTURY

Historian Robert Nisbet has argued that the nature–nurture distinction dates from the fifth century B.P.E. (before present era) in the Greek distinction between *physis* (equivalent to nature) and *nomos* (meaning a pasture for cattle, and hence nurture) (see his entry "Anomie" in the 1982 *Prejudices: A Philosophical Dictionary*. Cambridge, MA: Harvard Univ. Press). Plato, in *The Republic*, spoke of three "types" of people based on their nature or "metal": gold (rulers), silver (philosophers, statesmen), and iron (artisans, soldiers, workers). No amount of training (nurture) could change one metallic nature into another (Plato recognized that this concept was a "noble lie" in that he did not believe people were so rigidly determined, but put it forward as a necessary ideology to preserve social order).

In his extended agricultural poem *The Georgics*, Virgil notes that plants of different types, or natures (willows, olives, myrtles, etc.), need different soils for their nurture (book II, lines 109–112). Shakespeare portrayed the crude Calaban in *The Tempest* as "a devil on whose nature nurture can never stick" (act IV, sc. 1). And the nurturist position was implicit in John Locke's conception of the newborn mind as a tabula rasa (blank slate) on which experience is recorded as the individual's development proceeds (*Essay on Understanding*, 1689). Juxtaposition of the terms in the modern, biological sense took form in Francis Galton's 1874 book, *English Men of Science: Their Nature and Nurture*, in which he argued that scientific geniuses were primarily the product of biological inheritance.

In the traditional formulation, nature refers to the sum total of internal biological factors that influence what an organism will be like: whether it is an animal or plant, a cat or dog, or white-haired or black-haired, and for animals, aspects of behavior. Nurture refers to the sum total of factors external to the organism that influence its ultimate (adult) structure and function: for example, the amount of food or nutrients available, and conditions such as temperature, humidity, and amount of oxygen or light during its development.

Within this definitional framework, all factors of nature are biological in that they are part and parcel of the organism's potential makeup from fertilization onward. However, only some factors of nurture are biological (food, the presence of other organisms) while others are physical or chemical (amount of moisture or sunlight).

In biological terms, the sum total of an organism's appearance—its structure and function—is called its phenotype. The organism's inherited potentials for developing one or another phenotype are called its genotype, or the sum total of genes the organism inherits from its parents. The genotype is thus equivalent to the organism's inherited "nature." As we will see later in this entry, the phenotype of an organism at any given time is the result of a complex interaction between its genotype and the various factors of its environment, past and present, to which it has been exposed (i.e., a complex interaction between nature and nurture over the course of the life history of the organism).

Although the nature–nurture or heredity–environment debate has a long history, the focus of the debate has changed over time as new types of evidence or new social concerns have arisen. From a biological point of view, the often mutually exclusive positions of either heredity or environment make little sense, since all organisms, including ourselves, are a product of the interaction of heredity and environment. However, since the debate persists, the critical question for any particular trait is the relative weight that heredity and environment each carry in that interaction. For example, genetic factors appear to have much more influence than environmental ones in the development of eye or hair color in human beings, while environmental factors appear to have a larger role than genetic ones in the development of a person's intellectual capacities or taste in music.

Since the claims for a greater contribution of either nature or nurture for human social behaviors, personality, and diseases have implications for a variety of social policies, the debate, and the search for evidence supposedly resolving it, has resurfaced time and again in western culture over the past several centuries. From the middle of the 19th century on, however, the debate began to reach an ever-widening audience both inside and outside the scientific community. It has become an especially important topic in recent years in the wake of the extensive genetic information emerging from the Human Genome Project.

Before examining how the nature–nurture debate has played itself out in past cases, it will be useful to put the whole question into the perspective derived from modern genetics. We know that heredity consists of both a conservative and a radical element. It is conservative in that it preserves basic hereditary information faithfully from one generation to the next (the old adage that "like begets like"), it is radical in that it constantly introduces variation into the heredity process. These variations derive from a variety of causes: point mutation (change within a single gene), chromosomal alterations (changes in the order and arrangement of genes on the chromosome), and polyploidy (addition of extra chromosomes to the genome), to cite only a few of the most important. Thus, only in the case of monozygotic (identical) twins are any two organisms in a natural population genetically identical.

A great diversity of genetic elements (alleles) among members of a species is also a characteristic of human populations. Yet, ironically, underlying this great genetic diversity is an enormous homogeneity. Members of the human species from as geographically diverse regions as Africa, Borneo, Turkistan, Paris, and New York all share about 99.5% of their genes; the diversity lies in the other 0.5%. Yet, it is the diversity that occupies center stage in the nature–nurture debate.

Most contemporary arguments about the importance of nature (i.e., genetics) thus attempt to account for major phenotypic differences between individuals or groups (races, ethnic groups) on the basis of the 0.5% genotypic differences. To be sure, *some* genetic differences between individuals do make a difference, for example, in certain diseases known to be caused directly by point mutations or chromosomal variations (sickle-cell anemia is a gene mutation, and Down's syndrome is the result of an extra no. 21 chromosome). Variational differences in genes are real. The problem on which the whole nature–nurture debate hinges is determining when phenotypic differences are largely influenced by genetic, as opposed to environmental, differences. We return to the biological aspects of the nature–nurture dispute in Part IV of this article.

III. THE NATURE–NURTURE CONTROVERSY IN THE 19th CENTURY

Although versions of the nature–nurture debate are found from the 16th century on (for example, in arguments about whether the indigenous peoples of Africa or the New World were members of the same species as Europeans), it was in the 19th century that such theories began to proliferate. Historically, the form the nature–nurture debate has taken at any one time is that a particular claim and set of evidence are brought forward on behalf of the naturist claim. These data or arguments usually become the object of scrutiny or attack by those who doubt the value of the data in its own right, or become suspicious of the claims from their own nurturist position. In many historical instances, radical hereditarian claims have been met with equally radical environmentalist claims, with the two positions gaining or losing support over time. As will be discussed later, economic and social conditions do tend to effect which position gains dominance at particular times and places in history.

Most of the traits on which the nature–nurture debates have focused have been social, intellectual, and personality traits, mostly the differences in these characteristics between the so-called "races," Europeans (Caucasian) and Africans (Negroid), and between the male and the female sexes (mostly limited to the European setting). Since genetics as we now understand it was unknown until the beginning of the 20th, those who argued the nature–nurture issue in the 19th century framed their arguments in a variety of other terms, most notably anatomical characteristics that were assumed to be indicators of inborn qualities.

One of the first of these characteristics to gain prominence was facial angle, that is, the angle formed by drawing one line horizontally along the jaw, and the other diagonally from the chin along the cheekbones and forehead (Figure 1). Such measurements were first attempted by Dutch anatomist Pieter Camper (1722–1789) and his followers in the mid-18th century. Although at first they tended to show a major difference between groups such as Africans and Europeans, problems soon arose with methods of taking the measurements and with seemingly irrelevant acts such as degree of protrusion of the jaw or eyebrow ridges, making any claims about the meaningfulness of angular differences subject to doubt. Moreover, failure of this measurement to hold up across varied racial and ethnic groups (i.e., failure of the measurement to correlate with existing subjective evaluations of intelligence or degree of sophistication of a particular group) led to more direct attempts to measure biological differences, namely, what seemed self-evident to be a valid measure, the capacity of the cranium itself.

One of the first large-scale attempts to measure cranial capacity was made by Philadelphia physician Sam-

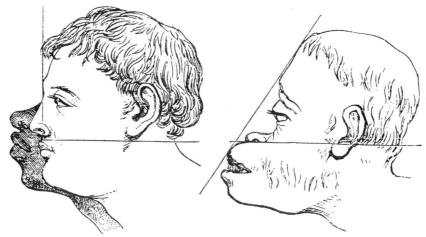

FIGURE 1 Facial angles from *The Races of Man* (1850) by Robert Knox. From J. S. Haller, 1971. *Outcasts from evolution: Scientific attitudes of racial inferiority, 1859–1900* (p. 10). Champaign–Urbana: Univ. of Illinois Press.

uel George Morton (1799–1851) in the 1840s and 1850s, on several hundred skulls that he had collected over a period of time. Using a variety of filler material (first mustard seed, and later BB shot) Morton determined that white Europeans had the largest cranial capacities, indigenous American (both North and South) people the next highest, and African-Americans the lowest of all. Morton's results were not easy to interpret, however, since he did not always determine accurately the age or sex of the skulls he measured, nor did his filler material (especially mustard seed) always give consistent results, partly because the seeds were very small and fell through the sutures in the skull and through the eye and ear openings, and also because the seeds can be variously compacted, thus yielding different volumes.

When actual cranial capacities were corrected for measurement error by age and sex (using BB shot, which gave more consistent values), the differences between groups became minuscule. But Morton's work was hailed by some proslavery forces as a biological justification for opposing abolition. For example, in a obituary of Morton appearing in the *Charleston Medical Journal* in 1887, it was said of Morton: "We of the South should consider him our benefactor, for aiding most materially in giving to the negro his true position as an inferior race." [Quoted from William Stanton, *The Leopard's Spots, Scientific Attitudes toward Race in America, 1815–1859* (Chicago, University of Chicago Press, 1960: p. 144] Morton's book circulated widely among southern politicians such as John C. Calhoun (Vice-President of the U.S. under both John Quincy Adams and Andrew Jackson, and later U.S. Senator from

South Carolina) and James Henry Hammond (Governor of South Carolina). [Also, Stanton, pp. 52–53].

Similar craniometric arguments were advanced in Europe for major social role differences between men and women. For example, French anatomist and anthropologist Paul Broca (1824–1880) used the circumference of skulls to show that women had a lower intellectual capacity than men (their emotional centers, however, were deemed to be larger). In the 1870s Broca and many of his contemporaries used these measurements to argue against the demands of the women's movement of the day: namely, the right to vote and admission to universities. Opponents of Broca's "naturist" claim pointed out that when Broca's measurements were corrected for body size, many women's brains were found to be larger in proportion to their height and weight than those of many males. This disturbing observation undermined the use of cranial measurements to argue for female intellectual and social inferiority.

Shortly after the demise of Broca's work, the Italian physician and criminologist Cesare Lombroso (1836–1909) undertook to propose a biological, or naturist, explanation for the widespread criminal behavior found in industrial European cities. Lombroso applied a broader set of measurements than merely skull capacity to the human body as a means of identifying biological indicators of what he called the "criminal personality." Lombroso employed the distance between the eyes, the shape of the nose, the length of the torso compared to that of the legs or arms, genitalia, eyebrow ridges, and a variety of other anatomical features. In a book of 1890, *L'uamo deliquente*, he claimed that such measurements gave accurate predictions of a criminal predisposition.

During the late 19th and early 20th century Lombroso's work was introduced into a variety of European and American legal trials as a basis for determining the type of sentence placed on convicted felons.

Critics of this sort of crude biological determinism pointed out as early as 1901 that a survey of anatomical traits of members of the British House of Lords showed as many of the apparent delinquent types as had been found in Lombroso's Italian prisons. As a result, by the next decade the field of "criminal anthropology" associated with Lombroso's name fell into disrepute, and with it, by the second decade of the century, the use of physical, anthropometric data to argue for a "naturist" position with regard to differences in human personality and social proclivities. By the end of the 19th century, then, it appeared that there was not one or even a collection of physical traits that appeared to correlate consistently with personality and behavioral characteristics over a wide range of human groups.

IV. NATURE–NURTURE ARGUMENTS IN THE 20th CENTURY: GENETICS AND EUGENICS

Failure of anthropometric data to justify existing social norms did not end the nature–nurture debate; it only changed the form of the naturist arguments. Among the most prominent naturist arguments to be advanced in the 20th century were those based on the then-new science of genetics. To one degree or another, most naturist theories since 1900 have referred their claims back to inborn genetic differences between individuals or groups to explain differences in personality, behavior, or social-economic position.

In 1900, three independent investigators rediscovered the writings of an obscure Augustinian monk, Gregor Mendel (1822–1884), who had lived and worked in Brno, which is now part of the Czech Republic. In 1866 Mendel had published a paper summarizing his experiments with the common pea plant and which laid down the basis for what was to become the new science of heredity. Ignored for 35 years, Mendel's work was quickly taken up by a new generation of investigators around the world during the first three decades of the 20th century. Central to Mendel's theoretical conception was the association of each trait in an adult organism (height or flower color in plants, coat color or spottedness in animals) with a specific hereditary unit that came to be called a gene (Mendel did not use that term, but rather called the units "factors").

Genes assorted and reassorted themselves from one generation to another by more or less random processes, and if large enough batches of offspring were obtained, it was possible to make predictions about what proportion of them would show a given form of the trait (for example, the proportion of pea plants from a particular cross would be tall versus short). Mendel's work provided biologists with a method of studying heredity experimentally and quantitatively in a way that had not been possible earlier. After 1910 biologists such as Thomas Hunt Morgan (1866–1945) and his research group at Columbia University showed that genes could be viewed as material components of rod-shaped structures in the cell nucleus known as chromosomes.

Mendel's work informed not only biologists concerned with understanding the theory of heredity, but also agricultural breeders whose work, previously, had been largely based on trial and error and certain rules of thumb. After Darwin, Mendel's work ranks perhaps as the second greatest revolution in biology in the past two centuries. Genetics was regarded as the cutting edge of biology at the turn of the century (the public hype surrounding it was not dissimilar to that surrounding molecular genetics in the 1980s and 1990s).

The rise of Mendelian genetics provided new avenues for reengagement of the nature–nurture debate. Naturists (hereditarians) quickly took up Mendel's ideas and developed a line of inquiry known as eugenics, or "the science of improvement of the human race by better breeding." (Subtitle of pamphlet, "Eugenics," published by Henry Holt & Co., New York, 1910) As practiced by Charles B. Davenport (1866–1944), intellectual leader of the movement in the United States, eugenicists sought to use Mendelian principles to determine what traits were inherited in human beings and what traits were not. The aim was to apply that knowledge to social programs in order to restrict the reproduction of people thought to harbor unfavorable genes (what was called negative eugenics) while at the same time encouraging the reproduction of people thought to have good genes (what was called positive eugenics). Eugenicists built a major movement throughout much of the world between 1910 and 1940, achieving the greatest prominence in the United States, England, and Germany.

Clearly on the naturist side, eugenicists claimed, based mostly on family pedigree analyses, that not only physical but also mental and personality traits (for example, feeblemindedness, alcoholism, pauperism, homosexuality, and criminality) were inherited in Mendelian fashion, and could be shaped by controlling who was allowed to reproduce. To this end, eugenicists lobbied in the United States (and elsewhere) for laws that would allow so-called genetically defective people to be involuntarily sterilized and that would restrict immigration of those with inferior genetic makeup. Much of eugenic ideology in the United States and in Europe was overtly anti-Semitic, antiblack, and strongly pro-Nordic in its thrust.

Those who stood on the more nurturist side, such as anthropologist Franz Boas (1858–1942), argued that although there might be some genetic "predispositions" to certain kinds of personalities or social traits, most complex human behaviors (such as those in which the eugenicists were most interested) were strongly, if not wholly, determined by environmental experiences (i.e., learning). Although many nurturists were skeptical of eugenicists' claims, eugenicists gained authority from then-current developments in the new and exciting science of genetics. Only after World War II, when Nazi atrocities carried out in the name of eugenics were revealed, did the oversimplistic and biologically naive nature of eugenic theories become fully apparent. By that time, however, millions of human beings had been sterilized, imprisoned, or eradicated because of their supposed genetic inferiority.

V. THE NATURE–NURTURE CONTROVERSY SINCE WORLD WAR II

In the years since World War II the nature–nurture debate has appeared and reappeared in various forms, although the reference to genetic differences has remained a major component of each argument (sometimes hormonal measurements or neurophysiological data have been invoked to explain, for example, broad-scale differences between men and women, or between heterosexuals and homosexuals, but ultimately these physiological differences are thought of as caused by genetic differences).

Thus, in 1969 Arthur Jensen, an educational psychologist at the University of California, Berkeley, claimed that African-Americans were genetically inferior in intelligence (on the average) to whites. His view, based on statistical analysis of I.Q. test scores of over 40 pairs of identical twins raised apart, suggested that I.Q. had a heritability of 0.8, or was 80% "heritable," and thus that the persistently lower I.Q. scores of African-Americans (compared to whites) must reflect genetic differences. Jensen's work had an immediate and major impact in the United States and western Europe. For one thing, it was a long and detailed article (over 100 pages), contained a vast array of references spanning much of the century, and was impressive in its use of quantitative data and statistical analysis. In the United States it was read into the Congressional Record and

copies were distributed to the presidential cabinet (under President Richard Nixon). It was also cited in a number of school busing cases to argue against the educational merits of school integration.

A word is in order about the statistical method of heritability, as it was a cornerstone of Jensen's argument connecting scores on I.Q. tests, race, and a genetical claim for a causal relationship between the two. Heritability was devised by the statistician and eugenicist Ronald A. Fisher (1890–1962) in England in the 1930s. It was intended by Fisher as a tool for animal and plant breeders to estimate how much of a given phenotypic trait was influenced by heredity for situations where it was difficult (for practical reasons) to carry out rigorous breeding experiments (for example, with cattle or pigs).

Heritability of a trait is defined as that portion of the total variance in a phenotype in a *population* due to genetic rather than environmental factors. For animal and plant breeders the technique is useful because both the genetic relationships between individual organisms (parent/offspring, siblings, etc.) and the basic environmental conditions (diet, living conditions, temperature) under which their stocks live are known. To carry out heritability studies, knowledge of *both* of these factors is crucial.

In human behavior, genetics studies of identical twins raised apart (the data set used by Jensen for his calculations), or comparisons of adoptive children to their adoptive and biological families, provide the counterpart to the breeder's genetic studies. But estimating components of human environments, especially in family situations which have not been directly and thoroughly studied, becomes virtually impossible. It cannot be said with assurance, for example, whether two identical twins raised "apart" live in significantly different or highly similar environments. The basic assumption behind heritability estimates in human populations is that if individuals who are more closely related (and therefore share more genes in common) are more similar in some behavior, for example, scoring high or low on an I.Q. test), than individuals who are more distantly related, then that similarity is more likely to arise from genetic than environmental causes. Using data from twin and other family studies, heritability of I.Q. has been estimated by various statisticians to run anywhere from 0.3 (30%) to 0.8 (80%); Jensen's estimate fell in the latter range. Such a large range in estimates suggests that heritability estimates in humans are subject to a variety of influences and therefore must be viewed with some caution.

In evaluating what a heritability estimate means, it is as important to understand what it does *not* say as well as what it does say. What it does say is that for a heritability of, say, 0.6, 60% of the differences observed *within* a given population (from which the data were taken) can be attributed to different genotypes within that population. So, first and foremost, heritability estimates apply only to a given population, and can never be generalized to other populations. This is because the technique requires knowing that all members of the sample population were exposed to the same environmental conditions (corn growers know that soil and weather conditions can be significantly different in two adjacent counties of the same state, making any heritability estimate from one locale invalid for the other).

Second, heritability estimates apply to populations, not to individuals within the population. A high heritability estimate for a trait does not mean than any one individual within that population has inherited the trait. A final important claim that heritability studies cannot make is that a trait, even with a high heritability value, is permanent. Phenotypes of organisms change dramatically when they develop in different environments, even if there is a distinct and clearly recognized genetic basis. Thus, a high heritability estimate for human I.Q. (for example, a low score) does not mean that individuals or the population as a whole cannot raise that value significantly. Despite the term itself, heritability says nothing necessarily about an actual genetic basis for a trait. It is only an estimate of what *fraction* of a trait in a given population *might* be attributed to differences in genotypes among individuals in that population.

Many people, including a number of geneticists who shared nurturist assumptions, called Jensen's claims into question by showing that, among other things, (1) he misapplied the statistical measure of heritability; (2) the twin data on which his finding was based were dubious in nature (in some cases the data were actually shown to be spurious); and (3) intelligence was not clearly defined and was treated as if it were a single entity, like height or eye color, about which independent observers could agree.

Jensen's work was strongly criticized by population geneticist Richard Lewontin at Harvard, beginning in 1970. Lewontin made the crucial point that Jensen misused heritability by using it to argue for a genetic basis of between-group rather than merely within-group differences. Thus, since it was clear that the vast majority of African-American populations in the United States did not share the same socioeconomic or educational environment as the vast majority of Caucasians, and since the twin studies on which Jensen's statistics were based were wholly Caucasian, it could not be claimed that differences in variability of I.Q. scores being due to genetic differences in "intelligence genes" between the two populations could apply.

Lewontin also criticized Jensen and others (such as physicist William Shockley and psychologist Richard Herrnstein, who strongly supported Jensen's work) for carelessly blurring the very important difference between the terms "heritability" and "inherited." Lewontin felt that such usage played on the lack of knowledge, especially among nonspecialists, of the statistical meaning of heritability, and thus gave a very wrong impression, namely, that 80% of a person's intellectual ability (or lack thereof) was genetically based.

It should be pointed out that two areas of confusion continue to abound in the discussion of heritability estimates of I.Q. The first is whether the data and analyses are themselves reliable, and the second concerns the meaning of heritability itself, i.e., its relationship to genetics, as previously described. There is little question that many traits in the human population can be shown to have significant heritability values; for example, certain vitamin deficiency diseases such as pellagra (vitamin B-complex deficiency) have been shown to have a high heritability in specific families, not because the disease is genetically determined, but because members of the family share environments (in this case diet) in addition to sharing genes. This has been a key point in the debate over the years, even when questions of the reliability of the data are not an issue.

The race–I.Q. controversy of the 1970s, as it was called, became one of the most widely publicized and contentious outbreaks of the nature–nurture debates in both the pre- and the postwar period. Ultimately it was undermined by a variety of scientific arguments and by an exposé of the work of the British psychometrician Sir Cyril Burt whose twin studies had served as primary data for Jensen's analysis. Several investigators determined that Burt probably fudged a good deal of his data, likely fabricated at least one of his coauthors, and in general had produced analyzed data (the raw scores were lost) whose validity could not be trusted.

Despite these and many other criticisms, the claims for high heritability of I.Q. and its significance for explaining interracial and interethnic differences in educational and socioeconomic standing have recurred periodically in the United States and western Europe over the past quarter-century. One of the most prominent revivals came in the fall of 1994, with the publication of Charles Murray and Richard Herrnstein's *The Bell Curve*. In that book, Murray and Herrnstein argued that since basic intelligence is highly heritable, and since socioeconomic advancement in the future is going to depend on increasing degrees of education and technical expertise (for example, computer-based work), it was an inevitable fact that African-Americans and other minorities would be increasingly excluded from the job market and from the place in society which such jobs provided.

The Bell Curve, like Jensen's work, contained a mass of statistics derived from a voluminous survey of the existing literature, and its massive size and bibliography brought it to immediate public and professional attention. Its conclusions were met by a storm of criticism from wide segments of the academic community—from biologists to sociologists to psychologists—but it still reached a large audience and garnered a lot of media attention, being the subject of numerous TV and radio talk shows, newspaper reviews, and magazine cover stories.

Those who support The Bell Curve's basic conclusions argue that the criticism is largely politically based—that is, derives from an unwillingness to examine the basic liberal premise of human equality. Supporters thus argue that such biases prevent many academic critics from studying the work carefully and following its basic logic. Thus, the issue of inheritance of mental capacity, and its differential distribution among different racial and ethnic groups, has been, and continues to be, one of the most controversial and hotly disputed claims in the field of behavior genetics.

Although the race and I.Q. issue had subsided by the middle or late 1970s, another biological theory, not seemingly naturist at first glance, came to center stage and soon generated a controversy almost as acerbic as its predecessor. In 1975 Harvard biologist Edward O. Wilson published a monumental book titled Sociobiology, the New Synthesis (Harvard University Press). Central to Wilson's thesis was the view that most important social behaviors, including altruism and cooperation, as well as basic male–female social role differences, have arisen in the human species by natural selection, and thus form a part of our general, biological makeup. What made sociobiology, as the new science came to be called, fall into the naturist or hereditarian camp was that, according to Darwinian theory, for any trait to be acted on by natural selection (either be eliminated or preserved), it had to be genetically based. Thus, in Wilson's scenario, stereotypic female traits such as staying at home and minding the children, passivity, and intellectual subjectivity, and male traits such as hunting and roaming, aggression, and intellectual objectivity, were all inherited and served adaptive roles in the social division of labor.

Wilson also argued that traits existing across cultures, such as religious feeling, ambition, ownership of private property, male promiscuity, and homosexuality, were also genetically determined and had been retained in the species because of their overall adaptive value.

Sociobiologists offered no genetic data to support the general assumption that such traits were biologically inherited, and so were often criticized for erecting an elaborate evolutionary paradigm on uncertain genetic ground. Critics often complained that sociobiology was just another way of dressing up social prejudices in quasi-scientific garb.

The application of sociobiology to human behavior has remained a controversial area of biology to the present day. On the other hand sociobiology has become an important method for the study of nonhuman animal behavior and its evolution, since in nonhuman species it is possible to carry out genetic experiments to determine whether there is a hereditary basis for certain behaviors. The new field of evolutionary psychology that has emerged in the past decade (at least since 1990) has largely taken over the claims of sociobiology with an added emphasis on human's biological ability to learn (which neither side in the nature–nurture debate disputes).

In more recent years (since 1985) a variety of hereditarian or naturist claims have arisen, each focusing on a particular human trait: alcoholism, schizophrenia, manic depression, shyness, infidelity, aggression/violence, criminality, homosexuality, and general personality traits such as fair-mindedness, and docility. The genetic evidence on which most of these are based has come mostly from studies of monozygotic twins raised apart (using different data sets than Jensen used in 1969), adoption studies, and in at least one case (homosexuality) the identification of molecular markers on shared chromosomes within family lines. Most of these data have not stood even a short test of time, and several of the studies have been withdrawn, or their conclusions contradicted. A Scientific American article in the June 1993 issue, surveying the current status of genetic determinist theories, included a prominent table titled Behavioral Genetics: A Lack-of-Progress Report (p. 125).

This is not to say that many human behaviors do not have some genetic basis—in one sense all do, since the human body as a whole develops under the guidance of genes and this is what, in part, makes our behavioral repertoire so different from that of other animals, including the other primates. But what does appear to be the case is that genes involved in the development of the nervous system, including the brain, have evolved by natural selection to require a wide repertoire of environmental inputs in order to produce some sort of normal development. In a sense, what has been selected for in human evolution is plasticity, not fixity of behavior. Thus, in many ways, from the biological point of view the persistent argument between nature and nurture makes very little sense, since each side has tended to emphasize only one component of what is an interactive system.

VI. BIOLOGICAL ASPECTS OF NATURE–NURTURE (GENE–ENVIRONMENT) INTERACTION

The general views that genes interact with each other and with their environment to produce a phenotype have been acknowledged for almost a century. What has not been clear is how that interaction takes place and how the interacting factors affect the final outcome. Thus, the strong claims made by both sides of the nature–nurture argument have come primarily from a lack of a basic biological understanding of the process of development of particular phenotypes from particular genotypes as expressed in different environments. There are several misconceptions at work in this confusion, including a failure to understand the nature of both genes and environment.

When a fertilized egg (of any plant or animal, including humans) begins to divide to form an embryo, the organism's genome (its whole collection of genes) already exists in an intracellular environment that includes the molecular components within the cell—from large proteins to small charged ions—that serve as signals to turn genes on or off, that is, to express their message (turned on) or not to express their message (turned off). Many factors both inside the cells (presence of proteins produced by other active genes) and in the organism's external environment—for example, temperature, ion concentration in the water or soil, humidity of the air, amount of sunlight, etc.—can influence the expression of genes (which genes are expressed or the nature of the expression itself). A familiar and relatively obvious example of gene–environment interaction can be seen in plant growth.

Plants with the same genetic constitution produce very different phenotypes when grown in restricted sunlight compared to abundant sunlight, with lots of water compared to little water, in rich soil compared to poor soil, etc. In some cases (Figure 2) the phenotypes are so different as to appear to be different species. Similar phenotypic alterations occur in animals raised under different environmental conditions: fruit flies (*Drosophila melanogaster*) exposed as larvae to temperatures just a few degrees higher than normal produce an extra set of wings that are highly modified from the normal shape (Figure 3). These phenocopies, as they are called, retain their genes for normal wing development, and can pass

FIGURE 2   Terrestrial (left) and aquatic (right) forms of *Sagittaria sagittifolia* . From Schmalhausen. *Factors of evolution* (p. 197). (Chicago, University of Chicago Press. Reprint of English ed., 1986).

these on to their offspring. But the expression of the genes is changed by an environmental signal.

The sort of observations just described have led geneticists in recent years to speak of genes as having a norm of reaction rather than a specified phenotypic effect. Norm of reaction refers to the variation in expression the gene displays over a wide range of environmental conditions. Thus, to understand how gene–environment interactions take place it is necessary to expose developing organisms systematically to as many different environmental conditions as possible and observe the range of phenotypic responses for given traits that result. Such experiments have not been carried out routinely by geneticists, who traditionally follow a converse plan: namely, they test different genotypes under highly controlled, uniform environmental conditions (so that all organisms are exposed to the *same* conditions). Thus, biologists know relatively little about the norm of reaction of most genes. The result is that the general impression abounds that the same gene always produces, with perhaps very minor variations, the same phenotype regardless of environment.

Such a concept of the gene gives rise to radical hereditarianism. At the same time, failure to recognize that even highly plastic phenotypes have some genetic basis has given rise to an equally erroneous view, namely, that

a

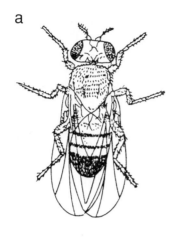

b

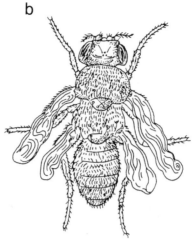

FIGURE 3   Tetraptera phenocopy in *Drosophila*. (a) Normal *D. melanogaster* male. (b) Abnormal *D. melanogaster* male showing the presence of an extra set of wings (tetraptera) produced by raising the larvae at higher temperatures than normal. From Farnsworth, 1978. *Genetics* (p. 70). New York: Harper & Row.

psychological or behavioral activities have no biological underpinning. This view gives rise to radical environmentalism. It is clear that by understanding every gene as defined by its norm of reaction, which, by definition, includes the interaction of that gene with a range of given environment(s), it is possible to begin to get beyond the otherwise apparently insoluble dilemma posed by the traditional nature–nurture debate and to understand the genesis of complex phenotypes, including behavior, in a more scientific way.

There is another issue in the modern debates in which nature and nurture are often confounded. Many naturist arguments make the assumption that if a given phenotypic difference between two individuals or groups can be shown to be biologically based, then it must therefore be genetically based. Many biological differences between two organisms can be measured clearly, and yet are not the result of corresponding genetic differences, but rather the result of the interaction of the same genes with a different environment. The norm of reaction concept makes it clear why this should be so. A normal green plant raised in the dark will grow long and spindly, and will have a smaller number of chloroplasts than one grown in full sunlight. This is a clear and distinguishable difference between the plants, but it has nothing to do with an innate genetic difference. This simple point, however, is often overlooked in nature–nurture arguments.

For example, a study in Finland in the early 1990s identified a number of families in which males displayed "impulsive" behavior, defined as the inability to control their emotions (it was exemplified in these subjects

by continually getting into barroom brawls). Medical studies of the subjects showed that their brain levels of the neurotransmitter serotonin were unusually low (serotonin is known to mediate various brain neuron signals, and thus preserves a kind of emotional equilibrium). The immediate conclusion was that the individuals in the affected families must all have inherited a gene (or genes) for defective serotonin production.

However, Michael McGuire and his colleagues at the UCLA Medical School have shown in monkeys that serotonin levels rise and fall as a consequence of a change in individuals' social position within their social group. While dominant males have low serotonin and subordinate males have higher serotonin levels, when a subordinate male become dominant, his serotonin level declines. Thus the measurable biological difference between dominant and subordinate males that some would take as reflecting a genetic difference actually turns out to be the result of a prior change in behavior.

VII. CONCLUSION

The long-standing nature–nurture debate can be seen at the present time to be the result of a naive misunderstanding of both genes and environment. In discussing mental, personality, and behavioral traits, naturists tend to view genes as rigid determiners of very specific phenotypes; even when gene interactions are acknowledged, the role of the environment is considered negligible or of minor importance. This view is very much reinforced by the conception of the gene presented the mass media, popular culture, and the like: genes are said to be "for" a given trait, or to "produce" a trait. Naturists often fail to recognize or investigate the nature of the environmental factors that influence gene action, paying only lip service to the importance of gene–environment interactions. Failure to investigate the expression of genes under a wide variety of environmental conditions (i.e., determining a gene's norm of reaction) is just one example of how the role of environment is so often taken for granted and consequently neglected.

Nurturists, seeing what appear to be oversimplistic claims for the effect of genes on complex behavior, often adopt an equally unrealistic "environmental determinist" view by claiming that many characteristics (especially mental development, personality, etc.) are determined solely by environment. In this view it is as if the specific biological makeup of the human organism did not matter. Such radical environmentalism also fails to take into account gene–environment interactions and the developmental processes by which human beings mature from early life on. Poor nutrition at early, critical stages of development can drastically affect brain development, and hence cognitive ability; the expression of genes guiding neuronal development can be altered in this way, and indeed the effects are often irreversible. The environment has played a role but so have genes, via their altered expression, and both contribute to the particular phenotype that results.

Biologists recognize that the only ways to rigorously separate the effects of "nature" vs. "nurture" are to carry out two distinct types of experiments on the organisms being investigated. The first is to make specific crosses (matings) between parents of known genotype and raise the offspring under as near as identical environmental conditions as possible; in this way differences in phenotype can be shown to reflect differences in genotype. The second way is to raise organisms of known genotypes in a wide range of environments to determine how that genotype responds to different conditions—i.e., determine its norm of reaction and thereby the range of phenotypic plasticity. Since these methods are impossible to impose on human beings, the resolution of issues in the nature–nurture debate is not likely to occur in the near future.

The different political alignments often associated with the nature–nurture debate are reflected in the historical fact that the prominence of the two positions has oscillated in a more or less parallel fashion with oscillations in economic (and associated social) conditions. In expansive economic times, as in the United States between 1945 and 1965, naturist arguments appeared to subside and nurturist ideologies prevailed: this was, after all the period that culminated in "The Great Society" and the expansion of a variety of social and educational programs. Beginning in the late 1960s, however, as the long-standing U.S. conflict in Southeast Asia took its economic toll, various naturist arguments began to reappear. And as various economic indicators (relative buying power of the dollar, loss of health care benefits, etc.) have continued to fall, the frequency of hereditarian claims has also increased. There is no clear reason for this relationship except the hypothesis emphasizing the strong, determinative effect of genes on human behavior. Naturist arguments place the blame for social problems on the defective biology of people, rather than the social and economic system. Thus, strong genetic arguments are likely to be favored by those with political and economic power because these arguments do not challenge the status quo. Historically, at least, emphasizing the strong genetic and determinist program has had the effect of preserving, or returning to, existing or previously-existing socio-economic conditions.

Thus, as a debate informing general social policies and ethical considerations about how human beings behave toward one another, the nature–nurture argument has never contributed anything of substance. It has, however, often been used by one side or the other of a given polemic to obscure the real social and political issues at stake, and thus has served to confuse, rather than clarify, the pursuit of human affairs.

Also See the Following Articles

EUGENICS • GENETIC RESEARCH • GENOME ANALYSIS • INTELLIGENCE TESTING • RACISM • SEXISM

Bibliography

Allen, G. E. (1994). The genetic fix: The social origins of genetic determination. In E. Tobach and B. Rosoff (Eds.), *Challenging racism and sexism: Alternatives to genetic explanations* (pp. 163–187). New York: City Univ. of New York, Feminist Press.

Allen, G. E. (1996). Science misapplied: The eugenics age revisited. *Technology Review*, Aug./Sept, 23–31.

Degler, C. (1991). *In search of human nature*. New York: Oxford Univ. Press).

Gould, S. J. (1996). *The mismeasure of man* (rev. ed.). New York: Norton.

Haller, J. S. (1971). *Outcasts from evolution: Scientific attitudes of racial inferiority, 1859–1900*. Champaign–Urbana: Univ. of Illinois Press).

Hubbard, R., & Wald, E. (1993). *Exploding the gene myth*. Boston: Beacon.

Stanton, W. (1960). *The leopard's spots. Scientific attitudes toward race in America, 1815–1859*. Chicago: Univ. of Chicago Press.

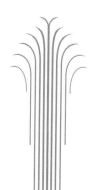

NUCLEAR DETERRENCE

Jeffery L. Johnson
Eastern Oregon University

GLOSSARY

deontology Moral theory in which considerations other than the consequences of actions are relevant to the determination of the rightness or wrongness of those actions.

deterrence Announced sanctions for certain courses of action designed to reduce the likelihood of those actions taking place.

game theory The formalized study of rational action in interactive and strategic settings where one actor's welfare is determined in part by the actions of other actors.

just war theory A historically significant part of Scholastic philosophy and political theory addressing the boundaries for a morally acceptable use of military force.

nuclear deterrence A strategy of nations possessing significant nuclear arsenals for deterring military actions, particularly the initiation of nuclear war, on the part of other nations.

nuclear war The massive use of nuclear weapons for military purposes.

utilitarianism Moral theory in which no considerations other than the consequences of actions are relevant to the determination of the rightness or wrongness of those actions.

NUCLEAR DETERRENCE is a strategy of nations possessing significant nuclear arsenals for influencing the behavior of other nations, usually also possessing nuclear arsenals. More specifically it is a strategy of putting in place incentives for other nations not to engage in certain kinds of military actions, in particular not initiating a nuclear war. These incentives are negative sanctions that are announced and are intended to be taken seriously. Basically, nuclear deterrence is a strategy of promising to retaliate against another nation for some military action with the use of nuclear weapons. The clearest case is a simple threat—if you use nuclear weapons against me, then I will retaliate and use them against you. The hope, of course, is that by clearly issuing this threat in a credible manner, you will come to the conclusion that it is not in your best interest to use nuclear weapons against me. Thus, I will have succeeded in deterring you from such a course of action.

Contemporary moral philosophy has shown much concern with nuclear war and nuclear deterrence. This is hardly surprising, given that everyone considers a full-scale nuclear war just about the worst thing that could ever happen. What may be surprising, however, is how complicated and contentious the normative analysis of the strategy of nuclear deterrence has proven to be.

I. WAR, NUCLEAR WAR, AND NUCLEAR DETERRENCE

For the purposes of this discussion, we should accept that fact that armed conflict between sovereign nations is both a historical, and contemporary, fact of the international scene. As regrettable as it may be, there is no reason to believe that things will change in the foreseeable future. War, therefore, will not be the subject of moral assessment, but a presupposed context for a normative analysis of war, and strategies for avoiding war, within the contemporary nuclear context. None of this should diminish the importance of, nor the intellectual interest in, moral defenses and condemnations of any sort violence inflicted by one nation upon another. Complete pacifism, although very interesting, has always been an extreme minority position. We will assume, therefore, that some sort of moral justification for war, in the abstract, is theoretically possible.

Nuclear war, however, is very different. Indeed, it is tempting to argue that the moral presupposition is in exactly the opposite direction. For the purpose of this discussion let us understand by the expression "nuclear war," the *massive* use of nuclear weapons for a clearly military purpose. This definition would rule out World War II as a nuclear war. I think it is important to do this, not for the purposes of excusing the decision makers for their choice to use atomic weapons against Japan, but because the level of destruction was on the same scale as that caused by conventional weapons. When moral philosophers, or Defense Department strategists, debate nuclear war they have in mind the use of thousands of these devices. The numbers—of warheads, of the dead and injured, of the economic loss—all quickly become so large that few, if any, can really comprehend them. One very modest Pentagon estimate from the early 1980s gives at least some sense of the relative destructive stakes at issue—100 nuclear warheads, delivered to the Soviet Union, could immediately kill 37 million and destroy 59% of Soviet industrial capacity.

It is very hard to see how an adequate moral defense of nuclear war could be mounted. We need not become distracted imagining such an argument, however, because everyone—hawks and doves, enemies and allies—agrees that nuclear war is so undesirable that it must be an absolute priority to avoid it. The key ques-

tion to be addressed is not about the normative status of nuclear war, which is pretty terrible, but the moral acceptability of the predominant strategy for avoiding nuclear war—nuclear deterrence.

Occasionally, the concept of nuclear deterrence is expanded to include threats to use nuclear weapons to deter other sorts of military action. We will spend little time discussing the wider understanding, because any sort of moral condemnation of the more narrow strategy will surely apply to the wider, and any judgment of the moral permissibility of narrow deterrence must be presupposed for discussion of the moral status of the wider strategy.

Several things are presupposed in a strategy of nuclear deterrence. I must really possess such an arsenal, or I must be very good at deceiving you that I do. I must also possess the technical capability of making good on my promise to retaliate, or I must fool you into thinking that I do. Finally, if my threat is to be at all credible, I must really intend to retaliate in the circumstance where my threat has failed to deter you, or, once again, I must bluff you into believing that I do.

Normative questions abound within a context of nuclear deterrence. The building and maintenance of nuclear arsenals is incredibly expensive. Moral philosophers and policy makers, alike, may well query whether this is the best, or most efficient, use of limited national resources. By all accounts, the continued existence of these arsenals, along with the technical capability to make use of them, significantly increases the risk that there will be a nuclear war. Given the horrors of nuclear war, it is reasonable to ask whether the strategy is worth the increased risk, from either a normative or a policy standpoint. There is a certain sense in which both of these concerns are empirical in nature. This, of course, in no way diminishes their importance, but it does suggest that behavioral perspectives like operations research, benefit/cost analysis, and the whole arena of contemporary social scientific research may have as much to say about these questions as traditional moral philosophy.

Particularly confusing from a moral perspective is the forming of intentions, or perhaps conditional intentions, to do something terrible in retaliation. My threat was to retaliate by using my nuclear weapons against you, if you used yours against me. I am asking you to believe that I am willing to carry through on this declaration. But the massive use of nuclear weapons against you is horrible, and probably immoral. Is it morally justifiable, therefore, for me to issue such a threat, set in place a mechanism to carry through with such a threat, and be willing to use nuclear weapons, should the treats fail to deter you from using your weapons against me?

There are a number of answers to these questions in the contemporary literature on the moral status of nuclear deterrence. I think its fair to say, however, that there is little consensus as to the correct answer. This is hardly surprising, but it is disquieting. Fortunately, there is at least a growing consensus about the parameters for a normative assessment of nuclear deterrence.

II. DETERRENCE, RATIONALITY, AND GAME THEORY

Deterrence presupposes rationality. If you are completely irrational, then my deterrent strategy will succeed only by accident. Economists understand rationality in terms of personal (some would say selfish) utility maximization. Mathematical decision theory is useful, therefore, in assessing the rationality deterrence as a strategy. Appreciating the dynamics of nuclear deterrence is further complicated by the fact that both you and I possess nuclear weapons, and each of us seeks to influence each other's behavior. My decisions seek to react to your decisions, while at the same time, they seek to influence your decisions. This sort of interactive strategy is helpfully modeled in contemporary game theory.

Consider the game of chicken illustrated in the payoff matrix in Table I, where my payoff is indicated before yours.

Clearly, from my selfish perspective, I desire that you not play Defect, because this results in the worst, and next worst, payoffs for me. It is in my best interest, therefore, to deter you from playing Defect. The obvious way for me to do this is to promise you (threaten you) with a conditional response—if you play Defect, then I will play Defect. Because both of our playing Defect results in the single worst payoff for you, it is rational for you (assuming that you believe my threat) not to play Defect. If my threat is credible, it will deter you

because you are rational and clearly see that playing Cooperate gives you the best payoff you can hope for.

You, of course, are faced with a mirror image problem. The payoffs give you exactly the same incentives to engage in strategy designed to deter me from playing Defect. You issue your articulation of the very same threat to me, and hope that I will take it seriously, and come to the rational conclusion that it is in my best interest to play Cooperate.

Two very different factors complicate the analysis just given. The first has to do with the single best payoff for each of us. Your single best outcome results in playing Defect, while getting me to play Cooperate. You have the incentive, therefore, to play Cooperate only as long as you take my deterrent threat seriously, otherwise playing Defect will maximize your utility. The same considerations apply to me—my preferred outcome is a Defect play while you play Cooperate. If either of us can get away with playing Defect, while the other plays Cooperate, there is rational incentive to do this. Indeed, both of us knew this all along in formulating our original deterrent strategies. If I did not worry that you had some rational incentive to play Defect in the first place, I would not have been nearly as concerned with deterring you from this move.

Much more disturbing, however, is a very plausible argument that seems to demonstrate that deterrence strategy is so fundamentally flawed that it is irrational, or even incoherent. In a world of perfect information, each of us has equal access to the payoff matrix in Table I. It can be argued that you would never take my deterrent threat seriously. After all, suppose you do play Defect, despite my best attempts to deter you. What is the rational play for me now? My best alternative is to not retaliate. Playing Cooperate after your play of Defect is not a particularly happy move for me—it results in my next worst payoff—but it is clearly better than playing Defect, which would doom to me to my worst payoff. It seems, therefore, that the strictly rational move is always to let you get away with playing Defect. And because you know this just as well as I do, why would you ever take my threats seriously? Once again, the same reasoning forces me to put little stock in your retaliatory threats. It now seems that assumptions of ideal rationality and perfect information guarantee that deterrent strategies will always fail.

Such a result has struck some as down right paradoxical. Defenders of the rationality of deterrence, as might be expected, have a number or responses. You will take my threat much more seriously, if I can convince you that extrarational considerations like pride and honor will influence my behavior—"Better dead than Red."

TABLE I

		Me	
		Cooperate	Defect
You	Cooperate	3 _3_	4 _1_
	Defect	1 _4_	0 _0_

Also, my announced intention to retaliate has greater credibility in a world where institutional complexity, or response time, makes my responding with Defect more automatic than freely chosen. Finally, some have argued that when "expected outcomes" are considered, and we calculate not just the payoffs, but also their probability of occurring, then a pure deterrent strategy can be rational.

Rational, or not, in this perhaps overly technical sense, deterrence is clearly puzzling. The strategy seems to depend on a stated willingness to undertake actions to bring about an objectively awful state of affairs, or more accurately, to make awful ones worse. Furthermore, most would agree that these actions are immoral. And, if this were not bad enough, the proposed actions seem at best futile, and more likely counterproductive. It is no surprise, therefore, that nuclear deterrence has attracted so much recent attention from moral philosophers.

III. JUST-WAR THEORY

A useful beginning point for discussing the morality of nuclear deterrence is an ancient part of Scholastic theology, moral philosophy, and political theory, called *just-war theory*. When the Catholic Church began to be a player in secular and political affairs there was a pressing need to square theological views with the realities of the international scene. Everyone realized that wars had always been fought, were being fought, and would continue to be fought. Western theism traditionally taught, however, that the taking of human life was wrong. The tension between the tacitly recognized right of nations to fight wars that were in their genuine interests, particularly the right of nations to defend themselves, and moral and theological teachings about the wrongness of killing, required some sort of theoretical compromise. The doctrines that emerged out of the natural law perspective have continued to exert great normative, legal, and political influence.

Classical just war theory distinguishes the conditions for justifiable recourse to war—*jus ad bellum*—from the conditions for the justifiable conduct during war—*jus in bello*. Both kinds of considerations have direct bearing on the moral assessment of nuclear deterrence.

Just-war theorists typically insist on a number of preconditions for entering into a just war. First of all the war, or warlike action, must be authorized in a politically appropriate manner. A nation's "leadership" must have decided to undertake military action against another nation, and historically they were required to

declare this intention. Much more important to our discussion, however, is the *jus ad bellum* requirement that just wars be fought only for just causes. The central notion in the just cause prerequisite is the principle of proportionality. Not any old national interest can justify military action. Because wars result in tremendous amounts of loss, they can only be justified in those circumstances where the national interests are so important that they outweigh, on some kind of normative scale, these losses. The purposes for engaging in war must be proportional to evil that will result from the war.

The principle of proportionality is, as one should expect, a central consideration in discussions of nuclear war and nuclear deterrence. The estimated affects of full-scale nuclear war are so horrible, that the compensating national interest would have to be very significant, indeed. The principle of proportionality is one of the reasons why most contributors to this literature simply assume that the actual use of nuclear weapons is immoral—they simply cannot imagine, nor can this author imagine, considerations of national interest that could possibly outweigh the death and devastation that would result from nuclear war.

If we assume that just-war theory covers, not just the conduct of actual wars, but military and defense strategy, as well, then nuclear deterrence raises some very interesting questions. The strategy of nuclear deterrence is expensive, dangerous, and seems to commit us to forming conditional intentions to perform immoral actions. Thus the principle of proportionality requires that the national interest that justifies undertaking such a military strategy be pretty important. But, of course, it is. The end that defenders of nuclear deterrence would argue justifies the highly problematic means, is the avoidance of nuclear war. Thus, the normative weighing that is required in assessing nuclear deterrence in terms of the principle of proportionality is subtle and interesting.

The principle of proportion reappears in *jus in bello* considerations. Just-war theorists insist that we must weigh, not just the national purpose for engaging in war, as a whole, against all the terrible effects, but also the military objective of some proposed action, an action or military strategy, against the loss that will result. Once again, the relevance to a nuclear context is obvious. Indeed, this application of just-war theory and this narrow application of the principle of proportionality is the theoretical basis for the sustained moral debate about history's one use of atomic weapons.

An additional *jus in bello* principle covers the moral status of innocent citizens and bystanders. The principle of discrimination prohibits attacks intentionally directed against noncombatants and nonmilitary targets. The destructive capabilities of modern conventional warfare have complicated the application, and to some degree the relevance, of this principle. Nuclear war raises even tougher questions. Nevertheless, the moral status of citizens, including children, of the nation against whom the deterrent threat is issued continues to occupy the attention of moral philosophers. Equally troubling, perhaps more so, is the moral status of citizens of nonbelligerent nations, who would certainly be affected by a full-scale exchange of nuclear weapons.

The principle of discrimination has particular relevance to debates about the strategy on nuclear deterrence. Intentions to retaliate are conditional, and inevitably refer to an uncertain future. Modern nuclear deterrence, nevertheless, requires that some decisions and actions be made and acted on in the present. They are not conditional intentions, but actual ones, with actual effects. Military decisions about the level of response to nondeterred aggressive actions must, to some degree, be made now. Choices about potential nuclear targets must be made in the present. Such actual decision making occupies the time and attention of defense strategists as full-time careers. Debates between national strategies of "mutually assured destruction," "countervalue," and "counterforce" are, at least to some degree, influenced by the traditional just war considerations like the principle of discrimination.

IV. DEONTOLOGICAL ARGUMENTS

A deontological perspective in moral philosophy commits a theorist to there being circumstances in which "the ends do not justify the means." Deontological arguments assert that other considerations besides a "simple" calculation of the consequences of some action or decision are morally relevant to its rightness or wrongness. Deontologists claim that objective values like duty, God's commands, or justice must be taken very seriously in making and justifying normative assessments. Most deontologists do not deny that consequences have considerable moral significance. They do insist, however, other considerations including the "intrinsic wrongness" of certain courses of action be given equal, or at least some, consideration in our moral decision making.

The first deontological principle that we need to review is in many respects the most important. It focuses on a right that is either collectively possessed, or more accurately that is in the possession of a purely

abstract entity. It is widely acknowledged that sovereign nations have a right to defend themselves with the use of military force. An explicit analogy is often drawn with the right of individuals to use deadly force in cases of self-defense. When people have good reason to believe that their physical safety and lives are in jeopardy because of the actions of an assailant they are granted permission to protect themselves through the use of physical violence. Very similar arguments have been used at the level of national defense.

Discussions of self-defense within the nuclear context often fail to distinguish the two very different senses in which sovereign nations might justify a strategy of nuclear deterrence by appeal to the above principle. Successful deterrence may save millions of innocent lives. We will examine this defense in a greater detail below. But, as significant as this consideration may be, the more common deontological appeal to national self-defense focuses on the continued existence of the abstract political entity—the nation-state—itself. Here the focus is on political and economic systems, culture and ways of life. Classical just-war theory always implicitly acknowledged this right of sovereign nations. Indeed, it seems presupposed in the entire discussion.

If a nation comes to a considered judgment that their existence is placed in real jeopardy by a rival nuclear power, if they have reason to believe that this enemy may desire to launch an attack and kill millions of their innocent citizens, if they believe this adversary will use the threat to attack to "blackmail" the nation into courses of action that are counter to its vital nation interests, many would say this nation has the right to defend itself. If, in its judgment a strategy of nuclear deterrence is the best means of protecting itself, such a normative defense of the strategy will always carry some significant argumentative force.

Moral opponents of nuclear deterrence have recourse to a number of deontological principles that point in an opposite direction. The first comes directly out of just-war theory. The principle of discrimination requires that military actions be directed away from noncombatants. It is plausibly argued, however, that the massive use of nuclear weapons will always have devastating effects on innocent people. Even if only military targets are considered, this will still include many large cities that function as military command posts. Basically, the use of nuclear weapons, even in a purely retaliatory context, would result in death and injury for innocent civilians on an unimaginable scale. Thus, this argument goes, because killing innocents is intrinsically wrong, and because nuclear deterrence commits a nation to these actions should all else fail, nuclear deterrence is intrinsically wrong.

Proponents of the strategy have at their disposal a very interesting response. They can argue that the whole purpose of nuclear deterrence is the avoidance of the death and destruction that innocent people would experience in a nuclear war. The deaths, everyone hopes, would not be actual deaths, but conditional deaths. No one dies from the use of nuclear weapons, *if* the strategy achieves its desired outcome.

The use of nuclear weapons in retaliation, and the death and destruction that would result, may only exist in our nightmares, and the world of subjunctive conditionals. The policy of nuclear deterrence has some actual effects, here and now. Many believe that both you and I having massive arsenals, planning national defense in a context of suspicion and distrust, and other obvious features of the contemporary nuclear scene, make it more likely that at some point in the future nuclear weapons will be used. This may come about because of mistaken calculations of strategic advantage, anger or irrational behavior on the part of national leaders, or by simple mistake. In any case, having such destructive power sitting there, armed with a hair trigger, seems by itself to make it frighteningly likely that the worst will eventually happen.

We consider it intrinsically wrong to put others, particularly innocent others, at great risk. It is wrong of me to drive my car in a state of intoxication, even if I am lucky enough to always get away with it. Negligent, or overly risky behavior, is wrong, and must be normatively condemned, whether or not it results in disastrous consequences. Because my engaging in a strategy of nuclear deterrence puts others, innocents in both of our nations, as well as innocents in nonbelligerent nations, at great risk, it is wrong. It is wrong, here and now, nonconditionally.

This argument is plausible, but once again it admits to a plausible response. Enthusiasts of nuclear deterrence can start by pointing out that society accepts high levels of risk, if they perceive that the benefit is great enough. We actively invest in, and make routine use of, national systems of highway and air travel. Clearly, driving the interstate, or flying in an airliner, is very risky business. Convenience, economic efficiency, and modern culture, simply force us to accept the risk of terrible accidents. We do not judge these risks as immoral, or even unreasonable. Nuclear deterrence does impose great risk, but its goal—avoiding nuclear war—is at least as important as ease of travel. Further, a world without nuclear deterrence might be even riskier. You still retain your nuclear weapons. If I do not make

it in your best interest not to use them through a policy of nuclear deterrence, my decision not to undertake this strategy, or to abandon it, may actually impose greater risk on innocents at home and abroad.

The final deontological consideration we will examine has received the most attention in the contemporary philosophical literature. It focuses on a controversial thesis in moral psychology. Let us grant that using nuclear weapons is wrong, on deontological grounds, and on a strict utilitarian calculation of positive and negative consequences. Many have taken it to be self-evident that if some action is wrong, it is intrinsically wrong to intend it. If I intend to murder you, indeed set my plan in motion, and you conveniently die before I can carry it out, most would agree that I am guilty of a significant moral wrong, although intuitions vary as to whether I am as wrong as if I had carried out the murder plan.

Let us assume that it would be wrong for me to retaliate against you for your use of nuclear weapons against me by using my nuclear weapons against you. It was very wrong of you, of course, to use them against me, but, because "two wrongs don't make a right," the wrongness of your action in no way justifies my action against you. Let us further assume that the wrongness of my using these weapons against you depends on deontological principles like the principle of proportionality—no possible military or political gain would outweigh the addition death and destruction—and the principle of discrimination—my retaliatory strike will inevitably target innocent noncombatants in your nation, as well as others. Is it wrong of me to say that I intend to use them against you, if you use them against me, if my whole purpose in issuing the threat is to ensure that neither of us ever use them in the first place? One way I might be excused from the charge of having wrongful intentions is if I am lying to you. Perhaps I am only bluffing, and have no intention to actually retaliate. Normative worries about truth telling aside, there is a huge problem with this strategy. In a world of international intelligence, public debate, and democratic decision making, my bluff is almost certainly guaranteed to be exposed. Suppose, therefore, that I steel myself to really mean what I say—I systematically form the real intention to use my nuclear weapons in the worst case where deterrence has failed. Am I acting wrongly? Is it wrong to form a robust intention to carry through with something that is wrong, even if the purpose is to avoid the wrong act?

It seems plausible to this author to argue that knowingly forming, and continuing to hold, an intention to conditionally do something wrong in the future, is itself wrong. This judgment is something of a discovery that has come out of the contemporary literature on the morality of nuclear deterrence. I am willing to grant, therefore, that my entire deterrent strategy violates a general deontological principle that sanctions the holding of wrongful intentions, even conditionally. This moral evaluation does not settle the question of whether I should discontinue my policy of nuclear deterrence, however. It can be argued, again with disturbing plausibility, that it would be even more wrong, to abandon the strategy.

One very widely accepted moral principle tells us that we should attempt to minimize evil. I have promised to go to the party with you, it's very important to you, and I know this; my promise was neither casual, nor trivial. It would be wrong to stand you up. Unfortunately, my best friend just called and is feeling down to the point of being suicidal. I need to be with him, it would be wrong not to do so. I can't keep my promise to go to the party with you, and at the same time fulfill my duty to my friend. I am stuck with doing something wrong, and the best I can hope for is that I will do the least normative damage. Perhaps forming the intention to retaliate with nuclear weapons is, indeed, wrong. It still may be argued that my duty to protect my national sovereignty, as well as my duty to take reasonable steps to prevent your using nuclear weapons, outweighs my duty not to form immoral intentions.

There is a common structure to the discussion above. Deontological theorizing seems to force us to a kind of moral balancing. Maybe in a world that is as complicated as this one we are not granted the luxury of formulating a morally acceptable nuclear defense strategy; maybe the best we can hope for is whatever policy minimizes the actual and possible evil.

V. UTILITARIAN ARGUMENTS

Talk by moral philosophers about balancing is more at home in the utilitarian tradition in moral theory. Utilitarians believe that whatever action will have the overall best consequences is morally correct. If, rather than abstract principles, it is the costs and benefits of possible courses of action that is measured and debated, we see the difficulty of the nuclear deterrence debate in its starkest terms.

When we carefully examine the books for nuclear deterrence, there are three huge entries on the debit side. The first is financial. A huge percentage of my gross domestic product, my resources, must be used for maintaining a credible nuclear threat. This is money

that could be used for health care and other social services, for buying down the national debt, or for lower taxes. Almost everyone agrees that there is something disturbing about making huge national investments in a class of things the whole purpose of which is to never be used. The context of our discussion has placed such heavy emphasis in future states of affairs, ones that can only be known in probabilistic or subjunctive terms. It is relevant to point out the obvious, therefore. These significant financial considerations are real costs, here and now, that make real differences in a nation's quality of life.

A second cost of nuclear deterrence, that is also very real, is psychological. Living in a world where national defense posture is predicated on strategies of a "balance of terror" must inevitably take its toll on ordinary citizens, and national leaders, as well. There is no reliable measure of how great a cost this really is, but it is safe to assume that everyone who lived through the 1950s, 1960s, and 1970s would agree that it is tangible.

The third cost, of course, is much more difficult to measure. It only becomes actual in a subjunctive future where deterrence has failed. You use your nuclear weapons against me, and I retaliate and use mine against you. Everyone agrees that this is the worst imaginable state of affairs possible. What is the cost of placing the world at increased risk of this "lose-lose" possibility? Many have argued that any situation would be better— even if this meant accepting increased risk of nuclear blackmail, or even the loss of national sovereignty. Without resolving these questions of detailed utilitarian balancing, we can all agree the international dynamics of nuclear deterrence create a very dangerous world, and that this increased danger is one consequence of the strategy that must be taken into account.

The other side of the ledger book for nuclear deterrence basically contains a single entry. The strategy has worked. The recent history seems clear. Humanity has possessed full-scale nuclear capability for more than 40 years without these weapons ever being used. For most of this period there was announced political and military hostility between the world's two "superpowers," without any kind of direct military conflict, conventional or nuclear. Judgments of causal efficacy will vary, of course. It can be argued that this was more blind luck than the stabilizing effects of nuclear deterrence. But proponents of the strategy can still point out how unlikely such a stretch of relative international stability has been in the last 100 years of international history.

A strictly utilitarian assessment of nuclear deterrence leaves us pretty much in the same place we were with the deontological approach. Both opponents and defenders of nuclear deterrence can point to consequences that are clearly relevant. Once again, unfortunately, intuitions vary wildly as to whether the strategy results in the greatest net balance of good consequences, or more likely in this case, the least net balance of bad consequences.

VI. SOME PUZZLES FOR THE FUTURE

Consider, once again, the game of chicken represented in Table I. What if the payoffs are changed so that any cell other than mutual cooperation results in payoffs of negative infinity for both players? In 1983 a group of close to 100 distinguished scientists issued published reports of a conference synthesizing empirical and theoretical estimates of the effects of even a "modest" use of nuclear weapons. The conclusions were quite startling, even for those who had long been concerned about the effects of nuclear war.

> There is a real danger of the extinction of humanity. A threshold exists at which climatic catastrophe could be triggered, very roughly around 500–2,000 strategic warheads. A major first strike may be an act of national suicide, even if no retaliation occurs. . . . No national or ideological confrontation justifies putting the species at risk (Sagan (1983). Nuclear war and climatic catastrophe: Some policy implications. *Foreign Affairs*, p. 159).

Discussions of nuclear war, nuclear deterrence, disarmament, and the like take on a very different tone when the real possibility of the extinction of our species must be entered into the moral equation. It is, of course, true that some dismiss the above estimates as empirically unsound, and alarmist in nature. Few, if any, of us possess the scientific competence to make the judgment, one way or another, as to how realistic the risk of species extinction is. One thing for sure, however, it is a morally relevant consideration. It will be interesting to see how the normative debate plays out in light of the "nuclear winter" hypothesis.

To conclude this discussion, suppose that my nation, due to economic and political instabilities, simply collapses. My nuclear weapons still exist, although successor nations that come to possess them make a commitment to dismantling them, or at least greatly reducing their number. Suppose that in everyone's considered judgment the chances of these weapons being used in a systematic first strike is significantly reduced. You have much less incentive to engage in a strategy of nuclear deterrence. What are the moral implications of your military and defense options with respect to your nuclear weapons? Obviously, in the judgment of many, we are living through just such a unique period of contemporary history. Assuming that this correctly describes international reality, and further assuming that this state of affairs persists, the agenda for the next generation of moral theorists concerned with nuclear war and nuclear deterrence seems clear. What will be a morally acceptable stance for nations possessing nuclear arsenals in a post cold war international scene?

Also See the Following Articles

GAME THEORY • NATIONAL SECURITY ISSUES • WARFARE, STRATEGIES AND TACTICS

Bibliography

Copp, D. (Ed.). (1993). *Nuclear weapons, deterrence & disarmament.* Concord: Paul and Company.

Hardin, R. (Ed.). (1986). *Nuclear deterrence: Ethics & strategy.* Chicago: Chicago University Press.

Holmes, R. L. (1989). *On War and morality.* Princeton, NJ: Princeton University Press.

Kavka, G. S. (1987). *Moral paradoxes of nuclear deterrence.* Cambridge UK: Cambridge University Press.

Lackey, D. P. (Ed.). (1989). *Ethics and strategic defense.* Belmont, CA: Wadsworth.

Lee, S. P. (1993). *Morality, prudence, and nuclear weapons.* Cambridge, UK: Cambridge University Press.

Shue, H. (Ed.). (1989). *Nuclear deterrence & moral restraint: Critical choices for American strategy.* Institute for Philosophy & Public Policy. Cambridge, UK: Cambridge University Press.

NUCLEAR POWER

Kristin Shrader-Frechette
University of South Florida

GLOSSARY

chain reaction A continuous, self-sustaining series of fission reactions in a mass of uranium or plutonium.

fission The only type of nuclear reaction that is controlled by people to produce energy. It occurs when a nucleus of uranium or another heavy element is split into parts.

half-life The time required for half the atoms of a radioactive substance to decay into another substance.

isotopes Different forms of the same element.

nuclear reactor A device for producing nuclear energy by means of controlled chain reactions.

radioactivity The radiation emitted by a radioactive substance such as uranium, radium, thorium, plutonium, iodine-131, strontium-90, cesium-137, or carbon-14. Radiation is ionizing when it is able to remove orbital electrons from other atoms or molecules. The ability of ionizing radiation to change

molecular structures is what accounts for its ability to cause cancer, genetic damage, and even death.

NUCLEAR POWER is a means of generating energy, mainly in the form of heat, by using either fission or breeder reactors. Fission reactors create energy by a self-sustaining chain reaction that splits the nuclei of atoms of uranium or plutonium. Breeder reactors convert a uranium isotope to fissionable plutonium and produce more radioactive fuel than they use. Both types of reactors control the heat energy they generate so that it can produce steam and run a turbine. Nuclear weapons such as bombs get their destructive power from uncontrolled fission.

Nuclear generation of electricity has several significant advantages. It avoids use of scarce oil and gas, it requires less fuel than other sources of power, and it releases only minimal chemical or solid pollutants into the air. At present, approximately 30 nations have more than 400 nuclear plants for generating electricity. More than 150 are in European countries, and the United States has the largest number (113 reactors) in the world. The first full-scale, commercial nuclear power plant was opened in England in 1956, and the second plant began operating a year later in the United States. Concerns about safety, however, have stopped the growth of commercial nuclear power in most nations of the world. Reactor accidents, cancer and genetic damage induced by the smallest amounts of radioactive material, and problems with disposal of the high-level radioactive waste (which remains dangerous forever) are the three most important nuclear-related safety issues. Cost overruns and public opposition—driven in part by the 1986 Chernobyl and the 1979 Three Mile Island accidents—also have contributed to the move away from nuclear power. Since 1974, no new commercial reactors (which have not been subsequently cancelled) have been ordered in the United States.

One reason that the health effects of ionizing radiation are so serious is that there is *no threshold* for increased risk as a result of exposure to even small amounts of radiation; all doses of ionizing radiation are harmful. Effects of radiation also are *cumulative*: successive exposures increase one's risk of harm. Exposure to radiation can cause cancer, reproductive failure, birth defects, genetic effects, and death. In 1989 the U.S. National Research Council argued that an acute dose of radiation is three times more likely to cause cancerous tumors and four times more likely to induce leukemia than risks calculated in 1980. Hence, despite the known consequences of radiation, even current standards may be too lenient. Identifying dangerous effects of radiation also is difficult because many of them are latent. For example, at the Oak Ridge National Laboratories, where many persons received high doses of radiation, it took 26 years for the cancer rate to exhibit a statistically significant increase. It took 4 years for thyroid cancers to show statistically significant increases near Chernobyl after the 1986 accident. Much radiation damage also remains undetected because few persons do epidemiological studies to measure its effects on humans, even though no amount of exposure to ionizing radiation is completely safe.

Because of the enormous capital expense of nuclear power and because it supplies about 3% of total global electricity, there is continuing ethical controversy over whether to build any new plants, whether to shut down existing reactors, and how to dispose of radioactive waste so as not to harm members of future generations. Most of these ethical issues focus on problems with equal protection from catastrophic reactor accidents, with due process in the event of nuclear-related harm, and with failure of the public to provide genuine informed consent to the risks associated with nuclear power.

I. HISTORY OF NUCLEAR POWER

In 1895, Roentgen discovered the x-ray, and in 1896, Becquerel and the Curies discovered natural radioactiv-

ity. Large volumes of radioactive waste were not created, however, until the atomic bomb program of World War II. During the war, both the United States and the former Soviet Union built uranium enrichment plants and started to develop light-water, nuclear fission reactors (that use enriched uranium fuel) because this was the technology already used in their military efforts. Canada, France, and Great Britain, however, began work on reactors moderated by graphite or heavy water. Using unenriched uranium, these reactors cost more to build than the enriched uranium reactors of the United States, but they were safer by virtue of being better able to withstand a loss of cooling.

The effort to collect the plutonium needed for atomic bombs during World War II was part of a U.S. defense effort, begun in 1942, known as the "Manhattan Engineer District Project." In December of that same year, Enrico Fermi directed a team that produced the world's first nuclear chain reaction. By January 1943, U.S. federal government researchers were overseeing the building of the first atomic bombs at Oak Ridge, Tennessee, and Hanford, Washington. On 16 July 1945, the world's first atomic bomb, using plutonium, was exploded in New Mexico. On 6 August 1945, the United States dropped the first nuclear warhead, employing uranium-235, on Hiroshima. Sixty-five thousand persons perished in the blast. Days later, another atomic bomb was dropped on Nagasaki.

Many of the ethical problems associated with decision making about commercial nuclear power stem from the military origins of the technology. The Manhattan Project, with its military focus, has left a legacy of secrecy, centralization, and technocracy which has dominated nuclear-related decision making for at least three decades. This three-part legacy led to haste, to temporary solutions, and to a lack of public participation in regulating nuclear energy. The legacy also contributed to institutional self-protection and to public policy that was neither properly debated nor scrutinized through scientific peer review. For example, in 1986, in response to public demand, the U.S. Department of Energy released 19,000 pages of formerly classified documents on the operations at the Hanford facility (used to develop the atomic bomb and to store radioactive waste) during the 1940s and 1950s. The documents reveal that U.S. military researchers had conducted radiological experiments on local people, without either their knowledge or their permission. In 1945 alone, the Hanford facility, devoted to wartime production of plutonium, routinely released 340,000 curies of radioactive iodine through its reactor exhaust stacks. (Current regulations permit less than 1 curie of iodine to be released each year at the facility, and even in 1945 this deliberate release far exceeded U.S. government environmental standards.) Numerous other accidents and deliberate releases occurred at Hanford, many of which were designed for the purpose of developing a monitoring methodology for intelligence efforts regarding the Soviet military program. Such experiments were made possible only because of the secrecy that shrouded the nuclear industry in all countries in its early years (U.S. Congress, 1994. *Human Subjects Research: Radiation Experimentation*. U.S. Government Printing Office, Washington, DC).

From 1940 to 1945, the United States spent $2 billion to develop the first atomic bombs used during World War II. Thereafter, the government took 20 years and more than $100 billion in subsidies to develop the first commercial nuclear reactors used to generate electricity. Scientists were optimistic about the Atoms for Peace program; it provided a nonmilitary rationale for continuing the development of nuclear technology and for obtaining weapons-grade plutonium that could be used for military purposes. Nobel-winning scientists, such as Henry Kendall (1991. *Calypso Log* **18**, 9), now claim that the present U.S. government subsidies for commercial reactors are running on the order of $20 billion per year; if these subsidies were removed from nuclear electricity, Kendall and others claim that the costs of fission-generated electricity would double.

In 1951, the Experimental Breeder Reactor at Arco, Idaho, produced the first commercial nuclear electric power. Between 1948 and 1953, the United States built and tested a submarine reactor at Idaho Falls under the leadership of Admiral H. G. Rickover. The submarine *Nautilus* went to sea in 1955, powered by a nuclear reactor using enriched uranium fuel. All of the Polaris missile-carrying submarines of the United States use nuclear reactors. In 1956, the first full-scale nuclear fission power plant began to operate at Calder Hall in northwestern England. Only after the passage of the 1957 U.S. Price–Anderson Act, limiting nuclear liability in the event of an accident, did the U.S. industry agree to begin using atomic energy for commercial generation of electricity. The first U.S. commercial nuclear plant opened in Shippingport, Pennsylvania, in 1957. Also in 1957, the United Nations established the International Atomic Energy Agency to promote the peaceful uses of nuclear power. In 1958, the former Soviet Union opened its first commercial reactor near Chelyabinsk. By 1970, nuclear plants had opened in Canada, France, Great Britain, India, Italy, Japan, the Netherlands, Spain, Switzerland, the United States, and the former Soviet Union. As this brief history of nuclear energy reveals, reactors came into use as part of military efforts to create a bomb. Despite widespread sponsorship and use of this technology, no country evaluated nuclear power, prior to its commercial employment, in order to determine whether or not it was a desirable means of generating electricity. Instead, driven by military applications, nations promoted commercial use of nuclear technology as a way to support weapons development.

In 1976, 20 years after commercial fission reactors began operating, the *Wall Street Journal* proclaimed them an economic disaster. Nuclear electricity has proved so costly that year 2000 projections for nuclear power plants are now approximately one-eighth of what they were in the mid-seventies. The few U.S. nuclear manufacturers still in business have remained so by selling reactors to other nations, often developing countries seeking fission-generated electricity as a way to obtain nuclear weapons capability, through the plutonium by-product. India exploded its first nuclear bomb, for example, by using plutonium produced by a reactor exported by Canada.

At least since the 1986 reactor core melt in Chernobyl, the future of nuclear power has been in doubt. Since the accident, republics such as Belarus and the Ukraine have been forced to spend 13 to 20% of their annual budget on Chernobyl-related problems. Scientists have confirmed a 100-fold increase in thyroid cancer in Belarus, Russia, and the Ukraine; increases in leukemia in Greece, Sweden, and Finland; and a doubling in germ-line mutations in Belarus children born after Chernobyl. In the face of such massive harms, controversy over continued use of nuclear power has accelerated.

II. TWO ETHICAL FRAMEWORKS FOR EVALUATING NUCLEAR POWER

Both this controversy over nuclear fission and decisions about how to assess societal risks and benefits from commercial reactors are unavoidably and fundamentally ethical. They both address what society "ought" to do in choosing a means of generating electricity, and they presuppose different distributions of the risks, costs, and benefits of generating electricity.

Most people who evaluate ethical issues concerning nuclear power follow variants of two main theoretical approaches, deontological/contractarian ethics or utilitarian ethics. In general, contractarian norms emphasize equity among persons and respecting individual moral rights. Utilitarians, however, typically do not recognize any individual moral rights or duties except to promote the best consequences for the greatest number of people. Often deontologists, such as Immanuel Kant, John Locke, and John Rawls, defend their appeals to duty by means of conceptual or logical analysis. Utilitarians, such as Jeremy Bentham, John Harsanyi, and John Stuart Mill, defend their claims by analyzing the consequences following from particular ethical positions. Contractarians and utilitarians each have important insights. Utilitarians tend to emphasize the economically desirable consequences that may arise from different standards for nuclear power and radiation-related hazards. Contractarians, however, tend to emphasize individual rights to protection from nuclear risks and to argue that any risk imposition is justified only in the context of individual consent, compensation, and equality of risk distribution.

III. NUCLEAR POWER AND THE NATURALISTIC FALLACY

Many scientists and engineers tend to assume that nuclear-related risks are ethically acceptable (or may be involuntarily imposed) if they present the same level of harm as voluntarily chosen risks. As contractarians point out, this assumption errs because ethical acceptability is not only a matter of risk magnitude but also a matter of risk distribution and risk compensation. As utilitarians point out, the ethics of nuclear power and radiation-related risks is also a matter of whether the dangers are associated with important benefits. Hence, when scientists and risk assessors such as Philip Abelson (1994. Reflections on the environment. *Science 263,* 591) erroneously argue that the public ought to be "consistent" in accepting radiation risks that are lower than other risks (such as driving an automobile), they are not really comparing consistent risks. Radiation risks imposed by commercial nuclear power, for example, are typically more catastrophic, less compensated, and less under voluntary individual control than are the risks associated with automobile accidents. Because of these ethical disanalogies, there is no "linear relationship" between risk magnitude and risk aversion. For example, because the radiation risks associated with a nuclear accident often are subject to a liability limit—the U.S. limit is approximately 5% of the total costs of the Chernobyl accident—many persons believe that ethically acceptable radiation risks require a much stricter evaluation than other threats that are

fully compensable (K. Shrader-Frechette, 1993. *Burying Uncertainty: Risk and the Case against Geological Disposal of Nuclear Waste,* pp. 9–23, 96–98, 157–158, 205–229. University of California Press, Berkeley).

Similar reasoning applies to the assumption that imposing additional nuclear-related risks of the same magnitude as typical background levels of radiation is always ethically acceptable. Of course, this assumption gains some plausibility because assessors often use "natural standards," in part, to evaluate the acceptability of various pollutants. Natural standards are based on existing or "natural" levels of pollutants. Determining acceptable levels of societally chosen risks on the basis of levels of unavoidable (background) risks, however, is not ethically defensible because the two classes of risks often are ethically disanalogous. They are associated with different levels of voluntariness, equity of distribution, benefits, compensation, and so on. Moreover, as G. E. Moore showed, to assume that a risk is ethically acceptable just because it is "normal" or "natural" is to commit the naturalistic fallacy (G. E. Moore, 1951. *Principia Ethica,* pp. viii–ix, 23–40, 60–63, 108, 146. Cambridge University Press, Cambridge). A normal rate of automobile accidents is not acceptable, for example, if it is possible and reasonable to lower the rate. Evaluating risks associated with nuclear power thus requires not only knowledge of risk magnitude, but also ethical decisions about issues such as how safe is safe enough, how safe is fair enough, and how safe is voluntary enough. Moreover, all these issues, in part, are matters of citizens' democratic rights to self-determination. They are not matters for only scientific experts to dictate because they are questions of ethics and because they affect human welfare.

Even definitions of "nuclear risk" often reflect the naturalistic fallacy. Some scientists and engineers who study societal risks—such as those associated with nuclear waste facilities—typically define "risk" merely as the probability that some harm, like death, will occur (see National Research Council, 1983. *Risk Assessment in the Federal Government: Managing the Process.* National Academy Press, Washington, DC). However, ethicists, especially contractarians, often argue that risk cannot be reduced merely to a mathematical expression because it also is a function of qualitative components such as citizen consent (K. Shrader-Frechette, 1991. *Risk and Rationality.* University of California Press, Berkeley; D. MacLean, Ed., 1986. *Values at Risk.* Rowman and Allanheld, Totowa, NJ). Thus merely probabilistic definitions of nuclear risk exhibit a "naturalistic fallacy" if they attempt to reduce ethical analyses to purely mathematical and scientific concepts.

IV. NUCLEAR POWER AND UNCERTAINTY

Many estimates and evaluations of nuclear power involve scientific and probabilistic uncertainty. There is, for example, uncertainty regarding actual radiation exposure levels, particular people's sensitivity levels, the likelihood of dangerous consequences in a specific case, the given causal chains of harm, and so on. U.S. Department of Energy (DOE) representatives admit that Chernobyl could cause up to 28,000 fatal cancers in the former Soviet Union, Scandinavia, and Europe over the next 50 years. Other scientists and policy makers claim that the number of fatal cancers caused by Chernobyl will be as high as 475,000. Also, U.S. Nuclear Regulatory Commission (NRC) data indicate that the United States has a 50-50 chance of having another accident the size of Three Mile Island or larger. For all these reasons, a fundamental ethical issue concerns how risk assessors ought to evaluate situations involving some sort of factual or probabilistic uncertainty. (1) Should one assume that a potential risk imposer is innocent until proved guilty or guilty until proved innocent? Should the burden of proof be on the alleged risk imposer or on the victim? (2) In evaluating uncertain radiation risks is one ethically bound to minimize false positives or false negatives? (3) In evaluating radiation risks, should one assume, in a situation of probabilistic uncertainty, that one is ethically required to follow the utilitarians' rules of maximizing average expected utility or the contractarians' rules of avoiding the worst outcome?

Many assessors evaluating nuclear-related risks in situations of factual or probabilistic uncertainty follow traditional norms of avoiding false positives (type-I error) rather than avoiding false negatives (type-II error). For example, the International Atomic Energy Agency (IAEA) and the International Commission on Radiological Protection (ICRP), which develop principles of radiation protection, require that radiation levels be kept as low as reasonably achievable, even below a particular exposure standard. In so doing, the ICRP and IAEA appear to follow the norm of avoiding false negatives, false assumptions of no harm (ICRP, 1991. *1990 Recommendations of the International Commission on Radiological Protection*. Pergamon, Oxford; IAEA, 1995. *Organization and Operation of a National Infrastructure Governing Radiation Protection and Safety of Radiation Sources*. IAEA, Vienna). However, when U.S. government risk assessors evaluated the radiation exposures of the late Orville Kelly, they avoided false positives and claimed that his death from leukemia was not caused by

radiation received when he was Naval Commander of Eniwetok Atoll. Kelly was within 5 miles of ground zero, unprotected, during 23 nuclear weapons tests on the atoll. He died in his thirties, leaving a wife and four children. Indeed, for virtually all of the leukemia and bone cancer victims among 500,000 U.S. servicemen exposed to fallout in nuclear weapons tests in southwestern United States and the Pacific during the 1950s and 1960s, government risk assessors claimed that their high radiation exposures did not cause their cancers (U.S. Congress, 1994). Part of the assessors' rationale was that, in cases of uncertainty, one ought to limit false positives, take a conservative approach, and avoid positing an effect where there may be none. Such a traditional scientific approach places the burden of proof on those—like Orville Kelly—attempting to confirm some harm.

Many deontologists or contractarians, however, claim that traditional scientific norms for dealing with uncertainty are inapplicable to nuclear risk decisions because they affect human welfare. They argue for minimizing type-II error (avoiding false negatives) because doing so gives greater protection to public health and places the burden of proof on risk imposers rather than risk victims. More generally, ethicists have challenged the traditional legal dictum that a potentially dangerous situation (such as exposure to high levels of radiation) is "innocent until proved guilty." They argue that fairness and citizens' rights to equal treatment require risk evaluators to place the burden of proof on the alleged risk imposer. Their reasoning is that causal chains of harm are difficult to prove and that risk victims are less able than risk imposers to bear the medical and economic costs of faulty risk evaluations.

Other ethical controversies concerning nuclear-related uncertainty focus on whether one ought to judge risk acceptability according to Bayesian or maximin rules. Should evaluators follow Bayesian rules and maximize average expected utility (where expected utility is defined as the subjective probability of some outcome times its utility)? Or should evaluators follow maximin rules and minimize the likelihood of the worst outcome (consequences)? Utilitarians like John Harsanyi argue for the Bayesian position on the grounds that "worst cases" of technological risk rarely occur (J. Harsanyi, 1975. Can the Maximin Principle Serve as a Basis for Morality? A Critique of John Rawls' Theory, *American Political Science Review 69*, 594–605). They say that maximin decisions are overly conservative, impede social progress, and overemphasize small probabilities of harm. Egalitarians or deontologists like John Rawls argue for maximin on the grounds that, in cases like radiation risks from commercial nuclear power, the subjective risk probabilities are both uncertain and dwarfed by potentially catastrophic consequences such as nuclear core melts (J. Rawls, 1971. *A Theory of Justice*. Harvard Univ. Press, Cambridge, MA). They also point out the essential asymmetry of zero–infinity risk problems: a small (close to zero) probability of catastrophe does not outweigh infinitely serious risk consequences. Hence, deontological ethical theory—with its emphasis on rights to bodily security and duties to avoid catastrophe—likely explains much aversion to commercial nuclear fission, despite the low probability of catastrophe.

V. EQUITY AND NUCLEAR RISKS

Even if the overall consequences of a nuclear accident are minimal, risk evaluators following deontological ethical theory point out that the hazard may be unacceptable if the risk is inequitably distributed. Psychological studies also reveal that, in their risk evaluations, laypeople are often more averse to a small, inequitably distributed societal risk than to a larger, equitably distributed risk. In general, both deontological and utilitarian ethical theorists argue that people ought not be discriminated against merely because they are in a different location in space and time. For example, Parfit argues that temporal differences are not a morally relevant basis for discounting future costs and thus discriminating against future generations with respect to risks such as radiation. He and others maintain that a risk imposition is less acceptable to the degree that it imposes costs on future persons but awards benefits to present persons. Commercial nuclear fission, for example, benefits mainly present generations, whereas its risks and costs also will be borne by members of future generations who may be affected by long-lived nuclear wastes (D. Parfit, 1983. Energy policy and the further future: the social discount rate. In *Energy and the Future* (D. MacLean and P. Brown, Eds.), pp. 31–37. Rowman and Littlefield, Totowa, NJ).

Every year, each 1000-MW reactor discharges about 25.4 metric tons of high-level waste as spent fuel. For 300 commercial reactors, worldwide, the annual high-level radwaste is 7620 metric tons. Only 10 μg of plutonium is almost certain to induce cancer, and several grams of plutonium, dispersed in a ventilation system, is enough to cause thousands of deaths. Moreover, as even industry experts admit, each of the 7620 metric tons of high-level waste produced annually has the potential to cause hundreds of millions of cancers for at least the first 300 years of storage, and then tens of millions of cancers for the next million years, in the unlikely event of its dispersal. These cancers could be prevented, of course, with isolation of the wastes for a million years. That is why most plans for high-level nuclear waste storage call for defense in depth, for sealing the waste in a ceramic material, and for burying it deep underground in stainless steel or copper canisters. Nevertheless, the U.S. Environmental Protection Agency and the U.S. National Academy of Sciences have warned that we cannot count on institutional safeguards for nuclear waste.

Many economists and utilitarians support the use of nuclear power. They say that policy makers should discount future costs such as deaths caused by radioactive wastes. They also question whether "geographical equity" or "environmental justice" requires risks to be distributed equally across generations, regions, and nations. Proponents of siting nuclear reactors and waste repositories in economically and socially disenfranchised areas argue that such risks have been voluntarily accepted and that they provide employment as well as tax benefits. They say that "a bloody loaf of bread is better than no loaf at all." Opponents of such risk impositions argue that life-threatening hazards rarely bring substantial benefits and that it is unfair for economically, educationally, and socially disenfranchised persons to bear larger burdens of societal and workplace risks. They claim that just as it was wrong, more than a century ago, for U.S. southerners to defend slavery on the grounds that it was necessary to the economy of the South, so also it is wrong for risk evaluators to defend inequitable distributions of radiation and other risks on the grounds that such inequities are necessary to the common good. Deontologists argue that "the end (economic welfare) does not justify any means (inequitable distributions of risk)." Rather, human rights to equal protection are inviolate. They argue that some risks should be kept lower than others and that uniform standards are too lenient in protecting only "average" people rather than those who are especially sensitive, such as children who are victims of the Chernobyl radiation exposures (R. D. Bullard, 1993. *Confronting Environmental Racism*. South End, Boston; K. Shrader-Frechette, 1991, 71–72; 1993).

VI. CONSENT AND NUCLEAR RISKS

Of course, ethics allows inequitable risk impositions if the victims give their consent. The difficulty, however, is that persons most able to give free informed consent to higher societal risks (the wealthy and well educated) usually do not, whereas those least able to give free informed consent are those who usually bear higher societal risks like those from nuclear power. In the United States, for example, the only communities willing to serve as compensated hosts for proposed high-level nuclear waste facilities are Yakima Indian Nation, Nye County (Nevada), and Morgan County (Tennessee), all areas with high unemployment, high poverty, and low levels of education. In such a situation, deontologists argue that it is questionable whether members of the proposed host communities—especially members of future generations—are able to give free informed consent to the radiation risks associated with the facility. Likewise, they argue that because of coercive social conditions, in general poor people ought not be allowed to trade bodily security for higher wages or economic benefits. If the deontologists' arguments are correct, then even small risks that are imposed on people who are unable to give genuine free informed consent are highly questionable. Most modern nations do not recognize the consent—allegedly given by children, the mentally ill, or prisoners—to higher risks of medical experimentation. Likewise deontologist risk evaluators argue that assessors ought not ignore the lack of genuine consent often associated with inequitable impositions of risks such as radiation (see, for example, MacLean, 1986; A. Gewirth, 1982. *Human Rights,* University of Chicago Press, Chicago; Shrader-Frechette, 1993, chap. 8–9).

Some utilitarian ethicists have argued, however, that risk-for-money trade-offs serve the greater good and that no instances of consent are perfect. They also believe that Adam Smith's "compensating wage differential," for example, gives unskilled workers (in riskier occupations) economic opportunities that they otherwise would not have. They claim that contemporary economies require a "politics of sacrifice" in which free informed consent (to all societal and workplace risks) is unrealistic and unattainable (J. Harsanyi, 1975. Can the maximin principle serve as a basis for morality? A critique of John Rawls' theory. *American Political Science Review 69,* 602).

Philosophers who argue for the ethical justifiability of the economics–safety trade-off tend to be utilitarians and to have more lenient conceptions of free informed consent. They also tend to underemphasize sociological differences among those who accept versus those who reject risky jobs and living conditions, and to believe that pursuing neoclassical economics leads overall to social and ethical benefits. Philosophers who argue against the economics–safety trade-off tend to be deontologists or contractarians and to have more stringent

conceptions of free informed consent. They also tend to overemphasize the sociological differences among persons allegedly choosing different levels of societal risks and to be more critical of the ethical assumptions underlying neoclassical economics. For example, in the United States most people who allegedly choose to be uranium miners are native Americans with high levels of poverty and unemployment and low levels of education and opportunity. Persons in more sociologically advantaged groups usually do not choose work that exposes them to risks from radiation.

VII. NUCLEAR POWER AND DUE PROCESS

Regardless of whether ethicists take a deontological or utilitarian position on questions of distributive equity, consent, and nuclear-related radiation risks, both groups of theorists generally agree that some form of compensation is required to justify imposing higher societal risks on particular groups, such as uranium miners. Psychological studies likewise reveal that people often are just as concerned about small, uncompensated societal risks as they are about larger risks for which they are certain to be compensated. If these concerns are legitimate, then ethicists ought to assess comparable uncompensated risks more negatively than less compensated risks. The rationale for such assessments is that lack of full compensation for a societal risk threatens victims' due-process rights and therefore harms them. As a consequence, the acceptability of radiation risks is in part a function of compensation.

At the beginning of the atomic era, industry was reluctant, both on economic and on safety grounds, to use fission to generate electricity. Worried about safety, all major U.S. corporations with nuclear interests refused to produce electricity by means of fission unless some indemnity legislation was passed to protect them in the event of a catastrophic accident. The top lobbyist for the nuclear industry, the president of the Atomic Industrial Forum, has confirmed what numerous government committee reports show. Commercial nuclear fission began mainly because government leaders wanted to justify continuing military expenditures and to obtain weapons-grade plutonium. Moreover, at least in the United States, fission-generated electricity began only because the government provided more than $100 billion in subsidies (for research, development, waste storage, and insurance) to the nuclear industry. Congress also gave the utilities a liability limit (in the Price–

Anderson Act) which protects licensees from most of the public losses and claims in the event of a catastrophic nuclear accident. The current U.S. liability limit is approximately $7.2 billion, less than 5% of the cost required to clean up Chernobyl, which was not a worst-case accident. Similar liability limits for commercial nuclear fission exist in other countries, such as Canada, where there is a $75 million government and industry liability limit for nuclear accidents. Since the costs of such accidents can run into the hundreds of billions of dollars, the constitutionality of these liability limits has been challenged in every nation in which they exist (Shrader-Frechette, 1993, 1–27).

At the proposed Yucca Mountain (Nevada) repository for U.S. high-level nuclear waste and spent fuel, site assessors have concluded that the location has met criteria for early site suitability. Nevertheless these evaluators have ignored the fact that the government has not met demands of the proposed host community for full liability for repository accidents. Indeed, the government is willing to compensate the host community for disruptions caused by site studies only if the community withdraws its opposition to the site. (80% of Nevadans oppose the facility. See P. Slovic, J. Flynn, and M. Layman, 1991. *Science* **254**, 1604.) At least part of citizens' opposition to the proposed repository has arisen because government has ignored their rights to full compensation and liability. If citizens' demands for such due-process rights are correct, and most deontologists would claim they are, then Yucca Mountain assessors ought not have ignored these demands. Some utilitarian moral philosophers also reason that if a nuclear waste facility is safe, as the government alleges, then risk imposers have little to lose from allowing full liability for accidents (Shrader-Frechette, 1991, 1993).

VIII. CONCLUSIONS

If the preceding survey of ethical considerations is correct, then several conclusions follow: (1) Evaluations of nuclear-related risk ought to be ethically weighted to reflect the value of deontological factors such as equitable risk distribution, compensation, and consent. Evaluations ought to reflect the fact that such ethical factors are just as important as risk magnitude in determining the acceptability of nuclear power. (2) Although technical assessment is necessary for an ethical evaluation of nuclear power, it is not sufficient. Ethical evaluation also needs to include components such as analysis of democratic preferences, citizen negotiation, and alternative assessments, so that the *procedures*, not merely the *outcomes*, of societal decision making regarding nuclear energy satisfy ethical constraints. (3) Although it is reasonable for good scientists to limit false positives, in evaluating nuclear-related uncertainties societal decision makers also need to limit false negatives and to protect the most vulnerable parties. (4) Although economically realistic risk evaluations, in a society of limited resources, ought not presuppose an infinite value for health and safety, neither ought risk evaluations to presuppose a zero value for even small threats to health and safety, particularly if compensation or consent is inadequate. At least for deontologists, consent and compensation are often necessary to justify risk trade-offs.

Because of the importance of ethical constraints, nuclear power ought not be evaluated by a technological "fix" that addresses only risk magnitude. Likewise, because the public has the right to determine how safe is safe enough, how safe is fair enough, and how safe is voluntary enough, societal risk evaluation cannot be accomplished by a public relations "fix" orchestrated by risk imposers or by the scientific community. Many controversies over evaluation of radiation risks can be solved only by ethical analysis and democratic process. Some of the most important aspects of nuclear power thus are not scientific but ethical.

Also See the Following Articles

ENVIRONMENTAL ETHICS, OVERVIEW • HAZARDOUS AND TOXIC SUBSTANCES • NUCLEAR TESTING • NUCLEAR WARFARE

Bibliography

Dubrova, Y. E., *et al.* (1996). Human minisatellite mutation rate after the Chernobyl accident. *Nature* **380**, 683–686.

Hogan, N. (1994). Shielded from liability. *ABA J.* **80**, 56–60.

International Commission on Radiological Protection (1991). "1990 Recommendations of the International Commission on Radiological Protection." Pergamon, Oxford.

Kendall, H. (1991). Calling nuclear power to account. *Calypso Log* **18**, 8–9.

Marples, D. R. (1996). Chernobyl: The decade of despair. *Bull. At. Scientists* **52**, 20–31.

National Research Council, Committee on the Biological Effects of Ionizing Radiation, Board on Radiation Effects Research Commission on Life Sciences (1990). "Health Effects of Exposure to Low Levels of Ionizing Radiation. BEIR V." National Academy Press, Washington, DC.

Shrader-Frechette, K. (1993). "Burying Uncertainty: Risk and the Case against Geological Disposal of Nuclear Waste." Univ. of California Press, Berkeley.

Shrader-Frechette, K. (1991). "Risk and Rationality: Philosophical Foundations for Populist Reforms." Univ. of California Press, Berkeley.

United Nations Scientific Committee on the Effects of Atomic Radiation (UNSCEAR) (1994). "Sources and Effects of Ionizing Radiation—UNSCEAR 1994 Report to the General Assembly, with Scientific Annexes." United Nations, New York.

U.S. Congress (1994). "Human Subjects Research: Radiation Experimentation." Hearing before the Committee on Labor and Human Resources, United States Senate, 103rd Congr., 1st sess., Jan. 13, 1994. U.S. Government Printing Office, Washington, DC.

NUCLEAR TESTING

Steven Lee
Hobart and William Smith Colleges

I. Is the Use of Nuclear Weapons Permissible?
II. Is Nuclear Testing Dangerous?

GLOSSARY

assured destruction A form of nuclear deterrence involving threats to destroy, and the capability of destroying, the opponent's society, if the opponent strikes first.

conditional intention An intention to do something, such as use nuclear weapons, only if some condition obtains, such as an opponent's aggression.

conventional weapons Nonnuclear weapons.

counterforce nuclear deterrence A form of nuclear deterrence strategy in which the threats are made against military rather than civilian targets.

credibility A measure of the effectiveness of deterrence based on the strength of the opponent's belief that the state would carry out its threats.

crisis (in) stability The ability (or inability) of a strategy of nuclear deterrence to ensure the avoidance of war during a political crisis between nuclear opponents.

just-war theory The traditional Western approach to assessing the moral status of military activity, which expresses a special concern for avoiding harm to civilians.

nuclear deterrence A policy of threatening the use of nuclear weapons in order to avoid an opponent's aggression.

nuclear proliferation The spread of nuclear weapons to nonnuclear states.

IS THE TESTING OF NUCLEAR WEAPONS morally permissible? The answer to this is more difficult than the answer to the same question asked about a conventional weapon. The reason is that there are important moral differences between nuclear and conventional weapons. Consider how one would respond to the general question about the moral status of weapons testing. It seems, in general, that weapons testing is permissible if the testing itself is not harmful and if the purpose of the testing is to increase the effectiveness of the weapon for its intended use, given that that use is itself permissible. This could be formulated as *the permissibility principle*: the testing of a weapon is permissible only if (1) its purpose is to make the weapon more effective for the weapon's intended use, which is itself permissible, and (2) the testing itself does not pose a serious risk of harm to others. Is it permissible to test a handgun? In general, the answer is yes, if it is tested at a safe firing range by a person intending to improve in the use of the weapon for legitimate acts of self-defense. But, if it is tested on a busy city street, or by someone intending to use it for an act of terrorism, the testing would not be permissible.

The question about the permissibility of testing conventional weapons is normally fairly easy to answer because it is usually not hard to determine if conditions

(1) and (2) apply. The difficulty in applying the permissibility principle to the testing of nuclear weapons is that it is not easy to determine if these conditions apply. This is the result of the moral differences between nuclear and conventional weapons. In the remainder of this article, I will consider in turn the difficulties in applying conditions (1) and (2) to the case of nuclear weapons testing.

I. IS THE USE OF NUCLEAR WEAPONS PERMISSIBLE?

In regard to condition (1), the main question is whether the intended use of nuclear weapons is permissible. Many have argued that it is never permissible to use nuclear weapons, even in self-defense. The reason, following just-war theory or related lines of argument, is that the destructive effects of the weapons are so vast that the use of the weapons would inevitably cause serious harm to innocent civilians, and that it is never permissible to cause such harm. Even if, the argument continues, the use of a single nuclear weapon would not cause serious harm to civilians, because the weapon was of a low yield and fired at an isolated area, still, given the vast number of existing nuclear weapons, the use of that one weapon would carry a serious risk of escalation, leading to the death of many civilians. Thus, the use of even one weapon would be impermissible. If this argument is sound, then, in the light of the permissibility principle, the testing of nuclear weapons is impermissible.

But matters are more complex than this. With the exception of the bombings of Hiroshima and Nagasaki, the way in which states have used nuclear weapons is not by firing them on an opponent, but by practicing nuclear deterrence, using the threat of a retaliatory firing of the weapons to keep an opponent from aggression. What if the purpose of testing the weapons is to make deterrence more effective? Well, in the light of the permissibility principle, the question to ask is whether or not it is permissible to use nuclear weapons to practice deterrence. Defenders of nuclear deterrence argue that it is permissible because the intention involved is not the making of war, but the avoidance of war. But there is a line of analysis, extending the argument of the previous paragraph, to the effect that the use of nuclear weapons for deterrence is impermissible. While nuclear deterrence may involve the intention to avoid war, implicit in the threat to retaliate is the conditional intention to

attack civilians, because nuclear deterrence, as practiced by the major nuclear powers, includes the ultimate threat to destroy the opponent's society, the threat of "assured destruction." But, because it is impermissible to attack civilians, it is impermissible to intend to do so, and so impermissible to adopt a military policy that has such an intention, even if the intention is conditional.

If we assume the soundness of this line of argument, the permissibility principle seems to entail the impermissibility of nuclear testing, even when undertaken for the sake of more effective deterrence. But there is one line of defense that proponents of nuclear testing could invoke. Because nuclear deterrence is practiced with two intentions, one permissible and one not, a defender of testing might argue that nuclear testing is itself permissible, if it is designed to support the permissible intention of deterrence, namely, that of avoiding war. Here is an analogy. The organizers of a prostitution ring may be said to practice their vocation with two intentions, to exploit the vulnerable individuals who work for them and to provide the public with a service. The latter intention, considered by itself, is permissible, but the former is not, because of the exploitation involved, and, for that reason, the practice itself is not permissible. Now, consider one organizer's decision to require that condoms be used in the sexual acts with the ring's clients. This could be said to be morally permissible (perhaps even morally required), even though the practice as a whole is impermissible. Why is this? Requiring condoms supports the permissible intention, in that it makes the service provided less risky and, in that sense, more effective, without making the nature of the practice in regard to the impermissible intention any worse. Requiring condoms does not deepen or extend the exploitation involved in the practice.

A generalization supported by this analogy is that when a practice has both a permissible and an impermissible intention, another activity that supports the permissible intention is not itself impermissible in virtue of the impermissibility of the practice as a whole. This principle may hold in the case of nuclear testing as well. Nuclear deterrence is like the prostitution case in that the practice is impermissible because a permissible end is pursued through impermissible means. But nuclear testing designed to make deterrence more effective, like the organizer's requiring of condoms, supports the permissible intention, the avoidance of war, without making the practice worse in regard to its impermissible intention, the conditional intention to attack civilians. Thus, even if nuclear deterrence is an impermissible practice, nuclear testing designed to make deterrence more effective may not be.

But here another complication arises. The idea of testing to make deterrence more effective disguises an important ambiguity. Nuclear testers may seek to make deterrence more effective in different ways, either (1) by impressing the potential opponent by making the capacity to retaliate more evident and the risks of retaliation more vivid, (2) by making the weapons more reliable, in order to lessen the risk of accidental detonation and increase assurances that the threats could be carried out, or (3) by developing new or more advanced weapons, in order to make possible a different, more effective form of deterrence strategy. All three of these intentions are intentions to make deterrence more effective, but there may be important moral differences among them. In particular, while the first two types of intention seem to raise no special moral problems, the third type of intention bears closer scrutiny.

In regard to the third type of intention, there are two kinds of cases to consider: weapons refinement and nuclear proliferation. First, a state that already has nuclear weapons may test new designs in order to develop weapons that are more advanced, for example, in their explosive yield or in the way in which the energy of the explosion is released, intending to use the improved weapons to adopt a more effective strategy of deterrence. Second, a state without nuclear weapons may seek to acquire them, and to test an initial nuclear device to ensure that it has developed a workable weapon, intending to adopt nuclear deterrence as a more effective form of military deterrence.

Consider the first kind of case, where a state tests a new weapons design in order to apply it to a different form of nuclear deterrence strategy. The example of this from our nuclear history is the development by the major nuclear powers of more advanced weapons that could support a strategy of counterforce nuclear deterrence, where the nuclear threat would be directed more toward military than civilian targets. Proponents of counterforce strategy believe that it would be a more effective form of deterrence, because it would increase the credibility of the nuclear threats. (They also argue that it would be a form of nuclear deterrence that would avoid the conditional intention to attack civilians, because it would allow the weapons to be aimed exclusively at noncivilian targets.) In a similar vein, in regard to the second kind of case, proponents of nuclear proliferation believe that the acquisition of nuclear weapons, and the consequent making of nuclear threats, would allow the state to practice a form of deterrence more effective than conventional military deterrence.

The truth of the beliefs that nuclear weapons refinement or acquisition would lead to a more effective form of deterrence is much debated. The argument that weapons refinement would not lead to a more effective form of deterrence is based on the claim that counterforce deterrence would increase the risk of nuclear war because it would increase crisis instability. In a crisis, counterforce strategy would make each side more likely to believe that the other side was about to strike first, and hence make each side more likely to strike, increasing the risk of war. While counterforce deterrence may make nuclear threats more credible, as its proponents argue, overall it would make war more likely, and hence deterrence less effective. There is a similar line of argument concerning the acquisition of nuclear weapons. The argument against nuclear proliferation is that the spread of nuclear weapons to states without them would make nuclear war more likely by making the military balance between opponents less stable, because, for one, each side may have a strong incentive to attack in a crisis to attempt to destroy the nascent nuclear capability of its opponent.

II. IS NUCLEAR TESTING DANGEROUS?

But one could argue that even if these criticisms of counterforce deterrence and nuclear proliferation are sound, they do not show that nuclear testing for the sake of weapons refinement or acquisition violates condition (1) of the permissibility principle. For the testing would be carried out with the intention to make nuclear deterrence more effective, even if the intention is based on a false belief. This is where condition (2), the requirement that the testing itself not pose a serious risk of harm, becomes relevant. Consider another analogy with conventional weapons. Imagine that my only intention in having a firearm is to use it in individual self-defense, but that I am testing a more advanced design of my own creation, an automatic weapon, in order to increase the effectiveness of my self-defensive capabilities. Despite the purity of my intentions, one might argue, it would be wrong for me to test the weapon, because automatic weapons pose a serious risk of harm to others. Presumably, this is why citizens in the United States are allowed to own handguns but not machine guns. Testing to create a machine gun is not permissible because they pose a great risk of harm to others.

So, nuclear testing is impermissible, due to condition (2), if the testing leads to a form of deterrence that is less effective, because a less effective form of deterrence creates a greatly increased risk of harm to others, in that it entails an increased likelihood of nuclear war. This is true whatever the intention with which the testing is carried out. The tester may seek to make deterrence more effective by impressing the opponent or by increasing weapons reliability, as well as by seeking to develop a new form of deterrence strategy, but if the result is a less effective form of deterrence, the testing is impermissible in any case. Let us assume for the moment that counterforce deterrence practiced by established nuclear powers and nuclear deterrence practiced by new nuclear proliferators are less effective than the forms of deterrence they replace. Does nuclear testing lead to these less effective forms of deterrence? Clearly it does in the case of new nuclear proliferators: for a state to test its first nuclear weapon is for it to begin to practice nuclear deterrence. While there is not the same tight link in the case of testing by established nuclear powers, our nuclear history suggests that a shift to counterforce strategy as a result of testing is the normal course of events.

But is it correct to assume that counterforce deterrence and nuclear proliferation are dangerous? Are the arguments that these represent less effective forms of deterrence sound? While there is disageement about whether counterforce deterrence is more dangerous, there is fairly strong consensus that nuclear proliferation is dangerous. But this is all the argument needs, for the only way effectively to stop the testing of nuclear weapons by nonnuclear states is to stop all nuclear testing. The reason is that an international ban on testing cannot be enforced against nonnuclear states alone. These states will not be willing to commit themselves not to test, however much they ought to do so, unless the established nuclear powers so commit themselves as well. Thus the testing by established nuclear powers is dangerous, if for no other reason than that it leads nonnuclear states to test as well, and that testing is itself dangerous. Thus there is a strong case, based on condition (2) of the permissibility principle, that nuclear testing is morally impermissible. This, along with other arguments, supports the adoption of a comprehensive test ban treaty, such as was approved by the United Nations in September 1996.

Also See the Following Articles

NUCLEAR DETERRENCE • NUCLEAR WARFARE • WARFARE, CODES OF

Bibliography

Arnett, E. (1995). *Implementing the comprehensive test ban.* SIPRI Research Report #8 Oxford: Oxford University Press.
Goldblat, J. & Cox, D. (Eds.). (1988). *Nuclear weapons tests: Prohibition or limitation.* Oxford: Oxford University Press.
Lee, S. (1993). *Morality, prudence, and nuclear weapons.* Cambridge: Cambridge University Press.
Shue, H. (Ed.). (1989). *Nuclear deterrence and moral restraint.* Cambridge: Cambridge University Press.

NUCLEAR WARFARE

Paul Viminitz
University of Waterloo

NUCLEAR WARFARE involves the use of highly destructive weapons employing the enormous force of nuclear energy.

GLOSSARY

counterforce The targeting of military sites.
countervalue The targeting of civilian populations.
existential deterrence Reliance on the deterrent effect of the simple fact that nuclear weapons exist.
mutually assured destruction The capacity of each party to a nuclear stand-off to inflict a level of damage on the other that would prohibit the rational initiation of an exchange.
no-deterrence deterrence Reliance on the deterrent effect of weaponless deterrence, notwithstanding one's having genuinely forsworn not to assemble them.
principle of tolerable diversion The principle that the gap between moral and prudential norms must not lead to the latter being ignored or revised.
special deterrence situation A situation in which, although it is wrong to retaliate, intending to do so would very likely deter provocation.
weaponless deterrence Reliance on the deterrent effect of being without nuclear weapons but able to assemble them.
wrongful intentions principle The principle that it is wrong to intend to do what it is wrong to do.

I. NUCLEAR WEAPONRY

The first nuclear weapon was tested at Alamogordo, New Mexico, on July 16, 1945. The only two "used"—a scant three weeks later—were over Hiroshima and Nagasaki on August 6 and 9, respectively. Still, the nuclear option has been "contemplated" in several conflicts since. It is widely believed we were at the brink of global holocaust during the Cuban Missile Crisis of October, 1962. Unidentified radar blips have occasioned innumerable alerts over the years. And the very real possibility of a madman precipitating Armageddon has been immortalized in Stanley Kubrick's 1964 film classic, *Dr. Strangelove.*

Defenders of the Manhattan Project—America's wartime push to develop the bomb—argue it was necessitated by reports of similar research taking place in Germany. And indeed throughout the war U.S. bombers repeatedly targeted the heavy water facilities at Penemunde. Defenders of the decision to use the bomb against Japan argue that doing so saved hundreds of thousands of lives, American *and* Japanese, lives that most certainly would have been lost had an invasion of the Japanese homeland been necessary. A mere demonstration for Japanese observers would have lacked specificity as to just what such a device could do to a densely populated area. And in the wake of such a demonstration Japan might have simply concentrated its air defenses to make delivery of the bomb just that much more costly. Critics, in turn, charge that Japan was known to be on the cusp of surrender anyhow; so the bombs were dropped either to wreak vengeance for Pearl Harbor or to dissuade Stalin from exploiting the superiority of his conventional forces in Central Europe. Historians and ideologues continue to bicker. But probably there is truth in *all* of the above.

What remains a mystery, however, is why, in the years immediately following the war, the United States did not exploit its monopoly to prevent the Soviets from following suit. Israel, by contrast, delivered just such a preemptive strike, albeit a conventional one, against Baghdad. In any event, the Soviet Union, the United Kingdom, France, and China joined the nuclear club in rapid succession. Today there are strong suspicions—suspicions Israel has been keen to fan—that it too has an arsenal. And a score of other nations, including India and Pakistan, Iraq and Iran, currently have weapons programs ranging from fledgling to all-but-delivery.

By the late 1950s the United States and the Soviets had achieved mutually assured destruction (MAD). That is, each had the capacity to ensure a level of damage on the other that the other deemed prohibitive. "Prohibitive" is a judgment, not a number. You and I might be "mad" to support a war in which our respective children will be the only two fatalities. But if the prospect of the same two deaths could convince the leader of our country to surrender to a foreign tyrant, he might rightly be assassinated. Moreover, the determination of MAD could be both relative and relational. A people with less to lose might be willing to lose more; and a nation might be prepared to absorb the loss of 10 million of its citizens provided the enemy absorbs a loss of 20.

At least 80,000 people died instantly in Hiroshima, and perhaps an equal number from wounds and/or radiation in the hours, days, and years that followed. Much has been made of the fact that this is not an order of magnitude greater than the conventional firebombing of Dresden. Today's warheads, however, are much more powerful. U.S. silos are strung out just south of the 49th parallel at 7-mile intervals to ensure that any preemptive strike against them will require a warhead each. But cities, unlike silos, cannot be "hardened." The same detonation over Chicago would kill millions. Moreover, at the height of the Cold War there were, and probably remain, at least 35,000 warheads in existence. Many commentators opine that they are all *present* would be less worrisome were they also *and accounted for.*

The Cold War came to an end with the break-up of the Soviet Union in 1991. In the wake of these developments the keepers of the "Doomsday Clock" moved their estimate of our prospects for survival from "only minutes to nuclear midnight" back a full half-hour. But it has been argued that, far from making the world safer, the end of the Cold War just put three more fingers on the button—Ukraine, Kazakstan, and Belorussia. And it may have released ready-for-use devices into a black market frequented by procurers of even more dubious moral reliability than U.S. presidents and Soviet premiers.

During the 1950s and early 1960s, American schoolchildren were taught, in the event of a nuclear detonation overhead, to "duck and cover," and survivalists stocked family-sized bomb shelters in their basements or backyards. It has since been decided there is no civil defense against a nuclear weapon. Few analysts predict there will be *no* survivors after a full-scale nuclear exchange. But many believe there can be no such thing as a "limited" nuclear war, much less a "winnable" one.

Still, unless one can entertain the possibility that a nuclear war *can* be won—or if not won then at least limited, or if not limited then at least protracted—she cannot understand the intricacies of nuclear strategy. Nor, therefore, could she understand the subtleties of nuclear deployment. To these I now turn.

II. STRATEGY AND DEPLOYMENT

Much has been made of the fact that there are enough nuclear warheads in existence to annihilate the human race several times over. This is rhetoric. As we will see, there are reasons for such redundancy. A more telling observation, however, is that it would take far fewer than 35,000 simultaneous detonations, *any*where on the land surfaces of the planet—although just how many is in dispute—to produce "nuclear winter." That is, enough debris will be tossed into the air, kept there and circulated by the winds produced by so many explosions, that the Earth will be shrouded from the sun for years. In short, long before radiation would have taken its toll, we will all have frozen to death. So this much is certain. Any stockpile in excess of this critical number, whatever it may be—adjusted, of course, for the number of warheads we can anticipate being destroyed in situ or en route—is morally and strategically irresponsible.

A peculiarity of nuclear weapons is that they continue to inflict casualties through radiation after hostilities have ceased, and *long* after through genetic mutation. They render vast tracts of land unusable and uninhabitable for decades, perhaps even centuries. And the winds carrying this radiation exhibit no respect for national borders. This and nuclear winter aside, however, there is nothing remarkable about *tactical* nuclear weapons, that is, smaller yields designed for battlefield use. They have changed the way fleets can maneuver, for example; but so did the Gatling gun change the formation of an infantry attack. Accordingly, I confine my analysis to *strategic* nuclear weapons.

By counter*force* is meant the targeting of an enemy's nuclear and/or conventional military capabilities. Counter*value* targets are its population centers, agriculture, industrial capacities, and religious and/or historical sites. These are included because an enemy might care about the quality of life of its surviving citizens as much as or more than how *many* survive. Some targeting is ambiguous. Both Hiroshima and Nagasaki were important munitions centers and mustering points. But it was probably the magnitude of civilian damage that was meant to, and did, induce the Japanese surrender. Moreover, a nation hoping to exploit the moral sensitivities of its adversary can *create* such ambiguity by, for example, locating its own launch sites in heavily populated areas.

Many ethicists would allow a nuclear power to target a nonnuclear adversary's conventional forces, provided it can do so without unacceptable levels of collateral civilian damage. Indeed, it was the failure to satisfy this proviso that made the attacks on Hiroshima and Nagasaki morally suspect. But unless the enemy's conventional forces are invulnerable, *and* the war is unambiguously defensive—both highly improbable—few countenance the targeting of the enemy's civilian population. Nor do they alter this judgment in the bilateral case, provided each can count on the other to share these moral constraints. And yet this is precisely what we *have* done. So, how came we to do it?

One answer is that our leaders are just evil. But this is unhelpful. Another is we came to this pass in increments, each of which seemed morally innocent at the time. But this belies history. Nuclear weapons were intended for cities from the outset. Countersilo targeting evolved much later.

A more instructive answer lies in the very *logic* of war, the object of which is to bend the enemy to our will. Or perhaps more accurately—because there are few uses one human being can make of another without *some* participation on his part—to bend him to bend *himself* to our will. To be sure, we achieve this end by first destroying his defenses. But we do *that* on the supposition that, once defenseless, he will succumb to our threat to do *further* violence to him.

Passive resistance, in turn, is the strategy of denying an aggressor that supposition. But it only works against an adversary too squeamish or unpracticed to counter it. Had the British in India been more selective in their violence, for example, by visiting it only on Muslims, the latter might have resented the Hindus taking a free ride on their suffering, and so their alliance might well have crumbled. So, similarly, were America to disarm and rely on passive resistance, the Soviets could induce the South to make a separate peace by declaring every city north of the Mason-Dixon line "open."

What *seems* to follow is that the principle of civilian immunity is logically incompatible with prosecuting a war in the first place. We can save the principle, short of outright pacifism, by modifying it to read that we can threaten the enemy's civilian population only *after* we have destroyed his defenses. But this sounds more ignoble than just rejecting the principle outright. So what *could* save the principle?

One plausible account of civilian immunity is offered by George Mavrodes. He suggests that over the millenia we decided, quite intelligently, to settle our differences through champions. (Note that passive resistance is incompatible with this convention.) So honoring the principle amounts to declaring our understanding that this is the practice in effect. By targeting civilians we withdraw that understanding, thereby putting our own civilians at risk. So, it would seem, mainstream ethicists are right to disallow countervalue targeting after all.

Still, what follows from this is that each nation is entitled to only as many warheads as the other has permissible targets. But because the latter include the other's launch sites, we are caught in an infinite regress. We can block this regress by agreeing to parity and then opening our arsenals to each other's inspection. But then what is to prevent the following scenario?

X mounts a full-scale attack on Y's permissible targets. Y detects this and decides it must either "Use 'em or lose 'em!" Because X's silos are now empty, all that remains to target are X's conventional forces. And then what? The war is over, without resolution of whatever was in dispute. Having lost all their "champions," X and Y have in effect exited the practice. Moreover, they are now both utterly vulnerable to any third party, be that third party nuclear or not.

So either each is entitled to *more* than as many warheads as the other has permissible targets, or else some of those targets are not permissible after all. Either way each must be left with the wherewithal to fight on. But *that* X has capacities in excess of those needed to ensure destruction of Y's permissible targets will indicate—rightly or wrongly, and attestations to the contrary notwithstanding—that X does *not* consider itself bound by the practice of civilian immunity. And if X is seen as, or even suspected of, intending a countervalue strike, then, on pain of inviting nuclear extortion, Y must be seen as so intending as well. So Y too will have to exceed its counterforce requirements. But what is worse is that if X's arsenal falls *short* of counterforce requirements it will be even *more* suspect, because Y will then rightly wonder by what means, other than nuclear hostage holding, X could be hoping to defend itself.

This fear of each other's fear is what Thomas Hobbes called "difference." The more contemporary term is the "security dilemma."

Some of the myriad paradoxes of nuclear security were manifest in the short-lived "Star Wars" program of the early 1980s. The United States, "innocently" seeking to escape its reliance on retaliation to deter Soviet provocation, sought instead to render itself invulnerable by mounting a laser cannon on a space platform from which it could then destroy a missile as it rose up from its silo. The Soviets interpreted this as the United States shielding itself from Soviet retaliation so it could strike the Soviet Union with impunity. That neither side *would* launch such a strike is beside the point. As we have already seen, it is that it *could* do so which backs up any lesser provocation it might employ, likewise with impunity, to bend the enemy to its will.

Nor do the subtleties end there. If the Soviet Union judged it could not match the Americans—and because, once operational, these platforms could defend *themselves* from any missile launched against them—it could have been forced into a preemptive strike against the facilities producing these platforms. Nor, save technically, would this have been an act of war, any more than the American blockade of Cuba was, save technically, an act of war. It would not, save technically, have been an act of war because its sole purpose, and effect, would have been the preservation of the very balance of threat and counterthreat that had been preserving the peace, and because it would have been directed against an initiative whose sole purpose could only have been to upset that balance. In short, expense and feasibility issues aside, Star Wars had to be abandoned because it was too destabilizing.

As was the Soviet attempt to place nuclear weapons in Cuba:

A Soviet warhead chafing in its silo 70 miles from American soil may raise hackles. But because, even in 1962, an intercontinental ballistic missile (ICBM) launched from the U.S.S.R. could have reached Miami in under an hour, what *strategic* difference could it make that from Cuba it could be reached in less than 10 minutes? Trivially the answer is—50 minutes. But, as we will see, 50 minutes is not trivial.

Five things can happen within 50 minutes of a first launch. The war can be (a) won, (b) lost, (c) drawn, (d) continued, or (e) none of the above. By the latter is meant MAD, which, by definition, is both morally and strategically unthinkable. But each of (a) through (d) supposes that, once initiated, a nuclear war can be stopped. Some say this is a delusion of idiocy. Or that nuclear war is morally unacceptable no matter how limited, and so, stoppable or not, believing it to be stoppable just increases its likelihood. If nuclear deterrence is to be practiced at all, say others, we should make it clear that any provocation will invite immediate, all-out retaliation. But if nuclear war, once initiated, is stoppable, we need flexibility in our responses—or, for that matter, in our own provocations—in order to stop it. Flexibility involves making choices. And in making choices, seconds, let alone minutes, are precious. For example:

Consider a lone missile detected incoming over the Pole and assumed to be carrying 10 multiple independent reentry vehicles (MIRV) warheads. If it is intercepted, then, in effect, we have just been put on warning, nothing more. We can do nothing, respond in kind, escalate, or even "cry uncle." Had we retaliated upon mere detection, however—and if the enemy fails to intercept us—then in effect, *we* have initiated. So, rather than run the risk of in-effect-initiating, we wait. And perhaps only if we fail to intercept do we then respond in kind. But how do we determine "kind" without knowing what of ours will be hit? So, once again, we need to wait. If only a few of our silos are hit, we can launch against an equal number of theirs. Or perhaps we can raise the bid. Or maybe we can signal our "concern" by deescalating—by, as it were, bidding *down*. But, once again, such deliberations take time. Time between detection and detonation to intercept and buy more time. Time between detonation and response to get that response just right. We might even want to offer our *adversary* time to deliberate. Or perhaps deprive him of it so he has to absorb the loss we have just inflicted on him and wait for the next interval to deliberate. In short, combatants in nuclear war are very much like partners in a game of bridge, each desperately trying to signal his strengths and weaknesses to the other by means of bids, leads, responses, and even body language.

Our common opposition is MAD. Thereafter, however, the analogy breaks down. For, unlike bridge, what constrains our communicating with each other is not a rule against talking. Rather it is that *what* is said may be disingenuous. And this is because we are also playing a subgame, against each other. Much as we would both rather lose to the other than lose to the opposition, our first choice is to emerge victorious over both.

Students of "game theory" will recognize this as a prisoners' dilemma, within which is embedded a bargaining dilemma, and within it, in turn, a game of chicken. One wins at Chicken by bluffing. But in this case one bluffs by *not* bluffing—for as long as he dares. But because we are also playing against MAD, at the same time as we are bluffing each other we need to cooperate to ensure things do not get out of hand. So, for example:

Had the Soviets been able to launch from Cuba, detection and detonation would have been virtually simultaneous. This would have undermined the credibility of the U.S. bluff that it would retaliate upon detection. Far from leaving the United States no time to deliberate, time to deliberate would have been imposed upon it. The Soviets, in effect, would have had a "free shot." So to match this immediacy of threat on Miami, the United States would have had to reassign Trident submarines from the mid-Atlantic to the eastern Baltic to pose a like threat against Leningrad. But in the Baltic they would be much more vulnerable. So they could not play the same role they had been serving, which was to assure the Soviets that no preemptive strike could hope to be fully successful. So, *mutatis mutandis*, not unlike the Star Wars scenario, had the Soviets persisted in arming Cuba, the Americans might have felt compelled to destroy those weapons before they became operational. So the Soviets had to withdraw them because, once again, not to do so would have been too destabilizing.

III. MORAL PARADOXES OF NUCLEAR DETERRENCE

Throughout the last section I have been oversimplifying by discounting both nuclear winter and radiation; and I will continue to do so here. But I have also been assuming—along with those in charge of our nuclear arsenals—that a nuclear war can be stopped. We could be wrong about this. And *if* we are wrong, then, it would seem, a first strike might just as well be all-out countervalue. One question—one I will leave completely unexplored here—is whether such a strike could ever be justified. We might suppose not. But nothing rides on this. For our question will be whether it could

ever be morally justified to *retaliate* in kind to such a first strike.

Prima facie the answer is no. I would be a poor U.S. president indeed who did not prefer American lives to Soviet lives. But I would be an even poorer human being if I did not prefer Soviet lives to no lives at all. If the entire Soviet arsenal is coming in, within minutes half the world's population will be dead. Only a moral monster could wish to see the other half dead as well. I might want revenge against whoever authored this tragedy. But surely not at the expense of billions of utterly innocent people. A reader may disagree. So let me put the case another way. Absent this sentiment there *are* none of the moral paradoxes of nuclear deterrence to which I now turn.

By *jus ad bellum* is meant the conditions under which it is morally permissible to go *to* war. Among these is that the war being contemplated does not necessitate a violation of one of the constraints on conduct *in* war, *jus in bello*. But, as we have already seen, among these, in turn, is that noncombatants cannot be intentionally killed. Some argue—among them Robert Holmes—that nuclear deterrence virtually guarantees nuclear war, and that a nuclear war is bound to escalate to countervalue targeting. So because one cannot conscionably fight a nuclear war, neither can she prepare for one. We ought, therefore, to disarm, if need be unilaterally.

That nuclear deterrence is inherently unstable, and that counterforce eventuates in countervalue, are both highly contentious empirical claims. Holmes' second line of argument proceeds by more a priori reasoning. Nuclear deterrence cannot be practiced disingenuously; so it must involve the genuine intention to retaliate. Retaliation involves the intentional killing of noncombatants; and this, we suppose, is wrong. It is wrong to intend do what it is wrong to do. So it is wrong to intend to retaliate, and so wrong too to practice nuclear deterrence.

Here the only premises that could be problematic are (1) it is wrong to intentionally kill noncombatants and (2) it is wrong to intend to do what it is wrong to do. Gregory Kavka calls (2) the wrongful intentions principle (WIP). But how can either (1) or (2) be rejected?

So the core paradox of nuclear deterrence is this. We seem to be saddled with three equally heartfelt, but logically incompatible, convictions. These are that

(1) it would be wrong to retaliate. That
(2) if it would be wrong to retaliate it would be wrong to intend to retaliate. And yet, in what Kavka calls a special deterrence situation (SDS),

(3) it would not be wrong to *intend* to retaliate.

We decided at the outset, recall, that without (1) we would have nothing to talk about. (2) is just an instance of the wrongful intentions principle. And without (3) we could no longer practice nuclear deterrence. But we have to reject one of them. So, which will it be?

Virtually alone in rejecting (1) is David Gauthier, not because he is a moral monster, but because he has commitments to a theory of rational choice that leave him no choice but to bite the bullet here. Both the just war theory behind (1), and the emphasis on intentions behind (2), are largely the products of Catholic theology. But Catholics are not alone in rejecting (3). Kavka however, rejects (2). His argument is as follows:

Normally we view intentions as constituents of the actions they author. But in an SDS, Kavka notes that

> the ground of the desire to form the intention is entirely distinct from any desire to carry it out ... [One] desires having the intention as a means of deterrence ... [S]he is willing, in order to prevent the offense, to accept a certain risk that, in the end, she will apply the sanction. But this is entirely consistent with her having a strong desire not to apply [it], and no desire at all to apply it. Thus while the object of her deterrent intention might be an evil act, it does not follow that, in desiring to adopt that intention, she desires to do evil, either as an end or as a means.

So because in an SDS it might even be morally *required* to intend to retaliate, the WIP must be rejected. And, along with it, the seemingly analytic assertion that "Doing something is right if and only if a morally good person would do the same thing in the given situation." This must now be rejected because, by hardwiring myself to retaliate—*ex hypothesi* what a morally good person would do—I will now retaliate—*ex hypothesi* what only an *evil* person would do. Last but not least, should it turn out that the only way I can acquire the intention to retaliate is to morally corrupt myself, then we might also have to reject the view that "It is wrong to deliberately lose one's moral virtue."

Kavka concedes that the loss of these three core moral intuitions—the WIP, the right-good principle, and the preservation of virtue principle—is a high price to pay. But SDS's are few and far between. Moreover, that our Cold War predicament *is*—or at least was—an SDS, requiring a retaliatory-intentions response, presupposes both (a) such intentions have a very high probability of deterring provocation, and (b) the dire-ness of Soviet domination and of nuclear holocaust are not an order of magnitude apart. Douglas Lackey takes Kavka to task on both scores. But these are matters about which reasonable people can disagree.

A more conclusive line of objection, perhaps, is that, under conditions of two-dimensional uncertainty—that is, where we know neither the direness of an outcome nor its probability—we should reject the advice of the *disaster avoider*. He tells us to court the small chance of the greatest disaster (mutual annihilation) both to preclude the more likely but lesser disaster (Soviet domination) and to access the even more likely *un*disaster (successful deterrence). Instead we should heed the counsel of the *maximiner*. She tells us to protect ourselves from the worst-case scenario (mutual annihilation) by forfeiting our first choice (successful deterrence) even if this means settling for our second last (Soviet domination). But some people are keener than others to avoid unnecessary losses, and some are more risk-averse than others. So perhaps that is all there is to say.

Not so, say feminist critics. As Helen Caldicott, *et al.*, have been telling us for years, there is any number of ways by which we might discourage puerile men from using our residential streets as a drag strip, including signage (moral persuasion), rumble strips (civil disobedience), and so on. But one way *not* to do so is to send their (and our) children out to play in the traffic! Moreover, there is strong evidence to suggest that such patterns of risk assessment are gender related. If so, and if no gender-independent case can be made for disaster avoidance over maximining, and because nuclear weapons are indifferent to the gender of their victims, perhaps women should be given equal representation in drafting our nation's nuclear policy.

Steven Lee shares this sensitivity to risk. The traditionalist abolitionist, recall, pegs her case to the WIP. To this the retentionist counters that conditional intentions have effects independent of the action conditionally intended. The abolitionist then cites the principle of moral dissociation: for an effect to count as independent, it must be unconnected with what the actor wants to achieve. The retentionist counters that because the killing of noncombatants would not be wanted were the threat to do so carried out, the deaths that are threatened *are* dissociated from the purpose with which the threat would be carried out. And so the debate continues. Lee avoids all this Jesuitry about intentions. The immorality of nuclear hostage holding lies not in the conditional *intention* to kill unwilling innocent civilians, but in putting them at risk of being killed either *un*intentionally or, perhaps, for reasons *dis*sociated from those driving the policy producing the risk.

Lee is anything but dismissive of the retentionist position. The deployment of nuclear weapons, says he, would seem to do violence to

> the *principle of tolerable divergence,* according to which what the moral norms of an institution prescribe [must] not greatly diverge from what [its] prudential norms prescribe.... The point of referring to the divergence as tolerable is that any divergence great enough to be *in*tolerable to those pursuing the institution's prudential goals would result in the moral norms being systematically disregarded, and so in time being revised or replaced.... [So b]ecause nuclear deterrence appears to be the only way in which such basic prudential goals as the avoidance of nuclear war and the maintenance of national sovereignty can be reliably achieved,

prudential reasoning would seem to countenance it. And yet, because nuclear deterrence is hostage holding, moral reasoning—at least deontological moral reasoning—would seem to eschew it. Lee's project, then, is to reconcile morality and prudence.

To this end he considers three approaches. *Moral* revisionism urges us to "alter the moral principle of respect for innocent civilians in [such a] way [that] the obligation not to practice nuclear deterrence would not exist." This is "clearly our last resort". *Strategic* revisionism argues for "forms of nuclear deterrence [that] avoid the deontological objections." By *existential* deterrence, for example, is meant the deferrent effect of there just *being* nuclear weapons in the hands of the enemy, even if he has sworn never to use them. But, Lee points out, all such *seemingly* innocent alternatives depend for their deterrent effect on the risk of either a) things getting out of hand, b) unintended but foreseen collateral civilian damage, and/or c) escalation to countervalue targeting. *Prudential* revisionism—Lee's own approach—attempts to show that "the consequentialist and prudential arguments for nuclear [over conventional deterrence] are unsound."

What is especially instructive, however, is his treatment of the problem of extrication. Here he concedes that "though there are serious instability problems with nuclear deterrence, those resulting from unilateral nuclear disarmament [may] seem to be worse." And even supposing unilateral, or even mutual, disarmament can be safely achieved, nuclear weapons cannot be *un*invented, nor can a nation divest itself of its own rebuild-

ing capacity. So abolition amounts to just one more species of nuclear deterrence, namely *weaponless* deterrence. Moreover,

> if a moral defense of impure counterforce deterrence, or of existential deterrence, on the grounds that no explicit threats against civilians are involved is not allowed, neither can such grounds be used to defend the nuclear threats inherent in the rebuilding capacity.

So how *can* a weaponless deterrence policy withstand the deontological objection? Lee's answer is that

> To threaten to hold hostages is not to hold hostages; so to threaten to threaten nuclear destruction is not to run afoul of the proscription of hostage holding. What puts civilians at risk is the *existence* of the weapons. So when a nation threatens to rebuild its nuclear weapons, it seeks to influence the behavior of the opponent's leaders, but it does not do so by putting civilians at risk.

It would put civilians at risk if and only if it carried *through* on that threat.

The problem with this is it runs afoul of Lee's own *credibility* principle. That is that:

> unless a nuclear strategy [leaves] something that is in [the nation's] interest to do if the deterrence fails, its threats will lack credibility, and the strategy will not be effective in achieving its deterrent end.

So by threatening to rearm we are announcing our willingness *to* rearm should our threat to do so fails to achieve its deterrent effects. This being so, one might see Lee's reasoning as analogous to that of the Gestapo interrogator who asks of his victim, "Now then, shall we do this the easy way, or the hard way?" all the while safeguarding his own virtue by only *displaying* his implements of torture—and displaying them in a state of preassembly.

One way to break the analogy between weaponless deterrence and the Gestapo interrogator is with reference to the time, effort, and expense involved in assembling a truncheon versus a nuclear arsenal. But what could make time, effort, and expense relevant, other than their relation to credibility? And yet having deontological acceptability vary inversely with credibility is a double-edged sword. If the time, effort, and expense involved in a nation's rearming itself undermines the credibility of its threatening to do so, its threatening to do so will be ineffectual. To achieve the requisite level of deterrent effect the nation would have to reduce the time, effort, and expense separating threat from execution. But the narrower the gap between threat and execution, the stronger the analogy.

And the same can be said if one cites instead the "intervening intentions" gap. If the number of people whose moral qualms have to be overcome in order to rearm is too high, the threat to rearm will prove ineffectual. So, once again, the solution will be to reduce that number; and so, once again, the analogy will be strengthened. Nor would it help to return to the notion of existential risk, because the gap in existential risk between assembled and unassembled nuclear weapons is neither greater nor less than that between assembled and unassembled truncheons.

But, Lee might counter, surely there is a greater risk of *un*intentional use of assembled nuclear weapons than of assembled truncheons. Unintentional uses can be divided into those which arise from irrationality and those which arise by accident. With respect to the former, the analogy clearly holds. After all, interrogators have been known to "lose their cool" too. But with respect to the latter Lee would be right. After all, how could there be an accidental truncheoning? But one can counter this counter by replacing the truncheon with a pistol. Do we not have far more evidence for the fallibility of gun safeties than of nuclear failsafes? And do we not have far more evidence for the possibility of disassembled firearms being accidentally reassembled than we do of disassembled nuclear weapons being accidentally reassembled?

So the only grounds for disanalogy that remain is what we might call the *morality* gap, that is, that it takes a greater, conscious, moral self-sullying to make good on a threat to assemble a nuclear weapon than it does to make good on a threat to assemble a truncheon (or a pistol). After all, anyone in a position to threaten to threaten to beat (or shoot) a defenseless prisoner is already in a morally suspect position, whereas … Whereas what? Anyone in a position to threaten to threaten a nuclear attack is not? But surely this is just to beg the very question at issue!

But even if the analogy stands, need we conclude that "nuclear weapons have [irrevocably] created a world in which one of our basic moral obligations must be [retired]"? Maybe not. For might not our virtue yet take a free ride, as it were, on the fortuitous misperceptions of others of our vice? That is, suppose that, to preserve our virtue, we privately but genuinely forswear any intention to rearm. Indeed, suppose we privately but genuinely swear *not* to rearm. For that matter, suppose we *publicly* and genuinely swear not to rearm. Because we will not be believed, it should make no difference. Let's call this *no-deterrence deterrence*. And, to distinguish it from the policy practiced by nations that are technologically *incapable* of arming themselves, call the latter *no-deterrence-at-all*. Can a no-deterrence deterrence policy fare any better than weaponless deterrence against the deontological objection?

Prima facie it can. Neither the enemy population nor our own are at risk. Nor do we invite greater risk of having to make territorial or political concessions, as a result of an adversary's preemptive rearmament, than we would had we *dis*ingenuously threatened *to* rearm. So no one has anything to fear from us save fear itself—a fear that is, to boot, self-induced.

But how fare our intuitions when tested against our interrogator analogy? Presumably the analogy would be the interrogator neither displaying his tools of persuasion, nor uttering any threats—in fact *assuring* his victim, genuinely as it happens, that whether she answers his questions or not no harm shall befall her—and yet relying on her appreciation of the *logic* of her situation to induce her nonetheless to answer. Would such an interrogator be entirely innocent?

Probably not. After all, most sexual harassment takes place by mechanisms very much like those just described. The harasser issues no threats; nor for that matter does he intend to make good on those he could issue. Rather he takes advantage of the fact—a fact known to his victim—that, were he less morally upright, he *could* issue them. And of the fact—a fact he himself cannot alter—that she feels herself unable to *rely* on his righteousness. Indeed it is for these very reasons that many institutions, recognizing a need for a more substantive interpretation of autonomy, have taken to building fences around the sexual autonomy of subordinates.

Whether rightly or wrongly need not concern us here. As with any attempt to repair one injustice, there are effects independent of that intention. But *our* interest, recall, is in the moral incumbency of the superior's *self*-restraint. Ought *he* to be satisfied by the purity of his own intentions? Or need he assure himself further that the logic of the situation has not likewise produced effects independent of his intentions? If I said the latter, would I be alone in my discomfort with the idea of, for example, prison inmates participating in medical studies, blood banking, or organ donation, notwithstanding that one autonomous effect of their exclusion is their being denied the opportunity to demonstrate a very likely genuine willingness to be of service to others?

Does this mean that, so long as torture remains even a *possibility,* there can be no such thing as morally innocent interrogation? If so, the difference between a merely *otherwise* innocent police officer in a country with a repressive regime, and a *categorically* innocent diplomat negotiating fish quotas for a nation practicing no-deterrence deterrence with a nation practicing no-deterrence-at-all, is just that in the case of the latter, but not the former, it is impossible for the state in question to divest itself of its status.

But does this not seem a bit odd? After all, it may be *as* impossible for the otherwise innocent police officer to divest his country of its repressive regime as it is for the categorically innocent negotiator to divest his country of its no-deterrence deterrence policy. Are we to believe that ought-implies-can operates at the gestalt level but not the personal? That the only way the police officer can escape a charge of moral complicity is to resign his commission?

One's only out, as we have seen, is to take it upon one*self* to level the playing field. Just as the otherwise innocent male professor can, and probably should, refrain from making advances to his female students in the first place so, perhaps, the otherwise innocent police officer should refrain altogether from interrogating his prisoner. But the problem in both cases is that such restraints might have effects independent of their good intentions. The professor takes it upon himself—perhaps contrary to both the interests and the wishes of his student—to forgo what very well might have been a deeply rewarding relationship for both of them. Similarly, the prisoner might *like* to have had the opportunity to bargain, say, for information leading to the arrest of a confederate in exchange for a lighter sentence for himself. So, it would seem, the intolerable divergence between morality and prudence remains.

Still, this result may have been skewed by our examples. Courting and interrogating are, for all intents and purposes, bivalent choices. One either courts or not. It is similar with interrogating. Negotiating fish quotas is another matter. There one *can* level the playing field. A nation with a no-deterrence deterrence policy, in negotiating with one with no-deterrence-at-all, *could* clean its hands by, for example, agreeing to the distribution of the cooperative dividend that it *would* have agreed to had either both parties or neither had the wherewithall for a no-deterrence deterrence policy.

Of course which account of counterfactuals we adopt will make a difference to whether it makes a difference whether we go for the "both" or the "neither." That is,

if by this "would have" we mean that everything about, say, the United States and Ethiopia remains just as it is, save that either (a) the Manhattan Project failed—this being the "neither" option—or (b) the Ethiopians were capable of mustering a nuclear arsenal—this being the "both" option—if, that is, apart from these minimal divergence and convergence miracles, the balance of conventional military power and/or potential between the two nations remained as it is—then the both/neither distinction would make no difference. Let's call this *narrow* counterfactualizing.

If on the other hand we mean to alter everything about the United States and Ethiopia that *would* be altered had either the Manhattan Project failed or the Ethiopians had had the wherewithall to build a bomb—let's call this *broad* counterfactualizing—then it *will* make a difference whether we are talking "neither" or "both." If the Manhattan Project had failed, the United States would still have been a world power, as assuredly as Ethiopia would not. If on the other hand the Ethiopians had had the wherewithall to build a nuclear device, then they would likewise have had the wherewithall to be at least a minor industrial power. In that case the balance of power between them and the Americans would be more akin to that between, say, *Iraq* and America.

What are the *moral* implications of these options? Broad counterfactualizing cleans our hands, but at the cost of penalizing ourselves for advantages that—at least within the scope of this discussion—are *not* morally suspect. By imagining that nuclear weapons had simply proven technologically impossible, we penalize ourselves less than by imagining that the Ethiopians had invented them too. But if we opt for the latter we reward them for that for which we would have penalized ourselves. Narrow counterfactualizing, by contrast, is more like giving our hands a quick rinse. But at least it is more discriminating about what gets thrown out with the bathwater.

But I raise these subtleties only to show why they can be dismissed. For the point is that, whether we opt for narrow counterfactualizing or broad—and *if* broad then for the "both" or the "neither"—the divergence between morality and prudence remains intolerable. Even the minimum concession that morality would allow—that is, that dictated by "narrow neitherism"—would be unacceptable to the American fishing industry, and so "would result in the moral norms being systematically disregarded, and so in time being revised or replaced."

So, to summarize: Prudential revisionism implies abolitionism. Abolitionism amounts to a species of strategic revisionism. And so the failure of strategic revisionism to meet the deontological objection drives us to some species of moral revisionism.

By moral revisionism, however, we need not mean "alter[ing] the moral principle of respect for innocent civilians in [such a] way [that] the obligation not to practice nuclear deterrence would not exist." We could instead buy the case for prudential revisionism, and so divest ourselves of our nuclear weapons. We could acknowledge that doing so amounts to adopting a no-deterrence deterrence policy, and so a species of strategic revisionism. We need then only deny that such a species of strategic revisionism runs afoul of the deontological objection by adopting a species of moral revisionism. But the moral revision we adopt need not be to the principle of civilian immunity. Rather we can simply revise the principle that it is wrong to profit from advantages that, but for the gestalt from which they arise, would be morally innocent. In short, far from having to choose *between* Lee's three options, we can opt for them all.

Of course, this way of making good on our respect for innocent civilians would incur costs. It would mean that neither prisoners, nor female students, nor Ethiopians would have grounds for moral complaint against, respectively, their otherwise innocent interrogators, amorous male professors, or militarily superior fish quota conegotiators. In light of our growing consensus on the immorality of such complicitous behavior, perhaps we should just be less intolerant of intolerable divergences between morality and prudence.

Also See the Following Articles

NUCLEAR DETERRENCE • NUCLEAR TESTING • WARFARE, CODES OF • WARFARE, STRATEGIES AND TACTICS

Bibliography

Beitz, C., *et al.* (Eds.). (1985). *International ethics.* Princeton: Princeton University Press.

Caldicott, H. (1984). *Missile envy: The arms race and nuclear war.* New York: Morrow.

Holmes, R. (1989). *On war and morality,* Princeton: Princeton University Press.

Kavka, G. (1987). *Moral paradoxes of nuclear deterrence.* Cambridge: Cambridge University Press.

Lackey, D. (1984). *Moral principles and nuclear weapons.* Towota: Rowman and Allenheld.

Lackey, D. (1982). Missiles and morals: A utilitarian look at nuclear deterrence. *Philosophy and Public Affairs,* **11.**

Lee, S. (1993). *Morality, prudence, and nuclear weapons.* Cambridge: Cambridge University Press.

MacLeon, D. (Ed.). (1984). *The security gamble: Deterrence and dilemmas in the nuclear age.* Towota: Rowman and Allenheld.

NURSES' ETHICS

Win Tadd
University of Wales Cardiff

practical reasoning Reasoning that leads to an act rather than a theoretical conclusion.

teleology A type of ethical theory which interprets morality in terms of an end or purpose.

virtue A settled habit or disposition of character.

virtue ethics A type of ethics which claims that agents should develop certain character traits rather than simply following rules or principles.

GLOSSARY

advocate A person who represents the interests of others, or who acts on the other's behalf.

consequentialism Types of ethical theory that judge what is right in terms of the consequences or expected consequences of actions.

deontology A type of ethical theory stating that certain acts must be performed, or certain rules or principles must be followed, without considering whether this will lead to the best consequences in the particular circumstances.

ethics of care An approach to ethics originating predominantly from feminist writing which focuses upon close personal relationships and emphasizes emotional commitment as a basis for acting rather than a reliance on abstract rules and principles.

impartiality The absence of favor or bias in moral decisions.

partiality The act or fact of making special allowances in certain instances.

"NURSING ETHICS" can be used in at least three senses. The first and perhaps most usual is when it is used to refer to the expressed norms of the nursing profession, that is, the values and principles that ought to govern and guide the day-to-day practice of the nurse.

The second sense in which the term can be used is a descriptive one when, rather than indicating an ideal action guide, it refers to the principles and values which in fact, or in reality, guide the practice of nursing. In the third sense, "nursing ethics" refers to the growing body of literature concerning the moral or ethical dimension of nursing practice and thus refers to a field or body of knowledge rather than to ideal or actual norms.

Before leaving the definition of nursing ethics it should be emphasized that there are two distinct viewpoints concerning the relationship of nursing ethics to that of bioethics generally. The first is that the term "nursing ethics" is itself controversial as "there is really very little that is morally unique to nursing" (R. Veatch, 1981. *Law Medicine and Health Care,* **9,** 17). Viewed in this way, nursing ethics is classified as a subset of bio-ethics in much the same way as medical ethics is.

The opposing view argues that nursing ethics is not simply a category of bioethics, but instead "[it] raises serious questions about the aims of theory formation in ethics, the meaning of philosophical principles of ethics, the nature of philosophical solutions to ethical problems and the modes of work necessary for progress in philosophical ethics" (A. Jameton, 1984. *Nursing practice: The ethical issues* (pp. xvi–xvii). Englewood Cliffs, NJ: Prentice-Hall).

For the purpose of this entry, this debate is largely, academic although it is worth highlighting that there are differences in practice between nurses and other health professionals which may lead to differences in one's judgments about the morality of various actions for the different agents. Thus although the same ethical principles might apply to all health professionals, the implications of these on the conduct of an individual may depend to some extent on the structure, power relationships, and conventions of a particular health care system. It is also worth pointing out that if nurses wish to have a voice in bioethics or the ethics of health care generally, then pursuing a separatist approach may prove unhelpful and isolate them from the mainstream of debate.

I. APPROACHES TO NURSING ETHICS

Contemporary discussions of nursing ethics in the field of applied ethics have until relatively recently been noticeable by their absence. It was not until the late 1970s that systematic analysis of the ethical dimensions of the nurse's role appeared in the literature, and in many ways the development of nursing ethics has followed a course which corresponds to the development of nursing as a profession.

Initial early approaches to the subject closely followed the recognized approaches to biomedical ethics in that major ethical theories such as consequentialism and deontology were applied to nursing situations. This has been termed the "Ethical Theory Approach" (T. Pence, 1987. *Philosophy in Context* 17, 7–16).

Following the publication of *Principles of Biomedical Ethics* by Beauchamp and Childress (1979), nursing literature soon followed suit with many texts exploring the dilemmas in nursing practice in relation to specific moral principles such as autonomy, beneficence, justice, and nonmaleficence.

One criticism of both such approaches is that they fail to take account of the context in which nursing is practiced, and this has led to Pence's claim that for ethical practice in nursing to become a reality, an approach based on the philosophical foundations of nursing must be adopted. Such an approach requires an understanding of the nurse's role and funciton, as well as of the prevailing social and political climate.

These are not the only approaches to nursing ethics, however. Again following general trends in both biomedical and professional ethics, nurses have shown an increasing interest in the subject of virtue ethics. Whereas consequential and deontological ethics have as their main focus the morality of certain acts, virtue ethics focuses on the character of the agent. Although interest in the moral character and qualities of agents has traditionally been an important feature of nursing, current interest stems from two sources. The first was the 1981 publication of Alasdair MacIntyre's seminal work on the nature of virtues, *After Virtue* (London: Duckworth), which brought a renewed interest in virtue ethics generally. The second source is the increasing dissatisfaction with traditional Western philosophy felt by growing numbers of feminist writers.

While the former approach emphasizes the importance of a number of core virtues claimed to be fundamental, feminist interpretations have tended to focus attention on the concept of human caring as the central virtue within feminist ethics.

II. VIRTUE ETHICS

Although the ethics of conduct has an important place in discussions of professional ethics, it does not provide the whole story. The application of principles or ethical theories of action depends on people being of good character and sound judgment. This is not to claim that there is no relationship between action and character, since, clearly, how an individual acts often provides important evidence about her character. Similarly, specific character traits lead to certain actions, for instance, when a compassionate person displays her compassion through compassionate acts. For a complete picture of morality, however, it is necessary to consider the internal qualities or characteristics which are essential for moral agency and which are at the heart of virtue ethics.

The main question in virtue ethics is, "What kind of person should I be?", and it has its origins in Ancient Greece. Although Socrates and Plato were both deeply concerned with virtue, it is invariable with Aristotle's account that contemporary philosophers commence their expositions. It should be emphasized that virtue is a complex concept; over the ages it has acquired certain connotations which were not originally present. For example, today, being virtuous implies that a person is wholesome, trustworthy, or a decent sort who puts others before herself. It also has uncomplimentary associations, such as being a "goody-goody." In Ancient Greece *areté*, or virtue, had a very particular meaning and certainly had no negative connotations. It was used to refer to a person who displayed excellence in whatever they did. Contemporary notions of virtue such as benevolence, meekness, or selflessness are in fact the antithesis of the virtue of classical moralists, and the modern word "virtuosity" more effectively captures the notion of excellence evident in early Greek accounts of virtue.

A. Aristotle's Ethics of Virtue

One idea which is crucial to understanding Aristotle's conception of virtue is that of teleology. The Greek *telos* means a goal or purpose, and Aristotle believed that everything had an innate purpose. This notion did not just apply to man-made objects such as a chair or table, where the purpose might be obvious and would have been in the mind of its maker from the outset. It applied to everything in nature, although it may not always be easy to determine the precise purpose of something. Aristotle claimed that to do so one must study what the object does best. If the object in question performed its purpose well, then it was virtuous. This approach was also applied to human beings, so raising a query as to what the human purpose might be.

The Greek word *eudaimonia* has been translated as "happiness," "flourishing," or "fulfillment," and again the same difficulties apply to these translations from the ancient Greek in that contemporary interpretations seem thin and superficial in comparison. For the ancient Greeks, *eudaimonia* was something that was extremely precious and rare and virtually impossible to achieve, although it had to be strived for. (Maslow's concept of self-actualization might capture something of its meaning.) For the ancient Greeks, *eudaimonia* was not the reward of virtue, but consisted of life lived in accordance with virtue. It was what everyone seeks for themselves and was thus the fulfillment of one's function as a person.

For Aristotle, not only did individuals have particular functions, but mankind itself had a unique function which would lead to the kind of life in which *eudaimonia* was achieved. Aristotle identified this unique function as the ability to reason. This supreme state cannot be achieved in one day and lost the next as his oft-quoted statement about one swallow not making a summer

suggests. Instead he states that we must consider a complete lifetime.

According to Aristotle the good person is one who uses his reason well by acting in accordance with two types of virtues: the "intellectual" virtues and the "moral" virtues. The intellectual virtues involve contemplation, or *theória*, rather than the mere acquisition of knowledge. He acknowledges that a life of total contemplation is beyond the reach of most humans, and thus the majority of people have to be satisfied with the secondary variety of rationality acquired through acting in accordance with the moral virtues—that of practical reasoning or wisdom (*phronesis*), which is reasoning that leads to action.

This notion of practical reasoning is important in Aristotle's account of virtue as it relates to the difference between the responsible actions of an adult and those of a child or an animal. According to Aristotle, the child or the animal is driven by passions such as hunger or anger while the voluntary actions of a responsible adult can be influenced by his or her own internal monitoring. This internal monitoring or evaluation involves awareness of the possible outcomes within a particular situation, awareness of the choice between these outcomes, awareness of the different ends which may be worth either attaining or avoiding in relation to the possible alternatives, and a deliberate act of judgment involved in choosing and acting.

Thus, good people will have the ability to reason well about what is good for their lives as a whole, and such deliberation will lead to the performance of actions in accordance with the virtues necessary for the good life. This aspect of reasoning is more practical, social, and political than is *theória*, as this activity necessarily involves others with whom we interact and how we behave toward them.

According to Aristotle, a virtue is a habit (*hexis*) or disposition of character—concerned with choice and manifested in emotions—to seek the mean in all things relative to us, where the mean is defined through reason as defined by a prudent man.

These dispositions are not inborn or natural, but are chosen and acquired through practice, and this, like the evocation of appropriate feelings, has implications for moral education, which should focus on the development of the individual's character by inculcating appropriate habits or dispositions.

Virtue is not, however, merely a matter of acting in a certain way—one must also feel in appropriate ways. Thus, a virtue or an excellence of character is a settled disposition, and any action which displays virtue will also involve the display of some emotion such as desire, anger, fear, confidence, envy, or joy. For example, courage is an excellence of character (virtue) displayed in relation to the emotion of fear, while cowardice is a defect of character (vice) displayed in relation to the same emotion.

For Aristotle, there is no emotion in itself which is either good or bad, rather it is the state of character or disposition to display an emotion either appropriately or inappropriately. What is necessary, therefore, is some way of deciding what is appropriate, and for a complete understanding it is necessary to consider what Aristotle calls the "doctrine of the mean."

Exercising a virtue involves the use of practical reasoning in judging the mean between two extremes, one of excess and one of deficiency. Courage, for example, is the middle ground between cowardice, which is too little, and foolhardiness, which is too much. This doctrine is often misinterpreted as implying "moderation in all things," but this is not what Aristotle had in mind. Displaying virtue involves finding the mean at the right times, on the right grounds, toward the right people, for the right motive, and in the right way. As to how one would determine the mean, Aristotle has much to say, and he emphasizes both the role of reason and observation of those who have practical wisdom. In particular he stresses three points.

First, one should try to always avoid excess, as it is the most erroneous position, so that, for example, in relation to modesty, shyness might be less evil than shamelessness. In this way one chooses the lesser of the two evils.

Second, everyone has a natural tendency to err on one side or other of the mean, and therefore we must try to steer ourselves in the direction of the other extreme. If an agent has a natural tendency to cowardice then she ought to make a deliberate attempt to veer toward foolhardiness, thereby moving closer to the mean.

Finally, one must always be aware or on one's guard against pleasure because our judgment of pleasure is not impartial.

Despite his practical advice, Aristotle acknowledges that hitting the mean is extremely difficult, and exact rules or comprehensive general principles cannot be laid down. It is more a decision which lies with perception and one has to be present in a situation to be able to judge or evaluate it. Only in this way can a person take account of the significant factors or values. Thus knowledge gained through experience is important in knowing how to act in accordance with virtue.

In summary, therefore, according to Aristotle, virtues are those excellences of character which are settled dispositions of choice, in a mean relative to the individual, such as a wise person would determine, in a particular context. For each excellence there will be some specific emotion whose province it is, and the mean is exhibiting the emotion to the right degree. If an individual displays too little or too much of an emotion then she is exhibiting a defect of character or a vice. Finally, there are no emotions that are good or bad in themselves.

B. A Contemporary Account of Virtue

MacIntyre, in *After Virtue* (second edition) defines virtue as "an acquired human quality the possession and exercise of which tends to enable us to achieve those goods which are internal to practices and the lack of which effectively prevents us from achieving any such goods" (1985, p. 191). He presents his concept of virtue in terms of three conceptual stages: practices, a narrative order of a single human life, and moral tradition. Although it is beyond the scope of this entry to provide a full account of MacIntyre's theory, it is important within the context of nursing to understand his description of practices.

Practices, in the sense in which MacIntyre uses the term, are complex and demanding socially established activities which have standards of excellence and goods internal to them. Examples of practices given by MacIntyre include chess, football, architecture, farming, physics, chemistry, biology, history, painting, and music. One could also include medicine, nursing, and teaching to his list. Each of these practices has a history or tradition as well as certain standards of excellence or performance, and each requires that the practitioner cultivate certain virtues. Although each practice can lead to goods which are external to them, such as great fame or fortune, they also have goods which are internal to them.

Internal goods can only be acquired by embracing a practice and conforming to its constraints and standards. They are internal because they can be achieved only by engaging in the practice and can be categorized only in relation to the practice itself. Although external goods may be acquired by submitting oneself to the standards and constraints of a particular practice, they could equally be achieved by participating in a range of practices. For instance, wealth can be gained through architecture, piano playing, or agriculture.

In relation to nursing, internal goods might include the gratification of being able to use one's knowledge and skills to promote health and individual well-being and to relieve suffering. Experiencing such goods can only come about by conforming to the particular rules and standards, developed over time, which are relevant to, and definitive of, competent nursing. Further, although technique might be important in a practice, MacIntyre is at pains to point out that a practice in his sense involves more than just the acquisition of a set of technical skills. It must involve a regard for the historical tradition of the practice and the internal goods derived from that tradition.

III. THE ETHIC OF CARE

A number of nurse writers claim that nursing needs a discrete approach to resolve the moral dilemmas and issues which arise as a result of the nurse's role and the current practice of nursing. The ethic of care offers a very alluring proposition for a number of reasons: nursing is a predominantly female profession and the ethic of care is frequently portrayed as a feminine ethic, and by focusing on care not only are medical toes not trodden upon as it is claimed that their main focus is cure, but also it offers nursing a distinctive function within the health care arena.

Generally theories of ethics of care suggest that women approach moral reasoning and moral activity in an entirely different mode than men in that rather than relying on abstract moral principles for guidance, they tend to focus on concepts such as care, responsibility, and interpersonal connections. Certain quarters in nursing have readily grasped these developments, for if it can be shown that a feminist ethic based on care does in fact operate, then as a largely female occupation, whose unique function it is to care, nursing not only has a theoretical basis, but also an ethical imperative on which it can establish its claims to a distinctive role and over which it can legitimately exercise supremacy.

The ethic of care favors the significance of interdependence in relationships where the specific situational and contextual demands are given due consideration along with values such as nurturing, caring, compassion, and empathy. A detailed exploration of this approach is not possible within the confines of this entry and readers are referred to texts in the bibliography which provide detailed accounts of the theory. However, some criticisms have been leveled at the approach which are important for nurses to consider.

A. Justification

It is important that when nurses are called to care, they know precisely what is expected of them. In other words, that they care about the right things; that they

do so effectively and with skill; and that they can explain and justify their actions. One important criticism of this approach is that currently the theory is underdeveloped and consequently it is very difficult to distinguish between the universally accepted notion of care in the everyday sense and those occasions when the term "care" is being used in a specific technical way as in philosophical writings on the ethics of care. This undoubtedly leads to confusion and a lack of clarity in the analysis of the term which makes justification of actions based on "care" questionable by those who do not subscribe to a similar orientation. Merely claiming that each situation is contextually dependent and therefore certain actions maybe wrong in one situation and correct in another is not satisfactory in professional ethics.

B. Guides to Actions

One difficulty with this approach concerns how boundaries or guides to an agent's actions can be established. In their rejection of principled approaches to ethics, many defenders of the ethics of care appear to miss the point that often moral principles and rules exist precisely because we care for others and wish to live in relation to them, and without some rules and principles, such as it is generally wrong to lie, it would be difficult for society to operate in anything other than an inconsistent arbitrary manner.

The assumption, by many advocating an ethic of care, that principles are applied in a cold, calculating, abstract way can also be challenged, as can the fact these proponents fail to see that they too are relying on principles, albeit different ones from those involved in more traditional approaches. For example, the importance of relationship could be claimed as a principle on which an ethic of care is based, and like other moral principles, would have to be defended on universal grounds.

C. Partiality versus Impartiality

In relation to this debate, at one end of the continuum impartialists argue that the only justification for preferential treatment is because close relationships impose particular types of obligations on agents, but that these are strictly limited. At the other end of the continuum, particularists, such as those advocating an ethic of care, claim that the demand for universal impartial principles is an inappropriate basis for morality. Occupying the middle ground are others who suggest that there will be times when private and public morality will collide with each other and in certain circumstances impartiality will be overridden.

It is often assumed by those who claim an ethic of care is an appropriate basis for a nursing ethic that the demand for impartiality requires that an agent stand back from the situation and adopt a dispassionate or disinterested view of the issues or dilemma. However, this does not mean either that emotions have no part to play in any deliberations or that one should assume that a disinterested position is an uninterested one.

Suffice it to say that that intimate relationships are different from those which are role based. For instance, husbands, wives, children, and friends would prefer to claim that they respond to each other out of love, rather than because of some particular type of duty or obligation, whereas impartial and abstract principles are necessary for a public morality where we are involved with strangers.

In nursing it would be extremely difficult to justify a morality based on particularity. Nurses should treat patients impartially by not showing favoritism, or giving certain people preferential treatment, but this does not mean they must adopt an indifferent or uninterested attitude. Nor does it mean that emotion plays no part in the delivery of care. In many cases, the nurse will be driven by powerful emotions such as compassion, empathy, and even anguish, but these emotions are not dependent on the identity of the particular patient; rather they emerge from her reasoning that when another human being is suffering, he or she ought to be helped.

D. General Criticisms

Because the ethic of care focuses to a great extent on women's experiences of caring involving relationship, responsiveness, and cooperation, there is a tendency for self-sacrifice, which has long been a traditional value in nursing and which should therefore raise alarms among nurses, since rather than being a force for empowerment, an ethic of care could reinforce the social and political structures which support dominant relations within health care.

A further difficulty is the frequent demand for exclusivity and intensity of the caring relationship. Although it may be the case that in the intimate caring relationships to be found within the family circle, receptivity, responsiveness, and relatedness pose no difficulty, one needs to take account of the fact that the nurse cares for many patients and it is far from certain that caring to such an extent is possible, or even desirable. The nurse cannot achieve high levels of intimacy and mutu-

ality with every patient for whom she must care, not only because of the numbers involved, but also because the average length of stay for a patient is hospital is falling rapidly, so that nurses have little time available to get to know patients. When the nurse cannot achieve the ideal portrayed, then she is left feeling inadequate in her relationship with patients.

One might also question whether patients want nurses to be closely involved to the degree suggested. Such intrusion could, for example, be seen as an invasion of privacy which has little to do with merely safeguarding dignity, or promoting or maintaining the person's health status. Although patients may expect sensitivity on the part of nurses and a willingness by them to carry out their duties in a caring and considerate manner, there is no evidence that patients wish or expect a relationship of such intensity. What patients do expect is competent care and being treated as people rather than objects.

Regardless of such limitations, however, one cannot escape the fact that for nurses to display caring behaviors toward their patients is a prevalent and reasonable expectation of their role. No one, for instance, would choose to be nursed by someone who behaves in a cruel and selfish manner.

IV. THE VIRTUES IN 19TH-CENTURY NURSING

This current interest in virtue ethics and the moral character of the nurse, although fashionable, can scarcely claim to be original, as any student of the historical development of nursing would testify. Concern that nurses should act in a professional and self-disciplined manner and that nurse education should address itself to moral as well as academic development is evident from the earliest days of professional nursing.

Professional nursing dates from the era of Florence Nightingale and the opening of her training school at St. Thomas's Hospital in London in 1860. Nightingale's views about the virtues required of a nurse are clear from her writing. For her, to be a good nurse one must first be a good woman, and what constituted a good woman can be found in the qualities she expected of recruits into nursing. These included sobriety, honesty, and truthfulness, which formed the foundations of moral character upon which nurse training would inculcate the habits of punctuality, trustworthiness, personal neatness, and obedience.

Until that time, nursing was considered to be an inferior, undesirable occupation with much of the care in hospitals being provided by women paupers, from the workhouses, who had neither the knowledge nor the inclination to deliver effective care. Charles Dickens immortalized this image of drunken, dirty, dishonest nurses in his portrayals of Sairey Gamp and Betsy Prig, and before Nightingale no respectable woman would have stooped to hospital nursing, which came under the category of domestic service rather than health care. It is therefore easy to appreciate that against this background Florence Nightingale's attention to moral character was an attempt to ensure that nursing would be viewed as an appropriate path for educated women to follow. It is also important to recognize that Nightingale's strong Christian upbringing and values influenced her views on nursing. The Christian ideal of service to others is echoed in much of her writing and explains her vehement warnings against nursing becoming a profession rather than a calling in which the performance of Christian duty is central to the conception of a good nurse.

Although Nightingale did much to improve the prevailing public image of the nurse, she also set crucial precedents in defining nursing as subordinate to medicine and in emphasizing that it was primarily women's work, precedents which are frequently claimed to have bedeviled nursing's advancement for much of the 20th century. From Nightingale's first claim that to be a good nurse it was necessary to be a good woman, nursing, perhaps more than any other profession, has been influenced by social conceptions regarding the nature of women. The Victorian values of the Nightingale era defined women's proper roles in narrow restricted ways while their actions had to be consistent with moral sensibility, purity, and maternal affection. In addition women were expected to subordinate all personal ambitions and desires to the maintenance of the home and family and to obediently serving men's needs, and this conception of a good woman influenced the virtues acclaimed by Nightingale as central to the practice of nursing. For her, a good nurse needed to be chaste, sober, honest, truthful, trustworthy, punctual, quiet yet quick, cheerful and hopeful, selfless, loyal, and obedient.

There is, however, an interesting dichotomy between the influence of Victorian and Christian conceptions of a good woman and Nightingale's beliefs about the importance of rationality and the intellectual virtues needed to practice as a good nurse. These included the ability to think clearly and independently about one's actions and to be able to demonstrate an understanding of one's business. This internal conflict between the 19th century virtues of the nurse is evident in Nightingale's stance on obedience. Although she taught loyalty and obedience to orders, whether given by nursing superiors or by doctors, she also claimed that true loyalty to orders must go hand in hand with independent judgment and a sense of responsibility, both of which were for Nightingale fundamental to trustworthiness.

The impact of such virtues on the nurse's values, her actions as a moral agent, and indeed nursing ethics is considerable, and the reflection of these virtues in nurses' ethical codes is clearly evident.

V. CODES OF NURSING ETHICS

The earliest attempts at developing a code of nursing ethics are to be found in the United States. The Nightingale Pledge, written in the 1890s and recited by American nurses until the latter part of the 1950s, included promises of a life of purity, abstention, confidentiality, loyalty to the physician, and devotion to duty. The requirement for obedience is apparent in a number of early nursing documents and codes. For instance, I. H. Robb, in *Nursing Ethics* (1900. Cleveland: Savage), wrote that "implicit unquestioning obedience is one of the first lessons a probationer must learn, for this is a quality that will be expected from her in her professional capacity for all future times" (cited in A. Jameton, 1984. *Nursing practice* (p. 34). Englewood Cliffs, NJ: Prentice-Hall).

Obedience and loyalty to medical staff were much more important than the concept of any obligation owed to the patient as evidenced by S. E. Parson's statement that should a mistake be made in treating a patient, this should be kept from him as the resultant anxiety and lack of confidence might be injurious to him and retard his recovery (1916. *Nursing problems and obligations* (p. 32). Boston: Whitcomb & Barrows; cited in G. R. Winslow, 1984. *Hasting's Center Report,* 14, 31–40).

These values and attitudes have endured in modern nursing until relatively recently as illustrated by the American Nurses' Association Code of 1950, which declared that nurses were obligated to carry out the physician's orders intelligently and must sustain confidence in the physician and other members of the health care team. Even as late as 1963 such expectations continued with the publication of the *Code for Nurses* by the International Council for Nurses, which asserted that the intelligent and loyal carrying out of the doctor's orders was an obligation of nurses.

Not until the 1970s were such clauses revised and replaced by the expectation that rather than obedience, nurses would sustain cooperative relationships with their colleagues. At the same time, emphasis on safeguarding patients from incompetent, unethical, or illegal practice began to appear in American codes of nursing ethics.

Until very recently therefore, obedience and loyalty were still the dominant values that influenced nurses' roles and relationships to others, and these virtues were emphasized in their professional socialization. Recent research into the nurse's role suggests that submissiveness to and respect for superiors still remains an element in the professional socialization of nurses, and just as there was considerable tension in Nightingale's values relating to Victorian womanhood and Enlightenment rationality, there is a similar tension in the ideals of professional nursing and the reality of day-to-day practice.

Even a cursory review of modern nursing literature leaves one in no doubt that nursing's most widely proclaimed values today are those of a just and unprejudiced service to humanity and a commitment to the dignity and well-being of the patient. Contemporary nursing codes such as those of the American Nurses Association (1985) and the United Kingdom Central Council (UKCC) for Nurses, Midwives and Health Visitors (1992) emphasize such values and leave the nurse in no doubt that the primacy of the patient is of paramount importance in relation to the nurse's obligations.

The nature of the nurse–patient relationship is fundamental to the expression of such values, and these documents claim that this ought to be one of individual trust and respect for persons. Today's codes along with current writings in nursing literature contain additional expectations in relation to the nurse's duty to her patient, namely, the demand that the nurse acts as patient advocate. Such a role involves accepting responsibility for one's own actions and decisions; having the authority to act in the patient's best interests; and, if necessary, challenging other health care professionals whom the nurse judges as threatening the patient's well-being.

This expectation requires that rather than occupying a subservient position, nurses will instead assert themselves and be recognized as autonomous practitioners. These changes reflect an interesting perspective of the virtues necessary in today's nursing profession, namely, assertiveness, compassion, honesty, courage, justice, and integrity.

VI. VIRTUES IN CONTEMPORARY NURSING

Before exploring in any detail specific virtues needed by contemporary nurses, a number of conclusions can be drawn from the foregoing discussion. The very idea of virtue must be thought of and pursued in relation to the goals or purposes of particular human endeavors. Thus although the emphasis may be on the individual's character it must be remembered that practices contribute to much wider human goods. The overall goal of nursing, wherever or in whatever type of institution it is practiced, must be to promote the health and well-being of the local population. Although achievement of this wider goal will sometimes involve other goals, such as cooperating with other professionals, or safeguarding the institutions where health work is carried out, it is the overall goal which must be viewed as primary.

A central concept of both Aristotle's and MacIntyre's accounts is the idea of wholeness or unity when considering a person's life, for it is only in this way that *eudaimonia* or flourishing can be attained. One needs to question therefore whether it is possible, or even desirable, to identify or separate what might be termed professional virtues from those that are necessary for everyone to live the "good" life. Nurses, like teachers, bankers, and shopkeepers, cannot leave their personal values at the entrance to their workplace and don an alternative mantle of professional values. The virtues which the majority of people come to accept during their early lives, such as honesty, reliability, integrity, courage, justice, and the like, are precisely the virtues expected in one's working life. Indeed this may well be part of the problem which besets many nurses in that they falsely believe that their professional role makes demands on them which in their private lives they would not countenance. Lying to patients might be just such an example. The effect of this segregation of personal and professional virtues is a denial and disintegration of the self, which often results in feelings of guilt and alienation.

Part of the reason for the perceived difficulties in relation to one's professional life lies in the fact that today the vast majority of people, including professionals, are employees of organizations and institutions, and this creates various tensions and conflicts. For example, not only may personal loyalties or obligations conflict with those of one's professional role, but also, there are often inconsistencies within an individual's role which seem to demand inconsistent courses of action.

It is for this reason that general rules and guidelines such as those offered by codes of professional conduct can appear to call for different actions when a nurse tries to follow their demands in a specific situation. For example, a ward sister faced with an unpleasant young doctor who is repeatedly rude and brusque with patients, thereby distressing them, must, according to the UKCC Code, ensure that nothing in her sphere of responsibility is detrimental to patients, and yet also work in a collaborative and cooperative manner with other health care professionals.

It is presumably for reasons such as these that Aristotle himself highlighted the importance of context, when he said that only the baker can tell when the bread is cooked. General rules about how long an average loaf takes might be useful, but this dough, made into this size loaf, in this particular oven, and burning that type of wood, may be very different from the average loaf. Nurses therefore cannot escape the responsibility of making judgments and they must consider how to do this wisely.

Also it emphasizes the fact that institutions must not only acknowledge the importance of individual virtues in its members, it must also cultivate the type of climate where people are expected to, and are supported in, the exercise of those virtues. At times this might well include displaying a sincere disagreement with institutional policies. Thus, political awareness and action cannot be separated from a moral life. Professional judgment is not only knowledge of a professional nature, but the practical wisdom of which, and how much, particular disposition to display to achieve the particular good to which one is devoted.

It is now appropriate to consider the virtues which might be pertinent for contemporary nurses to adopt. In doing this it is important to emphasize that within the confines of this entry, such a list cannot be complete or even comprehensive, as this could range across a host of human dispositions or qualities. First it seems important that nurses are not callous or selfish, dishonest or untrustworthy, or timid or cowardly. Thus it seems appropriate to start with compassion, honesty, and courage as important virtues. Secondly, virtues do not exist in a vacuum and so the moral environment of nursing practice must be such that appropriate virtues can be both fostered and practiced. This has obvious implications for health care institutions.

A. Compassion

Compassion is an altruistic virtue which involves a regard or concern for the good of others. It is therefore pertinent to nursing (an altruistic activity), which has as its goal the promotion of health and well-being of those who are in need. Merely recognizing that someone is suffering considerably is not in itself sufficient to describe a person as compassionate, as this can be associated with either indifference or simply intellectual interest. Also, even a genuine interest in relieving suffering can stem from attitudes other than compassion, such as meeting a professional challenge or duty. This point seems particularly important for the nurse. Aloofness or professional distance was until quite recently claimed as befitting the nursing role. Becoming too involved was thought to interfere with one's professional judgment and nurses were socialized into adopting a detached, impersonal approach to patients. Indeed there is such a strong public perception of this that one of the greatest anxieties of patients entering hospital is that they will be depersonalized and treated simply as a "case."

A critical constituent of compassion then involves viewing patients and their suffering in such a way that their humanity is recognized. In other words, there is a poignancy which stems from the fact that one is faced with a suffering human being and that such suffering could happen to anyone, including oneself. One can easily imagine a nurse lacking in this ability, merely performing her duties with little or no regard for the person on whom she is effecting her ministrations. Nursing care then is reduced to doing things to people, without taking into account that one is in fact dealing with people.

Compassion also involves concern for the other's good, as it is such concern which motivates us to alleviate suffering. This should not be confused with pity which involves separating oneself from the object of one's pity on the basis of why the person is suffering. In other words, pity is closer to condescension as it often focuses on social inequality rather than on human equality. For example, one may feel pity for a tramp while believing that he has brought his misfortunes on himself. The compassionate person, on the other hand, may feel concern that any human is cold, hungry, or without shelter, regardless of how he or she came to be in the situation.

Pity is also inappropriate for the nurse because it lacks the impetus to feel and act from concern for the person's good, as well as being divisive and alienating. For instance, a nurse may feel pity for a dirty and unkempt tramp who is brought into the casualty ward with hypothermia in much the same way as she might feel pity for a homeless, uncared-for mongrel with a mangy coat and bones sticking through its skin. People with AIDS, those who are dying, the elderly, the demented, and the mentally handicapped, like lepers, are often pitied when what they need is compassion, as it is this which generates the impetus to beneficent action.

A further element is the strength and degree of compassion, which must be at such a level of intensity and endure for long enough to motivate the individual to either act in a way which will alleviate or reduce suffering, or demonstrate concern for the needy individual in some other appropriate way. It is important to stress here that the impetus or motivation to beneficent action must stem from altruistic reasons, such as concern for the other's good, and not from personal interest or inclination, in so far as this is possible. The nurse who appears to give selflessly of her time and is always at the beck and call of patients in the hope that she will be praised is not acting out of compassion but out of self-interest. Similarly the nurse who is superficial in her concern for patients, who, for example, asks clients how they are while never listening to their replies, is not compassionate but has simply learned how to pretend to show interest.

Aristotle himself emphasizes that the strength of the disposition is what distinguishes between real and apparent virtue, the implication being that the stronger the disposition, the more likely one is to act for another's benefit.

However, it is not always possible for nurses to undertake beneficent actions which will automatically relieve suffering, for instance, when someone is terminally ill with cancer, a new mother has been told that her child is mentally handicapped, or a relative is told that their loved one has some progressive chronic condition, but this does not mean that compassion is inappropriate. By demonstrating understanding and concern, showing a willingness to listen or talk about someone's fears, and treating them with respect and dignity, one can indicate that they are worthwhile human beings who matter, and that is an important human good. This is especially so in illness, which tends to strip individuals of their dignity and self-respect.

There are dangers of compassion. First, an over-concentration on someone's plight can both alarm the individual and cause him to see himself as someone who is of interest simply because of his plight, rather than for himself. Second, compassion can be misguided, grounded in a superficial understanding of the situation. It is very easy for nurses to be so caught up in the tragedy of a situation that they are unable to cope. Also, there are many occasions when a superficial understanding of another's problems has led some nurses to intrude where they are not welcome. Such superficial

understanding can also lead the misguided nurse into undertaking interventions for which she lacks competence, albeit for altruistic reasons. Compassion, like most virtues, needs to be exercised with intelligence and wisdom.

B. Honesty

Truthfulness or honesty is essential in every society, as without it daily life as we know it would not be possible. Thus honesty is a universal virtue. However, when one considers the fiduciary nature of any professional-client relationship, the virtue of honesty is crucial for anyone who purports to be a professional. Clients place a special trust in professionals with whom they come into contact. Likewise professionals expect their clients to be truthful. For example, it would be pointless to consult a doctor if one lied about one's symptoms. Similarly nurses could hardly provide nursing care if patients lied about being in pain or needing assistance in their activities of daily living.

With this in mind it is therefore surprising to find that in the United Kingdom there is no direct expectation placed on nurses by their professional body to be honest in their dealings with patients, although there are a number of indirect references, such as justifying public trust, maintaining the profession's reputation, and avoiding abuse of the privileged relationship with patients.

Professionals have no automatic right to public trust; instead, they must earn it, and nurses are no different in this respect. To warrant such trust, certain standards of behavior are expected of people who occupy positions which allow them access to patients' person, valuables, or property. Honesty is therefore an essential disposition in the nurse, and for this reason nurses in the United Kingdom are not exempt under the Rehabilitation of Offenders Act, which means that any criminal convictions are never spent and must be declared.

Honesty, however, involves more than resisting the temptation to steal. It also requires candor, which can be described as a subclass of honesty. Candor is concerned with truthfulness and demands more than the avoidance of lying. For example, it is possible to avoid lying by refraining from answering a question, but this would involve a lack of candor, which requires full disclosure or the absence of deceit.

The trust which exists in the nurse–patient relationship makes truthfulness extremely important and many problems can result when practitioners are economical with the truth, not least the damage to public trust and confidence. If a nurse withholds information that is sought by the patient, or deliberately acts in a deceitful manner, then she is displaying a lack of respect for his judgment and autonomy, and is also manipulating his actions. This changes the fiduciary nature of the nurse–patient relationship to one with the added dimension of *paternalism*.

There are many reasons why nurses may decide to be less than candid with patients. The patient may have requested not to be informed of a poor or disturbing diagnosis, although in such a situation it is unlikely that the patient will then seek information.

The range of reasons or justifications offered for being less than honest with patients is very wide and may be based less on altruism than with concern for self-interest. One of the most common is that of benefi-cence, but it must be emphasized that sometimes dis-honesty or deception is the easy option in that it saves a great deal of distress for the health professionals as well as for the patient. A doctor or senior nurse may rationalize that to tell the whole truth will cause harm or distress to the patient, and this poses problems for junior members of the team who are then ordered not to disclose.

Harm is, however, a loose concept, and the distress caused by knowledge of a poor prognosis may be short-lived when compared with the effects on the individual and his family and friends of living a lie. The nurse who is ordered to lie must ultimately ask herself whether she will act from self-interest or patient interest and whether coercion is a justifiable reason to lie.

A second reason offered for dishonesty is the appeal that total truth is not possible because of the knowledge gap which exists between patients and professionals. The professional may reason that so little is known about the treatment or disease that the truth would be impossible. This justification is still inadequate, how-ever, as the issue does not concern absolute truth but the truthfulness of the professional involved. In situations such as these it is the intention to deceive which is crucial. Patients are likely to have more trust in those involved in their care if they are told honestly that no definitive answers can be given. Nurses must distin-guish between complete and accurate information and between intentional and inadvertent deception because someone has mistakenly claimed something which is untrue.

Justifications offered in some cases of deliberate de-ception, such as in the use of placebos, involve overrid-ing a person's autonomy, while in others, for example, treating children, the mentally ill, or mentally handi-capped without informed consent, the claim is often that such patients have impaired autonomy. Caution is needed, however, as claims involving autonomy can be used by professionals to ensure that their goals, rather than the patient's, are met. An easy test to apply in such cases is to ask oneself that if the patient agreed with the professional's decision, would the patient still be viewed as displaying impaired autonomy.

Lying to hide institutional mistakes or safeguard in-competent colleagues is sometimes justified by appeals to professional loyalty. Nurses who speak out about poor standards of care or incompetent colleagues are often vilified and discriminated against in terms of their future careers. This is a thorny problem as not only does no one like to tell tales, but also loyalty is often claimed to be a virtue and one then has to balance a clash between virtues. However, such a clash is not between loyalty and honesty. If it does exist, then it is between loyalty to the patient and loyalty to one's colleague or to one's employer. It is always wrong for individuals or institutions to *needlessly* harm patients, and therefore loyalty to the patient must be given prece-dence by a professional.

Reporting individual or institutional incompetence does not necessarily involve being disloyal, as ignoring such occurrences could be a greater disservice to either one's colleague or an institution. A colleague might continue in her incompetence until she kills someone and is the subject of litigation, whereas if steps to high-light her deficiencies had been taken sooner the tragedy might have been prevented. Similarly had an employee brought the inadequacies in care to the attention of those managing the institution then the distress and disgrace of a scandal could have been lessened if not pre-vented.

The need for honesty and the pressures which it can bring to bear does highlight the importance of a third virtue for those in the nursing profession, namely, courage.

C. Courage

Internal inhibitions such as fear, lack of confidence, or timidity may play a major role in how someone acts in a morally difficult situation. Such considerations indicate that personal strength is necessary if an agent is to fulfill her moral commitments and act ethically.

Aristotle's account of courage suggests that the cou-rageous person possesses a range of qualities. First, she is capable of independent thought; she can assess situations accurately; and she chooses to act responsibly for an appropriate ideal or end, despite personal impli-cations. This is not intended to imply foolhardiness on the part of the nurse in that she rushes into a situation without considering the implications for herself. Rather, she has thought about and is willing to face the outcome of her actions. Such qualities are needed by the nurse, perhaps more so today than at any other time in nursing's history. This is true of both physical and moral courage.

Physical courage is needed in a number of nursing situations. Nurses frequently have to face dying patients, many of whom are children or young adults; they work in stressful, dangerous situations where as well as the arduous nature of the work, the nurse also has to face significant personal dangers. Nurses need courage to face the hopelessness of many patient situations such as when nursing those suffering from severe mental illness or chronic progressive diseases. Tending people with Ebola virus in Africa is hazardous and requires considerable courage in the face of significant risks to one's own personal health.

Moral courage is perhaps even more essential than the physical variety. Technological advances, increasing specialization, routinization, and economic constraints along with a philosophy which favors a market economy can, if taken to extremes, result in health care being dehumanized so that both patients and nurses are reduced to the status of objects. In such a climate, irresponsibility flourishes alongside feelings of personal powerlessness. Commitment to personal and professional ideals and principles founders through lack of use, and courage is necessary to prevent being engulfed by such a social milieu. The nurse must resist the negative effects of such an environment and strive to maintain her personal ideals of nursing while creating a reality in which the patient is treated and respected as a unique person. Awareness of the effect that such a state of affairs can have on her as a person as well as on others is essential, and the nurse needs to confront the impersonality of the system not only for the sake of the patient's dignity and individuality, but also for her own. Humane nursing is possible if the nurse chooses it; however, she must be willing to embrace the autonomy which she has and use it wisely and responsibly. Thus the nurse needs courage to accept responsibility for her actions and also to overcome her own indifference.

It is in relation to moral courage that one can readily see why Aristotle thought confidence to be so closely involved with courage. Moral courage needs a sound knowledge base which comes with experience, maturity, and self-knowledge of one's own moral principles and commitment to an ideal end. It stems from the nurse's attitude to her work and her role in client care. By utilizing morally sensitive, practical reason, the nurse not only thinks and feels rightly about her actions,

but she also has the confidence and courage to pursue appropriate courses of action, which lead her to feel fulfilled not only as a person, but as a good nurse. Therefore, moral courage is a critical requirement for the nurse.

D. Justice

Justice is an essential personal virtue which the nurse should cultivate and display. Indeed it is often the case that when an individual's sense of justice is offended that she is motivated to act in such a way that other virtues (courage, compassion, honesty, and the like) are displayed.

Aristotle claimed that justice, unlike the other virtues, does not correspond to a particular desire or emotion, but that its lack results from a deficiency of motivation. For Aristotle, justice, or rather injustice, is not so much about a failure to view others as having an equal right to some goods, but more about the individual herself being motivated by self-interested ends.

Justice as fairness or equity is certainly important for the nurse. It is necessary in her dealings with patients and colleagues, just as it is in dealing with friends and family members. Nurses are in positions of trust in relation to their treatment of both patients and junior colleagues. If a nurse acts unfairly by giving more attention to certain patients because of personal preference, or gives one student a better report than another because of racial inclination, then she is not acting justly and is betraying the professional trust invested in her.

If the nurse is to meet demands of justice she must allocate her time between patients according to the patient's condition and his or her need for care. Patients with the greatest need should receive the greatest attention. A nurse, for instance, who spent time with patients on the basis that they were important members of the community or because they bought her gifts would be acting unjustly toward other patients.

Professionals who stick together when something goes wrong are not only dishonest but also unjust if by their wall of silence they prevent patients receiving compensation.

There is, however, another way in which the nurse can act unjustly and that is by failing to recognize the unequal nature of the relationship which exists between herself and her patients. In other words, justice is essential in the context of the community of nursing. Nurses who abuse the power vested in them by bullying, punishing, lying, or deceiving patients are, whatever else they maybe guilty of, acting unjustly. Likewise with junior colleagues, senior nurses should not exploit students by using them as a pair of hands without adequate support, supervision, or training.

It can be seen that the virtue of justice is essential to any communal enterprise, not merely in the sense of being unselfish, but in displaying the personal excellences of character which go to make one an ideal associate or colleague.

There is a final quality which appears central to any discussion of virtue ethics, and this is integrity.

E. Integrity

Integrity is a complex concept which embraces the notion of not only possessing a range of virtues such as honesty, loyalty, and fairness, but also a sense of wholeness, of being true to one's own moral principles or commitments. If there is dissonance between what one feels personally committed to do on one hand and what one feels professionally required to do on the other, one's ability to act as a moral agent will be severely impaired and this brings to mind Aristotle's claim that as well as a person thinking and choosing rightly, an agent must also feel rightly about her actions.

An important element of integrity is coherence, which exists when there is consistency between one's principles and one's actions. This would preclude insincerity by, for example, claiming that truth telling is an important principle while invariably lying. Also, consistency between one's principles and one's motivation is important. For example, a nurse may hold that it is important not to harm patients, but if she deliberately keeps a distressing prognosis from a patient, not because of her belief that to do otherwise would cause harm, but because the doctor has ordered her to lie, then it would be difficult to say that she has acted with integrity.

Integrity demands: (i) that a person subscribes to a set of principles or commitments which are consistent in themselves; (ii) that the person upholds these principles or commitments when challenged or tempted to relinquish them; and (iii) she does so for the right reasons.

Integrity is concerned with principles which are crucial to the individual and it is this ability to keep what is essential to the self intact, which makes integrity a special type of virtue. This specialness concerns integrity being a second-order virtue, as it seems to involve possessing another set of virtues such as honesty, courage, fidelity, and justice which indicate a range of excellences of character and a lack of confusion and weakness. When the person who possesses integrity is faced with temptations, challenges, or dilemmas she is able

to remain intact because she possesses the qualities of character which enable her to sustain her person. She will be honest, particularly with herself, about her actions and motivations; she will possess strength of will in upholding and defending important principles; she will display moral courage when required; and she will be consistent, reliable, and able to resist temptation.

Possessing integrity is essential for empowerment and effective moral agency, in that such a person will be genuine and true to herself rather than self-deceiving, shallow, or insincere. She will be committed to defining her own life, acting on her principles, and refusing to compromise them in order to conform. She will be willing to take responsibility and answer for her choices, even when this is difficult or results in personal cost.

Many nurses work in a highly traditional, routinized, and bureaucratic systems which encroach upon the individual and which result in increasing powerlessness and oppression. The problem facing the nurse is how she can respond to such a social climate in such a way whereby she can remain in touch with her moral principles and commitments and retain her sense of moral agency, while resisting institutional pressures for indifferent, inappropriate, or unethical practice.

Integrity will assist her to remain alert to the danger of growing immune to the needs of patients who are ill, might be suffering pain, or may be dying. It is integrity which will help to prevent her from abdicating responsibility and accountability for her actions. Because the nurse who possesses integrity rejects self-deception, she will engage in reflection and examine her nursing actions closely, ensuring that she does not indulge in behavior which is merely compliant and unquestioning without regard for how it impacts on herself as well as on patients. She will remain in touch with herself and be committed to a particular way of regarding herself, others, and life itself. In other words, her ethical behavior will be a mode of living which pervades both her personal and her professional life. Indeed, rather than believing that she can maintain a schizophrenic existence between the personal and the professional domains of her life, she will realize that her effectiveness as a nurse reflects the nature of her personal commitments. Nursing will be an activity in which she engages in an ethical nursing practice because she is an ethical person.

VII. CONCLUSION

This entry has explored the topic of nurisng ethics through the perspective of virtue ethics. Although other approaches to nursing ethics have been described and are of great significance in discussions of professional morality, the concept of virtue has a long tradition in nursing. In the 19th century the virtues of the good nurse were the virtues of the good woman, and qualities such as obedience, loyalty, self-sacrifice, and devotion to duty were emphasized.

These virtues were reflected in the early codes of nursing ethics, but they have gradually been replaced by virtues which reflect human goodness rather than a confining and outmoded female stereotype. Having said that, virtues such as courage, justice, honesty which were proclaimed by Aristotle to be vital to the moral life and human flourishing are still critical in contemporary professional ethics.

Having explored both ancient and contemporary approaches to virtue ethics, the ethics of care was discussed as it too can be described as a virtue-based approach. Unlike the other approaches, however, this one focuses on one virtue, that of caring, and has been claimed as being of particular relevance to nurses. This may well be the case, and certainly caring is an important behavior for nurses to demonstrate. Until this theory is further developed, however, there are some criticisms of which nurses should be aware, and until they are answered, perhaps compassion might be a more appropriate virtue for the profession to develop.

Although nursing remains a female-dominated profession there are now considerable numbers of men choosing it as a career. It seems fitting therefore that the virtues relevant to the nurse should be those that are relevant to being a good person, rather than those associated with being a good women.

Also See the Following Articles

ARISTOTELIAN ETHICS • CONSEQUENTIALISM AND DEONTOLOGY • INFORMED CONSENT • MEDICAL CODES AND OATHS • PATIENTS' RIGHTS • PROFESSIONAL ETHICS

Bibliography

Beauchamp, T. L., & Childress, J. F. (1994). *Principles of biomedical ethics* (4th ed.). New York: Oxford University Press.

Chadwick, R., & Tadd, W. (1992). *Ethics and nursing practice: A case-study approach.* Houndsmills, Basingstoke: Macmillan.

Larrabee, M. J. (1993). *An ethic of care.* New York: Routledge.

Soothill, K., Mackay, L., & Webb, C. (1995). *Interprofessional relations in health care.* London: Edward Arnold.

Tadd, W. (1995). Moral agency and the role of the nurse. Ph.D. thesis, University of Wales Cardiff.

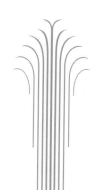

OBJECTIVITY IN REPORTING

Judith Lichtenberg
University of Maryland at College Park

GLOSSARY

bias The slanting of news reporting according to the personal views or professional interests of the journalist or the political, economic, and technological interests or constraints of the news organization.

objectivity A guiding principle of contemporary journalism according to which news should be reported without bias; held by many critics to be an impossible and undesirable ideal.

social construction A prominent contemporary theory, deriving from the sociology of knowledge, according to which the political, economic, and social circumstances of a society determine what constitutes reality and knowledge in that society.

OBJECTIVITY is a cornerstone of the professional ideology of journalists in liberal democracies. The distinction between news, where objectivity is thought possible and desirable, and opinion, where objectivity is thought impossible, is deeply entrenched in the journalistic culture. Objectivity is inextricably intertwined with truth, fairness, balance, neutrality, the absence of value judgments—in short, with the most fundamental journalistic values.

Yet the objectivity of journalism has come increasingly under fire in recent years. The criticisms come from a variety of quarters and take several forms. Some say that journalism *is not* objective; others that it *cannot* be objective; and still others that it *should not* be objective. Odd as it may seem, sometimes the same critic seems to be making all of these charges at the same time.

One challenge comes from critics—from across the political spectrum—who claim that the media have misrepresented their views or have not reported their activities impartially. Some say that the media have a "liberal bias," that they overemphasize unrest and dissent, or look too hard for muck to rake. Other critics contend that, on the contrary, the press serves the conservative interests of government and big business. Aggrieved individuals and groups of all kinds charge that news coverage of this or that issue is unfair, biased, or sensational.

Those who attack journalism on these grounds seem to share one crucial assumption with those they criticize. The complaint of bias seems to presuppose that *unbias* is possible. But many contemporary critics, not only of journalism but of every other form of inquiry, reject this assumption. Journalism is not objective, they say, nor could it be. As one recent textbook puts it, objectivity "is a false and impossible ideal," and although all media writers claim it in some way, "they are all wrong."

This view has its roots in the sociology of knowledge and today finds its fullest expression in postmodernism; it is shared by many sociologists, humanists, legal scholars, and other social critics. They believe that the idea of objectivity rests on an outmoded and untenable theory of knowledge, according to which objective knowledge consists of correspondence between some idea or statement and a reality "out there" in the world. "Objectivity," in the words of a former journalism school dean, "is an essential correspondence between knowledge of a thing and the thing itself." But according to the critics, reality is not "out there"; it is, as James Carey has put it, "a vast production, a staged creation—something humanly produced and humanly maintained." Reality, on this view, is "socially constructed," and so there are as many realities as there are social perspectives on the world. There is no "true reality" to which objective knowledge can be faithful.

Perhaps paradoxically, those who believe objectivity is impossible sometimes think at the same time that it is an undesirable and even a dangerous aspiration. According to Catherine MacKinnon, objectivity is a strategy of hegemony used by some members of society to dominate others. Gaye Tuchman calls objectivity a "strategic ritual" enabling professionals to "defend themselves from critical onslaught;" while Dan Schiller describes it as, at best, "a cultural form with its own set of conventions."

I. THE COMPOUND ASSAULT ON OBJECTIVITY

On the face of it, there is something odd in this compound assault on objectivity—that journalism is not objective, that it could not be, that it should not be—for the charges do not seem compatible.

1. The complaint that a particular piece of journalism is not objective makes sense only against the background assumption that objectivity is possible.
2. The insistence that journalism cannot be objective makes the view that objectivity is undesirable seem superfluous.
3. The assertion that objectivity is not desirable makes senseless the complaint that journalism is not objective.

But although the combination of these charges may seem confused, the appearance is somewhat misleading. For the different charges leveled against objectivity, we shall see, are really charges leveled against different understandings of objectivity.

Let us begin with a rough reconstruction of the chain of reasoning leading to the conclusion that objectivity in journalism does not, could not, and should not exist:

• Experience continually confronts us with examples of clashes of belief (between individuals, between cultures) that we cannot resolve—we do not know how to decide which belief is true.
• No one can totally escape his or her biases; no one can be completely objective.
• Therefore, the idea that there could be an objective, true account of things is a fiction.
• Anyone who sincerely thinks there could be such an account is deluded by a faulty understanding of the relation between mind and world.
• This faulty understanding has significant practical consequences; belief in objectivity and adherence to practices thought to be implied by it reinforces existing power relations and cultural and political chauvinism.
• Therefore, the aspiration to objectivity, whether innocent or not, serves as a prop in an ideological agenda.
• So, in other words, real objectivity is impossible and its attempted manifestations are either naive or insidious or both.

The enemy that makes such strange bedfellows—uniting critics from left and right and bringing together abstruse academics with practical politicians, advocates, and journalists—is not a single entity. In elevating objectivity to an ideal one may be endorsing any of several different ends or the supposed means of attaining them. Thus the attack on objectivity can represent a variety of different complaints. Because the values captured by the term "objectivity" vary greatly—in the extent to which they are possible, probable, actual, or desirable— the legitimacy of the complaints varies as well. In what follows we explore the most significant of these values and complaints.

II. METAPHYSICAL QUESTIONS

Our most fundamental interest in objectivity is an interest in truth. We want to know how things stand in the world, or what happens, and why. In this sense, to claim that a particular piece of journalism *is not* objective is to claim that it fails to provide the truth or the whole truth. And to deny that objectivity is *possible* is to say that there is no way to get at the truth, because all accounts of things are accounts from a particular social, psychological, cultural, or historical perspective and we have no neutral standpoint from which to adjudicate between conflicting accounts. To deny that objectivity is possible is often also to insist, not only that we can never get at the truth, but that for precisely this reason it makes no sense to think there is any such thing. Even to speak of "truth" or "the facts," these critics strongly suggest, demonstrates a certain naiveté.

To doubt that objectivity is possible, then, is to doubt that we can know how things *really* are or what *really* happens, where "really" means something like "independently of our own perspective." But there is a crucial ambiguity in the phrase "our own perspective." One way to doubt the objectivity of a story or an account of things is to challenge the particular perspective from which it is told. So, for example, one might doubt that American news accounts of the Persian Gulf War told an objective story. When our worries take this form, we may be doubting that a particular account or set of accounts is objective—that is, true or complete—but we need not be denying that it is possible to tell an objective, or at least a more objective, story. Indeed, we typically have specific ideas about how to go about getting one. We seek out foreign press reports of these events, compare them to each other and to American news reports, and evaluate inconsistencies within and between stories in light of a variety of standards. We inquire into a news organization's sources of information, likely obstacles to the reliability of its judgments, whether it has interested motives that might give it reason to distort the story. So, for example, in attempting to understand what happened in the Gulf War, the cautious inquirer will question the American media's reliance on U.S. military reports and press conferences as a source of credible information, and will attempt to find other sources of information with which to compare and assess U.S. reports. These sources will be subjected to the same kind of scrutiny.

Defenders of objectivity can point, then, to a multitude of standards and practices for evaluating the reliability of information. They do not need to claim that we are often or even usually in a position to determine the whole truth and nothing but the truth, particularly in the hurried and chaotic world that journalists cover. But it is rare, they will say, that we have no guidance whatever. We generally know how to distinguish between better and worse, more or less accurate accounts.

Often, however, the challenge to objectivity connects to deeper philosophical worries, to the centuries-old debate between realists and idealists. The metaphysical realist says that there is a world or a way things are "out there," that is, independently of our perspective. Traditionally, "our" perspective meant not yours or mine or our culture's, but the human perspective, or even the perspective of any possible consciousness. The ideal of knowledge presupposed by this view holds that objects or states of affairs in the world are "intrinsically" or "independently" a certain way, and that knowledge consists in somehow "mirroring" the way they are.

The metaphysical idealist denies that we can know what the world is like intrinsically, apart from a perspective. The world is our construction in the sense that we inevitably encounter it through our concepts and our categories; we cannot see the world concept- or category-free. Kant, the father of the contemporary idealist critique, described universal categories shaping our perception of the world that are necessary for human beings to experience the world at all. The sense for Kant in which we cannot get outside our perspective is unthreatening, because by "our" perspective Kant meant not that of our clan or culture but that of all human consciousness. So understood, idealism poses no threat to objectivity. The idealist can make all the distinctions the realist can make: between the real and the illusory, what is "out there" and what is "in here," the objective and the subjective. Lions are real and unicorns mythical; trees and sky are "out there" and stomachaches and beliefs are "in here." Idealism leaves everything as it is (D. Luban, 1986).

But Kant opened the door to a more threatening relativism. For having admitted that our knowledge of the world is relative to a framework, it was a natural step to the view that the categories molding our experience depend partly on concrete and particular conditions that vary from culture to culture, community to community, even person to person. When twentieth-century thinkers took this step, arguing not simply that reality is constructed but that it is socially constructed—constructed differently, therefore, by different groups and cultures—they repudiated Kant's consolation that we could accept idealism while preserving objective, because universal, knowledge.

III. GLOBAL DOUBTS AND LOCAL DOUBTS

We need a better understanding of what critics of objectivity mean when, in support of the view that our news accounts of events are not objective, they tell us that reality is socially constructed. Perhaps they mean that our culture, our political and other interests do much to structure and determine the way we (whoever "we" may be) look at the world, and that our news reports reflect, reinforce, and even create these biases. There can be little doubt that this is true. Yet some of the sharpest critics of the press make this argument without calling into question the possibility of objectivity; indeed they rely on it. The assertion that reality is socially constructed suggests something more than that we are strongly influenced by our surroundings, for no sensible person would deny this. There is a finality and inevitability about the claim: we believe what we believe because of our gender or class or cultural attachments; others with other attachments believe differently, and there is no adjudicating between our beliefs and theirs, for there is no neutral standpoint.

Perhaps objectivity's critics mean that we can never get outside the particular worldview in which we have been raised, that we can never look at it, criticize it, judge it. But this seems implausible, because they themselves seem to have succeeded in doing so. The judgment of bias rests partly on other sources of information, which taken separately or together have, the critics believe, proved more consistent or coherent.

The defender of objectivity argues, then, that we can criticize a statement or description as biased or unobjective only against the background of some actual or possible contrast, some more accurate statement or better description. We have a variety of means to settle differences between conflicting beliefs or to establish one view as superior to another. We get more evidence, seek out other sides of the story, check our instruments, duplicate our experiments, reexamine our chain of reasoning. These methods do not settle all questions, but they settle many. In showing us how, say, British news stories construct reality, critics of necessity depend on the possibility of seeing and understanding alternative versions of the same events. And if no means existed to compare these alternative "realities," the charges would have no bite. For the critics' point is not that these alternative "realities" are like so many flavors of ice cream about which *de gustibus non disputandum est* but that those who see things in one way are missing something important, or getting only a partial view, or even getting things wrong.

The social constructionist critique seems to vacillate between two different and incompatible claims: the *general*, "global" assertion that objectivity is impossible because different people and cultures employ different categories and there is no way of deciding which frame-

work better fits the world; and the charge that *particular* news stories or mass media organizations serve ideological interests or represent the world in a partial or distorted or otherwise inadequate way. But it can be argued that insofar as objectivity is impossible there can be no sense in the claim—certainly none in the rebuke—that the media are ideological or partial, for these concepts imply the possibility of a contrast. Conversely, the defender of objectivity may say, insofar as we agree that the media serve an ideological function or bias our vision, we implicitly accept the view that other, better, more objective ways are possible.

IV. TRANSCULTURAL COMMUNICATION

Implicit in the critique of objectivity is the assumption that different cultures possess worldviews so different they are impermeable to outside influence. On this view, different cultures cannot engage in genuine conversation with each other, because they speak different conceptual and evaluative languages and employ different standards of judging. And there are no available yardsticks external to the culture by which to judge these internal standards of judgment.

Against this claim the defender of objectivity can bring two objections. First, despite differences in worldview we share a great deal even with those from very different cultures. Second, even where we see things differently from those of other cultures often we can see *that* we see things differently and we can see *how* we see things differently. So our worldviews are not hermetic: others can get in and we can get out. As we shall see, the two points are not wholly separable: the distinction between sharing a perspective and being able to understand another's perspective is not sharp.

It is easy to fall under the sway of the doctrine of cultural relativism. At a certain point in our intellectual development—often in late adolescence—we are struck with the realization that language plays a crucial role in shaping the experience and worldview of individuals and even whole cultures. But it is easy to misunderstand and exaggerate the truth in this insight. For one thing, what impresses us depends partly on the premise that different "worldviews" take the same underlying stuff, the same data of experience, and shape it differently. The "aha experience" of relativism depends, then, on the commonsense recognition of one world out there—something that, paradoxically, the relativist is often at pains to deny.

Furthermore, the differences between worldviews can be overstated. Even those from very different cultures can agree, despite their deeply different conceptions of time, to meet at ten and to come together at what all recognize as the negotiating table. Intractable disputes between cultures arise sometimes because their values diverge; equally often, however, such disputes arise precisely because their values coincide. Both the Israelis and the Palestinians invest Jerusalem with sacred and irreplaceable value. Do their worldviews clash? As Francis I is supposed to have said about Henry VIII: "Henry and I agree about everything: we both want Calais."

Even where our points of view clearly differ, it's not clear what we should make of this fact. As Donald Davidson puts it:

> Whorf, wanting to demonstrate that Hopi incorporates a metaphysics so alien to ours that Hopi and English cannot, as he puts it, "be calibrated," uses English to convey the contents of sample Hopi sentences. Kuhn is brilliant at saying what things were like before the revolution using—what else?—our postrevolutionary idiom (D. Davidson, 1984).

Worldviews, then, are not hermetic. We can and do come to see things as others see them—not just others from our culture but from radically different ones. Thucydides brings the agony of the Athenians' war to life; Ruth Benedict gets us to see "the uses of cannibalism"; Faulkner shows us how things look to an adult with the mind of a child. The possibility of communication between cultures is perhaps inseparable from the first point: from the outset different cultures possess points of commonality and contact, and these enable us to travel back and forth. There could not be a point to history, anthropology, literature, journalism, biography, if this were not so.

V. ON THE SOCIAL CONSTRUCTION OF REALITY

If other "realities" are not hermetic and impermeable, that deflates the significance of the assertion that reality is socially constructed. For the usual connotations of the word "reality" are exhaustive and exclusive: reality is all, and all there is. If instead there are many possible realities, and ways to get from one to the other, then we can see into each other's worlds, and our realities can thereby be altered.

Perhaps critics of objectivity mean that even when we seem to escape the determination of our perception by a particular social construction, even when we seem to see things in a new light, that new perception is also socially constructed. Suppose, for example, that, partly as a result of changes in American news accounts, over the last 25 years Americans have come to understand the Palestinian point of view in the Middle East conflict better than they had before. (A New York Times/CBS News Poll found evidence of such a change in American attitudes.) It might be argued that this evolution results from differences in the American political establishment's view of its own geopolitical interests. On this view, the change is itself socially constructed out of the web of American ideology.

No doubt changing American interests partly explain the changes in perception. But to insist that apparently divergent views *always and only* derive from the push of the dominant culture's interests, from the powers that be, amounts to an unfalsifiable conspiracy theory. And the claim that reality is socially constructed is then in danger of becoming empty. If, on the other hand, it is acknowledged that other sources, apart from the powers that be, can be responsible for changes in our views, then the question is what work the concept of social construction is doing. Is the point simply that ways of looking at the world do not come into being *ex nihilo,* but are rather the product of ... of *something*—the total social-political-economic-cultural-psychological-biological environment? And is this anything more than the claim that everything has a cause? It is not clear what, beyond these extremely general assertions, the view that reality is socially constructed adds. For if every view is socially constructed but no view could *not* be socially constructed we learn nothing of substance when we learn that reality is socially constructed.

This is not to deny that the media often present events in a distorted, biased, or ideological way. It is rather to say that we can only explain this fact on the assumption that there are better and worse, more and less faithful renderings of events, and that, despite our own biases, preconceptions, "conceptual schemes," we can sometimes escape our own point of view sufficiently to recognize how it imposes a structure or slant on events.

The word "reality" is to blame for some of the confusion. In an influential article on objectivity and the media Gaye Tuchman argued that "the act of making news is the act of constructing reality itself rather than a picture of reality" (G. Tuchman (1978) *Making news: A study in the construction of reality*, p. 12. New York: Free Press). Tuchman's point trades on ambiguities in the term "reality."

News can illuminatingly be said to construct reality rather than a picture of it in two senses. First, some events are genuine media creations. When *Newsweek* in the 1980s proclaimed on its cover that "Nixon Is Back," then in a crucial sense Nixon *was* back. To have arrived on *Newsweek*'s cover is to be back from whatever realm of nonbeing one formerly inhabited. We have here a variation on the Pirandellesque insight that "It's the truth if you think it is": "It's the truth if they (the major media) say it is." But this rule applies to only a very limited fraction of our beliefs and a tiny portion of the total news product.

Second, the act of reporting news is an act of constructing reality in the sense captured by the sociological commonplace that "if a situation is defined as real it is real in its consequences." If people believe that news stories of an event are accurate, they will behave accordingly, and for certain purposes those stories function as "reality." This is sometimes simply a matter of the bandwagon effect: when a news story describes college-bound students' scramble for admission to elite institutions, more students may panic and start scrambling.

But journalists purport to represent an *independent* reality. Defenders of objectivity argue that although journalists often fall short, without the concept of a reality independent of news stories we undermine the very basis on which to criticize the media's constructions, as well as the motivation for journalists to do better.

VI. THE EXISTENCE AND MEANING OF FACTS

Clearly, whether or to what extent objectivity in journalism is possible depends on what we mean by "objectivity." Belief in objectivity need not mean that every question that can be posed or about which people might disagree has a single determinate right answer.

What, then, does belief in objectivity commit one to? At the very least it means that *some* questions have determinate, right answers—and that all questions have wrong answers. So, for example, it is a fact that in 1992 and 1996 Bill Clinton was elected President of the United States, and that in 1995 the New York State legislature reinstated the death penalty.

Presumably objectivity's critics do not deny that Clinton is President or that the death penalty was reinstated in New York. How, then, do they reconcile these facts with their repudiation of objectivity? We find several strategies.

1. One is to insist that nevertheless such facts are socially constructed. The question is what this means. No one would deny that for there to be such a thing as a President of such a thing as the United States, a variety of complex social institutions must be in place. If that is all it means to say this fact is socially constructed, nothing significant turns on admitting it. But typically the point of emphasizing the constructedness of a fact is to undermine its truth or credibility. Yet however constructed "Bill Clinton is President" may be, it is no less true or credible for that.

A variation on the theme that all facts are socially constructed is the claim that they are all "theory-laden." Certainly every factual statement can be understood to imply decisions about the usefulness or appropriateness of categorizing things in one way rather than another. Should even the most commonsensical of such categorizations be dignified with the label "theory"? If so, we must keep in mind that there are theories and theories. "The human fetus is a person" and "The PLO is a terrorist organization" are laden with controversial theories; "The earth revolves around the sun" and "The lion is a mammal" are laden with theories not seriously contestable in modern times. Facts, then, may be theory-laden; but whether they therefore lack objectivity depends on the particular theories they carry as freight. "Bill Clinton is President" may in some sense rest on a theory or conceptual framework, but it is one so widely shared and innocuous that the label "theory-laden," usually brought as an accusation, loses its bite.

It may be said that the facts just mentioned are not interesting facts, and that this weakens the point they are used to illustrate. In what sense are they not interesting? Surely New York's reinstatement of the death penalty is in many respects interesting. The critic must mean that it is uncontroversial that these *are* facts. But because the social constructionists sometimes seem to include all facts, however humdrum, in the realm of the constructed, this might itself be viewed as a concession to objectivity.

2. A different strategy for the relativist is to exempt such facts from the realm of the socially constructed, but to insist that they are trivial and that all nontrivial "facts" of the kind prominent in news stories are socially constructed in an interesting sense. Yet this is a significant concession. First of all, there will be a very large number of these trivial facts. Second, they will serve as

a crucial check constraining all the nontrivial, socially constructed "facts" that are supposed to make up the bulk of the news. Finally, having admitted the existence of some non-socially constructed facts, the relativist may find it difficult to draw the line between these and the socially constructed ones, especially given the constraints the former place on the latter.

3. A third strategy is to admit that some facts are independent of socially produced theories but insist that nevertheless these facts will be interpreted differently by members of different groups or cultures, and that these interpretations, themselves social constructions, will invest the same facts with different meanings. This claim can be understood in at least two ways.

(a) In one sense there is no disputing that these facts will be interpreted differently by different people. We all agree that the New York State legislature reinstated the death penalty, but we disagree about the reasons for it and about the agents ultimately responsible, its consequences, its symbolic significance.

Yet our disagreements about these matters of "interpretation" will in turn depend partly on other facts, such as people's beliefs about crime and about the efficacy of capital punishment. The constraint of facts will rule out some interpretations as wrong, even if it typically leaves room for reasonable disagreement about which interpretation is right. The web of expectations on which everyday life depends rests on the possibility of knowing all sorts of things "beyond a reasonable doubt." So although there is generally room for disagreement, interpretations of the facts are not wholly outside the reach of objective assessments. Some interpretations are better than others, and some are simply wrong.

(b) A second sense in which it may be said that different people and groups will invest the same facts with different meanings is best understood through an example. A study of British, American, and Belgian coverage of elections in Ireland found that the BBC story focused on the potential consequences of the vote for British–Irish relations; the CBS story used the election as a peg to talk about Irish unemployment and its potential consequences for immigration to the United States; and the Belgian account focused on the role of the Catholic Church in Irish politics, the relation between church and state being an important issue in Belgium (M. Gurevitch et al., 1991). It makes sense to say that each story began with the same set of data but interpreted them differently, selecting certain facts for emphasis or interpretation.

The point is important, and the significance of this "meaning construction" function of the mass media should not be underestimated; it bears extensive exami-

nation. But those who stress this point often seem to misunderstand its relevance (or lack of it) to the question of objectivity. The British, American, and Belgian news reports invest the Irish election with different meanings—they see it as signifying different things—but they all refer to the same set of events. Indeed, the three stories may not disagree about the truth of basic facts; rather they emphasize different facts as being important. It is no surprise to find that the same events have different significance for people of varying histories, cultures, or interests. We might put this point by saying that the issues raised here go *beyond* the question of objectivity, but they do not subvert objectivity.

VII. BEYOND OBJECTIVITY?

Belief in objectivity need not mean that to every question we might ask there must be a single right answer, or that there is one right way for a reporter to tell a story. Imagine a continuum of objectivity along which to locate the variety of subjects and statements news reporters investigate. At one end we find the relatively straightforward and uncontroversial facts of the kind just discussed. In the middle we find statements about which clearly there is a truth, a "right answer," but where to a greater or lesser extent the answer is difficult to discover. How did the dinosaurs become extinct? Who were the high-ranking Communists in British Intelligence? Did O. J. Simpson murder Nicole Simpson and Ronald Goldman? The answers to some of these questions may depend partly on what we mean by certain terms (like "murder"), but even assuming consistent usage we may reasonably disagree about the answers. Still, no one doubts that there are definite answers.

The line is sometimes thin between cases where clearly there is a truth about the matter although we have difficulty finding out what it is, and those where it cannot be said that there is a truth about the matter. For many of the complex goings-on between people, both at the "macro" political level and at the "micro" interpersonal level, the language of truth and objectivity may be thin and inadequate. When, for example, we have heard in detail "both sides of the story" from two quarrelling lovers or friends, we may sort out some clear truths about what happened, but in the end we may still be left with a residue of indestructible ambiguity, where it is plausible to say not simply that we do not know for sure what happened but that at the appropriate level of description there is no single determinate thing that happened.

Examples of this kind of ambiguity and indeterminacy abound for the most interesting and important subjects covered in the news. Did Clarence Thomas sexually harass Anita Hill? Uncertainty may depend partly on insufficient evidence and doubts about the credibility of witnesses. But disagreement may depend on other things as well: on different understandings of how sexual harassment should be defined and on related questions about the meaning of certain gestures, expressions, and interactions. Depending on the framework in which we embed the bits of evidence, the gestures and utterances, we will get different answers. And the question "Which framework is the appropriate one?" may not always have a determinate answer.

On the other hand, these matters are not always up for grabs. Once we know the context of a given utterance or action, the ambiguous often becomes unambiguous. Did he or didn't he? The answer may be yes or no.

So the defender of objectivity can perfectly well agree with Stanley Fish that "no degree of explicitness will ever be sufficient to disambiguate the sentence [for example, what he said to her] if by disambiguate we understand *render it impossible to conceive of a set of circumstances in which its plain meaning would be other than it now appears to be*" (S. Fish, (1980). *Is there a text in this class?* pp. 282–283. Cambridge: Harvard Univ. Press). But as long as we can know what context, framework, or set of conventions actually governed the circumstances—which we sometimes can—we will be entitled to conclude that in *these* circumstances he meant x or did y.

Questions about the application of concepts such as sexual harassment or racism reside in the murky area where fact meets value, description meets evaluation. Some who would describe themselves as objectivists would deny that values are objective; to the extent, then, that sexual harassment and racism are evaluative rather than descriptive concepts, they would part company with other objectivists who say there can be a truth about such matters as whether a remark is racist or a person has sexually harassed another. Facts can be objective, the first group would say, but value judgments cannot be. Yet our commonsense understanding of concepts like racism and sexual harassment supports the view that they can be applied or misapplied: that it can be true or false that a remark is racist or that one person sexually harassed another. Facts and values are not so neatly separable. The inseparability of facts and values is commonly taken to support the anti-objectivist position: facts are not that "hard," because they are infused with values. But the shoe can be placed on the other foot: values are not that "soft," because they are infused with facts.

The larger question lurking here of the objectivity of value judgments goes beyond the scope of this essay. But two points are worth making. First, the realm in which this question is relevant forms a limited part of the object of journalistic investigation. Journalists are typically concerned with issues at the more factual end of the continuum. Second, the journalist (and indeed anyone who hopes to understand the world) must arrive at the conclusion of indestructible ambiguity or indeterminacy very reluctantly, only after the arduous search for the truth has been found not fully realizable.

This suggests that the journalist must proceed on the assumption that there is objective truth, even if sometimes in the end she concludes that within a particular realm the concept of truth does not apply, or that in any case we will never discover it. It is not irrelevant to note that the vehemence with which defenders of both Thomas and Hill (a group that came to include a large number of Americans and other observers) made their respective cases reveals that *they* had no doubt that there was a right answer to the harassment question. Perhaps they were deluded. But it is significant that people behave and think as if there were a truth about these matters.

Some would argue that they cannot do otherwise, that the concepts of objectivity and truth function for us as "regulative principles," in Kant's sense—ideals that we must suppose to apply, even if at the limit they do not, if we are to possess the will and the ways to understand the world.

VIII. THE POLITICS OF OBJECTIVITY

In the foregoing sections we have seen why critics have thought objectivity is impossible, and also why others find the concept indispensable. But we still do not have a complete answer to the question why many critics not only deny that objectivity is possible but believe it is a pernicious idea.

The main reason is that they see the claim of objectivity as the expression of an authoritarian, power-conserving point of view. Michael Schudson describes this attitude as it arose in the 1960s:

"objective" reporting reproduced a vision of social reality which refused to examine the basic structures of power and privilege. It was not just incomplete, as critics of the thirties had contended, it was distorted. It represented collusion with institutions whose legitimacy was in dispute (M. Schudson, (1978). *Discovering the news. A social history of american newspapers,* p. 160. New York: Basic Books).

There are a variety of accusations implicit here that need to be sorted out.

First, the assertion of objectivity seems to heighten the status of claims to which it attaches. To insist not only that the enemy is winning the war, but that this statement is objective, seems to elevate it to a higher plane of truth or credibility. The assertion of objectivity then appears to involve a certain arrogance, a setting up of oneself as an authority. Now in one sense this concern seems unwarranted. Ordinarily when we say "The sky is blue" we imply "It's an objective fact (for all to see) that the sky is blue." My belief that what I say is true or objective adds nothing to the belief itself. At the same time, to the extent that we are convinced of our own objectivity or that of others, we are less likely to be open to other points of view. Belief in one's own objectivity is a form of smugness, and may lead to a dangerous self-deception. Belief in the objectivity of others—including the news media—enhances their credibility, often unjustifiably.

So acceptance of the ideology of objectivity—the view that institutions like the news media are generally objective and are sincerely committed to objectivity—has significant political consequences. A person's belief that a newspaper always and only publishes true and objective information will serve as an impediment to her political and intellectual enlightenment, whether she is a consumer or a producer of news. But for the ideology of objectivity to have the political consequences critics suggest, we must add a further premise: not only that people believe the press is objective, but also that the news provided favors the powers that be. (We can imagine an alternative: an opposition press with a great deal of authority and credibility.)

Is the press biased in favor of the powers that be? One reason to think so is that mass media organizations are vast corporate entities; they are *among* the powers that be, and so have interests in common with them. We can also raise a different question, however. Does the commitment to objectivity *itself* create biases in favor of the conservation of political power? This is the implicit claim of some of objectivity's critics: that the methods associated with the ideal of objectivity contain an inherent bias toward established power.

One reason for thinking that objectivity is inherently conservative in this way has to do with the reporter's reliance on sources. Among the canons of objective journalism is the idea that the reporter does not make claims based on her own personal observation, but instead attributes them to sources. Yet sources must seem credible to perform the required role, and official, government sources—as well as other important decision makers in the society—come with ready-made credentials for the job. In addition, they often have the skills and the resources to use the news media to their advantage. Yet such sources are not typically disinterested observers motivated only by a love of truth.

Journalists therefore confront a dilemma. If they provide to such sources an unfiltered mouthpiece, they serve the sources' interests. To avoid this outcome, journalists must make choices about which of the sources' statements are sufficiently controversial to call for "balancing" with another point of view, and they must choose those balancing points of view. And if, where the official view is doubtful, they merely balance the official source's view without even hinting at the probable truth, they mislead the audience. Each of these policies raises troubling questions about objectivity.

The first alternative, simply to provide an unfiltered mouthpiece, characterizes the press's response to Joseph McCarthy in the 1950s. This example, widely cited by objectivity's critics, has helped tarnish its reputation. But although we can see why journalists might have worried about challenging McCarthy's accusations, it seems clear that leaving them unanswered does not satisfy any intelligent conception of objectivity. Objectivity is supposed to be a means to truth; giving credibility to baseless charges—whether by commission or omission—should not count as objective.

If this is so, it follows that journalists must always make judgments about the credibility of sources and what they say. But when does a source's statement invite challenge? The obvious answer is: when it seems controversial. Yet what seems controversial depends on the consensus existing in the culture at a given time. And that consensus derives partly from powerful ideological assumptions that, while unchallenged in the culture, are by no means unchallengeable. So it is that I. F. Stone argues that "most of the time objectivity is just the rationale for regurgitating the conventional wisdom of the day." What goes without saying may be dogma rather than truth.

Supposing, however, that the journalist does recognize that an official view is sufficiently controversial to invite challenge, she must choose which opposing sources to cite and how to frame the debate between the opposing points of view. Is the dispute taken to span a fairly narrow range of the political spectrum?

If so, the press may be criticized for simply reproducing the conventional wisdom. Is the opposing point of view chosen an "extreme" one? (Obviously what we take to be extreme depends again on the prevailing consensus at the time. For a hilarious parody, see A. Cockburn (1987). The Tedium Twins. In *Corruptions of Empire*. London: Verso.) In that case the press may sensationalize the issue or marginalize the opposition by making them seem eccentric or irrational. Either way, the journalist cannot avoid exercising judgment.

These dilemmas explain another of the standard criticisms of journalism's commitment to objectivity: not that it necessarily favors established power, but that it leads to a destructive agnosticism and skepticism. Objectivity must be "operationalized," and this is achieved through the idea of balance. In exploring controversial issues, the journalist does not himself commit to a view, but instead gives voice to different sides of the story. The reader is left to judge the truth. But if the journalist truly balances the views, there may be no rational way for the reader to decide between them. And so he concludes that "there's truth on both sides," perhaps that every view is as good as every other. Rather than connecting with truth, objectivity, according to this way of thinking, leads to cynicism and skepticism.

Yet it might be argued that both these criticisms—that objectivity favors established power, and that it leads to skepticism and indecision—suffer from too mechanical a conception of objectivity. It is easy to see how the problems they address arise in the transition from objectivity-as-an-ideal to objectivity-as-a-method. In part, they may proceed from a confusion between objectivity and the appearance of objectivity. Questioning the remarks of an important public figure may look partisan, while leaving them unchallenged does not; but the appearance is misleading and only skin deep. Similarly, leaving two opposing points of view to look equally plausible where one has the preponderance of reason and evidence on its side is a charade of objectivity. It reflects the common mistake of confusing objectivity and neutrality. The objective investigator may *start out* neutral (more likely, she is simply good at keeping her prior beliefs from distorting her inquiry), but she does not necessarily *end up* neutral. She aims, after all, to find out what happened, why, who did it. Between truth and falsehood the objective investigator is not neutral.

The confusion between objectivity and neutrality may arise because of the belief, alluded to earlier, that "values" are not objective, true, part of the "fabric of the universe." According to the positivist outlook of which this is part, the objective investigator will therefore remain "value-neutral" and his inquiry will be "value-free." But the identification of neutrality and objectivity within a given realm depends on the assumption that there is no truth within that realm. Leaving aside the question whether values are objective, if facts are objective the objective investigator will not be neutral with respect to them.

As a journalistic virtue, then, objectivity requires that reporters not let their preconceptions cloud their vision. It does not mean that they have no beliefs, or that their findings may not be significant and controversial. Nevertheless, it is easy to see why many people confuse objectivity and neutrality. Often the outsider cannot easily tell the difference between a reporter who has come to a conclusion based on a reasoned evaluation of the evidence, and one who was biased toward that conclusion from the start. The safest way to seem objective, then, may be to look neutral.

IX. CONCLUSION

There are good reasons to suspect claims to objectivity. People who insist on their own objectivity protest too much; they are likely to be arrogant, overconfident, or self-deceived. In fact, those who acknowledge their own biases and limitations probably have a better chance of overcoming them than those who insist they are objective. Those who have faith in the objectivity of others may be complacent or dangerously naive. They fail to see the many obstacles—inborn and acquired, innocent and insidious, inevitable and avoidable—on the way to truth.

Often, furthermore, the press can rightly be accused of ideological or other bias. Sometimes these biases result from overt economic or political purposes, as when news organizations suppress damaging information about corporations to which they belong; sometimes from structural or technological features of media institutions, such as television's reliance on good pictures. But it is also true that, paradoxically, the aspiration to objectivity can contain biases of its own, by advantaging established sources or by encouraging an artificial arithmetic balance between views and tempting reporters to maintain the appearance of neutrality even in the face of overwhelming "nonneutral" evidence.

Finally, we must mention one further way in which, perhaps more than any other, the media shape our thinking. As one observer has put it, "The press doesn't tell us what to think, but it tells us what to think *about*." Journalists select from the innumerable events taking place in the world those to report, and, by giving them more or less prominence in a newspaper, magazine, or program, imply a great deal about their significance. As we saw earlier in the example of the Irish elections, even once an event has been chosen for coverage, there are crucial questions about which aspects to emphasize and how to interpret them. Whether these matters of selection fall squarely within the sphere of objectivity may be debatable; clearly they are intimately related.

Despite the variety of barriers to and limitations on objectivity, however, there are reasons for thinking that insofar as we aim to understand the world we cannot get along without assuming both its possibility and value.

Also See the Following Articles

KANTIANISM • MEDIA OWNERSHIP • MORAL RELATIVISM • POSTMODERNISM

Bibliography

Davidson, D. (1984). The very idea of a conceptual scheme. In *Inquiries into truth and interpretation*. New York: Oxford University Press.

Gurevitch, M., Levy, M., & Roeh, L. (1991). The global newsroom. In P. Dahlgren and C. Sparks (Eds.), *Communication and citizenship: Journalism and the public sphere in the new media age*. London: Routledge.

Luban, D. (1986). Fish v. Fish or, some realism about idealism. *Cardozo Law Review* 7.

Schiller, D. (1981). *Objectivity and the news*. Philadelphia: University of Pennsylvania Press.

Schudson, M. (1978). *Discovering the news: A social history of American newspapers*. New York: Basic Books.

Tuchman, G. (1972). Objectivity as strategic ritual. *American Journal of Sociology* 77.

ORGAN TRANSPLANTS AND DONORS

Ruth Chadwick and Udo Schüklenk
University of Central Lancashire

GLOSSARY

anencephaly Literally meaning "without brain," a congenital absence of all or part of the brain. Babies born with this condition have no hope of normal life or of long-term survival, but may have a functioning brainstem when they are born and thus are not brain dead in accordance with brainstem death criteria.

immunosuppression The reduction of the body's rejection of transplanted organs, for example, by drug therapy.

organ transplantation The act of removing an organ, such as a kidney or heart, from one individual and grafting it into another individual.

xenotransplantation The transplantation of animal tissue between species.

ORGAN TRANSPLANTATION is the surgical removal of a body organ, such as a kidney, from one individual (the organ donor) and placement of the organ in another individual for the purpose of improving the health of the recipient.

I. INTRODUCTION

The first successful kidney transplant between human identical twins took place in 1954, followed by the first successful transplant between fraternal twins in 1957. Subsequent development of antirejection drugs led to successful transplants between nonrelatives. The first heart transplant took place in 1967, when Dr. Christiaan Barnard transplanted a heart from a women into Mr. Washkansky, who died 18 days later.

Since those early experiments not only have now well-established heart transplant facilities been put into place (e.g., at Papworth and Harefield in the U.K.), but there have been developments in a number of areas, including liver transplants, heart-lung transplants, and transplants of tissue into the brain. In 1982 a team of doctors in Salt Lake City implanted an artificial heart into Dr. Barney Clark. The prospect of artificial hearts seemed initially to offer hope of an answer to the perennial problem of shortage; attention has subsequently turned to animals as an organ source.

There have been particular issues surrounding specific organ sources, for example, from fetuses and anecephalic babies. In 1989 in the United Kingdom following considerable discussion of the use of fetal tissue transplants, a Code of Practice on the Use of Fetuses and Fetal Material was published. There have been arguments to the effect that anencephalics should be defined as a distinct category of human being, which it is permisible to use as organ sources.

The practical problems surrounding organ transplants have been of several kinds. Rejection occurs in all cases except identical twins, although tissue typing improves chances of success. Immunosuppressive drugs suppress the rejection reaction but also have side effects. In the early days there were psychological problems, associated in particular with heart transplants, because of the symbolism associated with the heart.

A major problem has always been the shortage in supply of organs. In countries such as the United Kingdom the compulsory wearing of seat belts in cars has reduced the organ supply. Donor card systems have not been entirely successful because even when an individual carriers a donor card, their wishes are not always respected. The wishes of relatives may be allowed to intervene.

Another issue that has surrounded organ transplantation, especially heart transplants, has been the expense. Some cardiologists recommended abandoning the British program in the 1980s, because although it was glamorous high-tech medicine, the opportunity costs were great where other forms of treatment were concerned. This is an aspect of a more general problem concerning priorities in medicine, and regarding whether doctors should "do all they can" to prolong life. Given the shortage in supply, difficult decisions have to be made about prioritization among recipients.

Where human organs sources are concerned (the word "donor" is not always entirely appropriate), there are two kinds: live sources and cadaver sources. The ethical issues require separate consideration. In the case of some organs, of course, live donation is not a practical possibility. In each case there are potential conflicts of interest to be addressed.

II. LIVE HUMAN DONORS

A patient who needs an organ such as a kidney clearly has an interest in the preservation of his or her life. The potential organ source has an interest in the preservation of her own health and bodily integrity, for donating an organ to someone else is not without risks to the donor. The donor is subjected to a nontherapeutic operation. It may be argued that this problem can be overcome by requirements of free and informed consent, but in intrafamilial cases, in particular, individuals may feel a burden of responsibility and guilt if they refuse.

It might be tempting to think that the interest in preserving life should always take precedence over other interests. After all, life is a necessary condition of having any other interests at all. This is true when we are thinking of the life of any one individual. Things become more complicated when we try to compare the interests of different individuals. Societies that grant the potential donor the chance to consent or refuse to donate do not, as a matter of fact, put the interest of one person in living longer at a higher level than the interests of another preserving health or bodily integrity.

The reasons for this can be given in the following arguments:

(1) The interest in having a say over what happens to our own bodies is central to what gives us a sense of having a life of our *own* that we can to some extent control. For some people it is even more fundamental than the mere continuance of life, but even if not, it is an interest that we have to accept is a very deep one.

(2) The consequences of abandoning the principle that people should be asked to consent to donate would be potentially far-reaching. We have to consider not only the interests of one potential donor and donee but also the interests of society as a whole. Once we undermine the freedom of people to say what happens to their own bodies we may be undermining respect for human life itself anyway.

There have been cases, for example, in the United States of people trying to use legal process to force others to be donors of bone marrow. In a case study discussed in the *Hastings Center Report* a Mrs. X had actually registered as a potential donor to help a relative (A. Caplan, *et al.* (1983) 13, 17–19). However, Mr. Head, who desperately needed a transplant, found out (through a breach of confidentiality) that she would be a possible suitable match for him, and tried to pressure her into agreeing. This attempt was unsuccessful. Such a precedent could in effect legitimate a new kind of body-snatcher, any time organs were needed.

Under English law, at least, it would be an assault upon the person to perform an operation upon an individual without consent, and there are good reasons for thinking that this belief in freedom to decide is not something that we should give up. To the discussion of this topic there are, however, two qualifications and one criticism. The qualifications concern possible limits to choose what happens to our own bodies.

First, it might be argued that we have a moral obligation, if not a legal one, to help others where we can. Others would say that itis beyond the call of duty to agree to donate but that it provides an opportunity to choose altriusm. If freedom of choice is to be a reality, however, it is necessary to be aware of the potential burden of moral pressure.

The second qualification concerns the possibility of a market in organs. In the 1980s there were a number of cases concerning sale of kidneys, for example. In 1989 the U.K. government passed legislation to outlaw this. There are arguments to suggest that our ability to control what happens to our own bodies should not extend to selling bits of them. One aspect of this is a veiw that human beings have an intrinsic worth that puts them beyond price, and that selling human beings or parts of them is incompatible with respect for human dignity. Immanuel Kant, though writing long before organ transplantation became an issue, had arguments for the view that it is wrong to sell parts of oneself—even a tooth. One argument was that this involved a logical contradiction. "Man", he said "cannot dispose of himself because he is not a thing; he is not his own property; to say that he is would be self-contradictory". In selling himself man makes himself a thing and is in effect selling freedom. "We can dispose of things which have no freedom but not of a being which has free will" (Kant, I. (1963) *Lectures on Ethics* Translated by Infield, New York: Harper & Row).

An objection to this view, however, would be that if we are entitled to sell our labor in the market, then where is the dividing line between this in physical work, for example, and selling parts of the body? Kant's argument seems ultimately to depend on a view about what is intrinscially degrading to human beings. It also depends on his interpretation of human beings as ends in themselves, an idea that Schopenhauer rejected persuasively as a *contradictio in adjecto* in *On the Basis of Morality*.

If we confine our attention to interests, however, the argument may be that it is not really in the interests of the seller, who may be forced into it because of dire circumstances, and that social change is what is needed to try to prevent such situations from occurring, so that people are not in effect coerced into such transactions. There are also arguments about the wide consequences of a market in organs, analogous to Richard Titmuss's arguments in *The Gift Relationship*.

The criticism of giving importance to control over our own bodies might be based on a view that life is more important than anything else. John Harris, in "The Survival Lottery" considered the possibility that whenever two or more persons need organs, one healthy person should be killed to provide them, thus maximizing the number of lives saved. One person would be "sacrificed" (and attitudes in society would need to be changed so that this would be viewed as a noble thing to do) for the good of the greater number. The question is, of course, which implications for society such a strategy would have. There are a variety of negative "side-effects" that are not easily quantifiable, such as the anxiety people might feel that they could be sacrificed at any time to save other peoples' lives. These utilitarian cost considerations, as well as the fact that many donees (e.g., in the case of heart transplants) do not survive very long, make Harris's proposal an interesting thought experiment but practically unrealistic.

III. CADAVER DONORS

On the face of it, it might look as if the reasons for giving potential donors the freedom to consent or refuse do not apply when the donor is dead, but this is a view not widely held. Here too there seems to be a potential conflict of interest. Thus there is a commonly held position that it is not acceptable to take a person's organs without first asking whether she carried a donor card, or whether she would gave has any objections to donation. What are the arguments for this position?

One reason behind this seems to be that there is an interest in controlling what happens to our bodies, even after our death. There is an opposing view, however, that the interests a person might have in what happens to her body after death are of less or no relevance when compared with the interests of a person currently alive, but who will not survive much longer without an organ transplant. Indeed, one needs to ask whether it makes much sense to apply the ethical concept of personhood to a dead body. Dead people by definition do not satisfy the typical criteria of moral personhood, and hence their alleged wishes, as put forward possibly by relatives or their advance directives should not be considered as having the same status of those of living donors. Thus there have been various proposals at various times and in various societies, from requiring that form of consent describable as "opting in," to other ways of handling things, such as "required request," or "opting out."

An "opting-out" scheme would indicate that unless a person had positively registered an objection, her organs would automatically be available for use after death. It should be noted that such a scheme still preserves the donor's freedom of choice, but it alters the balance away from the interests of the donor and toward the interests of the donee.

A possible objection to this proposal may be that while it may be irrational to think that we can experience any harm after we are dead, nevertheless while we are alive we do not like to think of certain things happening to our bodies after death. This point is an extension of the point that we have an interest in having a say over what happens to our bodies. After all, they are our bodies.

But if this is all it is, it is not clear that such an interest can withstand the competition from those who have an interest in the preservation of their lives. Perhaps we should realize the weakness of the interest in controlling our own dead bodies and move toward an opting-out scheme.

But there are further arguments to consider. First, we must take into acocunt the fear, not of what will happen to our bodies after death, but of premature death. There is concern not only that mistakes do sometimes occur in determining whether someone is dead, but that the demand for organ transplants has in itself affected the way that death is defined, in leading to the establishment of criteria that maximize the chance of retrieving healthy organs suitable for donation. The obvious conflict of interest here is between a person's interest in not being declared dead, or even kills, before her time, and a potential donee's urgent need of an organ.

An unsentimental realist might suggest that if the potential donor, who is not quite dead, is so near death that she is never likely to lead a normal life, then the interests of the potential donee should still prevail. But the case is more complicated than this. For all members of society have an interest in people not being killed before their time (with possible limited exceptions such as voluntary euthanasia). For one thing, faith in the medical profession would be very rapidly undermined if it was thought that doctors viewed patients as potential sets of resources. What we do have to ensure is that the need for organs does not color in an unacceptable way people's judgments in elaborating and applying criteria of death.

An objection to an "opting-out" scheme is that it might reduce the possibility of displaying altruism. On the other hand it might be interpreted as "push" toward a more altruistic, rather than apathetic, society. It does not deny the possibility of choice but more directly confronts people with it while demanding less than is demanded of a living donor. Both types of conflict of interest considered as far could be much alleviated if the gap between demand and supply was not so wide where organs are concerned.

IV. ORGAN TRANSPLANTS AND PERSONAL IDENTITY

Moral problems surrounding organ transplants are not concerned solely with the interest of one person in staying alive as against the interest of another in having a say in what happens to her own body. Much depends on how we view the human person, and how we regard the relationship of ourselves to our bodies. People have widely varying views about this, of both religious and secular origins. For example, even within the Judeo-Christian tradition, against the Old Testament view of the human being as basically an animated body—a body into which God "breathed life," we may place some views that have seen the embodied person as an imprisoned soul. Others, again, have thought that the body is needed intact for the Resurrection, and thus have opposed cremation and regarded dismemberment as a terrible punishment. Such a view could rule out organ transplants altogether. How one views one's relationship to one's body thus has a great impact on how one regards certain forms of medicial treatment. They provide worldviews within which we must consider the conflicts of interests.

The modern secular philosophical debate about personal identity tends to concentrate on the merits of the opposing physical and psychological criteria of personal identity. To take the physical criterion: if I think of myself as basically my body, how much of my body can change before I am no longer than same person? There is a standard comparison in the literature here with a physical object such as a ship, of which over the years, various parts wear out and are replaced. Eventually none of the original parts remain. Is the end result the same ship? If so, what has remained the same? If not, at what point did it cease to be the same ship?

In the case of human beings, the predominant view of the physical criterion of personal identity holds that one remains the same person as long as one has the same brain. This of course would raise problems for the possibility of brain transplants. On the psychological view, it does not matter how many bits of one's body are replaced as long as there is psychological continuity between the person at various stages.

On neither of these views does a kidney transplant raise a deep philosophical problem of personal identity. What may be a problem is how donees feel about their personal identity. So it may be a matter of an interest in feeling secure about what one's identity is, rather than in the problem of personal identity itself. Of course, in the event of the theoretical possibility that at some time in the future we could gradually replace all human parts as they wear out we should have a problem like that of the ship. In such an event we may have to accept that questions of personal identity are unanswerable.

V. XENOTRANSPLANTATION

Another more recent issue pertains to the potential future possibility of successfully using animal organs for humans in need of replacement organs.

A. Science

Xenotransplantation is the transplant of animal tissue between species. For this entry only the issue of transplanting animal organs into humans will be discussed. Xenotransplantation is a means considered to bridge the gap between the organs needed by people and those available to them. The supply of human organs is handicapped by a wealth of ethical, economic, and legal problems, the latter of which apply in most part of the world. Serious attempts to implant animal organs into humans have been actively researched and tested since the early 1960s, even though early but equally unsuccessful trials date back to the end of the last century. More than 30 organs have been transplanted, without any of the human recipients being able to return to health. The ultimate scientific question is whether it will ever be possible to use animal organs in humans. The problems pertain to the risk that the human body might reject the animal organ, but also to the risk that infections might be transmitted from the source animal to the tissue recipient, and from the tissue recipient to her immediate contacts and the wider population. Current research tries to modify the genetic make-up of pigs by adding human genes, in order to research whether the scientific problems in xenotransplantation can be solved. At this point it is impossible to predict whether this will succeed or fail.

B. Ethics

The research into the possibility of xenotransplantation, and xenotransplantation itself give rise to a variety of ethical problems.

1. The Use of Sentient Nonhuman Beings as Involuntary Organ "Donors"

Several animal rights activists and philosophers providing a theoretical backing for their positions have argued that it is unethical to inflict pain upon sentient nonhuman beings for the sake of helping suffering human beings. Their arguments are either of a utilitarian nature or they are based in one type or another of deontological moral theory. The utilitarian approach to the use of animals in xenotransplantation argues that the equal consideration of interests requires us to use humans with a similar intellectual capacity than animals we might wish to use for xenotransplantation, too, or to use neither of these. Should we decide that we do not wish to use mentally handicapped people, or newborns, or senile people as organ banks, then it would be incoherent to suggest that we should be ethically entitled to use other higher mammals for this purpose. The reasoning consequentialist ethicists employ is that there is no morally relevant difference between some humans and higher mammals. For instance, they would suggest that we are ethically entitled to use anencephalic babies in which the cerebral hemispheres of the brain are absent, in order to provide organs for transplantation purposes. Deontologists, on the other hand, have argued that what qualifies human beings for personhood is also present, to some degree in other species. Every being that satisfies Tom Regan's "subject of a life" criterion has an inherent value and should not be used merely as a means to certain ends. Regan is clearly attempting to widen the scope of Kantian thinking to include nonhuman animals. He follows Leonard Nelson's line of argument who proposed to distinguish between subjects of duty who have a variety of rights and obligations, and subjects of rights, who have certain rights, but no duties because they are incapable of fulfilling these duties. Animals and humans who do not fulfill the criterion of full personhood may well fall into the latter category. Proponents of this view would argue that to treat animals as means to the end of extracting organs from them is ethically unacceptable. The British *Nuffield Council on Biethics* was particularly concerned about the use of primates for transplantation purposes because of the closeness of humans and primates in evolutionary terms. The Council deemed the use of pig organs less problematic simply because society uses these animals already for the purpose of food and clothes production.

2. The Use of Humans in Xenotransplantation Trials

Given that the majority of reports tend to be in favor of research into the possibility of xenotransplantation, and given that these views are supported by public opinion, the question is inevitable when trials involving human beings might be ethically justifiable. The history of research on human organ transplantation suggests that early recipients of animal organs have a low chance of survival. On the other hand, there is a large number of patients in desperate need of organs, and many of these patients would die before suitable organs become available. It seems, however, that no special ethical requirements for the conduct of such trials do exist, once the ethical decision to go ahead with such trials at all has been made. Voluntary first-person informed consent is a necessary condition just as the approval by an appropriately selected research ethics committee. No unique ethical problems occur in regard to such trials.

C. Religion

Christian theologians have argued that human beings are fundamentally superior to nonhuman animals. This view is certainly widely shared among most people in Western societies, as a variety of surveys of attitudes toward xenotransplantation indicate. It is based on Genesis 1:27, where human beings are said to "have unique significance and value because only they are made in the image of God." In view of, for instance, the British Christian Medical Fellowship the painless killing of animals for the purpose of saving human life, or for improving its quality would be considered as ethically justifiable. On the other hand some Christian theologians have argued that humans become less and less human the more animal parts we implant into people. They also pointed out that it would be somewhat frivolous to change God's creation by breeding animals into something more and more human by changing the genetic make-up through the infusion of human genes. Islamic theologians on the other hand are not opposed to xenotransplantation per se. However, they would find unacceptable the use of organs taken from so-called forbidden animals such as pigs.

VI. SUMMARY

A variety of practical problems in regard to live donor organ donations occur that seem to indicate that great care should be taken that no unethical practices arise.

In particular vulnerable populations (i.e., poor living donors selling their organs in order to survive) need to be protected from exploitation. On the other hand, it seems that cultural objections to the use of dead peoples' organs stand in the way of the effective use of such organs for the greater good of a large number of potential donees. It has been suggested that animal organs could help us to avoid the ethical problems raised by the use of human organs. However, to harm sentient nonhuman beings in order to avoid taking organs of nonsentient (i.e., dead) humans seems to be a policy that is a result of irrational beliefs. Irrespective of these concerns remains the problem of how to allocate scarce medical resources. As yet the costs of heart transplants stand in a disproportionate relation to the actual quality adjusted life years gained in this procedure when compared to other medical expenditure.

Also See the Following Articles

ANIMAL RIGHTS • DEATH, DEFINITION OF • FETUS • MEDICAL CODES AND OATHS

Bibliography

Advisory Group on the Ethics of Xenotransplantation. (1996). *Animal tissue into humans.* London: HMSO.

Allan, J. S. (1995). Xenotransplantation at a crossroads: prevention versus progress. *Nature Medicine* 2, 18–21.

Chadwick, R. F. (1989). The market for bodily parts: Kant and duties to oneself. *Journal of Applied Philosophy* 6, 129–139.

Chadwick, R. F. (1993). Corpses, recycling and therapeutic purposes. In R. Lee and D. Morgan (Eds.), *Deatrites: Law and ethics at the end of life.* London: Routledge.

Jones, D. G. (1991). Fetal neural transplantation: placing the ethical debate within the context of society's use of human material. *Bioethics* 5, 23–43.

Lamb, D. (1990). *Organ transplants and ethics.* London: Routledge.

McCarrick, P. M. (1995). Organ transplant allocation (Scope Note 29). *Kennedy Institute of Ethics Journal* 5, 365–383.

Nelson, L. (1971). *System der philosophischen Ethik und Pädagogik.* Hamburg: Felix Meiner.

Nuffield Council on Bioethics. (1996). *Animal to human transplants: The ethics of xenotransplantation.* London: Nuffield Council on Bioethics.

Regan, T. (1983). *The case for animal rights.* London: Routledge & Kegan Paul.

Singer, P. (1995). *Animal liberation.* London: Pimlico.

Truog, R. D., & Fletcher, J. C. (1990). Brain death and the anencephalic newborn. *Bioethics* 4, 199–215.

PACIFISM

Anne Seller and Richard Norman
University of Kent

GLOSSARY

absolute pacifism The view that participation in war could never, in principle, be justified.

anarchism The doctrine that all government is illegitimate because it limits the autonomy of the individual. It is commonly linked to the belief that governments are the source of violence and crime within society, through the maintenance of unjust systems, and without their influence people would live together in peace, harmony, and justice. It should not be confused with anarchy, which simply means no rule and is usually associated with violence and chaos.

civil disobedience Breaking a law publicly and nonviolently, and with no attempt to evade the penalty for so doing, as a form of political protest. The aim can range from mobilizing public opinion over an issue to putting direct pressure on government to change its mind.

consequentialism The view that all actions should be morally assessed on the basis of their good or bad consequences.

conscientious objection The refusal to conform to a regulation on the grounds of conscientious scruples, usually by appealing to a legal clause that allows such exemptions, and most commonly to refuse service in the military.

contingent pacifism The view that participation in war could in principle be justified but that in practice a sufficient justification will never be available.

federalism A system of government whereby several states form a political unity, bound together by treaties or laws, that they have agreed to, while maintaining control over their internal affairs. The most common form is an agreement not to go to war with each other, to enact a common foreign policy, and to have no trade barriers between each other.

feminism A widely disputed term, covering many theories, all arguing that men and women are equal and ought to be treated as such. A common strand is the perception that men as a group exercise power over women as a group, and that this relationship of dominance is institutionalized and is part of the social structure, so that it persists despite attempts to evade it in personal relationships.

"just war" theory A tradition of moral thinking about war that attempts to specify the conditions that must be satisfied if war is to be just.

nonviolent direct action An action or campaign of noncooperation, which is also nonviolent, and is aimed at bringing about change in government or social policy. It usually also has the long-term revolutionary aim of developing a society based on cooperation and autonomy, rather than coercion and dominance.

pacifism The view that participation in war can never be morally justified.

passive resistance The refusal to obey, without active opposition or resistance, a law or order.

peace This has a range of meanings from the cessation of hostilities to the idea of living in concord or harmony. Since open hostilities can be replaced by a steady and settled design on one's life (as, for example, in the Cold War) the contrast between peace and war depends upon the context, and the two terms are better understood as characterizing a continuum of human relationships from hostility to harmony, rather than as diametric opposites.

war The organized use of force by states or would-be states, or the steady and settled intention to use it.

THE MEANING OF THE TERM PACIFISM has developed over time and has become increasingly specific. In a broad sense it has been used to refer to a general disposition to advocate and promote peace rather than war, or, slightly more precisely, an active commitment to work for the abolition of war. However, the history of the twentieth century has forced a distinction between those who, although generally opposed to war, are prepared to recognize exceptions in extreme circumstances, for example the need to resort to war to defeat an appalling evil such as Nazism, and those who adhere to an absolute rejection of war in all circumstances. It is to that absolutist position that the term pacifism has come to be more precisely applied. Pacifism in this precise sense is exemplified by the "peace pledge," which the London clergyman Dick Sheppard, in 1934, invited people to sign, and which led to the foundation of the Peace Pledge Union: "I renounce war, and never again directly or indirectly will I support or sanction another."

Pacifism is thus at the extreme end of a spectrum of moral attitudes to war. It can be contrasted with:

> **militarism:** the view that war has a positive moral value, for example, because of the qualities of courage and heroism which it fosters, and that military solutions are the obvious ones;
> **"just-war" theory:** the view that, although the actions typical of war are of a kind that would normally be regarded as morally evil, waging war can sometimes be just, provided that certain strict conditions are satisfied;

> **pacific-ism:** the view that all war is an evil, and one that we can and should try to eliminate from human life, but that in the meantime it may sometimes, in exceptional circumstances, be a necessary and unavoidable evil.

The term "pacific-ism" has been usefully coined to mark the contrast with the absolutist position of "pacifism." The latter, in its most precise sense, then, is not simply the view that war is a bad thing; that belief is shared with pacific-ism and to some extent with "just-war" theory. What is distinctive of pacifism is the belief that participation in war can *never* be right.

With that definition, then, we reach a kind of precision, but the precision disappears again when we look at the variety of routes by which pacifists have reached that conclusion. Rather than attempt to reduce that variety to some kind of uniformity, it is better to regard pacifism not as a single moral position but as a family of moral positions. They all converge on the shared practical conclusion—the absolute rejection of war—but they reach that conclusion on the basis of a range of different moral and political theories and arguments. The remainder of this article will explore the variety of justifications invoked to support the shared practical conclusion.

I. JUSTIFICATIONS

One distinction standardly made in the literature on pacifism is between

> **absolute pacifism:** the view that participation in war could never, *in principle,* be justified; and
> **contingent pacifism:** the view that participation in war could in principle be justified but that *in practice* a sufficient justification will never be available.

This may seem thoroughly confusing, for we have just defined pacifism as itself an absolutist position. It looks as though we now need a distinction between the "absolute absolutist" and the "absolutist-who-isn't-really-an-absolutist!" The important contrast, however, is between the phrases "never in principle" and "never in practice." The principle to which the absolute pacifist appeals is the principle that human life is sacred. The term "sacred" need not imply a religious point of view (although it may do so). It refers to the idea that killing another human being is always morally wrong. The absolute pacifist is likely to maintain that the most fundamental of all moral principles, and the starting point for all moral thinking, is that it is wrong to take human life. Participation in war, however, is by definition participation in the activity of killing other human beings, and can therefore never be morally justified. That is the simplicity of the position of absolute pacifism.

Putting it that way may make it sound like the mechanical application of an abstract principle. That is why the language of life as "sacred"—even though the religious connotations could be misleading—is perhaps preferable. It points to the underlying moral attitude that animates pacifism—an attitude of reverence and respect for each individual human life. Pacifism strips away the stereotype of "the enemy" and recognizes that the enemy soldier is a human being like oneself, a human being who has his own life to live, and whose death is always an irreparable loss. (This recognition is exemplified in Wilfred Owen's poem of the First World War, *Strange Meeting*.) Killing an enemy soldier is murder, and war is murder on a massive scale. That attitude of respect for human life is the moral attitude underlying the varieties of pacifist belief. For the absolute pacifist it is decisive.

Notice, however, that the absolute pacifist will in addition have to appeal to some version of what is called the "acts-and-omissions" distinction. There are inescapably tragic situations in which the life of one person can be saved only by killing another. Suppose that person A is attacking person B with the intention of killing B. A third party, C, may then be confronted with the dilemma of whether to kill A in order to prevent B being killed. The absolute pacifist will have to say that even in that circumstance, killing A would not be permissible. C may attempt to save B's life by other means, but if the alternatives fail and B is killed, C will, by refusing to kill A, have failed to save B's life. The absolute pacifist must therefore be committed to the view that C's moral obligation not to kill A overrides the moral obligation to try to save B's life. The absolute pacifist is thus committed to the belief that there is a morally relevant distinction between "killing" and "failing to save life." Although we have a moral obligation not to kill and a moral obligation to try to save life, the former is the stronger obligation and always takes precedence over the latter. We should save life when we can, but we must never kill another human being.

BOX 1

——— *STRANGE MEETING* ———

It seemed that out of battle I escaped
Down some profound dull tunnel, long since scooped
Through granites which titanic wars had groined.
Yet also there encumbered sleepers groaned,
Too fast in thought or death to be bestirred.
Then, as I probed them, one sprang up, and stared
With piteous recognition in fixed eyes,
Lifting distressful hands, as if to bless.
And by his smile, I knew that sullen hall,
By his dead smile I knew we stood in Hell.
With a thousand pains that vision's face was grained;
Yet no blood reached there from the upper ground,
And no guns thumped, or down the flues made moan.
'Strange friend,' I said, 'here is no cause to mourn.'
'None,' said the other, 'save the undone years,
The hopelessness. Whatever hope is yours,
Was my life also; I went hunting wild
After the wildest beauty in the world,
Which lies not calm in eyes, or braided hair,
But mocks the steady running of the hour,
And if it grieves, grieves richlier than here.
For by my glee might many men have laughed,
And of my weeping something had been left,

Which must die now. I mean the truth untold,
The pity of war, the pity war distilled.
Now men will go content with what we spoiled,
Or, discontent, boil bloody, and be spilled.
They will be swift with swiftness of the tigress.
None will break ranks, though nations trek from progress.
Courage was mine, and I had mystery,
Wisdom was mine, and I had mastery:
To miss the march of this retreating world
Into vain citadels that are not walled.
Then, when much blood had clogged their chariot-wheels,
I would go up and wash them from sweet wells,
Even with truths that lie too deep for taint.
I would have poured my spirit without stint
But not through wounds; not on the cess of war.
Foreheads of men have bled where no wounds were.
I am the enemy you killed, my friend.
I knew you in this dark: for so you frowned
Yesterday through me as you jabbed and killed.
I parried; but my hands were loath and cold.
Let us sleep now ...'

WILFRED OWEN

To see the appliation of this rather abstract analysis to the dilemmas of war, consider the example of the Second World War. The Nazi regime in Germany embarked on a program of genocide—the extermination of the Jews. Many people who would have been resolutely opposed to war in most circumstances felt that here was an exception—that these genocidal policies could be defeated only by the military defeat of Germany. In accepting this conclusion they were accepting that it was necessary to kill members of the German armed forces. It was, in other words, necessary to kill in order to save lives. The absolute pacifist would have to reject that judgment. She or he would have to say that, although the genocidal policies of the Nazis were evil and had to be resisted, they must not be resisted by waging war and killing other human beings.

We shall encounter later some ways in which the absolute pacifist might elaborate and defend the acts-and-omissions distinction—for example, by appeal to some religious notion of conscience and responsibility—but for the moment we note that something like this must lie behind the absolute refusal ever to take human life. Turning now to the *contingent pacifist,* we find that the arguments are more complex. The simple appeal to principle is not enough. The contingent pacifist will allow that there are circumstances in which the taking of human life could conceivably be justified, but will argue that those circumstances do not include the taking of life in war. This will have to be argued on the basis of certain features of the nature of war. For example, the contingent pacifist might accept that killing in self-defense could in principle be justifiable, but argue that killing in war is not sufficiently like individual self-defense to provide a justification. Or, she or he might allow that on consequentialist grounds killing might sometimes be necessary to prevent terrible consequences, but argue that modern war is so immensely destructive that the costs in terms of consequences will always be unacceptable. Or, she or he might allow that killing could sometimes be justified at the individual level, but argue that to kill on the orders of the state is to surrender one's conscience in an unacceptable way. We shall explore these lines of thought shortly, but for the moment we note that they all count as versions of contingent pacifism. They all allow that the moral presumption against killing could in principle be overridden, but then invoke other considerations to show that it cannot in practice be overridden in war. The diversity of these further considerations helps to generate the variety of positions within the family of pacifist beliefs.

Cutting across this distinction between *absolute pacifism* and *contingent pacifism* is another important distinction: between those justifications for pacifism that *accept the framework of the state system,* and those that *challenge the assumptions of that framework.* We have defined pacifism as the view that participation in war can never be morally justified. That formulation puts the emphasis on the moral question faced by the individual: "Should I participate in, or support, a war being waged by my country?" For some pacifists, the answer will depend on a prior question: "Should my country itself go to war?" If it is wrong for the individual agent to support or participate in war, this will follow from the fact that it is wrong for states to go to war. That way of seeing the argument presupposes the framework of states as moral agents. It assumes that the question whether states should or should not go to war is an intelligible and legitimate question, and one that is prior to the question of what the individual agent should do.

Other pacifists question that framework. They may question the legitimacy of the state as a moral agent. They may say: "It is not for me to say what the state should do; I am not responsible for the actions of the state, I am responsible for my own actions as an individual, and that is the point from which I start." This kind of pacifism, as we shall see, encompasses a range of political views critical of the nation-state, and a range of views about individual responsibility, about "conscientious objection" and "civil disobedience," and other such concepts.

The division between these two kinds of pacifism is not a sharp one. The pacifist might hold views about the limits of state authority, or about the desirability of an international order to supercede the framework of nation-states, while recognizing that at present nation-states exist and that the question of what they ought morally to do is therefore pertinent. So it is possible to combine justifications for pacifism falling into both these categories. Nevertheless, the distinction is useful as a way of classifying the arguments, and it will provide the division between the remaining two main sections of this article.

II. JUSTIFICATIONS THAT ACCEPT THE FRAMEWORK OF THE STATE SYSTEM

A. Engagement with Just-War Theory

We have previously contrasted pacifism with the moral perspective standardly referred to as "just-war" theory.

This is a tradition of moral argument that accepts that the waging of war imposes a heavy burden of moral justification, and attempts to specify conditions that have to be met for war to be morally justified. The implication of the theory is that those conditions can sometimes be met, and hence that war can sometimes be just. One line of argument for the pacifist, therefore, is to take issue with just-war theory, and to argue that the theory's proposed conditions are inappropriate, or that they can never be met. We do not have space here to review all the proposed conditions for a just war, and the responses that the pacifist might make to them, but two points are especially worthy of attention.

1. The Self-Defense Condition

Modern versions of just-war theory have come to focus particularly on the requirement that a war cannot be just unless it is a *defensive* war. Wars of aggression cannot be justified, but war may be justified as defense against aggression. This requirement rests on an analogy with individual self-defense. If there are any exceptions at all to the moral prohibition of killing, then the most plausible case seems to be that of killing in self-defense. We have seen that the absolute pacifist rejects even this exception, but most people would see it as a legitimate exception. The point can be put in terms of the idea of a "right to life." If someone deliberately threatens my life, he violates my right to life, and in doing so he has in some sense negated his own right to life; it is therefore morally permissible for me to kill him if this is the only way in which I can protect my own life. To put it another way, the right to life carries with it a right to protect one's life, that is, a "right of self-defense." By extension, also, if I have a right of self-defense, then third parties have the right to help in defending me against an attacker. Modern versions of just-war theory present states' rights as the collective analogue of the individual right of self-defense. As individuals have the right to defend themselves against lethal threats (and other individuals have the right to help defend them), so also states have the right to defend themselves against aggression (and other states have the right to help in their defense). The analogy is familiar at the level of popular moral argument. Pacifists are regularly asked, "What would you do if someone were trying to kill your mother (or your wife, or your grandmother, or some other favored female relative)?" The implied answer is "You would defend her—by killing her attacker if necessary." And the suggestion is that by the same token you ought to defend your country, and you would be morally justified in doing so.

The analogy has a lot of moral work to do, and the pacifist can plausibly question whether it can do it effectively. There are two points at which the analogy seems to break down. First, it is important for the case of individual self-defense that the attacker is threatening my *life*. This is what makes it plausible to suppose that I might be justified in killing my attacker. It is my life or his, and because he is the attacker it is right that, if one life has to be lost, it should be his. It is much less obvious that I would be justified in killing my assailant in order to prevent him, for example, from taking my property. Some would argue that I do have such a right, but the claim is contentious, and the just-war theorist who appeals to that analogy is choosing to locate the argument on weaker ground. Much more plausible is the claim that I may justifiably kill an attacker to defend my own life.

However, we then have to recognize that a state's war of defense against aggression is not, as such, the defense of the right to life. It may in particular cases be that, but it need not be. When the armed forces of an aggressor state attack another state, their aim is not necessary to kill the inhabitants of the invaded state. They may perhaps be engaged on a war of genocide, but such cases are the exception, and the more likely case is that of aggression with the aim of exercising political power over the invaded state, or taking some of its resources, or some other such aim. It remains an open question whether military defense against aggression of that kind might be justifiable, but it cannot be decisively justified simply by appeal to the self-defense analogy. What is being defended in such cases is not a literal "right to life," but at most a metaphorical life, "the life of the nation." The right in question is more literally describable as the state's right of *sovereignty*. What the just-war theorist has to argue is that states' rights of sovereignty are of comparable moral importance to the right to life, and can justify killing in their defense. Further argument is needed to show this, the onus is on the just-war theorist to provide the argument, and in the absence of such an argument the pacifist can say that war has not been justified.

2. Noncombatant Immunity and Killing the Innocent

There is a second point at which the self-defense analogy becomes questionable. The supposed right of self-defense, in the individual case, depends crucially on the idea that the person whom I have a right to kill is the person who is *deliberately threatening* my life. It is his *responsibility* for the attack on my life that negates his own right to life and gives me the right to kill him.

I do not have a comparable right to kill an *innocent* person simply on the grounds that doing so will preserve my own life. Just-war theory recognizes this point by formulating the principle of "noncombatant immunity"—the principle that the only persons who may justifiably be killed in war are combatants. Killing civilians, for example by bombing cities, is morally wrong because it is the killing of the innocent, and a war cannot be a just war if it is fought in such a way as to involve the deliberate targeting of noncombatants.

This is a very demanding condition, and most modern wars have failed to satisfy it. In the Second World War both sides adopted the strategy of bombing enemy cities. The first German bombing raid on Britain in 1940 was immediately followed by a retaliatory raid on Germany, and thereafter the British and in due course the American air forces deliberately targeted centers of population with the aim of undermining civilian morale. The American war in Vietnam in the 1960s and 1970s involved both the bombing of cities in North Vietnam and the carpet bombing of rural areas in the South where guerilla forces were known to be active, killing guerillas and peasants indiscriminately. The Gulf War in 1992, fought to reverse the Iraqi invasion of Kuwait, began with a 43-day bombing campaign by American and allied forces against Iraq. The bombing was ostensibly aimed at "military targets," but this was interpreted widely to include, for example, roads and bridges, power stations and communication systems, in or near populated areas, and the bombing resulted in heavy civilian casualties. In all these and many more cases, recent wars have violated the principle of noncombatant immunity.

What the pacifist may go on to argue is that any modern war is bound to do so. The armed forces of any country depend crucially on the country's industrial and economic base. They depend on the production of weapons from the munitions factories, on supply lines, on effective communication systems and power supplies. Winning a modern war is likely to require attacking and disrupting the other side's economic base, and that means attacking populated areas and killing civilians. If that is indeed the inescapable character of modern war, then we have here a powerful argument for contingent pacifism. It is "contingent" pacifism because it may allow, at least for the purposes of the argument, that war could be just if it could be fought without killing the innocent. That condition, however, cannot be satisfied in the modern world.

This argument can be reinforced by a further feature of modern war. Most such wars are fought at least in part with conscript armies. Conscripts have not chosen to fight. They are not normally responsible for their government's decision to go to war, or for the military command's decisions about how the war should be fought. They are compelled to fight, and to obey the orders of their political leaders and military commanders. They are not in any strong sense responsible for the war. Therefore, the pacifist may argue, if a war cannot be fought without killing conscript combatants on the other side, this is another reason for thinking that it cannot be fought without killing the innocent.

The just-war theorist is likely to argue that conscript combatants are not "innocent" in the relevant sense. Innocent means, literally, "not harming." All combatants, including conscripts, are engaged in the activity of waging war and therefore in the activity of harming, and as such they are legitimate targets in war. This, however, is to understand the concept of innocence in a somewhat technical sense, and it is doubtful whether it can do the moral work which the just-war theorist needs it to do, especially if she or he is relying on the self-defense model of just war. As we have seen, the plausibility of a right to kill in self-defense depends on the fact that the person you may have to kill is deliberately attacking you and is, in some fairly strong sense, responsible for doing so. You cannot kill just anyone, such as someone who is an innocent threat, in order to preserve your own life. So, if the plausibility of just-war theory depends on the idea that those whom it is morally permissible to kill are those who are responsible for aggression, the pacifist can argue that this condition cannot be met in a war of conscript armies. This is a further dimension to the argument for contingent pacifism.

On these grounds, then, the pacifist who is prepared to argue with the just-war theorists in their own terms about the moral acceptability of states' resort to war may claim that war cannot be justified in those terms. The self-defense analogy is too imperfect an analogy, and the requirement of not killing the innocent, which is central to just-war theory, cannot be fulfilled in modern war. Apart from just-war theory, the other main kind of argument likely to be invoked by those who are serious about trying to provide a moral justification for war is a consequentialist argument. We turn now to such arguments.

B. Consequentialist Arguments

As the label indicates, arguments of this kind appeal to the consequences of waging war or refusing to do so. Common-sense justifications of war are often of this kind. It is said that though war may have terrible consequences, the consequences of a refusal to go to war may sometimes be even worse. If the alternative is acquiescing in violent conquest or tyranny or injustice, war may sometimes be the lesser evil.

It is difficult to respond to such arguments at the general level. By their very nature, consequentialist arguments tend to come down to claims about the consequences in the particular case. Some might say that to argue in those terms is already to abandon the standpoint of respect for human life, because it involves being prepared to sacrifice the lives of some for the good of others. However, we have seen that the absolute pacifist can rule out the possibility of ever having to sacrifice some lives to save others only by invoking the acts-and-omissions distinction, and that distinction is contentious. Consequentialist justifications for war do therefore have an undeniable intuitive plausibility. Is there anything that the pacifist can say in reply? Two general points, at least, can be made.

1. Means and Ends

Consequentialist justifications for war appeal to the principle that the end justifies the means. This is meant not in the sense that victory in war justifies all possible means; although politicians and military commanders do sometimes act on that basis, such an interpretation represents the abandonment of moral argument altogether. What can plausibly be meant by saying that "the end justifies the means" is that means have to be assessed according to how effectively they promote or prevent the achievement of desirable ends. War, too, the consequentialist will say, has to be assessed in those terms.

The general point the pacifist can make in reply is that means in turn tend to shape ends. The ends that people actually achieve may turn out to be very different from the ends that they originally intended, if the latter are distorted by the means that are employed. War, it may then be said, is likely to have that distorting effect. When employed as a means to combat tyranny or injustice, it may impose its own unintended character on the end result. War achieves its ends by terrorizing the defeated. On the side of the victors, it is liable to establish habits of ruthlessness and coercion that are hard to abandon once the war is over. On the side of the vanquished, it is liable to create feelings of humiliation and resentment, and a desire for vengeance, and in that way to sow the seeds of a future war. A classic example is the First World War. The settlement established by the Treaty of Versailles in 1919 humiliated Germany, and imposed intolerable burdens on the German economy. It led directly to the rise of Hitler and Nazism,

and thus to the Second World War, a war even more destructive than the first. Pacifists would say that this exemplifies the way in which violence breeds violence, and war perpetuates itself. The famous novelist and pacifist Aldous Huxley put the point thus:

> The means determine the ends; and however excellent intentions may be, bad or merely unsuitable means must inevitably produce results quite unlike the good ends originally proposed.... Once war has been adopted as a regular instrument of policy, once the idea that violence is the proper way of getting things done has become established as a truism, there can be no secure and lasting peace, only a series of truces between wars. For war, however "just" it may seem, cannot be waged without the commission of frightful injustices; frightful injustices cannot be committed without arousing the resentment and hatred of those on whom they are committed, or on their friends or successors; and resentment and hatred cannot be satisfied except by revenge. But how can military defeat be avenged except by a military victory? The successive wars to which the historian points are the strongest possible argument against war as a method of securing peace and justice. The means determine the ends, and the end achieved by war is not peace, but more war. ((1936) *The case for constructive peace.* London: Peace Pledge Union. Republished 1984, pp. 9–10)

2. The Unpredictable Destructiveness of Modern War

A second point that the pacifist can make about consequences is to refer again to the particular features of war in the modern era. Modern weapons are immensely destructive. Modern wars are therefore likely to be correspondingly devastating. Nuclear weapons are of course the ultimate in destruction; a single bomb can destroy a city, and a full-scale nuclear war, fought with existing nuclear arsenals, could wipe out human civilization and perhaps even the human species altogether. So long as wars have the potential to escalate into nuclear war, that danger is with us. This ever-present possibility has been seen by some as, in itself, a sufficient reason for thinking that war is always too dangerous to be entertained as an option. This version of contingent pacifism has sometimes been called "nuclear pacifism."

So-called "conventional" wars, however, are in themselves hugely destructive. The Second World War left thousands of cities and towns and villages reduced to rubble, many millions of people killed, and the economies of many of the participant nations devastated. The American bombing of Vietnam, using defoliants and other kinds of chemical weapons, left large areas of land contaminated and unusable perhaps for generations. These are the costs of modern warfare, and pacifists can reasonably ask whether anything that might be achieved by war is likely to be worth that kind of price.

A further dimension of the destructiveness of modern war is its unpredictability. This is true both of its physical consequences and its political consequences. At the beginning of the Second World War, many predicted, from the experience of the First World War, that gas would be used; it was not. No one could have predicted the use of the two atomic bombs dropped on Hiroshima and Nagasaki in 1945. Armies have always been difficult to control, but a modern war is a social upheaval on a huge scale. As an instrument of policy war cannot be used with precision or with predictable results. To take again the example of the Second World War, the extent to which the allies achieved their original aims is debatable. Nazism was defeated; but war was declared by Britain in 1939, not with the avowed aim of overthrowing Nazism, but because Poland had been invaded. Poland in 1945 was nominally liberated, but left with a government imposed by the victorious Soviet army. The real outcome of the Second World War was the Cold War—the division of Europe into two massively armed power blocs, Soviet hegemony in Eastern Europe, and the threat of nuclear war hanging over the world for at least a generation. Those results were quite unforeseen.

At the level of consequentialist arguments, then, the pacifist can reasonably cast doubt on the claim that war can be justified by its results. War, as a means, is by its very nature liable to subvert in the long term the desirable aims that may be intended. The massive destructiveness of modern war, allied to the unpredictability of its outcomes, makes it difficult to rely on any prediction that the good achievements of waging war will outweigh the costs. These arguments, although not decisive in themselves, provide powerful support for contingent pacifism.

Both the engagement with just-war theory and the engagement with consequentialist justifications for war accept at face value the initial question: "Can it be right for states to go to war?" That question presupposes the framework of the state system. It acknowledges the existence of states as moral agents. Within this framework, the pacifist's reasons for thinking that it is wrong for individuals to participate in war will tend to follow from the reasons for thinking that it is wrong for states themselves to go to war. We turn now to justifications for pacifism which proceed primarily by questioning that framework.

III. JUSTIFICATIONS THAT CHALLENGE THE LEGITIMACY OF THE SOVEREIGN STATE

So far the arguments examined have assumed the existence of the state, and understood it on the model of an autonomously acting individual, morally responsible for its actions. At the same time, they have tended to assume that responsibility for wars can be assigned to such bodies. This model of the state presupposes that it is sovereign both internally and externally. That is, it is answerable to no external body, and relates to other states as to other autonomous bodies: it can argue with them to try to force them to its view of things. Internally, it is equally unanswerable. Whether an oligarchy, composed of only some of its members, or a democracy composed of all, it makes the laws, it is the arbiter of whether or not those laws have been obeyed, and all citizens are subject to it. Pacifists have challenged both senses of sovereignty, particularly when they discuss the major challenge to the pacifist position: how to respond to violence. They challenge both the state's right to resolve disputes by violence, and its right to command its citizens to commit violence on its behalf. Thus, they challenge the ideas of both internal and external sovereignty, arguing for at least a limited sovereignty which is often extended to the idea of a federated world order on the one hand, and government by the federated councils of directly participating citizens on the other. In this section, we will look at how the pacifist position develops, often from a private religious commitment, into such revolutionary positions.

Many of these arguments also challenge the idea that war can be morally judged, not merely because, as the previous section argues, the consequences of declaring war can never be known, but because war is such a complex event, the outcome of what often retrospectively looks like the inevitable concatenations of actions, misunderstandings, and accidents, that it should be seen as more like a volcanic eruption or the outbreak of famine than the outcome of a deliberate action (as Tolstoy so dramatically showed in *War and Peace*). To look for who is responsible for a war is thus seen as a sort of category mistake, and instead, as with natural disasters, we should seek ways of changing or controlling the conditions which lead to war.

A. Federalist Arguments

These commonly claim that as long as sovereign states treat their own interests as paramount, and seek their unbridled self-interest, there will be conflict between them. However, they also argue that because states can recognize that such conflicts are not in their interest, they can be rationally persuaded to form agreements to abide by international laws, settling their disputes by discussion or, where this cannot be achieved, submitting them to international courts or tribunals. There have been several such proposals, perhaps the most famous being Kant's *Plan for Perpetual Peace*, published in 1795 in response to the horrors of the continental wars of that period. The ideas are often closely linked to liberal and enlightenment projects, which are committed to the view of a universal human nature that recognizes universal rules of reason and morality. Because these definitions of universal reason and right have often been used to disguise particular interests, especially in colonial contexts, it is understandable that they have been met with considerable scepticism, which may partly account for the current failures of the United Nations. Pacifists may reply that a world order or government can only be effective if it is a genuine parliament in which differing perceptions and values can be argued out, rather than the hegemonic imposition of one particular culture's views. This raises the other major difficulty with such proposals. The first international attempt to put them into effect, the League of Nations, came to grief because it did not have the means to contain the aggression of, first, Japan, and then Italy and Germany in the 1930s. Such a world order seems to require the means of violence in order to contain violence.

After the Second World War, the United Nations was founded with theoretically the right to call upon such means. However, it seems scarcely more successful in containing armed conflict. Many argue that this is because the continued existence of sovereign states that treat their own interests as paramount has led to the use of the United Nations as a tool by the most powerful, and certainly the attempt to learn from the errors of the League of Nations and recognise realities by institutionalizing power differentials within the United Nations has made this possible. But here the argument sticks between ineffectual idealism on the one hand, and ineffectual realism on the other. On the whole, pacifists now seem to pay less attention to these federalist ideas than they did in the twenties and thirties, when they were seen as the main hope for world peace, turning from legal solutions in favor of direct involvement by populations. Appeals to an international legal system are now seen less as *the* solution to violence and oppression, more as one possibility that can only work alongside more profound changes within our conceptions of the state and world citizenship.

B. Passive Resistance

In its simplest form, this consists in the refusal to comply with laws or orders considered to be wrong, but without engaging in active opposition to the government. It is thus strictly nonviolent, and suggests the idea of going quietly about your own business while avoiding doing what you consider to be immoral. Although the term seems to have been coined relatively recently (the Oxford English Dictionary gives a novel by Walter Scott, published in 1819, as the first reference), the idea is an ancient one, with Socrates' refusal to desist from his questioning and teaching as perhaps the most famous example. It occurs in a variety of forms, both theoretical and practical, and has been developed by nonpacifists as well as pacifists as a way of resisting violence and opporession.

1. Conscientious Objection

Conscientious objection is really just another term for passive resistance, but is most commonly witnessed in the refusal to serve in the armed forces at the demand of the state. It is thus one of the pacifist's most striking acts of faith, consisting in the claim that their conscience forbids them to kill. It was a feature of the early Christian church within the Roman Empire:

> I cannot become a soldier
> I cannot do evil,
> I am a Christian.
>
> Maximilianus

and later became a defining feature of many Protestant sects, such as the Quakers and Anabaptists.

> Christ Jesu the Prince of Peace who paid tribute to Caesar gives the word of command to his followers to love their enemies, do good to those who hate them and despitefully use them and persecute them. And your command to your followers is to kill your enemies. So that I choose rather to obey the captain of my salvation than you, whatever he may suffer you to inflict upon me for so doing.
>
> Phillip Ford, Quaker, appearing before the Lieutenancy at Guildhall for his refusal to bear arms, 1679.

It is the obvious move for a pacifist to make: if your conscience forbids you to kill, all that you can do is refuse, and suffer the consequences. The action appears to be personal, and apolitical. But although these resistors claim their willingness to "render unto Caesar that which is Caesar's," such behavior effectively undermines the idea of allegiance to the state and is highly political. The individual does what she or he considers to be right, and refuses to make her or his actions hostage to state decisions. If this were universalized, only laws with universal moral consensus would be operable. Traditionally, states have recognized this challenge to their authority. Maximilianus was decapitated and Phillip Ford was fined. But liberal states in the twentieth century, with an enshrined respect for religious rights on the one hand and a pragmatic approach to their authority on the other, generally allow conscientious objection on a narrow religious basis. This effectively confines conscientious objectors to the private religious sphere, and limits the extent to which their resistance might be seen as a challenge to the state and its right to wage war and use force. Such confinement is consistent with the pacifist objection that *he* ought not to kill. But, as has already been pointed out, modern warfare usually requires the collaboration of the entire population, for example, in placing the economy on a war footing and financing the venture through taxation, while at the same time liberal democratic states claim that they act in the people's name. Thus, even if his aim is to do more than keep his conscience clear, it would appear that the pacifist needs to do more than refuse to use weapons, since he is willy-nilly part of and responsible for a war machine. The Peace Tax Campaign, which campaigns to allow citizens to redirect that part of their taxes that is currently used to fund the military into peace-making purposes, is just one attempt to meet this objection. Given that modern war is generally seen to be total war, involving the total population in all its activities, it looks as if pacifists cannot confine their protest to exempting themselves from just one area of the state's activities.

This becomes even clearer when the narrowness of the grounds that the state allows for conscientious objection are considered. Conscientious objection is not confined to pacifists. For example, American conscripts refused to serve in Vietnam on the grounds that they considered that particular war immoral, and members of the Socialist Party of Great Britain refused to serve in the Second World War on the grounds that it was a capitalist war.

But once the state allows its citizens to decide which wars they will support, and which not, it effectively renounces what has hitherto been considered one of its defining rights. On the other hand, it seems unjust to allow religious people some, but not all, of their scruples, and not to allow the nonreligious any.

2. Anarchistic Noncompliance

This carries the ideas developed under conscientious objection to their logical conclusion, asserting on the one hand that the individual ought *always* to consult and follow his or her conscience, regardless of what the state requires and on the other that because the state is based on force and coercion, it is antithetical to the law of love, and therefore its authority should be rejected. This latter move develops the grounds for the pacifist's objection to killing. It is not simply that it is forbidden, but that this injunction follows from the way that individuals ought to relate to each other: through love and care for each other as unique and invaluable creations. Tolstoy is one of the most famous proponents of this view, claiming in his extremely bad-tempered old age that:

> Government is violence, Christianity is meekness, non-resistance, love. And therefore government cannot be Christian and a man who wishes to be Christian must not serve government.
>
> Tolstoy: *Letter to a Hindu*

Such an argument can only appeal to those Christians who hold their own lives lightly, presumably because of their commitment to eternal salvation, and at the same time believe that the force of their love will ultimately defeat evil. Thus, Tolstoy could claim that it was better to be killed by a madman than to restrict his liberty, but few under genuine threat are likely to share this view.

However implausible it may appear, the view is important because of its attempt to apply New Testament morality to public affairs, and thus make clear the revolutionary implications of at least one pacifist position. But, of course, many pacifists stop short of this, arguing that although they have a duty to try to change state behavior as well as keep their integrity, they remain committed to the idea of law and government.

3. Civil Disobedience

Civil disobedience generally consists in the disobedience of a law on moral grounds, usually nonviolently and publicly, and with a willingness to suffer the penalty or at least not to resist or evade it. It can look like a theatrical or rhetorical device, when, for example, highways are blocked in order to call attention to injustices completely unrelated to the traffic laws violated, or it can look like direct conscientious disobedience of a law, for example when Blacks and Whites sat in together at segregated lunch counters in the American South. Accepting the penalty enables protesters to demonstrate their general commitment to legal processes, especially important in the Civil Rights Movement in the United States, when the aim was to get Jim Crow laws recognized as illegal. It thus appears as a device which enables protesters to be proactive in making their moral dissent from a government's policies known, rather than merely passively refusing to obey when they happen to fall foul of them, and at the same time to stop short of anarchist noncompliance. This is significantly more restrained than the suggestions of one of its most famous proponents, Thoreau. Although neither an anarchist nor a pacifist, he argued that if a government committed immoral or unjust actions, then the conscientious citizen should simply dissociate himself from it, refusing to have anything to do with it by, for example, not paying taxes, claiming that:

> Under a government that imprisons any unjustly, the true place for a just man is also in prison.
>
> (Thoreau, *Civil Disobedience*)

This was not a matter of persuading governments to change policy: his view was that he did not have the time for that, merely the duty not to be a party to injustice. But he also argued that it would only take a few living their lives in this way to make government just, so his argument could easily develop either in the direction of seeing civil disobedience as a tool for persuading governments, or in the direction of anarchistic noncompliance. He himself concluded his famous essay with the thought that the most free and enlightened state is that which recognizes the individual as a higher and independent power, from which its authority is derived, and treats him accordingly. He thus indicates one of the most popular defenses of civil disobedience in twentieth-century democracies: that it is best understood as an extension of the democratic process, enabling the populace to inform governments of their most deeply held commitments when the electoral processes fail them. Indeed, Rawls argues in one of the most compelling defenses of civil disobedience that it is a way of reminding the rest of the community of the conditions of one's membership, particularly in the form of basic rights, and calling attention to the fact that these conditions are being violated (John

Rawls, *The justification of civil disobedience,* in Bedau (1969)). Opponents claim that it is destructive of democracy, which can only survive if people are prepared, once they have lost the argument, to abide by rules with which they disagree. However, such an argument can only work if the government is in fact operating in accordance with principles of justice agreed by all in the society, and if all are able to make their voices heard. These conditions are unlikely to be met in modern states that are complex, multicultural, and bureaucratically organized, and civil disobedience has become for many in Western advanced capitalist states the only way that they feel that they can plausibly engage in the political process.

C. Nonviolent Direct Action

Nonviolent direct action (NVDA) consists of taking direct action to change something, but in a way that is supposed to be nonthreatening and nonviolent, and that often effectively makes a particular policy unworkable. Examples range from the entire population donning the yellow Star of David that Jews were ordered to wear in Nazi-occupied Denmark, to the boycotting of products that are marketed in a harmful way, such as certain baby foods. It is thus a clear extension of the idea of civil disobedience, and it can be understood as the political activation of passive resistance, and the political coming of age of pacifism.

The theories so far discussed have all been based, in varying degrees, on the belief that the moral integrity of the individual is paramount, that there is an order of reality, either religious or metaphysical, more important than the political or the social, whereby attention to individual conscience regardless of the consequences will work out for the best, through the persuasive power of the example of love, and that the state is at best irrelevant, and at worst an obstacle, to the development of relationships of peace and harmony between people. It was the genius of Gandhi to take these beliefs (largely, but not exclusively, held by him in the form of Hinduism) and to politicize them. Indeed, he saw political involvement as the outcome of his religious beliefs, not a distraction or impediment to them (as for example Thoreau seemed to think at times).

Gandhi's philosophy began with belief that the main purpose in life is the pursuit of Truth, understood as a state of enlightenment, the realization of the soul's yearning for peace and harmony. For him, Truth was God, and hence many atheists were as godly as devout Hindus, because of their attachment to the truth. He was fond of quoting the parable of the blind men and the elephant, whereby each feeling a different part gives a different, but true, account of the animal. We always see Truth in fragments, from different angles, so the use of force is self-defeating, the only way to acquire truth is through tolerance, and active goodwill and attention to others. He took the Hindu notion of *Ahimsa*, a personal spiritual technique of self-suffering combined with love of others, and turned it into the political idea of nonviolent action. He believed that such action does not seek power, but power accrues to it, because humans unfailingly respond to the advances of love. He therefore trained his followers to be *Satyagrahi*, literally holders-on-to-truth, who would actively practice *ahimsa* or nonviolence in the effort to bring about reform. He described this as working by a kind of moral jujitsu. The violence practiced by oppressors against completely nonviolent resisters, who offered them no threat and treated their persons with love and respect, would ultimately rebound on themselves, and they would no longer be able to tolerate what they were doing. Thus British soldiers would weary of cracking open unresisting heads, and hence the importance of discipline and training for the *satyagrahi*. Not everyone could practice this form of nonviolence.

Gandhi was not only a great religious reformer. He was also politically astute, and noticed that the reason a tiny minority of British could control a population of 200 million could only be because that population cooperated. Hence, withdrawal of that cooperation would lead to the collapse of British rule, and the independence of India. Again, he politicized religious concepts; *dharna* for example, the practice of fasting to death at the door of your opponent, so that he would fear your ghost, became the hunger strike, a way of profoundly embarrassing the British government. Noncooperation could be practiced by any one, for even a child could refuse to wear British manufactured cotton, or join in a political strike by staying away from school. Thus the entire population could be involved. For Gandhi this meant that a genuine independence would be achieved, not simply the replacement of the British Raj by an Indian Raj. To engage in the struggle was to become educated and liberated into the ways of nonviolence and the search for truth, so that autonomy and self-sufficiency would be realized at the level of the individual and the village as well as at the national level. Thus Gandhi saw an intimate link between means and ends; India would only truly be liberated through the active nonviolent participation of all the people in the independence movement, and a genuinely cooperative and self-governing collective life could only be achieved in this way.

NVDA gets over many of the objections to the pacifist position: that it opts for an apolitical, nonresponsible life, leaving others to organize the world and defend the weak. It offers a way for the pacifist to engage actively and responsibly with the problems of the world, and seems to unite the best elements of the forms of passive resistance previously discussed. Indeed, Gandhi read and was influenced by both Tolstoy and Thoreau. Of course, at this point we have ceased to talk about passive resistance and moved into the idea of action for change, and it is this that makes it so attractive to populations in the second half of the twentieth century, particularly those who have either lost faith in the political processes, as in the antinuclear protests in Western Europe and the United States, or have no opportunity to join in them, as in the former Soviet Union or the Philippines under the Marcos regime. Looking at the range of its occasions and aims, it may be tempting to regard it as having moved away from its pacifist roots. But it reflects two important insights of pacifism, which have not so far been explicitly discussed.

(1) That peace does not consist simply in the absence of armed hostilities, and that peace based on injustice is not so much peace as quiet violence, as Martin Luther King said. The pacifist commitment to peace thus implies an opposition to relationships of domination and force, and a people can be more or less at peace depending on the degree of injustice within their society.

(2) That relationships of peace and harmony require changes not only in the organization of states and their relations, but in our persons and the way that we live our lives and resolve our conflicts. If exploitation is implicit in our patterns of consumption, for example, we cannot expect peace.

The main objection to NVDA, as with pacifism generally, remains: can it work? Indian independence is taken as weak evidence for Gandhi's success because it is argued that the British were anxious to leave anyway, that the terrorist tactics being simultaneously employed were equally effective, and that given the violence accompanying independence and the history of India and Pakistan since, Gandhi failed catastrophically in his aims.

These arguments can never be finally resolved because they involve claims about what might have happened, and these can never be substantiated. However, if the main alternative to NVDA is considered to be terrorist or guerrilla activity, as it is by many nationalist and oppressed groups, then its attractions become apparent. Given an increasing integration into a global economic system that appears irresistible by the usual political processes, and a fairly widespread disillusion, particularly among the youth of the West, with the promises of liberal democracy, together with the opportunities for global campaigns such as boycotts, we are probably yet to see the full potential of NVDA.

D. Feminist Challenges

Throughout the twentieth century, a common argument employed by feminists has been that if women were to enjoy the same power as men, this would put an end to the relationships of dominance and competitiveness that appear to make wars an inevitable feature of human history. The argument varies as much as the different theories of feminism, and not all feminists are by any means pacifists. But there is a recurrent theme, that women understand and form human relationships in a different way to men, and that if they had an equal influence on public affairs, the world would be a more peaceable place.

1. Arguments from Motherhood

Arguments from motherhood were part of the suffragette case for claiming that giving women the vote would make the world a better place. At their simplest, they claim that because women give birth, and devote a large part of their energies to nurturing life, they are far more likely to seek ways of preserving it. Unfortunately, the evidence is at best ambiguous. Women in Britain were "rewarded" with the vote for their enthusiastic support of the First World War, and female world leaders have not been noticeably less warlike than male ones. Of course, there are many ad hoc explanations of this: war gave women the opportunity to break out of the restrictions of private life; to succeed in the public world, women have to become like men, and like Lady Macbeth distrust their nature; and so on. A more serious objection is that if war is to be explained by the biological nature of men, then it is a bleak outlook for both peace and women. Nature can, however, be taken out of the argument with the suggestion that whatever our biological natures, the sheer variety of the human experience shows that our possibilities are a complex outcome of the interplay of biological givens, social influence, and sheer creativity, to the point where we can no longer delineate the brute givens. This argument suggests that masculinity and femininity are in some sense structured, and therefore open to changes, and that femininity has been structured by the function of

caring to which women have been traditionally assigned, at least in Western and probably in most societies. This suggests an ethic of care and sensitivity to the needs of others, which is a more promising culture for peace-building than that of a commitment to abstract principles and ideals that, it is claimed, characterize masculinity.

2. Aggressive Male Sexuality

The aggressive structure of male sexuality is cited by feminists as a reason why the world is likely to remain conflict-ridden as long as men, as now, continue to dominate in it. This argument looks like the obverse of the "women as natural peace-makers" one, and is open to the same strictures. Theories behind the claim range from the chemical (e.g., it is due to testosterone) to the psychological (e.g., it is due to the way in which little boys are taught to see themselves as separate from their mothers).

Whatever one thinks of the descriptions and theories of masculinity (and there is not space to examine them here), feminist writers have drawn attention to some striking coincidences between war and sex. Firstly, there is the common use of sexual imagery to talk about weapons and strategies ("vertical erector launchers," "deep penetration," "getting rid of all your stuff," "hardening missiles," "releasing 70% to 80% of our megatonnage in one orgasmic whump"). Phallic imagery and the promise of sexual domination not only dominate in weapons talk and arms sales catalogues, the same metaphors and images together with woman-hating language are used to develop aggressive attitudes in military recruits (e.g., the least offensive is to humiliate recruits by calling them "girlie"). Second, male sexual activity is often represented as violent or aggressive, particularly in pornography. Thus war is sexy, and sex is warlike, and masculine identity and war become intertwined. Thus, for example, General Noriega's "virility is proven by remaining in power," or General Robert H. Barrow, arguing against allowing women into combat: "It tramples the male ego. When you get right down to it, you have to protect the manhood of war."

Finally, rape seems to be a feature of war, as has been most recently and wretchedly demonstrated in Bosnia. The significance of this connection has been variously interpreted: for example it demonstrates that women are seen as property to be seized, the possessions of the enemy rather than protagonists, or it shows the way in which males prove their masculinity (which *does* appear to be a more fragile affair than feminity) through violence. Graphic examples have been provided not only in behavior but in the language soldiers themselves use in just about every theater of armed conflict this century. Thus in Vietnam a "double veteran" meant one who had raped and killed a "native" woman, and in Guatemala members of a civil patrol involved in a "pacification" program were told to prove their masculinity by killing the men and old women and raping the young women in a massacre in the town of Parraxtut.

Such arguments lead to the conclusion that there is a close connection between the way that our personal lives are organized in society and the continued risk of war, and that looking at safer ways of conducting international relationships, or disarmament programs, will be insufficient to guarantee peace as long as control and violence are considered "natural" ordering principles in the relations between men and women. This is not as paralyzing an insight as it first appears, because, as has been argued above, masculinity and femininity are as much social constructs as biological givens, and therefore could be reproduced differently.

3. Women's Restriction to the Private Sphere

Women have been confined to the private sphere, and this gives them insight into the causes of war. Because they are either excluded from, or subservient within, most of those public institutions that shape the state (e.g., universities, governments, courts, and churches) women are able to see them from an outsider's perspective, and particularly to see how they reproduce relationships of hierarchy and dominance. Virginia Woolf, writing on the eve of the Second World War, pointed out the failure of the (male-dominated) disarmament movement to notice the similarities between Mussolini's and Hitler's ideas about how society should be ordered, and those of Church of England clerics and Oxford dons. She argued that, excluded from the male clubs and rituals, mostly dependent, impoverished and vulnerable women should use this vantage point to derive a deeper understanding of militarism and to develop alternative ways of living together, concluding with this message to men:

> You are fighting to gratify a sex instinct which I cannot share; to procure benefits which I have not shared and probably will not share; but not to gratify my instincts; or to protect either myself or my country. 'For', the outsider will say, 'in fact as a woman I have no country. As a woman I want no country. As a woman, my country is the whole world.'

> (Woolf, *Three Guineas*)

Woolf's book provides a persuasive account of how

the exclusion of women in Britain in the twenties and thirties developed not only a scepticism about the state, but an ability to understand the underpinning of the causes of war as relationships of hierarchy and dominance, and this has become a common theme of both feminist and peace movements in the latter half of the twentieth century. Thus, Barbara Deming, a Quaker peace activist on a peace march through the southern United States in 1962 came to realize that the issue of racism could not be kept separate from the peace issue:

> For the issue of war and peace remains fundamentally the issue of whether or not one is going to be willing to respect one's fellow man.

and later, in 1971, that:

> one finds the causes of war in any society that encourages not fellowship, but domination of one person by another. *We must resist whatever gives encouragement to the will to dominate....* Bullets and bombs are not the only means by which people are killed. If a society denies to certain of its members food or medical attention, or a political voice, the sense of their own worth, the freedom to exercise their talents—this, too, is waging war of a kind.

Thus, definitions of war and peace shift through experiences of protest, and some strands of feminism come to look very similar to some forms of anarchism, while feminist agendas, pacifist agendas, and revolutionary or liberationary agendas, often overlap and/or argue with each other. In this way, the apparently private, religious pacifist evolves into a political critic of contemporary societies.

4. Distinctive Forms of Protest

Women in the peace movement have been inspired in their development of NVDA, perhaps because it is a much easier tool for them to use. The security forces tend to be male, and find female protestors both less threatening and more embarrassing than male ones. Thus, the Gandhian image of men lining up to have their skills split open by baton-wielding police, and bandaged up by their attendant women folk, has been replaced by security forces helplessly chasing women dressed up as teddy bears having picnics on bomb silos while their men folk make sandwiches. Women have proved effective not only in poking fun at the apparatus of the state, but also in showing its limits and fragility, entering high-security areas almost at their pleasure.

They have partly achieved this through the development of nonhierarchical forms of cooperation and communication, so that, for example, it was impossible for the authorities to disrupt or stop the actions against the nuclear base at Greenham Common by arresting leaders or seizing means of communication. There were no leaders, and communication was done by networking. The women moved in all areas of society, and could not be isolated, as was vividly demonstrated by the appearance of cards at one of the Queen's Garden Parties proclaiming "Greenham Women are Everywhere."

Because women were behaving politically in what are usually considered private places (laundromats can be political forums, for example), their activities tended to be unnoticed. This is a pattern of political resistance that has been used in many anticolonial movements, as well as movements in Eastern Europe opposing the hegemony of the Soviet Union, and demonstrates Gandhi's perception that the official organs of the state only survive with the cooperative tolerance of their citizens. Feminists have sought to demonstrate the dependence of the state on women's cooperation, and that regardless of their exclusion from public positions, this dependency gives women power.

Women's Peace Camps founded in the 1980s to protest against the acceleration of the nuclear arms race reflected the richness and ambiguity of both the peace movement and the feminist traditions. There was no single commitment or ideal that all had to subscribe to (as, for example, with the Peace Pledge Union). Rather, they provided a forum where people with a more or less agreed-upon core of values came together to discuss and protest. These values included a rejection of violence, a sceptical attitude towards the state, a rejection of domination, including the dominance of men over women, of class, of race, a rejection of neocolonialism and a sympathy with the oppressed wherever they struggled, and an openness to experimenting with new forms of political action. The camps reflected the range of the peace movement.

V. CONCLUSION

We have tried to show how pacifism is best understood as a family of beliefs and values, ranging from a concern that the state should act justly to a fundamental questioning of the state's legitimacy, and from personal religious conviction to active revolutionary doctrine. Likewise, we have seen that passive resistance covers a variety of experiments in consistently living as a pacifist in different contexts. In the twentieth century, as government action has become progressively identified with the peoples in whose name it is taken, and as war involves more of the civilian population, the ideal of pacifism seems to have moved away from a primarily religiously inspired idea, into a political idea inspired by the evils of war, and passive resistance seems correspondingly less concerned with issues of personal redemption, and to have developed into a people's movement of direct nonviolent action concerned to create a safer and more just world.

Also See the Following Articles

CIVIL DISOBEDIENCE • CIVILIAN POPULATIONS IN WAR, TARGETING OF • FEMINIST ETHICS • GENDER ROLES • NUCLEAR WARFARE • TERRORISM • WARFARE, CODES OF

Bibliography

Bedau, H. A. (Ed.). (1969). *Civil disobedience: Theory and practice.* Indianapolis: Pegasus.

Bondurant, J. V. (1965). *Conquest of violence: The Gandhian philosophy of conflict* (Revised ed.). Berkeley: University of California Press.

Ceadel, M. (1987). *Thinking about peace and war.* Oxford: Oxford University Press.

Deming, B. (1984). *We are all part of one another.* Meyerding, J. (Ed.). Philadelphia: New Society Publishers.

Harris, A. & King, Y. (Eds.). (1989). *Rocking the ship of state: Towards a feminist peace politics.* Boulder and London: Westview Press.

Holmes, R. L. (1989). *On War and Morality.* Princeton: Princeton University Press.

Norman, R. (1995). *Ethics, killing and war.* Cambridge: Cambridge University Press.

Parekh, B. (1989). *Gandhi's political philosophy.* London: Macmillan.

Teichman, J. (1986). *Pacifism and the just war.* Oxford: Blackwell.

Walzer, M. (1977). *Just and unjust wars.* Harmondsworth: Penguin and New York: Basic Books.

PAINISM

Richard D. Ryder
Tulane University

I. What Is Painism?
II. Painism and the Environment
III. Free Will
IV. Why Is Pain Bad?
V. Rights and Duties
VI. What Is Morality?

GLOSSARY

painience The capacity to experience pain or other suffering.
painient (Adj.) Capable of experiencing pain or other suffering; (Noun) One capable of experiencing pain or other suffering.
speciesism Hurtful discrimination on the grounds of species

PAINISM is a term proposed by the author to describe his attempt to bring together the utilitarian emphasis upon pain with the emphasis upon the individual that is found in rights theory. He rejects attempts to aggregate the pains of several individuals and argues that the chief moral task is to reduce the suffering of "the maximum sufferer." This article includes the author's views on such issues as environmentalism, free will, rights, and duties, and the nature of morality, in the context of painism.

I. WHAT IS PAINISM?

Painism is a term coined by the author, Richard Ryder, in 1990 to describe the theory that moral value is based upon the individual's experience of pain and that pain is the only evil. Ryder uses "painient" and "painism" to denote, respectively, endowment with the capacity to feel pain (and those possessing this capacity) and the principle that the moral code should be based upon this capacity. Ryder interprets "pain" broadly to include *all* negative experiences, that is to say, all forms of suffering, "mental" as well as "physical." Furthermore, morality is defined as being concerned with the treatment and experience of *others* and not of oneself. As pain is perceived as the only evil, the main moral objective, therefore, is to reduce the pain of others.

Other great moral objectives such as liberty, equality, and fraternity are important, Ryder asserts, only because it is believed (often correctly) that they reduce suffering. For example, why do people want justice? Because it will make them feel less aggrieved; it will reduce their pain. All aims such as justice, equality, and liberty are good only as means toward this end.

Acknowledging that utilitarianism is based upon the recognition of the importance of pain, Ryder nevertheless rejects the aggregation of pains and pleasures among individuals that is a central feature of utilitarianism. Utilitarianism will justify torture if the sum total of benefits to several others is considered to be greater than the pain inflicted. Ryder considers that around each individual is the boundary of its own consciousness and so such aggregations of pains and pleasures across individuals make no sense. There exists a barrier between individuals through which consciousness cannot pass. Ryder states that "however much I empathise or sympathise with your pain I can never feel that *same* pain. So, if there are a hundred people each suffering x amount of pain, the significant pain score is x, and not 100x. If there is one painient suffering 10 units of pain and one suffering 5 units of pain, the meaningful pain score is 10, not the sum total of 15. In other words the morally significant measure of pain in a group of painients is the *maximum* felt by any one of them." Ryder concludes that the moral imperative is to try to reduce the pain of the *maximum sufferer* in each case. If there is a choice between protecting many from mild pain or reducing the severe pain of just one individual then the latter course should be taken.

Painism concentrates upon the conscious experience and Ryder sees consciousness as an emergent property of the individual brain, being anchored to it. The individuality of consciousness is one of its strangest attributes. The question "why is my consciousness mine?" remains unanswered. Ryder tries to reconcile the individuality of consciousness with his support for those physicists who argue that the natural world is interconnected by "fields" that unify apparently distinct entities. "Consciousness, however, is a matter for individuals; we are not aware of being part of any field of consciousness."

The theory of painism was developed as an attempt to reconcile aspects of utilitarianism (viz its emphasis upon *pain*) with the rights tradition (viz its emphasis upon the supreme importance of the individual). Ryder, as the creator of the term "speciesism" is not, of course, speciesist in his use of the word "individual"; this refers to any imaginable painient thing; human, nonhuman, biological, mechanical, terrestrial or alien. As Ryder puts it: "Pain is pain regardless as to who or what experiences it."

The theory of painism has emerged from what was sometimes previously termed "sentientism." Andrew Linzey and Ryder had used this term approvingly while John Rodman had attacked it on the grounds that it established too narrow a moral circle. Ryder eventually rejected "sentientism" in favor of "painism" on three grounds: (1) that sentientism might be deemed to refer to *any* sort of feeling or sensation—"or even to sentient beings incapable of experiencing pain at all," (2) that "sentientism" and "sentient" were words not popularly understood whereas "painism" and "painient" could be easily grasped and thus be of greater use in applied ethics, and (3) that these words usefully fill some significant gaps in the English language.

The Belgian philosopher Johan Braeckman has used the term "pathocentrism" in rather the same sense. Ryder has argued against Braeckman's term on the grounds that the Greek word "pathos," from which pathocentrism presumably is derived, is rather wide in its meaning as it covers not only suffering but also emotion (some of which may not be painful) and disease.

II. PAINISM AND THE ENVIRONMENT

In his classic 1980 paper J. Baird Callicott described a triangular relationship between animal liberation, the land ethic of Aldo Leopold, and conventional humanism. Ryder suggests that all three are subordinate to painism and rejects any form of environmentalist ethic that gives rights to nonpainient things such as rocks and rivers. Such things have undoubted value, but this lies solely in the pain and pleasure that they give to painients. Ecosystems and species are also, per se, nonpainient so their protection is not a moral end in itself.

Ryder divides environmentalism into seven types, nearly all of which are anthropocentric, and calls these, respectively, *thrifty* environmentalism, *aesthetic, scientific, historic, health conscious, compassionate,* and *mystical* environmentalism, according to their principal psychological motive. The thrifty environmentalist is concerned to save energy and resources, the aesthetic to preserve beauty, the scientific to protect what is of scientific interest, the historic to do likewise for things of historic value, and the health conscious is concerned about threats to human health caused by pollution, radiation, and so on. Only the last two types of environmentalism, the compassionate and the mystical, escape the narrow confines of anthropocentrism and show a broader concern for the suffering of creatures for their own sakes, and for nature generally. Basically, there are four alternative ethical positions revealed by these approaches: a concern for all *natural features* (including rocks and rivers and other nonpainients), a concern for the *whole environment,* including human-made features such as buildings, a concern for all *life* (including nonpainient plant life) and Ryder's own position, a concern for all *painient* things. Environmentalists of other types need not fear painism, because all their concerns are subordinate to painism in the sense that damage or destruction of rocks, rivers, beautiful, historic, or scientifically valuable objects, are bound to cause suffering to the animals who inhabit these features or to humans such as themselves. They are thus all issues of concern to painists.

III. FREE WILL

Ryder addresses various problems, common to all moral theories. On "free will" Ryder says: "Decisions to act are made in our brains and are entirely dependent upon the physical state of our brains at the moment the decision is made. However, and this is where complication sets in, notions of what is right and wrong affect the physical condition of our brains and so may affect our decisions. Furthermore, the laws of nature are not at all straightforward but extremely subtle. In as complex a structure as a brain, where the laws of quantum mechanics operate, we do not yet begin to understand how decisions are made. The apparent element of 'free will' which we experience subjectively and, indeed, observe daily in the unpredictable waywardness of others' behaviour is mirrored by the behaviour of subatomic particles. Electrons and photons, for example, behave as if they, too, enjoyed free will. If free will exists, then it manifests as an element of apparent unpredictability throughout the Universe."

IV. WHY IS PAIN BAD?

Another problem for painism is also shared by other theories. On what is its premise based? In the case of painism, why is pain considered to be bad? Ryder replies, "The answer is circular. Morality is about good and bad. In one definition bad simply means painful. Pain itself is always bad even if, *indirectly,* it may lead to benefits. Always we return ultimately to the conscious experience of pain. The lives of all painient creatures are dominated by the twin experiences of pleasure and pain, of reward and punishment, of positive and negative stimuli. These are the two great principles which shape our lives and underlie the main theories of psychology. Morality derives from this fact. What is it that good things have in common? They all give pleasure. What property is it that all bad things share? They all cause pain (in its broad sense). Killing, lying, cheating and stealing are bad because they cause pain. Injustice, inequality, and lack of liberty are bad because they, too, cause pain. Neglecting and rejecting are bad for the same reason. Pain is the common feature of all bad things. A bad thing is that which causes pain."

Ryder adds, "Some may feel puzzled that I emphasise pain rather than pleasure. I admit that I do see them (provided both are defined in their broadest meanings) as opposite ends of the same dimension. Of course, one can experience simultaneously several different sorts of pains and pleasures. (Although it does not make sense to aggregate the pains and pleasures of several individuals it can be quite proper *within the same individual* to do so). But I have chosen to concentrate upon pain rather than pleasure for the reason that the avoidance of extreme pain matters more to us than the achievement of extreme pleasure. At its extreme, pain is more powerful than pleasure can ever be. Pain overrules pleasure within the individual far more effectively than pleasure can dominate pain."

V. RIGHTS AND DUTIES

Scruton, and others, have attacked painism on the grounds that it is allied to rights theory. Ryder replies, "Occasionally, I use the concept of rights and this needs a short explanation. I believe that 'rights' are a human creation and that we bestow them upon others. Rights do not exist on their own. The concept of duty is a similar human invention. Some people like to use the word 'duty' and some prefer the word 'rights.' This depends upon their psychology. Duties and rights are, in my opinion, opposite sides of the same coin. But there *are* different sorts of rights. Legal rights are enshrined in law whereas moral rights are not (yet). Then there are *active* rights (e.g., the right to do something such as vote or own property) and there are *passive* rights (e.g., the right to be tried before a jury). When I speak of rights I am normally speaking of passive moral rights and, principally, *the right not to be deliberately subjected to pain.* Animal rights are, in principle, no different from human rights. In practice, they are based upon degrees of suffering. Therefore, as individuals and species differ in what hurts them, rights will differ between individuals and, quite markedly between species. Equality of concern is for the pain suffered—humans suffer if denied the right to vote so this is important for humans but it is not so for other species. Access to eucalyptus leaves is, however, very important for koalas and so the right of access to eucalyptus leaves is an important right for them." Ryder sees such qualities as self-consciousness, the capacity for abstract thought, autonomy, the capacity for observing duties and so on as morally irrelevant. "Painience is all that matters."

VI. WHAT IS MORALITY?

Ryder has also addressed the fundamental question: "What is morality itself?" He replies, "As a psychologist I see it as a set of rules which assist in the difficult and, indeed painful, business of deciding what we are going to do. Morality is a program which constrains the potential chaos of our complex brains. Morality aids us in making decisions. It reduces the pain of decision-making. Some sort of moral code is a feature of all human societies and, probably, of many nonhuman ones. A sense of right and wrong is closely linked to the experiences of pleasure and pain, of joy and guilt. Morality is something natural; it does not require a god. My dog, Guinevere, has learned what is right and wrong; she knows that her basic impulse to eat the food on the kitchen table has to be restrained by her moral impulse not to do so. Morality, generally speaking, constrains our basic sexual, aggressive, and acquisitive impulses and those moral codes that have tended to produce behaviors with high social survival value have, obviously, tended to survive. Hence, no doubt, the survival of societies that value certain altruistic behaviors. Only one sort of impulse, basically just as unlearned as the others, can sweetly harmonize with morality, and that is our sense of compassion. It is unfashionable to regard compassion as an instinct, but it can be seen in other primates, in elephants and in dolphins; they have sometimes been observed trying to help their stricken comrades. In its more narrow and intense manifestation, compassion is found as parental behavior, which is one of the most powerfully driven of all animal instincts.

Compassion can, of course, be directed and augmented by experience or indeed suppressed or poisoned by it. It can be smothered by the almost universal cult of machismo that teaches people that it is weak or, in some other sense, *wrong* to express compassion. Thus, this side of our natures is frequently concealed and stultified. Habituation, too, to the sight of blood and pain, can dull our compassion."

Ryder has summed up his position thus: "We all have known that twinge of fellow feeling for other painient individuals. We need to build upon it a rational moral code aimed at the conquest of pain. Pain is, after all, the common enemy for all of us who live in the great transpecies community of pain. Our consciousness on this planet does not last long but, while it does, we should try to help one another to reduce the suffering it contains."

Also See the Following Articles

ANIMAL RIGHTS • ANTHROPOCENTRISM • ENVIRONMENTAL ETHICS • GAIA HYPOTHESIS • LAND USE ISSUES • RIGHTS THEORY • SPECIESISM • UTILITARIANISM

Bibliography

Callicott, J. B. (1980). Animal Liberation: A Triangular Affair. *Environmental Ethics* 2, 311–338.

Regan, T. (1983). *The case for animal rights.* University of California Press: Berkeley.

Ryder, R. D. (1989). *Animal revolution: Changing attitudes towards speciesism.* Oxford: Basil Blackwell Ltd.

Ryder, R. D. (1991). *Painism: Ethics, animal rights and environmentalism.* University of Wales.

Ryder, R. D. (1992). Painism: Ethics, animal rights and environmentalism. *Global Bioethics,* 5 4, 27–35.

Ryder, R. D. (1992). *Introduction to animal welfare and the environment* (Ed Ryder). London: Duckworth.

Ryder, R. (1995). Speciesism. In *On the Side of the Animals.* RSPCA Leaflet. And in *Concerns for Animals,* RSPCA Leaflet, (Jennings, M. J., and Silkock, S., Eds. for both).

Ryder, R. D. (1996). Non Lethal Control. In *Report to the Ministry of Agriculture from the Wildlife Conservation Unit,* Oxford University.

Ryder, R. D. (1997). Speciesism and Painism. Andrew Mellon Lecture. New Orleans: Tulane University.

Scruton, R. (1996). *Animal rights and wrongs.* London: Demos.

Singer, P. (1975). *Animal liberation: Towards an end to man's inhumanity to animals* (1st ed.). New York: New York Review of Books.

PALLIATIVE CARE

Robert Twycross
Oxford University

GLOSSARY

analgesic Drugs that reduce the perception of pain without loss of consciousness; colloquially called painkillers.

distancing behavior A form of behavior by which a carer avoids becoming psychosocially involved with a patient, usually without being aware of it, for example, by selective attention to physical problems or by saying, when faced with a distressed patient, "Don't worry, everyone in your position feels upset" instead of inquiring into the specific causes of the distress.

hope In this context, an expectation greater than zero of achieving a goal. Without a goal or focus, there is no hope. Hope is an essential part of palliative care.

opioid A generic term to describe drugs with actions similar to codeine (weak opioids) and morphine (strong opioids). Uses include pain relief, cough sedation, and control of diarrhea.

opiophobia A term used to describe the irrational fears of many physicians and drug regulatory authorities about the medicinal use of morphine and other strong opioids. Opiophobia stems from fears about addiction (which virtually never happens in cancer patients in pain) and about diversion into the black market (which is minimal or nonexistent in countries where medicinal morphine is readily available). As a result, most countries still do not have oral preparations of morphine available for cancer pain management.

rehabilitation The process of enabling disabled individuals to achieve their maximum potential for normal living, physically, emotionally, socially, and vocationally.

religion A shared framework of theistic beliefs and rituals that gives expression to spiritual concerns.

spiritual Relating to values (ultimate issues and life principles) and to a person's search for meaning and purpose in life. The term also refers to experiences and relationships that transcend sensory phenomena. The spiritual dimension may also be viewed as the integrating component, holding together the physical, psychological, and social dimensions.

Encyclopedia of Applied Ethics, Volume 3

PALLIATIVE CARE is the active total care of patients and their families by a multiprofessional team at a time when the patient's disease is no longer responsive to curative treatment and life expectancy is relatively short. The word "palliative" is derived from the Latin word *pallium*, meaning a cloak or cover. Thus, if the cause cannot be cured, symptoms are "cloaked" with or "covered" by specific treatments, for example, analgesics and anti-emetics. Palliative care, however, is far broader and deeper than mere "symptomatology." The term implies a holistic approach that considers not only physical but also psychological, social, and spiritual concerns. Its main goals are to provide

- relief for patients from pain and other distressing symptoms;
- psychological and spiritual care for patients so that they may come to terms with and prepare for their own death as fully as they can;
- a support system to help the patients live as actively and creatively as possible until death, thereby promoting autonomy, personal integrity and self-esteem;
- a support system to help families cope during the patient's illness and in bereavement.

Palliative care both affirms life and recognizes dying as a normal process. It seeks neither to hasten nor to postpone death. Thus, while not limited by "the tyranny of cure," palliative care is steadfastly opposed to euthanasia.

I. PHILOSOPHY OF PALLIATIVE CARE

Palliative care has developed largely as a result of the initial vision and inspiration of Dame Cicely Saunders who founded St. Christopher's Hospice in London in 1967. (Hospice care is essentially synonymous with palliative care and the two terms will be used interchangeably here). Centuries ago, "hospice" meant a resting place for travelers or pilgrims. The word survived in connection with several convent hospitals or nursing homes. Dame Cicely was attracted to the name because of her desire to provide a type of care that combined the skills of a hospital with the more leisurely hospitality and warmth of a home. In the hospice, the center of interest shifts from the disease to the patient and family, from the pathological process to the person.

Patients with terminal disease often need more care than those whose sickness is curable. Thus, palliative care offers "intensive terminal care." Professional skills of a high order are required; expert care that is individual to the patient, detailed, sensitive, and time-consuming. Palliative care is distinct from geriatric medicine and the care of the chronically sick, two specialties with which it is frequently compared:

It contains many of the rewards of surgery, since it operates in a setting of crisis intervention; of internal medicine, since it calls for the fine titration of drug regimens against troublesome symptoms; and of psychiatry, since it deals with the anxious, the depressed and the bereaved (Mount, B. M. (1980). Hospice care. *Journal of the Royal Society of Medicine*, 73. 471–473).

Palliative care developed as a reaction against the limitations of modern high-technology medicine. Halina Bortnowska, a Polish philosopher, author, and hospice volunteer, has contrasted the ethos of cure with the ethos of care. She defines ethos as a "constellation of values held by people." The ethos of cure encompasses the military virtues of fighting, not giving up, and endurance, and necessarily contains a measure of hardness. In contrast, the ethos of care has human dignity as its central value and stresses the solidarity between the patient and the caregivers, an attitude that results in "effective compassion." In curing, "the physican is the general," whereas in caring "the patient is the sovereign." It is important to give the patient the power to decide as much as possible for as long as possible.

Thus, palliative care seeks to prevent *last* days becoming *lost* days by offering a type of care that is appropriate to the needs of the dying. Although it has been described as "low-tech and high-touch," palliative care is not intrinsically against modern medical technology. Rather, it seeks to ensure that love and not science is the controlling force in patient care. High-technology investigations and treatments are used only when their benefits clearly outweigh the probable burdens. Science is used in the service of love and not vice versa. Palliative care is an attempt to reestablish the traditional role of doctors and nurses "to cure sometimes, to relieve often, to comfort always."

II. ORIGINS

A. Medieval Hospices

The original hospices go back to Fabiola, a Roman matron who opened her home for those in need in the fourth century, setting out to fulfill the Christian "works of mercy"—feeding the hungry and thirsty, visiting the sick and prisoners, clothing the naked, and welcoming the stranger. The word "hospis" then meant both host and guest, and "hospitium" included both the place where hospitality was given and the ensuing relationships. That emphasis is still central to hospice care today. The church subsequently attempted to carry the burden of caring for the poor and the sick, and continued this throughout the Middle Ages. In Britain this came to an abrupt end with the dissolution of the monasteries in the sixteenth century. None of these early hospices set out specifically to care for the dying but they welcomed people to stay as long as they needed help and would have included many who died. After the dissolution, many must have died at home in great poverty and discomfort.

B. Hospices for the Dying

The first hospice founded specifically for the dying was possibly in Lyons in 1842. After visiting dying cancer patients in their homes, Madame Jeanne Garnier opened what she called both a hospice and a Calvaire. She went on to open several others, most of which still exist. In Britain, the first revived use of the word hospice was in 1905 by the Irish Sisters of Charity at St. Joseph's in Hackney. Their founder, Mother Mary Aikenhead, had previously opened a hospice for the dying in Dublin in 1879 but there was no connection between her and Madame Garnier. Other homes were opened in London about the same time, including St. Columba's in 1885, the Hostel of God in 1892, and St. Luke's Home for the Dying Poor in 1893.

St. Luke's Home was the only one founded by a physician, Dr Howard Barrett. Of all the homes, Dr Barrett's was the most similar in principle to today's "modern hospice," full of particular and personal interest in the patients. Dr Barrett left a series of Annual Reports in which he writes not of "the poor" or "the dying" but of individual persons and their desolate families left at home without support. Subsequently, the National Society for Cancer Relief was founded in 1911 by Douglas Macmillan, a civil servant, to provide financial grants to families of cancer patients dying at home, enabling the purchase of extra comforts such as blankets, heating, and food.

C. St. Christopher's Hospice

Perhaps the next significant event was the increasing interest of a lady almoner (medical social worker) in the needs of dying patients at St. Thomas' Hospital in London. Her name was Cicely Saunders and her interest had been sparked by her encounter in 1948 with David Tasma, a Jewish refugee from Poland, who was dying of cancer. Together they discussed the type of institution that would best satisfy his needs. In addition to pain relief he wanted "nearness to someone who saw him as another person." He bequeathed £500 to Cicely "to be a window in your home."

The road from 1948 to 1967 was long and hard. Cicely Saunders worked as a volunteer nurse in the evenings at St. Luke's Home for 7 years. While there, she learned the value of regular "round-the-clock" oral strong opioids, notably morphine and diamorphine, for relieving severe cancer pain. It was necessary for the former Oxford English graduate to study science and gain entry into medical school. After qualifying Dr. Saunders became the first full-time doctor to work at St. Joseph's Hospice where she introduced the regular "round-the-clock" use of oral analgesics instead of "as required" injections. She also developed other aspects of symptom management, and began to plan her own hospice.

St. Christopher's Hospice opened in South London in July 1967 with 54 beds and associated accommodation for 16 elderly frail persons. It attracted much outside interest and soon became a rallying point in a protest movement for those who yearned for a better deal for the dying—rejects from a health system that, during the middle years of the twentieth century, had become progressively seduced by the glamor of curative treatment and the glitter of high technology.

D. Cancer Relief Macmillan Fund

Cancer Relief Macmillan Fund (formerly National Society for Cancer Relief) corporately became the major influence in the development of palliative care in Britain during the late 1970s after it had become involved in the development of the first hospices within the British National Health Service. In the 1980s several initiatives were greatly facilitated by financial "pump-priming" by Cancer Relief, including

- the development of a community hospice nursing service (Macmillan nurses);
- the establishment of academic posts in palliative medicine and palliative nursing;
- support for senior registrar posts to train future specialists in palliative medicine.

There were many local initiatives that often drew on the public relations and fund-raising skills of Cancer

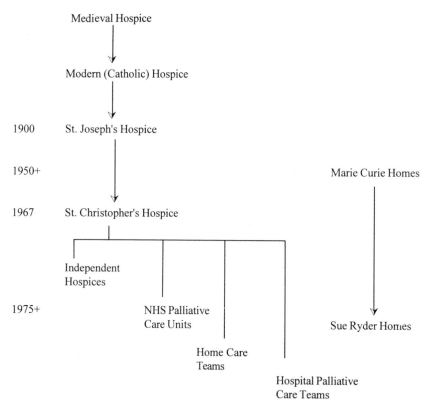

Medieval Hospice

Modern (Catholic) Hospice

1900 St. Joseph's Hospice

1950+   Marie Curie Homes

1967 St. Christopher's Hospice

Independent
Hospices

1975+
                        NHS Palliative
                        Care Units
                                                                   Sue Ryder Homes

                                    Home Care
                                    Teams

                                              Hospital Palliative
                                              Care Teams

FIGURE 1   The evolution of palliative care in the UK.

Relief Macmillan Fund. Simultaneously, Marie Curie Cancer Care upgraded its nursing homes to modern hospice standards, paralleled by the establishment of several Sue Ryder Homes (Figure 1). As a result, there are now few communities in the United Kingdom that do not have access to some form of specialist palliative care. Because it has not always been possible or desirable to build a separate institution, other approaches have been adopted including home care programs and hospital palliative care teams. Coordination is now facilitated by the National Council for Hospice and Specialist Palliative Care Services.

E. Further Developments

Because of the often distinct physical and nonphysical needs of people with AIDS, separate palliative care services have been set up in several major cities. In most localities, however, AIDS patients are cared for alongside those with cancer. An increasing number of hospices are also caring for patients with end-stage respiratory, cardiac, and renal disease, although the numbers are still relatively small.

Since the mid-1980s several children's hospices have been established. Helen House, situated in the grounds of an Oxford convent, was the first. It was built as a result of the enthusiasm and commitment of Sister Frances Dominica, then Mother Superior of her order. Children's hospices are very different from adult ones. Typically, there will be only some eight beds with more facilities for family members. Many of the children have degenerative neurological diseases, often associated with congenital metabolic disorders. Most admissions are for family respite and recur at regular intervals every 2 to 3 months over several or many years. The number of deaths per annum is relatively small. In contrast to adults, children with leukemia or cancer if not cured are mostly cared for until death within the specialist (paediatric) departments of major hospitals, often with extended care into the home when desired and if feasible.

The Association of Palliative Medicine of Great Britain and Ireland was formed in 1985 and two years later the United Kingdom became the first country to recognize palliative medicine as a medical specialty. All U.K. nursing and medical schools include palliative care in their curricula. Postgraduate palliative care training programs have also been established, including several diploma and degree courses.

III. INTERNATIONAL DEVELOPMENTS

A. United States of America

Cicely Saunders' influence spread progressively to other countries and her "torch" has been picked up and carried even further afield by an increasing army of second and third generation enthusiasts. Inevitably and rightly, what has developed has often differed substantially from the British model. In the United States, despite the early development of an inpatient facility at the Connecticut Hospice, most hospices provide only home care support. Further, whereas the British hospice medical director is usually a full-time (or nearly full-time) physician, in the United States the hospice medical director has been very much part-time and sometimes nominal. Indeed, within the U.S. hospice movement initially and for many years, the prevailing ethos was strongly antiphysician. In the late 1970s and early 1980s, hospice U.S. was very much a grass-roots, community-based, volunteer- and nurse-led organization that frequently actively discouraged or limited physician input.

This initial reaction was partly because nurses in the United States were quicker to catch a vision for hospice and partly because the medical establishment generally was antipathetic. Health care in the United States is largely insurance-based and there were considerable financial disincentives for both physicians and hospitals because hospice care was not initially covered by health insurance schemes. This meant that offering palliative care resulted in a loss of income for the physician, and for a hospital if a patient needed to be admitted. Although hospice care is now a legally required component of health insurace schemes in the United States, old attitudes and prejudices linger on. Part of the reluctance of the American medical profession to embrace palliative care wholeheartedly appears to stem from the reluctance of the American Medical Association to acknowledge the achievements of the hospice movement in the United States over the last 20 years. Some 2000 individual hospice programs are presently affiliated to the American National Hospice Organization.

B. Poland

In contrast, palliative care in Poland was sparked in the early 1980s by the banning of the workers' union, Solidarity, by the then-communist government. Senior doctors in the medical academies who had become members of Solidarity were removed from their posts and obliged to work in less prestigious government hospitals. Several of these doctors in Gdansk—the home of Solidarity—decided to develop a hospice program under the protection of the Roman Catholic church as one way of giving substance to their opposition to the government.

In this and in similar voluntary organizations, doctors fulfilled most of the necessary roles. Thus in practice, the original Polish hospice doctor was akin to a cross beween a substitute general practitioner and a specialist community palliative care nurse. Now there are many hospice groups in Poland and some inpatient facilities. Medically, however, it is still largely voluntary with doctors earning their living in their original specialty and working mainly after hours for the hospice.

C. A Widening Network

In other countries, developments have also reflected local needs, opportunities, and resources. In some, palliative care provision mirrors the British model to a greater or lesser extent (e.g. Canada, Australia, New Zealand); in others it reflects more the model in the United States and Poland. Everywhere it has met with initial resistance from oncologists and indifference in the medical establishment. The reasons for this are debatable but Halina Bortnowska's contrast between the ethos of cure versus the ethos of care probably provides the key to the answer. Many countries have founded national multiprofessional associations for palliative care. In addition there is a Nordic association and a European one.

D. The World Health Organization

A second powerful lobby for palliative care since the mid-1980s has been the World Health Organization. Under the visionary leadership of Dr. Jan Stjernsward, the Cancer Unit of the World Health Organization has campaigned for countries to develop comprehensive cancer control programs comprising

- prevention;
- early detection and curative treatment;
- pain relief and palliative care.

The publication of *Cancer Pain Relief* (Geneva: World Health Organization) in 1986 proved to be a major catalyst. This book, which incorporates the WHO Method for Relief of Cancer Pain, is the second most translated WHO publication ever. In addition to English, it is available in 19 other languages: Arabian, Brazilian, Bulgarian, Chinese, Croatian, Czech, French, German, Gujarati, Hindi, Hungarian, Italian, Japanese, Portuguese, Russian, Spanish, Thai, Turkish and Vietnamese. This publication, with over a quarter of a million copies sold and distributed, reflects the growing awareness of the problem of cancer pain. The WHO Method emphasizes that a small number of relatively inexpensive drugs, including morphine, are the mainstay of cancer pain management. Field testing has demonstrated the efficacy of the guidelines in most cancer patients. The original WHO Method has now been updated and published in the second edition of *Cancer Pain Relief.*

IV. OVERALL STRATEGY

In practice most patients cared for in hospices or by palliative care teams have cancer. Palliative care is part of a comprehensive approach to cancer control. Curative treatment with surgery, radiotherapy, and/or chemotherapy often has to be aggressive ("radical") if it is to be successful. Such treatment is justified only

- when cure is possible;
- when there is a realistic chance of worthwhile prolonging of life;
- in a clinical trial of a new, potentially effective method of treatment.

The decision to withhold curative therapy and to offer palliative care is a crucial one; attempts to cure the incurable are not in the best interest of patients who really need palliative care.

Even nonradical anticancer treatment (called palliative *treatment*) should not be offered unless there is a real possibility of the physical, psychological, and financial burdens of treatment being more than offset by the potential benefits for the patient. Prolonging life by a few weeks or months is generally not adequate justification from the patient's point of view if the cost is a markedly reduced quality of life for much of the extra time because of adverse treatment effects or financial ruin because of the cost. In most developed countries, despite overall 5-year survival exceeding 50%, some 70% of all cancer patients still need palliative care sooner or later. In developing countries, the figure is at least 90%. In practice, there are some patients who benefit from palliative *treatment* and palliative *care* concurrently. Here it is appropriate to offer a package

of "shared care" with both oncology and palliative care teams involved.

V. SPECIALIST PALLIATIVE CARE SERVICES

Specialist palliative care services in the United Kingdom now embrace

- community nursing services (Macmillan and Marie Curie nurses);
- medical consultations (palliative medicine specialists) both at home with the general practitioner and on other wards and in neighboring hospitals;
- outpatient clinics;
- day care;
- inpatient care;
- bereavement support;
- education (usually);
- research (sometimes).

Typically, about 95% of patients have cancer. AIDS and motor neurone disease (amyotrophic lateral sclerosis) account for most of the others. Although each service has a contract with one or more local health authority, additional money is obtained by fundraising in the community to provide anything from 30 to 70% of the total cost of the service. Palliative care in the United Kingdom is therefore free of charge to the patient whether it is provided directly by the National Health Service (NHS) or by an independent hospice or charity.

A. Home Care

The first community palliative care team began at St Christopher's Hospice in 1969. There are now over 400 home care teams, of which about a third are attached to an inpatient unit. Most have been initially funded by Cancer Relief Macmillan Fund. Specialist home care nurses (Macmillan nurses) liaise with the primary health care team and offer advice on treatment and care. A survey conducted by the Hospice Information Service at St Christopher's Hospice has shown that annually in the United Kingdom some 100,000 new patients are seen at home by palliative care nurses. This is more than 60% of all patients dying of cancer. Because they provide support for the whole family, more patients are able to remain at home until death.

B. Support Teams

Most palliative care units offer a consultation service (doctor, nurse or both) for patients in the community or in hospital. In over 300 hospitals, consultation has evolved into a palliative care support team—or has been established ab initio. The first such team was set up in 1976 at St Thomas' Hospital, London.

C. Day Care

The first purpose-built palliative care day center opened in 1975 at St Luke's Hospice, Sheffield. There are now over 230 day centers, of which about two-thirds are attached to inpatient units. Typically, a day center receives from 10 to 15 patients a day. Patients are driven to and from the center by volunteers. Patients attend for social support and to give the family a break. Medical and nursing care is also available. Services include bathing, hairdressing, manicure, massage, chiropody, and dentistry. Day patients often find new meaning and purpose in living as they make new friends, explore opportunities for creative expression, and enjoy cultural activities together. A day center also enables many patients to remain at home for much longer than would otherwise be possible.

D. Inpatient Care

There are more than 3200 inpatient beds dedicated to palliative care in the United Kingdom and Ireland distributed among some 220 units (Table 1). Only about 25% of these are within the NHS; the rest are in independent hospices. The number of beds per unit ranges from 2 to 63. Patients are admitted for symptom management, for family respite, or to die. A high nurse–patient

TABLE 1

Inpatient Palliative Care Units in the United
Kingdom and the Republic of Ireland
(January 1997)

Category	Number	Beds
Independent Hospice	148	2218
National Health Service	56	595
Marie Curie Cancer Care	11	289
Sue Ryder Foundation	8	151
	223	3253

Source: Hospice Information Service, St. Christopher's Hospice, London, U.K.

ratio is maintained because the physical and psychological needs of the patients are often considerable. Even so, about half of all admissions end with the patient returning home or to relatives. Rehabilitation is facilitated by occupational therapy and physiotherapy. The median length of stay is typically from 8 to 10 days. Less than 20% of all deaths from cancer in the United Kingdom occur in palliative care units.

E. Bereavement Support

This may be provided in various ways, often by trained volunteers under the supervision of a social worker. Support is offered to bereaved close relatives and other key carers if considered to be at risk of high psychological morbidity. Support may also be continued after bereavement by a Macmillan nurse.

F. Voluntary Help

Volunteers are involved in many aspects of palliative care, and are usually selected and monitored by a paid voluntary services coordinator. Volunteers receive initial and continuing inservice training. At some hospices, certain volunteers are trained for more specific tasks such as helping within a patient's home and bereavement support.

G. Education and Research

Education is an important aspect of specialist palliative care. Courses of various duration and intensity give opportunity for other health care professionals to learn how to care better for dying patients. Research is important if the care of dying patients is to be improved further. It is time consuming and costly, however, and is undertaken by only a small number of palliative care units.

In relation to pain and symptom management, there is the added difficulty of evaluating treatments in patients who are not physically stable, and who often have to be withdrawn from studies because of rapid deterioration and/or death. This means that data from formal randomized controlled trials will always be hard to come by in patients receiving palliative care. Yet, despite the humanitarian and practical difficulties, the volume of research being undertaken is increasing and it embraces both quantitative and qualitative approaches. Research is actively encouraged by the increasing number of academic departments of palliative medicine and palliative nursing, and by the establishment of the Palliative Care Research Forum of Great Britain and Ireland.

VI. PARADOX

Those visiting a hospice for the first time often comment that it is not the gloomy and depressing place they had imagined it to be. Instead they find a place which reeks of life and even joy. A strange discovery—life and joy in the midst of death and distress—but it is perhaps in this paradox that the "secret" of palliative care resides.

To set out to create a paradox of this nature is probably impossible. Life and joy in the midst of death and distress, however, is the end result of more down-to-earth activities—like nursing care, symptom management, and psychological support—stemming from *practical human compassion*. This, in turn, is the outworking of an attitude of respect for the patient and of corporate activity in which individualism is balanced by teamwork and vice versa. The "House of Hospice" model is a good way of expressing this (Figure 2), with its foundation stones of *acceptance* ("Whatever happens, we will not abandon you") and *affirmation* ("You may be dying but you are important to us"). The cement which binds the various components together comprises hopes, openness, and honesty.

Caring for the dying is not easy. One physician described it as "extremely harrowing but very rewarding." It is difficult but, paradoxically, it often has a positive "spin-off"—and not just for the professional carers. A journalist wrote the following after his wife's death:

Of course terminal cancer is unspeakably awful. That aspect needs no emphasis. More dif-

ficult to imagine is the blessedness which is the corollary of the awfulness ... I think my wife learnt more of our love during those dreadful months than she did at any other time, and we of hers ... The suffering of a long and terminal illness is not all waste. Nothing that creates such tenderness can be all waste. As a destroyer, cancer is second to none. But it is also a healer, or an agent of healing.

A patient dying of motor neurone disease (creeping paralysis) spoke of terminal illness as "coming together illness." After many weeks as an inpatient at St. Christopher's Hospice, he said, "I've seen it time and time again. Patient and family; patient and patient; patient and staff—coming together illness."

VII. ETHICS OF PALLIATIVE CARE

The ethics of palliative care are, of course, those of medicine in general. Perhaps the biggest challenge facing doctors globally in relation to palliative care is the question of truthfulness with patients who are terminally ill. Reluctance to share the truth with the patient about his/her condition ultimately stems from the doctor's own fear of death and associated cultural pressures. It is still often stated that to tell patients that they are terminally ill will destroy hope and lead to irreversible despair and depression. In reality the opposite is more often the case—lying and evasion isolate patients behind either a wall of words or a wall of silence that prevents the therapeutic sharing by the patient of fears, anxieties, and other concerns. It is not possible to offer good palliative care without a prior commitment to openness and honesty. The primary ethical challenge for many doctors, therefore, is to equip themselves with good, sensitive communication skills. Fortunately, awareness of this need is growing but globally lack of training in this area is still widespread.

A. Appropriate Treatment

Doctors have a dual responsibility, namely to preserve life and to relieve suffering. At the end of life, however, relief of suffering becomes of even greater importance as preserving life becomes increasingly impossible. Part of the art of medicine is to decide when sustaining life is essentially futile and, therefore, when to allow death to occur without further impediment. A doctor is not obliged legally or ethically to preserve life "at all costs." Rather, life should be sustained when from a biological

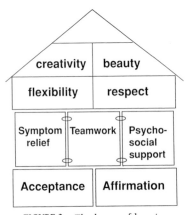

FIGURE 2   The house of hospice.

point of view it is sustainable. Priorities change when a patient is clearly dying and there is no obligation to employ treatments if their use can best be described as prolonging the process of dying. A doctor has neither duty nor right to prescribe a lingering death (Box A).

Thus, it is not a question of "to treat or not to treat" but "what is the most appropriate treatment?" given the patient's biological prospects and his personal and social circumstances. Appropriate treatment for an acutely ill patient may be inappropriate in the dying (Figures 3 and 4). Nasogastric tubes, intravenous infusions, antibiotics, cardiac resuscitation, and artificial respiration are all primarily support measures for use in acute or acute-on-chronic illnesses to assist a patient through the initial crisis toward recovery of health. To use such measures in patients who are close to death and in whom there is no expectation of a return to health is usually inappropriate (and therefore bad medicine).

Medical care is a continuum, ranging from complete cure at one end to symptom relief at the other. Many types of treatment span the entire spectrum, notably radiotherapy and, to a lesser extent, chemotherapy and surgery. It is important to keep the therapeutic aim

conditions and what are the prior expressed wishes of the patient and attitudes of the family or those who have responsibility for the custody of the patient. Even if death is not imminent but a patient's coma is beyond doubt irreversible and there are adequate safeguards to confirm the accuracy of the diagnosis and with the concurrence of those who have responsibility for the care of the patient, it is not unethical to discontinue all means of life-prolonging medical treatment.

Life-prolonging medical treatment includes medication and artificially or technologically supplied respiration, nutrition, or hydration. In treating a terminally ill or irreversibly comatose patient, the physician should determine whether the benefits of treatment outweigh its burdens. At all times, the dignity of the patient should be maintained. (Dickey, N. (1986). Withholding or withdrawing life-prolonging medical treatment. *Journal of the American Medical Association, 256,* 471.)

---

clearly in mind when employing any form of treatment. In deciding what is appropriate, the key points to bear in mind are

- the patient's biological prospects;
- the therapeutic aim and benefits of each treatment;
- the adverse effects of treatment;
- the need not to prescribe a lingering death.

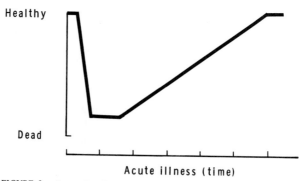

FIGURE 3   A graphical representation of acute illness. Biological prospects are generally good. Acute resuscitative measures are important and enable the patient to survive the initial crisis. Recovery is aided by the natural forces of healing; rehabilitation is completed by the patient on his own, without continued medical support. (Reproduced with permission from Radcliffe Medical Press.)

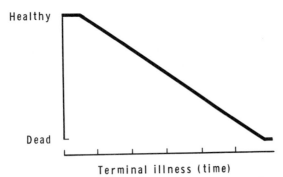

FIGURE 4   A graphical representation of terminal illness. Biological prospects progressively worsen. Acute and terminal illnesses are therefore distinct pathophysiological entities. Therapeutic interventions that can best be described as prolonging the distress of dying are both futile and inappropriate. (Reproduced with permission from Radcliffe Medical Press.)

Although the possibility of unexpected improvement or recovery should not be ignored, there are many occasions when it is appropriate to "give death a chance." Many doctors, however, find it extremely difficult to switch from a cure modus operandi to comfort care. This is perhaps one reason why the use of advance directives is becoming increasingly popular in many countries.

B. Opposition to Euthanasia

The almost unanimous opposition to physician-assisted suicide and euthanasia by palliative care doctors and nurses stems from the reality of looking after countless dying patients. Rather than soften attitudes towards these options, it appears to harden antagonism. Reasons for this are manifold but include patient vulnerability, patient ambivalence, and the fact that almost all patients who request physician-assisted suicide or euthanasia change their minds when provided with good quality palliative care. There is also the seeming impossibility of containing practice, if legalized, within secure limits.

The term "indirect euthanasia" has been used to describe the administration of morphine to cancer patients in pain. This is incorrect; giving a drug to lessen pain cannot be equated with giving an overdose deliberately to end life. Should life be marginally shortened by the use of morphine or related drugs, this is an acceptable risk in the circumstances (principle of double effect). Correctly used, however, such drugs are much safer than commonly supposed. There is circumstantial evidence that those whose pain is relieved may outlive those whose nutrition and rest continue to be disturbed by persistent pain.

C. Nutrition and Hydration

As the patient nears death, food and fluid intake generally diminish. It is at this time that the question is raised whether to administer fluids by artificial means. The traditional hospice view is that when interest in food and fluid becomes minimal, a terminally ill patient should not be forced to receive them. Indeed, eating and drinking at this time may no longer be relevant to the patient who has already withdrawn and whose attention is now inward or "beyond." Nonetheless, many dying patients automatically receive intravenous fluids when no longer able to maintain a normal fluid balance. The main reason for this appears to be a belief that dehydration in a person close to death is distressing. Hospice staff, however, have generally taken the view that dehydration may well be beneficial, and hydration often detrimental. It is claimed that with dehydration there is decreased urine output and less need for urinal, commode, or catheterization, and fewer bed-wetting episodes. A reduction in pulmonary secretions is said to result in less coughing and a decrease in choking and drowning sensations, with less need for suctioning. Likewise decreased gastrointestinal secretions result in fewer bouts of vomiting in patients with intestinal obstruction. Pain may also decrease due to a reduction in tissue swelling around tumor masses.

Intravenous hydration also has negative psychosocial effects in that the infusion acts as a barrier between the patient and the family. It is more difficult to embrace a spouse who is attached to a plastic tube, and doctors and nurses tend to become diverted from the more human aspects of care to the control of fluid balance and blood chemistry. Families are often distressed as patients near death drastically decrease their oral intake. Their feelings on intravenous therapy and its significance to them should be established and the rationale for discontinuing intravenous therapy explained. The decision regarding rehydration should focus on the comfort of the patient, rather than on the goal of providing optimal nutrition and hydration.

On the other hand, others claim that the administration of hypodermic fluids (500–1500 ml/24h) circumvents many of the objections to other artificial methods of hydration. To date however there is no evidence that rehydration generally makes patients more comfortable. Hypodermic fluid has also been reported to relieve delirium in some dying patients. On the other hand, improved cognition has also been reported after the withdrawal of hydration.

Among suggested indications for rehydration are a patient feeling dry despite good mouth care. Dry mouth is common in cancer patients and is related not only to dehydration, but to other causes such as drugs, oral infection, local radiotherapy, oxygen therapy, and mouth breathing. Thus, artificial hydration alone is unlikely to resolve the symptom of dry mouth in most patients. On the other hand, dry mouth can be relieved to a great extent by conscientious mouth care and 1 to 2 ml of water delivered by pipette or syringe into the dependent side of the mouth every 30 to 60 minutes.

VIII. REHABILITATION

Although probably surprising to the outsider, rehabilitation is an integral part of palliative care. Many terminally ill patients are unnecessarily restricted, often by relatives, even though capable of a greater degree of activity and independence. A patient's maximum potential will be achieved, however, only if troublesome symptoms are relieved and gentle encouragement is given by an attentive physician.

Not all physicians appreciate the opportunities that exist for rehabilitation in advanced cancer. This stems partly from relative inexperience in palliative care, but possibly also from excessively negative attitudes toward cancer. It is possible to live for 5 or more years with bone secondaries from breast cancer. Hormone therapy can radically alter prognosis in the patient with newly diagnosed disseminated prostatic cancer. The median survival after diagnosis of cancer of the pancreas may be less than 6 months but this means that half the patients live longer, and a few much longer. Further, symptom relief alone may well bring about considerable short-term improvement.

As mentioned already, in many palliative care units about 50% of first admissions end in discharge back to the patient's home or to relatives. This illustrates that the goal of palliative care to provide a support system to help patients live as actively and creatively as possible until death is not empty sentiment. The concept of living with cancer—until death comes—is still foreign to many patients and their families, and to many physicians and nurses as well. Cancer is a spectrum of disorders and, even when incurable, rates of progression vary.

Not all palliative care units, however, adopt a rehabilitative approach to patient care. Some adopt a "cocoon" approach rather than a "cradle." The cocoon provides a total sanctuary for the patient; admissions tend to be longer and discharges fewer. In contrast, the cradle invites progression toward independence.

TABLE 2

Factors That Influence Hope in the Terminally Ill

Decrease	Increase
Feeling devalued	Feeling valued
Abandonment and isolation: "conspiracy of silence" "there is nothing more that can be done"	Meaningful relationship(s): reminiscence humor
Lack of direction/goals	Realistic goals
Uncontrolled pain and discomfort	Pain and symptom relief

(Reproduced with permission from Radcliffe Medical Press.)

At its best, palliative care encourages patients to be creative, thereby restoring or enhancing self-esteem. An emphasis on "doing" rather than "being done to" helps the patient to live and die as a whole person. In many cases, gentle and imaginative encouragement is all that is needed to entice a patient into an activity that leaves him with an increased sense of well-being. Some palliative care units encourage creativity through writing poetry and art.

IX. HOPE

Agreeing on realistic goals with a patient is one way of restoring and maintaining hope. In one study, physicians and nurses in palliative care units set significantly more goals than did their counterparts in a general hospital. Hope is also related to other aspects of life and relationships (Table 2). Communication of painful truth need not equal destruction of hope; hope of recovery is replaced by an alternative hope. Thus, in patients close to death, hope tends to become refocused on

- being rather than achieving;
- relationships with others;
- relationship with God or a "higher being."

It is possible therefore for hope to increase when a person is close to death, provided care and comfort remain satisfactory. When little else is left to hope for, one can still hope not to be left to die alone and for a peaceful death.

X. SKILLED COMPANIONSHIP

The fear has been expressed that palliative care could become just one more "technique" within contemporary high-technology mainstream medicine: a technique behind which professionals can hide and through which they could soullessly exercise "power." This danger can be avoided provided palliative care continues to mean companionship—the skilled companionship of professional staff with those who are dying.

In a crisis we all need companions. When dying we need a companion who can explain why there is pain, or shortness of breath, or constipation, or weakness, and so on—someone who can explain what is happening in simple terms. Explanation is a key modality of treatment because it cuts the illness and the symptoms down in size psychologically. The situation is no longer shrouded in total mystery because there is someone who can explain what is going on. This is reassuring.

People sometimes comment to palliative care staff, "I suppose you become hardened to it in time and develop a protective shell." The answer to that is an emphatic "No!" Obviously, the palliative physician or nurse becomes more familiar with the many and varied practical challenges of terminal illness, and acquires a certain confidence from this. However, this is not the same as becoming hardened. For many, the opposite is true—feeling more vulnerable as each year passes. Palliative care is, and always will be, extremely demanding of the carers' emotional resources. It is hard to tell a patient, "Yes, it is a cancer," or "Yes, the illness does seem to be winning." It is especially hard if the patient is 16 or 26, but even at 76 or 86 it is not easy. Indeed, if ever it seems easy, a physician can be sure that he is no longer of much use to his patients.

How one person gives support to another person is ultimately a mystery. Research in the field of counseling has shown that for a therapeutic relationship to be maximally beneficial, it is necessary for the counselor to manifest *empathy*, *warmth* and *genuineness*. In addition, the value of touch should be emphasized. In *Anatomy of an Illness*, the author writes of:

> The utter void created by the longing - ineradicable, unremitting, pervasive - for warmth of human contact. A warm smile and an outstretched hand were valued even above the offerings of modern science, but the latter were far more accessible than the former (Cousins, A. (1979). *Anatomy of an Illness*. New York: Norton).

A nurse observed that there are two kinds of physician: "Beside-the-bed doctors who are interested in the patient, and foot-of-the-bed doctors who are interested in the patient's condition."

Unfortunately, many physicians use specific "distancing behaviors" in their dealings with patients. Physicians need to modify their behavior if they are to be truly supportive of dying patients and their families. It is necessary to learn how to "listen actively" in order to facilitate the expression of negative emotion and fears. One way of unlocking the door to the patient's unspoken concerns is to ask open-ended questions. For example:

"How are you today?"
"How have you been since we last met?"
"How is the family coping with your illness?"

XI. TOWARD FULLY PERSONAL CARE

Relief of pain and other distressing symptoms is rightly seen as the primary goal of palliative care. Where palliative care has been introduced, expertise in symptom management means that patients can expect to be almost free of pain. A high measure of relief can also be expected with many other symptoms. No longer distracted and exhausted by unrelieved pain, patients may become distressed emotionally and spiritually as they contemplate their approaching death. Few do this with equilibrium; most defend themselves psychologically in various ways; and some are overwhelmed with anguish, rage, or fear about what is happening to them. In consequence, it has been suggested that a hospice is "a safe place to suffer." Patients need to know that their turmoil and distress are a sign that they are making a major adjustment and not that they are going mad, because the fear of madness is often even greater than the fear of death.

It is necessary to offer fully personal care (Table 3). The staff seeks to help the patient do his best given his personality, his family, his cultural background, his beliefs, his age, his illness, his symptoms, his anxieties, and his fears. There is need for flexibility; patients must be met where they are socially, culturally, psychologically, and spiritually as well as physically. There is no such being as a typical dying patient.

XII. SPIRITUAL ASPECTS OF CARE

The modern hospice is historically rooted in Christian belief, although in practice it is more broadly theistic. A Jewish involvement has been evident from the early days and there is now a Buddhist Hospice Association. To work with the dying demands a belief in life. This is true whether expressed or not. Life is seen as having

TABLE 3
Needs of the Dying

Dimension	Need
Physical	Relief of symptoms.
Psychological	
safety	Feeling of security.
understanding	Explanation about symptoms and the disease; opportunity to discuss the process of dying.
self-esteem	Involvement in decision-making, particularly as physical dependency on others increases; opportunity to give as well as to receive.
Social	
acceptance	Noncondemnatory attitude in the carers regardless of one's mood, sociability, and appearance.
belonging	Feeling needed and connected; *not* a burden.
disengagement	Opportunity to take leave of those people or things to whom one is attached; to "tie up loose ends" in business and family matters; to hand on responsibility to others.
Spiritual	
love	Expressions of affection; human contact, e.g., touch.
reconciliation	Opportunity for healing damaged relationships; and to seek forgiveness.
self-worth	Knowledge that one is loved and valued.
purpose	Feeling one's life still has meaning and direction.

meaning and purpose throughout the terminal illness. This conviction is manifested more by attitudes and deeds than by words; more by how we respond to the dying and care for them than by what we say.

There is much written about the emotional needs of the dying; far less about spiritual aspects of care. Human life, however, is not governed simply by instincts and hormones. Human desire extends beyond the basic human needs of food, comfort, and companionship. People are questioning and questing creatures who ask, "Why?" As Nietzsche said, "He who has a why to live can bear almost any how." When dying, many people take stock of their lives for the first time:

"I have lived a good life."

"I never did anyone any harm."

"Why should it happen to me?"

"What have I done to deserve this?"

Only a minority of patients discuss these matters with their physician, although the majority do so with a nurse, a social worker, or with relatives and close friends. People are perceptive, and patients are unlikely

to embarrass a carer if they sense that communication at this level will cause discomfort.

"Spiritual" embraces the essence of what it means to be human (Box B). It includes those experiences in human life that transcend sensory phenomena. These experiences often give rise to theological reflections, religious responses, and ethical beliefs. Several features of the "House of Hospice" (see Figure 3) relate to man's spiritual dimension—acceptance, affirmation, beauty, creativity. For those nearing the end of life, there is often an associated need for forgiveness and reconciliation—for "right-relatedness."

XIII. TEAMWORK

Teamwork is an essential component of palliative care. Teamwork means integrated practice. It is naive, however, to bring together a highly diverse group of people and expect that, by calling them a team, they will behave as one. Just as there is a science of symptom management and of psychosocial support, so there is a science of teamwork. Teamwork implies coordination of effort.

Box B

Glimpses of Spirituality at Sobell House

In talking together at Sobell House about spirituality, a rich mixture of experiences, insights and feelings has emerged which defies simple definition. There is both meaning and mystery, a sense of interconnectedness and relationship alongside an awareness of our individuality.

We may connect with the spiritual dimension through the beauty of the natural world, through our relationships with others, through religious practices, through painting or music, or other forms of art. But there is also a sense of awe and aloneness on this journey. We may have faith, and we may search and question. Our feelings may shift from courage and hope to fear—and back again. There may be joy, love, forgiveness and truth, as well as pain and suffering. Through all, a dynamic energy takes us along our different paths. It is an area of experience where we may have more to learn from patients and relatives than we have to teach, more to receive than to give. (Spiritual Care Working Group, 1994, Oxford: Sir Michael Sobell House.)

It facilitates the identification of available resources and avoids wasteful duplication. In hospice care, the core clinical team most commonly comprises nurse, doctor, social worker, and clergyman. Although each profession has a specific contribution to make, there are inevitably areas of overlap. This is particularly true of nursing and medicine. "Role blurring" is an inevitable feature of teamwork; so too is conflict—and the need to handle it constructively and creatively.

Having a common purpose unifies. Yet, although the overall goal of the highest possible quality of life for the dying person may be easily agreed, consensus about what constitutes good quality life may be more difficult to achieve. One advantage of teamwork, however, is that the patient's situation is perceived more comprehensively than is usually the case by an isolated professional.

When hospice workers function well as a team, pooling their skills and resources—caring for one another as well as for patient and family—there seems to be almost inevitably a sense of rightness about it, a kind of joy and fulfilment that is all too rarely found in the workplace today (Stoddard, S. (1989). Hospice in the United States: An overview. *Journal of Palliative Care* 5, 10–19).

XIV. CHARISMA VERSUS ROUTINIZATION

It has been suggested that any society alternates between charisma and routinization through bureaucracy, but with charisma erupting as a recurrent phenomenon. In this context, charisma refers to the ability of exceptional individuals to act as a catalyst for social change, and is a recognition of the impact of personality in bringing about radical innovation in institutions and established beliefs. In relation to the evolution of palliative care in the United Kingdom over the last 25 years, Dame Cicely Saunders was clearly the initial charismatic influence—though subsequently replicated by similar leadership in other local settings:

Inherently unstable, charismatic leadership is one which has no organized "machine" at its disposal and whose power has not been gained through institutional procedure ... Essentially creative and disruptive, it promotes a new "value-orientation" that inevitably collides with the existing one ... According to Weber, leadership can remain charismatic only so long as the number of followers is small, that is to say at the very beginning of a successful movement. When exposed to everyday demands charismatic movements inevitably become confronted with the need to create an administrative machine; the acquisition of funds; and the problems of successions - and so the process of routinization begins (James, N., & Field, D. (1992). The routinization of hospice: Charisma and bureaucratization. *Social Science Medicine*, 34, 1363–1375).

Is palliative care moving from the creative and disruptive influence of charisma to the cosy ambience of routinization? Hopefully not. Most palliative care programs have not yet reached the goal of fully personal care. If palliative care is to continue to develop, an ongoing creative tension between charisma and routinization is necessary. Otherwise the hospice movement of the late-twentieth century will, like so many others before it, degenerate into a monument resting evermore precariously on faded laurels.

Also See the Following Articles

AIDS • BIOETHICS, OVERVIEW • DEATH, SOCIETAL ATTITUDES TOWARD • EUTHANASIA • MEDICAL CODES AND OATHS • NURSES' ETHICS

Bibliography

Armstrong-Dailey, A., & Goltzer, S. Z. (Eds.). (1993). *Hospice care for children.* Oxford: Oxford University Press.

Doyle, D., Hanks, G. W., & MacDonald, N. (Eds.). (1997). *Oxford textbook of palliative medicine* (2nd ed.). Oxford: Oxford University Press.

Du Boulay, S. (1994). *Cicely Saunders: The founder of the modern hospice movement.* London: Hodder & Stoughton.

Infeld, D. L., Gordon, A. K., & Harper, B. C. (Eds.). (1995). *Hospice care and cultural diversity.* New York: Haworth Press.

Keown, J. (Ed.). (1995). *Euthanasia examined: Ethical, clinical and legal perspectives.* Cambridge: Cambridge University Press.

Kubler-Ross, E. (1970). *On death and dying.* London: Tavistock Publications.

Lewis, M. (1989). *Tears and smiles. The hospice handbook.* London: Michael O'Mara Books Ltd.

Mann, R. D. (Ed.). (1988). *The history of the management of pain: from early principles to present practice.* London: Panthenon.

Mor, V. (1987). *Hospice care systems: Structure, process, costs and outcome.* New York: Springer Publishing Co.

Sims, R., & Moss, V. A. (1995). *Palliative care for people with AIDS* (2nd ed.). London: Edward Arnold.

Stedeford, A. (1994). *Facing death: patients, families and professionals* (2nd ed.). Oxford: Sobell Publications.

Stoddard, S. (1992). *The hospice movement: updated and expanded. A better way of caring for the dying.* New York: Vintage Books.

Working Party Report. (1991). *Mud and stars. The impact of hospice experience on the Church's ministry of healing.* Oxford: Sobell Publications.

World Health Organization. (1990). *Cancer pain relief and palliative care report (technical series no. 804).* Geneva: World Health Organization.

Worswick, J. (1993). *A house Called Helen.* London: Harper Collins.

PATENTS

Michael Wreen
Marquette University

I. Overview and Basic Concepts
II. Criteria of Patentability
III. Infringement
IV. Philosophical Issues

GLOSSARY

anticipation A bar to patentability involving prior patent, prior invention, prior printed publication, prior knowledge, or prior use by someone other than the alleged inventor.

claim Assertion, on patent application, of the novel, useful, and nonobvious features of an invention; the assertion of what is patentable about an invention.

criteria of patentability Novelty, utility, and nonobviousness.

diligence The pursuit of the perfection of an invention; the pursuit of patent protection.

idea/application A general notion respecting laws of nature, principles, mathematical formulas, etc.; A device that employs ideas in a product or process.

invention A product or process that satisfies the criteria of patentability.

junior inventor Absolutely, a nonsenior inventor; relatively, the second of two inventors to invent.

patent The exclusive right to make, use, or sell an invention.

process An invention that is a series of steps; a means for producing a product or effect.

product An invention that is a physical object; subcategories of products include machines, manufactures, and compositions of matter.

reduction to practice The successful production or application of an invention—for practical purposes, patent application.

senior inventor Absolutely, the first to invent; relatively, the first of two inventors to invent.

specification A description, on a patent application, of how an invention works.

statutory bar A bar to patentability on the basis of a failure to proceed at reasonable speed toward the patent, public use, public sale, or public description of an invention by its inventor.

PATENTS are of great practical and theoretical interest, but have received very little—in fact, virtually no—philosophical attention. The legal situation is very different, of course, but even the law, with its mountains of literature on patents, finds the concept somewhat elusive. Unlike an item of real property—land, bicycles, lamps, and the like—a patent is abstract and hard to get a firm conceptual grip on. The problem is that patents are intellectual property, and both the notion of property and that of the intellectual are vague, not concrete, and morally and legally contestable. As has been said, patents and their conceptual kin, copyrights, are "nearer than any other class of cases belonging to

Encyclopedia of Applied Ethics, Volume 3
Copyright © 1998 by Academic Press. All rights of reproduction in any form reserved.

435

forensic discussion to what may be called the metaphysics of law" (J. Story, *Folsom v. Marsh*, C.C.D.MASS.1841, no. 4901). Philosophical neglect is not due so much to a fear of metaphysics—metaphysical speculation and argumentation predate Socrates, after all—as to the, historically speaking, relatively recent development of the very idea of a patent, and the fact that philosophers have found it difficult enough just to understand the nature and justification of property per se.

I. OVERVIEW AND BASIC CONCEPTS

Historically, the modern notion of a patent began to evolve in the 17th century. British monarchs, wishing to secure certain benefits, granted exclusive rights to manufacture selected items, or ply certain arts. Patents concerned commerce, not invention, and effectively created monopolies. The situation could not last. Competition was stifled by such patents, and, in addition, the English common law tradition has antimonopolistic strands running through it. Still, even today, with an invention-based concept of a patent securely in place, patents have strong monopolistic tendencies: at least in theory and very often in practice, the granting of a patent shifts the balance of trade in a single direction, toward the holder of a patent. Recognized now is that the antimonopolistic pressure of the common law (and morality) must be balanced by the incentive for progress—and profit—that patents provide. Common sense favors the development of the new and useful, and equally favors the granting of limited-term patents to encourage invention.

In the United States, the power of Congress to grant patents is part and parcel of the Constitution (Article 1, Section 8, Clause 8), and there is a strong Constitutional presumption in favor of federal, as opposed to state, regulation of the area. The first patent statute was enacted by Congress in 1790, and since then, there have been only three major revisions of the Patent Act. They occurred in 1793, 1836, and 1952. The Patent Office, however, was not created until 1836. Its function is to determine whether patent applications meet the requirements for patentability.

An applicant for a patent must prove that he or she has developed a *new, useful,* and *nonobvious* process or product (35 U.S.C.A., sec. 101). A description of how the process or product works—a *specification*—must be provided, and must be accompanied with a claim (or claims) which details how the process or product goes beyond the existing state of the art. The claim is so called because it details—makes a claim about—what is

patentable about the described product or process. If all goes well, a patent is issued in due course. Until then, though, while the Patent Office is considering the application, no monopoly rights in the product or process are granted. "Patent pending" on an article thus affords no protection whatsoever until a patent is actually granted.

When a patent is issued, the patentee is granted exclusive rights to make, use, or sell the invention for the period of the patent. In the United States, that period is currently 20 years (35 U.S.C.A., sec. 154). However, because of governmental regulatory restrictions on certain products, especially on drugs and food additives, Congress amended the Patent Act (in 1984) so that under certain conditions, patent terms on some products can be extended for up to 5 years.

Patents are not renewable, and after a patent has expired, the invention (product or process) enters the public domain. Before that time, the patentee's rights are exclusive and, for all intents and purposes, absolute. Patents can be sold (to a single party) or licensed (to one or more parties), but they need not be. Nor need they be put to use at all: a patentee could "sit" on a patent, for all the law requires.

A fundamental distinction in patent law is that between an *idea* and an *application*. An idea is not patentable; the application of an idea is. The difference between the two shapes the somewhat hazy border of patent law. That potential energy can be turned into kinetic energy is an idea, and is not patentable; that a particular device, based on this idea, provides a new means of generating electricity may well be. Thus the three general criteria built into the Patent Act—novelty, utility, and nonobviousness—are not, by themselves, sufficient to guarantee patentability. They could be satisfied by an idea alone.

The Patent Act itself states that a patentee may invent or discover what he or she patents, and that the patentable divides into four categories: processes, machines, manufactures, and compositions of matter. A process is a way of doing things, a means to an end. It is the most abstract of the four categories. The other three—all of which fall under the general rubric of products, or ends in themselves—can be roughly distinguished as follows. A machine is an invention which produces a certain specified product; a composition of matter is a product created out of preexisting materials, as, paradigmatically, a new chemical is; and a manufacture is a fabricated product that otherwise satisfies the requirements of patentability. Products are physical things, and, as far as patentability is concerned, it does not matter that the three categories of products are somewhat vague and may overlap. What matters is that a product falls into at least one of them.

One restriction on all four categories is that a naturally occurring process or product is not patentable. (Substantially modified versions of a naturally occurring substance or thing may be, however, such as a genetically altered breed of plant or animal.) Another exception is printed matter, i.e., a printed form. Printed matter is not as such patentable, but if realized in a novel, useful, and nonobvious structure, that structure may be. A unique, novel, and functional coupon, for example, may be patentable, even if the written content on it is not. The general idea is that a manufacture must have a definable structure, and it is the definable structure that is patented. A third exception is business techniques and methods, construed broadly so as to include such things as teaching methods.

None of the classes of exclusions is sharply divided from the patentable, however. The courts have been reluctant to exclude a product of nature from the realm of the patentable if humans have had *something* to do with transforming it into a new, useful, and nonobvious product (in extracting or distilling a naturally occurring substance, for instance), and the discovery/invention of new drugs has frequently shown how fine a line there is between a natural object and a man-made product.

In effect, all three exceptions point to the difficulty of drawing a sharp and readily applicable idea-application distinction. Conceptually speaking, the problem is formidable. Practically speaking, though, the distinction can be and has been made workable by appeals to statutes and to the overarching purposes of patent law.

One particularly interesting area patent law has extended to in recent years is computers. Software has forced the courts to consider more closely the distinction between mathematical formulas or algorithms— which, like laws of nature, are not patentable—and their realization and utilization in software—which may be. (Laws of nature, principles, physical phenomena, and the like are not patentable for either of two reasons (or for both reasons): first, they are objects of pure discovery, and second, patenting them would seriously retard scientific research as well as the development of future products and processes.)

The problem is particularly pressing because mathematical formulas abound in software. What the court has done is hold fast to the view that algorithms are sufficiently like laws of nature to be, as such, unpatentable. Any software that is in essence an algorithm, then, is unpatentable, since a patent would remove a law of nature from the public domain and monopolize scientific truth. Required for patentability is a demonstration of novelty, utility, and nonobviousness independent of an algorithm or law of nature employed. Even the essential use of an algorithm in a piece of software, then, does not preclude patentability, and software is not *ipso facto* unpatentable.

Still, the line between idea and application can be especially thin with objects as abstract as software. Finally, it should be noted that, regardless of considerations respecting mathematical formulas, a software program as such is not patentable, though it may be copyrightable.

All of the patents considered so far have been utility patents, but there is also a slightly different breed of animal—or, better, plant—known as plant patents. Plant patents require novelty and nonobviousness, just as utility patents do, but distinctiveness is substituted for usefulness as a third criterion for patentability. Only plants which reproduce asexually are eligible for plant patents, and what is granted is an exclusive right to reproduce the plant.

Also slightly different are design patents. New and original ornamental designs for items of manufacture are protected by design patents, and again, only two of the three criteria for utility patents apply with such patents. In this case, though, ornamentality replaces usefulness. For two reasons, however, design patents are somewhat legally problematic, at least on the level of theory. First, they tend to blur the distinction between copyrights and patents to some extent, since the protection afforded by a design patent is against copying. Second, they can also threaten the notion of a utility patent by protecting, because of its design, a product that would not otherwise qualify for patent protection. This potential loophole has been plugged, however, by requiring that the design in question not be functional.

As the last two paragraphs indicate, the distinguishing characteristic of utility patents is simply utility as an essential requirement for patentability.

II. CRITERIA OF PATENTABILITY

A. Novelty

1. Anticipation

Each of the three criteria for utility patents presents complications of its own, and some are worth noting, even in a brief overview of the subject.

Lack of novelty precludes patentability, and, as far as the law is concerned, failures of this sort fall under one of two general headings. The first is anticipation. A claim of novelty is anticipated, and so defeated, if there is a prior patent on an invention, of course, but anticipation need not take this form.

If a product (or process) is invented first, it anticipates a later product that is substantially identical to it, but only if the senior inventor—the first person to come up with the product—has not abandoned, suppressed, or concealed it. This requirement not to abandon, suppress, or conceal is not as strict as it may at first seem. An inventor need not reveal his invention immediately after its creation—the law recognizes that delays may occur, and that an invention may need to be developed and perfected before a patent is applied for—but it does require that an inventor pursue *reduction to practice*—basically, patent application—with diligence. The rationale behind the concept of anticipation in general is, as both the exclusionary ground of prior patent and the exclusionary ground of prior invention make evident, the need to adjudicate competing claims of priority, and so novelty.

Another form anticipation can take is *prior printed publication*. If substantially the same product is already described in the relevant literature—a chemical engineering magazine or journal, for instance—patentability is barred. Weaker forms of printed publication are also sufficient to defeat patentability, however. Since a patent must advance the state of the art, a crucial test for anticipation, and so patentability, is whether a reference—a piece of relevant literature—would enable a person with ordinary expertise or skill in the art to reproduce the product. If it does, there is anticipation, and patentability is again defeated.

Two other forms which anticipation can take are prior knowledge and prior use. Prior knowledge of the product (or process) must be publicly available to bar patentability; secret or private knowledge, e.g., of a building material intended for use in national defense, does not preclude patentability. Similarly with prior use, meaning prior use by someone other than the inventor: public availability of such use is necessary for a claim to patentability to be invalidated. In general, in fact, the requirement that prior knowledge or prior use be publicly available serves the same function that a requirement that a prior invention not be abandoned, suppressed, or concealed does: that of disclosure.

There are, then, basically five major grounds for anticipation: prior patent, prior invention, prior publication, prior knowledge, and prior use.

2. Statutory Bar

The second failure defeating patentability concerns statutory bar. Whereas the conditions constituting anticipation (e.g., prior invention), and thus defeating patentability, can occur any time prior to invention, statutory bar is limited to a period of 12 months prior to application. Although similar in some ways to anticipation—grounds include prior patent, printed publication, public use, and sale—there are substantial differences. Public use of a product by the inventor, for example, and not public use by another, invokes statutory bar. Statutory bar is inventor-centered; it is geared to motivate the inventor to apply for a patent within a short period of time—12 months—of invention.

Abandonment, for instance, which is not limited to abandonment in the usual sense of the term but includes failure to pursue patent rights with diligence, raises statutory bar. An inventor who does not pursue a patent on his product for more than a year after invention is liable to lose a claim to patentability—and possibly lose it to a later junior inventor who, inventing substantially the same product independently of the senior inventor, pursues a patent with alacrity. Thus delaying patent application, in all likelihood an effort to extend the effective life of a patent, can result in the loss of patent rights altogether.

Note that, unlike anticipation, statutory bar does not preempt a claim of novelty so much as require that a claim of novelty—more generally and accurately, a claim of patentability—be pursued with reasonable promptness. Otherwise put, anticipation concerns novelty or invention priority, while statutory bar concerns claim or application priority. Anticipation encourages invention without undue delay; statutory bar encourages patenting without undue delay. Together, they encourage progress in making, and in making publicly available (disclosure), and so encourage orderly progress in the advancement of useful technology.

The rationale behind statutory bar being what it is, not just failure of diligence, say, in sitting on an invention, raises the legal barrier, but public use, sale, or description of a product by an inventor does as well. Statutory bar is itself qualified, however, by legal recognition of the fact that some products may require testing, of a confined but public nature, prior to patent application. Public use, then, is subject to a limited exception; it need not raise statutory bar if experimentation beyond the 12-month grace period is needed to perfect a product.

Since patents are many times lucrative, questionable attempts to extend them are inevitable. Statutory bar blocks one kind of illicit extension, and a prohibition against double patenting—patenting the same item twice—does another. The connivance of double patenting involves "saving" some properties of a product for later use, and then reapplying for a second patent. Deceit might not be involved, however, if the product were later discovered to have additional novel, useful, and nonobvious features. Still, attempted fraud or no, double patenting is *verboten*. The rationale is simply that no one, not even the original inventor, may patent the same item twice. Invalidity is due to prior patent.

3. Priority

One nest of particularly interesting—and vexing— questions respecting novelty concerns competing claims to *priority*. Two or more inventors may lay claim to priority, and so novelty and patentability. Priority is determined by three factors: time of conception, diligence, and reduction to practice. Time of invention refers to the unequivocal time of mental discovery of a product (or process); diligence to both the perfection of the invention and the pursuit of patent protection; and reduction to practice to proof that the product was successfully produced or applied, or to (what, for practical purposes, this usually amounts to) patent application.

A senior inventor—the first to conceive—has priority for patent protection, but subject to two qualifications. First, he must apply continuous diligence from the time just prior to the junior inventor's conception until the time of reduction to practice—note that he need not apply continuous diligence from the time of his conception until the time of reduction to practice.

Second, a challenge to priority must be based on a prior reduction to practice by the junior inventor. The rule of priority is therefore this: a senior inventor has priority unless (1) he did not apply continuous diligence from the time just prior to the junior inventor's conception to reduction to practice, and (2) the junior inventor reduced to practice first ("unless" is to be understood strongly here, as a biconditional). As a matter of sheer logic, this rule is guaranteed to yield a clear result if two applicants compete for priority: one has to be unambiguously prior to the other.

Unfortunately, though, there is no such guarantee if there are three or more applicants: paradoxically, given the conditions specified in the rule, it is possible for A to be prior to B, B prior to C, and C prior to A. This is because the rule invokes only a two-termed comparison respecting date of conception, a two-termed comparison respecting reduction to practice, and a two-termed requirement respecting continuous diligence. No absolute criteria respecting conception, diligence, or reduction to practice are invoked. Thus three or more items (claims to priority), serially considered two at a time, will yield three unambiguous judgments of priority of the form X is prior to Y. Since all

such judgments establish only the priority of one claim over another, however, and since there are multiple criteria for priority specified in the rule and all criteria are relative rather than absolute, there is no guarantee that the resulting three comparative judgments will be well ordered. As mathematicians would say, patent priority is not a transitive relation.

What the law is forced to do in the admittedly extremely rare case of paradoxical priority is to decide among competing claims on the basis of overall policy considerations, and especially the overarching purposes and functions of patent law.

B. Utility

Utility, the second of the three requirements for patentability, is somewhat less complicated than novelty. Utility is a qualitative, not a quantitative, consideration. The amount of utility or usefulness provided by a product is thus of no moment; that it provides utility of some *quality* is. Quality, in fact, is probably conveyed by the very notion of an invention itself: an invention that serves no useful purpose is no invention at all. Immoral and illegal products (for example, a new and potent form of marijuana) are also ruled out by the concept of quality, as are products of no significance. The White Knight (of *Alice Through the Looking-Glass*) may be able to boast that his new pudding, made of blotting paper, gunpowder, and sealing wax, is indeed "his own invention," but lacking quality altogether, it would end up on the shelf—and not the shelf in a grocery store.

Also entailed by the concept of quality is a requirement of effectiveness. The product must actually do what it is supposed to do. Convincing frightened and credulous victims of cancer that laetrile will cure them is not enough to prove effectiveness, and without effectiveness, there is no quality. An ineffective product, then, is *ipso facto* without quality.

Perhaps the most important point about utility is that it is never *presumed*. It must always be proven. Thus if a new drug is very similar in structure to another drug whose usefulness has been demonstrated, there is no presumption that the new drug will have similar useful effects. (In fact, drugs that have identical chemical formulas can have very different effects. In some cases, for example, if a chemical group attached on the right side of a chain in one compound is attached on the left side in the other, one, but only one, of the resultant two drugs is effective.)

The purposes of not presuming utility are to ensure that the useless and harmful do not enter the market and to put a cap on the range of applications that a patent is issued for. If utility were ever presumed, the applications of a product might turn out to be so numerous and wide ranging that a patent would constitute a monopoly on an aspect of nature. Inventors are thus forced to limit their claims to the proven usefulness of their products: a specific utility must be identified, and such utility is never speculative but demonstrated.

C. Nonobviousness

1. Background

While novelty and utility have been explicit components of patent law from the beginning, and appear under exactly those rubrics, nonobviousness is, at least as so described, a latecomer. Implicit from the start has been that minimal novelty and utility are not enough. It would be silly, wasteful, and counterproductive to issue patents on obvious extensions or developments of already patented items. Something like nonobviousness, then, seems to be required. Indeed, it almost seems to be required by the concept of novelty itself. In any robust sense of the term, slightly changing—minimally adding to, subtracting from, or modifying—a product does not result in novelty. The problem is how to conceptualize and implement the needed extra element.

One attempt to distinguish the merely novel from the patentable involves the concept of *invention*. Products that embody only skill, even highly trained skill, are one thing; products that embody ingenuity—true creative ability—are another. Only the latter are patentable. This early effort (associated with *Hotchkiss v. Greenwood,* 1850) to pin down the needed extra condition, even if only in a "suggestive" manner, eventually ran into great difficulties. Most of them stemmed from the fact that an implicit criterion of ingenuity, of more than mere skill in plying an art, is subjective and inventor centered. It concentrates on the psychology of development of a product, and inevitably invites subjective speculation. It also focuses on the inventor, and not his product, in relation to the state of the art. (To some degree, *Hotchkiss* smuggled the romantic notion of creative genius, a prevalent and powerful concept in the 19th century, into the legal domain under the guise of ingenuity, or creative ability.)

On a more practical level, the absence of a statutory definition of "invention" left the court to "bloweth where it listeth" as far as standards of invention were concerned. Sometimes it moved toward broad standards, and sometimes it moved toward narrow ones. The direction and speed depended on the composition of the court, as well as the nature of the requirements being imposed by the Patent Office. The end result was the development of so-called negative rules of invention.

Couched in general terms, such rules were intended to rule out specific innovations as truly inventive. Merely using lighter-weight materials to make a machine, for example, is not truly inventive, according to one negative rule. In time these rules multiplied. Dissatisfaction with them grew, due to their ad hoc nature, and so unpredictability, and due to the fact that they were sometimes overly inclusive and eliminated, by accident, products which were clearly and intuitively inventive. Despite a late court decision with even more subjective tendencies—"flash of genius" being declared the operative test for inventiveness (*Cuno Corp. v. Automatic Devices Corp.*, 1941)—it was recognized that subjective standards needed to be replaced with more objective ones.

Nonobviousness, a concept that first appeared in the Patent Act in 1952, was introduced to satisfy this need. However, the court has made plain and emphasized from the beginning that nonobviousness merely interprets and codifies the requirement of invention that has always been essential to patent law. "The general level of patentable invention," it has said, has not changed. Negative rules thus still have force. Still, their influence has weakened, and there has been a decided turn from subjective concerns, such as the method by which an item is invented, and to objective concerns, such as the properties of the invention itself, in relation to the state of the art.

2. Determination

A determination of obviousness or nonobviousness proceeds in three stages. First, there is a survey of the scope and content of the prior art. Second, the invention is examined in relation to the prior art, in order to note and gauge relevant similarities and differences. An overall judgment of obviousness or nonobviousness concerns the differences revealed at this stage. Third, an assessment is made of the level of ordinary skill in the art.

The prior arts relevant to the first stage are those either pertinent to the invention or analogous to those clearly pertinent to the invention. The basic idea behind including analogous arts is that a relevant art is one of technical or functional similarity to any art that is clearly relevant to an invention. If analogous arts were not surveyed, distorted judgments of nonobviousness would result, as borrowings from related technical or functional fields could mask obviousness.

Stage two inevitably involves a reconstruction of the state of prior art from an inventively more advanced position. Retrospection is inescapable, given the nature of the examination undertaken. So, too, is asking a hypothetical "reasonable man" question: What would the reasonable man versed in the art(s) have known at the time of invention? Since hindsight is the only form of vision that is invariably 20/20, such reconstructions always court the danger of making all discoveries appear obvious. Human beings being the sorts of creatures they are, knowledge of a new invention is all too readily read into the past, thereby making even the least obvious of discoveries appear mundane, evident, and no very significant achievement. Great caution must be exercised at this stage, then.

Measuring the level of ordinary skill in an art, the third stage of inquiry, is always undertaken with the invention in mind. The question of ordinary skill in relation to the invention is, moreover, functional in nature, not structural or technical. That a product can be constructed in a certain way may be obvious, but irrelevant. It is novel functional use, irrespective of questions of ease or obviousness of construction—and, for that matter, irrespective of questions of difficulty or nonobviousness of construction—that matters. The development of a new and useful chemical clearly illustrates the point. At a given time, it could be (so to speak) patent to researchers in a field that chemical substance XY could be synthesized, but far from patent that XY will interact with a number of the other chemicals in a novel and useful way, say, as an efficient catalyst. The very obviousness of a machine's construction, or the very obviousness of a manufacture's structure, may even be a good reason for thinking that its novel and useful function is nonobvious.

The nonobvious, then, need not be many technical steps away from the state of the art, or what, technically speaking, the ordinary skilled worker in the field could reasonably be expected to know. It could be many steps away, though, and if it is, persistence may pay off. Genius, as Edison said, is 1% inspiration and 99% perspiration. Edison was issued 1093 patents, more than anyone who ever lived.

Nonobviousness is (again, so to speak) obviously a matter of degree, and no invention is or could be completely nonobvious. All inventors draw upon a background of history and knowledge, and nothing, no invention, is created *ex nihilo,* culturally speaking. We all stand on someone's shoulders, and usually many people's. Still and all, nonobviousness is a *sine qua non* of patentability. Like many other concepts which are somewhat vague and differ from their contraries only by incremental degrees, it can be and has been made operational.

The differences between an investigation of prior art in a determination of novelty and an investigation of prior art in a determination of nonobviousness may not itself be obvious, but differences there are, and they are important and substantial. With novelty, prior art is investigated with an eye to determining whether, in some sense, substantially the same product already exists. Only substantially the same product is an object of inquiry, but a search for it could proceed virtually anywhere. The operative concept to rule out for patentability is anticipation.

With nonobviousness, prior art is investigated with an eye, not to substantially the same product, but to the level of ordinary skill in an art vis-à-vis the invention. Related to this task is a hypothetical test. Not so for novelty: no hypothetical questions are asked. Moreover, with nonobviousness, the prior arts investigated are limited to those in the fields of the invention—pertinent fields—and those in analogous fields. The operative concept to rule out is obviousness, in particular, obviousness in respect to novel and useful functional properties. Substantial identity is not in question. In addition, there is an evidential difference: secondary considerations, a concept explained in the next paragraph, are relevant to a determination of nonobviousness, but they are irrelevant to a determination of novelty.

Secondary considerations refer to so-called objective tests of nonobviousness (or obviousness), at least once a "nexus," or connection to the inventive characteristic of a product, is established. Generally speaking, secondary considerations are empirical facts that, if present, provide seemingly strong although indirect evidence of nonobviousness (or obviousness). For example, the commercial success of a product (especially if such success is immediate and strong), the failed attempts of others to invent the product, a long-standing but unmet felt need for the product, an expression of disbelief by skilled practicioners at successful invention of the product, and large amounts of money expended in research on the product are all secondary considerations. Although their exact legal status is still somewhat uncertain, an investigation of secondary considerations is becoming increasingly accepted as a fourth stage in determinations of nonobviousness. They are especially useful as an objective corrective to the subjective and very possibly distorted "Monday morning quarterbacking" that may occur at stage two.

A great deal of care and caution is needed when dealing with secondary considerations, however, for they are subject to market manipulation, and are sometimes better explained by factors other than nonobviousness. The instant and resounding success of a product, for example, may be due to aggressive promotion or complicated business practices rather than an indirect linkage to nonobviousness.

III. INFRINGEMENT

Infringement of a patent depends on whether a putative infringing item "performs substantially the same function, in substantially the same way, to obtain substantially the same result" as the patented item (*Pennwalt Corp. v. Durand-Wayland,* 1987). Direct infringement is basically making, using, or selling a patented item without permission; indirect infringement is basically encouraging another to make, use, or sell a patented item without permission; and contributory infringement is knowingly selling or supplying a nonstaple item, the only or predominant use of which is in connection with a patented item, without permission. Direct infringement may be innocent or inadvertent, but contributory infringement, which can be committed only in relation to the sale of a component of a patented item, requires knowledge (of the unique, specific function of a nonstaple part) on the part of the infringing party.

Remedies for infringement include injunctions to prevent manufacture, use, and sale; damages to compensate the patentee (which must amount to at least "a reasonable royalty," but under certain conditions may also include what, in effect, are profits enjoyed by the infringer); and attorneys' fees (but only if the infringer knowingly infringed, or "the plaintiff acquired his patent by fraud or brings an infringement suit with no good faith belief that his patent is valid and infringed" (*Arbrook, Inc. v. American Hospital Supply Corp.,* 1981)).

IV. PHILOSOPHICAL ISSUES

A. Ontology

Patents can raise some difficult philosophical questions: What is patented? Are patents—and other intellectual property—really property at all? Is the social institution of patents morally justifiable? Descending from the high plane of the last question, but still remaining in the realm of ethics, more specific questions can also be asked, such as, Should human genes or gene sequences be patented?

The answer to the first question might seem obvious: toasters, chemicals, hand brakes, and any number of other commonplace (and esoteric) products and processes are patented. Not everything can be or could have been patented; natural objects are excluded, and anything that has been in the public domain for as long as can be remembered, or prior to the advent of modern society, might be excluded as well (arguably, the wheel never could have been patented). With the possible exception of the class of artifacts just mentioned, however, every artifact is or has been logically susceptible to patentability. While correct as far as it goes, the answer here is not complete. It tells us something about the range and kind of objects that are patentable, but nothing, in a deep sense, about the nature of those objects.

Not just my particular VCR falls under patent protection; others, of the same make and model, do as well. If, however, only one VCR of its kind had been made, it alone would have been protected—even if it were destroyed shortly after it were made. In fact, even if no VCR of its kind had ever been manufactured, there still would have been patent protection—protection against infringement and against items of its kind being made, used, or sold without permission.

Suggested by this is that individual items—particular physical objects or processes, particular spatiotemporal occupiers—are accorded patent protection in a sense correlative with, but conceptually derivative from, a sense in which a kind of item as such is accorded patent protection. In other words, and in the usual philosophical terminology, a type of (artifactual) object is the logically primary object of a patent; it is what is patented in the conceptually primary sense. However, in at least the usual run of cases (if not all cases), a type does not exist without or independently of its tokens. A token is an actual physical object or event instantiating a type; a type, as an abstract object—a kind as such—is a design, in the broad sense of the term that includes material as well as formal elements.

Token products and processes are also patented, of course, or, better, patent protected; that is why the reconstruction of a patented product—the making of a new product from an old, patented one—is legally prohibited, while the repair of such an item is not. The patentability of tokens, however, is always conceptually derivative, because always conceptually dependent upon instantiating a patented design or type. The intellectual part of intellectual property resides in the logical priority of the abstract, conceptual, non-spatiotemporal notion of a design—a (man-made) type—to the concrete, physical, and spatiotemporal notion of an object—a token.

B. Patents and Property

It is just such priority and abstractness, in fact, that may give rise to doubts about whether patents in particular, and intellectual property in general, are really property at all. "Property" is somewhat ambiguous, alternating between meaning the object as such and the object-cum-a-package-of-rights. In the full sense of the term, as a rights-saturated concept, or even more abstractly (and in a third sense of the term) as a bundle of rights as such, our basic conceptual fix and criteria for applying the term is mediated by the notion of possession, a concept that entails physicality, or spatio-temporal occupancy.

This emphatically is not to say that property rights have to include possession rights. That certainly is not true, for it is perfectly possible to have property rights without possession rights, and, as theft makes evident, it is also perfectly possible to have property rights without possession. The point is a very different one. It is that our initial conceptual fix on or understanding of the very idea of property is mediated by the idea of possession, and even more basically, that of physicality. For the issue at hand, what is important is not so much the fact that possession, in the literal sense (the sense that derivative and metaphorical senses are built upon), entails physicality; what is important is physicality, or spatiotemporal occupancy, itself. If our notion of property is fundamentally mediated by spatiotemporal occupancy, then individual, concrete objects are and have to be the primary objects of property.

The conceptual difficulty this poses for patents and intellectual property in general is simply that, since their primary objects are types, not tokens (even if, derivatively, tokens are patented or intellectual property), it could be argued that intellectual property strays too far from the concept of property to merit the title. The proper objects of property and intellectual property are fundamentally different, and so our bases for understanding them, simply as concepts, also have to be fundamentally different. The result is two fundamentally different notions.

That they are two fundamentally different notions shows up in, because it has implications for, any number of facts, the argument would continue. One is that the rights that constitute a patent are exclusive rights to manufacture, use, and sale. None of these rights is *directly* applicable to the proper object of a patent, a type; all have to be understood derivatively, as rights concerning tokens of a type. The type as such is not manufactured or used, and the sale or licensing of a patent, for example, has to be understood in terms of the sale or licensing of the exclusive rights to make, use, or sell tokens.

A related fact is that many of the concepts which surround property do not find easy application with intellectual property. I can steal a VCR, a token VCR, but such theft does not constitute patent infringement—or patent theft. Patent theft as such would involve stealing a type, and the only way to make sense of that is derivatively, in terms of "taking" the abstract object. Even then, the concept is strained: How could X be stolen when the owner still has everything he previously had? If applicable at all, theft would thus have to be construed analogously, as intelligible only because of certain features shared with theft in the usual sense.

Discussion of this argument is not possible here, but suffice it to say that it is more suggestive than definitive. The notion of property may be more open ended and flexible than the argument would make it appear, and the conceptual correlativity of type and token may further strengthen the case for intellectual property as bona fide, full-blooded property.

C. Justifiability and Social Utility

The most basic and important moral question about patents is simply whether the institution is justifiable.

Even without the assumption that intellectual property, patents included, is truly property, all of the major arguments that have been advanced in support of the institution of private property in general can also be advanced, in slightly modified form, in support of patents. Only one major argument can be considered here, however.

The argument from social utility begins by noting that one of the main goals of social institutions is to make possible, and perhaps also to promote, the happiness of the populace. The institution of private property—the varying collections of rights which compose property rights—serves this purpose well. Property enables the needs of individuals to be met in an orderly and relatively trouble-free way. This is because property effectively means that the pursuit of the acquisition, possession, and use of items needed for happiness is regulated by rule-governed directives in the form of exclusive rights. The nature and strength of such rights provide strong social incentives for security, order, and progress.

More particularly, in an advanced industrial society happiness is, more than anything else, a function of technology and technological development. Patents, as exclusive rights of a certain distinct sort, provide individuals and corporations with the incentive needed to devote massive amounts of time, money, training, skill, and labor to the uncertain and frequently futile (if only because the competition can be quite stiff) task of invention. Given the prerequisites of technological advance, then, and given human nature—human beings will not take large risks or undertake substantial labor without sufficient compensation—patents are an attractive social institution.

This is especially true when the immense benefits of new inventions for the public are taken into account. The exclusive rights to make, use, and sell that are patents are also the most efficient social mechanism of technological advance, and so the furtherance of human happiness. The cost of invention—the investment of resources, human and otherwise—is substantial, and the risk is great, but the payoff, for the public, is enormous.

While there is undoubtedly a great deal to this argument—which may be a good thing, for unless the argument from social utility is fairly strong, patents probably cannot be justified—it can be questioned at several points. First, there is an unavoidable tension, due to the nature of the concepts, between rights and utility, even in a rule-utilitarian argument such as this one. The concept of a right is basically anti-utilitarian, and allows a person to ignore (within limits) considerations of general utility. Rule utilitarianism tries to make room for rights, but does so by, as it must, predicating rights on considerations of utility. The question that advocates of rights would ask is, Do we really have rights, if their justification is based on a concept that is fundamentally antithetical to our normal notion of rights? Are such moral concerns rights, or are they utilitarian surrogates, liable to evaporate if, unlike rights as usually understood, the causal matrix in which they operate were to yield a different utility output?

Still and all, a proponent of the argument from social utility would say that as interesting as this objection is, it operates on the level of pure theory. Practically speaking, we can and do smooth over theoretical tensions and difficulties in an effort to secure desirable results. There is no reason why that cannot be done with patents, as it has already been done in other spheres of social concern.

Secondly, and focusing more on patents, there is the empirical question of whether the same or better results—high general utility—could be achieved without the institution of patents. Perhaps other social arrangements would do a better job, and would not have the drawbacks of patents. Certainly, the absence of patent protection in the past did not prevent the develop-

ment of farm technology or herbal medicine; nor did it hamper the invention of all sorts of useful technical devices, such as sundials and mirrors. While this objection must remain sketchy and incomplete, in that entire alternative social systems must be envisioned and shown to be viable in order for it to have full force, weaker, less sweeping versions of it command our more immediate attention.

Why, even in the social circumstances we find ourselves in, exclusive rights? Why not nonexclusive rights, to be shared with the government, say? Why rights at all? Why not other social privileges or monetary compensation for inventors, with the kind or amount of privilege or compensation to be determined by an independent social agency? And why such a long term period for patents? In short, why would not more minor modifications of current social arrangements provide the incentive needed for invention, plus the social utility desired? There may be good answers to these and other questions of a like sort, but the point is that such questions need to be asked and, if the argument from utility is to survive, successfully answered.

Third, apart from the other two objections, there is the question of equity. Patents are monopolistic; there is no getting around that. They are thus in tension with antitrust legislation and moral sentiment respecting fair competition. The point is underscored by the fact that the majority of patents issued today are to large corporations. Even worse, though, considered globally, patents make for great discrepancies in standards of living and unfair competition between highly industrialized and emerging nations: invention is much more likely in developed nations, so to invest inventions with the exclusive rights of patents is to ensure the unavailability, in any realistic terms, of the valuable products of medicine, electronics, chemistry, and every other area of technology in third-world countries.

Moreover, the effect of this is that already limping third-world nations will be further hobbled in their efforts to draw abreast of first-world nations as inventors. Lack of wealth means the inability to invent; which means the inability, because of patent protection, to improve standards of living; which means falling even further behind first-world nations in terms of ability to invent. Because of patents (among other things), the distance between first-world and thirld-world countries continues to grow.

The upshot of this objection, then, is that even if the argument from social utility is correct in saying that patents do make for appreciable social utility, such utility is not enough to show that patents are justifiable.

There are considerations of equity having to do with intranational competition that have to be taken into account, and there are considerations of equity—and utility—having to do with international competition that also have to be taken into account.

Proponents of the argument from social utility usually respond to such objections by arguing that we have to choose among the available candidates of social institutions with the aim of creating the best overall system. Patents cannot ensure that there is a level playing field at all times, or even at any time (and that is true of rights in general), but in the long run, they do make for a better world than otherwise, and, as far as can be seen, a better world than any other social arrangement makes for. Patents may contribute to inequalities of wealth and development, but all realistic alternatives to patents make everyone—including third-world peoples—poorer and slower to progress (and may well contribute to inequalities of wealth and opportunity as well).

Today's wonder drug may not be available in third-world countries right now, but it will be available tomorrow, just as yesterday's wonder drug is available in such countries today. The alternative is that everyone, in all countries, lives with a three-days-ago wonder drug. As the main engine of invention, patents may not move all parties at the same rate, but they do move them all, and they do get them to any given destination faster than otherwise. So, at least, proponents of the argument from social utility would contend.

D. The Human Genome

Even if the institution of patents is justifiable, patents raise a number of specific moral questions. One particularly pressing one concerns patenting genes, and especially human genes and gene sequences. Research on the nature of human genes is international and enormously expensive. It holds out the promise of enormous benefits for mankind, however, and also of great financial rewards for potential patent holders. Legally speaking, though, there is a prior question that needs to be asked: Are genes and gene sequences patentable? Do they, or could they, meet the requirements of patentability? Morally speaking, there is a different and much more important question: If genes and gene sequences are patentable, should they be patented?

The answer to the legal question is probably "Yes." Although the only case to reach the Supreme Court resulted in the denial of the patent application—the National Institutes of Health applied for a patent on a sequence of human genes and was turned down in 1993—the negative decision was based on technical grounds. More sophisticated and better-drawn patent applications will probably succeed in the future. The court has already made it clear that animals can be patented—the patentability of oil-eating bacteria (created by splicing gene sequences from several different bacteria) was upheld by the court in a 1980 decision—and, appearances aside, the fact that genes and gene sequences are natural products, not human inventions, is no insuperable barrier to patentability. This is because what is patented is not raw genetic material but novel "purified and isolated" genes and gene sequences derived from naturally occurring objects—human beings—but otherwise unavailable and thus useless. Recombinant DNA cloning processes make possible the extraction of the purified and isolated genetic material, and thus make available a new and useful product.

More difficult is the ethical question: Should genes and gene sequences fall under patent law? A number of arguments for a "No" answer have been offered.

Some people in the European community have argued that they should not, because genes and sequences are part of our "universal heritage" and so belong to all mankind. An argument as hazy as this one, however, is not likely to carry much weight. As stated, it appeals to general nostalgia and warm feelings for our forefathers more than anything else. Still, it may be a rather confused attempt, wrapped in a little too much rhetorical dress, to get at the "public domain/collective property" argument discussed below.

Another argument that has been offered, especially on the European front, is that the human body and its parts are not property, and therefore should not fall under property law, and especially patent law. The usual response to this argument is that it is not the gene or its parts in their natural state which are patented but, as indicated earlier, sequences of nucleotides obtained by genetic engineering, sequences which are thus available and useful, which naturally occurring genetic material is not. While this reply may meet the letter of the objection, it is doubtful that it meets its spirit. The essence of the argument is that the human body, a natural object, should not be made available as property in any form, and to reply that it is not, only its clone is, is largely sophistry, however well-received such an argument might be in a court of law. No one would be taken in by a similar argument if the matter under consideration were, say, enslavement; no one would find the claim that it is wrong to enslave human beings (since human beings are not property) but, of course, since cloned human beings are not natural objects, there is nothing to be said against enslaving them—no one would find such a claim at all convincing.

A better reply to the objection would emphasize the type/token distinction explained above and note that moral and legal prohibitions on considering human bodies and their parts as property concern only token bodies and their parts. Not being physical objects, types fail to fall under such prohibitions. More than that, though, the rationale for not regarding human bodies or their parts as property, having to do with such phenomena as slavery and the sale of human organs, is clearly geared to apply to tokens, not types, and would protect cloned tokens as much as natural ones.

Two other arguments against allowing patents concern collective property (although many times this is oddly called a consideration of privacy) and risk. Genes and gene sequences, it has been argued, are our collective property; they belong to the whole of mankind. Therefore, exclusive rights to them cannot be assigned to any one individual or corporation. In fact, it has also been urged, genes and gene sequences fail of patentability from the start, for they are in the public domain, and always have been. The two sides of this argument actually go in different directions, however, and are at odds with one another: what is in the public domain is nobody's property, not everybody's. Even so, the argument deserves an extended response.

The claim that the human gene is collective property is hard to make out for lack of clarity. In and of itself, the fact that genes have been with us from the start is of little significance, as so have many other patentable products made available only by human effort, for example, drugs extracted from plants. That such drugs should be regarded as collective property just because the plants that contain them have been around as long as we have, or longer, is unclear at best and counterintuitive at worst. Nor is the fact that we, all of us, carry around the human genome with us, and always have, decisive. *Ceteris paribus,* possession may be the better part of property if there is no morally valid prior claim on an item, but possession by everyone is no possession at all. Property is, after all, an exclusionary concept. The whole idea of collective property is, in fact, a confused one if the so-called property is universally owned. To paraphrase a remark of Hobbes': everyone's having a right to *x* is very nearly equivalent to no one's having a right to *x*. Rather, what the argument seems to be getting at, even if in rather confused terms—and this brings us to the "public domain" side of the

argument—is that the human genome is like the air above us or the sea around us: too vital to fundamental and universal human interests to allow a monopoly by any one organization or individual, even for a limited period of time. (This is probably what the "universal heritage" argument is getting at as well.) So understood, the argument may well have a great deal to it, but its assessment takes us beyond the scope of this article.

Last, the argument from risk is that mapping human genes and gene sequences may not be dangerous in itself, but encourages all sorts of abuses and will ultimately lead to trouble, and maybe even disaster, in the future. The argument from risk, in short, is really a slippery-slope argument against genetic engineering in general. As such, patents figure as a concern only insofar as allowing them will speed up or abet the development of genetic engineering, or make it a less cautious endeavor than otherwise. Such an argument is best considered, then, in a discussion of the ethics of genetic engineering in general.

Also See the Following Articles

COMPUTER AND INFORMATION ETHICS • CONFIDENTIALITY, GENERAL ISSUES OF • TRADE SECRETS AND PROPRIETARY INFORMATION

Bibliography

Becker, L. C. (1977). "Property Rights: Philosophical Foundations." Routledge and Kegan Paul, London.

Becker, L. C. (1993). Deserving to Own Intellectual Property. *Chicago-Kent Law Review* 68, 609–629.

Benko, R. P. (1987). "Protecting Intellectual Property Rights." American Enterprise Institute for Public Policy Research, Washington, DC.

Bugbee, B. (1967). "Genesis of American Patent and Copyright Law." Public Affairs Press, Washington, DC.

Foltz, R. D., and Penn, T. A. (1988). "Protecting Scientific Ideas and Inventions." 2nd ed. Penn Institute, Inc., Cleveland, Ohio.

Foster, F. H., and Shook, R. L. (1993). "Patents, Copyrights, & Trademarks." 2nd ed. John Wiley and Sons, Inc., New York.

Gabor, D. (1970). "Innovations: Scientific, Technological, and Social." Oxford University Press, London.

Gadbaw, M. R., and Richards, T. J., Eds. (1988). "Intellectual Property Rights: Global Consensus, Global Conflicts?" Westview Press. Boulder, CO.

Gilfillan, S. C. (1970). "The Sociology of Invention." MIT Press, Cambridge, MA.

Honore, A. M. (1961). Ownership. In A. D. Guest, Ed. "Oxford Essays in Jurisprudence (pp. 107–147)." Clarendon Press, Oxford.

Kahin, A. (1989). Software Patents: Franchising the Information Structure. *Change* (May/June), 24–25.

Machlup, F., and Penrose (1950). The Patent Controversy in the Nineteenth Century. *Journal of Economic History* 10, 1–29.

Merges, R. P. (1992). "Patent Law and Policy." The Michie Company, Charlottesville, VA.

Miller, A. R., and Davis, M. H. (1990). "Intellectual Property: Patents, Trademarks, and Copyright." 2nd ed. West Publishing Company, St. Paul, MN.

Moore, A. D. (1997). "Intellectual Property: Moral, Legal, and International Dilemmas." Rowman and Littlefield Publishers, Inc., Lanham, MD.

Toulmin, H. A. (1939). "Patents and the Public Interest." Harper and Brothers, New York.

Weil, V., and Snapper, J., Eds. (1989). "Owning Scientific and Technical Information." Rutgers University Press, New Brunswick, NJ.

PATERNALISM

Heta Häyry
University of Helsinki

I. The Definition of Paternalism
II. The Value of Liberty and Autonomy
III. The Morality of Paternalism
IV. Maternalism
V. Summary and Conclusions

GLOSSARY

The terms listed here are used in the following limited or nonstandard senses throughout this article. The definitions given in the list should not, however, be understood as universally accepted among ethicists, lawyers, or philosophers. The terminological variation in the field is too wide to allow for legitimate claims of linguistic consensus.

autonomy The potential or actual ability of individuals and groups to govern themselves, an ideal of character derived from the conception of self-government, or the right to self-determination in matters that solely or mainly concern individuals or groups themselves.

coercion Constraint by intentional threats or the intentional use of force.

constraint A restriction of an agent's options, or action alternatives.

freedom A state where an agent's options, or action alternatives, are not restricted.

hard paternalism Paternalism that involves at least initial restrictions of liberty or violations of autonomy.

liberty *See* Freedom.

paternalism Practices and actions are paternalistic when those in positions of authority refuse to act according to people's wishes, or they restrict people's freedom, or in other ways attempt to influence their behavior, allegedly in the recipients' own best interest.

self-determination *See* Autonomy.

soft paternalism Paternalism that does not involve restrictions of liberty or violations of autonomy.

strong paternalism Hard paternalism that cannot be justified.

weak paternalism Hard paternalism that can be justified.

IT IS AN OLD TRADITION in political life and medicine to think that because the rulers and doctors know best what is good for their citizens and patients, they should be allowed to make decisions for other people without their consent. This model of making choices for others allegedly in their own best interest came to be called, at the end of the nineteenth century, *paternalism*. The term—the latin word *pater*, meaning father—refers to the patriarchal family model where the father makes all the choices, especially when it comes to the affairs of his children. The paternalistic attitude has been widely discredited in the political ideologies of the affluent West, but it can still be detected in many areas of legislation and social policy, and most notably in medicine and health care.

I. THE DEFINITION OF PATERNALISM

A. The Historical Starting Point: J. S. Mill

The best place to start an analysis of the concepts involved in paternalism is John Stuart Mill's classic antipaternalistic statement in his famous essay *On Liberty* (1859). At the outset of the work he defined his position as follows:

[The] only purpose for which power can be rightfully exercised over any member of a civilized community, against his will, is to prevent harm to others. His own good, either physical or moral, is not a sufficient warrant. He cannot rightfully be compelled to do or forbear because it will be better for him to do so, because it will make him happier, because, in the opinion of others, to do so would be wise, or even right. These are good reasons for remonstrating with him, or reasoning with him, or persuading him, or entreating him, but not for compelling him, or visiting him with any evil in case he do otherwise.

In this oft-quoted passage Mill manages to introduce most of the justificatory and conceptual questions related to paternalism.

The quotation reveals that there are six principles that can be evoked in attempts to justify coercion, constraint, and violations of a person's autonomy or self-determination. These principles are presented in Table 1.

B. The Harm Principle and the Offense Principle

The *harm principle* provides, according to Mill, the only feasible justification for exercising power over individuals who are capable of making decisions for themselves. People's freedom can be legitimately restricted, if what they intend to do threatens the physical safety of others. As for the *offense principle,* however, other people may think that what the individual does is not wise or right, and they can be offended by the individual's choices, but the feelings of others are not in themselves a sufficient ground for coercion or constraint.

It is important to notice already at this stage that the harm and offense principles stand diametrically opposite to the doctrine of paternalism in that they make appeals to what happens to *other* people if an individual makes unwise choices. The core idea of paternalism is to justify restrictions by referring to the recipients' *own*

TABLE 1

Principles Evoked in Attempts to Justify Coercion and Constraint

Reason given for restrictions of liberty or violations of autonomy or morality:	Principle or ism:
Harm inflicted on others	The harm principle
Offense caused to others	The offense principle
The recipient's physical (or mental) good	Paternalism
The recipient's moral good	Moral paternalism
Rationality	Prudentialism
Morality as such	Moralism

good in matters which regard solely or mainly *themselves.*

C. Paternalism, Prudentialism, and Moralism

It has been clear since Mill's time that there are many closely entangled principles and "isms" at work in the justification of what are generally regarded as paternalistic attitudes and practices. When people's choices are restricted because their own physical or mental well-being is otherwise in danger, the action can be called paternalistic in the narrow sense. When an appeal is made to the recipient's moral good, the ism in question is *moral paternalism.* Some public authorities have thought, for instance, that because people can be morally corrupted by exposing them to rock music, it is in the people's own best (moral) interest not to be led to temptation in the first place. Attempts to ban concerts or to censor radio and television programs can in these cases be defined as morally paternalistic.

In addition to the straightforward attempts to protect people from self-chosen harm there are also two isms that can be evoked when the narrow or moral forms of paternalism are not adequate, namely, *prudentialism* and *moralism.* While the argument of the genuine paternalist is of the form "This is for your own good," the simplest prudentialist line is "You would be irrational to do that," and the moralist response, "It would be immoral." The alleged irrationality or immorality of the constrained choice cannot be further justified by appeals to harm, as this would mean a return either to the harm principle or to paternalism in the narrow sense. Especially "morality as such," the reason given by moralists for their interventions, must be defined in terms of ethical intuitions or categorical rules of conduct rather than in terms of concrete injury or unpleasantness to specified individuals.

D. Three Ways of Defining Paternalistic Interventions

In different contexts philosophers and ethicists have employed slightly different definitions of paternalism.

Legal paternalism has usually been defined in terms of state coercion. Laws have been considered as paternalistic if they interfere coercively with people's liberty of action, and if they are justified by appeals to people's own welfare, good, happiness, needs, interests, or values. Laws requiring motorists to use crash helmets to protect their skulls in case of an accident are an example of such legislation.

Medical paternalism has sometimes been defined as behavior that is intended to benefit patients or clients without their consent, but that also involves violating moral rules such as the prohibition against killing, causing pain, disabling, depriving of freedom, or cheating. According to this approach, the possible wrongness of giving a blood transfusion to an unconscious Jehovah's Witness (the members of this Christian denomination are forbidden by their religion to receive blood) is based on the fact that the physician in charge must eventually violate a moral rule, not on the fact that the transfusion was given against the patient's will. The violation of the moral rule takes place after the treatment has been successfully completed and the patient is conscious again. The physician must then either deceive the patient by lying, or cause painful feelings by telling the truth.

A *wide* definition of paternalism does not make confining references either to coercion or to violations of moral rules. It states that practices and actions are paternalistic when those in positions of authority—legal, medical, or otherwise—refuse to act according to people's wishes, or they restrict people's freedom, or in other ways attempt to influence their behavior, allegedly in the recipients' own best interest. This is a wide definition in the sense that it covers both practices that can be regarded as strictly authoritarian and policies that would be accepted by the most extreme liberals. A refusal to operate on a person who asks for sterilization belongs to the obviously restrictive type of control. On the other hand, attempts to influence people's behavior by providing them with truthful information are not normally seen as constraining.

II. THE VALUE OF LIBERTY AND AUTONOMY

A. The Definitions of Liberty and Constraint

Because the perceived immorality of paternalism is based on its ill effects upon the freedom and self-determination of individuals, it is necessary to define these concepts and to assess the value of liberty and autonomy before the morality of paternalism can be properly evaluated.

The most neutral definition of freedom is that individuals are free when—and to the degree that—their options, or action alternatives, remain unrestricted. The restriction could be imposed by other people's actions, or their inactions, or by natural causes over which human beings have no power. In the first case, I am free to leave the room if nobody has locked me in or threatened to shoot me if I come out. In the second case, I am free to use public transportation if the authorities have established such a system. In the third case, I am free to take a walk outside without the fear of getting my feet wet if it is not raining.

In a similar vain, constraint can be defined as the restriction of options. I am unfree to leave the room, to use public transportation, or to take the sunny walk if somebody or something prevents me or deters me from doing so.

B. The Definition of Autonomy

The notion of autonomy has two main interpretations, which are related to what have been called the positive and negative concepts of liberty. Those who uphold the *positive* concept of liberty believe that freedom means the presence of certain rationally, emotionally, politically, or morally correct restrictions. Their idea of personal autonomy is that individuals can achieve genuine self-determination only by subjecting their lusts and desires to the universal human will to be moral, or to their own vital need to live in an organized society. The former, moral solution was advocated by Immanuel Kant, and the latter, more political model can be found in the works of Jean-Jacques Rousseau.

The defenders of the *negative* concept of liberty agree in the main with the analysis presented in Section II.A. and argue that freedom means simply the absence of restrictions. If this view is taken to refer only to positive, external restrictions such as locked doors and explicit threats, then the content of personal autonomy is reduced to freedom from coercion. But if the restrictions in question are also extended to negative and internal constraints such as a lack of self-control, then autonomy can be seen in a different light. Joel Feinberg, for instance, has given four meanings to "autonomy" when the term is applied to individuals. These are "the *capacity* [or potential ability] to govern oneself"; "the *actual condition* of self-government and its associated virtues"; "an *ideal of character* derived from that conception"; and "the *right* of self-determination" (Feinberg 1986. *Harm to self,* p. 28. Oxford: Oxford University Press). In this model autonomy can be seen, depending on the context, either as a potential, an actuality, a value, or a norm.

C. The Link between Liberty and Autonomy

There are many ways to defend the claim that liberty is of value to individuals, and ought to be protected. Standard liberal views of the nonconsequentialist type include, first, the idea that freedom is symbolically valuable, and, second, the claim that there is a "presumption of liberty" that entails that freedom should never be interfered with unless there are good grounds for restrictions.

Another way of looking at the value of liberty is instrumental. The idea is that freedom is a necessary condition for achieving other good things, notably autonomy. It is true, of course, that not all restrictions of action alternatives are likely to violate autonomy, and it is also true that no amount of open options can in themselves make a person autonomous. But on the other hand, frequent restrictions, especially if they happen to accumulate on important areas of an agent's personal life, do have a strong tendency to affect the agent's ability to make autonomous decisions. And because there is no way of telling beforehand which restrictions will have an evil effect, there is at least an initial reason to suspect all of them of violating autonomy. If this way of thinking is accepted, the value of liberty becomes conditional on the presumably more fundamental value of autonomy.

D. The Instrumental Value of Autonomy

Autonomy, like freedom, can be valuable either as a means to something else or as an end in itself. A prominent option is to claim that the self-determination of one's actions, choices and life-plans is essential to the pursuit of well-being and happiness. John Stuart Mill, for instance, argued in *On Liberty* that "a state which

dwarfs its men, in order that they may be more docile instruments in its hands even for beneficial purposes, will find that with small men no great things can really be accomplished." Mill's point seems to be that the promotion of liberty and autonomy is a causal factor without which it would be impossible to bring about genius and industriousness, which in their turn are necessary prerequisites of material welfare and cultural greatness.

The problem with this approach is that the causal connections it presumes defy any real proof. It can be claimed that people are, in the end, happier and healthier if they are allowed to make their own choices in matters that concern solely or mainly themselves. But it can equally well be argued that the welfare of the population is best secured by paternalistic interventions and benevolent manipulation. The instrumental value of personal self-determination remains, therefore, largely unproven.

E. The Intrinsic Value of Autonomy

The intrinsic value of autonomy (the value of autonomy in and by itself) can be elucidated by considering what societies would look like if they did not allow their members to be self-governed. Some philosophers have thought that it is helpful here to think about the imaginary social order described by Aldous Huxley in his satirical novel *Brave New World* (1932). Huxley's New World is a peaceful and stable society from which all standard sources of conflict have been removed by eliminating family ties and other close human bonds, natural reproduction, restrictions of sexual freedom, pain, anguish, suffering, illness, old age, and the experience of death. Instead, human embryos and fetuses develop in a hatchery during their prenatal period, after which they are hypnopaedically programmed to the tasks, opinions, and values of their caste. Adult inhabitants of the New World lead a happy life in the sense that they are content, and there are always pleasures available to them when they want or need them. The main forms of recreation are sensual entertainment, games, promiscuous sex, and the use of psychoactive drugs. Because the society has rather conclusively determined every decision an inhabitant is apt to make, the very idea of autonomy, however, is alien to the new order.

Most people would presumably not think that the society described by Huxley would be an ideal place to live in. One of the main reasons for this is that the happiness enjoyed in the Brave New World does not seem to be the kind of happiness that makes human life worth living. Pleasures, admittedly, could be experienced by individuals, but not in a considered manner, not in a manner that would enable the individual to be proud of a good choice, thereby multiplying the value of the experience. It seems that contentment without autonomy would be less valuable than happiness accompanied by self-government, and this connection can be seen to give autonomy its intrinsic worth.

III. THE MORALITY OF PATERNALISM

A. Paternalism, Liberty, and Autonomy

There are two philosophical schools of thought concerning the ethical status of paternalism. One school insists that all forms of benevolent control are immoral, and that any definition of paternalism should therefore include a reference to coercion, constraint, violations of autonomy, or immorality in general. The other school, in turn, holds that although coercion and the rest of the evils may be present in most paternalistic behavior, this is not universally true and decisive. There are also modes of paternalism where the evils are either absent or small enough to be overridden by other considerations.

For the sake of conceptual clarity and variety, it is in the present context best to assume the wider notion, and to take it that there are both acceptable and unacceptable forms of paternalistic behavior. Furthermore, it shall also be assumed here that the demarcation line is drawn between autonomy-respecting and autonomy-violating types of caring control over others.

The different branches of paternalism, their relationship to freedom and self-determination, and their moral statuses according to the assumed, generically liberal, interpretation are depicted in Figure 1.

B. Soft and Hard Paternalism

The first type of benevolent control over people's affairs can be called *soft* paternalism, and it consists of caring

FIGURE 1   The Liberal View on Paternalism.

action that does not even initially constitute violations of the recipient's autonomy. Examples of this kind of control—if that word can be used—include, on the societal level, truthful and nonsensational health education, warning labels on dangerous products, and improvements in the social security system. Soft paternalism does not normally need any separate legitimization.

Hard paternalism, by contrast, does violate people's self-determination, at least according to the strictest interpretations of what constitutes a violation. This form of paternal protection must therefore be deemed wrong unless other, more weighty ethical reasons can be provided for overturning the judgment.

C. Weak Paternalism

Hard forms of benevolent constraint can be further divided into two groups. The first can be labelled *weak* paternalism, and it consists of caring control that at first glance seems to violate the recipient's autonomy but that, in the last analysis, does not. The cases where hard paternalism can be justified are presented schematically in Figure 2.

There are four main kinds of situation where the recipient's self-determination is ultimately secured even though an apparent violation of liberty or autonomy will inevitably be required. The following points were first presented by C. L. Ten in his pioneering article "Paternalism and Morality," which appeared in 1971 (*Ratio* **13**: 56–66).

1. C. L. Ten on the Justification of Paternalism

First, instances of weak paternalism take place when *special categories of persons* such as children, the mentally subnormal, or the mentally ill are involved. Children, for instance, can quite legitimately be prevented from taking poison although the preventive act is in many cases constraining and may seem to constitute a violation of their autonomy. Children and the mentally defective do not have the same capacities as normal adults, and their decisions are therefore generally subject to vitiating factors.

Second, when *lack of knowledge* prevents agents from making fully informed decisions, they sometimes ought to be temporarily held up for a briefing. If their actions are not checked, they can do things without being aware of the harmful consequences of their acts, or fail to understand their true nature. An example of the first category would be a person who intends to take a medicine without knowing about its harmful side-effects. The second condition would be satisfied by a person

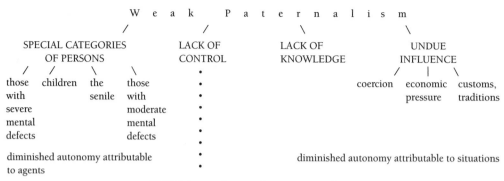

FIGURE 2 Justifications for Hard Paternalism.

who inadvertently sits on a gravestone honestly thinking that it is a bench for the visitors of the cemetery. Lack of knowledge may be due to the deceptive influence of others, or the result of negligence on somebody's part, or it can be simply accidental.

Third, *lack of control* may be involved in decisions that justify paternalistic interventions. This means that while agents know about the consequences of their actions, they can, because of temporary emotional unbalance, be unable to appreciate the full significance of these consequences and to exercise rational judgment with respect to them. This emotional unbalance, or lack of control over one's decisions, can be the result of grief, distress, or severe strains, and it has often been referred to as a potential justification for denying the possibility of legalizing voluntary euthanasia.

Fourth, people's decisions can be impaired because of *undue influence* on them from the outside. Undue influence takes many clearly perceptible forms, most notably the explicit use of coercion, but there are also less-conspicuous pressures that stem from religion, economic inducements, traditions, customs, and the like. Duelling for reasons of honor in the past has often been given as an example of the tyranny of custom that could have called for legitimate paternalistic interventions.

2. The Central Role of Impaired Decisions

The core idea of all weak paternalism is to interfere with the actions of individuals when—and only when—two conditions are met. The conditions are, first, that the individuals in question would otherwise harm themselves, and, second, that their decisions are impaired because they belong to a special category of persons, lack knowledge, lack control over their actions, or act under undue influence.

The important justificatory point here is that because the autonomy of these persons has not yet been fully developed or will never be fully developed or has been temporarily or permanently lost, seeming violations of their self-determination are not necessarily immoral, because the interventions can actually support their autonomy instead of suppressing it. Voluntary decision-making is not possible without certain mental abilities or under certain less-than-optimal circumstances, and involuntary choices are not entitled to the full respect of other agents.

D. Strong Paternalism, Moralism, and Prudentialism

Those who advocate *strong* paternalism, however, want to go further and control what they see as self-destructive, immoral, or irrational behavior even if the decisions leading to these are not, in any detectable sense, impaired. There are three types of justification for strong paternalistic interventions, but none of them can be accepted in the liberal framework sketched in Section III.A.

1. Utility

The first attempt to justify strong paternalism makes an appeal to the *utility* of benevolent control, both for the foolish decision-makers themselves and for other people. According to this view, interventions are justifiable every time the person interfering with the actions of others has good grounds to believe that the welfare of the recipient or the universal well-being of humanity will be better served by the constraint. This appeal makes, of course, perfect sense against the background of classical utilitarianism—the nineteenth-century ethical doctrine that requires us under all circumstances to maximize human happiness in the form of pleasure, preference fulfillment, or need satisfaction.

Within the liberal model the argument is, however, erroneous in two ways. On the one hand, the well-being of others is *not* a justification for *paternalistic* interventions. It can undoubtedly be a justification for interventions, but the principle that applies to this case is the *harm principle*. If individuals are about to inflict harm, for no good reason, on other individuals unless they are stopped, then their behavior may be checked, but the legitimation must come from the other-regarding harm principle, not from paternalistic considerations of any kind.

On the other hand, if the actions in question are solely or mainly self-regarding, then it does not matter what the outcome facing the free and competent agent is. If people's decisions are not impaired in the manner described in Section III.C., then there are no sufficient liberal grounds for interventions, whatever the consequences of the actions to the agents themselves may be. Individuals are, according to the originally Millian view, the rightful masters of their own fates, including their lives and deaths.

2. Morality

The second attempt to justify strong paternalistic interventions is to refer to *morality as such,* which is according to the proponents of this defense known to all decent people by intellectual or emotional intuition. Our actions are not, they argue, self-regarding in the sense that it would not genuinely matter to the rest of humanity what we do in our privacy. If, for instance, there are religious rites or sexual practices that all decent people think or feel are wrong, then they should be forbidden even if they would not harm anybody and even if the moralistic segment of the population would never have to see or experience them.

This argument is, self-evidently, valid to those who believe that morality is something that can be divined only by purely intellectual calculations or immediate emotional reactions. But it does not make sense in the context of Millian liberalism where the problem of paternalism was originally introduced. If the test for the legitimacy of control is what other people think or feel, then the true justificatory maxim is the offense principle. If, on the other hand, the point is to argue that those who act differently corrupt themselves in some moral manner, then the question is, why are the individuals involved not allowed to be the judges of their own morality?

3. Rationality

The third way to defend constraints that genuinely violate people's autonomy is to state that it is *irrational* to act in certain ways, regardless of the morality or immorality of these actions, and regardless of their effects on others. The idea is that all people are, to some degree at least, irrational, and that it is prudent for us to collectively ensure that our lack of reason cannot drive us to courses of action that we could in our more clear-headed moments regret.

This argument can be interpreted in two ways. If it is assumed that the lack of reason that human beings suffer from is temporary, then the justification for at least some interventions can be found in weak paternalism. Surely there is always an explanation for our irrationality, and if it involves references to lack of knowledge, emotional disturbancies, or undue influence, then control is appropriate because our decisions are, for the time being, impaired.

If, however, it is assumed that the lack of reason is permanent, then it is difficult to see how this deficiency could be employed to justify purely paternalistic constraints in the case of individuals who cannot be classified as retarded or mentally ill. The line of reasoning seems to be that people can be competent in any given technical sense but yet irrational due to the content of their choices. This view, while comprehensible and popular in some philosophical quarters, clearly contradicts the Millian position stated in Section I.A.

IV. MATERNALISM

A. The Sexism of the Discussion on Paternalism

The term "paternalism" carries with it many sexist connotations. One is the idea that the father is the rightful ruler of the family, and that, more generally, men in positions of authority can legitimately control women and lesser men, because they—the male authorities—know what is in the best interest of the ruled. This enhances the false view that at least some men are, because of their sex, wiser and more fitted to leadership than any women.

A diametrically opposite but also sexist aspect of the discussion is that the use of the term "paternalism" seems to imply that only men are likely to coerce other people, or restrict their liberty and violate their autonomy. The unsubstantiated implication is that men are meaner and more inclined toward totalitarian attitudes and behavior than are women.

Both views are, of course, blatantly skewed. There is no evidence indicating that men as a group would be either wiser or meaner than women, and even if there were, this would not prove anything about particular individuals. Some persons are undoubtedly more prone than others to believe in the usefulness of paternalistic control, but these persons can, for all we know, be women as well as men.

B. Paternalism and Maternalism

The belief that men are more paternalistic than women is usually based on two assumptions. The first is that not all restrictions of liberty can be counted as genuine constraints, and the second is that women are more likely to confine their actions to the nonconstraining field. The second assumption is shamelessly stereotypical, but if it is accepted for the argument's sake, an often invisible kind of strong paternalism is brought to light. This form of benevolent control can be labeled as *maternalism*—bearing, however, in mind that there is no reason to believe that it would be practiced by women more frequently than by men.

The main differences between paternalism in the traditional sense and maternalism are the following. Customary forms of paternalism consist of control by threats of punishment or by lies and evasiveness. An example of the first kind would be the state's decision to withdraw social benefits from those who refuse to assume healthy life-styles as defined by the public authorities. The paradigmatic cases where lies and evasiveness play a central role are the situations where physicians try to protect their patients by withholding information, or by telling comforting half-truths or lies.

The core idea of maternalism, in its turn, is to control people's actions by emotional blackmail. This form of control can perhaps most naturally be exercised in face-to-face circumstances such as family life, social work, or nursing. An example would be a social worker who persuades customers to conform to the rules set by the authorities by claiming that unless they do so, the social worker will be blamed for it. It must be assumed that the claim is designed to make the customers feel guilty and, eventually, to make them alter their behavior.

To put the matter in the original stereotypical terms, the paternalist is supposed to be the father who threatens to send his children to bed without supper if they behave self-destructively. Following the same logic, the maternalistic is the mother who lets her children know that she will be heartbroken if they go and hurt themselves.

C. An Attempt to Justify Maternalism

Paternalism in its traditional forms is usually defended by appeals to the greater knowledge and experience of the public and medical authorities, who see themselves as acting in a parental role as regards the rest of society. Arguments for maternalism, in their turn, are based on the claim that emotional persuasion cannot be considered genuinely coercive or constraining.

If this claim is valid, then maternalism is not a form of hard caring control at all, and no separate justification is, according to the view presented in Section III.B., required for it. The theory of freedom and constraint underlying this kind of reasoning states that only physical hindrances and coercion by threats of physical violence can restrict human liberty. Emotional persuasion, according to the model, does not curtail liberty because the recipient can always refuse to yield to the wishes of the persuader. The customers of the social worker, for instance, are not truly forced into conformity by their possible guilt.

D. The Immorality of Maternalism

But the account of freedom and constraint on which the defense of maternalism is founded is not tenable within the Millian view. Granted that psychological pressures cannot in fact restrict individual freedom because they can be rejected, the same argument can be applied to physical hindrances and coercion as well. Prisoners must, admittedly, adjust their spatial movements and daily routines to the prison walls and prison rules, but they can refuse to repent their deeds. And those coerced by threats of physical violence are always free to choose the physical violence instead of submitting to the coercer's wishes. Surely it should not be inferred from these observations that force and coercion have no influence on human liberty.

The theory of freedom and constraint outlined in Section II.A. gives, in the framework of paternalism, a more balanced view of the relationship between coercion, force, and restrictions of liberty. According to this theory, individuals are free when—and to the degree that—their options, or action alternatives, are unrestricted. People who are imprisoned have only few of their preconviction options open to them, and they can therefore be regarded as substantially unfree. Those who are faced with threats of physical violence are free in the sense that the combined choice that consists, first, of rejecting the demands of the threatener and, second, suffering the consequences is open to them even after the threat.

On the other hand, individuals who are faced with threats of violence are not free to select the combined option that was available to them before the threat and that consisted of, first, ignoring the threatener's wishes but, second, remaining unharmed. Drawing an analogy to this latter case, maternalistic actions can be seen as threats of psychological harm. The recipients of maternalistic interventions are free to reject the directives given to them, but the rejection makes them unfree to live without the awareness of the pain they may have inflicted on another person.

Consider, for instance, the case of the social worker who persuades the customers to conform to the rules by attempting to evoke guilty feelings in them. The first effect of this maternalistic action, whether in the end successful or not, is that the recipients realize that by doing what they want to do they will potentially hurt the person who tries to help them. The implications of this realization may vary considerably depending on the mental constitution and moral views of each customer. But the initial awareness concerning the situation is unavoidable, and the seeds of guilt are therefore always sown. As for the constraint caused by the intervention, the recipients are unfree to return to the state of pleasant ignorance that was unconditionally available to them before they were subjected to maternalistic action.

V. SUMMARY AND CONCLUSIONS

According to the view presented in this article, paternalism can be defined as actually or allegedly benevolent control over people's behavior and choices. Paternalistic interventions can under this wide definition be divided into three main categories. The first category, which is called in the article *soft paternalism,* is not even initially constraining, and it does not require any moral justification. The interventions in the second category, referred to as *weak paternalism,* are seemingly condemnable as restrictions of liberty, but ultimately are justifiable, because the controlled decisions are impaired. In the third category, *strong paternalism,* all attempts to alter people's behavior by repressing their unimpaired decisions constitute genuine violations of personal autonomy and are, accordingly, immoral.

The view presented in this article is based on an interpretation of John Stuart Mill's liberalism. Seen from other ethical viewpoints, the results would be drastically different. If, for instance, the central normative role is given to utility, morality as such, or rationality instead of autonomy, instances of strong paternalism could easily be justified. And if a limited view of constraint is assumed, the form of control labelled as *maternalism* must be accepted, because emotional persuasion does not constrain human actions. But these are conclusions that cannot be drawn in the Millian framework where the problem of paternalism was originally detected.

Also See the Following Articles

AUTONOMY • CHILDREN'S RIGHTS • COERCIVE TREATMENT IN PSYCHIATRY • EUTHANASIA • GENDER ROLES • INFORMED CONSENT • MEDICAL CODES AND OATHS • SAFETY LAWS

Bibliography

Childress, J. F. (1982). *Who should decide? Paternalism in health care.* New York and Oxford: Oxford University Press.

Feinberg, J. (1986). *Harm to self.* Oxford: Oxford University Press.

Häyry, H. (1991). *The Limits of Medical Paternalism.* London and New York: Routledge.

Häyry, H. (1991). A critique of the paternalistic theories of correction. *The Canadian Journal of Law and Jurisprudence* 4, 187–197.

Häyry, H. (1992). Legal paternalism and legal moralism: Devlin, Hart and Ten. *Ratio Juris* 5, 191–201.

Kleinig, J. (1983). *Paternalism.* Manchester: Manchester University Press.

VanDeVeer, D. (1986). *Paternalistic intervention: The moral bounds of benevolence.* Princeton, NJ: Princeton University Press.

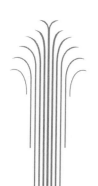

PATIENTS' RIGHTS

Bernard Dickens
University of Toronto

GLOSSARY

AIDS Acquired immune deficiency syndrome; a medical condition leaving a person liable to infection and death.

autonomy Making one's own decisions; independence.

bioavailability The effect of drugs on the body, influenced by factors such as distribution of body fat, hormones, and body chemistry.

diagnosis An examination to find the nature of a person's disease and its cause.

doctors' orders Physicians' advice to patients regarding medications and health-care practices that will assist patients' well-being.

elective treatment Medical treatment that patients may choose to undertake but the refusal of which will not endanger life.

euthanasia The deliberate causing of death in order to spare the deceased person from pain and suffering that are unavoidable by other means.

fiduciary duty A person's duty recognized by law on the grounds of the person's moral commitment or obligation.

gametes Sperm and ova.

HIV Human immunodeficiency virus, infection with which leads to AIDS.

learned professions Professions such as medicine and law, qualification in which requires lengthy study.

litigiousness An undue inclination to start legal proceedings.

natural law A concept of right reason based on nature that humans can understand through correct reasoning. St. Thomas Aquinas made natural law the foundation of theology of the Roman Catholic Church in the 13th century.

palliative care The control of pain that patients would otherwise experience from their cause of death.

paternalism Father-like or parent-like regard, now considered demeaning when it treats adults as children.

pathology Disease; the science of finding the origin, nature, and course of diseases.

pre-embryo An embryo formed by fertilization of an ovum by a sperm before it becomes implanted in the lining of the womb.

therapeutic Intended to treat disease or disability.

THE RIGHTS OF PATIENTS are applicable to the extent of different theoretical approaches to ethics. Common themes of approaches are often found in the ethical principles of respect for persons, the duty to do good (beneficence) and not harm (nonmaleficence), and justice. Rights afford patients equality in dealings with health-care practitioners when they depend on them for well-being, and empower patients to act according to their views of their interests. Rights are applicable at the individual level of relations between a health-care practitioner and a patient (micro ethics) and at the communal level of public health services (macro ethics). Approaches and principles may have different effects and priorities when applied at different levels. For example, a patient's consent is usually required for individual treatment, but public health practices may be undertaken ethically with social or political approval. Patients as citizens have rights to adequate public health services as well as to proper individual treatment. Not every person may become a patient of a chosen health-care practitioner or facility, or for a favored service.

I. THE ORIGIN OF PATIENTS' RIGHTS

The movement to require health-care professionals to recognize patients' rights and to practice their professional skills within the limits of respect for patients' rights is relatively modern. Historically, physicians, with lawyers, clergymen, and military officers, occupied positions of dominant authority in European and many other societies, and expected those who received their services to have faith and trust in their wisdom and judgment. Physicians today still often base their ethical integrity on variants of the physicians' Hippocratic oath, developed in ancient Greece by the physician Hippocrates. In its early and many later forms, the oath prohibited physicians from explaining to patients what their medical conditions were and the nature and purpose of the treatment physicians intended to give those who requested their assistance. The elite status of physicians grew in the 18th and 19th centuries when medicine transformed itself from an art into a science, as science was growing in popular prestige. Medicine came to be practiced less at patients' bedsides and more in hospitals and university schools of medical science. The move from patients' homes to centers of medical care, education, and research added to the social, intellectual, and scientific status and aloofness of physicians. It also reinforced patients' tendencies to treat physicians with deference and to not contest or question their conduct or advice. Doctors and patients accepted that "doctors' orders" should be followed, and that doctors should act in a caring parent-like or paternalistic role.

In more modern times, concepts of human equality and social democracy have eroded unquestioning faith in traditional sources of authority. The status of members of learned professions and practitioners of sciences and vocations no longer places them above having to explain and justify what they do. Physicians are no longer considered social or intellectual superiors or natural leaders of their societies, but equal participants. Medical paternalism has become discredited in ethics now applied to medical treatments, often called "bio-ethics," and patients claim and assert their rights to be treated by physicians and other health-care providers as equal adults and key makers of the health-care decisions that affect them most directly.

II. THE FUNCTION OF PATIENTS' RIGHTS

Rights can be approached from several directions and possess sophisticated philosophical, religious, legal, and other qualities. Health-care professionals and their patients commonly address patients' rights at a more immediately recognized level based on law and professional discipline. Rights of patients considered fundamental reflect claims to innate human rights, founded on moral or ethical instincts. These instincts to acknowledge rights are sharpened in reaction to the history of physicians' violations of human rights recorded at the Doctors' Trial at Nuremberg in 1946, and to later evidence of outrages in other countries, including our own.

In legal analysis, rights depend on duties. A patient has a right only against a provider of a health-care service who is compellable by a court or professional disciplinary authority to observe the duty to respect the right. For instance, a patient has a right to confidentiality of his or her health information because the health professional in whom it is confided is legally bound by courts or a professional licensing authority not to disclose such information to strangers. The patient has no similar right against, for instance, a parent, because a parent is not usually legally prohibited from informing others of a child's health status, including an adult child's. Accordingly, identification of patients' rights depends on identification of health professionals' duties that courts or other disciplinary authorities will enforce.

Many patients' rights have come to be guaranteed by legislatures through enactment in statutes. Not all legislated rights are based on ethical or moral rules, and ethical conduct often requires behavior that the law allows but does not compel. Legal rules are usually applied in ways aimed not to offend ethical rules, and not to compel individuals to act in ways they consider unethical. Reciprocally, an important ethical rule is that laws be respected, although when laws are considered seriously unethical they may be ethically challenged and even defied provided that no person or interest not willingly involved in the conflict is forced to suffer. Laws often recognize that some accommodation should be made for individuals' conscientious objection to them and for legitimate dissent. A challenge for patients is to decide whether it is ethically appropriate for them to invoke their legal rights when doing so may impose unconscionable burdens on others.

Where there is equality of all people before the law, rights empower vulnerable, disadvantaged, or dependent individuals to enjoy at least a basic equality in their dealings with others. Rights reduce the privileges that powerful or advantaged people may claim, because such people can be compelled to respect others' rights at least at the minimum level required by law. Individuals may receive treatment that exceeds the basic level of their rights, but they are equal in that no one should receive less, and anyone who delivers less than the service to which the recipient has a right will face legal and/or professional liability.

Patients' rights empower patients to be treated as health-care professionals' equals when patients recognize that such professionals possess the power of medical and related knowledge. Patients approach them for diagnosis of their sickness and for treatment and care when they are ill and vulnerable, and are at the disadvantage in their relationships with physicians and other professionals of depending on them for future well-being. Because of the tradition of medical paternalism, health-care professionals were conscientiously restrained from exploiting their power and patients' dependence, but the historical relationship was nevertheless unequal. Patients' entitlement to rights renders the relationship more equal, in that rights afford patients the power to compel those on whom they depend for health services to discharge the duties they owe.

Rights may be divided into positive and negative rights, although at times the distinction is unclear. Negative rights are rights to be left alone—to do as one wishes without interference. Individuals have negative rights, for instance, to refuse to become patients. They may remain untreated or treat themselves if they become sick or, for instance, fracture a limb. Only if they are dangerous to others, for example, due to a disease that they may spread to others or to forms of mental disorder, may they be obliged to accept medical management. Within this limit, patients have the right to

disregard medical advice and discharge themselves from hospitals against their physicians' recommendations. Positive rights are rights to receive assistance. Patients have rights, for instance, to competent diagnosis and care when they seek it from their physicians, to prescriptions for drugs available only on prescription, and to be referred to alternative service providers if they seek a legally available health service to which their health-care provider has a conscientious objection.

III. ETHICAL ORIENTATIONS TO PATIENTS' RIGHTS

There are several types of ethical theory, each of which will address patients' rights according to its own orientation. Similarly, the approach taken to the claim of a particular right of a patient will reflect one or more ethical theory of rights. A simplistic distinction, inadequate for a sophisticated understanding of ethical theories but sufficient to explore applications of theories to patients' rights, is between theories based on key abstract philosophical principles, such as natural law, duty, or virtue, which require behavior that is "right" in itself, and those based on the significance of practical experience or consequences, such as utilitarianism, which require behavior that achieves "right" results. A medical technique that achieves patients' purposes may satisfy consequentialist approaches and be considered ethical to use, but offend principles of other theories. Similarly, applications of abstract principles may lead to preventable harms in practice and offend ethical approaches based on accountability for consequences.

A. Principle-Based Theory

Many ethical theories distinguish right from wrong according to categorical rules that take little account of their practical consequences. The natural law approach, embraced for centuries, for instance, by the Roman Catholic Church, teaches that good results cannot come from evil practices, and that their ends cannot justify wrongful means applied to achieve them. Similar deontological theories, meaning theories that invoke duty or virtue, focus on the inherent conformity of conduct to required standards of behavior assessed without regard to its practical effects. Any suffering to which virtuous conduct leads is considered the price that virtue demands to be paid. The effects of conduct that violates duty, even if pleasing for some purpose, are considered corrosive of the moral order and to diminish the moral stature of persons and societies. Accordingly, patients do not possess rights to require health-care services that offend categorical rules, even if violation of such rules would achieve some goal or satisfaction for them. For instance, if use of contraceptive pills and devices and also abortion are considered wrong, rights to use contraceptive pills and devices will be denied even to limit unplanned pregnancies that cause women to have abortions. Patients' rights can exist only within the confines of the theory that defines correct behavior.

B. Pragmatic or Consequence-Based Theory

An ethical theory that assesses the merit of behavior by its practical effects on human happiness may be described as pragmatic or utilitarian. Such approaches to the application of ethics accept that it is proper to promote and maximize happiness in a given society, and that conduct that reduces human pleasure in society is wrongful. This approach to patients' rights seeks some means to assess the balance of benefit of proposed conduct against its risks within the common framework of social happiness, and praises or condemns health-care professionals according to the impact of their treatment of patients on society at large. The denial of easily delivered care that would relieve patients' sufferings, in obedience to some abstract principle, would be considered wrongful. Patients' rights would be denied to receive treatments even to save life that compromised availability of care for many others, such as by exceptionally expensive drugs paid for from the limited budget of a public hospital, or prolonged surgery that made surgical personnel and facilities unavailable to many others in need.

C. Contrasts in Approaches

Principle-based approaches focus on how patients should want to be treated, and attribute the fact that they may want to be treated differently to, for instance, their weakness of ethical resolve, lack of receiving correct education or guidance, or sin. Consequence-based approaches focus more on how patients tend to be as representatives of their societies and regard approaches to their rights that do not take account of patients' wishes and values as inadequate and flawed. A number of instances of health-care options illustrate how different ethical orientations result in different approaches to patients' rights.

The issue of elective medical termination of preg-

nancy, or abortion, has been a continuing source of social controversy between adherents to categorical rules that protect the sanctity of human life and those more concerned with protecting the quality of life that women and families experience in fact. It has been seen that a natural law approach is to consider not only abortion as prohibited among patients' rights, but also access to means of artificial contraception, since every act of sexual intercourse, which is considered proper only in marriage between husband and wife, must be open to the possibility of conception. Abortion is frequently requested by patients who experience unplanned pregnancy, and a utilitarian approach to reduction of the incidence of unplanned pregnancy is the practice of artificial contraception. Accordingly, the utilitarian view is that patients possess rights to contraceptive treatment to reduce unplanned pregnancy and their resort to abortion, and that denial of patients' access to contraceptive means they want is wrongful. The natural law view is that the reduction of resort to abortion by this means is unacceptable and cannot be considered virtuous because good cannot result from the wrongful act of artificial contraception. Sexual abstinence within as well as outside marriage and the ethical fortitude to continue unplanned pregnancy are considered correct approaches to reduction of abortion that patients have no rights to resist.

Similarly divisive are patients' rights to use condoms to reduce the spread of sexually transmitted diseases, including HIV infection and AIDS. Utilitarian orientations not only include condom use among patients' rights, but favor promotion of access to condoms among healthy people who are not patients, such as adolescents who are sexually active or liable to become so. Some principle-based theories would accommodate this means to reduce the spread of infection, but some authorities taking their guidance from interpretations of natural law oppose the use of condoms for this purpose as a right, in the same way that they reject a right to condom use for contraceptive purposes.

Medically assisted reproduction, including by sperm, ovum, and pre-embryo donation, is considered a right of patients according to some pragmatists who recognize its beneficial effect of overcoming unwanted childlessness among infertile patients. Indeed, they may consider its denial a violation of the human right to nondiscrimination on grounds of disability, since infertility is a reproductive disability. Medically assisted reproduction is not accepted as a right of infertile patients by those opposed to any artificial methods of human reproduction, but some adherents to principle-based ethics consider medical assistance of reproduction a right of married couples. However, they may consider the introduction of sperm, ova, or pre-embryos donated by third parties to be a violation of genetic coherence within families, even analogous to adultery. Some utilitarians too may consider gamete and pre-embryo donation not to be a right, because it may result in genetic confusion in society and leave its child products distressed by ignorance or uncertainty of their genetic origins. A utilitarian response is that gamete and pre-embryo donation may be included among patients' rights, provided that the resulting children have means to acquire information about their genetic parents if they wish.

Even among favorably disposed utilitarians, medically assisted reproduction may be considered only a negative right in that, while patients are entitled to have resort to it at their own expense, no health-care practitioner such as a urologist or gynecologist is bound by any duty to provide the service, and no public agency providing health care or private company providing financial insurance for health care is obliged to pay for it. This is because many forms of medically assisted reproduction depend on costly skills and drugs, increased when gamete donors have to be tested to preclude their transmission of harmful genetic conditions and infections, and the effectiveness of some procedures is uncertain.

Medically assisted suicide and euthanasia are unlawful in all but a very few countries, but are coming under increasingly widespread public discussion. They divide protagonists of different ethical orientations to patients' rights in much the same way, and on many of the same grounds contrasting the sanctity of life and quality of life, as the abortion issue. Many ethical orientations accept patients' rights to decline and discontinue medical procedures that postpone death, although some deny a right arbitrarily to end by death the discharge of duties that patients owe to others. At the other extreme, no ethical orientation recognizes that patients have rights to have their lives ended, because none accepts health-care professionals' duties to kill patients. However, particularly utilitarian theories may recognize patients' rights to ask for help in controlling the circumstances of death, whether through acts that directly result in death or facilitation of patients' means to end their lives when they cannot accomplish this result themselves in circumstances of dignity and of respect for the lives they have lived that they find suitable. Principle-based approaches tend to priorize the sense of sanctity in human life and deny that patients are entitled to request the infliction of death even when it anticipates by only a short time the occurrence of natural death. Utilitarian approaches may recognize that the final phase of dying may be a time of pain and distress, physical and mental, for both patients and those who love them, and that patients have rights to make requests that the suffering that may accompany natural dying be mitigated by medical means. Pragmatic hesitation about recognition of such rights may be based on any deterrent effect that medically assisted suicide and euthanasia may have on developments of palliative care, difficulty in distinguishing terminal anguish from severe depression, and apprehension that patients may be conditioned consciously and subconsciously by caregivers and family members to make requests.

Gene therapy is in its early stages, and many formal codes of medical and research ethics prohibit germ-line genetic therapy, meaning treatment that would change the genetic inheritance that patients transmit to their children. Gene therapy currently undertaken and in prospect is called somatic cell gene therapy, which does not change patterns of genetic inheritance but repairs some genetic deficits from which patients suffer. Genetic conditions that compromise survival and lead to premature death are clearly deficits, but other conditions are more contentious, and their treatment may be more cosmetic than therapeutic. Short stature is relative, for instance, and may be viewed differently among ethnic groups and families. Whether gene therapy to enhance a child's stature is therapy to which there is a right, an indulgence of a parental preference that may be tolerated, an intervention in a child's natural development that should be discouraged, or a risk to a child's well-being that should be prohibited are matters on which adherents to various ethical orientations are likely to differ. A consequentialist approach might find a right to seek genetic enhancement acceptable if it increases parental and family satisfaction and children's integration into their families and communities. Approaches favoring minimal intervention with nature, except for treatment of pathology, and opposed to medical enhancement that affords individuals competitive advantages over others' natural endowments might consider genetic enhancement of trivial value and at best tolerable, but not a right that may be claimed by or on behalf of a patient. Similar approaches may be taken to cosmetic surgery in general, which even the most favorable views would not elevate above a negative right of patients.

D. Comparisons in Approaches

Different ethical theories of patients' rights might find wide areas of common ground regarding many claims that patients assert. The rights of patients capable of decision making to autonomous and appropriately informed choice of treatments to which different theories consider them to have rights are widely and even universally agreed. Patients' choice is consistent with theories of virtue that hold patients responsible for the medical treatment they receive and, within limits, their health status, and with consequentialist theories that find it an enhancement of personal satisfaction and self-esteem and of patients' social standing that they should have control of medical choices.

Similarly, it is widely agreed that patients have rights not only to informed choice of their medical care, but also to control who gains knowledge of their confidential health status and medical treatment. Privacy entails control of disclosure of health and medical information, and patients do not have full rights to privacy because it is sometimes considered in the public interest that disclosure be allowed. Patients with diseases that may be spread to others, for instance, are often reportable to public health authorities, which are responsible for protection of the public and for being aware of growing pathologies that medical schools and hospitals must supply trained personnel, facilities, and means such as drugs to contain and cure. Whether information of patients' health status and medical treatment is shared with patients' consent or without their consent under the compulsion or authorization of the law, health-care professionals who receive it must treat it as confidential and exercise care against unjustified and undue disclosure. Their duties to preserve the confidentiality of patients' information they receive in the performance of their functions affords patients rights that are almost invariably legally enforceable. Ethical theories may differ on the proper scope of patients' privacy, since some would allow a wider range of nonconsensual sharing of patients' health and medical information, but almost all agree that health care professionals who receive such information, with or without patients' consent, must respect patients' rights to have their information treated as confidential.

More recently recognized but also widely agreed upon are patients' rights to be informed if the care they have received was substandard, omitted a promised element that would have contributed to their well-being, or included an avoidable or previously undisclosed element or risk prejudicial to their health. Health-care professionals' inclinations not to provide this information have historical roots and a modern reinforcement in apprehension of malpractice claims and professional disciplinary proceedings. Nevertheless, principle-based ethical theories concerned, for instance, with truth tell-ing and acceptance of moral responsibility, and consequence-based theories concerned that patients receive information they need to repair defects in care and protect themselves against future harm, agree that patients have rights to such information. Utilitarian approaches may be less certain about disclosure that treatment was substandard when health-care practitioners have taken restorative measures. It may be of no positive consequence to a patient to know, for instance, that surgery was unduly prolonged, or that a drug dosage had to be adjusted because the initial prescription or administration was too high or too low, when the surgical or drug treatment has been successfully concluded and the shortfall in care has no implications for the future. Utilitarians may find this truth telling counter-therapeutic in demoralizing patients or raising undue apprehensions, and therefore not to be a patient's right.

E. Feminist Theory

Of growing concern in consideration of patients' rights are women-centered approaches. They have arisen in reaction to the absence and frequently the exclusion of women from the historical sources of ethical discourse and authoritative pronouncements, including religious ministries, universities, medical, legal, and other professional institutions and legislative assemblies. The modern inclusion of women in many of these institutions, sometimes holding high office, has not remedied centuries of patriarchal or male-centered conditioning of the ethical influences they project. Feminist approaches to patients' rights spread across a wide spectrum, but have in common an awareness that women have been afforded fewer entitlements and less respect as authoritative decision makers in their health care than men, and that women's interests and health have been subordinated to the interests of men. Except for differences in reproductive functioning between the sexes, medical care has been based on a male model of physiology and pathology, women's health dysfunctions historically being considered not interesting or explicable by failure to meet male standards of physical and mental health or temperament ("the weaker sex").

Feminist approaches to patients' rights address the rights that women are perceived to require in order to occupy their due status and to enjoy their due respect as patients. Feminist analysts disagree about whether such rights should aim at simple equality of the sexes, which might apply male-centered duties to women's care, or at taking account of their differences. Special concerns are the disregard of women patients' well-being in application of the new reproductive technologies, the neglect of research into women's health needs at all stages of life, and nonconsensual interventions in pregnancy and childbirth justified by the belief that officials and others can protect fetuses and children better than the women who bear them.

IV. ETHICAL PRINCIPLES

Ethical theories have evolved as reactions to earlier theories and have developed in interaction with others, so that they tend to be in conflict among themselves and define themselves by their differences from others. Some are diametrically opposed to others, but even those that appear akin to each other in many respects are in fundamental disagreement in others. To overcome the contradictions and complexities in theories, attempts have been made to identify a core of basic principles that are common to leading theories. A small number have been established that are commonly, but not uniformly, recognized. Feminist analysts, for instance, may treat the principles with caution because they were identified before feminist theory was elaborated. Critics rarely claim that the principles are not common, but rather find that they do not present a full or adequate account of the ethics of patients' rights, or that mechanical application of principles ("principlism") does injustice to the merits of separate theories.

The principles are presented below in a widely followed sequence, but the principles rank equally with each other. The challenge of applied ethics of patients' rights is to assess the competing claims of different principles and to justify the ascendancy of one over others to resolve a particular conflict.

A. Respect for Persons

Patients' rights to be respected as persons are widely agreed upon. A conflict concerns which persons are entitled to become patients, and a wider conflict involves approaches to "personhood" and status of the unborn. The abortion issue becomes intractable when those who hold opposing views show no respect for each other. Those who attribute personhood to embryos and fetuses may describe those who perform abortions out of conscientious convictions as common murderers, and those who believe that women must be allowed their own choice of abortion may accuse opponents of disrespecting women's dignity and treating women only as means to the ends of fetal life. The principle of respect for persons includes two elements.

1. Autonomy

Patients capable of making health-care decisions for themselves should be enabled to do so. Decision-making capacity requires insight into and foresight of the implications of health-care options, and an ability to understand the information that health-care professionals have a duty to provide. Respect for patients' autonomy requires that they be treated on their individual merits as persons, and not be denied autonomy simply because, for instance, they are below a given age or suffer from a mental disorder. Autonomy includes the right to make decisions upon the basis of relevant information, emotion, intuition, or belief, and to make decisions that health-care professionals and others consider ill-judged. Autonomy is served when capable people anticipate times when they will lack decision-making capacity, either temporarily such as when under anesthesia or chronically such as when suffering from advanced Alzheimer's disease, and make advance medical directives of their treatment preferences that are to be respected when they are unable to express or form preferences. A limitation of patients' autonomy is that persons cannot insist on becoming patients of particular health-care practitioners or facilities but may have to meet conditions of eligibility, and may not be able to require the administration of scarce or futile treatments.

2. Protection

Persons incapable of giving effect to autonomy should be protected against abuse, exploitation, and indignity. Historically, infants, children, and mentally impaired patients were considered vulnerable and to have the right as patients to protection by an appropriate guardian. Parents and family members of such patients are often suitable guardians, but at times may use their powers of control to authorize unproven medical procedures that risk irreversible harmful effects. Historical examples include sterilization procedures and experimental brain surgery and drug treatments. Modern concerns include female genital mutilation and invasive experimentation. Adult patients of ordinary competence can also require protection of their rights, such as when they are prisoners or in the custody of police officers who want to acquire their tissue samples for genetic testing.

B. Beneficence

Beneficence, meaning the duty to do and to maximize good, seems a self-evident principle of ethics, but it presents difficulties in application to patients' rights.

Each patient has a right to have a health-care practitioner seek his or her good, but pursuit of one patient's good may be at the cost of good to another, equally entitled patient. For instance, a physician's admission of a patient to an intensive-care unit may require another patient to be removed or to forego the chance of admission when equally eligible to benefit from the unit's care. Patients have a right to their health-care provider's loyalty in pursuit of the patient's best interests, but providers often have duties toward more than one patient. When their duties are to several patients, each patient has a right not necessarily to care that priorizes his or her care alone, but to care and resources allocated according to the principle of justice; that is, the duty to do good and the right to have good rendered are applied at a communal rather than an individual level. When health-care providers are compromised in their pursuit of the good of all of their patients by inadequate resources, patients' rights arise to providers' advocacy of their interests before public and private suppliers of the resources on which patients' welfare depends.

C. Nonmaleficence

The principle to "Do no harm" is sometimes considered an element of beneficence and is described as the first rule of medicine. Patients may claim rights not to be harmed and to have the risk of harm minimized in the course of receiving care. The concept of harm extends beyond physical injury and includes harm, for instance, to dignity, respect in the community, and self-esteem. Harm is sometimes an unavoidable risk in medical care, since, for instance, surgery exposes patients to risks of anesthesia and of being accidentally injured, and therapeutic drugs expose patients to risks of previously unknown adverse reactions. Patients' rights are to health-care providers' disclosure of the likelihood of benefit, known risks, and side effects of the proposed and alternative treatments and the range of unknown risks, and to assistance but autonomy in assessing the risk-to-benefit ratio in deciding whether or not to consent. In types of medical research, there may be no intended benefit to participants, who may or may not be patients of the investigators. Further, harm such as piercing of a vein or artery for blood sampling may be deliberate. Patients invited to participate in research, and other participants, have rights to minimization of deliberate harm and the risk of unintended harm, and to full information. Participants who face no physical risks, for instance, because only their medical records are intended to be consulted, may still risk the disre-

spect of lost confidentiality if their autonomy of choice is not observed.

D. Justice

Although patients' rights are primarily concerned with principles of distributive justice, corrective or punitive justice is implicated when health-care professionals accept or are required to bear responsibilities in capital punishment, prisoners' health-care in solitary confinement, and hunger strikes undertaken in protest against alleged wrongdoing. Distributive justice requires that like cases be treated alike and different cases with due regard to the difference, but criteria of likeness and difference require justification. Rights to the just allocation of scarce resources, for instance, may indicate that patients closer to death are more deserving of care that is their last means of survival than patients with less urgent needs and several choices, because their proximity to death renders their care different and of higher priority. Equally, patients with a better prospect for recovery of all normal functions may claim to be different from, and a higher priority than, those likely to die, or to survive with severe impairments. Resource allocation that favors more severely ill patients closer to death may devote scarce resources to the least promising patients and prejudice those capable of recovery. Allocation to achieve the most promising outcomes of care may abandon patients to comfort measures only until death when, due to age, poverty, or other factors outside their control, their future prospects fail to satisfy a test of adequacy.

Organ distribution programs for transplantation frequently have to resolve difficulties of meeting patients' rights justly. For instance, nonalcoholic and reformed alcoholic patients may claim rights to priorization over nonreformed alcoholic patients for liver transplantation because they have better prospects of survival of liver disease. Nonreformed alcoholics may claim a right to equal entitlement as a matter of social justice, because their addiction is involuntary and they should not be disqualified from eligibility for indicated treatment on the ground that they suffer the illness of addiction. The priority to maximize utility of scarce resources is incompatible with the priority to help patients at greater risk of death. The justice of either priority will be contested by patients and their family members who feel prejudiced by it, and who may advance claims based on beneficence and nonmaleficence. This raises issues in the applied ethics of patients' rights of whether favor toward selected patients is discrimination against others, and of the level at which analysis of the problem is to be undertaken.

V. LEVELS OF ETHICAL ANALYSIS

Development of medical and wider health-care ethics on the basis of personal conscience and the intimate, person-to-person nature of the relationship between health-care provider and patient has conditioned conventional ethics of patients' rights to be pitched at the individual or micro-ethical level. The proposition that an ethical physician will consider first the well-being of the patient is honorable when the interest competing against that of the patient is the physician's. In modern health care, however, providers frequently have therapeutic responsibilities to several or many patients. When health-care services are privately purchased, patient purchasers may claim protection and priorization of their interests through legal doctrines of contract law and fiduciary duty. When health care is delivered through publicly funded services or facilities, or through collective insurance or other institutions in which individual patients consent to participate, the ethics of patients' rights may be approached by reference to collective or public interests, or macro ethics.

A. Micro Ethics

The respect a health-care provider owes a patient and the patient's ethical entitlement to that respect are addressed in every ethical theory applied to patients' rights. Views differ on whether the micro-ethical relationship is to be governed by respect for the patient's autonomy or whether another principle warrants priority, such as beneficence or nonmaleficence. For instance, a patient may confide an intention or disposition to act in a way that endangers an identifiable third party, such as by having unprotected sexual intercourse with an unaware partner when the patient is infected with a sexually transmissible disease. Some claim that the duty of confidentiality owed to the patient should not be betrayed, and that the health-care providers' powers should be limited to offering the patient advice on the implications of behaving in the way disclosed. Others claim, however, that such advice should be given and that, if the patient remains recalcitrantly committed to the harmful conduct, the health-care provider, after duly informing the patient, may warn the party at risk. The micro-ethical dilemma may accordingly be resolved by priorizing the principle of respect for persons through the patient's autonomy, through beneficence

affording the third party protection, and through nonmaleficence in minimizing the patient's commission of harm. The latter two responses may be favored because they also protect the interests of the patient in not becoming responsible for causing harm. However, it may be disrespectful and paternalistic for a health-care provider unilaterally to undertake to enforce the ethical duty that a patient owes another.

In fact, many societies have anticipated and addressed the dilemma of observing the duty of confidentiality or the power (or at times the legal duty) to warn by laws that compel health-care providers to notify public health authorities of patients' transmissible diseases. Health-care providers who act under such laws that limit patients' privacy may then observe patients' rights of confidentiality in good conscience by not making further disclosures, and public health authorities that undertake, for instance, contact tracing and warning of those at risk must usually also observe confidentiality in not disclosing the identities of warned persons' sources of risk. In some cases the identities of such sources are obvious, and in others innocent persons may fall under unjustified suspicion. In either case, however, the issue is not left for resolution at the micro-ethical level but is tackled at a social or macro-ethical level.

B. Macro Ethics

Public health services approach patients primarily as participants in the affairs of the societies they affect, which are often those in which they reside, rather than as individuals who have obtained health-care services. Public health officers often prefer emphasis on the health service they perform, but their constitutional status and ethical capacity arise from a state's police powers. Like other police, they sometimes appear in uniform and frequently have powers of involuntary detention of suspected persons (quarantine), can interrogate them for information (contact tracing), and may be empowered to compel treatment to protect and cure when there is danger to the community. The practice of epidemiology (classically meaning the study of epidemics) is a routine instrument of public health care that may include consultation of patients' identifiable medical records without their consent or knowledge, and as seen above, health-care providers' duties to report patients' information given in confidence. The need for information is to know the prevalence of disease in order to provide protective and preventive health care for communities at risk.

The ethical justification for many public health practices is that they are not governed by principles that are applied at the micro-ethical level of analysis, where involuntary detention and data disclosure are usually considered unethical, but at the level of macro ethics. Here, the social principle of justice has priority. Societies decide at a collective or political level what measures of individual restraint and individual and collective protection are required, and how conflicts between patients' individual rights and collective rights as citizens are to be resolved. Patients dissatisfied with how the balance between their rights as private persons and as citizens have been resolved are free in democracies to have resort to political action to change the balance.

Hospitals and clinics are also able to apply ethical principles at the macro-ethical level to address patients' interests as citizens. Both public facilities and private hospitals and clinics, including nonprofit facilities and those operated commercially, may apply ethical principles to decide which services to offer and how they propose to allocate their resources. As its population ages, for instance, a community hospital may reduce pediatric services in order to expand geriatric care. Hospitals may determine by what application of justice organs are to be allocated for transplantation, or with which organ-sharing arrangement they will collaborate, and teaching hospitals responsible for training future health-care practitioners may decline to provide the volume of services for which there is a local demand in order to expose students to a full experience of treatments and not just those for which demand is greatest. The interests of patients proposed to be served by these policies are rights in only a moral sense, since they are not enforceable by legal or disciplinary means, unless governments operate public facilities or licence private facilities in ways that afford individuals means of legal resort to enforce ethical accountability.

C. Meso Ethics

Between the private and the public planes of micro and macro ethics are meso ethics. These address the administrative or bureaucratic level of application of ethics. They often frame the context in which patients' rights are applicable at the micro-ethical level, because they allocate resources with which health-care practitioners are able to meet the needs of individual patients. Meso ethics arise after decisions have been made at the macro-ethical or political level to furnish, deny, or amend services for communities. They may not involve patients' rights in a direct sense, since patients often lack legal or disciplinary means to compel any particular allocation of resources, but they may involve patients'

rights to procedural fairness in that patients may have enforceable rights to know what resource allocation decisions have been made or are available to be made, and the grounds on which they were or may be made. Moreover, human rights laws may be available through national and international instruments, the latter applying at universal or regional levels, that open administrative decision-making processes to scrutiny to enquire whether decisions have the purpose or effect of violating antidiscrimination provisions and to apply sanctions against offending decisions. Not all administrators of health-care resources are affected, but those in the public and quasi-public sectors who are required to observe principles of administrative law may be compelled to respect the rights of patients, their family members, and prospective patients to open and fair processes of decision making.

VI. SPECIFIC ELEMENTS OF PATIENTS' RIGHTS

A. The Right to Become a Patient

Where governments undertake to provide citizens with health-care services, citizens usually acquire rights of reasonable access to medically necessary care, and to any additional care governments choose to make available such as preventive services. Health-care providers and administrators usually bear duties to ensure that this standard of care is available. Provision may be made through the funding of public hospitals, national health insurance plans, or, for instance, services made available to patients on the basis of their particular needs due, for instance, to advanced age, infancy and childhood, disability, or poverty. Patients who acquire rights under such programs have rights to a general level of care, but in most cases cannot claim treatment of any nature or cost, by any particular health-care provider or facility, or within any time unless perhaps if delay would exceed anticipated survival time without treatment. Further, patients with access to a health-care provider of their choice cannot usually insist that the practitioner admit them to any hospital of their choice, since most hospitals are "closed" rather than open to any practitioner who wishes to admit patients to them and treat them there. Admission of patients to a particular hospital is a privilege the hospital grants to physicians and sometimes others such as dentists, and is not a right of patients except perhaps in emergency cases. Similarly, a hospital that admits a person as a patient does not usually grant the right to treatment through any particular member of its staff of the patient's choice, nor to treatment that the practitioner in charge of the patient considers futile or not indicated by the patient's condition or circumstances. These limitations of rights severely confine patients' claims to be treated according to the ethical concept of autonomy. Autonomy is most significant at the micro-ethical level of observation of individual patients' rights, and has a lesser role at the macro-ethical or social level of application of rights.

Patients may acquire rights to health care under private arrangements such as health insurance contracts and employment-based provisions. They will then enjoy rights against contracting parties and perhaps others bound to give effect to those arrangements. Not all interactions with health-care professionals are for therapeutic reasons alone or are governed by the same ethics as the conventional doctor–patient relationship. A practitioner who examines employees in order to monitor their fitness and health and safety in the workplace, for instance, may assume duties to assist them to obtain indicated therapeutic services, but is not bound by duties of confidentialty not to disclose unfitness to the employer when reporting is an essential purpose of the examination.

In some cases the right to become a patient does not exist. Even under government-funded schemes, some persons may be ineligible, such as noncitizens and illegal immigrants and those who fail to meet criteria of coverage such as age or low income. Persons without the means to purchase the care they want may then be unable to become patients. Those who have the means may also be unable to be patients, however, because accessible practitioners decline to accept them on grounds that do not violate applicable antidiscrimination laws. It may be an offense to reject a person on the ground of race, color, or, for instance, HIV-positive status, but not if the practitioner has ceased accepting any new patients due to pressure of existing commitments. Practitioners may also decline to accept applicants as patients for procedures to which they have conscientious objections, such as abortion, without assuming duties owed to patients to refer the applicants to other practitioners who do not share their objections.

More contentious is whether refusals may be based on applicants' litigiousness and history of suing practitioners for malpractice. It may be ethically defensible to decline to accept such persons if practitioners' insurers or the hospitals where they hold treating privileges will discontinue relations with them regarding their acceptance of such applicants. Distinctions may have to be drawn between *bona fide* litigation and nuisance or vexatious proceedings that lack a reasonable basis

in law or fact since the former may not be an ethical ground to refuse care. Although an individual practitioner may have no micro-ethical duty to accept as a patient a person who has sued other practitioners, the profession itself may have a macro-ethical duty to ensure that those who genuinely believe they have suffered malpractice not be denied competent care.

B. Medical Research

Much medical research involves participants who are not properly considered to be patients. They may be described as subjects of research or as participants for whom physician-investigators have no transcending therapeutic responsibilities. They must be afforded due care during research procedures, of course, and be provided for if injured as a result of their participation, but they do not enter studies because they are patients. However, many patients are invited to take part in research, sometimes because they are conveniently accessible to investigators by reason of attending hospitals, clinics, or health-care practitioners' offices, and sometimes because of the very conditions for which they seek diagnosis and appropriate treatment. Further, at times the investigators inviting patients' participation in research will be the health-care practitioners to whom they have gone for care.

Codes of medical research ethics invariably limit therapists' abilities to ask their own patients to become participants in their research, because of their conflict of interest and the risks of coercion and patient's fears of offending those on whom they depend for care. At times, however, research justifies patients taking part in their therapists' investigations. Patients' rights must then be carefully protected, since research does not simply depart from the physician–patient relationship, but inverts it. In therapy, a patient seeks help and a physician assists the patient. In research, an investigator seeks help and a subject assists the investigator. This inversion may not be apparent to a patient-subject, and it may equally not be apparent to the therapist-investigator.

A patient has the right, however, to the therapist's recognition of inversion of the usual relationship, to a full explanation that a departure from usual therapy is proposed in the invitation to participate in research, and to noncoerced, noninduced, autonomous choice of participation. The inversion may be masked in therapeutic innovation, which is designed to assist a patient for whom conventional care is unavailable or inappropriate, and when the research offers one of two or more conventionally indicated forms of care to be allocated according to a research design. In the latter case, the research consists not in the care itself but in the suspension of the practitioner's clinical judgment exercised in the patient's best interests in favor of impersonal allocation set by the study.

It has recently been recognized that, while individual patients have a micro-ethical right not to take part in medical research, patients in a collective sense have a macro-ethical right to require that research be conducted. Patients living with AIDS and HIV infection have been vocal and forceful in demanding that research be conducted into their condition, condemning the refusal to fund and conduct research as discrimination. They have asked that they participate in drug, vaccine, and selected studies designed to develop means to treat them and to find a cure for their infection.

Women's groups have noted the lack of studies into conditions that affect women except those concerned with pregnancy and infertility and the historical omission of women from studies to develop treatments given to women. For instance, some drug treatments modeled on studies of men are ineffective or unsafe for women because of the different bioavailability of drugs in men and women. Women may have been excluded from studies because women were not considered different from men, because of uncertainty about the risk to unborn life if they were pregnant or became so, or because their different stages in the menstrual cycle introduced hormonal variables that made results of study difficult to interpret and required a larger sample size, and so greater research expenditure, to obtain statistical validity for women subjects at different stages of their cycle. Now, however, it is required that women be appropriately included as research subjects in studies in order to ensure that therapies intended for both sexes are as effective and safe for women as for men. Women have a collective right as patients to know that treatments proposed for them have been researched on women subjects.

VII. ETHICS COMMITTEES AND PATIENTS' RIGHTS

Several types of committees make decisions on ethical matters that affect patients' rights. Hospitals have ethics committees at central and sometimes departmental levels that address issues of patient care, and those where research is undertaken on human subjects have research ethics committees named, for instance, institutional review boards in the United States and research ethics boards in Canada. Alternatively and sometimes in addition, hospital-based research is reviewed by university-based human subjects ethics review committees. Other health-care facilities such as nursing homes and specialized clinics are increasingly creating ethics review committees, and independent committees exist which are composed of members with suitable backgrounds and who review the ethics of research proposals, for instance, from drug and medical device manufacturers. Ethics committees have been created by many health-care professional organizations and licensing authorities, and governmental departments and agencies concerned with health care and, for instance, social services sometimes constitute such committees. Also concerned with patient care, although not primarily with ethical aspects, are health-care institutional risk management committees and adverse incident review committees. These may recommend reforms that affect how their institutions handle patient care, usually in the interest of increased safety but sometimes by sacrificing some patients' interests for promotion of the interests of others.

Individual patients do not have rights to sit on these committees, but they may have rights to require institutions and agencies to constitute committees or to have their practices, policies, and proposals considered by committees at appropriate levels, to require patients' interests to be represented on committees in an adequate manner, and to make representations that will be heard and to which committees will have to respond. Views differ on whether committees should consider individual cases and deal with them prospectively or only retrospectively. Committees are not licensed to practice medicine and are subject to patients' expectations of confidentiality, so they may not have powers to review patients' medical records. Hearing cases anonymously, however, they may make recommendations for future management. Their best function is probably retrospective review of patient care, perhaps making remedial recommendations, and consideration of policy matters such as assisting administrators in making meso-ethical decisions.

Committees often sit behind closed doors to preserve confidentiality and frankness of their deliberations, although policy matters may be aired in public. Advance notice of their meetings may not be publicized, but their conclusions and recommendations are often circulated in their institutions and sometimes in the community, including by news media releases. Patients can usually obtain information of committees' activities, findings, and recommendations.

However, findings of health-care facilities' risk management and adverse incident review committees may not be accessible, even by legal proceedings. Such committees may identify errors in patient management and care that indicate their institutions' and staff members' legal liability or make recommendations for safety on which institutions have refused or negligently failed to act, leading to repetition of injuries to patients. Some laws and courts will compel production of such committee reports to litigants in proceedings against institutions, but most will not, holding the reports to be internal documents privileged from production to third parties. This is because it is considered in the interests of the public in general and patients in particular that institutions critically review their practices and correct them when necessary. Review might be deterred or compromised if institutions that conduct them thereby create instruments that can be used against them, while institutions that do not care to conduct reviews of incidents of harm to patients are protected. Patients may have a right to be informed of their substandard care, shown perhaps by internal hospital reviews, but may not obtain the assistance of such reports in legal proceedings.

Also See the Following Articles

ADVANCE DIRECTIVES • AIDS • EUTHANASIA • GENE THERAPY • HUMAN RESEARCH SUBJECTS, SELECTION OF • INFORMED CONSENT • MEDICAL ETHICS, HISTORY OF • PATERNALISM • REPRODUCTIVE TECHNOLOGIES

Bibliography

Annas, G. J., and Grodin, M. A. (1992). "The Nazi Doctors and the Nuremberg Code: Human Rights in Human Experimentation." Oxford Univ. Press, New York/Oxford.

Beauchamp, T. L., and Childress, J. F. (1994). "Principles of Biomedical Ethics," 4th ed. Oxford Univ. Press, New York/Oxford.

Dickens, B. M. (1994). Legal approaches to health care ethics and the four principles. In "Principles of Health Care Ethics" (R. Gillon and A. Lloyd, Eds.), pp. 305–317. Wiley, Chichester.

Dworkin, R. (1977). "Taking Rights Seriously." Harvard Univ. Press, Cambridge.

Gillon, R., and Lloyd, A. (Eds.) (1994). "Principles of Health Care Ethics." Wiley, Chichester.

Leary, V. (1994). The right to health in international human rights law. *Health Human Rights* 1, 24–56.

Sherwin, S. (1992). "No Longer Patient: Feminist Ethics and Health Care." Temple Univ. Press, Philadelphia.

PERFECTIONISM

Douglas B. Rasmussen
St. John's University

GLOSSARY

agent-neutral Describes any value, reason, or ranking V for which, "if a person P_1 is justified in holding V, then so are P_2–P_n under appropriately similar conditions.... On an agent-neutral conception it is impossible to weight more heavily or at all, V, simply because it is one's own value" (D. Den Uyl, 1991. *The Virtue of Prudence*, p. 27. Peter Lang, New York). Sometimes referred to as "impartialism" or "impersonalism."

agent-relative Describes any value, ranking, or reason V for which its description includes "an essential reference to the person for whom the value exists, for whom the ranking is correct, or who has the reason" (E. Mack, 1989. "Moral Individualism: Agent-relativity and deontic restraints." *Social Philosophy & Policy* 7, 84). Thus, a good, G_1, for a person, P_1, is *agent-relative* if and only if its distinctive presence in a world, W_1, is a basis or reason for P_1 ranking W_1 over W_2, even though G_1 may not be a basis or reason for *any other* person ranking W_1 over W_2.

cognitive realism The epistemological position that holds that human beings can know what things really

are. This position is opposed to the claim that the mode or manner of human knowing determines the character of the content of human knowledge.

consequentialism Any theory in normative ethics that attempts to determine obligations simply by whether an action or rule produces the greatest, net, expected "good" (or least "bad") consequences.

contractarianism Any ethical theory that attempts to determine normative and/or political obligations by an appeal to what is (or would be) agreed upon by actual or hypothetical persons, considered apart from their social situation. It is usually assumed that conflict resolution is the central aim of ethical theory.

deontology Any theory in normative ethics that holds "duty" and "right" to be basic and defines the morally good in terms of them. Such theories attempt to determine obligations apart from a consideration of the good. For Kantians, this is accomplished primarily by a universalizability test.

eudaimonia The ultimate good for human beings and goal of human conduct as understood in terms of an examination of human nature. Traditionally translated as "happiness," meaning "satisfaction of *right* desire" or "good feeling *plus* well-being," but more recently expressed by such terms as "human flourishing," "self-perfection," "self-realization," or "self-actualization."

naturalistic fallacy The alleged fallacy of deducing a statement of what *ought* to be from a statement of what *is* the case, or of a statement about a *value* from a statement about a *fact*.

phronēsis A form of practical reasoning in which there is intellectual insight into the particular and contingent that determines the proper course of conduct at the time of action. It is not simply means–end reasoning or cleverness, but it is usually translated as "prudence" or "practical wisdom."

utilitarianism A consequentialist theory of obligation whose aim is neither altruistic nor egoistic, but universalistic. One's own good should be considered, but not more than any other's—hence, it is an agent-neutral theory.

virtue ethics Any theory in normative ethics that attempts to determine obligations by an appeal to what the virtues require. Usually, the virtues are understood as features of the human good.

———————————————————

PERFECTIONISM refers in ethics primarily to normative theories that treat the fulfillment or realization of human nature as central to an account of both goodness and moral obligation. If we understand normative ethics to ask two questions, (1) "What is inherently good or valuable?" and (2) "How ought persons to conduct themselves?", the respective answers of perfectionism are that *eudaimonia*, that is, happiness, human flourishing, or self-perfection, is the ultimate good or value and that human beings ought to live virtuously. "*Eudaimonia*," however, is an unfamiliar term, and "happiness" as a translation of *eudaimonia* does not, as it does for many modern ethicists, mean a subjective good. Rather, it is understood to mean an objective good. Thus, "human flourishing" may more accurately signify what is meant. Further, "perfect" comes from the Latin *perfectus* and its Greek counterpart *teleios*. *Perfectus* implies that a thing is completed or finished and thus involves the idea of a thing having a nature which is its end (*telos*) or function (*ergon*). To "perfect," to "realize," or to "actualize" oneself is thus not to become God-like, immune to degeneration, or incapable of harm; it is rather to fulfill those potentialities and capacities that make one human. Finally, the notion of a thing functioning well or with excellence is the completion or attainment of its *telos*. This is the basic idea of virtue (*aretē*). *Eudaimonia* is an activity according to virtue.

I. PERFECTIONISM IN CONTEMPORARY ETHICS

Perfectionism has had a strong influence throughout the history of ethics. From Plato, Aristotle, and Aquinas

to Hegel, Marx, and Nietzsche, various conceptions of the good life, as defined by human nature, have been a central part of normative ethics. During most of this century, however, perfectionism has not fared well. It was thought to embody a "naturalistic fallacy," to entail commitments to controversial ontological and epistemological views, and simply fail to offer sufficiently determinate advice for ethical conduct. Deontology, contractarianism, and consequentialism (usually in some utilitarian form) have dominated the ethical scene. However, with John Rawls' discussion of theories of goodness and perfection in part three of *A Theory of Justice* and Alasdair MacIntyre's criticisms of consequentialism and deontology in *After Virtue*, as well as Bernard Williams' criticisms of impartialism in *Ethics and the Limits of Philosophy*, interest in perfectionist and virtue theories in the last quarter of the 20th century has greatly increased. Further, the explosion of works on Aristotelian ethics and politics as well as the efforts of such scholars as Ackrill, Foot, Cooper, Maslow, Norton, and Miller have helped to bring such terms as "self-perfection," "self-actualization," "self-realization," "human flourishing," and "eudaimonism" into current philosophical usage.

Perfectionism in contemporary ethics has moreover taken an interesting turn in that it is understood increasingly to be a radical departure from Kantian, contractarian, and utilitarian modes of theorizing. This is especially so with a neo-Aristotelian version of perfectionist thought. This theory, the many interrelated features of which generate an elaborate conception of the human good and obligation, illustrates well how perfectionism represents a fundamental alternative to this century's more dominant views in normative ethics. The following outline and discussion will provide a basis for understanding the challenge to Kantian, contractarian, and utilitarian outlooks presented by contemporary perfectionist thought. It will also provide a point of departure for a discussion of the ontological and epistemological presuppositions of perfectionist ethics.

II. A NEO-ARISTOTELIAN VERSION OF PERFECTIONIST ETHICS

Before embarking on an outline and discussion of this contemporary perfectionist theory, a comment is necessary about the use of the term "neo-Aristotelian" to describe it. "Neo-Aristotelian" is used "for modern theorizing which incorporates some central doctrines of

Aristotle.... Such theorizing should critically assess his claims in light of modern philosophical theory, scientific research, and practice experience, revise or reject them where necessary, and consider their application to . . . contexts not envisioned by him" (F. D. Miller, Jr., 1995. *Nature, Justice, and Rights in Aristotle's* Politics, pp. 336n1. Clarendon Press, Oxford). Though often interconnected, there is a difference between neo-Aristotelian theorizing and an exegesis of Aristotle's texts. It is, then, in the foregoing sense that this perfectionist theory is neo-Aristotelian.

Central to understanding this neo-Aristotelian version of perfectionism is the account that is given of human flourishing. Accordingly, the basic, interrelated, features of human flourishing should be examined.

(a) Human flourishing is a way of *living* and is thus not intelligible apart from a biocentric context. But it is nonetheless a *way* of living. It is thus something more than self-preservation or survival. Further, it is not the mere possession of needed goods and virtues. *Omne ens perficitur in actu:* flourishing is to be found in action. Basic or "generic" goods would not exist *as goods* (or virtues *as virtues*) if they were not objects or manifestations of a person's effort. Flourishing is an activity, not a static or passive state.

(b) Human flourishing is an object of desire. Yet, in terms similar to Socrates' question to Euthyphro, flourishing *is* an object of desire, because it is desirable and choiceworthy, not simply because it is desired. Thus, flourishing is understood to be an objective value. This is, however, not to say that it is an agent-neutral or abstract universal value. Rather, it is because of what flourishing is that makes it an objective value. It is an actuality, as well as an activity, and thus ultimately the standard by which desires, wishes, and choices are evaluated.

(c) Human flourishing is an inclusive end, not a single dominant end. Human flourishing is "the *most* final end and is never sought for the sake of anything else, because it includes all final ends" (J. L. Ackrill, 1980. "Aristotle on Eudaimonia" in *Essays on Aristotle's Ethics,* (A. O. Rorty, Ed.), p. 23. Univ. of California Press, Berkeley). Human flourishing comprises basic or "generic" goods and virtues—for example, such goods as knowledge, health, friendship, creative achievement, beauty, and pleasure, and such virtues (or rational dispositions) as integrity, temperance, courage, and justice—that are valuable not merely as means to human flourishing but as expressions of it. As such, these goods and virtues are regarded as final ends and valuable in their own right. Thus, human flourishing is not an

ultimate end that reduces the value of everything else to that of simply an instrument.

(d) Human flourishing is individualized and diverse. "Human flourishing" is not some abstract universal. There is only individual human flourishing, but individuals do more than provide spatial differentiation. Human flourishing achieves determinacy and reality only through a joint engagement of the individual's unique talents, potentialities, and circumstances with "generic" goods and virtues. Human flourishing is dependent on *who* as well as *what* one is, and is thus not interchangeable, but is unique. Thus, this account of human flourishing offers a version of moral pluralism that is not simply subjectivism.

(e) Human flourishing is agent-relative. It is always and necessarily the good for some person. It is not merely that flourishing occurs or takes place within some person's life. Rather, it arises and obtains *in relationship* to some person's life. There is no such thing as human flourishing *period.* There is no flourishing-at-large that is not essentially the good-for-some-person. As a result, it is illegitimate to hold that ethical reasoning requires one to be indifferent to whose good is being achieved. One person's good cannot be substituted for any other. Contrary to an agent-neutral view, it is legitimate to weight more heavily a good because it is one's own—for example, the well-being of one's children as opposed to those of others.

(f) Human flourishing is achieved with and among others. "Only a beast or a god would live outside the polis," as Aristotle notes (*Politics*, 1253a27–29). Human flourishing is not atomistic. It does not require gaining the goods of life exclusively for oneself and never acting for the sake of others. Indeed, a significant part of human potentialities is other-oriented. *Philia* (friendship) is an integral feature of the self-perfecting life. Further, there are no a priori limitations on relationships. Though relationships with others are based on values that form the basis for a continuum of relations—from close friends to acquaintances to the development of communities and cultures—human sociality is open-ended. The interpersonal dimension of human flourishing demands that consideration be made for how it might be possible for different individuals to flourish and to do so in different ways (in different communities and cultures) without coming into moral conflict. Thus, natural sociality opens perfectionism, which sees flourishing as always lived in some community and culture, to questions of frameworks and modern political issues—particularly to the problem of finding a political framework that is both compatible with the moral propriety of pluralism and yet based on something that can be mutually advantageous to everyone involved.

(g) Human flourishing is self-directed. Practical wisdom, which will be discussed next, is the central integrating virtue of human flourishing. Yet, practical wisdom is not passive. It is not something that happens to the individual. The functioning of one's reason or intelligence, regardless of one's level of learning or degree of ability, does not occur automatically. Rather, it is something the individual initiates and maintains. It requires effort or exertion. Effort is needed for reason to discover the goods and virtues of human flourishing as well as for it to achieve and implement them. Practical wisdom is fundamentally, at its very core, a self-directed activity. Thus, "self-perfection" suitably describes the nature of human perfection, because not only is the *object* of perfection the individual human being, the *agent* of perfection is the individual human being as well.

III. THE ROLE OF PHRONĒSIS OR PRACTICAL WISDOM

The foregoing outline makes it clear that for this perfectionist theory human flourishing is something plural and complex, not monistic and simple. There is a basis for this view in Aristotle, for when criticizing the Platonists he states, "of honor, wisdom, and pleasure, the accounts are distinct and diverse. The good, therefore, is not some common element answering to one idea" (*Nicomachean Ethics*, 1096b23–25). But whether this is Aristotle's final view or not, there is, in this account of perfectionism, no single good or virtue that dominates all others and reduces them to mere instrumental values. Such goods as health, creative achievement, friendship, beauty, pleasure, and knowledge, and such virtues as integrity, courage, temperance, and justice, are essential features of human flourishing and as such are valuable in themselves, not merely as means.

Each is only one of the features, however. Each, like all the other necessary features of human flourishing, must be achieved, maintained, and enjoyed in a manner that allows it to be coherently integrated with everything else that makes up human flourishing. Moreover, since human flourishing is individualized, these goods and virtues must be achieved in light of a consideration of the set of circumstances, talents, endowments, interests, beliefs, and histories that descriptively characterize the individual—what is called his or her "nexus"—as well as the individual's community and culture. Thus,

an examination of human nature may reveal basic or "generic" goods and virtues, but it does not reveal what the weighting or balancing of these goods and virtues should be. As Ackrill observes regarding Aristotelian eudaimonism,

> [Aristotle] certainly does think that the nature of man—the powers and needs all men have—determines the character that any satisfying human life must have. But since his account of the nature of man is in general terms the corresponding specification of the best life for man is also general. So while his assumption puts some limits on the possible answers to the question "how shall I live?" it leaves considerable scope for a discussion which takes account of my individual tastes, capacities, and circumstances. (J. L. Ackrill, 1973. *Aristotle's Ethics*, pp. 19–20. Humanities Press, New York)

In other words, what human flourishing *concretely* amounts to for any particular individual is not something that can be simply "read off" human nature in some a priori or recipe-like manner.

Since knowing what human flourishing "generically" consists of does not solve the question of how people should conduct their lives, the charge of underdetermination has, as a result, often been leveled at perfectionist ethics. The neo-Aristotelian perfectionist response is, however, to turn this seeming flaw into one of the theory's principal advantages. If it is indeed the case that self-perfection is the aim of human conduct and if human flourishing is a highly individualized, agent-relative activity, then a large measure of individualism must be factored into the process of determining what a person should do. The Kantian (and utilitarian) supposition that the *sine qua non* of ethical reasoning is providing impersonal prescriptions is simply wrong-headed. The attempt to provide a set of specific and equally suited rules of conduct for all persons regardless of their nexus, which has characterized so much of 20th century ethics, confuses agent-neutrality with objectivity and law with ethics, and forgets the open-endedness of ethics. Such ethical rationalism ignores the central integrating role of the virtue of *phronēsis*, translated as "prudence" or "practical widsom," to an ethics of self-perfection.

If the foregoing respone is to be appreciated, however, the nature and role of prudence within this perfectionist ethics must be understood. Practical reason is the intellectual faculty employed in guiding conduct. This faculty can be properly or improperly used, while prudence or practical wisdom is the excellent or virtuous use of this faculty. That prudence is *the* intellectual virtue for ethics is shown by considering Aristotle's definition of moral virtue. "Virtue or excellence is a state of character involving choice and consists in observing the mean relative to us, a mean defined by a rational principle, *such as a man of practical wisdom would use to determine it*" (*Nicomachean Ethics,* 1107a1–3, italics added). It is thus difficult to overstate the importance of prudence for this view. Yet it is not merely cleverness or means–end reasoning. Instead, it is the ability of the individual at the time of action to discern in particular and contingent circumstances what is morally required. Since there are for this view no a priori universal rules that dictate the proper weighting of the goods and virtues of human flourishing, a proper weighting is only achieved by individuals using *phronēsis* at the time of action to discover the proper balance for themselves. Abstractly considered, there being a plurality of ends that compose human flourishing does not logically entail that these ends are incompatible. Concretely considered, keeping them from becoming incompatible by discovering the proper weighting or balance of these ends is an individual's central task.

Achieving proper weighting or balance is needed as well for the moral virtues or rational dispositions that define an individual's character. When considered as a class, moral virtue is necessary for the coherent achievement and use of multiple basic human goods, but when considered not as a class but as one good among many, a virtue can be given more or less emphasis—for example, a soldier's emphasis on the virtue of courage. Thus, the outcome from this consideration remains the same. Individuals need to determine the proper balance in light of the unique facts that pertain to them and through a consideration of the contingent circumstances. As Aristotle notes, "the mean is relative to us." The entire process is one in which the particular and contingent are ineliminable.

It is admitted that there may indeed be times where though the principles are clear, the situation precludes achieving all the necessary goods. Tragedies are possible. Ethics is understood as being concerned with what is, in principle, within the realm of human agency, and then it is only concerned with what is for the most part. Human lives are not numbers that can be neatly fit into a mathematical equation. Though there is no abstract incompatibility among the goods and virtues of flourishing, making them compatible is not necessarily guaranteed. There is no single path or set formula. Despite what theologians, politicians, philosophers, and even

friends may offer—and sometimes this can be valuable—only individuals exercising their own prudence or *phronēsis* can make themselves whole.

According to this neo-Aristotelian version of perfectionism, the role of prudence in the self-perfection process not only moves practical reasoning away from a concern for basing conduct on impersonal prescriptions, but also away from consequentialist, utilitarian, and contractarian reasoning. This occurs in the following ways:

(a) It is not necessary to calculate what the expected consequences of every proposed course of conduct might be in order to determine what is good and ought to be done. Though such calculation would be appropriate for dealing with matters that are entirely instrumental to self-perfection, this is not so when it comes to the features of self-perfection itself. The first principle of practical reason is, as Aquinas noted, pursue good and avoid evil. Thus, the major concern is determining what in the particular and contingent is really good or virtuous. Once one discerns what is good or virtuous, one knows what ought to be done. It is in this respect that an ethics of self-perfection is also a virtue ethics, because virtues are seen as activities that characterize our human flourishing, not simply as external means.

(b) Yet the proper use of practical reasoning is not simply a process of maximization. The chief appeal behind consequentialism is that given that something is a desirable goal, it seems irrational to choose a course of conduct that gives one less of it. But if it is the case that desirable goals are never pursued in isolation from other such goals, then practical reasoning has to involve more than simply maximizing a good. It has to determine how to weight the pursuit of one necessary good or virtue relative to another so as the achievement of one does not eliminate the achievement of another. Indeed, practical reason properly used, which is the virtue of prudence, is the intelligent management of one's life so that all the necessary goods and virtues are coherently achieved, maintained, and enjoyed in a manner that is appropriate for the individual human being.

(c) The utilitarian conception of practical reasoning as a process of comparing proposed acts or rules in terms of which produces "the most" human flourishing is mistaken. The utilitarian confuses abstractions with realities and treats one person's version of human flourishing as comparable to another's. It is as if the pursuit and achievement of human flourishing were a race in which everyone competes for the same prize. There is no unified race, however, with a single standard of swiftness. There is no flourishing-at-large, no agent-neutral best end. Versions of human flourishing are only valuable relative to some individual; thus the attempt to aggregate "total outputs" of actions or rules in terms of some agent-neutral conception of human flourishing is not something at which practical reason can engage.

(d) The procedure by which practical reasoners momentarily distance or put themselves outside their current situation in order to either abstractly consider what is the best that is possible for human beings or to relate to others does not show, as some advocates of contractarian (and discourse) ethics contend, that an agent-neutral conception of human flourishing is required. Taking a perspective other than one's own—whether it be ideal, that of a friend, or of any human being—is a valuable tool for prudence in an agent-relative view of self-perfection. An individual's moral growth, in both its personal and its interpersonal dimensions, requires that this procedure be used, because self-perfection requires learning about one's potentialities and understanding others. However, it is a mistake to equate the value of taking such perspectives with the idea that values and reasons for conduct should or must be agent-neutral. After using such perspectives, an individual needs to return to his or her own case to determine what ought to be done—that is, to determine how to achieve the highest level of excellence with respect to various potentialities that is compatible with the most complete enjoyment of the other necessary goods and virtues. Human flourishing remains individualized and agent-relative.

(e) Since neither individualism nor agent-relativity imply that human flourishing is subjectively determined, and since humans are naturally social and need to live with and among others to flourish, there is no radical worry why individuals should be concerned for others or about setting the context for their own flourishing. Despite whatever heuristic value they might have, the value of state-of-nature thought experiments as a basis for moral analysis and understanding is very minimal. It is not necessary to (1) posit atomistic individuals, who conduct themselves solely according to instrumental reason, and (2) take as the problematic to be solved why these alleged beings should have any concern for others. Nor is it necessary to launder the nature of reasoning through such devices as "veils of ignorance," "impartial ideal observers," or an agent-neutral view of practical reason to show why individuals can have concern for others or for the character of their political/legal frameworks. Yet such natural concern remains individualized and agent-relative, and thus any attempt to formulate foundational political principles would need to be both consistent with the diverse forms of human flourishing and based on something in which each and every person in the concrete situation has a necessary stake. Such political principles, unlike normative ethics, would need to be both universal and minimal. This perfectionist theory would seem, then, to support political principles that facilitate mutually advantageous compossible flourishing, such as a system of individual rights. Contrary to Rawls, there would seem to be at least one version of perfectionism that would not lead to illiberal political institutions.

IV. ONTOLOGICAL AND EPISTEMOLOGICAL PRESUPPOSITIONS

The foregoing account of perfectionism has two basic ontological presuppositions and one major epistemological one. They are, respectively, natural teleology, essentialism, and cognitive realism.

Undoubtedly, the most important feature of this neo-Aristotelian perfectionist ethics is its claim that human flourishing (or self-perfection) is the end (*telos*) or function (*ergon*) of human life, for it is this claim that allows this theory to avoid the "naturalistic fallacy." It is, however, its most controversial feature. This claim is often associated with dubious metaphysical views, which MacIntyre termed "metaphysical biology"—namely, that there is an end of the cosmos, that species are fixed and do not evolve, and that there is a *scala naturae* ascending from simple elements to an unmoved mover. Moreover, teleology is associated with such positions as theism, vitalism, ineluctablism, and genericism as well as the fallacy of anthropomorphism. Indeed, there are some advocates of contemporary perfectionism, such as MacIntyre and Hurka, who seek to avoid making ontological commitments when it comes to understanding human flourishing.

Present-day advocates of natural teleology argue, however, that their position does not require them to uphold any of the foregoing views or commit any fallacies. It is not necessary to hold that the cosmos, history, society, or the human race is directed toward some grand *telos*. Instead, it is only necessary that individuals have ends. Moreover, there are individuative potentialities that are actualized. It is not true "that all developmental processes are generically equivalent across individuals such that individuals come to be little more than repositories of generic endowments" (D. Den Uyl, 1991. *The Virtue of Prudence*, p. 36. Peter Lang, New York).

Neither does teleology require ineluctability. Human

beings actualize their ends through their own self-directed action. They are not driven to it. Nor is it necessary to hold that God has created the universe or individual things to serve some end to which they are drawn. There need only be a *naturalistic* teleology.

Further, it is not necessary to deny evolutionary theory or posit a separable force, an *élan vital*, within an organism that provides direction and motivation. Rather, teleology can be understood as an internal directive principle that is an irreducible feature of the developmental processes of the living organism itself. The process is irreducible in the sense that the movement from potentiality to actuality is inherent in the structure of the organism in such a way that other forms of explanation (e.g., mechanical or chemical) are insufficient to account for the phenomenon. It is thus argued that minus Aristotle's account of the physical mechanisms through which end-oriented behavior takes place, the theoretical core of Aristotle's teleology—namely, that life-forms are self-directing in virtue of inherent forms or structure—is vindicated by modern biology.

The claim that human flourishing is a *telos* is also closely connected with the idea that there is a distinct human nature in terms of which this *telos* is defined. As noted earlier, to "perfect," "realize," or "actualize" oneself is not to become God-like, immune to degeneration, or incapable of harm, but is to fulfill those potentialities and capacities that make one human. The idea here is complicated, because it is not, as some critics think, that an entity's function is determined by what is peculiar or unique, but, instead, it is by what is "proper" or "essential" to human beings. In terms of Aristotelian logic, it must be considered to what the "genus" refers as well as the "differentia" in understanding the essence of something, and for human beings, it is animality and all that goes with it. Moreover, it needs to be realized that any definitional statement of an entity's essence is a condensation of a vast number of facts and is meant to provide the means by which it is sorted conceptually from other things. It thus implies the presence of many other qualities and features than those explicitly noted by the definition. For the neo-Aristotelian theory we have been describing, then, fulfilling our human function is "the practical life of man possessing reason," not disembodied reasoning. Fulfilling our function includes the faculties shared by other animals such as pleasure and health, and, as has been already discussed, many other things as well. What the distinguishing characteristic does is to characterize the *modality* through which the development of these other faculties will be successful.

According to this view, the character of human flourishing or self-perfection is not discovered by a scientific study of human nature alone. Considerations of the requirements and conditions for human choice and action, cultural and social practices, and common-sense observations are part of the process. Yet any account of human flourishing, if it is to function as a basis by which the status quo is evaluated, requires an understanding of what is a human being is. Otherwise, there is no limit on what is ultimately included or excluded from the account. The foregoing account of perfectionism is thus essentialistic in the following minimal sense: what and who human beings are is not entirely a function of social or cultural forces, linguistic and conceptual schemes, or systems of interpretation. In other words, there are individual realities of a certain kind to which the term "human being" refers.

Whether human beings can know human nature, or indeed the nature of anything, has been an issue in modern philosophy for some time. It is argued, however, that a commitment to cognitive realism does not require that human knowing be God-like or that our understanding of things, including human nature, cannot change. Thus, our conception of human flourishing could change as well. Of course, possibilities cannot be merely asserted. However, the central area of dispute in contemporary epistemology for cognitive realism is the question, "Does the very manner and mode of human knowing itself determine the character of the content of human knowledge?" The fate of this neo-Aristotelian version of perfectionism rests on the answer to this question, but of course so does much more.

V. CONCLUSIONS

Certainly, some regard the dependence of this form of perfectionism on controversial ontological and epistemological positions to be a weakness. However, it is not clear that a normative ethical theory can avoid having controversial presuppositions, and if a theory can, it is also not clear that it can be of any use.

By offering an account of the human good that is not agent-neutral, while still objective, and a view of prudence that avoids the hubris of ethical rationalism, while still allowing a place for reason, this theory offers a defensible form of moral pluralism. This theory also seems to have use when it comes to foundational political questions, for it offers the possibility that liberalism might have a perfectionist foundation after all. Though perfectionism is certainly one of the oldest normative theories, it remains to be seen how this most recent incarnation will fare.

Also See the Following Articles

Bibliography

Cooper, J. (1975). *Reason and Human Good in Aristotle.* Harvard Univ. Press, Cambridge, MA.

Den Uyl, D. (1992). "Teleology and agent-centeredness." *The Monist,* 75, 14–33.

Hurka, T. (1993). *Perfectionism.* Oxford Univ. Press, New York.

Norton, D. L. (1976). *Personal Destinies.* Princeton Univ. Press, Princeton, NJ.

Rasmussen, D. B., and Den Uyl, D. J. (1991). *Liberty and Nature.* Open Court, La Salle, IL.

Rasmussen, D. B., and Den Uyl, D. J. (1998). *Liberalism Defended: The Challenge of Post-Modernity.* Elgar, Cheltenham, UK/Lyme, NH.

Salkeaver, S. G. (1990). *Finding the Mean.* Princeton Univ. Press, Princeton, NJ.

Veatch, H. B. (1971). *For an Ontology of Morals.* Northwestern Univ. Press, Evanston, IL.

Veatch, H. B. (1992). "Modern ethics, teleology, and love of self." *The Monist,* 75, 52–70.

Whiting, J. (1988). "Aristotle's function argument: A defense." *Ancient Philosophy,* 8, 33–48.

PERSONAL RELATIONSHIPS

Andrew Gilman
Andover Newton Theological School

GLOSSARY

civility Behavior in public that is due to others generally.
civil sphere The social region that lies outside of the state and beyond the family in which individuals can meet in public as private persons.
fidelity The deep commitment of a person to be trustworthy and faithful.
friendship A companionable relationship built on some valued commonality.
practice A socially instituted rule or way of doing things that helps people realize important ends.

PERSONAL RELATIONSHIPS refer to one sort of connection that people have with other people. These are associations which one enters voluntarily and which are usually of some duration, although this is not always the case. Of course, most, if not all, of one's ties to others are personal relations insofar as they exist between persons. However, as an ethical topic, personal relations should be distinguished from other ties such as those arising from kinship or official roles. While these are certainly morally significant, they are qualitatively different from personal relations, primarily because of the element of choice. For instance, family ties have a quality of givenness to them. They are a function of one's position in a network based on consanguinity more than individual volition. This means that one has duties and claims that grow out of one's preestablished status as a child or parent or cousin, not on the basis of one's own will. Similarly, one's obligations as a professional or as an employee are related to one's official position. These duties exist by virtue of one's role rather than because of one's volition, as tends to be the case with personal relations. Personal relations, even in this circumscribed sense, are a matter of importance to every community. Every culture has some sort of guidance it offers its members for appropriate behavior in this area. Often such guidance is based on custom and tradition or is understood primarily as a matter of etiquette. In the West, there has also arisen an ethics of personal relationships, by which is meant rational reflection on these connections. This is really a branch of moral philosophy and is concerned with articulating ideals and standards appropriate to these relations. What follows is written primarily with reference to the contemporary Western context.

I. INTRODUCTION

It is analytically useful to describe three general categories into which personal relations fall. These classifications are neither absolutely independent of one another nor are they all of one piece. Relations tend to be quite varied and dynamic in their makeup and so these categories do not really characterize discrete realms. Rather they identify three very broad ranges of connections that people have with one another. These categories are analytical tools which help highlight important moral issues. Few personal relationships fall purely within the bounds of a single classification, although they often reflect one more than another.

The first category covers those relationships that we have with nonacquaintances. These are associations we have with people whom we do not know but with whom we interact in public settings. Examples of such nonacquaintances are the people we pass by on sidewalks, those we stand next to on platforms, or those with whom we chat as we wait for appointments. We often call such people strangers, because we have not been introduced, even informally, but they are not aliens or outsiders in any strong sense. They are simply people who are unknown to us but with whom we deal on a level above mere impersonality. We are expected to acknowledge them as persons even though they are unfamiliar to us. We know that we share public space with them and thus are fellow participants in at least some minimal sense. As a consequence, we have ethical duties toward them, usually known under the rubric of civility, which describes the standards of personal conduct appropriate in society at large.

A second category of personal relationships refers to associations with people with whom we are acquainted, often quite closely. These are people we know and with whom we have some sort of bond usually formed on the basis of a shared interest or experience. Our connections with these people may be extensive or they can be somewhat distant. In either case we are sufficiently familiar with them to know that they have some important interest or experience in common with us. They may be cohobbyists. They may be fellow alumni. They may simply be people who habitually have coffee at the same time and place as we do. Whoever they are, they share a significant aspect of our lives and to some extent reflect our own concerns. The ethics of this sort of personal relationship is often discussed under the heading of friendship.

The third ethical category of personal relations deals with those which are predicated on a high degree of commitment and trust between persons. Here we share more than an interest with another; we share ourselves. Our lives are tightly intertwined with one another and we draw on a sense of commitment that transcends the bonds of civility or friendship. Marriage is the most common form of this sort of personal relation, but by no means is it the only form it takes. Best friends, long-term associates, and partners of various sorts can also embody this personal relation. The ethical dimension of this category is discussed primarily under the notion of fidelity.

II. RELATIONS WITH NONACQUAINTANCES

A. Background

Of the two major roots of Western ethics, only one has a significant regard for strangers. The philosophical traditions of classical Greece tended to have a fairly strong sense of boundaries and a penchant for exclusion. Outsiders, whether by place of residence, language, or gender, were not accorded the same respect as full citizens. This is true of the Platonic, Aristotelian, and Epicurean traditions. Only the later Stoics approached a universal regard for all persons. The biblical perspective, on the other hand, did emphasize ethical duties to outsiders. In part this is attributable to the stress on hospitality appropriate for a nomadic culture. For people whose herds led them from one pasture to another, the ready provision of shelter and food was an important safety net and numerous stories in the Bible are predicated on this duty. There was more than this, however, in the biblical perspective. Obligations to strangers had a sacred quality which was connected to the historical experience of the people of Israel. As resident aliens in Egypt who understood themselves to have been protected by God, the people of Israel preserved a sense of the vulnerability of outsiders and the need to treat them fairly. They also maintained a sense of their own distinctiveness, especially in the writings from the period after their Exile. But a minimal sense of responsibility for strangers was also maintained.

The Stoic universalism and the biblical stress on duties to aliens provide some basis for the morality of personal relations to strangers. However, in the modern era, there has been a qualitative change. New possibilities have emerged in our relations with nonacquaintances largely because of social evolution. The growing complexity of society has produced spaces for interactions between persons who are not related by kinship or office. Rather, they are connected to one another as private individuals in the public realm. This new space is called the civil sphere. The thinkers who first took note of this development were often interested in economic activity. This is true for the Scottish Enlightenment figures Adam Ferguson and Adam Smith. It was also true for G. W. F. Hegel, who gave added philosophical depth to the concept of civil society in his *Philosophy of Right*. In the recent past, Jürgen Habermas has helped reinvigorate interest in this notion, particularly in his *The Structural Transformation of the Public Sphere*. The essential idea refers to that realm of society which is neither fully private nor formally public. It does not include the state, with its official apparatus, nor does it include the family, which is the location for more intimate relations. The civil sphere includes groups and associations, theaters and taverns, religious institutions and schools, places of employment and centers of recreation, and so on. Clearly, not all of these arenas are equally open to all; however, they share the common attribute of being places where one encounters others with whom one is not acquainted, but with whom one has some degree of social interaction.

In the 17th and 18th centuries, when the civil sphere emerged in western Europe, it was centered in such places as London coffeehouses, Parisian salons, and German literary societies. While admission to these was certainly limited, they were still unprecedented in the breadth of their inclusion. They were spaces where people who did not know each other were held accountable to some level of duties to one another. At the very least, they were expected to listen to each other. Today we are not limited to these particular settings. In fact much of our lives are lived in the civil sphere, especially in developed nations, where a strong tradition of limited government as well as circumscribed authority of the family exists. Much of what fills the expanding social space between these two realms is the civil sphere in which we are in public but as private individuals. Our behavior to one another as we wait for buses or gather at sports events or stand in lines at checkout counters is not a matter of interest to the state, nor is it dependent on family standing. We are neither public officials nor entirely private individuals, but we are not really strangers either. Consequently, there is a degree of behavioral expectation that applies to us all. This is identified as civility, understood not in its broad sense of considerate conduct toward others, but more narrowly as the behavior appropriate generally in the civil sphere.

B. Norms of Civility

Civility has rarely been an explicit topic of moral reflection. It is generally expected that people will accord one another the minimal regard that is due universally to all persons, but there has been little attention by ethical thinkers to the bonds of personal relationships between nonacquaintances. Writers of etiquette manuals sometimes address this matter when they discuss our behavior to others in public. However, the moral requirements of civility go beyond mere politeness. It is not enough that we not be rude to one another, although this is a fine start.

A useful indication of the norms of civility can be gained from rules which were posted on the walls of a 17th century London coffeehouse. These were written in verse and included the following:

> Pre-eminence of place none here should mind,
> But take the next fit seat that he can find:
> Nor need any, if finer persons come,
> Rise up for to assign to them his room.
>   *   *   *
> Let noise of loud disputes be quite forborne,
> Nor maudlin lovers here in corners mourn,
> But all be brisk and talk, but not too much,
> On sacred thing, let none presume to touch,
> Nor profane Scripture, nor saucily wrong
> Affairs of state with an irrevent tongue: ...

(Quoted in J. Timbs, 1899. *Clubs and Club Life in London*, pp. 272–273. Chatto and Windus, London)

1. Bracketing of Status

These few lines indicate some of the dominant normative themes of civility. Four expectations should be noted. The first is that one's place in civil space is allocated on a first-come, first-served basis. One's personal or official status is of little weight. Rather, there is a rough equality among participants. Once one has a seat, he or she does not have to cede it to another, regardless of the other's position. This norm is commonly reflected today in our behavior in lines, where the order of service is established according to the time of one's entrance rather than on the basis of one's social standing. Once we have taken our position, we do not have to give it up to another, and those who attempt to cut into the line are both resented and usually rebuffed. There is a fundamental notion of fairness based on equality of status. In the civil sphere we are private individuals in public, sheared of our status either within our families or in our official capacities. It is certainly true that we do engage in relations in public where status plays a part. In some situations we defer to those who occupy certain roles. If we arrived at a buffet table at the same time as our boss, we would probably let him or her go ahead of us. In a general discussion where an authoritative figure is present, we would probably permit him or her to have the first word. However, on the whole, in the civil sphere, where our ties are truly a matter of personal relationship, one's status outside of the sphere is bracketed.

2. Inclusiveness

By the same token, we are expected to extend to one another some minimal level of respect to all. We do not have to give up our place to another, but we are to permit whoever shows up after us to occupy the next position. We may be able to reserve some number of spaces in our line, but we are not permitted to limit the sort of person who can occupy unreserved spaces. An open seat at the coffee house was legitimately available to the next patron who showed up. The place in line behind us is there for anyone who wants it. This feature reflects a low-level expectation of inclusion. As public space, the civil sphere is open to all. Sometimes, this explicit openness does carry within it implicit exclusions. For instance, the London coffeehouses were the province of males, generally of the middle social classes. However, this indicates a less than complete realization of the norm that should hold. Barriers of this sort are contrary to the basic expectations of this realm. Just as all are roughly equal by virtue of their status as private individuals in the public realm, so all merit the same possibility of inclusion.

3. Propriety

A third normative standard reflected in the coffeehouse rules is the limitation of conduct to the sort of behavior appropriate for the civil sphere. One should adjust the way one acts to take into account the fact that one is acting in a public space. Lovers, maudlin or otherwise, are not to sit off in a corner thinking deep thoughts. This behavior is too private. It is appropriate for the intimacy of one's home, where such private concerns are to be pursued. In a 17th century coffeeshop such conduct is out of place. One owes to the others a self-restraint that reserves such highly personal matters to other places. In the civil sphere one is expected to participate, at least somewhat, in the common life of the location. Of course, in contemporary settings, one may certainly sit and think of whatever he or she wants. However, in a public event such as a concert or athletic contest, a fellow member of the audience who kept harping on his or her own personal concerns would be considered a bore, if not worse. Similarly, revelations by a fellow passenger of highly private matters is usually seen as inappropriate. In any interactions that take place, one is expected to limit him- or herself to matters of general interest, and not raise personal issues.

4. Adjustment to the Context

A fourth norm is similar. It is that one should accommodate one's participation to the general level of interests and backgrounds. Just as one should not focus on one's own private concerns, so one should fit one's comments and conduct to the public context. The coffeehouse rules prohibit talk of either religion or politics (or at least "saucy" comments about the state) because these topics are both highly charged and appropriate to other spheres. Religion is both otherworldly and personal. Governmental matters are official. As topics of conversation, they should be pursued elsewhere. The civil sphere is a distinct space. It is a realm of public relations among private persons. One should adjust one's talk accordingly. There is a range of appropriate topics to which one should limit oneself. In today's world sauciness is not viewed as negatively as it was in the 17th century. However, irreverence of a certain sort is still understood as contrary to the norms of the civil sphere. We do not observe a strict prohibition on political or religious issues, but we do expect that people will observe limits. For instance we think that people should not insult another person's deeply held beliefs. Similarly, some values (such as the dignity of all persons) are not appropriate to disparage. By and large, we limit ourselves much more than this. We do not discuss ideals or highly charged values as we stand in lines or sit next to one another on buses. Except for very unusual circumstances, we limit our conversation in the public realm to topics which will not offend others. In a culture which emphasizes as strongly as we do each individual's right to personal expression, this can be quite a discipline. The fact that we observe this limit on our comments even minimally is an indication of the importance of this norm.

These four norms apply to our personal relations with nonacquaintances. They are the expectations on us as participants in the civil sphere. They are fairly low-level, but they are still significant. Among strangers we are still subject to demands that apply to our relationships with one another. We are not to call upon our status in spheres other than the civil sphere, we are not to prevent the general inclusion of all participants, we are not to engage in conduct appropriate to other spheres, and we are not to act in a way that offends general sensibilities. These normative standards are obviously quite basic, so much so, in fact, that they are often overlooked in ethical reflections. Certainly few moral philosophers have given much attention to them. In the past one of the few places these norms have been raised is in discussions about conversation. Here one can find explicit attention to these expectations, but such treatments are often seen more as matters of etiquette than ethics. They often appear in literary essays (for instance, Henry Fielding, Jonathan Swift, and William Cowper have all written about conversation) which tend to be nontechnical and so may be taken less seriously by ethical thinkers. Some modern scholars have given attention to conversation (for instance, Bruce Ackerman and Seyla Benhabib have argued about the range of topics that is appropriate for public discussion), but only a few have done so. On the whole, however, the normative standards appropriate for our relations with nonacquaintances have not been given a thorough consideration in recent years.

C. Concerns

1. Pluralism

There are two general concerns that complicate the normative standards for personal relations among nonacquaintances. The first is that the norms can be expressed in a wide variety of ways. While the general expectation that all people in the civil sphere be granted roughly equal standing, the definition of that standing may vary quite a bit. Different people may have quite divergent understandings of the accepted boundaries of a private individual in public life. What is included? For instance, traditionally, the range of legitimate topics was limited to reason giving; however, many people in the contemporary world would want to include feelings. Another area of difference concerns the people with whom one is closely related. For many persons, one has standing in the civil sphere as an individual, stripped of all ties and connections. Others have a sense of themselves that includes their close relations. The same concern arises in connection with other aspects of one's background. Is one's religion or race or ethnic makeup or sex a legitimate part of one's identity as a private individual in the public realm? Different persons may arrive at various answers, a fact which complicates the ethical picture.

Another aspect of this sort of pluralism is the style of discourse which people normally employ. Much research has been done that indicates that people from different backgrounds tend to use dissimilar linguistic patterns. Sociability may be expressed by some through an argumentative speech while others do so by being quite restrained. Some people show respect through directness, others through indirectness, and so on. These styles are rarely so extreme that a person from a different background cannot decode them, but the interactions of the civil sphere are often so ephemeral and peripheral to one's attention that misreadings are actually quite likely. When this happens the personal relations one has with strangers tend to be undermined.

2. Privacy

The increased emphasis on privacy is another potent influence on personal relations in the civil sphere. While there has always been a realm of private life which counterbalances our social relation, it has traditionally been fairly limited. In the modern world, the private realm has expanded dramatically. It is no longer limited to the domestic realm, as it has been for much of our history. Many areas of our life are now oriented to personal discretion and individual autonomy. Especially as this latter notion is understood by John Stuart Mill, it reinforces an expanded role for privacy in our lives. When Mill advocated the freedom of the individual to pursue his or her own plans, he had in mind the opposition of public opinion as much as governmental restriction. In either case he sought to give each person great discretion in choosing his or her own path in life. This is an idea which resonates widely in the modern world. People are quite interested in personal freedom, understood as the lack of restraints by others, be they neighbors or the state. This sort of liberty is a very appealing idea, and it finds expression in our daily lives by such commonplace features as the wide use portable radios with individual headsets or the great appeal of support groups. Rousseau worried about the destructive effects of the theater, because each person enjoyed the show in the dark, alone. He would be even more nervous about the modern innovation of home theaters which enable one to enjoy the show without ever leaving one's own residence. Of course, the most prevalent and significant encouragement to privacy is the automobile, which has profoundly altered our world far beyond its function as a personal form of transportation. It has changed the way we do errands, eat meals, organize our commercial areas, and so on. In all these areas it has heightened our ability to insulate ourselves from one another. By no means is this necessarily a negative development. There are ethically defensible reasons for endorsing a heightened emphasis on privacy in our lives. However, there is also certainly a price. In general, whatever else any of these developments have done, they have affected our sense of relationship to one another. By increasing our insularity, they have made it more difficult for us to realize our relationships with nonacquaintances. They have diminished the number of actual interactions we have with such people, thereby weakening the civil sphere. The result is that we tend to have fewer resources for establishing such relations. When opportunities do present themselves, we are less able to take advantage of them. Erving Goffman used the term "civil inattention" for the modern obligation in a public setting not to notice others. In elevators we are to look at the doors rather than other passengers. As we pass on the street we are expected to drop our gaze. In doing this we respect the privacy of the other person by maintaining the fiction that we do not see them. The challenge such a heightened sense of privacy poses to our relations with nonacquaintances is powerful indeed.

III. RELATIONS WITH CLOSE ACQUAINTANCES

A. Background

Unlike civility, the ethics of our personal relationships with close acquaintances has been a topic of great interest throughout most of the history of Western moral philosophy. The classical authors wrote on this matter, as did many figures in the early modern era. Although the biblical corpus does not give much attention to this topic it does appear there as well, for instance in the story of David and Jonathan, whose relationship was of equal, if not more, importance to them than the authority of King Saul, Jonathan's father. The centrality in the Bible of the love of neighbor also touches on this theme, although not in a direct way. While the sort of concern that is envisioned is of the intensity usually identified with friendship (one is to share thoroughly with one's neighbor and to care for him or her), it is clearly the case that a neighbor can be a stranger. In the paradigmatic story of the Samaritan (Luke 10:29–37), neighborly love transcends historic enmities. This sort of relation is an approximation of theological ideals. As such, it is perhaps best understood in terms of one's relation to the divine, rather than as a matter of personal relationships.

The classical philosophers gave sustained attention to relations between close acquaintances. Beginning with Socrates in the *Lysis,* moral philosophers have addressed a range of questions surrounding this topic. They have inquired into the basis for such bonds, the relative importance of these connections, the ethical

weight they should bear for each of us, and the social significance of this sort of relationship. By far the most influential of these thinkers is Aristotle, who devoted a significant portion of the *Nicomachean Ethics* to this topic. Although several other important thinkers such as Montaigne, Kant, Kierkegaard, and Emerson deal with this topic, Aristotle remains the dominant author. On the one hand he saw friendship as a matter of broad importance. For instance he advanced the notion of civic friendship, asserting that political bodies were held together by personal bonds between citizens. On the other hand he also understood friendship as an ideal restricted to a fairly small elite. It was more like an extra bonus to a good life than an essential ingredient. This is especially true for the best form of friendship which is focused on moral goodness. Other bases for close relations are pleasure and utility as when we connect with those who amuse or benefit us. In Aristotle's view these are less than satisfactory foundations for they are superficial and unstable. The most durable basis of friendship is also the most morally significant. It is virtue. One is friends with another whose character one admires. Since only those who are themselves good can truly appreciate the goodness of others, this sort of friendship is limited to those who are virtuous. This seems to restrict friendship unduly, but the real liability to Aristotle's view is connected to his understanding of the approximate self-sufficiency of truly good persons. Since they are not deficient, they cannot be said to *need* friends, an observation which leads Aristotle to wonder about the real importance of friendship. He concludes that although relations with close acquaintances are not essential ingredients of a good life, they are a positive addition. One tends to be happier with them than without them.

The contemporary discussion of relations between close acquaintances draws much of its impetus from the work of Carol Gilligan and others who have emphasized the moral importance of personal qualities of care and concern. Some earlier moralists, including David Hume, Adam Smith, and Arthur Schopenhauer, had given significant attention to the role of sympathy or compassion in morality. However, these suggestions have not been widely pursued among ethicists, who have preferred to stress such elements as impartiality and universality in their moral systems. In reaction to this tendency some contemporary figures have drawn attention to the neglect of relationships in ethics. They have pointed to the moral importance of emotional attachment as well as rational disinterest, to particularity as well as to universality, and to responsibility for one another as well as rules. In Gilligan's phrase, many have advocated an "ethics of care." While very few of these authors have connected this newer theme with the traditional discussion of friendship, both are addressing the same general area of interest.

B. Norms of Friendship

The literature on friendship and the attention to an ethic of care point to four norms of close relationships. They are freedom, commitment to one another as a particular person, an approximate sense of equality between the closely related persons, and reciprocity among them.

1. Freedom

The first attribute is that those related must have something in common that they value. As with any relationship there needs to be a tie that binds people together, but here the tie is not a matter of kinship or an ascribed feature *per se*. People do not become closely connected simply because they are from similar backgrounds or have similar physical attributes, unless, of course, those elements become objects of value. Personal relationships that are close emerge from common interests or shared experiences that are seen as significant. One's occupation can be the focal point for such a relationship with a colleague, as can one's hobby. As Aristotle's analysis indicates, we can build close associations with those who participate in our sense of amusement, with those whose interests are more pragmatic, and with those whose ideals reflect our own. Whatever sort of relationship we build, it emerges on the basis of a common regard for some feature of our lives which we have chosen.

The ethical corollary of this feature is that one must recognize the need for a degree of choice and freedom in the other. If part of the foundation of a close relationship is some value that is chosen, then the other must be granted the opportunity to choose. By virtue of the connection, one is bound to acknowledge a degree of space for the other. It would not be right, even if it were possible, to control or program the other person. A robot cannot be a friend. A genuine relationship of familiarity with another entails the commitment to recognize some sphere of independence in the other person in order for him or her to choose the value or experiences that are the basis for friendship.

2. Particularity

One of the deficiencies of Aristotle's analysis of friendship is his understanding of the other as a sort of extension of oneself. He calls the friend a "second-self," a reasonable designation given that he assumes one will choose someone not from any need of company but to see the ideals one already holds reflected in another. Modern commentators have been helpful in reminding us that part of a genuine relationship is a regard for the particularity of the other person. One does not establish a close bond with another person as a type or an icon. Relationships of this sort may exist, but they are not really close and hardly personal. Authentic connections are between individuals who have unique identities, and it is the uniqueness that is at the heart of the association. The quirks and idiosyncrasies of the other person are central to their appeal because they help define who the other person is in his or her concrete existence. When a friend does us a favor, he or she may say it is what anyone would do for a friend, but ideally it is more than that. It is what my friend does for *me*.

Just as one is morally obligated to grant one's companion a degree of free space, so one is bound to attend to his or her distinctiveness. One cannot expect the other person's individual needs or interests to be submerged under some generic pattern. It is wrong to see others with whom one is closely connected simply as members of categories. Instead, one must make the effort to notice their particularity.

3. Equality

Friends must be roughly equal. Obviously, they are not the same, nor they equal in every way. They do need to be similar in the terms that matter most to them. If the basis for their relationship is their interest in a hobby, they should have roughly equivalent levels of interest and knowledge. If they are connected because of a shared experience, they must occupy more or less the same status. If their association is founded on professional ties, they ought to be in approximately parallel positions. One can be friends with one's classmates, one's partner, or one's fellow team member. It is much less likely that one have a close personal relationship with one's teacher, one's boss, or one's coach. A consequence of this approximate equality is that one should not seek to dominate or disempower one's close acquaintance. Similarly, one should not accede unduly to the other's wishes. Of course, arguments will be won and lost. Moreover, deference will be voluntarily granted. As an overall pattern, however, rough equality of power must be maintained.

4. Reciprocity

By the same token, a genuine close relationship has an aspect of mutuality. Friends not only maintain a balance of power, but also engage in give-and-take. Their association is reciprocal. It is not unidirectional. Close acquaintances share the spotlight as well as the shades. They exchange gifts and they return favors. People do not keep strict accounts, but something like a balance of payment is observed. Morally, this feature requires that each person in the relationship make the effort to preserve the mutuality. One cannot be forced to do this without distorting the very relationship such reciprocity is meant to sustain. Mutuality must be pursued voluntarily, but it must be pursued. Without it, the close relationship decays.

C. Concerns

1. Gender

There are two general issues that complicate the ethics of close personal relationships. The first is the general question about friendship and gender. For instance, a question that is raised in popular culture is whether it is possible for men and women to be friends. This is a question which moralists have also raised, with no clear conclusions. In part this is a matter of deeply ingrained power differentials. To the extent that society has established patterns of inequality between males and females, one of the essential ingredients in close personal relationships is missing. Similarly, strongly delineated roles tend to frustrate the reciprocity that is necessary. There is more, however, to the matter than this. Even if these factors could be accommodated, a question remains about whether men and women tend to have different patterns of perception and expression to an extent that makes genuine friendship impossible. A similar issue is whether close relationships between males are different from those between females.

2. The Ethical Status of Friendship

A second set of issues is raised about the ethical legitimacy of close personal relations. To the extent that morality aspires to universality, the inherent preferential orientation of friendship strikes some as ethically suspect. According to many perspectives, Kantian, utilitarian, and Christian, one is obligated to all people. According the scheme of moral development associated with Lawrence Kohlberg, the highest level of ethical sensitivity is a concern for all that does not take into account one's own associations and bonds. Close personal relationships clearly pull in another direction. They ask us to take into account, and to be limited by, the sort of exclusive relations that moralists often bewail. This is a source of some perplexity. Most ethicists are not willing to deny the validity of universal concern. Those who also want to preserve the moral importance of close relationships may try to work out such relations as a concrete expression of tendencies which should be more generally applied, at least theoretically.

IV. RELATIONS WITH INTIMATE ACQUAINTANCES

The boundaries between the three sorts of personal relationships are not at all hard and fast. The distinctions are drawn to highlight significant issues but they do not represent a real categorical differentiation. For instance, there is a gray area in which the nonacquaintance in the civil sphere becomes more and more familiar until he or she is a virtual colleague. Similarly, a good friendship sustained over time produces an association that takes on additional features. Indeed, the relationship may be slowly transformed. The other person becomes a best friend or an intimate partner. When this happens, new demands arise. The relation is qualitatively different from what it has been. It is now a new occasion which teaches new duties.

A. Background

When the Bible addresses this kind of close relationship, it most often has marriage in mind. Certainly there are other instances of intimate bonds in other relations, for instance the relation between Abraham and his son Isaac or between Ruth and her mother-in-law Naomi. Nevertheless, the usual reference is to marriage. As reflected in the very first writings of the Bible (sequentially, not chronologically) as well as in its last additions, the relation between a man and a woman is informed by an ideal of profound fidelity. The husband and the wife are bound to one another to a very intimate degree. The model goes beyond the notion of being a second-self. Rather, one and one's partner become a new unit, a sort of expanded self. The two become "one flesh" (Ephesians 5:31). This is not primarily a romantic notion (although that element does appear in the Song of Solomon). Instead it points to a sense of enlargement of one's identity. It is an acknowledgment that the two persons are so intertwined that their welfare is now a common project. The Bible does not always articulate this ideal perfectly, but this is the essential notion that it supports.

In the classical world marriage was not the focus of ideals of this sort. Domestic matters were customarily relegated to a secondary status. Friendship was a matter philosophers addressed, but marital bonds were not. However, attention was given to intimate personal relationships. For instance, Sophocles' play *Antigone* deals with the duties which a sister owes to her brother, even though he has been a traitor. Despite Creon's order to leave the body of her brother where it has fallen, Antigone felt bound to prepare it for a proper burial. Her obligations to her brother took precedence over her allegiance to the state as well as her regard for her own safety. It would be a violation of what she holds most dear, indeed a violation of herself, if she were not to offer him the respect she felt he was due. In this connection he is a virtual extension of herself. The service she renders him is also an effort to maintain her own integrity.

B. Norms of Fidelity

1. Promise Keeping

There are three normative standards of intimate relations. The first is promise keeping. Such a close connection demands reliability from its members. Because the intimacy heightens the vulnerability of the partners, they depend on the constancy of one another. A pledge given must be observed. One's word must be one's bond. This is also true of friendships as well as some impersonal relations that one has, but in the context of intimate personal ties it is of great importance. Such an association is a relationship which is often of great intensity, and there is a profound need for dependability. Uncertainty tends to undermine the relationship, or at least hinder its progress. For the other person to be not simply a second-self but an enlargement of one's own self, one must know the other well and have confidence in his or her words and commitments.

The moral importance of the trust that promise keeping sustains is reflected in the legal concept of fiduciary obligations. This idea applies most generally to matters of finance where it often refers to a trustee who is bound to work for the well-being of his or her client. At its core, however, the fiduciary relationship is a rough approximation of an intimate personal relation. This is so because the fiduciary relationship is one of vulnerability and care. One depends on another for some significant portion of one's welfare. Indeed, although the relationship is not symmetrical, the two parties are closely bound up with one another and this leads to the ethical responsibility to look out for one another. As Chief Justice Benjamin Cardozo said,

Many forms of conduct permissible in the workaday world for those acting at arm's length, are forbidden to those bound by fiduciary ties. A trustee is held to something stricter that then morals of the marketplace. Not honesty alone, but the punctilio of an honor the most sensitive, is the standard of behavior.

B. Cardozo, 1929. In *The North Eastern Reporter,* vol. 164, pp. 545–546. West Publishing Co., St. Paul, MN.

This statement was made in reference to two real-estate partners. It is even more true of other relations. In many areas of life the dependence and requirements of the other person require the trustee to exercise great care. This is the heart of the fiduciary relationship, the core of the fidelity which intimate personal relations demand. Because two partners are so closely bound up with one another, they rely on one another, to some extent, for their well-being. By the same token, they are bound to pursue this as a goal.

2. Exclusivity

Similarly, the partnership must be exclusive. The openness and high degree of communication that are entailed in an intimate relation tend to restrict sharply the number of participants. Whether one can have only one such intimate acquaintance at a time or not is unclear, but it is the case that there must be some boundary of intimacy. This is not simply a practical matter of the time and energy involved in such relations. It is also the case that a connection demands some form of restriction and focus in order for true intimacy to occur. Obviously, the demand for exclusivity applies most clearly to relations of sexual intimacy. We are accustomed to think of this sort of partnership in terms of strong boundaries. In nonsexual relations the emphasis on exclusivity is not so clear-cut. However, even here there is some sense of limit. While one can certainly have a number of close acquaintances, one cannot be best friends with everyone, or even with many people. This sort of intimacy requires a degree of exclusivity.

The need for boundaries has, of course, not been without its challenges. In recent years some people have advocated the notion of an "open" marriage, that is, a marriage without sexual exclusivity. Of course, various patterns of sexual liaison have been tried through the years, including polygamy and free love. What is relatively new is the proposal that an "open" relationship is a form of personal intimacy which still embodies the distinguishing marks of trust and fidelity. This seems highly debatable. Nevertheless, whether the exclusivity of an intimate relationship is sexual or not, it must be present in some form. The association itself must entail some degree of separateness or isolation in order for it to be a sufficient locus of shared identity.

3. Loyalty

The third normative standard of intimate relations is loyalty, an element which points to the importance of transpersonal ideals. The moral center of intimate relationships is a personal commitment. It is a commitment to the other person, but it must also be more than that. If a partner truly seeks the other's good, he or she needs to seek something more as well. He or she needs to realize the ideal that is reflected and embodied in the relation. Implicit in our intimate associations is a commitment to the importance of intimacy. Our moral obligation is not simply to the other person, but to the form of the relation itself. This is so because the form makes the closeness of the relation possible. In Josiah Royce's language, a fundamental loyalty in life is to loyalty itself.

This point touches on the concept of practices as used by the ethicist Paul Ramsey. In reflecting on the importance of rules, Ramsey observed that certain standards were significant for the social possibilities that they made possible. For instance, only if particular regulations are observed can a person participate in a game. He observed that "a man can slide into a bag of sawdust any time and anywhere he pleases; but he can slide into first base only in a game of baseball. (P. Ramsey, 1967. In *Deeds and Rules in Christian Ethics,* p. 139. Scribner's, New York). Ramsey was clearly drawing on rule utilitarianism, but he goes beyond this. His notion of practices is meant to indicate that rules have a constitutive role. In his view some rules had to be obeyed not because they tended to produce benefits over time, but because of the possibilities they created. The relevance of this point here is that one must have a regard for the importance of intimacy itself if one is to sustain an intimate relation with another. Richard Lovelace's statement that he could not love his mistress much if he did not love honor more is true beyond the way that he meant it. Although an intimate personal relationship seems to be determined by nothing but the personal qualities of the partners involved, there is, in fact, more required. In order for the closeness to be well-founded and secure, each person in the relationship must have confidence in the durability of the commitment of the others. Each must be able to trust the other deeply. This means that the discipline of such trust must be respected. Thus, the primary

ethical demand of intimate partnerships is not really a matter of how one treats the other person (although this is surely important). Rather, the essential moral obligation is a commitment to fidelity itself.

C. Concerns

One concern that this sort of personal relationship evokes is similar to the concern raised in connection with friendship. In both areas, the relationship is a matter of preference. Like a friend, a partner is chosen above others, and one's relationship depends in some measure on excluding others. This aspect of the relationship stands in tension with ethical imperatives that stress disinterested regard for others in general.

A second concern that relates primarily to intimate relations has to do with their termination. Since such relations depend fundamentally on an assurance of loyalty and fidelity, the primary ethical problem is connected to the ending of such relations. When is it legitimate for one to end such a relationship? Of course, terminating personal relations exacts a price in all circumstances. If one is deciding to cut short a conversation with a fellow passenger or to drop a friend, one faces some degree of loss and needs to justify the act, at least marginally. For intimate partnerships, however, the ethical stakes are much higher. One is not only breaking a connection with another, one is also making a statement about fidelity itself. Divorce is the most obvious instance of this sort of act, but it occurs elsewhere as well. The problem of ending a close relationship can apply to couples who are not married, to business partners, or to best friends. In such cases, we often say that the breakup "feels like a divorce." We mean that it involves the severing of a tie that is more far-reaching than that involved in close acquaintances. We mean that we feel extremely vulnerable because we have been so thoroughly involved. We also mean that an ethical question is raised about fidelity itself. There are, of course, occasions when ending an intimate relationship is not only personally necessary, but morally called for. No matter what conditions precipitate this step, however, certain ethical concerns are also present.

V. CONCLUSIONS

Personal relations not only come in various forms and degrees of intensity, they also are inherently complex. They involve us physically, emotionally, and intellectually, just as we are creatures of body, heart, and mind. As many books of practical advice point out, there are various commonsense techniques and skills that are important ingredients of successful personal relations. One needs to be a good listener and also able to express oneself. One needs to be aware of the feelings that are present, both in oneself and in others. One should manage one's schedule and balance various commitments and responsibilities. One does well to be polite.

Personal relations are also an ethical matter. They entail not only our comfort and sense of self-fulfillment, but our aspirations toward the good and the right. They involve our standing as moral as well as interpersonal beings. Different forms of relations do this in different ways. Our relations with nonacquaintances draw on our deference and respect for one another, those with close acquaintances on our powers of friendship, and those with intimate acquaintances on our ability to keep faith with one another. Civility, amity, and fidelity are the moral centers of our various relations with one another. The way these qualities are applied will certainly vary according to individual situations, but they will generally be present in some form because whatever else they are, our personal relations are matters of ethical concern.

Bibliography

Blum, L. (1980). "Friendship and Altruism and Morality." Routledge & Kegan Paul, London.

Cohen, J. L., and Arato, A. (1994). "Civil Society and Political Theory." MIT Press, Cambridge, MA/London.

Farley, M. (1986). "Personal Commitments: Beginning, Keeping, Changing." Harper & Row, San Francisco.

Fletcher, G. P. (1993). "Loyalty: An Essay on the Morality of Relationships." Oxford Univ. Press, London.

Meilaender, G. (1981). "Friendship: A Study in Theological Ethics." Univ. of Notre Dame Press, Notre Dame, IN/London.

Oldenburg, R. (1989). "The Great Good Place: Cafés, Coffee Shops, Community Centers, Beauty Parlors, General Stores, Bars, Hangouts, and How They Get You Through the Day." Paragon, New York.

PLACEBO TREATMENT

Jos V. M. Welie
Creighton University

I. Introduction
II. The Psychosomatic Context of Placebos
III. Placebos in Experimental Research
IV. Placebos as Therapy
V. Placebos and the Doctor–Patient Relationship

GLOSSARY

double-blind study Research protocol in which a new drug is compared with a placebo (or an established drug when available), whereby neither the patients nor the researcher/physician knows in advance which patients receive which pills.

impure placebo A placebo that contains chemically active substances, but not for the particular condition of the patient (notably, vitamin tablets).

nocebo effects The undesired, harmful side effects of a placebo.

paternalism The attitude of physicians and other care providers to behave in a fatherly manner in the best interests of their patients but without the latter's active involvement and consent.

patient autonomy The ethical notion that patients have a right, and (barring manifest exceptions) are able to determine which medical interventions to undergo and which to refuse on the basis of information provided by the physician.

placebo A pill, capsule, injection, or other medical intervention that the patient believes to directly affect her condition and that, for that very reason, is likely to contribute to her healing indeed, but that the physician knows to be chemically or surgically inert for the patient's particular condition.

pure placebo A placebo that contains no chemically active ingredients.

THE MORALITY OF PLACEBO TREATMENTS has been challenged ever more frequently in the past three decades. Placebos' presumed immorality can be attributed first and foremost to the physician's concealing the true nature of the prescribed drug. This article examines whether placebo treatment is a form of patient deception and, if so, under what circumstances—if ever—such deceit can be justified. Comparisons will be made with the application of placebos in a research setting where their use is more accepted because patients are given a chance to consent to placebo administration. It will be concluded that the morality of placebos hinges on the model of the doctor–patient relationship adopted.

I. INTRODUCTION

The term "placebo" is derived from the Latin verb "placēre," to please, and literally means "I shall please," or "I shall be pleasing, acceptable." A placebo once may have been understood as any "commonplace method or medicine" (Motherby's New Medical Dictionary, 1785).

But as early as 1811, its pejorative connotation was fixed in Hooper's Medical Dictionary as "an epithet given to any medicine adopted to please rather than to benefit the patient." The opposition "... rather ..." is significant. As Fagge and Fye-Smith admit in their 1885 *Principles of Medicine* (2nd ed.), even if a medicine is a "mere placebo, ... there is every reason to please as well as cure our patients." Nevertheless, the general sense is that placebo treatments are not kosher. Placebos are not proper medical treatments. They are dummies. In fact, they are deceptive forgeries.

Indeed, the typical contemporary placebo is either a tablet that contains no pharmacologically active chemicals (a pure placebo), or chemicals that have some known benefit but not for the particular condition for which they are prescribed (an impure placebo, notably vitamin tablets). The typical instance in which a physician may be tempted to prescribe a placebo concerns the patient who suffers from a nonserious, self-limiting affliction. Given the potentially harmful side effects of virtually every drug, the physician will advise the patient to be patient for a few days. But the patient demands a prescription anyway. Knowing that refusal may induce the patient to shop around for drugs elsewhere, the physician may decide to "please" the patient and prescribe a placebo. Obviously, the patient is kept in the dark about the "true" nature of the prescribed pills.

Placebos are deceptive sops. In fact, placebos are intentionally manufactured for the purpose of deceit, mislabeled as drugs, and knowingly prescribed to trick the patient. Moreover, health-care insurance companies must be misled because they are not likely to reimburse the patient for "nothing." And because placebos are relatively inexpensive drugs, insurers are bound to end up overpaying for nothing. Finally, the public at large is deceived into believing that medicine has a remedy for all ailments. While intended to decrease the use of potentially harmful drugs, placebos may end up fostering reliance on and use of drugs.

The conclusion seems evident: The prescription of placebos is unprofessional and immoral. It is at odds with patients' right to honesty and information; it unduly contributes to the rising health-care costs; and it fosters the medicalization of society. And yet placebos have been in use for centuries. Placebos have even survived the recent rise of patient autonomy and demise of physician paternalism. The physician is no longer the captain of the ship, but she or he continues to prescribe placebos. The current prevalence of placebo prescription is unknown, but the vitamin version is probably rather common. Physicians are less likely to feel uncomfortable prescribing "at least something" rather than "nothing at all," even if they have no clue whether and how this "something" will contribute to the patient's healing.

Can this practice be justified notwithstanding its deceptive character? Is it really as deceptive as it seems at first sight? Is the deceptive connotation of placebos itself deceptive? Let us reflect for a moment on the earlier definitions of placebos. We have already seen Hooper's 1811 Medical Dictionary defining the placebo as "any medicine adopted to please rather than to benefit the patient." We pointed out that the opposition "... rather ..." is significant. Yet it seems odd to oppose (rather than juxtapose) "pleasing" and "beneficial." Even though some beneficial medical interventions are all but pleasant, what is pleasing is at least in some sense beneficial as well. If patients requesting drugs and receiving placebos are satisfied, less anxious, and more at ease, they are less dis-eased—which is the primary goal of medicine.

More importantly, it is equally problematic to oppose (rather than juxtapose) placebo and cure, as did Fagge and Fye-Smith in 1885 and as many have done since. Generally, placebos not only contribute to patients' ease and relaxation, they contribute to the healing of the diagnosed illness as well. Granted, their effect is indirect because placebos do not contain chemicals that are known to possibly affect the patient's illness directly. They do not kill microorganisms as do antibiotics; when added in a laboratory to a culture of echoviruses, nothing happens. But when prescribed to a patient suffering a common cold caused by those very echoviruses, the patient is likely to heal faster than she or he would without taking the placebo. The causal chain from placebos to health necessarily includes the patient, but the placebos are a necessary part of the causal chain as well. In that sense, placebos can be said to genuinely "cure" patients.

Why, then, are placebos condemned? They effectively heal; they do not have the same potentially harmful side effects as so many other drugs do; and they are probably the least expensive therapies on the market. Granted, the patient has no idea what she or he is taking, but that is true for most drugs taken by patients. Granted, the physician does not know either how the placebo is contributing to the patient's healing, but even that is true for numerous physicians who prescribe drugs. And it would be rather shortsighted for insurance companies not to reimburse placebo prescriptions because else they are likely to end up paying for more expensive "real" drugs in the long run.

In order to shed additional light on this deceptively deceptive practice, we will first examine medical and psychological explanations of the placebo effect. While we may not understand, and never be able to understand, the first link in the causal chain (i.e., the booster effect of chemically inactive pills on a patient's biological self-healing resources), the remainder of the pharmaco-neurological chain has been explored in depth. Next, we will examine the area of placebo use that is the least controversial, experimental medical research. Because patients participating in such research are told in advance and consent to the fact that they may or may not receive the tested new drug, but a placebo instead, it is felt that patients are not deceived. We then discuss the more controversial therapeutic prescription of placebos whereby patients are kept in the dark. In a final concluding section, we will attempt an evaluation of different arguments and assess the overall justifiability of placebos in medical practice.

II. THE PSYCHOSOMATIC CONTEXT OF PLACEBOS

A. The Paradoxic Nature of Placebos

To understand the pejorative connotations of placebos, notwithstanding their proven effectiveness, we have to understand the particular scientific "bias" of contemporary physicians. Ever since the rise of medicine as an empirical science (rather than a practical art), physicians—as well as patients!—have come to understand illnesses as detectable changes in the body's biochemical regulatory mechanisms or, preferably, its anatomical, histological, and cellular structures. Patients' complaints and subjective symptoms are relevant in the diagnostic localization of the disease, but they are not intrinsic to the nature of the disease. Patients may be diseased without having any complaints or symptoms; conversely, patients complaining about pains or aches that do not seem to point to localizable disorders are sick, maybe even ill, but not diseased. Likewise, drugs that do not seem to operate according to understood and acknowledged localizable mechanisms, fail to qualify as genuine drugs, even if they clearly influence genuine diseases.

This particular understanding of medicine has resulted in awkward inclusions and exclusions. Effective but poorly understood therapies may end up being dismissed as unorthodox medicine; thoroughly researched drugs with a moderate effectiveness may nevertheless be hailed by medical professionals when insurers intend to ration because of poor efficiency. Patients suffering from mental illnesses that can be correlated with neurological pathology tend to be taken more seriously by physicians as well as insurers, employers, and society at large, than are patients suffering from even more serious mental illnesses that lack a localizable component.

This skewed development has evoked such counter-developments as holistic medicine, anthropological medicine, and psychosomatic medicine, all of which have tried to restore the primacy of the ill subject as opposed to abnormal (sub)cellular structures and mechanisms. Although constituting another extreme, the World Health Organization's defining health in terms of physical, mental, as well as social well-being poignantly reflects the same belief that presumably objective, localizable disorders are secondary to patients' subjective symptoms and dis-ease.

The particular definition of disease and the consequent labeling of patients and therapies as genuine and scientific, respectively (or imagined and unorthodox) is always relative to the theory of medicine espoused. The therapeutical effect elicited by needle pricks may be a complete mystery to those operating from one theoretical paradigm, but it may be perfectly understandable and reasonable in another paradigm. The paradoxic quality of placebos is that they presume two incompatible paradigms. In order to be effective, patients must strongly believe in the superiority of bioscientific medicine and the power of chemical drugs versus their own personal impotence and dependence. Yet the effectiveness of placebos can only be explained in a theoretical model that emphasizes the restorative resources of the human subject, while assigning to biomedical drugs a "mere" supportive function.

B. The Effects Elicited by Placebos

It is extremely difficult to uncover the effects of placebos. How to distinguish between the natural course of the disease, or the healing effects of the visit to the doctor's office, the physician's physical examination, and his reassuring advice on the one hand, and the effects of taking the placebo on the other? Normally, if one intends to uncover the effects of a new drug, the research protocol will include two categories of patients. One group is given the new drug, the other a placebo. Neither the patient nor the researcher will know in advance who gets what pill (see also Section III). But it is extremely difficult to examine the effects of a placebo in such a double-blind study, comparing placebos with placebos.

Placebos seem to be most effective in relieving pain, whether it be the blunt aches in the low back or the sharp pains caused by dental treatment. But the list of reported beneficial effects of placebos is considerably longer and includes mental complaints such as anxiety and depression, and somatic symptoms related to angina pectoris (pain in the chest), asthma, common cold, cough, hypertension, nausea, seasickness, and many other conditions. Placebos have been found to lower blood-sugar levels in diabetics and to affect tumor growth. And it has been reported that a legally blind girl's vision improved to normal when she was prescribed fake glasses.

While some studies have reported an almost 100% response to placebos, on average placebos have a 35% chance of relieving pathological phenomena. Some studies report different responses depending on the color of the pill. Bitter pills work better than flavorless placebos. The higher the number of pills to be taken at once, the stronger the responses. Capsules elicit a stronger response than pills, but injections—notably when they hurt—do even better. Surgery seems to be an especially powerful placebo. However, other researchers have concluded that the primary effects are not related to the pills (and the like) as such, but the encompassing context in which they are given.

The literature does not present a clear picture as to what kind of patients respond best to placebos. But it is clear that even such presumably sophisticated and well-informed subjects as medical students are likely (30%) to respond to placebos. Even more remarkable, psychiatric patients who were told in one study that the drugs they were given contained only sugar but that the physicians knew it would work, without knowing why and how, improved as a result of the placebo treatment. Naturally, like the physicians in the latter example, those prescribing placebos must at least impart a sense of strong belief onto their patients in the effectiveness of the pills prescribed. And other care providers involved in the administration of the placebo (notably the pharmacist and the administrating nurse) will have to radiate the same confidence.

C. The Pharmacology of Placebos

Given the difficulty in differentiating between the effects of the "inert" placebo proper, the mode of administration, the accompanying explanations and recommendations, and other potentially significant factors, it is also very difficult to discover the secondary, pharmacological processes elicited by the primary, psychological impact of placebos. In view of the potent analgetic effects of placebos it has been suggested that endogenous opiate-like substances (endorphins) may be the first biological link in the healing process. If true, placebos would work similarly to acupuncture and hypnosis. However, at present research results remain inconclusive. Given the wide variety of placebo effects—other than pain relief—immunological and hormonal processes may be involved as well.

D. The Side Effects of Placebos

As mentioned earlier, the prime justification of prescribing and administering placebos rather than "real" drugs is the damage that the latter may inadvertently do. Virtually all pharmacological substances have side effects, hence the attractiveness of chemically inert yet effective pills.

Awkwardly, placebos can have side effects and may harm as well. The "nocebo" (I shall harm) effects of placebos are less frequent than the beneficial effects (5 to 10%) and generally a bit vaguer as well, but they certainly are important to consider. Reported side effects include collapse, diarrhea, irritability, insomnia, itching, hypotension, palpitations, rash, somnolence, temporal headache, and weakness. Moreover, placebos can be addictive with patients suffering from withdrawal symptoms when administration is discontinued.

III. PLACEBOS IN EXPERIMENTAL RESEARCH

The most common and ethically least problematic use of placebos occurs in double-blind experimental research. As mentioned earlier, to be able to distinguish between the beneficial effects of a new drug's chemical content and the placebo effects of administering the drug, researchers use so-called double-blind studies. In these studies neither the patients nor the administering researcher knows who will receive the "real" drug and who will get the placebo. Upon concluding the observation of the effects of the administered drugs, it is revealed to the researcher which patients received which drugs. Next, statistical analysis will show whether the new drug is significantly more effective than the placebo.

The use of placebos in double-blind studies is not without ethical problems. If there is already an established drug on the market, it is difficult to justify comparing a new drug with a placebo and withholding from patients the older, yet effective, drug. One will have to compare the new drug with the established drug. A similar moral problem occurs when no established drug is on the market but the new drug is very promising.

If in the course of the study preliminary results confirm the beneficial qualities of the new drug, it is improper to continue placebo control for the sake of research accuracy, thereby withholding a beneficial drug from sick patients.

The major moral advantage of placebo use in an experimental setting over its therapeutical use is the explicit consent granted by the patients involved. Research subjects will be informed in advance that they may be receiving a placebo rather than the experimental drug. Hence, they are not deceived into believing they are taking a chemically active drug when they are not. In fact, if properly informed about the possible side effects of the drugs and the potential nocebo effects of the placebo, research subjects voluntarily undergo those risks as well and cannot be said to be harmed by the researchers.

IV. PLACEBOS AS THERAPY

A. Limitation of the Consequent Analyses

It is commonly argued that the effectiveness of premodern medicine—if any—was mostly a matter of placebo effects. Likewise, many home remedies concocted by patients and even most "over-the-counter-drugs" that do not require a physician's prescription would qualify as placebos because the dose of potentially active chemicals in such pills is far too low. However, these examples disregard one important aspect of placebo treatment proper that has also prompted its dubious moral status: the intentions of the prescribing physicians. Placebos have been criticized most harshly because physicians knowingly deceive patients by prescribing dummy pills and concealing that fact.

For the sake of argumentative clarity, the consequent discussion will be limited to an ethical analysis of instances where a clinician provides his patient with a prescription of what the patient assumes to be pharmacologically active drugs but that the clinician assumes *not* to have any pharmacological impact on the patient's particular affliction. This practice raises the question whether the clinician is deceiving the patient, and if so under what circumstances—if ever—such deceit can be justified.

B. Placebos as a Quick Fix

Not unlikely, at times placebos are given to patients who continue to demand some kind of prescription from their physician although the latter has informed the patient that his ailment is self-limiting and requires no medical intervention. Foreseeing that the patient may be back in a few days complaining about the persistence of his symptoms, or may shop around for a more compliant physician, the physician may "give in" and prescribe a placebo. Of course, this solution may be counterproductive if the patient returns after two weeks and, quite satisfied about the effects of the drug on his back pain, demands a new prescription. If the physician continues to "give in," he may end up with a patient genuinely addicted to placebos. If he reveals the truth to the patient, the latter may feel betrayed and seek medical help elsewhere.

The examples show that placebo treatment, even if to enlighten the patient rather than to get rid of hateful patients, is a precarious undertaking. In the consequent paragraphs, we will examine the ethics of placebo prescription in greater detail. However, it should be emphasized at this point that the prescription of "real" drugs in order to get rid of demanding patients is morally just as troublesome, if not more so. Catering to patients when certain diagnostic procedures, medications, surgeries, or other interventions are not medically indicated, may not involve as apparent a deception as does placebo treatment. After all, the patient got what he asked for. Moreover, the physician can warn the demanding patient that the requested drug is really not effective, while in prescribing placebos, the physician has to impart the belief that the pills *are* effective. Hence, the patient's consent can be said to be fully informed, which it never can be in case of a placebo. But the patient clearly does not believe the physician's warnings about the drug's ineffectiveness. It is at least questionable whether such a patient is competent to consent to the proposed medical intervention. While physicians are no longer expected to paternalistically guard over their autonomous patients' well-being, incompetent patients constitute the acknowledged exception to this rule.

Furthermore, giving in to patients by prescribing "real" drugs as opposed to placebos generally entails greater risks to more serious side effects than the nocebo effects of placebos. Nobody has the moral right to harm his fellow human being, not even at the latter's own request, when the benefit expected—if any—will not outweigh the harm. This prohibition applies ever the more to health-care professionals who have a sworn duty first and foremost not to harm (*primum non nocere*). In a world in which quick fixes will continue to occur, placebos are still to be preferred over "real" drugs.

An analogous counterargument can be made against those who worry that the availability of placebos may increase laxity among physicians in diagnosing complicated conditions or locating targeted remedies—after all, a simple fix is always available. While this danger certainly exists, the same danger is present—if not greater—when physicians prescribe "real" drugs as quick fixes. At least, the placebo-prescribing physician knows he is walking a narrow path; the drug-prescribing physician may consider his quick solution standard medical care.

C. Nondeceptive Uses of Placebos

The primary cause of the placebo's dubious moral status is the deception that is necessarily involved in its prescription. Physicians may avert outright lies by such vague explanations as "this pill has been proved to work really well for your kind of condition" or by simply refraining from volunteering any kind of explanation. But these obfuscating strategies cannot change the ethical nature of the act, which is to intentionally conceal the truth from the patient in an attempt to mislead the patient into believing she or he is taking chemically active drugs.

(1) One obvious way around the problem of deceit is to simply tell patients that the pills contain no ingredients that are known to be chemically effective, and yet they work. Although some researchers apparently have managed to successfully prescribe placebos to patients while informing them about the chemical inertia of the pills (see Section II.B), generally patients are not informed about the real ingredients of the prescribed drugs in an attempt to boost the placebos' effectiveness.

(2) A second manner of averting deception would be for the practitioner to inform patients in advance that in due time she or he may prescribe a placebo. This could be done orally in a first introductory meeting with new patients, in a brochure handed out to visiting patients, or on a poster on the wall of the waiting room. If patients continue to frequent the practitioner's office notwithstanding this revelation, one may assume that they have consented to the possibility of receiving a placebo when medically indicated.

However, this strategy is not likely to be enacted. The mere prospect that patients could be scared away by the idea of being prescribed "fake" pills rather than "real" drugs will keep many physicians from announcing their faith in placebos. More importantly, if patients start wondering every time they are prescribed drugs whether the drugs are "real" or "fake," the "real" drugs may turn out to be *less* effective.

(3) A variation on the former theme would be for the physician to tell the patient that he is contemplating a new kind of therapy. If the patient continues to ask questions, the physician could try to evade informing the patient by an excuse along the lines of "if you have no objections, I would like to first wait and see if it works before I tell you what it is—but believe me, it's not a very aggressive drug that is certainly not likely to have any unpleasant side effects." If the patient is willing to wait and see as well, she or he has consented de facto. However, the more inquisitive and assertive patient is not likely to wait and see. Conversely, those patients who do go along may do so out of timidity: When the doctor says it's better to wait and see, one better wait and see. Yet such acquiescence does not qualify as a proper consent.

(4) The fourth strategy to inform patients and yet prescribe placebos, is to mimic experimental research studies. This is called a $n = 1$ trial, whereby a single patient consents to and is daily given either a placebo or a "real" drug according to a schedule unknown to both patient and physician. The physician can inform the patient that the purpose of the $n = 1$ trial is to find out whether the "real" drug is really more effective in the patient's case. If the drug turns out to be more effective indeed, the patient will be prescribed only real drugs.

The interesting question is of course what to do if the placebo turns out to be equally effective and, on top of that, elicits fewer side effects. In order to be able to continue prescribing the placebos, the physician would have to conceal the truth. Alternatively, the patient can consent in advance to a $n = 1$ trial protocol according to which the patient will never be told what turned out to be most effective. It is unlikely, however, that patients will be able to resist the urge to ask anyway, at which time secrecy would have to be broken.

A version of the $n = 1$ study that is self-limiting and hence does not run into the problems described above is the weaning of an addicted patient. One could arrange with the patient to substitute the pharmacologically active drug (e.g., pain killers) with a placebo at unknown but ever more frequent moments. While ethically sound and practically feasible, this strategy is only applicable in rare cases and cannot easily be expanded to cover the more common cases in which placebos tend to be prescribed.

D. Nondeceptive Alternatives to Placebos

The previous examples have shown that it is not very easy to prescribe placebos in a therapeutical setting without concealing some information from the patient. This fact has led many authors to conclude that placebo use is at odds with the bioethical principle of respect for patient autonomy and the related patient right to informed consent.

Granted, patient autonomy has only recently risen to unparalleled moral significance. Indeed, prior to the 1960s, not much ethical reflection was devoted to the use of placebos. Granted, patient autonomy is not universally acknowledged either as the single most important ethical principle guiding health care. But it certainly has redirected medical practice away from its more traditional paternalistic format and it has resulted in a rather extensive body of legal rules and regulations affirming patients' decision-making rights. While few cases involving placebos have been tried in courts, the legal consensus (among American health lawyers) holds that it will be rather difficult for physicians to successfully defend their placebo prescriptions in court.

The emerged moral significance of patient autonomy has led many authors to oppose any and all uses of placebos that involve inaccurate or limited information to the patient. It is pointed out that there are many strategies available to foster the patient's own healing resources other than deception. Not only is there the apparent healing power of the placebo that remains even if patients are informed of its true nature. There are also such nonmedical interventions as extended communication, a caring doctor–patient relationship, and behavior modification techniques that do not require deceiving patients or withholding relevant information from them.

The proposed alternative strategies to foster the patient's own healing resources have obvious advantages (and some obvious side advantages, notably increased investment of professionals' time). But it is not as obvious that these strategies are entirely beyond the same reproach as are placebos. Is it possible to sharply distinguish between (i) taking the patient seriously, being attentive, informative, and comforting; (ii) verbally boosting the patient's self-confidence by suggesting a good outcome without really knowing that a good outcome is probable and how it will be realized medically; (iii) prescribing a healthy diet to foster a patient's grip on her own condition when there is no particular medical need for the patient to change her diet, and (iv) prescribing daily doses of vitamin capsules when the patient is not suffering from a vitamin deficiency? Or do they all involve an infringement on the patient's autonomy?

All four strategies are motivated by a concern that the patient has additional resources within herself but is unable to tap into them. Hence, the patient cannot be approached as a fully autonomous medical consumer but needs some professional, benevolent "coaching."

The choice of which medical interventions to undergo and which to decline is not fully left to the patient. Some patients (still) put their faith in the white coat and the authoritative adhortations by their physician, and so they are counseled. Others have a blind faith in pills and potions, and so they are administered placebos. Still others believe one's diet is the key to a healthy and happy life, and so a healthy diet is prescribed. The physician does not deceive the patient; it is the patient who does so. Or rather, neither deceives anybody. It is part of the human psychosomatic condition never to be in complete rational power of all available mental and somatic functions. Comforting adhortations, behavior modification, as well as placebos are all based on this "limitation" in the human condition.

E. Secrecy

Notwithstanding the apparent similarities between the different "motivational" strategies described in the former section, opponents of the placebo are likely to object that "fake" pills, as well as impure placebos, still differ because of the secrecy involved. Placebos seem to demand secrecy more so than caring attentiveness, counseling, and prescribing diets. Most likely it would reduce the effectiveness of placebos if the physician informs the patient that the pills really do not contain any chemically active substance and are only prescribed because research has shown that everybody taking pills, even dummy pills, improves. At best, the physician can explain that the prescribed pills have scientifically been proved to be effective although it has yet to be discovered how exactly they work. But even then, the physician is not completely honest because research has revealed (at least in part) how placebos work.

But what about prescribing a diet to bolster a patient's sense of control and empowerment? The physician may explain that the diet is not intended to directly affect the patient's condition, but it would be medically beneficial for the patient to work on her life-style more generally. But the physician cannot speak his true mind; he cannot frankly admit that the prescribed diet is irrelevant from a dietary perspective and could be substituted by any other diet as long as it requires the patient's own active involvement.

And what about providing a more optimistic interpretation of the situation than is scientifically warranted in an attempt to boost a patient's self-confidence? It is commonly argued that such a "violation" of the patient's right to honest disclosure of her own condition can only be justified if the so called "therapeutic exception or privilege" applies. That is, withholding the full truth from the patient must serve an overriding patient benefit that cannot be realized otherwise. The classic example is the patient who is expected to suffer significantly from the proposed disclosure, for example, by sliding back into a major depression. Naturally, the therapeutic exception can only be invoked as long as the danger to the patient continues to exist.

Even though scholars as far back as Plato (*The Republic* 389b–e) have granted physicians—and physicians only—the right to use an untruth as medicine, the therapeutic exception is itself not underwritten universally. Courts have been rather restrictive in allowing physicians to invoke this defense. Nevertheless, there can be no doubt that in some form or another it is rather common in daily clinical practice. Physicians routinely hold back on information, notably when they are not explicitly requested to provide the information. They postpone informing patients until more certainty has been gained, and in the mean time they try to relax patients with comforting words. After all, patients have a tendency to only hear the worst of all that is said, to misinterpret probabilities as certainties, and to assume they are going to be the rare exception to the rule. Why then is there so much more resistance, also among physicians, to the prescription of placebos?

F. Known Effect—Unknown Cause

While all four motivational strategies outlined in Section IV.D are only indirectly therapeutical, at least the causal links from intervention to effect make sense in the first three. The problem of placebos is not that we do not fully understand all the links in the causal chain. The causal chain of many recognized medical and psychological interventions is partially, largely, or completely unknown. Moreover, unraveling the missing links often has no impact on their clinical applications. The problem with placebos is one of presumably sensible causal links. It makes sense that comforting words relax the patient, thereby decreasing muscle tension and relieving headaches. It makes sense that actively monitoring one's own diet restores a feeling of control and thus decreases the sickening feeling of dependence that tends to accompany disease and loss of function. But in case of placebos the physician has no clue how taking dummy pills can increase the brain's endorphin production. It just looks too much like magic, tricks, and deception.

It is the same paradoxical character of placebos granting them their healing power that also causes their apparent immorality. When consoling and counseling, physicians operate within a strictly psychological paradigm; when administering pills and potions, they think in terms of biochemical processes. But placebos seem to defy these paradigmatic barriers. Centuries-old Cartesian dualistic divisions hamper physicians from thinking along holistic, psychosomatic lines. Pills are used to administer biochemically active ingredients into the body. It is simply irrational and incorrect of patients to have faith in the shape, color, and taste of pills. It is unscientific for physicians to rely on patients' irrational beliefs. And it seems unprofessional to encourage those beliefs by prescribing placebos.

G. Paying for Nothing

Before we turn to a final analysis of the ethical justifiability of placebo prescriptions, one thorny question may not go unnoticed. Even if we were to agree that in certain circumstances placebo treatment can be justified, is it justifiable as well to charge patients for "nothing"? Surely, the physician's invested time in explaining the prescription and its proper use are to be reimbursed for they are but a form of acknowledged counseling and behavior modification. But is it fair to charge for the pills themselves and all that is related to them (such as packaging, the pharmacist's investments, the nurse's time dispensing them)?

It should be noted that it is only when placebos are deemed a dubious treatment that payment becomes a problem. If, on the other hand, placebos are acceptable as a motivational strategy not unlike counseling or diet prescription, the biochemical inertia of the pills is quite irrelevant. On the other hand, prescribing impure rather than pure placebos so that patients at least get something for their money is always deceptive because patients end up paying for more expensive chemicals (e.g., vitamins) that they do not need. This is ever the more true if the physician resorts to the prescription of even more costly diets when an inexpensive placebo could have yielded the same results.

Genuine moral quandaries arise when the price of placebos is artificially increased to match those of "real" drugs. No doubt, many drugs and treatments obtain their therapeutical effectiveness in part from their high prices. But this does not justify artificially increasing the price of placebos, nor the price of "real" drugs for that matter.

V. PLACEBOS AND THE DOCTOR–PATIENT RELATIONSHIP

The justifiability of placebo treatment hinges largely on the ethical model of the doctor–patient relationship adopted. Four varieties will be examined briefly.

(1) For much of medicine's history, the physician has been viewed as fatherly guard of the incompetent patient's interests. This paternalistic authority can be attributed to a variety of phenomena, such as the social status of physicians or their unusual skills and knowledge. Less commonly noted but equally important is the phenomenon of the sick patient presenting an obliging call to his fellowmen to minister and heal. The therapeutic exception discussed above is best understood in reference to the latter phenomenon. Irrespective the ultimate foundation of this model, placebos are a morally acceptable option when they are medically indicated and serve the patient's interests. However, three decades of bioethics and a strong patient-rights movement have undermined this model in much of the Western world.

(2) A more prevalent understanding of the contemporary doctor–patient relationship is one in which the physician is an acknowledged medical expert with limited delegated authority for the sake of the patient's medical well-being. This delegation can be explicit, for example, when the patient tells the doctor to go ahead with whatever she or he feels is medically indicated. For the most part, however, it is implicit. Emergencies, unconsciousness, and serious illnesses all limit the competence and responsibility of the patient and care providers are expected to assume a greater responsibility and authority. But even in everyday situations patients can only be informed about and consent to the generics of the proposed therapies. They will have to rely on physicians to select and execute all the proper tests and interventions involved. Hence, it could reasonably be argued that a patient who has been treated for a condition (either with "real" drugs or with counseling) but unsuccessfully so, and who continues to resort to her physician, is delegating authority to the physician. When medically indicated and in exceptional circumstances, physicians may make full use of this delegated authority by prescribing placebos.

(3) A similar conclusion would follow if the physician is viewed as the patient's educator. Some patients—most patients—are not fully autonomous when they enter the doctor's office and it is the primary function of medicine to restore patients' autonomy, somatically, mentally, and personally. Informing patients about unhealthy life-styles and counseling them toward greater awareness of their own condition is as much part of medicine as is combatting a sickening infection or debilitating headache. And if, again in exceptional circumstances and only when educationally indicated, placebos are a necessary part of this healing process, there is no a priori reason not to utilize them. The obvious difference with the former model is that in the end patients must be told about the prescribed placebos if there is to be any educational value in prescribing them.

(4) Last, but ever more prevalent among bioethicists and health lawyers, is the modern view of the physician as autonomous provider of requested services to autonomous patients. While illness may incapacitate the patient's decision-making autonomy, he nevertheless remains standing as the captain of the ship. Advance directives allow patients to be in control even in a state of persistent unconsciousness. In this model, there is no place for physicians concealing relevant information from patients and controlling patients' decisions by deception and tricks. It unduly infringes on the rights of patient as free consumers of medical goods.

Notwithstanding its popularity among bioethicists and lawyers, this fourth model still is largely an ideal. In the real world of daily clinical practice, patients' active involvement still is only moderate. Efficiency-boosting mechanisms imposed by conditions of fiscal scarcity only seem to limit the time available to physicians and their patients to develop a relationship of mutual respect and shared responsibility. Nevertheless, those planning on prescribing placebos should be aware that patients are ever more eager and clever in obtaining second opinions, checking medical books and pharmaceutical guides in public libraries, or searching the ever-more informative electronic net for revelations. Irrespective of the model of the doctor–patient relationship adopted, placebos are justifiable within the context of a sound, fiduciary relationship only. The more assertive and informed the patient, the more openness will be required for this relationship to remain one of mutual trust, and the less room there will be for concealed placebo treatments.

Also See the Following Articles

AUTONOMY • INFORMED CONSENT • MEDICAL ETHICS • PATERNALISM • PSYCHOPHARMACOLOGY

Bibliography

Bok, S. (1978, November). The ethics of giving placebos. *Scientific American, 231,* 17–23.

Brody, H. (1980). *Placebos and the philosophy of medicine: Clinical, conceptual, and ethical issues.* Chicago: University of Chicago Press. Originally published in 1977 as a doctoral dissertation.

Jospe, M. (1978). *The placebo effect.* Lexington: D. C. Heath.

Kapp, M. (1982). Placebo therapy and the law: Prescribe with care. *American Journal of Law and Medicine.* 8, 4: 371–407.

Nielsen, J. R. (1989). The doctor, the pharmacist, the patient, and the placebo, or you're not my mother, doctor. *Food, Drug, Cosmetic Law Journal.* **44**, 6: 639–657.

Pinto, H. A. (1983). *Ethical guidelines for the use of placebos in clinical practice.* Thesis, Yale University School of Medicine, New Haven, CT.

Rothman, K. J., & Michels, K. B. (1994). The continuing unethical use of placebo controls. *The New England Journal of Medicine.* **331**, 6: 394–398.

Spiro, H. M. (1986). *Doctors, patients, and placebos.* New Haven/ London: Yale University Press.

White, L., Tursky, B., & Schwartz, G. (Eds.). (1985). *Placebo: Theory, research, and mechanisms.* New York: Guilford Press.

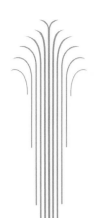

PLAGIARISM AND FORGERY

Denis Dutton
University of Canterbury, New Zealand

GLOSSARY

aesthetic empiricism The thesis that the artistic value of an art object is grasped in immediate auditory or visual experience.

forgery An artistic or literary work created and spuriously attributed to another, usually more famous, creator.

pastiche An artistic or literary work that borrows motifs or stylistic elements making it resemble the defined style or the style of a particular artist.

piracy The unauthorized use of copyrighted material such that the original rights holder is given credit for the work but deprived of profit from its use or sale.

plagiarism The passing off as one's own work the work or ideas of another.

provenance The origin and proof of authenticity, including previous owners or whereabouts, of a work of art.

FORGERY AND PLAGIARISM are both forms of fraud. In committing forgery I claim my work is by another person. As a plagiarist, I claim another person's work is my own. In forgery, someone's name is stolen in order to add value to the wrong work; in plagiarism someone's work is stolen in order to given credit to the wrong author.

I. THE PROBLEM OF FORGERY AND PLAGIARISM

The art world is as much infected as other areas of human enterprise by greed and ambition. Artists and art dealers seek recognition and wealth, and they often deal with art collectors more interested in the investment potential of their acquisitions than in intrinsic aesthetic merit. In this climate of values and desires, it is not surprising that poseurs and frauds will flourish. Works of sculpture and painting are material objects whose sometimes immense monetary value derives generally from two aspects: (1) the aesthetic qualities they embody, and (2) who made them and when. The reputations of artists are built on what history and taste decide is high aesthetic quality; forgery is an attempt to cash in on such established reputations.

Forgery and plagiarism are normally defined in terms of work presented to a buyer or audience with the intention to deceive. Fraudulent intention, either by the artist or by a subsequent owner, is necessary for a work to be a forgery; this distinguishes forgeries from honest copies and merely mistaken attributions. But while unintentional forgery is impossible (I cannot simply out of mistake sign a painting I have just finished with "Rembrandt"), it is possible to unintentionally plagiarize. Without realizing what I am doing, I might remember and carry over into my work elements (verbal, musical, pictorial) I have experienced in works by other people: if my unwitting borrowing is quantitatively sufficient, I can be accused of plagiarism, although I may not be fully aware of the extent of my borrowing. Even self-plagiarism, both intentional and unintentional, is possible. The Vermeer forger Han van Meegeren was once offered money for a prize-winning drawing. Unwilling to part with it, he copied it and sold the second drawing as the original prize winner; as van Meegeren was using his own name and lifting existent artistic content, this would be a rare case where the definitions of forgery and plagiarism both apply. Robert Schumann, when he was on his death bed, heard in his mind a melody that he believed to be new, but that was actually the slow movement of his violin concerto; copying it down, he could be said to be guilty of self-plagiarism, although it was clearly unintentional.

Normally, however, a forger simply paints a work in the style of a famous artist and tries to sell it, often in connivance with a crooked dealer, claiming it is from the hand of the famous artist. Very seldom do forgers try to execute exact copies of existing authentic paintings, as such works are difficult to sell.

Ordinary plagiarism involves the passing off as one's own the words or ideas of another. Paradigm cases of plagiarism are instances where a writer publishes a text that was originally written by someone else. This type of fraud is unequivocally discoverable if the original is published, although it may be impossible to prove if all original copies of a text are hidden or destroyed. Because the publication of plagiarized work opens it to wide scrutiny, it is, unlike forgery, a difficult fraud to accomplish as a public act without detection.

Both forgery and plagiarism must be distinguished from piracy, in which unauthorized copies of a work are made and sold, depriving an original author or manufacturer of profit. A pirate edition of a novel or textbook will credit the author's name, and will presumably be word-for-word accurate, but its manufacture and sale keep the author from enjoying rightful royalties. The same can be said of pirate computer programs and manufactured items, such as brand clothing items and wristwatches.

Forgery in the arts has been an issue since fakes of Greek works started showing up in the art market of ancient Rome. The market value of a work normally falls if it is shown to be a forgery, and museums will relegate to their basements paintings that are shown to be forgeries, despite the fact that they may have delighted generations of museum goers. Is this justifiable? If a work of art remains the same visual object after we know its status as a forgery, why should it be repudiated? Arthur Koestler and Alfred Lessing have both insisted that only confusion could underlie the rejection of forgery; it amounts to nothing more than hypocrisy and snobbery. If a viewer cannot tell the difference between two aesthetic objects, so this argument goes, there can be no aesthetic difference between them, since the aesthetic value of art is a function of immediate auditory or visual experience. This stance, which has been termed "aesthetic empiricism," applies to (1) forgery that exactly copies an existing art work, (2) forgery that presents new work in the style of another artist, but is directly attributed to that artist, and can be extended as well to (3) a legitimate copy of an existing work or a new work in another artist's style that is honestly attributed.

The third category could suggest plagiarism, were the copyist to put his or her own name to the copy. Because plagiarism involves the theft of content of a work, rather than the theft of the author's name, it is less philosophically interesting, although even more legally ambiguous and complicated. It is also more common than forgery. The history of copyright is a story of the continuing struggle by authors, artists, musicians, and cultural producers in general to protect the contents of their work, as in forgery artists struggle to protect their names. In the realm of copyright, then, it is for courts to determine the point to which borrowing counts as infringement, what can count as independent invention, and what kinds of intellectual production should be subject to protection. In forgery, on the other hand, it is not content that is in question, but simple authorship.

Because the tradition of basic copyright law is more frequently to protect not ideas expressed, but the particular expression of ideas—that is, the specific words of a poem or prose passage, or the specific notes of a melody—plagiarism is less infected with theoretical problems than forgery. Plagiarism involves the extension of property rights to the ownership of writing, and its consideration therefore lies more with copyright than does forgery. Because forgery can involve the misapplication of a name to what is quite new—and perhaps independently valid—work, it raises some of the thorniest issues in value theory. Carried to its extreme, the results of perfect plagiary is completely worthless, as the plagiarized work already exists somewhere else in its original, authentic form. But at least in principle, a perfect forgery could possibly be a new and important work of art.

II. PRACTICES OF FALSIFICATION

The most celebrated forger of the twentieth century was the Dutchman Han van Meegeren (1889–1947). As his promising artistic career faltered in the 1920s, he turned to forgery. It was in faking the work of Johannes Vermeer (1632–1675) where he achieved his greatest notoriety. Van Meegeren's pseudo-Vermeer, *Christ and the Disciples at Emmaeus*, which he finished in 1937, was described by the eminent art historian Abraham Bredius as perhaps Vermeer's greatest masterpiece at its unveiling (see Fig. 1).

Van Meegeren went to on to forge another half-dozen Vermeers. He was arrested shortly after the war for having sold a Dutch national treasure to the enemy. It turned out that one of his forgeries had ended up in the private collection of Reichsmarschall Hermann Göring. He confessed to the lesser crime of forgery, and in jail painted yet another pseudo-Vermeer to prove that he has indeed produced his claimed paintings. Van Meegeren was treated as a hero in the popular press and given a light sentence by the court. However, he died in prison before his release.

Another exemplary modern forger was the British artist Eric Hebborn (1934–1996). While still a student, he went to work for a London picture restorer named George Aczel. Restoration, it developed, meant much more than cleaning and retouching, and soon Hebborn was painting large areas of old works, cleverly extending cracking into newly painted surfaces, and even "improving" old paintings by augmenting them. An insignificant landscape became, with the addition of a balloon in its grey sky, an important (and expensive) painting recording the early history of aviation. As Hebborn wrote, "A cat added to the foreground guaranteed the sale of the dullest landscape.... Popular signatures came and unpopular signatures went.... Poppies bloomed in dun-colored fields."

Such "improved" pictures went straight into gold frames and the plush surroundings of a dealer gallery whose sale often netted Aczel a 500% profit. Before long Hebborn realized that there is little need to begin with an old painting: talent and old inks and paper were enough, and talent was something Hebborn demonstrated in abundance. Hebborn began to produce "masterpieces" to take important places in the collections of the British Museum, the Pierpont Morgan Library in New York, the National Gallery in Washington, and innumerable private collections. These were not trifles, but mainly Old Master drawings authenticated by noted art historians, such as Sir Anthony Blunt, and sold through Christie's, Sotheby's, and especially the respected London dealer Colnaghi.

By the time his career as forger concluded, Hebborn had produced by his own account approximately 1000 fake drawings, purportedly by such hands as Castiglione, Mantegna, Rubens, Bruegel, Van Dyck, Boucher, Poussin, Ghisi, Tiepolo, and Piranesi. In addition, there was sculpture, a series of "important" Augustus Johns, and works by Corot, Boldini, and even David Hockney. A Renaissance bronze *Narcissus* was authenticated by Sir John Pope Hennssey, and a "Parri Spinelli" drawing was purchased by Denys Sutton, editor of *Apollo*, for £14,000.

In 1978, Colnaghi's realized that they had been sold fakes by Hebborn and a general panic set in, depressing prices for Master Drawings. A curator had noticed that the Pierpont Morgan's "Cossa" was on paper identical to the National Gallery's "Sperandio." These drawings had been obtained from the same source. Doubts multiplied and Hebborn's reputation was destroyed. His reaction was to vow to flood the Old Master market with yet another 500 drawings, which he claimed to have accomplished between 1978 and 1988. Given the quality and diversity of his known output, there is no reason to doubt this claim. Hebborn's life ended in Rome where he was murdered in 1996 by persons unknown.

The creation of plausible forgeries is a difficult and demanding procedure. An old painting requires actual old canvas and a knowledge of old paint formulas. Simply painting over an old work is problematic because X-rays will reveal the underpainting. As it is sometimes impossible to remove old paint, which might have fused with the canvas, forgers have left parts of the underpainting and incorporated them into the layout of the forgery. In the forging of drawings, a knowledge of ink formulas is required, along with a supply of suitable paper, usually taken from the endpapers of old books. A good forger will carefully avoid any paints that would be anachronistic. For example, ultramarine and Prussian blue are both nineteenth-century pigments. Hebborn collected old drawing and writing sets for his purposes and van Meegeren used only badger hair brushes, so that not a single modern bristle would ever be found embedded in the paint of his forgeries.

FIGURE 1   Han van Meegeren: *Christ and the Disciples of Emmaeus* (1937). Forgery in the style of Vermeer (Museum Boijmans Van Beuningen, Rotterdam).

Style, of course, is of the greatest importance. A forger of painting needs to have an adequate grasp of period brush techniques, producing a typical subject matter for a specified target artist. Most forgeries tend to be pastiche works: paintings or drawings that bring together miscellaneous elements from authentic paintings in a way that will allow them to fit comfortably into an accepted body of work. However, it is almost impossible for a modern painter to think himself completely back into the representational conventions of a previous epoch. Even so careful a forger as van Meegeren produced paintings that displayed elements of the style of his own time: for example, the faces in his *Christ and the Disciples at Emmaeus* are clearly influenced by photography; one of them actually resembles that of Greta Garbo. Hebborn, on the other hand, displayed more than van Meegeren an ability to think himself into another artist's style and effectively to imitate it. Beyond that, many of his fakes are disarming in their life and grace: as basic visual objects, beautiful to look at.

Once a forged painting or drawing has been produced, the forger faces the difficult task of establishing a provenance for the work—a narrative about where the work came from and why it has remained undiscovered until now. This is not so different from what goes on in other fields of fakery: whether one is promoting the newly discovered burial cloth of Jesus, a metal fragment of a flying saucer, or a mermaid preserved in formaldehyde, it is necessary to invent a provenance for the object. Museum certificates, which are themselves easily forged, are common, as are wax seals on the backs of paintings. Many invented provenances have been variations of this story: "An old European family, which has owned this masterpiece for generations, has fallen on hard times, and with tears of regret, has been forced to sell it. They have insisted on the utmost discretion and do not want to be named." (We may imagine this sales pitch delivered, perhaps with an upper-class British accent, to an oil millionaire in the plush and soothing surroundings of a metropolitan dealer gallery.)

Because plagiarism involves theft of another's work, rather than attributing one's own work to a famous artist or writer, it tends to be less important to the literary historian. If an unknown writer publishes a plagiarized novel, it will probably be discovered and make little difference in the long run. It is only the career and reputation of an individual that is affected by plagiarism, not our understanding of an important body of work. For example, the Australian writer Helen Darville won a major literary award for her novel, *The Hand That Signed the Paper*, which, it was revealed in 1995, had sections copied from the work of Thomas Keneally. Despite the notoriety this occasioned, Darville later became a columnist for an Australian newspaper. However, she resigned in 1997 when her column was shown to have reproduced writings taken off the Internet. Because it is only the reputation of a relatively unknown writer that was at stake, such an episode could never invite the same excitement as the possibility of someone placing in museums faked paintings by Vermeer or drawings by Piranesi; such forgeries could alter our understanding of figures whose historical importance is already established.

The most common cases of plagiarism are, in fact, entirely private, between students and their teachers. This form of fraud in education has been made easier by the availability from Internet sources of essays to fulfill high school and university assignments. One of the results of this has been the increasing tendency of teachers to assign highly specific topics for essays, topics so specialized that they defy finding a source from which to plagiarize. However, the same Internet technologies that make available essays for the asking may also enable teachers to detect plagiarism. Internet search engines commonly in use can be employed to determine if an essay has been plagiarized from one submitted to another university course or available on the Internet. All that is required is that university faculty keep in computer memory every student essay ever written for a course; this would enable a search for duplicated material in new essays submitted.

III. RESPONSES TO FORGERY AND PLAGIARISM

Discussions of forgery sometimes invoke the notion of a "perfect," indistinguishable fake or copy of a work of art. The philosopher Nelson Goodman has argued, however, that the idea of a so-called perfect fake is deeply problematic. Just because I cannot today tell the difference between an original and an apparently indiscernible copy, it does not follow that I will be unable ever to see a difference between them. Goodman says that although a copy might be indistinguishable from its original to a newsboy, the two works might be easy to tell apart when that newsboy has grown up to become a museum director. For Goodman, the very fact of knowing that a work is a forgery, along with the possibility that one might someday be able to see a difference, makes a justified difference to how the forgery is seen today. Knowledge that work is forged "assigns the present looking a role as training toward ... perceptual discrimination." Trying to detect subtle qualities that distinguish an original from a fake, we learn to see such differences. This explains why for the serious art lover, there is an enormous gulf between an original art work and an apparently indistinguishable forgery or other copy.

Goodman's ideas apply both to identical twin copies and to works produced with the intention to include them falsely in an existing body of works. His emphasis on the importance of the educated eye is supported by van Meegeren's forgeries. Although they looked to many people like perfectly acceptable Vermeers in 1930s, such paintings as *Christ and the Disciples at Emmaeus* were by the 1950s far less plausible. Today it seems surprising that any of the van Meegeren forgeries were once thought of as Vermeers.

In fact, the acceptance of the van Meegeren fakes was a gradual process. Once the *Emmaeus* was included in the body of authentic Vermeers, van Meegeren did not need to work quite as hard with his next effort: it had only to seem plausible, given the new understanding of Vermeer's output, which was now modified by the inclusion of the *Emmaeus*. So each new van Meegeren-Vermeer distorted the historical view of Vermeer by adding yet another forgery to the accepted works, and van Meegeren found it increasingly easy to get away with his fraud. His final, flagrant pseudo-Vermeers thus more resembled twentieth-century German expressionist paintings than seventeenth-century paintings by any artist. (Still, it should not be forgotten that there was a minority of experts who had doubts from the beginning: the Dutch agent for the New York dealer Duveen attended the first showing of *Emmaeus* in 1937 and telegraphed his boss that it was a "rotten fake.")

The art philosopher Arthur Danto has provided one of the most penetrating responses to aesthetic empiricism. Danto agrees with Goodman that there is an important difference between an original and an indiscernible fake, but he denies that it lies in the possibility of being able in the future to see a difference undetectable at present. Forgery for Danto is a matter of a falsified history of an object, and works of art do not always "wear their histories on their surfaces." Danto regards art works as constituted by the ideas they embody and express; they are surrounded by an "atmosphere is theory" that makes them what they are. It is therefore impossible that an original work and its perceptually indistinguishable forgery could ever have the same value, even if they were to remain forever indistinguishable: art is less what you see and more what you know.

Jorge Luis Borges's celebrated story, "Pierre Menard, Author of *Don Quixote*," presents an odd thought-experiment to help illustrate Danto's position. In it, a modern poet produces passages of prose that are word-for-word identical with passages in Cervantes' seventeenth-century novel. Despite this identity (which is not plagiarism, because Menard acknowledges it), there are important aesthetic differences between the two texts, with the later one "almost infinitely richer," as described in the story. For instance, in the two texts, history is called "the mother of truth." When Cervantes writes this, it is a conventional rhetorical gesture of little significance; when Menard writes the same thing, it suggests the pragmatism of William James or the historicism of Marx. The historical context in which a text—or by extension any work of art—is created therefore determines meaning and value.

The justification for demanding authenticity is located by Denis Dutton in the notion of artistic performance. Concepts of achievement and failure are intrinsic to the idea of art as human activity. Undiscovered forgeries excite admiration through a form of fraud: they systematically misrepresent artistic achievement. This is not just a moral question for Dutton, but an aesthetic one as well. Consider the excitement of hearing a brilliant recording of a Liszt étude; the listener's excitement evaporates as soon as it is learned that the recording has been accelerated electronically. In the field of piano performance what counts as "brilliance" or "beautiful tone" is assessed against a background tradition of normal expectations and conventions of the art form. The point can be applied to other arts and their value terms, such as "inventiveness" or "originality." It follows from this that a forger's achievement can never be the same as that of the original artist, even if the forgery is indistinguishable from an original, or seems to fit well in a body of original work.

Michael Wreen has pointed out, however, that this position is unable to distinguish between an original work and a forgery if they are both products of the same historic context—for example, a contemporary Picasso forger who lived in France at the same time as Picasso—because the original artist and the forger face essentially similar technical problems. In fact, it might well be that the forger's problems will be even more difficult than the original artist's, because the forger faces the additional difficulty of trying to execute a passable imitation of another artist's style. Another theorist, Jack W. Meiland, stresses the excessive concern with artistic originality that he thinks infects discussions of forgery. Meiland insists that originality is a "derivative," rather than primary aesthetic value. For Meiland, originality of the kind that initiates a tradition or genre has value only insofar as later works in that established tradition can lay claim to primary aesthetic value. Like the first telephone or phonograph, original art can command interest as historical curios, but if they continue to retain much aesthetic interest at all, it will be through their achieved formal qualities.

IV. AT THE MARGINS OF FORGERY

Many cases that might come to be treated as forgery are not clear cut. Suppose a Renaissance nobleman admires a painting owned by a neighboring duke, and instructs his court artist to paint a copy of it. If neither the original nor the copy is signed, they will both pass later scientific tests as belonging to the Renaissance. A later owner of the copy may surreptitiously sign it with the original artist's, not the copyist's, signature. Thus, what began as an honest copy is transformed by a later owner into a forgery. Perhaps the original itself was unsigned; in such a case a later owner may forge on it the signature of the original artist in order to protect the reputation and value of the painting. In such a foggy and confused historical context, it may be impossible ever to distinguish the original from the copy.

Moreover, many paintings, such as those of Peter Paul Rubens (1577–1640), were workshop products.

In this situation, the primary artist may have painted no more than the most important parts of the work, leaving filling in and minor detail to assistants. It has sometimes happened that workshop assistants have falsely signed their own work with names of their famous employers. To add to the complexities, Rubens often used as assistants artists of the stature of Van Dyck, Teniers, and Jan Breughel. The tradition of the workshop continues in our time, with Andy Warhol and the contemporary artist Jeff Koons among those who use assistants to produce work to which they have themselves applied little or no hands-on effort.

Jean-Baptiste-Camille Corot (1796–1875) was a popular and prolific artist, whose loose and sketchy style is relatively easy to forge. It has been said only half in jest that of the 3000 or so paintings he produced, about 10,000 are now in the United States alone. Actually, the number of Corot forgeries exceeds even this figure: it has been estimated at more than 100,000 paintings. Corot was a generous man who occasionally signed his own signature to paintings of his students. The body of work claimed for Corot is now so clogged with fakes, some obvious, but others quite subtle and apparently respectable, that it will never be possible precisely to sort out in every case the authentic from the forged paintings. However generous Corot was, he did not match Salvador Dali, who in his old age signed sheets of white paper to be used for prints, either for his own work or anybody else's.

Finally, a word must be said about the cultural dimensions of forgery and plagiarism. The western European demand for originality in thought and expression is not universally shared, nor was it even found in its modern degree all through Western history. In the Middle Ages, the copying and memorization of traditional texts was a stronger element in education than it is today, and such purely reproductive thought is still an important element in many non-European cultures. For example, plans have been announced in Osaka, Japan, for a museum of painted reproductions of European masterpiece paintings. Europeans would doubtless consider this a travesty of an art museum, and the very idea does indeed suggest serious cross-cultural divergences in the attitude toward copying. In another example, many North American university faculty members will have encountered situations of trying to make clear to a foreign student, quite possibly Asian, the importance of originality, the use of quotation marks, and of the rewording of source material in the writing of essays. Even students raised in North American culture often have little understanding of the extent to which they must credit ideas and words on which

they depend for their own written work. Given the increasing internationalization of all world cultures, it may be surmised that the European demand for originality and crediting of sources will be diluted or compromised by competing cultural ideas as what counts as legitimate borrowing. However, because of the rise of digitization of information, and with it the spread of copyright protections, it seems more likely that other cultures will come more in line with Europe and North America, rather than the other way around. In other words, the demand for legal protection of intellectual property worldwide will alter norms of individual cultures.

V. THE HARM OF FORGERY AND PLAGIARISM

Forgery is a form of fraud, and is therefore as blameworthy as any other fraud that involves the production and sale of misrepresented goods. So much is uncontroversial. What is disputed is the extent to which the moral question ought to be allowed to affect the aesthetic response. One of the most useful treatments of this question has been supplied by Francis Sparshott who has written, "In seeking to appreciate a work we rely on its promise of a human significance and loyally entrust ourselves to that promise." What the art forger "exploits and betrays is just the self-giving on which all human relationship depends." Sparshott's analogy has us imagine making passionate love in the dark to another who in the event turns out to be the wrong person. Anyone who claims that it makes no difference whether a painting one appreciates is forged is rather like the champion of free, indiscriminate sex, or making love to anyone in the dark. Sparshott thinks that authentic aesthetic experience, like sexual experience, "depends on imaginative construction and association, for only an imaginatively funded vision detects and responds to the meaningful structure of a picture or a musical piece. And, because all social and personal bonds are reciprocal but directly known from one end only, all the relationships we know or think we know ourselves to be living in are as fragile and subject to illusion as the art lover's confidence in the authenticity of a work and the integrity of its artist."

This suggests that the enjoyment of the arts is in part a transaction between artistic creator and audience, a transaction that needs good faith and trust. There might, therefore, be mounting confusion in the future over what counts as a fake, given that technologies may enable a proliferation of copies and altered performances. Digital technologies allow not only the easy alteration of news photos and other visual material, they also make it possible to improve a singer's pitch or increase a pianist's speed. Such doctoring may come to be considered normal procedure, ot it may remain a kind of cheating. If the copying technologies for painting and sculpture can catch up with the digital transformations of sound, which may happen in the next decades, our view of creativity in the visual arts may thereby change.

The existence of greed and profiteering in the art marketplace has prompted some forgers to try to mount a moral justification for their activities. Van Meegeren's original intention, so he later claimed, for his activities was to avenge himself on critics who had humiliated him. The idea was that he would wait until the *Emmaeus* had been lauded by critics and experts, and then he would announce, to their cost and embarrassment, that he was the artist. However, there is good reason to doubt that this is something he ever seriously considered. He had produced forgeries before that painting and was making so much money as a forger that he had little incentive to stop simply for revenge's sake.

Eric Hebborn contrived to justify himself by quoting Ernst Gombrich that because pictures do not assert anything, they cannot be true or false. It follows, Hebborn claims, that his works cannot be false, and he is guilty of no crime. In answer to this, we can agree that a drawing is a drawing. It is the forger's claim that it is by Tiepolo or Mantegna that is false. Pictures do not lie: it is only the people who make and sell them, such as Hebborn or van Meegeren, who do that. Hebborn's justification fails.

The situation with regard to historical understanding and plagiarism is different. Because forgery is usually attributed to a historically important figure, forgery distorts and falsifies our understanding of art history. The historical damage of plagiarism, on the other hand, is normally minimal because the plagiarist is stealing contemporary work for his own designs, to help his own reputation. The successful forger, in contrast, affects our view of historically important artists and creators.

For some cynics, the only real damage done by forgers is what they inflict on the bank accounts of rich art investors. However, it is a mistake to see forgery in this way. Art is not just about beautiful things, it is about the visions of the world recorded in centuries past. The illustrated record of those visions can be corrupted by the skill and subterfuge of a contemporary faker. The extent to which this subtly distorts our grasp of our forebears' understanding of their world remains to be seen. But the skilled handiwork of people like van Meegeren and Hebborn, when it succeeds, will distort our understanding of the history of graphic representation just as surely as a document forger's skill might alter our understanding of the history of ideas. Forgery is not a victimless crime, even if the forger is successful and "no one knows." For the real victim is our general understanding of the history of art and of human vision. As noted earlier, many forgeries are recognized for what they are only by later generations. But is a perfect, undetectable forgery possible? We can never be certain. The perfect forgeries exist among us as unknown, undetected aliens.

Bibliography

Arnau, F. (pseud. for H. Schmitt). (1961). *The art of the faker.* Boston: Little Brown.

Borges, J. L. (1964). Pierre Menard, author of *Don Quixote* J. E. Irby, Trans. In D. A. Yates & J. E. Irby (Eds.), *Labyrinths.* New York: New Directions.

Bulley, M. H. (1925). *Art and counterfeit.* London: Methuen.

Cebik, L. B. (1995). *Nonaesthetic issues in the philosophy of art.* Lewiston, ME: Edwin Mellen Press.

Coremans, P. B. (1949). *Van Meegeren's faked Vermeers and de Hooghs.* (A. Hardy and C. Hutt, Trans.) London: Cassel.

Danto, A. (1981). *The transfiguration of the commonplace.* Cambridge: Harvard University Press.

Dutton, D. (Ed.) (1983). *The forger's art: Forgery and the philosophy of art.* (Contains articles by Rudolf Arnheim, Monroe C. Beardsley, Denis Dutton, Nelson Goodman, Alfred Lessing, Joseph Margolis, Jack W. Meiland, Leonard B. Meyer, Mark Sagoff, Francis Sparshott, Hope Werness, and Michael Wreen.) Berkeley: University of California Press.

Godley, J. (1967). *Van Meegeren, master forger.* New York: Charles Scribner's Sons.

Goodman, N. (1976). *Languages of art.* Indianapolis: Hackett.

Grafton, A. (1990). *Forgers and critics: Creativity and duplicity in Western scholarship.* Princeton: Princeton University Press.

Hebborn, E. (1991). *Drawn to trouble.* Edinburgh: Mainstream Publishing Projects. (Also published under the title *Master Faker.*)

Hoving, T. (1996). *False impressions: The hunt for big time art fakes.* New York: Simon and Schuster.

Jones, M. (Ed.). (1990). *Fake? The art of detection.* Berkeley: University of California Press.

Koestler, A. (1964). *The act of creation.* New York: Macmillan.

Koobatian, J. (Compiler). (1987). *Faking it: An international bibliography of art and literary forgeries (1949–1986).* Washington: Special Libraries Association.

St. Onge, K. M. (1988). *The melancholy anatomy of plagiarism.* Lanham, MD: University Press of America.

Van Bemmelen, J. M. *et al.* (1992). *Aspects of art forgery.* The Hague: Martinus Nijhoff.

Woodmansee, M., & Janszi, P. (Eds.). (1994). *The construction of authorship: Textual appropriation in law and literature.* Chapel Hill: Duke University Press.

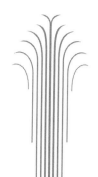

PLATONISM

Timothy Chappell
University of Manchester

GLOSSARY

akrasia Deliberately doing what I believe I should not do.

city/soul analogy Plato's view that the proper parts of the state and the soul are analogous, as are their proper relationships.

democracy A society organized in the manner of classical Athens or the modern United Kingdom or United States, on the basis of the maximum practicable freedom of speech, belief, and practice.

elenchus The Socratic method of addressing philosophical issues, by asking precise and logical questions from a point of view of real or feigned ignorance.

the Forms The world-transcending standards of reality by which alone, according to Plato, everything in the world is to be judged and understood. Thus, for example, it is impossible for me to know what justice really is, unless I am aware of and understand the Form of Justice.

guardian A member of the ruling class in the utopian state that Plato describes in the *Republic*: a "philosopher ruler," a person characterized by his exemplary rationality and justice, and his awareness of the Forms.

holism Plato's own political philosophy; the view that the only direct concern of political science is to bring about the well-being of the *whole* state, because if that is looked after, the well-being of the individuals who compose the state will also be achieved by this.

individualism The denial of holism; the view that, to bring about the individual's well-being, it is not sufficient to bring about the well-being of the state in which he lives. (Extreme individualists add that it is not necessary either, or even that the two ends are incompatible.)

moral dilemma Any ethical predicament in which every option available is a moral impossibility.

relativism The thesis that there are no standards of right and wrong, truth and falsity, rationality and illogicality, which are anything more than the products of some particular historical tradition.

rhetoric The art of persuasive utterance, highly prized by most Greek thinkers, but condemned by Plato, despite his own proficiency in it, as insufficiently responsive to truth.

sophistry The practice or profession of being a sophist—a professional teacher of rhetoric, statecraft, and related matters including, sometimes, ethics, logic, and metaphysics. Plato regarded sophists as fake philosophers, dangerously imbued with relativism, and with no real interest in the truth, but only in personal aggrandizement.

statecraft Knowledge and understanding of how to live in and run a state, a human political community. The Greek term is *politikē tekhnē*: it includes everything from political science, via legal and social philosophy and sociology, to one's own ethical beliefs.

unity of the virtues The thesis that the different respects in which anyone can be a good human being (= the virtues) are compatible.

PLATONISM is a name for a wide range of philosophical views, most of which were first developed by Plato (427–347 B.C.) out of the teachings of his master Socrates (469–399 B.C.). Various sorts of Platonism have subsequently been developed and defended by such famous figures as Plotinus (205–270 A.D.), Augustine (354–430 A.D.), Boethius (480–524 A.D.), and the seventeenth-century Cambridge Platonists. Platonist lines of thought continue to be deeply influential in many areas of philosophy today, often showing up as it were by surprise even in the thought of those who like to think of themselves as archetypal anti-Platonists. (Take, for example, Russell's and Quine's views about numbers and sets, respectively.)

Views covered by the name "Platonism" include positions about most important philosophical topics. As a result, the word "Platonism" and its cognates have come to have many different senses, in and indeed beyond philosophy. One familiar colloquial use of "platonic" is to describe nonsexual friendships (see Section V). Platonism can mean a certain view about what it is for there to exist things like numbers, or sets, or universals, or other abstract objects—perhaps even including objective, nonrelative moral values. It can also mean the view that minds or souls are naturally separate from and superior to bodies; or the view that the same mind or soul can be reincarnated in a succession of different bodies (see Section VI). Platonism has been associated with various sorts of utopian idealistic political programs, with elitism, and with women's rights (Section V); with religious mysticism and religious ethics (Section IV); with a poetic sort of philosophy, and with an absolute rejection of all the arts (Section IV).

All of these different uses and expositions of Platonism are interesting to the applied ethicist. There is also an interesting question about how systematically the different sorts of Platonism can be connected. However, perhaps the strongest reason for Platonism's enduring importance is its powerful critique of democratic liberalism, first developed in Plato's own philosophical dialogues. This Platonist critique of liberalism raises central issues in applied and political ethics, and is still very much a live issue today. I therefore focus on it here. (It is Platonism, not Plato, that I wish to talk about. Nonetheless, for reasons of space I here restrict myself largely to offering one possible interpretation of and extrapolation from Plato's own writings, although other Platonist writers are quoted occasionally. Nor shall I go into the vexed historical issue of how Socrates' views relate to Plato's.)

To understand the Platonist critique of liberalism, we need to look at the particular liberal society that was the original target of Plato's own critique: the Athenian democracy, in which Plato lived at least during the earliest and most formative years of his life, and Socrates during the whole of his life. This is worth doing, not only for its own interest, but also because of the striking parallels between that society and modern Western democratic societies such as the United Kingdom and the United States, which enable us to make a reasonable guess as to what Plato would have thought of such societies. (Briefly, the guess is that he would have been appalled!)

I. DEMOCRACY, TEACHING, AND KNOWLEDGE

The historian Thucydides gives us a beautifully exact portrait of the Athenian society in which Socrates and Plato lived, in a speech that he puts in the mouth of the great statesman Pericles (Thucydides 2.35–46), and that Plato ridicules by parody in the *Menexenus*. Thucydides' Pericles (2.41) describes Athenian society as "an education to all Greece." Athenians felt deep pride in the way they ran their society, and a modern liberal is likely to share their enthusiasm. From about 480 B.C. onwards, Athens was run as a democracy that was, for its citizens anyway, direct, participatory and egalitarian to a degree unequalled even by any modern society. At Athens, all male adults with Athenian parents who were not slaves or immigrants were Athenian citizens: in Plato's lifetime this meant a citizenry of about 6000 people. All such citizens were equally entitled to vote in the Athenian Assembly, to speak in person on every political or military decision that Athens took, and even (if they had the time and the inclination) to attempt to become major political figures in their own right.

Plato is an unsparing and unceasing critic of such a radically democratic constitution. His most basic objection to egalitarian democracy is very simple, and it highlights a central concern of Plato's, namely the business of education. The objection is that there is no justification for the democratic way of running a state—as if all men are equal—unless all men *are* equal in the vital respect: that is, in respect of *statecraft*.

In Plato's *Protagoras* (322e), Protagoras of Abdera is made to defend the view that men are at least roughly equal in statecraft. All men, says Protagoras, must share in expertise in statecraft, because if they did not, no state (*polis*) would even be possible. It is clear in Plato's later works, for example, the *Republic*, that he is not prepared to grant that *anything* exists that deserves the name of *polis* (Plato even questions whether any such *polis could* exist). So he presumably thinks that Protagoras' argument depends on a false assumption. In any case Plato argues plausibly that it is a truth we should hold as self evident that all men are *not* equal in statecraft—not even *approximately* equal. Statecraft is not a gift of nature, as (say) language is. Rather, says Plato, it involves special knowledge, which can only be acquired by a very special sort of education. Not the sort of education that Protagoras offers, either, which Plato regards as sophistry in the worst sense of the word (Section III). Protagoras' sort of teaching is refuted partly by its failure in practice—Plato repeatedly cites Pericles' failure to teach statecraft to his notoriously dissolute sons by Protagorean methods. It is also undermined by an incoherence in Protagoras' whole project that Plato discerns. Plato argues that Protagoras ought, on his own principles, to hold that anything in the category of virtue or excellence—in which category statecraft is preeminent—is not genuinely knowledge. Now what is not knowledge is not teachable, and statecraft seems not to be knowledge: yet Protagoras sets up to teach it.

As for Plato's alternative to a sophistical education, he gives various accounts of this. In early dialogues, it often looks as if, on Platonic or Socratic principles, it will not be possible to learn anything at all (*Meno* 80d). The earliest Socratic inquiries (e.g., *Laches, Charmides, Euthyphro*) typically proceed in a rigorous question-and-answer form (*elenchus*), but fail to establish any firm conclusion—not at least of the sort originally intended. However, Socrates' scepticism is always moderated by his certainty about some basic ethical views, some of which will be clear already. In Locke's phrase, Socratic scepticism is a broom to sweep the rubbish out of the way of the progress of knowledge. It is a propaedeutic to finding the truth, not an attempt to say that the truth cannot be found. In this sense Socratic scepticism is like Cartesian scepticism and unlike the Academic scepticism of later antiquity—despite the Academic school's habit of claiming Socrates as their founding father.

Thus, Plato always has some positive doctrine to offer, especially about education. By the time of writing of the *Protagoras* (356d) he is offering a rather simple utilitarian education in the comparative measuring of pleasures and pains. In *Republic*, Bks. II-III, VI-VII, the picture is markedly different and much more complex. The central idea is now that real knowledge is knowledge of the transcendent standards that govern everything else—the Forms, as Plato calls them—and that the various components of the education of a ruler-to-be are of no value in themselves unless they provide ways of getting towards the knowledge of the Forms. It is this progression toward reality that justifies Plato's educators in spending so long training the minds of their elite charges in geometry, astronomy, and so forth. Such studies are no more than steps along the way to that contemplation of reality that alone fits a man to rule over others.

There again, once he has thus contemplated the superb beauty of the highest realities, a man will not *want* to engage in the far less pleasurable task of ruling over others (*Republic* 519e): contemplation is always, for Plato, a higher calling than action. But the philosopher's unwillingness to rule is precisely what qualifies him to rule. Compare the sophist's or democrat's dangerously avid greed for power, and the indifference to it affected, for example, by Julius Caesar. Plato's picture of what a ruler's education should be is a radical one, and would have seemed eccentric to his contemporaries in its neglect of such elements of a traditional education as poetry and rhetoric; above all in its insistence that the only person fit to rule the state is *the philosopher* (*Republic* 473d), who alone has any true knowledge of statecraft, or indeed of anything else.

To sum up, Plato holds that the very idea of a democracy runs flatly counter to readily observable facts about the distribution of *knowledge* among men. The democrat's central assumption—that all men are or can become equal in their knowledge of statecraft—is plainly false. Therefore, egalitarian democracy is a foolish way to run a state. To take Plato's own analogy, it is as foolish as sailing a ship by the majority vote of everyone in the crew from captain to bottle-swabber (*Republic* 488ab). It makes more sense to be, like Plato, an unashamed elitist.

Plato thinks that this democratic mistake about knowledge is not simply a mistake in its own right. It breeds other mistakes as well. One mistake thus bred is what Plato calls *polypragmosynē* (*Republic* 434b): Jack-of-all-tradery, specious versatility. Democracy fosters the error of thinking that just anyone can dabble in just any pursuit they care to try, statecraft included, and hope for fair success. This kind of versatility is explicitly praised by Thucydides' Pericles (2.40), but Plato thinks it simply unnatural. No human has the capacity to do everything equally well. Therefore, they should not be allowed to try. They should concentrate on what they do best. In the utopia that Plato describes in his *Republic,* they are *compelled* to; it was Plato who gave us the proverb "The cobbler should stick to his last" (*Republic* 370c, 434a).

Third, by encouraging *polypragmosynē,* democracy also encourages *relativism.* The democrat prizes two thoughts: first (as we have seen) that all men alike have the same potential (at any rate) for various sorts of expertise, especially about statecraft; and therefore, second, that all alike may be tolerantly left to make their own choices about how to live. (Again, Thucydides' Pericles exemplifies both attitudes. So does Ronald Dworkin's claim that "political decisions must be, so far as is possible, independent of any particular conception of the good life, or of what gives value to life. Because the citizens of a society differ in their conceptions, the government does not treat them as equals if it prefers one conception to another" (Dworkin, *A Matter of Principle,* p. 191).) From these tolerant or optimistic views it is a short and familiar step to two relativist views, both of which Plato thinks absurd: that any choice about how to live is as good as any other, and that so is any view about statecraft. In Plato's *Theaetetus* (162–172) Protagoras himself, one of the great spokesman of Periclean democracy, is accused—apparently with some historical justification—of making these steps into relativism explicit. His relativism is then attacked as self-refuting or self-defeating.

Fourth, to encourage *polypragmosynē* is to encourage the view that just anyone, however ignorant or stupid, can fairly be judge of anyone else's actions, however expert or wise. Sometimes at Athens this meant *literally* judges. Two notorious verdicts had been handed down by popular courts at Athens, neither of which was ever forgiven or forgotten by Plato. (See *Theaetetus* 200d ff., *Republic* 516e.) One of these verdicts was passed on the Athenian admirals who had just won a brilliant naval victory against Sparta at Arginusae, off Lesbos (406 B.C.). The admirals were unable to rescue survivors from the sea in the tempest that followed the battle. For this understandable omission, they were put to death— despite their triumph, despite the fact that Athens was desperately in need of military success at the time, and also incidentally despite objections from Socrates. The other was the verdict that, on equally unreasonable

grounds, sentenced to death Socrates himself (399 B.C.). Plato would ask: How can a motley of landfarers be fit to judge decisions taken, in the heat of battle and sea storm, on the other side of the Aegean, by acknowledged and proven masters of naval warfare? Or how can a mob of semiliterates, who know of Socrates' philosophical practice only from the comedian Aristophanes' parodies of it (which are on the level of *Sesame Street*)—how can such people be thought fit to decide whether Socrates' activities make him unworthy to live? Democracy means submitting everything to the test of popular opinion. But that is to say that the most expert in any field has to accept the advice of those who know least about it: as if Einstein should have to take physics lessons from Kermit the Frog, or as if research budgets should be settled by popular vote or market forces (as they are in our own society). The objection here is not merely that democracy leads to relativism, to the leveling out of the distinction between the expert and the ignoramus. Worse, the charge is that democracy actually turns that distinction upside down by setting the ignoramus up as judge of the expert.

II. THE WILL TO TRUTH AND THE WILL TO POWER

Precisely because democracy by definition involves counting everyone's opinion as worth the same, it also and equally by definition involves the sidelining of the concept of knowledge, and therefore of *truth* as the object of inquiry. This indifference to truth is the uniting theme of a second group of Platonic objections to democracy.

Plato thinks democracy's attitude to truth central to the disasters that must befall it: "He who is to be a true and noble character must necessarily and primarily be directed *by the truth.* If he is not to be a mere charlatan, with no trace of the true love of wisdom in his character, it is the truth that he must pursue, at all times and with all his powers" (*Republic* 490a). We have already seen how Plato thinks the wrong attitude to truth can lead a society toward Protagorean relativism, or even toward the situation where the expert must answer to the know-nothing. There is another consequence to be borne in mind as well. This is the possibility, famously noted by Nietzsche, that a quite different sort of inquiry might come to be, of which the object is not at all **the truth**, but **power**. (Curiously, Nietzsche takes Socrates' use of elenchus—the "knife-thrust of the syllogism" as Nietzsche calls it—to be the exemplar of a peculiarly vicious and perverted form of the will for power, and Socrates' aristocratic opponents, who did not argue but coerced, to be much more nearly examplars of the will to truth. Like much else in Nietzsche this seems a willfully improbable judgment, however entertainingly it may be presented.)

Consider the contrast between Socrates and his prosecutors, noted at the beginning of his first speech in his own defense that Plato gives us in the *Apology*. In the popular assembly, in a law court, or in a philosophy seminar, I can do what Socrates does there: argue a case with the truth in mind, and aiming at nothing but a true and reasoned understanding of how things really are. This aim may of course prove embarrassingly hard to achieve, because in Oscar Wilde's words, the truth is never pure and rarely simple. As noted already, the Socrates whom Plato depicts is put to pretty well constant embarrassment by his own high standards of inquiry—especially in the earlier dialogues. He is not afraid to seem foolish—even though, as Plato emphasizes, that appearance of folly finally helps to get him executed.

On the other hand, I can avoid all danger of embarrassment by doing what Socrates' prosecutors did: by arguing just to *win*—to get a majority of the verdict on my side, and so to get my enemy convicted. (Compare English, Scottish, and American criminal trials, where the point at issue is not at all *what actually happened,* except insofar as what can be *proved* to have "actually happened" can be used to convince a jury to bring in one verdict or another.) But notice what happens if we do go down this road. If *victory* becomes the goal of argument, there is a danger that truth and rationality will cease to be its goals. They can become mere instruments to the attainment of victory.

Now the importance of victory in debate, as indeed in everything else, had always been central to the Greek tradition. To win was glorious, honorable, a reason to be remembered by posterity and to dedicate statues to the goddess *Nikē* (Victory). To lose was shameful and disgraceful, unfit for a gentleman: witness the behavior of Achilles when he is routed in debate by Agamemnon in *Iliad* I. Plato denounces the Greeks' preference for winning the argument—*looking* like good arguers— over discovering the truth—*being* good arguers (*Apology* 1ab)—just as later Platonists like Augustine were to denounce the Romans for their "lust for domination" and their "love of glory" (*City of God* Bk. V). Again, Plato gives Homer famously short shrift. But at least a Homeric debate was likely to be settled by aristocratic considerations about "who was the better man" (*Iliad* I. 186-187)—by notions of honor that were at least

cousins of notions of true worth. By contrast, Plato thought, argument at Athens was *altogether* debased, by the combination of this desire for honor with one further factor: namely, that, in a democracy, the vital consideration in any debater's mind is always and necessarily his need to please the electorate. This, as Steele noted in *The Spectator* (No. 394, June 2, 1712), can only mean those who are baser than the candidate himself: "You see in Elections for Members to sit in Parliament, how far saluting Rows of old Women, drinking with Clowns, and being upon a Level with the Lowest Part of Mankind in that wherein they themselves are lowest, their Diversions, will carry a Candidate. A Capacity for prostituting a Man's self in his Behaviour, and descending to the present Humour of the Vulgar, is perhaps as good an Ingredient as any other for making a considerable Figure in the World."

Democracy turns debate away from the will to truth and toward the will to the power won through victory in debate. Because in a democracy victory is won by pleasing the electorate, it thus corrupts both the politician and the people. It trains the people to expect the politician to tell them what they want to hear instead of what is true; it trains the politician to suppress all that is best in himself, and pander uncritically to their desires. This is a training that leads headlong toward tyranny (*Republic* 562e).

Moreover, because a democracy is a state where the pleasant is more influential than the true, and where power is what counts, not being right, it follows, first, that there is apt to be no room in a democracy for unpalatable truths; and second, that a democracy is necessarily a state that is preoccupied principally with making money to provide the power to satisfy, not its citizens' *needs*, but their *whims*. Hence, the great, and (Plato admits) attractive, *variety* to be found in the democratic state (*Republic* 557c). Because the democracy is the state where people do whatever they feel like doing (and can afford), its shops are stuffed with the greatest possible range for consumer choice; its range of possible lives from which individuals choose one to live (off the peg, as it were) is the greatest of all societies'; and its external relations are characterized by just that willingness to take on indefinitely many expansionist projects at once, which (Thucydides 2.39) Pericles praises, and Plato condemns, as *polypragmosynē*.

As for unpalatable truths, it is an observable fact that in a democracy true and important news that is bad is driven out by false or trivial news that is good, by a sort of Gresham's Law, which makes information itself a commodity for financially driven consumer choice.

(Consider the control exerted by the present-day media over which stories count as *news*, and why.) Hence, Plato's contrast (*Gorgias* 454e ff.) between medicine, which seeks the body's well-being, and cookery, which seeks only its pleasure. The democrat is the man who treats his doctors (i.e., his statesmen) like his cooks (i.e., the providers of his pleasures): if he doesn't like what one of them is telling him or doing to him, he simply spends money on a second opinion or treatment that he *will* like. Hence, in a democracy it pays the doctor of the constitution to behave like a cook to the constitution and not like a true doctor—attending to its whims instead of to its needs. (Of course, it is also possible for a literal doctor to behave like this—to behave, in fact, like a cosmetic surgeon.) Compare the modern notion of "political impossibilities", that is, those policies that no elected politician will implement even if he admits that they are necessary or just or right, because doing so will make him unelectable: for example, tight environmental controls on private cars, or a welfare policy that successfully meets the needs of the desperate but nonvoting poor by heavy taxation of comfortable middle-class voters.

III. SOPHISTRY, PRETENSION, AND AGGRESSION

Democracy not only encourages public debate to develop in ways that are not (to adapt Robert Nozick's phrase) "truth-tracking" but "power-tracking" (or pleasure- or wealth-tracking). Worse, it elevates power-tracking (etc.) methods of debate and persuasion to the level of a *system*, a *science* (or rather, as Plato might have said, a pseudoscience). In Plato's day this kind of system was what was being offered by the *sophists*— men like Protagoras, Thrasymachus, Callicles, and Gorgias. Their claim was to make good citizens out of anyone who came to them (*Protagoras* 318a), by instruction in such things as "statecraft" and oratory (Gorgias' speciality). But in Plato's view, they were simply the means whereby the decadence and corruption of Athenian democracy perpetuated itself. It was the *sophists* who were really guilty of the "impiety and corrupting the youth of Athens" for which Socrates was executed when, by what Plato saw as a terrible irony, his society became so drunk on sophistry that it could no longer distinguish the true philosopher from the imposter. To a sophistic relativist, of course, this distinction is not even *available* (*Sophist* 235c–236e): hence, the importance of being able to make this distinc-

tion, as Plato tries to in the *Sophist*: cp. *Protagoras* 313d ff.

One reason why Plato held the sophists to be corrupters of the aristocratic youths of whose education they were often put in charge had to do with the deliberate and systematic inculcation of the already-noted emphasis on victory in debate, rather than on truth. Such an education leads the young aristocrat to regard the pursuit of truth or wisdom in itself as an amusing schoolboys' exercise, like boy scouting or holding class debates (*Gorgias* 485bd). It is fine for juveniles, but a contemptible and worthless pastime for those old enough for the serious business of politics. This, for Gorgias as much as for Machiavelli, is simply the seeking and retaining of the power that is necessary if one is to live well. (Contrast *Gorgias* 492bc and Machiavelli, *The Prince*, p. 101. There is an interesting parallel between classical Athens and Italian city-states in the Renaissance such as Machiavelli's Florence.)

Hence, second, the sophists' teaching also leads the young aristocrat to be most interested not in rationality, but in whatever kind of argument *works*— not the rational appeal but the emotional, if that is more successful; not the laborious, painstaking minutia of Socratic elenchus, but the quick, neat, and stylish argument that wins immediate approval—even if this argument has some hidden flaw: that is, in the modern sense, a *sophistry*. (For a showcase of sophistries, v. the *Euthydemus*.) The sophists also encourage their pupils to view the "wisdom" that they offer as a commodity by charging payment for their instruction—a point that Plato regards as a scandalous indictment of their practice.

Third, in two ways sophistic teaching encourages the primary democratic vice of *pleonexia*—pathological acquisitiveness, *haben und mehrwollhaben*, as Nietzsche translated it. First, because the desire for victory that we have just seen encouraged by the sophists is itself a form of the pleonectic desire to have *more* (more honor and more power, in this case). Second, because in a democracy, a crucial necessity for a statesman who wants to please the people is that he should satisfy their *pleonexia*. At Athens, popular *pleonexia* was not only expressed by material acquisitiveness within the marketplace. It was also expressed by a desire for an overseas empire, met above all in those imperialist policies which Thucydides' Pericles (2.41) praises not only for their *polypragmosynē*, but also for their aggressive daring and ambition: in brief, for their *pleonexia*.

Thus, *pleonexia* is necessarily an aggressive and predatory disposition. Thinkers as diverse as Hobbes and modern game theorists have taken this sort of aggressive predation to be a natural human trait. In his famous account of the Melian Debate Thucydides (5.106) reports Periclean Athenians as arguing that "it is a general and necessary law of nature to rule wherever one can"; Machiavelli writes that "the wish to acquire more is admittedly a very natural and common thing" (*The Prince* p. 42); Plato's own character Glaucon questions whether anyone, however virtuous they might seem, would really turn up the chance to get away with murder, if they thought the murder sufficiently advantageous and its discovery sufficiently unlikely (*Republic* 359b ff.). Again, Plato has the sophist Thrasymachus argue that "justice is the advantage of the stronger" (*Republic* 338c; cp. *Laws* 714d), meaning by this that that we call "justice" is really a confidence trick, not a virtue—a device for the powerful to keep the upper hand over the weak. (Compare Callicles (*Gorgias* 492b), who thinks that *conventional* justice is a confidence trick that the *weak* use to keep down the *strong*; he contrasts this with *natural* justice, which demands that the naturally strong should reject all conventions and displace the naturally weak.)

The sophists' exaltation of *pleonexia* is not only a natural result of their position in a democratic milieu. It is also, and above all, an attack on the notions of *justice* and (once more) *truth*. Justice has come to be seen by the sophists, not (as Plato thinks it is) an indispensable and utterly central social good, but as a device for exerting control over others. The "justice" of the Thrasymachean ruler is not his concern for those he governs; it is his concern for *himself*. But this, Plato argues (*Republic* 342e), is the exact opposite of what real justice means in a ruler. Just as in argument what matters to the sophist is to *look* like you have proved your point—never mind whether you really *have*—so too with justice: what matters to the sophist is not to *be* just, but to *seem* just. "A prince need not ... have all these good qualities, but he should certainly appear to have them ... indeed if he has these qualities and always behaves accordingly he will find them ruinous; if he only appears to have them they will render him service" (Machiavelli, *The Prince*, p. 100).

Plato takes it to be a dire judgment on democracy that it should engender and foster these sorts of attitudes. To treat justice as a mere pretense, a cloak for power-hungry aggression—this is an attitude that leads straight to tyranny. (As Callicles would have agreed: but he evidently approved of tyranny.) Plato's response to the sophistic assault on justice is to argue that it is better to die than to be unjust. His first attempt to argue this is in the *Crito*, where Socrates refuses to run away

to escape execution on the grounds that this would be unjust because it would mean refusing to recognise the authority of the laws of Athens. The conclusion seems to be that nothing could justify civil disobedience, and that a legal verdict of punishment is always just, provided it is passed under the proper legal forms, even when it is passed by unjust men. (The conclusion is *not*, as Nietzsche insinuates, that Socrates was suicidal: Socrates held suicide to be expressly forbidden by one of the very few unbreakable moral rules he knew of (*Phaedo* 62a)).

Plato argues in the *Gorgias* too that it is better to die (however painfully or unjustly) than to act unjustly, and that it is better to be punished for one's wrongdoing than to get away with it: for the person who acts unjustly is less just than the person who suffers injustice, and the person who acts unjustly and is not punished is less just than the person who acts unjustly and is punished: and no one who is unjust can possibly be *happy*. Such arguments are ridiculed by the sophists (*Gorgias* 473c), and they lead Plato into a very specific and perhaps counterintuitive account of what happiness is, on which it follows from the definition of "happiness" that only the truly just man is truly happy (*Gorgias* 507d).

In the *Republic*, Plato takes a third shot at the same target, arguing that it is always better for a state or an individual to be just because true happiness only comes to those who are truly *just*: this time it is Plato's account of what justice is that is the innovation, and once again the charge can be made that his new account is a counterintuitive one. This charge Plato would perhaps admit—but would add, characteristically, that the reason for the counterintuitiveness is the confusion of our intuitions.

Another common and traditional Greek intuition that Plato fiercely opposes is the view that it is part of being just to take revenge, to render good for good and evil for evil (*Republic* 332ab: cp. Thucydides 4.63). Plato thinks that this attitude is indicative of a tyrannical and destructive temperament that has nothing to do with justice. Justice is a virtue, and so naturally connected with *being beneficial*; so it can be no part of my being a just man for me to harm anyone at all, no matter what they may have done to me. (*Crito* 49bc, *Gorgias* 507a ff., *Republic* 335be). It is not of course accidental that this very Christian-sounding point (cp. *St. Matthew's Gospel* 5:38–44) about revenge is most clearly made in just the same contexts as those where Plato argues that it is always better to be just than unjust. Unlike previous Greek thinkers, Plato is moving towards *defining* "injustice" in terms of harm.

IV. ART, TRUTH, AND DILEMMA

What led the democrat toward sophistry, and toward the dangerous attitude that real (as opposed to apparent) justice is not of central importance, was his willingness to compromise on the centrality of truth. Another potentially dangerous form of compromise about truth, in Plato's view, is representative art—any sort of art that involves representation. (The principal forms of representative art known to Plato were Homer's narrative epics and the Greek tragedies; he also speaks of sculpture and painting.) In the *Republic* Plato argues that such art can be dangerous in at least five ways.

First, drama and epic, and painting and sculpture too, present us with *fictions*: which of course means they present us with what is *not true*. This obvious and—to many earnest minds—troubling point is doubly to be insisted upon if like Plato you believe that even the particular things that art imitates themselves have an air of uncertainty and unreality. Plato believes that the very world of fact is something we can only make sense of, or find truth in, with the help of standards that themselves appear in the world of fact only in contradictory and not fully coherent fashion—in pale imitations of their true reality. (These standards are Plato's famous "Forms.") If we can only make sense of the *factual* world with the help of the Forms, those standards of truth and reality that lie beyond it and that it palely imitates, how are we to make sense of what lies in the same relationship to the factual world as the factual world lies to the Forms? Will not such fictional worlds be "at the third remove" from truth (*Republic* 597e)? Hence, will they not be at best mere distractions from the transcendent truths on which we ought to focus our attention—and at worst will they not tend to be yet another way in which our grip is loosened on the whole distinction between the true or real and the false or unreal?

Second, the person who acts or paints is imitating a nature that is not actually his, and may actually be worse than his—as for example if he plays or otherwise imitates a villain. (Notice that nearly every good story or drama needs a villain.) What is more, he is also engaging in a sort of *polypragmosynē*, and thus breaking the basic rule of justice that applies in Plato's ideal state (Section VI), that each part of the state should perform its own function and no one else's: that everyone should specialize in whatever they are best at. An actor or painter is not specializing in this way, for his aim is to be able to *mirror* whatever everyone else does—"like a most miraculous sophist," as Plato dryly observes (*Republic* 596d; cp. *Sophist* 234b). Moreover, the artist

does not even perform the functions of others *properly*: cp. the last point.

Third, Plato argues that art—or most of the art that was found in his own society—feeds the wrong emotions. It teaches us fear and dread where we should be courageous; its frequent depiction of extremes of emotion makes it harder for us to greet disaster in our own lives with restraint or sobriety, rather than "pouring out great laments and threnodies even over the smallest misfortunes, shamelessly and unrebuked" (*Republic* 388e). Then there is the paradox of tragedy, famously described by another great Platonist—St. Augustine. "The more the spectator of the tragedy is grieved, the more he applauds its actors" (*Confessions* III). Augustine and Plato can see no rational justification for these upside-down emotional states; still less for the conscious decisions whereby we choose to be exposed to them. How then can they be good for us? The enjoyment or practice of art as it stands is, in Plato's view, quite incompatible with the proper control of emotion by reason in the soul, or in the state. Much of the appeal of art is not rational at all, but subliminal and instinctive. It is incalculable, uncontrollable, and therefore, Plato argues, incalculably dangerous.

Fourth, Plato holds that the arts tell us lies not only about the way the world is, but also about the gods. Greek drama, based as it is on the myths of Homer and Hesiod, gives us a view of the gods as (among other things) cruel, arbitrary, lecherous, dishonest, and superbly indifferent to human suffering. In this way Greek drama seems blasphemously false to Plato: he argues vehemently that the gods are not as the traditions and the tragedians depict them—and moreover that accepting the traditional view is disastrous for the development of a good character. "After all," someone might say, "if Zeus is an irrational tyrant, what point is there in *my* trying to be controlled by reason?"

Finally, Plato accuses the arts of blasphemous untruth for another reason. Much of the best art, in particular Greek drama, is above all an examination of moral *dilemmas*—insoluble problems confronting practical choice, which Greek tragedians often resolved only by the expedient of a *deus ex machina*—that is, by the intervention of a divinity's direction into an otherwise irresoluble uncertainty. This is objectionable to Plato for at least two reasons. First, because Plato proposes an ethical theory according to which there is no possible practical problem that is truly insoluble. To him, the idea of a situation where *nothing* right can be done, like that of Sophie's choice, is a nonsensical and (once more) blasphemous idea. Second, even if there were such a situation, to add a divine command to it would resolve nothing. (In fact the tragedians seem to have recognized this. As Alasdair MacIntyre has observed, the whole point about a *deus ex machina* "resolution" of a dramatic dilemma is that it does not *resolve* it at all: "The action is interrupted rather than completed . . . the intervention of a god in Greek tragedy often signals the disclosure of an incoherence in moral standards and vocabulary" (*After Virtue*, p. 132).)

But Plato is not content, as the tragedians are, simply to note such moral dilemmas. Plato wants to solve them—but not primarily by artistic means. Not by bringing the gods in either: for any attempt to base ethical decisions on divine commands faces the famous logical dilemma of *Euthyphro* 10a. Do the gods command what they do command because they recognize the same standards of justice and holiness as us? If the answer is yes, then we already have reason to do what is commanded, without there being any need of a divine command. If the answer is no, then we have no reason to do what is commanded, even if there is a divine command. Hence, we need to look in another direction to solve moral dilemmas.

Plato's suggestion is that we look once more to the Forms, and in particular their relations to one another. A moral dilemma such as that of Sophocles' Antigone, who is caught between an act that goes against family piety and an act that goes against civic loyalty and justice, is for Plato a problem about the interrelations of the Forms of the relevant virtues. But relations among the Forms are always clear-cut and definite, because, to put a complex theory very crudely, the Forms are arranged in a hierarchy with The Good at the top of it (*Republic* 509b), and The Good is what gives every other Form its place in the hierarchy and its definition. Hence, no one who actually understood how the standards of Piety and Justice were interrelated, by the relation of each to The Good, could possibly suppose that any moral dilemma they might find themselves in was anything more than apparent. There could be real moral dilemmas only if the thesis of the unity of the virtues was false: only if it was possible for one virtue to conflict with another. But the fact that there is a Form of the Good shows that it is not possible. (On the other hand, we should also notice that the Form of the Good is itself highly mysterious, and could only be properly known by someone who had completed the education of the philosopher ruler. Plato admits that no one has done this (*Republic* 506c). But until someone *does* do it (and no one yet has), the idea of a complete ethical knowledge or science of how to resolve all possible moral dilemmas is no more than a research program.)

To sum up on art: it is not that Plato wants to *abolish* art, or (in Iris Murdoch's phrase) "banish the artists" without exception. All too commonly this is taken to be his wish, but other Platonists such as Plotinus (*Enneads* 1.6) have clearly rejected that alternative, and even Plato himself is much more flexible about art than some people take him to be. Just like Plotinus, Plato speaks at times (*Philebus* 51c) of the legitimate pleasures of nonrepresentative art—delight in pure forms like simple shapes or sounds (what the Bloomsbury aesthetician Clive Bell called "significant form"). Nor does Plato condemn *all* representative art: there is room in his republic at least for the depiction of heroic and saintly characters (*Republic* 401b). Socrates himself seems to have had some intimation that to attack poetry was to risk impiety (*Phaedrus* 243b); indeed Plato tells us that Socrates actually wrote poetry in the last few days of his life (*Phaedo* 60de). Again, Plato does not shrink from proposing the invention of a "noble lie," a foundation myth for his utopia (*Republic* 414b), so that even his abhorrence of the falsehood of fiction is decidedly qualified. The only artists whom Plato certainly banishes are Homer and the tragedians. And even his decision to expel them from the republic is qualified by an invitation to them to appeal against their expulsion by defending their own practices: "For our part, we will happily admit into our city imitation and the sort of art which aims at pleasure, if it can provide a good argument as to why it is needed in a well-governed city. For *we ourselves are conscious of art's enchantments*; but it would be impious to betray the truth as it appears to us" (*Republic* 607c; italics added).

Plato, then, is not exactly the out-and-out foe of art that some take him to be. Certainly he would like to censor or even ban much of the art that appears in societies like his own (such as our society). But this is not because he hates art, or artists. It is because he hates what societies like ours *do* to art, and to artists. (Take, for instance, an industry that flourishes in our society, but that Plato would surely have thought sleazy and contemptible: the making of what are called "controversial" films. A "controversial" film—the term appears to be a compliment—is one that is not quite shocking enough to get banned, but is still shocking enough to create waves of free publicity in the form of outraged protests and half-witted chat-show twitter about whether or not it is "art.") For this reason there is no point in protesting, against Plato, that the artist must be free to produce what he wants, and what seems good to him. Plato will simply retort that, in a corrupted society like the typical democracy, the artist is unlikely to know what he wants, or what is good. He is likely to produce art that displays, celebrates, and perpetuates the values that his society has warped and twisted in him. If, that is, he is not actually so corrupted that he ceases trying to produce things for their *artistic* value, and instead—whether or not he notices the difference—starts producing merely what will sell well: gross pornography, or graphic violence, or mindless "light entertainment," or whatever the current fashion dictates.

V. TRANSCENDENCE, SEX, AND EUGENICS

So it would be nearer the truth to say not that Plato aims to abolish art, but that he aims to reconstruct it. The same is clearly true of his attitude to another central phenomenon of human life, sexuality. In his *Symposium* and *Phaedrus* we see these two reconstructions going forward together. The phenomenon of erotic love—the fascinated longing for one other human body and person, usually, in Plato's Athens, for another *man*—is put to the question in these dialogues. What gives erotic love its peculiarly bewitching power and pleasure? What is the lover really seeking, and why does physical conquest and satiation so often lead to immediate disenchantment on both sides? Plato's answer is that sexual desire in its lower forms is desire for one person's particular beauty. But the enlightened lover will aim higher than that particular, realizing that bodily beauty is no more than a clue to beauty of character, and one character's beauty no more than a clue to "the great ocean of beauty" (*Symposium* 211c):

"Beginning from visible beauties he must, for the sake of the beautiful itself, go on and on upwards, using one beauty, then two, and then all beautiful bodies like the rungs of a ladder: then all beautiful characters, and then all beautiful sorts of wisdom; until finally he arrives at that one sort of wisdom of which the concern is nothing but beauty itself, and so is made perfect by his knowledge of what is itself beauty."

The lover's desire for the beloved is not complete in itself—as is shown by his dissatisfaction when he gets what he thought he wanted: his desire is both too deep and too high for any other *individual* to satisfy. It is a desire that goes beyond its (apparent) object in a way that Plato sees as leading the lover to the Forms, and that a Christian Platonist like Augustine will similarly see as leading him toward God himself: in Augustine's words, "you made us for yourself, and our hearts are restless till they find their rest in you" (*Confessions* I.1).

Thus, his sexuality can itself play a part in the philosopher's education, his rise from the deceptive particularities of the world to the pure truth of the divine Forms, just as much as we saw his study of (say) mathematics or astronomy could (*Republic* 528c). We are very far here from the picture of Plato as a body-hating ascetic that is so often put about. True though it is that Plato regards the body as potentially a dangerous distraction from what really matters for humans (*Phaedrus* 246ab), and true though it is that he takes *merely* bodily life to be little better than death (*Phaedo* 66c), and philosophy as a kind of training for death (*Phaedo* 64a), it should also be noted that, as the *Phaedrus* and *Symposium* make clear, Plato is willing to give the body and its sexuality a crucial role even in his account of the soul's salvation. (To revert to art for a moment: If this is so even of sexuality, then any intelligent Platonist ought to be able to add the inference that Plotinus explicitly draws: How much more so of art. Art too can lead us, if it is used aright, beyond itself to what it stands for. Perhaps, indeed, how much its lower aspects prove a distraction to us depends not on its potentialities, but on our own. In Clive Bell's words, "Let no one imagine, because he has made merry in the warm tilth and quaint nooks of romance, that he can even guess at the austere and thrilling raptures of those who have climbed the cold white peaks of art.")

The first notable feature of Plato's reconstruction of sexuality is, then, this insistence that the best sort of homosexual friendship includes no sexual consummation, but rather a chaste, almost monastic, quest together after the Forms that the lovers first glimpsed in each other. This idea was a kind of extrapolation from normal Athenian thinking about homosexuality, which—inconsistently—held that it was honorable to seduce, but dishonorable to *be* seduced. (For a farcical presentation of the whole theme, see Alcibiades in *Symposium* 215a ff. Meanwhile John Donne's *The Good-Morrow* turns Plato on his head: "If ever any Beauty I did see, which I desir'd and got, 'Twas but a dream of thee.")

Heterosexual love is for Plato a lower form of love than (chaste) homosexual love (*Symposium* 208e). It certainly seems to be more tightly policed than homosexual love in Plato's utopia. Marriages, at least among Plato's elite class of philosopher rulers (the guardians), are arranged on a strict eugenic basis: it simply seems obvious to Plato that any well-ordered state should do at least as much as is done by any breeder of dogs or birds to improve its genetic stock, and to control the state's population (*Republic* 460a; *Theaetetus* 150a).

One objection to such a proposal is the individualist retort that people should be allowed to marry whomever they want. To this Plato would reply, first, with the point made above about "what artists want": that in a typical individualist democracy most people have no idea of what they actually want, because their desires are so much manipulated by the various sorts of propaganda that Plato symbolizes as the "puppeteers" in his famous image of the Cave (*Republic* 514b). Sophists, rhetoricians, advertising men, astrologers, double-glazing salesmen, and quack evangelists of every sort are so busy brainwashing the average inhabitant of an individualist democracy that the notion of "what he or she wants" simply lacks any clear content. Second, Plato would add that the long-term well-being of the entire state should not be sacrificed to the short-term and often illusory satisfaction of the individual. Thus Plato can see no reason why "the best men" should not be "united with the best women as often as possible, and the worst men with the worst women as rarely as possible—the offspring of the first unions being raised, but not that of the second unions—if the human flock is to be at its best" (*Republic* 459de).

Here his eugenic proposals commit Plato to the further view that some children should be secretly *exposed* (left to die) at birth. Elsewhere, for example, *Theaetetus* 148 ff., he also countenances the use of *abortion* to bring about the same sort of ends. His proposals also commit him to bringing about the end of the family. Among the guardians in his ideal society, even wives and children are to be held in common, and every member of any given age group is to have his relations to other age groups entirely defined by which age group he belongs to. Thus, Plato proposes, any man of (say) 20 will have a reason of filial piety to obey any man of 40, and a reason arising from the incest taboo to avoid having sex with any woman of 40. For any 40-year-old man might be his own father, and any 40-year-old woman might be his own mother. (Whether anyone could have reasons for caring about filial impiety or incest in a state such as Plato describes is a question he does not discuss.)

There is one concession to individualism that Plato makes in this context. He concedes that it would be so difficult to get his eugenic program accepted, even in his ideal state, that it is better not to try to do so directly. Instead, he suggests, the rulers among the guardian class should engage in a further sort of systematic deception of the other guardians, besides "the noble lie" (*Republic* 414c). At each of the "mating seasons" or times for sexual activity that his guardians will enjoy, there should, he suggests, be a lottery for choice of sexual partners, which the rulers will rig so as to serve their own eugenic ends. Moreover, those eugenic ends will further be served if greater access to sexual activity is offered to those who show courage in warfare: the pretext (*prophasis*) of a reward will be used to bring about the result that the brave have a better chance of reproducing.

What lies behind these suggestions is a rejection of individualism that is taken to the point of abolishing the very notions of "yours" and "mine." Thus, in the *Republic*, 462ab, although not in the *Laws*, we have Plato arguing for complete *communism*—the holding of all possessions in common among the guardians, and not merely the community of husbands and wives:

> Nothing is worse for the state than whatever causes it to be disunited, and makes it many constitutions rather than one; and nothing is better for the state than whatever binds it together and unites it. Sharing in pleasure and grief unites us, when all the citizens, so far as is possible, mourn the same deaths and rejoice at the same births. Contrast the privatisation (*idiosis*) of such feelings, when the very same experiences of the city or of its inhabitants bring about extremes of woe in some and of joy in others: this dissolves the city's unity. But the main cause of this sort of effect is this: that the people in the city do not apply such words as "yours" and "mine" in the same way....

Plato also has some radical proposals to make about the role of women in his society. His main proposal is simply that because "women have just the same natural ability as men to be guardians over the city, although they are weaker than men," women too should "be chosen to live together with the male guardians, and share in their work as guardians" (*Republic* 456ab). Plato adds, daringly given his own society's conventions, that women guardians should even partake, virtually on equal terms, of the musical and gymnastic parts of the education of guardians. This may sound like *feminism*, but we should notice Plato's main argument for allowing that there should be women guardians as well as men: (i) *if* women were better than men at anything, then that would be what women were naturally fitted to do—their naturally distinct role; (ii) but there is nothing that women are better at than men; (iii) so women have no naturally distinct role; (iv) so if some men are naturally fitted to be guardians, there is no good reason to deny that some women are naturally fitted to be guardians too (*Republic* 455c ff.). As the argument depends on the assumption (ii) that women are not only inferior to men, but inferior to them in every possible respect, it hardly gives us grounds to call Plato a feminist. (Two other examples of Plato's attitude to women include *Timaeus* 91a: reincarnation as a woman as Destiny's way of punishing a bad man; and *Symposium* 208e: those men who procreate "merely physically" by sexual intercourse with women unfavorably contrasted with those men who procreate "spiritually" by social intercourse with other men.)

VI. SOULS, CITIES, AND AKRASIA

A central theme of the Platonic critique of democracy is, as has doubtless become clear, Plato's *political holism*—his belief that individualism is self-defeating, and that the only way to achieve the ends of individuals effectively is not to attempt to do so directly at all, but concentrate rather on the good of the state seen as a single unified whole. Thus we have already noted Plato's image of the statesman as a doctor, tending an organism, the state. In the *Republic* Plato develops this image, at great length and in great detail, as the *city/soul analogy*—a parallel between the composition and parts of the individual's constitution and the city's constitution. (Notice, by the way, this double sense of "constitution": here Plato has left his mark on the English language.)

Plato's analogy divides both the city-state and the individual's soul into three parts. In the individual's soul the three parts are (i) the highest part, the reason (this is the part that is capable of contemplating the Forms); (ii) the lowest part, the desires and passions of the body; and (iii) an intermediate part, which Plato calls "the spirited part," and which is responsible for such emotions as anger, pride, and daring.

Plato holds that no individual can be happy or just unless (i) their reason rules (ii) their passions with complete authority, and with (iii) the assistance of the spirited part. To be so ruled is what is meant by *justice* in the individual. (This is Plato's famous redefinition of justice: Section III.) Likewise, he holds that no city can be happy or just unless (i) its rational members, the philosopher rulers or guardians, have complete authority, with the support (iii) of the military and police establishment, over everyone else, and in particular those members of the city whose principal concerns are (ii) money-making and pleasure-seeking.

Thus, the city/soul analogy is used by Plato to justify a kind of rationalist authoritarianism, both in politics and in personal ethics. It also enables him to explain

a number of phenomena. One such phenomenon so explained is the differences between different races, which Plato proposes to explain as a difference in the admixture of the three elements in their souls. Another is the differences between different people's ability to be taught: this Plato explains by reference to the part of them that is dominant. He thinks that someone dominated by their reasoning or rational element is best able to be educated, whereas someone dominated by their desires can learn nothing except obedience. (Hence Plato's explanation of the Athenians' rejection of Socrates: he believed that they had rejected Socrates because they were dominated by the ill discipline of the lowest parts of their souls—"the rabble of their desires.")

Third, the analogy is also used, in *Republic* VIII-IX, to generate a tightly controlled essay in political pathology. Plato uses his theory of the soul to explain how a state can decline from aristocratic rule, via the forms of (mis-)government he calls timocracy, oligarchy and democracy, into tyranny. This happens as the state comes to be dominated in turn by characters who value, first not truth, but honor; then not honor, but wealth; then not just wealth, but complete freedom; and finally not just freedom, but power. His account of this decline is not only a philosophical and rhetorical *tour de force*: it is also one of the first attempts in history to make political science truly scientific. It clearly had a profound influence on the methods and thought of at least one other great pathologist of society: Karl Marx.

Finally, fourth, the city/soul analogy helps Plato to provide an explanation of *akrasia*, the phenomenon of someone's deliberately doing what they hold to be wrong. This phenomenon had seemed inexplicable to Plato when he wrote the *Protagoras* (357e). He then held that any desire was necessarily a desire for some good, and so could not see the pursuit of any desire as anything but a form of seeking the good that was misdirected because of the agent's ignorance. But in later works like the the *Phaedrus* (246b ff.) and the *Republic* (Bk.IV) Plato develops a view of the soul as having parts the desires of which are not necessarily always directed at any good at all. Such desires, therefore, can conflict in ways not simply reducible to mere ignorance.

Besides all this, Plato's view of the soul and its parts is interesting for at least two other reasons. The first is because of the detail and intricacy of Plato's psychology, and his view of the person as composed of an amalgam of conflicting causal systems at a subpersonal level, some of which (as cases like *akrasia* show) are more responsive to the body's controlling influence, and others to the reason's. In this sense Plato's view is reminiscent of Freud's psychology, with its tripartite scheme of id, ego, and super-ego.

The second point, however, is that, on the other hand, there is another line of thought in Platonism that is at least equally important, and that emphasizes the *unity*, not the multiplicity, of the self (*Phaedo* 70c ff.; *Phaedrus* 245c ff.; *Theaetetus* 184d; contrast *Symposium* 208ab). Often this means the unity of the self seen as *over against* the kind of bodily dominated causal systems that are taken to be part of the self in the theory given in the *Republic*; although perhaps the truth is that in the *Republic*, such systems are only *ideally* parts of the self—only parts of a fully virtuous and fully integrated self (*Republic* 443e.) However that may be, the main lines of Plato's thought on this matter are clear. What he gives us in such texts as *Phaedo* 115c is the concept of the *person* as distinct from their body—for the person in Plato's sense is the kind of thing that could be reincarnated in many bodies: *Republic* 617e ff. For the same reason Platonic persons are distinct also from the concept of the *human animal* that is central, for example, to Aristotle's thought in his *de Anima*. In this respect Plato's thought about the nature of the person is still enormously influential. A concept of the person that owes as much to Plato as to Cartesian dualism is still very firmly in place in many philosophers' thinking, not only in philosophy of mind, but also in such issues in applied ethics as abortion, euthanasia, and animal rights. Here then is one more legacy of Plato's thinking about applied ethics—and perhaps the most important of all.

Also See the Following Articles

ARISTOTELIAN ETHICS • GREEK ETHICS, OVERVIEW • MACHIAVELLIANISM

Bibliography

Aristotle. *de Anima.* Translated by W. S. Hett for *Loeb Classical Library,* 1986.
Augustine, *Confessions.* (E. B. Pusey, Trans., 1938). London and New York: Nelson.
Augustine, *City of God.* (Henry Bettenson, Trans., 1984). London and New York: Penguin Classics.
Bell C. *Art,* London, G. P. Putnam's Sons, 1914.
Boethius, *The consolation of philosophy.* (H. F. Stewart, Trans., 1936.). *Loeb Classical Library.*
Chappell, T. D. J. (1996). *The Plato reader.* Edinburgh/New York: Edinburgh/Columbia University Press.
Dworkin R. (1986). *A matter of principle.* Oxford: Oxford University Press.
Ferguson J. (1970). *Socrates: A source book.* London: Macmillan (Open University).
Hesiod. *Works and days.* Many translations available.
Hobbes T. *Leviathan.* (Ed. E. Curley, 1994). Indianapolis: Hackett.
Homer. *Iliad.* Many translations available.
Jowett, Benjamin. (1954). *The dialogues of Plato.* (4th ed., Vol. 1–5). Oxford: Clarendon Press.
Machiavelli. *The prince.* (George Bull, Trans., 1961.). London and New York: Penguin Classics.
MacIntyre A. (1981). *After virtue.* London: Duckworth.
Murdoch. (1977). *The fire and the sun: Why Plato banished the artists.* Oxford: Clarendon Press.
Nietzsche F. *Twilight of the Idols.* (R. F. Hollingdale, Trans., 1968.). London and New York: Penguin Classics. (Pp. 29 ff. especially relevant.)
Nozick R. (1980). *Philosophical explanations.* Oxford: Clarendon Press.
Plotinus, *The Enneads.* (A. H. Armstrong, Trans., 1966). In *Loeb Classical Library* (Vols. 1–6). Cambridge, MA: Harvard University Press.
Popper, K. (1945). *The open society and its enemies*: Vol II: Plato. London: Routledge.
Sophocles. *Antigone.* Many translations available.
Thucydides. *Histories.* Many translations available.
White, N. C. (1979). *Companion to Plato's Republic.* Indianapolis: Hackett.

PLAYING GOD

William Grey
University of Queensland

GLOSSARY

DNA Deoxyribonucleic acid. The molecular vector of genetic information which determines the attributes and development of organisms.

genetic engineering The deliberate alteration of the structure or hereditary characteristics of organisms, especially by the direct modification of DNA.

germ cells Reproductive cells containing the DNA genetic blueprint which determines the structure, character, and development of an organism. Modifications to an organism's germ cells are passed on to its descendants.

hubris Human overconfidence, arrogance, or overweening pride.

negative genetic engineering Also called therapeutic or corrective engineering. Genetic engineering that aims to rectify some defect, disease, or disability.

positive genetic engineering Also called eugenic or enhancement engineering. Genetic engineering that aims to improve character traits of organisms, for example, increasing disease resistance, robustness, or fertility.

somatic cells The body tissues of an organism apart from the reproductive or germ cells. Somatic changes are not passed on to an organism's descendants.

PLAYING GOD is a phrase frequently used to describe acts or decisons about matters which the speaker believes should either be treated with extreme caution or left well alone. Often, as the phrase suggests, the implied objection to a proposed course of action is based on religious beliefs. Such use of the phrase usually presupposes, or at least alludes to, a divinely ordained order in the physical or moral universe which it would be reckless or impermissible to transgress. There are also secular uses in which the phrase is used metaphorically to indicate that the consequences of an act are exceedingly serious or far-reaching and must therefore be considered with very great care. The phrase may also be used to describe paternalistic or authoritarian decisions, often resented, made by individuals in positions of power.

The most familiar applications of the phrase are in discussions in bioethics, especially in describing decisions about the termination of life. Accusations of "playing God" are frequently encountered, for example, in connection with decisions which have serious and irreversible consequences for individuals, such as decisions about abortion or euthanasia. The expression is also used to describe proposals for genetic manipulation, especially in discussions about the permissibility of modifying human germ cells. What is common to all the various uses of "playing God" is the idea that there is a natural order or structure, perhaps divinely ordained, and that proposals to exceed the limits which this natural order defines should be rejected out of hand—or at least considered very carefully.

When a phrase is used to characterize actions or behavior as morally blameworthy, there is an implicit appeal to an underlying moral principle. It is important to state the principle explicitly, so that its application can be adequately assessed. The major problem with the accusation of "playing God" is the danger that it operates as a rhetorical device to obfuscate rather than to illuminate discussion.

I. SECULAR AND RELIGIOUS APPLICATIONS

The phrase "playing God" is usually encountered in descriptions of acts or decisions which involve arrogating power or control over matters of profound or far-reaching importance, such as decisions about the termination of life. Sometimes the phrase is used rhetorically to indicate that the topic under discussion raises momentous issues which must be addressed with great care. Doctors who have to allocate scarce life-saving medical resources, or decide which fetuses to terminate in unsustainable multiple pregnancies, face invidious decisions which may be characterized as "playing God." Edmund Erde has provided a useful survey of uses of the phrase in biomedical discussion (1989. *Journal of Medical Philos.* **14**, 593–615).

A somewhat different colloquial use of the phrase is to decide the inflexible exercise of authority or "laying down the law," for example, when a supervisor insists on a particular approach to a task, perhaps riding roughshod over the feelings or suggestions of subordinates.

These essentially metaphorical and secular uses of the phrase "playing God" must be distinguished from its use to mark out a zone of choices which supposedly involve overstepping a boundary of legitimate human activity. It is the latter literal and generally condemnatory use of the expression which needs to be examined. This pejorative sense is the one used, for example, in the book title, *Who Should Play God?* (T. Howard and J. Rifkin, 1977. Delacorte, New York).

Often, but not always, the implied objection to a proposed course of action is based on religious belief, and the proposed action is found objectionable because it allegedly involves a morally culpable or *hubristic* transgression into the prerogatives of the deity. As well as being used to indicate that a supposedly divinely ordained limit has been transgressed, the phrase may also be used to indicate a "natural" order. When appeal is made to naturalistic considerations it is suggested that a proposed course of action would upset some supposedly natural cosmic or world order which, it is supposed, should be left undisturbed. In these cases the suggestion is typically that we have a power to act which is not matched by the knowledge required to act wisely.

The accusation of playing God, however, is unhelpful and serves to darken rather than to clarify discussion. If it is being used as shorthand to indicate the will of God then an immediate problem is posed by the abundant diversity of opinions about God and the moral order which supposedly receives God's sanction. It is not helpful to be told that an action transgresses the prerogatives of the deity unless we know what these prerogatives are. "Playing God" is equivocal and unhelpful precisely because divine prerogatives are conceived so disparately by different religious authorities. Larue, for example, has recorded an immense diversity of religious opinion both between and within Christian and non-Christian denominations concerning the acceptability of euthanasia or physician-assisted suicide (G. A. Larue, 1996. *Playing God.* Moyer Bell, West Wakefield, RI). There is in general no unified Christian, Jewish, or other denominational position on this issue.

Appeals to divine authority as a basis for moral principles are in any case problematic. Objections to this sort of strategy for establishing secure foundations for morality go back at least as far as Plato's *Euthyphro*.

II. THE MORAL PRESUPPOSITION

Because there is no agreement among the authorities about which acts are divinely sanctioned, there may be argument about whether a particular course of action is serving or usurping the will of God. The confusion generated by the accusation of playing God is well illustrated by the fact that it can be confidently deployed by both sides of a dispute. It can be used, for example, to criticize a decision to withhold life-saving medical treatment as well as to criticize the decision to administer heroic medical treatment. If appeal is made to a divinely sanctioned principle which constitutes the basis of a moral proscription then it is important to state that principle explicitly so that its probity can be properly evaluated.

Serious uses of the phrase "playing God" thus presuppose a moral framework or appeal to a moral principle, and therefore to avoid confusion it is important for the presupposed principle to be stated explicitly so that its application can be properly assessed. The importance of stating the underlying principle can be demonstrated by uncovering the implicit moral principle which lies behind the application of the phrase in its central applications, which concern the domains of bioethics and genetic engineering.

III. APPLICATIONS IN BIOETHICS

The most widespread application of the charge of playing God is in connection with medical technologies, in particular those involving decisions to terminate human life. Most theologies speak of the sanctity of human life. The most significant procedures criticized for not paying proper respect to God's law are euthanasia and abortion, and sometimes also, associated with the latter, prenatal testing. The charge of playing God has also been leveled against the use of new reproductive technologies concerned with establishing pregnancy, such as *in vitro* fertilization (IVF) and gamete intrafallopian transfer (GIFT).

A common basis for objection to applications of medical technology is the belief that allowing something to happen, even though we can control it technically, is to leave it to God's providence, acknowledging that exercising control wisely in some circumstances is beyond our power.

It is difficult, however, to provide a rational justification for this position. After all, much of modern medicine aims precisely to prevent mortality and morbidity which would eventuate if left to providence. Suffering is reduced by the elimination of noxious pathogens such as smallpox, and this is not usually thought of as a violation of God's providential design. If we are prepared to act to prevent disability and disease caused by environmental pathogens, then why balk at measures such as therapeutic abortion which also aim to prevent disability and suffering caused, for example, by severe genetic disorders?

One response is to claim that there is crucial difference between the destruction of pathogens and the destruction of innocent human life. Even if the decision to terminate a human life is motivated by compassion, that does not, on a view widely endorsed by many religious authorities, alter the character of the act as an act of killing. Abortion involves the destruction of a being with an immortal soul, and such an act presumes on the prerogatives of the deity. This objection to abortion may also be extended as an objection to prenatal genetic testing, since a major motivation of prenatal testing is to detect genetic defects with a view to therapeutic abortion if genetic mishap is detected.

Making sense of the relationship between soul and body is notoriously problematic. But even if it is granted that fetuses have immortal souls it is hard to understand how the destruction of a fetus with genes, for example, for Tay-Sachs disease or Lesch-Nyham syndrome is anything but an act of kindness. A physical life will be ended, but a truly immortal soul would continue, perhaps to be reunited with its maker. Indeed precisely this consolation is often provided to parents on the premature death of a child.

It is sometimes suggested that suffering is good for the soul, but this is an implausible way to defend the continuation of a life that will be wretched. It amounts to an objection to virtually the whole institution of modern medical practice, which exists largely to alleviate suffering. Of course this is not a dominant view, and many religious authorities see little or no spiritual merit in suffering, and regard it rather as an affront to human dignity.

It is important to distinguish religious objections to abortion from objections based on the claim that it is absolutely impermissible to terminate innocent human life because that involves the destruction of persons or potential persons. The present concern is only with explicitly religious objections to abortion. Objections based on secular considerations are considered elsewhere.

The other major category of medical practice which attracts the charge of playing God in the termination of life is euthanasia. Sometimes it is alleged that it is contrary to the will of God to fail to treat the terminally ill; but, confusingly, it is also claimed that permitting the terminally ill to refuse heroic medical treatment, that is, to permit what is sometimes called "voluntary passive euthanasia," is precisely to *decline* to play the role of God (Larue, 1996, 10). There is also a more controversial claim, supported by some progressive religious thinkers, that personal autonomy is a God-given right, and that a merciful and compassionate God would have no objection to a terminally ill patient choosing a quick, painless, and dignified death.

Once again confusion surrounds the charge of playing God, and rather than appealing to God's will or God's law it is essential to state explicitly what principle this claim alludes to so that it can be systematically examined. Taking innocent life is always a morally grave matter which needs justification. The justification of end-of-life and ending-life decisions typically involves addressing important distinctions between acts and refrainings, and between killing and letting die, and consideration of the role of individual autonomy. Whether or not moral justification can be provided in particular cases, it certainly cannot plausibly be provided simply by appeal to religious authority.

IV. APPLICATIONS IN GENETICS

Molecular biologists have developed a variety of techniques of genetic engineering to manipulate and control the development, structure, and hereditary characteristics of organisms. In particular manipulation of the genetic material itself (deoxyribonucleic acid or DNA) by gene splicing has led to the development of powerful tools for modifying life-forms and creating new ones. The allegation of playing God has almost become a cliché in the field of genetics and is used, in particular, to describe proposals to modify the human genome.

There are several important distinctions which need to be kept in mind when considering arguments about genetic engineering. First, there is the human–nonhuman distinction, and the question of whether there are special considerations which constrain the manipulation of human genetic material which do not apply in the case of other species. Secondly, there is a distinction between somatic and germ cell genetic modification: somatic changes affect only the subject organism; modifications to germ cells are passed on to an organism's descendants. Thirdly, there is a distinction between negative (therapeutic or corrective) engineering, which aims at rectifying some disease, defect, or disability, and positive (eugenic or enhancement) engineering, which might aim, for example, to produce a healthier, smarter, more capable, more robust, and longer-lived individual or population.

One way that misgivings about genetic engineering are expressed is in terms of the religious belief that the gene pool is God's sacred creation and should be preserved. Genetic engineering is sometimes characterized as a dangerous Promethean adventure which involves appropriating knowledge which is properly the province of the deity. In our post-Enlightenment state of knowledge this view does not survive inspection. Gene pools are more plausibly seen not as the product of divine providence, but as the piecemeal accretions of billions of years of accident, mishap, and good fortune.

A more secular and more persuasive argument is that biological processes and products have evolved over billion-year geological time scales and have thereby proved their robustness. Natural life-forms come with the quality assurance of exceptionally prolonged testing under the most searching conditions.

There are also self-interested considerations based on the desirability of maintaining biodiversity, which entail that we should take care to ensure that we not reduce biodiversity through genetic tinkering—or any other way.

The argument against the substantial genetic modification of any species which alludes to the alleged wisdom of the evolutionary process is summed up in the phrase, "Nature knows best." This is a modern secular expression of an older religious belief in divine providence. Not everyone, however, is impressed by the result of several billion years of evolution, and it is sometimes suggested that its products might well be improved. Why should we favor the slow, fitful, chancy, piecemeal, small-scale, incremental processes of natural evolutionary change above the rapid and radical changes made possible by genetic technology?

Some critics, such as Howard and Rifkin (1977), suggest that it would be best if genetic engineering were completely prohibited. Howard and Rifkin argue that genetic engineering is inherently dangerous and threatens to transform organisms, including humans, into technologically designed products, and may lead to a new caste system in which social role is linked to genetic makeup.

This alarmist assessment ignores or plays down the fact that genetic engineering of a kind has been practiced by selective breeding in animal husbandry, horticulture, and agriculture for thousands of years. Indeed the principal plant and animal food sources in the human diet are all products of selective breeding.

It is certainly legitimate to be apprehensive about the possible dangers posed by recent genetic technologies, but rather than talk of playing God we need once again to examine what motivates these worries. There may be a serious basis for concern, such as a possible deliberate or accidental release of synthetic pathogens which might devastate a community or ecosystem. Risk should always be assessed prudently, bearing in mind that if there is a potentially hazardous solution to a problem it is always advisable to seek less hazardous alternatives. But the potential benefits of genetic engineering cannot be dismissed, and objections to it need to be selectively directed to particular proposals.

In the case of human genetic modification, negative engineering is generally thought to be ethically unproblematic, while positive engineering in general is not. A basic aim of therapeutic medicine is to eliminate serious disability and *ceterus paribus,* any measures which can help with this project, including genetic technologies, are to be welcomed. A proposal to use gene therapy for the topical treatment of lung tissue of sufferers of cystic fibrosis, for example, seems unexceptionable. But the situation is not always straightforward, and benefits must always be measured against risks.

Michael Ruse accepts negative engineering in principle but argues against producing radical changes through positive genetic engineering, claiming that enhancement engineering could degrade much of what is distinctively human (1984. *Zygon* **19**, 297–316). There is, however, a problem defining the boundary between positive and negative genetic manipulation which features centrally in the discussion by Ruse and others. Negative engineering is corrective, and its aims are spelled out in terms of rectifying dysfunction, disease, or abnormality. While these notions provide a rough guide, they are problematic in particular cases. To take a fairly trifling example, is correcting male pattern baldness a therapeutic treatment or cosmetic enhancement? Ruse may nevertheless be right about the need to restrict or proscribe radical enhancement proposals.

There is no precise, universal, objective criterion which determines what constitutes either a dysfunction or an enhancement. In the case of therapeutic somatic treatment, it may be unexceptionable to allow individuals to make informed autonomous choices about self-regarding changes, though the case of genetic enhancement modification of somatic tissue is less clear. However, if we allow people to change their appearance with breast implants or plastic surgery—and even to mutilate themselves up to a point, for example, with body-piercing and tattoos—perhaps we should allow them to genetically program themselves to grow green hair, or to make even more bizarre choices.

Germ-line modifications are less straightforward because deciding the destiny of others without their consent seems to be precisely one of the objectionable features of an action censured by the charge of playing God. Germ-line engineering, including enhancements, involves making choices for others without their consent, though it is difficult to know exactly how much weight to put on this, since choosing to reproduce at all apparently involves that anyway.

While a strong case can be developed for negative germ-line engineering to eliminate such debilitating genetic disorders as cystic fibrosis, Tay-Sachs disease, and Huntington's chorea, systematic attempts to improve

or perfect a species presupposes that we know what constitutes an improvement or perfection. The value of a gene depends on the environmental situation in which it is expressed. Eliminating genetic traits may weaken a species, or make it unable to adapt to changing environmental circumstances which may arise from unforeseen contingencies.

Whereas improving the shelf life of tomatoes does not generate any obviously serious hazards, tinkering with the complex system of the human genome—with an estimated complement of 100,000 genes operating in a sequential and coordinated fashion—may have unforeseen serious or even catastrophic effects, some of which may not be expressed for several generations. This uncertainty argument applies of course to germ-line, but not somatic, genetic engineering.

There are, then, serious considerations which need to be addressed in deciding what forms of genetic engineering to allow; but we need to get behind the rhetoric of the phrase "playing God" and examine the underlying principles to evaluate how seriously these concerns are to be taken.

V. CONCLUSION

The phrase "playing God" is used to characterize actions or behavior that is deemed to be morally blameworthy, and typically it is intimated, but not explicitly stated, that some immutable moral principle has been violated. It embodies the notion that there are possibilities which should not be realized—choices which should not be made. The accusation also often expresses concern about the *hubris* of tinkering with the sacred.

The power and resonance of the phrase derives ultimately from a deep conviction that there is a providential divine or natural order. This conception of a hierarchically structured benign cosmic order reaches back to Plato, and its classic exposition is *The Great Chain of Being* by Arthur Lovejoy (1936. Harvard Univ. Press, Cambridge, MA). It is deeply entrenched in Western thought and is associated historically with what Lovejoy called the principle of plenitude, according to which every genuine possibility is realized. If inexhaustible divine productivity has left no gaps in nature then we should seek neither to add to nor subtract from the natural order.

This is a potent conception which still has the power to exercise a subtle but substantial subterranean influence on our thinking. The danger presented by this seductive image is that it can come to dominate our thinking and provide a substitute for serious moral thought.

"Playing God" is an expression which is unhelpful as an analytic tool because it suffers from vagueness and multiple ambiguity, and in any case alludes to a dubiously secure foundation for moral principles. Apart from the unexceptionable metaphorical and rhetorical uses of the phrase, noted at the outset, the phrase does more to obfuscate than to clarify.

Also See the Following Articles

ABORTION • DO-NOT-RESUSCITATE DECISIONS • EUTHANASIA • GENETIC ENGINEERING • GENETIC SCREENING • GENOME ANALYSIS • REPRODUCTIVE TECHNOLOGIES

Bibliography

Erde, E. L. (1989). Studies in the explanation of issues in biomedical ethics. II. On "Playing God." *Journal of Medicine and Philosophy,* **14,** 593–615.

Howard, T., and Rifkin, J. (1977). *Who Should Play God? The Artificial Creation of Life and What It Means for the Future of the Human Race.* Delacorte, New York.

Kitcher, P. (1996). *The Lives to Come: The Genetic Revolution and Human Possibilities.* Simon & Schuster, New York.

Larue, G. A. (1996). *Playing God: Fifty Religions' Views on Your Right to Die.* Moyer Bell, West Wakefield, RI.

O'Donovan, O. (1984). *Begotten or Made?* Oxford Univ. Press, Oxford.

Ruse, M. (1984). Genesis revisited: Can we do better than God? *Zygon,* **19,** 297–316.

Scully, T., and Scully, C. (1987). *Playing God: The New World of Medical Choices.* Simon & Schuster, New York.

PLURALISM IN EDUCATION

Eamonn Callan
University of Alberta

GLOSSARY

assimilation The integration of individuals or groups who belong to a particular culture into another culture through educational or other social pressures.

celebratory pluralism The thesis that societies are ethically enriched by the realization of many incompatible but worthwhile ways of life.

common schools Schools whose admission requirements, curricula, and educational aims are designed with the intention of meeting all students' educational needs, irrespective of cultural differences among them.

ethnocentrism Action or judgment corrupted by cultural bias.

multicultural education The thesis that education in pluralistic societies must respect cultural differences among students.

patriotism Emotional identification with a polity as a community of citizens within which one's own good is at least partly constituted by the common good.

pluralism The coexistence under common political institutions of groups divided by ethnicity, language, religion, or other cultural criteria that may generate conflicting political demands.

rights-based pluralism The thesis that respect for rights is the moral basis for distinguishing the politically acceptable limits of pluralism.

separate schools Schools whose admission requirements, curricula, and educational aims are designed with the intention of meeting the particular educational needs of culturally distinct groups.

toleration The willingness to afford political protection to conduct regarded as undesirable on moral, prudential, or religious grounds.

PLURALISM raises many questions, the most important of which is a moral one. How do we find terms of cooperation that are both just and stable, given the circumstances of pluralism? One important arena in which the question arises is education. Pluralism is central to many familiar controversies about the content of education, such as disputes about racial and cultural bias in the curriculum. Similarly, the proper limits of state support and regulation for common and separate schools is a matter of ongoing conflict in many societies where culturally distinct groups have inconsistent views on sponsorship and regulation.

Although the main question posed by pluralism is moral, it does not follow that the more citizens are alike in their fundamental ethical beliefs the easier it must become to find an answer to the question. This is so because citizens may disagree in the application of basic values in ways that strongly reflect other differences.

Those who agree about the foundational role of human equality in any decent polity may yet disagree sharply in their views about the school's role in opposing racism partly because their experience of racism as members of different racial groups is so markedly different. People who share a general commitment to religious tolerance may yet differ about the justice of state control or sponsorship of denominational schools because of differences in the importance of religion to their own identities. A cogent answer to the question of pluralism must acknowledge the great variety of human differences that can stand in the way of consensus on a just and stable political order.

The question of pluralism asks about the justice and stability of a polity under certain general social conditions. The focus on justice and stability requires some clarification. Political regimes can often achieve stability by means that make some accommodation to pluralism but are nonetheless profoundly unjust. Some of the great empires of history sustained political institutions that survived for generations and owed their stability in part to a qualified toleration of religious and cultural diversity. But their stability also depended on systematic oppression of large social groups, such as slaves. On the other hand, the ideal of a just social order becomes utopian if the ideal is constructed so that it cannot inform any regime we could reasonably expect to endure, given what we know of human psychology and culture. If justice is to be a realistic political aspiration, we cannot seek justice alone without regard to stability.

The question of pluralism is especially troubling if it is asked within the context of liberal democratic politics. That context is a loosely demarcated tradition of political thought and practice which insists on the necessity of certain conditions to any just society. The relevant conditions are the consensual core of the tradition, even though their implementation admits much variation from one society to another, and in any given society disagreement about their interpretation may be severe. The conditions include universal suffrage, the rule of law, liberties of conscience and expression, and the right to assembly. The freedom citizens enjoy under a liberal democratic regime can be exercised in ways that not only make the society increasingly pluralistic, but that endanger the continued vitality of free institutions. Some groups may demand in the name of liberty of conscience the right to educate their children in a way that runs counter to the legitimate ends of civic education. Acceding to their demand may leave their children without the skills or virtues that competent political participation requires, and to that extent, the stability of the polity seems threatened. Rejecting their

demand discounts what is claimed on the basis of one of the cardinal freedoms of liberal societies, and to that extent, the justice of the polity is put in doubt. Under illiberal government, the challenge of pluralism can be addressed through massive coercion in educational and other areas of policy. But that response is self-defeating in a liberal democracy because even if coercion succeeded in bringing about social concord it would do so only at the cost of violating the constitutive moral principles of government. How can the question of pluralism be answered while keeping faith with the values of a free society?

I. CELEBRATORY PLURALISM AND EDUCATION

Pluralism is commonly seen as an unfortunate fact of social life which must be overcome or at least mitigated if the good society is to be realized. But even if pluralism often makes the achievement of justice and stability harder than it would otherwise be, it can also be regarded as something that enriches all our lives. That thought is the nerve of "celebratory pluralism." Many different ways of life, all sustained within the embrace of a single polity, attest to the power of human creativity and give each citizen a richer sense of the variety of worthwhile human lives than any culturally monistic society can afford.

Celebratory pluralism is an animating principle in certain strands of feminist thought and is invoked by some postmodern theorists who have elevated the idea of "difference" to a position alongside freedom and equality in the pantheon of democratic ideals. Celebratory pluralism is also the moral stance at the core of much of the literature on multicultural education. It is commonly adopted in arguments about the expansion of the literary canon, as defined within the curricula of schools and universities; it also figures prominently in debate about how the story of minority groups is to be integrated into the historical self-understanding of future citizens. Celebratory pluralists would oppose circumscribing the curriculum according to the cultural predilections of the most powerful group. They would insist that the history we teach the young must reflect the full range of cultural difference within the societies we inhabit. That means history in schools must heed the voice of the relatively powerless and marginalized, and not merely the perspective of the cultural mainstream. If we accept the premises of celebratory pluralism, its welcoming attitude to diversity must also become a paramount aim in the moral and political education of the young. The same premises would also seem to justify concessions to groups who sue for state support for separate forms of schooling designed to transmit minority values from one generation to another.

A. The Justification of Celebratory Pluralism

What justifies a celebratory attitude to pluralism? A cogent answer might appeal to the idea that many valuable but incompatible ways of life are possible for human beings. Their incompatibility consists of the fact that the distinctive values that define such lives cannot be harmoniously combined within a single life. Under the conditions of cultural diversity that characterize most contemporary societies, the fullest feasible realization of human good depends on the active encouragement of pluralism.

Although that conclusion might seem at odds with monistic ethical theories, such as utilitarianism, that is not necessarily so. A utilitarian can agree that many incompatible ways of life are conducive to human happiness, and that happiness in general thrives best when political authority accommodates the widest range of ethical diversity compatible with respect for rights. The utilitarian defense of pluralism was offered by John Stuart Mill in his celebrated essay *On Liberty* (J. S. Mill, 1956, 1859. Bobbs-Merrill, Indianapolis, IN). Mill also thought that commonality of ethnic identity and language was typically necessary to the political stability of free societies (J. S. Mill, 1962, 1861. *Considerations on Representative Government*, p. 309. Gateway Editions, South Bend, IN). But we might take a more sanguine view than Mill's on the viability of multiethnic or multilingual liberal democracies and yet concur with his utilitarian defense of pluralism.

A different and less philosophically partisan line of defense is offered by John Rawls. Rawls argues that a crucial element in the best argument for a liberal democratic constitution is the idea of the "burdens of judgment" (J. Rawls, 1993. *Political Liberalism*, pp. 54–58. Columbia Univ. Press, New York). These burdens are the many sources that stand in the way of ethical agreement among people even when we reason as skillfully and as impartially as we feasibly can under conditions of freedom. Even in that ideal case, we would continue to disagree because of differences in personal history, for example, as well as the many hard cases to which ethical concepts are susceptible. Therefore, pluralism with its conflicting political demands is not

to be regretted as a sign of irrationality or selfishness; instead, we should regard it as the natural and appropriate outcome of the free exercise of human reason.

Part of what makes Rawls' argument especially interesting is its broad appeal. The argument may be acceptable to many utilitarians or other ethical monists as well as those who reject such views. Similarly, the argument may be endorsed by religious believers and nonbelievers, and nationalists or cosmopolitans, given that all accept the rational humility and spirit of accommodation that goes with acceptance of the burdens of judgment in political deliberation.

B. Celebratory Pluralism and Moral Discrimination

Regardless of its philosophical defense, celebratory pluralism faces a fundamental question that is commonly evaded. How do we distinguish between instances of pluralism that warrant a celebratory response and instances that do not?

Consider how making that distinction correctly is at the very heart of the controversies about education to which pluralism gives rise. History is taught in a more morally inclusive way when the experience of traditionally marginalized or oppressed groups is addressed than when the self-glorification of political and economic elites is its driving force. But history cannot be responsibly taught so as to be equally welcoming to the perspectives of all groups because some will inevitably seek to distort the historical reality of oppression. The great educational benefit of historical study in a pluralistic society is that it may teach the young both to understand the social roots of injustices that linger in the present and to appreciate the moral resources of the political institutions they inherit in order to address those injustices. By these means, the political morality they will come to share as citizens can be shaped in ways that are conducive to justice and stability in the midst of diversity. But these laudable outcomes are blocked unless historical study is informed by a morally discriminating response to pluralism.

Similarly, if children are to learn to celebrate pluralism appropriately, part of that learning must entail an evolving ability to discriminate the pluralism that is rightly accommodated under a liberal democratic constitution from that which is not. Finally, state sponsorship or at least toleration of alternatives to common schools may well be warranted in many cases. But sponsorship is certainly inappropriate, and even toleration may be misplaced, when separate schooling is wedded to educational aims that are flatly opposed to pluralism, such as the promotion of racism or religious bigotry.

The last point highlights an important general issue that is sometimes overlooked by celebratory pluralists—namely, the issue of toleration. The moral discrimination that must characterize a wise response to pluralism cannot only be a matter of determining which differences deserve to be celebrated and which have to be opposed through political coercion. Those two options do not acknowledge the possibility that many sources of diversity might call for moral condemnation in light of liberal democratic norms and yet the case for political protection is strong by virtue of the same norms. Instances of pluralism that we rightly condemn but rightly protect are the appropriate sphere of toleration. Sexist speech is morally reprehensible in light of democratic ideals of equality. But much sexist speech is also politically protected by principles of intellectual liberty and freedom of conscience. Even if we accepted the arguments of some feminists for prohibiting certain kinds of currently tolerated sexist speech—the products of the pornography industry, for example—there would still be much sexist speech we should continue to condemn and to protect politically. Similarly, a pluralistic society may contain educational practices that we rightly condemn but protect politically, and the idea of celebratory pluralism cannot help us to identify what these might be.

A tendency to favor a celebratory attitude to diversity, rather than the precarious balance of disapproval and acceptance that "toleration" connotes, is easy to understand because toleration may appear to be a less generous and inclusive virtue than its celebratory alternative. But the appearance is deceptive. If all children were required by law to be taught to celebrate religious diversity, the law would thereby fail to tolerate the many religious traditions that insist on the exclusive truth of their own creed. No doubt celebratory pluralism is often morally preferable to toleration. Teachers who respond to racial diversity in their classrooms with a grudging tolerance are not more virtuous than those who evince a welcoming attitude. But a blanket generalization about the superiority of that attitude to toleration is untenable. The moral propriety of toleration or its alternatives is too dependent on variable contextual factors for any such generalization to be credible.

The questions that have been raised about celebratory pluralism do not make it irrelevant to the question of pluralism. The point has only been that a complete answer to the question cannot be found in the proposal that pluralism is something to be celebrated rather than suppressed or tolerated. All three responses—celebration, suppression, and toleration—must be a part of a morally discriminating accommodation of pluralism. The difficulty is to specify the moral reasons that properly guide the necessary discriminations.

II. RIGHTS-BASED PLURALISM AND EDUCATION

Moral debate about pluralism in education often takes the form of argument about rights. A common claim in such debate is that people can have a right to pursue a vast plurality of conflicting educational ends in a free society. That claim is the nerve of rights-based pluralism.

Rights-based pluralism can be understood as a way of addressing our need to discriminate cases in which celebration, suppression, or toleration is the morally best political response to pluralism. One reason to endorse a polity grounded in the principle of respect for rights is that rights can provide a framework of political order within which diversity can flourish. Therefore, celebratory pluralism may support rights-based pluralism. The idea of rights can also guide us in determining when suppression or toleration is warranted. For example, many religious traditions that shape the education of children in a pluralistic society will inevitably be viewed by some citizens with profound disapproval insofar as the traditions are seen to embody religious error, and ardent nonbelievers will view all religions as so much corrupting fantasy. But disapproval in any such case can be muted by the thought that people have a right to practice their religion, regardless of its truth or falsity, and that the right properly includes the liberty to teach the faith to one's children. So a wide variety of forms of religious education must be tolerated as a matter of parents' rights. Nevertheless, some religiously motivated educational choices may encroach unacceptably on children's rights and thus warrant political intervention on the children's behalf.

But even though rights give us a framework within which we might make the moral distinctions that an adequate answer to the question of pluralism demands, the framework admits many rival interpretations. We disagree about the scope of parents' rights to educational choice; we argue about the educational rights of children; and we often cannot reach consensus on how to adjudicate among such rights when they come into conflict. Pluralism also gives rise to some controversial arguments about so-called group or collective rights.

A. Parents' Rights in Education

According to Article 26 of the Universal Declaration of Human Rights, parents have a right to choose the kind of education that shall be given to their children. In this context, "parents" presumably refers to those who are morally entitled to occupy a particular social role rather than those who just happen to stand in a certain biological relation, even though there is ordinarily (and rightly) a close correspondence between the social role and the biological relationship that procreation establishes. The social role is defined by the primary and more or less permanent responsibility that individual adults may have for rearing particular children as their own.

To claim on behalf of parents a right to educational choice is to say that they have an interest in the education of their children of sufficient weight to warrant the imposition of duties on others regarding the protection or promotion of that interest. To discharge the requisite duties is to respect the corresponding right. Two questions must be distinguished straightway: Are we justified in thinking there is such a right? What is the moral content or scope of the right? The really interesting question is the second one. Moral conflict about the significance of parental choice in education arises from rival answers to the second question, and an affirmative answer to the first does virtually nothing to overcome the conflict. Agreement that there is a parental right to educational choice coincides with profound differences about its scope.

Those differences are intensified by pluralism. The right to educational choice may be taken largely for granted in homogeneous societies where everyone would tend to choose virtually the same kind of education. Like religious liberty in cultures that revolve around a shared faith, the right to educational choice may fade into the moral background without ceasing to be when all can agree on the kind of education their children should receive. But pluralism tends to pull the right of parents to educational choice into the foreground of public debate, where it becomes a lightning rod of moral controversy.

The scope of any right is indicated by specifying what it is a right to—that is, by enumerating the particular duties it imposes on others, by identifying who these others are, and by noting the general conditions in which the duties have application or might be waived by the right-holder. The relevant duties are conveniently classified as either negative, when they require only noninterference toward the right-holder, or positive, when some action of support or protection is de-

manded. Similarly, rights or facets of rights are positive or negative depending on the duties with which they are correlated, although a given right may comprise an amalgam of positive and negative facets.

A negative right to educational choice, which nonetheless comes with some strings attached, forms part of the agreed context to disputes about parents' role in education. No one supposes a totalitarian state that dictates the course of education in all its fine detail could respect whatever right to choice parents have. Nor does anyone think that someone who makes gravely harmful choices about the education of her children by depriving them, say, of the benefits of language is nontheless acting within her rights. Yet the content of the duty of noninterference that correlates to the right remains strongly contested. State regulation of home schooling and denominational education may frustrate parental choice, especially in states where substantial minorities are alienated from the dominant public culture; whether such regulation fails to comply with the negative duties that the parental right to educational choice entails is another, and far less obvious, matter.

If we lack much consensus about the negative duties we have with regard to parents' choices, we also share little common ground on whatever positive duties might be binding on us. Many libertarians assume that we can rightfully interfere with parents' choices regarding the teaching and learning of their children in only the most egregious cases of irresponsibility. But libertarians cannot acknowledge rights to positive provision of more than minimal scope without abandoning their libertarianism. Conversely, a conception of parents' rights that accords a much narrower range to negative duties than libertarians would countenance can also assign exacting positive requirements. Some theorists have argued for parity of state funding for students in common and separate schools as a requirement of respect for parental rights in culturally diverse societies. But that argument is consistent with the view that parents have no right to send their children to schools, whether common or separate, that do not meet stringent, politically enforced educational requirements. These criteria might be justified by the rights of children or the common civic ends that education must serve in a pluralistic society. So even though we might agree that morally weighty parental rights are the lodestar of educational policy in all rights-respecting societies, our agreement might still be virtually empty because we conceive the scope of that right in utterly different ways.

Achieving consensus on the scope of parents' rights depends on the resolution of more general problems about the nature of justice. So long as libertarians and devotees of the welfare state exist we cannot expect agreement on whatever duties of positive provision might be entailed by the parental right to educational choice. Nevertheless, at least one strong moral reason may support a reading of the right to educational choice that would give it substantial scope and weight, regardless of these wider controversies.

Child-rearing is commonly undertaken as one of the basic meaning–giving tasks of human life. The task resembles religious practice or the expression of erotic love because it is likely to be both central to the pursuit of our good, given that we choose to become parents, and yet vulnerable to disruption through the coercive intervention of others. Rights seem crucial here precisely because they serve as a bulwark against such interference. Further, success in the task of child-rearing is typically understood by parents in terms of broadly educational ends of some sort. They hope to rear children who will sustain a cherished ethnic identity, practice the one true faith, or excel in certain culturally prized social roles. This is the "expressive interest" that parents have in child-rearing: the interest in shaping the child's education in order to achieve ends that express deeply held parental values. Under the conditions of pluralism, the interest necessarily pulls in contradictory directions because different parents will want an education suited to different religious creeds, ethnic affiliations, first languages, and so on. So if the expressive interest in child-rearing can underpin a parental right to educational choice, it must also support, as a pressing matter of social justice, some political accommodation with the many different demands to which the interest inevitably leads in pluralistic societies.

B. Children's Rights in Education

Suppose we accept a parental right to educational choice of substantial scope. That gives us reason to respect parents' divergent educational choices in the determination of policy in a pluralistic society. But other moral reasons may tell against deference to their wishes on some occasions. One such reason might be the right of children to an adequate education. Whether or not children have a right to an adequate education is not widely disputed, but the basis and scope of the right certainly are.

One influential line of argument locates the normative source of rights in the ideal of individual autonomy, and that argument generates a case for children's rights in education that may conflict with parental choice. The conflict arises when parents want an education

that would insulate the child from all influences that threaten fidelity to some creed or tradition the parents regard as crucial to their child's well-being. Unfortunately, the same influences might be regarded as educationally beneficial for the child, given the ideal of autonomy.

People are autonomous to the degree that they have developed powers of practical reason, a disposition to value those powers and use them in giving shape and direction to their own lives, and a corresponding resistance to impulses or social pressures that might subvert self-direction. The concept of autonomy is open to different interpretations. But irrespective of which interpretation is best, a tight link seems clear between the development of autonomy and an education that encourages critical scrutiny of the different ways of life that exist within a just and stable pluralism. To be denied a sympathetic understanding of diversity by parents who seek to instill unswerving identification with the culture of the family is to be denied the deliberative raw material for the independent thought about the right and the good that a developed autonomy necessitates.

But even in technologically advanced and culturally variegated societies, a seemingly fulfilling human life without a high degree of autonomy continues to be a viable possibility. On any credible account of the criteria of human well-being, they are a heterogeneous bunch. Satisfying many of them might be compossible with a renunciation of strong autonomy. Happiness is certainly possible without Socratic self-scrutiny, as are rewarding personal relationships and many kinds of creativity and aesthetic accomplishment. Even if all such goods would tend to flourish better with a highly evolved level of autonomy, their presence in a life without it may be contingently inseparable from its absence: someone's happiness may depend decisively on the unquestioning security of the faith her parents' educational choices instilled.

If all this were true, a child whose education forecloses a broad understanding of ethical diversity may yet grow up to live a good life, and the educational choices her parents make may be in large part the cause of what is good in that life. Autonomy is perhaps only one ideal among others that people permissibly pursue through the exercise of their rights, rather than the ideal that is foundational to all rights. This makes it tempting to infer that children have no right to an education that would be conducive to autonomy, and hence none that might conflict with the right of parents to choose an education that would insulate their child from all that might cast doubt on parentally approved values. Therefore, the rights of parents must prevail when they want an education for their children that repudiates autonomy, or so it might be argued.

Two considerations should make us wary of this conclusion. First, even if the open-ended development of autonomy through education could not be reasonably claimed as a matter of any child's rights, it does not follow that parents are morally entitled to shape their children's upbringing so that autonomous development is utterly thwarted. Some degree of autonomous development may be integral to the education to which all children have a right, and some forms of child-rearing may be so restrictive of imagination and criticism that the requisite degree of autonomous development is blocked. Second, even if no violation of children's rights occurs when their education takes a culturally insular form, the fact that insularity may militate against the civic virtues needed in a pluralistic society will favor an education that is more open to diversity. These virtues are incompatible with an ignorant antipathy to all values beyond the boundaries of some tightly circumscribed cultural group. The educational importance of these virtues is discussed at greater length in Section III.

C. Group Rights in Education

Although the interpretation of parents' and children's rights in education is very controversial, the claim that there are such rights is widely accepted. That is not so with group rights. Many people are skeptical about the justification and even the intelligibility of group rights. Yet they commonly figure in public debate about educational policy in some liberal democracies. The moral force of the appeal to group rights, as well as the difficulties it must address, can be explored through the example of linguistic rights and educational policy in a pluralistic society.

Under the Canadian Charter of Rights, state support for francophone schools is guaranteed as a right in specified circumstances to French-speaking communities in predominantly English-speaking provinces. This is a group right in that one comes to possess it not by virtue of one's humanity or even citizenship but through membership within a specified group within the citizenry. The right has an additional collective dimension in that the interest it protects—the interest in linguistic security for long-established and linguistically defined cultural groups—can only be enjoyed in the context of group activity. But notice that the right limits no one's freedom. Members of the selected minority may or may not choose to make use of the francophone schools to which they have a right to send their children.

The justification of group rights in cases like this one is sometimes questioned on the grounds that the rights bestow privileges on some but not all citizens and thereby constitute discrimination. But discrimination of an invidious kind is not inevitable in such cases. The right in question may simply reflect the morally relevant fact that certain interests which all citizens share—such as the interest in linguistic security—are under greater cultural threat for some than for others, and therefore special group rights might be a way of upholding the basic moral equality of all citizens.

But consider now the provision under Quebec provincial law which denies all francophone parents, as well as all others who did not receive an education in English inside Quebec, access to anglophone schools for their children. The point of the law is to safeguard the future size and cultural vitality of the francophone community in Quebec against the possible corrosive effects of permitting parents to choose an education in English for their children. But is any group—in this case the francophone majority in Quebec—morally entitled to curb the free choice of its own members, as well as other citizens, for the sake of cultural ends? The trouble with appeals to group rights of this kind is that they argue for curtailing rather than enlarging the scope of individual choice, and for that reason a heavier burden of justification must be borne by those who would make the appeal. Unlike the case of choice-enhancing group rights, it is not clear that such arguments can be squared with the democratic truism that all citizens are free and equal.

D. The Limits of Rights-Based Pluralism

The chief problem of rights-based pluralism is finding reasoned consensus on the interpretation of rights even when we can agree on some abstract list of rights. To the extent that we fall short of consensus, many citizens will regard the polity as unjust—perhaps with excellent reason—and its stability will be in jeopardy.

This problem suggests that the concept of rights by itself cannot answer the question of pluralism. For if what we need is reasoned consensus on the interpretation of rights, we must instill in our children whatever civic virtues would dispose them to such consensus, given the fact of pluralism, and this will require much more than teaching them to understand and cherish some determinate catalog of rights. On any plausible account of what that larger educational task involves, it is complex and onerous. Each future citizen needs to develop some imaginative sympathy for compatriots whose experience and identity incline them to see political questions in ways that differ systematically from one's own. A respect for reasonable differences and a concomitant spirit of moderation and compromise have to be nourished. A vivid sense of the responsibilities that the rights of others impose on the self, as well as the dignity which one's own rights secure for the self, must be engendered. All these accomplishments may be subsumed under the idea of the virtue of justice so long as we bear in mind that that idea captures no simple, unitary virtue. The virtue that is relevant here is rather an intricate composite of many psychological capabilities and inclinations that citizens must coordinate appropriately in discharging their civic responsibilities.

However, if the civic education that befits liberal democracy is a burdensome endeavor that revolves around an array of morally substantial aims, its compatibility with an inclusive respect for pluralism may be doubted. Imaginative identification with culturally distant compatriots may dissolve wholehearted identification with the religious creed or cultural practices learned in the family. A respect for reasonable differences and a spirit of compromise in politics may undermine ways of life that stress the unique moral purity of some received tradition outside politics.

The civic education that rights-based pluralism would seem to support thus pushes us toward an education that significantly constrains pluralism in the name of social unity. Therefore, we should expect those whose way of life is threatened by this kind of civic education to oppose its implementation as a violation of parents' or group rights. How far can a liberal democracy pursue moral unity through civic education without betraying the value of pluralism itself?

III. ASSIMILATION AND EDUCATION

The proposal that civic education might legitimately pursue robust educational ends at variance with the values of some citizens will be rejected by many as an affront to the pluralism that liberal democracies must honor. Such an education will seem but another example of the policies of assimilation that dominated the practice on civic education throughout most of the 20th century in some countries. In the USA and Canada, civic education as cultural assimilation was often espoused and practiced in ways that evinced open contempt for the cultures of immigrants and aboriginal communities. The unseemly moral visage of civic education as assimilation is exemplified in the following words of the distinguished American educator Ellwood Cubberley, writing near the beginning of the century about immigrants from eastern and southern Europe: "Illiterate, docile, lacking in self-reliance and initiative, and not possessing the Anglo-Teutonic conceptions of law, order and government, their coming has served to dilute our national stock, and to corrupt tremendously our civic life" (E. Cubberley, 1909. *Changing Conceptions of Education*, p. 15. Houghton Mifflin, Boston). According to Cubberley, civic education is necessarily and literally an act of cultural conquest: the customs of immigrants are to be eradicated and their children absorbed into a single race whose values are as thoroughly Anglo-Saxon as such unpromising human material will allow.

The evil here is partly Cubberley's ugly stereotype of Europeans who do not belong to the "right" racial stock. He also confuses the particular conception of public morality and government that liberal democracy entails with the ethnic identity of those who first brought that conception to America. Given that confusion, civic education must become a wholesale assault on diversity. But if this was indeed the mistake of Cubberley and many who were and are like-minded in their ethnocentric vision of civic education, we overreact to their error by rejecting all assimilation. Cubberley was right to insist that future citizens of a democratic community have to be assimilated to a common political culture that affirms shared understandings of law and government. He was also right to say that future citizens needed to be literate and capable of self-reliance and initiative. Where he went astray was in thinking that cultural homogenization had to penetrate every aspect of life if civic corruption was to be forstalled. But as advocates of human rights across the globe show every day, a passionate commitment to the values of free and equal citizenship is not the unique preoccupation of any race or ethnic group. Furthermore, that commitment may cohere with an equally strong adherence to a particular religious creed or ethnic identity. That being so, we may reasonably expect that the assimilation necessary to sustain liberal democratic norms across generations may coincide with a generous, although not an indiscriminate, openness to cultural diversity. Celebratory pluralism and assimilation are not mutually exclusive alternatives.

Liberal democracies rightly pursue cultural assimilation to the extent that cultivating a particular family of civic virtues is needed for justice and stability, even if policies that give effect to that purpose may restrict pluralism somewhat. This is not to say that the laudable end of encouraging civic virtue will justify whatever means might be used in its pursuit. A concern for the rights of conscientious dissidents under a liberal regime will certainly weigh heavily against the more intrusive methods of advancing civic virtue, however effective those methods might be. The legitimate public interest in the ends of civic education is merely one reason among others that properly shape educational policy; it supplements rather than supplants a commitment to respect rights.

A. The Problem of Patriotism

An important residual question about civic education under pluralism is whether or not patriotism belongs within the family of civic virtues that we might legitimately pursue through public policy. Like assimilation, the idea of patriotism is often confused with its most morally unsavory manifestations. But even when we acknowledge that not all patriotism takes the form of a repellent chauvinism, deeper suspicions may persist about its status as an educationally legitimate end of civic education.

Patriotism entails emotional identification with the political community of all citizens. The history of that community is integral to the self-understanding of the patriotic citizen, and its future prospects are entwined with her own hopes and aspirations. An obvious difficulty here is that attempts to inculcate patriotic allegiance may run into conflict with more local group loyalties, and unlike attempts to evoke the minimal requirements of a sense of justice among future citizens, efforts to teach patriotism against the current of dissent may lack a compelling moral justification. That problem is not unique to some religious minorities who repudiate attachment to secular political communities altogether. A more pervasive difficulty is the fact that the different groups who compose a pluralistic society may have very different conceptions of their relationship to the state, even when they are in broad agreement on abstract principles of justice. These different conceptions often surface in opposing historical perspectives, and hence in conflict about the teaching of history. That is to be expected since the history of a pluralistic society is not the story of a single people but a cluster of overlapping stories of many peoples. Episodes of oppression and conquest, accomplishment for some and humiliation for others, are often the points at which the stories overlap. Finding a basis for a common patriotic allegiance in that context without falsifying the moral complexity of the past is often a daunting challenge.

But it is not clear that all this requires a civic education that would not include patriotic allegiance among its aims. First, a shared sense of history is as necessary to the common exercise of justice as it is to patriotism be-

cause how we understand the demands of justice at a given moment in history necessarily depends on our understanding of the past that has shaped the present. For that reason, we cannot simply agree to disagree about our history and then proceed with the task of constructing a just society. Second, if justice and stability are to prevail in a pluralistic society, some secure emotional attachment to the particular, historically situated political community within which justice is pursued is surely necessary, and education will have to play a role in cultivating that attachment. The force of this point becomes apparent once we acknowledge that a pluralistic society is sure to harbor powerful centrifugal civic pressures by virtue of its pluralism. Citizens who differ substantially in ethnic background or moral and religious conviction will face large difficulties in understanding and giving due weight to the political claims of others where these are prompted by the differences that divide them. The truth in celebratory pluralism must not obscure the considerable strains that pluralism is likely to impose on the maintenance of a shared sense of justice. That being so, an education that aspires to encourage patriotism alongside the virtue of justice will be justified so long as the sense of political community it conveys is duly sensitive to the plurality of ways of life that may rightfully flourish within the community.

Patriotic allegiance to a centralized state may not always be the political attachment that is of paramount concern. As demands for power among minorities in pluralistic states acquire increasing salience on the international political agenda, trends toward political decentralization may gather pace, and the traditional patriotism of the modern nation-state might become decreasingly relevant in that environment. Yet such developments would also create an urgent need for federal institutions and other international political structures to secure justice across boundaries in what might otherwise become a dangerously tribalized world. Then we would be faced with the task of encouraging through public education emotional attachment to new institutions that transcend the particularities of group identity. The problem of patriotism would thus be replicated in a somewhat different form.

IV. CONCLUSION

Celebratory pluralism, rights-based pluralism, and assimilation are not rightly understood as alternative educational responses to the question of pluralism. They are instead complementary elements within a liberal democratic answer to that question. Without widespread acceptance of celebratory pluralism, citizens will tend to be alienated from the polity because diversity will at best evoke an attitude of grudging tolerance. Given that alienation, the justice and stability of the polity cannot be secure. Without rights-based pluralism, the necessary moral discrimination cannot be made between pluralism that warrants political protection and that which does not. Without a civic education that assimilates the individual to a shared public morality and a political community that encompasses pluralism, the moral cohesion of the just society cannot be achieved.

Also See the Following Articles

AUTHORITY IN EDUCATION • CHILDREN'S RIGHTS • RELIGION IN SCHOOLS • THEORIES OF JUSTICE: RAWLS

Bibliography

Bull, B., and Fruehling, R. T. (1992). *The Ethics of Multicultural and Bilingual Education.* Teachers College Press, New York.

Fullinwider, R. K. (1996). *Public Education in a Multicultural Society: Policy, Theory, Critique.* Cambridge University Press, Cambridge, UK.

Friedman, M. (1995). Multicultural education and feminist ethics. *Hypatia, 10,* 56–68.

Galston, W. (1995). Two concepts of liberalism. *Ethics, 105,* 516–534.

Giroux, H. (1992). *Border Crossings: Cultural Workers and the Politics of Education.* Routledge, New York.

Guttman, A. (1987). *Democratic Education.* Princeton University Press, Princeton, NJ.

Macedo, S. (1995). Liberal civic education and religious fundamentalism: The case of God v. John Rawls? *Ethics, 105,* 468–496.

McLaughlin, T. H. (1992). Citizenship, diversity and education: A philosophical perspective. *Journal of Moral Education, 21,* 235–250.

Raz, J. (1994). Multiculturalism: A liberal perspective. In *Ethics in the Public Domain: Essays in the Morality of Law and Politics.* Clarendon, Oxford, UK.

Sigel, R. S., and Hoskin, M. (Eds.) (1991). *Education for Democratic Citizenship: A Challenge for Multi-Ethnic Societies.* Lawrence Erlbaum, Hillsdale, NJ.

Strike, K. (1994). On the construction of public speech. *Educational Theory, 44,* 1–26.

POLICE ACCOUNTABILITY

Neil Walker
University of Aberdeen

GLOSSARY

external accountability The accountability of the police to nonpolice agencies.

internal accountability The accountability of police officers to others within the police organization.

police The specialist agency or group of agencies charged with performing policing functions within a community.

police accountability The obligation on the part of the police to provide a satisfactory account of their actions to another agency or agencies.

policing The set of activities aimed at preserving the security of a particular social order.

POLICE ACCOUNTABILITY is but one aspect of political accountability, whose demand arises from the fact that some individuals and institutions assume responsibility or have responsibility conferred upon them to perform certain functions on behalf of their fellow citizens. Police accountability refers to the set of relationships through which the institutions authorized to carry out policing functions are subject to oversight, influ-

ence, or direction with a view to ensuring that these functions are performed to the satisfaction of the accountee(s). In its narrowest sense, accountability is synonymous with *answerability,* involving nothing more than a commitment on the part of the accountor to answer questions. More broadly, accountability may imply not only the duty to provide a satisfactory account, but also a power on the part of the accountee to sanction past performance and shape or direct future performance. Police accountability has been aptly described as "one of the thorniest conundrums of statecraft" (R. Reiner, 1993). In *Accountable Policing: Effectiveness, Empowerment and Equity* (R. Reiner and S. Spencer, Eds.), pp. 1–23 IPPR, London), as it involves a commitment to "watching the watchers"—monitoring the very institutions which are engaged in potentially coercive supervision of the social order on behalf of the state.

I. THE NATURE OF POLICE ACCOUNTABILITY

A. Introduction

There are a number of different important aspects, or dimensions, to the relationships through which police accountability is secured. The present section involves an examination of each of these dimensions through a series of focused questions. This examination will reveal in greater detail the nature and dynamics of police ac-

Copyright © 1998 by Academic Press. All rights of reproduction in any form reserved.

countability and demonstrate the variety of forms that accountability relationships can take within political communities.

B. Accountable to Whom?

1. Internal Accountability

A basic distinction may be drawn between internal accountability and external accountability, depending upon whether the accountee is located inside or outside the police organization. Internal accountability is a pervasive feature of police organizations. Police organizations tend to be hierarchically structured, with a series of reporting and supervisory relationships linking the senior ranks to the junior ranks. Junior ranks are held accountable by senior ranks for their standards of performance and for the compliance of their conduct with legal rules and other organizational rules, which in many accountability systems include a Discipline Code. Senior ranks have at their disposal a number of positive and negative sanctions to encourage high levels of performance and rule compliance and to discourage inefficiency and misconduct.

2. External Accountability

Police accountability to external agencies is a much more controversial matter. The adequacy of the system of external accountability is often treated by politicians and commentators as an important index of the degree of subordination or otherwise of the police to a constitutional system of government. The issue of police accountability also tends to provide a focal point for conflict between police interests and perspectives and the interests and perspectives of other constituencies, whether politicians, bureaucrats, or civilians. D. Bayley has drawn a useful distinction between "external-exclusive" forms of accountability, where the control mechanism is of a specialist nature, and "external-inclusive" forms of accountability, where the control mechanism covers a range of other institutions as well as policing institutions (1985. *Patterns of Policing.* Rutgers Univ. Press, New Brunswick, NJ).

a. Exclusive Forms of Accountability

i. Government or Nongovernmental? As Bayley indicates, external-exclusive forms of accountability vary along a number of axes. To begin with, accountees may reside within government or, less commonly, in agencies outside government. If the former, they may be situated either within central government or within local government.

Accountability lies primarily to one or more specialist departments of central government (Departments or Ministries of Justice, Interior, Defense, etc.) in policing systems based on the European *continental* model of policing, which is distinguished by the wide-ranging responsibility of the police to maintain order and to carry out a variety of administrative functions on behalf of the state. The preeminent role of central government also characterizes accountability relationships in policing systems based on the *colonial* model. This is the model of policing originally applied by the British state in Ireland, and then gradually extended to other parts of the British empire, and, to a lesser degree, to the empires of other powerful European states. While the significance of the colonial model is now mainly historical, its legacy remains apparent in a number of postcolonial states. Under the colonial model, the police derive their legitimacy less from the indigenous population than from the colonial power, and a centralized system of command and control is developed as a means of maintaining "imposed" rule. In contrast, policing systems based on the *American* or *British* models, which have traditionally been highly decentralized and less directly concerned with upholding the authority of the state than the continental and colonial models, locate accountability primarily within local government.

Where accountability lies to agencies outside government, it may again take a number of forms. One popular option is the police or public safety commission, which is not directly elected but instead is appointed by an official body or bodies which themselves may be elected. Such commissions typically have a broad role, often monitoring a wide array of police policies and practices ranging from recruitment and deployment to discipline. This has traditionally been the main form of accountability in states as culturally disparate as Canada and Japan.

A less common type of nongovernmental accountability agency is concerned more narrowly with investigating or supervising the investigation of individual complaints against police officers. Members of such an agency may be central government appointees, as with the Independent Police Complaints Authority for England and Wales, and the South Australian Police Complaints Authority. Alternatively, such a body may adopt the model of the civilian review board, which was briefly favored in the United States in the 1960s and is now enjoying a resurgence of popularity. Under this model, the investigatory or supervisory role is performed by lay representatives of the local community, often appointed by local government members.

Another type of local civilian-centered accountability agency is the local consultative committee, which, as its name suggests, is restricted to a purely advisory role and possesses no compulsory powers in respect of policing. There are also some examples of hybrid structures, partly within and partly outside government, such as Police Authorities in England and Wales whose membership includes both elected members of local government and appointees nominated by members of central and local government.

ii. Unitary or Multiple? A second main variation within external-exclusive forms of accountability is between unitary and multiple systems. Unitary systems of accountability tend to be predicated upon a single centralized policing structure, as in Ireland or Israel. Multiple systems of accountability are much more common. In part this is explained by the fact that multiple-force policing structures are much more common than single-force structures, with each force accountable to a different agency. For example, European continental systems tend to be characterized by a multiplicity of national forces, each accountable to a different department of central government, whereas the United States, with its mixture of national forces and local forces, has a corresponding mix of national and local agencies of accountability. The preponderance of multiple systems of accountability is also due to the fact that accountability for particular forces may be divided between different agencies. In England and Wales, for example, central government, through the Home Office, shares with the local Police Authority the responsibility for holding each local police force accountable.

iii. Elected or Appointed? External-exclusive forms of accountability also differ from one another in terms of the nature of the personnel involved, and in particular, whether they are elected or appointed. As already noted, nongovernmental bodies tend to be staffed by (usually part-time) appointees, in some cases chosen by central government representatives and in others by local government representatives. Within governmental agencies of accountability, the balance of influence tends to vary between elected politicians on the one hand, and full-time appointees who belong to the government bureaucracy, or civil service, on the other. In European continental systems, the professional bureaucracy plays a significant role within the accountability system, whereas in systems based upon the British or United States models, politicians are much more to the fore.

b. Inclusive Forms of Accountability

i. Courts. External-inclusive forms of accountability also take a variety of forms. To begin with, the courts

of justice have a key role to play. In many legal systems, the courts may try and may punish police officers for infringements of the criminal law, and may also award financial compensation to parties who raise successful actions against the police for breach of the civil law. Courts may also seek to sanction the conduct of police officers through more indirect means, such as the exclusion of evidence required to convict an accused person of a criminal offense on the basis that the evidence was obtained by the investigating police officer in an unfair or illegal manner.

The use of the ordinary courts to sanction police behavior is the norm in legal systems based on the Anglo-American common law model. In contrast, in legal systems based on the European civilian model, actions must be pursued in a special set of administrative courts. Administrative courts offer advantages from the point of view of effective accountability to the extent that their personnel have the opportunity to develop more specific expertise about the operation of public administrative bodies such as the police, and to the extent that they often have the power not only to provide redress for the aggrieved individual in the particular case but also to amend administrative rules with a view to modifying undesirable *patterns* of police practice. On the other hand, administrative courts may confer immunities on police action in circumstances where ordinary courts would not.

Finally, it should be borne in mind that in all legal systems, but particularly common law systems, the role of the courts extends not only to applying settled law but also to developing the law through creative interpretation of existing rules. Thus, for example, the U.S. Supreme Court has been highly influential over the last 40 years in developing new standards for the regulation of police practices of search, detention, and interrogation by reference to the Fifth and 14th Amendments of the U.S. Constitution. Similarly, in England and Wales the preeminent role of the courts until 1984 in formulating a code of conduct for police officers in their dealings with suspects was symbolized in the name given to this code—the Judges' Rules.

ii. Prosecutors. Prosecutors supply a form of external-inclusive accountability closely linked to that of the courts. Whereas courts are responsible for the application of the criminal law in any particular case, prosecutors, as the "gatekeepers" to the formal criminal justice system, are responsible for the decision to bring criminal charges against a police officer or other accused person in the first place, and for preparing the case for the consideration of the criminal court.

iii. Ombudsmen. Another important form of external-inclusive accountability is the ombudsman. Originating in Scandinavian countries, the ombudsman is an agency, independent of the executive branch of government, which is charged with receiving and investigating complaints from citizens of misconduct or maladministration on the part of government officials. While sharing many of the investigatory and evaluative functions of the judge, the ombudsman, strictly speaking, is a nonjudicial agency. As such, it tends to be more popularly accessible and visible than many judicial agencies, but also to lack the compulsory powers of disposal available to judicial bodies. In its classical form, the ombudsman has jurisdiction to investigate across the broad range of government functions. However, there are also examples of ombudsmen with more restricted roles, as in the case of the Queensland Criminal Justice Commission which investigates official conduct across a wide range of criminal justice matters, including policing, as well as police-specific ombudsmen, including the police complaints authorities and civilian review boards referred to in Section I.A.2.a.i.

iv. Legislatures. A final main type of external-inclusive police accountability agency is the legislature or Parliament. It exercises influence in two main ways. In the first place, the main constitutional function of the legislature is to pass laws—or statutes—which may include laws for the regulation of policing. Statute law, which in the regulation of public matters, such as policing, tends to be a far more significant source of contemporary law law than judge-made law—or common law—provides the ultimate authority for the various forms of accountability already set out. Statute law may also influence policing more broadly, through specifying matters as diverse as rates of pay for police officers, qualifications for employment, and criteria for the allocation of resources both between police and other public services and within the police.

The capacity of the legislature to alter the legal framework of policing confers upon it not only a measure of direct control over the matters in question, but also a degree of leverage where it operates as an agency of accountability in its own right, which is its second main channel of influence over policing. Where it is operating in this second mode, the legislature typically employs methods such as the questioning of government ministers with responsibility for policing, investigation of aspects of police conduct or policy by specialist committee, and oversight of police spending.

3. Informal Accountability

The agencies and mechanisms of police accountability considered so far are formal in character. That is to say, they are part of an explicit framework of regulation underpinned by the authority of law or officially sanctioned organizational rules and procedures. There are, however, other less formal sources and channels of police accountability. Internally, police officers are guided and constrained by early socialization within the organization, by peer pressure, by the positions adopted by police unions and employee associations, and by a sense of professional commitment to the police mandate. Externally, the police are susceptible to the influence of the communities within which they work, the investigatory activities and the opinion-forming capacities of the mass media, and the policies developed by political parties and other pressure groups which have a political stake in policing, such as civil rights organizations and minority interest organizations.

These informal sources of accountability may be just as significant as the formal sources. Moreover, the relationship between formal sources and informal sources is complex. In some circumstances they may be in harmony, while in others they may be in a state of mutual tension. Some of the ramifications of this are explored in Section I.C.

B. Accountable for What?

Police agencies engage in a wide variety of practices and make decisions across a broad range of situations. The requirements of accountability may differ depending upon the type of practice or decision in question. In order to explore this matter, we draw upon a typology developed by Reiner. This groups police activities according to whether they relate, first, to law enforcement or internal organizational matters, and, secondly, to general policy or individual cases. Variation along these two dimensions produces a matrix of four different areas of police activity.

To begin with, broad law enforcement policy refers to matters of general *policing style*. This may include the fundamental method and philosophy of policing (e.g., a reactive "fire-brigade" approach or an interventionist, community-based approach), the pattern of deployment of staff to different areas and different functions (e.g., criminal investigation, general patrol, or traffic patrol), and the priority given to some offenses over others. Secondly, the focal point of law enforcement activity by individual officers is the decision to use or not to use coercive *legal powers*. These include powers of stop and of search of persons and of property, and also powers of arrest, detention, and questioning. Thirdly, internal organizational policy concerns *housekeeping* decisions and arrangements. These include matters as diverse as controls on petrol consumption and overtime, and policy concerning the acquisition of weaponry and communications equipment. Fourthly, *personnel management* refers to internal organizational matters concerning individual officers, such as career development, redeployment, and discipline.

Each of these four areas of police activity tends to be regarded differently in debates over police accountability and to attract its own distinct accountability arrangements. Matters of general policing style concern fundamental policy choices about the kind of policing a community should receive. Accordingly, insofar as external policy accountability is provided, it tends to be owed to bodies such as central or local government, which are explicitly constituted along political lines, or to police commissions or local consultative committees, which comprise individuals whose qualifications for holding the police to account rest upon their experience of policing or public affairs or their representativeness of local communities.

The operational exercise of individual legal powers tends to attract a more investigatory and complainer-centered mode of accountability. Insofar as this is located externally, it tends to be found in courts, ombudsmen, specialist police complaints authorities, and civilian review boards.

Internal organizational activities are less likely to give rise to demands for external accountability arrangements, but to the extent that they do, there is again a distinction between general housekeeping matters and individual-centered personnel management decisions. Many housekeeping decisions, including decisions about the purchase of equipment, patterns of shiftwork, and distribution of operational substations provide a framework which influences the formation and impact of law enforcement policy. Accordingly, the case for political accountability of law enforcement policy may be extended to cover such framework decisions.

Similarly, there are areas of personnel management, particularly the enforcement of discipline, which may have a strong bearing upon the capacity of the police organization to ensure compliance with standards of legality by individual officers exercising powers of arrest, search, and questioning. Decisions about internal discipline, therefore, are often closely linked to the findings of external accountees charged with investigating the validity of the exercise of legal powers by individual police officers.

Notwithstanding the previous analysis, it should be stressed that there is no necessary relationship between types of police activity on the one hand and actual or optimal accountability arrangements on the other. In part, this is because the boundaries between the various types of police activity are blurred. We have already noted this in respect to the relationship between externally directed law enforcement activity and internal organizational activity. It is also true of the relationship *within* the sphere of law enforcement activity between general policy and individual operational activity. General policy, whether it be the targeting of particular offenses or the discouragement of public stop and search tactics in communities hostile to the police, can affect the conduct of individual police operations. Equally, the conduct of many individual police operations can create a pattern of activity which for all practical purposes amounts to a policy, and which indeed may challenge or confound officially formulated top-down policy. This conceptual overlap between policy and operations complicates arguments about the *proper* scope of broad political accountability on the one hand and narrow investigatory accountability on the other.

The absence of any necessary relationship between types of police activity and types of accountability arrangement is also partially attributable to the fact that the optimal accountability relationship remains deeply contested for *all* areas of police activity. The reasons for this are explored below.

C. Which Regulatory Strategy?

The idea that within any community there exists a single coherent strategy for holding the police to account tends both to overestimate the rationality of the legal and political systems and to underestimate the strength of the arguments set out in Section I.B for treating different areas of police activity differently. Nevertheless, there are a number of broad options available at the overall strategic level, and different policing systems can be distinguished more or less neatly by reference to their position with regard to these options.

In turn, these positions reflect two different types of consideration. The first consideration is the underlying set of values that any police accountability system is supposed to serve. This is a key question in its own right, and is the subject of Section II. The second and equally important consideration is the enforceability of particular accountability arrangements. Which regulatory strategy is most likely to be successfully implemented? This question is addressed in the present discussion.

Let us now examine two central strategic issues which different systems of police accountability are required to resolve.

1. The Balance between Internal and External Accountability

All policing systems contain elements of both internal and external accountability, with external accountability tending to be concentrated upon the law enforcement activities of the police. However, there is considerable variation between policing systems in the balance struck between internal and external mechanisms.

Although many of the underlying values associated with police accountability support a strong system of external regulation (see Section II), internal mechanisms of accountability tend to be more easily enforceable than external mechanisms. Given the professional background of the accountees, internal regulation is likely to be better informed than external regulation. As policework is a highly dispersed activity which often takes place in regions of "low visibility," internal regulation can also be more comprehensive and thorough. Furthermore, it is able to draw upon informal allegiances and a common sense of vocation or professional identity in ways not available to external mechanisms.

As well as being less effective on its own terms, reliance on external mechanisms may actually undermine the capacity of police organizations to engage in effective self-regulation. As external regulation suggests an unwillingness to trust the police to monitor themselves, it can breed disillusionment and a defensive "siege mentality" among police officers, together with a propensity to avoid or undermine the external mechanisms in question. As reduced commitment among police officers to publicly acceptable standards and goals accentuates the gap between public expectation and police performance, this may lead to further demands for external regulation, which are likely to be even more vigorously resisted within the organization, so producing ever-diminishing returns.

On the other hand, even if the danger of a downward spiral of mutual disillusionment between police and public is conceded, external mechanisms may still have to take precedence on grounds of enforceability alone. In certain circumstances, an exclusive or preponderant reliance on internal accountability mechanisms may be insufficient to ensure that the police conform to publicly acceptable standards of behavior and performance. This may be because the cultural "schism" between senior police officers and junior officers which has been noted in systems as disparate as the United Kingdom, the United States, and the Netherlands encourages junior officers to subvert internal control mechanisms (M. Punch, Ed., 1983). *Control in the Police Organization.* MIT Press, Cambridge, MA). Alternatively, it may be because the internal control system represents a "mock bureaucracy" in which senior management creates an elaborate facade of internal controls but in the final analysis shares, or at least is prepared to defer to, the interests of the rank-and-file. In either case, a robust assertion of external accountability will, at the very least, serve the symbolic function of reaffirming the subservience of policing to a wider public interest.

Beyond that, external accountability may serve a more specific communicative function. For reasons already set out, in the face of a hostile rank-and-file, external accountability mechanisms may be even more vulnerable to subversion than internal accountability mechanisms. Nevertheless, the operation of an external accountability mechanism, however imperfect, may be effective in highlighting both to the police and to the public the seriousness of concerns over police performance and in stimulating a broader process of internal and external reflection and reform.

An example of this process at work is provided by police disciplinary arrangements in England and Wales. Prior to 1976, this was a matter entirely for internal accountability mechanisms. Lack of public confidence in the system led to the institution of the Police Complaints Board, an external body with a responsibility to oversee internal investigations of police misconduct. The performance of the Board highlighted both the scale of the problem of misconduct and the inadequacy of its powers to tackle the problem. There was pressure for further reform from various sections of the public, supported ultimately by police representative groups who came to appreciate that public confidence in the fair and thorough investigation of complaints would only be restored if a stronger mechanism of external accountability was established. As a result, the Independent Police Complaints Authority was set up in 1984. It has much broader powers of oversight and direction of the investigation of complaints, although it still falls short of an independent investigatory agency. However, the publicity that the new body generates and the incidents that it highlights means that, like its predecessor, it serves as a beacon in the campaign for further reform.

Clearly, the appropriate balance between internal and external accountability is a complex and contested matter, offering no definitive solution. According to Bayley, whether a particular accountability system gravitates toward one pole rather than the other depends instead upon wider cultural considerations. In countries where the citizenry has a cautious and contractual attitude toward the limits of the authority of government and its bureaucracy, where individualistic attitudes prevail, and where the population is socially heterogenous, internal controls are insufficiently trusted and external accountability mechanisms tend to come to the fore. The United States is the clearest illustration of this proposition. On the other hand, in countries where the citizenry has a more deferential attitude toward government authority, where communitarian attitudes prevail, and where the population is socially homogeneous, internal accountability mechanisms may come to the fore. Japan is the clearest illustration of this proposition.

2. Degrees of External Accountability

Just as controversial as the balance between internal and external accountability is the degree of external accountability. In discussing the various models available, R. Morgan identifies three key points along a continuum of accountability relationships (1985. *Setting the P.A.C.E.: Police Community Consultation Arrangements in England and Wales*. Centre for the Analysis of Social Policy, Bath). At one extreme, there is the *stewardship* model. Under this model, the police are largely autonomous. They are delegated general responsibility for police policy and operations and external accountability is understood in narrow terms as answerability. Beyond providing an explanatory account of their activities, and satisfying the external accountee that they are performing honestly and competently, the police are not required to follow the instructions of the external accountee. At the other end of the continuum is the *directive* model. Under this model, control over policy ends vests in the external accountee. The main purpose of procuring an account is prospective rather than retrospective. It enables the external accountee to engage in an informed evaluation, and, where necessary, redirection of policy, rather than merely to sanction past performance. Between these two poles, a significant third option is the *partner* model. Under this model the importance of dialogue and negotiation between accountor and accountee is accentuated. The flow of information is two way and emphasis is placed on the joint resolution of policy objectives.

As with the proper balance between internal and external accountability, the choice between these various models of external accountability involves addressing the fundamental values underpinning accountability systems (see Section II) as well as questions of enforceability. In line with the general difficulties facing external accountability mechanisms, each of these models attracts its own particular enforcement problems.

The stewardship model is highly dependent upon an efficient flow of information from the accountor to the accountee in order for monitoring to be thorough, but it is difficult to ensure the accuracy and comprehensiveness of information when its ultimate source is the very body which is the object of critical scrutiny. Similarly, the directive model, and, to a lesser extent, the partner model, challenges the professional autonomy of police agencies and so cannot be guaranteed the good-faith cooperation of these agencies.

As is true of regulatory strategy more generally, the arrangements for external accountability which apply in any particular system are unlikely to conform neatly to any particular model, and it is difficult to observe any clear relationship between underlying political culture and accountability preference. The most that can be said is that in systems where internal accountability mechanisms predominate, those external accountability mechanisms which do exist are likely to reflect the underlying deference to professional autonomy and so resemble most closely the stewardship model. Equally, in systems where external accountability mechanisms dominate, these mechanism are likely to reflect the underlying assertiveness of the culture of external scrutiny and so resemble most closely the directive model. Examples of the partner model are less common, but, as will be discussed in Section III, this type of approach is increasingly prevalent in recent innovations.

II. THE VALUE OF POLICE ACCOUNTABILITY

The manner in which police accountability is provided has implications for a number of core values associated with policing. Analysis of these values helps to explain why particular accountability systems have developed as they have and also provides a critical standard against which the merits of particular systems may be evaluated.

Basically, police accountability systems may be measured against three distinct but interconnected sets of values. First, there are values associated with *democratic legitimacy*. Secondly, there are values associated with *impartial treatment*. Thirdly, there are values associated with *effectiveness* and *efficiency of performance*.

A. Democratic Legitimacy

The most fundamental justification for police accountability is that it is required in order to ensure the democratic legitimacy of the police. The police constitute one of the most central services of the modern state. They sustain the order necessary for the preservation of the state, including, where applicable, its democratic institutions and its guarantees of individual freedom. Accordingly, it is appropriate that this vital service should itself be properly accountable to the public it serves.

Democracy can be broken down into a number of more specific values, each of which is relevant to police accountability. First, democracy requires that a service be responsive to public opinion. Secondly, and relatedly, democracy requires that adequate redress is available when dissatisfaction with overall performance of the service and the conduct of individuals within it is registered. Thirdly, democracy requires that power should not be overconcentrated at any point within the political system. A broad distribution and balance of power is necessary so that no single agency or network acquires undue influence in public decision making or the means to accumulate power at the expense of other agencies within the political system. Finally, democracy requires a degree of public participation. This may be direct participation or, more commonly, indirect participation through elected representatives. These last two values—distribution of power and participation—are of broader significance inasmuch as their pursuit through forms of police accountability serves not only to affirm the democratic credentials of policing, but also to enhance the democratic culture of the political system more generally.

On the face of it, these various democratic values would appear to be best pursued through external accountability agencies staffed by elected representatives or the appointees of elected representatives. Paradoxically, however, there is a danger that democratic institutions of police accountability might undermine democratic values. In the first place, such are the powers and resources of the police that unscrupulous members of an external accountability agency may be tempted to draw the police into a web of corruption. That is to say, elected or appointed accountees may seek to use their leverage over the police to persuade them to enforce (or refrain from enforcing) the law in a manner which serves narrow personal or political interests.

Secondly, democratic institutions of accountability may produce the "tyranny of the majority." In the attempt to meet the aspirations of their electorate, external accountees may seek to secure the application by the police of policies which systematically favor the sectional interests of the majority over those of minorities. For example, an accountee whose election or ap-

pointment reflects the preferences of a white middle-class majority within a community might support policies which allocate disproportionate resources to the protection of the personal security and property of that majority at the expense of the equivalent protection of ethnic minority neighborhoods. If, as many would argue, it is strongly implicit in the definition of democracy that there should be some minimal guarantee of equal protection of the interests of all, then partisan majoritarianism of this type offends against democracy.

B. Impartial Treatment

In seeking to maintain order and protect life and property, the main resource and guide available to the police is the universal framework of criminal law. In order to remain faithful to its universal premise, police officers must treat like cases in a like manner. Therefore, just as it is important that general policing policy does not systematically discriminate in favor of or against particular sections of the public, so too the evenhanded treatment of individual cases is a requirement of fair policing.

Investigatory accountability mechanisms can help to meet this requirement by ensuring that the treatment of individuals by police officers conforms to certain general rules and standards established through law or formal organizational rules. Optimally, such accountability mechanisms should be externally situated and be predominantly judicial or quasi-judicial in character. External mechanisms are preferable to internal mechanisms as the process of investigation and judgment may be insufficiently thorough and critical if it is entrusted to an internal agency whose officers may share the same values and institutional commitments as the officers under scrutiny. Judicial or quasi-judicial scrutiny is preferable to scrutiny by a politically appointed or elected agency, as a body chosen for its political beliefs may be ill-suited to disposing of particular cases in a disinterested fashion.

C. Effectiveness and Efficiency of Performance

As policing is a purposeful activity, the pursuit of these purposes in a manner which is both effective and not unnecessarily wasteful of scarce public resources is clearly a key priority. Accountability mechanisms, particularly external accountability mechanisms, can contribute to effectiveness and efficiency in a number of ways.

To begin with, the accountee can bring additional knowledge and expertise and a different perspective to the task of improving police effectiveness and efficiency. Relevant knowledge and expertise may be provided by both internal and external accountees, but independence of perspective is more likely to be provided from an external vantage point. Secondly, the provision of external accountability mechanisms, through increasing public influence over and understanding of the police, may lead to improved relations between police and public, and in turn to an increased willingness on the part of the public to cooperate in providing information about criminal incidents to the police. As such information is the most valuable and least costly resource available to the police in solving crime and detecting offenders, any increase in the quantity or quality of its flow will enhance effectiveness and efficiency. Thirdly, the improved relations between police and public which may result from external accountability arrangements may also increase public respect for and observance of the law, and diminish the prospects of flashpoints between police and public which precipitate public disorder. Again, this improves the prospects of police attaining their objectives and frees resources for deployment elsewhere.

On the other hand, external accountability mechanisms may also threaten effectiveness and efficiency. Ill-informed interference in police policy can upset well-considered lines of internal strategy while restrictions on the conduct of individual officers may reduce their capacity to pursue criminal investigations. Also, if the responsibilities of servicing the demands of the external accountee are burdensome, they can result in a significant diversion of resources from the primary policing task.

D. An Ideal Framework of Accountability?

On the basis of the above analysis, a framework of police accountability which sought to optimize values associated with democracy, impartiality, and effective and efficient performance would have to reconcile divergent pressures and build in a number of checks and balances. In the cause of democracy, a robust system of external political accountability for general policy would be warranted, but safeguards would have to be included to minimize the dangers associated with corrupt self-interest and crude majoritarianism. In the cause of impartiality in the treatment of individual cases, an equally robust system of external investigatory accountability would be warranted, although it should

be judicial or quasi-judicial rather than political in character. Finally, while considerations of effectiveness and efficiency may reinforce the case for external accountability in general, there are particular dangers. Measures would have to be provided to ensure that accountability agencies were well-informed and that accountability mechanisms were not unduly restrictive of operational autonomy or wasteful of police resources.

Clearly, this leaves much scope for argument about the design of an ideal accountability framework. Furthermore, this discussion makes no allowance for considerations of enforceability, which, as discussed in Section I.C, tend to favor internal accountability over external accountability. The additional complexities involved in trying to accommodate enforceability questions ensure that the design of optimal accountability arrangements is likely to remain a hotly contested matter in the foreseeable future.

III. TRENDS IN POLICE ACCOUNTABILITY

Although attitudes toward and arrangements for police accountability differ significantly between different states, it is possible to discern a number of recent developments in the relationship between policing and political systems which may have a long-term impact on the design of police accountability systems generally.

A. The Growth of Nonstate Policing

Prior to the development of professional state-authorized policing on a large scale in the 19th century, policing services were mainly provided on a private basis. Throughout the 19th and 20th centuries private policing continued to provide a parallel system alongside state policing, but from the 1960s onward the private policing sector has undergone such a significant revival that in many states it has come to rival or even outstrip the state sector in terms of numerical strength. For example, it has been estimated that by the year 2000 the ratio of private security employees to public police in the United States will stand at 3 : 1. Figures for Canada, the United Kingdom, France, Spain, and Germany suggest that in these countries also employment in the private security industry already exceeds that for sworn police officers, while there is more informal evidence of similar trends elsewhere.

Alongside explicit privatization, there has been a complementary movement toward a more diversified public sector. New types of "hybrid" policing, including state organizations which sell police services on the private market and specialist agencies which have a narrower clientele than the general public (e.g., policing of nuclear installations or military sites), are assuming a more prominent position beside the traditional public police. These various developments reflect a number of broad sociological changes, including a growing skepticism about the capacity of the public police to achieve satisfactory levels of crime control, a new mood of financial austerity in government, and an associated movement toward applying market-based techniques in the operation and supervision of public services.

There are also new challenges to the policing authority of the state from beyond its frontiers. After the Second World War Interpol succeeded the International Criminal Police Commission (founded in 1923) as the primary agency of international police cooperation, providing a medium of information transfer and exchange for national forces faced with the developing problem of international crime. More recently, the supranational political entity known as the European Union (comprising 15 Western European states) has extended its remit to include policing and related issues, culminating in the establishment in 1994 of the Europol organization. Its brief is to develop general policing strategy and criminal intelligence on drug trafficking, illegal immigration, automobile theft, and money laundering, with the prospect of this list being greatly expanded in due course.

Europol, although still lacking its own executive powers of arrest, search, etc., is the most ambitious form of international policing agency yet conceived. This reflects not only the intensification of the international crime threat in an era of global travel and communications, but also the particular security concern arising from the European Union's policy of open borders between member states and, most importantly of all, the growing self-image of the European Union as a political community to rival that of the state.

Both of these sets of developments raise questions about the adequacy of existing accountability arrangements, which are largely focused on traditional forms of state-authorized public policing. Private and hybrid policing tend to be unregulated or subject to relatively light regulatory frameworks. Arguably, however, policing is an activity with such broad ramifications for general order that accountability arrangements should always acknowledge and reflect a broader public interest, even when the immediate client represents a more specific interest.

As for policing beyond the state, this has traditionally attracted mainly internal forms of accountability. Insofar as the need for external accountability is acknowledged, this has tended to center upon the national government or agency with responsibility for the international initiative. However, particularly in the case of Europol, there is a strong argument for external accountability to bodies situated at the same institutional level as the police agency itself (e.g., European Parliament). This reflects the fact that the new policing agency is as much if not more under the responsibility and control of the European Union considered as a separate political entity as it is under the responsibility and control of the 15 members states considered separately.

B. The Externalization of Audit

One significant development in internal accountability arrangements over the 1970s and 1980s was the application to policing of increasingly sophisticated forms of financial and managerial audit. In the United States, this trend was marked by the emergence and application of management theories such as policing by objectives and problem-oriented policing. Approaches such as these, which are subsequently adopted in many other countries, stressed the need to move beyond vague generalizations in the formulation of policing objectives. They sought instead to develop a more systematic approach to the identification of goals, backed up by performance indicators to measure the extent and costs of goal achievement together with procedures to allow critical feedback and informed reassessment of policy.

During the 1980s, governments, which for reasons set out in Section III.A were seeking to impose new disciplines on public policing, gradually sought to extend the new methods of auditory control to the accountability relationship between police and external agencies. This new approach, which involves external agencies in budgetary control and in the development of policing plans and systems of performance appraisal, has been developed in a comprehensive fashion in England and Wales since 1994, but elements of it are influential on a broader international front.

External audit is open to the criticism that it threatens to elevate financial efficiency over other public concerns about policing. On the other hand, it may encourage a more reflective attitude to police policy by all parties involved. Further, by emphasizing the importance of verifiable performance indicators, the approach seeks to address the problems of inadequate information and poor enforceability which plague all external accountability systems.

C. The Externalization of Grievance Procedures

There is also some evidence to suggest a gradual shift from reliance upon internal mechanisms in the investigation of individual grievances to a mixed approach in which external mechanisms have an important monitoring or directive role to play alongside internal mechanisms. It was argued in Section I.C that, whatever their shortcomings, external mechanisms of review become difficult to resist when public confidence in the efficacy of internal procedures is low. More specifically, where public disquiet over policing stems from events which attract numerous individual complaints, the internal investigatory mechanisms will fall under heightened critical scrutiny, and the demand for external regulation will increase correspondingly. This helps to explain why the growth of civilian reviews boards in the United States followed urban race riots in the 1960s; the development of the Independent Police Complaints Authority in the United Kingdom followed urban disorders in 1981; and various external accountability initiatives in Australian states in the 1970s and 1980s, most notably the recent establishment of the Queensland Criminal Justice Commission with its own Official Misconduct Division, followed widespread revelations of official corruption and police misconduct.

Moreover, once a climate of mistrust of internal mechanisms has been established and external mechanisms have been embraced, this trend is unlikely to be reversed. Therefore, although the first generation of civilian review boards in the United States were mostly short-lived, the underlying complex of attitudes which encouraged their emergence was more enduring. Civilian review has gradually become reestablished, and in 1990 was present in some form in 30 of the country's 50 largest cities.

A related development has been the important role accorded to external procedures for investigating grievances in some societies where there are pronounced social divisions in terms of class, race, or ethnicity. Examples include the National Police Commission appointed in India in 1979 and the Goldstone Commission appointed in South Africa in 1992. In such deeply divided societies, disadvantaged minorities often have a long experience of confrontation with and oppression by the national police. If they are to develop or regain a measure of confidence in the state policing system they require an independent forum in which their complaints and criticisms may be candidly voiced and will be accorded serious consideration.

Some of these examples reveal a further subtrend in the movement toward external grievance procedures, namely the location of these grievance procedures within a broader review mechanism. For example, the Queensland Criminal Justice Commission does not simply react to individual complaints, but can act proactively in investigating official misconduct and can inquire into patterns of misconduct. In the case of the South African Goldstone Commission, the hearing of individual complaints is part of a broader investigation into the causes of public violence and intimidation and the means necessary to their eradication. In both cases, the emphasis is not only upon satisfying the individual complainer—a procedure which in isolation can heighten confrontation and division—but also upon identifying and seeking to remove the underlying causes of conflict and abuse.

D. Participation and Partnership

Finally, there are some radical developments and suggestions for development in the provision and oversight of forms of security which question the basic premise of the police accountability relationship. As we have seen, the accountability relationship presupposes two distinct agencies—the accountor and the accountee—and the various accountability mechanisms available must grapple with the considerable difficulties of reconciling the distinct interests and perspectives of these two agencies and of ensuring the supply of relevant information to the accountee.

Participation is one way of overcoming the accountability division. Although it would be unrealistic to conceive of a system of policing in a modern complex society which did not involve some degree of professional specialization, some commentators have suggested an arrangement in which professional policing is reserved for the national level, while, building on informal arrangements and practices, security at the local level is designated as a communal responsibility. For example, such a system of "dual policing" has been suggested by M. Brogden and C. Shearing for South Africa as a means of ensuring that all racial groups retain confidence in and influence over the policing system in the transition to a democratic society (1993. *Policing for a New South Africa.* Routledge, London).

The partnership approach is less radical in that it does not advocate a comprehensive form of community self-policing. Instead, it envisages a model of "discursive policing" (I. Loader, 1996. *Youth, Policing and Democ-*

racy. MacMillan, Basingstoke), involving a genuine dialogue between the professional police and the community it serves, and a commitment to develop policy in an open and consensual manner. In this regard, local consultative committees represent an interesting development. Although they lack formal authority over policing policy, are often insufficiently representative of the entire range of community interests, and are rarely fully committed to consensual solutions, their growing popularity worldwide may be an early sign of the viability of the partnership approach.

Also See the Following Article

POLICE AND RACE RELATIONS

Bibliography

Anderson, M., den Boer, M., Cullen, P., Gilmore, W. C., Raab, C. D., and Walker, N. (1995). "Policing the European Union: Theory, Law and Practice." Clarendon Press, Oxford.

Bayley, D. (1985). "Patterns of Policing." Rutgers Univ. Press, New Brunswick, NJ.

Brogden, M., and Shearing, C. (1993). "Policing for a New South Africa." Routledge, London.

Goldsmith, A. (Ed.) (1991). "Complaints against the Police: The Trend to External Review." Clarendon Press, Oxford.

Goldstein, H. (1990). "Problem-Oriented Policing." McGraw–Hill, New York.

Jefferson, T., and Grimshaw, R. (1984). "Controlling the Constable; Police Accountability in England and Wales." Muller/Cobden Trust, London.

Johnston, L. (1992). "The Rebirth of Private Policing." Routledge, London.

Jones, T., Newburn, T., and Smith, D. J. (1984). "Democracy and Policing." Policy Studies Institute, London.

Lubans, V. A., and Edgar, J. M. (1979). "Policing by Objectives." Social Development Corp., Hartford.

Lustgarten, L. (1986). "The Governance of Police." Sweet & Maxwell, London.

Marenin, O. (1996). "Policing Change, Changing Police: International Perspectives." Garland, New York/London.

Mawby, R. (1990). "Comparative Policing Issues. The British and American System in International Perspective." MacMillan, Basingstoke.

Morgan, R. (1985). "Setting the P.A.C.E.: Police Community Consultation Arrangements in England and Wales." Centre for the Analysis of Social Policy, Bath.

Skolnick, J. H., and Fyfe, J. J. (1993). "Above the Law: Police and the Excessive Use of Force." The Free Press, New York.

Tonry, M., and Morris, N. (Eds.) (1992). "Modern Policing." Univ. of Chicago Press, Chicago.

Walsh, D., and Dickson, B. (1994). "Police Accountability in Divided Societies: A Literature Review," Ulster Papers in Public Policy and Management, No. 35. Univ. of Ulster, Jordanstown.

POLICE AND RACE RELATIONS

Trevor Jones
Policy Studies Institute

I. Relationships between Ethnic Minorities
and the Police
II. Measures to Address Problematic Relationships
III. Conclusions

GLOSSARY

Black people African Caribbeans in Britain, and African Americans in the United States.

discrimination The outcome of social processes that work to the disadvantage of particular social groups.

empiricism An approach that aims to avoid untested theoretical speculation and to examine hypotheses by reference to experience and the available evidence.

ethnic minorities A term commonly used in Britain to denote groups of people with family origins in the countries of former British colonies in the Caribbean, the Indian subcontinent, Africa, and the Far East.

phenomenalism The doctrine that phenomena (things that appear, are observed, or are perceived) are the only objects of knowledge

prejudice An individual attitude of active hostility toward another social group, in this context racially defined.

racism The determination of actions, attitudes, or policies by beliefs about racial characteristics.

South Asian People with family origins in India, Pakistan, and Bangladesh.

the police The body of officials empowered by the state to enforce the law and maintain order.

THE SUBJECTS OF POLICING, CRIME, AND ETHNIC MINORITIES have provided a controversial focus within debates about law and order for many years in both Britain and in the United States. Commentators range between those at one end of the spectrum who suggest that Black people are more likely to commit crime than people of other ethnic groups, and those at the other who argue that "Black criminality" is an illusion created by a racist criminal justice system. Despite fundamental disagreements about causes of crime, there is, however, wide consensus that the relationship between the police and many racial minorities has been long characterized by mutual suspicion, mistrust, and, at times, hostility. These problematic relationships have manifested themselves in a number of ways, ranging from lower ratings from ethnic minority people in surveys of public satisfaction with the police, to violent mass confrontation in deprived inner-city areas. This chapter summarizes some of the main themes arising from research into the nature and causes of problematic relationships between the police and racial minorities. It draws primarily on the British literature, although it also makes some references to U.S. research. While there are important variations between different national contexts, the central question applies almost universally. That is, why is it the case that in many different

Encyclopedia of Applied Ethics, Volume 3

countries, certain ethnic groups are much more likely than others to be caught up in the criminal justice system? Although some reference has been made to other ethnic minority groups, it is Black people who have been the primary focus of research on ethnicity and policing. The relationships between the police and other minority ethnic groups, such as Hispanic Americans in the United States and South Asians in Britain, show some elements of similarity with the Black experience, but also important areas of difference that can often become submerged within discussions of "police–Black" relations.

I. RELATIONSHIPS BETWEEN ETHNIC MINORITIES AND THE POLICE

A. Police Attitudes and Behavior toward Ethnic Minorities

1. Urban Unrest

Attention to problematic relationships between the police and Black people in the United States grew during the 1960s, following serious inner-city urban disturbances, and with the rise of the civil rights movement. Official investigations, such as that undertaken by the National Advisory Commission on Civil Disorders in 1968, cited police misconduct as the key factor behind the unrest. The relationship between the police and racial minority groups has been the subject of comment ever since, often emerging to the forefront of public debate. This was particularly evident after the filmed assault by Los Angeles police officers on Rodney King and the officers' subsequent acquittal, which led to serious urban riots. More recently, the trial of O.J. Simpson again focused attention on racial tensions, in particular on allegations of police racism. It was during the 1970s that police–Black relations emerged as a focus for public debate in Britain. Since this time, serious urban disorders involving Black people have again been crucial in highlighting the issue. Perhaps the most significant watershed came in 1981, when serious rioting in Brixton, South London, was followed by outbreaks of violence in other major cities. An official public inquiry into the disturbances by Lord Scarman (1981) found that police behavior toward Black people had been one of the main causes of the riots. Public attention was again focused upon hostile relationships between the police and Black people (along with unemployment and economic deprivation) by further serious outbreaks of urban disorder in several of Britain's larger cities during the mid-1980s.

2. Ethnic Minorities as Suspects—Stops and Arrests

Black people are substantially more likely to be stopped, searched, and arrested by the police than White people. This is the overwhelming conclusion of the research in both Britain and North America. The subsequent discussion focuses mainly on Britain, although makes some reference to the United States where appropriate (Wilbanks (1987) provides a comprehensive summary of the U.S. evidence). British studies showing disproportionate police stop rates of Black people have been based both on analysis of police records, and on survey data. Surveys have found that a much higher proportion of Black people report having been stopped by police in the past year. Of those people stopped by the police, Blacks tend to have a much higher average number of stops than Whites. Most British studies have shown people of South Asian origin (Indians, Pakistanis, and Bangladeshis) have lower overall stop rates than all other ethnic groups, including Whites. The ethnic differences in overall stop rates in such studies are reduced when age is taken into account (ethnic minority groups tend to have a younger age profile, and as offending is more common among the younger age groups, the police are more likely to stop young people). Controlling for other factors such as car ownership and unemployment rates also tends to reduce, although by no means eliminate, ethnic differences in stop rates. Studies that are confined to more homogenously deprived inner-city areas consequently tend to find smaller ethnic differences in rates of being stopped (Jefferson, T., & Walker, M. A. (1993). Attitudes to the police of ethnic minorities in a provincial city. *British Journal of Criminology* 33:2, 251–266). Thus, it is possible to argue that, as Black people are more likely to live in areas of greater social deprivation, the different styles of policing adopted in such areas (rather than the ethnic group of suspects) may explain a large part of the ethnic differences in stop rates. One interpretation of such findings is that the differences in other surveys "are almost certainly accounted for by the fact that whites tend to live in more well-to-do areas, and are likely to have fewer experiences of the police of any kind (and certainly fewer unpleasant experiences) than non-whites" (Jefferson & Walker, 1993). Other interpretations see comparisons between Black and White people living in the same small areas as rather unhelpful, because of the unusual characteristics of the relatively small number of White people living in areas of high ethnic concentration compared to the general population.

The high stop rate for Blacks only partly explains the higher overall arrest rate, because less than a quarter of all arrests arise from police stops. There are no national data in Britain on the ethnic origin of arrested people, but local studies show that Black people form a much higher proportion of people arrested than they do of the general population, whereas South Asian people form the same proportion of the two groups. The figures show that the proportion of those arrested who are Black varies little between offense categories, but is extremely high for robbery. As outlined below, these findings have been used to argue that rates of offending are higher in the Black population. However, the overrepresentation of Black people in police stop and arrest statistics have also been explained by reference to racial prejudice and discrimination.

3. Police Prejudice and Discrimination

Police racism, according to some commentators, is the primary cause for the higher stop and arrest rates of Black people. All major ethnographic studies of policing in Britain and the United States to date have found that expressions of negative, stereotyped, and hostile attitudes toward Black people are commonplace among working groups of police officers. Although no major ethnographic studies of policing have been undertaken in Britain since the mid-1980s, some recent studies and official reports have indicated that this problem has persisted into the 1990s. What actually causes the development and articulation of such attitudes, and how far and in what ways they shape police behavior, is more difficult to determine.

Various arguments have been employed to explain the origins of such attitudes. Some focus on the character of the individuals who join the police. For example, it could be argued that the police occupation attracts unusually conservative and authoritarian personalities. Another view suggests that police officers simply reflect the prejudices of the social group from which most recruits are drawn. More generally accepted explanations focus on the process by which social *groups* propagate and entrench within their individual members certain beliefs and attitudes. There is good evidence that occupational culture and on-the-job experience are crucial in fostering racial prejudice within the police organization. For example, perceived higher rates of offending in the Black community (see below) are sometimes used to explain police prejudice toward Black people, or at least justify the greater police attention directed towards them. Explanations of ethnic differences in stop and arrest rates that are set largely in terms of police racism come up against the strikingly different findings for South Asian people. A large body of research on the housing and labor markets has suggested that racial discrimination is just as prevalent against South Asians as it is against Black people. This suggests that an undifferentiated and generalized notion of racism cannot by itself explain differential police treatment. It may be that different forms of racism are directed against Black people from those directed against South Asian people. In Britain, a growing body of work presents racism as something far more complex than undifferentiated color discrimination. For example, some authors have argued that during the 1990s there was a growth of specifically anti-Muslim prejudice, partly reflected by a growing divergence in the circumstances of Muslim and non-Muslim South Asians. An important question for future research is the degree to which the acute levels of economic deprivation being experienced by Pakistanis and Bangladeshis are manifesting themselves in problematic relationships with the police in some areas.

The high levels of stated racial prejudice among police officers do not, however, translate into observable behavior patterns in a straightforward or simple way. A pioneering study of the police and ethnic minority groups in London was carried out by the Policy Studies Institute (PSI) during the 1980s (Smith, D. J., & Gray, J. (1985). *Police and people in London*. Aldershot: Gower). This study found that despite the pervasiveness of racial prejudice within the police organization, many police officers appeared to have relaxed and friendly relationships with individual Black people. Another interesting finding was that when the police were called upon to provide a service, the action taken by the police (in terms of making a proper investigation, acting quickly, and attempting to catch the offender) was similar for all ethnic groups. These apparently paradoxical findings have been explained with reference to the relative independence of individual and group levels of perception and cognition. Thus, friendly relationships with people at the individual level can coexist with strongly negative attitudes towards the group to which they belong as a whole.

The police might argue that the high stop rate of Blacks is related to the higher incidence of criminal offending in that group. The law requires that a police officer must have "reasonable suspicion" that an offense has been, is being, or is about to be committed, in order to justify stopping or searching a person. Thus, it could be argued that if the high stop rate arose from racial discrimination, then a lower proportion of Black people who are stopped would be arrested, whereas the proportion for stopped Blacks and Whites is about the same.

Against this, however, the criteria for arrest is the same "reasonable suspicion" as that for a stop, and thus it could be argued that police officers simply put more effort into finding an offense with which to charge Black people once they have stopped them. One recent study, however, found that ethnic origin had little impact on whether a person is positively treated after being stopped (in fact, slightly more of the Whites were subject to hostile or negative treatment from police officers). Overall, the data suggested that in routine policing by uniformed patrol officers, prejudice does not significantly lead to differential or discriminatory police action once a stop is in progress (Norris, C., Fielding, N., Kemp, C., & Fielding, J. (1992). Black and blue: An analysis of the influence of race on being stopped by the police. *British Journal of Sociology*, 43:2, 207–224).

This is not to argue that unequal treatment of Black people does not occur. It clearly does. The problem is to decide how far such treatment constitutes unfair discrimination in this context, especially given the vague and unenforceable criteria that determine whether a stop is justified. For example, it is generally accepted that the police will tend to stop more young men. However, this approach is essentially discriminatory because individuals are being targeted because of their membership in a particular group, even though such discrimination may be partly justified by evidence of higher rates of offending in this group. The PSI study referred to above found that police officers tend to make "a crude equation between crime and black people," a finding that has been confirmed by a number of studies. Thus, racial prejudice is one of a number of factors that can lead to unjust discriminatory behavior by police officers. Observational research of police stops has suggested that, where there is no obvious reason for the stop, the criteria that police officers use are ones that, in their view, are associated with the chance of getting a "result" (i.e., finding some evidence of a criminal act). Thus, officers tend to stop young males, especially if they are Black, but also people who look poor, dirty, have long hair, or unconventional dress.

4. Lack of Police Protection

The heavy-handed policing experienced by some ethnic minority groups is, it is argued, compounded by a lack of effective police protection. Analysis of the most recent British Crime Survey suggests that Black and South Asian people are substantially more likely than Whites to be victims of crime, and have significantly greater fear of crime. Not surprisingly, risk of actual criminal victimization tends to be closely linked to the characteristics of the area of work or residence. It is clear that

experience of crime, and the fear of crime, provide strong constraints on the quality of life for ethnic minority groups as a whole.

Particular concerns about inadequate police protection are raised with regard to racial violence and harassment. It has been alleged that racial violence has been the subject of police indifference, or in some cases, even hostility. Over recent years, there has been a large increase in the number of racially motivated crimes recorded by the police in Britain. It is difficult to know how far this represents an increase in actual incidence, and how far it is due to increased reporting rates, and changes in police recording practices. Compared with police statistics, victim surveys indicate a smaller increase over recent years, but a much higher absolute level of racial harassment. There are important differences within the ethnic minority population, in that South Asian victims are more likely than Black victims to report that a crime has been racially motivated, and have substantially higher rates of *fear* of racial attack than do Black people.

Victim surveys have important limitations when it comes to attempting to estimate the extent and nature of racial harassment. Although survey evidence will indicate experience of discrete criminal acts such as racial assaults, they cannot measure the sequence of incidents, ranging from verbal abuse to criminal assault, which blight the lives of many ethnic minority people. Racial harassment is the term given to such patterns of repeated racially motivated incidents, within which many of the events taken alone would not constitute crimes, but the cumulative effect of which is to substantially reduce the quality of life of the victims. The police have been criticized for the way they define and conceptualize the problem of racial violence and harassment. Racially motivated attacks are not aimed purely at individuals, but rather they constitute attacks against people as members of a particular group. Thus, the police have been criticized for subsuming racial harassment under any criminal incident when the victim and offender happened to be of a different ethnic group. The police in some areas have attempted to address some of these criticisms, including modifying their definitions of racial incidents, and setting up specialist units to deal with racially motivated crime.

5. Unrepresentative Police Forces

Whatever the disagreements about the extent to which ethnic minority people are simultaneously "overpoliced" and "underprotected," there is little doubt that they are significantly underrepresented in the police service itself. In Britain, after more than a decade of official concern about this problem, ethnic minorities still make up less than 2% of the police service, even though they form 5.5% of the general population. Similar concerns have been raised about underrepresentation of Black people in U.S. police forces. In the United States, hiring quotas and affirmative action policies helped to increase Black representation within police departments after the 1960s. However, recent studies have shown that despite these advances, Black officers are underrepresented in many police departments in the United States.

B. Ethnic Minority Attitudes and Behavior toward the Police

1. Negative Attitudes toward the Police

There is strong evidence from public satisfaction surveys that Black people are more likely than White people to hold negative views of the police. This finding is generally true, although not to the same degree, for people of South Asian ethnic origin. Lower proportions of Black and South Asian people in general express confidence in the police in victimization and public satisfaction surveys. Of those who have themselves initiated contact with the police (to report a crime or an incident, or to provide information), both Black people and South Asians are substantially more likely than Whites to express dissatisfaction with the police response. With regard to police-initiated contact, it is again true that both South Asian and Black people are more likely than Whites to express dissatisfaction with the police, although the proportion is much higher for Blacks, particularly for young Black men. Most surveys have found a strong positive correlation between the amount of contact with the police (of any kind), and critical views about the police. The more contacts a person had with the police, the more negative were their views, with police stops being the main adversarial contact associated with critical views of the police.

As with the issue of police prejudice, it is important to remember the distinction between attitudes and behavior. It is not necessarily the case that negative attitudes are reflected in a simple or straightforward way in the everyday behavior of Black people toward the police. There is some evidence from the United States suggesting that Black people are more likely than Whites to show antagonism to the police. Research for the Presidential Crime Commission in the 1960s explained the higher proportions of Black people arrested partly by a supposedly greater tendency among Blacks to show disrespect for the police. In Britain, there is some limited evidence (on the basis of hypothetical questions in surveys) that Black people are less willing to help the police by reporting incidents or appearing as a witness in court. A few British studies have suggested that a more hostile demeanor of young Black men toward police officers contributes to greater arrest rates. However, more recent research has found that it is unlikely that higher arrest rates can be explained by more hostile attitudes among young blacks (Norris *et al.*, 1992). Contrary to earlier research, the findings showed that Black and White people were equally likely to be calm in interactions with the police, and that police encounters with Black people are not particularly confrontational or difficult. This is not to argue that negative or hostile attitudes toward the police are unimportant. Such attitudes, along with rank-and-file police views about Black people, provide a mutually reinforcing potential for conflict, which may be activated when other precipitating factors lead both the police and Black people to switch into antagonistic group identities.

2. Generalized and Police-Specific Hostility

More negative attitudes among Black people toward the police may of course simply be part of a generalized disaffection with society and its institutions, in which the police are perhaps the most potent symbol of social authority. Thus, problematic police–Black relations can only be understood within the broader social context that strongly influences the attitudes and behavior of both police officers and Black people. In Britain, the urban disorders and industrial conflicts of the 1970s and 1980s contributed to a growing sense that the legitimacy of the state itself was coming under question. Antagonism toward the police may in this sense be a broader expression of tension between Black people and the main centers of power and authority. However, this will inevitably lead to conflictual contacts between the police and subordinate groups, which compound the hostility, and perhaps focus it upon the police as an institution. Hostile group attitudes toward the police are formed in the wider context of important developments that have led many Black people to see themselves as under attack (as a group) from White society. These include increasingly restrictive immigration controls which identify Black people as unwanted, the growing incidence of racial attacks and harassment (see above), and high levels of socioeconomic deprivation.

There is, however, strong evidence that hostility may be police-specific, rather than simply due to a general alienation from society. Research during the 1980s found that young Black people's views of the police were largely independent of their views of British society in general. Young Black people were actually more positive than their White counterparts about some institutions such as the law courts, Parliament, and local government. Thus, "generalized negativity" was not the primary factor behind the negative views about the police held by young Black people. These negative views were related only indirectly to personal experiences of policing. Although contacts with the police were more frequent and hostile for Black than for White youths, young Blacks' hostility to the police was based more on shared stereotypes, relatively independent of particular personal experiences. Thus, there was a clear "police-specific" focus of the disaffection of young Black people, but related only indirectly to actual experiences of the police (Gaskell, G., & Smith, P. (1985). Young Blacks' hostility to the police: An investigation into its casues. *New Community* 12:1, 66–74). Similarly, analysis of the PSI findings from London led David Smith to argue that hostile views were not anarchic, and that Black people "want a police force and in practice they make use of its services like everyone else, while being highly critical of it in some respects' (Smith, D. J. (1991). The origins of Black hostility to the police. *Policing and Society* 2, 1–15). Even the strong hostility toward police found among many young Black men does not amount to a complete rejection of the policing system. The association between critical views and experience of adversarial encounters with the police is much less strong among Black people than it is among Whites. This provides further evidence to suggest that hostility toward the police is a group-level phenomenon rather than related directly to particular experiences of individuals. Thus, even Black people with no personal experience of the police tend to form hostile views on the basis of information from friends, acquaintances, the newspapers, and television. Smith concluded that "(b)lack hostility to the police is akin to a political force: it is part of the assertion of identity by a social and cultural group."

Thus, group-based belief systems that are related to negative individual experiences, but not in a simple or direct way, are important factors shaping *both* rank-and-file police attitudes toward Black people, *and* Black people's views of the police.

C. Ethnic Minority Involvement in Crime and Disorder

In both Britain and the United States, debates about ethnicity and crime have been highly controversial. At one end of the political spectrum, there are commenta-tors whose work implies that some ethnic groups are innately more likely to offend, and in particular that there is a growing Black "criminal class" (for example, Herrnstein, R. J., & Murray, C. (1994). *The bell curve: Intelligence and class structure in American life.* New York: Free Press). Against this, radical theorists have argued that Black criminality is simply a "folk devil," constructed by racist White society as a scapegoat to divert attention from the growing crisis of the capitalist state (see, for example, Hall, S., Critcher, C., Clarke, J., Jefferson, T., & Roberts, B. (1978). *Policing the Crisis.* London: Macmillan). Between these polarized views, the "new realist" criminologists have focused on a cyclical sequence of interactions, in which higher rates of offending, racial prejudice, and economic deprivation mutually reinforce each other. Thus, economic disadvantage contributes to increased offending by some Black youths, which in turn fosters police prejudice and discriminatory behavior by police officers against Black people (higher stop and arrest rates). Black youths are further marginalized by this, leading to a greater propensity to commit crime, and so the cycle continues (Lea, J., & Young, J. (1984). *What is to be done about law and order?* Harmondsworth: Penguin). Although radical criminologists have strongly criticized such a thesis, it is now quite widely accepted that discrimination by the police and criminal justice system on one hand, and increased offending by some Black people on the other, reinforce and feed off one another in a vicious circle. This general argument is now quite widely accepted as the basis for a more thorough (and realistic) explanation of the crime profiles of some ethnic groups.

There is much controversy surrounding attempts to measure statistically the degree to which higher stop and arrest rates amongst Blacks outlined above can be explained by higher offending rates. Some radical commentators dismiss any such studies as "empiricist haggling" that at best fails to tell us anything useful, but at worst "give intellectual support to racist stereotypes of the black community" (Gilroy, P. (Ed.). (1982) *The myth of black criminality.* London: Merlin). Such a position has been criticized for dismissing any rational basis for debate about ethnic minority involvement in crime. However, there is broader agreement about the main limitations of empirical studies. The main limitation is the inadequacies of crime statistics and victim reports. It is widely accepted that only a small fraction of crimes are reported, and that victim identifications only apply in a fraction of offenses. This suggests that the "unknown" crime figure is so large that the "real" rates of offending by different groups can never be known. Another problem with the purely empirical approach is that a variety of factors contribute to a greater likelihood of criminal involvement, and it is extremely difficult to disentangle the effect of each. For example, the police arrest higher proportions of working-class people, and a greater percentage of Black people than White people are working class. So higher arrest rates for Blacks will reflect this "social class effect." Similar arguments apply for a range of other variables such as age and gender distribution, and measures of economic deprivation such as unemployment. Thus, the process whereby researchers attempt to control for all the relevant variables in order to identity the residual "pure discrimination" has been compared by Tony Jefferson to "sieving flour with ever finer meshes" (quoted in Gelsthorpe & McWilliam, 1993).

The division between empiricism and phenomenalism in studies of ethnicity and crime is an important one. Each approach, taken alone, has important weaknesses. The avowedly empiricist approach often fails to examine the wider social context of offending, and does not take account of how racialized relationships develop and change over time. Furthermore, there are clearly serious limitations on the available data. Some authors see these criticisms as a basis for either rejecting empirical studies completely, or regarding their findings as no more than speculation. The problem with this kind of argument is that it is not always consistently applied. If the empirical evidence (for example, about disproportionate police stops and arrests of Black people) cannot be used to evaluate hypotheses about differential offending rates, then neither can it provide an adequate basis for assertions about the existence of police racism. In this view, the anti-empiricist approach wrongly presents social science as aspiring to "god-like certainty" rather than the more modest aim of making decisions in light of the best available evidence. Although clearly it is important to be explicit about the weaknesses of the various statistical studies, they remain an important part of the available evidence.

As outlined in an earlier section, most available research has shown that Black people are overrepresented in the police stop and arrest statistics. However, this was not always the case. It was not until the 1970s that the debate about "Black criminality" really surfaced in Britain. In fact, early studies (based on the "race" of people in police arrest statistics) suggested that the then largely immigrant communities in British cities were equally (or less) likely to be arrested than White people. By the mid-1970s, however, such figures were showing a different picture. The Metropolitan Police published statistics that showed higher than average "offending rates" (measured by arrests) among the "West Indian/

African" population. These rather raw data did not take age or gender distributions into account, and the ensuring public debate thus paid little attention to the fact that ethnic minority communities tend to have higher proportions of people in the "peak-offending" age groups. However, later research commissioned by the Home Office found that variables such as age structure and economic deprivation explained some but not all of the ethnic differences in arrest rates. Although some of the remaining differences could be explained in terms of police behavior (for example targeting particular kinds of crime, neighborhood, or even ethnic minority groups), the findings also suggested higher than average offending rates within certain groups.

The finding that young Black men are overrepresented in the arrest statistics for certain kinds of crime, even when a number of relevant variables have been controlled, is supported by most other studies. The problem with using such figures as evidence of higher offending rates, or of police racism, is that they represent the outcome of a sequence of interactions between a range of variables. Although useful in illustrating the effect of broader structural factors, for example, the association of unemployment and crime, this kind of study is unable to shed any light on the interactional processes between such factors. Furthermore, such studies focus only on the fraction of offenses that result in an arrest. The overall picture is highly dependent upon the kind of offense being considered, because ethnic minority groups are relatively underrepresented in arrests for certain kinds of offense, such as company fraud or tax evasion.

A more recent addition to the available evidence about ethnicity and offending has come from self-report studies. A recent Home Office study of offending and drug use among young British people found White and African Caribbean respondents reported very similar rates of overall participation in offending, and each of the South Asian groups had substantially lower rates of participation, with the findings broadly consistent across offense type. Although this provides a significant counterfinding to the main body of research on ethnicity and crime, it is important to note that self-report studies, as with the other empirical studies, have a number of significant weaknesses when it comes to making quantitative estimates.

In general then, it is clear that Black people are overrepresented in the arrest statistics for certain kinds of crime. On the balance of the available evidence, it is likely that this results from a combination of factors, including higher actual rates of offending among Black groups. This should not be a surprising or contentious finding, given the link between certain kinds of crime with deprivation and unemployment, and the overrepresentation of Black people in such disadvantaged groups. Given what we know about the attitudes that characterize police occupational culture, it is probable that racial discrimination is also important, although we should beware of drawing simple causal connections between attitudes and behavior. Thus, there is a vicious circle in which both police and Black youth deviance are amplified. Attempts to statistically "measure" how much unequal treatment of minorities relates to pure racism provide important evidence about this vicious circle of amplification, but are only a part of the picture. The focus should also be on the ways and forms in which racialized relations arise and develop over time. The challenge for future research is to combine the various approaches to the subject, in order to understand better the social processes that result in constructions of racial difference such as stop and arrest rates.

II. MEASURES TO ADDRESS PROBLEMATIC RELATIONSHIPS

A. Improvements in Wider Society

Although commentators strongly disagree about the extent to which problematic police–Black relationships are caused by police discrimination or higher offending rates, there is wider agreement that the prejudice and inequality of wider society operates as the basic trigger that sets the cycle in motion. In Britain, there was some evidence at the end of the 1980s of some improvements in the overall socioeconomic positions of certain ethnic groups. However, these did not include the "Black" groups that are the particular focus of problematic relationships with the police. An equally significant development is the divergence of economic circumstances within the South Asian population. On average, Muslim South Asians (Pakistanis and Bangladeshis) in Britain found themselves in substantially poorer living circumstances than the Black population by the end of the 1980s. Research has yet to shed light on the ways in which such developments are effecting relationships between the police and members of these particular groups.

Although police involvement in conflict is to a large degree determined by forces outside of police organizations, certain styles or aspects of policing may well exacerbate already-present trends and encourage conflict to become entrenched and endemic. Robert Reiner (1992) has argued, "the police are reproducers rather than creators of social injustice, although their prejudices may amplify it" (Reiner, R. (1992). *The politics of the police.* (2nd Ed.). Hemel Hempstead: Harvester). It is this amplification effect to which reformers must address their efforts, and the development of measures that can be taken to address problematic relationships within the framework of policing.

B. Police-Specific Improvements

1. Policing Policy—Changing the Pattern of Policing

It is possible that problematic relationships between the police and certain sections of the community reflect ineffective mechanisms of police accountability. It could be argued that the police (and policing policy) have become distanced from the communities that they police, with resulting increases in tension and hostility with some groups. There is clearly a need for policing to be broadly congruent with the needs and wishes of the community to be policed, while retaining adequate safeguards to ensure adequate law enforcement, and to prevent control of policing by partisan interests. Accountability to the "community" is a central theme in British police rhetoric, although the notion of exactly what is meant by community in this regard is highly problematic. In particular, as far as policing is concerned, there are many "publics" upon which policing impinges in totally different ways. There is strong evidence that certain policing policies and strategies are more likely to bring the police into conflict with Black people. This was most clearly illustrated by police actions prior to the Brixton disorders, when police stop-and-search operations targeted a very large number of Black youths, contributing to an explosion of resentment and hostility. It has thus been suggested that changes in the pattern of policing are a precondition of reduced tension and hostility between the police and some ethnic minority groups. In this view, an important policy objective should be to reduce the number of conflictual encounters between the police and Black people, to try to bring about a gradual reduction in the base of experience in which Black criticism of the police is grounded. This would mean a careful consideration of the use of policies such as stop and search in areas of significant racial tension and hostility. A second matter of "policy" that might improve police–Black relationships concerns the symbolic significance of the police, as the most visible sign of social authority. If the police were required to make major public gestures to help Black people, for example by taking strong and effective action against racial attacks, this might help to reduce hostile relationships.

The opportunities for external bodies to influence the pattern of policing are, however, rather limited. The very nature of police work, an often-invisible process involving the extensive discretion on the part of individual police officers, makes it a very difficult process to control. In both the U.S. and British police systems, there is a degree of accountability to local elected bodies. In the U.S. city police departments, the chief of police is answerable to the elected mayor, and can be sacked from post. Political mobilization of Black people was far greater in the United States following the 1960s disturbances than was the case in Britain following the 1980s. This growth in Black political influence may have led to some improvements in police–Black relations in the United States. In England and Wales, police forces are administered by police authorities, of which the majority are locally elected representatives. Black involvement on these bodies has remained rather limited, and in any case, police authorities have traditionally had little influence over police policy-making, and chief police officers have retained a large measure of independence.

The debate following the inner-city riots in Britain during the 1980s highlighted the need for policing policy to be more closely in tune with the wishes of local people. One attempt to address this was the development in Britain of local "police consultative committees," which provide a regular forum for discussion of policing policy and exchange of views between local police commanders and representatives from a variety of community groups, and often from the general public. Most research on these committees has, however, suggested that they have yet to have any major effect on the pattern of policing locally, although they have some uses as information sharing forums. In many cases, these committees are rather unrepresentative, and have too few resources, and too little information and experience to influence the pattern of local policing substantively.

2. Addressing Occupational Culture—Recruitment and Training

Although the relationship between prejudiced attitudes and behavior is not straightforward, there is evidence that police occupational culture helps to foster and reinforce racial prejudice. One way of addressing this problem could be to improve recruitment procedures in order to remove prejudiced individuals from the process, and also to increase the number of police officers from ethnic minority groups. Another widely used response to problematic police–Black relations adopted by Western police forces has been the introduction of training programs designed to counter racial ignorance and prejudice.

a. Recruitment

One critical distinction between Britain and North America is that there is no British equivalent to the "Contract Compliance" legislation in the United States. This kind of legislation restricts federal funding for projects that fail to meet "formal hiring quotas" for minority groups. A number of police departments across the United States responded to problems in their relationships with Black people by introducing recruitment campaigns to increase ethnic minority representation on their staff. It was argued that positive effects for police–Black relations would follow from the use of officers familiar with the social and cultural norms of the area to be policed. For example, Black officers are more familiar with the nonverbal signals of other Black people that may often be interpreted by White officers as threats, thus exacerbating conflictual relationships. There has been a growth in the number of Black officers in U.S. police departments since the 1960s, which has been related to wider societal changes, antidiscrimination laws in local government, recognition of the political value of Black officers in the police, and the increasing willingness of Black officers to organize and fight discrimination. As noted earlier, though, there remains an underrepresentation of ethnic minority officers among the staffs of U.S. police departments.

In Britain, concern about the low levels of ethnic minority representation within police forces dates back to the mid-1970s, but really gathered pace following the 1981 inner-city disturbances. In particular, the Scarman report following the Brixton riots recommended prominent and committed police policies to improve relationships with Black people, including those directed at recruiting more people from ethnic minority groups to the service. This has led to various initiatives; some forces have changed height restrictions which were seen as discriminating against some ethnic groups, and others have introduced special access courses to increase the number of ethnic minority people passing the initial police recruitment assessment test. Other schemes include the organization of public meetings about joining the police, special advertisements directed at people from the ethnic minorities, and leafleting in areas of high ethnic minority concentration. Progress has been slow, and by the mid-1990s, ethnic minority people remained significantly underrepresented in British police forces compared to their proportion in the working-age population. Research has suggested that one of the most important factors preventing the recruitment of more ethnic minorities to the police is the expectation of prejudice from future colleagues.

In the British context, hiring quotas and affirmative action policies of the North American kind would be unlawful, although special training and hiring campaigns can be designed to target racial minority groups. There is evidence that many currently serving ethnic minority police officers oppose hiring quotas and positive discrimination, fearing that such policies would stigmatize them as "second class" police officers. Recruitment campaigns by British police forces have generally failed to address the main factors inhibiting minority applications; namely, race relations within the organization and relationships with the local Black and South Asian communities. Increased ethnic minority recruitment to the British police service has thus been constrained by the British legal tradition (which does not allow positive discrimination) and by the structure of ethnic relations within contemporary British society.

In general, the available research suggests increasing the recruitment of minorities, unless done at very significant levels, has rather limited effects on police culture. Making police forces more ethnically representative is better justified as a good in itself, or by reference to some other reason, such as improving employment prospects for ethnic minority people. Most research suggests that it is unrealistic to expect such initiatives by themselves to bring about significant improvements in relationships between the police and Black people. Studies have shown that many Black officers come to adopt the organization's *status quo,* including the working assumptions of other police officers. Black officers can face the double-edged sword of discrimination and racism from their own colleagues, and isolation and vilification from some members of their own community who regard them as turncoats.

b. Training

There is a general trend within Western European and North American police forces, away from training based mainly on legalistic enforcement, to a much broader and socially aware interpretation of the police role. This is partly intended to train recruits in wider social skills to counteract the perceived negative side effects of the occupational culture. Similar arguments apply to these developments as apply to reforms of recruitment policies. Although it may have some beneficial effects, it is perhaps unrealistic to expect training alone to change police occupational culture. In particular, it is argued that such approaches "individualize" racial prejudice,

which is not so much a product of the dispositions that the recruit brings to the job, but rather is produced or entrenched by particular experiences as police officers. Arguably, it is the practice of police work in the company of fellow police officers that produces prejudiced attitudes. Job-based culture may be too resilient to be significantly affected by training.

There have been many training initiatives in Britain and the United States, including human relations training programs aimed at reducing the propensity for racial prejudice among officers, and through encouraging an improvement in the general educational level of police officers by introducing special college-training programs. As with recruitment intiatives, while improved training may be beneficial for a variety of reasons, it is important to remain aware of its limitations as a cure for the ills of racial prejudice and discrimination. As noted above, such programs often fail to recognize the social nature of racial prejudice, which is a learned pattern of beliefs and behaviors. Although training can play an important part in improving service delivery, it cannot be effective in isolation from wider organizational commitment and support within a positive framework of equal opportunities. Training remains a low-status activity within police forces, reflecting the commonly held view by police officers that policing is basically learned on the job. Much of the available research on training has been focused on evaluation via psychological measures of attitudinal change. However, as outlined earlier, the relationship between attitudes and actual behavior is an indirect and complex one. Thus, even if training programs are successful in reducing the amount of stated racial prejudice among groups of police officers, this will not automatically translate into improved relationships between the police and Black people. Although studies of police training have provided some limited indications about positive short-term effects on attitudes, only longer-term qualitative approaches will provide evidence about more fundamental changes in policing behavior.

3. Redress

a. Formal Complaints Systems

Complaints mechanisms in Western police systems vary in terms of their degree of independence from the police, and the extent to which they have the power to impose decisions upon the police organization. On a general policy level, many complaints mechanisms are limited to reporting back to legislatures and councils that can have only a limited and indirect impact on the dynamics of the police organization. The key critical feature of such systems is that they tend, like the criminal justice systems they mimic, to operate reactively in response to complaints from individuals and to solve problems by blaming and punishing individuals. Critics of such systems have argued that calls for complaints systems should focus upon the police organization itself, rather than individuals within it.

In Britain, the 1984 Police and Criminal Evidence Act established the independent Police Complaints Authority (PCA). It supervises the investigation of incidents referred to the Authority by the police because of their gravity. The PCA also comments on a regular basis on certain police practices and policies. The standard of proof in disciplinary cases has traditionally been that the case must be proved "beyond reasonable doubt," which makes it extremely difficult to substantiate a case against a police officer. However, it has been decided to change the standard of proof to one of "reasonableness," which is expected to lead to more disciplinary cases against officers being successful. Research on the operation and "effectiveness" of the PCA suggests that the system is some distance away from working to the satisfaction of its "users"—be they complainants or police officers. There is doubt about whether the existence and operation of the complaints system applies sanctions in such a way as to constitute a genuine deterrent to rude or aggressive behavior by police officers. Studies suggest that the majority of complainants are dissatisfied by the response to and outcome of their complaints and that, partly as a consequence, the system fails to meet one of its main objectives—winning public confidence in the system. The general conclusion from the research in Britain is that without either more effective means for facilitating police–public consultation and/or mechanisms of accountability that involve more than post hoc explanation of individual actions, whatever means are used for handling complaints will have little impact.

Recent surveys have suggested that the level of knowledge about the police complaints system is significantly lower among ethnic minorities than among White people. There is also evidence that ethnic minority people hold more negative views of the effectiveness and fairness of the police complaints procedure. Statistics about relative overall rates of usage of complaints systems are, however, very difficult to interpret. For example, a low tendency to make complaints may be interpreted as being indicative of either high levels of satisfaction with police actions, or very low levels of confidence in the complaints system. Research has suggested that complaints by Black people have a lower substantiation rate than those of other ethnic groups, although substantiation rates for all groups is low.

b. Legal Redress

It has been suggested that the increasing use of civil litigation in the United States has been a major factor influencing improvements in police behavior towards racial minorities. During the 1960s there was simultaneously a large increase in the supply of lawyers, and a narrowing in the scope of sovereign immunity. Although direct effects of civil litigation on police practice are difficult to prove, such developments may have reduced the sense of powerlessness felt by many Black people in dealings with the police. In Britain, there has been a growing tendency for people who feel they have been unfairly victimized by the police to take civil action in the courts rather than pursue a formal complaint. The large amounts of money paid by the Metropolitan Police, either in civil damages or out-of-court settlements, is testimony to the growing popularity of this avenue of redress. A number of high-profile damages cases have involved Black people, the effect of which may be to increase the pressure on police organizations to improve policy and practice in race relations.

III. CONCLUSIONS

There is clear evidence along a number of dimensions of problematic relationships between the police and some ethnic minority groups. Black people in particular are subject to a high degree of unequal treatment by the police in that they are disproportionately stopped and arrested. However, it has proved extremely difficult to establish how far this is due to racial discrimination by the police, and how much is due to higher offending rates among Black people. The strong evidence of past studies about the pervasiveness of racist views among rank-and-file police officers suggests that discrimination is a factor, although the connection between attitudes and action is indirect and complex. Such prejudiced views appear to be encouraged and entrenched by occupational culture, and the day-to-day experience of police work in societies characterized by ethnic tensions. The available evidence also suggests that some ethnic groups are disproportionately involved in particular kinds of crime. This has led to contentious debates about "Black criminality" on the one hand, and racism within the criminal justice system on the other. The most trenchant positions are adopted by those at one end of the spectrum who argue that Black people are inherently more likely to offend, and those at the other who see "Black crime" as an illusory construction of a racist society. However, the most generally accepted view is that both police (and societal) racism and higher offending rates reinforce and feed off of each other in a cycle of amplification. One problem for those who explain higher rates of police stop and arrest of Black people purely in terms of an undifferentiated color racism, is how to explain why such an affect appears not to apply to the South Asian groups. If the explanation is to be couched in terms of racism, it appears that different forms of racism are being applied to different groups. Major improvements in relations between the police and ethnic minorities ultimately lie in an easing of racial antagonism in wider society. However, within the framework of policing, Western societies have seen a number of developments intended to address such problematic relationships. Much faith has been placed in better recruitment and training procedures, to increase ethnic minority representation within the police organization, and to reduce the racial prejudice within police occupational culture. Taken alone, such reforms can ultimately have only a rather marginal effect (although in themselves they are undoubtedly beneficial). Perhaps the best hope of improvement lies in controlling the pattern of policing, so as to reduce the antagonistic base of experience that fosters much hostility between Black people and the police.

Also See the Following Articles

DISCRIMINATION, CONCEPT OF • ETHNOCULTURAL MINORITIES, STATUS AND TREATMENT OF • POLICE ACCOUNTABILITY

Bibliography

FitzGerald, M. (1993). *Ethnic minorities and the criminal justice system.* Research Study No. 20. Royal Commission on Criminal Justice. London: HMSO.

Gelsthorpe, L., & McWilliam, W. (Eds.). (1993). *Minority ethnic groups and the criminal justice system.* Cambridge: Cambridge University Institute of Criminology.

Holdaway, S. (1996). *The racialisation of British policing.* Basingstoke: Macmillan.

Jones, T. (1993). *Britain's ethnic minorities.* London: Policy Studies Institute.

Skogan, W. G. (1994). *Contacts between police and public: Findings from the 1992 British crime survey.* Home Office Research Study No. 134. London: HMSO.

Smith, D. J. (1994). Race, crime and criminal justice. In R. Reiner, R. Morgan, & M. Maguire (Eds.), *The Oxford handbook of criminology,* pp. 1041–1117. Oxford: Oxford University Press.

Wilbanks, W. (1987). *The Myth of a Racist Criminal Justice System.* Monterey, CA: Brooks/Cole.

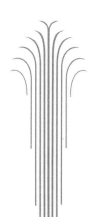

POLITICAL CORRECTNESS

Edward Johnson
University of New Orleans

GLOSSARY

cultural left/right Vague labels for the various individuals, forces, and practices that lend cultural support to social theories associated with the political viewpoint of "radicals" (and, sometimes, "liberals") or "conservatives" (and, sometimes, "liberals"), respectively.

hegemony A complex idea, influentially developed by the Italian Marxist Antonio Gramsci, concerning how social power is exercised through political, economic, and, especially, cultural forms which collectively shape and manipulate individual consent; emphasis may be put either on the determinative power of such cultural forms or on their contradictory and contestable nature.

identity politics The idea that politics is, and perhaps should be, based on the particular social identities of individuals, typically as defined by group membership.

natural lottery The distribution of (socially valuable) natural characteristics among individuals; associated with the idea, defended by American liberal theorist

John Rawls, that advantages founded on this arbitrary distribution are properly subject to the constraints of a theory of justice.

oppositional discourse Texts and other cultural products that call into question the dominant framework of values and assumptions; the opposite of hegemonic discourse.

repressive tolerance The idea, articulated by Herbert Marcuse, that "tolerance" for behavior (including, especially, speech behavior) can operate as a sophisticated means of preventing it from effecting real social change.

social constructionism The idea that key features of personal identity are artifacts based on social preconceptions rather than biologically or metaphysically given; the notion that, in previously unsuspected areas, controllable "nurture" takes precedence over uncontrollable "nature" in carving out an individual's (socially significant) identity.

POLITICAL CORRECTNESS became a popular term at the beginning of the 1990s as a negative characterization by members of the political/cultural "right" of restrictions on speech and behavior imposed by the "left." The term has a history, however, going back several decades. In its most general sense, it refers to a phenomenon as old as politics itself: adherents of a particular political position criticizing each other for acting in ways inconsistent with the spirit of their shared commitment (not adhering to "the party line"). In the 1960s, if not before, members of the left came to apply the standard of political correctness (PC) to each other's actions somewhat *ironically,* in a spirit of self-mockery. But the term was also used as a serious form of criticism as far back as the 1940s and 1950s, and perhaps even earlier. The term figured in later leftist-influenced movements, such as feminism, in the 1970s and 1980s.

I. THE POPULAR DEBATE ABOUT POLITICAL CORRECTNESS

As Stanley Fish notes, "in 1989, 'political correctness' had not yet become a code phrase for the supposed sins of the academic world." By the end of 1990, however, the media had picked up the phrase, and in May 1991, President George Bush, in a commencement address at the University of Michigan, attacked "political correctness" by name. Social critics at that time, in such works as Roger Kimball's *Tenured Radicals: How Politics Has Corrupted Our Higher Education* (1990) and Dinesh D'Souza's *Illiberal Education: The Politics of Race and Sex on Campus* (1991), claimed to discern a tyranny of politically correct speech, thought, and behavior imposed on students by professors who themselves had been radical students in the 1960s. These "tenured radicals," having failed to transform society, had retreated to the academy, where they were busy corrupting the next generation.

Many in the academy have responded by denying that political correctness in this sense really exists (except, of course, for the occasional aberration). Anti-PC media critics such as George Will view this denial as itself merely another PC phenomenon: "... the new tenet of political correctness is that political correctness does not exist."

Despite such denials, the term caught on (perhaps because of its widespread employment in the communications media and for marketing purposes) and entered the language. It has been defined as "intolerance of intolerance"—with all the ambiguity those words imply. Most often, the term has come to serve as a catchall phrase for the debate between left and right about the substance of education and the proper path for social progress.

During the first half-dozen years of the 1990s, political correctness became the subject of widespread commentary, analogized to everything from Elliot Richardson's "mild pressure ... not unlike that re-

sulting from parental insistence on politeness" to the slide during the French Revolution from the Rights of Man to the Terror, in Richard Bernstein's *Dictatorship of Virtue* (1994). Conservatives argue that the student radicals of the 1960s became the professors of the 1970s, were tenured and promoted in the 1980s, and now control academia. Many leftists dismiss the charges as false; or, if not false, then exaggerated; or, if not exaggerated, then irrelevant, an attempt to divert attention from social injustice. They point out what little influence they have in the academy compared to conservatives.

Others who explicitly avow a leftist political agenda are themselves critical of political correctness and identity politics. Political correctness, Richard Ohmann says, is often "a self-indulgent substitute for politics"; identity politics may simply "mirror the ideology of the marketplace." In his view, "our aim is not to affirm cultural identities and enforce correct attitudes; it is to scrap the tired yet violent project of capitalist patriarchy." This is, however, to construe political correctness very narrowly, and does not address what anti-PC critics, politics aside, find most perplexing—namely, the fact that politics does not seem to get put aside.

Many examples have been reported, though the details and the frequency of the incidents are commonly disputed by anti-anti-PC critics. An often recounted instance involved a University of Pennsylvania student on a "diversity education" committee who wrote a memo in which she mentioned her "deep regard for the individual." An administrator marked the word "individual" and suggested, "This is a 'RED FLAG' phrase today, which is considered by many to be RACIST. Arguments that champion the individual over the group ultimately privilege the 'individuals' who belong to the largest or dominant group." A second example is recounted by D'Souza, who after a presentation was accused by an Afro-American Studies professor of advancing racist views. The professor denied, however, that he was calling D'Souza a racist. "You are a person of color. *You cannot be a racist.* You don't have power in this society. Only whites can be racist."

It is this rejection of familiar standards (such as the value of individualism), combined with the invocation of double standards, which provokes many anti-PC critics. The deep issue raised by debates about political correctness relates to the pervasiveness of politics. This can be seen most easily in one of the central documents in the radicalization of the left—Herbert Marcuse's famous essay, "Repressive Tolerance" (1965). As he put the point in his 1968 postscript:

The Left has no equal voice, no equal access to the mass media and their public facilities—not because a conspiracy excludes it, but because ... it does not have the required purchasing power. And the Left does not have the purchasing power because it is the Left. These conditions impose upon the radical minorities a strategy which is in essence a refusal to allow the continuous functioning of allegedly indiscriminate but in fact discriminate tolerance. ... Not "equal" but *more* representation of the Left would be equalization of the prevailing inequality.

It is a short distance from this to the philosophy professor who defended using the classroom to move students toward Marxism by saying, "If they want the other side, they should watch TV or read the newspapers." Over the course of time, this idea metamorphoses into crude leftist slogans, such as "No freedom of speech for fascists." If instances of political correctness were nothing more than bad behavior, the subject would hold limited interest. What makes it an important topic in social theory and applied ethics is the question of whether this asymmetry can be justified.

II. THE UNDERLYING PHILOSOPHICAL ISSUES

A. Two Rationales for Multiculturalism

To understand the rationale for multiculturalism is to be in a better position to comprehend the surface phenomena associated with political correctness. It will be useful to distinguish between a positive and a negative rationale.

1. The Positive Rationale

The positive rationale for multiculturalism appeals to ideas about democratizing education and everyday life. This idea was explicit in Paolo Freire's widely celebrated efforts to develop in South America a "pedagogy of the oppressed" (described in his 1968 book of the same name), as well as in "liberation theology" which was, as Phillip Berryman has characterized it,

Freirean in spirit ... focusing on those who are marginalized, calling for a "liberating education," and stating that education should be "democratized." Education should not mean incorporating people into existing cultural structures but "giv-

ing them the means so that they can be the agents of their own progress."

A secular analogue—liberation without the theology—has been pursued by many social critics in the United States during the past three decades; indeed, in its "socialist" guise, since the 19th century. One of the traditional problems with socialism was that it threatened to replicate in its organization the very hierarchical structures it criticized in traditional society. The positive rationale reflects an uncertainty about the "imperialism" of imposing on a subject culture—even in the guise of aid—the practices and preconceptions of one's own culture, as though one knew everything about the other's problems. It is the anthropologist's guilty conscience, the suspicion that it would be better to approach an intercultural interaction with questions rather than answers. This democratizing impulse remains a powerful legacy of the 1960s, if not indeed of much older traditions claimed by both the left and the right.

2. The Negative Rationale

In earlier times the appeal to democracy was usually thought to involve some universal truth (such as the "Rights of Man"). That such an appeal is no longer unproblematic is related to the negative rationale for multiculturalism, which involves an alleged overthrow of the very idea of hierarchy in human life.

Behind this negative rationale lies a long philosophical debate, indeed one as old as that between Plato and the sophists. Western philosophy has been, as Alfred North Whitehead said, a series of footnotes to Plato because it has consisted of a series of attempts to find the best place from which to see how things really are; it has sought an "epistemologically-privileged position." At the end of the 19th century, Nietzsche called this whole idea into question—with what success is disputed, but his influence on the 20th century has been, for good or ill, decisive. Many thinkers in the present century have seen Nietzsche, perhaps along with Marx and Freud, as having unmasked the "rationality" of culture and exposed the power struggles beneath the deceptive surface. When Allan Bloom, in his surprise bestseller *The Closing of the American Mind: How Higher Education Has Failed Democracy and Impoverished the Souls of Today's Students* (1987), suggested that Nietzsche was somehow responsible for the decline of American education, it was this turn—from Plato to the sophists, from logic to rhetoric, from reason to relativism, from truth to power—he was lamenting. From his perspective, just thought must reside in the canon of truth-bearing texts history has bequeathed to us. Precisely these views, however, are called into question by the philosophical attitudes which underlie the negative rationale for multiculturalism.

B. Three Philosophical Theories

1. Antiessentialism

An important trend has been the emergence of antiessentialism. From Socrates on, philosophers largely assumed that the things a word named must share some common property or properties, some "essence." The nature of this essence and the character of our epistemological access to it have been defined in various ways by different philosophers, but the quest for certainty about the essences of things has persisted. The rejection of the idea of essence, in the present century, can be presented in many ways. (Perhaps the simplest, and one of the most influential, is found in Wittgenstein's discussion of "family resemblance," which seems to show that there does *not* have to be a single property shared by all instances of a given concept.) With the idea of essence goes the notion of a timeless, unchanging framework of both knowledge and reality. Historicism is a natural companion to this new contingency of things.

In the 19th century, the Enlightenment picture (exemplified in Kant) of essential human nature gave way to increasingly historicist (and, especially in the Romantic movement, localist) viewpoints. Kant's fixed categories gave way to Hegel's vision of the shifting constellations of the spirit. Marx materialized Hegel's spirit, and searched for the shaping forces in class structure and the relations of production, but still clung to the idea of a teleological (goal-given) social dynamic. When this teleology is lost, so is the notion of progress, and with the idea of progress disappears the ability to claim that one cultural condition is superior to another. History ceases to be seen as the revelation of divine meaning, or as the unfolding of the mind, or even as a groping toward utopia. What is left but the characterization of cultural change as a series of power struggles between interest groups, between "us" and "them"?

2. Social Constructionism

The course this complex intellectual heritage has taken in recent decades underlies the negative rationale for multiculturalism. One legacy is the idea of social constructionism. From this point of view, various aspects of life are understood not as expressions of a timeless human nature, but rather as something created by particular social interactions. Thus, an expression of gender may be viewed as the product of a certain set of social understandings, power relations, etc. But if a trait or a practice is socially constructed, rather than given by nature, then it may seem to be open to change (though this assumption requires careful scrutiny). Under the influence of Michel Foucault, among others, there has thrived the project of unmasking apparently neutral, natural givens as in fact socially constructed obfuscations of power relations. As Foucault put it,

> The real political task . . . is to criticize the working of institutions that appear to be both neutral and independent; to criticize them in such a manner that the political violence which has always exercised itself obscurely through them will be unmasked so that one can fight them.

3. Indeterminacy of Meaning

Another legacy is the idea that meaning is indeterminate; thus, the meaning even of these social constructions is ultimately determined by the one who does the interpreting. This view is decisively expressed in the thinkers who began in the 1960s to speak of the "death of the author." In other words, instead of there being a determiner of meaning outside of the process of interpretation (the "author's intention"), human creators are obliged to participate in a system of meaning over which they have little control, since the meaning of one's words depends on their place in a structure larger than one's life.

With a postmodernist philosopher such as Jacques Derrida, this notion of the radical indeterminacy of meaning, and the inescapability of the process of interpretation, acquires new power, as we learn how the text may work against itself, and may in fact speak most eloquently about what it omits. (Of course, what it omits is almost everything, so we need another theory to tell us to which omissions we should pay most attention.)

C. American Cultural Relativism

1. Thomas Kuhn

Among American philosophers, Richard Rorty has had an influence on the multiculturalism debate, though, as a "liberal" defender of "ethnocentrism," his political relationship to multiculturalism is complicated. Rorty's position can be very roughly characterized as, among other things, an extension to culture at large of the attitude pioneered in Thomas Kuhn's *The Structure of Scientific Revolutions* (1962, rev. 1970), which decisively revised the philosophical (and, to some extent, the popular) conception of how science functions.

Before Kuhn, there had been a tendency to see science, or at least natural science, as the model of rationality, proceeding through careful accumulation of evidence and logical deduction to conclusions which, if they failed of certainty, did so only because of mistakes (which we can correct) or the limits of the evidence (which we can hope to improve). Kuhn made an influential but controversial case that science actually works in a much more complicated way, in which dominant ideas and practices (which depend on, and partly constitute, "paradigms" of "normal" science) play a decisive role in determining what is counted as evidence and how the evidence is construed. The precise nature of a "paradigm" was much controverted (one critic noted 21 different senses of the term), but out of Kuhn flowed a new approach to the philosophy of science, one in which virtues traditionally ascribed to science, such as "rationality" and "progress," were increasingly viewed as contestible, historical concepts subject to change.

2. Richard Rorty

In *Philosophy and the Mirror of Nature* (1980), Richard Rorty explicitly generalized Kuhn's notion of normal science into the concept of "normal discourse," defined as any discourse embodying agreed-upon criteria for reaching agreement (a version of Kuhn's notion of paradigm). He argued that "the attempt (which has defined traditional philosophy) to explicate 'rationality' and 'objectivity' in terms of conditions of accurate representation is a self-deceptive effort to eternalize the normal discourse of the day." The broad influence of this book and several subsequent ones, including *Contingency, Irony, and Solidarity* (1989), played an important role in undermining the traditional *essentialist* case for liberal values.

At the beginning of the 1990s, Rorty was still inclined to claim that some political engagement was a necessary feature of a vital humanities program, though he counted on "academic freedom and collegial good manners" to prevent undesirable suppression of unpopular political persuasions. In *Essays on Heidegger and Others* (1991), he said,

> There are already indications that leftist political correctness is becoming a criterion for faculty hiring. But, with luck, these injustices will be no worse than those which contemporary academic leftists endured from exponents of "traditional humanistic values" in the course of their own rise to power.

Already in the late 1980s, however, he had registered his discomfort with important elements of the negative view of American society popular among members of the "cultural left." Though he joined in the criticism of Allan Bloom, he saw merit in E. D. Hirsch's "cultural literacy" project. By the mid-1990s he was sharply distancing his views from multiculturalism (and from postmodernism as well), arguing on the Op-Ed page of the *New York Times* that left-wing academic supporters of multiculturalism are "unpatriotic."

Rorty's experience provides a useful case study of the frustrations encountered even by antiessentialist liberals in remaining sanguine about political correctness. As David Hollinger recounts, in *Postethnic America* (1995):

> Rorty, as a defender of human rights, had managed by 1993 to distance himself dramatically from a syndrome criticized by the Aristotelian philosopher Martha Nussbaum ... [who had] heard anthropologists attack "Western essentialist medicine" for its "binary oppositions" such as life and death, and health and disease. One lamented the introduction of smallpox vaccination to India by the British because it "eradicated the cult of Sittala Devi, the goddess to whom one used to pray in order to avert smallpox," and thus exemplified "Western neglect of difference."

3. Stanley Fish

Some would doubt whether it is possible to be an antiessentialist liberal. Stanley Fish, who has been called the "high priest" of political correctness, is one of the most vocal critics of liberalism, which he considers incoherent. In his criticism of liberal values, Fish is an important source of the view that notions such as "free speech" and "discrimination" have a different meaning for victims and for oppressors.

It is in the critique of liberal values that the negative rationale for multiculturalism takes its most powerful, and perhaps disturbing, form. Politics is seen as pervasive because notions of neutrality, impartiality, objectivity, fairness, and so on have no absolute character. For Fish, there is no neutral standpoint to be occupied. Accordingly, the claim of traditional values to proceed from an impartial process should (sometimes) be unmasked; everything is political already, since "the truths any of us find compelling will all be partial, which is to say they will all be political."

Aside from being associated with the "bad company" of a long history of anti-immigration racism, the attack on political correctness is in Fish's view misconceived:

> Political correctness, the practice of making judgments from the vantage point of challengeable convictions, is not the name of a deviant behavior but of the behavior that everyone necessarily practices. Debates between opposing parties can never be characterized as debates between political correctness and something else, but [only as debates] between competing versions of political correctness.

Despite his critique of the attack on political correctness, Fish himself resists "the invocation of diversity as a principle, as a new theology." Though he has argued for the pervasiveness of politics, he has also defended the autonomy of professional standards ("professional correctness") against the demands for political relevance/action; he is "for politics and against Politics (the new transcendence)." For Fish, postmodernist stories about the constructed character of disciplines and their dependence on interpretive communities are correct, but the construction still creates a reality, albeit a partial and impermanent one.

Though Fish's views were apparently formed independent of Kuhn's influence, it is instructive to see them as a version of Kuhn's normal–revolutionary dichotomy. Kuhn, Rorty, and Fish are all figures who have, in various ways, helped to popularize the notion that what we know, or the truth to which we have access, depends crucially upon the ongoing functioning of communities which serve as interpreters of meaning, evidence, and argument. Their work was helped to smooth the way for an American version of social constructionism.

III. POLITICAL CORRECTNESS IN THE ACADEMY

A. The Curriculum Wars

1. Black Studies and Women's Studies

The war over the "canon" began with the perception that the set texts of the tradition often harbored language which expressed a low opinion of, or hostility to, previously subordinated social groups. As the civil rights movement led to programs devoted to the sympathetic exploration of blacks (for the term "Afri-

can-American," see further on), so the women's liberation movement gave birth to programs dedicated to women's studies. As these programs developed, their study of the character and effect of racism and sexism grew bolder. Soon, it seemed insufficient merely to catalog and repudiate earlier prejudice. Omission seemed a form of subordination, too; so scholars began to listen for the silenced voice of the oppressed throughout history: the voice of the slave, the voice of the wife. These interests were influenced by new directions in historiography, which sought the voice of the silent classes and searched for the trace of the everyday life of common people, rather than the epic exploits of heroes. They were also influenced by theoretical developments such as the deconstruction of Jacques Derrida, Paul de Man, and others, which offered new ways of discovering what a text *failed* to say, a failure which spoke volumes.

2. Gay and Lesbian Studies and Postcolonial Studies

Such studies expanded naturally to include other histories of systematic oppression. The movement for homosexual rights, under the labels of "Gay" and "Lesbian" scholarship, detailed millennia of "compulsory heterosexuality." Edward Said and others pointed out the West's longstanding misrepresentation of the Orient in books such as *Orientalism* (1978) and *Culture and Imperialism* (1993). The study of "postcolonialism" explored the ravages and vestiges of imperialism.

3. Cultural Studies

The proliferation of programs devoted to the study of the oppression/subordination/marginalization of various groups or conditions has natural links with the cultural studies movement. Patrick Brantlinger holds that "the best short definition of cultural studies" is Raymond Williams' characterization of "cultural materialism": "the analysis of all forms of signification ... within the actual means and conditions of their production." Ideology begins, says Brantlinger, "when ideas appear to be severed from the social conditions which produce them." Cultural studies had roots in the earlier "Frankfurt School" of Theodor Adorno, Max Horkheimer, Leo Lowenthal, Herbert Marcuse, and other social critics who explored the politics of popular culture, moving beyond the limits of "highbrow" culture to examine the ways in which popular ideas, products, and practices embodied, communicated, and supported preconceptions about the nature and value of human life. As Horkheimer succinctly put it, "It is not that chewing gum undermines metaphysics but that it *is* metaphysics."

4. New Lessons

In each of these new studies, what was at stake was perceived to be more than simply a set of forgotten, overlooked, or repressed facts. These studies held out the promise that understanding racism and imperialism, sexism and heterosexism, required a recovery of the point of view of "the Other," who had been systematically excluded from the culturally and epistemologically "privileged" conditions of social life.

Gradually, the liberal ideal of consistency and inclusion gave way before the challenge of epistemological separatism. The perception that the "voice" of, say, women in men's novels was often distorted, and in systematic ways which revealed the collusion of male self-interest, led naturally enough to the idea that women should be allowed to speak for themselves—and similarly for other groups. It is only a short trip from this to the idea that *only* a woman can speak as a woman, and that anything else is a kind of fraud. Furthermore, one might claim that a woman should speak only (or, always primarily) as a woman, a black as a black, etc. The impact of such doctrines on identity and, in the case of artists, productivity, is incalculable. In the case of minority authors, Richard Costa has asked, how much writer's block "can be assigned to fear of 'incorrectness,' to paranoia about daring to write against what was and is fashionable?" He notes that "in many of his essays, [Ralph] Ellison lamented that his life both as a man and as a writer changed when Negroes began to be referred to as blacks."

B. The New "Sensitivity"

Beyond the debate about curriculum, multiculturalism has challenged and changed the tone of campus life: new demands have been made for greater "sensitivity" in treatment of, and comment about, protected groups. Some institutions have adopted "speech codes" which define and restrict what can be said in and out of the classroom. These codes have excited widespread comment because of their tendency to define new, and sometimes surprising, forms of censurable conduct, as well as their tendency to attempt to apply relatively explicit, rigid, and codified rules to subtle and complex human interactions. (The sexual harassment policy adopted by Antioch College is a notorious example.)

C. Three Approaches

1. Prescriptive Approaches

One way to view the traditional approach to curriculum and campus climate is to see the university as civilizing students by showing them what they need to learn and how they need to act in order to assume their place as adults in "the great conversation." In at least some of its versions, the radical's displacement of traditional values is equally prescriptive: students need to "unlearn the lies" of Western civilization and adopt liberatory values. What the idea of *ignorance* is to the first approach, the idea of *false consciousness* is to the second.

2. Student Demand

There is a third approach, however, which rejects precisely the prescriptivity of both. According to this approach, the business of a university is to provide students not with what (according to some normative theory, conservative or radical) they "need," but rather simply to give them what they want—i.e., what they are willing to pay for. This is, roughly, the customer-is-king principle gone to college. On this view, what is transforming the academy is simply changing demographics. As society becomes *de facto* more multicultural, multiracial, and multilinguistic, businesses (including universities) must adapt.

For some, the elimination of racial, sexual, and other bias in determining who is well-off and who is not represents the vindication of capitalism. For others, the fact that inequalities of wealth and power continue—even, grow worse—under the new multicultural regime demonstrates the moral bankruptcy of less-than-radical critique. Underlying this dispute is a longstanding debate over *opportunity* versus *result*: Does equal treatment under the law mean that all individuals are ensured an equal opportunity to have access to social goods, or does it mean guaranteeing that everyone actually gets the same social goods?

D. Sponsored Research

Those who emphasize equality of result (in theory or in practice), as well as those who hold that equality of opportunity has yet to be attained, are apt to see the attack on political correctness not only as a restatement of conservative antiegalitarian ideals, but as in fact a diversionary tactic to draw attention away from what they see as the *real* political invasion of the university—its takeover by the money (and therefore the research agenda) of big business. (This argument has a conservative analogue, according to which it is big government that has distorted the university, as concern with grant money has displaced the traditional educational mission.)

Some analysts trace the chief features of higher education's decline to the influence of "sponsored research," where the bill is being paid by a corporation with a vested interest in specific results (for example, studies sponsored by tobacco interests to cast doubt on the health hazards of cigarette smoking). To the extent that specific results are being sought, the integrity of the research process may be questioned, especially if unwanted results are suppressed. In a media-driven society, there is a fine line between suppressing results and failing to give them due publicity.

It is also easier, in such a society, to blur the line between impropriety and the appearance of impropriety. Each side in the PC debate has pointed an accusing finger at the political connections and funding sources of its opponents—as though discovery of an interest amounted to a demonstration of bias.

A striking emblem of this ambiguity at the heart of the culture wars is the fact that Arthur Schlesinger's *The Disuniting of America: Reflections on a Multicultural Society* (1991) first appeared as a slim volume published by Whittle Communications, with numerous full-page magazine-style advertisements for Federal Express scattered throughout the volume. An earlier report on the canon debate, James Atlas's *The Book Wars: What It Takes to Be Educated in America* (1990), appeared in the same series. The philosophy of Chris Whittle, the politically well-connected man who headed Whittle Communications, was, "The biggest contribution business can make to education is to make education a business."

E. Four Factors in the Transformation of Higher Education

It is true that *faculty,* some of whom as students in the 1960s dismissed traditional educational values as "irrelevant," now exert some influence in the academy. But it is also true that the past three decades have seen enormous and complex changes in the substantive philosophical views of many professors, changes which call traditional justifications into question.

It is true that *students* who come to college now often seem less "literate," by conventional standards. Some critics insist that these students are merely "*differently* literate"—they know *other* things—and argue that the attribution of "illiteracy," cultural or otherwise, obscures generational, ethnic, or class disagreements about the relevant standards. If a decline exists, it may

have been caused by the political and cultural woes of the elementary and secondary education systems; or by changes in family structure or values; or by recent technological and economic shifts in society: television, malls, cyberspace, etc. Whatever the causes, students seem unable, or unwilling, to fit into the old definitions and fulfill the old expectations. A broader range of the population is going to college, but whether this should be seen as a triumph of "access," or as "dumbing down," has been hotly debated. David Berliner and Bruce Biddle, in *The Manufactured Crisis* (1995), argue that widespread claims of decline in American education seriously misrepresent the available evidence, which shows "that, on average, today's students are at least as well informed as students were in previous generations and that education in America compares favorably with education elsewhere."

It is true that the *government*—after World War II, and particularly after Sputnik raised the temperature of the Cold War—infused large sums into the academy, thereby to some degree altering its character. But the growth of the universities was also fueled by the postwar Baby Boom.

It is true that *business* has increasingly turned to universities, not only for training future and current employees (and retraining them), and not only to tap expertise, but especially to pursue "proprietary research" and lend (supposedly impartial) academic authority to what may be little more than market ploys. Yet often it is the universities which have come, mortarboard in hand, seeking funding to make up for cuts in state and federal funding, and decreases in student enrollments.

Clearly the simplest stories, whether of the right or the left, cannot explain the complex transformation in higher education.

IV. BEYOND THE ACADEMY

A. Social Injustice and Advocacy

1. Conflicting Ideals

The influence of the PC agenda, and of its critique, has been as multifaceted beyond the academy as on campus. American society has traditionally conceived of itself as, ideally if not actually, "indivisible, with liberty and justice for all." The right has seen these values as implicit in the status quo. The left has tended to see these values as deformed in practice by influence, wealth, race, sex, and other forms of bias. For the right, the heart of the American promise is equality of opportunity.

For the left, inequality of result has usually seemed presumptive evidence of absence of equal opportunity.

For the right, human inequality can be taken for granted. Individuals differ in ability, desire, commitment, perseverance, and luck, and these differences lead some to succeed in life and others to fail. To deny these differences is to fail to respect people as individuals, who make different choices and thereby earn different degrees of merit. For the left, in contrast, the presumption of equal worth means that we should be *very* suspicious about supposing that different choices reflect anything other than differential conditions.

For the right, the central element in freedom is social mobility—i.e., the ability of equality of opportunity to yield differential reward. Everyone has the (same) chance to get rich and rise to the top of society. For the left this is false. It is false, in the first place, because the chances are not in fact the same, but are skewed by various factors. But suppose, for the sake of argument, that these distorting factors could be overcome—that society could become colorblind, gender-blind, etc. (like the lady with the scales of justice). Some leftists might be satisfied with such a world, but many would not. For even if anybody could become rich, it would not follow that everybody can. A society with a built-in structural unemployment rate, for example, will not have full employment, even if the best jobs are fully open to merit (however that is defined). Conservatives who refute the claims of the poor by pointing to the want-ads overlook this obvious fact; that jobs are always available does not show that jobs are available for all.

Some leftists want a world in which the inequality between the rich and the poor disappears, or at least becomes minimal. To them, this difference (unless justified in some way, as, for example, by appeal to Rawls's "difference principle," which permits disparities that would make the worst-off members of society better off) is the ultimate injustice, since it is difficult to link any results of the "natural lottery" to desert. For this view, it is the job of society (within reason) to sit in judgment on natural assets, since no one deserves his natural assets (or hers either). For the radical egalitarian, what is yours is yours only because society is better off because it is yours. For the conservative inegalitarian, on the other hand, possession is presumptive evidence of right—unless it can be demonstrated that you have unjustly deprived others.

What the conservative views as the unfortunate, *but not unjust,* disparity between the lucky and the unlucky, the theorist of political correctness sees as the unjustified, and unjust, rejection of difference.

2. Critical Legal Studies

At the beginning of the 1980s, roughly a decade before the discussion of "political correctness" became popular, there appeared in the law schools and journals a precursor movement to multiculturalism. Critical Legal Studies (CLS) had roots in the early work of Roberto Unger—*Knowledge and Politics* (1975) and *Law in Modern Society* (1976)—but took decisive public shape in the 1980s, e.g., in David Kairys' *The Politics of Law* (1982) and Unger's 1986 *The Critical Legal Studies Movement* (1986). Drawing inspiration from Marxist theory, especially Gramsci, CLS embraces radical democracy and rejects the idea of the neutrality of law. Gramsci's notion of hegemony is seen as expanding the notion of the state to include civil society, so that it becomes possible to see the legal structure which supports the state as pervading, and being supported by, the culture at large. Particularly striking in this connection is Robert Gordon's explanation of the desire to move away from large-scale social theories:

> It may be that the place to look is somewhere quite different—in the smallest, most routine, most ordinary interactions of daily life in which some human beings dominate others and they acquiesce in such domination. It may be, as Foucault's work suggests, that the whole legitimating power of a legal system is built up out of such myriad tiny instances.

Out of CLS, and to some extent in criticism of it, grew Critical Race Theory, under the influence of Derrick Bell and others. Holding racial tension to be ineliminable, and neutrality impossible, this theory promotes a race-conscious advocacy approach to legal interpretation.

These forms of advocacy reach beyond the academy into the world of litigation, politics, and business in a more direct fashion than most academic disciplines.

B. Discrimination and Preferential Treatment

It is sometimes fair and appropriate, even laudable, to show "discriminating" taste. Exactly when such differential treatment is justified is one of the central questions of ethics. The phrase "preferential treatment" is approximately neutral. Those who strongly disapprove of a given preferential treatment policy often stigmatize it as "reverse discrimination," while those who approve of it often praise it as "affirmative action." Under the latter heading, the topic is discussed more fully elsewhere; our brief treatment is required because of the centrality of this topic to the concerns of political correctness.

The basic liberal defense of preferential treatment or affirmative action is simple. Some people have been the victims of seriously unfair treatment earlier in their lives. In many cases, the result of this maltreatment has been to put the individual at a competitive disadvantage with others whose social placement has been more fortunate. It would be morally idle to pretend that one can run a fair race against a man who has recently been unfairly beaten up—and this remains true even if one is in no way individually responsible for that beating.

This familiar appeal to "level playing fields" makes the justification of affirmative action apply to present individuals, rather than past groups. It also makes it apply regardless of any personal wrongdoing or responsibility on the part of those whose interests a policy of affirmative action weighs against. In addition, affirmative action on this account usually applies to matters where neither party can be said to have any specific right to the good at stake.

Despite these appealing analogies, however, the idea of "preferential treatment" remains unsettling, even to many liberals who support the idea of affirmative action, because the deviation from formal neutrality (itself a contested concept) is worrisome in such a complicated area of life, where the dangers of special pleading and self-deception seem very great. As a policy, affirmative action seems perpetually unstable since, by the very nature of the case, the question must constantly arise: Is it time to stop? Have we done enough to ensure a level playing field? (This instability does not bother those who, like Stanley Fish, view it as the unavoidable concomitant of any policy.)

Indeed, how are we to tell? If equality of opportunity is different from equality of result, then disparities of wealth and social influence will not be a reliable guide to the availability of fair opportunity. Those who see the gifts of nature as inequitably dispersed among the population will be more likely to explain patterns of success and failure in terms of those natural gifts. Those committed to equality may be tempted to view this as prejudice (racism, sexism, etc.), but the other guys are going to insist that they are just recognizing the way things are. Much can be done, to be sure, by way of discovering flaws and bias in the way relevant assessments of ability are made. But it will be hard to deny, in the end, that the question of how abilities break down in terms of groups is finally an *empirical* question. A commitment to the moral equality of, say, all human beings does not imply—and may even be empirically inconsistent with—an *a priori* judgment of factual equality.

Of course, after one has heard a lot of bad arguments for racial or sexual disparities (in intelligence, or whatever), it will not be surprising if patience grows short and suspicion grows long. But though suspicion may be useful (or even, perhaps, necessary) as a rule of thumb, it is not in itself a demonstration of the truth of what is suspected.

Some critics argue that engaging in debate with a morally repugnant position lends it intellectual respectability and misleads the indiscriminate public. If it is legitimate to refuse to debate those who argue that the Holocaust never occurred, as some claim, why is it not equally legitimate to decline engagement with those whose claims about race, sex, or whatever seem only another version of the old prejudice?

Such considerations lead critics such as Stanley Fish to argue that discrimination can only be fought by discrimination. If no one would want to call any post-Holocaust clannishness on the part of Jews racism, because it is an understandable reaction given their history, then why should one not say the same sort of thing about antiwhite sentiment on the part of blacks? Since neutrality is impossible, Fish thinks one should choose whichever side one thinks is morally right.

Many advocates of political correctness, however, go further and argue that since neutrality is impossible, one should side with the victim. This is far from the liberal position, where it is precisely respect for neutrality that justifies siding with the disadvantaged. With a little simplifying, this becomes the view that prejudice is only possible in one direction. We are told by Tom Lewis, for example, that " 'racism' requires the *power* to oppress—a power that blacks, Latinos, and other minorities do not possess in this society." This view is based on the reasonable idea that people in different situations may behave in ways that look the same, and yet remain morally very different. But the argument seems to assume that issues of power are more homogeneous than they really are. It is not the case that members of a given minority race are in every situation in life less empowered than whites, simply in virtue of race; or that women are always less empowered than men, because of sex. To claim otherwise is not only to override most people's real life experience and appeal to arbitrary theorizing, but is in fact to demean the status of all of those who are seen as automatically disabled simply because of their group status. And that seems itself racist, sexist.

V. CULTURAL CHANGE AND THE INTEGRITY OF LANGUAGE

During the two dozen centuries that separate Thucydides and George Orwell, many social critics have warned about the dangers of linguistic corruption. The difficulty lies in determining *which* changes in language are problematic, given that change is an inevitable part of the nature of language. Many issues raised by the debate over multiculturalism relate specifically to questions of language use, and the contentious social debates over multilingualism constitute a natural development of those issues.

A. Proper Language

1. Hateful and Offensive Speech

Language is cognitive and expressive, but it is also a weapon. Because speech is also an act, the law has always recognized certain limitations: "freedom of speech" does not justify my using a loudspeaker to damage your eardrums. In certain circumstances, e.g., under conditions favorable for a riot, the act aspect of speech may loom larger than its cognitive or expressive functions. The liberal position on such matters emphasizes the importance of giving individuals wide latitude in the absence of clear and present danger.

Stanley Fish has argued that the university should be viewed primarily as a workplace, subject to the sorts of restraints on expression common to the workplace, where what counts is people's being able to perform their jobs.

Certainly, if hate speech is permissible, speech that is merely offensive or "insensitive" would be hard to exclude. On the other hand, if even the ideal of academic freedom is thought not to exempt the university from policing its forms of expression in the name of correctness, then we will not be surprised to see, as we have, an increase in the imposition of new standards of feminist and multicultural sensitivity in society at large.

2. Good English

Thinking about the political correction of speech habits and linguistic practices raises the question of the character of language itself. Many writers have lamented the decline of English grammar and usage. Though these complaints have a point, they tend to overlook the fact that language is not static.

Feminist critics, for example, have suggested a variety of ways in which familiar English usage could be improved in order to diminish linguistic sexism. Such correction can be faddish and polemical at the expense of etymological sense—"herstory," for example. In other cases, the issues are more substantive. English is a language that to some degree marks gender. Is this a problem? Is there a *universal* meaning of "man" and "he," in addition to a *male* one? Should there be?

Many "PC" innovations flow out of concern about the power of language to stigmatize individuals or groups. But often it seems as though no language could ever be satisfactory, because of the perennial need to flee from unwanted connotations. Terms concerning disability are an example: "crippled," "handicapped," and "disabled" have yielded to "physically challenged," or even "differently abled." The same has been true of terms for race and sex. As Henry Louis Gates, Jr., put it in 1969, "My grandfather was colored, my father was a Negro, and I am black." More recently, "black" has in turn fallen into disfavor, replaced by "African-American" (even, sometimes, "person of color"). "African-American" has the advantage of seeming on a par with ethnic labels such as "Italian-American," but the analogy is false, as can be seen by asking whether Americans of Egyptian descent count as African-Americans. What the trip from "colored" to "people of color" may have accomplished is open to debate.

The discussion about good English also has been altered by the tendency to translate what used to be seen as issues about "proper" usage into claims about dialect alternatives. Beginning about 1970, a number of linguists argued for reconceptualizing many instances of "bad English" into legitimate forms of "Black English." For this reason, among others, elementary and secondary education has tended to deemphasize the correction/normalization of writing and talking in favor of approaches (praised and vilified under the name of "self-esteem") which allegedly encourage individuality and creativity. Critics claim that such an approach does native speakers of "Black English" a disservice, since it ill prepares them to compete linguistically in a society where "standard English" is the norm. This oft-repeated argument may be correct, though it is open to the reply that changing population demographics may mean that "standard English" is (or soon will be) no longer the standard.

Who determines the standard—i.e., what political interests are at work in linguistic domination—and whether there has to be a standard at all are important questions. When we look at Shakespeare—a man who spelled his name in a variety of ways—we may be reminded that great periods of literature have not necessarily required uniformity of spelling, grammar, or usage. Then again, maybe that lesson does not apply to the powerful, complex, highly integrated, modern world.

3. Multilingualism

The question, Why not many forms of English?, leads to the even larger question, Why not many languages? This question is most pressing in societies, such as Canada or India, where multiple languages have long had official recognition. But the question is increasingly urgent in supposedly monolinguistic societies such as the United States. In fact, the challenge of secondary languages has been so strong that, in many parts of the country, public functioning has had to be done in Spanish as well as English, and there has been a strong movement in favor of educating children in their home language as well as in English. All this has generated a vocal countermovement in favor of English only.

Because language is a central component of identity, the struggle for or against linguistic diversity connects to the arguments about multiculturalism and political correctness.

4. Representative Speech

The politics of language are part of the politics of identity, which insists on the importance and ineliminability of difference. Liberal individualists also talk about respecting individual differences, but in the politics of identity these differences are seen as tied to group membership. Therefore, respecting individual differences is seen as requiring due respect for the claims to autonomy of the community—what some call the *ethnos*—which supports a particular kind of identity. The politics of identity thus approximates a rejection of sheer liberal individualism, which is often seen as the imposition of the norms of a particular ethnos (e.g., white, Anglo-Saxon, Protestant, male).

In light of this conception, the question becomes very important: Who speaks for whom? The tendency—based on the appeal of radical democracy as well as on a suspicion formed by the long history of stereotyping and distortion—is to insist that members of a given group or community can only speak for themselves. But this raises again the difficulty about how multiple identity is to be dealt with. To deal with this in a merely confessional manner is not adequate, as Jodi Dean recognizes in *Solidarity of Strangers: Feminism after Identity Politics* (1996):

> … the contexts and discursive practices informing and determining the words "I" use (as well as the "I" who uses them) are multiple, overlapping, and contradictory. Were I to assert my

identity, listing the appropriate categories, I would risk installing a foreclosure that ends discussion, that establishes my authority to speak or write for those who share these categories with me. I would be excusing myself for what I have excluded, suggesting my inability even to imagine the possibility of another perspective. Instead of taking responsibility for my silences and omissions, I would conceal them behind proclamations of who "I" am—all the while knowing that "I" am, of course, more than that, that this "I" is no defense.

Similarly, for David Hollinger's version of "postethnic America,"

> a postethnic perspective recognizes that most individuals live in many circles simultaneously and that the actual living of any individual life entails a shifting division of labor between the several "we's" of which the individual is a part…. Multiculturalism breeds an enthusiasm for specific, traditional cultures that can sometimes mask a provinciality from which individuals are eager to escape through new, out-group affiliations. Welcome as is the cultivation of difference against the conformist imperative for sameness too often felt in American society, that very imperative for sameness can all too easily be reinscribed, in yet more restrictive terms, within the cultures of smaller, particular communities. Postethnicity projects a more diverse basis for diversity than a multiplicity of ethnocentrisms can provide.

Society presumably cannot function without categorizing people in some ways. Which ways are reasonable? And how should we deal with complex categorical crossings and multiple identities/loyalties? This subject has only begun to be addressed, in works such as Ruth Colker's *Hybrid: Bisexuals, Multiracials, and Other Misfits under American Law* (1996).

5. The Voice of the Deaf

We noted earlier some of the terminology through which the disabled have sought to escape from the confinements of language. An alternative is to see disability itself as due not to nature but to society. For example, Harlan Lane argues, in *The Mask of Benevolence: Disabling the Deaf Community* (1992), that what disables the deaf are the preconceptions and demands of a hearing society.

If we respect the right of people in other cultures, including those within our borders, to have their own constitutive rules, which may differ from ours (and we can refuse to do so only at the risk of being impossibly naive), then we must recognize that the deafness of which I speak is not a disability but rather a different way of being.

Congenital deafness is not a matter of disability, but of culture. Deafness is not to be understood as an infirmity, but as membership in a cultural minority. "Members of the deaf community believe, as do members of other cultural minorities, that one should marry within one's minority: marriage with a hearing person is definitely frowned upon." But, other matters aside, would this attitude not make the passing on of deafness more likely? No matter. Lane quotes with enthusiasm the mother who says, "I want my daughter to be like me, to be deaf," and reports the view of the deaf that "research in genetics to improve deaf people's quality of life is certainly important ... but must not become, in the hands of hearing people, research on ways of reducing the deaf minority."

To those who think of the inability to hear as a defect, involving some serious disadvantages, these views will seem remarkable. It is an interesting question how far this style of interpretation can be extended. And yet, it is clear that the improvements the deaf have recently enjoyed in their social and legal status have been premised on the disability model.

In July 1996, actor Jeremy Irons was described as "trampling all over the notion of political correctness" for having insisted at a reading he gave that the sign language interpreter be moved to the side of the stage so as not to distract the hearing audience. Two dozen deaf fans stormed out as a result. Irons' comment expressed his mystification: "Why would deaf people attend a reading? It's like a blind person wanting to attend ballet."

The action may imply, and the comment says outright, that the deaf do not belong at this public event. Aside from marginalizing the deaf, Irons' reaction assumes that the only legitimate reason people would have for attending the reading would be to hear his spoken interpretation. They might, however, be interested in the content of what is read, just as the blind might be interested in listening to a ballet. But if we view the deaf community as merely a different culture, with a language of its own, then the very justification for requiring a sign language interpreter disappears. (No one would expect for the audience to be provided

with interpreters to render Irons' words into French or Swahili.)

IV. KNOWLEDGE AND POWER IN THE AGE OF INFORMATION

Perhaps the largest issue raised by the debate over political correctness (broached earlier in connection with "sponsored research") is the question of the definition and control of knowledge in the new electronic age of information and communication. For some, the central problem is the privatization of information. Thus, the leftist critic Len Masterman, in *Teaching the Media* (1985), worries that "the turning of information into a commodity and the growth of transnational corporative data systems threaten the very future of all public information systems, not least the education system itself." This is because the "production of *socially* useful information is undermined by the production of *profitable* information." According to this vision, culture workers—especially media teachers—play a special role, because privatized info-vendors cannot produce "*an expansion in critical consciousness.* . . . Only a fully autonomous public educational system will be able to do that."

Such a vision is a common one among those who are eager to transform departments of literature or history into programs in cultural studies. It is a view which has many versions; one of the most powerful is that associated with the critique of "the society of the spectacle" described by Guy Debord and other members of the Situationist International movement in the 1960s. This successor to the politics of surrealism continually reconfronted the difficulty of sustaining oppositional discourse against the omnivorousness of postmodernist capitalist culture. When the Beatles' "Revolution" has become the theme song for a brand of athletic shoes, when Jimi Hendrix's fierce version of the National Anthem has become the tune for a beer commercial, and when *philosophy*™ means a line of skin-care products, how can radical political expression resist being coopted and marketed for its "style" rather than its content?

Many have seen the crusade against political correctness as a conservative substitute for the anticommunism which defined American political culture for most of the 20th century, and particularly during the half-century of the Cold War. But the deepest kind of leftist criticism has always concerned itself primarily with the human cost of the triumph of capitalism. Its difficulty has been the fact that this story has increasingly required a denial that consumer "consent" is really consent. Here appeal is routinely made to Gramsci's concept of hegemony, whereby a society's dominant ideas aid, in a wide variety of concrete cultural interactions, in "reinscribing" subordination in the "free choices" of those placed by society in a subordinate position. What makes the consent seem spurious is that it is not fully informed consent because it has been formed in terms of conceptions that are "myth" in the sense articulated by Roland Barthes in *Mythologies* (1957): they rest upon a repression of both history and politics. Commodities appear as possessible things, bereft of a history (how did they come to be produced?) and of a politically contestable future (whose interests do they serve?). Reflection on such matters leads to the popular leftist conception of the intellectual as a facilitator in the creation and recreation of a "counterhegemonic" cultural force. As Masterman puts it,

> One of the primary tasks of media education ... is to challenge the media's common-sensed representations by asking whose interests they serve, by demonstrating how they neutralize contradiction, by exploring alternative representations and by developing a critical consciousness that will seek to restore the history, the politics and the struggle to the processes of representation.

All this requires, however, confidence that, beneath the spurious overlay of hegemonic discourse, we can uncover the true voice of those who have been subordinated. For some, that voice must be a group voice. Thus, Masterman worries, "dominant discourses do more than simply mask the facts both of class exploitation and of class or collective interests. They *fragment* us, representing us, not as classes, but as ... individual citizens and consumers."

It is a general feature of many forms of countercultural politics that they presume that the true voice of individuals is determined by their relevant group membership. For those Marxist-inspired analyses which take class as the central fact, individuals' true interests are understood to be the interests they have as members of a certain class. And similarly for race, sex, etc.

Militating against the persuasiveness of such analyses, however, is the sense of individuals as bound each by a unique, elected, and changeable array of group loyalties. This is the very individualism celebrated by liberal theorists. The group theorist, however, insists upon group loyalty, alleging that the individualist view is naive, if not disingenuous, because in the real world we are *not* free to pick and choose our associations, precisely because of the prevalence of prejudice and inequality.

From this point of view, the racist delusion that races exist, and matter, is only to be met with the counterracist assertion that, e.g., "We blacks (or, perhaps, African-Americans) have to stick together." And so, on this account, the racial discrimination of antiracism is not racism, but merely a recognition that "the powers that be" have defined the terms of discrimination; the social subordination defined in those terms can only be rejected in those terms.

Of course, the antiracist liberal will urge that "we human beings have to stick together," and stress the irrelevance of race. But this is open to the challenge that in a society long dominated by white racism, thinking race to be irrelevant is a luxury reserved to those who are white—whose views and traits have been built into the definition of what is "color-blind." In such a situation, a white man's race *is* irrelevant, because whiteness is taken as the norm, but a black man is constantly being confronted with the fact, and therefore the "relevance," of his race. And similarly for someone who is "only a woman" against a male-defined norm, someone whose sexual orientation is "deviant" against a norm of heterosexual reproduction, etc. If "neutrality" is not a real option, then the temptation to advocacy for the oppressed (which motivates political correctness) is understandable. As Hilary Putnam once put it, to be "neutral" in a mugging is to side with the mugger.

The realities of power in social life, however, are more complicated and less monolithic than the simpler versions of leftist theory would suggest. A lesson can be learned from another event of the summer of 1996. In June, a rally of the Ku Klux Klan in Ann Arbor, Michigan, was interrupted by a massive number (over a thousand, according to one report) of anti-Klan demonstrators, some of whom proceeded to chase down and viciously assault (hit, kick) a Klan member who was wearing Confederate flag clothing and who had apparently been shouting "white power" slogans. A young black woman, Keshia Thomas, got down on top of him to shield him from the attackers who, no doubt astonished, soon desisted. "Just because you beat somebody doesn't mean you are going to change his mind," she said later. "You'll only make him worse." She did not consider herself a hero. "I was just doing what my parents taught me to do—just doing what's right."

Maybe this case is a harbinger of a postethnic America. Or maybe it is just a vestige of the moral imagination lost as inevitable sophistication displaces the very idea of wisdom.

Also See the Following Articles

AFFIRMATIVE ACTION • CENSORSHIP • DISCRIMINATION, CONCEPT OF • IMPERIALISM • INTELLIGENCE TESTING • LIBERALISM • MEDIA OWNERSHIP • PLURALISM IN EDUCATION • RACISM • SEXISM

Bibliography

Arthur, J., and Shapiro, A. (Eds.) (1995). *Campus Wars: Multiculturalism and the Politics of Difference.* Westview, Boulder, CO.

Aufderheide, P. (Ed.) (1992). *Beyond PC: Toward a Politics of Understanding.* Graywolf, Saint Paul, MN.

Beard, H., and Cerf, C. (1992). *The Official Politically Correct Dictionary and Handbook.* Villard Books, New York.

Berliner, D. C., and Biddle, B. J. (1995). *The Manufactured Crisis: Myths, Fraud, and the Attack on America's Public Schools.* Addison–Wesley, Reading, MA.

Brantlinger, P. (1990). *Crusoe's Footprints: Cultural Studies in Britain and America.* Routledge, New York.

Denby, D. (1996). *Great Books: My Adventures with Homer, Rousseau, Woolf, and Other Indestructible Writers of the Western World.* Simon & Schuster, New York.

Edmundson, M. (Ed.) (1993). *Wild Orchids and Trotsky: Messages from American Universities.* Penguin, New York.

Fish, S. (1994). *There's No Such Thing as Free Speech: And It's a Good Thing, Too.* Oxford Univ. Press, New York.

Gitlin, T. (1995). *The Twilight of Common Dreams: Why America is Wracked by Culture Wars.* Metropolitan Books/Owl, New York.

Gutmann, A. (Ed.) (1994). *Multiculturalism: Examining the Politics of Recognition.* Princeton University Press, Princeton, NJ.

Hollinger, D. A. (1995). *Postethnic America: Beyond Multiculturalism.* Basic Books, New York.

Johnson, E. (1995). Beauty's punishment: How feminists look at pornography. In *Nagging Questions: Feminist Ethics in Everyday Life* (D. Bushnell, Ed.), pp. 335–360. Rowman & Littlefield, Lanham, MD.

Kurzweil, E., and Phillips, W. (Eds.) (1994). *Our Country, Our Culture: The Politics of Political Correctness.* Partisan Review, Boston.

Levine, L. W. (1996). *The Opening of the American Mind: Canons, Culture, and History.* Beacon, Boston.

Patai, D., and Koertge, N. (1994). *Professing Feminism: Cautionary Tales from the Strange World of Women's Studies.* Basic Books, New York.

Rieff, D. (1993). Multiculturalism's silent partner. *Harper's* Aug., 62–72.

Soley, L. C. (1995). *Leasing the Ivory Tower: The Corporate Takeover of Academia.* South End, Boston.

Taylor, G. (1996). *Cultural Selection: Why Some Achievements Survive the Test of Time—And Others Don't.* Basic Books, New York.

Williams, J. (Ed.) (1994). *PC Wars: Politics and Theory in the Academy.* Routledge, New York.

Wilson, J. K. (1995). *The Myth of Political Correctness: The Conservative Attack on Higher Education.* Duke Univ. Press, Durham.

POLITICAL ECOLOGY

John P. Clark
Loyola University

GLOSSARY

anthropocentrism The view that only human beings and human experience have value in themselves, that only the human good deserves moral consideration, and that nonhuman beings have only instrumental value for humans.

communitarianism A social theory that focuses on the central importance of the community in the achievement of the social good and personal self-realization, and often emphasizes the communal nature of meaning and value.

deep ecology An ecophilosophy and social movement that rejects anthropocentrism in favor of a biocentric (life-centered) or ecocentric view, and that stresses the importance of a fundamental and rapid change in social values and policies to reverse the human devastation of the planetary ecosystem.

dialectic A form of reasoning that sees reality and

thought as processes of transformation and development, and that stresses both the unfolding of potential that is immanent within beings and the mutual determination between beings that constitute parts of larger developing wholes.

ecocentrism The view that nonhuman beings, including members of other species, ecosystems, and the biosphere, have intrinsic value or a good, and that human experience and value should be interpreted within their larger ecological context.

ecofeminism An ecophilosophical tendency and social movement that links the patriarchical domination of women to the hierarchical and dualistic values legitimating the domination of nature, and often stresses the importance of feminine values in attaining an ecological perspective.

globalization The dominant tendency in contemporary society toward a unified world market, the elimination of protectionism and trade barriers in general, the concentration of economic power in transnational corporations, and the growth of a global economic culture.

green movement An international political movement based on an ecological perspective and committed to such social values as grassroots democracy, social justice, nonviolence, feminism, decentralization, and cooperative economics.

holism The philosophical theory holding that wholes have qualities, meaning, and value that may not exist in the parts and that cannot be expressed as a summation of the attributes of the parts; and that entities in nature have the quality of being both parts and wholes in relation to other entities.

intrinsic value The value or worth that any reality (e.g., a being or an experience) has, not as a means toward some other end, but in itself.

THE FIELD OF POLITICAL ECOLOGY has developed rapidly in recent times as political theorists and philosophers have sought to redefine their subject matter in response to an increasing interest in environmental issues, to the intensifying ecological crisis, and to the emergence of the ecological worldview as a major paradigm in contemporary thought. In recent ethical theory, these same factors have produced forms of "moral extensionism," in which the principles and methodologies of various traditional ethical theories are applied to environmental questions, and have also inspired ethical theories that are more fundamentally transformed through ecological thinking. Similar developments are now taking place in political theory and social ethics, producing a spectrum of positions that express ecological concerns and embody ecological concepts to widely varying degrees.

I. THE EMERGENCE OF POLITICAL ECOLOGY

The term "environmentalism" is sometimes used to refer to the traditional human-centered approach that sees the natural world as that which *surrounds* human beings, while "ecology" is reserved for a more holistic view that attempts to rethink the place of humanity *within* a larger system or whole. At present, most ventures into "political ecology" have remained at the "environmental" level. Most discussions of ecological questions from conservative, liberal, libertarian, and socialist perspectives have merely applied their preexisting categories to "environmental" issues with little or no reflection on the implications of ecology for these categories. Some Marxist theorists have, however, moved further in an ecological direction by exploring the affinities between dialectical and ecological thought. Furthermore, social ecology, bioregionalism, and radical environmentalism have taken as a primary task the development of a new politics grounded in an ecological world view. As a result of these efforts, political ecology has become a vibrant and rapidly evolving field. Nevertheless, the literature in ecological political theory is only

beginning to emerge, and no major work presenting a strong theoretical defense of any position has yet appeared.

The discussion of issues in political ecology has expanded enormously in recent times. This development has been influenced by the growing concern about far-reaching ecological problems that seem to require a political response in the near future. These problems include global warming, ozone depletion, biodiversity loss, species extinction, desertification, massive loss of topsoil, depletion of global fisheries, disposal of nuclear waste, global population growth, environmentaly related illness, acid rain, and decline in air and water quality. Official estimates of the cost of cleanup and "containment" of nuclear wastes in the United States alone range up to $500 billion. Even this problem pales into insignificance when projections of possible social, economic, and ecological disruptions caused by global warming are considered. In addition, the massive global loss of biodiversity poses an indeterminate but ominous threat to the planetary ecosystem. And finally, humanity may be facing the final doubling of its population before ecological limits are reached, and unprecedented stresses are imposed on the biosphere.

In view of the enormity, complexity, and global nature of such problems, the need for a political approach to them has gained wider recognition. The growth of political ecology has perhaps been evident in no area more than in the rapid emergence of environmental justice movements. Widespread public attention has been given to the Chipko movement in India, to the struggles of the rubber tappers of the Amazon basin, and to the movement against environmental racism in the United States. Two important figures in the development of a Third World political ecology are Indian writers Ramachandra Guha, who takes a social ecological approach in his widely reprinted critique of American environmentalism, and Vandana Shiva, who presents an ecofeminist viewpoint in several important recent works. The transformation of the American ecology movement has been particularly striking. While it was once thought to be the exclusive preserve of the White middle class, a large proportion of environmental activism in the United States now occurs in poor, working class, and minority communities, as demonstrated in Jim Schwab's 1994 study of the environmental justice movement. Around the world, political movements among peasants and the urban poor that once seemed focused on social justice issues are increasingly becoming both social and ecological in their focus. The growing international green movement has also been an important expression of interest in political ecology.

While the United States has lagged behind many other counties, ecological politics in much of the world is now represented through strong green political parties and movements, a few of which have entered into governing coalitions, and many of which have exerted a significant influence on ruling parties. Such political developments have been accompanied by a rapidly growing literature in green political theory. In view of such developments, the field of political ecology promises to become an important area of political theory and social ethics, just as environmental ethics has moved to the center of discussion in applied ethics.

As political ecology develops, a number of reasonably well-defined, though sometimes overlapping theoretical orientations have emerged. In the following discussion, eight of these positions will be outlined.

II. FREE MARKET ENVIRONMENTALISM

Free market environmentalism applies to environmental issues the general principle that the good of all can best be promoted through the unrestricted operation of the market economy. Its proponents contend that the proper function of government is the protection of life, liberty, and property rights. They support a minimal state in which governmental activity consists primarily of police powers, a judiciary, and a stable monetary framework within which the market can operate smoothly. In one sense, free market environmentalism is a critique of political ecology, because it contends that ecological issues should be addressed primarily by the market, rather than in the civic realm.

Free market advocates reject the view that market forces have led to significant ecological degradation in the past or that they will produce any severe ecological crisis in the future. Terry L. Anderson and Donald R. Leal, in the best-known defense of free market environmentalism, contend that predictions of severe environmental problems are inaccurate because they do not consider the ability of human beings to adapt to scarcities in certain areas through the creation of substitutes and through increasing productivity. They develop an environmental analysis that echoes the "cornucopian" antiregulatory position most associated with economist Julian Simon. Simon has argued that all basic natural resources and services will be available in the future at prices comparable to present-day levels.

Theorists such as Anderson and Leal maintain that clearly defined property rights are the best assurance of optimal environmental decision-making (indeed, of the best decision-making in every area). In their view,

ecological problems seldom result from the exercise of property rights in ways that are, as critics of the market charge, individually rational but socially and ecologically irrational. Rather, these problems result from an inadequate definition of property rights or the absence of such rights over certain natural resources, which are consequently not protected. They accept the economic model of human beings as self-interested rational calculators and consider a reliance on altruistic motivation such as civic responsibility or moral values to be ineffectual. They argue that because of the complexity of ecosystems they cannot be effectively managed by the state, but only by private owners who are more familiar with particular natural resources. Owners will make good decisions if they are allowed to benefit fully from their property, if they are expected to pay the costs incurred in their use of the property, and if price mechanisms are not "distorted" through political intervention. Furthermore, it is claimed that political decision-making will be biased in favor of groups that are more organized and better informed than the majority, who may not have a strong interest in most decisions and are "rationally ignorant" concerning the issues. According to this analysis, the market assures efficiency (which is taken as the major criterion by which to judge decision-making), while democratic electoral processes do not.

As a major alternative to government regulatory agencies, free market advocates support the idea of holding polluters legally responsible for the effects of their actions. Under such a system, the government would register pollutants, monitor levels of environmental pollution, and hold the polluters liable for damages to others. Governmental activity would thus follow the minimal state model of using policing powers and the court system to protect life and property rights from invasion.

While most free market approaches exhibit little evidence of fundamental influence of ecological thought, the recent work of Gus diZerega is an exception. DiZerega claims, following Hayek, that societies with very limited governmental activity constitute self-regulating systems comparable to naturally functioning ecosystems. The social system is thought to operate according to natural processes that maintain order and balance, which are upset by governmental regulatory activity. DiZerega is also atypical of free market advocates in his rejection of certain property rights. He argues that there are no property rights that can justify various ecologically destructive consequences such as the creation of wastes that cannot be recycled or the reduction of genetic diversity. In general, free market advocates contend that such activities do not violate any rights if they are carried out by legitimate property owners, but argue that they will be eliminated to the extent that the public develops a demand for such environmental goods, so that it will be in the interest of owners to "produce" these commodities.

III. CONSERVATIVE ENVIRONMENTALISM

Conservative environmentalism has not been limited to the free market variety, which, as its exponents often point out, is in fact a form of neoliberalism or libertarianism. There exists a conservative environmentalism that sometimes diverges greatly from the former approach. Conservative political thought is often divided into "libertarian" and "traditionalist" varieties, the former of which has been overwhelmingly dominant in the United States. While libertarianism may be generally equated with a free market position, traditionalism (like much of European conservatism) is sometimes quite skeptical of the operations of an unrestricted market. It is often inspired by a Burkean social philosophy or by traditional religious values, puts a heavy emphasis on the importance of local community, cultural traditions, and nonmaterialistic values, and exalts the virtues of prudence, piety, restraint, and moderation in personal life.

This variety of conservatism has, not surprisingly, a strong conservationist impulse. It is more open than are free market approaches to environmental protection laws, to green taxes, and to public ownership and protection of lands considered to be an important historical and spiritual legacy. It accepts a stewardship ethic that may be expressed in concern about the destruction of species and ecosystems. John R. E. Bliese contends that the conservative historical vision implies a duty to carry on economic activity in ways that protect the earth, so as to provide for the welfare of future generations. In addition, he argues that the traditionalist virtue of piety requires veneration for the earth itself. Such a conservatism has some goals that are not distant from those of liberal environmentalism, although it differs from the latter in its fundamental distrust of the bureaucratic state as a means of achieving its ends.

IV. GREEN MARKET ENVIRONMENTALISM

The best-known advocate of "greening the market" is Paul Hawken, who proposes a market-based approach that differs considerably from that of the free market theorists. Hawken contends that the ecological crisis is much more severe and the risks for the future much greater than the latter are usually willing to admit, and he argues that the unregulated market inevitably creates ecological crisis. The reason this occurs, in his view, is that enterprises have an economic incentive to reduce expenditures and gain a competitive advantage by externalizing costs as environmental damage. Hawken believes that extensive government action is necessary, but he argues that as little of it as possible should consist of administrative regulation and government planning. Rather, he sees the most desirable policy to be the enactment of "green taxes" that would internalize ecological costs through prices. In this approach, he follows the British economist A. C. Pigou, who proposed the idea of a tax on producers equal to the costs they avoid by passing on to the public the expenses related to pollution. Under such a system, producers would have the same kind of incentives as at present to produce profitably and efficiently, but the incentives would work to produce cleaner, more ecologically sound products. In Hawken's view, such a system would make sustainability profitable, while harnessing what he sees as the vast creative ability of the competitive market and individual initiative. It would also permit the phasing out of much of the present tax system as green taxation is introduced over a 20-year period.

There are several other elements in Hawken's green market system. One is what he calls "an intelligent product system," in which products are licensed to the consumer for use, while the producer retains ownership and responsibility for ecological consequences during the life of the product. He claims that such a system would result in the design of products for maximum reuse and recyclability. Another of his innovative economic proposals is the formation of public "utilities" that are a hybrid of public and private interests in areas of important natural resources. These entities would receive levels of return on investments proportional to their fulfillment of needs in an ecologically sound manner. The result of all these policies would be a market that is both substantially "free" in its principles of operation, and ecologically sustainable in its functioning.

V. LIBERAL ENVIRONMENTALISM

Liberal environmentalism rejects the idea that unrestrained market activity can solve ecological problems, and contends that significant governmental regulatory activity is necessary to prevent environmental damage while respecting human rights and maintaining justice. Liberalism (in the American sense of a moderate social democracy) is the guiding ideological orientation of much of contemporary environmental thinking. This is exemplified, for example, in the extensive publications of the Worldwatch Institute, including the annual editions of *State of the World*, which focus heavily on expanded government regulatory activity and more effective international environmental agreements. Robert C. Paehlke's often-cited analysis of the possibilities for a "progressive environmentalism" is typical of the somewhat greener, less bureaucratic version of liberalism that has increasingly been adopted by environmentalists. And while Gregg Easterbrook's widely discussed and controversial work has been attacked by many environmentalists as part of a conservative backlash against the ecology movement, its author contends that it is in fact a defense of environmental liberalism. Easterbrook notes that public investments produce not only long-term benefits but also significant improvements in the lives of the taxpayers who fund them. He claims that environmental protection programs are the best example of social progress through governmental activity. Easterbrook's views are a good example of the persistence of an older liberalism that sees evidence of a general amelioration in human society and has faith in a march of progress that encompasses both humanity and the earth.

In view of the fact that mainstream environmentalism in the United States and many Western countries has remained steadfastly in the liberal tradition, it is rather surprising that a significant literature in liberal environmental political theory has not yet developed. A notable exception is Avner de-Shalit's recent forthright defense of liberal environmentalism, in which he makes the case for governmental environmental regulation combined with a strong welfare state based on an expanded version of the liberal conception of the general good. He contends that "antichauvinism" is basic to liberalism and that an extension of liberal principles yields an effective environmental politics. He proposes that the liberal principle of concern for the interest and welfare of others can reasonably be amended to include other species, all sentient creatures, entire ecosystems, and even all living beings.

De-Shalit rejects the green market approach to ecological problems on the grounds that Pigovian taxes are regressive and therefore unjust. In his view, if producers are charged for "externalities," they will pass the cost on to consumers, and the poor will bear a disproportionate burden, because they spend much more of their income on energy and other goods that will be taxed most heavily. Advocates of green taxes respond that other taxes and even some of the green fees themselves could be made progressive to offset the undoubtedly regressive nature of taxes on energy and other necessities. Equity could thus be reconciled with full-cost pricing, as some liberals are willing to admit.

However, de-Shalit has a stronger criticism against the very idea that "costs" can be internalized in the market price of a commodity. He points out the difficulty of placing a price on sickness and suffering, and the obvious impossibility of assigning a cost to human lives and destruction of animal life, not to mention species loss and ecosystem destruction. He also points out the fact that cost-benefit analysis irrationally "discounts" the value of the lives and experience of future generations. His point, like that of many critics of cost-benefit analysis, is that determination of value is an ethical and political question. Neither an unrestricted market nor even a market that theoretically internalizes estimated external costs can assess value in any "objective" manner.

De-Shalit's version of liberalism advocates a process of public debate and political decision-making to limit the amount of pollution and environmental destruction in accord with the public's view of its own interest, whatever the market might otherwise have dictated. He rejects the idea that the community's interest is served by the free market approach of suits after the fact by specific individuals whose "property rights" are violated by polluters. He asks why the public should not act to limit pollution before there is serious damage to human health or to environmental quality. De-Shalit espouses a liberal concept of citizenship that has a significant communitarian dimension. He holds that environmental questions involve issues of ethical and political principle that cannot be reduced to matters for narrow economic calculation, and he stresses the importance of people's role as citizens concerned with the public good. He strongly rejects the value neutrality of the kind of liberalism popularized by John Rawls, Bruce Ackerman, Ronald Dworkin and other recent theorists. Instead, he believes that there must be a commitment to a common "idea of the good" flowing from a theory of value that guides moral and political reasoning by a conception of intrinsic and instrumental value.

However, other recent liberal theorists have tried to construct a liberal environmentalism based on Rawlsian principles. Rawls's own recent restatement of his position gives little encouragement to those interested in developing his theory in an ecological direction. He states that his idea of justice as fairness can account for obligations to future generations, but it does not offer guidance concerning obligations to other species and to the rest of nature. He also notes that his principles would justify appeals to present and future human survival, health, aesthetic, recreational, and intellectual needs on behalf of protection of animals and the natural world. Beyond this, he says, we enter the realm of "natural religion," in which "public reason" can be of no assistance. Nevertheless, some theorists, including Brent A. Singer, have presented the case for a Rawlsian environmental liberalism. Singer attempts an environmentally oriented reformulation of Rawls's "original position" in which hypothetical contracting agents determine the nature of just political institutions and social practices. According to Rawls, there are certain primary goods that any rationally self-interested person will desire. Singer argues that these will include a quality of air, water, food, and shelter that is dependent on healthy environmental conditions. Such goods, in Singer's view, are as fundamental as such political liberties as free speech or the right to vote, in that they cannot rationally be traded for any social and economic privileges. Singer contends further that Rawlsian assumptions require consideration of future generations in an assessment of the need for these primary goods, in addition to a consideration of the interests of many animal species as well. Finally, he argues that because many people consider places of great natural beauty to have spiritual value, a Rawlsian liberal argument can be made for preserving wilderness and various natural sites on grounds of freedom of religion and liberty of conscience, unless there are overriding considerations of justice. Such an attempt to apply liberalism to environmental issues may have a somewhat more ecological dimension than the free market approaches they hope to correct, yet the concern for nature seems much closer to the "moral extensionism" of animal rights theories than the more thoroughgoing ecological (ecocentric or holistic) viewpoints.

It is noteworthy that while neither free market environmentalism nor liberalism have been at the center of discussion in political ecology, their theoretical assumptions remain dominant in most analyses of the political dimensions of environmental issues. Most approaches have assumed that some balance between the decision-making processes within a corporate capitalist market economy, planning and regulation by centralized nation-states, and agreements between such states is the context in which approaches to environmental issues and growing ecological crisis must be discussed. However, there are several tendencies in ecological thought that propose deeper changes in political and economic systems and a more radically ecological rethinking of political categories.

VI. SOCIALIST ECOLOGY

As environmental issues began to move to the center of political discussion, efforts were made by writers such as Howard L. Parsons to defend the fundamentally ecological nature of Marx's thought. These analyses were questioned by various critics, who pointed out serious obstacles to such an endeavor, in view of Marx's conceptions of nature, historical progress, industry, and technology. Many ecosocialists now recognize the problematical character of Marx's concepts of society and nature, and are attempting a more sophisticated approach to ecology based on a development of the holistic, dialectical, and systemic aspects of Marxian thought and of the socialist tradition in general. A growing body of theoretical work has emerged in the process. Much of it can be found in the journal *Capitalism, Nature, Socialism*, which has become a major forum for the development of socialist ecology. In fact, its level of ongoing theoretical discussion of issues in political ecology is unsurpassed by any English-language publication dealing with such issues.

One of the most notable developments in eco-Marxist theory is James O'Connor's application of Marx's analysis of conditions of production to environmental issues, and his resulting thesis that the ecological crisis is "the second contradiction of capitalism." O'Connor proposes a "red green politics" based on the view that ecological crisis requires a radical transformation of capitalist relations of production and that economic crisis requires a radical transformation of capitalist forces of production. Ecosocialists contend that global competition has led to an externalizing of social and environmental costs, which has resulted in a deterioration of environmental and labor conditions. Because these problems are widespread and overstep regional and national boundaries, they cannot be solved through action at the local level to the extent that many greens, bioregionalists, and social ecologists contend. Even seemingly local problems such as transportation, housing costs, and drugs are in fact global issues related to the operations of international capital, and therefore require globally coordinated political action. O'Connor concludes that the only political form that can cope adequately with both the global dimensions and local specificity of such issues is a democratic state; that is, one that succeeds in democratically organizing and administering the division of labor.

David Harvey has also developed one of the most sophisticated versions of ecological Marxism to date. Harvey traces environmental problems in a capitalist society to the nature of a money economy. He notes that in such an economy much of what is thought of as "the environment" is assigned a monetary value that has no necessary relationship to any other kind of value it may have. Monetary value has a privileged position over forms of value in a capitalist social system: it is the only universal standard of value available, and is the one given most recognition by those who hold decision-making power. This dominance of monetary value does not result from its adequacy as a means of evaluation. It is generally agreed that many realities cannot be quantified in monetary terms if in any way at all, and many find a morally objectionable quality in the assessment of human life, species survival, or ancient ecosystems in monetary terms. Harvey argues that the inappropriateness of economistic values becomes increasingly obvious the more we consider realities that are complex wholes, rather than discrete entities. While monetary values can be attributed, however inadequately, to individual parts of an ecosystem, ecological value is a function of the complex relationship between the various parts of the whole, and the relation of all these parts to the whole. Harvey argues that economistic value also fails when we expand our evaluation over time. He contends that the economic practice of discounting the value of goods that might exist in the future is irrational ecologically because certain goods in nature are the precondition for any other kind of value. Finally, Harvey argues that the fundamental economistic conceptualization of environmental consequences as "externalities" is in basic contradiction to an ecological analysis, which looks upon processes as intrinsically interrelated parts of a whole.

Harvey focuses much more directly on the project of a radically dialectical approach than most thinkers in the Marxist tradition, for whom issues of class, economic exploitation, ideology, social crisis, historical agency, and revolutionary social transformation often take theoretical priority. This emphasis gives Harvey's analysis a strongly ecological flavor that is missing in many versions of political ecology. He points out that dialectical thought concerns itself more with processes, flows, and relations than with things, structures, and organized systems. Ecological thinking gives priority to these same realities. Harvey's efforts to make a connection between the two makes his approach one of the most successful attempts at ecologizing Marxism.

David Pepper presents an extensive defense of an ecosocialism that remains much closer in many ways to more traditional Marxism. Marxism is "ecological," in Pepper's view, precisely because of its completely anthropocentric concern for human welfare. Because socialist economic growth will be a form of rational, planned development that is for the benefit of all, it must be ecologically responsible. Pepper claims the Enlightenment heritage of Marxism and rejects the "green postmodernist" critique of anthropocentrism and the project of the domination of nature. Marxism, he says, rejects a "mastery" of nature that implies subjection or destruction, but espouses a "domination" that will in fact solve ecological problems. This "domination" consists of humanity's achievement of conscious control over its relationship to nature. Such a process results in careful stewardship rather than destructiveness. The problem is thus not with anthropocentrism, but with a narrow, short-sighted, individualist form of anthropocentrism, which is ecologically destructive.

Pepper notes that socialists have divergent proposals for social reorganization. Some advocate greater or lesser levels of state planning, size of market sectors, and use of monetary exchanges. What is clear to him is that centralized planning must play a large role in social decision-making and that purely decentralized solutions are naively utopian. Pepper believes that such planning can only be instituted if a majority of a society believes it to be necessary. For this to take place, a large-scale social movement must espouse socialist goals. He places heavy emphasis on working-class organizations in the development of such a movement, although he also sees an important role for such transitional steps as municipal socialism and local currency systems.

While ecosocialist thinkers such as Pepper seek to hold on to much of traditional Marxism while attempting to introduce an environmental dimension, more strongly ecological socialisms continue to emerge. Perhaps the most promising is the expansive synthesis of ecosocialism with aspects of psychoanalytic theory, phenomenology, social ecology, and Eastern and Western spirtual traditions presented by Joel Kovel. Robyn Eckersley has recently explored the possibility of a convergence between deep ecology and ecosocialism, based on her view that the two share common principles of entitlement and responsibility.

The fact is that with the collapse of "actually existing socialism," Marxist and socialist ideas of praxis are in a state that one might see as either disarray or creative ferment. Accordingly, we find some ecosocialisms that sound much like environmental liberalism or social democracy, others that propose radical decentralism and participatory democracy reminiscent of social ecology, some that incorporate more traditional Marxist ideas in the concept of an ecologically responsible centralized workers' state, and still others that propose an eclectic "postmodern" socialism inspired by environmentalism and other "new social movements."

VII. SOCIAL ECOLOGY

Social ecology is the other major dialectical approach to ecopolitics. This ecophilosophy comes out of the tradition of social geography and ecological regionalism of Elisée Reclus, Patrick Geddes, and Lewis Mumford, the libertarian communitarianism of Peter Kropotkin, Gustav Landauer, and Martin Buber, and the teleological and dialectical philosophical tradition of Aristotle, Hegel, and Marx. It is also related to recent evolutionary and process philosophies, and holistic traditions of both East and West.

Contemporary social ecology is best known through the works of social theorist Murray Bookchin. Some commentators, such as Peter List, have identified the theory narrowly with Bookchin's ideas, while others, such as Carolyn Merchant, subsume under social ecology much of the ecological left, including ecosocialists. In contradistinction to both these views, however, there is a coherent social ecological tradition that is much larger than any one writer's ideas, but that that is still quite distinct from most (but not all) socialist and Marxist views.

Social ecology applies an evolutionary, developmental view of history and a holistic conception of social unity-in-diversity to social and political issues. As a dialectical holism, it sees beings in nature as *holons*, that is, as both wholes relative to their parts and parts relative to larger wholes. A fully holistic account attempts to give adequate consideration to both of these dimensions. Thus, social ecology is concerned with the development in society of both individuality and community, so that each member can achieve personal self-realization while developing a sense of identification with and responsibility toward the larger social and natural whole.

Social ecology sees politics as a branch of ethics, that is, as the pursuit of the good life and of self-realization both for the individual person and for the entire community. It interprets this community not only as the various forms of human community in which we participate, but also as the diverse ecological communities of which we are also members, up to the level of the biosphere or earth community. Social ecology has sometimes been thought to construct naively a view of ethics or politics on the model of what is found "in nature."

Rather, a social ecological view reinterprets ethics in the light of a holistic outlook that attempts to avoid a dualistic split between humanity and nature. A social ecology of value situates human processes of self-realization and value-experience within a wider context of self-realization, experience of value, and attainment of good in nature. It holds that there is no purely external nature that can serve as a model for human activity or social organization, because both the person and society are thoroughly ecological in their fundamental nature.

A major project of social ecology is the critique of all forms of domination that hinder the evolutionary processes of human and planetary self-realization. The objects of this critique include the centralized state, concentrated economic power, patriarchy, the technological megamachine, and various authoritarian and repressive ideologies. While social ecologists hold that there is a *system* of domination in which various hierarchical and authoritarian institutions interact, they find some to be more central to the social and ecological crisis than others. They see the dominance of economic power as the major force producing both social injustice and ecological crisis today, and find this power to be embodied in a vast economic and technological machine (globalized corporate capital), and in an all-pervasive, nihilistic culture of consumption.

The political goal of social ecology is the creation of a free, communitarian society in harmony with the natural world. In developing its vision of such a society, social ecology looks back to a long history of human experiments in mutual aid, cooperation, decentralized production, direct democracy, human-scaled institutions, and communitarian values. These include the Athenian polis, many tribal traditions, medieval free cities, antiauthoritarian revolutionary movements, the New England town meeting, many communitarian experiments, the cooperative movement, and various other historical examples.

While social ecologists agree on the ideal of a free, decentralized, democratic, and ecological society, the means to this end are vigorously debated. The politics of social ecology has sometimes been identified with Bookchin's "libertarian municipalism," which aims at creating a movement to establish libertarian municipalities governed by municipal or neighborhood assemblies. While the municipalities are to remain politically sovereign, they will form voluntary "confederations" to organize themselves politically and economically beyond the local level. In Bookchin's view, these confederations will eventually create a condition of "dual power" in which they will be able to challenge the power of the nation-state and the global corporate economic power with which it is allied. A system of libertarian communism, in which distribution will be according to need, will then be established. Private ownership of the means of production will be abolished and replaced by community-controlled enterprises. Hierarchical social institutions, including patriarchy, will be destroyed and the quest for human domination of nature will come to an end.

Many social ecologists question libertarian municipalism as both an effective practical politics and as an adequate vision of a future society. Rather, they incorporate some aspects of Bookchin's municipalism in a broader ecological communitarianism. There is general agreement among social ecologists that there must be a decentralization of political power away from the centralized state and of economic power away from large corporations, and that more human-scale technologies are essential both socially and ecologically. However, many support a variety of social, political, and economic strategies as a means of working toward a free ecological society. Social ecologists are often interested in creating and promoting producer and consumer cooperatives, land trusts and housing cooperatives, ecological agriculture, ecologically sound technologies, municipal citizens' movements, Green political parties, environmental justice groups, publishing projects, environmental defense groups, and many other efforts at social and ecological regeneration.

Social ecologists often take a comprehensive, theoretically grounded but experimental approach to social transformation. They base their efforts on the needs and interests of local communities, the possibilities for social creativity that exist in a historically determinate situation, and the relationship between such diverse particularity and the evolving global whole. Such a nondogmatic, experimental social ecology takes as the measure of its success the organic growth of a compassionate, cooperative, ecological culture, rooted in the specificity of history and place, but developing growing interconnections within the entire earth community.

Over the past decade, social ecology has gained some notoriety through Murray Bookchin's often bitter attacks on other philosophical positions, including most notably deep ecology, but also ecofeminism and ecosocialism, and more recently bioregionalism, ecocommunitarianism and various forms of ecoanarchism. Bookchin gained some attention for his views through his claims of links between deep ecology and racist and politically reactionary ideas. His argument was based primarily on statements by several deep ecologists that supported the withholding of aid to famine victims,

opposed immigration on both ecological and cultural grounds, and held that AIDS and other diseases were a natural process of controlling human overpopulation. Interestingly, Bookchin's attack was directed at deep ecological theorists, very few of whom support any of the views he attributes to them, rather than a thinker like Garrett Hardin, who is well-known for his opposition to immigration and aid to famine victims, and who has proposed a world government with powers to control population.

The most salient political distinction between social and deep ecologists has not in reality been any supposed ecofascist tendencies of the latter. Rather, social ecologists have undertaken a more systematic analysis of social institutions and their relationship to ecological problems. Deep ecologists have in general devoted little attention to social analysis, and have adopted a spectrum of political positions, ranging from a rather apolitical emphasis on the need for changes in personal values and "lifestyle," to a liberal and reformist politics, and even to a revolutionary opposition to the megamachine that aims at the overthrow of industrial civilization. Recently, however, deep ecologists have begun to undertake quite serious analysis of social and political issues, as exhibited in important works by Robyn Eckersley and Andrew McLaughlin, and the theoretical gap between social and deep ecology is narrowing considerably. In addition, social ecologists have begun to discuss commonalities with some aspects of deep ecology, and useful dialogue has begun to replace sectarian quarreling.

VIII. BIOREGIONALISM

Bioregionalism is the tradition in political ecology that has gone furthest in taking account of the ecological in the most concrete sense. Bioregionalism differs from other ecological approaches in that it goes beyond respect for, identification with, defense of, and general understanding of nature. While it recognizes the importance of all of these goals, it focuses on the process of "reinhabitation": the creation of a culture and way of life based on a very specific, detailed knowledge of the ecological realities of the larger natural community in which the human community participates. Furthermore, it explores forms of governance based on such a bioregional consciousness. Bioregionalism's values call into question the concept of the nation-state and political boundaries on the one hand, and the homogenizing culture of consumption on the other. Its vision of social transformation does not appeal to any abstract principles of rights or justice, or contentious ideas of individual or group interest. Rather, it is rooted in realities that are very concrete and experiential and that, in its view, might form a strong basis for personal and communal identification.

For two decades there has been an organized bioregional movement advocating the rediscovery of a sense of place, the rooting of culture in the particularities of natural regions, and the development of social and political institutions reflecting bioregional realities. The term "bioregionalism" was first used in this sense by Peter Berg and Raymond Dasmann of the Planet Drum Foundation in San Francisco. The organization's journal, *Raise the Stakes*, has been the most important ongoing arena for discussion of bioregional ideas. In addition, a series of semiannual Turtle Island (North American) Bioregional Congresses have contributed to the movement's growing cultural and political significance.

Bioregionalism is sometimes described as a "watershed politics," in view of its focus on bioregions (typified by watersheds of rivers and streams) as the context of political activity. Bioregionalism does not stress politics in the electoral and other traditional senses as much as it proposes a broader cultural kind based on the development of local bioregional institutions. However, there have been efforts to draw out its more specific organizational implications. For example, Kirkpatrick Sale compares the "bioregional paradigm" and the dominant "industrio-scientific paradigm" and finds the former's conception of "polity" to stress values such as decentralization, complementarity, and diversity, as opposed to the latter's emphasis on centralization, hierarchy, and uniformity.

Sale's conception of bioregional political institutions is very similar to that of social ecologist Murray Bookchin (despite harsh attacks on Sale by Bookchin and his colleague Janet Biehl). Sale states that bioregionalism rejects social hierarchy and domination as unecological, and proposes an egalitarian, decentralized form of social organization. This would include community ownership of productive enterprises, and decision-making at the local level, with the local units ranging from villages of perhaps 1000 people up to larger towns and neighborhoods of 5 to 10,000 inhabitants. Bioregional politics is to be based on informal decision-making by those with competence and experience, the election of a small number of community officials, and the retention of ultimate power by the whole body of citizens. As in Bookchin's municipalism, Sale envisions cooperation on a larger scale through voluntary confederations, although their boundaries would be determined biore-

gionally. Unlike Bookchin, Sale foresees the persistence of some market exchange between communities alongside barter and cooperative sharing. He does not present any detailed picture of how such a decentralized cooperative economy might operate. He assumes, however, that bioregionalism would require a decentralization not only of political and economic power, but also of population. He advocates the voluntary resettlement of the urban population into ecologically sound cities of much smaller scale than at present.

Donald Alexander argues that there is a need to overcome the split between those who see bioregionalism in sometimes rather reductive scientific terms, and those who see it primarily as an ethic and a sensibility. Alexander sees Lewis Mumford as the inspiration for a more expansive bioregionalism that dialectically synthesizes the divergent geographic, economic, and cultural aspects of regionalism. While bioregionalists could certainly benefit from more study of Mumford, the kind of regional vision that he expresses is already present elsewhere within the tradition. The work of Gary Snyder, the major intellectual influence on the bioregional movement, expresses such a rich conception of natural and cultural regions. Snyder plays a very important role in contemporary ecophilosophy and political ecology. While he is a major figure in bioregionalism, he has also had enormous influence on many deep and social ecologists. His broad ecological vision, his exploration of the complex interconnections between nature and culture, his critique of centralized power, and his synthesis of Eastern, Western and indigenous traditions help one find the common ground in ecophilosophy. Snyder encourages us to learn from the wisdom of societies that do not create a sharp division between culture and nature and for whom education includes songs, stories, myths, rituals, and practices that arise out of the experience of the local ecological community and its diverse members. Bioregional reinhabitation means becoming part of such a culture of nature rooted in a specific place. Snyder does not spell out the political implications of his regionalism in a programmatic manner; however, a strong political critique is implicit in it. For Snyder, it is wild nature and organically rooted local and regional culture that are the source of ecological and social order. On the other hand, forms of hierarchical and centralized power are inherently disorderly and disruptive. The political question thus becomes how a disenfranchised humanity can regain its power of self-determination, so it can creatively express itself, in cooperation with nature, in diverse cultures of place.

IX. RADICAL ENVIRONMENTALISM

Radical environmentalism is a form of political ecology that has emerged from grassroots ecological activism, especially the wilderness preservation movement and the organization Earth First! It is a distinctive approach to political ecology, first, because it has an explicit ecophilosophical basis in deep ecology, and secondly, because of its support for an uncompromising politics of direct action. The term "radical environmentalism," like "radical ecology," is often used in a generic sense to refer to a number of ecophilosophies and ecological movements. However, the concept is also used in a more specific sense to refer to groups such as Earth First! (which calls itself a "radical environmental movement"), and is employed by Christopher Manes in his theoretical defense of the movement.

Manes explains the philosophical basis for radical environmental politics as the identification with a larger self proposed by some forms of deep ecology. He argues that if one identifies oneself with such a larger self that is thought to pervade the entire ecological community of which one is a member, then an attack on that community or any part of it will be seen as an attack on oneself. Manes argues that ecodefense is thus a form of legitimate self-defense, because defense of oneself would certainly justify activities that damage only inanimate objects (as in the case of tree-spiking or the disabling of equipment). There is some ambiguity, however, in this concept of ecodefense. If defense of the wild is quite literally interpreted as self-defense, then one might conclude that it would justifiably include injury not only to instruments used by attackers, but to the attackers themselves, because these aggressors actually kill trees, wolves, and sometimes whole ecosystems. However, radical environmentalists overwhelmingly reject such retaliation and strongly oppose any sort of injury to human beings. The ethical basis for doing so has not yet been clarified. If the concept of the larger self and self-defense is not to be taken so literally, further discussion of the nature of such expanded selfhood is necessary.

What is clear is that radical environmentalism is grounded in a strong ecological sensibility that has usually been expressed most strongly in a love of and identification with wilderness. At one time radical environmentalism was identified almost exclusively with wilderness defense. More recently, however, there has been within the radical environmental movement (particularly in the case of Earth First!), a strong shift toward concern with social and economic issues, and even attempts to combine wilderness preservation

and ecodefense with labor organizing and campaigns against transnational corporations. The gap between deep ecology-inspired radical environmentalists and social ecologists has therefore narrowed.

Radical environmentalists take two primary approaches to direct action. Civil disobedience, as Manes describes it, is based on respect for others, nonviolence, acceptance of possible penalties, and refusal to damage property. It is thus in the classical tradition of Thoreauvian and Gandhian nonviolent protest. The other form of direct action, "monkeywrenching" or "ecotage," has produced much more controversy, focused especially on the alleged activities of Earth First! members. Dave Foreman, cofounder of Earth First!, has defined such activity as a form of nonviolent resistance to the destruction of biodiversity and wilderness. It is based on an anarchic, nonhierarchical approach in which small groups of activists prevent ecodestruction by using the simplest, safest, and most effective methods. These methods usually include the damaging or disablement of equipment used in the ecodestruction. Such actions are aimed neither at effecting social change by example nor at influencing the public, but rather at achieving pragmatic results. According to Foreman, the activist who practices ecotage has no obligation to accept punishment for such activity, but rather should be looked upon as a kind of guerrilla fighter for nature, whose success depends on avoiding capture and continuing the struggle. Both the ethics and the pragmatic value of such tactics of ecodefense continue to be debated in the radical environmental movement and among environmental ethicists.

Foreman sees the major concern of radical environmentalism to be the defense of the wild. Manes agrees but argues that defending it successfully requires far-reaching social, economic and political changes. Foreman has said that radical environmentalism does not have the aim of overthrowing any social, political, or economic system. However, Manes depicts its goal of social transformation as more far-reaching in many ways than that envisioned by most revolutionary movements. Radical environmentalism, he says, proposes the restoration of extensive areas of wilderness areas, the banning of all toxic substances, the abolition of commercial logging, automobiles, coal-fired power plants, petrochemical-based industries, and monoculture in agriculture, and a considerable reduction of human population. In short, radical environmentalism is willing to contemplate the destruction of the entire modern industrial system. As much as ecosocialism or social ecology, it foresees a fundamental transformation of the global power structure, in that its goals, in Manes' view, will require the abolition of the multinational corporation, the driving force behind global ecodestruction.

X. THE FUTURE OF POLITICAL ECOLOGY

There are two overriding factors in the future development of political ecology. The first is the high likelihood that global ecological crisis will become more severe. As ecological problems continue to intensify, efforts to find solutions within the existing global market economic system will continue, and the literature of free market environmentalism will no doubt grow. Furthermore, in view of the extensive tradition of liberal political thought, much more serious attempts to develop liberal environmentalist theory can be expected. Ecosocialism already has one of the most highly developed bodies of theory, and its evolution in diverse directions is likely to continue as socialist thought in general takes a more pluralistic turn. If social ecology can successfully follow much of ecosocialism in overcoming its political sectarian tendencies, its comprehensive approach could make it one of the most important political ecologies. Both ecofeminism and deep ecology have played important roles in contemporary ecological thought, and both can be expected to express themselves in various political ecologies.

The second major factor in the development of political ecology will be the continued growth of economic globalization, with its enorous impact on the international balance of power. There is an increasing awareness that just as ecological problems must be approached in their local, regional, and global dimensions, the political and economic issues that are intertwined with them require a politics that addresses all these levels. It is likely that there will be a convergence between the goals of the environmental justice movement, the concerns of Third World environmentalism, and certain issues in mainstream social ethics. While in the past the environmental justice movement has focused on disproportionate environmental impacts on minority communities, it is likely that in the future it will place greater emphasis on injustices against the larger community also, and will express itself more in terms of the public interest and the general good. The corporate abuse of power and the development of corporate environmentalism and "greenwashing" has been a growing concern of political ecologists. There has already been some discussion of the political implications of "astroturf" movements, in which heavy corporate

spending generates letters and telephone calls to legislators, in order to artificially create the impression of grassroots support or opposition to targeted legislation. One might expect more systematic reflection on the fate of democratic decision-making in a media-dominated society in which advertising and public relations campaigns are increasingly effective in shaping public perceptions and policy. It is also likely that discussions of environmental justice will devote more attention to the issue of influence on legislatures and regulatory agencies through lobbying and corporate ties of members of such bodies.

The direction in which political ecology is developing is indicated by the emergence of the concept of "environmental security" to stress the centrality of ecological issues to global political concerns. It is argued that environmental issues will have increasingly greater influence in conflicts within nations, in internatonal disputes, and in controversies involving corporations, nation-states, and international organizations. Relevant factors include disposal of hazardous wastes, population pressures, exhaustion of arable lands, toxic emissions crossing national borders, global climate changes, possible changes in ocean levels, effects of nuclear accidents, effects of weapons testing, ecodestruction in armed conflicts, global effects of biodiversity loss, exhaustion of fisheries and marine life in international waters, epidemiological effects of ecological disturbances, and numerous other issues that extend beyond national boundaries. Such issues point to the necessity of a rethinking of traditional political categories.

Thus, the crucial issue in political ecology today is the extent to which a critical conception of "the ecological" can lead to a fundamental reconceptualization of "the political."

Also See the Following Articles

ANTHROPOCENTRISM • COMMUNITARIANISM • DEEP ECOLOGY • ECOLOGICAL BALANCE • ENVIRONMENTAL JUSTICE

Bibliography

Anderson, T., & Leal, D. (1991). *Free Market Environmentalism*. San Francisco: Pacific Research Institute for Public Policy.

Athanasiou, T. (1996). *Divided planet: The ecology of rich and poor*. Boston: Little, Brown and Company.

Benton, T. (1996). *The greening of Marxism*. New York: Guilford Press.

Bliese, J. (1996, Fall). The conservative case for the environment. *Intercollegiate Review*, 28–36.

Bookchin, M. (1982). *The ecology of freedom: The emergence and dissolution of hierarchy*. Palo Alto, CA: Cheshire Books.

Brown, L. et al. (Eds.). (1984–present). *State of the world*. New York: W. W. Norton & Co.

Clark, J. (1997). A social ecology. In M. Zimmerman, et al. (Eds.), *Environmental philosophy: From animal rights to radical ecology* (2nd ed.). Englewood Cliffs, NJ: Prentice Hall.

Coleman, D. (1994). *Ecopolitics: Building a green society*. New Brunswick, NJ: Rutgers University Press.

de-Shalit, A. (1995). Is liberalism environment-friendly? *Social Theory and Practice* **21**, 287–314.

Dickens, P. (1992). *Society and nature: Toward a green social theory*. London: Harvester Wheatsheaf.

diZerega, G. (1995). Empathy, society, nature, and the relational self: Deep ecology and liberal modernity. *Social Theory and Practice* **21**, 239–269.

Dobson, A. (1991). *Green political thought*. London: HarperCollins.

Eckersley, R. (1992). *Environmentalism and political theory*. Albany, NY: SUNY Press.

Foreman, D. (1991). *Confessions of an eco-warrior*. New York: Harmony Books.

Goodin, R. (1992). *Green political theory*. Oxford: Polity Press.

Harvey, D. (1993). The nature of environment: The dialectics of social and environmental change. In R. Miliband & L. Panich (Eds.), *Real problems, false solutions: Socialist register 1993*. London: Merlin Press.

Hawken, P. (1993). *The ecology of commerce: A declaration of sustainability*. New York: HarperBusiness.

Kovel, J. (1991). *History and spirit: An inquiry into the philosophy of liberation*. Boston: Beacon Press.

List, P. (1993) *Radical environmentalism: Philosophy and tactics*. Belmont, CA: Wadsworth Publishing Company.

Manes, C. (1990). *Green rage: Radical environmentalism and the unmaking of civilization*. Boston: Little, Brown and Company.

McLaughlin, A. (1993). *"Regarding nature: Industrialism and deep ecology*. Albany, NY: SUNY Press.

Merchant, C. *Radical Ecology: The search for a livable world*. New York: Routledge.

Morrison, R. (1995). *Ecological Democracy*. Boston, MA: South End Press.

O'Connor, J., et al. (Eds.). (1988–present). *Capitalism, nature, socialism: A journal of socialist ecology*. New York: The Guilford Press.

Paehlke, R. (1989). *Environmentalism and the future of progressive politics*. New Haven, CT: Yale University Press.

Parsons, H. (1977). *Marx and Engels on ecology*. Westport, CT: Greenwood Press.

Pepper, D. (1993). *Ecosocialism: From deep ecology to social justice*. London: Routledge.

Sale, K. (1985). *Dwellers in the land: The bioregional vision*. San Francisco: Sierra Club Books.

Schwab, J. (1994). *"Deeper shades of green: The rise of blue-collar and minority environmentalism in America"*. San Francisco: Sierra Club Books.

Singer, B. (1988). An extension of Rawls' theory of justice to environmental ethics. *Environmental Ethics* **10**, 217–231.

Snyder, G. (1990). *The practice of the wild*. San Francisco: North Point Press.

Tokar, B. (1992). *The green alternative: Creating an ecological future*. Philadelphia: New Society Publishers.

Watson, D. (1966). *Beyond Bookchin: Preface to a Future Social Ecology*. New York and Detroit: Autonomedia and Black & Red.

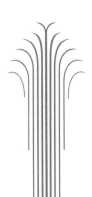

POLITICAL OBLIGATION

Terry Hopton
University of Central Lancashire

GLOSSARY

anarchism Rejection of political authority in any form as immoral.

consent Self-assumed, voluntary obligation of obedience to political authority.

contract Historical or quasi-historical, formal act of consent to establish political authority, which is held to be binding on subsequent generations.

hypothetical consent An obligation inferred from the belief that we ought to consent to political authority because it is legitimate, or because to consent would, in any case, be rational.

legitimacy Conformity of political authority to an independent criterion of rightness in terms of origin, procedure, or performance.

nonvoluntarist theory A form of theory of the Right that identifies obligations as a duty binding on individuals, irrespective of their own acts of commitment or consent.

philosophical anarchism An anarchist theory based on the failure of theories of political obligation that, nevertheless, accepts that there may be moral reasons for compliance.

political obligation Obligation of the individual to political authority, such as the law, government, or state, which is a moral reason for obedience.

pseudoproblem A philosophical "problem" that arises as a result of conceptual confusion and that is, because of this, incapable of solution.

tacit consent Consent given without an explicit or formal act, but that can be conventionally inferred from absence of dissent.

theory of the good The theory that certain acts are obligatory or right because they contribute to a state of affairs independently defined as morally good.

theory of the right The theory that certain acts are obligatory or right in themselves, irrespective of their consequences.

utilitarianism A form of theory of the Good that uses the pleasure or happiness consequent on acts as the criterion of what counts as morally good, and as a means of identifying what is right or obligatory by means of their contribution to this.

voluntarist theory A theory that identifies obligations as self-assumed by individuals by means of their acts of commitment or consent.

I. THE CONCEPT OF POLITICAL OBLIGATION

A. The Meaning of Political Obligation

The expression *POLITICAL OBLIGATION* has come to stand for a number of related problems concerning the relationship between politics and morality. Its central question is taken, variously, as asking why the individual morally ought to obey the law, government, state, or political authority generally. But it has also come to include other, more detailed, questions, such as those concerning the role of state intervention in specific areas and, at the other extreme, to include the most general pictures of political life and the human situation.

B. Origin of the Concept

The term "political obligation" only came into use in political theory after T. H. Green's *Lectures on the Principles of Political Obligation* of 1895. Green took political obligation as the core problem of political thought, both as constituting the newly reestablished academic discipline of political theory and as identifying a canon of classic texts from earlier periods. Although Green took the problem to be characteristic of individualist theories, which he was concerned to criticize, by extension it came to represent at a highly abstract level *the* theme of the history of political thought, from Plato's *Crito* to the present. (This was despite the enormous variety of political thought and practice that this encompassed). Green also sought to show how a theory of political obligation could be used to provide practical moral guidance on a range of practical political issues. These ranged from state regulation of the sale of alcohol to the justification of the death penalty. Few subsequent thinkers have shown a similar practical concern, being concerned with the problem at a more abstract level. Nor has much interest been shown in Green's solution to the problem, which consisted of a reinvigorated form of citizenship exemplified in practical service to the community.

C. Political Obligation and Ethics

It is important to emphasise that the problem of political obligation is concerned with *justification,* asking why people *ought* to obey the law, government, and so on, and not with the *explanation* of why, in fact, most people *do* obey. This is so even if their belief that they are justified in obeying is an important cause of their obedient behavior. In this sense some empirical theories, and "realist" theories, which might interpret such beliefs as an ideological sham to legitimate coercive power, are *not* about the problem of political obligation.

D. Classification of Theories

There is a considerable variety of potential solutions to the problem of political obligation, and although it is possible to classify these in different ways for different purposes, it is suggested that the following classification at least has the virtues of simplicity and clarity. It also accords with very general distinctions employed in contemporary ethics, which, given the insistence that the problem is a moral one, seem appropriate. Even so, two reservations must be made for reasons that will soon become apparent. First, the classification is not intended to be hard and fast, but as merely providing some signposts in a difficult landscape. Second, although it is possible to identify most theories with the name of a classical political theorist, because it seems that we have the entire history of political thought to draw on, this retrospective recruitment of contributors will inevitably be at the cost of insensitivity to their particular historical context. Moreover, pigeonholing into even the general classification suggested here might suggest that each thinker had only one solution to the problem. In fact, thinkers like Locke employ elements of different types of theory in an ensemble that seeks to achieve a structure of argument in order to influence a defined audience in a particular ideologically charged context.

It is possible to arrange theories of political obligation into three groups corresponding to basic responses to the question of obeying the law, government, and so on. First, those that claim that we *do* have a political obligation, a view which can be cautiously ascribed to most political thinkers of the past. Second, those that claim that we *do not* have a political obligation, a view identified with anarchist thinkers in the last 200 years. Third, those that claim that the problem has no clear answer because it is a result of conceptual confusion, or a *pseudoproblem,* a view explicitly held by some recent philosophers.

II. THEORIES OF POLITICAL OBLIGATION

A. Arguments for Political Obligation

The pattern of argument employed by theories seeking to show that we have a *political* obligation, is to take a familiar *moral* obligation and attempt to show that the former is analogous to, or a special case of, the latter. Our puzzlement about political obligation is thus solved by the use of a moral principle "writ large" as a model taken from the private to the public sphere. Given the diversity of possible moral principles in history that have come to constitute the substance of our modern moral thought, there are plenty of potential models available, not to mention many possible paradigm examples of each one. These may be broadly grouped into two categories corresponding to the contemporary distinction, popularized by Rawls, between Theories of the Right and Theories of the Good. Roughly translated into terms of political obligation. Theories of the Right would claim that I ought to obey the law, government, and so on, because it is my duty, and that it is right to do so *in itself*. Theories of the Good would claim that I ought to obey because it will bring about a good state of affairs in consequence.

B. Theories of the Right: Voluntarist Theories

1. Consent

The most influential voluntarist theories have been consent theories of various types. These tend to model our political obligation to the government or other institutions on obligations that arise from promises or voluntary agreements, and to see the state as a voluntary association. They emphasize that obligations are self-assumed individual commitments. Hence, although we have a duty to *keep* promises or agreements that we have made, there is no duty to *make* them. We can bind ourselves, or not, if we choose. Whatever the merits of consent theory in general, it is strongly concordant with modern notions like individual autonomy. Hence, if we believe both that we are politically obligated *and* autonomous, something like consent as a free and rational restriction of one's own freedom *must* be assumed. Similarly, if we believe that people are in some sense politically equal, the exercise of authority as a form of political inequality can only be comprehended as a result of consent if it is to be legitimate. While few doubt that political obligation could be created by consent, the problem is in indentifying when, where, and how this occurs. It is possible to distinguish several forms of consent theory according to their different stipulations of which of our acts count as our political consent.

a. Consent: Contract Theories

The first consent theory, and the theoretical paradigm for later versions, is the idea of a historical contract. By means of a contract, or similar agreement, men had passed from a prepolitical state of nature into a civil society, and this agreement was held to be binding on subsequent generations in that society. This type of theory, generally termed *social contract,* became dominant in the 17th century, when it accorded with the pervasive assumption that historical origins settled questions of legitimacy. Some thinkers were cautious

about asserting the actuality of such a historical event. This was understandable because contemporary critics pointed to the lack of evidence for a contract, to its absence from scriptural accounts (taken as historically true and divinely sanctioned), and to the uncertainty of the *terms* of the contract (evidenced by the variety and number of contracts used by different thinkers). Critics also objected to the idea that we could be bound by the consent of our ancestors (or at least that we could without invoking a separate duty of inheritance). In part, it was a tribute to the genius of contract theorists, to its concordance with new ways of thinking like individualism, and to its ideological value, that it was dominant in the face of such serious objections. In part also, theorists, such as Hobbes and Locke, employed other forms of consent theory alongside the contract. And it is these other forms that have become central to contemporary thinking about consent, while the historical contract idea lost its influence during the 19th century. These forms seek to retain the force of a contract and its conditions of validity, like absence of coercion and deception, without its formality and historicity.

b. Consent: Tacit Consent

In the *Second Treatise,* Section 119, Locke famously claimed that people tacitly consent to their government simply by living within its jurisdiction, although he was careful to indicate that this was so only if it was legitimate. Legitimacy here was defined as respecting and maintaining rights. This argument appears to be more plausible now than in Locke's time, because more people today have a degree of choice of living elsewhere, if they object to a government, in a way that was open to few then. The main objection to this account is that it robs consent of its meaning. Any act by any person, even done unwittingly, is taken as their consent. This is not to deny that there *is* such a thing as tacit consent, whereby even the absence of action, such as dissent, can be taken as consent. This is familiar in group meetings where actual votes are absent. But these cases exist because there are well-understood conventions about the moral significance of inaction at a given juncture. Locke, however, merely asserts that there is a binding convention about residence that takes *all* action at *any* time, or simply the absence of emigration, as constituting consent. There are strong grounds for doubting the existence of a convention, especially when those allegedly acting in compliance with it are unaware that they are doing so. (They may be said to follow the convention, but they cannot be acting in accordance with it.) The consequence would be that people, paradoxically, would be surprised to hear of their own "consent" when, elsewhere, consent conventions normally entail a self-conscious choice. In fact, Locke's tacit consent appears both unavoidable and deceptive in a way that would undermine the validity of more explicit formal acts of consent like contract.

c. Consent: Hypothetical Consent

An alternative form of consent theory, advanced by Pitkin, and attributed by her to Locke, is that of hypothetical consent. This directs our attention even more to the legitimacy of government. If government is fulfilling its moral purpose, however defined, then we ought to consent to it. Actual consent is reduced to the role of providing evidence of legitimacy, rather than creating it. An alternative formulation claims that consent to a legitimate state is simply *rational*. While a degree of rationality is normally required for a person to be counted as capable of consenting, to claim that rationality *is* consent is every bit as dubious as claiming that residence is. That people *ought* to consent, or rationally *would* consent, is simply not *actual* consent, but (at best) a background to it. Moreover, the problem of political obligation is, on this account, merely relocated to the problem of legitimacy, without answering the obvious questions of what makes a government legitimate and why I should obey one legitimate government rather than another, (that is, why is one *my* government?).

Looking at the three versions of consent mentioned so far, all meet the absence of actual consent to government by individuals by postulating a dutiful "double," who consents on our behalf, and yet over whom we have no control.

d. Consent: Voting

A more promising possibility, not widely available to earlier theorists, is to identify our *actual* consent with voting. Because voting is the one conspicuous and "official" political act that most contemporary citizens do every few years, this would go a long way toward the universality of obligation that most theories seem to seek. True, there are those who do not, or cannot, vote, and these presumably are not obligated (mere opportunity of voting cannot be consent). The problem here, as with tacit consent, is whether there is a well-established convention that identifies voting with consent to government. Voters think that they are choosing a representative and a party of government, but are they, at the same time, acquiring or confirming an obligation to obey even if "their" party loses? It could be argued that, by taking part, freely and deliberately, in elections their consent is *implied*. Consent to a procedure is consent to its outcome if it could reasonably be foreseen, as is the case with majority decisions. But such a suggestion seems quite idealistic in view of what we know about voting behavior, the electoral process, and democratic systems generally. And if one votes *against* a party, say the Nazis in 1933, does this obligate you to their government if they win?

e. Consent: Reformist Consent

One response to the difficulties of both the absence of actual consent, and of counting other things as its equivalent, is to admit that the political system cannot be interpreted to fit the theory. Instead, the system must be changed in practice so that it relies on actual consent and also provides the encouragement and reasons for people to consent. This reformist theory, suggested by Beran, for example, requires things like the establishment of "dissenter's territories" to ensure that there is a genuine alternative in order to make consent a reality. It would not be overly cynical to suggest that governments are unlikely to carry out such reforms, preferring nonactual consent that can safely be taken for granted.

A more radical theory, like that of Pateman, insists that a yet more fundamental change is required. Here, the suggestion is that consent is not enough, implying as it does, acceptance of something presented *to us*, rather than a participation *by us*, in creating and shaping it. This leads in the direction of direct participatory democracy.

2. Fair Play

Alongside consent theories it is worth considering another theory that can be conveniently classified as a voluntarist Theory of the Right. This is the fair play theory that originated in the work of H. L. A. Hart and Rawls. It likens the state to a voluntary scheme of cooperation where the benefits of the scheme are made possible by the contributions of the members. It suggests that if one is a beneficiary of the contributions made by others, then one has an obligation to reciprocally contribute and, by so doing, to continue the scheme. By analogy, it is argued that if one benefits from the state in the form of, say, security, and this is made possible by contributions by others in taxation and keeping the law, then one has, in turn, an obligation to pay tax and keep the law when the occasion arises. However, as Simmons points out, this only appears plausible if we are voluntarily members of the scheme, or have become so by voluntarily *accepting*, rather than passively *receiving*, benefits. These requirements serve as the equivalent of consent. While this element does appear to be needed for political obligation to arise, it is difficult to make a distinction between acceptance and receipt when the state's benefits, unlike smaller schemes, are unavoidably open to all (for example: defense). This makes it impossible to identify noncontributing beneficiaries or deliberate free-riders who could be excluded, or conversely, to identify those willingly committing themselves. In effect, the benefits are compulsory, because unavoidable, and few would accept that they create an obligation in return. A commercial equivalent would be receiving unsolicited goods followed by coercive demands for payment. A possible exception suggested by Klosko are "presumptive" benefits, for example: security that we can assume people *must* want (and would *accept* if a convention for doing so was available). However, one might ask whether they want them at *this* cost, and from *this* source (that is, political obligation to the state), especially if there are alternative suppliers. And, in any case, this merely reiterates the problem of hypothetical consent where if we "must" means that we "ought" to consent. And this does not create a political obligation. Moreover, it is important that the scheme *is* fair for fair play to arise. This means that there should be an accepted fair allocation of contributions and benefits across the scheme and some relation between the two in the case of each member. It is neither obvious nor uncontroversial that this is the case with the state, given persistent and undeniable inequalities in society.

C. Theories of the Right: Nonvoluntarist Theories

1. Duties of Obedience

In contrast to the voluntarist theories just considered, nonvoluntarist theories argue that we have a duty of obedience irrespective of our choice. Many of these fail to correspond to modern ideas of individuality, and they presuppose a world view that has largely disappeared from Western societies. For example, highly influential theories that argued for unquestioning obedience to the king on the basis of divine right, by scriptural injunction (especially Romans 13), by appeals to natural hierarchies, or by analogy with children's duties to parents (patriarchalism), have all lost their force. (This does not, however, necessarily apply outside Western societies.) A more sceptical suggestion might be that they have been replaced by consent only in a form that, despite its voluntarist credentials, proves to be as unavoidable as duty ever was. Despite this general picture, two types of duty have been suggested as models for political obligation in recent years, although both contain voluntarist elements.

a. Gratitude

It has been argued by A. D. Walker that our political obligation arises as a debt of gratitude, owed to government, for the benefits that it has bestowed upon us. This may also prove to be the basis for the family duties of children to parents employed in earlier theories like patriarchialism. Gratitude is normally *warranted* when a benefactor bestows an unquestioned benefit, at the cost of some sacrifice on his part and without seeking a return of benefit. Gratitude is normally *expressed* in degree and kind according to conventions of appropriateness that, nevertheless, leave much discretion to the beneficiary. Paradigm cases tend to be of highly personal debts of gratitude such as that owed by someone who had been drowning to his rescuer. Some deny that an institution, for example a hospital, rather than an individual within it, can be treated as a benefactor. Even if a government is not ruled out for this reason, it is difficult to see it as making sacrifices to provide benefits, especially when these are paid for by the taxation of the recipients. It would also be naive to see this provision as disinterested, rather than designed to generate feelings of gratitude and, hence, support. This might be compared with commercial sponsorship, or even bribery, rather than pure beneficence. Another reservation about the gratitude model is that government, in contrast to normal benefactors, demands the degree and kind of gratitude that it expects (namely: political obligation). And although this model drops the idea of a scheme as used in the fair play theory, it does rely on the benefactor–beneficiary relation being continuous in a way that is relatively rare in modern society. It also shares with the fair play model the difficulty of distinguishing acceptance and recipience. This is not normally a difficulty in paradigm cases of gratitude, such as life saving, where acceptance is obvious (albeit in dire necessity). But it may well be so in the case of "open" state benefits.

b. Natural Duty of Justice

The second nonvoluntarist duty suggested as a model for political obligation is that of natural duty. In traditional versions this would crucially depend on shared foundational assumptions about the moral significance of "nature" in a wide sense. In the recent version found in Rawls' *A Theory of Justice* there is a natural duty to obey *just institutions,* including states, on entirely different foundations. This is because parties in Rawls' "original position," a hypothetical situation of fairness, would base their rational political obligation on this. (They would, as hypothetically rational individuals, decide to make obedience to a just state their duty.) It is also, supposedly, in accordance with out intuitions about the necessary arrangements of a just society. The plausibility of this account crucially depends on the plausibility of Rawls' theory as a whole, and here one can only say that the debate continues. However, it seems that even if this account does not actually turn into a hypothetical consent theory, it will suffer from the same problems.

D. Theories of the Good

Having looked at Theories of the Right, both voluntarist and nonvoluntarist, and found them deficient as theories of political obligations, it is necessary to turn to Theories of the Good. Here the obligation is generated by its contribution to a good state of affairs.

1. Utilitarianism

This is by far the most familiar and influential contemporary version of a Theory of the Good, where goodness is defined as utility (itself defined as pleasure, happiness, welfare, and so on). Here the right action depends on the net utility it produces in consequence (after deduction of its disutility). This appears to rule out action done in accordance with obligation as having any independent or special worth. But in one variety of utilitarianism—rule utilitarianism—obligations are reinstated as rules, the following of which have been found to have indisputable utility. Here it is argued that obligations have to be kept, even when specific breaches would produce seemingly greater utility, because otherwise uncertainty and disappointed expectations (both disutilities), would result. Obligations, including political obligation, are thus justified as contributing to "the greatest happiness of the greatest number." In fact, apart from this, utilitarianism has very little more to say on the subject. It takes the utility of government, and the obedience to it, for granted, by assuming that it is indispensable as a means to the utilitarian end.

The utilitarian account of political obligation is entirely dependent on the validity of utilitarian theory in general. While it was used by Bentham and his successors as a public philosophy, and might be suitable on that account for *political* obligation, it does have major disadvantages. This is in spite of its admission of voluntarism, either in the form of individual choice or discovery by individuals of what makes them happy. (The plurality of many different individual pursuits is "cashed" into the common currency of utility.) It is this individualism, and a kind of economic rationality, that seems to accord with widespread modern ideas.

Although it has not lacked for ingenious defenders, utilitarianism is widely thought to have severe limitations. Many are unconvinced that its account of obligation is really satisfactory. Others doubt that one can really *calculate* utility—especially when only the vaguest examples are offered by utilitarians. Others, too, object to the assimilation of moral reflection to a form of calculation as being a distortion. This is particularly so as it suggests that deep convictions, that form our moral identity, are also merely the contingent product of calculation. And if utilitarianism is meant to uncover the logic of our moral beliefs, there seem to be examples where the sacrifice of individuals for the greater happiness is promoted in a way rejected by common morality. For these reasons, utilitarianism is probably an insecure foundation for political obligation.

2. Other Theories of The Good

Of course The Good need not be defined in utilitarian terms. It could be defined in more specific terms, but this would be at the cost of more general acceptance. This difficulty can be evaded by invoking ideas like *the common* or *public good,* but when these are unpacked they tend to lose their plausibility. In terms of political obligation, this move will still rely on the state as a necessary, or uniquely effective, way of promoting whatever counts as The Good. However, it must be conceded, because many ideas of The Good presuppose political order for their attainment, the role of the state is not obviously easily dispensed with. Hobbes, in particular, was anxious to remind men of this.

3. Aristotle's Theory of The Good

A much older theory of The Good is that of Aristotle, although to call this "a theory of political obligation" is stretching the definition a good deal. Here, participation in the life of the state as a citizen is seen as *intrinsic* to the good life for any human being of full rationality. It is not a *means* to something else, such as an individual's privately chosen good. To be political, for Aristotle, is part of what it means to fulfill the function of a human being, as cutting is to fulfill the function of a knife. The idea of obligation seems out of place here for two reasons. First, the morality is one of virtues or excellencies of character, rather than the modern morality of duties and obligations. It is a human excellence to be a citizen. Second, the state is not something *other* than the citizen, to which he needs to be bound by an obligation. Rather the state *is* the citizen body. This represents an ideal where each rules, and is ruled in turn, as equals. In practice, as Aristotle knew, there is a distinction between being a good citizen and being a good man in any state, short of the ideal. It is this distinction that makes the arguments of Plato's *Crito,* concerning the acceptance by Socrates of the death penalty imposed on him by Athens, seem so central to the problem of political obligation.

Although the recovery of the importance of The Political, that some contemporary theorists call for, would contribute to making a revival of Aristotelian citizenship possible, it is not at all clear how this could be done without the most massive changes in modern society. (This would apply to Green's idea of citizenship also, even if he does not seem aware of this.) Not only that, but a new metaphysical foundation would be required to establish the idea of a human "function." This would be something that is quite alien to modern ways of thought.

III. ANARCHIST THEORIES

A. The Form of Anarchist Theories

Having looked at theories that claim that we *do* have a political obligation, it is worth pointing out that none of them claims that this obligation is absolute. The absence of moral reasons for obligation becomes the grounds for refusal or even for a duty of resistance. It is the defining feature of anarchist theories that they claim that we *never* have a political obligation to government. However, because most envisage anarchy as a form of society rather than chaos, other obligations or communal ties are accentuated to *displace* political obligation, or to *become* political obligation in a nonauthoritarian form. The pattern of argument that emerges is one in which one form of obligation, familiar in everyday morality, is taken as the model, *not* for obedience to government, but for the operation of an alternative form of society. In fact, it can be suggested that every obligation that has been used as a model for government, can be used as a model to replace it.

B. Philosophical Anarchism

A recent type of anarchism, which explicitly addresses the problem of political obligation, philosophical anarchism. In Simmons' version it is a *last resort* following the failure of all other theories. After examining most of the theories mentioned above (citizenship being a notable absentee), and finding none adequate, he concludes that there is *no* political obligation. His argument depends on the list of candidate theories being exhaustive and exclusive of each other. It is

thus vulnerable to the production of an additional theory, or to the (admittedly faint) possibility that a composite theory might not suffer from the defects of its constituent theories. It is also vulnerable to counterargument in support of the theories that he rejects.

In fact, the consequences, of Simmons' position are insignificant in practice, because he believes that our ordinary, everyday various moral obligations, *not* treated as models of political obligation, are sufficient to tie us to our political society. At the very least, government is left in place as a significant nonmoral fact of life. Much the same is true of Wolff's theory, where philosophical anarchism is a *first resort.* Wolff argues that the quest for a theory of political obligation is doomed from the start. In a devastatingly simple argument, he claims that to be a moral agent is to be autonomous, but that to obey authority is an abdication of autonomy (and by definition immoral). It follows that autonomy and authority are incompatible, and any theory of political obligation "justifying" obedience *must* fail, because it is necessarily immoral. Wolff's critics, of whom there are many, have pointed out that this idea of authority is so strong that it preludes *any* commitment, because it is a loss of autonomy. Authority, in turn, is defined as something that is obeyed *because* it is authority and for no other reason. There is no compelling reason to accept these definitions, which take common understandings of them to extremes. Wolff's attempts to fill out his argument become quite confused. He does make clear that there is an exception to his claim that a legitimate state is a "logical impossibility," and that exception is a unanimous direct democracy. This is, however, eventually dismissed as utopian. Surprisingly, despite the radical sound of this theory, it will, Wolff believes, have little effect in practice. He believes that philosophical anarchists will autonomously find good reasons of their own to *comply with* rather than *obey* "their" government and state.

C. Classical Anarchism

In the classical anarchist theories and their contemporary descendants, there is a rejection of the state, accompanied by suggested measures for its abolition. They propose an alternative form of society based on the strength of a moral principle, such as nonviolence in Tolstoy, or collective solidarity in Bakunin. Such arguments rely on the possiblity that a moral principle that some people adhere to some of the time, will be adhered to by just about everyone just about all of the time.

This would then serve as the basis for a new society. If this possibility was dismissed, anarchist writers would still serve to remind us that even governments and states that are normally thought of as legitimate have many morally dubious features. And this only goes to emphasize the difficulty of the problem of political obligation.

IV. POLITICAL OBLIGATION AS A PSEUDOPROBLEM

The final response to the problem of political obligation is that of what could be called "conceptualism." This argues that the problem is incoherent and that no justification of obligation is either possible or necessary. This argument was developed as a response inspired by 20th-century analytical or linguistic philosophy to the diversity of previous theories, and to the failure of any to gain wide acceptance. The reason for this scandalous state of affairs was held to be due to the imprecision of the problem, and to the craving for a general theory—when there could only be different reasons for obedience, for different people, in different cases. (Asking why I should obey the state was analogous to asking why I should read books.) While there is much force in these objections, a stronger group of arguments was advanced, which purported to show that the problem could not even arise. The state was compared to the rules of a game like chess. Objections made to following laws, or rules, can only show that we have not understood that *that* is precisely what membership of the state, or playing the game, means. But this obviously depends on an untenable analogy between states and games. A second argument, related to the first, pointed out that a legitimate state *ought to be obeyed* because that is what *legitimate* means. One has, simply by definition, an obligation to a legitimate state. But even were this true, and the meaning of legitimacy is hardly clear-cut, this only displaces the problem to one of deciding what counts as legitimate, as was noted in the case of hypothetical consent earlier. A final argument asserted that seeking a justification of the state went beyond the bounds of meaningful justification. By analogy, while we can doubt our senses *on occasion* it does not, contra Descartes, make sense to doubt them *always*. We may, then, doubt particular obligations, but not that we are still obligated to the state. But the morality of obedience is hardly as indubitable as the veracity of our senses. Certainly, to doubt specific political obligations presupposes that there can be genuine political obligation, but it does not, *of itself,* establish that there is.

Two things make the conceptual argument persuasive. One is the implied limitation to liberal democracies, where legitimacy is taken for granted. The other is the assumption that any justification of political obligation must be metaphysical and thereore unacceptable in the new philosophical climate. The consequence of the argument is, by denying there is a genuine problem, to assume that there *is* political obligation, but that it is something about which we must remain silent and leave as it is.

V. CONCLUSION

Recently there have been some indications of a new direction in thinking about political obligation. Dworkin has suggested that political obligations most resemble those generated in friendships and other groups that can be classed as neither the result of a voluntary decision or as nonvoluntary. These "associative" or "communal" obligations suggest a move from the individualism that most contemporary theories presume. A related suggestion is made by Horton who argues for a richer understanding of what membership of a polity entails than can be captured by analogy with one particular model of obligation.

None of the theories considered are without difficulties. This is true of theories that seek to show that we *do* have a political obligation, or that we *do not*, or that it is *not a genuine problem*. Yet it is clear that people act as if there was an obligation. The practice of obeying political authority seems to persist, while theories come and go. Perhaps even if no theory is successful, each raises considerations that should have a place in any moral reflection by individuals about politics. Rather than *solve* the problem, such considerations make us aware of the difficulties involved. This applies also to actions and relationships in respect of institutions and practices not normally thought of as political, in our more general social and economic lives, for instance, areas normally thought of as private.

Also See the Following Articles

ARISTOTELIAN ETHICS • CITIZENSHIP • CONTRACTARIAN ETHICS • MORAL DEVELOPMENT • RIGHTS THEORY • THEORIES OF JUSTICE: HUMAN NEEDS

Bibliography

Beran, H. (1987). *The consent theory of political obligation*. London: Croom Helm.

Gans, C. (1992). *Philosophical anarchism and political disobedience*. Cambridge: Cambridge University Press.

Harris, P. (Ed.). (1990). *On political obligation*. London: Routledge.

Horton, J. (1992). *Political obligation*. London: Macmillan.

Klosko, G. (1992). *The principle of fairness and political obligation*. Lanham, MD: Rowman and Littlefield.

Marshall, P. (1993). *Demanding the Impossible: A history of anarchism*. London: Fontana Press.

Pateman, C. (1985). *The problem of political obligation* (2nd ed.). Oxford: Polity Press.

Pitkin, H. (1992). Obligation and consent. In P. Laslett, W. G. Runciman, & Q. Skinner (Eds.). *Philosophy, politics and society* (4th series). Oxford: Basil Blackwell.

Simmons, A. J. (1979). *Moral principles and political obligations*. Princeton, NJ: Princeton University Press.

Walker, A. D. (1989). Political obligation and gratitude. *Philosophy and Public Affairs, 18*, 359–364.

Wolff, R. P. (1976). *In defense of anarchism* (2nd ed.). New York: Harper and Row.

PORNOGRAPHY

Susan Easton
Brunel University

I. Defining Pornography
II. The Regulation of Pornography
III. The Harm Principle: The Liberal Defense
of Pornography
IV. The Harm Principle: Critiques of Pornography

GLOSSARY

erotica Erotica represents the world of the sensual and depicts sexual activity but, unlike pornography, does not present sexual relations in a degrading or dehumanizing way.

harm principle The principle that the only ground on which intervention is justified is to prevent harm to others; the individual's own good is not a sufficient justification.

moral independence The concept that the individual should not be prevented from freely expressing ideas, provided that no tangible harms to others result directly from their expression, even if others think those ideas are foolish, mistaken, or offensive.

obscenity Material that is indecent, offensive to modesty or decency, expressing or suggesting lewd thoughts, and tending to deprave and corrupt. Obscene materials appeal to a prurient interest in sex and portray sexual conduct in a patently offensive way.

pornography The word "pornography" originates from Greek and means writing about prostitutes. It has

also been defined as sexually explicit material that subordinates women through pictures or words.

PORNOGRAPHY has been described as hard to define but easy to recognize. Justice Stewart said in *Jacobellis v. Ohio* (1972, 378 U.S. 184) that he was unable to define pornography but he knew it when he saw it. The word "pornography" originates from Greek and means writing about prostitutes. Pornography should be distinguished from obscenity, which means filthy or disgusting. Obscenity rather than pornography is the term normally found in legal instruments. The *Oxford English Dictionary* defines "obscene" as filthy, indecent, offensive to modesty or decency, expressing or suggesting lewd thoughts. It defines "pornography" as the description of the life and manners of prostitutes and their patrons. Legal usage does not conform to everyday language or to dictionary definitions.

I. DEFINING PORNOGRAPHY

Schauer favors a definition of pornography in terms of sexual depiction rather than obscenity, as obscenity could, but need not, be pornographic, and pornography may, but need not, be obscene (1982. *Free Speech: A Philosophical Inquiry*. Cambridge Univ. Press, Cambridge). In England the Obscene Publications Act 1959 has been used to prosecute leaflets extolling drug use

Encyclopedia of Applied Ethics, Volume 3
Copyright © 1998 by Academic Press. All rights of reproduction in any form reserved.

but has been deployed primarily to control pornography.

Obscenity is defined in the Obscene Publications Act in terms of its tendency to deprave and corrupt, that is, its impact rather than content. In considering whether the material in question is obscene, the court will consider whether its effect is, taken as a whole, such as to tend to deprave and corrupt persons who are likely, having regard to all relevant circumstances, to read, see, or hear the matter contained or embodied in it. The material may include books, pictures, films, and videocassettes. However, the future medium for the dissemination of pornography is likely to be computer disks or CD-ROMs, and as Manchester notes, there may be problems in controlling the electronic transmission of material under existing legislation (C. Manchester, 1995. *Crim. LR,* 546). Does a computer disk constitute an article as defined in section 1(2) of the 1959 Act? If information is transmitted electronically does it constitute a "publication" under the Act? The Home Affairs Committee's report (*Computer Pornography* (1994), H.C. 126) recommended amending the legislation so that the electronic transmission of information from one computer to another constitutes publication.

The Obscene Publications Act includes a public good defense if it can be proved that publication of the article in question is justified as being for the public good on the grounds that it is in the interests of science, literature, art, or learning, or of other objects of general concern. The focus in English law is on the state of mind of the consumer, rather than on harms to others. The legislation was criticized by the Williams Committee for its inconsistency. It noted the difficulty of finding a reliable criterion for separating work of no value from valuable work, and of relying on juries to reach decisions on such matters (B. Williams, 1979. *Report of the Committee on Obscenity and Film Censorship.* Cmnd 77. HMSO, London). It has also been criticized by feminist campaigners because it does not take account of the effects of pornography on women.

Child pornography is covered by the Protection of Children Act 1978 which makes it an offense to publish, distribute, or take an indecent photograph of a child. Section 160 of the Criminal Justice Act 1988 makes it an offense to possess an indecent photograph of a child. The Criminal Justice and Public Order Act 1994 tried to strengthen the law relating to adult and child pornography and to restrict children's access to harmful videos. It amends the Protection of Children Act to cover data stored on a computer disk or by other electronic means which is capable of conversion into a photograph or pseudo-photograph. The question of harm is also recognized by sections 89 and 90 of the 1994 Act which amends section 2 of the Video Recordings Act regarding the classification of video recordings, so that an authority in reaching a decision regarding the suitability of a video recording should have special regard to any harm which may be caused to potential viewers, or through their behavior, to society by the manner in which the work deals with criminal behavior, illegal drugs, violent behavior, or incidents, horrific behavior or incidents, or human sexual activities.

In the United States Catherine MacKinnon and Andre Dworkin, in drafting Minneapolis and Indianapolis ordinances, defined pornography as sexually explicit material which subordinates women through pictures or words. It includes scenes of women enjoying pain, humiliation, rape, and penetration by objects or animals, or shown as bruised or hurt in a context which makes these conditions sexual. It would also include scenes of men and children being treated in sexually dehumanizing ways.

Recurring themes found in pornography include multiple rape, men planning and executing a rape which the victim enjoys despite initial resistance, sadism, and the profaning of the sacred. The latter dimension has received less attention in current debate, but in the past has been used as a strong motif in pornographic works, featuring in the writings of de Sade. The view of pornography as liberating, radical, and challenging has partly developed because of the shock and outrage caused by profanity.

Feinberg distinguishes three definitions of obscenity. Obscenity may be used in a pejorative, judgmental way, to suggest the offended state of mind of the maker of the statement. It is also used by the courts to refer to material aimed at producing an erotic response in the consumer. Thirdly, obscenity may be used in a neutral way to classify material, for example, describing the fact that it contains certain words (J. Feinberg, 1987. *Harm to Others.* Oxford Univ. Press, London). Obscenity is seen by Feinberg as a particular form of offensiveness, suggesting disgust, producing what he calls a "yuk" reaction, and allurement.

He is critical of the identification of pornography with obscenity. Although the two may overlap they are not identical. Because pornography is used descriptively to refer to sexually explicit writing and pictures, he says it is narrower than the obscene. Pornography is confined to sex, while obscenity is more than sex. But it may be difficult to maintain such a sharp distinction since disgusting materials might still be intended to produce a sexual response and have that effect, however bizarre the taste or the audience.

The U.S. Supreme Court's analysis of obscenity has developed in the context of assessing challenges to the constitutionality of laws passed by state legislatures to control obscenity. Prior to 1957 the Court used the Hicklin Test, the tendency to deprave and corrupt, when considering obscene materials. In *Roth v. United States* (1957, 354 U.S. 476) the Supreme Court excluded obscene material from the protection of the free speech principle, but since then the Court has had difficulties in defining what constitutes obscenity. The test of whether material was obscene was whether the dominant theme of the material taken as a whole appeals to a prurient interest. The effect on the average person is taken into account, applying contemporary community standards to the work. Each of these concepts has raised problems of interpretation. In *Stanley v. Georgia* (1969, 394 U.S. 557) the possession of obscene material at home was held to be protected by the right to privacy.

In *Miller v. California* (1973, 413 U.S. 15) the court defined obscenity to mean works which appeal to a prurient interest in sex, which portray sexual conduct in a patently offensive way, and which, taken as a whole, do not have serious literary, artistic, political, or scientific value. The court affirmed that prohibitions on obscenity do have constitutional validity, but subsequent attempts to ground regulation in harm, such as the Indianapolis ordinance, have received little support from the court.

The aim of the ordinance was to hold pornographers accountable for injuries to others; to provide remedies, including damages and injunctions, for proven injury; and to prevent unjust enrichment from that injury. Men, children, and transsexuals injured by pornography would also have been able to obtain remedies under the ordinance. It encompassed a number of issues, including trafficking, assault, coercion, and the forced consumption of pornography. The Indianapolis ordinance was struck down in the Supreme Court as a violation of First Amendment free speech rights.

In considering the ordinance in *American Booksellers v. Hudnut* (1986, 475 U.S. 1001), the Supreme Court acknowledged the harms caused to women by pornography. But the harms were seen as outweighed by the need to protect free speech rights, and the ordinance was seen as a content-based restriction, which discriminated on the basis of viewpoint. It amounted to "thought control" in defining an approved view of women and it was stressed that the feminist view of pornography was one standpoint among others. Perceptions of pornography varied according to standpoint, and the ordinance could therefore not be justified. While a civil rights ordinance was favored by reformers in the United States, in England consideration has been given to other possibilities, including a criminal offense of incitement to sexual hatred.

A distinction is also often drawn between erotica and pornography, the former representing the world of the sensual and depicting sexual activity, but unlike pornography, not presenting sexual relations in a degrading or dehumanizing way. However, while this distinction is well established in Western culture, in other cultures such as China, erotic or even romantic material may be seen as pornographic.

A useful classification was given in *R. v. Butler* (1992, 89 Dom LR 449) where the Canadian Supreme Court distinguished between materials depicting the following: (i) explicit sex with violence; (ii) explicit sex without violence, but which subjects people to treatment that is degrading and dehumanizing; and (iii) explicit sex without violence which is neither degrading nor dehumanizing. Feminist campaigns for regulation and prohibition are directed at the first two categories.

Demands for the regulation of pornography raise philosophical, empirical, and legal questions. The philosophical issues include the question of whether pornography constitutes speech, the boundaries between speech and conduct, the nature and scope of the free speech principle, and the relationship between the state and the individual. The empirical problems center on the measurement of the effects of pornography. Legal problems have arisen over the drafting of appropriate legislation, evidentiary problems regarding the burden and standard of proof, the appropriate remedies for those harmed by pornography, and procedural issues concerning the responsibility for determining the impact of pornography in a particular case (whether this should lie with expert witnesses, the jury, or the judiciary). Problems have faced the courts in determining the scope of free speech protection and framing appropriate legislation in England and the United States.

II. THE REGULATION OF PORNOGRAPHY

The dispute over pornography and censorship has split both liberals and feminists. The role of pornography in legitimating and perpetuating violence against women has been of great concern within feminism. As well as stimulating theoretical debates, the problem of pornography has also generated political activism, culminating in pickets of sex shops, "off the shelf" campaigns directed at high street retailers, and vigorous demands for legal constraints on the free market in pornography.

The emancipatory potential of pornography in liberating sexual inhibitions and providing affirmation to sexual minorities has also been considered. The demands for the regulation of pornography have been seen as raising the issue of censorship of ideas and publications by the state. Once the regulation of pornography is in place, it is feared that there is a risk of censorship of political, religious, and artistic works, including gay and lesbian literature. There are many literary, artistic, and educational texts which have been suppressed in the past but which have later been recognized as valuable. The risk of suppression is that unconventional political views and artistic expression will be crushed, and the effect of state censorship is to stifle radical thinking.

The problem of pornography has been a central issue within liberalism, and arguments both for and against the regulation of pornography may utilize classical liberal ideas. Mill's "On Liberty" offers a useful source of concepts and methods, including the harm principle, which are used by both sides in the pornography and censorship debate. Liberal defenders of pornography have deployed Mill's notion of moral independence, his plea for toleration, and his focus on the importance of a range of opinions for social and individual improvement to allow for the possibility of learning through errors and experience.

Millian arguments have dominated debates on free speech and censorship. The major justifications of free speech found in English and American jurisprudence, including the democracy and truth justifications, are advanced in Mill's writing and have been used by defenders of pornography. The harm principle has underpinned this debate.

III. THE HARM PRINCIPLE: THE LIBERAL DEFENSE OF PORNOGRAPHY

Mill's objective in "On Liberty" was to chart "the nature and limits of the power which can be legitimately exercised over the individual" (1970, 126). What is needed, said Mill, is one very simple principle to govern the relationship between society and the individual. The principle he offers is the harm principle: the only ground on which intervention is justified is to prevent harm to others, and "his own good, either physical or moral is not a sufficient warrant" (1970, 135).

The feminist demand for regulation of pornography, a matter which properly concerns only the passive consumer, would be seen by defenders of pornography as a clear example of the unwarranted intrusion of public opinion and constraints into the self-regarding sphere. Pornography is seen as "harmless" in so far as no compelling evidence has been offered of any tangible harm to others. Of course one might argue that it is in the consumer's interest to refrain from this activity, and therefore to restrict access to pornographic materials because they are demeaning to users and they divert them from more worthy self-enhancing occupations. It is precisely this type of argument for restriction which is ruled out on Mill's principle, for here the focus would be on the consumer, and "in the part which merely concerns himself . . . over his own body and mind, the individual is sovereign" (1970, 135). For Mill, no matter how degrading and depraved an activity is, if no one else is affected by it, the fact that others may think that foregoing this activity would make an individual a happier or better person is not sufficient to justify the imposition of sanctions.

Mill exempts from his doctrine immature and mentally impaired individuals, so children and those who are incapacitated are excluded, but adults' preferences clearly fall within the principle of liberty. Within this domain of personal liberty lie the realms of consciousness, thought, and feeling. Where opinions are concerned, whatever the subject matter, absolute freedom is essential.

The appropriate guardian of the individual's mental, spiritual, and physical health is the individual. If the effect on others infringes their rights or substantially affects their interests, then regulation of the harmful activity might be appropriate, but otherwise the appropriate sanction would be mere criticism.

On this argument, legal regulation of the kind embodied in the Indianapolis Ordinance would seem to be an unjustified intervention, as sexuality is the most private area of self-expression and self-realization. Consequently attempts to control pornography, other than by persuasion, have been firmly resisted by liberal theorists. Any increase in state power is seen as an evil in itself and the specter of state officials investigating private activities and thoughts accounts for much of the liberal fear of feminist protest. This fear has also characterized some feminist approaches, and partly accounts for skepticism over the use of the law as a feminist strategy.

In defending the realm of personal sovereignty, Mill stresses that he is not undervaluing the exercise or development of higher faculties, or treating all pleasures as equal. But the "lowest" preferences deserve protection: no one is warranted in preventing other adults from adopting a particular activity—from doing what they like with their own lives—when they are the best judges of their own feelings. The outsider may offer observations on more edifying pursuits and seek to persuade, but ultimately individuals must decide for themselves.

Mill recognizes that there may be hard cases which lie on the boundary between self-regarding and other-regarding action, but this is precisely why a free and wide range of opinions are necessary, in order to find the best policy to adopt consistent with respect for the individual's rights and interests. If activities such as drinking and gambling are acceptable in private, why should we condemn them because they operate as a business, governed by commercial considerations? Similarly one might argue that if sexual relations conducted by consenting and loving adults constitute a social good, then individuals working in the sex industry should not be attacked simply because the cash nexus is involved. However, Mill recognized that commercial motives and financial interests could lead proprietors to encourage excessive use of drink and gambling.

The fear for the liberal defender of pornography is the prospect of disapproval being hardened into legal and physical restraints on actions—into civil or criminal sanctions. Even if *some* pornography is used for improper means, for example, as an aid to rape by an unbalanced individual with a prior disposition to harm others, this does not justify denial of access to pornography to the vast majority of law-abiding consumers who use pornography for private noncriminal activities, for example, as harmless fantasy or sexual aids.

Claims of a causal link between the circulation of pornography and violent crime have met with considerable skepticism from pornographers, commentators, and investigators, including the President's Commission (The Report of the Commission on Obscenity and Pornography, 1970. Washington, U.S. Government Printing Office, Washington, DC), in the United States and the Williams Committee (1979) in the United Kingdom. But some defenders of pornographers further argue that pornography has positive benefits in contributing to individual and social well-being, including liberating individuals from taboos and constraints at the harmless level of fantasy, promoting personal growth and awareness, and providing a catharsis for individual sexual tensions. Pornography may also be used in therapeutic programs to reeducate sex offenders away from negative perceptions of sexuality into more positive attitudes and behaviors.

Restrictions have found more favor than prohibition with liberal commentators. The Williams Committee (1979) advocated restricting the public display of material which others find environmentally unattractive and denying access to sex clubs to minors, while leaving adults a free choice whether or not to buy the goods or to enter those clubs. Restrictions were also imposed by the Indecent Displays (Control) Act 1981.

Millian principles have often been invoked in defense of free speech. Free speech has been seen as essential to the functioning of democracy and representative government, the promotion of autonomy, and the pursuit of the truth. Applying these justifications of free speech to pornographic materials has proved difficult. Pornography does not constitute political speech and does not contribute to the democratic process, so it is hard to justify it by appealing to the democracy justification. The point was made forcefully by Justice Stevens in *Young v. American Mini-Theatres* (1976, 427 U.S. 50) that every schoolchild can understand the duty to defend the right to speak in relation to political or philosophical discussion, but "few of us would march our children off to war to preserve the citizen's right to see Specified Sexual Activities exhibited in the theater of our choice."

The autonomy justification is also difficult to apply since pornography contributes little to the self-fulfillment of the consumer or to the promotion of autonomy, and the truth justification is problematic since pornography makes no obvious contribution to the pursuit of the truth. In fact it may prevent the discovery of the truth about women's abilities. Some might argue that pornography should not be seen as speech because it lacks the dimension of communication, but is simply a sexual aid, but others would argue that what is pernicious in pornography is precisely the message it communicates about women. If it is seen as speech it might be seen as a form of commercial speech which contributes to sex discrimination and therefore justifies a much lower weighting than political speech.

Nonetheless pornography has attracted considerable and vigorous support from defenders of free speech. Freedom of thought is meaningless without the freedom to publish. A slippery slope argument is also invoked in support of the pornographer's right to publish. If sexual material is restricted, then sex education in schools may be exposed to the risk of control and political ideas, and literary and artistic works will also be under threat. Moreover, it is argued that a free market in ideas and opinions is essential to the public good in affording the possibility of acquiring knowledge of satisfying ways of living.

In modern liberal thought the right to consume pornography has been defended by Ronald Dworkin, who bases his defense on the right to moral independence, that is, the right not to suffer disadvantages in the distribution of social goods and opportunities or in liberties just because others think that one's opinion about the best way to lead one's own life is flawed. He says the right to moral independence demands a permissive legal attitude toward the consumption of pornography in private. His argument would permit a restriction scheme similar to that advocated by the Williams Report. The individual's right to moral independence cannot be breached simply on the grounds that the community as a whole will benefit. For Dworkin the right trumps utilitarian demands for prohibition when the majority find the idea of consuming pornography offensive.

Dworkin's critique of the Williams Report and his defense of the right to consume pornography has been subjected to criticism from within feminist theory, but some feminists have used Dworkinian ideas to support an argument for regulation. For example, if one begins from the premise of mass culture, one might accept a Dworkinian rights-based argument and yet reach an opposite conclusion to Dworkin. One might argue that the effect of a free market in pornography is to violate women's right to autonomy, self-fulfillment, and equal concern and respect, and that the free speech of pornographers silences women's speech. A free market gives more weight to the preferences of producers and consumers of pornography than to women's rights to autonomy and equality. If women's right to autonomy is given more weight, the case for regulation does not rely here on the condemnation of the consumer as a bad person and so does not violate the consumer's right to moral independence.

One could also appeal to Dworkin's notion of integrity in adjudication which demands that consistency be achieved so that moral and political principles held by the community apply equally to all members of the community in all areas of the legal system. The principle of integrity demands equal consideration of women's interests and this encompasses the regulation of pornography (see S. Easton, 1995. Taking Women's Rights Seriously: Integrity and the "Right" to consume pornography, *Res Publica*, *1*(2), 183). On this argument the regulation of pornography could be construed as compatible with existing principles, in terms of the established limits on free speech.

Acknowledgment of the other-regarding nature of speech is reflected in the civil law of defamation and the criminal law of incitement. The harms of words, as Schauer argues, may in certain cases far exceed harms from physical injuries, if one's whole livelihood, for example, is affected by a libelous statement. The effects of speech may be extensive, affecting community relations or gender relations, for example, in the cases of "hate speech" directed at ethnic minorities and women, as well as inciting immediate violence or hatred. Mill recognizes that effect of speech on others and formulates the problem of free speech in terms of calculating the negative consequences of speech against the ill effects of speech suppression. As Schauer observes, the protection of free speech in American law and jurisprudence may be given not because it is self-regarding, but despite the fact that it is other-regarding and in some cases harmful or offensive to others. Offensiveness will not always justify restraints on speech, and toleration of offensive speech may be the price to pay for living in a democratic pluralist society. Pornography can be seen as communicating powerful ideas and statements about the nature of women and the legitimacy of their abuse and degradation. If seen as communicative it is more likely to be included within the scope of the First Amendment.

If speech is seen as other-regarding and resulting in harm, this does not resolve the issue of regulation. The type and extent of harm would have to be sufficiently serious to warrant intervention and one would need to take account of the nature and strength of the opposing rights and interests. Consequently, the pornography and censorship debate has focused on the identification of harms; measuring the extent of harms and their proximity and remoteness; and balancing these harms against the harms arising from suppression of pornography.

However, even if the harmful effects of pornography are accepted, harm may not be the conclusive factor in the determination of regulation as illustrated by the case of *American Booksellers v. Hudnut* (1986, 106 S.C. 1172). Here the Supreme Court, in considering the constitutionality of the Indianapolis Ordinance, affirmed the opinion of the Court of Appeals in *American Booksellers v. Hudnut* (1985, 771 F.2d, 7th Cir.), which had accepted evidence of harms to women and objective causation, but concluded that the harms to women were outweighed by the need to protect First Amendment speech rights. This contrasts with the approach of the Canadian Supreme Court in *R. v. Butler* (1992, 89 Dominion Law Reports 449) where it was held that section 163 of the Criminal Code, dealing with obscenity, did violate the Charter of Rights and Freedom, but was justified as a reasonable limit prescribed by law.

Although it was difficult to establish the precise causal link, it was reasonable to presume that exposure to pornography affected attitudes and beliefs, including women's own self-perceptions: "Materials portraying women as a class worthy of sexual exploitation and abuse have a negative impact on the individual's sense of self-worth and acceptance." The Court said that, "Among other things, degrading and dehumanizing materials place women (and sometimes men) in positions of subordination, servile submission or humiliation. They run against principles of equality and dignity of all human beings." Legislation aimed at preventing harm to women and children and to society as whole was of fundamental importance and could justify infringement of the right to freedom of expression. So in *Butler* the Court accepted that the harms to women, children, and society arising from pornography could justify constraint on the free speech rights of pornographers. Pornography appeals only to the basest aspect of individual fulfillment, physical arousal, and is primarily economically motivated. Obscenity legislation is directed at the avoidance of harm caused directly or indirectly to women or other groups by the distribution of materials. Although education may be a helpful way to deal with negative attitudes to women, it is insufficient and legal measures may also be required.

IV. THE HARM PRINCIPLE: CRITIQUES OF PORNOGRAPHY

To elucidate the question of harm in relation to pornography, one needs to be clear whose interests are being harmed: the consumer's, whose capacity for self-development could be undermined by consumption, and the interests of women and society as a whole. Here we might distinguish among women's interests as participants in pornographic productions, as real and potential victims of sexual assaults, and as citizens of a society in which pornography flourishes as part of a general pattern of gender inequality. When considering the interests of society as a whole, the impact of pornography on community morality and the quality of the environment is relevant.

The types of harm may include physical or psychological effects along the dimensions of minor or serious, direct or indirect, and proven or speculative. Psychological effects were recognized by Mill as grounds for regulation.

These distinctions are important both at the level of philosophical debates and in terms of the specific problems in construing legislation in England and the United States. For example, considering *who* is liable to the depraved and corrupted is important in interpreting and applying the Obscene Publications Act 1959 in England and in determining community standards using the test formulated in *Miller v. California* (1973, 413 U.S. 15). There may also be difficulties in applying legal concepts of harm, based on tort models, when considering the impact of pornography on women as a group—as tort models are essentially atomistic and linear models. If we are dealing with harms to women as a class, the harms may be indirect rather than direct and the concept of a group injury is undeveloped in English law. If the consumer's interest is the only issue, then there is no ground for social intervention, no matter how degrading the effects of the activity. The key question in considering the regulation of pornography is whether a free market affects the interests of others sufficiently to justify constraint. The case for regulation has principally relied on the claim that obscene or pornographic materials may cause antisocial or illegal acts, including sexual offenses. A number of claims and counterclaims have been advanced, and attempts to establish a causal link raise methodological and evidential problems.

The major sources of evidence in the debate have been the results of experimental studies to test the impact of pornography on subjects' attitudes and behavior undertaken by social psychologists, the President's Commission on Obscenity and Pornography (1970), and the Meese Commission, and the testimony of victims at the Minneapolis hearings.

A review of the research on the impact of pornography was commissioned by the Home Office in Britain and undertaken by D. Howitt and G. Cumberbatch (1990. *Pornography: Impacts and Influences.* HMSO, London), who in their report could find no compelling evidence in the materials surveyed of a causal link between pornography and sexual violence: "Inconsistencies emerge between very similar studies and many interpretations of these have reached almost opposite conclusions" (p. 94). They point to major methodological difficulties in the experimental studies raising doubts regarding their internal and external validity. There are also gaps in our knowledge of the relevant variables; for example, not enough is known about the attitudes which may encourage sexual attacks or the role of pornography in psychosexual development. We do not have sufficiently detailed records of sexual offenses to plot changes through time in relation to changing patterns of pornography consumption. Most of the available research is based on Canadian and American experience rather than European studies. Although reluctant to infer a causal link, the authors were nonetheless skeptical regarding claims of the advantages of pornography:

... it would be overgenerous to the research evidence to argue a case for the benefits of pornography. The idea that pornography might serve as a substitute for the direct expression of sexual violence has not really been subject to the necessary empirical tests.... However, it is probably unrealistic to believe that there is a major contribution made by pornography in this respect since there is no substantial evidence of any reduction in sexual crime where pornography circulation rates have increased. (1990, 95)

The President's Commission on Obscenity and Pornography was set up in 1967 and reported in 1970. It made a number of recommendations which reflects the liberalization of sexual morality at that time. It reviewed the effectiveness of the existing laws on pornography and obscenity, examined methods of distribution and its effect on the public and its relation to crime, and made recommendations accordingly. The Commission could find no empirical research to firmly establish a causal relationship between the consumption of pornography and criminal behavior. It therefore recommended the repeal of existing legislation prohibit the sale, exhibition, and distribution of sexual materials to the consenting public. It could find no grounds for state interference with the reading or viewing materials of adults. The Commission's report was criticized for its selective use of statistics, and a further study undertaken by the Meese Commission came to quite different conclusions.

The question of harm was central to the Meese Commission's inquiry. This federal commission was briefed by Edwin Meese, the attorney-general, in 1985, to find new ways of controlling pornography. It reported in 1986 and recommended stronger enforcement of existing obscenity legislation as well as enactment of new civil remedies. The Report concluded that pornography does cause individual, social, moral, and ethical harm and proposed further restrictive measures. Sexually violent pornography, it concluded, is causally related to antisocial and possibly unlawful acts of sexual violence. The Commission also supported the work of citizen action groups seeking to use nonlegislative measures to reduce the availability of pornography. While the Meese Commission did not undertake its own research, it did examine research undertaken by others, including that of Malamuth and Donnerstein, who testified to the Commission.

The claim that pornography is harmless has been challenged on a number of grounds.

A. Imitative Harms

The assertion of a link between pornography and sexual crime is one of the most controversial claims advanced by critics of pornography. Murder and rape trials in the United States and the United Kingdom have, in some cases, revealed instances of apparent imitation of particular practices found in literature on the accused's person at the time, or identical to those shown in films seen by the offender. The influence of pornography on sexual offenses has been referred to in a number of English and American cases by judges, counsel, expert witnesses, and defendants [see, for example, *R. v. Taylor* (1987, 9 Cr. App. R. (S) 198) and *R. v. Holloway* (1982, 4 Cr. App. R. (S) 128)]. Pornography may be shown to the victims of sexual offenses, as in the case of *Liddle* (1985. 7 Cr. App. R. (S) 59), where the accused had a history of sexual offenses which included showing the victims pornography. In the United States, in *Hoggard v. State* (1982, 27 Ark. 117 640 S.W.2d 102), for example, which concerned the sodomy of a 6-year-old boy, the court recognized that pornography could have an instrumental role: "the pornography was used as the instrument by which the crime itself was solicited—the child was encouraged to look at the pictures and then encouraged to engage in it" (at 106).

B. Harms in the Production Process

Harm may also be involved in the production of pornography if participants suffer bodily harm as part of the filmmaking process or are coerced into taking part. Once individuals have been persuaded to appear, the film itself may be used as proof of their participation to ensure further compliance, or by threats to tell parents where minors are involved. Substantial evidence of coercion, including physical coercion and blackmail to ensure further cooperation in pornographic productions, was admitted at the Minneapolis hearings in 1983. The harms caused to the victims in these cases may be exacerbated by the repeated showings of the film. For this reason the use of injunctions where coercion has been proven was seen as a key component of the Indianapolis Ordinance.

C. The Credibility of Victims of Sexual Offenses

The effect of a free market in pornography on particular groups, namely, child and adult survivors of rape, abuse, and violence, for whom a major problem is gaining credibility, also needs to be considered. The relationship between pornography and the credibility of survivors of sexual violence is complex. Although to defenders of free speech it might seem too remote to warrant intervention, the issue needs to be addressed. It is only relatively recently that the extent of child sexual abuse has been acknowledged. New doubts regarding the credibility of child witnesses have been expressed following the Cleveland and Orkney investigations. Numerous challenges to children's evidence have been mounted, including the contentious "discovery" of false memory syndrome. Complaints of rape by adult women have for long been treated with suspicion by the police, judges, juries, and the general public. Until recently both children and women were subject to corroboration warnings when giving evidence. Proving absence of consent in rape cases has been a major problem for prosecutors, which has resulted in a reluctance to proceed with complaints from certain categories of women who are unlikely to be believed in the witness box.

If women and children are portrayed in pornography as acquiescing and enjoying violence and abuse—if these assaults are portrayed as normal sex—then it becomes harder for the survivors of sexual violence to establish their credibility and to be taken seriously.

The legitimation of nonconsensual violent sex is an important dimension of pornography. Women's subordination is portrayed as natural and normal; their rape is depicted as having a "positive outcome."

A number of small-scale studies have been undertaken to ascertain the effects of exposure to pornography on tolerance of sexual crimes and the process of desensitization (see, for example, D. Zillman and J. Bryant, 1982. *J. Comun.* 32(4), 10–21; 1989. *Pornography: Research Advances and Policy Considerations.* Erlbaum, Hilsdale, NJ). If sex is defined in pornography as violence, then the tolerance of crimes of sexual violence may increase. This may be more pronounced as pornography becomes more violent. Some experimental studies have found that men exposed to pornography become more tolerant of rape and violence against women than men who have not been exposed to pornographic stimuli. The former are more likely than the latter to accept rape myths, seeing rape victims as having less worth and suffering fewer injuries. Social psychologists also gave evidence at the Minneapolis hearings in 1983. Laboratory experiments on "normal" males have found that exposure to pornography increases acceptance of rape myths and of violence against women (Malamuth and Donnerstein, 1984). While these studies on their own might be seen as inconclusive, the impact of pornography may be further corroborated by the experi-

ence of victims on the "receiving end" of pornography, although their experience has been underresearched.

D. The Effects on Community Morality

Constraints on pornography might also be seen as a means of upholding a community's moral standards. The focus on using law to enforce a society's moral standards has its roots in the 18th century but is associated more recently with Lord Devlin, who advanced a view which contrasts sharply with that of Mill.

Lord Devlin challenged the assumption that morality was a matter for private judgment. Society may pass judgment on moral issues and society may use the law to protect and preserve morality to enforce its moral judgments. Without this morality, society could not survive but would disintegrate. A common morality is the price paid for social cohesion. If we accept society's right to make moral judgments and that common morality is necessary to society, then society may use the law to protect morality. In practice the law should accord the maximum freedom to individuals which is compatible with the integrity of society. Privacy should be respected as far as possible but the law may justifiably intervene to protect society.

On this argument, then, if a community decides that it does not wish to live in a culture where pornography freely flourishes, it would be legitimate to use the law to express this view. Here we are taking account of the effects on society as a whole as well as on participants. A similar argument was used by Justice Burger in *Paris Theatres v. Slaton* (1973, 413 U.S. 49) where he referred to the adverse effect of pornography on "the mode,... the style and quality of life, now and in the future."

At the time Lord Devlin's view seemed out of tempo with the mood of sexual liberation. But in recent years the right of society to intervene in the private sphere has gained more support from the courts.

E. Environmental Harms

Environmental harms have also been cited in support of the case for regulation. Various ways of dealing with the environmental effects have been proposed, including limiting the number of shops which sell pornography, dispersing them through the city, or confining them to particular streets or areas through planning controls. One form of regulation used in the United States is zoning, which is usually justified in terms of offensiveness. Because it restricts rather than prohibits access to pornography, it meets with more support from defenders of pornography and free speech. Pornographic bookstores have been subject to zoning laws in the United States.

The Supreme Court in 1976 upheld a Detroit ordinance confining the bookstores to certain areas. Municipal zoning ordinances will be upheld if they permit the bookstores to survive, but not if access to them is significantly restricted. In *Young v. American Mini-Theatres* (1976, 427 U.S. 50) the court held that the Detroit ordinance prohibiting the location of adult cinemas and bookshops in certain locations has a valid means of regulation because of the city's interest in protecting the character of its neighborhoods, and this interest supported its classification of films, although it included some films which might be constitutionally protected. In England a form of zoning has been deployed through planning regulations and controls on sex shops and cinemas. The Williams Report also favored the use of restriction rather than prohibition.

Although the environmental effects of sex clubs, shows, and shops may be contained by zoning, some neighborhoods are protected at the expense of others so that residents in the selected areas suffer loss of their property values as well as a poorer quality of life and a decline in their visual environment.

From a Millian perspective, a liberal feminist could advocate regulation on the harm principle on the ground that it is other-regarding and harmful to the interests of others. But even if the link between pornography and physical harm were refuted, other arguments might be advanced on which to ground a claim for regulation, including the argument from autonomy, which builds on the perfectionist strand in liberalism, associated, for example, with Joseph Raz, which sees the government having an obligation to provide a range of options which enable individuals to lead autonomous lives, to encourage those options which promote autonomy, and to discourage those which negate or undermine autonomy.

From a perfectionist standpoint, pornography may be seen as undermining women's capacity to develop their human faculties by circulating images which emphasize their unreflective nature; instead of generating new ideas pornography reaffirms women's subordination and passivity. The depiction in pornography of women as creatures lacking autonomy contributes to the perpetuation of gender inequality.

Some liberal feminists have focused on pornography as a violation of women's civil rights, including the right to equality. MacKinnon in recent writings has argued that even if pornography is deemed to be protected by First Amendment speech rights, it nonetheless violates the equal protection clause of the 14th Amendment. The Supreme Court, she argues, should acknowledge that pornography raises a conflict between two fundamental principles of liberty and equality. The use of government intervention to promote equality is accepted in other areas, such as sexual harassment, so the prohibition of pornography may be justified by an appeal to equality. The Indianapolis ordinance aimed to protect the civil rights of women and construed pornography as a civil rights violation and a practice of sex discrimination. If the pornography issue is approached from the standpoint of emphasizing the autonomy and self-fulfillment of women as moral agents and their rights to dignity and to equal concern and respect, then the argument for a free market in pornography may be effectively challenged.

Also See the Following Articles

CENSORSHIP • FEMINIST ETHICS • FREEDOM OF SPEECH IN THE USA • SEXUAL CONTENT IN FILMS AND TELEVISION • SEXUAL HARASSMENT • VIOLENCE IN FILMS AND TELEVISION

Bibliography

Abel, R. (1994). "Speech and Respect." Sweet and Maxwell, London.
Butler, J. (1997). "Excitable Speech." Routledge, London.
Dworkin, R. (1996). "Freedom's Law." Oxford Univ. Press, Oxford.
Dworkin, R. (Mar. 3, 1994). Pornography: An exchange. *N.Y. Rev. Books,* 48–49.
Dworkin, R. (Oct. 21, 1993). Women and Pornography. *N.Y. Rev. Books,* 33–42.
Easton, S. (1994). "The Problem of Pornography, Regulation and the Right to Free Speech." Routledge, London.
MacKinnon, C. (Mar. 3, 1994). Pornography: An exchange. *N.Y. Rev. Books,* 47–48.
MacKinnon, C. (1993). "Only Words." Harvard Univ. Press, Cambridge, MA.

POSTSTRUCTURALISM

Todd May
Clemson University

GLOSSARY

antirepresentationalism A moral principle stating that certain ways of being and acting should not be represented as being inherently superior or inferior to other ways.

deconstruction The view that language is a project of bringing to presence that necessarily excludes an absence which helps constitute it.

otherness of the other That in other beings that cannot be brought into one's own conceptual or linguistic categories.

poststructuralism The dominant movement of recent French thinking that emphasizes a rejection of the traditional project of unified founding theories.

post-structuralism The complex of views that emphasize the multiplicity of practices that constitute our experience.

POSTSTRUCTURALISM is the set of dominant approaches within French philosophy that arose in the wake of the decline of existentialism and structuralism.

Poststructuralism refers to a wide variety of philosophers, which can be grouped roughly into two types. The first type, called for the purposes of this piece "poststructuralism," consists of the work of Michel Foucault, Gilles Deleuze, and Jean-François Lyotard. It emphasizes the diverse and local nature of the practices that make up our experience, and seems to be tacitly committed to the principle of antirepresentationalism. The second type, called deconstruction, consists of the work of Jacques Derrida and Emmanuel Levinas. It emphasizes an otherness in language which cannot be brought to presence and the strategies of exclusion that language itself brings to bear upon this otherness. Although divergent, both strains of poststructuralism converge in their rejection of unified founding accounts of experience.

I. WHAT IS POSTSTRUCTURALISM?

People often think of poststructuralism as a single, unified approach to philosophy. Poststructuralism, as a movement, seems to propose a way of thinking, to defend certain claims and commitments, and to be distinguished from other philosophical views by that way of thinking and those claims and commitments. There is some truth to this view, but only some. Within poststructuralism, there are deep divisions, a couple of which we will consider more closely. It is perhaps best, then, to think of poststructuralism in the plural rather than the singular. In that sense, poststructuralism is like

Encyclopedia of Applied Ethics, Volume 3

postimpressionism, which was united in its rejection of the impressionist approach, but divided about how that rejection was to be carried forward. Both Foucault and Derrida reject important structuralist commitments, to be sure, but their rejections place them in very different philosophical places. Before turning to poststructuralism's relation to morality, we need to get a grip both on the common poststructuralist rejection of structuralism and on the divergent paths that rejection has taken.

A. The Prehistory of Poststructuralism

Poststructuralism is a deeply French phenomenon. Although it has adherents and practitioners everywhere in academics, its major thinkers—Michel Foucault, Jacques Derrida, Emmanuel Levinas, Gilles Deleuze, and Jean-Francois Lyotard—are French, and developed their views within the context of the post-World War II French intellectual context. To understand poststructuralism, then, it is necessary to understand a bit about the movement that more-or-less preceeded it: structuralism. And to understand a bit about structuralism, it does not hurt to have some existentialism under one's belt. So we turn first to existentialism.

Existentialism, the philosophy most popularly associated with the writings of Jean-Paul Sartre (although the influence of Maurice Merleau-Ponty has probably been more deeply felt over the years), starts from the premise that there is no inherent purpose in human (or any other) life. We are born into this world—tossed into it really—with no plan to fulfill and no goals it is our duty to realize. Life is without meaning, except for the meaning we happen to confer upon it. And that meaning can receive no justification other than the justification we happen to give it. Moreover, since life is without meaning or ultimate plan, we are radically free to do or be what we want. There are no constraints, human or divine, that are placed upon us. With meaninglessness, then, comes freedom.

One can see how a philosophy like existentialism might get a toehold in Europe during the period of Nazism and the dictatorships, when one could not help feeling a sense of cosmic abandonment. However, there is a gap in existentialist philosophy between the meaninglessness it recognizes and the commitment to absolute freedom it derives from that meaninglessness. One way to view structuralism is as inserting itself within that gap.

The gap is this: The fact that there is no ultimate purpose in life does not entail that there are no constraints on human action. It could be the case that we have no cosmic purpose, and yet have constraints on

who we can be and what we can do that are as arbitrary as the goals we give ourselves. An example of this can be seen in Darwinian theory, where evolution constrains biological possibilities although those constraints are not linked to any larger purpose. Structuralism, while converging with existentialism in jettisoning the idea of an ultimate purpose, nevertheless discovers constraints that limit—and sometimes even define—who we are and what we do.

For the structuralists, the task is to discover the limits and definitions of our experience. Most of the central structuralists—Claude Lévi-Strauss and Jacques Lacan especially, and Louis Althusser less so—turn to the work of early 20th-century linguist Ferdinand de Saussure in order to orient their own views. Saussure claims that, at least for most purposes, language is best grasped as a systematic structure of differences. By this he means that a sound's phonetic value or a word's meaning are defined less by what they are in themselves and more by the differences between them and the other sounds or words in that language. For instance, the meaning of the word "tree" is not given by anything that matches the word, but the role the word "tree" plays in the language as distinguished from "bush," "flower," and the like. Such a view sees meaning as an intralinguistic matter rather than a matter of language matching up to the world or to prelinguistic ideas.

Saussure's view was appropriated by structuralists in order to show how people's lives are structured by forces outside of them. For Levi-Strauss, for instance, many of our cultural activities are unconsciously structured by differential symbolic elements that have a systematic relation to one another. As we engage in these activities, we are not aware of the structural relation among those elements. Nevertheless, our activities are guided by them. Jacques Lacan offered a similar viewpoint, although for him the structural elements were given by Freud's psychoanalytic view. Louis Althusser proposed an understanding of Marx as delineating the structure of social relationships such that people are unconsciously constrained and defined in their actions and relations. (Althusser, however, did not appropriate the Saussurean idea of differential elements as deeply as did Lévi-Strauss and Lacan.)

The structuralists, then, sought "structuring" elements of our experience that did not require a commitment to any of the kinds of cosmic transcendence that the existentialists rejected. At the same time, however, they jettisoned the existentialist privileging of subjective experience and subjective freedom. The poststructuralists accept both the existentialist/structuralist rejection of cosmic transcendence and the structuralist embrace of external structuring elements. What they reject is the idea that one can give some kind of unified founding account of what it is that structures our lives, whether that founding account be anthropological (Lévi-Strauss), psychoanalytic (Lacan), Marxist (Althusser), or any single competing alternative.

Although the poststructuralists are bound by this rejection, they are divided on the reasons for and the implications of the rejection. In what follows, I will distinguish, in an oversimplified way, between two major lines of poststructuralism. This distinction misses the nuances of the thinkers discussed, but does capture what I hope are the essential moves of each. On the one side there is the group I will call the "post-structuralists" (adding a hyphen to distinguish them from poststructuralism generally). They include primarily Michel Foucault, Gilles Deleuze, and Jean-François Lyotard. Their deepest problem with structuralism is that a unified founding account of the structuring of experience is too few—there need to be many rather than one. On the other side, there is the group I will call deconstructionists, and who will be exemplified by Jacques Derrida and Emmanuel Levinas. Their problem is not that a unified founding account is not enough—rather it is that such an account is already too many.

B. Post-structuralist Poststructuralism

For the post-structuralists, the idea that one can give a unified founding account of what it is that structures our experience—who we are, what we do, and how we grasp the world—is both misguided and pernicious. It is misguided because, in fact, many—often disparate—things structure our experience. It is pernicious because such an idea fosters the view that everyone can be understood and their experience modified in order to bring them under the same conceptual umbrella, which will result (and has resulted) in reinforcing a blind conformism and a marginalization of that which is different.

In order to understand the post-structuralist approach to accounting for our experience, we need to grasp a term that informs the work especially of Foucault and Deleuze. That term, borrowed from Nietzsche, is "genealogy." To give a genealogy of an object of study—of a word, a practice, or a way of looking at things—is to give a history of it; but this history is of a certain type. It is not the unfolding of the object, as though history were tending toward it throughout its course; nor is it the descent of the object from a single original wellspring. Neither ends nor origins are unitary, and neither are they grand affairs. A genealogy cites the manifold sources of the object of study, the intersections through which those sources produce the object, and the accidents along the way without which those intersections would not have happened or would not have produced what they did. (It would be a mistake to think of the sources of an object as origins; the sources are themselves derived from yet other sources, which makes the starting point of any genealogy necessarily a bit arbitrary.)

Post-structuralists differ on the kinds of sources they use when constructing a genealogy. For Foucault, the sources are social practices; for Deleuze, they are Nietzschean forces; for Lyotard, both, depending on what stage in his writings one chooses. Nevertheless, post-structuralists converge in their use of genealogies to account for the objects they wish to treat, and this convergence opens out onto two central post-structuralist commitments. First and foremost, unified founding accounts of our experience (or of much else worth accounting for) are misguided. Such accounts fail to capture what is significant in our experience because they misascribe it to a single origin. The structuralist attempt to offer a key to unlock the structuring of our experience, then, is bound to be mistaken. Second, since many theoretical studies, and philosophy especially, attempt to offer unified founding accounts, perhaps the proper objects of genealogical study are the accounts themselves, or at least crucial aspects of them.

Examining the work of Foucault, Deleuze, and Lyotard, one finds that many of their objects of study—psychology, psychoanalysis, sexuality, capitalism, and linguistic meaning—try to stand in one way or another as keys to unlock our experience, as cornerstones for any accounting of who we are. The genealogical approach taken by the post-structuralists shows that these supposed cornerstones are not so much true origins as they are the product of historical intersections and accidents. This is not to say that they do not play important roles in structuring our experience. They do, although none of them in a singular, founding way. Instead, their importance is a result of the (partly arbitrary) convergence of practices or forces that has bequeathed to us the situation we find ourselves in. Moreover, part of their staying power lies in the mistaken belief that these phenomena are indeed cornerstones. And herein lies the perniciousness of unified founding accounts. As long as we elevate psychology, psychoanalysis, capitalism, or whatever object one wants to the role of experiential wellspring, we will allow that "wellspring" to dictate to us who we are and what we can become. It is by recognizing the genealogy of that wellspring that it begins to lose its hold on us, and we, in turn, can begin to recognize other ways to structure our experience—and thus other ways to become and to behave.

C. Deconstruction

As with post-structuralism, the label "deconstruction" covers thinkers who, in some ways, have profound divergences. The thinkers I subsume under this label—Derrida and Levinas—are certainly not of a piece in their thinking. However, they are bound by a commitment that importantly distinguishes them from the post-structuralists, and thus I put them under a separate heading. For both Derrida and Levinas, the philosophical difficulty that attaches to unified founding accounts is that such accounts misunderstand an important aspect of language that undercuts the pretensions of those accounts to be founding in any way. Levinas is particularly concerned with the ethical aspect of founding accounts, and Derrida with the structure of founding accounts more generally. Let me start with Derrida and then turn to Levinas' approach.

Derrida notes that an important aspect of any unified founding account is that it must be given in a language that is transparent to the accounter. The reason for this is, roughly, that in order to serve as a foundation for everything else, an account must not let anything escape conceptually. And, in order to know that nothing has escaped conceptually, one must be in control of one's language, which is the form in which concepts appear in accounts. How can I be sure that I have given you a foundational account if I cannot be sure of the language in which I give that account? I cannot, of course. Therefore, my language must be transparent to me in order to ensure that my account is a proper foundational account.

The problem, as Derrida argues, is that language does not possess the kind of transparency required for a foundational account to be given. Although the reasons for this are complex, we can at least get a picture of them here. In order for language—or, more accurately, linguistic meaning—to be transparent, that meaning must be fully present to the one who is speaking (writing, etc.). People familiar with Descartes will recognize this idea as a derivation of the Cartesian idea that only that which is clear and present to my consciousness is indubitable. However, as Derrida argues, linguistic meaning cannot be fully present to one, since it is always inhabited by an absence that cannot be made fully present. Therefore, any account of linguistic meaning will reveal that meaning is always internally riven by an absence that is partially constitutive of it. Meaning is

a product of the play of presence and absence, a play that Derrida calls *differance*.

Derrida makes his claim based not upon an analysis of language itself, but in a series of case studies of specific philosophers of a foundational bent. Perhaps the most famous of these case studies—or deconstructions—is the study of Husserl. For Husserl, the indubitability of linguistic meaning is founded on an unmediated presence of meaning to a subject (the accounter, in the terms of the previous paragraph). However, if one turns to Husserl's analysis of time, one finds that the idea of full temporal presence is only an ideal point; the present is constituted not only by presence but by the no-longer-present state of the immediate past and the not-yet-present state of the immediate future. Thus, in order for there to be presence, there must be the absence of immediate past and future. These latter cannot be brought to full presence, and thus the transparency of linguistic meaning is lost.

Levinas' approach is not unlike Derrida's. His concern is less with linguistic meaning, though, and more with ethics. Like Derrida, Levinas believes that something is lost in foundational philosophical accounts. What is lost, however, is not the recognition of *differance*, but rather the experience of the other (or the Other), which cannot be reduced to my own conceptual understanding (or the categories of the Same). What is characteristic of otherness (and here one can think of the otherness of other people or the otherness of a deity) is that that otherness is beyond my conceptual grasp; it eludes my attempt to make it an object of knowledge. The recognition of what Levinas calls the infinity of this otherness is the beginning of ethics. Indeed, it is the only basis ethics can have. Alternatively, the failure to recognize this infinity is the beginning of violence, in the deepest sense of violence. In order to grasp this idea, it might be helpful to point out that in the background of Levinas' thought is the Holocaust, which might be interpreted as a denial of the otherness of others and an attempt to impose sameness by eliminating that otherness.

II. POSTSTRUCTURALIST VIEWS OF MORALITY AND ETHICS

The relationship of poststructuralism to morality is a controversial one. In the section following this one, when I present a view of poststructuralist moral commitments, I will not be presenting a generally agreed-upon view. Although I believe that my views can be substantiated by close readings of poststructuralist texts, I cannot pretend that that reading—or any other reading—is one upon which scholars of poststructuralism have converged. Although the proper interpretation of poststructuralist morality may yet be in question, the poststructuralists' own views of morality are not. It is true that, aside from Levinas, poststructuralists have not written extensively on morality. However, their relationship to morality and moral discourse is often given in their writings.

A. Post-structuralist Views of Morality and Ethics

If we think of morality—or better, moral discourse—as a practice which centrally involves the creation and delimitation of universal prescriptives, then it can be said that the post-structuralists' view of morality ranges from leeriness (Foucault) to disdain (Deleuze). (More recently, Lyotard has embraced a Levinasian view of ethics, so we can lay his work aside for a moment.) This is not to say that the post-structuralists have shied away from something they have called, and we might call after them, "ethics." But ethics is a different kettle of fish. I will first discuss the relation to morality and then turn to ethics.

The post-structuralist reservations about moral discourse have to do with their reservations about the idea of universal prescriptives. The potential problem is that philosophical approaches to moral discourse have traditionally grounded themselves in unified founding accounts; one only needs to recall here the Kantian and utilitarian accounts of morality to recognize this. For such accounts, that which is good to do or to be falls within severely constraining limits. Now there may be ways to mitigate the force of such constraints, for instance, by drawing distinctions between duty and supererogation. However, it remains the fact that under such accounts, what is considered to be really good is something limited in scope.

It is not difficult to see why post-structuralists will be uncomfortable with such limitations. Recall the worry post-structuralists have about the perniciousness of unified founding accounts: they tend to force a blind conformity and marginalize those that do not conform. If this is true of general accounts of our experience, it will certainly be more so of constraining moral accounts. In fact, one can at times see a collusion between unified accounts of experience and unified theories of morality that produce just such narrow constraints. Foucault, in the first volume of his history of sexuality, argued that the collusion between the idea of sexuality

as the key to one's identity and the project of normalization as a moral ideal produces many of the patterns of conformity and marginalization that we see around us today.

It is no surprise, then, that post-structuralists have shied away from engaging in moral discourse. When broaching moral issues, Foucault has tended to hold the position that those who are oppressed ought to be allowed to speak their desires for themselves, rather than for him to speak for them. Deleuze has ridiculed morality as a police action that constrains thought and strangles life. For Deleuze, a true Nietzschean in this respect, that which allows life to flourish in all its differences is good, and that which funnels life into narrow channels is bad.

A rejection of morality, however, is not a rejection of ethics. Both Foucault and Deleuze have contrasted the ethical with the moral, and found value in the former. The contrast between ethics and morality can be seen as a contrast between universal prescriptives and aesthetic appreciation. Consider, for a moment, Deleuze's view that life in all its differences ought to flourish. If this is so, then the project of universal prescriptives (with some exceptions which the post-structuralists neglected and I discuss in the next heading) will, in all likelihood, undercut rather than foster such flourishing. If we are seeking *the* good life, then all those lives which are not that will be less than good, and should not be pursued. Of course, we may expand our idea of the good life to include all sorts of lives, but if we do that, then we begin to move away from universal prescriptives and toward something more like aesthetic appreciation. By aesthetic appreciation, I mean the enjoyment of a life in the individual qualities it possesses or the particular vision it instantiates. This kind of appreciation is what Foucault and Deleuze mean by the ethical, and its contrast to the constraints of traditional morality could hardly be sharper.

B. Deconstructionist Views of Morality and Ethics

Levinas and Derrida share the post-structuralist reservations about moral discourse. This may seem a bit odd, particularly in the case of Levinas, whose major works are recognizably moral tracts. However, the central theme of many of those tracts is the worry that direct moral accounting will do more harm than good to the attempt to construct a moral life. Like the post-structuralists, the deconstructionists use the term "ethics" instead of "morality," but the use to which they put that term is quite different. I want to discuss Levinas' view in more detail, and then show how Derrida's views are closely aligned with his.

For Levinas, the true object of ethics—the other in his/her/its infinite otherness—cannot be captured in one's own conceptual categories. Indeed, we can go further and say that (a) the other is precisely that which cannot be captured in one's conceptual categories, and (b) one's moral responsibility to the other lies in its being irreducible to one's conceptual categories. On the first point, briefly, it is the unique otherness of the other that makes it infinite, conceptually unapproachable. The second point is crucial for Levinas. The problem with traditional moral accounts is that they make our responsibility to the other dependent on being able to render that other—or what is significant about him/her/it—in concepts we can understand. We give moral accounts which tell us what categories the other falls into that are relevant for moral evaluation and moral respect. It is, for example, that the other is capable of suffering or of autonomy that grounds our moral treatment of that other.

What this misses, however, is that it is the other in his/her/its uniqueness that calls for recognition and respect. Levinas here inverts the traditional idea that it is our similarity to others that grounds moral treatment. It is not that you are like me in some significant way that I owe you the respect that I do; it is precisely because you are not. Levinas thinks of this respect as something one experiences, as a calling to which one is compelled to respond, a calling that is grounded in the face of the other. One can certainly deny or refuse that experience, for instance, by trying either to assimilate the other into one's own categories or to eliminate the otherness of the other by exterminating him/her/it. But such a denial or refusal, which for Levinas is the fundamental form of violence, already presupposes the experience of the other it is trying to escape.

There are deep affinities between Levinas' view of ethics and Derrida's. Like Levinas, Derrida is concerned with the other that cannot be brought to conceptual presence. And like Levinas, he is worried that the attempt to bring the other to conceptual presence is form of violence against him/her/it. Where he diverges from Levinas is in his general characterization of the otherness of the other. (We have to take the notion of a general characterization a bit loosely here, since one cannot directly characterize that which resists conceptualization.) In Derrida's view, the philosophical project of bringing-to-presence is also an (always failed) attempt to exclude that which cannot be brought to presence. And in our history—that is, the history of the West—examples of that which cannot be brought to

presence are writing, metaphor and poetry, and women. In the last case, it is obviously not physically gendered women that cannot be brought to presence. Rather, it is the idea of women's essence, an idea that has been created by, marginalized from, and yet recurs within the Western philosophical tradition.

Derrida's concern, then, like Levinas, is to protect the other in its otherness. For him, that involves a rethinking of the philosophical project, one that often takes the form of a "double-writing" in which the inevitable attempt to write in such a way as to bring-to-presence is doubled by a writing (often within the same text) that gestures at the absence or otherness which is constitutive of the text which is being written. In keeping with his view that the issues involved in foundational philosophy and in ethics are linguistic ones, Derrida seeks to intervene in them by proposing linguistic usages which respect the issues he raises.

III. POSTSTRUCTURALIST MORALITY

From the preceeding summaries, we can glean important affinities between post-structuralist and deconstructive approaches to morality and ethics. First, there is a discomfort with traditional moral discourse, rooted in the belief that such discourse fails to respect important phenomena that deserve respect. In the case of post-structuralism, it is the failure to respect multiplicity and particularity that are the source of discomfort; in the case of deconstruction, the failure concerns uncategorizable otherness. If we pushed these affinities deeper (which we will not), we might see affinities between particularity and uncategorizable otherness in their resistance to universal prescriptives. Moreover, both approaches seek to develop action-guiding views that do not come in the form of universal prescriptives, and thus to connect their views with our lives without falling into the trap of traditional moral discourse.

None of what I have said so far will be very controversial within the community of poststructuralist philosophers. What I am about to say will be, although I think it is defensible and enlightens important aspects of poststructuralism in both of its forms. I believe that there are recognizable universal moral prescriptives in both post-structuralism and deconstruction, and that the acknowledgment of those prescriptives does nothing to diminish the force of their work (although whether it will involve a rethinking of some of their commitments is an issue I leave aside).

Both post-structuralists and deconstructionists seek to create a space for protecting that which does not fall easily into the traditional forms of moral discourse. But they seek not only to offer their own protection, they want us, their audience, to offer our own protection (recognition, respect, etc.). In that sense, there are universal prescriptives nascent in their work. These prescriptives are different in the two approaches, however. What I propose to do is offer a central prescriptive for each approach that captures a significant aspect of what each seeks.

A. Post-structuralist Morality: Antirepresentationalism

Post-structuralism is concerned about the historical emergence of what Foucault has called "normalization." Normalization is the process by which people are classified as more or less normal relative to a chosen category or activity; moreover, a classification of abnormal is held to constitute justification for intervening in order to make a person more normal. The distinction between the normal and the abnormal works differently from the distinction between the permitted and the forbidden. The latter distinction is binary; intervention is called for only when one has crossed a clear line between the permitted and the forbidden. The former distinction is gradational; one is more or less normal and more or less abnormal. Thus, on the latter distinction, intervention is almost always justified, and the area in which one is left alone can become small indeed.

The effects of normalization are to hold up certain, very constrained, ways of being and acting as justified, with all others requiring at least monitoring and perhaps intervention. Foucault details such constraints regarding psychology, sexuality, and medicine; Deleuze concentrates on psychoanalysis and philosophy; Lyotard, in his early work, focuses on psychoanalysis as well, and in his later work turns to the constraining forms language can take. For all three, the process of normalization is insidious, both because it narrows the possibilities for living that people might engage in and because it reinforces other oppressive social relationships. Deleuze, for example, discusses the ways in which psychoanalysis reinforces capitalist oppression and shows how the freedom from traditional social constraints that capitalism has promoted has, with the advent of psychoanalysis, turned into a new set of constraints that hold capitalist relationships together—individualism, inattention to social conditions, conformism, etc.

Given their concern about normalization, the post-structuralists can be seen as embracing a moral principle that we might call "antirepresentationalism," and which states roughly that certain ways of being and acting ought not to be represented as being inherently superior or inferior to others. (This use of the term representation may ring a bit odd in Anglo-American ears, but it appears fairly often in Continental and Continentally inspired writing.) This principle does not imply that no way of being or acting is better or worse than any other—for example, that harming people is no worse than helping them. Rather, it implies that no way of being is *inherently* better or worse, aside from the effects that it has. By ratifying anti-representationalism, one becomes leery of practices of normalization; a process of normalization can be morally justified only by the effects of normalizing, and not by the standard of normality to which one is being constrained.

Post-structuralist reluctance to embrace a principle like antirepresentationalism can be seen, ironically, as a way of trying to act in accordance with it. Foucault, Deleuze, and Lyotard have, as noted, always shied away from prescriptives. I believe that their implicit commitment to antirepresentationalism is the reason why, although I do not see how an explicit commitment to the principle would harm their position.

B. Deconstructionist Morality: Respect for the Other

Deconstruction, too, has implicitly embraced a moral principle, although its embrace is perhaps closer to the surface than that of post-structuralism. Levinas is clearly committed to a respect for the other, and for what might be called a respect for the otherness of the other. The otherness of the other, as distinct from just the other, can be thought of as the other in his/her/its difference from me. To see this distinction, let us consider two ways of thinking about respect for the other. In the first, non-Levinasian way, I respect the other because the other is, in the end, another me; just as I would like respect from the other so I should treat the other as worthy of respect. This form of respect is broadly Kantian. In the second way, I respect the other precisely because the other is not another me—he/she/it is not like me and cannot be thought of as being like me without violence being done. What calls forth my respect is precisely that otherness to which I can have no analogical relation.

Although a principle of respect for the otherness of the other seems straightforward, both Levinas and Derrida have avoided positing the principle as such.

Their reluctance to do so has to do, as does the post-structuralists', with trying to respect the principle at issue. In keeping with their more general philosophical commitments, however, their reluctance has to do more with language than with historical-political processes. Recall that for both Levinas and Derrida (although for different reasons), the otherness of the other cannot be brought directly into discourse—it cannot be made present. The attempt to do so both misses the very otherness it seeks to capture and risks doing violence to that otherness. Therefore, the positing of a straightforward philosophical principle of respect for otherness risks, in their eyes, repeating the problem it counsels against. Better, then, to gesture at otherness and promote respect more allusively and indirectly than to engage in the formation of more traditional philosophical principles. Although I do not believe that the worry that motivates their reluctance to engage in the formation of principles is indeed a philosophical problem, one can see how their philosophical views could lead to such a worry.

It should be noted that, in his later writings, Lyotard also embraces a Levinasian view of morality. He does hold, in a more post-structuralist fashion, that there are different language games—different "genres" in his terms—and that the genre of obligation is only one among them. But when he turns his attention to the genre of obligation, he endorses the Levinasian view that obligation comes from an otherness that cannot be directly spoken of or discursively justified. In that way, Lyotard's later moral view partakes both of the post-structuralism of Foucault and Deleuze and of the deconstruction of Derrida and Levinas.

Before turning to the political implications of post-structuralist moral commitments, let me call attention to something the reader has likely already noticed—that antirepresentationalism and the principle of respect for the otherness of the other have some similar implications. Most striking of all, both counsel a recognition that the terms in which one thinks about the world and the views one takes on it are not shared by everyone else, nor should they be. A world of different, and perhaps even conflicting, viewpoints is better than a world of conformity. This does not mean that any viewpoint (or better, acting on any viewpoint) is fine—poststructuralist principles, like almost all moral principles, have limits of application. But it does mean that there are points of convergence between the moral commitments of post-structuralism and deconstruction. As long as the differences between them are not obscured, a recognition of convergence is not theoretically harmful.

IV. POLITICAL IMPLICATIONS

In France, philosophy is almost always done with an eye to the political implications of the position one takes. This is true not only for overtly normative areas of philosophy, but also for such areas as ontology and philosophy of language. I will close this piece by calling attention to several significant political implications of the moral and ethical views of the poststructuralists.

A. Post-structuralist Politics

For the post-structuralists, there are at least three crucial—and intertwined—political implications to their work. First, politics is everywhere; second, people need to speak for themselves more than they are generally allowed in both political theory and practice; and third, the idea of a "grand" politics is at best misguided and more often dangerous.

The idea that politics is everywhere is consonant with the post-structuralist view that analyses of our experience cannot be had by recourse to unified foundational theories. If what makes us who we are happens as a result of a variety of often accidentally intertwined practices, then we need to look to those practices to see how the constraints and restraints on our lives have developed and how they currently operate. Power is not a matter simply of what the state or the economy does; it has to do as well with the ways I have been formed sexually, philosophically, psychologically, linguistically, etc. This idea, of course, is not unique to post-structuralism. Other philosophical perspectives, perhaps most notably feminism, have called our attention to it. However, it is a staple of post-structuralist thought, and much of the current recognition of this idea can be traced to the influence post-structuralism has had.

The implication that people need to speak more for themselves derives both from general post-structuralist commitments and specifically from the commitment to antirepresentationalism. If people are, for the most part, not to be told where their good lies, then they need to be able to express their own needs and desires. Instead of consulting philosophers or psychologists on human nature or economists on efficiency and rational desire, political activists need to listen more to the people themselves. Foucault fostered this listening by helping, after his work on the birth of the prison, to start a prison newspaper written by prisoners.

The final implication derives fairly straightforwardly from post-structuralist thought. If power is not centered in a single source, then the attempt to locate a "grand" politics—a politics that seeks change solely from some privileged point, hoping that all will be well when that privileged point (the state, the economy) is changed—is hopeless. Engaging in such an attempt will only replay the various local oppressions within a different context. Lyotard was perhaps the first to call attention to the demise of what he termed the "grand narratives" of Western society. Deleuze, in collaboration with Félix Guattari, once described the social realm as a rhizome, a plant with no central root and with stems shooting out all over in intersecting patterns. Conceived thus, power can accrete at various points, some perhaps more than others, but cannot be derived or changed simply by an intervention at any one point.

B. Deconstructionist Politics

The politics of deconstruction is a bit more elusive than that of post-structuralism. The main reason for this is that Derrida and Levinas are not primarily political thinkers. Their texts, unlike those of the post-structuralists, rarely engage in topical debate or political analysis. (However, in Derrida's recent writings, more overtly political themes are emerging.) Nevertheless, there are implications for how we *think* politically in deconstruction. Two of them are worth noting here.

The first is that we need to recognize the political dangers of the linguistic categories we use. Specifically, since those categories are necessarily exclusivist, they must be used with caution and with an eye to periodically undermining their exclusivist pretensions. We must be constantly self-reflective about our language in the field of politics—not in order to develop another, better language, but in order to recognize the exclusions in which it is engaging. Just as deconstruction works by citing the limits of our language, so must a deconstructive politics work by citing the limits of our political categories.

The second implication is that the opposite of political exclusion is not political inclusion. The object of a just politics is not to be able to bring others into our linguistic categories, nor is it to expand our categories to include them. Recall that for deconstruction, there is a necessary absence haunting all presence, and to try to bring that absence to presence is to do violence to it. We must learn a political form of respect without assimilation, and recognition without recovery. It is, in Levinas' terms, the infinity of the other, the otherness of the other, that needs to be accommodated. That accommodation occurs not by conceptual comprehension but by recognizing the limits of one's own discourse and being sensitive to what may lie beyond it.

Also See the Following Articles

EXISTENTIALISM • KANTIANISM • MORAL DEVELOPMENT • UTILITARIANISM

Bibliography

Caputo, J. (1993). *Against Ethics: Contribution to a Poetics of Obligation with Constant Reference to Deconstruction*. Bloomington: Univ. of Indiana Press.

Critchley, S. (1992). *The Ethics of Deconstruction: Derrida and Levinas*. Cambridge: Blackwell.

Martin, B. (1992). *Matrix and Line: Derrida and the Possibilities of Postmodern Social Theory*. Albany: SUNY Press.

May, T. (1995). *The Moral Theory of Poststructuralism*. University Park: Penn State Press.

Scott, C. (1990). *The Question of Ethics: Nietzsche, Foucault, Heidegger*. Bloomington: Indiana Univ. Press.

Wychogrod, E. (1990). *Saints and Postmodernism*. Chicago: University of Chicago Press, 1990.

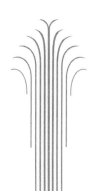

POVERTY

Paul Spicker
University of Dundee

I. The Nature of Poverty
II. Poverty in Different Societies
III. Responsibility for Poverty
IV. The Stigma of Poverty
V. The Causes of Poverty
VI. Responses to Poverty

GLOSSARY

dependency A state of reliance on the support of others, especially social services, which may be physical, financial, or psychological.

exclusion Social relationships in which people are excluded from participation in the normal pattern of social life.

inequality Disadvantage in a social context.

pathological explanations Explanations that attribute the causes of social phenomena to the people who experience them.

poverty A general term used to refer to conditions of material deprivation, insecurity, inequality, social exclusion, and dependency, associated with the lack of resources.

reciprocity The norm that requires some return to be made for goods or services that are received.

solidarity Responsibility to others in society.

stigma A complex pattern of social rejection and condemnation, commonly experienced by people who are poor or dependent.

structural explanations Explanations that attribute the causes of social phenomena to the nature of the society in which they occur.

subculture A distinctive pattern of behavior and values shared by a group of people within a society.

underclass A term variously used to refer to the lowest social class; people who are economically nonproductive and in receipt of benefits; people who are marginal to the labor market; or people who are socially undesirable.

POVERTY is a contested concept, subject to many different definitions. Because the term is used morally to refer to conditions that are unacceptable, the definition is much disputed. The extensive empirical research that has been done on the topic has led to a proliferation of attempts to operationalize the concept—that is, to translate it into measurable terms—and these in turn have tended to shape the way in which the concept is understood.

I. THE NATURE OF POVERTY

Poverty might be understood, in the first place, as a form of material deprivation. People may be said to be poor when they are in need—that is, when they lack material goods or services, such as food, clothing, fuel, or shelter, which people require to live and function in society. This has widely been taken to mean that people lack the resources to obtain these things, and poverty is often measured in terms of a lack of resources; but over time, lack of resources (and particularly, lack of income) has often been taken as evidence of poverty in its own right. The use of a "poverty line"—a threshold of income used as a measure of resources—may be presented as a measurement of the numbers of people who are poor or, depending on where their income stands relative to the poverty line, a measurement of the depth of their poverty.

Second, poverty is represented as a condition of life, associated with material needs but mainly characterized by the range of problems rather than the needs themselves. Vulnerability is a key element: Charles Booth referred to poor people as "living under a struggle to obtain the necessaries of life and make both ends meet." Research in the United Kingdom has developed the idea of a "web of deprivation"—a shifting constellation of deprivations associated with limited resources and experienced over a period of time. Poverty is not defined, on this account, by any specific need (like hunger or homelessness), but on the existence of a pattern of deprivation.

Third, poverty may be understood as the social conditions that produce deprivation. It has been argued both that deprivation and lack of resources reflect lack of entitlements, rather than the absence of essential items in themselves. Homelessness results from lack of access to housing or land, not from lack of housing; J. Drèze and A. Sen argue, in *Hunger and Public Action* (1989). Clarendon Press, that famines result not from lack of food, but from people's inability to buy the food that exists. Poverty can also, then, be described in terms of a lack of social rights.

Fourth, poverty may be seen in terms of exclusion—a set of social relationships in which people are excluded from participation in the normal pattern of social life. This extends beyond the experience of deprivation to include problems that result from stigmatization and social rejection. The European Community has defined poverty as exclusion resulting from limited resources:

> The poor shall be taken as to mean persons, families and groups of persons whose resources (material, cultural and social) are so limited as to exclude them from the minimum acceptable way of life in the Member State in which they live.

Fifth, poverty has been defined as a form of severe inequality. Inequality consists of disadvantage in a social context; poverty is a condition of extreme disadvantage. People may be held to be poor because they are disadvantaged by comparison with others in society. The Luxembourg Income Study uses income inequality as a measure of poverty; poverty is experienced when income falls significantly below the median income prevalent in that society. The designers of the study identify poverty with "economic distance."

Sixth, poverty has been identified with a different set of social relationships, concerning people who are financially dependent. Poor people are sometimes taken to be those who receive social benefits in consequence of their lack of means. The sociologist Georg Simmel argued that poverty, in sociological terms, referred not to all people on low incomes but to those who were dependent. The receipt of services itself seems not to be a sufficient condition to constitute dependency; there is the implication first that only certain services imply dependency (particularly social assistance, and perhaps public housing, but not public education), and second that the receipt is of long duration.

These uses of the idea of poverty are discrete, but there is a considerable overlap in practice between them, and there is no reason why they should not all apply simultaneously to certain sets of conditions.

II. POVERTY IN DIFFERENT SOCIETIES

A. Absolute Poverty

The conditions of the Third World—countries with limited economic development—are often taken as paradigms of poverty, because they represent extremes of material deprivation and lack of resources. The idea of "absolute poverty" has been used to represent a minimum subsistence level based in essentials for survival. Absolute poverty has been characterized in an OECD report as a definition "in terms of some absolute level of minimum needs, below which people are regarded as being poor, for purpose of social and government concern, and which does not change over time." The idea that absolute poverty does not change over time, and is not affected by social circumstances, is untenable; basic necessities, like what people eat or where they live, are defined in social terms. Homelessness, for example, is directly affected by access to housing and entitlement to land, and the squatting that is the dominant tenure in many Third World cities is not available to homeless people in developed countries. Sen has referred to an absolutist core in the idea of poverty; people need certain "capabilities," or ability to function, such as transport, food, and so forth. These elements of the definition of poverty are universally applicable, irrespective of the social circumstances in which they are applied. The variation which occurs relates to the "commodities" that serve these functions.

Absolute poverty is principally operationalized by an assessment of the resources necessary to maintain subsistence, in the form of a poverty line. The poverty line in the United States is based in the cost of a minimum diet determined by the Department of Agriculture. The World Bank currently measures world poverty with a poverty line of $372 per annum. This line is arbitrary, and is not based on any assessment of minimum need: the figure is equivalent to $31 a month, or a dollar a day, multiplied by 12. The figure is an indicator of poverty—a signpost to circumstances—and not a definition of it.

B. Relative Poverty

The concept of absolute poverty is commonly taken not to apply in much of the developed world, and it has been supplanted in much of the literature by a concept of "relative poverty." Relative poverty defines poverty in terms of its relation to the standards that exist elsewhere in society. This is linked to three discrete propositions: the social definition of poverty, the definition of poverty in comparative terms, and the description of poverty as a relational issue. The first proposition, that standards are socially defined, is not disputed. The second proposition is that poverty must be understood in terms relative to the condition of others who are not poor. This used to be understood primarily in terms of inequality. Townsend uses the term in a different way, more closely related to the idea of exclusion. He refers to poverty as a form of "relative deprivation," by which he means the lack of goods, resources, and activities that are an accepted part of social life. He denies that this defines poverty as a form of inequality, but if poverty is defined as a form of disadvantage in a social context, and inequality is the name given to disadvantage in a social context, then poverty is defined as a form of inequality. The central problem with a definition of poverty in these terms is that it is possible to reduce inequality while increasing insecurity, dependency, or the incidence of material need.

The third proposition is that poverty has to be understood in relational terms. Economic distance is treated as a definition of poverty, not because people are unequal, but because the consequence of extreme inequality is social exclusion. Social exclusion leads necessarily to material deprivation, because there are "positional goods," whose value is determined at least in part by the worth of other goods around them. Housing and access to education are examples. This means that poverty in this sense can only be understood in terms of the pattern of social relationships in which it is applied.

The absolute model of poverty has been dominant in the study of developing countries, because without some external standard it is difficult to identify poverty in different countries. The relative model has increasingly been adopted in studies of developed industrial countries, because material deprivation in developed countries is strongly related to inequality and because the problems with which social policy in these countries are concerned are problems, like dependency and social exclusion, best described in relative terms.

III. RESPONSIBILITY FOR POVERTY

If the term poverty itself implies a moral judgment, the suggestion that poverty calls for some kind of response or intervention is tautologous. Some commentators have sought to resist the application of the term poverty, on the basis that they see no moral responsibility to alleviate the circumstances. Equally, the argument that poverty is relative has been taken to mean that "real" poverty does not exist.

The basis of the responsibility to alleviate poverty is commonly represented in four ways.

- *Virtuous conduct.* Charity and altruism can be seen as virtues, justified not in terms of the consequences for the poor but rather as an indicator of moral worth in the donor. This justification was important in feudal societies and the development of medieval poor relief.
- *Altruism and solidarity.* Altruism is action to help others, based in concern for their situation or a sense of obligation. It has also been described as an "ultraobligation"—conduct that goes beyond obligation—but in that case it falls under the category of virtuous conduct rather than obligation. The obligation is not necessarily felt to the poor person; it may be held to society, or to God. Catholic social teaching describes the general responsibility in terms of "solidarity." This is a dominant theme in the social policy of the European Union.
- *The rights of poor people.* Poor people have a claim to the same rights as others. Rights are sometimes represented in negative terms, as injunctions against the conduct of others; equally, they can be represented in positive terms, which imply obligations on others. A

right to freedom, for example, may be seen in the positive sense as implying the freedom to do an action, and poverty precludes possibilities for action. "Rights to welfare"—sometimes referred to in the philosophical literature as "welfare rights," although that term is also used to refer to legal rights—are claim rights, because they rely on the delivery of resources that are outside the capacity of the person who holds them.

• *Consequentialist arguments.* Poverty implies a lack of welfare, and positions that are concerned with improving welfare, such as utilitarianism, argue for the reduction of poverty. Contractarian arguments that depend on anticipated consequences might equally be seen as consequentialist; the relief of poverty can be related to the minimization of suffering (an application of Rawls' maximin principle). Redistribution from richer to poorer people can increase the aggregate of happiness (because with diminishing marginal utility, the value of resources is greater to poorer people than it is to richer people).

The arguments against relieving poverty are primarily based either in consequentialist arguments (Herbert Spencer, for example, saw poverty as an essential and desirable aspect of a competitive society in which only the fittest would survive) or in judgments about the moral desert of the poor. The effect of some other arguments (e.g., Nozick's arguments against redistribution) is to deny the legitimacy of intervention on behalf of the poor, but few have taken this position; even Hayek accepts the necessity of some residual welfare system.

IV. THE STIGMA OF POVERTY

A. Exchange and Stigma

The obligation to support the poor is subject to an important corollary: that poor people who receive support are liable to be condemned morally on that account. In most societies, if not in all, there is a norm of reciprocity: people are obliged to make a return for the things they receive. Richard Titmuss argued that people are prepared to give to others in the understanding that they would ultimately benefit. Reciprocity is not necessarily balanced; it may be "generalized," in which the person who contributes receives from someone different than the person who has received. An example is support for elderly people, which is delivered, not on the basis that old people have supported the working population, but that they supported the previous generation of elderly people, and the current generation of workers will be supported in turn by the generation that follows it. Generalized reciprocity is closely related to the principle of solidarity.

The main response to this, made by Robert Pinker, is that society expects a more direct form of exchange: poor people who are unable to make a return for the help they receive suffer a loss of esteem or status. Some forms of dependency are more acceptable than others: pensioners, for example, are widely accepted on the basis that they have previously contributed to society, while children may be seen as potential contributors. Others, by contrast, are liable to be rejected; unemployed people, outsiders (like gypsies), and people with long-term illnesses are subject to a strong social stigma. The combination of generalized and balanced reciprocity has a paradoxical effect—the simultaneous acceptance and rejection of the poor.

B. The Moral Condemnation of the Poor

The moral condemnation of the poor is one of the enduring features of discussion of the subject. In medieval times, poverty was linked with deviance, and in industrial society, the link was reinforced by its association with punitive policies. Nineteenth-century policies distinguished the "deserving" from the "undeserving" poor; the deserving poor were those who worked or who became dependent through unavoidable misfortune, and the "undeserving" were those who had failed to exercise thrift, had not sufficiently attempted to escape from poverty or who had condemned themselves to poverty through their actions (for example, through bearing children). The condemnation of the undeserving, however, was extended to "degenerates," including people with birth defects or mental illness.

The central features of the condemnation are that poor people have inflicted their circumstances on themselves; that their conduct leads to rapacious dependency, with no appropriate sense of shame; that they are at the root of a range of social problems, including crime; that their conduct is immoral, both in relation to honesty and to sexual conduct; and that they are dirty. (These arguments are reviewed in P. Spicker, *Stigma and Social Welfare*, 1984. Kent: Croom Helm) Defenders of the poor have sometimes accepted the criticisms, while arguing that it is not the responsibility of the poor; in Victorian times, reformers like Charles Booth or Octavia Hill argued that the conditions of poverty themselves caused immorality. Contemporary social scientists have argued that the accusations are false, an example of stigmatic labeling or ideological bias. The moral condemnation of the poor is seen, in consequence, as a way of blaming the poor for the ills of society.

V. THE CAUSES OF POVERTY

Explanations for poverty are generally classified in three main ways. Pathological explanations are those that explain poverty in terms of the circumstances of poor people. Subcultural explanations identify factors that lead poverty to affect groups of people who share particular circumstances and values. Structural explanations explain poverty in terms of the society in which it occurs.

A. Pathological Explanations

The most important pathological explanations are individualist, genetic, and familial. Individual explanations attribute poverty to the conduct of the individual who has become poor: poverty may be represented as the result of laziness, personal inadequacy, making the wrong choices, or some kind of shortcoming or handicap. This is often seen as cause for moral condemnation; Charles Murray's influential book *Losing Ground* (1984). New York: Basic Books is an example.

Genetic explanations for poverty were prominent at the turn of the nineteenth century. They rely on the proposition that the structure of rewards in society in some way reflects the inherited capacity or behavior of its citizens. In the later nineteenth century, mental defects and "degeneracy" were seen as the root of crime, insanity, pauperism, and social pathology of all kinds. The argument of eugenicists was that such problems could be bred out of society through isolation of degenerates. The argument was largely discredited only through their association with Nazism in the 1930s and 1940s, but survived in arguments about "problem families" and later in arguments about the hereditability of intelligence.

Familial explanations overlap with genetic explanations, but are discrete. The argument has been made that upbringing and heredity are primary reasons for the persistence of poverty and that intergenerational continuities in poverty persist. The importance of this argument in the United Kingdom led to extensive investigation of the problems, and the contention has been firmly contradicted by the empirical evidence: a summary of the main findings can be found in M. Brown and N. Madge, *Despite the Welfare State* (1982). London: Heinemann. Despite increased vulnerability to poverty, deprivation is not in general transmitted between generations. The effect of intermarriage, social mobility, and changing economic conditions over time is such that even if the familial circumstances produce disadvantage, it does not persist in most cases. Later research on the dynamics of welfare has shown that poverty is not a fixed condition but a constantly changing condition that people move into and out of during their life cycle: an example is R. Walker, *Poverty dynamics* (1994).

B. Subcultural Explanations

Subcultural explanations constitute an intermediate category between pathological and structural explanations. The best-known example is the formulation by Oscar Lewis, in the 1950s and 1960s, of the concept of a "culture of poverty," a pattern of behavior, values, and circumstances that led to poor people being locked into poverty. Lewis's views, based on analyses in Mexico, Puerto Rico, and New York, were particularly influential in the U.S. War on Poverty. They were subject to extensive criticism, because Lewis's description confused aspects of deprivation, behavior, and attitude with culture; because the derivation of the theory was based on questionable generalisations, tinged with elements of sensationalism; and because Lewis had no basis for the argument that the culture he described was either distinctive to poverty or persistent.

The strongest argument for a subcultural adaptation of this type seeks to explanation variations in family structure in terms of poverty. The economic marginality of poor men means that although they can at times fulfill conventional social roles, they cannot do so consistently, and women cannot afford to form permanent ties with them. William Julius Wilson, in *The Truly Disadvantaged* (1987). Chicago: University of Chicago Press identifies economic factors as the basis for a breakdown in familial norms; he points to a shortage of "marriageable" or economically stable males. The marginality of men implies higher rates of relationship breakdown, illegitimacy, serial relationships rather than stable partnerships, and fragile family structures.

The arguments about subcultural adaptation have reemerged recently in debates about the "underclass." The term is infused with the same stigmatic elements as the "culture of poverty," and some commentators have refused to use it.

C. Structural Explanations

Structural explanations attribute poverty to the society in which it takes place, rather than to individuals who experience it. If society is unequal, then some people will fall to the bottom. This does not mean that people must be poor, unless poverty is seen directly in terms of inequality, but poverty is likely to be produced in an unequal society. Similarly, the effect of an economic system that does not provide enough work for all who wish to work, or more specifically of a labor market divided between secure and precarious employment, is to put some people in the situation where their resources will be inadequate. Titmuss saw poverty as a form of "diswelfare," the natural outcome of a competitive social structure. This view can coexist with individualist explanations; if people fail to survive in a competitive environment, it may be attributed either to their personal characteristics or to the fact that they are in a competitive environment. Titmuss argued that the production of diswelfare by social arrangements created an obligation on society to offer social protection against diswelfare.

Poverty is also represented in some quarters as the product of social divisions: the class system, the division of status, or the structure of power in society. Status refers to social esteem or honor; it is typically conveyed by education, occupation, or breeding. Class refers in social science to the economic position in which people find themselves: Marxists attribute class to position in relation to the means of production, conventionally seen in terms of employers and workers, while Weberians define class in terms of common economic positions (which could mean, for example, that home owners constitute a class distinct from tenants, or that salaried workers are in a class different from people on casual wages). Class is popularly linked with "socioeconomic status," which brings together economic position with occupation as a primary indication of social standing. Poverty represents the lowest class, and the term "underclass" may be taken to refer to those who are at the bottom of the status hierarchy.

The division of power in society is more controversial, because it seems to link the position of the poor to oppression by others who are more powerful than them. Power is understood, by Weber, as referring to might, influence or authority; poor people lack all three. "Nondecisions"—lack of interest, and a refusal to countenance some issues as belonging properly on a policy agenda—can perpetuate the status quo. Marxists have also written of "hegemony," which legitimates a set of values and beliefs favoring the status quo and the powerful.

The different perspectives are not exclusive; within a structural perspective, it is possible to use pathological explanations to explain which individual becomes poor. If this is unusual, it is because pathological explanations have been strongly linked with the moral condemnation of the poor, while structural explanations have been used to emphasize their status as victims.

VI. RESPONSES TO POVERTY

Responses to poverty are not necessarily linked to its causes; the way into a problem is not necessarily the way out of it. Pathological problems, like unemployment through limited competence, may still be alleviated by structural responses in the labor market; structural problems, like the exclusion of women, may be responded to by programs aimed at furthering the position of individual women.

By contrast, the response to poverty does depend strongly on the way in which the term is understood. If poverty is based in material deprivation, then strategies to deal with poverty that do not address material deprivation—for example, through education—cannot have a direct effect. If poverty is based in dependency, increasing benefits will not reduce it. If poverty is based in inequality, then policies for economic growth that promote inequality cannot address poverty.

There are six main classes of response to poverty.

• *Poor relief.* Poverty is characterized by problems relating to deprivation, and it is possible to respond to these issues by making provision for deprivation, like lack of food or housing, or general income support. This may be seen as treating the symptoms rather than the disease, but its importance is far from negligible; addressing deprivation does not necessarily deal with all the issues, but it contributes to the alleviation of poverty, and problems of deprivation are serious issues in their own right.

• *Respond to individual circumstances.* The second response is individualistic: to respond to the circumstances of poor people on a case-by-case basis. This implies some process of selection by which poor people can be identified, most usually in the form of means testing. There are problems associated with means testing: it is widely perceived as stigmatizing, administratively cumbersome, and it can have perverse consequences—a "poverty trap" is created because benefits are withdrawn when income increases.

• *Provision for contingencies.* It is possible to respond to poverty by addressing the circumstances in which people become poor—old age, sickness, or unemployment. This is the basis on which many social security systems have been organized.

• *Approximate responses.* A response may be made

not to poverty, but to circumstances associated with poverty. The World Bank has argued, in the context of provision in developing countries, for "indicator targeting"—directing resources not to poor people, because it is expensive and impractical in that context, but to poor regions or defined demographic groups (like old people, women, or new mothers).

• *Key intervention.* Complex social phenomena can be represented as "systems," in which different issues are interrelated. Intervention at certain points of the system affect other parts, and the choice of key factors may be held to have crucial effects on associated social problems. This argument has previously been made for education and political participation.

• *Prevention.* Measures can be taken to prevent deprivation from arising—for example, through the promotion of economic development, employment, education, or improved housing.

Also See the Following Articles

GENETIC RESEARCH • HOMELESSNESS • PATERNALISM • SOCIAL ETHICS, OVERVIEW

Bibliography

Room, G. (Ed.). (1995). *Beyond the threshold.* Bristol, UK: Policy Press.
Spicker, P. (1993). *Poverty and social security.* London: Routledge.
Townsend, P. (1993). *The international analysis of poverty.* Hemel Hempstead: Harvester Wheatsheaf.
World Bank. (1990). *World development report 1990: Poverty.* Oxford: Oxford University Press.

PRECAUTIONARY PRINCIPLE

Jenneth Parker
The Hastings Center

GLOSSARY

anthropocentrism The concept that the human species is unique and that environmental issues should thus be examined in the context of human interests and needs.

biocentrism The concept that the human species is one among innumerable species on earth, and that environmental issues should thus be examined in the larger context of all living things rather than within a specifically human context.

biosphere The entire community of living organisms inhabiting the earth, and the physical environment supporting this life.

cocktail effect A term for the principle that certain substances, though not individually deleterious to the environment, may prove harmful in combination.

ecosystem A localized community of diverse organ-

isms and their environment, interacting as one biological unit.

GMO genetically modified organism, an animal or plant whose genetic makeup has been altered through the introduction of foreign genetic material by some laboratory or industrial technique.

indicator species A particular species whose presence (or absence) is regarded as characteristic of a given environment, and whose ability or failure to thrive there is thus thought to be indicative of the overall ecological status of this environment.

In the face of highly uncertain outcomes philosophers should develop alternative systems of ethics which promote environmental quality and are ethically sensitive in the absence of firm ecological knowledge Lemons 1983.

We should recognise our incomplete knowledge of nature and therefore exercise caution and special concern for natural values.

MRS TOBY VIGOD

THE PRECAUTIONARY PRINCIPLE (PP) is wide ranging with many different interpretations and formulations: despite this uncertainty and ambiguity it is incorporated into international law and some domestic laws concerned with the environment. Besides taking a specific form in various laws, the PP in its wider form resembles sustainable development as being an umbrella term covering the growth of a whole discourse and also in that commitments have been made to a principle still in development. The PP also resembles sustainable development in that it is an area of intense contestation in the realm of interpretation in relation to specific decisions and in more theoretical statements attempting to define its scope and commitments. I shall attempt to define the key parameters of the discourse and indicate some of the conflicts, while making my own position clear. I shall argue that, from the perspective of environmental ethics, the principle should be taken in its widest form.

The historical context within which the PP developed was a "permissive" attitude to the environment. Environmental life-support systems were taken for granted as "externalities" and the environment generally was thought to be robust and capable of absorbing the impact of human activities. The growing recognition of a number of dramatic environmental problems began to change these perceptions, and governments who had to license new technologies and substances began to use ecological science to attempt to establish "critical loads" and "safe thresholds." It then became apparent that the task set was impossible since ecological science cannot declare that a new substance or technology is "safe," and equally causal links between actions and effects may either be impossible to establish or else take a very long time to establish, by which time great harm may already have been done.

I. LEGAL FORMULATIONS: STRONG AND WEAK

Overall, in its various legal forms the PP insists that where a substance or a technology is potentially damaging to the environment, regulation should be considered irrespective of "final scientific proof" (B. Dickson, in press. In *Proceedings, International Jacobsen Conference, Feb. 29–Mar. 2, 1996.* Harare: Univ. of Zimbabwe Press).

Within this general legal approach Dickson has identified stronger and weaker versions.

• *Stronger:* For example, the London Declaration of 1987 on the Protection of the North Sea states that substances will be regulated "when there is reason to assume that certain damage or harmful effects on the living resources of the sea are likely to be caused by such substances, even where there is no scientific evidence to prove a causal link between emmissions and effects."

• *Weaker:* For example, the Rio Declaration states that "where there are threats of serious or irreversible damage lack of full scientific certainty shall not be used as a reason for postponing cost-effective measures to prevent environmental degradation." This formulation is weaker as it does not unambiguously commit the parties to regulatory action and implicitly suggests that, *although there may be other valid reasons against regulatory action,* scientific uncertainty should not be taken as one such valid reason.

Not only do the various legal forms differ but they are also open to stronger and weaker forms of interpretation; this can be seen even in interpretations of the stronger, less ambiguous form. For example, according to one commentator, Greenpeace has in effect interpreted the principle as meaning that no activity that might impact on the environment should be allowed unless it can be proved to be harmless.

The principle will inevitably be subject to different views of what might constitute environmental harm. For some environmentalists the fact that a substance is not naturally occurring is a *prima facie* reason to suppose that it may have harmful effects on complex natural systems—including the human body: organic farming is, for example, premised upon this view of the precautionary approach. Other interpreters will hold that the "reason to assume... damage" clause requires some good reason supported by some scientific evidence: what constitutes sufficient scientific evidence to give reason for concern will be contested. The dialogue over these interpretations can be seen played out in the recent controversy over the dumping of oil platforms in the North sea. Greenpeace insists that there is now a presumption against any dumping, while Shell insists that there is no reason to fear any resulting harm.

II. WIDER USES OF THE PP: "WAKING UP IN THE EXPERIMENT"

It is clear that various legal formulations do differ, and yet a range of commentators, lay environmentalists, and NGOs (nongovernmental organizations) insist on referring to *the* precautionary principle. In so doing, I will argue, they are referring to a prototypical ethical principle with important links to other areas of environmental thought.

Some commentators, Dickson in particular, argue for the restriction of the PP to its narrower legal formulations. Fortunately as even applied moral philosophers cannot effectively legislate against the development and use of concepts in the wider world, the PP is developing a life of its own within the range of professional, general environmentalist, and lay discourses that I hope to show will repay attention from environmental ethicists.

For example, in setting out the debate around the release and labeling of genetically modified organisms (GMOs), one lay environmental group, the "Natural Law Party," describes the context of technological intervention in natural systems, including human bodies, as a vast experiment; only unlike more limited medical experimentation, informed consent does not have to be obtained. This change of perspective moves from regarding intervention as unproblematic technological "advance" toward viewing intervention as a potential violation of the natural world and of the rights of humans conceived as part of that world. The PP, while not encapsulating this kind of perspectival shift, is certainly within the same frame of discourse. Concerns about GMOs are formulated within the context of the existing natural system: "The genetic structure of plants has been nourishing mankind for millennia. Tampering with the genetic code of food... could upset the delicate balance between our physiology and the foods we eat...." (Natural Law Party, 1996). "Dangers of genetically engineered foods." Buckinghamshire, UK: Mentmore).

This perspective of the "vast experiment" indicates a useful possible approach to the PP as a wider application of the degree of precaution that usually prevails in a scientific laboratory—only with the enormously increased complexity obtaining where the whole of the living world constitutes the experimental subject.

In speaking of their concerns about the decision not to label genetically modified foods, the Soil Association claims that this decision shows that "a GMO food is assumed to be harmless unless proved otherwise," viewing this as "a shameless abandonment of the 'precautionary principle.'" Here the principle is viewed as a shifting of the burden of proof: instead of environmentalists having to demonstrate damage after the fact, the PP is viewed as shifting the onus onto the potential polluter to demonstrate that what they propose will not cause damage. In a survey of biologists, lawyers, and administrators it was found that 80% supported this interpretation of the PP. The survey also showed support for varying interpretations and confusion about the status of the principle. I suggest that this does not so much show a lamentable ignorance of the "real"

legally limited PP but the emergence of a prototypical ethical principle whose status and assumptions I shall further explore below.

Dickson has claimed that it is in the interests of pragmatism to restrict the PP to the legal forms that have been ratified by states in the real world. In fact the environmental agenda is increasingly set by civil society in its various forms: citizens' organizations, NGOs, and the wider new social movements. For example, the Rio conference itself was initiated by the civil associations of the UN which are to be found around the world. Pragmatism thus dictates that applied ethicists should take note of the debates and perspectives developing in these sectors as these are likely to shape the policies of tomorrow. Equally if current precautionary policies have been "grafted onto a body of policy still based on the presumed assimilative capacity of the environment," as MacGarvin (1994. In T. O'Riordan and J. Cameron, Eds., *Interpreting the precautionary principle*) claims, "the result will be a contradictory mess." Insofar as applied philosophers seek to clear up contradictory messes, we had better look beyond the current legal actualities.

In summary, therefore, as I have argued, the limited legal form does not express the breadth of the import of the PP in wider environmental discourse, which is the legitimate concern of environmental ethicists. In what follows I will be considering the wider PP—that representing an ongoing debate around the implications of environmental science for the current pattern of our interventions in nature.

III. ENVIRONMENTAL SCIENCE AND THE PP

The PP has been partly founded upon a growing acknowledgment by environmental science of its own limitations. One potent example is that of marine ecology, described with admirable clarity and directness by Malcolm MacGarvin (1994). It has been found to be impossible to establish critical loads of pollutants due to the multiplicity of factors involved in the health of marine ecosystems. The validity of using so-called "indicator species" to judge ecosystem health is now seriously suspect. MacGarvin concludes that "monitoring programmes designed to protect marine habitats do not have a firm scientific foundation." One consequence of this is that there is now a presumption against dumping of *any* pollutants in the ocean—a much stronger precautionary attitude than that based on an earlier (more optimistic) science. The same downshifting of expectations has occurred throughout the whole of environmental science.

A large number of scientific considerations support the PP. Many commentators stress uncertainty, but in order to give an accurate account of the PP it is necessary to place the unknown and the unknowable in the context to what *is* known.

A. Uncertainty

Uncertainty is the product of both the actual current limits of science and the "in principle" limits: the unknown and the unknowable.

Factors currently limiting science (the unknown) include:

- The lack of detailed long-term research in many areas of concern
- The underfunding and marginalization of ecology
- The lack of interdisciplinary research

Factors which limit environmental science in principle (the unknowable) include:

- The intrinsic difficulties of field science in the open system of the environment
- The logistical difficulties of multivariate analysis, e.g., testing for the "cocktail effect"—possibly synergistic effects of chemicals thought to be safe when tested singly
- The impossibility of a "control" environment for comparison as human effects are ubiquitous
- The chaotic nature of many natural processes, e.g., population dynamics and climate
- The intrinsic limits of any intentional process— science designs experiments to look for effects that are expected and information gathering is always limited with respect to a hypothesis (for example, ozone testing equipment in the stratosphere was originally programmed to treat any holes merely as "noise" in the data set)

It should be stressed that this negative assessment of the ability of environmental science to deliver the safety assurances that technological society requires is not just made by a few dissenters: this is the current mainstream opinion. Although it may be understandable that environmental science as a profession has not been proclaiming this from the rooftops, many scientists believe that the situation must be made clear since current unrealistic expectations are threatening to destroy the overall credibility of environmental science.

Dickson emphasizes the dictinction between *risk* and precaution; whereas risk applies where there are reliable scientific predictions on the basis of which probabilities can be assigned, precaution applies where uncertainty is prevalent. In view of the previous assessments of environmental science, it seems that situations of risk must be in the minority; this has the interesting corollary that many situations currently referred to in terms of risk (and perhaps a substantial amount of the literature on risk) should be reread in terms of precaution.

B. The Context of Knowledge and Experience

Reasons for supporting precautionary action include the following:

- The overview or model of life as a complex system of mutually interacting subsystems and organisms
- The awareness that ecosystem damage may be irreversible
- The repeated experience of harm being caused in ways that have not been predicted or suspected
- The fact that natural systems do not produce "waste"

The previous limitations of environmental science must be set, against the broader picture that environmental science has been able to assemble. As precaution may be seen as denying benefits, it requires justification. It is the knowledge produced by environmental science that does enable us to rationally state the reasons for concern which are needed to justify precaution.

IV. PRECAUTIONARY IMPLICATIONS OF ENVIRONMENTAL SCIENCE

The implications are many and diverse, and I must refer the reader to the main sources at the end of this article. However, I will here summarize some of the more basic implications to help set the context for discussion. It should be noted that drawing out the precautionary implications of environmental science involves practical judgment guided by an overall aim of preserving life.

- A presumption against any technology at a scale to disrupt natural systems

- A presumption against synthetics (MacGarvin, 1994)
- A presumption in favor of clean production rather than regulation of emmissions
- A general presumption in favor of reducing human impacts on natural systems

V. IS THE PRECAUTIONARY PRINCIPLE A SCIENTIFIC PRINCIPLE?

The exact nature of the relation between environmental science and environmental ethics is controversial and I will only claim here that the PP as a developing ethical principle is *informed* by science. But may it not be that the PP is a scientific principle? I will argue that the PP makes implicit assumptions to do with "taking care" and thus cannot be a purely scientific principle. I will now explore the idea that the PP could be viewed as a form of ecological rationality rather than as a specifically ethical principle.

A. The Precautionary Principle as Ecological Rationality

The concept of "ecological rationality" has been persuasively outlined by Robert V. Bartlett (1986, *Environmental Ethics, 8*). Lynton K. Caldwell proposes that the test of rationality should be "that which is consistent with continuing health and happiness of man and with the self-renewing tendencies of the planetary life support system" (1971. *Environment.* New York: Doubleday. Quoted in Bartlett, 1986).

It may be that the PP could be seen as a rational principle rather than primarily as ethical: the PP could support an ecological rationality formulated on the recognition of the limits or "bounded" nature of rationality. "Bounded rationality" proposes that "the capacity of the human mind for formulating and solving complex problems is very small compared to the size of the problems whose solution is required for objectively rational behaviour in the real world" (H. A. Simon, 1957. *Models of man.* New York: Wiley. Quoted in Bartlett, 1986). The PP replaces the concept of the *size* of a problem (after all, computers can deal with huge data sets) with that of its unconscionable *complexity*. Thus the PP proposes that a precautionary attitude based on what we do know is rational in the face of unknowns.

Bartlett draws upon Simon's distinction between substantive rationality, "the extent to which appropriate courses of action are chosen," and procedural rationality, "the effectiveness of the procedures used to choose actions." Looked at from this perspective, the wider PP can be seen as proposing procedural ecological rationality, challenging the prevalent procedure of permissiveness toward the environment and implicitly characterizing it as reckless.

Bartlett proposes that ecological rationality will have to be considered along with other forms of rationality (e.g., economic) in any particular decision context. This view would support Dickson's contention that the PP will always be balanced with other considerations in any decision context—that is, it is not absolute. However, Bartlett contends that ecological rationality is in some sense more basic than other forms of rationality, such as economic rationality, in that it provides the ground for other forms to exist.

While the notion of ecological rationality is an interesting conception, it is so precisely because it is a value-enriched conception of rationality where life systems are seen as valuable. The ethical presumptions of ecological rationality are shared by the PP and it is to these that I must now turn to inquire into their status, justification, and relation to environmental ethics.

B. Ethical Assumptions of the PP

Perhaps the most general ethical presumption of the PP is that we ought to exercise rational prudence or take care of things we regard as valuable. This may seem obvious but is not necessarily so: we might take the view that something is valuable precisely in its ephemeral nature and prefer to be fatalistic or whimsical about it; e.g., "Life is just a party and parties weren't meant to last." In this respect arguments in favor of an ethic of care can support the PP (see further on for ethics of environmental care).

A further ethical presumption of the PP (that without which it could not get going) is that living systems are valuable. I do not think that at present there is any clear agreement on exactly on what basis they are valuable (see further on for a reputation of the PP as embodying intrinsic value). This may not matter since, as varieties of moral pluralism such as pragmatism hold, a wide range of values may all legitimately contribute to our ethical decisions without having to be grounded in one overall principle or theory.

We may ask about what environmental science is adding to these general ethical principles. I would say that environmental science has produced knowledge which is helping us to understand some of the ways in which the functioning biosphere is valuable as well as fostering an increased degree of respect for the complexity, longevity, and integrity of the biosphere. I do hold that coming to care for something or someone does involve taking the time to appreciate the relevant qualities. This is not to say that the arts do not also alert us to environmental qualities.

It is against this background of the positive contribution of environmental science that the warnings of the limits of that science have their impact. The PP tells us that caring for our environment is going to involve restraint and details specific presumptions against certain kinds of action. I conclude that the PP represents procedural rules for rational decision making guided by a commitment to environmental care. It is therefore an ethical principle in this sense but is not an ethical *first principle*. I have already claimed that an ethic of care is a necessary presumption for the PP but that this care perspective can accommodate a plurality of views on value. This approach thus avoids the reduction of these values to expressions of a common principle as do monistic and hierarchically ordered systems of ethics. In this way I would propose that an ethic of care has the dual advantage of expressing a broad ethical attitude and accommodating a variety of perspectives. This would seem a very suitable kind of basis on which to found a principle of social decision and conduct which has to be substantive and yet have wide agreement.

Robin Attfield has proposed that there are important relationships between the PP and questions of justice. To value the biosphere is to recognize it as a valuable common inheritance, and this inevitably raises questions of just distribution and "ownership." I do not, however, think that the PP is committed to a particular position on justice. The PP does seem to assume a joint responsibility for environmental care that is not restricted to traditional attributions of moral responsibility. Traditional (Western) models of moral responsibility assume that we are responsible for things that have come about as a result of our actions, or that we have specifically contracted to do (of course there are many forms of mitigation but these need not concern us here). The PP, and, I would argue, the concept of care on which it is based, assumes that our connectedness with living systems involves a necessity to care for them *irrespective* of the relevance or not of traditional moral responsibility. In this way the PP assumes that we all share the problem of excessive human impacts on living systems and the presumption is that we should act to reduce these impacts *whenever we can*—not just when we feel that we are particularly responsible. From

my perspective it is care which provides the real support for burden sharing in a time of environmental change, not justice.

C. Support for, and Consistency with, a Biocentric Ethic

In what way can the PP be seen to support a biocentric ethic that views nonhuman species and ecosystems as intrinsically valuable? One might argue that the ethical assumption of care for the environment supports the notion of intrinsic value. This seems an unjustifiable assertion if, as I claim, the PP does not take a particular position as to why the environment should be valued. We could suggest, consistently with the PP, that it would be a good thing if people acted *as if* nonhuman species and ecosystems had intrinsic value—the kind of instrumental use of a biocentric approach or "sanctity" appealed to by a large number of people who apparently believe that this is an argument for instrinsic value.

Equally it would seem possible to have an attitude of "respect" for the qualities of nature without being committed to intrinsic value: one might respect nature in the same way as one respects a potential enemy with whom one wishes to keep on good terms. Insofar as the PP is upheld by science that might be held to limit its possible use to support intrinsic value. If intrinsic value is adopted then it seems that it would be held that the life of least intervention in natural systems and with other species would be morally preferred with or without scientific support.

I do not therefore consider that the PP provides any particular support for intrinsic value as such. However, this is not to say that the PP is not thoroughly *consistent* with a biocentric ethic in that following such an ethic does entail adopting principles of minimum impact or "living lightly."

D. Support for, and Consistency with, an Anthropocentric Environmental Ethic

The PP is clearly consistent with an ethic which takes concern for humans to be central, as we may be morally recommended to take precautionary action merely to protect human interests. However, it could be argued that the science supporting the PP also supports an almost infinite extension of the concept of human interests. On the strong interpretation of the PP the intricacy and interconnectedness of the biosphere together with the intrinsic limits on our knowledge of its workings are such as to justify an *identification* of human interests with the interests of every other aspect of the biosphere. This view is particularly supported by the sometimes spectacular inadequacy of our attempts to pursue human interests by intervening in natural systems; many projects such as dams not only fail to deliver the expected benefits but have negative consequences often unforeseen by planners (but not always unforeseen by local people).

E. Environmental Virtue Ethics

Geoffrey Frasz has claimed that "the thrust of environmental virtue ethics is to foster new habits of thought and action in the moral agent—not just to get the immediate decision made right, but to re-orient all actions henceforth in terms of a holistic, ecologically based way of thinking" (1993). *Environmental Ethics,* **15**). Such an ethic requires much input from the ecologically based sciences in order for agents to be able to think and act within a new environmental paradigm. In this sense a precautionary habit of mind with respect to environmental intervention, based on "respect" for nature, could be seen as an integral part of environmental virtue ethics. Further, proper attention to the PP may begin to clarify the different senses of "virtue" required.

Frasz uses Thomas E. Hall's concept of "humility" as the cardinal environmental virtue. Frasz himself highlights the problems with this formulation when he interprets environmental "humility" as continuous with our human social conceptions of humility, proposing that the appropriately humble person might unfortunately be too reticent to adequately defend nature. Attention to the PP and its scientific underpinnings points to the difference between our ordinary social conceptions of humility (by no means an uncontroversial social "virtue") and the notion that we ought to maintain a properly restricted view of our capacity to knowledgeably intervene in nature as a *species* (or perhaps more accurately as a specific culture). It could be argued that this collective "humility" in the face of nature would be properly expressed in the habitual attitude that the PP could inculcate. The confusion between collective and individual "humility" is a crucial one for Frasz's account; it leads him inevitably to the individualistic conclusion that environmental virtue ethics seeks "workable ways of living with nature that foster changes in personal virtue rather than larger societal changes."

I have argued that the PP is ethically supported by an assumption of care for the environment. An ethics of environmental care can be seen as a form of virtue ethics; for example, Joan C. Tronto discusses the virtues of care. Berenice Fisher and Joan C. Tronto define care

as "a species activity that includes everything that we do to maintain, continue and repair our world.... [T]hat world includes our bodies, our selves and our environment, all of which we seek to interweave in a complex, life-sustaining web" (1991).

This suggests that, in parallel with the previous discussion, a care-based environmental ethic may need to beware the transfer of concepts of care drawn from human social contexts to "care for the environment." However, Tronto does not make this error; her concept of "attentiveness" certainly corresponds to the spirit of the PP interpreted in its wider form as a general requirement to exercise caution in intervening in functioning life systems. In that the "care" approach involves a general injunction to look at the widest possible consequences of our actions, seeing them as part of a web of associations and relations, the PP is an harmonious part of an environmental ethics of care.

VI. THE PRECAUTIONARY PRINCIPLE AND THE STATUS QUO

Robin Attfield has made the important point that the PP is not necessarily in favor of the current status quo and may necessitate changing it, giving the example of keeping running "Chernobyl style" reactors. This raises the whole question of the nature of the valued states which we seek to protect, preserve, or reintroduce (ecological restoration). It is indeed true that there are many states and processes which the PP would seek to change. However, this should not lead us to overlook the positive judgment that immensely complex life support systems have been functioning extremely well for millennia and it behooves us to be cautious in bringing about changes. In this sense the PP is for the "status quo" or continuing life.

In this respect it might be argued that humans have been changing ecosystems for a long time, apparently without causing catastrophes (though this is arguable as some environmental historians seek to show that the collapse of at least some civilizations has been brought about by reckless treatment of natural systems). It is at this point that considerations of qualitative changes or discontinuities are relevant. It can be reasonably argued that there is a qualitative change—in both the nature and the scale of our technologies. I argue that the PP must apply to both: to the nature of our technologies in the ways already reviewed and also to the sheer scale of our interventions in nature. This latter point means that even "traditional" practices may need to be subject to precaution.

Commentators on the PP have sought to include natural and social systems within its remit. I will now argue that this is a mistake which if persisted in gives rise to socially conservative conclusions which are not necessarily implied by the PP. This is important for environmental ethics as it is in part a reforming project—seeking to open up new ethical perspectives on the environment within our culture. The relationship between environmental ethics and environmental social movements has not been openly explored by many writers; there is a lack of attention to the politics of our own discourse. At present there is assumed to be some kind of symbiotic relationship between environmental ethics and related movements attempting to bring about social change. If as environmental ethicists we accept that we should be precautionary in the same way about social change as we are in relation to the environment, this would render our practice highly problematic.

If the PP applies to societies we would then be mandated to respect the complexity and fragility of social systems in the same way as we are told we should respect natural systems. For example, O'Riordan and Cameron claim that "liability and onus of proof shift more and more onto the promoter of social change" (1994. *Interpreting the precautionary principle*); their argument seems to be that this is because scientific uncertainty is "mediated via social contexts." However, it is quite possible to accept the social construction of science without thereby holding that social science can be used in exactly the same way to formulate policy as natural science. This is one of the reasons that it is important to place uncertainty in environmental science against the background of what is known. Notions of a healthy environment are much less problematic than notions of a healthy society. As we have noted, the PP does not just support the status quo; it may support environmental restoration in line with a broad knowledge of environmental health.

To return to the science underpinning the PP, I would argue that there is a *prima facie* case against moving from environmental science to principles that are held to apply to society. But this case can be made much more strongly with the help of a realist philosophy of science. A critical realist perspective (such as that propounded by Bhaskar or Sayer, among others) proposes the objective reality of the structures of the natural world in distinction to the demireality of the structures of the social world while also recognizing the social construction of science. The structures of the social world are viewed as real insofar as they are causal (e.g., the monetary system), but they are subject to human intentions. The structures of the natural world cannot simply be altered by human intention—even genetic engineering and reproductive technologies have to work with natural structures.

The distinction between the realities of the natural world and the human constructs of the social world is at the heart of environmentalism shown, for example, in the New Internationalist dictum, "only when you have killed the last fish and poisoned the last river will you realise that you cannot eat money." This distinction is extremely important in that it implies that a conservative (in the ecological sense) attitude to nature may actually necessitate a radical (in the political sense) attitude toward reforming society. Any conflation of the natural and the social completely undermines the message of environmentalism. To say this is not at all to deny the complexities of social change, but it is to maintain the possibility that human beings can intentionally change society and their relationship to nature—indeed the PP itself is evidence of the belief in this possibility.

The notion that social systems are self-organizing and should be left to do so is most famously associated with Hayek and his concept of "catallaxy." The "new right" has developed this idea in various ways and it does contain some pertinent observations about human societies and the place of regulation. However, it is broadly accepted that Hayek's critics have refuted the extreme claim that human society can be seen as a totally unconscious self-creating phenomenon. In opposition to those who would present the PP as simply the embodiment of a natural conservatism (which might be taken as unproblematically transferable to the social sphere), I have argued that the PP does seek to draw upon our existing knowledge of natural systems to *justify* precaution.

At this point we must return to Attfield's comments about the environmentalist mission to change at least some aspects of the existing situation. Indeed were the PP to be unproblematically extendable to human society there would be a severe dilemma for environmentalists. The fact that some environmentalists believe they do find themselves in this dilemma testifies to the prevalent confusion in this area.

There is an important coda with respect to the previous argument regarding development projects. Development critics, environmentalists, ecofeminists, and indigenous people themselves have sought to present the "other side" to "development." They have stressed the ways in which development projects have often resulted in the destruction of forms of human living which maintained a healthy environment. In the language of ecological rationality, some cultures provide us with "examples of functioning ecological rationality" (Bartlett, 1986).

However, it is precisely because we do have some positive criteria by which to judge ecological rationality that we can argue for the preservation of such forms of living—as well as on the grounds of care, justice, and human rights. With respect to these cultures we might well apply a precautionary principle—but even then it would be different because we would be dealing with human beings who have a perspective which we would have to take into full account. To apply the PP in the same way to such cultures as we might apply it to an ecosystem would be to comply in the oppressive "naturalization" which has operated throughout colonial discourse. In fact political conservatism tends to be equally choosy about which forms of "catallaxy" should be preserved, traditionally holding that subsistence forms of life do not constitute anything worthwhile. An ecological rationality, of which I have argued the PP is a part, leads to a revaluation of such cultures, thus demonstrating the depth of the challenge to at least some traditions of valuation in Western society.

VII. CONCLUSION

The PP rests upon two ethical statements: firstly that we should "take care" of valued things, and secondly that natural living systems (including human bodies) are valuable. The PP interprets these ethical statements in the context of environmental science to deliver a form of procedural rationality—a rule which should help make decisions about our interventions in natural systems. This can also be interpreted as a form of "vir-

tue" or a pattern of caring behavior toward natural systems.

I have interpreted this broad environmental ethics of care as open to a variety of different approaches to environmental value, including, centrally, both biocentric and anthropocentric approaches. This is consistent with the wide approach of the PP which should be retained on pragmatic grounds. The PP is a procedural rule for decisions to do with natural, not social, systems, and hence the association of the PP with conservatism is fallacious. Environmental science has helped us to discover what "taking care" might mean in relation to natural systems and has also enriched our sense of the value of these systems through attention to their specific characteristics.

Also See the Following Articles

ANTHROPOCENTRISM • BIOCENTRISM • BIODIVERSITY • ECOLOGICAL BALANCE • ENVIRONMENTAL JUSTICE • SPECIESISM • VIRTUE ETHICS

Bibliography

Attfield, K. (1994). The precautionary principle and moral values. In T. O'Riordan and J. Cameron, Eds., *Interpreting the precautionary Principle.* London: Cameron May.

Light, A., & Katz, K. (1996). *Environmental pragmatism.* London: Routledge.

O'Riordan, T., & Jordan, A. (1995). The precautionary principle in contemporary environmental politics. *Environmental Values,* 4, 191–212.

Parker, J. (1995). Enabling morally reflective communities. In Y. Guerrier, N. Alexander, J. Chase, and M. O'Brien, Eds., *Values and the environment: A social science perspective.* New York: Wiley.

Warren, L. M. (1993). The precautionary principle: Use with caution! In K. Milton, Ed., *Environmentalism: The view from anthropology.* London: Routledge.

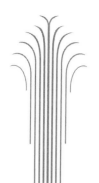

PREVENTIVE MEDICINE

Nina Nikku and Bengt Erik Eriksson
Linköping University

GLOSSARY

informed consent An ethical rule developed in the context of medicine and biomedical and behavioral research. It involves the physician's or researcher's obligation to give information and the recipient's understanding of and consenting to the treatment, or to participating in the research. The practice of informed consent has developed in order to protect the right of patients and research subjects to self-determination.

paternalism The notion that an authority acts toward adults like a father acts toward his children. The paradigm case is the good father's behavior toward his children when he is acting in their best interest but without their permission. It includes a beneficial intention but is at the same time an act without the recipient's informed consent.

privacy The condition of having a zone of private life. This includes one's body, its parts, and objects intimately associated with the person, but also his or her intimate relationships. To respect privacy is to respect the limits of the private zone in the way

that personal knowledge is not possessed by others, information is not spread, and others are not given access to the private sphere without the individual's permission.

screening A selection procedure applied to a population. The aim is to detect disease in presymptomatic individuals in order to provide more effective treatment in the early stages of disease, or to identify risk factors or carrier states.

social steering The forms and strategies to influence society at large and social groups within it from what is defined as not wanted, to wanted or favored conditions. Restrictions, regulations, laws, and information are examples of instruments for social steering.

stigmatizing The accusation of a person or group of deviant behavior or a deviant condition that is recognized as a threat against the social order. It stresses the negative characteristics and discrimination against the person or group as a consequence of the deviation.

CENTRAL TO PREVENTION is the notion of reducing the risk of the occurrence of a disease process, illness, injury, handicap, or other unwanted phenomenon. A classical way for distinguishing the preventive measures is the classification of prevention in primary, secondary, and tertiary prevention. The classification considers the natural progress of disease, that is, disease without ther-

TABLE I

Definition of Preventive Medicine

Primary Prevention	Secondary Prevention	Tertiary Prevention
Measures that promote health	Early diagnosis and treatment	Prevention of relapses and complications
—Health information	E.g., screening and health controls	Restriction of handicap
—Health legislation		Rehabilitation
—Health protection		
Prepathologic stage	Pathologic stage	

apeutic intervention. A preventive effort undertaken before the disease has developed is classified as primary prevention, early detection and measures directed toward a manifest disease is described as secondary prevention, while tertiary prevention consists of actions directed toward the disease after it has become chronic and has developed perhaps into a handicap. The latter includes, for instance, measures such as rehabilitation. This article focuses on primary prevention, which includes measures that enhance positive health, prevent risk of disease, and prevent the first onset of disease (see Table 1).

The notion of prevention in this article and in the classification presented above is aimed at a broad field of activities whose purpose is to prevent disease and to promote positive health. Others have chosen another vocabulary for distinctions between disease-preventive efforts and the enhancing of positive health. For instance, health promotion may be used as a generic term for a number of connected activities of which prevention is only one part and aims exclusively at disease-preventive measures.

I. THE FIELD OF PREVENTIVE MEDICINE

Preventive and health-promotive actions, such as hygienic and sanitary measures, improved nutrition, and better housing, have contributed to increased health among people in those places where such things have been accomplished. Some of the efforts have been directed toward the environment, but doctors and other health workers have also provided important advice on healthy behavior.

Although in the past epidemics of infectious diseases were the main cause of illness and early death, the disease panorama looks different today. Infant and child mortality rates have decreased, and today cancer, diabetes, accidents, and cardiovascular diseases are examples of the major health problems in a modern population.

As the health problems have changed, the targets and the means of the preventive measures have shifted from the environment toward the individual's life-style and behavior. During the twentieth century a new medical view has appeared that includes not only the sick person but also the potentially sick person. The preventive measures include changes in behavior where the interest may of the individual be subordinated to the interest of society.

Prevention is truly an international trend. Establishing the active participation of the population in health questions is a central issue in the strategy of agents such as the World Health Organization. Information measures and a focus on positive health are highlighted as the determining factors in the work toward such a development. In basic policy documents there is an emphasis on the necessity of influencing people's attitudes and behavior toward a healthy life-style and using preventive measures to minimize health risks.

In recent years preventive measures have begun to focus on the people's life-styles and their total way of living. Behind this strategy lies the understanding that a larger and larger portion of the panorama of disease in society has its origin in the way that individuals treat their own bodies and minds. Poor diet, lack of exercise, and alcohol and tobacco consumption are intimately woven together with an individual's total life-style, and the damages he inflicts upon himself are being identified as related to his way of living; these are conditions that can be helped only to a limited degree by traditional biomedical treatment. Thus, to reach political goals for health and social welfare, authorities and practitioners find themselves developing methods on different levels that should have the effect of leading the population to changes in life-style. At the same time, life-styles and healthy behavior are areas that are characterized by an individual's own notions and his or her willingness and desire to live in a certain way. The drive for autonomy and self-control in an individual's everyday life could thereby be threatened by preventive measures.

II. THE ETHICAL DIMENSIONS OF PREVENTIVE MEDICINE

The ethical dimension of preventive medicine concerns the problems of anticipated intervention and the paternal way in which authorities act toward the public. The beneficent value of preventing disease may come into conflict with other values, such as the recipient's self-determination and privacy. In spite of the fact that the intention is beneficent the measure may lead to negative consequences, or even to harm.

There are a number of circumstances that distinguish the preventive measures from treatment in curative health care, for example, and contribute to another kind of ethical question. In some cases preventive measures are directed toward healthy persons and toward individuals who have not demanded the intervention. Further, because many preventive efforts are directed toward a population whose recipients are unidentified or are unknown persons, sometimes not everyone who is affected by the action will derive benefit from it.

Because measures are directed toward healthy persons the reason for intervention may not be as obvious and clear as in the case of curative care, where there is a suffering patient in need of treatment. It is often thought to be better to prevent the occurrence of disease than to cure it afterwards, if that is at all possible. However, this may not be true in all cases. The cure may be quite simple compared to prevention. Consider, for instance, the case of directing a mass vaccination for influenza toward the entire population of a country. In addition to the financial costs the measure also would involve a lot of inconvenience, discomfort, and even harm among the recipients. This will not, so it seems, be motivated just to reduce the effects of an influenza epidemic on a national level. It may be better to focus on preventive measures toward high risk groups, such as the old and weak.

Directing preventive measures toward healthy persons involves the risk of negative consequences. In spite of good intentions to prevent disease, it may also be necessary to consider the risk of harm to the recipients. Screening for cancer in the prostate has been the subject for several recent studies. It was learned that tumors are found in quite a large number of men after a certain age. However, because the disease often progresses slowly it means that the majority of men who have prostate cancer never will exhibit any symptoms. They will most likely die for other reasons before the cancer develops. Screening and early detection means that they may be worried and treated unnecessarily. Informing these men that they have prostate cancer means that they will have to live with that knowledge and with the anxiety that this causes. The negative consequences of screening must, of course, be compared to the beneficent consequences of the early detection of the disease, because this eventually leads to a better prognosis.

Preventive measures work as a diagnostic tool. The patient in most situations has not demanded the preventive measure. Unlike curative care, where the patient generally actively demands the treatment, in preventive medicine it is health care personnel who approach the healthy person. It is the professional health worker who defines the good that will eventually come from the preventive measure, at least for some of the recipients. The recipient, who has not asked for the intervention, may be offered a preventive measure, or this could be directed toward him without his agreement. In certain cases the preventive measure is seen as a standard procedure, in others (as with small children) the informed consent is given by others than the recipient. In all such situations ethical questions come to the fore.

Consider, for instance, screening to prevent diabetes in children. The screening procedure involves a large number of children who will never get diabetes and many others who will test positive but will never develop diabetes. On the other hand, the act of screening, which involves blood sampling, could violate the child's privacy, it could be painful, and it could cause anxiety in both child and parent without producing any beneficial effect. Furthermore, the economic cost in relation to medical value might be doubtful, which is in itself an ethical question in terms of priority. Considering the ethical objections to such a general screening perhaps we can choose an alternative action. It may be a reasonable option to screen a clearly definable risk group. An analysis of the consequences may show the procedure to be an ethically defensible alternative.

The recent trend that focuses the preventive measures on the individual's life-style, targeting changes in everyday behavior, highlights the relationship between prevention and autonomy. Here, health promotion and information are given a key role in bringing about the changes that for one reason or another are seen to be desirable. According to the ideal that dominates the area, the preventive measure shall be given in such a form that the individual feels that his eventual change in behavior is the result of a voluntary choice. Nevertheless, the changes in life-style must be the "right" ones, in line with the preventive goals defined by the health workers. This brings about a kind of paradox, where the individual's self-determination is regarded as positive only if he determines his change of life-style is in line with the goals of the preventive measure.

On a macrolevel it has been noticed that preventive medicine in many instances has the tendency to increase the disparity in health between social groups. The better-off groups have benefited the most from preventive measures. There are two reasons for this. Because those who formulate the messages in health information are members of the same social groups, these groups find it easier to understand the messages contained in health information. At the same time these groups have greater abilities to change their way of life than do others. The ethical question in preventive medicine is thereby also often a political question.

If this is true on a national level, it would be even clearer as an international or global trend. Inequalities in health care between the so-called first and third worlds is also inequality when it comes to applying preventive strategies and achieving preventive goals. Furthermore, partly because of funding, preventive measures in several developing countries have a tendency to reproduce and favor Western values and ideals on healthy or good behavior. Some practices of preventive medicine, for instance certain campaigns favoring specific reproductive techniques for producing the ideal (or good) family, are not free from ethnocentricity. This could be analyzed in ethical terms.

Nor is preventive medicine free from valuations of the sexes, so that sometimes men and women explicitly or implicitly are given different levels of attention or different roles in preventive measures. Often, this disparity is not based on the facts and the consequences are not analyzed. Until now, gender issues in preventive medicine have not been given much attention. Here, ethical analysis can also make a contribution.

III. SOCIAL STEERING AND PREVENTIVE MEDICINE

The measures used by the authorities for directing the health behavior of the population can be presented as three classes of instruments for influencing people's lives: administration, economy, and information. The administrative measures consist of laws and regulations, for instance, about the use of safety belts or the prohibition of drugs. Price policy and taxes are examples of economic influence, which can be used for regulating such things as the consumption of alcohol and tobacco. Information provided through education and advisories issued through the mess media are instruments used in efforts to focus attention and to provide knowledge, or to change the attitudes and behavior of the population.

The authorities often act paternalistically toward citizens. This is similar to the way that good fathers behave toward their children, and it includes both the father's beneficent intention as well as his acting without the children's consent. To act toward someone without his

or her informed consent is an infringement of the right to self-determination. Further, it may lead to such consequences as the recipients' negative feelings for being treated like children. Through instruments of social steering the authorities hope to benefit their citizens, but this behavior is directed more or less without their permission.

On the other hand, if the authorities do not intervene in the case of harmful food additives, for example, this could lead to negative consequences. Accordingly, there are situations where almost everyone would agree to the morally right for the authorities to intervene on behalf of their citizens, and in many cases, citizens will demand this sort of paternalism. However, a disagreement exists concerning the limit between the morally right and the morally wrong intervention.

IV. TARGET GROUPS OF PREVENTIVE MEDICINE

Preventive medicine is aimed at undifferentiated populations, identified risk groups, or focused individuals. The ethical questions are influenced by which target group the preventive measure addresses.

Many preventive measures are directed toward an entire population. In the case of a curative treatment the action is directed toward an identified individual who will have personal contact with the promoter; however, here the opposite holds true. Consider the example of fluoridating the water. The purpose of adding fluoride to drinking water is to strengthen the teeth of the citizens, improving their dental health. This measure is applied in several countries. When fluoride is added to the water system the entire population is reached by the measure, so avoiding fluoride may be impossible or very difficult. The intentions of the authorities are beneficent, with the improved dental health of the population in mind. However, the authorities must pay attention to the fact that the population is a heterogeneous group of people. This means that some will benefit from the measure and have an improved dental health, some will not be affected, and a few may be harmed by allergic reactions, for example.

The preventive measure may also be directed toward a certain group of persons. The fact that they are approached and are made the target of this effort means that attention will be focused on a particular behavior or condition. This is because the behavior or the condition are identified as having the potential for an increased risk of disease. However, giving attention to this behavior or condition may involve stigmatizing these groups. Consider preventive information about HIV. In some countries authorities have chosen an information strategy that describes HIV as a potential threat to the whole population, thus trying not to stigmatize certain high-risk groups. This has been criticized as creating anxiety within groups that have an extremely low risk of getting HIV. In other countries the information strategy has been directed primarily toward identified groups, such as homosexuals and drug addicts. This strategy represents a realist perspective, focusing on certain groups. At the same time these groups can be stigmatized, harming them in everyday life.

Still other preventive actions may be individually directed, focusing on certain individuals. An individually directed measure, such as giving face-to-face information, is often considered to be ethically unproblematic, and in many cases it does not present any moral problem. However, a few examples will show that in certain cases individual health information may not be that ethically unproblematic. Information about health risks may create anxiety. As a consequence, individuals may feel that they are at risk, and this can influence their everyday life. The information may be frightening or it may be incomplete or formulated in a confusing way. The individual's right to self-determination is not as recognized as it is in ordinary health care. Moreover, informed consent, which is a fundamental principle in ordinary health care, may be difficult to maintain in individual health information.

Consider the case of genetic information or counseling. Progress in genetics increases the possibility of identifying those who are at risk for inherited disease. It may happen that the genetic counselor becomes aware of the occurrence of a hereditary disposition for disease in a family whose members may be unaware of the risk. The ethical problem concerns whether to inform these persons.

There are special circumstances in this topical problem. First, the health care organization searches actively for those at risk. The act of contacting people and offering them a test is an indication that they have a genetic disposition for disease. Second, the health care system identifies these people only because they run the risk of having inherited a genetic disposition. This puts health care professionals in a difficult situation. They are forced to be paternalistic if the decision is to inform those having an increased risk of developing a disease. In this case, it is not possible to obtain an informed consent from the individuals because providing the information itself is the action to be consented to.

V. PREVENTION AND EDUTAINMENT

A fairly new trend in international preventive work that has interest for ethical analysis is "edutainment." The main thought here is to combine health information with entertainment. Thus, a strategy for altering behavior through hidden or nearly hidden messages in pure entertainment settings such as television, radio, published material, and popular music is used to transfer health information that is integrated into an entertainment context. It is common to exploit so-called soap operas on television for this purpose. In several countries soap operas have been constructed so that they contain hidden health messages that concern sexual behavior, for example. The villain, who is a permanent ingredient in these series, is the one who follows everything that is unhealthy in life. Several of these series have become great public successes. In the same way, pop music has been used successfully, primarily for reaching young people. Putting health information to music, engaging popular artists, and allowing radio stations to play the melodies without any fee has created quite a few number one songs. In the evaluations that have been made of such efforts, the results in general seem to be very good from the viewpoint of spread. Only when the informational and preventive side has been overly obvious have they not been successful. In these cases they have elicited negative public reactions or the reaction has been one of total disinterest. Effective edutainment is built upon the invisibility of the preventive measure within the shell of entertainment. The ethical analysis must compare the goals of such measures with the way those goals are reached.

VI. THE APPLIED ETHICS OF PREVENTIVE MEDICINE

Without doubt, everyone would agree with the beneficent intention of preventing disease and promoting positive health. Furthermore, there is a positive evaluation, in general terms, of the World Health Organization's goal of not only increasing life expectancy but also increasing the level of good health. Still, as we have shown, promotive measures raise some fundamental ethical issues and could be grounds for social, cultural, and political conflicts. This will be controversial when it is the case that the preventive action is directed not toward a certain disease but toward preventing an identified or supposed risk factor. The preventive measure may involve an uncertain health gain for the recipient in exchange for a change in his former life-style and behavior and as a consequence, it may restrict his freedom.

The fact that preventive measures often are not directed toward identified persons in a population is not an argument against the need for ethical analysis. Instead, it involves the need to take into consideration the ethical balance where the benefit to both the individual and to society receives attention. This means that the individual's rights and values as well as the consequences in form of the utility for society must be respected.

Also See the Following Articles

AUTONOMY • GENETIC COUNSELING • INFORMED CONSENT • PATERNALISM • PATIENTS' RIGHTS • SAFETY LAWS

Bibliography

Doxiadis, S. (Ed.). (1990). *Ethics in health education.* Chichester: John Wiley & Sons.

Downie, R. S., Fyfe, C., & Tannahill, A. (1996). *Health promotion. Models and values* (2nd ed.). Oxford: Oxford University Press.

Eriksson, B. E. (1993). Social steering of lifestyles. In Boje, T. E., & Olsson Hort, S. E. (Eds.). *Scandinavia in a New Europe.* Oslo: Scandinavian University Press.

Liss, P-E., & Nikku, N. (Eds.). (1994). *Health promotion and prevention. Theoretical and ethical aspects.* Stockholm: Department of Health and Society, Swedish Council for Planning and Coordination of Research.

Nikku, N. (1997). *Informative paternalism. Studies in the ethics of promoting and predicting health.* Linköping: Linköping Studies in Arts and Science.

Tones, K., & Tilford, S. (1994). *Health education: Effectiveness, efficiency and equity* (2nd ed.). London: Chapman & Hall.

Townsend, P., Davidson, N., & Whitehead, M. (1988). *The health divide.* London: Pelican Books.

PRIVACY

Edmund F. Byrne
Indiana University

GLOSSARY

consequentialism An approach to ethical assessment that prioritizes the consequences of an act or course of action.

deontology An approach to ethical assessment that prioritizes the inviolability of principles from which conduct may not deviate.

encryption The process of rendering a communication unintelligible to outsiders, by means of either hardware or software.

harm principle No action is morally justifiable if it causes more harm than good (a consequentialist version) or if it causes any avoidable harm whatsoever (a deontological version).

insiders/outsiders Persons who are, respectively, included in or excluded from some undertaking on the basis of a requirement for access.

name-linked (data) A characteristic of data that explicitly identifies the person or persons to whom the data refers, as opposed to anonymous collective or summary data.

private sphere The set of all institutions and activities whose principal if not only purpose is maintenance and enhancement of one or more individual's well-being.

public sphere The set of all institutions and activities in and through which the affairs of the people as a whole are dealt with (a subset of which is the political public sphere, or government).

right to privacy Negatively, a right to be left alone; positively, a right to others' respect for one's intimacy and autonomy.

secrecy The practice, often mandated and sanctioned for insiders, of excluding information and conduct from outsiders.

PRIVACY denotes a zone of inaccessibility. Ordinarily attributed to an individual, it encompasses others whom an individual invites into this zone. Thus it may also be attributed to a group as a whole, and the group may be of any size, including even corporations. This zone of inaccessibility is a social construct, however, and as such varies in scope inversely to that of the public (especially political) sphere. Given this public–private dynamism, privacy is commonly defended as a prima facie but seldom as an inviolable right.

I. PRIVACY IN SOCIAL DISCOURSE

The meaning of privacy in a social context depends on determinations as to what is public. This may mean governmental, but it ordinarily refers more generically to whatever is beyond the private, however conceived, for example, all that is beyond the home. Other correlative usages include an institution's place in the "public sector" or "private sector" or an individual's acts "in public" or "in private." Either alternative may be perceived as being independent of the other, as is true of "the public" or, simply, "privacy." Sometimes one alternative is viewed as being in competition with the other, as in controversies over surveillance versus privacy. Similar controversies arise with regard to secrecy.

Privacy and secrecy are complementary in some contexts, but they cover different ground. Each characterizes certain information as the property of designated insiders from which outsiders are excluded. But respect for privacy is meant to obligate outsiders, whereas it is insiders who are called upon to respect secrecy. Normative claims regarding insiders' and outsiders' options are often stated as though factually given. The facts, though, include different levels of power and of compliance.

Similarly, one who uses the public–private distinction may believe it to be factually based; but it is ultimately normative, as when used to limit women's life experiences and opportunities. In this respect, it is comparable to, and at times overlaps, the secret–public partition: each imposes constraints on access to or dissemination of information. What is at stake, though, is not simply information about, but interference with activities of insiders.

Acts one performs "in public" are observable by others whom one ordinarily has not preselected but still might not wish them to report. Whether they may be reported or not depends on accepted rules, the severity of which varies with time and circumstances. Acts performed "in private" are supposedly observable only by others who respect one's interests.

A. Privacy as a Zone of Inaccessibility

In effect, privacy talk announces a zone of inaccessibility, the parameters of which are determined collectively. Rules establishing this zone of inaccessibility may, however, be acceptable to insiders but not to an outsider. A private party may be "crashed." A private organization is one whose membership list need not be "made public." A "private club," intended for a select clientele, is closed to the "general public." Balancing concerns about discrimination against the also valued right to assemble freely, some jurisdictions in the United States establish an arbitrary number of members (variously set at 400–600) beyond which a club cannot claim to be private.

A claim to a zone of inaccessibility imposes no limit on dissemination of information, but secrecy requirements do. Concealment of information by insiders is a necessary condition of secrecy. This concealment may be contested, however, in which case privacy would be at issue. The resulting challenge to cognitive disequilibrium may affect different levels of social organization—according to Stanton Tefft, the intimate (privacy), private life, and public life—and secret-searching is operative on each of these levels.

Public affairs are accessible by definition because they are matters of broad concern about which people should learn and communicate as much as possible. Uninvited access to information about private affairs is, by contrast, considered inappropriate except in unusual circumstances and in accordance with reasonable procedures, such as obtaining a warrant to search a house in which someone is believed to be committing a crime.

Constraints on intrusion into an individual's zone of inaccessibility are commonly associated with a "right to privacy." Various exclusionary claims are asserted under this rubric, sometimes with the support of law or popular opinion, but not always. Claims made about personal materials illustrate particularly well how contested an exclusionary claim can be. "Private papers" are written materials whose possessor has no obligation to make them available to others—unless they are legally adjudicated not to be private (see *U.S. v. Nixon* further on). Institutionally controlled materials are commonly made available on a "need-to-know" basis. To this end, U.S. government documents may be classified (i.e., restricted as to use) in one of three ways: confidential, secret, or top secret (Federal Register 37, 98 and 5209 [1072]).

B. The Public Domain

The availability of information, then, falls along a continuum. At one end of this continuum is secrecy, and at the other, full accessibility. Materials "in the public domain" are deemed available to anyone, not being subject to any proprietary restriction based on state or trade secrets, national security, or religious or political censorship. But reality is often less accommodating. Totalitarian authorities in particular find reason to impose constraints on human discovery and creativity. The old Soviet Union's ban on Mendelian genetics, the writings of dissidents, and bourgeois attitudes in general is paradigmatic in this respect. But censorship is not unknown in democracies.

In the United States, if government tries to keep expressions of opinion out of the public domain without showing that imminent harm would result from publication, courts usually rule this to be unconstitutional infringement of freedom of speech ("prior restraint"). An exception is now made, however, for activities and practices of the intelligence services: an author who does not obtain a CIA imprimatur may have all royalties confiscated (*Snepp v. U.S.* [1980]). The British government blocked domestic publication of a similar book about its MI5 that was available in the United States, contending that a book is in the public domain only if it is public property (R. Wacks, 1989. *Personal Information: Privacy and the Law,* p. 55. Clarendon Press, Oxford).

Comparable secrecy behavior is now a common feature of legal processes, much of which is treated as inaccessible to the public. Caucusing or going into "executive session" are practices widely used by public bodies that no "sunshine law" has eradicated. Similarly, litigants take their cases before private judges, public courts agree to sequester discovered documents introduced into evidence, and settlements are entered into that make plaintiff's silence a condition for being awarded damages. Some states now back the public's right to know, at least in cases that have health and safety implications, but some defendants insist that these disputes are essentially private.

Confidentiality is similarly recognized as an appropriate prerogative of professional–client relationships. Law and medicine offer much discussed examples in this regard, but similar exclusivity obtains in other professions, notably in the business world. Regulatory efforts to prevent selective leakage of price-sensitive "insider" information prior to its public announcement are usually serious but much is left to ethical codes.

Interpretations of libel law establish an area of respect for personal privacy while making exceptions for "public persons" such as politicians. But the rules of media distancing are arrived at somewhat less formally, for political as well as commercial reasons. Journalists used to accept the liberal insistence that one's private life has no bearing on the quality of one's public performance. Today, however, politicians face not reportorial alternatives but a continuum. And at least in electoral democracies the career of an elected or appointed official may be ended by revelations about his or her private life that may show unfitness for the office held. Nominees to high political office, especially women, have been discredited by even the most inconsequential evidence of their being scofflaws. The effectiveness of public service is too easily undermined, however, if political ruin can be brought about just by publicizing an allegation about a politician's private life.

In short, the scope of a zone of inaccessibility is ever challenged by claims as to what is in the public domain. That such a zone exists at all is commonly tied to a right to privacy. In an advanced democracy, this right is likely to be codified in law, but its basis is in morality.

II. PRIVACY IN LAW AND MORALITY

Many questions arise in connection with a legalized concept of privacy. For example, does the law *establish* a right to privacy or merely confirm its existence? If the latter, is this right derived from rights defined in property law and tort law or from extralegal considerations? In either case, what is the public counterpart to this privacy? Such questions, according to libertarians, are answered by defining one's "negative liberty," that is, the extent to which one has a right to be left alone. This cannot be done, however, without somehow deciding which moral values, if any, law should enforce. For this reason, the Hart–Devlin debate a generation ago is a microcosm of the perennial issues involved.

The British Parliament was considering decriminalization of prostitution and homosexuality, as recommended in the Wolfenden Report, which relied heavily on a distinction between public and private acts. Patrick Devlin, a judge, retorted that if public policy adhered to this distinction society would be unduly at risk. H. L. A. Hart, a philosopher, acknowledged the need to limit risk, but, echoing John Stuart Mill's advice a century earlier, he urged a much sterner test to justify intervention. First he distinguished between a social group's actually accepted and shared morality ("positive morality") and general moral principles ("critical morality") used to criticize actual social institutions including positive morality. Then he warned that blanket enforcement of positive morality without regard to the distinction between acts performed privately and those done in public exposes all popularly disapproved conduct to punishment. Like the Wolfenden Report, then, his "critical morality" approach recognizes a private sphere. This private sphere is not impregnable, but merely acknowledging its existence is a first step towards clarifying its scope.

A. Legalization of Privacy

Standards of privacy are elaborated in a social context, and law codifies these standards. This it may do by means of constitutional analysis, statutes, or common law. In France the components of one's private life have been specified in statutes, and the French constitution has been interpreted as recognizing the right to respect for one's private life as a public liberty. In Great Britain, interests elsewhere protected in the name of privacy are dealt with especially under the legal tort of breach of confidence, which covers not only personal but also artistic and literary confidences, government information, and trade secrets. In the United States, a right to privacy has emerged in both constitutional analysis and statutory law, primarily to protect information, but a constitutional variant also protects procreation-related decisions.

The U.S. Supreme Court asserted a constitutional right to informational privacy as early as 1886 (*Boyd v. U.S.*), and defense of this right is commonly traced to an article by Samuel Warren and Louis Brandeis that defended private life against publicity (1890). Later, as a Supreme Court justice, Brandeis defined the right to privacy in a pivotal dissent as "the right to be left alone—the most comprehensive of rights and the right most valued by civilized men" (*Olmstead v. U.S.* [1928] at 478).

Before the 1960s, American judicial rulings did not recognize decisional privacy in words, although several cases were consistent with the assertion of such a right. Then the U.S. Supreme Court began appealing explicitly to a constitutional right to privacy not only, for example, to exclude illicitly obtained evidence from court but to invalidate prosecutions for the use of contraceptives. Reflecting on this evolution of the right to privacy into a constitutional doctrine, Justice Abe Fortas repeated Brandeis's definition but made it subject to "the clear needs of community living under a government of law" (*Time, Inc. v. Hill* [1967]).

The right to privacy thus understood attributes to a person a zone of inaccessibility from which uninvited others are excluded. This zone, however, is anything but secure, especially as to decisional privacy, so its defenders are wary but pragmatic. Anita Allen, for example, prefers a restricted-access definition of privacy. But, she notes, controversies about the best definition of privacy concern "not so much what is at stake, but how what is at stake is to be labeled" (1988. *Uneasy Access: Privacy for Women in a Free Society*, pp. 32–34, 97–101, 190 no. 4. Rowman & Littlefield, Totowa, NJ).

Also for pragmatic reasons, many scholars warn against letting a right to privacy become an inviolate protector of harmful behavior. Both feminists and critical legal theorists, with varying emphases, argue that, as often interpreted, this right unduly protects coercive contracts and sexual harassment in the workplace and "domestic" violence in the home. Conservative scholars, analogously, dislike legal determinations that hinder law enforcement by precluding government intrusion into social and personal matters or that limit freedom of the press by protecting informational privacy. Robert Bork, a strict constructionist constitutional law scholar, once called decisional privacy a "loose canon [*sic*] in the law." And U.S. Chief Justice Rehnquist thinks personal decisions are constitutionally entitled only to the procedural protection of liberty guaranteed by the Fourteenth Amendment.

B. Privacy in Legal Theory

Noting this revisionist trend, some advocates of personal choice seek alternative justifications that are not tied to the concept of privacy. Others consider a right to privacy an indispensable part of the individual's legal defense against oppression, because a system of law that lacked a right to privacy would be less equipped to maintain socially important values. This disagreement is embodied in an ongoing debate among legal scholars over proposals to supplement tort and criminal law with separate privacy rights.

So-called reductionists insist that a remedy for every harm identified as a violation of privacy is already provided by more traditional components of criminal law and the law of torts. The paradigmatic view in this respect is that of tort law expert William Prosser, who identified four types of privacy cases, each of which, in his judgment, is appropriately disposed of under existing tort law. Privacy cases, according to Prosser, involve any of four distinct torts: (1) intrusion; (2) public disclosure of private facts; (3) presenting someone in a false light in the public eye; or (4) misappropriating (and exploiting) a person's name, likeness, or identity. According to him, a plaintiff can, without invoking any right to privacy, be compensated under the law for any privacy-invading harm that would be so considered by "a reasonable man of ordinary sensibilities" (F. Schoeman, Ed., 1984. *Philosophical Dimensions of Privacy*, pp. 104–115. Cambridge Univ. Press, New York). This position was subsequently endorsed by the American Law Institute as a model for tort law and has been adopted, sometimes in modified form, in a number of states.

Reductionists not only would reduce privacy to a short list of torts, as does Prosser, but also favor reducing Prosser's list. Several writers favor just three categories; others endorse two, namely, intrusion and disclosure of the private. Some devoted defenders of freedom of the press want only one, covering only the most intimate details about a person, disclosure of which would be tortious only if it caused an average person distress, or humiliation, or deep embarrassment.

Opponents of this reductionism insist that a distinct concept of privacy clarifies what the U.S. Supreme Court defends when it appeals to a right to privacy. The Court often considers the degree of liberty to be assigned to activities entitled to privacy; but nonreductionists seek a more basic value from which to derive such liberty. Alan Westin once identified four "states" of privacy, but a univalent privacy is most often defended. This has been described, for example, as an "aspect of dignity" (Edward Bloustein), or "an autonomy or control over the intimacies of personal identity" (Tom Gerety), or a group-binding intimacy that combines privacy and some type of "close and familiar personal relationship that is in some significant way comparable to a marriage or family relationship" (Kenneth Karst). All these nonreductionists defend an extralegal concept that provides "protection of one coherent value—privacy—in all branches of the law." In so doing, they develop three different arguments, each of which accentuates some function of privacy. One ties it to a need for freedom from physical access; another, to limiting censure and ridicule; and a third finds privacy necessary for the maintenance of personhood. All, says Ruth Gavison, are instrumental, in that they relate privacy to some other goal. And so is her own two-step argument that democracy requires autonomy, and privacy is important for autonomy (Schoeman, 1984, 361–81).

Jurists' talk about liberty, personhood, and autonomy may be, as Gavison says, extralegal. But so are unstated preferences with regard to human relationships that find their way into constitutional interpretation. This is illustrated by responses to the U.S. Supreme Court's decision in *Bowers v. Hardwick* (1986). In that case the court upheld a statute criminalizing sodomy because it found no strong protection of the practice in the state's legal history. This decision, according to one critic, amounts to an "evisceration of privacy's principle" in that the majority abandoned value-neutrality to impose moral limits on personal identity. Another took the ruling to mean that at the heart of the right to privacy "there has always been a conceptual vacuum" (Jed Rubenfeld).

C. Privacy and Intimacy

No friends of conceptual vacuums, philosophers have been attentive to the right to privacy, especially as it relates to personhood. This person-oriented right to privacy is explained by reference to the behavior, communications, relationships, and even property that contribute to one's self-fulfillment, but all this may be subsumed for purposes of discussion under the concept of intimacy.

Proprivacy jurists counted on autonomy, intimacy, and personhood to justify a privacy right—at least until *Bowers v. Hardwick*. Philosophers, similarly, have defended a right to privacy along the lines of Gavison's instrumental trio: physical access limitation, embarrassment avoidance, and personhood maintenance. In 1975 Judith Jarvis Thomson defended a minimalist claim that access constraints on information can be based solely on nonprivacy rights, especially those tied to ownership, and two respondents traced a separate right to privacy to, respectively, a person's special interests or special relationships (Schoeman, 1984). In time, privacy came to be defended as the guardian of intimacy.

Intimacy is certainly important for personal growth and fulfillment. But a claim to privacy based on intimacy is voidable by a counterclaim that respecting that intimacy may cause greater harm. In its generic usage, the term "intimate" qualifies a relationship as one that involves close association, contact, or familiarity. But these may be attained without the relationship being warm or friendly or reciprocal. In fact, a right to privacy might well be claimed by two individuals who live thousands of miles apart, have never met, but send messages to one another electronically. And so might it be if they merely belong to the same organization, or subscribe to the same journal.

Inversely, it is not obvious that a couple having sexual relations should be protected by a right to privacy. According to one philosopher, they should because while so doing they are vulnerable (Richard Wasserstrom). But so is anyone who is preoccupied with any endeavor and has not taken adequate precautions against possible intruders. In any event, sexual intercourse does not in and of itself justify a privacy claim. One partner may be brutalizing, even raping, the other. Even if they have been having consensual sex together over an extended period of time, one may be stealing from, or slowly poisoning, or transmitting an incurable disease to, the other.

These objections might be neutralized by requiring that the privacy-protected relationship be not just physically intimate but emotionally caring as well. Thus, in an effort to identify what kind of intimacy merits decisional privacy, Julie Inness requires relationships to be motivated by love, care, or liking. Taking these three qualities as reducible, for purposes of discussion, to caring, one is left with a normative criterion for limiting the intrusions upon intimate relationships.

This criterion clearly rules out at least the harm-indifferent exclusivity that an unqualified intimacy test would allow, for it would shield only those intimate relationships imbued with caring, preferably reciprocal. But intimacy as such, with or without caring, is neither a necessary nor a sufficient condition for immunity from intrusion. For it must ultimately yield to responsibility expectations.

D. Privacy and Responsibility

Privacy is quite rightly understood as a protector of intimacy and caring, and yet this very understanding implies responsibility as a limiting condition. This limiting condition invites intrusion, but in what circumstances?

First, one *individual's* appeal to caring as a defense against intrusion may be both self-serving and harmful to another, for example, if in fact he or she is engaging in spouse abuse. To say that only "real" caring makes a relationship deservedly private is an improvement in theory, but this still leaves unresolved such operational problems as assessing that reality and assigning the burden of proof.

Second, even if those in an intimate relationship are mutually caring, the relationship still might not be entitled to privacy. For, they may be harming a third party, perhaps their own child or any number of outsiders. Thus has the problem of child abuse led to the establishment of child protection mechanisms which make a couple's familial autonomy conditional at best. Similarly, a couple's capacity to harm outsiders diminishes their claim to inviolability. Concern about a capacity to harm has long been a factor in public responses to contagious disease and is becoming no less so with regard to genetic defects. In response to the AIDS epidemic, recognition of the harm principle as a limit on privacy is sweeping away all objections save that intrusion take the form of the least restrictive alternative. Attempts to analogize voluntary transmission of AIDS to freedom of religion have floundered, as have attempts to treat as private rather than public commercial enterprises such as bath houses where homosexual encounters are accommodated or blood banks where HIV-positive blood might be donated. But AIDS-inspired inroads into privacy claims encounter greater resistance when professional prerogatives are at stake.

Emphasis is usually put on the benefits of confidentiality to clients, but even if professional career salvaging is the focus, the social desirability of professional autonomy is the basic issue. Other things being equal, the interest of outsiders in knowing what goes on in a socially beneficial professional service relationship may be disregarded. But the claims of professionalism do not invalidate the harm principle with regard to either parties in the relationship or to outsiders.

Professional relationships may be regulated in various ways, either by a profession-enforced code of ethics or by externally imposed legal standards. Medical practice, for example, is subject to the "standard of care" test and to informed consent requirements. The latter have been legalized in various countries, however, less to protect a woman who wants an abortion than to put obstacles in the way of her having one. Most such obstacles have been ruled unconstitutional in the United States, but in any event the cases themselves show that a professional relationship is not immune from public scrutiny.

A professional relationship may also be subject to intrusions if the interests of a third party are at stake. Opposition to such intrusions is usually based on an appeal to confidentiality. But confidentiality may be overridden by invoking a duty to warn. This issue surfaced in *Tarasoff* v. *Regents of the University of California* (1976), a case involving a murder that might have been prevented if a counseling clinic staff had warned the victim of a client's hostile intentions.

This notion of a duty to warn points to another limitation on the intimacy thesis, namely, that one intimate relationship, however caring, may overlap another, and the interests of each relationship may be incompatible. The *Tarasoff* case in particular involved not just a counseling relationship but a parent–child relationship as well: the victim's parents contended that if warned they could have gotten word to their daughter, who was abroad at the time, that she would be in grave danger upon her return. A comparable point is made with regard to the question of whether a physician–patient relationship involving a minor child is subject to oversight by the child's parents, for example, in cases involving birth prevention advice and treatment.

A personal relationship is even more likely to be invaded if one or both parties in the relationship is employed, since the employer may be motivated by concerns about profit and loss, productivity, favorable public image, or tort liability. Indeed, these commercial concerns are responsible for many recent developments in privacy-related law in the United States. In its role as employer the government may invade its employees' privacy in ways it cannot with regard to citizens who are not in government employment, but its employees can draw upon the full range of constitutional constraints on government intrusiveness. Employees of a private employer lack such constitutional protections. Both public sector and private sector employees may, however, challenge their employers' intrusions on the basis of common law torts and various statutes. In general, though, courts are more sympathetic to an employee's privacy violation claim if the employer's intrusion has occurred outside the workplace, or if the complainant is a member of a union. Details aside, these policies point to an emerging doctrine that a nonintimate relationship, such as that of employer and employee, is subject to restraints on the basis of privacy.

While acknowledging a public employer's right to invade its employees' privacy if doing so is "reasonable," the U.S. Supreme Court also endorsed employees' rights to sue the employer to prove the employer's policies led them to expect that their privacy would be respected. A private employer, by contrast, may need only show that it has violated no protectable privacy interest. Such an interest may arise out of statutory protections against sexual harassment, disparate impact discrimination, including discrimination on the basis of marital status, or wrongful discharge. The burden of proving that an employer's invasion of privacy was not justified is usually on the employee. Employees have nonetheless prevailed in a number of cases.

E. Privacy and Politics

The counterclaims others can reasonably make against one's claim to privacy obviously limit its effectiveness as a bulwark against unwanted intrusions. From this perspective, the privacy–intimacy linkage is circular, and hence unavailing in a social context that is deficient in respect for human dignity. In such a context, however, those who control social arrangements may appeal to privacy, or the private sphere, as a justification for denying women any opportunity to exercise public responsibility. Such privacy-based infantilization of females has been practiced in Poland and Palestine, for example, but has been overcome in Norway and, for a time, in Nicaragua (J. M. Bystydzienski, Ed., 1992. *Women Transforming Politics.* Indiana Univ. Press, Bloomington and Indianapolis.). Thus an appeal to privacy may be a tool of political oppression. Yet privacy as analyzed above is a legitimate and deservedly defended cultural value. How vigorously it should be defended is, accordingly, debatable. So even in a liberal democracy it is a political matter. Indeed, some who subscribe to democratic principles seem to think of it as being almost entirely political.

Charles Fried agrees with the intimacy defense of privacy. But he weakens that defense by creating a procedural concept of privacy out of John Rawls' theory of justice as fairness. In a work entitled *Right and Wrong* (1978), Fried said law should protect privacy because privacy is a prerequisite to the components of intimacy ("love, friendship, and trust"), and these are impossible in modern society if one lacks privacy. But he qualified this right to privacy as being limited by the rights of others. Limits, in turn, require standards, which are to be set by "a political and legal process," the results of which will be just if (1) the process itself is just and (2) the outcome of the process protects basic dignity and "at least some information about oneself."

This proceduralization of privacy reduces intimacy to government's transitory acceptance of limitations on its hegemony. Indeed, Fried demonstrated how weakly fair procedures might protect intimacy in the *Webster v. Reproductive Health Services* case, in which he argued that abortion decisions should not be protected under the right to privacy, even though birth control should. This position having been advocated by his executive branch employer, he was merely doing his job. But he admits that people in positions of power strive to move courts to rulings they deem politically preferable. Such activist intervention, he says, is based not on value-neutral criteria but on "organized society's value judgments" as articulated by "knowledgeable people [who] can tell good from bad law" (1991. *Order and Law;* pp. 17–20, 237 no. 43, and *passim* Simon & Schuster, New York.). This deontological approach to public policy may not meet with universal approval, as witness responses to any culture-determining decision of a high court.

Neither the intimacy nor the caring approach, then, provides a sufficient condition for defending privacy because each presupposes a level of personal autonomy that is acontextual and potentially dangerous. Each also assumes that privacy can be contained within the discourse regarding the private sphere. But the right to privacy is defined in a public context. By acknowledging this public side of privacy, one admittedly accepts the risk that its scope may be narrowed or enlarged more than one considers appropriate. But privacy cannot be immunized against this dialectic by ignoring the public alternative while arguing for the private (Inness, 1992, 86–90). Decision-making privacy must be defended on the grounds that it is advantageous to society as a whole and not just to an individual or group deserving respect. This defense cannot be effected merely by combining allegedly fair procedures with an a priori sense of moral propriety. It must also include a truly participatory process of deliberation that is comprehensive in its consideration of relevant standpoints and Hartian in its consequentialist application of the harm principle.

Of no less importance, neither intimacy nor caring is a *necessary* condition for privacy. For example, a right to privacy may be claimed to prevent harm to activities that are not in any ordinary sense in the personal sphere and may involve only the most superficial and transitory relationships. An electronic communication between distant strangers, as already noted, is also entitled to privacy—but on what basis? Certainly not by virtue of any intimacy, at least not in any accepted sense of the word. Similarly, a company whose profitability depends on certain trade secrets is entitled to exclude industrial spies from its facilities even if neither intimacy nor caring is characteristic of its workforce relationships. Such a claim is sometimes indefensible, though, not because it is based on nonintimate or even noncaring relationships, but because honoring the claim would on balance cause more harm than good. Arriving at such an assessment is not just a matter for experts, however, but should come out of a democratic process sensitive to the necessary and sufficient conditions for society's fundamental well-being. What this might involve is clearly illustrated by attempts to assess the impact of technology on privacy.

III. PRIVACY AND TECHNOLOGY

Modern technologies, for all their advantages, threaten privacy in many ways. Information and communications technologies in particular require major adjustments in our expectations as to what can be kept private. Institutions and individuals alike are affected, but individuals have fewer defenses.

The record of concern about technological intrusions began when public figures—rulers and celebrities—asked courts to endorse their right to privacy; now even noncelebrities may win legal protection of their privacy if commercial gain is involved. Early cases involved etchings and tintypes, and then photographs and recordings. In time just about every new device used to collect or disseminate information has been brought before the bars of justice as a violator of someone's privacy. Taken in its totality, this ongoing confrontation has helped keep in focus the problem of balancing privacy against the public's right to know (q.v.). This problem, however, has been raised to a higher order of magnitude by the emergence of information and communications systems that are in common use but are controlled primarily by dominant institutions.

A. Privacy and the Media

In the United States, First Amendment protection of speech and press has been applied for the most part only to print media, which were in place when the U.S. Constitution was adopted. Newer communications technologies were regarded as scarce resources that require government regulation in the public interest. In the 19th century telephone and telegraph were kept under separate ownership, and under the 1934 Federal Communications Act, local ownership of disparate media (press and radio, plus, in time, television and cable) was kept divided by a formula that remained intact until passage of the Telecommunications Reform Act of 1996. This legislation finally recognized that various new communications technologies are rendering the old assumption of media scarcity technically untenable.

Congress and the Federal Communications Commission (FCC) were slow to relinquish the FCC's role as overseer and even censor of the media. And the courts carefully avoided saying that electronic media are as deserving of constitutional protection as is print. To justify this seeming inconsistency, they built a circular agreement on, for example, Alexander Meicklejohn's dubious distinction between public (protected) and private (unprotected) speech, which was meant to show that the government protects a family's right to privacy by censoring television. This "game of mirrors," warned Ithiel de Sola Pool in 1983, would generate a constitutional crisis, because electronic technologies were blurring all the old distinctions between print, wire, and wireless means of transmitting information. The issue facing the Court, however, was not constitutional niceties but market stability, and now that the interests of newly dominant major players have been sorted out, their commercial freedom has been greatly enhanced. But the emergence of still newer technologies such as the Internet and its refinements and revolutionary improvements in television leave us no reason to assume that the list of technological challenges to privacy rights is now complete.

A key reason for this projection in the United States is the juridical determination that the communications industry has First Amendment rights. Already in 1886 the Supreme Court had found that corporations are persons under the Fourteenth Amendment. When reminded of this early ruling, already prominent in other business-favoring decisions, it moved quickly in the late 1970s to liberate "listeners' rights" from the shackles that had limited the number and variety of messages marketers could beam in their direction. First came decisions that linked the First Amendment and personhood to protect information dispersed by some public interest organizations. Then came probusiness decisions that effectively surrendered the media to the major corporations. Business now not only advertises but engages in "advocacy advertising" and even provides the media with prepackaged and nonattributed "news" items. This "free flow of commercial information" leaves the audience "encapsulated in a corporate-message cocoon" (H. I. Schiller, 1989. *Culture, Inc.* ch. 3, pp. 164, 168. Oxford Univ. Press, New York).

B. Privacy and Surveillance

Commercial control of large-audience telecommunications is not duplicated in the area of focused information/communications technologies, especially because law enforcement agencies want access to these for surveillance purposes. Private individuals as well as businesses use various monitoring devices to inform themselves about and/or record unwanted activities of insiders and outsiders alike. Similarly, public concern about collective dangers and threats has led to selective acceptance of government surveillance. So long as credible enemy or criminal activities are being targeted, such surveillance, e.g., via satellites in orbit or metal detectors at airports, is accepted as a socially necessary inconvenience. Not all government surveillance, however, is narrowly targeted, and some may even jeopardize important business interests. Regarding these, government has had to exercise more restraint. This can be illustrated by comparing earlier struggles in the United States over government surveillance with the recent Clipper chip controversy.

The telephone and its progeny have transformed the way we communicate, but they have also stimulated the invention of devices to intercept communications. The success of such devices has led to efforts to limit their effects, and out of these efforts came the introduction of a concept of privacy into U.S. constitutional law. It was, however, a long slow process. The first step was Justice Louis Brandeis's insistence in dissent that wiretapping, though not a trespass of tangible property, does violate Fourth Amendment rights (*Olmstead v. U.S.* [1928]). In 1967 the Supreme Court abandoned its trespass test for electronic surveillance and held, as Brandeis had argued, that the practice requires a warrant because "the Fourth Amendment protects people not places" (*Katz v. U.S.* [1967]). Congress legalized wiretapping in 1968, but information thus obtained continued to be excluded as evidence, and in 1972 the Court ruled unanimously that evidence obtained by warrantless wiretapping is inadmissible in a federal court. But it also ruled two years later that not even the President may withhold specific taped conversations subpoenaed as part of a criminal investigation (*U.S. v. Nixon* [1974]). At the same time Congress adopted standards for disseminating government-held data.

The U.S. Privacy Act of 1974 endorsed openness (of federal agency records), individual access, and participation, but it imposed limits on collection, use, and disclosure. It applies only to the federal government, exempts most intelligence gathering agencies, and leaves the gathering of information unregulated. Minimal redress was authorized under both civil and criminal law, but no compliance monitoring mechanism was provided. The definition of personal information in this law is fairly broad, but it is constructed by enumeration, so can be expanded only by questionable analogies or by amendment. It also conflicts with the Freedom of Information Act (1966, as amended), which while exempting nine categories of information from disclosure, leaves implementation to agency discretion. Other countries, notably Germany and Canada, have since enacted much stronger laws. Bills introduced into Congress to bring U.S. privacy protection up to their standards (especially by adding a compliance monitoring body) have not moved past the hearing stage, except for an enhancement in 1996 of civil and criminal penalties for unlawful disclosure of wiretapped information. Short of a police state, however, no system of enforcement can ever guarantee the privacy rights of electronic data subjects: once data are collected, their use is limited for the most part only by technology and ingenuity (D. H. Flaherty, 1989. *Protecting Privacy in Surveillance Societies.* Univ. of North Carolina Press, Chapel Hill).

Legal reform, then, is meant to minimize the socially disruptive potential of communications technologies, but law is generally unable to keep up with technology. Regulating telephone use, for example, does little to limit surveillance made possible by the cooperation of one participant without the knowledge of the other. Nor does it prevent agents of one country from tapping communications originating in another country, or prevent a private individual from using relatively inexpensive eavesdropping devices that work remotely or by being planted on or near the person under surveillance. Such devices are, however, far less challenging than are those that permit essentially undetectable intrusions. But even these may be blocked by sophisticated cryptographic technologies, which are at issue in the Clipper chip controversy.

The U.S. National Security Agency (NSA) wants to have access to any communication whatever. But competing private sector providers of cryptographic devices have emerged in recent years, and the forces of commerce are gaining ground over those of sovereignty. The NSA worries that commercial computer security systems could prevent it and other intelligence agencies from intercepting messages, so it wants to have a Clipper chip installed in every instrument of electronic communication to provide a "back door" for warrant-authorized surveillance. This technological back door would work in combination with an NSA-developed algorithm to create a third-party decipherable message encoding system. Transmission of an encrypted message is done by means of an electronic public key, which a sender and a receiver access by means of their respective private keys. Clipper-facilitated access requires yet another key, which would be divided into two parts, each to be stored by a different government agency. In 1994 presidential support for this plan met with objections so intense and widespread that this support was amended to embrace only surveillance of telephones—a position itself now complicated by a comparable dispute over mobile (cellular) phones.

The Clipper chip proposal is opposed for many different reasons, including questions of feasibility, efficiency, and cost. But beyond these are basic questions about privacy rights and government responsibility in a nonbelligerent democracy. For one thing, the technology of Clipper is neither exclusive nor even competitive without government backing because of both software and hardware alternatives available in the private sector. Even a limited Clipper system would be more expensive than its commercial competitors, because the Clipper system utilizes technologies on which crucial patents are held by private entities.

C. Privacy and Data Banks

Actually, the U.S. government's case for Clipper is undermined by the existence of important alternatives, including the virtual equivalent of a national database that is rapidly emerging under the aegis of the U.S. Department of the Treasury. Tended by the Financial Crimes Enforcement Center, this database already consolidates some 35 databases including reports of all currency transactions over $10,000, suspected drug traffickers' profiles, money laundering investigations and trends, and bank reports of possible criminal activity, and it will soon add another hundred databases, one of which would provide access to every bank account in the country. It will also be linked to an artificial intelligence system which has already been used to uncover irregular banking habits of a mole in the CIA and bombers of the World Trade Center.

Governments do need information, of course. But unconstrained record-keeping is not in the public interest. In particular, a computerized national database would not be an unmixed blessing, even if useful for some legitimate purposes. In France, for example, the equivalent of a national database has existed since a 1951 decree called for "the collection and centralization of political, social, and economic data about which government needs to be informed." This originally paper-stored database now consists of files on over a million persons, half computerized and half on hard copy. Such name-linked files may be maintained, under a 1978 law, for purposes of national defense and public security, if authorized in accordance with certain administrative reviews. Appealing to this law, the Mitterand government announced in 1990 that law enforcement and the RG would be adding name-linked "sensitive data" about individuals' racial origin, political, philosophical, or religious opinions, and union affiliations. Public and political response was almost uniformly negative, so the government canceled the RG's mandate. But for all practical purposes it has existed since 1988 in the form of identity cards tied to a National Identity Register (Flaherty, 1989, 226–229).

As the French experience illustrates, public opposition to government-controlled data banks is severely compromised by government's legitimate need for information for both administrative and law enforcement purposes. Similarly, Americans' organized opposition to the Clipper chip has been effective at least in the short run. This opposition included groups all across the political spectrum, but the most effective of these were business interests. Many of the latter, of course, also maintain massive data banks that generate complex privacy-related problems, notably in the health insurance and credit rating industries. These too require effective monitoring. Some legal constraints have been enacted, but justifications based on business necessity tend to be even more insurmountable than those based on government responsibilities.

IV. CONCLUSIONS

Concern about personal privacy no doubt increases in direct proportion to the extent of its vulnerability. Even dominant institutions and those who run them are likely to claim a right to privacy if by so doing they can exclude outsiders more effectively. They tend to have little respect for personal privacy, though, if this is taken to imply any restriction on their access to information of value to them. Such unbridled curiosity, once associated primarily with journalism, is increasingly a by-product of technical, especially computer, capacity for collecting and cross-referencing large amounts of information. Precedent offers little survival training for this emerging world. But it does motivate individuals to collaborate in defense of personal privacy—preferably in such a way as not to unduly restrict anyone's access to the public sphere.

Also See the Following Articles

CENSORSHIP • COMPUTER AND INFORMATION ETHICS • CONFIDENTIALITY, GENERAL ISSUES OF • CONFIDENTIALITY OF SOURCES • INFORMATION MANAGEMENT • PRIVACY VERSUS PUBLIC RIGHT TO KNOW

Bibliography

Branscomb, A. W. (1994). "Who Owns Information? From Privacy to Public Access. Basic Books, New York.

Byrne, E. F. (1995). The two-tiered ethics of EDP. *Journal of Business Ethics,* **14,** 53–61.

Inness, J. (1992). "Privacy, Intimacy, and Isolation." Oxford Univ. Press, New York.

Schoeman, F. (1992). "Privacy and Social Freedom." Cambridge Univ. Press, Cambridge, UK.

Wacks, R. (Ed.) (1993). "Privacy." New York Univ. Press, New York.

Weintraub, J., and Kumar, K. (Eds.) (1997). "Public and Private in Thought and Practice." Univ. of Chicago Press, Chicago.

PRIVACY VERSUS PUBLIC RIGHT TO KNOW

Darren Shickle
University of Sheffield

GLOSSARY

physical privacy Freedom from search and seizure, for example, as protected under the Fourth Amendment of the U.S. Constitution.
decisional privacy Freedom to make choices without interference by third parties.
informational privacy Freedom to limit access to personal information through confidentiality and record secrecy.
confidentiality This relates to information that has been confided and duties that affect disclosure to a third party.

PRIVACY may have a narrow or a wide definition. In its narrow formulation it relates exclusively to personal information about an individual and the degree to which third parties have access to this information. In an even more restricted definition there is a requirement that this information should be "undocumented." Thus, if all information about an individual were published in the public domain, it would be impossible to infringe privacy, although there would be no privacy to invade because there would be nothing that was kept secret. In its widest sense privacy extends beyond control over information (informational privacy) to include decisional privacy and physical privacy. Many of the most controversial legal cases that have led to significant changes in social policy in the United States have been based on privacy claims, usually involving decisional privacy (e.g., over the right to make private decisions about abortion, free from societal interference). However, the more usual context of rights to privacy (especially outside the U.S.), is confidentiality (i.e., informational privacy). It should be noted, however, that privacy, even if restricted to its informational context, is a broader concept than confidentiality. In addition to restricting access to information to third parties, the right of privacy may also be used to defend the person against the intrusion of unwelcome information.

I. PROFESSIONAL CODES OF ETHICS AND THE DUTY OF CONFIDENTIALITY

A. Medical Profession

Within medical practice there is an expectation that confidentiality will be maintained. For example, the Hippocratic Oath contains the phrase:

Whatever, in connection with my professional practice, or not in connection with it, I see or hear, in the life of men, which ought not to be spoken of abroad, I will not divulge, as reckoning that all such should be kept secret.

Principle IV of the American Medical Association's Principles of Medical Ethics states that:

A physician shall respect the rights of patients, of colleagues, and of other health professionals, and shall safeguard patient confidences with the constraint of the law.

The American Medical Association (AMA) has further stated that the information disclosed by a patient to a physician

... is confidential to the greatest possible degree. The patient should feel free to make a full disclosure of information to the physician in order that the physician may most effectively provide needed services. The patient should be able to make this disclosure with the knowledge that the physician will respect the confidential nature of the communication. The physician should not reveal confidential communications or information without the express consent of the patient, unless required to do so by law.

In the United Kingdom, the General Medical Council (GMC) has also stipulated that:

Patients have a right to expect that you [the doctor] will not disclose any personal information which you learn during the course of your professional duties, unless they give you permission. Without assurances about confidentiality patients may be reluctant to give doctors the information they need in order to provide good care.

Both the AMA and GMC codes of conduct provide exemptions to the strict observance of confidentiality. For example, in addition to any requirements stipulated in law the AMA permits the following exceptions:

Where a patient threatens to inflict serious bodily harm to another person or to himself or herself and there is a reasonable probability that the patient may carry out the threat, the physician should take reasonable precautions for the protection of the intended victim, including notification of law enforcement authorities. Also, communicable diseases, gunshot wounds, and knife wounds should be reported as required by applicable statutes or ordinances.

The GMC guidelines state that:

Disclosures may be necessary in the public interest where a failure to disclose information may expose the patient, or others, to risk of death or serious harm. In such circumstances you should disclose information promptly to an appropriate person or authority.

The British Medical Association have also laid out the exceptions to the standard of care on confidentiality. Thus, disclosure by a doctor would be permissible if:

- the patient consents;
- it is in the patient's interest to disclose information, but it is either impossible or medically undesirable to seek the patient's consent;
- it were required by law such as the statutory requirement to notify certain communicable diseases;
- the doctor has an overriding duty to society to disclose information, e.g., following a serious crime;
- it were necessary to safeguard national security;
- it were necessary to prevent a serious risk to public health, for example, if a patient is suffering from a serious infectious disease and refuses to take precautions;
- it were for medical research approved by a local research ethics committee.

However, terms such as "reasonable probability," "reasonable precautions," "serious harm," and "appropriate person" are subjective, and a doctor may be unclear as to whether the specifics of the case that he or she is dealing with would meet these exemption criteria. The GMC have given examples of circumstances where disclosure would be acceptable.

For example, where:

- A patient continues to drive, against medical advice, when unfit to do so. In such circumstances you should disclose relevant information to the medical adviser of the Driver and Vehicle Licensing Agency without delay...;
- A colleague, who is also a patient, is placing patients at risk as a result of illness or another medical condition...;

• Disclosure is necessary for the prevention or detection of a serious crime.

B. Legal Profession

Similar approaches to confidentiality are taken by other professions, that is, an "absolute" duty to maintain confidentiality except in specified circumstances. For example, rule 1.6 of the American Bar Association states that:

(a) A lawyer shall not reveal information relating to representation of a client unless the client consents after consultation, except for disclosures that are impliedly authorized in order to carry out the representation, and except as stated in paragraph (b).

(b) A lawyer may reveal such information to the extent the lawyer reasonably believes necessary:

(1) to prevent the client from committing a criminal act that the lawyer believes is likely to result in imminent death or substantial bodily harm; or

(2) to establish a claim or defense on behalf of the lawyer in a controversy between the lawyer and the client, to establish a defense to a criminal charge or civil claim against the lawyer based upon conduct in which the client was involved, or to respond to allegations in any proceeding concerning the lawyer's representation of the client.

As in the medical professional codes, the legal profession recognizes that:

the observance of the ethical obligation of a lawyer to hold inviolate confidential information of the client not only facilitates the full development of facts essential to proper representation of the client but also encourages people to seek early legal assistance ... The client is thereby encouraged to communicate fully and frankly with the lawyer even to embarrassing or legally damaging subject matter.

II. PUBLIC INTEREST EXEMPTIONS AND THE COURTS

In most societies the boundaries of acceptable medical practice will be established by the courts (not by eth-

icists) although the judgments will be heavily influenced by codes of conduct devised by the profession itself, and by evidence of expert witnesses as to customary behavior.

In *R v. Crozier* (1990), a psychiatrist called by the defendant handed his report to the counsel for the Crown because he was concerned that his opinion would not be presented to the court. His client appealed against his conviction on the grounds that the breach of confidentiality between doctor and patient had denied him the opportunity of deciding whether or not the evidence should be submitted. The Court of Appeal considered that there was a stronger public interest in the disclosure of the psychiatrist's views than in the duty of confidence owed to the appellant; the psychiatrist was found to have acted responsibly and reasonably in a very difficult situation.

The "public interest exception" was also considered by the British courts *in W v. Egdell* (1990). A patient (W) convicted of manslaughter and detained in a special hospital applied to a mental health tribunal for his discharge. He engaged an independent consultant psychiatrist (Dr. Egdell) to report on his mental state. The application was withdrawn when the psychiatrist's report did not support discharge. The doctor felt that if the patient were released there would be a substantial risk to the public. Dr. Egdell notified the hospital and the Home Office of his findings despite the patient's solicitors refusal to grant permission. The patient's application to prevent release of the report was refused. W brought a case against Egdell alleging breach of a duty of confidence. However, as the trial judge pointed out: "The question in the present case is not whether Dr. Egdell was under a duty of confidence; he plainly was. The question is as to the breadth of that duty."

The judge concluded that a doctor has a duty not only to the patient but also to the public and that the latter would require him to disclose his concerns to the proper authorities if, in his opinion, the public interest so required.

A. Appropriate Disclosure

1. In the United Kingdom

The Court of Appeal in *W v. Egdell* provided guidance on the circumstances when disclosure of confidential information is permissible. Firstly, disclosure should only be made to those whom it is necessary to tell so as to protect the public interest. Secondly, the risk must be "real" rather than hypothetical. Thirdly, the risk should be of "physical" danger to the public.

It has been suggested that if a doctor who knew that one of his or her patients was an unsafe driver, failed to report the danger to the driver licensing authorities, then the doctor may be sued for negligence if the patient was responsible for a subsequent road accident. In the United Kingdom, a doctor is required to notify the Driver Vehicle Licensing Agency of any patient who experiences an epileptic fit. The patient's driving license is only returned after a fit-free period has elapsed.

2. In New Zealand

A doctor in New Zealand acted in what he believed was in the public interest when he had concerns about the ability of one of his patients to drive safely (*Duncan v. Medical Practitioners Disciplinary Committee* (1986)). The patient, who worked as a bus driver, had undergone a triple coronary bypass operation but had been subsequently certified as fit to drive by his surgeon. His general practitioner (Dr. Duncan), however, asked that his driving license be withdrawn and furthermore, warned the bus driver's passengers of their supposed danger. Dr. Duncan was reported to the Medical Practitioners' Disciplinary Committee and was found guilty of professional misconduct in that he breached professional confidence in informing lay people of his patient's personal medical history. Following the verdict Dr. Duncan compounded the breech by seeking publicity in the national news media. Dr. Duncan sought judicial review of this decision. The High Court accepted the principle of breaching medical confidentiality in cases of clear public interest but refused the application because Dr. Duncan had not ensured that the recipient of the information was a responsible authority.

3. In the United States

The most well-known American case analogous to *W v. Egdell* and *R v. Crozier* is *Tarasoff v. Regents of University of California* (1976). The Student Medical Center at the University of California was sued for failing to warn a young woman of the risk posed to her by one of their patients. The woman's former boyfriend had sought psychiatric help at the Center. During the consultation he revealed his violent intentions toward the woman and that he had a gun. The staff at the Center notified the police of their concerns (who decided to take no action). The woman, however, was not informed. She was murdered by the patient shortly afterwards. The dead woman's family sued the University for negligence. The U.K. and New Zealand cases may suggest that by informing the police, the Medical Center had fulfilled any duty of appropriate disclosure. However, the University was found liable for failing to breach

their patient's confidence and warn the woman of the threat to her life.

The Tarasoff judgment seems to impose duties to disclosure in order to protect third parties that would not apply within the United Kingdom. The judgment suggested that this duty may apply only when there is an identifiable third party who is in imminent danger. However, subsequent cases within the United States have extended the principle so as to impose liability on psychiatrists who fail to detect and warn of more general danger. For example in *Perreira v. State of Colorado* (1989), the spouse of a police officer killed by a released psychiatric patient successfully sued the state mental hospital and psychiatrist for negligence. The court held that the psychiatrist had not adequately assessed whether the patient had a propensity for violence and posed a risk of serious harm to others, even though he had made frequent threats against the police and would have access to a gun after release.

III. PUBLIC INTEREST IN MAINTAINING CONFIDENTIALITY

A. Privacy and Confession

The Court of Appeal in *W v. Egdell* unanimously confirmed the trial judge's decision to dismiss the action but did so with rather more reservation. The concept of a private interest competing with a public interest was rejected in favor of there being a public interest in maintaining professional duties of confidence. The Court noted that Section 76 of the Mental Health Act 1983 showed a clear parliamentary intention that a restricted patient should be free to seek advice in confidence: "Preservation of confidence would be conductive to the public safety; patients would be candid, so that problems such as those highlighted by Dr. Egdell would become known."

In the case of *X v. Y* (1988), it was also recognized that there were circumstances in which the public interest would be served from protecting privacy. The HIV status of a doctor had been disclosed to the press. However, the judge found that "the very important public interest in the freedom of the press" and an informed public debate was outweighed by the public interest in ensuring that people with AIDS should be able to come forward for treatment without fear of their identity being revealed.

As Lord Wilberforce has pointed out, "there is a wide difference between what is interesting to the public and what is in the public interest" (*British Steel Corporation v. Granada Television* (1981)).

The benefits to the public from being seem to maintain confidentiality was also recognized with the American Bar Association guidelines:

> However, to the extent a lawyer is required or permitted to disclose a client's purpose, the client will be inhibited from revealing facts which would enable the lawyer to counsel against a wrongful course of action. The public is better protected if full and open communication by the client is encouraged than if it is inhibited.

B. Disclosure: Potential Benefits and Certain Harm

One argument for breaching confidentiality is that the harm recognized by the confidant is significant (at least of a magnitude greater than the value of losing trust) and possibly can be averted by disclosure. However, according to Kottow, "breaching will relentlessly harm the confider, subjecting him or her to precautionary investigations and constraints of some sort, perhaps even with unavoidable defamatory consequences. The harm purportedly averted is merely potential.... Furthermore, the practice of confidentiality is in itself damaged by breaching because its trust-worthiness is disqualified."

According to Kottow even gravest dangers did not justify breach because "the more exorbitant and preposterous the threatener's claims are, the less likely they are to occur," and Kottow's argument depends on balancing the possible against the certain.

> Ultimately, degrees and probability of harm are so difficult to assess, that they will hardly deliver an intersubjectively acceptable argument for or against confidentiality, except one: breaching confidentiality can not be a significant and enduring contribution against harmful actions, for these are no more than potential, whereas the damages caused to the confidant, to the practice of confidentiality, and to the honesty of clinical relationships are unavoidable.

Kottow's arguments are reminiscent of those of Kant in an essay "On an Supposed Right to Lie from Benevolent Motives." Kant asserted that it was wrong to lie to a potential murderer who came to your home asking about the whereabouts of your friend who had taken refuge in your house. Although Kant conceded that telling a lie to the potential murderer in order to protect your friend may not be a legal crime, he saw it as a crime to humanity, because the trust on which society depends will be damaged: This is a theme that appears throughout Kant's works. For example, in a lecture on ethical duties toward others he wrote: "Although I do man no injustice by lying to him when he has lied to me, yet I act against the right of mankind, since I set myself in opposition to the condition and means through which any human society is possible."

It is possible to paraphrase Kant as arguing for a duty to tell, while Kottow is arguing for a duty not to tell, yet there is a consistency in their stances. Both argue that the greatest harm from lies/disclosure is to society rather than to the individual who is deceived or whose secret is not kept. Kant, just like Kottow, argues that this harm is certain while any benefit from lying/disclosing is not.

Kant wrote his essay in response to criticism by Constant. While Constant accepted that there may be a duty to tell the truth, he went on to explain that:

> The notion of duty is inseparable from the notion of right. The duty is what in one being corresponds to the right of another. Where there are no rights there are no duties. To tell the truth then is a duty, but only towards him who has a right to the truth. But no man has a right to a truth that injures others.

Similarly, if the secret relates to some harm that the confider wishes to inflict on a third party, then any absolute right to confidentiality is lost. Kottow seems to concede this when he says "excessively vicious menaces may well be uttered by psychotics who are rationally incompetent and therefore not protected by a pledge to confidentiality they can neither honor nor demand."

C. Privacy and "Little White Lies"

The public interest may be served by allowing individuals to maintain privacy. For example, there is a reduced incentive for an inventor to work on his or her ideas if the competition is shown the plans before a patent can be put in place to protect any financial rewards. If the idea is commercially viable, the public will benefit by having access to the new idea. It would be an inefficient use of resources if individuals had to take excessive measures to protect themselves from surveillance.

Similarly, there may be public interests in allowing conversations to be kept private, even if these conversations are between public officials. When devising public policy, many options may be considered. If all these discussions were in public, then these debates may be constrained by political correctness, and the discussants may be less likely to suggest novel ideas.

Even communications between private individuals would be inhibited without privacy. A referee asked by an employer to provide a reference for an applicant for a job, may feel obligated to provide a complimentary report if the applicant is to see what is written. The reference becomes of limited use, because the employer will assume that any negative aspects have been withheld. This is not in the interests of suitable applicants who would otherwise benefit from a positive reference, and it is not in the interests of society because jobs may not be filled by the most appropriate people.

Everyday conversations would also be very different if all were reported publicly, with the use of more formal language. People would be less likely to say what they think. Thus, when Posner wrote about an economic theory of privacy he observed that:

> The principal effect of publicity will be to make conversations more formal and communication less effective rather than to increase the knowledge of interested third parties. Stated differently, the costs of defamatory utterances and hence the cost-justified level of expenditures on avoiding defamation are greater the more publicity given the utterance. If every conversation were public, the time and other resources devoted to ensuring that one's speech were free from false or unintended slanders would rise. The additional costs are avoided by the simply and inexpensive expedient of permitting conversations to be private.

It would be nice if people could be more honest with each other, but there are undoubtedly benefits to society from "little white lies."

IV. THE POTENTIAL ABUSE OF A RIGHT TO PRIVACY

Posner believed that "few people want to be left alone. They want to manipulate the world around them by selective disclosure of facts about themselves." As Posner has pointed out:

> The other side of the coin is that social dealings, like business dealings, present opportunities

for exploitation through misrepresentation … The strongest defenders of privacy usually define the individual's right to privacy as the right to control the flow of information about him. A seldom-remarked corollary to a right to misrepresent one's character is that others have a legitimate interest in unmasking the misrepresentation.

An individual intent on antisocial behavior is endangering his or her right to the benefits of community membership. In such circumstances, different rights to confidentiality may apply, because duties to other members of society may not have been fulfilled. The degree to which an individual jeopardizes his or her right to privacy will depend on the form of the misrepresentation and underlying motives. For example, even the most ardent libertarian would concede that criminal activity should be detected and if possible prevented. However, a reformed criminal who, following punishment, now wishes to become an upstanding member of the community, should be allowed to keep his or her past private if it is no longer of consequence. Privacy in such circumstances is in the public interest, otherwise there would be less incentive for a criminal to reform.

A hypocrite's private moral conduct may be at variance with a moral standard that they profess in public. Privacy may conceal this deception, although the circumstances of the case may affect whether he or she should alter the private conduct in line with public pronouncements, or vice versa. Alternatively, it may be that the difference in public and private stances is a consequence of a narrow-minded and intolerant society, and thus the deception is necessary to avoid persecution.

"White lies" are not in themselves intrinsically bad, but Bok, as indeed had Kant before her, condemned such deception for altruistic motives because they represented the slippery slope to maleficent lies.

V. THE RELATIONSHIP BETWEEN THE INDIVIDUAL AND SOCIETY

A. Balancing Rights and Duties

The balancing of rights and duties has been enshrined in a number of statutes on human rights. For example, the United Nations Universal Declaration of Human Rights (article 29) indicates that the exercise of a person's rights and freedoms my be restricted for the purpose of meeting the "just requirements of morality, public order and general welfare in a democratic society." Similarly, the European Convention on Human Rights states that:

there shall be no interference by a public authority with the exercise of this right [to respect for private and family life, home and correspondence] except such as is in accordance with the law and is necessary in a democratic society in the interests of national security, public safety or the economic well-being of the country, for the prevention of disorder or crime, for the protection of health and morals, or for the protection of the rights and freedoms of others (article 8).

Thus, social control over an individual's reproductive autonomy may be legitimate if it is necessary to prevent harm to other individuals. As John Stuart Mill argued in his essay "On Liberty," freedom means "doing as we like, subject to such consequences as may follow: without impediment from our fellow creatures, so long as what we do does not harm them" nor "attempt to deprive others of theirs, or impede their efforts to obtain it."

Beauchamp and Childress recognized that as with all moral principles, the principle of autonomy "has only prima facie standing." They go on to say that:

it is always an open question which restrictions may rightfully be placed on choices by . . . subjects when these conflict with other values. If choices endanger the public health, . . . it may be justifiable to restrict exercises of autonomy severely. The justification . . . being some competing moral principle such as beneficence or justice.

B. A Society of Individuals or the Individual as a Part of the Whole

As Bentham pointed out in his *Introduction to the Principles of Morals and Legislation,* "the community is a fictitious body, composed of the individuals who are considered as constituting as it were its members. The interest of the community then is, what?—the sum of the interests of the several members who compose it."

The connection between the individual personality and social solidarity was of interest to Durkheim. In his study of *The Division of Labour in Society* he explored "how does it come about that the individual, whilst becoming more autonomous, depends ever more closely upon society":

We believe this is sufficient to answer to those who think that they can prove that in social life everything is individual, because society is made up only of individuals. Undoubtedly no other substratum exists. But because individuals form a society, new phenomena occur whose cause is association, and which, reacting upon the consciousness of individuals, for the most part shapes them. This is why, although society is nothing without individuals, each one of them is more a product of society than he is the author.

Communitarians recognize the importance of individuals including a consideration of public interest when making moral decisions. For example, Sandel believed that it is necessary to regard the common good rather than deontological principles of right. In order to be sustainable, moral principles should be congruous with the values and practices of the society in which they are to be applied. Thus when an individual attempts to define their personal moral code they ask "who am I," "how am I situated," and "what is to my benefit" as well as establishing "what is good for the community," because, as Sandel pointed out, we are "partly defined by the communities we inhabit" and are therefore "implicated in the purposes and ends characteristic of those communities." Liberal theories give priority to the rights of the individual above those of society. They attempt to define an individual out of the social context even though it is the community that nurtures and sustains the individual's capacity for autonomous choices.

Privacy is culturally defined. In the most restricted definition of privacy outlined at the start of this essay, it was suggested that "if all information about an individual were published in the public domain, it would be impossible to infringe privacy, although there would be no privacy to invade because there would be nothing that was kept secret." However, another apparent contradiction exists for a hermit or someone stranded on a desert island. If there is no one to keep a secret from, then there is no privacy. As Benn pointed out, the concept of "private" is both norm-dependent and norm-invoking, and hence the boundaries of privacy will vary from one culture to another.

One can imagine cultures, for instance, . . . where to say that someone had done something in private would be to accuse him of acting inappropriately—perhaps cutting himself off from a collective experience and cheating others of their right to share in it. Or again, "privacy" might apply mandatorily; that is, anything private *ought* to be kept from the knowledge of others.

Thus, in most Western countries it is expected that defecation, genitalia, sexual intercourse, and so on should be kept within the private sphere. However, these "rules" will differ between cultures but also with context. For example, wearing clothes would not be the norm in a nudist colony. Topless bathing may be acceptable on some beaches, but not on others, but even on these latter beaches it would be acceptable for a young child to play without clothes.

VI. A NEED FOR A POSITIVE CONCEPTION OF PRIVACY

A. Privacy and Human Dignity

In George Bernard Shaw's *Pygmalion*, Eliza Doolittle complains when she notices that Professor Higgins is recording her speech in Covent Garden. Her resentment, and that of the people around her is based in part from the invasion of informational privacy, but also because of a lack of respect for her dignity: "See here: what call have you to know about what never offered to meddle with you? ... You take us for dirt under your feet, don't you?" Higgins is treating people as objects or specimens, means to further his studies rather than as ends, people with feelings and dignity.

According to Bloustein intrusions on privacy threatens the liberty of the individual to "do as we will, just as an assault, a battery or imprisonment." He believed that because these latter torts are an offense to the reasonable sense of personal dignity, so too should privacy be regarded as a dignity tort. Defenses of the importance of privacy based on a regard for human dignity are appealing to such conditions as moral integrity, individuality, or consciousness of oneself as a moral being.

In a report to the Norwegian Parliament, rather than autonomy, respect for human dignity and human rights and the principle of solidarity were stressed. The Norwegians recognized that it is "necessary to find a balance between protection of integrity of the individual and freedom of choice, and the limit society sets for this choice on the basis of fundamental and overriding values" (Ministry of Health and Social Affairs, Norway. (1993). Biotechnology Related to Human Beings Report No.25 (1992–1993) to the Storting. Oslo: Ministry of Health and Social Affairs, 8.)

B. Love, Respect, and Privacy

Others have argued that privacy is integral to our understanding of ourselves as social beings within varying kinds of relationships. Having a private life is central to the development of a personal identity.

Rachels observed that we may adopt apparently different identities in different circumstances. For example, a man may be affectionate at home, while businesslike at work. Rachels rejected criticisms of such different behaviors as being hypocritical. He believed that privacy is crucial to the individual's ability to maintain various kinds of relationships. For example, a married couple may be intimidated from being intimate if observed by a third party. Such a concept of privacy is wider than relating purely to information. As Reiman has pointed out:

> Intimacy is not merely the sharing of otherwise withheld information, but the context of caring which makes the sharing of personal information significant. One ordinarily reveals information to one's psychoanalyst that one might hesitate to reveal to a friend or lover. That hardly means one has an intimate relationship with the analyst.

According to Fried privacy is

> necessarily related to ends and relations of the most fundamental sort: respect, love, friendship and trust. Privacy is not merely a good technique for furthering these fundamental relations; rather without privacy they are simply inconceivable.

However, Fried recognized that one:

> element in love is a spontaneous relinquishment of certain entitlements of one's own to the beloved, a free and generous relinquishment inspired by a regard which goes beyond impartial respect ... Persons love, hoping to be loved in return, and thus the fulfilled form of the relationship is one of mutual relinquishment ... The fulfilled form is the mutual relinquishment of rights in favor of new, shared interests which the lovers create and value as the expression of their relationship.

Fried believed that friendship differed from love only in the "degree of absorption in the relationship and of significance which the relationship has in the total economy of a person's life and interests."

C. A Positive Conception of Privacy

Privacy should not be a negative concept whereby the individual is left alone and becomes isolated. If privacy is to be worthwhile it should enable the individual to be an active member of society with a range of social relationships. To this extent, despite arguments that privacy is a fundamental human right, privacy should be a means rather than an end. It is for this reason that an account of privacy incorporating love and respect is attractive: if we love, hoping to be loved in return, perhaps we should consider the common good in order to have our own interests recognized. There are analogies here with Kant's Categorical Imperative:

> Act as if the maxim of your action were to become through your will a universal law of nature.... Act in such a way that you always treat humanity, whether in your own person or in the person of any other, never simply as a means, but always at the same time as an end... So act that your will can regard itself at the same time as making universal law through its maxim.

As Beauchamp and Childress have pointed out, "when a person voluntarily grants others access, this act is an *exercise* of the right to privacy, not a *waiver* of the right. For example, a patient's decision to grant a physician access for diagnostic, prognostic, and therapeutic procedures is an exercise of a right to control access that includes the right to grant access as well as to exclude access.... We exercise our right to privacy by reducing privacy in order to gain other goals."

"Man is by nature a social animal." Prehistoric humans came together to form communities for mutual protection and hunting, but also companionship and love. In exchange for these community benefits, the individual exchanges some of his or her privacy. It is for this reason that the individual should retain some measure of privacy. Indeed it is also right that the individual should place great importance upon the privacy that they do have, because what value is a gift that is given without any cost to the giver?

There will however, still be those who are understandably concerned about the "tyranny of the majority." As a last resort, the individual should have the right to negative privacy, by opting out of a community to join a new society, as did the founders of the United States, or an even more extreme choice of the isolated existence of a hermit.

In his essay "On Liberty" John Stuart Mill argued that "there is no one so fit to conduct business, or to determine how or by whom it shall be conducted, as those who are personally interested in it." The best way of maximizing the utility (happiness) of a community is therefore to maximize the utility of its constituent members. Similarly, the best way of ensuring the public interest is by endeavoring to fulfill the interests of the individual.

In extreme circumstances, there will be exceptions to this rule. However, the arguments that society benefits from protecting individual privacy are strong and when this utility is added to the individual's interests, then the degree to which the public would benefit from disclosure would need to be very large to justify infringing privacy. Thus, when individual and public interests appear to conflict, privacy of the individual should be maintained, and the onus should be on those who advocate the public interest to prove their case.

Also See the Following Articles

CONFIDENTIALITY, GENERAL ISSUES OF • LEGAL ETHICS, OVERVIEW • PATIENTS' RIGHTS • PRIVACY

Bibliography

Areen, J. A., King, P. A., Goldberg, S., Gostin, L., & Capron, A. M. (1996). *Law, science and medicine.* (2nd ed.). Westbury, NY: The Foundation Press.

Beauchamp, T. L., & Childress, J. F. (1994). *Principles of Biomedical Ethics* (4th ed.). New York: Oxford University Press.

British Medical Association. (1993). *Medical ethics today.* London: BMJ Publishing Group.

Council of Europe. (1992). *Human rights in international law: Basic texts.* Strasbourg: Council of Europe Press.

Grad, F. P. (1990). *The public health law manual* (2nd ed.). Washington, D.C.: American Public Health Association.

Kennedy, I., & Grubb, A. (1994). *Medical law: Text with materials* (2nd ed.). London: Butterworths

Kottow, M. H. (1995). Medical confidentiality: An intransigent and absolute obligation. In C. Levine (Ed.) *Taking Sides: Clashing views on controversial bioethical issues* (6th ed. pp. 153–161). Guilford, CT: The Dushkin Publishing Group.

Schoeman F. D. (Ed.). (1984). *Philosophical dimensions of privacy.* Cambridge: Cambridge University Press.

Wing K. R. (1995). *The law and the public's health* (4th ed.). Ann Arbor: Health Administration Press.

PROFESSIONAL ETHICS

Timo Airaksinen
University of Helsinki

I. The Primacy of the Sociological Definition
   of Professionalism
II. The Types of Professional Ethics
III. Values and Service in Professional Life
IV. Engineering as a Pseudoprofession
V. Truth, Science, and Information as
   Professional Fields

GLOSSARY

audience That segment of society that is not influenced by given professional practices.

classic profession One of the traditional service-orientated professions such as education, law, and medicine, characterized by its members' theoretical knowledge and training, service ideal, autonomy, authority, and relatively high status.

client A direct recipient of professional services.

code of ethics In this context, an officially accepted document that spells out the values and obligations of a given profession, from the point of view of the profession itself.

exclusivity A status of professional practice in which (i) it is licensed and (ii) professionals treat outsiders as charlatans or impostors.

paternalism The attitude that a professional knows better than a client what is good for him or her.

professional ethics The considerations that determine the good conduct of professionals together with, or independently of, legal and prudential factors.

professional knowledge Abstract and theoretical knowledge, often measured in terms of a Ph.D., that (i) forms the basis of professional work and explains its efficiency, and (ii) whose possession is a necessary condition of entering into the profession.

professional power The ability of a member of a profession to make his working environment promote his own varied goals; professional authority.

pseudo profession A profession that has no classic value-based service ideal.

subprofession A professional group whose work is under the jurisdiction of another.

theoretical profession A profession that serves truth, knowledge, and information.

the public Those who are influenced by professional practices without being clients.

PROFESSIONAL ETHICS govern the work of professionals in addition to more specific legal considerations. In many cases legal constraints must be supplemented with ethical norms so that professional life can be better understood, and controlled. Most professions publish their own codes of ethics for this purpose. Philosophical ethics studies professional life, and tries to understand the foundations of professional values and obligations. Other important philosophical questions concern the analysis of the power of professions in a democratic society, professional authority, paternalistic practices, clients' rights, and the nature of professional knowledge. Professional ethics as a general field can be supplemented by such disciplines as the ethics of work, medical ethics, bioethics, legal ethics, and environmental ethics. Another important aspect of professional ethics is the criticism of professions that it affords. Some radical theorists, such as I. Illich, claim that professional power and privilege are unjustifiable. Professional ethics as an independent field of philosophy is still underdeveloped in the sense that not much theoretical unity can be found among the wealth of practical examples and social problem cases. However, there is no question that professional ethics is an important field of study, especially for the public. The public and the audience of the professions cannot leave the regulation of professional work and service in the hands of professionals alone. Legal controls have limitations as well, mainly because the law steps in only after the harm is done. Ethical practices prevent harm and other problems before they occur.

I. THE PRIMACY OF THE SOCIOLOGICAL DEFINITION OF PROFESSIONALISM

Life in modern society is in many ways dependent on professionals and their work. The terms "professional" and "professionalism" may be understood either as technical terms or everyday ideas. Usually, "profession" is used in the latter way to denote a paid occupation, in contrast to a mere hobby. In this sense a professional ballplayer is different from an amateur one. A car mechanic is a professional in the sense that he earns his living by working on cars instead of only on his own vehicles. Here the term "professional" has a contrastive rather than an independent and well-defined meaning.

"Professionalism" is often taken to mean one's serious and conscientious attitude towards one's own work. A professional works hard to achieve her goals. She is persistent and yet flexible when she confronts problems. A professional attitude towards one's work is clearly a virtue in modern societies, which are permeated by the "Protestant work ethic."

Professional ethics can be understood in two different ways: first, by focusing on paid occupations, and second, by utilizing the sociological definition of a profession. The first approach leads to the ethics of work, which governs the practices, rights, and duties of the members of paid occupations, or workers. We shall not discuss them here because the ethics of work is a field that is only marginally relevant to professional ethics proper. Workers have no autonomy or power in the same sense as professionals. Therefore, it seems advisable to leave the ethics of work out of the field of professional ethics because, by starting from the technical definition, we find a rich field of problems that are only remotely connected to work as such. In other words, we have two different fields here, work and professionalism, each of which leads to very different considerations and theories.

Such a commonsense usage of the term is clearly a problem when discussing professional ethics from a philosophical point of view. Therefore, we may want to use the technical definition borrowed from the sociology of the professions. No exact definition exists, of course, although something like the following can be suggested: a professional is a member of an exclusive group of individuals who possess a value-based service ideal, and an abstract knowledge of their own field. Professionalism is the relevant ideology with its behavioral and policy-orientated counterparts. It must be emphasized that the concept of a profession is an essentially contested one in the sense that no single meaning emerges from the literature. It is difficult to select the single correct one among the countless sociological suggestions of a definition. Such a state of affairs must be simply accepted in philosophy that cannot create for it its own definition.

A simple way to understand what professions are is to consider examples of professionals, such as certified public accountants, physicians, teachers, lawyers, social workers, and psychologists. Their occupations can be called the classic professions. Other occupations, such as nursing, engineering, and various business jobs can also be mentioned. The following classification can be suggested. We call the members of first list "classic professions," or "professions" for short. Nursing has traditionally been a subprofession because it has been under the authority of another profession, namely medicine. The same can be said of psychology. Engineering is a pseudoprofession for reasons that are related to its service ideals: engineers do not seem to have their own values in the sense to be explained below. Business is not a profession and, therefore, business ethics is an independent field for the simple reason that business is not an exclusive occupation. However, the business community must comply with the standards of related professions, such as law, accounting, and medicine. Anyone can start a business or apply for a job in a corporation or enterprise. Moreover, no abstract knowledge is required. Science and research have also been professionalized, and it is interesting to ask what kind of profession they form.

Understood as a theory of professions in general, professional ethics is not a unified field of study. The philosophical study of professional ethics has suffered from such definitional difficulties as those mentioned above. The understanding of the term "profession" has been too wide. This leads to fragmented views without any underlying unity, for instance, when professions, business, and work become confused. On the other hand, if a sociological definition is adopted, it may lead to overtly technical considerations and to a narrow perspective. Moreover, the sociology of the professions is a very complicated field. It seems advisable to narrow down the field of study, but at the same time to keep it simple and intuitive.

II. THE TYPES OF PROFESSIONAL ETHICS

A. Codes of Ethics

Professional ethics can be studied from several points of view. Most professions have their official codes of ethics. It is possible to focus on these codes, in order to criticize and develop them. Professional practices can be understood as embodiments of their codified values and obligations. What such codes are and how they work is indeed an interesting question.

B. Quandary Ethics

Professional practices are often controversial. Therefore, professional ethics includes the criticism of professional malpractice and in general the kinds of dramatic problems and dilemmas associated with a given professional field. Professions are open to criticism; for instance, psychiatrists may have sexual relations with their incompetent, but consenting clients. Medical experiments with animals are often condemned even when they have beneficial consequences for people. Such a focus belongs to an approach that can be called "quandary professional ethics," is a new term is needed.

The quandary approach is diametrically opposed to the view that focuses on codes of ethics, which are highly idealistic documents. The quandary approach is at the same time useful and dangerous. It is useful because professionals often hide behind their official declarations of values even when their practices are dubious. Quandary ethics wants to go beneath the facade to uncover the most dramatic problem areas. This, however, is the weakness of the approach: by focusing on some dramatic examples, a more balanced picture

is lost. The teaching of professional ethics becomes difficult, because no professional is enthusiastic about cases in which negative interpretation may stigmatize their own field of work.

This criticism of quandary professional ethics must be taken seriously. Professional ethics cannot be just a theory based on negative rhetoric where the purpose is to degrade professionalism. Many aspects of professionalism deserve criticism, but the quandary approach runs the risk of exaggerating this need. Professional ethics imply positive ethical standards. It cannot be expected that professionals listen to moral experts outside their own field, if their message is exclusively problem-oriented. The professionals' negative response means that promoters of professional ethics have lost their following. For example, this may be true in the accounting profession in United States because companies expect internal accountants and auditors to have as their first priority being loyal to their company and not to their profession. The professionals may study professional ethics independently without the help of ethical experts. But this tends to lead them back to their official moral codes and their self-serving idealism. The media tend to use the quandary approach because it is often entertaining.

C. The Standard Approach

Instead of focusing exclusively on dramatic problems in professional life, it is possible to develop standard professional ethics. By this term we mean an approach that first lays out the features of the field of professional practices, and then applies ethical concepts of duties and rights. In this field it is often claimed that there is no professional ethics as such, but only an ethics applied to everyday social relations in professional life. For instance, a teacher has obligations to pupils and parents, but he or she also has various rights, such as the right to evaluate the pupil's progress in the classroom, or to discipline the pupil within some well-defined limits. Like all professionals, the teacher has the right to make decisions that promote his or her own success both professionally and extraprofessionally. Such an extraprofessional right is strong in the case of the legal professions and in medicine, but less so in teaching or in social work.

It is evident that normal moral considerations apply to professional life. This fact should make one cautious in using the term "professional ethics" because one may think that the term refers to a special type of ethics. This is not plausible, although it must be admitted that some professional practices may look morally extraordinary, even supererogatory. A doctor has a stronger duty to provide help than a member of the public. Professionals may have the right to do things that nonprofessionals cannot be expected to do. For example, a teacher can punish his students, unlike a member of the public. In Great Britian, social workers have had the right to decide where a young delinquent should be placed within the child-care system. No parent, as a member of the public, has such a right. The existence of such rights and duties is one of the reasons why professionalism is such an important social category.

D. Professional Virtues and the Demise of Obligations

The most recent approach to professional ethics is through virtue ethics, which focuses on the good life of a professional who is able to find fulfillments as a professional. The motivation of such an approach is clear. In philosophical ethics, this trend clearly leads away from the deontology of duties and obligations via rights toward virtues and character ethics. The body of literature on ethical rules, understood as universalized prescriptions, has recently been labeled as dubious, especially by postmodernists. While we need not decide whether their relativism and value nihilism is justified, the challenge must be recognized.

Such an applied field as professional ethics has a strong practical influence and therefore its development must be taken seriously. It seems true, however, that the codes of professional ethics must not be left as too dispersed and underdeveloped to follow the trends of ethical theory. As a corrective, one can focus on the practices of the professional and compare them to those of other professionals. One need not pay too much attention to those unattractive quandaries, nor play with unrealistic descriptions of idealized values and obligations. At the same time the theory can locate professional life within the structure of a modern democratic society.

What are the virtues of a good nurse or a good lawyer? It seems that they are different simply because their characteristic practices are so different. The virtue approach should also look attractive to the professionals themselves, including students. Such an approach uses the first person in a way that is not egoistic. A young and aspiring professional sees the importance of becoming a good professional and a happy person, in the Aristotelian sense of the term, according to which happiness is fulfillment, or reaching one's goal. Indeed, the first and most important message of professional ethics to professionals should be that they not only aim at their own success but at competent service. According to virtue ethics, these two goals are not in conflict, as they would be from some other ethical viewpoints. Professional practices are goal-oriented so that the success and happiness of professionals can be measured in terms of their ability to reach the goal, defined in terms of their service ideal. If, on the contrary, success is measured, say, in money, a good professional practice may be detrimental to success.

III. VALUES AND SERVICE IN PROFESSIONAL LIFE

A. Characteristic Professional Values

If professional ethics is going to be more than a collection of particular considerations taken from the law, medicine, and education, among other fields, an account of the values that the professions promote should be provided. In their philosophical study, some complex issues must be simplified so that their logic becomes visible, while at the same time the real world is kept in sight. A simple method of doing this is to list the values of different professions using the shortest possible name for each key value. The truth of this presentation can be checked from the accepted code of ethics of the profession. It seems that it is possible to do so. Among the benefits of this method is its teachability and its connection to virtue ethics, as we shall see in due course.

In Table I the name of a profession is accompanied with its ideal value and goal, together with its real function in social life. Another consideration that must be taken into account separately is the dysfunction of a given profession; in other words, what the clients and the audience are afraid of, as well as the characteristic factor of the individual success of an individual professional. These two factors may be more or less detached from the real function. All the characterizations in Table I are tentative and should be used with caution, keeping

TABLE I

Profession	Value	Real function (example)
Law	Justice	Utilization of law
Medicine	Health	Medicalization of life
Education	Human growth	Socialization
Psychology	Autonomy	Social adjustment
Social work	Welfare	Stigmatization
Accounting	Fairness	Measurement of income and assets

in mind that professional ethics involves the study of the above-mentioned issues.

B. The Gap between Facts and Values in Professional Ethics

Lawyers value the goal of justice, but in real life they may merely utilize the law in the following sense. If a society is unjust, like Hitler's Nazi Germany or Stalin's Soviet Union, its laws are also unjust. In such a situation, lawyers may have no other choice but to do what the law says and thus pretend that they act justly. In most real-life cases, lawyers pay more attention to the law itself than to the justice of the law. In normal democratic conditions, this is justifiable, but it is also dangerous if the social conditions degenerate. A standard counterargument, for instance, is that the Nazi laws are not laws in the full legal sense. It follows that the law professionals of Nazi Germany were not lawyers at all, surprising as this sounds.

In order to see how the emphasis on values and on the service ideal work in professional ethics, let us briefly review an interesting quandary in legal ethics. A defense attorney defends successfully an accused person whose guilt is evident to everybody, including the attorney: Is this a moral problem? Such a case cannot be understood properly if some abstract deontological principles are applied to the case, because then one must say that both the principle of social utility and the Kantian obligation of justice are violated. If a guilty person should go free, why should the attorney try to free him? The answer must focus on the concept of justice that is the goal of the attorney, namely, on the moral fact that every person has the right to defend himself and the right not to be punished before he is found guilty by the court. These rights cannot be realized without the help of the attorney who, therefore, needs not refuse to defend his client. It may happen that he helps to set the guilty party free, but this is irrelevant to the service ideal understood as justice.

Medicine is one of the strongest of the professions. This is shown, for instance, by the fact that its service ideal and real function prima facie coincide. Of course, values and reality, ideals and facts never really meet, but in the case of medicine one needs to develop a complicated and problematic theoretical account of what the facts of medicine are. It indeed looks as if everything physicians do is supposed to take care of the health of clients. However, it is possible to argue that a hidden real function of medicine is to medicalize the social environment, in the following sense. The definition of health is so broad that more and more

human physical and psychological conditions can be classified as illnesses for which cures should be found. Human life becomes open to medical intervention in all of its stages. The advancement of medical science is taken to support such a view, often uncritically.

Teaching as a profession is troubled by the wide gulf between its ideal and its reality. If teachers' moral sensitivity and self-knowledge are sharp enough, they cannot avoid noticing this gulf, and professional ethics requires such awareness. The rift is between the needs of society and the rights of individual pupils. The task of education is the reproduction of culture so that the new generation can find its place in that process of history that leads to an open future from an unalterable past. This means, at the same time, the socialization of youth who, when they learn about the features of their own culture, not only continue it but become socialized by it.

Yet, from the point of view of pupils, they have the right to expect their education to make them flourish as persons. It might seem as if these two faces of education would be compatible, at least in normal cases. However, radical theorists of education have suggested that the task of education is to make pupils accept the social norms of injustice. In social life injustice is unavoidable, so that those who do not accept the relevant norms are troublemakers and self-destructive individuals. As logical as this argument may sound, it is hardly possible to maintain that an ideal ethical teacher should participate in such an educational system. Yet, teachers are expected to do so. According to this radical argument, there is a moral dilemma at the core of the teacher's work: socialization is not enough and yet human growth is an unrealistic ideal. An ethical teacher recognizes the problem and tries to do whatever he or she can to overcome its negative effects.

Psychology aims at the autonomy of the client. What this means is perhaps easiest to understand via the opposite of autonomy. People have unrealistic fears, neuroses, and addictions. One may conceptualize the situation by saying that such factors do not allow one's mind to work autonomously, in the sense that one's decisions are one's own. On the contrary, they are determined regardless of his or her free will, making the person at the same time less responsible as an agent. This condition need not be classified as an illness and, therefore, cannot be located within the jurisdiction of psychiatry.

Regardless of such a service ideal, which can be expressed in terms of moral psychology, the reality may be different. A psychologist helps the client to adjust to society even in cases where the person is troubled because of the imperfections of the norms of social life. For instance, working life in society may make unjustified and unrealistic demands on the worker whose ability to cope becomes more and more difficult. A psychologist helps him to adjust even in such cases where adjustment is personally undesirable in the long run. Perhaps it is too difficult to change the dynamics of the social structure so that such a possibility is never even conceptualized. Another example is marriage and divorce: in modern society a life-long marriage may be simply too demanding a norm and yet the clients may seek help to allow them to continue their married life. A psychologist cannot change the social institution, but she may be able to help the client to adjust to it.

Social work has a value ideal that may be understood in the minimalistic sense of the concept of welfare. Clients receive support, which allows them to avoid the final disaster that would make them unable to return to a normal, self-supporting lifestyle. A system of welfare is a safety net that catches those who would otherwise fall into the void. In other words, social work opposes marginalization and, therefore, its service ideal is not, like that of the majority of professions, a perfectionist one. However, the facts are disturbing. It has been argued, especially by conservative theorists, that welfare systems are highly stigmatizing in the sense that they consolidate the social positions of those caught in the safety net. The system makes the clients dependent on it so that they are not willing or able to live a life without it. The social welfare machinery produces its own clients and their life-style. What should be a brief interlude in their lives becomes their stable social position from which they have no escape. Whether such a description is valid or not is, of course, an open question whose political relevance is obvious.

The discussion above has focused on the key aspect of professional ethics, the virtue of self-understanding, which makes the professional a better person in his or her chosen social role. He or she should be aware both of the values, of the service ideal, and of the social reality of the profession.

C. Professional Practices and Their Virtues

To make the argument for the importance of virtue ethics for professional life more interesting, the following thesis can be presented. Professional values are both objective and internal to professional practices. Such a view is necessarily controversial. The concept of objective values is far from clear as is also the idea of practice-internal values. At the same time it seems important to

indicate certain steps that virtue ethics of the professions might take.

Objective values: Such values as health, autonomy, human growth, welfare, and justice are objective in the following limited sense. One cannot sensibly maintain that one does not want to be healthy, which is to say that the denial of such values is false. It follows that these values are unavoidable, and this can be taken to indicate their objectivity. At the same time, it must be admitted that at the individual level, some people maintain that they are not interested in, say, justice or health. Perhaps such values are social values in the sense that in general, and at a policy level, it cannot be supposed that people would reject these values.

Internal values: Professionals work in order to realize social values that are generally perceived as unavoidable and as such objective. These values are internal to the work of professionals in the following sense. A physician who does not recognize health as the goal of his work is no longer a physician, in the intended sense of the term. The Nazi "physicians" were impostors for this very reason when they performed cruel experiments with prisoners of war. Abortions can be criticized from the point of view of professional ethics in the same way, because it requires the killing of a fetus that may be perfectly healthy, in a situation in which the mother has no valid medical reason to want an abortion. If health is the internal value of the medical profession, abortion as well as euthanasia present crucial problems.

Teaching as a profession is anchored to the development of personality so that mere socialization is not the goal of a teacher. The same argument can be repeated in the case of each of the professions. The definition of professional work is offered in terms of the value that defines the relevant service ideal.

D. Professional Power and Responsibility

Such a description of professional ethics in terms of practice-internal values allows us also to understand professional power and responsibility. Professional values, although they are objective, are always open to redefinition. What "health" or "justice" means is neither self-evident nor unchangeable. Historical studies show that both concepts have developed in the course of time. For instance, "health" can mean the absence of disease, a negative and perfect concept, although the current meaning is more like "optimal function of the mind–body unity," a positive and imperfect concept. The former kind of health can be perfected in the sense that a person is free from illness. In the latter sense, no one is ever perfectly healthy. Professions have the ability and power to redefine the relevant value concepts. For instance, "autonomy" is a psychological notion. Such value terms are often naively supposed to be natural and unproblematic so that their meaning is fixed independently of the professional work as if the meaning were independent of professional power.

In an almost paradoxical manner, professions make value-based goals internal to their practices and, consequently, to their work, but the meanings of these values are their own product. This fact emphasizes not only the power of professions but the difficulty of controlling them in modern, democratic societies. In fact, as has been argued, professions wield invisible and uncontrollable social power. At the same time, such a power must be balanced by the responsible behavior of professionals. They should realize that their position is unique in the sense that their profession enjoys an exclusive status; because there is no challenge to their expertise, they should use their own definitional power with caution. They should understand that the value terms that they use are not only based on their scientific theories or abstract learning, but that the meaning of such value terms always reflect some social factors that are difficult to specify. As a recommendation it makes sense to say that professional groups should not isolate themselves from the public discourse. Their members should remain open to external opinions and questions. This is a part of professional virtue.

E. Service and Success: Is There a Conflict?

To put these issues in a sharper focus, we may discuss briefly the application of the social contract theory of ethics to professional life. It seems plausible to suggest that professionals and their clients make an implicit social contract that regulates their relations. Professionals commit themselves to the service ideals that are beneficial to their clients and acceptable to the audience. Their level of cognitive competence is high. Professionals may be required to perform supererogatory acts, or to do more than is normally required, demanded, or expected. In exchange they gain the permission to pursue their own success, which may look less than desirable to clients. Professional fees may be expensive, the availability of services may be relatively scarce, and their status may be artificially high.

A counterargument shows the weak points of this application of the social contract theory. The clients can argue that the contract is invalid because it is based on coercion. Because the clients need the services provided by professionals, these services are necessary for them. Moreover, if they reject the services, they cannot find an alternative source. In other words, if professional values are objective and the profession is an exclusive provider of the relevant services, the clients have no choice but to accept the contract as it is defined by professionals. This is, technically speaking, coercion that invalidates the contract. The alternative sources are named impostors and charlatans who are unable to provide services for clients.

To make the contract work, professional ethics should dictate that an open attitude be adopted toward alternative services offered by other providers. It seems unlikely that any official professional code of ethics would include such norms. The reason is easy to understand on the basis of the idea of professional competence based on abstract knowledge. There is no alternative knowledge, according to professional cognitive objectivism. It follows that the professionals' benefits are high and the opportunities of social success very attractive.

The clients and the audiences of professions must tolerate their success-oriented claims. This is to say that professional ethics cannot be based solely on the service ideal, however important that seems to be. The service is always exchanged for money, status, and privilege. This is evident in law and medicine, but much less so in education and social work. In these latter fields, professionals have not been very successful in their efforts to transform their services into success and benefits. It is not easy to explain why this is so even if the problem certainly deserves studying.

A service ideal entails professional altruism that conflicts with the demands of success. This fact creates the peculiar moral atmosphere that surrounds modern professional life. The standard argument as presented by professionals is that their services are so valuable that they deserve their success. From the clients' and the audience's point of view, this may sound dubious. If the professional ideology is service-oriented and so altruistic, it does not seem to contain any right to claim excessive benefits. The case of those professionals who work for a company or organization is different and must be treated separately.

If the professionals' own argument is utilitarian, the other side represents the deontology that makes it the professionals' duty to provide the relevant services. Such a view is also reflected in official codes of ethics, although the right to success then becomes something of a mystery. A utilitarian may argue that the right to success is based on the maximization of the public good measured in terms of the services provided to clients. The maximization of social good follows from large benefits and good services. However, if professionals have a duty to provide the services, it is difficult to see what is the basis for their claims to success. The performance of one's duty does not entitle one to a reward.

Obviously, the ethical aspects of the relations between professionals and their clients deserve our careful and critical attention. It seems that in philosophical literature, too strong an emphasis has sometimes been placed on the notion of professional obligations. Certainly, professionals have many obligations, but it may be unrealistic to suppose that deontology is the ultimate explanatory theory of professional life. For example, a professional has a moral obligation to be honest when he or she deals with clients. However, he or she has no duty to provide special services. A professional exchanges the services for benefits, a fact that entails freedom-rights. There are exceptions, of course, like emergency medical treatment and an occasional free legal service for the poor.

IV. ENGINEERING AS A PSEUDOPROFESSION

A. The Nature of Engineering Ethics

It has been remarked that engineering is a profession that failed. Such a judgment might be unrealistically harsh considering that engineering is one of the major professions of industrial society. However, it is true that engineers' relationships to a service ideal and its values are problematic, or at least they must be understood differently from the classic professions discussed above. Because the engineering profession faces tremendous challenges in our time, it is sensible to ask whether this profession is able to assume the responsibilities of the leadership role when pollution, war, and the overuse of natural resources become a problem. It is unlikely that engineers want to claim that such issues do not belong to their expertise.

The key issue here is the service ideal. What kind of value-based service is provided by engineers? It is clear that they provide some kind of service. For instance, when people move from one place to another, they use automobiles, trains, and airplanes instead of their own legs, horses, or homemade carriages. When nations go to war, they use highly sophisticated weapons. When soldiers come back from war, they often need medical care, which again is made possible by the

achievements of engineers. The engineers first design factories that pollute, and then they design water- and air-cleaning equipment. The blessings of engineering seem to be mixed. It is, however, clear that the modern world is a technological world.

The engineers' code of ethics mentions the safety, health, and welfare of the public as their service ideals, or as is said in the code, those factors should be held "paramount." It is not easy to specify the intended meaning of such a word. Certainly, for instance, a car should be safe. Cars also promote human well-being by allowing us to travel from place to place with the maximum ease. One can, of course, ask whether the notions of health, safety, and welfare are the same as those mentioned by medical professionals, the police, the armed forces, and social workers. The answer must be in the negative. Therefore, it seems plausible to suggest that such values are side-constraints rather than goals in engineering. Their main task is to produce good designs, when the goodness is evaluated according to standards that are internal to the practice of engineering.

The concept of side-constraint can be understood as follows. The physician must promote health. But though an engineer must take care that his design does not risk health, the design need not promote health. Cars may be good, but they are never healthy in the medical sense.

The following can be suggested as a blueprint for engineering ethics. An engineer is responsible for serving an employer by producing good designs that allow the employers to achieve their goals. The designs must be safe and, say, economical. Unlike the second, the first requirement is self-evident. Yet it is obvious that safety alone is not sufficient for a good design. The exact characterization of the sufficient condition must be one of the main tasks of engineering ethics. Certain additional observations can also be offered. Engineers are responsible for providing good designs for an employer, but they should also keep the interests of the public in mind. Here it is important to see how different their relation to employers and clients are, compared to, say, lawyers or teachers. The latter professions have their clients and audience; engineers have their employers and the public. Teachers provide only one type of service, regardless of their employer, unlike engineers who serve many employers with different goals. A teacher's audience is an external one, unlike the public that, say, buys cars. The idea of externality means that the audience is not directly influenced by the work of teachers: they are not taught and they do not learn anything.

B. The Need-Based Service Ideal

Engineers provide a service that is based on needs and desires, not on objective values. The following practical syllogism illustrate this point:

Medical profession:
I believe that the only way to stay healthy is to follow medical advice and do X.
I want to stay healthy.
Therefore, I do X.

Engineering:
I believe that the only way to build a bridge is to use engineering knowledge and to do Y.
I want to build the bridge.
Therefore, I do Y.

We notice that in the first syllogism we cannot reject the first premise, simply because health is an objective value, in the special sense of the word explained above. In the second syllogism, the second premise can be rejected because it is possible simply not to want to build the bridge. The engineer's employer may offer a bridge to his client who, after considering it, refuses to buy it. But if he wants to build the bridge, we can interpret Y as follows:

Y: let a responsible engineer design a bridge so that it is safe, beautiful, practical, ecologically viable, and economical to use and maintain in the long run.

In sum: the engineers provide a service to the public by creating designs that the public wants and that are safe and "good," in the special sense of the word, and that the employer will offer to the public.

Engineers serve also their employers whose goals vary widely, and in some cases are ethically problematic. An example is the weapons industry where, for instance, the infamous neutron bomb was supposed to kill people but leave material objects intact. Such a weapon was considered by the public as morally repulsive because it implied ideologically that people are less important than material objects. Engineers succeeded in reaching their employer's goal but they offended the public. This example shows how difficult it is to pinpoint the exact nature of the ethical side-constraints of engineering designs, which can be offensive almost in the same sense as pornography.

C. From Paternalism to Clients' Rights

A useful way of approaching some recent trends in professional ethics is to start from engineering ethics and then focus on the classical professions. These have tended to be, at least to some degree, paternalistic in the sense that a professional is supposed to know what is good for a client independently of the client's own opinion. Such a position of authority is evident especially in medicine. In recent years the client's rights have become stronger and stronger so that a kind of breakdown point has been reached. In this situation the professional can only advise the client without possessing any authority over his or her decisions. The patient, for instance, can insist on unnecessary treatment that is futile and ineffective. The same phenomena can well occur also in education where parents may want to bypass the teacher's expertise and insist on a certain kind of teaching that the professional sees as ineffective and potentially harmful to a child.

We may then ask what is the difference between "body engineers" and physicians, between "mind engineers" and psychologists, or "socialization engineers" and teachers. It is a useful exercise in professional ethics to try to answer these questions because then one can focus on the nature of the goals and responsibilities that constitute the basis of professional authority. It seems that the basic intuition suggests that medicine cannot be a matter of body engineering, although physicians are highly dependent on engineering designs. In other words, those who design the tools are yet incapable of using them because of some ethical, goal-orientated reasons.

What would happen if physicians were body engineers? One way to accept this is to focus on patients' rights. Suppose a cancer patient wants to try a new treatment that was promising some time ago, but that is now ineffective. The patient has a right to the treatment, if he can afford it financially. It is his physician's duty to inform him that the treatment does not work; but he does not have the right to withhold the treatment from the patient, simply because the patient has the right to determine what happens to his own body. According to such examples, the physician's role approaches that of a body engineer. In engineering the employer may want results so that he insists on working on the technical side of the problem even when engineers deem it futile. An example is the American Star Wars defense program. Interestingly, engineers may have more authority over such a decision than the physicians have. In both cases the clients may make an effort to find more compliant professionals if those whom they originally contacted want to refuse.

Notice that such an example indicates clearly why medicine, unlike engineering, is an ethical profession. Even when physicians are body engineers, their patients have the moral right to the treatment they choose, unlike the employer of an engineer who has no such right over the engineers' projects. Unlike a physician, an engineer can refuse much more easily.

An even more illuminating example is cosmetic plastic surgery, which seems to present a moral problem from the point of view of the medical code of ethics. In this type of case, a person wants to have a more beautiful face, just as he may want to have a more beautiful car. In such a case, the doctor does not violate a code of ethics. Instead, he bypasses his moral role as a member of the medical profession, because the patient has no moral right to the treatment. Compare this case to that of the cancer patient.

It is possible that the nature of the classical professions is changing along with the recognition of strong patients' rights. This means that professionals provide the services requested by their clients without having any authority over those decisions. They do what they are hired to do on the basis of their technical expertise. Nevertheless, these professions retain their moral basis simply because a client's rights are moral rights, which create a strong obligation to the professionals to provide the service in question. The expertise of the professional becomes more technical in nature.

Another related trend is the emergence of alternatives to the services provided by the classic professions. It seems that their members have difficulties in defending their exclusive epistemic status. The concepts of charlatanism and fakery become more difficult to apply. This is evident in medicine where the ideas of faith healing and of alternative medicine are gaining ground. In the legal professions, the law has been compared to literature. In education, different minority groups have successfully argued against the mainstream educational ideas under the banners of political correctness. In such a process, educators have not much authority and certainly no motive to be paternalistic.

V. TRUTH, SCIENCE, AND INFORMATION AS PROFESSIONAL FIELDS

A. The Concept of Theoretical Profession

An important segment of professionalism can be found among the information professions. These are different both from the classical professions and engineering. Their key concepts are truth, knowledge, and information. We can mention librarians, who are the oldest of them, as well as scientists, journalists, and information-management people.

Let us first suggest why such professionals are not to be classified together with those in the classical professions. The main reason is that truth, knowledge, and information are not ethical terms. In fact, they have no practical value component built into them. The fact that lay people miss this point creates confusion when they discuss professional ethics in this field. It is easy to see why this is so. Truth is either logical or empirical, and empirical truth is simply the property of a sentence such that a true sentence corresponds with facts. Accordingly, "Snow is white" is true if, and only if, snow is white. Knowledge is, according to its classical definition derived from Plato, a justified, true belief. In this definition "justification" means epistemic acceptability, according to some more or less exact but always theoretical criteria. "Information" has many meanings, but the general idea is that information is a variation of a signal.

Some of the related ethical concepts are "truthfulness," "reliability," and "honesty." The idea that the truth must not be concealed or twisted seems to give some credibility to the thesis that truth as such is a value. It is also clear that from the pragmatic perspective, it is easy to accept the proposition that knowledge is useful. The Marxists claim that knowledge is a force of production. However, one should not forget in this context the standard fact-value distinction, or the distinction between theoretical and practical considerations and, indeed, values. There are theoretical values and also theoretical virtues, according to Aristotle.

In what sense are scientists professionals? The answer to this question allows us to understand the ethics of science from a specialized perspective. It is clear that scientists are in most cases professionals, in contrast to the amateurs of the Royal Society of 17th-century England, for instance. It is also interesting to recall that the first famous philosopher who was a professional in the sense of being a university professor is Immanuel Kant at the end of the 18th century.

We can argue that even if truth and knowledge are not values, access to them is. Therefore, the scientific profession has its own service ideal that is based on values. The main question is: What has science to do with truth and knowledge? It is notorious that neither the above-mentioned definition of truth nor the definition of knowledge applies to modern science. The offered definitions must be scientific in nature, so that science seeks for scientific truth and knowledge, which are not unproblematically related to the everyday notions of truth and knowledge. Perhaps the best way to put it is to say simply that scientists serve science in the sense that they try to add to the body of literature concerning certain disciplines and theories. Their aim is the advancement of science, which indirectly seems to entail the betterment of knowledge. It is not easy to characterize the goals of the scientific enterprise, if one takes the ideas of the philosophy of science seriously. Nevertheless, it seems obvious that scientists provide an access to something that is called scientific knowledge, and which is valuable in a modern technological society.

Scientists as professionals have no clients, if their students are not regarded as such. Consequently, they have no obligation to produce useful or entertaining data for the consumers of knowledge. Of course, society at large, or its political segment, often criticizes science for remaining in an ivory tower, which is to say that science is not useful enough and that scientists have too much autonomy in matters of science. Such a challenge should be taken seriously, of course, although it may be difficult to see how modern science could be more consumer-friendly. The scientific enterprise is supremely difficult to understand anyway.

Consequently, the ethics of science must focus mostly on the obligations of scientists toward each other, although the relations to various funding agencies are important as well. At least two levels are relevant here: norms between master and disciple or teacher and student, and between equal colleagues. At the first level, it is important, for instance, that the teacher does not exploit the ideas of the student. At the collegial level, it is important to avoid plagiarism. But what about forging the data that seems to be a growing concern in a present-day competitive scientific environment? Do scientists have a duty to the public not to do that, or do they have a duty toward each other? The answer must depend on the specific view of science one takes, which also determines one's ethics of science. An easy example is a case where forged data are used in an effort to gain a grant from public funds. This case has the moral status of stealing.

Perhaps it is possible to apply the Aristotelian notion of theoretical virtues to the professional ethics of science. The classic practical virtues are wisdom, courage, moderation, justice, and benevolence. Their theoretical counterparts can be listed as follows: theoretical understanding, creativity, logical consistency, criticism of others and oneself, and clarity. A good scientist should

possess all of these virtues, and his training must facilitate their acquisition.

B. The Obligations of Journalists

Journalism is an important profession in modern society. Its service ideal is to provide access to information about society to the public. It seems that it has a direct responsibility to the public rather than to its employer. It is often said that the public has the right to know. This is taken to be a moral right, although it is not easy to see how such a right should be understood.

Here, just as in science, the idea of the professional serving truth seems to prevail. In the case of journalism, this may be misleading. It is hardly the responsibility of a journalist to find out whether publishable material is true or not, although he or she must be reasonably certain that what he or she writes is reliable information. It can also be argued that there is no value-free knowledge or information. All knowledge is contaminated by some social interests and background values. This is also to say that the transmission of information and knowledge is tied to social power. How all this happens is not at all easy to understand. It seems clear, however, that journalists cannot pretend that they just serve the truth. On the contrary, it is part of their moral responsibility to understand the aspects of social interest and power that are connected to the information they create and transmit to the public. The professional ethics of scientists and journalists are different, although the work of both focuses on knowledge, truth, and information.

Also See the Following Articles

BIOETHICS, OVERVIEW • CODES OF ETHICS • LEGAL ETHICS, OVERVIEW • MEDICAL CODES AND OATHS • SCIENCE AND ENGINEERING ETHICS, OVERVIEW

Bibliography

Abbott, A. (1988). *A system of professions.* Chicago: Chicago University Press.

Airaksinen, T. (1994). Service and science in professional life. In R. Chadwick, (Ed.), *Ethics and the professions.* Avebury, U.K.: Aldershot (pp. 1–13).

Bayles, M. D. (1989). *Professional ethics* (2nd ed.). Belmont, CA: Wadsworth.

Cohen, W. (1995). *Ethics in thought and action: Social and professional perspectives.* New York: Ardsley House.

Harris, E. C., Jr., Pritchard, M. S., & Rabins, M. J. (Eds.). (1995). *Engineering ethics.* Belmont, CA: Wadsworth.

Shrader-Frechette, K. (1994). *Ethics of scientific research.* Lanham, U.K.: Roman & Littlefield.

Sprinkle, R. H. (1994). *Profession of conscience.* Princeton, NJ: Princeton University Press.

Windt, P. Y., et al. (Eds.). (1988). *Ethical issues in the professions.* Englewood Cliffs, NJ: Prentice-Hall.

Wueste, D. E. (Ed.). (1994). *Professional ethics and social responsibility.* Lanham, U.K.: Roman & Littlefield.

PROPERTY RIGHTS

John Christman
Virginia Polytechnic Institute and State University

GLOSSARY

free market (competitive market) System of exchange that displays the following properties: full information and rationality (on participants' parts); no transaction costs; no monopolies; and no externalities.

liberal conception of ownership A view of ownership according to which owners enjoy the full list of rights associated with ownership unregulated by state interference. Such rights include rights to possess, use, destroy, consume, trade, bequeath, alienate, and gain income (from exchange) from their property.

libertarianism A political theory that claims that the state's only obligation is to protect the individual rights of citizens, including their rights to property. This view implies that political institutions should not interfere with the private market transactions of citizens.

natural rights Rights persons have independent of social conventions, legal institutions, or other institutional relationships.

ownership Rights, liberties, powers, and related legal modalities a person has against others in relation to some tangible or intangible thing. Rights of owner-

ship often involve rights to possess, use, consume, trade, and gain income from the thing owned.

private property System of ownership where individuals tend to be the primary holders of ownership rights, in particular full liberal rights to use and trade their goods.

public ownership System of property where public bodies, such as the state, are the primary holders of ownership rights over goods.

self-ownership The enjoyment of rights associated with ownership over one's body, talents, and labor.

PROPERTY RIGHTS are the rights, liberties, powers, and liabilities that give a person or collectivity particular power over some tangible or intangible thing. Such rights form a complex array of legal modalities holding between the owner and (generally) all other persons in relation to some item. These rights can be held by individuals, groups, communities, or the state. Typically, property rights involve the rights to possess, use, consume, destroy, transfer or bequeath, and gain income from some good. Such a bundle of rights can be held by individuals (private ownership) or the state (public ownership) or some combination. The specification of who may own goods, the particular kinds of things that are protected by property rights, and the extent of the rights and liberties included in the ownership bundle, are all matters to be determined by principles of justice more generally.

I. THE STRUCTURE OF OWNERSHIP

The word "property" is often used to denote both the thing owned by someone as well as the set of rights held by such owners over their goods. The subject of discussion here, however, is the latter usage, more precisely, "ownership." It is also often assumed that property is simply a right that a person has over a particular thing. This is a simplification: first, ownership is neither a single nor a simple concept. Ownership refers to a varying array of legal modalities—rights, privileges, powers, liabilities, immunities, and the like—that owners have over some thing. Second, the object of ownership may not be best described as a "thing" at all, but rather a kind of abstraction such as stocks, corporations, or insurance policies. Some have argued that because the objects of ownership are often difficult to specify, ownership holds over the rights bundle *itself*. Some legal analysts have approached the concept this way, arguing that all one "owns" in having property rights is the rights themselves. This, however, creates a rather cumbersome redundancy: ownership then comes to mean having a certain bundle of rights over a certain bundle of rights relative to some tangible or intangible thing.

Ownership is best seen, however, not as a relation between a person and a thing at all, but rather as a relation holding between a person and all others, protected by the state, in relation to some item or asset. This relation is neither a simple nor invariable one, even within systems of "private" ownership. A wide array of legal modalities, or "incidents," can be enumerated as generally associated with ownership: the right to possess; the right to use; the right to the capital (which breaks down into the power to make valid disposition of the thing owned as well as the power to transfer title—that is, the rights of alienation, consumption, and modification); the right to manage (a cluster of powers to contract with others concerning control over various uses of the thing); and the right to the income (the right to increased benefit from ownership, where this benefit flows from exchanges with others). In traditional parlance these modalities can be grouped under the rights of *usus*, *abusus*, and *usus fructus*. Connected to this system of rights must be various correlative legal rules for the determination of title, regulation of transmissibility (after death), as well as enforcement and redress procedures in cases of contested ownership.

It must also be recognized that one can talk either about property systems or about particular property claims. The system of property that reigns for a particular society can actually be rather difficult to pinpoint, because the statutory and constitutional provisions for the society may leave much room for a variety of patterns of ownership structures within it. It is often assumed, for example, that private property is the rule in the United States, but nothing in the U.S. Constitution would prevent a scenario where all of the socialists in some area pool their assets into a collective scheme, creating a pattern of collective holdings in that area. To find out what sort of ownership structure is dominant in a society, we may often have to analyze not just the rights that people have but how they are in fact exercising them.

Indeed, many writers have argued that the complexity of ownership is such that a single concept of "ownership" is actually otiose. On that view, the various rights and liberties associated with ownership are so variable, disparate, and unrelated in particular contexts that the concept of ownership has now gained the status of a legal fiction. In addition, many economists have argued that for efficiency's sake, the only important right in a property bundle is the right of alienation, enabling individuals to trade any other "sticks" in the bundle in order to achieve maximally optimal outcomes (although see Section II.B below).

At the other end of the spectrum, however, are those that claim that the *only* coherent sense of property is one that includes the full rights to possess, use, consume, trade, and gain income from property, what could be called "full liberal ownership." But in both cases, it can be pointed out that the particular package of rights afforded to owners of property for a society cannot be determined by conceptual analysis, but rather is the result of normative argument, in particular arguments from principles of distributive justice (see Section III below).

A. A Framework for Ownership

Whether ownership is fully reducible to its constituent rights or whether the only coherent conception is the full liberal view, it is clear that actual property schemes vary widely. The most salient distinction between kinds of property systems holds between "public" ownership (socialist) systems and "private" ownership (capitalist) ones. But there are also many kinds of "mixed" property systems, including ones that recognize a variety of collective ownership rights. Moreover, whoever is the title-holder in the system, the array of rights and liberties held by any given owner may vary greatly within a society. (Indeed, it may well be unclear how exactly to delineate the "owner" of an item in question, especially

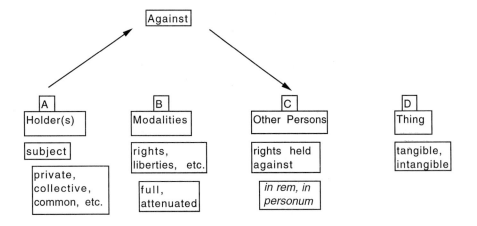

Rules:
1. **Fixing title (determining best title) and determining lesser interests.**
2. **Regulation of transmissibility (intestate rules).**
3. **Effective enforcement mechanisms (rights to security in holdings).**

FIGURE 1

when the variety of rights associated with the item is shared with other individuals, groups, and the state.)

A "framework" for ownership is a template into which the various forms of ownership for a given society (and following from a given set of principles of distributive justice) may fit (See Fig. 1). Although the elements in the framework vary widely, the organization of those elements—hence the "relation" of ownership—can be seen to hold constant. The framework presented in Figure 1 is divided into four cells: Cell A refers to the class of persons (and person-like legal entities) who are recognized as potential owners in a society. As listed below A, this can range from individual persons, to collectivities, to entire communities. So-called "private-property" regimes will have individual persons as the predominant holders of goods. Cell B indicates the various modalities (legal rights, liberties, powers, immunities, and liabilities) that might be granted to owners in a jurisdiction. Cell C refers to the fact that one's property rights may be held against everyone (*in rem*) or against particular persons (*in personum*), the former being the norm for property but not the only possibility (sometimes particular rights and duties to specific individuals are part of an ownership package, such as a duty to bequeath property to a particular heir). Cell D refers to the kind of thing recognized as "ownable" in a society—physical objects are the paradigm case here but more abstract entities are more often the norm. (Also, some objects may be declared as not properly the subject of property rights at all, such as one's internal

organs.) So-called "intellectual property" refers to the rights people may hold over less tangible items such as designs, logos, texts, and other materials—those items covered by patents, copyrights, and trademarks. The rights granted to individuals or corporations over such material is quite variable, although most of the issues that arise over traditional property rights apply to such resources as well.

In addition to the "relata" of ownership, there must exist certain background rules that stabilize and help define the property system. These include, normally, rules that determine title to property in contested cases, rules that regulate the transmission of goods after death (called "intestate" rules), and laws establishing the background security for the enjoyment of other property rights. (In fact, some include the "right to security" as one of the elements of ownership itself.)

Determining the *proper* structure of ownership for a society, then, will be a complex process, involving various questions of distributive justice. Traditionally, the justification of "private property," however, has assumed that the ownership structure in question is one where individual persons hold the full bundle of rights and liberties against all others in relation to the things they own (full liberal ownership). Such an ownership structure has usually been associated with free market capitalism, in that, it is assumed, if owners hold the full liberal rights over goods, they are then able to trade resources freely without interference from the state.

B. Private Property, Markets, and Capitalism

In discussions of various ownership schemes, it is often assumed that "private property" is conceptually equivalent to "capitalism" and hence conceptually connected with the operations of free economic markets. However, the relation between private property and economic markets is, in fact, more complex than this picture assumes. A "market" is any system of social interaction that allows for the exchange of goods. A "free market" or "perfectly competitive market" is one that meets a variety of (rather stringent) conditions. These include: (1) full information (participants in trades have full knowledge all relevant information about available goods, technology, prices, and costs); (2) no transaction costs (all exchanges of goods or information are costless); (3) full rationality (all participants are perfectly rational in the sense of always choosing the optimal means to advance their own ends, where these ends do not include consideration of the welfare of those with whom they are trading); (4) no monopolies; and (5) no externalities (no positive or negative effects on parties not covered in the price of goods traded in particular exchanges).

A basic tenet of microeconomics is that such a market will reach an efficient equilibrium (where further trades can make no one better off without making at least one person worse off). An assumption often made in discussions of property rights is that full liberal ownership structures will coincide with perfectly free (and hence maximally efficient) markets. But there are several ways in which this correlation is not precise.

First, a condition of perfectly free markets is that no stable monopolies exist—no one controls all of the resources of a particular type in an area. But to prevent monopolies from occurring (or remaining in place) it often will be necessary to *curtail* the (full liberal) property rights of the owners of the resource in question. Liberal ownership allows owners to withhold goods as long as they wish, and to sell them at whatever price they wish, but dismantling a monopoly will often necessitate restricting these rights on the part of present owners.

Second, a fully free market with no transaction costs should allow individuals to trade not only bundles of goods but also particular *rights* over those goods, rights separable from the full bundle specified by the full liberal structure. So in this way, perfectly free markets may conflict with the maintenance of liberal ownership, for owners will be moved to trade separable aspects of their ownership.

More generally, it should also not be thought that liberal private property is a necessary condition for competitive markets, at least not a conceptually necessary condition. If participants in a market have the right sort of motivations (to trade goods efficiently even if they retain no individual rights over those goods), then a fully competitive market could operate even if no one held liberal ownership rights over the goods traded. It is not a necessary truth that individuals are only motivated by the economic aspects of ownership rights, because they can well engage in "efficient" trading behavior while not holding property rights to the goods traded at all (they may do so on another's behalf, for example, or for a noble cause). Competitive markets are also consistent with certain kinds of taxation (lump sum taxes for example), and hence do not necessitate full ownership, as long as participants are motivated to trade optimally despite lacking rights to the "full" economic return on their trades.

But the reality of markets in the real world never succeeds in meeting the conditions of perfect competition just described. In reality, then, markets will operate despite the presence of positive transaction costs, externalities (positive and negative ones), less than full information, and many local monopolies. Protecting the "full" individual ownership rights of owners of goods in such environments will guarantee, then, that resources will eventually be distributed unequally, as those who face lower transaction costs or have more information will take advantage of their situation and make the best deals. If full liberal ownership is recognized then such trades will be left relatively untouched by taxation and hence the unequal outcomes will be left to stand.

In these ways, the relation between private property systems and capitalism is also more complex than is often assumed. Capitalism is often defined as a system where the means of production are privately owned. The alternative—socialism—is then thought of as the public ownership of such productive resources. But as we have seen, the complex nature of ownership, and the somewhat variable relationship that exists between ownership and economic markets, gives rise to various ambiguities in these standard definitions. What, for example, counts as "the means of production" exactly? And where is the line between public regulation of the use, possession, and trade of a resource and public "ownership" of it? And to what degree must economic markets be "free" and unregulated for a society to be labelled "capitalist"?

Nevertheless, in the philosophical literature on property ownership, it is usually assumed that a private property system will include generally free markets, capitalist relations of production, and a distribution of property that leaves some with more than others (and many with little external property at all, giving rise to the institution of wage labor). With these assumptions in the background, then, let us now turn to the traditional strategies for justifying private property, in something like the full liberal sense. To simplify, we will assume that "private property" refers to the rights to possess, use, consume, trade, and gain income from property, relatively unregulated by state interference, held generally by individuals or individual-like entities. Most discussions of property systems have centered on the question of the justification of private property, assuming that lying in the wings as an alternative are more redistributive property structures (if not complete public ownership of all productive goods).

II. JUSTIFICATIONS FOR PRIVATE PROPERTY

First, arguments for private property can be either "direct" or "indirect." Direct arguments connect the right to own property directly with some moral principle or value, claiming that such a right follows from certain premises concerning one's liberty, or self-ownership, or desert (together, perhaps, with auxiliary premises concerning certain actions a person might have taken in relation to the object). Indirect arguments, on the other hand, justify property in virtue of its connection with other structures or institutions, most notably, economic markets. The prime example of such an argument is the Utilitarian one, which claims that private property gives rise to free market capitalism and that this mechanism serves to advance aggregate utility more than relevant alternatives. In such an argument, property is justified instrumentally and hence indirectly.

Arguments for property may also be "general" or "specific": general arguments are aimed at justifying whole systems of property, while specific arguments focus on particular claims by particular (kinds) of people. One may favor, for example, the system of private property capitalism, but argue that everyone ought to be afforded property rights over equal amounts of wealth at the initial stage of production and trade. Specific arguments also may be aimed at the particular rights and liberties that owners—whoever they may be—enjoy over their property. For, as we have seen, ownership is an exceedingly complex legal relation.

Questions about the justification of property surround issues concerning whether and on what basis private property claims ought to be recognized and protected in a society, and if there is such a basis, what is the particular structure of the property claims so justified. We have to look, therefore, at a variety of questions: first, at what level is this justification taking place (are we asking about the justification of a "system" of property or a particular claim or kind of claim); second, are these justifications attempts to support the conclusion that this or that property structure is *optimal*, merely *permissible*, or justified on balance. And finally, even if the entirety of a property system (or some of the elements of a single property claim) fails to be justified, it still may be possible to claim a "partial" justification—that is, that some aspect of the property claim is supported by the moral arguments in question.

Justifications for property rights can be categorized into "historical," "consequentialist," and what can be called "constitutive" arguments. Historical arguments include as a premise a condition that makes reference to some act or event that has taken place in the past relating a person with a piece of property (for example, that he or she acquired the good under certain justifying conditions). Consequentialist strategies make reference to the effects of private property systems, most notably the economic efficiency they allegedly make possible. What I am calling constitutive arguments are those that claim that the ownership of property helps constitute some valued phenomenon or state of affairs, in particular, some aspect of the owner's personality or a virtuous life. I describe examples of each of these strategies in turn.

A. Historical Arguments

There are many attempts to justify private ownership based on historical circumstances or events. What they all have in common is a premise to the effect that property is justified (under certain conditions) because some individuals took some action in relation to the goods in question at some point in the past, usually acquiring the goods under conditions of nonownership. The specification of what such actions had to have been for ownership to have been established range from mere first declaration of ownership to complex stories about mixing one's labor with the good, incorporating the good as part of one's projects, and so on. Generally, however, such premises rest on claims either about people's *liberty*, what they morally *deserve*, and/or what their natural *rights* are.

The least plausible kind of historical argument is what we can call a "first declaration" account. Few philosophical arguments have ever rested on the view that merely declaring oneself the owner of a good could justify a title to it (even if there are others around who, in Rousseau's phrase, "are stupid enough" to respect one's claim). Although "first come first served" has some currency as a principle to decide disputes, it cannot stand alone as a justification of property. Therefore, such accounts are usually enriched by various conditions concerning the proper manner in which first acquisition had to have taken place for the property claim to be justified.

The most famous of such attempts to set out more robust conditions for the rightful appropriation of previously unowned goods is that of John Locke. Locke's much discussed argument centered on the claim that even in a state of nature, prior to the creation of civil society, everyone enjoys a natural right to his or her self and labor. The argument then proceeds as follows: "Labor being the unquestionable property of the laborer, no man but he can have a right to what that is once joined to, at least where there is enough, and as good left in common for others" (Locke's *Second Treatise of Government*, sec. 27). This states both the positive requirement—that labor be mixed with some unowned thing—as well as the proviso that limits this requirement—that enough be left for others (actually a second proviso was required by Locke, that the goods in question do not spoil while in the possession of the owner). Under these conditions, if a person "mixes" his or her labor with some unowned thing, the person acquires a natural right of ownership over that thing.

There are, in effect, two distinct ways this argument can be understood. In one version, the fact of self-ownership plays the crucial role, where because one mixes what one owns (one's self or labor) with some object, improving the condition of the latter, the object cannot be expropriated from one without a violation of right. In another version, labor and self-ownership are not crucially relevant to the justification; rather, the argument rests on the exercise of the natural right to "liberty," where this is construed as the right to act in ways that do not violate others' rights (and in this case, others' rights are defined according to the conditions set out be the proviso). The argument is that if one takes any action, such as appropriation of unowned material, that does not infringe the rights of others—in this case specified by the proviso that enough and as good be left for others—then one has a natural right to engage in that action, and hence one secures ownership rights over the object.

Many have raised questions about both these strategies. On the one hand, it is unclear what is meant by the "mixing" of labor with an object, in any but the simplest cases (why doesn't the person lose his or her labor rather than gain the new item; and what exactly is "mixed" with the object?). Moreover, it will be objected by all those unfree to use the appropriated item that the new owner did not secure their consent before engaging in the labor-mixing activity itself. It is therefore unclear why the appropriator should gain the new right that will be denied to the bystander, despite there being other material nearby of similar value.

As for the version of the argument based on the right to liberty, the major difficulty is drawing the "baseline" of welfare that defines the rights of those unable to acquire the new good. The idea behind the argument is that even for those left unable to acquire resources for themselves, the past acts of appropriation did not violate their liberty to appropriate if such past actions (and the system of private property built up around them) has not left them worse off than they would have been otherwise. But how is "otherwise" to be specified? It may be quite unclear just how much worse off those first acquisitions have actually made those bystanders, for it may be quite indeterminate what the various counterfactual events might have been if *they*—both the bystanders and all future people not then able to appropriate goods for themselves—had been the ones to first engage in the labor mixing with that particular bit of property, or if systems of property other than private property had been set up at the outset. Therefore, it will be unclear whether those first acts of acquisition violated the natural rights of nonowners.

One other important species of historical argument that does not rest on claims about our natural rights (to our labor or selves) has a structure quite similar to the ones just mentioned; these are arguments based on claims of moral desert. (Not all desert arguments, by the way, need be historical: one could claim that only a system of private property effectively awards deserving behavior as a general rule. Such an argument would belong in another category) The general form of such historical desert arguments is this: when a person has performed labor on some property, he or she has engaged in an activity that either displays some sort of human excellence (such as working hard) or confers a needed benefit on surrounding others (like making an object they may want to buy); and when nothing but property rights in the thing labored upon is a fitting and proportional reward for the beneficial behavior, then the person in question ought to be assigned property rights to those goods. The basic intuition motivating this argument is that "I worked on this, I've benefitted others in doing so, I therefore deserve to own it."

Briefly, the problems with this kind of argument that have been mentioned are the following: First, the benefit that might be afforded to others by an act of appropriation is a highly variable quantity, and is subject to a variety of interpretations. I have benefitted greatly from the efforts of those who discovered oil (whoever did that) and decided to manufacture it into gasoline. But it is not at all clear that I might benefit even more if the property rights of oil companies were to be heavily restricted, say through taxation and redistribution. Second, the proportionality requirements that all desert claims carry with them—that the good claimed as deserved is somehow proportional to the value of the beneficial activity engaged in—are notoriously indeterminate. Calibrations of proper rewards and punishments only seem determinate when they appear within a well-developed system of rules backed up by various cultural practices that give substance to intuitive associations between this or that act and this or that reward or punishment. Why do we give medals, for example, instead of free massages to our Olympic athletes? So without a determinate specification of which acts of first acquisition might deserve which kinds of benefits, arguments to the effect that it is ownership that is the deserved reward are not very promising.

For *all* historical arguments, however, a major objection will also be raised: the actual events of the history of resource acquisition in the real world has not conformed to the stringent conditions of acquisition spelled out by the arguments. Present-day titles to land and natural resources are sullied by a history of theft, military domination, fraud, and the like, so that even if conditions of first acquisition could be worked out that *would* justify property ownership, the actual history of property appropriation does not come close to meeting those conditions.

An exception to this last observation could be in the area of intellectual property, however. For those creations covered by patent and copyright law, it could be claimed that the creative act was undertaken under conditions free from force or fraud. Even there, however, for a right to such property to be grounded in historical framework just outlined, it must be the case that the "materials" used in the creative process—the labs, computers, musical instruments, and even the various ideas being shared and discussed in the society at large—must be fully owned by the creator or granted to her or him for that use.

B. Consequentialist Arguments

The most famous consequentialist strategy for defending private ownership is comprised of utility-based arguments that turn on the claim that a system of private ownership (or a particular claim by this or that owner) will yield the greatest net utility as compared to all other alternatives. Usually such arguments take an economic form and put emphasis on the incentive effects of the free markets that result from the protection of private ownership. These strategies turn on a range of assumptions concerning the connection between private ownership and free markets, the efficiency of such markets (either under ideal or less than ideal conditions), the preferences and motivations of market participants, and a positive moral appraisal of the goal of efficiency itself.

In the utilitarian version of this argument, it is claimed that social policy should be measured by the standard of maximizing utility (preference satisfaction, for example). Free, or nearly free, economic markets are the best mechanism for producing results that embody the greatest utility for participants. Private property systems are necessary for such competitive markets to operate. This is because, among other things, individuals are motivated to act in rational ways only if they can enjoy full control over the goods they own and can look forward to maximum—that is unregulated and untaxed—returns on their exchange behaviors. Therefore, private property ought to be protected with minimal interference by the state.

This argument is subject to a variety of standard criticisms. First, the question of whether efficient outcomes (defined in economic terms) should be used as a primary standard of morally valued states of affairs is open to debate. Many have questioned the austerity of the value categories that such arguments utilize for the measurement of outcomes. More generally, this argument is vulnerable to all the standard objections to utilitarianism as a moral theory. According to utilitarianism, all that counts in our moral appraisals is the degree to which maximal preference satisfaction, pleasure, or happiness has been produced. But many have argued that considerations other than simply consequences should bear on such judgments, or that, even if only consequences matter, it is not merely the *utility* involved in the resulting states of affairs that matters morally. Moreover, the standard of maximal utility is insensitive to the *distribution* of goods or utility in a society, and so a maximally efficient but highly unequal distribution of resources (of the sort even ideal markets will produce) is of questionable moral value.

Indeed, some economists have argued that for fully free markets to operate efficiently, owners must be allowed to trade not only any good they may own but also any particular right or set of rights they have over those goods. Now such claims are themselves subject to the criticisms of markets as a tool for optimal social policy, but, as pointed out above, they nevertheless suggest how free markets may in fact result in the dismantling of private liberal ownership—where owners tend to maintain the full spate of rights, liberties, and powers over their property. In many scenarios involving market trading, property rights may well become separated and diffused among various individuals, leaving none of them with full, private rights over particular goods.

In addition, *restricting* the exercise of ownership rights of particular persons will be necessary for competitive activity to be maintained. And as I suggested above, systems other than full liberal ownership can, allegedly, produce efficient economic outcomes. For these reasons, even if it is accepted that the operation of efficient markets are to be valued, it is not clear that private ownership will thereby be justified in the general array of cases, because the degree to which efficiency requires private ownership varies from situation to situation and depends on a number of variable factors.

Also, one can be a consequentialist where property is concerned without being either a utilitarian or an economist. One can claim, for example, that private property structures optimally maximize such things as liberty (political freedom for example), virtuous character, the reward of deserving behavior, or some other goal. One example of such a nonutilitarian, consequentialist argument is one that claims that a system of private property is uniquely effective in making possible a diverse and decentralized political environment, one which in turn produces the widest opportunities for nonconformist activity and the exercise of political liberties. (This is an argument associated with Milton Friedman: see *Capitalism and Freedom* (Chicago, IL: University of Chicago Press, 1962).) Such arguments will be convincing, however, only if the predictive premise that private property—and only private property—*best* produces the desired result. Skepticism about this premise will generally plague all manner of consequentialist defenses of property ownership.

C. Constitutive Arguments

What I am here labelling "constitutive" arguments are those that claim that the ownership of private property in some way helps constitute some valued state of af-

fairs. For example, it could be claimed that property ownership is part of the life of a virtuous or independent person. One of the most influential arguments of this sort connects private property with one of the components of personhood itself, or at least with the achievement of the highest potential of the (free) person. Such a claim is associated with the work of Hegel, who saw a connection between the acquisition and/or ownership of property and the full embodiment of the subjective self in the objective world. Freedom, in an idealized and positive sense, is only possible through property, on this view.

The tradition of philosophy which has put special emphasis on the enjoyment of "positive freedom"—the freedom to govern oneself and to effectively carry out one's plans and desires—has generally seen property in this manner. Another way to couch such an argument is in terms of autonomy: autonomy or "self-government" is a basic human good, basic to the idea of a dignified human existence; the control of one's material environment, in particular goods that make up one's personal life and domestic existence, is necessary for such autonomy. Private property affords individuals the fullest degree of such control and independence. Hence, private property should be protected.

The first thing to note about such arguments, however, is that insofar as the good in question—freedom, autonomy, a dignified existence—is a *universal* human value, and insofar as private property of some sort is necessary to realize that value, then it follows that property ought, as far as possible, be distributed to everyone, and insofar as the same amounts of property produce the same degree of freedom, and so on, then *equal* amounts of property should be given to all. The radically egalitarian nature of this conclusion may well conflict with the typically inegalitarian patterns of resource distribution which result from systems of private ownership, in particular capitalism. (This can also be said of arguments connecting property with virtue.)

Moreover, as has been pointed out by many commentators (Waldron, Christman, Radin), the enjoyment of autonomy or positive freedom may well be connected with some elements of property ownership, but by no means is it connected with all the incidents of private liberal ownership. The rights to use and control one's goods might be necessary for the full development of self-government, but the right to bequeath, exchange, and gain income from goods—those elements of private property most directly connected to capitalist economic markets—bear only a distant relation to that characteristic.

These are some of the traditional attempts to justify private property. Some philosophers have also argued, however, *against* the institution of property, not only because the arguments in its favor are seen as wanting, but also because property ownership is seen as somehow negative in itself. Instrumentally, private property could be viewed as a means to corruption and materialistic thinking. The rights afforded to owners, as well as the competitive markets that are built up around them, are seen as inimical to a virtuous, cooperative personality, and just social relations, and tend to produce social ills such as poverty and inequality. Although provocative, this argument suffers from the weakness in its speculative psychological premise, namely that individuals will be corrupted by the activities that their property rights make possible for them. Whether such results would ensue (or have ensued in capitalist settings) is the subject of much debate.

III. OWNERSHIP AND DISTRIBUTIVE JUSTICE

In most discussions of the right to private property, the question at issue is whether a particular individual or type of individual ought to be allowed to have rights over certain objects in the world. This issue is very much tied up, however, with the question of how resources ought to be distributed in a just society. The question of whether goods should be distributed according to need, desert, natural rights, virtue, or some other standard is very much connected to the question of what sort of property system is justified for a society. Property rights are intertwined with principles of distributive justice in at least two ways: the question of who should own what just *is* the question of distributive justice, and the question of what rights citizens ought to be afforded over their property—what ownership structure ought to be adopted for particular owners—is also a matter covered by principles of just social institutions.

In the arguments surveyed in the preceding section, it was assumed that if claims of ownership by certain classes of individuals could be justified, then the particular pattern of holdings in the society at large, no matter how unequal the distribution of those holdings might be, was itself justified. In this way, the justification of private property is seen as "distribution insensitive." However, if those arguments, and all similar arguments for private ownership, are seen as insufficient, then that gives greater credence to a "distribution sensitive"

system of property. Moreover, insofar as specific arguments for private property systems are seen as wanting, then more general principles of distributive justice—those demanding that goods be distributed according to some pattern of characteristics in the society—will provide the fundamental justification of property. In this way, the justification of property rights will merely be derivative from those more general distributive principles.

The assumption that private property will inevitably produce radically unequal distributive patterns is one shared by both defenders and critics of private property. Egalitarian critics of private property argue that distributive justice demands that resources be distributed according to patterns that run counter to those which would result from a private property regime, in particular that justice demands some measure of equality of wealth and unregulated private property systems produce inequality of wealth. From this observation, egalitarians mount a critique of the institution of private property. Defenders of private property similarly assume unequal distributive implications of that scheme but argue that *because* private property is justified, such inequalities are not inimical to social justice.

While it is surely the case that full liberal ownership of property, of the sort we have been considering, will produce such inequalities, it is a mistake to think that this package of property rights is the only kind available (or that the only alternative to liberal ownership is the complete public ownership of all goods). But many thinkers insist that to properly understand the relationship between principles of distributive justice and rights to property one must consider various elements in the property bundle separately, and evaluate the relationship between the different elements and the individual and social values being promoted.

For example, some philosophers and legal theorists have argued that some values, such as positive freedom, autonomy, and the achievement of one's full "personhood," are associated with particular elements in the property bundle but not others—with rights to use and control the items, for example, but not necessarily with the rights to trade and gain income from property. The argument is that putting special emphasis on those individual liberal values such as autonomy and freedom will not necessarily justify the systems of private property and capitalism traditionally associated with liberal societies, but rather they may well justify far more egalitarian systems of economic justice. In particular, such egalitarianism follows from the premise that such values should be universally protected in the population.

The rights to trade and gain income from property, however, serve different, and more social, purposes. Allowing individuals the rights to exchange and to retain the income from trades, gifts, or inheritance will have specifiable effects, especially on the distribution of resources for a society. Therefore, the particular property rights structures that are justified (or, correspondingly, particular sets of regulations and tax structures) will depend on the the kinds of distributive patterns thought to be acceptable or required. This connection, in turn, will depend on the behavioral and motivational assumptions being made about the participants in the economy. Moreover, economic outcomes may well be measured in terms quite different from the standards of efficiency and productivity (defined in narrowly economic terms) that are usually assumed. The effect of particular property structures on the nonhuman environment, for example, as well as on the culture and social institutions of society, may well be considered.

Therefore, the complexity that is evident in the structure of ownership demands that the rights and liberties enjoyed by owners be evaluated according to the varying values to which these various property rights give rise or express. This is especially true if one rejects all of the arguments for affording individuals *full* liberal ownership rights of the sort that traditional private property systems, and traditional models of free market capitalism, have assumed.

Also See the Following Articles

CONSEQUENTIALISM AND DEONTOLOGY • DEVELOPMENT ISSUES • DISTRIBUTIVE JUSTICE • MARXISM • PATENTS • UTILITARIANISM

Bibliography

Becker, L. (1977). *Property rights: Philosophical foundations*. Boston, MA: Routledge and Kegan Paul.

Bromley, D. W. (1991). *Environment and economy: Property rights and public policy*. Oxford: Blackwell.

Buckle, S. (1991). *Natural law and the theory of property: Grotius to Hume*. Oxford: Clarendon Press.

Christman, J. (1994). *The myth of property: Towards an egalitarian theory of ownership*. New York: Oxford University Press.

Epstein, R. (1985). *Takings: Private property and the power of eminent domain*. Cambridge: Cambridge University Press.

Gordon, W. (1993). A property right in self-expression: Equality and individualism in the natural law of intellectual property. *Yale Law Journal*, **102**, no. 7, 1533–1609.

Munzer, S. (1990). *A theory of property*. Cambridge: Cambridge University Press.

Penner, J. E. (1996). The "bundle of rights" picture of property. *UCLA Law Review*, **43**, no. 3, 711–820.

Radin, M. J. (1993). *Reinterpreting property*. Chicago, IL: University of Chicago Press.

Reeve, A. (1986). *Property*. Atlantic Highlands, NJ: Humanities Press.

Simmons, A. John (1992) *The Lockean theory of rights*. Princeton, NJ: Princeton University Press.

Waldron, J. (1988). *The right to private property*. Oxford: Oxford University Press.

PROSTITUTION

Igor Primoratz
Hebrew University

I. What Is Prostitution?
II. Prostitution and the Law
III. The Morality of Prostitution
IV. The Politics of Prostitution

GLOSSARY

blocked exchange The sale of a good that must not be bought and sold according to the understanding of that good prevailing in a society.

double standard The standard that makes one and the same action permissible, or at least excusable for a man, and impermissible for a woman.

harm principle The principle justifying legal restriction of individual liberty for the sake of preventing the individual from harming others.

legal moralism The view that the law may restrict individual liberty for the sake of enforcing positive morality.

legal paternalism The view that the law may restrict individual liberty in order to prevent the individual from harming himself/herself.

liberal feminism A trend in feminism combining feminist concerns with the liberal commitment to individual liberty as a paramount value.

offense principle The view that the law may restrict individual liberty in order to prevent acts that offend the feelings of others.

positive morality The set of moral beliefs, rules, and values accepted and enforced in a society.

prostitution The granting of direct sexual access for payment on a relatively indiscriminate basis.

radical feminism A trend in feminism calling for radical social change, and willing to countenance significant curtailment of individual liberty in order to eliminate the inequality and oppression of women.

sex industry The services catering to sexual needs and interests of consumers, including prostitution, pornography, sex shows, and sex surrogacy.

sex work Work in the sex industry.

surrogate motherhood The bearing of a child by a woman with the aim of turning it over to another woman. The embryo may have been conceived by the surrogate mother and a man (usually the partner of the woman who is to receive the child after birth) either by sexual intercourse or by artificial insemination, or it may have been conceived *in vitro* and transferred to the womb of the surrogate mother, who then carries the pregnancy to its termination.

PROSTITUTION is probably the most widespread variety of commercial sex. It seems to be a universal phenomenon, and more often than not a controversial one. In the past two centuries, in particular, there has been a continuing debate about its nature, causes, moral status, and the prospects of ridding society of it, as it has been widely considered, albeit for many different reasons, to be a "social evil." The central if not the sole means of continuing attempts to suppress, or at least regulate, the practice of prostitution has been legal coercion. But such attempts have had very limited and transitory success at best, and the advantages and disadvantages of criminalization or legal restriction of prostitution are still very much an open question.

The debates about prostitution in applied ethics have focused on two questions: Assuming it is socially undesirable, is there a sufficient justification for prohibiting or restricting it by law? And if it is indeed undesirable, is that because it is held to be immoral? If so, just why should it be thought immoral?

These debates have sometimes overlapped with the controversies about prostitution that have taken place in the political arena. Various movements for social and political reform have taken on the issue of prostitution. In modern feminism, in particular, there has been strong opposition to it, as it has been seen as a practice that both displays and reinforces the inequality, oppression, and degradation of women.

I. WHAT IS PROSTITUTION?

Prostitution is sex engaged for commercial reasons, rather than for its own sake; it is commercial or mercenary sex, sex as work. But the word "prostitution" does not merely refer to commercial sex; more often than not, it also carries a strong negative connotation which reflects the opprobrium of the practice felt by modern Western society (and other societies). Those who do not want to endorse this opprobrium, and in particular many prostitutes, have lately taken to using the expression "sex work" instead. While this may indeed be more appropriate in certain contexts, it cannot replace the older term in any discussion aiming at discernment and accuracy. For "sex work" is a much wider term covering, beside prostitution, other types of work in what may be called the "sex industry": pornography, sex shows, sexual surrogacy, etc. Prostitution is a type of sex work that involves granting the client direct sexual access. This may involve fully fledged sexual intercourse, but even if it does not, it differs from sex shows, for example, in that it normally provides sexual satisfaction to the client through direct physical contact of some sort.

Moreover, the provision of such service is relatively indiscriminate: just like any other type of service, within certain limits, anybody willing to pay the price asked will be accepted as a client. This distinguishes the prostitute from the mistress (kept woman) and the gigolo (kept man), as well as from the spouse in what used to be called a marriage of convenience. In the latter arrangements, sex is just as commercial as in prostitution, but is confined to a relationship with a single partner (client) over a period of time. The prostitute differs from them in being promiscuous, and indiscriminately so.

Prostitution, then, can be defined as the granting of direct sexual access for payment, on a relatively indiscriminate basis.

II. PROSTITUTION AND THE LAW

A. The Principles Involved

The legal status of prostitution today differs from one country to another. In most Western countries it is not against the law as such. Nevertheless, it is usually restricted or regulated by law. The extent of restriction and regulation varies, but in some countries the law prohibits certain activities closely, and even inevitably associated with prostitution, so that the overall effect on the practice is almost crippling. The basic question is whether the law should be interfering at all in the liberty of individuals to sell and buy sex. The answer will depend on the way one answers the even more basic question about the proper limits of legal restriction of individual liberty in general.

1. The Harm Principle

Those who accept only the harm principle will be likely to oppose the legal proscription of prostitution as such, as long as it involves only competent and consenting adults. But they may allow for a measure of legal regulation of the practice with a view to protecting public health. Moreover, their conception of public harms may be wide enough to call for certain restrictions on soliciting.

2. The Offense Principle

The offense principle is likely to lead to a similar stand on prostitution. In a society where the feelings of the average person tend to be seriously offended by encounters with the various aspects of prostitution, the principle will justify the imposition of certain legal restrictions in order to prevent such offense. This can be ensured by confining the practice and its attendant activities to certain venues, so that those who wish to engage in it can do so without much difficulty, while others need not be exposed to its manifestations unexpectedly and against their will.

3. Legal Paternalism

Unlike the two preceding principles, legal paternalism does provide arguments for making prostitution illegal. These arguments point to the various hazards to which the prostitute exposes herself: the high chance of contracting venereal and other disease (including AIDS), abusive or violent behavior of clients, exploitation by pimps and owners of brothels, extremely low social status, and ostracism by most of society. But such arguments are flawed: they assume the validity of the legal prohibition of prostitution (as well as of its conventional moral condemnation to which the law gives expression). But all these hazards are either caused or greatly enhanced by the illegality of prostitution. If prostitution were not a criminal offense and those who engage in it were not considered criminals, they could enjoy the same level of health protection as well as the same level of police protection from violence, exploitation, and fraud as everybody else; their social status would not be so low; and they would not be treated as social outcasts. To bring up the extremely adverse effects the legal prohibition of prostitution has on those who practice it as an argument supporting the prohibition is circular, and tantamount to adding insult to injury.

There is, however, one paternalist argument that is not circular in this way: the argument referring to the damage commercial sex is liable to inflict on the personal sexual and emotional life of those who provide it. This hazard is not a repercussion of society's condemnation of prostitution and the illegality of the practice, but is rather inherent to it. The prostitute normally performs her job with considerable detachment; but this detachment may spill over into her personal sex life, and perhaps bring about alienation from her sexuality and various emotional problems. However, there are other types of work that expose the individual to certain serious psychological and physical hazards, but which have not been made illegal on account of them.

The most that any plausible version of paternalism can justify are legal provisions ensuring that minors or incompetent persons do not engage in such hazardous work, and that competent adults are not forced or manipulated into it. This is no minor task, for prostitution has often involved minors, and has often been an occupation engaged in only under extreme pressure of social and economic circumstances, without full understanding of its nature and hazards, and sometimes even because of fraud or coercion. On the other hand, if a competent and well-informed adult makes a free choice of prostitution as a line of work, and the law prohibits her from engaging in it for paternalistic reasons, that

will presuppose an explicitly moralistic type of paternalism that claims to define and impose the "real" or "true" interest or welfare of the individual against the individual's own informed and free choice. But this type of paternalism will be unacceptable to anyone who accords any great value to individual liberty.

4. Legal Moralism

Finally, legal moralism will readily justify the criminalization of prostitution in those societies whose morality condemns it seriously enough. If one of the main tasks of the law is to express and enforce positive morality, and if the average person in a society (i) considers prostitution a moral issue, (ii) considers it to be of general, rather than merely personal, relevance, and (iii) condemns prostitution strongly enough, and responds to it with feelings of intolerance, indignation, and disgust, that will provide a case for making it illegal in that society. How many contemporary societies would satisfy these conditions is a question for the sociology of morals. But it is not an urgent one, since legal moralism is a philosophy of law unlikely to be adopted by anyone who considers liberty a basic moral and political value.

B. Practical Problems

Most contemporary societies (albeit not for the same reasons) respond to the phenomenon of prostitution by means of law and either make it illegal in order to eradicate it or impose various legal regulations and restrictions on it.

1. Criminalization

The criminalization approach, which is today best exemplified in the United States (with the exception of the state of Nevada), is plagued by a host of very serious problems. It flies in the face of experience of many centuries, which shows that prostitution cannot be legislated out of existence. Criminalization merely drives prostitution underground. This is true even of societies, such as the former Soviet Union, which made it a criminal offense and enforced the law vigorously, and then proclaimed that prostitution no longer existed within their boundaries. Whatever the rationale behind the criminalization approach—whether it is motivated by moral condemnation of the practice, by considerations of public health, or by paternalistic concerns for prostitutes themselves, and whether the aim is to eradicate prostitution or only to suppress it as much as any criminal behavior can be suppressed—the approach proves to be self-defeating. Prostitutes are practically forced to join forces with criminal elements in order to avoid apprehension, prosecution, and punishment on the one hand, and to cope with the problems posed by aggressive customers and extortionist landlords on the other. Making prostitution illegal also provides additional opportunities and temptations to police corruption. Finally, an important, and perhaps even unavoidable, method of enforcing the law and making arrests is the morally highly dubious one of entrapment: a plainclothes police officer poses as a potential customer in order to get the prostitute to offer her service, whereupon she gets arrested for doing so.

2. Restriction and Regulation

In countries such as Italy, France, or the United Kingdom, prostitution is not illegal as such, but various legal restrictions make it very difficult, if not impossible, to practice it in a law-abiding way. This casts doubts on the good faith of its decriminalization. Thus the law prohibits soliciting on the street (in France this includes "passive solicitation," so that a woman standing on the street doing nothing but "looking as if she is a prostitute" can be fined). Various provisions about "immoral earnings," "aiding and abetting prostitution," "cohabitation with a prostitute," etc., make it extremely difficult for a prostitute to live with a roommate, set up a family, and even rent an apartment for living and/or working.

In still other countries, such as Germany and Austria, prostitution is neither illegal in itself, nor crippled by the laws against various attendant activities, but is rather very thoroughly regulated by law. In particular, prostitutes must be registered; their work is then tolerated in certain "zones" in large cities, and off limits everywhere else. This approach has the drawback of making prostitution a long-term occupation for many who would otherwise engage in it only for a while but, having been formally labeled as prostitutes, find it very difficult to leave "the life." In general, the enforcement of the many provisions of the registration and zoning system tends to greatly circumscribe human and civil rights of prostitutes.

3. Legal Disengagement

In view of the extremely limited success of all the main approaches to prostitution in achieving their proclaimed objectives, and their many social disadvantages and moral flaws, some authors have suggested consistent legal disengagement. They propose that prostitution should be decriminalized, and that there should be no licensing, zoning, or any other restriction or regulation of the practice and its attendant activities, as long as it involves only competent adults. Only the

laws against force and fraud should apply, just as in any other occupation or commerce. As this approach has not been tried widely and consistently enough, it is still not possible to pronounce on its merits.

III. THE MORALITY OF PROSTITUTION

The other major question prostitution raises for applied ethics is that of its moral status. Many societies have morally condemned prostitution—some in very harsh terms. Western societies, in spite of the general liberalization of their sex mores in recent decades, still tend to see it as a serious moral wrong. This condemnation exacts a heavy toll on most prostitutes in all the main aspects of their working and private lives, both directly and indirectly, in so far as it affects the laws relating to the practice. Since the immorality of prostitution is not obvious beyond any doubt to any serious and decent person, its condemnation should be supported by argument. This section is a brief critical review of the main arguments advanced to establish its immorality.

A. Positive Morality

Many of these who view prostitution as morally wrong would, if challenged, refer to the condemnation of the practice by the morality of their society. But there are obvious philosophical reasons against accepting positive morality as the authority in moral questions. Indeed, if it were to be accepted as such, moral philosophy would have to be replaced by a sort of descriptive sociology of morals, whose findings would make independent and critical moral thinking both unnecessary and out of place.

One of the reasons against recourse to positive morality in settling moral questions is that this morality is a very unreliable guide, as its adoption would result in a sort of moral relativism. One and the same action or practice would be both right and wrong: right in one society, and wrong in another. Indeed, prostitution has been considered wrong in many societies, but there have also been societies that considered it morally indifferent.

Positive morality is also morally suspect, since it sometimes makes moral distinction where such distinctions should *not* be made. Prostitution is a case in point. Historically, its condemnation has been bound up with the double standard: positive morality that condemns prostitution also condemns the prostitute, but *not* the client, although both, equally and necessarily, participate in the proscribed action. This double standard informs not only conventional moral judgment on prostitution, but also legislation and law enforcement relating to the practice. Another morally unacceptable discrimination typical of positive morality has to do with the internal social and economic structure of the occupation. Social historians of prostitution have remarked that its conventional moral condemnation "varies significantly from the high-paid courtesan or call girl to the low-level prostitute, and generally the higher the fee the less the stigma" (V. and B. Bullough, *Women and Prostitution: A Social History,* p. 313. Prometheus Books, Buffalo, NY).

B. A Blocked Exchange

The shortest and probably most popular argument for the immorality of prostitution is that some things simply are not for sale, and that sex is one of them.

The first step of this argument will surely be granted; the view that not everything is fit to be bought and sold is most likely universal, although the list of what Michael Walzer has termed "blocked exchanges" (M. Walzer, 1983. *The Spheres of Justice,* pp. 100–103. Basic Books, New York) differs from one society to another. But the second, critical step makes sense only against the background of a conception of sex that explicitly blocks its exchange for money. There are two such conceptions.

1. Sex, Procreation, and Marriage

The traditional Judeo-Christian view ties sex to procreation as its natural purpose, and confines it to marriage as its proper framework. Adherents of this view will obviously think ill of prostitution as sex that is both extramarital and deliberately and consistently nonprocreative. But this does not mean that they should morally condemn it very harshly. The proper attitude for them to take is rather one of tolerance. For, as many thinkers have pointed out, although commercial sex is extramarital, it is not necessarily opposed to marriage or dangerous to it. On the contrary, it can be seen as a complementary and supporting practice, for it provides an additional outlet to a force that, in its sheer intensity and its pursuit of novelty and diversity, might otherwise endanger marriage and what it stands for.

This conclusion is supported by sociological research: in the United States, for example, up to 75% of clients of prostitutes are men who are and intend to remain married, and who seek in commercial sex the gratification they do not find with their wives.

2. Sex and Personal Relationships

In another influential view, sex is an important component of some highly significant personal relationships characterized by mutual feelings of closeness, concern, friendship, love, and the like. Those who subscribe to this view tend to deprecate and condemn prostitution for its impersonal and mercenary character. Sex as part of close personal relationships is a distinctively human, complex, rich, and fruitful experience, and a matter of great significance, while commercial sex is merely casual, a one-dimensional, barren experience that can give only a fleeting satisfaction and pertains to our animal nature.

If this were ground enough to morally condemn commercial sex, it would also be enough to condemn all casual sex. But it is not a valid ground for condemning either. It cannot even justify the denial of all value to casual sex in general, and commercial sex in particular. If A is much more valuable than B, that does not entail that B lacks any value whatsoever. And the understanding of sex as bound up with important personal relations can be plausibly advanced only as a (moral?) ideal, not as a moral norm that should, or indeed could, be legislated for all and sundry and enforced by the threat of moral sanctions for noncompliance. The only negative implication this, or any other ideal, can have concerning those who do not live in accordance with it is that they are missing out on something valuable. And even this conclusion would be established only if it could be shown that human beings cannot experience and enjoy, at different times and with different partners, both sex as part of significant personal relationships and casual (including commercial) sex.

C. The Marxist Critique of Prostitution

The Marxist account of prostitution is part and parcel of the Marxist analysis of capitalist society. It makes two main points about prostitution, each bringing out its continuity with another, more basic social practice characteristic of capitalism: with the bourgeois marriage, on the one hand, and with wage labor, on the other.

1. Prostitution within and without Marriage

Marxists depict the prostitute as a woman typically born and raised in a working class family and subjected to the same inequality, oppression, and exploitation that is the fate of her class in capitalism. She is forced into selling sex by economic necessity. But so is the woman in capitalist society who belongs to the other, exploiting class, albeit on somewhat different terms. Bourgeois marriage is no less a product of capitalist social and economic relations; therefore it is typically a relationship based on economic interest, rather than on mutual personal attraction—a marriage of convenience, not of love. This type of marriage

> turns often enough into the crassest prostitution—sometimes of both partners, but far more commonly of the woman, who only differs from the ordinary courtesan in that she does not let out her body on piecework as the wage worker, but sells it once and for all into slavery. (F. Engels, 1985. *The Origin of the Family, Private Property and the State.* Trans. A. West. p. 102 Penguin, Harmondsworth)

The wording is too strong, but it makes a valid point: while conventional morality legitimizes bourgeois marriage and condemns prostitution, both are basically types of mercenary sex.

But the moral import of this sociological point (which has also been made by feminists) is ambiguous. Those not already committed to morally rejecting commercial sex may take it as showing that prostitution is no worse than marriage of convenience, and since such marriage is perfectly legitimate, so is prostitution. Those who already condemn commercial sex will draw the opposite conclusion: since marriage of convenience is not much different from prostitution, it ought to be rejected too. While some liberals would draw the former conclusion, Marxists opt for the latter. In a truly human society as they depict it, people would both have sex and marry out of mutual personal attraction, not for extrinsic economic or social reasons. Such a society, of course, can evolve only after the dismantling of capitalism.

2. The Work of Prostitution and the Prostitution of Work

Marxists also argue that prostitution in the usual sense is but a special case of prostitution in a wider sense of "use of one's capacity is an unworthy way," which is the fate of wage labor in general in capitalist society. The capacity of working, and indeed the need to work, is a defining trait of human nature: it is in work that a human being expresses both his or her generic humanity and his or her personality. In a truly human society, therefore, humans would work in order to express themselves in their work, rather than in order to earn

money to support themselves and their dependents, as they must do in capitalism. In other words, in a truly human society, work (just like sex) would be an activity performed and experienced as valuable in itself, while in capitalism it is "alienated," reduced to a means to something else, and thereby "prostituted" in the wider sense of the word.

This point, again, lends itself to different moral interpretations. Liberals would construe it as saying that prostitution is merely a type of wage labor, a service, an occupation morally on a par with any other. Marxists, on the other hand, see it as a condemnation of all wage labor as on a par with prostitution, which is taken to be morally repugnant.

> Prostitution is only a particular expression of the general prostitution of the worker, and because prostitution is a relationship which includes both the person prostituted and the person prostituting—whose baseness is even greater—thus the capitalist, too, . . . is included within this category. (K. Marx, 1977. *Selected Writings.* Ed. D. McLellan. p. 90. Oxford Univ. Press, Oxford)

While liberals see the prostitute as but a wage worker, Marxists see the capitalist employer as but a pimp.

3. Critical Comments

An evaluation of the Marxist contribution to the debate about prostitution will largely depend on the assessment of the accuracy of the sociological analysis of capitalism and of the appeal and relevance of the Marxist ideal of a truly human society. Such large questions cannot be properly discussed in this article—two brief remarks must suffice.

The claim that women in capitalism take up prostitution out of sheer economic necessity is too simplistic. What research shows is that in some cases prostitution is indeed the only way out of circumstances of extreme need (and, today, the need for money generated by drug addiction in particular). But it is also often chosen as the line of work that enables women to earn much more than any other available option, or because of the relative independence and flexibility it allows, when compared to other types of work.

On the other hand, the ideal society in which there is no need and no occasion for the use of sex as a means to an ulterior purpose and in which, accordingly, people engage in sex solely out of mutual attraction has no prospect of ever coming true in our world. The ideal involves a sort of sexual preestablished harmony in which every desire meets with a complementary desire, while no persons too unattractive to be sexually desired by others exist.

D. The Feminist Critique of Prostitution

Today, the discussion about the morality of prostitution is largely a debate between those who consider it a service, morally legitimate like any other and those who hold that it is deeply morally flawed, since it is essentially bound up with the inequality, degradation, or oppression of women. The concern for the suffering of, and the injustice done to, women is definitive of feminism, while the former position can be termed liberal. But the positions cannot be delineated so neatly. Feminism is a wide and varied school of thought; it includes liberal feminism, which does not share the radical feminists' rejection of prostitution. And one need not subscribe to the tenets of feminism in order to appreciate some of the arguments concerning prostitution usually put forward by feminists.

To be sure, one might question the feminist approach to prostitution (and the way prostitution is being discussed in this article) as an occupation of women. A prostitute is not by definition a woman; there are male prostitutes also. But this is not a weighty objection. Historically, prostitution has been overwhelmingly a woman's line of work. Moreover, most male prostitutes have catered to the needs of other (homosexual) males.

1. Degradation of Women

Many feel that the selling of sex is degrading. There are four main arguments for this claim: (a) mercenary sex is impersonal, (b) the client's attitude to the prostitute is purely instrumental, (c) sex is an intimate matter, and (d) the prostitute sells her body or herself.

(a) The argument from the impersonal nature of prostitution is incomplete. The impersonal character of a social transaction as such does not make that transaction degrading. Indeed, we have personal relations only with a limited number of other people: our family, friends, and acquaintances. All our remaining social transactions and relations are, and must be, impersonal. And one's impersonal attitude to another person, e.g., to one's barber, implies no disrespect and in no way degrades that person. If it is objected that giving others sexual satisfaction is not at all like giving them haircuts, the objection will only display that it is assuming what needs to be shown by argument, namely that sex ought always to be personal. Among the main theories of the nature and value of human sexuality, only the "personal relationships" account might seem to imply this—and that, as we have seen (III.B.2), is a false impression.

That account can be plausibly advanced only as a sexual ideal. Those who adopt that ideal rightly point out that commercial sex is not at all like it; but falling short of an ideal is by no means tantamount to being degrading.

(b) A second argument is that the client relates to the prostitute as but a means to his sexual gratification, thus reducing her to a mere means—a thing, a sex object—and that is surely degrading.

If he were to rape the prostitute, he would certainly be treating her with utter disregard for her autonomy, and thus reducing or degrading her to a mere means. Being a customer rather than a rapist, he gets sexual gratification from her for a charge, on the basis of a mutual understanding, and she does her part in the bargain willingly. No coercion or fraud is involved. Therefore the prostitute's autonomy, her status as a person, is not denied or violated, and she is not degraded on that count.

Just as most of our social transactions and relations are and must be impersonal, so most of them are and must be instrumental. And just as the fact that A relates to B in an impersonal way does not amount to a violation of B's personhood, so the fact that A relates to B only in an instrumental way does not amount to A's reducing B to a mere means. In both cases B's free and informed consent removes the ground for any such charge, and therefore also for the charge of degradation.

(c) Sex is indeed an intimate part of our lives. But if commercially motivated disregard of the bounds of intimacy is to be judged degrading, we shall have to say that a paid nurse who attends to the intimate hygiene of disabled patients is also doing something degrading.

(d) The claim that prostitution degrades is also present in the traditional view of the prostitute as a woman who sells her body—indeed sells herself. This view can be explicated by saying that sex and sexuality are constitutive of the body. Sexuality and the body are inseparable from one's conception of one's gender. And all these are constitutive of one's sense of identity—one's understanding of who one is. Therefore, when sex is sold, so is the body and the self.

However, if we accept this line of argument as showing that the prostitute sells her body and herself, and thereby does something degrading, we shall have to maintain the same about the wet nurse and the surrogate mother, for their bodies and gender are no less involved in what they do, and they too do that for a fee. This conclusion seems clearly unacceptable in the case of the wet nurse. The practice of surrogate motherhood is controversial, but the concerns that have been voiced about it do not relate to the argument that links body, gender, and the self.

Indeed, if we attend to what actually goes on between the prostitute and the client and on what terms, it is clear that the transaction is most accurately described as the sale of a sexual service, rather than the sale of a body, let alone of a self. (The latter two descriptions might be appropriate only in the case of a person selling himself or herself into slavery.)

2. Inequality of Women

Another standard feminist objection to prostitution is that it both epitomizes and reinforces the inequality of women. The mere fact that the overwhelming majority of prostitutes are, and always have been, women catering to the sexual needs and preferences of men might be thought evidence enough for this claim.

According to a more elaborate version of this objection, prostitution is "an inherently unequal practice defined by the intersection of capitalism and patriarchy" (C. Overall, 1991/1992. *Signs, 17*, p. 724). Unlike other types of woman's work which can, but need not, be performed on a commercial basis, prostitution is essentially an exchange between a socially inferior seller and a socially superior buyer. This relation of inequality is multidimensional, but its central dimensions are those of class and gender. The social and economic conditions of capitalist patriarchy make a reversal of this relation quite unlikely, and equality of men and women in the sex industry an utterly unrealistic goal. On the other hand, with the demise of capitalist patriarchy, prostitution would no longer be needed nor, indeed, possible.

This argument has obvious flaws. Prostitution both predates and survives capitalism, while this account defines out of existence all prostitution taking place in other types of society. And it does not do justice to the complexity of the practice in capitalist patriarchy, which also includes much sex commerce between members of the same social class.

3. Oppression of Women

According to Simone de Beauvoir, the prostitute "sums up all the forms of feminine slavery at once" (1988. *The Second Sex*. Trans. and Ed. H. M. Parshley. p. 569. Pan, London). This may not be very plausible with regard to prostitution as such, but it has been argued that the practice is indeed implicated in the oppression of women in modern Western societies.

Prostitution in these societies is said to both express and reinforce certain assumptions about men, women, and sex that have far-reaching implications. The most important of these assumptions are that men are "naturally" dominant and that sex with men pollutes and harms women. The latter view is implicit in the use of

four-letter verbs for sexual intercourse, which assumes that the male is the active and the female the passive side. The same verbs are also used in nonsexual contexts to refer to the taking advantage of, or harming, somebody. This points to a conception according to which when a man and a woman have sex, the man is the active side causing the pollution or inflicting harm, and the woman the passive side being polluted or harmed.

These assumptions determine the meaning of sex in general, and commercial sex in particular, in modern Western society. They justify the oppression of women and harm both prostitutes and women in general.

However, it is not at all clear that modern Western society still subscribes to these assumptions about men, women, and sex as strongly as it may have done several decades ago. The view about men as "naturally" dominant has surely lost much ground. As for the conception of sex implied in the vulgar language about it, such language has never been used universally, and cannot be considered the standard way of talking about sex. Therefore, the conception of sex embedded in it cannot be *the* conception of sex in modern Western society. And if it is not, the above no longer amounts to an argument against prostitution in modern Western society; it is at best an argument against certain instances, or types, of commercial sex in it.

E. Conclusion

It seems, then, that none of the main moral arguments against prostitution are entirely convincing. If so, and if the traditional moral condemnation of the practice is not self-evidently true—as it certainly is not to many intelligent and decent persons—the conclusion must be that prostitution is not necessarily immoral— immoral in itself.

To say this is not to commend prostitution. Even if it is not positively immoral, most of the time it surely leaves much to be desired in comparison with both sex people have just for the enjoyment of it on the basis of mutual attraction and sex as part of a more complex and significant personal relationship. But it does mean that the conventional moral condemnation of prostitution, and the pressure of the moral sanction many societies have brought to bear on the prostitute (but almost never on the client), at a great human cost to her, lacks rational justification and is morally suspect.

Many Marxist and feminist critics of prostitution insist that we should not be trying to understand and judge it in the abstract, but rather within its social and cultural context. When approached in this way, they argue, it can be seen to be symptomatic of, and implicated in, the inequality, exploitation, and oppression of women. Now this is not true of many noncapitalist societies, nor of all types of prostitution in capitalist societies. But it may well be true of many varieties of commercial sex to be found in contemporary capitalist society. Thus this line of criticism, when appropriately refocused, does make important points—not about prostitution as such, but about a considerable part of the practice as it exists in our society. When we look closely at prostitution as it actually exists in our own society, we find that much of it is bound up with such legal, social, and economic conditions that it does express and tend to reinforce the inequality, exploitation, or oppression of women. In so far as it does, it is indeed morally unacceptable.

IV. THE POLITICS OF PROSTITUTION

Prostitution is also a political issue. Legal and moral considerations such as those already reviewed have played a part in the debates about the way society should relate to the practice that have been particularly intense in the past two centuries.

A. The Feminist Position

In the 19th century prostitution was a major issue for the emerging feminist movement, in particular in Britain. There feminists initially opposed the laws regulating prostitution, felt to be discriminatory on the basis of both class and gender. Later on their efforts focused on attempts to do away with involuntary and child prostitution. This eventually evolved into a movement for the eradication of all prostitution. By that time feminists were pursuing their objectives in a somewhat problematic coalition with reactionary "social purity" movements, and were involved in a crusade against a wide array of practices considered morally suspect.

On the issue of prostitution, contemporary feminists are, by and large, heirs to their predecessors. Advancing arguments such as those already canvassed (III.D), they tend to strongly oppose all prostitution. However, this rejection of prostitution is not shared by liberal feminists who, on this issue, side with other liberals, rather than with radical feminists. Another important qualification concerns the methods: while 19th century feminists wanted to abolish prostitution by means of criminal law, contemporary feminist critics of prostitution usually do not support its legal repression, but propose to eliminate it in other ways.

B. The Liberal Position

Liberals hold that there is nothing morally wrong with prostitution as such, and that it should accordingly be treated simply as a service like any other. But they are by no means oblivious to the moral and social problems plaguing much of the practice as it actually exists in contemporary society. They tend to call for moral, legal, and social change that would alleviate, if not completely eliminate, such problems, and make it possible for prostitutes to work in much healthier social conditions.

A characteristic example of this approach is the argument for "sound prostitution" in Lars O. Ericsson's seminal 1980 article (*Ethics, 90,* 335–366). As most, if not all, moral and social ills affecting prostitution as it is practiced today are direct or indirect consequences of its harsh condemnation by conventional morality, the first and most important precondition of a sound prostitution is that we abandon this attitude to commercial sex. It should be abandoned for two reasons: because it cannot withstand rational scrutiny and therefore turns out to be mere prejudice, and because of the human misery it causes. Prostitution should be decriminalized. The law should recognize that prostitutes have the same rights as anyone else, including the right to rent premises for their work. They should be given the same legal protection from economic exploitation enjoyed by those pursuing any other line of work. Steps should be taken to eliminate prostitution of minors (on paternalistic grounds), and to ensure that it is practiced only by competent adults who choose to do so as freely as any other occupation may be said to be freely chosen. Finally, prostitution—as an occupation and as a service—should be equally available to men and women (Ericsson, 1979/1980, pp. 361–366).

C. The Prostitutes' Position

There is, of course, no single understanding of the nature and status of prostitution that can be ascribed to prostitutes in general. But with the emergence of the international movement for prostitutes' rights in the past two decades, prostitutes now have a venue for articulating their position on the questions concerning their work and their lives. This development is especially significant because, historically, those who have participated in the debates about prostitution and the proper social response to it, including both 19th century and contemporary feminists, have as a rule taken a paternalistic attitude to prostitutes, and presumed to speak on their behalf without making any sustained effort to enable them to speak for themselves.

Politically active prostitutes resent this, as well as the assumption that their occupation is necessarily degrading and never freely chosen, and that their work and their lives are but examples of social pathology. According to a statement issued at the Second World Whores' Congress in 1986

> many prostitutes identify with feminist values such as independence, financial autonomy, sexual self-determination, personal strength and female bonding. However, prostitutes reject support that requires them to leave prostitution; they object to being treated as symbols of oppression and demand recognition as workers. Due to feminist hesitation or refusal to accept prostitution as legitimate work and to accept prostitutes as working women, the majority of prostitutes have not identified as feminists.... (G. Pheterson, Ed., 1989. *A Vindication of the Rights of Whores,* p. 192. Seal Press, Seattle, WA. Quotations used by permission of the publishers. Copyright © 1989 Gail Pheterson.)

On the crucial issue of rights, they describe the existing state of affairs in the following way:

> At present, prostitutes are officially and/or unofficially denied rights ... [...] ... Denial of human rights to prostitutes is publicly justified as a protection of women, public order, health, morality and the reputation of dominant persons or nations. Those arguments deny prostitutes the status of ordinary persons and blame them for disorder and/or disease and for male exploitation of and violence against women. Criminalization or state regulation of prostitution does not protect anyone, least of all prostitutes. Prostitutes are systematically robbed of liberty, security, fair administration of justice, respect for private and family life, freedom of expression and freedom of association.... They suffer from inhuman and degrading treatment and punishment and from discrimination in employment and housing. (Pheterson, 1989, p. 103)

Politically active prostitutes want society to acknowledge that a prostitute is "a worker like any other worker" and "a woman with rights" (Pheterson, 1989, p. 68). They affirm "the right of all women to determine their own sexual behavior, including commercial exchange, without stigmatization or punishment" (Pheterson, 1989, p. 194). And they oppose criminalization and state regulation of prostitution, while calling for positive measures basically similar to, but much more specific than, those favored by liberals (Pheterson, 1989, pp. 40–42, 103–108, 141–143).

Also See the Following Articles

AUTONOMY • FEMINIST ETHICS • LIBERALISM • MARX AND ETHICS • PATERNALISM • SEX EQUALITY • VICTIMLESS CRIMES • WOMEN'S RIGHTS

Bibliography

Bullough, V., and Bullough, B. (1987). "Women and Prostitution: A Social History." Prometheus Books, Buffalo, NY.

Ericsson, L. O. (1979/1980). Charges against prostitution: An attempt at a philosophical assessment. *Ethics* **90**, 335–366.

Jaggar, A. M. (1991). Prostitution. In "The Philosophy of Sex: Contemporary Readings" (A. Soble, Ed.), 2nd ed. Rowman & Littlefield, Savage, MD.

McLeod, E. (1982). "Women Working: Prostitution Now." Croom Helm, London.

Overall, C. (1991/1992). What's wrong with prostitution? Evaluating sex work. *Signs: J. Women Culture Soc.* **17**, 705–724.

Pateman, C. (1988). "The Sexual Contract," chap. 7. Polity, Cambridge.

Pheterson, G. (Ed.) (1989). " A Vindication of the Rights of Whores." Seal Press, Seattle, WA.

Primoratz, I. (1993). What's wrong with prostitution? *Philosophy* **68**, 159–182. Reprinted in "Human Sexuality." (1997). (Primoratz, I., Ed.). Ashgate, Aldershot.

Richards, D. A. J. (1982). "Sex, Drugs, Death, and the Law," chap. 3. Rowman & Littlefield, Totowa, NJ.

Schwarzenbach, S. (1990/1991). Contractarians and feminists debate prostitution. *N. Y. Univ. Rev. Law Social Change* **18**, 103–130. Reprinted in "Human Sexuality." (1997). (Primoratz, I., Ed.). Ashgate, Aldershot.

Shrage, L. (1994). "Moral Dilemmas of Feminism: Prostitution, Adultery, and Abortion," chaps. 4–6. Routledge, New York/London.

PSYCHIATRIC ETHICS

Jocelyn Y. Hattab
Eitanim Mental Health Center

GLOSSARY

borderline A pathological condition characterized by affects lability, poor reality testing, and poor social relations; considered a personality disorder.

conscious (subconscious, unconscious) According to psychoanalytical theory, the topics of the mind with separate functions in conflict emergence and resolution. Conscious is mainly the "place" of the ego and its functions in solving real or imagined problems and conflicts.

hallucinations Perceptions by senses (hearing, seeing, touching, smell, and taste) of nonexisting objects.

neurotransmitters Chemicals that play a role in transmission between neurocells. Some of them are serotonine, dopamine, and so on. These are thought to play a crucial role in psychopathology.

psychotherapy All therapeutic procedure that uses nonbiological technics, such as speaking, playing, arts, sports, and so on, to treat mentally disturbed persons or to improve mental functioning.

psychotropic drugs Chemicals that influence mental functions and disorders, such as antidepressants, neuroleptics (antipsychotics), and sleeping drugs, but also "bad drugs."

schizophrenia A severe and chronic pathological condition characterized by thought and affect disorders and deterioration of personality.

PSYCHIATRY is the part of medicine that deals with mental disorders. As with every other medical discipline, psychiatry involves research, training, and prophylaxis. Psychiatry is specifically related to psychology, human development, law, anthropology, culture, and ideologies, and in certain aspects, politics.

This article will cover the ethical issues relevant to all aspects of psychiatry. The history of psychiatry is the history of the attitudes of societies toward their mentally disturbed members. As such, it is also the history of ethics. "Tell me how you treat your fools, I will tell you who you are!" The mentally ill have been and are still the object of our lowest human instincts. During World War II, mentally ill persons were among the first to be deported and exterminated. In ancient Greece, they were executed at the moment of diagnosis. During the Middle Ages they were used by nobles for their entertainment. In the former Soviet Union psychiatric disorders were an excuse for political harassment. In most modern societies, psychiatric patients are the victims of stigmatization and to some degree of segregation. Psychiatric hospitals are generally built outside of the cities because of the general fear of the mentally ill. This historical survey will be described extensively and will stress the relevant ethical issues.

Mental health and mental disorders have given rise to many theories, but none is fully satisfactory. Alexander and Selesnick in their *History of Psychiatry* propose three main theories: mental functions and disorders are brain functions and disturbances, as such, brain research and psychiatric research overlap but the holistic view of the human being is eluded; second, human beings have an inorganic mind, with the brain being only a tool for translating mind functions into reality. The third theory relies on magic, gods, and witches for explaining mental functions and disorders. More modern theories, such as the antipsychiatric movement, Thomas Szasz's positions, and Foucault have modified society's view considerably and focused concern on psychiatry. All theories have ethical implications that are relevant to the care of and approach toward people who behave and think differently. But, to what extent! Cultural, developmental, and individual factors are highly significant in this determination of normality and abnormality. These factors must be considered carefully. According to these theoretical considerations, nosographic systems are established that define by vote, as in the DSM (*Diagnostic and Statistical Manual*) system, or by consensus, as in the ICD (International Classification of Diseases), who is ill and must be treated. In one system the homosexual is a patient, in another, a normal person. These statements have also political and economical consequences. The prophylaxis of mental disorders is a controversial issue. No single measure has been proved to be as efficient as immunizations are for infectious diseases! However, it seems to be possible to reduce some disorders by adequate policy measures such as the improvement of early infant–mother relations, the involvement of fathers in child rearing, genetic counseling, and so on. But as stated by Gerald Caplan, the cost of these dubious measures on a large scale, is by no means incomparable to the cost of the treatment of a few patients.

Research in the medical sciences in general and in psychiatry in particular has been well codified. However, informed consent, freedom of participation, confidentiality, dependency versus autonomy of patients and so on, must be reconsidered and elaborated in psychiatry. Because the animal model is hardly useful in psychiatric research most experiments have to be done with human subjects who are by definition not in the normal state of mind to give consent and to understand information. It is well known in psychiatric hospitals that psychotic and borderline patients have a subconscious influence on staff relations and functioning.

Relations between professionals in mental health and in other systems have to be open to an ongoing discussion, in order to prevent the misuse of patients and burnout in workers. Staff meetings are an ethical requirement in hospital and other residential settings. The therapeutic community model established by Kernberg is more efficient and respectful to ethical duty for open and free expression by patients and staff members. There is no etiological treatment for mental disorders. However, neuroleptics and psychotherapeutic procedures have revolutionized psychiatry. Although the efficacy of psychotropic drugs no longer has to be proved, they all have side effects that must be considered. Every prescription must be carefully weighed according to its potential advantages and disadvantages.

Psychotherapies are expensive and time consuming but they offer real relief to most patients and on some occasions, they can be considered an etiological treatment.

A society must protect itself and each of its members. Some psychiatric patients can be "dangerous to themselves and/or others". These people must be treated and protected, even if in a compulsory way. Compulsory hospitalization must be strictly ruled and supervised by law. These regulations, although necessary, are contrary to basic civil rights. Law and psychiatry share many concerns that must be clarified in order not to confound roles and responsibilities. Psychiatrists should not judge their delinquent patients, and judges are not allowed to treat the accused.

Child and adolescent psychiatry share the same concern for ethics as general psychiatry. Being dependent upon their parents and other adults, children must be protected from all sorts of abuse. Children are the first victims of divorce disputes and they are the focus of adoption procedures and other placements. Ethical concerns should be a part of all such decisions.

We are strongly opposed to the idea of relying on ethicists to make decisions in place of the firstline physician. The ethicist will be at best a referral for better understanding and relevant knowledge, but the ethical decision must be made by whoever is in charge of the specific case.

Training in ethics cannot be only formal and academic. It must include the personal example of seniors for younger trainees and also by joint meetings with peers and experienced colleagues.

All of these and other issues will be discussed extensively, not only by questioning, as is normal in ethics literature, but by making recommendations and taking positions on these issues.

I. DEFINITION OF ETHICS

There are many definitions for ethics and every author uses his or her own understanding of this complicated concept. These differences sometimes lead to misunderstandings and even to accusations of unethical behavior or thoughts, which is by itself unethical.

To be understood and followed in my discussion, I first have to explain my conception of ethics. It is based on the Talmudic sentence proposed by Hillel: "The Wise Man." Once, a Gentile came to him and asked to convert him (to Judaism) while he stood on one foot! Hillel answered: "Don't do to your fellow what is hated by you; now, go and learn!" Hillel's answer has two facets that are equally relevant to ethics. Whatever you propose or decide for your patient, whether medication, hospitalization, psychotherapy, or a court report, you have to ask yourself first if you were this patient or his family, would you appreciate or agree with this proposition and the way it is given? My understanding of ethics is mainly practical rather than philosophical or scientific. Do I behave in a way that is acceptable to me if I were the patient or the patient's family, but also as a citizen and a member of the human race? This conception causes many problems. My patients sometimes do not understand their own well-being and in some cases I have to impose on them their treatment or other dispositions. I will discuss this issue further. This is to say that ethics can never be a clear-cut decision. Ethics is formulated by dilemmas. If an ethical proposition is clearly and generally accepted it has to be legislated and formulated as a law, and then it is no longer ethical. For many years it was ethical to report on child abuse in the family; now in most Western countries it is legally required. To obey the law is not to be ethical, but observant or afraid either of God, the judges, or the police. In this example we can see the core of the ethical dilemma. On one hand we have the obligation to protect a child under threat for his or her life, and on the other hand we have the fundamental right to privacy in the family. But because this dilemma has been resolved, and a law enacted, there is no more room for ethical discussion.

Must a society reach such an ideal that all ethical issues are resolved and lawful? As is apparent in traditional Jewish law (the Halacha), who deals with affects like "loving the other as himself" or forbids jealousy or hate? Judge Barak, president of the Israeli Supreme Court, defends the statement that every human act is or has to be included in the legal system, the power of the Court, "even dreaming." If dreaming is not yet subject of law it is because there are more urgent issues to deal with. Barak's former vice-president, Judge Elon, claims the opposite. Only behaviors and acts that are relevant for the given society are of interest for legal system, certainly not dreaming! It is in the best interest of a society to have laws that regulate the well-being of its members and prevent delinquency, abuses, and suffering. However, ethical dilemmas will reflect the changes in a developing society.

Ethical issues are formulated as dilemmas between two good solutions, between two values that are more or less equally justified. The first and obligatory step in any ethical discussion is to formulate the questions raised by the given problem. To be ethical is first to question any issue, to acknowledge that there can be many possible answers to the same problem, and that many people can defend various, equally valuable opinions. This statement implies liberalism and open-mindedness. But to only ask and formulate questions is not enough to behave ethically. It can be even unethical to leave questions open. As stated by Hillel the Wiseman, "go and learn!" Ethics implies involvement in action and continuous learning, for there cannot be definitive answers, the world is changing, new problems arise, societies develop, and solutions have to be adapted to this evolution. The second and unavoidable step in an ethical behavior is to give answers, to cut on only one hand and not stay forever in a "two-handed" approach. Unfortunately, most publications on ethics contain a list of "two-handed problems" and questions. That is certainly important by itself, but is not enough to be ethical. Patients and families, a society as a whole, cannot function on questions alone, even if they are wonderfully formulated. They need clear-cut solutions and recommendations. It is unethical to leave a patient, a family, or a society without clear responses to their ethical dilemmas. Their free choice will be to accept or reject these solutions. It is the responsibility of the physician or of the health professional to give the expected answer. I am strongly opposed to relying on ethicists, or on specialists in ethics, to make decisions. Of course, some people have more knowledge on ethics through their readings and participation in specific seminars and conferences. They only can function as advisors, but they can never make decisions in the place of the directly involved doctor in a given case. In some situations, such as resuscitation of impaired premature newborns, research or compulsory hospitalization, a committee can be appointed to take these decisions, but the most important member of these committees has to be the family doctor or the professional directly involved in this case.

II. DEFINITION OF PSYCHIATRY

"Psychiatry is part of medicine." This statement has to be repeated, because it is still being questioned by many, including medical doctors. "It is the bridge between the *soma* and the *psyche*, between the physical, humanistic, and behavioral sciences, with the difference that the measuring apparatus is inductive and subjective (Bernal y del Rio). Whatever our conception on mind/brain relations, human beings have psychic functions, including cognitive, affective, and fantastic functions. These functions are explored and learned by psychology as physiology learns somatic functions. These functions can be impaired quantitatively and qualitatively. Assessment, diagnosis, care, and treatment of these impairments are the role of psychiatry in medicine. That is a narrow definition of psychiatry; as such, the ethical duty of the psychiatrist is reduced to the functions listed above.

However, psychic functions are activated and sometimes affected in any human condition and specifically during development and illnesses, and during social and family changes. The person is made of soma and psyche, they are continuously activated one by each other. In this broad concept, the scope of psychiatry is extremely large and as such, the ethical duties of the psychiatrist go beyond psychopathology to development, culture, social issues, and somatic illnesses.

Psychiatry is strongly linked to anthropology. Psychopathology is influenced by social, cultural, and religious features. Christians hallucinate Jesus, and Jews, Moses. Assessment, diagnosis, and especially treatment have to take into account these crucial elements. It is unethical, and professionally stupid, to use in an indifferent way the same tools for all people. This problem is more pressing in this era of mass migration from the Third World to Europe and North America. Very few centers have as members of their staffs professionals from different cultural origins who speak different languages. Migrants have to cope with a new culture, a new language, and new norms in a time of deep stress for having left behind the familiar.

III. ETHICS OF HISTORY AND THEORIES

Alexander and Selesnick, in their *History of Psychiatry,* describe three main strands in explaining mental functions and disorders: the *organismic theory* in which the brain is the mind, and all psychic functions are expressions of brain disorders or damages. In the *animistic theory,* the brain is only the translator of mind. The third theory is linked with *magic, sorcery* and in our modern world, sociological and philosophical theories. The first two of these theories confront us again with Brain/Mind relations and as such with bioethics.

Bioethics acknowledges that human beings, in their biological dimension, are the subject of moral consideration, from at least the time of birth until their death. Both the spiritualistic approach, where mind is the person's *primum movens* and only specificity, and the materialistic one, where one's psychic functions are but brain interactions, defend the basic human right to be respected in the body. This seems evident, but nothing can be accepted as is evident after the *Shoa* (holocaust), and nothing is evident in human mental functioning. Nothing is evident for an ethical discussion. All evidence must be questioned.

Bioethics can be discussed in two different ways, either by approaching human beings as a whole or by considering every new technique or science as such and discussing the ethical problems that are raised by this technique or science.

Psychiatry has a long tradition of moral concern toward people. Mental health professionals do not have to be told about the uniqueness of each person. Given this, a patient should be involved in any procedure, whether clinical or research or social or educational, only if this procedure is of direct interest for him as a person, if he understands and accepts it, and if it does not cause any harm.

Neurology and psychiatry developed hand in hand for many years, but they separated even though they were never definitively divorced. Today, it seems that they are ready to live together again. They are both mature enough and have enough self-assertiveness to cope with each other. They are no longer threatened by the long-living brain/mind dichotomy.

In our analyses of the brain, we are caught between two basic and opposite fantasies. The first one can be called the "*total control fantasy.*" According to this fantasy, all human behaviors, feelings, affects, values, fantasies, and mental expressions can be completely understood and controlled. The best and easiest way of control is through our senses, mainly our eyesight. We would like to locate each of these functions in our brain. The fact that some of them have been already located is very encouraging and it enables us to believe that sooner or later they will all be precisely located in our brain and through our neurotransmitters, including the "locus of ethics." The champion of this fantasy and belief was Sigmund Freud. He believed that "biology is a domain of unlimited possibilities." He added: "We have to be ready to receive from it [biology] the more striking enlightment and we cannot predict which responses it could give us in few decencies to the questions we ask it. Maybe, these answers will destroy all our artificial theoretical edifice." More recently, Changeux in his *L'Homme neuronal* proposes to build a bridge over the gap that separates human sciences and neurology. "This bridge can be perceived as abusive and exaggerated."

The second basic fantasy is the *"total freedom fantasy."* This claims that every human being is the only master of all his or her psychic functions, and the brain is only the tool to express these functions. Spirit or mind or psyche is of another nature, immaterial, specifically human, linked or not linked to God. During human life, it elaborates thoughts and fantasies through cerebral functions. According to this fantasy, man is totally free in his will and other psychic productions, limited only by his somatic nature. Into this psychic nature, man can be limited by conflicts inherent to psychic functioning. Every mental production is the result of instincts, drives, and the solution of conflicts between different topics of the mind at different levels: conscious, subconscious, and unconscious. The champion of this position is Sigmund Freud. He elaborated this genius theory, called psychoanalysis, and specifically its metapsychology that explains and interprets man's behavior and psychic functioning into itself.

It seems to be very hard for human thinking to rid itself of this basic dichotomy between *psyche* and *soma.* Brain research tries to bridge this gap. Its results give more and more evidence of the brain's complexity, not only in its motor, sensory, and vegetative functions, but also in its cognitive, affective, memory, drives, and so-called higher functions. This knowledge can be interpreted in different ways according to the basic belief of the researcher; either in a materialistic or psychic mode. By doing so, we make a serious confusion between our "two brains": the anatomic/physiologic brain and the metaphoric brain.

Brain anatomy, histology, genetics, physiology, biophysics, and biochemistry give us information on the brain as an organ. The fact that a lesion in a specific place modifies or neutralizes a psychic function does not prove anything but that this function, let us say memory, is impaired when such a lesion occurs. This has nothing to do with memory as such, differentiated from recalling. In his book, *Matter and Memory,* the French philosopher Bergson used Broca experiences on memory to establish the disconnection between brain and memory. Memory over goes the "matter," the brain. If a lesion that impaired memory disappears or improves, memories will come back. Bergson used Winslow's descriptions in his work, *On Obscure Diseases of the Brain,* to establish his position. The example is of a man who forgets a foreign language that he knows prior to his illness, and who composed afterward the same poems he wrote few years earlier.

We have the tendency to take the part for the whole and to go faster than scientific findings so that we can realize our basic fantasies. The metaphoric brain has its vicissitudes. According to this logical concept that the more important functions have to be placed at the most important place in the body, psychic functions were localized in the heart.

When speaking of brain research and functions we have the tendency to confuse these "two brains." Today, no one will confuse the heart and love except in poetry, and no one will confuse the choleretic canal and melancholia. Brain fantasy is very resistant, because we need it to determine our human specificity as totally free and totally controlled or controlling.

This confusion has been expressed by the question if brain cell grafts will also transmit the donor's personality. This question did not occur in heart transplants! On the same coin, brain imaging provides only brain blood perfusion and the brain's intactness (Salvatore) and not "brain quality" or the patient's personality. People could be selected according to their "brain quality" in PET (positron emission tomography) or MRI (magnetic resonance imaging) images as they were 50 years ago according to the shape of their nose or ears!

We speak about the organic brain and think about the metaphoric brain. The same difference exists between self-representation and self. One can be described anatomically, physiologically, and so on, but perceives oneself quite differently. Self-representation as brain representation can be seen as an anthropomorphism. I speak about my body, my brain, my self, as if it were a total human being somato-socio-psychic, as if this body or this brain has a soul. Does the brain think, feel, hallucinate, love, or memorize?

Brain research progressively closes the gap between brain representation and the organic brain. Will this gap be totally erased someday, will this research ultimately succeed? The answer can be only based on belief and not on the knowledge that is available today. Every answer is an extrapolation. This confusion is expressed in almost all fields of brain research.

In order to respond to the concept of "brain death," some authors, such as Goldenring or Sass, have developed the concept of "brain life." As is well known today, "brain death" is a necessary concept when the heart and the lungs are still alive, because it gives doctors the right to take organs from the donor for transplantation. This concept of "brain life" is much less necessary or even useless. Hans-Martin Sass claims that "brain life I" occurs around the 44th day following conception and it "shows the first living cells, some of which will develop into the human cortex." "Brain life II" begins around the 70th day after conception and is characterized by the first formation of synapses, which provide the possibility of "ever-growing networks of interconnections." For Sasz, brain-life II is the point "after which fetal life should be morally recognized and legally protected."

Kushner offers a psychological argument for brain life. She distinguishes between a biological (zoe) and conscious (bios) life: The first, zoe, for organic structure, the second, bios, for biography, referring to existence as "the subject of a certain life with its accompanying history." The brain-life theory simply stated is: "whenever a functioning human brain is present, a human being is present, that is, when the thalamus becomes connected to the cortex around the 20th week, the nervous system is then physically integrated. According to these theories, Tauer proposes a third definition of human being: "the psychic person who has the present capacity to retain experiences as 'memories' through the building of pathways in the CNS (central nervous system); and the potential to become a person 'in the strict sense.'"

These developing concepts help us understand the critical interest raised by brain research and brain peculiarities, not only for neurologists but also, perhaps mainly, for psychiatrists and all people concerned with the nature of their psychic functions.

The CNS is among the first systems to begin development and probably the last to complete it. It is characterized by its "autistic nature": among its 10^{10} cells, 99.98% are connected among themselves and only 0.02% are connected with the outside (Bourguignon). This to say that the brain invests almost all of its energy and capacities in elaborating, in a close system, the little information it receives, and in sending messages, motor or others, to the outside world. As such it is also painless. On the other hand, it is extraordinarily adaptable to external changes. The experiments on vision in newborns and young children are convincing proof of it. Platoon himself explained the beginning of deficit in memory function by the development of writing and reading. Cicero knew all his conferences by heart, "even forward and backward!" We foresee even a bigger loss of memorized information due to the development of computerized knowledge.

Do these facts modify the brain organ or only the brain concept? If it is generally thought that structures reflect functions in biology generally and in human beings specifically, the brain seems to be an exception. Nothing in its macro- and microanatomy lets us imagine what its functions are. Knowing how it functions does not mean *ipso facto* that all psychic functions take place in these cells and their connections.

This discrepancy between our "two brains" becomes explicit in the different modalities of intervention on brain: psychosurgery, embryo cell transplants, psychotropic drugs, psychotherapy, and brainwashing.

Monitz's psychosurgery technique to treat gravissime mental disorders had its successes and it is still used, in some countries quite intensively. Without denying its scientific basis, this technique is linked to the "Dibbuk" fantasy. Trepanations had been performed by ancient Greeks and others to take away the wrong part of the psyche out of the brain; in this case, it was thought to be the mind. If this fantasy is not necessarily the surgeon's fantasy, it is certainly the referents and the family's fantasy. The fantasy of "take it (bad ideas, bad behavior, insanity, bad spirit "Dibbuk," etc.) out of your/his/her head!"

The transplant of embryonic cells to Parkinson's or Alzheimer's patients is relevant to other fantasy processes. Again, all this has nothing to say about the proved efficiency of this technique nor about the ethical dilemmas it raises. Moving part of one brain to another one is an old fantasy. The wish to mixing personalities between friends, allies, and spouses was formulated by mixing blood. The fantasical "real proof" that mind and brain are one will be shown by brain transplantation!

Psychotropic drugs revolutionized psychiatry in the sixties. Mood, hallucinations, thoughts, and cognition are all drastically modified by these molecules. Today, their pharmacokinesis and sites of action are well known. Does it mean that mood, hallucinations, and so on are products of biochemical processes? Or are such processes only the condition for expression of these psychic functions, from psychic elaboration to external expression?

Psychotherapy raises the same question. By no doubt, psychotherapies (being, speaking to, and listening to someone according to a certain theory and technique), modify one's thoughts, mood, cognition, behavior, and so on. Is this psychotherapeutic process entirely dependent upon neurological processes, listening, seeing, cortex projection, frontal integration, and thalamic regulation, or is it "only" a "mind-to-mind dialogue"? Modern technics of brain imaging show clear changes in brain blood flow after psychotherapeutic intervention in obsessive-compulsive disorders. The same changes also occur after medication.

Brain washing is of the same vein; it differs in its aims, intensity, and techniques. It proves how adaptable the brain is and how flexible, as stated by Dagognet.

All of these examples cannot convince us of the organic nature of the mind, nor of the opposite. We cannot replace a "theory of mind" with a "theory of brain." They are still two different theories. The challenge is to bridge the gap between them by joining brain and psychological research walking.

This uncertainty on the one hand, and the extraordinary specificity of the brain, the "cerebrality" (Dagognet), on the other hand, confront us with specific ethical duty. Because we know so little about brain/mind relations and because we cannot manage totally every manipulation of brain and mind, from psychosurgery to psychotherapy, we have to be extremely careful and humble when coping with the brain and the mind, and we must make a clear differential diagnosis between reality and fantasies, between the organ brain and the metaphorical brain.

This discussion is highly relevant for our topic, ethics and psychiatry. The way psychiatrists relate to their patients is influenced by their understanding of mental illnesses, among many other important factors: personality, education, beliefs, and so on. A supposedly brain-damaged individual is considered less responsible and as such, less able to modify his behavior and thoughts by his own will than a supposedly fully independent person. According to the first assumption, the patient–doctor relationship is aimed only at convincing the patient to take the drugs that will modify his brain metabolism and giving him support during this hard period of his life. Even within this framework of reference, the psychiatrist grants some independence to his patient who can either agree or refuse to take medications, and who suffers psychically from an illness and does not only feel pain.

As psychiatrists, we are or we have to be more aware of the social dimensions of diseases, development, affective disorders, and conduct disorders. A biochemical explanation of all of these diseases is surely important but is not sufficient to solve them and to lessen their impact upon families and society. There is a need for the psychiatrization of neurology.

More and more voices in the United States call for the unifying of psychiatry and neurology. The arguments for it emerge from what has been said previously, and they are convincing. However, we have to weigh the ethical price of this unification, or in other words, the "neurologization" of psychiatry. Even if there is no longer a place for the brain/mind dichotomy, human being cannot simply be a body, or an admirable complicated nervous system, even if it is scientifically correct. We also have social obligations, and our societies need other considerations toward their subjects beyond neurological explanations. For a long time, psychiatrists have pleaded for a multidisciplinary approach; joining neurologists will be of great benefit to our patients and it will be ethically correct. The key word today is to consider human beings as psycho-bio-social individuals.

Psychoanalysis postulates human freedom and responsibility. Psychoanalysis can be conducted only with the full consent of informed patients. When proposed to borderline or even psychotic patients, psychoanalysis is always a relational mode of treatment, between two free and equal persons. That is its more ethical statement. The other face of this coin is that patients and families have been falsely considered as responsible for their own and their relatives' illnesses, without any consideration for their suffering. This is due to a misunderstanding of psychoanalytical theory. Causality differs from responsibility and responsibility is not guilt. The core of the ethical dilemma in psychoanalysis is the transference/countertransference issue. "One of the axes of psychoanalytical ethics is drawn by the transfer theory. In the course of an analytical cure, the practitioner understands the development of a patient's discourse whether associations are transmitted by language or, in the younger child, by different modalities of play as determined by movements of love and hate directed to his person and provoked by the framework of the treatment. The choice of the conceptual system of the psychoanalytical metapsychology leads to this form of knowledge. The psychoanalytical framework implies that the psychoanalyst is constantly aware of what the patient produces without taking anything literally, that is, at the first degree, but also without neglecting anything. He strives to establish links between the different sequences. The relations he constructs in this way will enable him to proceed further in the reconstruction of the patient's psychic history. For his part, the patient, confronted by a situation that is totally new in both its satisfying and frustrating aspects, tends to transform the unknown into the known, in the registers of both love and hate. The psychoanalyst can thus construct the following theory: the patient expects everything from him, for better and for worse, since he projects onto him the idealized image of the parents of his early childhood, precisely the one that is overlain by amnesia. Whether his patient is an adult or a child, this experience tests the psychoanalyst's ability to analyze his countertransference. He must continue to analyze the links without taking himself for the object of ideal love that the adult patient projects onto him, and without taking himself for a better parent than the parents of his patient, if he is treating a child. In any event, he must not allow himself to be carried away by the fantasy of omnipotence that every patient tends to make him take for a natural reality, even though the patient, at the same time knows that this is not so, and that he can unmask his therapist's impotence in no time. Since the first decades of psychoanalysis, love transference has been a well-known form of resistance to the psychoanalytical process, but the illusory feeling of power remains tempting. The terrifying passage in *Amok,* where Stefan Zweig describes the intoxication of the doctor overcome by the conviction that the lady who is asking a favor from him is in his power, comes to mind here. In the course of the treatment of children, the tragic dimension is less obvious, but their are many traps that can give rise to the abuse of power. In truth, psychoanalysts are not the only ones who risk showing a lack of moderation. Psychiatrists and psychologists often consider themselves sure of their knowledge when they make decisions or give advice that influences the patient's fate in a manner that, at the very least, is uncertain. But psychoanalysts possess a conceptual tool that enables them to criticize their own attitudes: one is thus justified in expecting from them the utmost rigor. Ensuring the consistency of the psychoanalytical framework is not sufficient for ethical exigencies to be fulfilled" (Diatkine, R. (1994). In Hattab, J. Y. (Ed) *Ethics and child mental health.* (p. 100–109.) Jerusalem: Gefen Publishers.).

The spread of psychoanalysis brought the banalization and a misuse of its principles. Even if it is not the direct responsibility of the psychoanalytic movement, psychoanalysts have to be careful when diffusing their knowledge and techniques. What Freud called "wild interpretation" is now used indifferently by people who are poorly aware of its dangers and insufficiently trained. Interpretation is a powerful therapeutic tool and as such has its own indications, contraindications, and harmful side effects. Besides this iatrogenic effect,

it is totally immoral to misuse interpretations. It is psychological rape to interpret behaviors or the speech of a person who has not been asked for and who has not given informed consent outside of the psychoanalytical setup.

At the opposite pole, the theory of conditioning and its behavior modification therapeutic application, describes man's behavior as a product of educational and situational influences. When considered as deviant, these behaviors will be modified by a powerful person other than parents and in another environment. In this approach the patient is mostly considered an object and not a subject. However, his acceptance and collaboration is highly recommended.

In the mid-sixties, along with the students' rebellion against the establishment and its social values, psychiatry as a medical discipline was questioned. This was the *antipsychiatry movement* lead by Laing, Cooper, and others. They claim that the so-called mentally ill person is "the healthier person in an ill society". As a consequence of this approach, many psychiatric institutions were closed and their patients were freed without any other rehabilitation program and/or settlement. Chronic "schizophrenic" and other patients found themselves in the streets in Italy, the United States, and elsewhere. From an ethical view, this approach was catastrophic for all these needy persons.

However, the antipsychiatry movement has the important distinction of having made the authorities and the psychiatric establishment aware of the abuses and misuses of psychiatry and mental illness.

The French philosopher Michel Foucault dealt with madness as an archetype of attitudes toward ideologies. Madness was first freely integrated in the medieval society. When it was then considered an illness it was used by those in power to place the mentally ill in asylums, for treatment and change. It was the era of positivism, scientism, and logic that led to measurement and description or control. As such, madness is the best example of how societies use their control and power over their weakest and most dependent members. Totalitarian societies still use psychiatry to express their power and domination. Perhaps because of the antipsychiatry movement it now seems that human rights, liberty and the "freedom to be a fool" are better accepted and encouraged. From an ethical point of view, this approach has considerably improved the status of the mentally ill in our societies. Charters of human rights include specific considerations for the mentally retarded and for mentally ill persons.

IV. ETHICS OF NOSOGRAPHY

The classification of diseases represent the standardization of treatment procedures for higher efficacy, the avoidance of harmful or useless procedures, the need for communication between professionals, and also the magic need for a name of the illness for patients and their families. Diagnoses are concepts and not reality. They are an attempt to organize and name the reality of pathology. Diagnoses change due to research, new theories, politics, insurance companies, and financial pressure.

But naming an illness is not the same as naming the person by this illness. Every person remains a totally free individual who is known by his or her name, and who is affected by and suffers from a specific illness. Mr. Brown is not a psychotic; rather, he is Mr. Brown who actually suffers from a psychotic state.

One of the great difficulties in psychiatry arises from the possible iatrogenic effects of nosological classification. Since psychiatry has become a medical science, the necessity of making a diagnosis is no longer open to discussion. This diagnosis implies an explanation, etiological or pathogenic, that enables a prognosis to be established and a treatment to be decided upon. In psychiatry two attitudes are possible: the treatment can be considered one that is designed to alleviate the suffering of the patient and his loved ones without changing anything fundamental in the psychic structure; or it can be designed to refute the prognosis that follows from the diagnosis.

A diagnosis is based on signs and symptoms gathered by the clinician. This assessment is highly influenced by whichever theory the clinician believes in. He will emphasize and pay attention to symptoms that fit his theory and minimize those that do not. Although the DSM system was intended to be a descriptive and unthe-oretical system, its underlying message is of phenomenology theory. The fact that co-morbidity reaches a range of 95% proves its weakness and its failure to be only descriptive. Even in DSM, most symptoms and signs are described by approximation and subjective facts such as, "qualitative impairment in social skills" in autism, thought disorders, hyperactivity, and so on, without paying enough attention to cultural and individual differences. As such, the ethical requirement of a nosology is to serve the patients and not only science.

The relation between diagnosis and treatment is not clear and certainly is not unified, because there is no one accepted etiology for mental disorders. Treatment, which is most important for patients, is planned according to the physician's understanding of the pathol-ogy and it relies heavily on his own beliefs. No single practitioner can know and use all techniques based on all theories, with each having its own advantages and disadvantages. From an absolute point of view, it is also unethical not to provide a patient with the best information and therapeutic protocol.

V. ETHICS OF PRACTICE

Lebovici says: "Our power over the souls, minds and bodies of those who have various types of contact with us in the course of our professional life is such that we have to accept no compromise in the field of Ethics. We would simply repeat, as others have done, "*Primum non nocere*". We would also say, "Science is of no value without conscience," and add, with Bacon: "I dressed his wound; God cured him." By following a certain French fashion, *panser,* meaning to dress a wound, could be written *penser,* to think: "I thought of him; God cured him." In fact, professional morals, in certain aspects, are difficult to distinguish from our morality in daily life, and they cannot be limited to advice not to harm our clients and their families. To abstain from action can run contrary to our elementary professional obligations, for example, in the case of maltreatment."

Every action must be measured by the pain or pleasure that it gives according to a number of criteria defined by "moral arithmetic," such as intensity, duration, fecundity, purity, and so on. This would seem to be a far cry from the deontological foundations of the Hippocratic oath. Are we to suppose that the respect of the rule will make the doctor who has respected this oath a man as happy as Hippocrates seems to have been, "projected by legend into the world of great men... He, of course, possessed all the virtues and qualities of the mind; he died at a ripe old age and covered in glory, and miracles are worked on his tomb." In the evocation of this illustrious example, we are a long way from the stipulations and prohibitions defined in the Code of Deontology. In France, this Code has regulated the conditions of medical practice since 1947, and some doctors have been the object of sanctions decreed by the disciplinary committee, which is independent of possible penal sanctions. In the United States and in some other countries, these rules enable litigation to be instituted against doctors for more or less obvious professional errors. But these situations generally have nothing to do with the stipulations of medical morals: they are "professional errors." Let us assume, at least provisionally, that these morals that specialists must not infringe upon are easy to define. This is not the case for ethics.

Compared with other medical disciplines, psychiatry is less confronted with death except in deeply depressed and suicidal patients. However, psychiatrists are confronted with chronicity, long-term treatment, which leads to a continuous relationship with their patients. Psychiatrists establish specific relations with their patients that involve dependency, transference, and countertransference.

These facts are real and active in any treatment including psychopharmacology, behavior therapy, counseling, and so on. The only difference is in the use and emphasis of the phenomenon of transference–countertransference.

A. In Psychopharmacology

The placebo effect, which is well-known and proved in all fields of medicine, is more effective in psychiatry with success in about 20% of cases. The therapeutic effects of drugs, both direct and side effects, will be enhanced by the way they are proposed, explained, and supported by the physician who prescribes them.

Psychopharmacological research has brought to practitioners a large range of powerful and effective drugs. Even if this same research helped make progress in understanding of the etiology of mental disorders, these drugs are still all but symptomatically effective and no one acts simply because of a supposed etiology. More than that, it has been clearly established that the effect of medication is greatly enhanced by supportive psychotherapy. In adolescent depression for example, psychotherapy has been proved as more efficient than medication alone. When confronted with agitated, delusional, or hallucinatory patients, practitioners are tempted to administer drugs as soon as possible. However, no medication can be administered before a minute and comprehensive assessment of the patient is completed. In many cases, such a procedure leads to refraining from medication and using instead less dangerous treatment procedures or postponing medication and its possible side effects. This is more important in child and adolescent psychiatry.

The ethical dilemma in psychopharmacological therapy can be expressed as follows: On one hand, patient and family are entitled to receive full explanations concerning the proposed medication, including all side effects, both at short- and long-term; on the other hand, these explanations can induce through suggestion these same side effects, or some of them, specifically with mentally disturbed and highly sensitive patients, who

can be frightened by the description of side effects. Refusal of treatment can lead to deterioration and sometimes can endanger the patient and his loved ones.

The only absolute in ethics is to raise ethical dilemmas and to solve them. Truth is, of course, a value but it is not the only one and in medicine, it may be not the most important. The higher value in medicine is the relief of suffering and the protection of the patients. In such cases, the psychiatrist is authorized to act in the best interest of his or her patient as express by this patient or the patient's family, who are considered as most likely to defend the patient's best interests. In any case the psychiatrist can discuss these issues with colleagues.

B. In Psychotherapy

Nearly 250 different types of psychotherapy have been described in the professional literature. That makes the choice for the best therapeutic approach for a given patient highly difficult. Theoretically and ethically, a therapist has to know and to be able to discuss all these therapeutic procedures, including medications and other biological treatments. The therapist must continue to learn new theories and techniques, and he should discuss with colleagues most of his patients.

Psychotherapy is not small talk with a needy person, even if that can also be helpful. Psychotherapy is a powerful therapeutic instrument that, as such, has its indications, contraindications, effects, side effects, and dangers. It must be practiced by highly trained persons.

All psychotherapeutic techniques and theories require special training. Psychoanalytic training, which is very intensive, includes the requirement that the candidate pursue by himself what is called a training analysis that can last 5 years or longer, with three to five sessions a week.

In all psychotherapeutic techniques one of the most powerful curative or iatrogenic factors is the psychotherapist's personality, mainly in its empathetic, caring, cognitive, and affective dimensions, whether consciously or subconsciously. Countertransference as well as transference are always enacted even if they are not interpreted and elaborated. For these reasons, there is an ethical requirement for all psychotherapists to elucidate and explore their own subconscious and experience transference–countertransference phenomena before they penetrate their patients minds and project their own unresolved conflicts.

This kind of projected conflict is expressed in child psychotherapy. Sooner or later, the child in psychoanalytically oriented psychotherapy will be confronted with his ambivalence toward his parents, enduring, perhaps, a period of opposition to them. Relations between the child and its parents can be compromised if they are not restructured at a better level. The parents consent to having the therapist take charge of the child. What of our childhood desires, our own parenthood, our own relations in such situations? It is not a matter of elaborating on transference and countertransference in the psychotherapy of children, but of discussing the relevant ethical dimensions. This is but one of the conflict aspects of psychotherapy. Individual or group control would guarantee against such misuses, whatever our experience.

The definition of ethics in behavior therapy, as with any psychotherapeutic enterprise, can be elusive and frustrating. The Association for Advancement of Behavior Therapy (AABT) developed a series of questions for behavioral interventionists to consider in their treatment programming. These included the following primary issues:

1. Have the goals of treatment been adequately considered?
2. Has the choice of treatment methods been adequately considered?
3. Is the client's participation voluntary?
4. When another person or an agency is empowered to arrange for therapy, have the interests of the subordinated client been sufficiently considered?
5. Has the adequacy of treatment been evaluated?
6. Has the confidentiality of the treatment relationship been protected?
7. Does the therapist refer the clients to other therapists when necessary?
8. Is the therapist qualified to provide treatment?

The American Psychological Association (APA) adopted its own set of ethical guidelines for its members. The APA has identified its major concerns in research as informed consent, cost/benefit ratios, free access to data, and other provisions for the protection of the subject's human rights, issues that apply equally to behavioral treatments. Other issues have been noted, including the powerlessness of clients who are institutionalized, incarcerated, and incompetent, and others who are not fully able to assert their rights; the shortsightedness of focusing on specific behaviors to the exclusion of the understanding of the whole child; the role of value systems; the limits of the concept and practice of least restrictive alternatives; the anti-aversives movement versus the right to effective treatment; the relationship between clinical decision-making and acceptable community practices; and claiming treatment effectiveness beyond supporting data. The definitions of both ethics and behavior therapy are so far-ranging that no simple encapsulation of the multiple factors is easily obtained. The general guidelines provided by the Association for Advancement of Behavior Therapy as well as those promoted by the right-to-effective-treatment advocates can serve as a basis for discussion and evaluation of the practitioner's own behavior. It is evident that the current climate demands careful attention to the effects of behavioral practices on the public conscience and an awareness of the role of cultural and societal norms.

As a therapeutic and medical process, psychotherapy has to be offered indiscriminately to every person who needs it, whatever their race, sex, religion, or ideology. However, due to the importance of countertransference in the therapeutic process, it is more ethical to refer a patient to a colleague if this patient evokes uncomfortable feelings or associations in the therapist. In any case, we have to ensure that this patient will be treated.

Confidentiality is a condition to fulfill a psychotherapeutic process. Some disclosures present the therapists with harmful dilemmas. When a child or a spouse tells us that another family member abuses him, whether somatically, sexually, or psychologically, the therapist has a responsibility, according to the law in most countries, to report the problem to the police or to a social officer. If this child discloses this fact in psychotherapy and asks the therapist not to reveal it, is there an alternative? It could be a patient who reveals during psychotherapy or counseling that he cannot handle his aggressiveness and sometimes hurts his child or his spouse. Another case is that of a father in psychoanalysis who acknowledges incest.

There are no simple answers to difficult questions. Each case needs its own special consideration and solution. It is most important to protect lives and those in danger of being hurt. We also have to take into account the future of the family, spouse, child, and siblings. No one has to pay or suffer for others. We must use our psychotherapeutic tools to help this child or any other victim, these parents, and this father cope with these terrible facts and resolve them.

From the very moment of disclosure the psychotherapist must focus only on the problem in order to help the patient strengthen himself. If, based on our knowledge of the situation, we think that the crime will stop that same day and does not require more active intervention, we can refrain from reporting it, but we need to work with the parties intensively and add more sessions until a solution is found. The first and compulsory duty is to protect every victim. Such cases should always be discussed with colleagues, so that everyone, including the therapist, is protected.

Every person infected by AIDS who refuses to reveal his terrible truth and continues to have unprotected sex is potentially a murderer. If a patient admits this in psychotherapy, you have no choice but to convince him or her to practice safe sex. In such cases, no one can argue that the patient is totally autonomic and can make his or her own decisions.

These are examples of cases when the psychotherapist can no longer be neutral.

C. In Hospitalization

Hospitalization is a very serious decision that when made can change the life of the patient, especially if the patient is a child. The need for hospitalization has to be weighed carefully against other therapeutic, less harmful, less detrimental, and cheaper procedures. However, hospitalization has its advantages and its limits.

The institution's therapeutic objective is not to achieve a superficial modification of the symptoms or to accumulate educative acquisitions that are not truly integrated into the personality; the aim above all is to put in place new modes of mental functioning and, correlatively, new modalities of exchange with others, and the patient's attainment of capacities of symbolization. This cure seeks to integrate them into the patient's personality so that he can use them in a way that is not purely mechanical or conditioned. As R. Mises clearly stressed: "There is no opposition between the educative and the psychotherapeutic process, and it is the dialectic articulation of these two levels which creates the originality of this type of institution. This assumes that everyone who lives and works within the institution feels involved in this therapeutic process more by what he is than by what he does. The educative actions he carries out count as much, if not more, for their therapeutic dimension as for their technical aspects." This does not mean, however, that the role of each is indistinguishable. Each member of the team preserves his function, his technique, and his own specificity. That is also an ethical requirement.

Another essential function of the institution is to constitute a protective and protected framework, to set up a kind of nondeforming but attenuating filter in relation to the outside world, which is designed to protect the patient from stimuli that are too strong, and to prevent a return to experiences whose traumatic character the patient's psyche cannot yet master. This

is not to say that the institution must be designed essentially to give satisfaction, to fill in or to compensate for what the patient has suffered, or to eliminate every frustrating experience or every confrontation with a distressing experience. What it must do is modulate all these situations as a function of what the patient's condition enables him to accept, to present them to him during a therapy session so that the patient is not alone when confronted with experiences that are too distressful. This is analogous to the function of protection from overexcitement that a mother gives her newborn child.

The institution also has a containing function that is absolutely essential: it assumes that the personnel possess a real capacity to receive, contain, and live the original, often disorganized emotions felt by the patients, and to give them meaning in order to restore them to a form the patient can assimilate. Only when the patient has felt within the institution this ability to receive and to contain his disorganized feelings and emotions is he then able, by regaining for himself this capacity to contain through a basic mechanism of introjective identification, to begin to establish a proper psychic space and to organize his emotional life. This containing function is analogous to the function of maternal daydreaming advanced by W. Bion: "The mother's ability to bear and contain the first sensorial and emotional elements of her child and to restore them to him 'detoxicated' in a form he can accept." As J. Hochmann stressed, this means presenting through words, and giving linguistic meaning to what the patient lives and feels, to help him construct a coherent historical whole in which he can place himself as subject, to enable him to derive pleasure from harboring thoughts and not to persist any longer in destroying and expelling his own thoughts as the psychotic process compels him to do.

The institution's maternal function is a function of exchange and communication through the channel of physical care, a function that is analogous, although it is not superimposable, to the relation created between mother and infant in the course of mothering. The time devoted to this care enables the patient to carry out a libidinal investment of his own body and to take possession of it. It is well known how frequently the psychotic person is ignorant of certain parts of his body or does not use them. This time is comparable to the body-to-body time a mother spends with her child, the time of "primary seduction," to use Freud's term, which roots the libidinal drive in the child's body by means of desire and maternal care, and comes to create zones of excitability of erogenic sensations in the child's body.

The institutional framework can constitute a "transitional area" in the sense that Winnicott defined it. By allowing the hospitalized person to develop transitional activities, by giving him the possibility of exercising his primary creativity while confronting him with the perception of the reality of objects and of the world, the institution makes possible this illusory correspondence between primary creativity at the source of the hallucinated object and the discovery of the object of exterior reality.

The close contact of the institution and the patient's family is maintained whenever this seems possible, that is, when the clinical condition of the patient, and the qualities and possibilities of the family to receive him, are good.

Hospital day care then appears to be the preferential formula, with schooling for children or rehabilitation workshops for adult patients within the hospital or, when possible, in normal settings. All clinicians know that the absence of family involvement seriously harms the continuity and effectiveness of treatment.

A psychic life and a relational life disturbed by mental illness are the source of suffering for the person, but they can be improved when the proper institutional therapy is offered to the mentally ill. This institutional therapy must give the patient all the curative, educative, reeducative, and pedagogical contributions that his condition requires, but they must be given within the framework of a meeting with an adult in which there is psychotherapeutic value and a structuring function for the patient's mental life. This action aims to reestablish the patient as a subject. This is the foundation of our ethics, which are based on an optimistic vision of the evolutive possibilities of the human psyche and on a solid, realistic humanism.

The decision whether or not to hospitalize and the evaluation of the result of hospitalization on social and professional grounds present ethical problems. Civil rights defenders, peer review boards, and members of other professions raise accusatory voices against too much hospitalization. Setting policies and rules for hospitalization creates endless ethical dilemmas.

In assessing the need for hospitalization, the psychiatrist has to take into consideration four factors: the clinical state of the patient; his or her family functioning and ability to participate in a community based therapeutic program; the resources of a given community in terms of outpatient clinics, staffing, halfway houses, daycare centers, foster families, and so on; and the adequacy of the hospitalizing department to treat a given patient. This point is ethically crucial. Hospitalizing today does not mean putting someone into an asy-

lum. This is an engagement of treatment and care. The institution has to evaluate at any given moment its functioning and its ability to receive new patients, and it has to make any effort to fulfill this duty.

Thus, psychiatrists may continuously move between their position as participant members of the community and their position as physicians to the patient. The decision whether or not to hospitalize is an ethical one, and it was not dutifully pursued when there was a concentrated national drive to reduce psychiatric hospital populations and to close hospitals.

Compulsory hospitalization has become a legal issue, but it actually affects an extremely small number of patients. Most developed countries have elaborate rules and laws limiting and supervising such compulsory hospitalization. Generally, lawyers and representatives of families are involved in this process and the lawful requirements meet the ethical ones.

However, it is unethical to suspect a priori that every psychiatrist is interested in hospitalizing his patients, regardless of their needs, and in placing them in the care of nonprofessionals.

The hospital has to offer to its patients humane facilities and security, including privacy, informed consent, ongoing explanations of treatment, free mail and phone calls, adequate living conditions, decent food, laundry, furniture, and so on.

VI. ETHICS OF TRAINING

The following are the principal goals and objectives of teaching medical ethics as defined by Steinberg:

- To increase awareness of, and sensitivity to, the ethical problems encountered in clinical and research medicine and in basic biomedical research;
- To identify ethical problems in medicine and in biomedical science that may not be immediately obvious, but that are nonetheless serious;
- To familiarize students with a fundamental knowledge of philosophy, religion, and law pertinent to biomedical ethics, and thereby enable them to analyze the ethical difficulties they will encounter as physicians or scientists, and to seek appropriate solutions;
- To sharpen the decision-making capabilities of the students in situations where medical/scientific and ethical dimensions of a given situation meet;
- To encourage the bringing together of scientific–technological knowledge and skill with human empathy and sympathy, i.e., the developing of an opti-

mal integration of the science medicine with the humane art of medicine;
- To inculcate in the students respect for different ideologies, viewpoints, and sensitivities in the area of biomedical ethics, as well as respect for the dignity and autonomy of the individual patient and colleague;
- To inculcate a fundamental philosophy of medicine: that treatment must always be of the patient, rather than merely of a particular illness and of an isolated organ or tissue.

When discussing ethics with psychiatric teams, are we obliged to demand of ourselves and of those who work with us this irrevocable recourse to the absolute? This question brings us back to moral and deontological imperatives. These principles could justify a prior selection of personnel specialized in psychiatry based on ethical requirements.

It foresees the elimination of some of them. This is true of those who have proven mental problems, in particular, states of severe, chronic depression or signs of psychotic disorders. Nevertheless, it should be noted that experience shows that the profession of psychiatry undoubtedly attracts subjects whose mental life may be troubled.

Mental health professionals and candidates for these professions, are supposed to be well educated and they should behave according to high moral standards. The perceptions that inherently decent persons working in health care will act ethically because they are so inclined, and that people cannot be trained to be good human beings are wrong. These perceptions ignore the fact that even the most benevolent individual is in need of intensive training to prepare himself/herself to confront the agonizing dilemmas of ethics that modern medicine so often presents, and that even "good" people can readily make ethically untenable decisions if they meet such dilemmas unprepared and unequipped.

However, as we see all along nothing can be taken for granted and values have to be taught and protected. Working with mentally ill persons of all ages can be very provocative for those with sadistic drives, for those who wish to exercise power over weak and suffering persons. The abused autistic girl will not be able to disclose the abuse she is victim of, and the allegations of a psychotic person will be denied too easily. The first and most important step in training will be to select the right people to work in mental health professions. Beside diagnoses of evident mental deviations, we have no reliable criteria for this crucial step. Many medical schools that tried to define such criteria gave up, and medical students are recruited based only on their intel-

lectual capacities as expressed by their records at end of high school. For other professionals, such as nurses and social workers, schools have established some requirements in addition to graduation.

Several methods for providing training in ethics have been proposed. Some schools include in their curriculum specific optional or compulsory courses on Ethics. These lectures are given by doctors who have devoted themselves to this subject. They include a review of the literature, case presentations and discussions, role playing, and so on. In this way the material presented can remain theoretical. This approach can be only in preparation for the more substantive and helpful ethical instruction for students: personal example. Whatever their future profession, students have to be trained to raise ethical issues in all they learn and see. Patrons do not like to be criticized. They are generally convinced that they are always right. But the Talmud already taught us that the pupil is the best teacher. These students' remarks should not be seen as offensive, but, on the contrary, as a real collaboration and identification with the profession. As we stated in the introduction, we are opposed to leaving ethics to the ethicists. Everyone who is charged with teaching, training, or influencing others must be an ethicist as well as a professional in medicine, psychiatry, psychology, nursing, and so on.

The role of ethicists in hospitals, for example, can be to support and back students who have been offended and troubled by what they have seen their teachers do. Ethical committees in hospital, which resolve ethical problems between patients, families, and staff, and also between staff members, can be used for the training of students under certain circumstances.

VII. ETHICS OF RESEARCH

"No devotion to science, no thought of the greater good to the greater number, can for an instant justify the experimenting on helpless infants, children pathetically abandoned by fate and untrusted to the community for their safeguarding. Voluntary consent by adults should, of course, be the *sine qua non* of scientific experimentation" (Klin, A., & Cohen, D. J. (1994). In Y. J. Hattab (Ed.) *Ethics and child mental health* (p. 217–233). Jerusalem: Gefen Publishers.). In 1941, for the first time, a scientific paper was rejected for ethical reason by the editor, Peyton Rous, of a professional publication: the *Journal of Experimental Medicine*. Throughout the preceding century, children, the mentally retarded, the mentally ill, and prisoners were used as guinea pigs for medical experimentation.

"In the past 15 years there has been an increasing awareness of the value of safeguards and regulations protecting participants of studies in the behavioral and medical sciences. Classic behavioral studies conducted in the 1960s and 1970s such as Milgram's research on obedience to authority, Zimbardo's research on role play, or even Harlow's and Gallup's studies involving nonhuman primates would probably raise concerns and might not be approved by most human investigation committees (Institutional Review Boards, IRBs) of today. This trend toward higher standards for approval of research was given regulatory status by the National Commission for the Protection of Human Subjects of Biomedical and Behavioral Research (National Commission, 1977), which defined the basic ethical principles that should guide research involving human subjects. Respect for persons and the inalienable rights of subjects to privacy, confidentiality and informed consent were established as the necessary requirements protecting individuals from being used merely as means to the researchers goals. In practice, investigators today are required both ethically and legally to assure that subjects provide informed consent, which signifies the participant's volitional embrace of the investigator's scientific goals. Procedures judged as entailing risk of any form, deception, samples that are not demographically representative of the distribution of gender or ethnicity among the general population, and the involvement of particularly vulnerable populations who are not able to fulfill the requirement of informed consent (such as children and the mentally impaired) are all scrutinized in order to prevent injustices that affront societal consensus on appropriate norms of scientific conduct. These moral values are obviously valuable counterweights against the thoughtless and potentially dangerous pursuit of studies that may harm individuals or distort the scientific search for truth. Yet, their implementation has not gone without some inadvertent deleterious impact on the field of human research. Also, by framing the questions primarily in terms of the protection of individuals, the protagonists of scientific research, the investigators, may be cast, as in science fiction thrillers, as more dangerous than beneficent. Yet, the goal of ethical regulations is not the needless burdening of scientific progress or the elimination of research. Rather, it is the pursuit of an acceptable balance between trying to assure that humans are not endangered nor is their autonomy reduced on the one hand, and the quest for understanding the unknown and the benefits that may accrue from knowledge based on empirical, systematic, and creative research on the other hand. Research is not supposed to be judged as

unduly intrusive, nor are investigators to be perceived as in need of scrutiny to prevent them in their unethical pursuit of dehumanized science. Nevertheless, the cultural pendulum may have swung away from the societal commitment to the fundamental value of the scientific enterprise: to probe the unknown responsibly and respectfully, but also unrelentlessly in order to make knowledge the property of not only a given culture but of those members of the society who are most in need of its benefits. In a field as young and uncharted as child and adolescent psychiatry, the balance between the known and the unknown still tilts heavily toward the latter. Its population is probably the one most in need of protection. Yet, a cultural aversion directed at research with children may leave whole areas of behavior, pathology, and potential treatments barred to systematic examination. An acknowledgment of the extent of the unknown carries with it a responsibility, indeed a moral mandate, to conduct research. The moral dictum, "First do no harm," goes hand in hand with striving to prevent or minimize harm, be it the result of congenital anomaly, disease process, or societal inequities. The dilemma defined by the equally valid ethical principles of the protection of subjects and the need for knowledge is nowhere more acute than when the subjects of research are children. Here, the uncertainty about the ethical propriety of clinical investigation has led to some ethically untenable results.

One extreme example of overconformance to safety considerations is provided by what Shirkey called the therapeutic orphans of our expanding pharmacopoia, a situation created by the great reluctance of investigators to conduct studies to determine the safety and efficacy of drugs in children. The use of drugs in childhood is often considered an orphan indication, as if childhood was an anomalous and rare state of being and the diseases of childhood were of secondary importance. As Levine points out, if we consider the availability of drugs proved safe and effective through the devices of modern clinical pharmacology and clinical trials a benefit, then it is unjust to deprive classes of persons, for example, children and pregnant women, of this benefit. At times, the use of a medication for an orphan indication may lead to quite surprising side effects that would not have been risked if the full implications were known beforehand, as was the case when desipramine was associated with sudden death among hyperactive children. But there is the danger that such principles might serve as self-justification for inaction, reinforced by an often unflattering portrayal of researchers and the fear of malpractice litigation. Our ethical sensitivities, however, should be as much aroused by the persistence of acknowledged ignorance as by the wish to avoid unethical research. For the ethical pride we might take in avoiding human investigation with children brings no solace to children (or their families) who are afflicted with developmental or psychiatric disorders, or whose lives and development are seriously burdened by disadvantaged circumstances. The assumption that protection of subjects and the research enterprise represent confrontative values is fallacious. Research inaction in clinical practice is not an ethically neutral stance; the lack of serious research may, and often does, signify a willingness for society to consign psychiatric patients to chronic suffering. Unexamined hypotheses about etiology and treatment, even if they represent the state of the art and the standard of care, demonstrate a willingness by clinicians and society to live with ignorance. This complacence belittles the value of those in need of valid knowledge and authenticated treatments."

Research is defined as the "systematic investigation designed to develop or contribute to generalizable knowledge." In medicine it ensures that "scientific medical practice should be based on formal studies of safety and efficacy and not solely on anecdotal clinical experience". Klin and Cohen even stated that it is an "ethical imperative to conduct research" in *Child Psychiatry*.

The ethical dilemma of brain research in psychiatry can be posed in the following terms:

1. People, children as well as adults, suffer from developmental and psychiatric disorders, which alters their mental functions and handicaps their full autonomy.
2. There is more and more evidence, although not totally grounded, that these impairments are brain based, either anatomically, biochemically, metabolically, and so on.
3. Proving these facts will lead to tremendous progress in understanding, and, more important, to treatment for these suffering people and their families.
4. The only way to improve knowledge is to conduct research. As stressed by Klin and Cohen there is a moral obligation to conduct research in psychiatry in order, at least, to adapt treatment to the special needs and nature of psychiatric patients, but not in a blind way, as is generally done today.
5. This research uses procedures that are intrusive but are the only way to really understand a fact or try a new promising treatment. This includes X-rays, venipuncture or lumbar puncture, and even normal control subjects.
6. Ethical duty obliges every scientist to consider the patient's rights to be questioned, it requires informed consent and assent, it respects the patients mind and body. The families are to be consulted, respected, and listened to.

This dilemma is generally answered by displacing the question onto the researcher and/or IRBs: "Responsible scientists must themselves balance the research question with an obligation to protect children," or: "The participation of children in research entails consideration of a variety of scientific and ethical principles. These include: the scientific validity of the question, the calculation of costs and benefits to the patient and to society; the necessity for the project to be done in patients; issues of assent, permission and consent; consideration of the special status of members of special groups (children, aged patients, mentally retarded, mentally ill, wards of the court)."

Clinicians and researchers all have their own biases and blind points. No one is perfect, we are all well meaning and we care for our patients. Beyond these statements, others like "human nature from its beginning," competition between research teams, publication, promotion, fear of change, routine, self-esteem, selfishness, self-assertiveness, self-serviceness, all have to be considered. No one alone can answer the ethical dilemma, certainly not the scientist, even the more moral; and not the clinician; nor the IRB, if composed only by scientists or clinicians from the same academic or hospital staff.

The answer can be approached only by an independent board composed by scientists, clinicians, representatives of families or advocacy groups, and a lawyer, and nominated for this specific research program. This procedure seems to be very difficult to manage. Ethical requirements are important enough to justify complex procedures, and it will not be so problematic if such standing committees are ready to meet upon request. Once these general statements are accepted, it will be simpler to consider every specific technique or procedure.

Autistic children are striking subjects for neurobiological research and at the same time they are more problematic from an ethical point of view. We are all eager to understand what happens in these children's brains to make them autistic. This knowledge will open the doors of early development, language, social skills, and so on. No one even supposes that an autistic child can give his or her assent and consent to a research procedure, and their families are generally either overprotective or they have already abandoned the child. Does this child really feel pain when pricked? Does he really feel manipulated when scanned? The temptation is strong to overcome or simplify ethical protocols. Rationalization and intellectualization are useful. On another hand, the cost/benefit calculation is almost obvious.

The ethical requirements and rules are established precisely for these cases. Because knowledge, even if meant for human well-being, cannot obliterate the higher value: respect for every person and specifically for those who cannot defend themselves. To be accepted by the adequate committees (IRBs or others) a research project has to answer to the following criteria: risks to subjects are minimized, risks to subjects are reasonable in relation to anticipated benefits to the subject (if there are any), and the importance of the knowledge that may reasonably be expected from the research selection of subjects is equitable. Informed consent from subjects will be obtained and documented, with certain exceptions to this rule. These exceptions relate to mentally retarded persons, psychiatric patients, and children.

"Though the idea of patients' consent has always been at the very heart of the therapeutic relationship, it is only in the course of the last few decades that it has become a fundamental element of the entire medical ethic. This important change reflects society's awareness of the powers linked to the practice of medicine and biomedical research. Under pressure from legal authorities, it also aims to ensure respect of the patient's autonomy, and to avoid the persistence of paternalism, which for so long characterized the practice of medicine. In the contract between doctor and patient, demands for the respect of the patient's consent counterbalance the basic inequality that marks the therapeutic relationship and the nature of the contract. In particular, the practice of adult psychiatry with its power and obligation to interfere actively and temporarily with the patient's freedom (especially by confinement to a mental hospital) ceaselessly confronts the psychiatrist with the problem of consent. The problems posed by obtaining the informed consent of adult patients undergoing psychiatric and psychotherapeutic treatments are dealt with in a large number of studies. The most important contributions in this field have been made by jurists in collaboration with developmental psychologists. Most of these studies come from the Anglo-Saxon countries, chiefly the United States. The study of consent depends in large measure upon the social contexts in which a more or less defensive form of medicine is practiced, and on the laws in force in different countries, or in states within the same country. The stress placed on certain aspects of consent (the fixing of age, for example) clearly depends on the criteria governing the laws applicable in each country. For many years the legal systems in many countries considered that psychotic patients, children, and adolescents were incapable of making important decisions concerning their life and hence, the management of their health. A discrepancy exists between the different rights granted to minors and the mentally ill. Thus, in many countries the courts have been more explicit and liberal when determining the rights of minors in criminal or penal cases, granting them rights and capacities of which they were deprived in the field of health. However, rights are regularly granted to minors in certain fields of health management: these rights, which vary significantly from one country to another, generally concern contraception, abortion, but also access to psychological treatments. Studies of the child's consent must therefore be placed in a far more general current of thought that reconsiders the status of the child within the family. Recognition that the interests of parents and children are not always coextensive, apart from situations of abuse or neglect, must lead to greater attention being paid to the opinions of persons with special needs. Thus, their participation in decisions that concern them should be encouraged and developed for ethical and legal reasons. The right possessed by a child capable of discernment to express his opinion is inscribed in the United Nations convention of child's rights. For a patient's consent to be considered informed, a number of conditions must be met" (Bachmann, J-P. (1994). In J. Y. Hattab (Ed.), *Ethics and child mental health* (p. 254–263). Jerusalem: Gefen Publishers.).

The patient must receive from the doctor all the necessary information liable to influence his decision about a treatment: that is, his illness (diagnosis and prognosis without treatment); the treatment suggested; and the possible alternatives. The patient must be capable of discernment, capable of understanding the information, of estimating and measuring the results he can expect from a treatment, and of grasping the future consequences of his decisions. The patient must also be in a position to freely express his will. As in any other medical discipline in which treatment is given to children or psychiatric patients, therapeutic measures in the field of mental health cannot be applied without the consent of the family or in their absence, legal representatives. Thus, the therapist must be sure not only that the parents are capable of meeting the requirements of free consent, but also, in the vast majority of situations, he must obtain the patient's consent or examine his ability to consent. In fact, the contract that links therapist and parents is accompanied by the therapist's moral contract with the patient, whose interests and rights he must defend.

"Though according to countries, the scope of the duty to inform is more or less defined by legal texts, it seems to us that in our social context at least, a considerable degree of reserve is often maintained regarding certain aspects of the information involved. Many parents are not informed of the precise diagnosis of the illness their child is suffering from. Some therapists fear the negative effects such information may have on the parents' image of their child, particularly when grave diagnoses are structurally conceptualized (for example, child psychoses). Others stress the difficulty of giving information whose value sometimes seems relative (uncertainty about the diagnosis and even the prognosis). Such reticence seeks to protect the patient or his entourage, but there is no doubt that it is not always justified, and may even be contrary to the expectations of most parents. Is not this reticence often another manifestation of the frequently ill-founded fear that the announcement of a diagnosis has regrettable repercussions on the patient? The dissatisfaction of our patients' parents often arises from the limited nature of the information they are given about the modalities of treatment rather than from the treatment's results. In Philippe Graham's view, the limitations imposed at present on research on the results of many forms of treatment pose ethical problems, and must incite us to prudence regarding the value of information given to parents about the benefits to be expected from certain treatments. This aspect of information plays a fundamental role in obtaining real consent. The obtaining of patients' consent must be perceived in a broader context which includes an understanding of the particular dynamic of each family, of the kind of efforts invested in the patient, and of the repercussions of the patient's symptoms on the family economy. It is often the outcome of a process which aims at creating a therapeutic alliance with the family and the patient" (Bachmann)

Clearly, in this analysis of the capacity of consent within a family, the clinician comes to ask himself questions about his own system of values, and about his countertransferential attitudes on this subject. Family therapies give rise to a particular problem because the risks and benefits differ from those of individual therapy. They can produce effects that one member of the family considers undesirable. A frequent attitude in which treatment of a family is refused, unless all the members of the family participate in it, is a potential source of pressure. Most forms of family therapy employ certain types of manipulation that limit a "true" informed consent and the freedom of choice of treatment (for example: the optimism which therapists decide to display about the results of the treatment in order to

alleviate the family's anxiety). Refusal of treatment after a period of investigation is one of the most frequent modalities of a breakdown in the relationship. Out of respect for the family's integrity and parents' autonomy, it is very rare that steps are taken to defend the interests of the child and his right to psychiatric treatment, unless other aspects of the family environment fully justify state intervention. This attitude is dictated by the fear of placing the child in a conflict of loyalty with his parents, a conflict that would have regrettable repercussions on the therapeutic process. Many psychotherapists are extremely reticent about undertaking treatments that are opposed by one of the parents, even when that parent no longer has parental authority, and this for the reasons mentioned above. Although the consent of both parents is always desirable, indeed indispensable, the seeking of this consent in cases of conflict between the parents sometimes obscures the desire and expectations of the child concerning treatment, particularly if he is not yet capable of giving real consent. In our view, the child should not be deprived of his right to psychotherapeutic treatment providing certain conditions are fulfilled: that the understanding which the parent requesting treatment has of that treatment is not an expression of the parental conflict. Further, the framework of the treatment must allow for a clarification, or even an interpretation of the child's conflicts in the face of his parents' disagreement.

This same dilemma can be raised when treating an adult patient who cannot fully understand the need for psychotherapeutic or any other therapeutic procedure. Generally, patient and emphatic explanations will evolve in him the acceptance for treatment; in other cases, family is generally considered to be the best defender of the patient's best interest but if the physician detects family conflicts. In these cases the court or official agencies will play this role of defender of patients rights.

VIII. ETHICS IN CHILD AND ADOLESCENT PSYCHIATRY

What has been said for general psychiatry is also highly relevant to child psychiatry. Child psychiatry has a privileged place at the heart of medicine and the human sciences. It is where the child is, and the child is everywhere. The child psychiatrist should not see his role limited to the care of mentally ill children, to diagnosis, and to establish programs of treatment, although this, too, is certainly within his domain, specifically. Anxious to serve as a prophylactic, the child psychiatrists have been called upon to intervene in assuring the mental hygiene of the pregnant woman. He knows what developmental problems await the newborn of the mother who smokes, drinks, takes drugs, overworks, suffers from mental problems, or lives within a conflicted conjugal relationship. He follows the child from its first steps at the center for maternal and infant care, or "well baby" clinics, then into the playground and later still into the school. He follows the child into the hospital when it falls sick, and helps to spot the psychological and psychosomatic dimensions activated in response to physical suffering. He follows the child into the family or institution, should the latter become necessary. His role is likewise to increase the awareness and comprehension of normal development and child psychopathology. He is called upon to adopt in each case the proper measures and modes of treatment. In addition to recognizing the inner and outer world of the child, the child psychiatrist must advise and influence those who may have a wider, political impact on the child and its family: in education, leisure, sports, as well as in the application of abortion laws, methods to help conception, or through procreation and filiation, of maternal and infant protection, of the work engaged by mothers and children, and so on. He will be solicited to help solve family problems, such as divorce and adoptive and foster-care placement. This field of action, as extensive as it is, also has its limits. The child psychiatrist must work as part of a team, choosing its members, cooperating with other professionals in the field of child and family mental health. Such teamwork is the modest recognition that others, at once similar to and different from us in their makeup, opinions, modes of thinking, are also close to the child's world and feel just as concerned for his well-being. We must know how to remain central to the team while managing the skills and personal sensibilities of each and every collaborator. Its limits are those imposed in resisting the temptations of omnipotence and megalomania. The ethical consideration is not a limit in itself, even though it may appear to be so.

IX. ETHICS IN PSYCHOGERIATRY

At least in the Western world, people live longer and longer. In the last decade, 70% of aged people died in their homes, compared with 30% in the previous decade. There is no doubt that this fact is highly relevant to the psychological distress suffered by these persons. It is most probable that mentally disturbed elders are the first to be removed from their own homes and deported to such institutions.

Elders are a financial and psychological burden for modern societies. They require expensive care, presence, and protection. They are not productive and during their long life after retiring they already make more from their insurance than they paid for.

As said before, ethics deals with difficult human situations. Ethics is the barrier in front of aggressive drives supported by smart rationalizations. Elders, like children, through their weakness and dependency, awake our basic sadism and raise our kindness and concern. But, unlike children, they also evoke death. Their presence represents at the same time success against death and fear of it. As such they are at risk to be rejected. The mentally ill elder is even more "dangerous." He or she is the living symbol of death and insanity, both highly frightening and rejected. Treating mentally ill elders is doubly difficult. They suffer roughly of two basic psychopathologies: depression and paranoia.

Old people who never suffered from psychic disorders develop atypical psychotic states with agitation, anxiety, paranoid ideations, generally jealousy toward the spouse or persecution from children concerning inheritance, and so on. Their psychic pain is so terrible and their arguments seem so stupid that it is quite difficult to manage their therapy. They are also highly sensitive to pharmacotherapy and the dangers of frequent side effects.

Even young depressive patients are sometimes hardly able to be convinced that life is worth living and their state is reversible. Depressive elders are not cooperative to our therapeutic efforts. They ask to die "as soon as possible," they refuse drugs and all forms of psychotherapy. Every therapist can easily be convinced by their call for death with dignity.

Among 225 non-demented elders aged 85 and above, 4% thought that "life was not worth living"; 4% expressed death wishes; and 0.9% thought of taking their lives but no one considered suicide seriously. But, 1.7% of those with mental disorders did seriously consider suicide; 9.2% thought about it; 27.5% expressed death wishes; and 29.2% considered life not worth living.

With aging, character traits become more prominent and accentuated. The suspicious become paranoid, the precocious become obsessional, the querulent become aggressive. The border with psychopathology is not clear and these attitudes are almost unbearable for the family. Is it more ethical to consider these persons as disordered and to treat them as such for the sake of their families, or to respect their basic identity and its changes? Experts in psychiatric gerontology have a crucial role in protecting these persons from rejection, neglect, and even abusive psychiatric hospitalization.

Systemic approaches and family therapies are not only efficient but also respectful of all participants rights.

In this article, we must also mention the psychological difficulties of elders who suffer from somatic acute, chronic, or terminal illnesses. At this age, the linkage between illness and death is magnified and is highly relevant. The threat is higher, the depressive features are obvious and the regression is deeper. Besides identifications, deep concern, and pity they also provoke anger and rejection. Ethics in psychogeriartry is the very confrontation between our basic values and our spontaneous tendencies.

X. ETHICS OF PREVENTION

Prevention in the field of mental health has more to do with sociology, politics and philosophy than with medicine. At the beginning of the communist revolution, it was thought that the newly established society would solve all problems " from alcoholism to sadness." So the founders of the Kibbutz movement claimed that they were establishing a "normal society that will solve all plagues." Religions also preach that such a behavior in their believers will make them always be somatically and mentally healthy. This has never been proved because these systems has never been perfectly observed.

"Prevention programs seek to reach out and intervene in relatively healthy populations in order to monitor their progress and in order to support them so that they will choose coping methods that contribute to a healthier outcome. They hope thereby to reduce the sum of mental suffering by influencing those who are passing through times of trial to choose what will be a healthier course, rather than haphazardly and unwittingly falling into a train of reactions that may bring not only that population to greater and more protracted disturbance, but that may, in turn, be communicated to the next generation when these children become parents. So large a task cannot be performed by mental health professionals alone. It requires the partnership of other community care givers: teachers, physicians, clergy, lawyers, public health nurses, welfare workers, probation officers, and so on, who are alerted, sensitized, and if necessary, supported by mental health consultants in dealing in their everyday work with those who are deemed to be at special risk. Fulfilling the purpose of prevention raises two major areas of ethical concern. The first involves the issue of whether, under current circumstances of limited budgets and relative ignorance about the psychic and social repercussions of even well-meant interventions, it is justified to inter-fere in the affairs of healthy people. The second involves an even more fraught question. As a mass movement, community psychiatry and its preventive component encourage and tacitly license thousands of care givers to enter, often uninvited, into the intimate psychological and psychosocial domains of individuals and families. Among the many well-meaning and well-trained workers in this field, there are a significant number of mediocrities, badly trained and poorly supervised, who in the name of prevention may wreak havoc in people's lives" (Caplan). To what extent are mental health specialists obligated and even able to control those they have unleashed? In the first place, it is unhappily axiomatic that programs of prevention are not cheap, and they do not save money in the short or long run. They do not cut treatment costs or rehabilitation costs down the road. There is no equivalent of a peace dividend to be garnered from an investment in preventive programs. While it is hoped, and even believed, that such programs, when properly implemented, save children and adults preventable suffering, they do not recompense the public purse for their cost by lowering the need for future appropriations for mental health services and facilities. To claim otherwise is unethical. And it is even more unethical to siphon funds away from treatment programs with the spurious argument that primary prevention is a better investment. Both types of services are necessary and complimentary. If programs of primary prevention are seen by the public as useful, they will be supported as long as professional promises and results seem congruent. The danger is of overselling and of subsequent public disillusionment. For in the history of psychiatry, claims were often made that if large sums were only dedicated to building mental hospitals according to the latest model, or invested in whatever other plan was currently fashionable in psychiatric practice, miracles of healing would take place and the public would save money as the number of sick was reduced, and as patients were rapidly returned to enrich society with their productive work. Unfortunately, this claim always proved false, since care is always more expensive than no care, and since the stream of need flows endlessly. The calls for funds never abated as sick replaced and outnumbered cured, and the cured relapsed and returned for more care. The public eventually caught on to the fact that it had been duped, and its resentment curtailed funds and withdrew sympathy from those it now saw as making exorbitant claims.

Requests for funding preventive programs, therefore, should be scrupulous in not making exaggerated promises. In this, as in all other areas of preventive psychiatry, the ethical stance is also the pragmatic one: tact, flexibility, modesty, and a noncoercive mien. Inherent in the community mental health model of prevention that is derived from public health is the danger that one may unintentionally harm those one sets out to help by tampering with healthy people who have only a statistical risk of developing pathology. This ethical issue is sharper in preventive psychiatry because, unlike public health, it can not base itself on cause and effect relationships between stressors and pathology and between intervention and outcome that have been exhaustively tested and proved. There are few psychiatric equivalents to the certainty that if one bars access to a contaminated well, the typhoid epidemic will be contained. Psychiatry deals in such complicated fields of social and psychic variables that it often relies on impressions of cause and effect and statistical probabilities, not on hard, proven facts like the observed interaction between micro-organisms and cells. Therefore, while ethical issues of inadvertently causing harm may be relatively resolved in public health, they must still be confronted in preventive psychiatry. In primary preventive psychiatry, individuals are being addressed by care givers while they are not only symptom free but may always remain so, despite exposure to potentially damaging forces. Any intervention at all in people who do not request or currently need it may do unnecessary harm. There is the danger of creating a self-fulfilling prophesy, for example, if care givers suggest future dangers that the individual might have never considered himself, through hysterical reactions or through obsessive fear on the part of that individual or his family of an apparently fated outcome. In programs of primary prevention as unimpeachable as warning children about the dangers of drug addiction, the information may excite the curious and rebellious with a hitherto unawakened desire to try it out for themselves. Or, conversely, it can make children fear even medication prescribed by physicians. In public health, a certain, albeit tiny proportion of those inoculated against disease may suffer fatal reactions. Individuals who might have escaped infection or residual damage from whooping cough or mumps, for example, may be infected or killed by the injection that was meant to protect them. The justification for campaigns of mass immunization that may cause such casualties is that diseases are contagious and epidemics cause far more widespread suffering and damage to individuals than measures to prevent them. The few casualties are seen as an inevitable lesser evil. In the area of psychological intervention, however, the weighing up of risk and gain may be less clear cut. Contagion and risk to society do not follow so simply here. Warnings about possible adverse reactions to ines-

capable situations may further heighten anxiety and stress, creating in their turn more problems for the already overburdened.

XI. ETHICS IN FORENSIC PSYCHIATRY

(This section is in large part reproduced from Diane Schetky's chapter under the same title in *Ethics and Child Mental Health* edited by the author.) Forensic psychiatry is a subspecialty that deals with the interface of psychiatry and the law. In contrast to the usual role of the clinician, the forensic psychiatrist's expertise is directed toward legal rather than therapeutic ends. Ethical problems may arise when the expert is not clear about his or her role or when competing parties attempt to influence the expert's testimony. This section will explore some common ethical dilemmas and offer guidelines for conducting forensic evaluations in an ethically sound manner.

"Unique ethical dilemmas arise in forensic psychiatry where the moral value systems of the legal and psychiatric professions are often at odds with one another. Hundert reminds us that law operates on the principles of liberty, justice, and what is right, whereas medicine focuses on what is good for the patient. Accordingly, the psychiatrist as expert witness may be tempted to slant testimony to the desired outcome especially if testifying as an adversary. As noted by Stone, "The problem is that helping the patient, which is the ethical thesis of the practitioner, becomes the ethical temptation in the legal context." Curran also cautions that, "The greatest danger to truth for a forensic scientist is in becoming an advocate." Further dangers lurk for the expert who blindly becomes an advocate for his own opinions and is not willing to entertain other possibilities even when confronted with new information. Additional pressures to alter testimony may come from the attorney who hired the expert and from the expert's need to please the attorney. It is easy for the psychiatrist to get caught up in the adversary system and the need to win. Another risk is that of becoming overidentified with any of the parties. It is often difficult to remain detached when one does extended evaluations and cases go on for many years awaiting settlement.

Role confusion may be lessened if the psychiatrist is clear about whom he serves. In contrast to a therapeutic relationship, the forensic psychiatrist is there not to help the patient but rather to testify as to facts and opinions. In so doing he helps the court determine the truth and answer the legal question at hand. Psychiatrists may bristle at the constraints of the legal system that exclude certain types of evidence from being heard. We need to remember that the adversary system has a long and honorable tradition, much better established than psychiatry, and that while on legal turf we must defer to that tradition and its rules of protocol. Most ethical guidelines do little to guide the expert through the quagmire of offering expert testimony.

The American Medical Association's Principles of Medical Ethics emphasizes the tenets of beneficence and nonmaleficence, that is, do no harm, in the doctor–patient relationship. Do these apply to the forensic psychiatrist who is not in a doctor–patient relationship? What about the harm we do to parents when we advocate terminating parental rights or we recommend waiver of a juvenile to the adult court? Appelbaum argues that beneficence and nonmaleficence do not obtain primacy for forensic psychiatrists and that offering any such promises could undermine the forensic process. Weinstock, chair of the American Academy of Psychiatry and Law's Ethic Committee, argues that although the forensic psychiatrist's priorities may differ, he or she still has a responsibility to adhere to medical ethical principles and to conduct evaluations with compassion and respect for human dignity. Unfortunately, the ethical guidelines of the American Academy of Psychiatry and Law, the American Psychiatric Association, or the American Academy of Child and Adolescent Psychiatry fail to expand upon this issue. Psychologists Koocher and Keith-Speigel note that many ethical codes of professional organizations ignore the special interests and needs of children and that some have no means of monitoring or enforcement capacity" (Schetky, D. H. (1994). In J. Y. Hattab (Ed.), *Ethics and child mental health* (p. 265–272). Jerusalem: Gefen Publishers.).

Conflicts of interest, if not recognized and avoided, can affect the neutrality and objectivity of the expert. For instance, is it possible to perform an objective custody evaluation on the children of a colleague? Certainly not, and even if the expert thought he was being objective his opinions would be suspect in the eyes of the court. Another example is the expert who is asked to testify against a colleague in a malpractice proceeding. If they are in any way in competition financially this could be viewed as a conflict of interest. Conflicts may also arise if one has current or past social interaction with any of the parties involved. The expert, out of regard for his own need for boundaries and comfort, might wish to avoid forensic cases in which there is likelihood of future professional or social involvement, for example, neighbors or the parents of one's children's classmates.

Basically, there is a conflict with ethical consequences inherent to fact that the psychiatrist is both a professional of mental health and a citizen of his own society when he has to give expertise on the responsability of a delinquent. The person he has to examine is either a murderer, a thief, a rapist, or a child sexual abuser. The fact that a judge asks for psychiatric examination does not mean that this person is no longer a criminal and such awareness in any moral, normal person may cause anger, disgust, revenge and maybe more.

Preaching for objectivity in such cases is an illusion. Psychiatrists are not likely to use pathological defense mechanisms like splitting. This conflict of interests can be approached by using a team who must first express all feelings and thoughts before they plan the professional examination, preferably through sitting with the suspected criminal.

The psychiatrist needs to consider whether his own strong personal beliefs preclude involvement in a particular case. Homophobia or bias toward mothers having custody would preclude an objective assessment of a gay father seeking custody of his child. If he has strong feelings against interracial adoption these could color his ability to objectively assess whether a child of a different race should be adopted by long-term foster parents. More subtle biases may enter in cases where professionals favor adoption by well-educated, middle-class parents over the return of a foster child to indigent birth parents. If in doubt, the psychiatrist should at least be up front about his biases at the onset with the referring attorney. Bias may be apparent if one is always testifying for one side or the other and attorneys are quick to point this out on the witness stand. For example, if an expert is always testifying on behalf of fathers versus mothers in custody proceedings or always finding sexual abuse, this maybe indicative of bias. A useful exercise is for the expert to ask, "How often do I give the side that hired me the opinion they want?" It is possible in some custody cases to be court appointed. While this infers more neutrality and often more cooperation from parties involved, it does not necessarily overcome the problems of the expert's personal biases.

Before accepting a case the psychiatrist needs to determine whether he has sufficient expertise in the area in which he is being asked to testify. Credentials should never be inflated and if they are, this is bound to be discovered during qualification of the expert and will only undermine his credibility. The neophyte need not be ashamed by lack of court experience and this may sometimes be used to advantage in negating the image of "hired gun." Attorneys are often willing to educate the expert as to the legal issues and sometimes even the relevant psychiatric literature. They should in all cases, no matter how experienced the expert, spend time with the expert as he prepares his report for court and his expected lines of questioning. Often expertise in one area may be parlayed into another. Having testified in several dog-bite cases the expert soon becomes conversant with the principles of tort litigation, and testifying about a child exposed to toxic waste is not that far afield. Likewise, the psychiatrist well versed in the psychodynamics of incest may be suited to testifying about the damaging effects of sex between therapist and patient. Special problems exist for the experienced forensic psychiatrist when attorneys attempt to impeach him by showing that the expert is contradicting himself.

Accepting fees on contingency is always unethical because it creates a vested interest in the outcome of the case. Attorneys who, in contrast, operate in an adversarial role commonly do this in tort litigation. For the expert witness to do so is to invite slanted or biased testimony.

Most forensic psychiatrists demand a retainer fee up front which is based upon estimated time spent in meeting with parties, attorneys, and reviewing records. The retainer not only assures payment, but also that one is being paid for time rather than for opinion. It is customary and acceptable to charge more for forensic evaluations. They are time consuming and taxing, and they can raise havoc with one's schedule. They call for a high level of skill and experience for which the expert should be adequately compensated.

Evaluation and treatment must be separated. When treating a person you can no longer give testimony for him or give any report on his behalf; you must never begin treatment of a person you first encounter in court. This absolute can seem harmful and sometimes stupid in the eyes of attorneys or even judges but it guarantees the total objectivity needed in such cases. An expert is entitled to interview the psychotherapist of the person he has to give a report on. It will be up to the therapist to decide whether to provide information on the patient, hopefully with the informed consent of the patient. Numerous pitfalls await the therapist who testifies in court on behalf of a patient. Privilege belongs to the patient and may only be waived by the adult patient, the minor patient's parents, or in some instances by court order. An exception is when the patient brings a malpractice action whereupon medical records are automatically tendered. Patients may waive confidentiality if they think their psychiatrist's testimony will be helpful to them. Confidentiality is lost once the witness is on the stand. He has no control over areas of inquiry and the patient may be damaged by his testimony. The therapist also lacks objectivity in that he is an advocate for the patient. This may tempt the therapist to slant testimony to a desired outcome or away from making statements that could hurt the patient. It may also lead him to be overly optimistic about the prognosis.

A thorny issue arises when the child psychiatrist is treating a patient whose parents decide to divorce. The court or attorneys may appeal to the therapist for direction in making custody recommendations, pointing out that he knows the family better than anyone else. This is a seductive ploy and if the therapist ventures into court he may lose the trust of his child patient. Another risk is that the parent against whom he testifies may undermine his continued therapy with the child. If forced to disclose statements made by the child, this could jeopardize the parent–child relationship. Parents may attempt to subpoena the therapist's records as part of a fishing expedition to see what they can turn up to use against the other parent. The American Psychiatric Association (1991) formed a task force to study the issue of disclosure of records in child custody disputes. It came up with recommendations that the party petitioning for the records must demonstrate the relevance of the material in the psychiatric records and that this material is not available from other sources, or through a court-ordered psychiatric evaluation. Another exception may be the child who has been threatened if she discloses information. There are numerous issues that involve trust in this case; these may not be surmounted in a limited evaluation.

To conduct a forensic evaluation, all parties, including children, need to be appraised of the purpose of the evaluation, the fact that it is not confidential, and which side, if not court appointed, has retained your services. For young children it may suffice to say that you will be helping the judge understand how they are feeling so that he can make the best decision for them. It is helpful to spell out that one is not acting in the role of therapist. Releases of information should be signed at the onset of the evaluation. Minors can not give consent for release of information but should at least be asked for their assent. The psychiatrist needs to avoid taking short cuts. Ample time should be spent with parties to arrive at opinions and recommendations that are supported by the data obtained. If there are opposing parties, as in custody evaluations, parties should be treated fairly and allowed to present their version of events in a reasonable amount of time. The expert needs to be able to tolerate ambiguity and should not rush to premature conclusions. If there are allegations of abuse against a parent, the expert should attempt to meet with the parents and to be open to the possibility of false allegations. It is irresponsible to offer opinions about parties one has not actually interviewed. Time also needs to be spent reviewing corroborating materials and to assess whether or not they are consistent with one's opinions. Is it ethical to perform a unilateral custody evaluation? It may be ethical, if one refrains from making comments about parties not seen and qualifies recommendations.

The forensic report should be addressed to the legal questions at hand. It should carefully document the foundations for one's opinions. Speculative comments usually have no place in a forensic report and psychoanalytic formulations should be used judiciously, if at all. It is important in jury trials not to invade the province of the jury by addressing the ultimate question such as a victim's credibility or the guilt of an alleged perpetrator. The expert may however, state with certainty that findings are or are not consistent with abuse. More latitude may be allowed to the witness in terms of what he may testify about in some family courts and those dealing with dependency issues rather than criminal or tort litigation cases. In commenting on issues of parental fitness, it is tactful to address strengths as well as weaknesses of respective parents. Deficits should be addressed with compassion if possible, for example, commenting that a mother's difficulty with bonding relates to her own neglect as a child. Pejorative statements should be avoided and their use should alert the expert and others to possible bias. The expert needs to be aware that she has no control over who sees that report once it is released. A forensic report will be most effective when it is written in clear language that is free of jargon, when it is balanced and fair, and when recommendations are reasonable and feasible. A well written report often leads to an out-of-court settlement, sparing the parties additional stress and expense.

XII. CONCLUSION

Ethics in psychiatry approaches the developing and suffering person and his family as a whole, in all their dimensions: neurological, biological, social, and the affective. It also must acknowledge this principle called *mind,* which is so important for a human being to be considered as such. It does not matter if the mind is real or not; it is an unavoidable concept, not only for understanding human behavior but also for understanding human history, human society, human laws, and what it means to be human.

Jewish Kabbale divides the creation into the inert, the vegetal, the alive and the speaking. Man was created by God from earth, which is altogether inert, vegetal, and alive, and he in insufflated in him spirit, which is his specificity and his condition to remain a speaking, mindful creation.

Bibliography

Alexander, F. G., & Selesnick, S. T. (1966). *The history of psychiatry.* New York: Harper & Row.

Cicchetti, D., & Cohen, D. J. (Eds.). (1995). *Developmental psychopathology.* New York: John Wiley & Sons, Inc.

Grodin, M. A., & Glantz, L. H. (1994). *Children as research subjects.* New York: Oxford University Press.

Hattab, J. Y. (1994). *Ethics and child mental health.* Jerusalem: Gefen Publishers.

Foucault, M. (1961). *Histoire de la folie à l'âge classique.* Paris: Plon Ed.

Maruani, G. (1976). *Psychiatrie et ethique.* Toulouse: Privat Ed.

Zadock, B. J., Kaplan, H. I., & Grebb, J. A. (Redford, D. C., Ed.). (1994). *Comprehensive textbook of behavioral sciences clinical psychiatry.* Baltimore: Williams & Wilkins Publ.

PSYCHOPHARMACOLOGY

Angus Dawson
University of Liverpool

GLOSSARY

a priori/a posteriori The a priori/a posteriori distinction relates to two different ways of obtaining knowledge. A priori knowledge is gained independently of experience; for example, through "logical" or "conceptual" clarification. A posteriori knowledge is gained through experience; for example, empirical work.

biological psychiatry Psychiatry that is concerned with exploring the possibility of a biological basis to psychiatry with the view to establishing scientifically valid treatments based upon an understanding of the way that the mind works, and what happens when it goes wrong.

neuroleptics Drugs used to relieve and prevent the recurrence of psychotic symptoms. They have many uses in psychiatry, but are most closely associated with the treatment of schizophrenia.

psychotropic drugs Those drugs that have an effect upon the mind. There are many different types, but they include neuroleptics, antidepressants, and anxiety-relieving drugs (anxiolytics).

psychopathology A general term used for things that go wrong with the mind, which may include mental illnesses and diseases.

psychopharmacology The study and use of drugs that have an effect upon the mind, with the aim of curing, or at least relieving, the symptoms of mental illnesses.

psychopharmacotherapy The general use of drugs as a form of treatment for mental illnesses.

tardive dyskinesia A distressing and sometimes permanent side-effect of neuroleptic drugs, that results in uncontrolled movements of the muscles, most commonly those in the face, including the tongue, and those controlling the limbs.

MENTAL ILLNESS is a widespread and debilitating affliction. The long-term aim of psychiatry is to provide, for mental illnesses, the range of successful explanations, treatments, and cures that mainstream medicine has provided for physiological illness. One of the central elements in contemporary psychiatric practice has been the role played by psychopharmacology. Psychopharmacology is concerned with the study, production and use of drugs that have an effect on the mind. Substances that have had a supposedly therapeutic effect upon the mind have been used since prehistory, but the modern age of psychopharmacology is usually held to date from 1952, when chlorpromazine was first used as an antipsychotic. This event was quickly followed by the development of the first modern antidepressants and tranquilizers. Despite extensive research, the classes of drugs introduced into psychiatric treatment during the 1950s still form the basis of available treatments today. Perhaps the only new group of drugs that have been developed more recently are the new class of antidepressants called selective serotonin reuptake inhibitors (SSRIs), which have been introduced since 1984 (the most famous of which is Prozac).

Despite the many criticisms that have been leveled at the use of drugs to treat mental illnesses, they have been widely prescribed and used throughout the world; and their use is expected to continue rising for the foreseeable future. The supporters of psychopharmacology will argue that this is justified because a great deal of progress has already been made in understanding the nature of the human brain and mental illnesses, and the role of drugs in treating mental illnesses. Psychopharmacotherapy, it is argued, has lead to the relief of much suffering, and the future holds the prospect of increased knowledge and new and more precise treatments. It is argued by its advocates that psychopharmacology provides the basis for a truly scientific approach to curing mental illness.

Given the supposed present, and possible future, benefits of psychopharmacology, we might ask why anyone would argue that drugs should not be used in the treatment of mental illnesses. There are perhaps three different types of argument against the use of psychotropic drugs, and we will consider each in turn.

i. We can call the first type of arguments "a priori arguments," because they seek to provide a "conceptual" or "logical" objection to the use of drugs in psychiatric treatments. Such arguments are largely the result of disagreements about the nature of the mind and how the philosophy of mind should be conducted.

ii. The second group of arguments are very different in that they seek to use empirically based findings as the justification for ethical conclusions. This means that much of the debate results from disagreement about the assessment of the empirical evidence relating to the supposed scientific study of the mind, to the action of drugs upon the mind, and to what effects drugs may have upon their users. It is suggested by opponents of psychopharmacology that the empirical evidence suggests not that drugs are useful in the treatment in psychiatry, but rather that on the contrary, they are dangerous and therefore should

not be used. The disagreement here is over the empirical evidence, so we can therefore call these "a posteriori arguments".

iii. The third class of arguments has to do with what we might term straight ethical issues related to aspects of the way that psychiatric practice, and psychopharmacotherapy in particular, is carried out. Again, the opponent of psychopharmacology will argue that either individually or jointly these arguments point to the unethical nature of drug use in psychiatry, and provide the basis for arguing that it should cease.

We will consider each of these three types of argument against psychopharmacology in the following discussion.

I. A PRIORI ARGUMENTS AGAINST PSYCHOPHARMACOLOGY

The advocate of the use of drugs in psychiatry argues that psychopharmacology will increasingly lead to a new understanding of the mind and of what occurs when it is ill, and to the development of new drugs to treat and cure mental illnesses. This idea is encouraged by the recent multidisciplinary advances in areas as diverse as anthropology, psychology, linguistics, artificial intelligence, neuroscience, genetics, biology, and the clinical sciences. Of course, it can be admitted that a unified scientific understanding of the mind does not exist at the moment, but the important point is that there is no reason in principle why it could not one day be achieved.

Some opponents of modern psychiatry and the use of drugs argue against this view, by claiming that a science of the mind is *in principle* impossible. This is an a priori argument, because it is not based upon empirical considerations, or anything else that is open to observation. It is supposed to be a "conceptual" or "logical" point. The thought is that there is something about the nature of the mind that means that it can never be a fit subject for science. It is held that this provides a reason to believe that drugs *cannot* possibly be effective in the treatment of mental illnesses. We will consider just one influential example of this type of argument here.

In 1960 Thomas Szasz famously argued that mental illnesses are "myths". This is not the place to look at all the details of his position, but it is worth noting that his argument rests upon the view that the so-called "mental illnesses" are not illnesses at all, because illnesses are *physical* things. Szasz argues that the group of behaviorial and verbal acts that are called mental illnesses are in fact what he calls "problems for living." Such behaviorial and verbal acts are expressions of meaning, and therefore "logically" not the fit subject matter for medicine. He holds that both medicine and meaning are governed by norms, but the two types of norms are radically different in nature. A failure to follow the norms that govern meaning cannot be corrected through medical intervention. Psychiatric treatments are held to be useless because they ignore this logical difference, and, therefore, physical intervention such as the use of drugs to treat mental illnesses can be ruled out in principle. His conclusion is not that drugs *do not* work; but rather the stronger claim that they *cannot* work.

Szasz's argument relies upon the idea that there is some "logical" difference between the mental and the physical that we are to accept a priori. The problem with this is that arguments advanced in the past as a priori have often been refuted by subsequent science; for example, it was once held a priori that space was Euclidean. This was later discovered to be untrue. It is always a possibility that an a priori argument may be refuted by advances in our understanding; for example, it *might* well turn out that a complete and unified scientific account of the mind becomes available in the future. However, even if this point is not accepted, we might also question whether such arguments rely upon an assumption about the nature of physicalism, which is not necessarily true. For example, recent discussions in the philosophy of mind have suggested how it might be possible to envisage sophisticated nonreductive forms of physicalism, which may be able to respond to the objection that they are too crude. The importance of Szasz's argument is that if it succeeds then the use of drugs in psychiatry is ruled out at this early stage on nonempirical grounds. If it is even *possible* that one day a unified science of the mind may exist, then his a priori assumption may be doubted.

II. A POSTERIORI ARGUMENTS AGAINST PSYCHOPHARMACOLOGY

"A posteriori arguments" are those based upon evidence gained through experience. The advocates of psychopharmacology can argue that there is strong empirical evidence to suggest that we are well on the way to understanding the nature of the mind, the causes of mental illnesses, and the actions of drugs in relieving symptoms. Opponents of drug use in psychiatry such as Peter Breggin challenge the scientific status of psychopharmacology by questioning the empirical evidence that supports these views, and suggesting that on the contrary, there is strong empirical evidence that drugs actually cause brain damage in the user. This idea is then used to suggest that psychotropic drugs should not be used. We will consider some of the a posteriori arguments for and against psychopharmacology.

A. Empirical Evidence of Drug-Induced Damage

Breggin offers a sustained argument that the drugs themselves do not cure a disease but cause one; and that the damage produced by the drugs is mistaken for the symptoms of the illness. He argues that neuroleptic drugs, for example, cause "brain dysfunction" characterized by what he terms lobotomy-like effects. He states that, "the neuroleptic drugs are chemical lobotomizing agents with no specific therapeutic effects on any symptoms or problems. Their main impact is to blunt and subdue the individual." Breggin argues that this view is supported by empirical evidence. If this is valid, then we are dealing with an a posteriori argument against psychopharmacology. Evidence in support of such a view may be drawn from two possible consequences of drug use: the threat of dependency and the severity of so-called "side effects."

1. Dependency

An important reason to hold that psychopharmacotherapy is harmful to the user is to consider the empirical evidence that many psychotropics induce dependency or addiction. Breggin discusses these issues by focusing upon drugs used to treat anxiety such as benzodiazepine. Such drugs can be addictive and besides producing the undignified loss of self-control that dependency induces, they also cause severe withdrawal symptoms when the patient ceases to use them. Breggin also argues that such drugs actually increase the very symptoms that were the reason to take the drugs in the first place.

The advocates of psychopharmacotherapy can of course reply to these points. For example, it could be admitted that there is always the possibility of dependency, but that it is important to see that the risk differs with different psychotropics. Many drugs used in psychiatry cannot induce dependence, whereas some others, such as some types of anxiolytics, can more easily bring about dependence. It is important to be aware of the various properties of the different drugs and prescribe accordingly. This is particularly important where drugs are to be used over long periods. Advocates can also argue that there are increasingly drugs available of all types that do not induce dependence, and that as psychopharmacology develops they will become the model for standard treatments; drugs such as benzodiazepines are either no longer used at all, or only in very special circumstances.

2. Side effects

"Side effects" can be defined as those consequences of a drug that are unwanted. Even though most side effects stop when the drug is withdrawn, they can still be disturbing to the sufferer. Psychotropic drugs are especially likely to cause at least minor side effects. For example, neuroleptics can produce a whole range of unwanted symptoms, which include different types of tremors, dry mouth, constipation, and cardiac problems. Perhaps the best-known side effect of psychotropic drugs, and certainly one of the most serious, is that of tardive dyskinesia. One reason why this is so well known is that it can have a permanent effect upon the patient, even after drug use ceases. It is especially common where the neuroleptic drugs are used over a long period to help prevent recurrence of the symptoms of schizophrenia. Breggin, and other opponents of psychopharmacotheraphy argue that there is plenty of empirical evidence that demonstrates the devastating damage that so-called "side effects" can inflict upon patients. This evidence provides strong grounds for the argument that because the harm done outweighs any possible benefits, psychotropic drugs should not be used.

The advocates of psychopharmacotherapy can also produce a response on this issue. For example, it might be argued that the nature of the damage that can result means that the benefits and risks need to be carefully weighed up where drug use is contemplated. Perhaps where the possibility of side effects exists, it is only in the severest of cases, and not where it is felt that the use of drugs will only bring about a slight gain, or where the chance of the desired effect is held to be slight, that drugs should be used. For example, perhaps it can be questioned whether neuroleptics should be used to suppress what could be considered merely embarrassing symptoms of something like Tourette's Syndrome in a child, given the potential long-term dangers of tardive dyskinesia.

The advocates of psychopharmacology could also argue that it is vital that there are improved methods for monitoring side effects, so that treatments can be fairly assessed and, if needed, modified or even rejected. One of the problems at the moment is that feedback from patients about side-effects is poor. For example, Edwards reports that it is estimated that only 1 in 10 to 1 in 25 side effects are reported. Finally, it might be held that where side effects exist they are an unfortunate, but unintended consequence of treatment, and that they should not prevent the use of the treatment as long as they do not outweigh the benefits of that treatment.

B. Empirical Evidence in Support of Psychopharmacology

Advocates of biological psychiatry can point toward a number of specific areas where our empirical knowledge has recently increased, such as the role of genetics, the importance of neurotransmitters, and the significance of physical brain changes. It is argued that this can be used as evidence in support of biological psychiatry, and psychopharmacology in particular. However, opponents of psychopharmacology, such as Breggin, challenge each of these supposed areas of progress, and we will consider each in turn.

1. Genetics

There is a new emphasis on trying to determine the relative extent of the role of genetic factors and the environment in mental illness. This regeneration of interest in genetics has occurred for a number of reasons. One is the reanalysis of family and twin studies; and another is because of new models of genetic inheritance that have shifted away from classical or Mendelian models of genetic inheritance toward the idea of looking for multi-gene contributions, and more complex interactions between genetic and environmental factors. The supporters of biological psychiatry argue that there is strong empirical evidence for a genetic basis for at least some mental illnesses.

Breggin attacks the empirical evidence from the family and twin studies, arguing that they do not in fact support the conclusions that the advocates of biological psychiatry suggest. There are difficult issues here about interpreting the data, and there is always a danger that more is claimed for such studies than is scientifically justified. However, it should be noted that Breggin's discussion of the empirical evidence is rather selective; for example, he does not look at the work of Gottesman and his co-workers on the role of genetics. If we look at Breggin's other arguments against a role for genetic explanations in mental illnesses, then we can perhaps ask whether he is being fair in his discussion of this issue. For example, he seems to hold that genetic explanations cannot be given because there is good evidence that mental illnesses are not caused by single genes. However, as suggested above most work is now being done on the assumption that genetic explanations are more complex than this, in that they involve multiple genes, and interactions between genes and the environment. His discussion is also colored by the rather emotive way that he associates genetics with eugenic policies. It seems perfectly possible to believe that genetics play a role in mental illness, without being committed to eugenic solutions.

2. Neurotransmitters

The present optimism of biological psychiatrists is also supported by apparent advances in recent research into the neurological basis of mental functions and mental illnesses, and by new understanding of the role and workings of neurotransmitters and inhibitors in normal brain function and in psychopathology. For example, there has been much work done on the role not only of dopamine, but also glutamate and serotonin in schizophrenia. However, Breggin argues that such observed changes in the brain chemistry are due to the effects of the drugs, and are not part of any mental illness.

3. Physical Differences

The advocate of biological psychiatry can also argue that there has been a revolution in the development and use of new technologies, and that these will increasingly lead to greater understanding of general brain functions, and of the role of neurotransmitters in particular. For example, some studies have suggested that the brains of schizophrenics show a characteristic pattern of damage or "shrinkage," and it has been argued that this could be a physical symptom of this illness. The development of such new technology as magnetic resonance imaging (MRI), positron emission tomography (PET), single photon emission tomography (SPET), and magnetic resonance spectroscopy (MRS) suggests that further discoveries of such physical symptoms will be made. However, once again, Breggin argues that the evidence from such studies actually suggests that these changes in the brains of schizophrenics are the result of neuroleptic drugs, rather than any illness.

C. Arguing with Empirical Evidence

Empirical evidence on any subject can be contradictory, and is often difficult to interpret. However, this is no excuse for not basing our views on what evidence is available to us. The empirical basis of psychopharmacology is not established beyond all dispute, but there seems to be strong grounds for at least not dismissing the idea. The fairest conclusion might be that the relative contributions of genetics and the environment to psychopathology, the role of neurotransmitters, and the implications of the physical changes in the brain are still not clearly established. Where there is contradictory evidence, perhaps the best solution is to admit this fact, and suspend a final judgment until more evidence is available. Empirical evidence should be approached with an open mind, and assessed in an objective manner, rather than being selected because it supports a favored initial viewpoint.

It is certainly the case that the uncertainties over the empirical evidence mean that any ethical conclusions should only be drawn tentatively and with care. For example, even if present psychotropic drugs do cause the type of damage Breggin suggests, this does not mean that future drugs need do so. Even if they did, perhaps that damage itself would have to be weighed against the possible benefits of treatment. Perhaps we can agree with Tyrer, who argues that on balance no fair observer could fail to accept that drugs have been beneficial. The advocate of psychopharmacology will also argue that new drugs are also likely to be more precise in their application, and less likely to induce dependency and produce side effects.

III. ETHICAL ISSUES IN PSYCHOPHARMACOTHERAPY

Now we have considered arguments against psychopharmacology in principle, we can turn to the many arguments about the nature of psychiatric practice involving drugs. These arguments are not directly related to the nature of drugs, nor the empirical evidence about their effectiveness, but more to how they are used. They are grouped here into a number of themes: issues that have to do with injustice in psychopharmacotherapy, informed consent, involuntary treatment, and issues that have to do with drug production. Besides considering the details of each of these issues, it is also important to decide whether there is unethical conduct, and if it is an essential feature of the use of drugs in psychiatry. If it were, then this could be used to argue that psychopharmaco-therapy is intrinsically wrong.

A. Injustice in Psychiatry

There have been a number of scandals in psychiatry that are often used as evidence to cast doubt upon the possibility of there ever being such a thing as ethical psychiatric practice. There is no denying that abuse has occurred in psychiatry in the past. One example would be where drugs have been used in nursing homes to sedate patients, and thereby allow the existence of less than optimum staffing levels. Other unethical treatment would include exploitation of a vulnerable population, as, for example, where abuse has occurred in an institutional setting.

B. Informed Consent in Psychiatry

The issue of informed consent is central to much recent discussion in applied ethics. An informed consent is held to be more that a mere act of consent. It is a decision based upon information provided to the consenting party, upon all aspects relevant to the decision. In the medical sphere this will include information on different therapeutic options, possible risks, and side effects. It is only when this information is understood and digested, and forms the basis of a free decision by a competent individual that it constitutes informed consent.

It is often assumed that informed consent will only play a minor role in psychiatry because of the nature of psychiatric illness, but there is no clear reason to think this is so. Certainly, it is important to be aware of the difficulties that might arise because of the nature of mental illnesses, and the very real possibility of temporary or permanent loss of competence. Many mental illnesses effect the ability to reason, and thereby the capacity to consent. However, it should never be assumed that just because an individual is suffering from a particular mental illness that they are incompetent. It might be better to think of moving from this idea of incompetence necessarily arising from particular illnesses, toward a notion of competence that is related to the task or decision that needs to be made. This would allow the specifics of the individual's illness and capacity relevant to that particular decision to be taken into account. As a general rule, it is worth noting that sufferers of mental illnesses are actually competent in far more situations than is presently realized.

There are also many practical benefits that can result from the provision of information as part of the process of gaining a consent in psychiatry. For example, patients can be warned of possible risks (for example, that certain foods interact with the monoamine oxidase inhibitors family of antidepressants. See Bernstein, J. G. (1995). *Handbook of Drug Therapy in Psychiatry* (3rd ed.), Appendix A. St. Louis: Mosby.) or possible side effects, so that they can be prepared to recognize likely reactions, and know that they should notify their psychiatrist. Bernstein argues that the good psychiatrist will anticipate, as well as respond to patient fears. He gives the example of weight loss as a symptom of depression, and the frequent assumption by the patient that this is a symptom of cancer, which the physician does not want to disclose. He recommends informing the patient of the nature of her illness in some detail, if possible. It can be explained, at the same time, that if any side effects do develop, the dosage or the drug itself can be changed, or the side effects themselves might be treated.

There is good reason to think that when patients are actively involved in decision-making in this way, they feel more comfortable taking the drugs, and they are also more likely to follow the prescribed drug routine. Bernstein also suggests that regular reviews of treatment are carried out, so that the patient can report any problems, worries, or side effects, and the psychiatrist can ensure that the regimen is being followed correctly. He sums up these points by stating that, "providing adequate patient education is one of the fundamental techniques of good pharmacotherapy."

C. Involuntary Treatment

This is one of the most discussed ethical issues related to the use of drugs in psychiatry. Some argue that it can never be justified, and this attitude places the emphasis upon a patient's right to refuse a treatment. In recent years this has been supported by some courts, particularly those in the United States. For example, it was held in *Rogers v. Okin* (738 F2d. 1 (1stCir), 1984) that patient incompetence to refuse treatment did not follow from the fact of that patient's involuntary detention. The issue of involuntary treatment raises wider issues, such as whether such a practice is paternalistic, and thereby unethical, or whether nonconsensual treatment can be given in certain circumstances. If so, some justified account of what those circumstances are must be provided.

Such an attempt to provide a justification for involuntary intervention may appeal to features such as the possible harm the patient might cause to himself or others. This is a real possibility in some severe cases of mental illness, for example, where a patient is severely depressed, and there may be a substantial risk of suicide. The performance of an act of involuntary treatment may be the best way of returning the subject to a position where their own views on the nature of treatment can then be the basis of future treatment. For example, Bernstein argues that even where an involuntary treatment is felt to be absolutely necessary, such as in a genuine emergency situation, there are still choices about the details of the action that make a moral difference. For example, it is possible to use a short-acting rather than a long-term drug. This would allow the possibility of the shortest and least invasive involuntary treatment, and would mean that informed consent could then be sought as quickly as possible.

In any case, it is interesting that research suggests that where a patient at first refuses treatment, they often consent at a later date. This suggests that, unless there is a genuine emergency situation, it might be as well not to enforce treatment, but attempt to understand the reasons for a refusal, and seek to respond to those reasons. Where this is unsuccessful there may need to be more thought given to the possibility of involuntary treatment, and whether it is justified in that particular case.

Bernstein points out that there may well be a contrary danger to that suggested by the opponents of drug use in psychiatry, and this is a tendency not to use drugs where a proven treatment exists, but is not given because of general worries about psychopharmacotherapy. He gives the example of depression where psychotherapy is a popular treatment rather than drugs, despite the evidence that drugs are effective and fast acting. Perhaps it is as well to emphasize that an interest in psychopharmacological treatments does not exclude other forms of psychiatric and psychological treatment.

D. Ethical Issues in Drug Production

1. Drug Research

There are, of course, a large number of ethical issues that arise from any research; but there are also a few special concerns with research in psychopharmacology. One important issue is whether there is a clear dividing line between research and treatment. In a sense, one of the strong attractions of psychopharmacology is that drug treatments not only supply beneficial treatments, but they also provide information about the workings of the physiology of the brain. One of the reasons for optimism among the advocates of psychopharmacology

is the relationship between drug development and the new understanding of the mind it can afford; examples might include the much discussed role of dopamine in schizophrenia, and monoamines and serotonin in depression. The use of drugs to explore these issues would seem to require a very high degree of informed consent on behalf of the patient. Is the degree of understanding required for nontherapeutic consent greater than that where the individual is likely to directly benefit? See the "Statement of Principles of Ethical Conduct for Neuropsychopharmacologic Research in Human Subjects" in Meltzer, which suggests that it should be. Perhaps such procedures may well be completely separated from treatment, but there is always the danger of confusion, and a possible conflict between the needs of the individual patient and the thirst for greater scientific knowledge. Can research be justified upon the incompetent when future sufferers may benefit, but perhaps the patient themselves do not directly benefit?

A practical issue about drug trials is that the patient body from which they are drawn must be representative; if it is not, then there are serious limitations to the scientific basis to that treatment. For example, Hamilton and Jensvold warn about the differential effects that drugs can have on men and women. Many trials have been done only with male subjects, despite the fact that women appear to have different drug absorption and excretion rates than men. This makes a difference when it comes to prescribing particular doses, and this may account for the apparent larger number of side effects suffered by women. Hamilton and Jensvold are keen to have these points acknowledged, so that women can benefit from drug treatments to the maximum extent. Similar points could be made about children or the aged as drug subjects.

2. Drug Marketing

Most of the research into drugs is financed by the pharmaceutical industry. The majority of drugs that are the subject of preliminary research never even go to initial trials, never mind onto the market. However, it should not be forgotten that drug production is ultimately market driven, and that the manufacturers aim to make a profit. There is a mass market for many psychotropics, particularly for antidepressives and anxiolytics. On the one hand the development of a new drug is a costly, lengthy, and risky endeavour, but the financial returns on a successful drug are huge. It is for these reasons that there are always supposedly new drugs coming onto the market; however, it is often the case that these "new" drugs are only slight variants of an existing treatment.

There are also ethical issues to do with the actual marketing of the drugs. For example, there is a strong possibility of a conflict of interest in psychiatry given the degree of funding that comes from drug companies to help with the funding of journals, conferences, books, research, and private individuals. Even if it were true that psychiatry as a profession is uninfluenced by the source of this funding, which would be little short of miraculous, it could be argued that the need to retain public trust should be a greater priority. Another issue to do with drug marketing is the well-documented over-representation of women in advertisements for psychotropic drugs, particularly antidepressants. There is always the danger that advertising for psychotropics actually reinforces stereotypes about who are the likely consumers of such drugs.

In conclusion, it is important to clarify the nature of such ethical problems in psychiatric practice. There is a strong case for psychiatrists to be made aware of such objections so that where necessary they can respond to their critics by changing their practice. However, while it is important not to belittle past and present unethical conduct by psychiatrists, it should be noted that to argue from the fact of such unethical behavior to the conclusion that drug use in psychiatry is fundamentally unethical, it would have to be held that such events are *necessary* features of psychopharmacotherapy. It is far from clear that this is the case, in that such events seem to result from the contingent unethical behavior of individuals. If this is true, then the existence of unethical conduct does not establish that drug use in psychiatry is essentially unethical.

IV. CONCLUSION

There is a need to distinguish the different types of arguments about psychopharmacology, so that they can be assessed fairly. If the a priori arguments are successful, then psychopharmacology is ruled out in principle. If such arguments can be questioned, then the next step is to consider a posteriori arguments, and this must involve a fair assessment of the empirical evidence about the effects of drugs. If this evidence fails to suggest that drugs are so damaging that they should not be used,

then we need to consider whether the use of drugs as part of psychiatric treatment is so unethical, it rules out psychopharmacotherapy in principle. However, it might be concluded that although there are many ethical problems with present psychiatric practice, there is no reason to think that they could not, in principle, be overcome. There is surprisingly little specifically written about ethical issues that has to do with psychopharmacology in the psychiatry textbooks. Ethical issues are something that psychopharmacologists need to urgently address in their writing as well as their practice.

Also See the Following Articles

DRUGS: MORAL AND LEGAL ISSUES • INFORMED CONSENT • MEDICAL CODES AND OATHS • MENTAL HEALTH • MENTAL ILLNESS, CONCEPT OF

Bibliography

Bernstein, J. G. (1995). *Handbook of drug therapy in psychiatry*. (3rd ed.). St. Louis: Mosby.

Block, S., & Chodoff, P. (1991). *Psychiatric ethics* (2nd ed.). Oxford: Oxford University Press.

Bloom, F., & Kupfer, D. (Eds.). (1995). *Psychopharmacology: The fourth generation of progress*. New York: Raven Press.

Breggin, P. (1993). *Toxic psychiatry*. London: Harper Collins.

Buchanan, A. & Brock, D. (1989). Deciding for others: the ethics of surrogate decision making. Cambridge: Cambridge University Press.

Edwards, J. G. (1995). Adverse reactions to and interactions with psychotropic drugs. In King, D. J. (Ed.), *Seminars in clinical psychopharmacology*. London: Gaskell.

Gelder, M., et al. (1996). *Oxford textbook of psychiatry* (3rd ed.). Oxford: Oxford University Press.

Gottesmann, I. (1991). *Schizophrenia genesis*. Freeman: New York.

Hamilton, J., & Jensvold, M. (1995). Sex and gender as critical variables in feminist psychopharmacology and pharmacotherapy. In J. Hamilton et al., *Psychopharmacology from a feminist perspective*. New York: Harrington Park Press.

King, D. J. (Ed.). (1995). *Seminars in clinical psychopharmacology*. London: Gaskell.

McGuffin, P., et al. (1994). *Seminars in psychiatric genetics*. London: Gaskell.

Meltzer, H. (Ed.). (1987). *Psychopharmacology: The third generation of progress*. New York: Raven Press.

Szasz, T. (1960). The myth of mental illness. *American Psychologist*, *15*, 113–118.

Tyrer, P. (1979). The basis of drug treatment in psychiatry. In P. Hill, et al. (Eds.), *Essentials of postgraduate psychiatry*. London: Academic Press.

PSYCHOSURGERY AND PHYSICAL BRAIN MANIPULATION

Jean-Noël Missa
Free University of Brussels

I. Historical and Medical Aspects
II. Psychosurgery Today
III. Ethical Aspects

GLOSSARY

amygdalotomy A psychosurgical operation that destroys the amygdala, a part of the brain located in the limbic system and involved in emotional experiences associated with fear and anger, fight and defense.

hypothalamotomy A psychosurgical procedure sometimes used in the treatment of violent, aggressive, or restless behaviors.

leucotomy or lobotomy A psychosurgical operation realized in the early period of psychosurgery that consists of extensive cutting of prefrontal cortical connections to the thalamus.

limbic system A neuroanatomical structure functionally concerned with emotional experiences.

obsessive–compulsive disorder Psychiatric disorder characterized by obsessions that are accompanied by the experience of subjective compulsion.

prefrontal cortex The anterior part of the cerebral cortex functionally involved in thought and emotions.

stereotactic subcaudate tractotomy A current psychosurgical operation for anxiety and obsessive-compulsive disorders resistant to conventional treatments.

stereotactic surgery A technique for precisely locating targets within the brain, thereby allowing destruction of specific areas with great accuracy.

PSYCHOSURGERY—sometimes called "functional neurosurgery for psychiatric disorders" or "psychiatric neurosurgery"—is the treatment of psychiatric disorders by means of cerebral neurosurgery. Psychosurgery is still limited to making lesions in the brain.

From the time of the first operation in the 1930s until today, psychosurgery has been a controversial treatment. The use of psychiatric surgery has been overshadowed by doubts about its usefulness, inadequate reporting of outcomes, and ethical questions.

After its introduction by Egas Moniz in 1936, psychosurgery became popular in the 1940s and in the early 1950s. Then, the advent of effective psychotropic agents and the rise of sociopolitical views of the causation of mental disorders led to a rapid decline of the surgical treatment.

Today, psychosurgery is not a common practice. Psychiatric surgery is carried out in a few medical centers where new stereotactic radiosurgical techniques requiring no opening of the skull are used. With time, its indications have also changed. In the forties and the fifties, thousands of schizophrenic patients received surgery. It is now generally accepted that schizophrenia cannot be helped by psychosurgery. Its current main indications are for treatment-resistant mental disorders, in particular severe anxiety, major depression, and obsessive–compulsive disorder.

I. HISTORICAL AND MEDICAL ASPECTS

A. Physical Treatments for Mental Illness in the 1920s and the 1930s

In the field of biological psychiatry, the first half of the century was the period of the "great and desperate cures" (Valenstein, 1986). In the 1920s and the 1930s, extraordinary physical treatment for mental disorders was introduced including insulin therapy, cardiazol therapy, and electric shock therapy. The theoretical principle of these therapies was very simple: in order to cure a mentally ill patient, it is necessary to give him a shock.

In 1928, Manfred Sakel introduced insulin therapy (Sakel, 1938). The Sakel method was a treatment of schizophrenia by means of an insulin coma. Insulin was used to induce hypoglycemic coma and seizures. In the thirties, other violent somatic treatments were used in psychiatry. A new method of inducing convulsions by the use of cardiazol was introduced by Laszlo von Meduna. These treatments were extremely risky and many patients died. In this climate of shock therapy, it was natural that the idea should occur to someone that electricity could be applied to patient as a convulsive stimulus. In 1936, Ugo Cerletti, a physician in Rome, undertook electrical convulsion experiments upon humans. It is interesting for our purpose to note that in this case of experimentation on humans, Cerletti did not think it necessary to obtain the consent of the patient. Like Moniz, Cerletti did not ignore the fact that "unexpected—perhaps terrible—surprises might be encountered with the new method of treatment" (Cerletti, 1950). The patient, a schizophrenic of about 40, was chosen for the first test. No one knew who he was. Nobody asked the patient for his permission. He had arrived in Rome from Milan by train without a ticket. The patient expressed himself in incomprehensible neologisms. According to Cerletti, "preparations for the experiments were carried out in an atmosphere of fearful silence bordering on disapproval in the presence of various assistants and some outside doctors" (Cerletti, 1950). For the first test, Cerletti and Bini used a reduced tension (70 volt) with a duration of 0.2 second. The patient suddenly jumped on his bed, but he did not lose consciousness. Cerletti thought that the voltage had been held too low and he wanted to continue the experiment with a second test. Someone got nervous and suggested that the subject should be allowed to rest until the next day. Suddenly, the patient exclaimed: "Not a second, it is deadly." The assistants began to insist upon suspension of the proceedings. However, Cerletti did not want to be influenced by "those superstitions," and he gave a second discharge of 110 volts for half a second. That is how the first epileptic fit experimentally induced in man through the electric stimulus took place. Electroshock was born.

The initial enthusiasm among psychiatrists for somatic treatments waned rapidly. These treatments, based on fanciful theories, were sometimes effective in bringing about a transitory improvement of psychotic symptoms. But these therapies were extremely violent and dangerous. Patients often died after insulin therapy. Cardiazol therapy and electroshock caused significant morbidity, due to fractures until curare was used to induce paralysis. After 1936, psychosurgery was offered to those who had already failed to respond to "shock therapy." Very often, electroshock was used before or after psychosurgery. The history of electroshock is strongly connected with the history of psychosurgery.

B. Psychosurgery: A Historical Analysis

1. Early Psychosurgical Interventions

In 1891, German psychiatrist G. Burckhardt removed the cortical areas responsible for language (Broca and Wernicke areas) from the brain of five persons suffering from psychoses. In 1910, Puusepp in Russia also carried out brain surgery for psychiatric reasons. But the real story of psychosurgery began in 1935 with Egas Moniz, professor of neurology at the University of Lisbon, who inaugurated a surgical procedure in the treatment of certain psychoses. Moniz was present at the Second International Neurological Congress in London in 1935. The central issue of the symposium was the frontal lobes. Fulton and Jacobsen reported their experiments upon the tranquilizing effect of frontal lobectomy in two chimpanzees. After the communication by Fulton and Jacobsen, Moniz asked if frontal lobe removal prevents the development of neuroses in animals, why would it not be feasible to relieve anxiety in humans by surgical means? Back in Portugal, Moniz asked his surgeon collaborator, Almeida Lima, to operate on psychotic patients from the Manicome Bombarda, a psychiatric hospital in Lisbon.

He suggested that by interrupting some of the connections between the prefrontal lobes and other parts of the brain, some modifications might be brought about in the mental processes of psychotic individuals.

The idea was to operate on the brain of the patient by interrupting the connecting fibers between cells of the prefrontal regions and the thalamus. The hypothesis underlying the procedure might be called in question. The surgical intervention might be considered very audacious. But Moniz, in the preface of his book, *Tentatives operatoires dans le traitement de certaines psychoses*, published in Paris in 1936, justified his standpoint on the use of psychosurgery.

In order to undertake his experiment Moniz needed some patients. He asked Pr Sobral Cid, director of the Manicome Bombarda, to help him choose some patients who were chronically ill. Moniz did not care to ask for the patients' consent. However, he knew that there were some risks in operating on the brain. In the introduction of his book, he explains his ethical principles. "Even if our conception is true, we are acting as the blind in this therapy. We must progress carefully, but with decision, when we are sure we don't jeopardize patient's life. As the first experiments must be undertaken upon incurable cases, the fact we could spoil their mental life doesn't matter. In the worse hypothesis, they keep on being insane persons" (Moniz, 1936).

2. Walter Freeman, James Watts, and the Standard Prefrontal Lobotomy

The neurosurgeon team of Walter Freeman and James Watts introduced Moniz's intervention in the United States. By the end of 1936, they completed their first series of operations on 20 patients. They developed a new technique of prefrontal lobotomy, which became known as the standard prefrontal lobotomy (Freeman and Watts, 1950). In this procedure, two burr holes are drilled laterally in the frontal bone, and incisions are made with a leucotome in the white matter of both frontal lobes to cut the connections between the thalamus and the frontal pole. Freeman and Watts advanced the hypothesis that "the frontal lobes are concerned with foresight and insight and that the emotional component associated with these functions is supplied by the thalamus." For the two neurosurgeons, the intervention cuts off the emotional component concerned with the abnormal ideas of the psychotic patient. The crude intention of the operation is to break the connection between the patient's thoughts and his emotions, thus relieving mental tension. Freeman and Watts admitted that prefrontal lobotomy was "an operation of last resort" that should be done with the knowledge of possible unfavorable results, including persistent inertia, flattening of emotional life, convulsive seizures, incontinence, and aggressive misbehavior. The long-time side effects were described as the "frontal lobe syndrome,"

which includes inertia, apathy, decreased attention, social inappropriateness, and seizures. In the late 1940s, prefrontal lobotomies were being adopted in many parts of the world: United States, Great Britain, continental Europe, Latin America, India, New Zealand, and so on. This operation was used in the treatment of depression, obsession-compulsive states, schizophrenic states, chronic anxiety syndromes, and in the treatment of pain due to organic disease (cancer, tabes, intractable causalgia, etc.).

3. Transorbital Leucotomy and Other New Procedures

In 1946, Freeman also introduced in the United States a new technique of prefrontal leucotomy, called transorbital leucotomy, which was performed immediately after two applications of electroconvulsive therapy (Freeman, 1949). This leucotomy was first carried out by Fiamberti in Italy (Fiamberti, 1952). Transorbital leucotomy was performed in the postconvulsive coma following the electroshock without further anesthesia. The lesion is produced through the roof of the orbit of the eye with a transorbital leucotome (an ice-pick-like tool). The eyelid on one side is elevated, and the prefrontal cortex is cut through the orbite by the leucotome. According to Freeman, the method is "simple, quick and safe." The whole operation is over in 10 minutes. And, as the French neurosurgeon F. Ody said in 1956, "the patient will ignore if it is judged appropriate not to reveal to him that he has undergone a leucotomy." Freeman felt that transorbital leucotomy was best recommended for psychiatrists in mental hospitals where major neurosurgical procedures were not available. This technique was widely criticized, even by some neurosurgeons. When Freeman introduced transorbital leucotomy, Watts, his associate, decided to terminate his collaboration. Despite the objections, the influence of Walter Freeman in the development of psychosurgery in the United States was considerable. In the late forties, J. L. Pool and W. B. Scoville described new, open procedures where Brodmann's areas 9 and 10 are removed or separated from the underlying white matter. In the early 1950s, lobotomies were being performed at the rate of 5000 per year in the United States.

4. Dissent and Decline

In the 1940s, the introduction of psychosurgery in the United States met vigorous opposition. Some physicians referred to it as medical sadism. The psychoanalysts objected to the lobotomy because it conflicted with their fundamental theoretical set. Even some nonpsychoanalysts were vehement in their opposition. Their claim is grounded upon the adverse effects of psychosurgery (modification of the personality, apathy, infection, hemorrhage, death) and upon a lack of understanding of the relation between the mind and the structure of the brain. The debate about psychosurgery was emotionally charged, with some opponents comparing psychosurgical patients to "patients without souls" or to "decerebrated robots."

By the early 1950s, tens of thousands of individuals had undergone prefrontal leucotomy. Later in the 1950s, enthusiasm for psychosurgery began to fade away. As an editorial in the *Lancet* put it in 1972, "such was the enormous pool of psychotic patients vegetating as chronic sick in the closed wards of mental hospitals, without effective drug control and without hope, that when it became possible to help them in any way, this new method was taken up with more enthusiasm than caution and with more technical skill than psychiatric and neurophysiological understanding. A wave of reaction followed and this was sustained by advances in drug therapy." When the French physician Henri Laborit introduced chlorpromazine, the therapeutic situation changed fundamentally. Chlorpromazine was approved for use as an antipsychotic in 1954. With the availability of the major tranquilizers and antidepressants, psychoses and depressions ceased to be a primary indication for psychosurgery.

5. Psychosurgery in the Past Three Decades: The Advent of Stereotactic Surgery

In the 1960s and the 1970s, psychosurgery used new stereotactic apparatus permitting the selective destruction of parts of the brain. This technique, called stereotactic surgery, was introduced by Ernest Spiegel and Henry Wycis in the late 1940s. Stereotactic surgery ushered in the new era of psychosurgery by allowing destruction of relatively small, precisely located areas within the human brain. With this new technique, psychosurgery became more precise and focused on other regions of the brain. Lesions in the frontal lobes (bifrontal stereotactic subcaudate tractotomy, capsulotomy) are still employed to treat anxiety states and obsessive–compulsive disorders. But lesions in other areas, such as the temporal lobes, the limbic system (cingulotomy, limbic leucotomy), and the hypothalamus have been introduced to treat affective disorders, violent behavior, hyperkinesis, and abnormal sexual behavior. Some of these indications were very dubious. Especially contro-

versial was the attempt to control abnormal aggressiveness (Narabyashi 1968, Sano 1988, Ramamurthi 1988) or sexual deviations (Roeder, 1972) by means of amygdalotomy or hypothalamotomy. Some neurosurgeons, for instance, have been severely criticized for performing stereotactic neurosurgery (hypothalamotomy, amygdalotomy) in young children to cure "hyperkinesis" or "aggressive behaviors" (Balasubramaniam, 1972).

II. PSYCHOSURGERY TODAY

Today, in Europe and in the United States, four procedures are generally used in the treatment of intractable anxiety and affective disorders: capsulotomy, stereotactic subcaudate tractotomy, cingulotomy, and limbic leucotomy. In these interventions, the neurosurgeon destroys some part of the frontal lobes, or their connections to the limbic system.

A. Indications

The patients selected for psychiatric surgery have severe, incapacitating, persistent, and treatment-resistant psychiatric illnesses, including anxiety states, obsessive–compulsive disorder, and major depression. Today, it is agreed that uncomplicated schizophrenia is not helped by psychosurgery. Currently, psychosurgery is generally considered a "treatment of last resort."

B. Techniques

Current psychiatric neurosurgery consists of producing lesions in the brain by heating electrodes in the target areas to coagulate the tissue, or by focused radiation utilizing either a linear accelerator radiation source or a focusable cobalt radiation source (the gamma knife). Contrary to the heating lesion, the radiation lesion requires no opening of the skull. The patient is simply exposed to a focused beam of radiation.

Leksell initiated the concept of stereotactic radiosurgery in 1951. This past decade has seen a rapid proliferation in the development of the methodology. By focusing the beams of hemispherically arrayed cobalt sources, the gamma knife delivers a high dose of radiation to a small target (Leksell, 1983).

In general, four surgical interventions have been utilized over the past 30 years. In these interventions, the neurosurgeon destroys some part of the frontal lobes, or their connections to the limbic system (the prefrontal cortex and the limbic system play a prominent part in emotional and cognitive functions).

1. Capsulotomy

Capsulotomy is an established psychosurgical intervention for anxiety disorders that are resistant to conventional treatments. This intervention was first realized by T. Herner (Herner, 1961). Today, fronto-limbic connections contained in the anterior limb of the internal capsule are intersected by way of radiofrequency heat lesions or gamma irradiation. Capsulotomy is currently used by P. Mindus (Karolinska Hospital, Stockholm) to treat anxiety disorder and obsessive–compulsive disorder.

2. Subcaudate Tractotomy

The target in subcaudate tractotomy was described by G. Knight in 1964 and popularized by P. K. Bridges in the United Kingdom (Knight, 1965). The lesions are made by implanting radioactive beads in the medio-postero-basal part of the frontal lobes. This procedure, a stereotactic variant of Scoville's orbital undercutting procedure, is indicated for anxiety states, obsessional symptoms, and depression.

3. Cingulotomy

Cingulotomy severs, through the administration of heating lesions, the anterior supracallosal fibers of the cingulate gyrus within the limbic system. This functional neurosurgical technique was popularized by H. Thomas Ballantine in the United States (Massachusetts General Hospital, Boston). Cingulotomy is used as a potentially effective treatment for patients with major affective disorders and anxiety disorders, and with severe and disabling obsessive–compulsive disorder.

4. Limbic Leucotomy

Limbic leucotomy combines cingulotomy with subcaudate tractotomy.

C. Toward a Renewal of Psychosurgery?

Today, psychosurgery is no longer a common practice, and is performed only to a limited extent in Europe and in the United States. In the United States, psychosurgery is still a rare treatment, despite approval by the Department of Health, Education and Welfare in 1978. In Europe, psychosurgery is mainly used in Sweden and in the United Kingdom, but not frequently. For instance, in the Geoffrey Knight Unit (the principal unit of psychosurgery in the U.K.),

nearly 1300 psychosurgeries have been performed since 1961. In Belgium, the actual rate of psychosurgery is 0.2 per million inhabitants per year. This low acceptance is perhaps due to the controversial aspects of the therapy. A review of the literature suggests that there are few facilities in the world that regularly perform operations, including the Geoffrey Knight National Unit for Affective Disorders (Brook General Hospital, London); Departments of Psychiatry and Neurosurgery (Massachusetts General Hospital, Boston); Department of Clinical Neuroscience, Karolinska Hospital, Stockholm; the Neuropsychiatric Institute, Sydney, Australia).

We could well observe a development in the use of psychosurgery in the next years. Two factors could play a role in the new interest for psychiatric surgery. The first factor is the development of new technologies in brain surgery. The gamma knife, in particular, is a new surgical tool that can produce localized lesions in the brain without requiring the opening of the scalp. The second factor is the change in the reaction to the use of psychosurgery: after the development of psychopharmacology in the 1950s psychosurgery saw a sharp decline. In the late 1970s and in the early 1980s, one might have expected the disappearance of psychosurgery. But today, some psychiatrists and neurosurgeons (including H. T. Ballantine, M. A. Jenike, P. Mindus, and P. K. Bridges) think that psychosurgery is still useful to treat "a small number of highly disturbed and suffering therapy-resistant patients." For P. K. Bridges stereotactic subcaudate tractotomy is "an indispensable treatment" (Bridges, 1994). In the future, we could well observe an increase in the number of psychosurgical interventions. H. T. Ballantine, of the Harvard Medical School, affirmed in 1988 that "there is a need for more surgical intervention in the treatment of intractable disorders of affect and more leadership in this direction from the psychiatrists" (Ballantine, 1988). In 1993, P. Mindus became enthusiastic about psychiatric surgery: "Given the remarkable progress in the diagnosis and the treatment of anxiety disorders in recent years, it is probable that, in the future, an even more refractory patient population will be referred for neurosurgical treatment.... In the heyday of lobotomy, it would appear that too many were operated on too soon. Today, as it would seem, too few are operated on too late. In both situations, the patients pay a price. It is therefore hoped that in this Decade of the Brain, physicians may overcome outdated attitudinal barriers and more often consider surgical intervention in their desperately ill patients" (Mindus, 1993).

III. ETHICAL ASPECTS

A. Psychosurgery: Cut the Brain to Save the Mind?

Psychosurgery is the most radical technique of physical brain manipulation. What does psychosurgery do? This question raises the ethical issues of how to balance its benefits and its hazards in making therapeutic judgments. Psychosurgery is a highly controversial therapy. Its promise to relieve great psychic pain must be balanced against the perils of impairing the personality, diminishing affect and creativity, and the ordinary dangers of a surgical intervention. Peter Breggin has argued that psychosurgery is the murder of the soul, that the physical destruction of any healthy brain tissue is an invasion of the sanctity of the person. I do not agree with those who insist that the intact brain should not be tampered with at any cost. This conception, which is at once mystical and emotional, is a tribute to the idea that the human body is somehow inviolate, and that it is sacrilegious to experiment upon it. Here, the objection approaches the dogma of religious conviction. There is some validity to the argument that states that if someone is in pain and we can help him, we should do it even if we do not know exactly what we are doing. But, in the long run, we need to know what we are doing so that we can take responsibility for it. With reference to psychosurgery this means that the relation between the somatic structures that are destroyed and the mental structures thereby affected must be understood. This is not yet the case.

B. Psychosurgery: An Experimental Therapy

The story of psychosurgery is the story of an experimental therapy. Despite technical advances in psychiatric surgery, the procedures are still experimental and irreversible in their effects on brain tissue. The term *experimental* has two meanings. In one sense, an experimental procedure stands in contrast to a therapeutic one: it is done with no expectation of benefit to the patient, but only to further knowledge. In the field of psychosurgery, there is no excuse for experimental procedure in this sense. Unfortunately, the story of psychosurgery offers some examples of such "cognitive experiments." For instance, we remember the operation of bilateral occipital leucotomy undertaken by the Norwegian neurosurgeon Arne Torkildsen in 1948. Torkildsen cut all the white matter of the occipital lobes of a blind, schizophrenic

patient who destroyed his eyes because he had heard the voice of God telling him to accomplish such an act. This experience was nonsense, even in the scientific context of the 1940s. Of course, the results of the operation were negative: "The experience with this case shows that the disconnection of both occipital lobes has no influence as far as can be judged from the psychiatric observations" (Torkildsen, 1948).

In another sense, a procedure is experimental if its effects are unpredictable, its risks highly variable, its mechanisms poorly understood, and its usefulness subject to widespread debate in the medical community. Psychosurgery has always been an experimental procedure in this second sense (for example, Moniz, Freeman, Scoville, Herner, and Knight).

The therapeutic effects of many of its procedures fall into a wide range of success and failure. The first operations were very dangerous. Many patients died directly or indirectly as a result of the operation. Especially hazardous were the operations of stereotaxic amygdalotomy and hypothalamotomy for aggressive or restless behaviors. In a report of 128 cases who had undergone stereotactic surgery over a period of 6 years (1964–1970), 9 of the first 50 cases died after the operation (Balasubramaniam, 1972).

Now with the new stereotactic procedures (anterior capsulotomy, subcaudate tractotomy) that are realized in specialized units carrying out regular interventions, the incidence of complications for each procedure is relatively low when compared with the morbidity and mortality in the early period of psychosurgery. There are fewer somatic side effects (epileptic seizures, intracerebral hematoma). Current psychosurgical operations can reduce disabling symptoms such as obsession or anxiety with minimal cognitive changes. But some behavioral side effects are still present. Perseverative behavior, for instance, often occurs after capsulotomy. The patient tends to repeat old patterns of behavior even in circumstances that demand change. It is not surprising, because the surgical operation cut some connections with the prefrontal cortex and perseveration is a distinctive disorder arising from prefrontal damage. The most distinctive disorder arising from prefrontal damage is the inability to initiate and carry out new and goal-directed patterns of behavior. The patient encounters trouble when forced to develop a new form of behavior based on deliberation and choice, especially if in order to reach the goal that behavior requires the organization of a novel sequence of acts. The frontal patient tends to repeat old patterns of behavior even in circumstances that demand change. Perseveration in old but inappropriate behavior is a distinctive trait of the performance of frontal patients in cognitive tasks (Fuster, 1989).

The risk of behavioral side effects must be weighed against the eventual clinical benefit of stereotactic psychosurgery. Unfortunately, postoperative assessment of psychiatric disorders is most difficult. Partisans of psychosurgery claim that the stereotactic procedure is followed by a significant improvement in measures of clinical morbidity and in psychosocial functioning, with preservation of personality. In about 30 to 60% of the cases of patients who suffer from obsessive–compulsive disorders, one of the modern form of psychosurgery will bring relief. It may not entirely eliminate the symptoms, but they become less intrusive and they no longer dominate the patient's life. However, the results of psychosurgery are not always as clear as crystal. In a long-term follow-up of 33 patients with severe and disabling obsessive–compulsive disorder, the team of Ballantine in Boston estimated that 25 to 30% of the patients benefited substantially from the cingulotomy procedure. But most of these patients did not receive all potentially effective therapies before psychosurgery. The treatment failures of future candidates—who will be required to undergo trials of other treatments before surgery—may represent a more refractory population.

The mechanisms of the eventual therapeutic effects are not well understood. "There is no accepted understanding of how psychosurgery works, but obviously it sometimes produces change and reduces certain biological vulnerabilities of the patient," writes the neurosurgeon, P. Cosyns (1988). What is very disturbing in psychosurgery is that neurosurgeons do not exactly know the mechanisms of the operations they undertake. The functions of the regions of the brain that are destroyed (prefrontal cortex, limbic system, amygdala) are far from being completely known. In the modern forms of psychiatric surgery, the neurosurgeon destroys some part of the frontal lobes, or their connections to the limbic system. The prefrontal cortex and the limbic system play a prominent part in emotional and cognitive functions (Damasio, 1995). The relationship of these neural structures with emotions is accepted, but the specific functions of the various areas have not been identified with any certainty. Moreover, the neurophysiological mechanisms involved in affective disorders are poorly understood. Therefore, the rationale for selecting targets for psychosurgical procedure is rudimentary and empirical. Neurosurgeons explicitly recognize that psychosurgery is still an experimental therapy. "There are no definite data resulting from animal experiments which could sustain the neurophysiological basis of psychosurgery.... Therefore, it is considered to be our neurosurgical duty to collect experimental data in human beings in a methodically proper manner and with respect to our ethical precepts," affirms the Belgian neurosurgeon A. Waltregny (1988). Thomas Ballantine agrees: "A current pressing need for more clinical investigation also exists. Sub-caudate tractotomy, limbic leucotomy, anterior capsulotomy and cingulotomy all have their proponents an critics. It must be determined whether there is really a specific limbic system interruption which is best for a specific disorder or affect or: Is the limbic system such a truly reverberating circuit that the location of a lesion within it is less important than its size and shape?" (Ballantine, 1988.)

Our knowledge of the brain is still very poor. Today, we can hardly understand the neurophysiological mechanisms of basic mental phenomena, such as visual perception or memory. The neurobiological bases of emotions and rational thought are weakly understood. In 1945, 9 years after the first prefrontal leucotomy, the great neuroscientist Donald Hebb affirmed that the functions of the frontal lobe were unknown. Today, we know that the prefrontal cortex intervenes in the so-called "higher mental functions," in memory, in planning, and in the temporal organization of behavior, but the precise role of the diverse areas of the prefrontal cortex is still mysterious (Fuster, 1989). Psychosurgery is an experimental therapy and, paradoxically, the neuroscientists learn about the frontal lobe functions and other brain regions from neurosurgical treatment of intractable psychiatric disorder.

The usefulness of psychiatric surgery is far from being unanimously agreed upon. Today, psychosurgery is not a normal practice; it is used in few institutions. In most neuropsychiatric hospitals, psychosurgery has disappeared from the therapeutic armamentarium. Moreover, psychiatrists familiar with this treatment disagree on the therapeutic indications. Most think that psychosurgery should be reserved for "highly disturbed and suffering therapy-resistant patients." But others argue that "psychosurgery may be a good indication for patients with post-traumatic stress disorder" and are convinced that "psychosurgery as ultimate resort is an out-of-date standpoint" (Haaijman, 1993).

C. Assessment of the Effects of Psychosurgery

Frequently it has been pointed out that the assessments of the effects of psychosurgery are inadequate (Valenstein, 1980). In the first era of psychosurgery, the studies about the long-term outcome of patients who had undergone psychiatric surgery had serious methodological problems. The efficacy of psychosurgery performed in this area is doomed to remain in doubt. More recently, better research methods have been developed for evaluating psychiatric symptoms and therapeutic efficacy. Psychometric instruments and rating scales are used to assess psychiatric symptoms and cognitive functions. Nevertheless, personality change and improvement of the psychiatric symptoms remain difficult to assess empirically.

D. Ethics of Psychosurgery and the Mind–Brain Problem

Nowhere does the relationship between mind and body take on a more practical aspect than in psychosurgery that pretends to alter the brain to improve the mind. The eventual improvement in mental health after a psychosurgical treatment is hard to evaluate because of the dual aspect of the mind–brain. The mind–brain is one entity with two faces: an objective one, the brain; a subjective one, the mind (Missa, 1993). It is an organ with both physical and mental aspects. As the philosopher Thomas Nagel says, "There seem to be very different kinds of things going on in the world: the things that belong to physical reality, which many different people can observe from the outside, and those other things that belong to mental reality, which each of us experiences from the inside in his own case." After a psychosurgical treatment, the neurosurgeon and the psychiatrist have to judge indirectly and behaviorally the therapeutic effects of the operation. They cannot see directly what happens in the mind of the patient. That is why the real effects of psychosurgery are so difficult to evaluate precisely.

E. Indications

The patients selected for psychiatric surgery should have severe, incapacitating, persistent, and treatment-resistant psychiatric illnesses, including anxiety states, obsessive–compulsive disorder, and major depression. Theoretically, psychosurgery today is generally considered a "treatment of last resort" that is utilized when all other treatments have failed. Unfortunately, this condition is not always respected. In a long-term follow-up of 33 patients who had undergone cingulotomy as a treatment for obsessive–compulsive disorder at Massachusetts General Hospital (Boston), only three had undergone behavioral therapy (Jenike, 1991). Most of these patients did not receive all potentially effective therapies for their disorder before surgery. Future can-

didates for psychosurgery should undergo trials of other treatments (psychotherapy, behavioral therapy, medications, electroconvulsive therapy) before surgery.

There are unacceptable indications. For instance, the operations of thalamotomy, hypothalamotomy, and amygdalotomy for aggressive behavior, sexual violence, and "sexual deviation" seem unacceptable to most people. In these circumstances, the aim of the "treatment" is to normalize the conduct of the patient, not to relieve his sufferings. Especially controversial was the attempt to cure aggressive or restless behaviors by amygdalotomy or by posterior hypothalamotomy. Some neurosurgeons (Narabyashi, Sano, Ramamurthi), for instance, have been severely criticized for performing a surgical destruction of brain centers (hypothalamotomy, amygdalotomy) in young children. The rationale, the methodology, and the neurophysiological theories underlying these operations were particularly dubious.

F. Informed Consent and Psychosurgery

In the field of psychosurgery, informed consent is so important and should be strictly observed. Does the patient consent to the treatment? Does he know the dangers of the treatment? But a real informed consent is extremely difficult to obtain from psychiatric patients. Often, close members of their families are the sources of consent. Is proxy consent acceptable as a substitute? It must be remembered that the closest kin are likely to be the ones who have suffered the most from the patient's behavior, and hence may have the greatest motive to seek a more drastic solution than is necessary.

G. Necessity of an Ethical Regulation of Psychosurgery: Criteria for the Selection of Psychiatric Patients

Psychosurgery should be considered as a kind of human experimentation, and, therefore, the psychosurgical operations and their theoretical background should be systematically examined by competent ethics committees. In practical terms, this means that a committee of some sort, composed of neurosurgeons, psychiatrists, physicians, and ethicists should be present to monitor the psychiatric or surgical treatment. National advisory committees should also regularly formulate opinions about psychosurgery. In most countries, no official regulations or restrictions are currently applicable to this treatment. There are some exceptions. In the United Kingdom, for instance, the Mental Health Act (1983) requires—in case of psychosurgery—competent consent and a second opinion (from a doctor appointed by the MHA).

Most of the units carrying out regular psychosurgical operations have developed general guidelines. The guidelines generally include the following rules:

1. It is a treatment of last resort. The patient is chronically disabled by a psychiatric illness that has not responded to all currently available therapies (psychotherapy, behavioral therapy, medications, electroconvulsive therapy).
2. The disorder is causing great suffering and severe reduction in the patient's psychosocial functioning.
3. The prognosis without psychosurgical intervention is considered poor.
4. The patient is required to have someone near and dear to him who agrees to give emotional support before, during, and after the surgical intervention.
5. The patient, along with his nearest relative, must be fully informed of the risks and benefits of the surgical intervention, and must give informed consent.
6. The referring psychiatrist agrees to be responsible for the postoperative long-term management of the patient.

These guidelines on psychiatric surgery are an example of the self-regulation of a delicate problem by professionals. Scientists have come to accept regulation of their work. The psychosurgery's topic is highly controversial and one in which regular national and international guidelines are highly desirable. Because of its controversial aspects and of its experimental nature, I think that the practice of psychosurgery should be strongly regulated by ethics and advisory committees.

Also See the Following Articles

INFORMED CONSENT • MENTAL ILLNESS, CONCEPT OF • PATIENTS' RIGHTS • PSYCHIATRIC ETHICS

Bibliography

Ballantine, H. T., *et al.* (1967). Stereotaxic anterior cingulotomy for neuropsychiatric illness and intractable pain. *Journal of Neurosurgery* **26**, 488–495.

Ballantine, H. T. (1988). Historical overview of psychosurgery and its problematic, psychosurgery and personality disorders. In *Personality and Neurosurgery, Acta Neurochirurgica* (Suppl. 44), 128.

Baer, L., Rauch, L., Ballantine, T., *et al.* (1995). Cingulotomy for intractable obsessive-compulsive disorder. *Archives of General Psychiatry,* **52**, 384–392.

Balasubramaniam, V., Ramanujam, P. B., Kanaka, T. S., & Ramamurthi, B. (1972). Stereotaxic surgery for behavior disorders. In E. Hitchcock, L. Laitinen, and K. Vaernet (Eds.), *Psychosurgery: Proceedings of the Second International Conference on Psychosurgery,* Springfield, IL: Charles C. Thomas, 87–111.

Blond, S., *et al.* (1993). Stereotactically guided radiosurgery using the linear accelerator. *Acta Neurochirurgica* (Suppl.), **124**, 40–43.

Bridges, P. K., Bartlett, J. R., *et al.* (1994). Psychosurgery: Stereotactic subcaudate tractotomy—An indispensable treatment. *British Journal of Psychiatry,* **165**, 599–611.

Cerletti, U. (1950). Old and new information about electroshock. *American Journal of Psychiatry,* **107**, 87–94.

Corkin, S. A. (1980), A prospective study of cingulotomy. In E. Valenstein (Ed.), *The psychosurgery debate.* San Francisco: Freeman.

Cosyns, P. (1988). Psychosurgery and personality disorders. In *Personality and Neurosurgery, Acta Neurochirurgica* (Suppl. 44), 124.

Council of Europe, Parliamentary Assembly. *Human rights and the mentally ill* (Research study prepared by Dinah Shelton and Thomaïs Douraki), Strasbourg, 23 March 1992.

Diering, S. L., & Bell, W. O. (1991). Functional neurosurgery for psychiatric disorders: A historical perspective. *Stereotactic Functional Neurosurgery,* **57**, 175–194.

Fiamberti, A. M. (1952). La méthode transorbitaire de la leucotomie préfrontale. *Encéphale,* **41**, 1–13.

Freeman, W., & Watts, J. W. (1950). *Psychosurgery in the treatment of mental disorders and intractable pain* (2nd ed.). Springfield, IL: Charles C. Thomas.

Freeman, W. (1945). Transorbital lobotomy. *American Journal of Psychiatry* **105**, 734–739.

Fuster, J. (1989). *The prefrontal cortex* (2nd ed.). New York: Raven Press.

Haaijman, W. P. (1993). Psychotherapy in patients with anxiety disorders: The supportive influence of psychosurgery. Abstract presented at the 6th Meeting on Controversial Topics: The Use of Psychosurgery in OCD and related disorders. Belgian College of Neuropsychopharmacology and Biological Psychiatry, Antwerp, 26 November.

Hebb, D. O. (1945). *Archives of Neurology and Psychiatry,* **54**, 10–24.

Herner, T. (1961). Treatment of mental disorders with frontal stereotactic thermo-lesions. A follow-up study of 116 cases. *Acta Psychiatr. Neurol. Scand.* (Suppl.), **158**, 36.

Jenike, M. A., Baer, L., Ballantine, H. T., *et al.* (1991). Cingulotomy for refractory obsessive compulsive disorder. *Archives of General Psychiatry,* **48**, 548–555.

Kiloh, L. G., Smith, J. S., & Johnson, G. F. (1988). *Physical treatments in Psychiatry.* Oxford: Blackwell Scientific.

Kleinig, J. (1985). *Ethical issues in psychosurgery.* London: Allen & Unwin.

Knight, G. (1965). Stereotactic tractotomy in the surgical treatment of mental illness. *Journal of Neurology, Neurosurgery and Psychiatry,* **28**, 304–310.

Leksell, L. (1983). Stereotactic radiosurgery. *Journal of Neurology, Neurosurgery and Psychiatry,* **46**, 797–803.

Mindus, P. (1993). Present-day indications for capsulotomy. *Acta Neurochirurgica* (Suppl.), **58**, 31.

Missa, Jean-Noël (1993). *L'esprit-cerveau. La philosophie de l'esprit à la lumière des neurosciences.* Paris: Vrin.

Moniz, E. (1936). *Tentatives opératoires dans le traitement de certaines psychoses,* Paris: Masson.

Narabyashi, H., Nagao, T., Saito, Y., Yoshida, M., & Nagahata, M. (1968). Stereotaxic amygdalotomy for behaviour disorders. *Archives of Neurology, 9,* 11–26.

Ramamurthi, B. (1988). Stereotaxic operation in behaviour disorders, Amygdalotomy and hypothalamotomy. *Acta Neurochirurgica* (Suppl. 44), 152–157.

Roeder, F., Orthner, H., & Müller, D. (1972). The stereotaxic treatment of pedophilic homosexuality and other sexual deviations. In E. Hitchcock, L. Laitinen, & K. Vaernet (Eds.), *Psychosurgery: Proceedings of the Second International Conference on Psychosurgery,* pp. 87–111. Springfield, IL: Charles C. Thomas.

Sachdev, P., & Hay, P. (1995). Does neurosurgery for obsessive compulsive disorder produce personality change? *Journal of Nervous and Mental Disease, 183,* 408–413.

Sakel, M. (1930). The nature and origin of the hypoglycemic treatment of psychoses. *American Journal of Psychiatry, 94* (Suppl.), 24–40.

Sano, K., & Mayanagi, Y. (1988). Posteromedial hypothalamotomy in the treatment of violent, aggressive behavior. *Acta Neurochirurgica* (Suppl. 44), 145–151.

Spiegel, E. A., Wycis, H. T., Marks, M., & Lee, A. J. (1947, October 10). Stereotaxic apparatus for operations on the human brain. *Science,* 349–350.

Swayze, V. W. (1995). Frontal leukotomy and related psychosurgical procedures in the era before antipsychotics (1935–1954): A historical overview. *American Journal of Psychiatry, 152,* 505–515.

Torkildsen, A. (1949). Notes on the importance of the occipital lobes in a case of schizophrenia, experience with a case of bilateral occipital leucotomy. *Acta Psychiatrica et Neurologica, 24,* 705.

Valenstein, E. S. (1986). *Great and desperate cures: The rise and decline of psychosurgery and other radical treatments for mental illness.* New York: Basic Books.

Waltregny, A. (1988). Regarding the experimental neurophysiological basis of psychosurgery, psychosurgery and personality disorders. In *Personality and Neurosurgery, Acta Neurochirurgica* (Suppl. 44), 134.

PUBLIC DEFENDERS

Adina Schwartz
John Jay College of Criminal Justice, and the Graduate School and University Center CUNY

GLOSSARY

accusatory system A legal system in which the prosecution has the burden of producing evidence of guilt.

adversary system A legal system in which the prosecution and defense engage in a contest before an impartial jury and judge.

assigned attorney An attorney in private practice who is appointed and paid by a court in the United States to represent an individual defendant in a particular case or stage of a case.

constitutional right A right that the United States Constitution ensures individuals against the United States government and/or the governments of the individual states. The federal and state governments may, but need not, grant individuals additional rights.

contract attorney A private legal practitioner under contract with a court system in the United States to represent indigent criminal defendants at either a fixed fee per case or a fixed price for a given time period regardless of the caseload.

court-appointed attorney An attorney whom a court system in the United States selects and pays to represent an indigent criminal defendant(s). Court-appointed attorneys may be either assigned attorneys, contract attorneys or public defenders.

Criminal Justice and Public Order Act (1994) An act of Parliament that allows judges and juries to draw negative inferences from a defendant's silence.

duty solicitor scheme A scheme ensuring suspects at English and Welsh police stations access to legal advice on a 24-hr basis.

inquisitorial system A legal system in which the judge assumes the prosecutorial role, and the suspect's confession is the preferred form of evidence.

legal aid The English and Welsh system for providing government payments to attorneys whom individual indigent litigants choose to represent them.

PACE The Police and Criminal Evidence Act, 1984, which entitles all suspects at English and Welsh police stations to advice from solicitors.

plea bargain A criminal defendant's agreement to plead guilty to a certain charge(s) in exchange for the prosecution's agreement to either (i) reduce the severity and/or number of charges against him or her and/or (ii) recommend a particular sentence to the judge.

public defender A salaried attorney in a law office operated by a government or nonprofit organization in the United States to provide representation to indigent criminal defendants.

Sixth Amendment An amendment to the United States Constitution that provides criminal defendants with various trial rights, including the right to the "assistance of counsel."

IN SOCIETIES where individuals are free to purchase the best legal services they can afford, governments use various methods to provide attorneys to indigent criminal defendants. In England and Wales, there is a system of legal aid payments by the government to attorneys whom individual defendants choose to represent them. By contrast, courts in the United States appoint attorneys for indigent defendants, taking both the selection and payment of the attorney out of the defendant's hands. There are three basic types of court-appointed attorneys in the United States. First, public defenders are the salaried legal staff of law offices established for the purpose of representing indigent defendants. Public defender offices are run either by government or by nonprofit organizations that the government selects and pays to provide indigents with legal representation. Second, contract attorneys are individual attorneys or groups or organizations of attorneys under contract with the government to represent indigent defendants. The contracts specify that representation be provided either at a fixed fee per case or at a fixed price for a given time period regardless of the caseload. Third, assigned attorneys are private practitioners who are appointed and paid to represent individual defendants in particular cases or stages of cases. Judges may assign particular attorneys in an ad hoc manner to represent particular defendants in particular cases or proceedings. Alternatively, court or other government officials may appoint individual practitioners to panels of attorneys, assigning individual panel members to represent particular defendants in particular cases or proceedings. Some court systems in the United States rely exclusively on assigned counsel to provide legal representation to indigent defendants. Other court systems, however, rely on public defenders and/or contract attorneys but also resort to private practitioners when conflict-of-interest or workload problems arise. The basic normative issue raised by all of these methods for providing attorneys is the extent and quality, if any, of legal representation that a government is obligated to provide to indigent criminal defendants.

I. THE NORMATIVE FRAMEWORK

A. Fairness and Equality Justifications for a Government Obligation to Provide Attorneys to Indigent Criminal Defendants

Both a fairness and an equality justification for a government obligation to provide attorneys are im-

plicit in the American case law defining the Constitutional right to counsel. In 1938 in *Johnson v. Zerbst* (304 U.S. 458), the United States Supreme Court held that the Sixth Amendment right to the "assistance of counsel" obligates the government to provide attorneys to indigent criminal defendants in federal court. Although the Sixth Amendment of the United States Constitution applies only against the federal government, in 1963, *Gideon v. Wainwright* (372 U.S. 335) established that indigent defendants in state courts are also entitled to court-appointed attorneys. *Gideon* reached this holding by reasoning that the Sixth Amendment right to counsel is "fundamental and essential to a fair trial" (*id.* at 342). As such, according to *Gideon,* the Sixth Amendment right is incorporated in the protections that the Due Process Clause of the Fourteenth Amendment affords individuals against the states.

Gideon and subsequent American cases ground the government obligation to provide counsel in claims about the nature of Anglo-American legal systems. First, Anglo-American legal systems are adversarial in that the prosecution and defense engage in a contest before an impartial jury and judge, and accusatorial in that the government has the burden of producing evidence of guilt. The contrast is to inquisitorial legal systems where the judge assumes the prosecutorial role, and the suspect's confession is the preferred form of evidence. Second, the adversary contests in Anglo-American courts are governed by technical legal rules and procedures that attorneys are especially able to understand and apply.

1. The Fairness Justification

An argument, which we will call the fairness justification, arises from the two premises above and the normative premise that an adversary proceeding cannot be fair if one party to the contest is vastly outmatched in skill. Due to the technical nature of court proceedings, such unfairness results if the prosecution is represented by an attorney while the defendant is forced, by lack of economic resources, to represent him- or herself. From the factual premise that American state and federal governments expend "vast sums of money" on attorneys to prosecute crimes (372 U.S. at 344), *Gideon* concludes that fairness demands government provision of attorneys to indigent criminal defendants.

2. The Equality Justification

While the fairnesses justification looks to case-by-case equality between the prosecution and the defense, systemic equality between defendants or, in other words, having "every defendant stand ... equal before the law" (*Gideon,* 372 U.S. at 344) is the norm invoked by what we will call the equality justification. Other things being equal, a defendant represented by an attorney is more likely to prevail in a formal legal proceeding than a defendant who represents him- or herself. From the factual premise that "there are few defendants charged with crime, few indeed, who fail to hire the best lawyers they can get to prepare and present their defenses" (*id.*), *Gideon* suggests that separate systems of rich and poor men's justice can be avoided only if the government provides attorneys to indigent criminal defendants.

B. Basic Normative Issues Raised by Government Provision of Attorneys

In 1995, the O. J. Simpson prosecution highlighted the fact that in the United States and Britain, a few wealthy individuals are able to hire attorneys who outmatch the government with no-holds-barred defenses. By contrast, "assembly line" legal services culminating in guilty pleas often, although not always, are provided by both the court-appointed attorneys who represent the overwhelming majority of defendants in the United States and the private law firms paid by criminal legal aid to represent the overwhelming majority of defendants in England and Wales. Scholars differ about both (i) the extent to which government-provided attorneys fail to be vigorous advocates for their clients and (ii) the explanation for such nonadversarial conduct. Proposed explanations include: (1) most indigents are factually and legally guilty and hence have no viable defense; (2) government-provided attorneys are burdened by overly large caseloads and/or fewer resources than the prosecution; (3) judges and other government officials use their appointment, payment and disciplinary powers to reward nonaggressive conduct by attorneys and impede aggressive advocacy; (4) socioeconomic differences prejudice attorneys against indigent defendants and/or hinder indigents from working effectively with attorneys; (5) government-provided attorneys have "crime control" values that prevent their assuming an adversarial stance on their clients' behalf.

Regardless of how nonadversarial the conduct of government-provided attorneys in fact is and of what the explanation(s) for such conduct may be, substantial government expenditures on criminal defense attorneys have not produced either systemic equality between defendants or case-by-case equality between the prosecution and the defense. The tension between ideal and reality raises fundamental normative questions.

First, can the equalizing of individuals' access to legal representation justifiably stop short of absolute equality? Is the requisite equality (i) case-by-case equality between the prosecution and defense and/or (ii) systemic equality between defendants?

Second, what is the status of the basic liberal assumption that formal equality before the law is compatible with an unequal distribution of wealth? For legal rights to be equal, must all members of society have exactly the same access to the services of attorneys who will assert their rights? Must economic resources be equalized across the board, instead of merely in regard to the ability to purchase legal services, if socioeconomic disparities are not to impede the legal representation of low-income clients?

Third, does the resolution of the overwhelming majority of cases in both the United States and England and Wales through plea bargaining imply that attorneys' conduct should be policed and/or legal procedures changed to restore adversarial behavior? Is the adversary ideal instead economically unviable and/or out of step with the need to control crime? If the adversary ideal is modified or rejected, what, if any, justification remains for government expenditure on attorneys for indigent criminal defendants?

Fourth, the adversary ideal implies that an attorney owes a primary duty of loyalty to his or her client and that effective representation must, accordingly, be conflict-free. Are conflicts of interest not inevitable, however, whenever government officials select and/or pay criminal defendants' attorneys? Are government attempts to provide attorneys to indigent criminal defendants thereby discredited by the very ideal of adversary justice that appeals to require such attempts?

These issues will be developed by considering the American and English and Welsh attempts to provide legal services to indigent criminal defendants. In discussing the relevant American law, our primary focus will be on the rights that the United States Constitution ensures individuals against the federal government and/or the governments of the individual states. These Constitutional rights contrast with additional rights that individuals may, but need not, be accorded by federal or state law. Although state and lower federal courts as well as the United States Supreme Court decide on the nature and extent of Constitutional rights, we will focus on the most authoritative decisions, those of the United States Supreme Court.

II. CONCRETE ILLUSTRATIONS OF THE NORMATIVE ISSUES

A. When Should Indigents Be Afforded Attorneys?

The landmark *Gideon* decision concerned the right to an attorney at trial. The likelihood of an acquittal or an advantageous plea bargain is substantially affected, however, by (i) the evidence, including confessions, that the prosecution obtains before trial and (ii) the evidence that the defendant's attorney obtains and the nature and extent of his or her pretrial preparations. Similarly, whether an attorney is available on appeal or for other postconviction proceedings substantially affects the likelihood of having a conviction reversed. Hence, a basic issue about the government's obligation to provide attorneys is the extent of pre- and posttrial representation to be afforded to indigent defendants.

1. Pretrial Access to an Attorney

a. Access during Police Custody

The general rule in the United States is that the Constitutional right to counsel attaches with the formal commencement of criminal proceedings. Thus, an uncharged suspect has no Constitutional right to the presence of an attorney during procedures, such as lineups, that may create crucial evidence for a conviction. The exception is that the Fifth Amendment right against compelled self-incrimination entitles any suspect—whether charged or uncharged—to the presence of an attorney during custodial police interrogation. In 1966, *Miranda v. Arizona* (384 U.S. 436) held that the police must deliver what have come to be called the *Miranda* warnings: that the suspect has a right to remain silent; that anything said can be used against him or her at trial; that he or she has a right to the presence of an attorney during interrogation; and that an attorney will be appointed at government expense if he or she cannot afford to hire his or her own. Unless the government proves that a suspect knowingly and intelligently waived these rights, any statements made in response to police interrogation cannot be used in the government's case at trial.

The Police and Criminal Evidence Act, 1984 (PACE) entitles all suspects at English and Welsh police stations to advice from solicitors. Although suspects are allowed to select their own solicitors, duty solicitor schemes have also been instituted to ensure that legal advice is available on a 24-hour basis. Legal-aid payments are available for police station advice even if the suspect is not indigent, and solicitors can precertify themselves to receive legal-aid payments. By contrast, English and Welsh criminal legal-aid payments for all other pretrial work are contingent on both means and merit testing.

A commitment to an accusatorial legal system as opposed to an inquisitorial one underlies both the *Miranda* and PACE provisions for legal representation.

b. Government Obligations in the Face of Suspects' Failure to Remain Silent

Notwithstanding popular perceptions, most suspects in the United States respond to police reading of their *Miranda* rights by waiving their rights and proceeding to talk. One commentator (Ogletree, Charles J., 1987, Are Confessions Really Good for the Soul?: A Proposal to Mirandize *Miranda, Harv. L. Rev.* 100:1826-1845) has suggested "Mirandiz[ing] *Miranda*" by instituting a nonwaivable right for suspects to consult with an attorney before police interrogation. If, as *Miranda* assumes, the custodial situation is so inherently coercive that attorneys are needed to prevent suspects from involuntarily incriminating themselves, then attorneys are also needed, he argues, to prevent suspects from succumbing to the pressures of the custodial situation by involuntarily waiving their right to an attorney and other *Miranda* rights. The nagging philosophical question, however, is whether there are normatively uncontroversial criteria for determining whether choices are coerced. Will one's views on the relative merits of accusatorial and inquisitorial justice necessarily infect one's judgments as to whether the widespread waiver of *Miranda* rights results from subtle psychological coercion by police or instead simply reflects suspects' desire to talk?

Different issues arise in England and Wales. While American suspects may be motivated to talk by the fact that the *Miranda* rights do not require police to provide attorneys promptly, English and Welsh duty solicitor schemes have reduced the typical waiting time for a legal adviser's arrival at the police station to 1 or 2 hours. However, even after the PACE codes were revised in 1991 to clarify that access to solicitors at police stations was free, only about 30% of suspects requested legal advice. In the United States, legal advice is rendered by attorneys who almost always advise suspects to remain silent during police interrogation. By contrast, nonlegal support staff from solicitors' offices, including many former police officers who continue to share police values, provide legal advice to between two-fifths and one-half of the suspects who request advice at English and Welsh police stations. These advisers, as well as the qualified solicitors who attend at police stations, advise suspects to remain silent in only about one-fifth of the cases. A Royal Commission Study (Leng, Roger, 1993, The Royal Commission on Criminal Justice, Research Study No. 10) found that the right to remain silent was exercised by only 4.5% of suspects at police stations in England and Wales, a far lower percentage than in the United States.

Parliament's enactment of the Criminal Justice and Public Order Act (1994), effective spring 1995, complicates the issue of whether, in view of suspects' overwhelming waiver of the right to remain silent, the British government has failed to fulfill its obligation to provide legal representation at police stations. The Act allows judges and juries to draw negative inferences from a defendant's remaining silent (i) at trial; (ii) during police interrogation about any fact relied on at trial that the defendant could reasonably have been expected to mention at the time of interrogation; (iii) in response to police requests for explanations of any suspicious marks, objects, or substances found on the suspect's person or clothing or otherwise in his or her possession; and (iv) in response to police requests for explanations of his or her presence at the time and place of the alleged crime. While these provisions for allowing defendants' silence to be used against them move England and Wales toward an inquisitorial system of justice, a commitment to an accusatorial system underlies and justifies the PACE provisions for solicitors' advice at police stations. Thus, the basic normative question of the relative merits of accusatorial and inquisitorial systems underlies the questions of (i) what extent and quality of legal assistance a government is obligated to provide during police interrogation and (ii) how, if at all, the conceptions of the solicitor's role in PACE and in the Criminal Justice and Public Order Act can be reconciled.

c. A Government Obligation to Motivate Pretrial Preparation

Defense attorneys' pretrial work does not only consist of protecting their clients from government attempts to obtain confessions and other evidence. In addition, there is pretrial preparation, including researching, framing, and arguing legal issues and conducting interviews and otherwise obtaining evidence on the client's behalf. Both court-appointed attorneys in the United States and solicitors paid by English and Welsh criminal legal aid tend to spend significantly less time on pretrial preparation than the private practitioners that wealthy defendants retain. In determining what, if any, wealth-based disparities in legal representation are justifiable, it is therefore necessary to consider whether and to

what extent a government is obligated to encourage pretrial preparation by indigents' attorneys.

Court systems in the United States increasingly resort to contract attorneys to represent indigent criminal defendants. Because the contracts provide flat fees per case or for a given time period, they save governments money at the same time as they make it economically disadvantageous for attorneys to spend time on pretrial preparation. A similar disincentive issues from differential fee schedules for in- and out-of-court work by assigned attorneys, such as the $25/hour for out-of-court work but $40/hour for in-court work that New York State courts pay in noncapital cases, or the $40/hour for out-of-court work but $60/hour for in-court work that federal district courts are allowed to pay. Similar fee differentials in the English and Welsh criminal legal aid scheme are correlated with solicitors' tendency to delegate interviewing and other crucial aspects of pretrial preparation to nonlegal support staff. The delegation occurs in both the magistrate's court cases where solicitors appear in court and the Crown Court cases where the solicitor's role is to prepare barristers for appearances.

It is questionable whether changed fee structures alone would significantly increase pretrial preparation by government-provided attorneys. If, in the United States, both contract attorney schemes and differential pay rates for in- and out-of-court work by assigned attorneys were eliminated, it might be economically advantageous for local governments to increase the caseloads of public defender offices. Even though the salaried lawyers in these offices would be paid equally well for in- and out-of-court work, they might still be motivated by heavy caseloads to forego pretrial preparation and dispose of cases rapidly through routinized plea bargaining.

Changes in caseloads and in fee structures are much easier to effect than the changes in solicitors' culture that a British study (McConville, M., Hodgson, J., Bridges, L., & Pavlovic, A. (1994). *Standing accused.* New York and Oxford: Oxford University Press) argues are needed to ensure adequate preparation of English and Welsh criminal legal aid cases. While not discounting the economic incentives, McConville and his colleagues argue that the delegation of crucial aspects of pretrial preparation to nonlegal support staff in solicitors' offices is also explained by: (1) crime-control values that lead solicitors to assume, without investigation, that criminal legal aid clients are guilty; (2) solicitors' desire to distance themselves from low-income people whom they view as unacceptable clients; and (3) solicitors' tendency to equate "real lawyer's" work with in-court representation. Government attempts to change these values might infringe unacceptably on the legal profession's autonomy. As a practical matter, any such attempts may be precluded by political pressures to "get tough on crime."

2. Access on Appeal and Other Postconviction Proceedings

a. Wealth-Based Distinctions in Access

On the same day as it decided *Gideon,* the United States Supreme Court held, in *Douglas v. California* (372 U.S. 353, 355 (1963)), that because "there can be no equal justice where the kind of appeal a man enjoys 'depends on the amount of money he has,'" indigent criminal defendants are entitled to court-appointed attorneys to appeal their convictions. Nonetheless, *Douglas* announced that "[a]bsolute equality [between rich and poor] is not required" (*id.* at 357). On this basis, *Douglas* and subsequent cases limited the Constitutional right to a court-appointed attorney to the first appeal from a conviction. While defendants with the economic wherewithal have a Constitutional right to retain attorneys for (i) subsequent appeals and (ii) collateral proceedings such as motions for a new trial and habeas corpus petitions, indigent defendants have no Constitutional right to court-appointed attorneys for such proceedings.

A further wealth-based distinction arose from the justices' concern that courts would become clogged with frivolous or meritless appeals if appellate attorneys were provided to indigents at the government's expense. In the United States, a court will hear the arguments of any attorney whom a nonindigent defendant retains on appeal, without asking whether other attorneys found no merit in the case and were therefore not retained. By contrast, *Anders v. California* (386 U.S. 786 (1967)) allows a court to use a court-appointed attorney's finding of no merit as a basis for depriving an indigent defendant of appellate representation and dismissing his or her appeal. To allay its concern that court-appointed attorneys would use claims of frivolity to excuse their own failure to advocate indigents' cases vigorously, the *Anders* Court held that an appointed attorney would not be allowed to withdraw from an appeal if he or she simply alleged that it raised no meritorious issues. Instead, a motion to withdraw must be accompanied by an "*Anders* brief," explaining why all seemingly meritorious issues in fact have no merit. The *Anders* Court required appellate courts to consider both the arguments that the court-appointed attorney advanced in the *Anders* brief and any reply that the indigent defendant might submit without the aid of an attorney. A court that accepts the arguments in the *Anders* brief is to grant the court-appointed attorney's motion to withdraw, refuse to appoint another attorney for the defendant on appeal, and dismiss his or her appeal.

b. Questions about the Limit to a First Appeal

The Supreme Court's attempted justifications for these wealth-based distinctions in legal representation on appeal fail to face the fundamental normative questions. One purported justification for not extending the Constitutional right to a court-appointed attorney beyond the first appeal is that instead of using attorneys to shield them from being stripped of the presumption of innocence, convicted defendants use attorneys as swords to overturn determinations of guilt by a jury or judge. In addition, the Court has reasoned that convicted defendants need attorneys less on subsequent appeals or collateral proceedings than on their first appeals because they can rely on the records, briefs, and opinions from the first appeal when they represent themselves in subsequent proceedings.

The "sword and not shield" argument does not prove, however, that indigent defendants may justifiably be deprived of court-appointed attorneys beyond the first appeal even though wealthy defendants remain free to retain their own attorneys. Instead, the logical implication is that the rights to appeal and to be legally represented on appeal should be vastly reduced, if not eliminated, for rich and poor criminal defendants alike.

Similarly, differences between the first appeal and subsequent postconviction proceedings create questions about how much, if at all, an indigent defendant's access to the records, briefs, and opinions from the first appeal reduces his or her need for an attorney in subsequent proceedings. While first appeals are won by showing that the law was incorrectly applied to the particular facts in a case, subsequent appeals are won by developing systemic legal or policy issues. While the purpose of an appeal is to show that a conviction is not justified on the facts brought out at trial, the purpose of a collateral proceeding is often to bring out facts not brought out at trial. Because the different kinds of postconviction proceedings thus call for different kinds of legal work and skills, an indigent defendant's access to the records, briefs, and opinions from the first appeal cannot remedy the absence of an attorney at subsequent proceedings. The Supreme Court's purported justifications for not extending indigent defendants' Constitutional entitlement to court-appointed counsel beyond the first appeal thus evade the question of whether and how the ideal of equality before the law can be reconciled with the view that "[a]bsolute equality is not required" (*Douglas*, 372 U.S. at 357).

c. Frivolous Appeals and the Adversary Ideal

The *Anders* brief requirement also raises troubling issues that the Supreme Court did not see. While the *Anders* Court assumed that a court-appointed attorney "acts in the role of an active advocate in behalf of his client" when he or she submits an *Anders* brief (386 U.S. at 744), the attorney in fact acts as his or her client's adversary. An *Anders* brief is supposed to show the court that any seemingly meritorious issues raised by the appeal in fact have no merit. Faced with such a brief by a competent attorney and the objections, if any, that an indigent defendant submits on his or her own, a court is highly likely to grant the attorney's motion to withdraw and to refuse to appoint another attorney to pursue the appeal. A new attorney might have succeeded, however, in having the indigent's conviction overturned by arguing creatively against the very precedents that the *Anders* brief invoked to convince the court that the appeal had no merit.

In addition to this potential damage to the individual defendant, the *Anders* Court also failed to recognize a systemic effect. Because it is often easier to brief some issue on a client's behalf than to canvas all potentially meritorious issues and show why they have no merit, the *Anders* brief requirement has the overall effect of motivating court-appointed attorneys to raise appellate issues that they otherwise might think too marginal or insignificant to raise. In view of these effects, an adequate evaluation of the *Anders* brief requirement must wait on answers to the empirical question of whether there is in fact little merit to most indigents' appeals or whether this appearance is instead created by attorneys' failure to raise or effectively litigate potentially meritorious issues.

B. Indigents and the Right to Effective Assistance of Counsel

The Sixth Amendment right to the "assistance of counsel" encompasses a right to the "effective assistance of counsel." Cases defining this right raise basic issues about the quality of representation that a government is obligated to provide.

1. Credentials or Performance?

The right to effective assistance of counsel entitles defendants to "actual effectiveness" in the performance of their attorneys during legal proceedings. In *United States v. Cronic* (466 U.S. 648 (1984)), the defendant's privately retained attorney had withdrawn shortly before trial and been replaced by a young court-appointed attorney whose practice was primarily in real estate, who had never tried a case before a jury before, and who had 25 days to prepare a case on which the prosecution had expended more than 4½ years On appeal, the defendant argued that these facts showed that he had been deprived of the effective assistance of counsel and was therefore entitled to a reversal of the fraud convictions for which he had received a 25-year sentence. The Supreme Court held that because Cronic had not "point[ed] to specific errors made by trial counsel," ineffectiveness had not been shown (466 U.S. at 666).

An "actual effectiveness" interpretation of the right to effective assistance of counsel is consonant with the fact that attorneys, like everyone else, may have paper credentials that are either superior or inferior to their performance on the job. If, however, Cronic's interpretation had prevailed, there would have been a constitutional mandate for setting fees for contract and assigned attorneys and salaries for public defenders high enough to make representation of indigent criminal defendants attractive to significant numbers of well-credentialed attorneys. The low pay rates for indigents' attorneys that currently prevail in England and Wales as well as the United States are likely to become still lower as demands for fiscal austerity and crime control increase. The question is whether such pay can be compatible with the underlying fairness and equality justifications for government provision of attorneys to indigent criminal defendants.

2. Actual Ineffectiveness

Rigorous judicial monitoring of the "actual effectiveness" of attorneys is another possible route to ensuring high quality representation of indigent criminal defendants. That route was foreclosed, however, by the performance and prejudice prongs for proving actual ineffectiveness that the Supreme Court established in *Strickland v. Washington* (466 U.S. 668), on the same day in 1984 as it decided *Cronic*.

a. The Prejudice Prong

Under *Strickland*, "[t]he defendant must show that there is a reasonable probability that, but for counsel's unprofessional errors, the result of the proceeding would have been different" (466 U.S. at 694). While the rationale for this requirement is that a defendant who was not prejudiced by his or her attorney's mistakes should not be able to use the mistakes to obtain a reversal, the mistakes themselves may make it difficult or impossible for a defendant to satisfy the prejudice prong. For example, the record of a trial will not enable an appeals court to determine that a seemingly impregnable prosecution witness appeared impregnable only because the defense attorney failed to bring out crucial facts on cross-examination. Nor will the record reveal that the weaknesses in the defense case resulted from the defense attorney's failure to investigate promising leads. Although new facts may be brought to the court's attention in the collateral proceedings that are the preferred vehicle for bringing ineffectiveness claims, evidence available at the time of a proceeding may have disappeared by the time ineffectiveness is claimed. An additional barrier to successful ineffectiveness claims by indigents is that the Constitutional right to appointed counsel does not extend to collateral proceedings.

b. The Performance Prong

The *Strickland* standard for determining whether an attorney's performance is effective is "simply reasonableness under prevailing professional norms" (*id.* at 688). The presumption that the legal profession maintains adequate norms goes hand in hand with the view that "[j]udicial scrutiny of counsel's performance must be highly deferential" (*id.* at 689). Thus, ineffectiveness is proved only if, in challenging specific acts or omissions by his or her attorney, a defendant overcomes a "strong presumption" that seeming mistakes are instead justifiable components of the attorney's litigation strategy (*id.*).

This deferential standard of review rests on the questionable assumption that the legal profession can be trusted to police the representation of criminal defendants. In assuming this, the *Strickland* Court avoided the requisite normative and empirical inquiry into (i) how to measure the quality of legal representation and (ii) the extent to which privately retained and court-appointed attorneys in fact act in their clients' best interests. In addition, the Court evaded the question of whether and to what extent the same standards of performance are appropriate for both privately retained and court-appointed attorneys.

C. Assistance or Imposition of Attorneys on Indigent Defendants?

1. Choice and Quality in Attorney–Client Relationships

Although the Sixth Amendment includes a right to choose one's own attorney, this right only entitles defendants to choose attorneys they can afford to pay. In practice, the Sixth Amendment therefore confers no choice on the great majority of criminal defendants in the United States. As indigents, they are relegated to the attorneys courts appoint. The question is whether choice can be valuable enough to be a component of the right to an attorney and yet not so valuable that limiting choice by wealth is incompatible with according rich and poor alike the right to an attorney to assist in one's defense.

Empirical findings raise important questions about the connections between choice and the quality of legal representation. Indigent criminal defendants in the United States tend to view court-appointed attorneys as government agents and to distrust them on grounds that "you get what you pay for." Consequently, court-appointed attorneys' relationships with their clients tend to depart from the ideal of mutual trust and confidence between attorney and client that case law sets forth. While American scholars have argued that these problems can be mitigated by allowing indigents to choose their own attorneys (e.g., Committee to Review the Criminal Justice Act, Report of the Committee to Review the Criminal Justice Act, reprinted in 52 *Crim. L. Rep.* (BNA) 2265 (Mar. 10, 1993); Flemming, R. B., 1986, Client Games, *Am. Bar Fdation Rsch J* 253-277), the English and Welsh experience calls this into question.

Although English and Welsh legal aid payments are made to attorneys whom indigents select, in practice, this system has arguably not produced either a broad or a meaningful choice of attorneys for indigent criminal defendants. A relatively small number of solicitors' firms does the bulk of criminal legal aid work. Instead of shopping knowledgeably for attorneys who will be aggressive advocates, suspects are often steered to particular solicitors' firms by police, either directly or through seeing firms' advertisements on coffee mugs or matchbooks that firms distribute around police stations. Solicitors' firms also attempt to exploit potential clients' vulnerabilities by hiring Black support staff to solicit business by driving around minority neighborhoods in flashy cars.

The English and Welsh experience also raises questions about the extent to which choice can improve attorneys' relations with indigent clients. The perception that criminal legal aid clients devalue them because they are free has been found to lead English and Welsh solicitors to devalue these clients in turn (McConville, *op. cit.*) Similar findings about court-appointed attorneys in the United States generate questions about whether adequate relations between indigents and government-provided attorneys can prevail in societies where the quality of representation is widely perceived to depend on the amount of money spent. In addition, English and Welsh solicitors have been found to view criminal legal-aid clients as the undeserving poor and to see themselves as devalued by this unacceptable client profile. This attitude arguably contributes to solicitors' tendency to distance themselves from legal-aid clients, at the cost of knowledge of their cases, by delegating interviewing and case preparation to support staff (McConville, *op. cit.*). Similarly, differences in socioeconomic background appear to decrease trust and hinder communications between court-appointed attorneys and indigent criminal defendants in the United States. This raises questions about whether, as socioeconomic disparities increase in Britain and the United States, government expenditures on legal representation for the indigent can possibly effect significant equality before the law.

2. Allocation of Decision-Making Powers between Attorneys and Clients

A basic issue in any attorney–client relationship is who controls the decisions about how to conduct the client's case. Market power may enable wealthy clients to control the allocation of decisions. Absent an allocation by the law, however, both indigents with government-provided attorneys and those who can barely afford to hire their own attorneys will have only as much power over decisions as their attorneys allow. An argument for legally according control to attorneys is that government expenditure on attorneys for indigent criminal defendants makes sense only if, as a rule, attorneys are more qualified than defendants to make legal decisions. Nonetheless, criminal defendants are arguably entitled to control on the ground that they, rather than their attorneys, stand to suffer imprisonment and other adverse consequences from legal proceedings. In *Jones v. Barnes* (463 U.S. 745 (1983)), the United States Supreme Court held that although criminal defense attorneys are obligated to consult their clients, virtually all decisions about the conduct of a case are decisions of strategy within the attorney's control. According to *Jones*, the Constitution entitles criminal defendants to control only four decisions: whether to plead guilty or go to trial; whether to waive a jury at trial; whether to testify in one's own behalf; and whether to appeal from a conviction. Although attorneys are obligated to advise their clients on these four fundamental matters, they are also obligated to leave the final choice to the client alone.

Differences in the backgrounds of attorneys and criminal defendants make it difficult to draw the line, however, between advising and coercing defendants in regard to legal decisions. Attorneys may need to engage in threatening conduct in order to bring the adverse consequences of decisions home to clients who do not understand the law and are unskilled at abstract reasoning. For example, a criminal defendant may only appreciate the risks of taking the stand if his or her attorney humiliates him or her by staging a "mock" cross-examination that highlights the inconsistencies in the defendant's story and confronts the defendant with his or her criminal past. Arguably, an attorney fulfills the duty to advise if he or she uses the threat of rehearsing until the defendant survives cross-examination to persuade a defendant with a long record and a weak story not to testify. It is also arguable, however, that the attorney has coerced the defendant into waiving the right to take the stand. The difficulty of distinguishing between advice and coercion is compounded by the fact that the awareness that their attorneys are government-selected and paid appears to lead indigent criminal defendants in the United States to experience their attorneys' conduct as coercive. Thus, privately retained attorneys who strenuously insist on certain choices may nonetheless be experienced as less coercive by their clients than court-appointed attorneys who explain the consequences of decisions but take care to insist that the choice remains the client's own (Flemming, *op. cit.*).

III. CRIMINAL JUSTICE VERSUS SOCIAL JUSTICE

The nature and extent of a government obligation to provide attorneys to indigent criminal defendants cannot be adequately determined by looking to norms of equality and fairness within the criminal justice system alone. Because the cost of government expenditure for this purpose is increased taxation and/or decreased expenditure for other purposes, broader questions of distributive justice arise.

A. Government Provision of Attorneys to Indigent Litigants Other than Criminal Defendants

In both England and Wales and the United States, government expenditure on legal services for indigent civil litigants is dwarfed by such expenditure for indigent criminal defendants. The classic justification for this differential funding is that the criminal defendant's stake in litigation is uniquely important. Arguably, however, the peril of being convicted and sentenced to imprisonment may not outweigh such perils of civil litigation as being rendered homeless through eviction proceedings or being deprived of parental rights. In addition, because government findings of criminal behavior have not haled them into court, indigent civil litigants may appear more deserving of government-provided legal representation than indigent criminal defendants are. Such a distinction between deserving and undeserving poor calls the very commitment to an adversarial legal system into question, however. To the extent that the merits of criminal and/or civil litigants' cases are knowable in advance, questions arise as to the justifiability of the continued, expensive operation of court systems in which attorneys' role is to act as advocates for opposing sides.

B. Government Expenditures on Attorneys for Indigent Criminal Defendants or on Other Social Services

Even assuming that the adversary system is the best system for resolving disputes and that the system's internal norms of equality and fairness dictate government provision of attorneys to indigents, it is questionable whether government funds are not better spent on other purposes. In particular, affording fair legal process to indigent criminal defendants might appear less important than providing housing, education, and career opportunities that will enable indigent youths to escape from crime. Aside from raising difficult questions about the causes of crime, this proposal may assume that the goals of preventing crime and fairly adjudicating guilt are more separate than they in fact are. Where, as in many African-American communities in the United States, the great majority of men are involved in the criminal justice system at some point in their lives, youths' perceptions of their own stake in society and consequent commitment to law abidingness may be affected by their perceptions of the fairness of their elders' treatment by the criminal justice system. Indigent criminal defendants' relations with their government-provided attorneys substantially affect their own and their community's perceptions of the fairness of the criminal justice system. These relations, however, are likely to be rendered difficult by the socioeconomic gaps between attorneys and clients.

Also See the Following Article

CRIME AND SOCIETY

Bibliography

Everitt, E. O. (Ed.). 1995. Symposium: Toward a more effective right to assistance of counsel. *Law and Contemporary Problems* 58, 1–125.

Flemming, R. B., Nardulli, P. F., & Eisenstein, J. (1992). *The Craft of Justice: Politics and Work in Criminal Court Communities.* Philadelphia: University of Pennsylvania Press.

Hanson, R. A., & Ostrom, B. J. (1993). Indigent defenders get the job done and done well. In Cole, G. F. (Ed.), *Criminal justice: Law & politics.* (6th Ed.). Belmont, CA: Wadsworth Publishing Co.

McConville, M., Hodgson, J., Bridges, L., & Pavlovic, A. (1994). *Standing accused: The organization and practices of criminal defense lawyers in Britain.* New York and Oxford: Oxford University Press.

McConville, M., & Mirsky, C. (1995). Guilty plea courts: A social disciplinary model of criminal justice. *Social Problems* 42, 216–234.

O'Reilly, G. W. (1994). England limits the right to silence and moves towards an inquisitorial system of justice. *J. Crim. L. & Criminology* 85, 402–452.

Walker, S. (1993). *Taming the system: The control of discretion in criminal justice 1950–1990.* New York and Oxford: Oxford University Press.

PUBLISH-OR-PERISH SYNDROME

Philip E. Devine
Providence College

I. Normative Issues
II. The Sociology of the Profession
III. Conclusion

GLOSSARY

academic freedom The principle that: (1) A professor should be free of academic sanctions, including but not limited to dismissal from his position, for things that are said and done in the course of his academic duties. (2) The academic profession is entitled to govern itself—to define and enforce its own standards—without external interference.

adjunct A part-time academic appointment, usually at far less than the appropriate fraction of a full academic salary (and no benefits).

false dilemma A false proposition of the form *p or q,* understood exclusively.

junior Not academically tenured.

nontenure-track Appointed for a year or term of years. Sometimes the appointment is renewable, but it does not provide eligibility for tenure.

postmodernism As characterized by Peter Novick, a condition of chaos, confusion, and crisis, in which everyone has a strong suspicion that conventional norms are no longer viable, but no one has a clear sense of what is in the making.

publish-or-perish syndrome Alleged overemphasis on publication as a requirement for tenure, undermin-ing the educational mission of colleges and universities.

senior Academically tenured.

student evaluations Forms by which students evaluate their teachers' abilities—in effect, their popularity—often in quantitative terms. They are used chiefly for the purposes of tenure decisions.

tenure A quasi-property right in an academic position, of which its holder can only be divested for serious cause.

tenure decision A decision to grant tenure or to dismiss, traditionally made in the sixth or seventh year of a professor's appointment.

tenure denial Equivalent to dismissal in present academic practice.

tenure track Eligible (at least nominally) for tenure.

THE PUBLISH-OR-PERISH SYNDROME, many critics of the academy argue, undermines its educational mission by requiring faculty to neglect teaching for scholarship. But others argue that this syndrome is a fable. There are two ethical issues: (1) the relative roles of scholarship and teaching in evaluating professorial performance; (2) academic freedom, particularly that of nontenured professors, when the intolerance in question is that of fellow members of the profession, rather than that of the larger socity. These issues are questionably illuminated by the expression "publish-or-perish syndrome."

I. NORMATIVE ISSUES

The phrase "publish-or-perish syndrome" expresses a common complaint, that the scholarly aspirations of the academy undermine its teaching mission. But many academics respond that this complaint rests on what philosophers call a false dilemma, that is, a proposition of the form *p or q* (*but not both*), when either *both p and q*, or *neither p and q* in fact obtains. It is often possible not to publish without perishing, and it is possible to publish and perish anyway.

Closer analysis reveals, moreover, that the phrase "publish or perish" conceals three different problems of academic ethics. One is the status of nontenured faculty, in a system that makes them vulnerable to pressures of all sorts. Another is the question of how the performance of faculty is to be evaluated in order to make decisions about appointment, promotion, retention, and job mobility. Yet another is a need for a more adequate understanding of academic freedom. When a bad academic decision is attributed to the publish-or-perish syndrome, a more accurate account will invoke one or more of these considerations.

A. The Status of Nontenured Faculty

The tenure system places nontenured faculty, and in particular the increasing number of those holding non-tenure-track and adjunct appointments, in an especially vulnerable position, because administrators and senior colleagues are reluctant to become saddled permanently with a difficult colleague. The remedy for this situation, if any, must be found in revisions of the tenure system, leading to a more nearly equal relationship between colleagues doing essentially the same work (and among whom, given the vagaries of the academic market, the less secure may be the better qualified).

B. Teaching vs. Research

Complaints about publish-or-perish raise the issue, whether colleges and universities should think of their mission primarily in scholarly or educational terms. In fact, there seems to be a general answer to the question, how to evaluate faculty for purposes of appointment, promotion, retention. To the extent that the mission of a college or university is research, faculty performance should be judged in terms of research; to the extent that is teaching, faculty performance should be judged in terms of teaching.

An influential view within the academy is that teaching and research are mutually reinforcing activities. Teaching helps scholarship, because it frees it from the obscure jargon, unexamined professional presuppositions, and quest for novelty at all costs, that frequently afflict academic discourse. Scholarship helps teaching, because it is evidence of ongoing engagement with a discipline. A college that wishes to support teaching and scholarship might consider separating tenure and promotion—retaining faculty who are good teachers without scholarly aspirations as permanent assistant professors.

In any case, "teach-or-perish" can be quite as lethal as publish-or-perish. Student evaluations favor professors who neither demand much work nor question their students' prejudices. Bizarre alliances are possible here: for example, fraternity members and fundamentalists can conspire to denounce a professor who presents unfamiliar, and for that reason difficult, ideas. (All examples used in this article are real, although not all are public knowledge.)

C. Academic Freedom

Academic freedom is an essentially contested concept, as the appearance with works with titles like *The Real Meaning of Academic Freedom* (Birely, 1972. *The Real Meaning of Academic Freedom*. London: World University Service) testify. Its sense, scope, and evaluative force are a matter of political and not merely philosophical debate. We need to distinguish, for example, the freedom of the individual scholar to advocate unpopular views—a freedom that approximates but is not identical to free speech in the larger society—from the freedom of the academic community to govern itself without external interference.

Academics can be as intolerant as anyone else. Where it is not possible to get a deviant colleague dismissed, ostracism will do the job almost as well: Alan Gribben of the University of Texas was ostracized by his colleagues in the English Department for voting against a master's program in ethnic and Third World studies and other ideological crimes. In the teeth of such considerations, John Searle maintains that, under a regime of faculty sovereignty, tenure would be unnecessary to protect academic freedom.

Despite Steven Cahn, questions of competence and those of creed are not independent of one another. For there are conclusions, such as the reality of astrological influences, that many academics believe could not be reached by a competent scholar. And, short of this, academics who offend entrenched sensibilities, whether in the academy or in the larger society, always have a tougher time than do others in convincing their colleagues of their intellectual credentials and teaching abilities. We neither are, nor should we be, as tolerant as our rhetoric sometimes suggests—which is not to say that we draw the needed lines in anything like the right places. The blending of professional and political judgment is both more pervasive and more acceptable than our pieties would lead people to believe. But this blending affects the evaluation of teaching quite as much as the evaluation of publications.

II. THE SOCIOLOGY OF THE PROFESSION

An accurate understanding of the sociology of the academic profession is essential to the resolution of issues of academic ethics. First, professors are not noted for their moral courage, and often deny appointment to a distinguished teacher and scholar on the ground that he is "too controversial." Second, professors can be as intolerant as any other group, sometimes in ways that harmonize with wider forms of intolerance and sometimes in ways that do not. Third, some academic forums are more prestigious than others, so that ideological pressures obliquely affect a professor's professional standing in a number of different ways. Fourth, a range of contemporary conditions, commonly known as "postmodernism," make it harder to draw the line between intellectual performance and political acceptability. Peter Novick has characterized the postmodern world as one "of chaos, confusion, and crisis, in which everyone has a strong suspicion that conventional norms are no longer viable, but no one has a clear sense of what is in the making" (Novick. (1988). *That Noble Dream,* p. 524. Cambridge: Cambridge University Press).

In consequence, although we sometimes handsomely reward publication, and some nontenured faculty do lose their jobs for failure to publish, the phrase publish-or-perish is misleading. Many colleges and universities require little or no publication for tenure, and extensive publications sometimes lead to tenure denial. Expressions such as "lack of communications skills"

and "social awkwardness" are available to secure the dismissal of junior colleagues whose scholarly aspirations are deemed excessive. Moreover, a professor denied tenure at a prestigious research institution seldom "perishes," in the sense of being obliged to leave the profession, if he has been able to acquire a good scholarly reputation and powerful patrons or cronies.

III. CONCLUSION

The phrase publish-or-perish is used to suggest that emphasis on scholarship undermines education. Equally arguably, however, it conceals three different sorts of problem. One is the dark side of the tenure system, which puts nontenure-track and adjunct faculty in a more vulnerable position than they would be otherwise. Another is the many complications involved in a fair evaluation of faculty performance, both instructional and scholarly, for purposes of appointment, promotion, and tenure. A third is the blending of professional and political judgment, which makes academic freedom a far more complicated matter than an earlier generation of academics would have had us believe. None of these issues is much illuminated by the phrase publish-or-perish syndrome.

Also See the Following Articles

Bibliography

Bernstein, R. (1994). *Dictatorship of virtue,* pp. 318–322. New York: Knopf.
Cahn, S. (1986). *Saints and scamps,* p. 5. Totowa, NJ: Rowman & Littlefield.
Devine, P. (1996, July). Academic freedom in the postmodern world. *Public Affairs Quarterly,* **10,** 3, 185–201.
Harvey, D. (1990). *The Condition of postmodernity.* Cambridge, MA: Blackwell.
Searle, J. (1972). *The campus war.* (Chaps. 7 and 4). Harmondsworth, Middlesex: Pelican.

QUALITY OF LIFE INDICATORS

Andrew Edgar
University of Wales

GLOSSARY

cost-utility analysis A measure of efficiency, calculating the resources (expressed in financial terms) needed to generate a unit of utility (such as one QALY).

epidemiology The branch of medicial science concerned with the distribution, occurrence, and transmission of disease.

health related quality of life The satisfaction or well-being that an individual derives from his or her life, insofar as that satisfaction is causally affected by his or her health.

health status A measure of an individual's physical, social, and mental functioning and well-being.

psychometrics A branch of psychology concerned with measurement of psychological conditions (and thus, in relation to health-related quality of life, the source of techniques for establishing individuals' relative preferences for different health states).

quality of life In health economics, psychometrics, and epidemiology a term that is typically synonymous with health-related quality of life.

quality adjusted life year (QALY) Evaluation of the outcome of health care produced by adjusting the value of a year of life by a factor that represents the utility that the person derives from that year, given his or her health state.

QALY league table A table ranking different medical interventions, in terms of the ratio for each intervention of its cost to the QALYs it yields.

utility The pleasure or satisfaction derived by an individual from being in a given state or situation (and thus, with relevance to health economics, from a given health state).

QUALITY OF LIFE INDICATORS are tools designed to measure the health status of individuals and populations. Research on what may more exactly be termed "health-related quality of life" is concerned, on the one hand, with determining the attributes or dimensions of an individual's life (such as everyday activities at home and at work, emotional states, and physical experiences) that are indicative of health, and, on the other hand, to attribute quantitive scores to the health states defined in terms of these dimensions. Quality of life indicators thereby give a richer and more complex picture of a patient's health than that typically given by physiological measures (such as temperature or blood pressure), and as such represent a challenge to the exclusive use of biomedical models of health and illness within medicine. Quality of life indicators have been developed for a variety of purposes, including the monitoring of changes in the health of individual patients, the assessment of the efficacy of medical treatments, and the efficient allocation of resources within a health care system.

I. QALYs

A. Derivation of QALY Measures

The Quality Adjusted Life Year (QALY) is the best known of the many quality of life indicators that have been developed, and the term "QALY" is frequently used as the generic name for, if not all, then at least a certain class of indicators. Perhaps most significantly, the QALY gained a certain notoriety thanks to the proposal that it could be used in determining the allocation of scarce health care resources. The form of QALY measure perhaps most typically cited in illustration of the concept is more precisely referred to as the Rosser or Rosser-Kind index. While this is a relatively simple form of QALY, and as such a simple form of quality of life indicator, it has a number of basic properties shared by all indicators, and may serve as an initial concrete illustration of those properties. For this reason, the discussion of quality of life indicators will be introduced by giving a relatively detailed but uncritical account of the QALY, and its potential uses. (This account is largely based on Gudex and Kind, 1988.)

The development of the QALY was motivated by a desire to produce a more subtle measure of the outcome of medical interventions on a patient's health than had previously been given by survival or mortality data. While the time that a patient survives after an operation may provide some indication of the success of the operation (especially in comparison to expected survival times without treatment or with alternative treatments), this information does not reflect the patient's health state during that time. A patient who survives for 5 years may enjoy good health, or may be confined to bed for the duration. It may be assumed that the patient would not typically be indifferent between these two alternatives. The concept of a Quality Adjusted Life Year therefore begins with basic data on survival, but rather than treating all years survived as being of equal value, in indifference to the state of health enjoyed by the patient, lower scores are given to years spent in poor health compared to those spent in good health.

The development of a QALY indicator involves two distinct stages. First, the concept of "health status" or

"health-related quality of life" needs to be operationalized. This will involve establishing the qualities, aspects, or "dimensions" of health that are considered relevant, and using them to define a series of distinct health states. Crucially, in the QALY no reference is made to specific diseases because, as a "global" or "generic" measure, the QALY is designed to be applicable to patients suffering from any disease. Second, scores are given to each of these health states, expressing the value of the health state to the person enjoying it. These two stages may be considered in turn.

In order to operationalize the concept of quality of life for her original index, Rosser consulted a small group of doctors, asking them to describe the criteria they used to decide on the severity of illness of a patient (independently of any consideration of the patient's prognosis). The two dimensions that emerged from this discussion were those of disability (constituting the objective dimension of the loss of function and mobility) and distress or pain (as the subjective dimension, reflecting the patient's experience of the health state). This framework was further confirmed by consulting groups of economists and health administrators. These groups were asked to recall two people they considered to be ill and two considered to be healthy, and to identify the characteristics that distinguished them. Further consultation with the group of doctors resulted in a classification of eight categories of disability and four of distress (see Table 1). This gave rise to 29 different health states. (It was argued that when the patient is unconscious—the lowest of the eight levels of disability—there can be no experience of pain, and so the differentiation of this level according to degrees of distress is irrelevant.) This classification was tested first by asking doctors if they could classify patients reliably using these discriptions of health related quality of life, and second by using the classification to rate 2120 patients (from various specialities) on admission to and discharge from hospital. In general patients shifted from intuitively poorer to intuitively better health states between admission and discharge.

The second stage in the development of the QALY entails going beyond the mere description of health states, and thus the classification of patients according to these descriptions, in order to evaluate each of the health states described. Evaluation of health states would result in an index score being given to each, indicative of the relative severity of a state in comparison to all the other states. In order to carry out this evaluation, structured interviews were conducted with 70 subjects. Six "marker" states were selected from the 29 available (being IC, IID, VC, VIB, VIIB, and VIID).

The respondent was first asked to order these states according to their degree of severity. He or she was then asked to consider the two states that had been ranked as least severe, and was asked "how many times more ill is a person in state two as compared with state one?" In making this judgment, the respondents were asked to consider, first that the ratio would determine the distribution of resources within the NHS between patients in the two states, and second that the ratio would define a point at which one would be indifferent between curing one patient in the more severe state, and a number of patients in the less severe state. This procedure was then repeated with the remaining pairs of marker states. Values of the remaining intermediate states were calculated from the valuations of the marker states. (The respondents were allowed to modify the valuation of any state at any time.) The median valuations of the 70 respondents were then subject to a mathematical transformation, so that the state of good health (IA) could be given a score of 1. Respondents were asked to indicate where they would place death in the series of health states, and a value of 0 was given to any health state of equivalent value to death. Negative valuations (and thus the valuation of states as being worse than death) are possible. The resultant matrix is reproduced in Table 2.

TABLE 1

Classification of States of Sickness

Disability

1. No disability.
2. Slight social disability.
3. Severe disability and/or slight impairment of performance at work. Able to do all housework except very heavy tasks.
4. Choice of work or performance at work very severely limited. Housewives and old people able to do light housework only but to go out shopping.
5. Unable to undertake any paid employment. Unable to continue any eduction. Old people confined to home except for escorted outings and unable to do shopping. Housewives able only to perform a few simple tasks.
6. Confined to chair or to wheel chair or able to move around in the home only with support from an assistant.
7. Confined to bed.
8. Unconscious.
A. No distress.
B. Mild distress. (Slight pain that is relieved by aspirin.)
C. Moderate distress. (Pain that is not relieved by aspirin.)
D. Severe distress. (Pain for which heroin is prescribed.)

(Source: Rosser and Kind, 1978, 349.)

TABLE 2

QALY Matrix (Marker states in italics)

Distress disability	A	B	C	D
1	1.000	0.995	*0.990*	0.967
2	0.990	0.986	0.973	*0.932*
3	0.980	0.972	0.956	0.912
4	0.964	0.956	0.942	0.870
5	0.946	*0.935*	0.900	0.700
6	0.875	*0.845*	0.680	0.000
7	0.677	*0.564*	0.000	−1.486
8	−1.028	—	—	—

(Source: Kind, Rosser, and Williams, 1982, 160.)

B. Application of the QALY

If it is assumed that the Rosser-Kind matrix represents accurately the valuation that a typical patient will give to his or her health states (and this is a large assumption, not least because the original survey of 70 people represented little more than a pilot study), then QALYs can give a more subtle and accurate indication of the outcome of a medical intervention than that given by simple survival rates. The benefit a patient receives from health care "is measured in terms of the effect on life expectancy adjusted for the quality of life" (in Williams's phrase). Five years of survival in state IA (the good health of no disability and no distress) would score 5 QALYs. Five years of survival in state VD (being unable to work and being in severe distress) would score only (5 × 0.7 =) 3.5 QALYs. One implication of this is that the typical patient would be indifferent between living 3.5 years in good health and 5 years in VD, or, to express this slightly differently, that a typical respondent will prefer a shorter healthy life to a longer life in poor health (so that 4 years of good health are preferable to 5 years in VD). (The qualification that a QALY matrix represents the evaluations of a *typical* patient is important. Because a QALY matrix is generated by surveying a population, the values encoded into it do not represent the values of any individual patient. QALYs are therefore not designed to determine the benefit that individual patients will derive from medical treatment, but rather the benefit that populations of patients will derive.)

Alan Williams outlined the potential application of the QALY method, using the Rosser-Kind matrix to evaluate the health states of patients, with specific reference to coronary artery bypass grafting. He proposed three problems to be considered: to compare the benefits that different groups of patients will gain from a given type of operation; to compare different health care interventions, within a specialty, in terms of the different quantities of resources used to achieve benefits; and to compare the benefits and efficiency of interventions in different specialties. The solutions to all three problems depend heavily upon the accuracy of the data used (concerning the evaluation of health states, survival times and costs of medical intervention), and precisely because of the uncertainty of the data available, Williams's argument provides only a sketch of the potential inherent in the QALY method.

1. Patient Benefit

In response to the first problem, Williams obtained data on the survival rates and health states of patients with severe, moderate, and mild angina. These three groups of patients were further subdivided, and appropriate survival and health state data obtained, according to cases with left main vessel, triple vessel, double vessel, and one vessel disease. For each group or subgroup of patients, comparisons could be made between the QALYs they would enjoy following a coronary artery bypass graft, and the QALYs resulting from mere medical management of their condition. The benefit of the operation is calculated as the total benefit from the operation minus the benefit that the patient would receive from medical management. Thus, while (typically) patients with severe angina and left main vessel disease gained 3.5 QALYs, (typically) patients with severe angina and one vessel disease gained only 0.5 QALYs, indicating that a bypass operation on the latter group may be of minimal benefit. The QALY method therefore may be used to establish the overall efficacy of a treatment and the type of patient to whom that treatment is most appropriately applied (at least where appropriateness is understood in terms of QALY benefit). This application of QALYs lies at the heart of the movement toward evidence-based medicine (i.e., the use of medical interventions that have proven efficacy, as opposed to those that have only anecdotal support, or worse that have been used traditionally without evidence of efficacy).

2. Cost Effectiveness and Resource Allocation

The second and third problems entail the use of QALYs to establish, not just the efficacy of a treatment, but more precisely its cost effectiveness. In being used to make such calculations, the QALY method comes to be seen to have direct implications for the allocation of resources within a medical specialty and within the health care service as a whole. This use of QALYs rests firmly upon the acceptance of the principle that resources available to a health service are always scarce (i.e., that there are insufficient resources available to meet all the actual or potential demand for treatment that is placed upon the health service). A calculation of the cost effectiveness of treatments gives some indication of how those scarce resources could be deployed in order to maximize the benefits (measured in QALYs) generated by the health care system. While this approach need not entail that cost effectiveness is the only criterion by which resources should be allocated, it does entail that cost effectiveness is an important consideration in the justification of the funding of any treatment.

The second problem involves discovery of the most cost-effective way to treat patients with a given condition, and thus facilitates comparisons within a speciality. To introduce cost into the QALY calculation (to give a cost per QALY figure, i.e., the cost in monetary terms of producing one quality-adjusted life year), entails recognizing that a treatment may not be the best simply because it generates the greatest benefit (or gain in QALYs) per patient treated. If a QALY gain is achieved only at a high cost, then it may be suggested that the resources represented by the high cost may be better used elsewhere, in more cost effective treatments. To offer a hypothetical example, assume that a cancer operation will cost £3,000. Palliative care for the same condition would generate fewer QALYs, but at a fraction of the cost of the operation. If the operation generates 5 QALYs, then the cost per QALY is (£3,000/5 =) £600 (i.e., for every £600 spent on cancer operations, the equivalent of one year of life without disability and distress is generated). If palliative care generates only 2 QALYs, but at a total cost of £500, then the cost per QALY is £250. Thus, if only £100,000 were to be allocated to a unit to treat cancer, and all these resources were to be put into operations, then approximately 165 QALYs would be generated (through 33 operations). If all the resources were put into palliative care, 400 QALYs would be generated. The second course of action would entail that 33 individual patients would be denied the operations that could extend the length and quality of their lives, and yet the total health gain would be greater. Underlying this is the philosophical point (to be discussed below) that the value of QALYs is indifferent to the number of people enjoying them. Thus, 10 QALYs enjoyed by 10 different people are equivalent to 10 QALYs enjoyed by a single person. Table 3 reproduces Williams's estimates of the costs and benefits of three treatments for kidney failure. Again, assuming the accuracy of the data used to compile this

TABLE 3

Summary of Costs and Benefits of Treatment for Kidney Failure

Treatment	Costs (£000)	QALYs gained	Cost/QALY
Kidney transplantation	15	5	3
Hemodialysis in hospital	70	5	14
Hemodialysis at home	66	6	11

(Source: Williams, 1985, 328.)

table, cost per QALY calculations give a strong prima facie case for increasing funding to a transplant program.

Table 4 reproduces Williams's estimates of the cost per QALY figures for the treatment of three different conditions. This represents a limited form of QALY league table. Such comparisons are possible because the QALY is non-disease specific. Because the discriptions of health states do not entail any reference to particular diseases, nor to symptoms typical of particular diseases, the QALY matrix can be used to evaluate the health gain of patients suffering from any disease and receiving any type of treatment.

C. Summary

The concept of the Quality Adjusted Life Year facilitates a more subtle measurement of the outcome of medical intervention than survival rates or appeal to clinical symptoms. Survival rates are largely irrelevant to inventions in non-life threatening treatments, while QALY measures may indicate improvements in the patient's health, independently of any change in his or her life expectancy. Insofar as quality of life measures reflect the patient's experience of illness and disease, they may indicate changes in a patient's health independently of changes in symptoms. As such, the concept of health-

TABLE 4

Summary of Costs and Benefits of Three Procedures

Treatment	Costs (£000)	QALYs gained	Cost/QALY
Heart transplantation	23	4.5	5
Hip replacement	3	4	0.75
Kidney transplantation	15	5	3

(Source: Williams, 1985, 328.)

related quality of life poses a challenge to cruder biomedical models of health and illness.

The QALY is an example of a utility measure, in that its matrix attempts to encode the preferences of a population over a range of health states. As such, the QALY is principally to be understood as a tool of health economics, with its main applications being confined to the comparison of the efficiency and cost effectiveness of different health care interventions. Such comparisons facilitate the efficient allocation of scarce resources. Such allocation is not, however, to be understood as an allocation between individual patients (for QALY calculations deploy data of averages of costs and responses to treatment). The allocation decisions that QALY calculations can aid are between alternative treatments within a specialty (e.g., kidney transplant against dialysis) or between specialties.

II. A CLASSIFICATION OF QUALITY OF LIFE INDICATORS, AND THEIR DERIVATION

A. Uses and Types of Indicator

In the last 20 years an intimidating number of quality of life indicators have been developed. In part, this explosion of research and development may be understood as an attempt to construct tools that measure "health-related quality of life" (HRQL) ever more accurately and sensitively. Different tools have different uses, and so in part the diversity is legitimately accounted for in the need to refine tools to specific purposes. The uses of economic utility scales, such as the QALY, in measuring efficiency and cost effectiveness, have been noted above. A concern with effectiveness, and thus with resource allocation, goes beyond the problem of funding medical units or specialties, to questions of the efficacy of (new and established) medical interventions (and thus to evidence-based medicine and medical technology assessment), and similarly to the clinical trialing of pharmaceutical products. The relevance of this work is indicated by the estimate that in the United States one-third of operations for endarterectomy, one-half of coronary artery bypass grafts, and two-fifths of pacemaker implants will be of no benefit to the patient treated.

In addition to the assessment of efficiency, quality of life indicators may play a role in the assessment of the health of populations. Mortality rates, either of the population as a whole, or of subdivisions of the population, as, for example, expressed in infant mortality rates, while widely used and relatively unproblematic to interpret (insofar as high mortality rates are bad, and low rates are good), give only a limited indication of the health of the population (which is to say, the cause of mortality). Similarly, they give little indication of nonfatal chronic disease and illness, that may yet adversely affect the lives and well-being of the population. More substantive data, such as statistics on the incidence and prevelence of particular diseases, give a more complex and detailed picture, but give rise to problems of interpretation. It is not clear, for example, whether a population with a high incidence of lung cancer is in better or worse health than a population with a high incidence of arthritis. Health-related quality of life measures, if following the model of the QALY—where possible health states are given scores indicative of the potential sufferer's evaluation of those states—could guide such interpretation.

Such uses are typically concerned with the responses of populations of patients to given medical interventions. In addition quality of life indicators may be used to measure the responsiveness, and thus change in health state, of individual patients, and to provide patients with better and more relevant information as to the likely progress of their disease and its treatment. Crucially, quality of life indicators go beyond physiological indicators, in terms of the more complex and subtle account of health and illness they provide, not least in being able to take account of the patient's subjective experience of illness and its treatment. Quality of life indicators thus provide a more complex account of the nature of the outcome of medical intervention. They cannot then replace physiological indicators, but they are being increasingly recognized as a necessary complement. Thus, measures that take account of (for example) the emotional state of a sufferer from arthritis, alongside levels of pain and functional mobility, may give a more accurate indication not just of the patient's health state, but also of his or her prognosis. Conversely, in the treatment of cancer, for example, patients may be able to make better-informed decisions about treatments if they have information about the impact of the treatment itself upon their quality of life, and they may be better able to articulate their preferences with respect to what may be a necessary trade-off between quality of life and life expectancy.

The range of quality of life indicators may usefully be classified through a simple typology. First, a distinction may be made between generic (or global) indicators and disease specific indicators, which is to say that indicators either are applicable to patients suffering from any disease or condition, or are constructed to capture the particular experience and evaluation of a specific disease or group of diseases (such as the cancers). The choice of indicator type will depend upon the use to which it is to be put. Generic measures are of use in monitoring general populations, and in making comparisons (for example in cost effectiveness) between treatments in different specialties. However, they may be insensitive to the changes associated with a particular disease. In consequence, a disease-specific measure will be more likely to give accurate and precise indications of both the effects of new therapies and drugs upon the disease, and the progress of an individual patient suffering from that disease. A generic measure may, however, be an important complement even in these two cases. In monitoring the effects of a therapy, the generic measure may be sensitive to a wider range of outcomes, and as such may be a better indicator of the treatment's side effects, when these are not typically associated with the disease. The generic measure may thus give a better indication of the net benefits of alternative treatments, and of the overall health of the patient.

A second distinction can be made between indicators that are indices and those that are profiles. An index will express the evaluation of the patient's health state in a single (index) number, while the profile will express the patient's condition across a range of different qualities or dimensions (such as physical mobility, pain, sleep, energy, social isolation, and emotional reactions, to cite the dimensions of the Nottingham Health Profile). In a profile each dimension may be given its own score or valuation (so that, for example, a patient may score well in terms of physical mobility, but poorly in terms of sleep and energy), but no attempt will be made to reduce the complexity of this picture to a single value. (The QALY is therefore an example of a generic index.) As a general characterization it may be suggested that indices, expressive of a population's preferences between health states (or the utility to be derived from them), are of relevance to problems of resource allocation (insofar as they facilitate ready comparisons between outcomes of different treatments or patient groups). The index thus offers a strong indication of which health states are preferable to others (thereby making interpretation relatively straightforward). Profiles are typically designed for the measurement of the HRQL of individual patients, or for providing more complex pictures of the health of populations than can be given by indices or more traditional health indicators. The profile does not seek to establish that one health state is unambiguously preferable to another, but rather to indicate in some detail the nature of any changes in a patient's or a population's quality of life.

B. Quality of Life Measurement

It is conceivable that quality of life could be measured by a single-item questionnaire. Two examples may be given: "Would you describe your health (for your age) as 'excellent,' 'good,' 'fair' or 'poor'?"; and "Here is a picture of a ladder. At the bottom of this ladder is the worst situation you might reasonably expect to have. At the top is the best you might expect to have. The other rungs are in between. Where on the ladder would you put your quality of life over the past four weeks? On which rung would you put it?" The first question allows four classifications (or more depending on the addition of extra categories, such as "very good") of quality of life, and the second a numerical score. While such an approach is simple and easy to administer, and may provide a useful summary question in conclusion to a more comprehensive questionnaire (such as the SF-36), it is of limited use unless precise implications can be drawn from responses (for example, it has been suggested that the first question is a valid predictor of mortality, and the patient's satisfaction with health). Crucially, such simple questions give little indication of what (health-related) quality of life is, and effectively sidestep two key problems in the development of quality of life measures. On the one hand, "health-related quality of life" must be operationalized into a usable measuring tool. This entails, at best, reflection upon the meaning of "health," and thus the qualities of the respondent's life that need to be addressed by the measure. In sum, the dimensions of health covered by the measure (be it a profile or an index) need to be justified. (Tables 5A and 5B summarize the dimensions of two indices and three profiles.) On the other hand, if the quality of life measure is going to go beyond the mere recording of changes in the various dimensions of the patient's health and quality of life, then the impact of those changes on the patient's life needs to be evaluated. In addition, if values are given to possible health states, then it is important to establish exactly what information those values convey. (For fuller details of the development and use the major quality of life measurement instruments, see Walker and Rosser, 1993.)

1. The Dimensions of Quality of Life

The Rosser-Kind index was seen to have only two dimensions, disability and distress. Measures of disability and function—including activities of daily living (ADL) indices that sought to measure such basic activities as bathing, dressing, toileting, continence, and feeding, as well as instrumental activities (including shopping, cooking, housekeeping, use of transport, managing money), and mobility—may be seen as the precursors of quality of life indicators. While the Rosser-Kind index crucially adds the subjective dimension of distress and the resultant evaluation of health states to the measurement (or at least the classification) of disability, and thus attempts to grasp quality of life as the patient's experience and evaluation of the condition, the concept of "health" upon which the index is based is a negative one. Health is understood merely as the absence of disease and disability. This may be criticized as too narrow a definition, and other quality of life indicators have been based upon more rigorous reflection upon the meaning of "health," and thus upon the meaning of "health-related quality of life" itself.

"Quality of life" may encompass a person's ability to carry out mundane social functions (for example, self-care, housework, recreation, and paid employment), opportunity for and competence in social interaction, psychological well-being, somatic sensation (such as the experience of pain), and the degree of satisfaction the person gains from mundane activity. Crudely, the person's quality of life improves as he or she is able to do more and to derive greater satisfaction from that activity. (This is broadly in line with a humanist model of health, where health is understood as a resource that a person exploits, creatively, in the setting and pursuing of goals constitutive of a worthwhile life.) To speak meaningfully of "health-related quality of life" entails, at least implicitly, appealing to ordinary language usage, where talk of one's "quality of life" suggests the general satisfaction that one has with one's life. "Quality of life" will thus depend upon such factors as one's housing, the environment in which you live and work, one's social relationships, and so forth. It may not be an exaggeration to suggest that talk of one's quality of life makes an implicit appeal to the degree to which one's life approaches one's personal image of an Aristotelian "good life." A quality life has certain inherent satisfactions that make it a life worth living. (While philosophers have carried out significant work on the concepts of "quality of life" and a "life worth living" (see Aiken 1982 and Glover 1977) the concept of "quality" remains elusive, and a significant tension exists between the evaluative concept of quality and a more technical, and value-neutral, use. The seventeenth-century English empiricist John Locke used the concept of "quality" in the sense of the properties constitutive of an object. In this sense, a HRQL indicator may be understood as

TABLE 5A

Structures of Two Generic Indexes

1. Quality of Well-Being Scale

4 attributes Weighting*	Examples of levels/CPX	
Mobility (3 levels)	No limitation in driving or use of public transportation for health reasons.	−0.000
	In hospital as a bed patient overnight.	−0.090
Physical activity (3 levels) 0.000	No limitations for health reasons.	
	Found it difficult to life, stoop, bend over or use stairs or inclines. −0.060	
Social function (5 levels)	Performed major role and other activities, with no limitations for health reasons.	−0.000
	Did not perform self-care activities for health reasons.	−0.106
(36) symptom/problem complexes (CPX)	Burns over large area of face, body, arms or legs.	−0.367
	Sick or upset stomach, vomiting or loose bowel movements, with or without fever, chills, or aching all over.	−0.290
	Breathing smog or unpleasant air	−0.101

* Weights may be aggregated, so that, for example, a patient with burns who is unable to perform self care has a quality adjustment of $(1 - (0.367 + 0.106) =) 0.527$.

2. EuroQol

6 dimensions	Descriptions
Mobility	1. No problems with walking about. 2. Unable to walk about with a stick, crutch or walking frame. 3. Confined to bed.
Self-care	1. No problems with self-care. 2. Unable to dress self. 3. Unable to feed self.
Main activity	1. Able to perform main activity (e.g., work, study, housework). 2. Unable to perform main activity.
Social relationships	1. Able to pursue family and leisure activities.
Pain	1. No pain or discomfort. 2. Moderate pain or discomfort. 3. Extreme pain or discomfort.
Mood	1. Not anxious or depressed. 2. Anxious or depressed.

(Combining one item from each of the six dimensions would lead to the description of 216 health states. 16 such states were chosen for weighting by survey populations.)

serving to identify those qualities, properties or characteristics that define "health." Such an approach to quality of life measurement therefore places emphasis upon the description of health states, and the derivation of the dimensions or parameters to be recognized in the measuring instrument. Crucially, it may be seen to including the social dimensions and consequences of health as qualities, alongside purely physiological conditions.)

To speak specifically of "health-related quality of life" suggests that it is possible to isolate from all the factors that impact upon one's quality of life those that are to do with health, or that may reasonably be considered to be the responsibility of the health care system and health care providers. Such distinctions can rarely be made unambiguously. Thus, Patrick and Erickson note that while "a safe environment, adequate housing, a guaranteed income, respect, love, and freedom" are all valued aspects of human existence, and as such contribute to overall quality of life, they are not the responsibility of the health care system. A causal relationship is thus established between health and quality of life. The direction of causality is from health to quality of life. Patrick and Erickson give the example of assessing "the well-being and disadvantage because of health among a group of persons with rheumatoid arthritis," noting that the disease affects social functioning. The point is that the consequences of being ill thus spill over into mundane life. "Health-related quality of life" thereby refers to those aspects of a person's mun-

TABLE 5B

Structures of Three Generic Profiles

1. Nottingham Health Profile
Part 1

6 dimensions	No. of items	Example statements	UK Weighting if "yes" *
Physical mobility	8	I find it hard to bend.	10.57
		I am unable to walk at all.	21.30
Pain	8	I'm in pain when I walk.	11.22
Sleep	5	I lie awake for most of the night.	27.26
Energy	3	I'm tired all the time.	39.20
		Everything is an effort.	36.80
Social isolation	5	I'm finding it hard to make contact with people.	19.36
		I feel I am a burden to people.	22.53
Emotional reactions	9	Worry is keeping me awake at night.	13.95
		I wake up feeling depressed.	12.01

Part 2

7 *dimensions* (single question, of the form: "Is your present state of health causing problems with your ...," requiring an unweighted yes/no answer)
Employment ("Job of work").
Social life ("Example; going out, seeing friends, going to the pub").
Household work ("Looking after the home").
Home life ("That is, relationships with other people in your home").
Sex life
Interests and hobbies (Examples: sports, arts and crafts, do-it-yourself).
Holidays (Examples: summer or winter holidays, weekends away).

* A score of 0 is equivalent to good health; 100 is the worst health condition within each dimension (i.e., the respondent answers "yes" to all the questions posed in that dimension.)

2. Sickness Impact Scale

12 dimensions	No. of items	Example statement
Ambulation	12	I do not walk at all.
Mobility	10	I stay at home most of the time.
		I stay away from home only for brief periods of time.
Self-care	23	I only get dressed with someone's help.
Home management	10	I am not doing any of the maintenance or repair work around the house that I usually do.
		I am not doing heavy work around the house.
Social interaction	20	I go out to visit people less often.
		I isolate myself as much as I can from the rest of the family.
Communication	9	I am having trouble writing or typing.
		I do not speak clearly when I am under stress.
Emotional behavior	9	I laugh or cry suddenly.
		I act irritably and impatient with myself, for example, talk badly about myself, swear at myself, blame myself for things that happen.
Alertness	10	I do not keep my attention on any activity for long.
Eating	9	I just pick or nibble at my food.
		I am eating no food at all, nutrition is taken through tubes or intravenous fluids.
Work	9	I am not getting as much done as usual.
		I often act irritably toward my work associates.
Sleep and rest	7	I sit down during much of the day.
Recreation	8	I am not doing any of my usual physical recreation or activities.

3. SF-36

9 dimensions	No. of items	Example question/answer
Physical functioning	10	Does your health now limit you in these activities? Lifting or carrying groceries. A lot; a little; not at all.
Role functioning Physical	4	During the past 4 weeks, have you had any of the following problems with your work or other regular daily activities, as a result of your physical health? Accomplished less than you would like. Yes; no.
Bodily pain	2	How much bodily pain have you had during the last 4 weeks? "None" to "very severe" (six categories).
General health	5	In general, would you say your health is: excellent; very good; good; fair; poor?
Vitality	4	How much of the time during the past 4 weeks did you feel full of pep? "All of the time" to "none of the time" (six categories).
Social functioning	2	During the past 4 weeks, how much of the time has your physical health or emotional problems interfered with your social activities (like visiting friends, relatives, etc.)? "All of the time" to "none of the time" (five categories).
Role-functioning-Emotional	3	During the past 4 weeks, have you had any of the following problems with your work or other regular daily activities, as a result of any emotional problems (such as feeling depressed or anxious)? Accomplished less than you would like. Yes; no.
Mental health	5	How much of the time during the past 4 weeks have you felt calm and peaceful? "All of the time" to "none of the time" (six categories).
Reported health-transition	1	Compared to one year ago, how would you rate your health in general now? "Much better" to "much worse" (five categories).

dane existence that are affected by his or her health state. "Health-related quality of life" thus attempts to grasp the experience of health and illness. This experience is not confined to the experience of somatic sensations (as is implied by the Rosser-Kind index), but is inevitably mediated by the impact that the physiological level of illness has upon the person, as an integrated social and psychological being. In contrast, such factors as the environment within which a person lives, and his or her income and social relationships will have a causal impact upon health (thereby reversing the order of causality under consideration). In sum, if quality of life measures are interpreted as indicators of a person's health (and if the Lockean qualities of health include the capacity to carry out social roles, and an experience of personal well-being and satisfaction), then the causal impact of health upon the conduct of one's life is most relevant.

The descriptions of health states, or the description of the relevant parts of their component dimensions, can be derived in a number of ways. For the designers of the measure to write their own list of health states may overly privilege the designers' perception of health and illness. Similarly, to draw classifications from the existing medical literature, or from medical experts, may overly privilege the medical profession's perception of health, so that the resultant set of descriptions will reflect objective, physiological measures of health and illness, and not the patient's experience. (The descriptions of functions in the Quality of Well-Being Scale, for example, were initially derived from reviews of medical reference works, to establish all the ways disease and injury can affect behaviour and role performance.) For the Nottingham Health Profile, 768 patients with a variety of chronic ailments were interviewed, thereby generating 2200 statements describing the effects of illness. (The Sickness Impact Profile was based upon 1250 responses to open-ended request forms, from health care professionals, patients, and those accompanying the patient.) The raw descriptions generated are typically scrutinized for redundancy, ambiguity, and comprehensibility, and may be subjected to pilot studies or further scrutiny by the designers in order to refine the statements in terms of the dysfunctions they describe, ensuring that they do not overlap and that they comprehensively identify real differences between health states.

Consulting patients or the lay public has the advantage of avoiding the designers' or the medical professions' preconceptions about the nature of health and illness, which may be of particular relevance to a measure (such as the Nottingham Health Profile) that is explicitly seeking to challenge the dominance of a biomedical conception of health and illness. In addition, the descriptions of health states generated are more likely to be readily comprehensible by lay people.

2. Measurement Theory

Perhaps the most dramatic aspect of a QALY measure is the attribution of scores to the different possible health states. For most uses of quality of life indicators, it is insufficient merely to describe health states. It is necessary to establish whether one health state is preferable to another, and thus to establish the impact that health states have upon the patient's quality of life.

The process of evaluating or weighting health states is referred to as scaling. Health states are being placed upon a scale. Not only the method of scaling, but also the properties of the scale need to be considered. Four types of scale may be identified: nominal, ordinal, interval, and ratio. A nominal scale merely classifies health states (for example, Florence Nightingale classified patients as "dead," "relieved," "unrelieved"), but does not necessarily express anything about the relative severity of the states described. An ordinal scale places items in order of severity or preference (for example, the responses of "excellent," "good," "fair," and "poor" as descriptions of one's general health). Ordinal scales do not, however, indicate anything about how much more severe one state is in comparison to another. (Hence, the degree to which "excellent" health is preferable to "good" health is not necessarily the same degree as the difference between "fair" and "poor" health.) In interval scales the differences between points on the scale can be compared. For example, in the Celsius temperature scale, the difference between 10° and 20° is the same as that between 20° and 30°. If a quality of life indicator uses an interval scale, then if one patient's health improves from 0.5 to 0.6, and another's from 0.8 to 0.9, then both patients have made the same health gain. A ratio scale has the additional property of having a nonarbitrarily defined zero point, so that, in contrast to the Fahrenheit or Celsius temperature scales where 0° is arbitrarily defined, it is possible to establish the ratios between different points on the scale. One cannot say that 10°C is twice as hot as 5°C. In contrast, one can say that 10 decibels is twice as loud as 5 decibels, if zero decibels is nonarbitrarily defined as silence. In the Rosser-Kind scale, death (as zero) and the absence of disability and distress (as 1) are defended as nonarbitrary points, so that a QALY score of 0.8 is twice as good as a score of 0.4. (A quality of life scale that does not have ratio properties is inappropriate for use in QALY-type resource allocation decisions.)

The evaluation of different health states may be carried out by a number of different weighting and scaling techniques. Thurlstone ranking (an example of scaling through the use of "paired comparisions") is a relatively straightforward weighting technique used for the first part of the Nottingham Health Profile. For each dimension of the profile, respondents are asked to rank the severity of each statement within the dimension against every other statement within the dimension. (For a dimension with five statements, the respondent is then asked to make 10 judgments.) It is argued that a weighting can be derived from the proportion of the respondents who judge each given statement as being more severe than another. An alternative to this use of paired comparisons is to confront the respondent with all the dimension's statements at one time, and ask them to place them in order of severity. While possibly faster to administer, this latter method may be less able to accurately weigh statements that are of a similar degree of severity.

The rating scale is a technique which facilitates the derivation of an interval scale. Respondents are presented with a scale with fixed endpoints (such as "death" or "worst imaginable health state" at 0 and "good health" or "best imaginable health state" at 1 or 100). They are then asked to place items on the scale, so that the intervals between items indicate the differences in their preferences for these states. EuroQol, among others, uses a visual analogue scale, in the form of a thermometer, to aid the response. In category scaling, respondents may be asked to place items into preexisting slots or categories (for example by allocating each of five items to categories marked 0 (the worst) to 4). A ratio scale may be secured by explicitly asking the respondents to estimate how much better or worse given states are in comparison to a standard or reference state (known as magnitude estimation). Similarly equivalence technique (or "person trade-off") may be used where the respondent is asked to decide on the number of people in one health state that would be equivalent to a given number in a reference state. In equivalence, the respondent might be presented with the scenario of so many people in one undesirable health state, so many in another, and then be asked, if only one group could be cured (say due to scarce resources), which should be chosen. The numbers in one of the health states can then be varied until the respondent is indifferent between the two groups. The ratio of the number of people in each group is then indicative of the respondent's comparitive evaluation of the two health states. (Magnitude estimation and an equivalence technique were seen above, in section I.A, to be used in the Rosser-Kind index.) Time

trade-off similarly requires the respondent to establish a ratio of severity between two conditions. In time trade-off the respondent must express his or her preference, not simply between two health states, but rather between being in two health states each for a given period of time (followed by death). The time may then be varied, until the respondent is indifferent between the two alternatives.

In standard gamble technique the respondent is asked to choose between two uncertain or risky alternatives. Two chronic health outcomes are presented, one of which is relatively good (e.g., good health) and the other relatively bad (e.g., death). The respondent is then asked to choose between two alternatives. The first alternative is a lottery, where the probability of achieving the good health outcome is p, and of achieving the bad health outcome is $1 - p$. The second alternative is the certainty of achieving a chronic health outcome that is intermediate between the good and bad outcomes. Probability p is then varied until the respondent is indifferent between the two alternatives. This probability gives the respondent's evaluation for the intermediate health state. (In effect, respondents are being asked to choose between remaining in a state of chronic poor health, and receiving a treatment that may either cure them or kill them. Varying "p" amounts to varying the probability of being cured as opposed to not surviving the treatment.) The standard gamble technique is well grounded in economic utility theory, and specifically in models of individual decision-making under conditions of uncertainty.

A problem for the derivation of quality of life indicators is that different scaling techniques, and indeed different approaches within a technique, yield significantly different results. It is thus unclear which technique is the best (or, more precisely, which is the most appropriate for the derivation of an indicator designed for a given use). A fundamental problem is that scaling techniques typically require respondents to carry out complex exercises that are not obviously grounded in their everyday experience and competences. (An extreme response to these methodological problems, but nonetheless one that deserves careful consideration, is the criticism of quality of life measurement for its excessively positivistic approach, insofar as the various scaling techniques assume an unrealistic, and excessively rationalist, model of the respondent.) Cultural and emotional characteristics of the respondent may then, unwittingly, have a distorting impact on results. Thus, an aversion to gambling or risk taking, or an inability to understand probabilities, may be more significant to the outcome of a standard gamble exercise than the respondent's health preferences. The results of rating scales, including the use of visual analogue scales, may be distorted by the respondents' tendency to spread items evenly across the scale. The phrasing of a question may also have cultural implications. For example, as Nord points out, the presupposition that "a state half way between good health and death" will have been situated on an ratio, or even an ordinal, scale by the respondent ignores the nuances of the phrase "feeling half dead." If being "half dead" is a serious condition, the weightings of other conditions will tend to be compressed into the upper half of the scale.

Perhaps more significantly, for it touches on certain presuppositions of the QALY methodology as a whole, respondents' attitude to time may influence results. Thus, a time trade-off exercise may be distorted because respondents will typically be less concerned with loses to be incurred in a distant future, so that they will be more willing to trade in life years, the longer the time horizon of the exercise. Similarly, if respondents are asked to evaluate different health states (as for example in magnitude estimation), then the amount of time the respondent imagines to be spent in that state will be important. In development of the Quality of Well-Being scale, respondents were asked to evaluate one day in a given condition. One day confined to bed was not percieved as being that much worse than one day with a stuffy nose. Such an evaluation seemingly offers little insight into the value of being chronically bed-bound. Thus, QALYs as a whole have been criticized for failing to take accont of the accumulative impact of chronic illness (for three weeks confined to bed is not simply three times as bad as one week confined to bed). The Healthy Year Equivalent is a measure proposed, in part, as a response to this problem.

Further, the link between the scaling exercise and the potential use of the resultant quality of life instrument is not always made clear to the respondent. (It may be noted that a point in favor of the Rosser-Kind index is that respondents were explicitly asked to consider the implications their evaluations would have for resource allocation.) Most significantly, while some techniques ask the respondents to consider alternative possibilities for their own health and life expectancy, others ask the respondents to consider the health and lives of others. Again, there may be distortion through an aversion to make such "life and death" decisions about others. However, respondents' evaluation of the lives of others will be more relevant if the quality of life instrument is being designed for resource allocation (as opposed to the clinical evaluation of medical interventions).

A further, and fundamental problem in the evalua-tion of health states is that different types of respondent will give different responses to the same scaling technique. Thus, in the early presentation of the Rosser-Kind index, six alternative matrices were presented, apart from that derived from the total sample population. The six represent subgroups within that total population (medical patients, psychiatric patients, medical nurses, psychiatric nurses, healthy volunteers, and doctors), and each showed small but significant differences in evaluations. (For example, doctors gave less importance to death compared to other health states, but greater importance to subjective suffering. While doctors' valuations were close to those of healthy volunteers, patients' valuations were closer to those of their nurses.) Similarly, research has been done on a number of quality of life indicators, most notably perhaps the Nottingham Health Profile, to establish the variation in weightings that will occur between nations. This becomes a crucial ethical (and political problem) of quality of life measurement, precisely because the ethos of most quality of life measurement centers about the desire to break away from the domination of the medical profession (and narrow physiological criteria) in the determining the value of health care outcomes. Quality of life measures increasingly derive both their definition and articulation of health states, and their evaluations and weightings from consultation with a wider public. However, if different sectors of that public have different preferences, and no simple consensus values can be discovered, the moral and political question is posed, as to whose values should be incorporated into the indicator?

3. Methodological Criteria

In conclusion to this section, brief notes will be given on both the statistical tests to which indicators should be subjected, and other issues of design and application.

An indicator is of value only if it actually measures what it claims to measure, and if it can make appropriately fine distinctions in the domain of objects measured. An indicator thus needs to be reliable, valid, and responsive. Reliability refers to the indicator's ability to produce the same results on different occasions (hence test-retest reliability is a statistical measure of the results of applying the indicator to the same subject on two or more occasions). Thus, an indicator designed to discriminate between groups of patients with better and with worse health related quality of life is reliable if it recognizes a greater difference between the groups than it does between patients within each group.

Validity refers to the degree to which an indicator measures what it purports to measure. It is perhaps the most difficult test of an indicator, precisely because there is no objective or generally agreed set of criteria (or "gold standard") against which to test indicators. Informally but rather vaguely, indicators may be assessed on "face" validity, which is to say, whether or not they appear, to experts, to measure what they purport to measure. More precisely, content validity tests the indicator in terms of the adequacy with which the indicator includes the relevant properties of the object studied. Construct validity compares the indicator to a theoretical model of the domain being studied. The indicator is tested in terms of specific hypotheses about how the instrument will behave if it is valid. Thus, an indicator designed to discriminate between groups of patients should be able to discriminate between, say, a group receiving a toxic chemotherapeutic regimen and one receiving a less toxic regimen. Similarly, it may be expected that patients with higher levels of physical symptoms will have a lower health-related quality of life. In effect, this entails that content validity entails testing an indicator against other instruments (such as physiological measures of severity of disease, or against existing quality of life indicators). Exact agreement would not be expected, as that would make the quality of life indicator redundant.

Responsiveness is used to refer to the ability of indicators to evaluate changes in the condition of patients over time (as opposed to comparisions between different patients or groups of patients). A responsive measure is sensitive to change. A lack of responsiveness may occur because of ceiling and floor effects. A ceiling effect occurs if a respondent reports that his or health has improved, despite the fact that he or she received the highest possible score on an earlier application of the indicator. A floor effect, conversely, is insensitive to deterioration in health beyond a certain point.

Reflection on the issues of establishing reliability and validity may reinforce the doubts raised above, as to exactly what quality of life measures do measure. In consequence, it may be suggested that quality of life measurement may benefit from recieving the same attention from philosophers of science and mathematics as it has to date received from ethicists. While quality of life indicators are discussed as if they refer to some external entity, validation procedures appear more closely to abide by a coherence theory of truth, rather than a correspondence theory, which is to say that measures are valid because they are coherent within the overarching framework of assumptions of the discipline, rather than because their results correspond to the properties of some independently identifiable entity.

Beyond its statistical properties as a measuring instrument, a quality of life indicator must still be practicable. Indicators that are designed for the assessment of individual patients, particularly on a routine basis (such as the Nottingham Health Profile or the Sickness Impact Profile), or to survey large populations, need to be relatively easy to administer, even if this comes at the cost of a loss in sensitivity and comprehensiveness of cover. An excessively long self-administered questionnaire may place too great a burden, not merely of time but also of physical or emotional energy, on a patient. (The issue of whether patients enjoy, or are distressed by, the act of completing such questionnaires is relevant.) Long and complex questionnaires are also less easy to interpret, and thus less appropriate to most clinical settings.

III. ETHICAL ISSUES IN THE DERIVATION AND APPLICATION OF QUALITY OF LIFE INDICATORS

A. Moral Justifications of QALYs

There has been an extensive moral debate over the use of quality of life indicators (and specifically QALYs) in the use of resource allocation. The main points of that debate will be reviewed (largely following the summary account given by Crisp (1989)), after an outline of two moral frameworks within which QALYs may be defended.

1. Utilitarianism

The most usual defense of the use of QALYs in the allocation of health care resources rests upon a utilitarian interpretation of QALYs. While classical utilitarianism, following Bentham, justifies social policy that aims to achieve the greatest happiness for the population, so it is argued that the dominant objective of health care policy is to achieve the greatest net health gain for the population. If health gain is defined in terms of QALYs, then cost per QALY calculations can serve to bring about an efficient use of inevitably scarce health care resources, precisely in so far as guidance will be given as to where those resources will be able to generate the greatest health gain. At the core of this approach is the assumption that, all other things being equal, a gain of one QALY is of equal value whoever enjoys it. This "standard rule," as Alan Williams calls it, "has a very strong non-discriminatory egalitarian flavour, it is free of judgements about people's worth, or deserts, or influence, or likeability, or appearance, or smell, or manners, or age, sex, wealth, social class, religious beliefs, race, colour, temperament, sexual orientation, or general or particular life style." The QALY is therefore defended, not merely on grounds of efficiency, and maximizing a population's health, but also on the grounds that consideration of health gain in terms of QALYs serves to screen out other prejudices that are irrelevant to the conduct of a just health care system.

2. Contractarianism

An alternative defense of the use of QALYs has been offered by Paul T. Menzel, from the position of a social contract theorist. Menzel's argument is not primarily concerned with the consequences of applying QALYs to resource allocation, but rather appeals strongly to the grounding of QALYs in public consultation and surveys, both in order to derive the relevant dimensions of HRQL, and in order to weigh or evaluate the resultant health states. Potentially, the QALY matrix can then be understood as expressing a population's "prior consent" to certain rules governing the allocations of health care resources. (In effect, the QALY is seen as articulating an otherwise implicit social contract between potential recipients of a given stock of scarce health care resources.) Scaling techniques such as the standard gamble or time trade-off, as was seen in Section II.B.2, allow the respondent to express a preference between a shorter life of good health and a longer life of poorer health. Thus, a QALY matrix might value a condition of severe chronic paraplegia less than one of good health. A consequence of this valuation might run as follows. Imagine two accident victims who will die without treatment. One victim can be restored to good health, but while the life of the other could be saved, he or she would remain a paraplegic. If resources are not available to save the lives of both victims, then the victim who can be restored to good health should be given priority. Menzel, in line with the doubts about the relevance of scaling techniques to resource allocation and the eliciting of preferences noted above, does not accept that current QALY matrices or the techniques used for their derivation are sufficient to elicit the community's "prior consent" to decisions such as this. He argues rather for respondents being confronted by a "QALY bargain," in the form of an explicit gamble concerning the availability of health care if they were the accident victim. The evaluation of health states would then have explicit consequences in terms of the different probabilities of the respondent receiving treatment, for given prognoses. In sum, the QALY bargain "would expose me to a greater risk of being allowed to die should I ever be [an accident victim who could only survive

with paraplegia], but in return I gain a better chance of being saved should I ever be a victim with prospectively normal health gain." On Menzel's interpretation, a suitably formulated QALY instrument would seek to establish the precise nature of the bargain into which respondents would be willing to enter (or, if they are willing to enter into such a bargain at all).

B. Moral Criticisms of QALYs

1. The Priority of Life Saving

Cost per QALY calculations may be criticized for failing to take account of the extra value that is inherent to the saving of a life, as opposed to the mere improvement of the quality of that life. QALY gain is indifferent to the identity or number of people enjoying those QALYs. The following example may be considered. A given quantity of funds may be extended to only one of two medical units. The first unit could save an additional 100 lives for an average of 10 QALYs each. The other unit could save 600 lives, but for an average of only 1 QALY each. The first unit would therefore generate 1000 QALYs, as against 600 QALYs from the other unit. On cost per QALY grounds, the funds will be given to the first unit, thereby sacrificing a net 500 lives. Similarly, QALY calculations suggest that an improvement in quality of life may be preferable to saving lives that are then maintained at a low quality. (The above example can be modified. The first unit does not save the lives of the 100 patients it treats, but raises the average quality of life of each patient from 0.4 to 0.9, and sustains that gain for an average of 20 years per patient.) QALY calculations therefore appear to contradict the moral intuition that live saving is of greater importance than merely improving quality of life.

The utilitarian may respond to this criticism by arguing that life is only of instrumental value. Life is only of value insofar as it is a condition of a person pursuing other, intrinsically satisfying goals. A low QALY score for a health state is therefore taken to imply that being in that state seriously inhibits the pursuit of otherwise satisfying goals. The starkest counter argument to this position would be a defense of the sanctity of life. Here it would be argued that all innocent human life, regardless of health conditions or any other factors, is of inherent and infinite worth. As such, the value inherent in the saving of life cannot be compared with, or traded off against, any value in merely improving the quality of life. Life saving and quality of life enhancement are incommensurable. A sanctity of life doctrine therefore entails the rejection of the QALY approach as untenable.

A more significant articulation of this criticism comes from John Harris, not least because he shares an instrumental view of the value of life. He argues that "it does not follow that where the choice is between three years of discomfort for *me* or immediate death on the one hand, and one year of health for *you*, or immediate death on the other, that I am somehow committed to the judgement that you ought to be saved rather than me." From this psychological insight, Harris argues that the comparison of two patients in terms of the number of QALYs they each may yield is irrelevant. A person with 10 QALYs left to live does not, for Harris, have more to lose than a person with only 1 QALY left. They both face the same loss, namely the rest of their lives. Thus, if someone wants to go on living, then a wrong is done to them by failing to save their life, because the "value of someone's life is, primarily and overwhelmingly, its value to him or her." In effect, Harris is arguing that the only conceivable grounds upon which two patients could be compared is the degree of their fervor to go on living. As this is unmeasurable, no such comparison should be made. The QALY approach is thus dismissed as iniquitous. Menzel's approach to QALYs makes an explicit reply to Harris, precisley insofar as the "QALY bargain" makes clear the trade-off to which one is committing oneself, between one's own long life of poor health and someone else's short healthy life. However, as Menzel acknowledges that this bargain can be rejected, he leaves scope for members of community to act upon something akin to Harris's psychological insight, and thus refuse to present a calculated trade off of one's own life against another's.

2. Ageism

Allocation according to cost per QALY calculations has been criticized as unjust, on the grounds that it entails a systematic and morally unjustifiable bias against the elderly. It is claimed that this bias follows because a group of patients is more likely to receive funding for its treatment if it can yield more QALYs than other comparable groups. The longer the patients are expected to live, the more opportunity they have to yield those QALYs. All other things being equal, groups of young and middle-aged patients therefore have an inherent advantage over groups of elderly patients. (This is not simply, or most acutely, a criticism of QALYs. To assess the success of a health care system merely in terms of post operative survival would incorporate a greater bias against the elderly. The QALY approach at least acknowledges that a few years of good health lived by the elderly, may outweigh many years of poor quality health lived by younger patients.)

The standard reply to this accusation appeals to the idea of a "good (or fair) innings." Drawing on a metaphor from cricket, and appealing to a phrase frequently used, at least in the United Kingdom, to comfort friends and relatives at the death of an elderly person (such that the deceased "at least had a good innings"), this argument holds that it is just to redistribute resources toward the young and away from the elderly. The elderly have already enjoyed a (long) life. If their lives are saved at the expense of those of the young, then the young are being denied the opportunity to have something (a "good innings") that the elderly have already had. In effect, the argument implies that it may be an obligation of a health care system to ensure, as far as possible, that everyone lives to a certain age (say "three score years and ten"), but that those who have the fortune to live beyond that age are no longer a priority.

An attempt to counter the "good innings" argument works as a reductio ad absurdum. While it might be accepted that a 80-year-old has less claim to resources than a 5-year-old, what then of a 20-year-old and a 40-year-old, or a 35-year-old and a 36-year-old? These extensions of the argument do not obviously work. Firstly, it may be suggested that no 20-, 30-, and 40-year-old has yet had a good innings, so the concept is irrelevant for distinguishing them. Secondly, and more significantly for QALY applications, it may be noted that QALYs are not designed to allocate resources between individuals, but rather between medical units (and thus groups of patients). While many diseases and conditions afflict the elderly and not younger groups, and so one can readily imagine situations in which a choice could be made between additional funding to a geriatric unit and a neo-natal care unit, a specialist unit that treats people up to, but not beyond, the age of 35, and another that only treats 36-year-olds and above are much harder to conceive. (This highlights an important point, insofar as certain criticisms of QALYs may in fact be better understood as criticisms of the misuse of QALYs, and these will be criticisms that the advocates of cost per QALY methods would readily endorse.)

Independently of the "good innings" argument (which may itself be subject to an inherent ageism, more insidious than any inherent in the QALY), the QALY can be defended against ageism on the grounds that, to be genuinely ageist, one must discriminate between people on explicit grounds of age (and where such grounds are inappropriate). The QALY method does not discriminate between groups of patients of grounds of age, but rather on grounds of survival and quality of life. The elderly are not thereby treated differently than any other patient group. Thus, a group of neonates with poor prognoses of survival would be of less priority than a group of elderly with prognoses of several years of good health. (Indeed, the QALY method would, on these grounds, give greater priority to the elderly than would an approach based on the good innings argument.) In effect, this appeals back to Williams's "standard rule." The QALY approach is not interested in the age of the potential recipients of health care, only in the QALYs they can yield.

It may further be suggested that if the community is unhappy with the allocations of resources that arise from QALY calculations, for example on the grounds that too few resources are being given to the elderly (and thus, say, that the elderly are not receiving the respect that is their due, or are not being fairly treated given the funds they have contributed through tax or insurance to the health care system), QALY scores can readily be modified (or weighted). Thus, each year of good health lived after the age of 70, for example, could be given a weighted score of 1.1, rather than 1.0 (and all other quality adjustments could similarly be modified by 10%). Weighting therefore allows the QALY matrix to express moral sentiments otherwise screened out by the "standard rule."

3. Double Jeopardy

If QALYs assess potential recipients of health care only on the grounds of the years and quality of life they are statistically likely to enjoy, it may be argued that they thereby serve to impose a second dose of misfortune upon someone already disadvantaged by disease or illness. For example, a person suffers from liver failure. If it is assumed that liver transplants are expensive and liable to failure, so that the QALYs liver transplant patients yield on average are low, then that person is likely to find that transplant facilities are not available. The bad luck of liver failure is thus compounded by the bad luck of having a poor prognosis (and indeed a condition that is expensive to treat).

An implication of this double jeopardy argument is that it is a core goal of a health care system to compensate for people's poor fortune (in health). This is intuitively attractive. However, it becomes problematic when the notion of compensation is interrogated. The argument suggests that adequate compensation is the mere availability and access to treatment, without consideration of the degree or probability of successful treatment. The sufferer from liver failure is thus compensated if he or she is treated, regardless of the period

of postoperative survival or the quality of life of that period. The argument appeals to the idea that what matters is the degree of fervor with which a patient wants to go on living. The operation, however successful or unsuccessful it is likely to be, meets, as well as possible, that fervent wish. It may be suggested that, if that is indeed all that matters, then it would be reflected in a suitable sensitive QALY matrix (as, perhaps, the community's "prior consent"), precisely because a surveyed population would make little or no differentiation in the value of a life of good health and, say, a life confined to bed. Further, this compensation policy would entail that medical units would receive priority for funding on the grounds of the severity of the condition they treat. If the QALY matrix did indeed fail to differentiate between health states, then possibly the severity of the preoperative condition would be a principal criterion of allocation. (This in turn begs the question of the criteria used to assess "severity." The only unambiguous criterion of severity would be threat to life. If one is indifferent as to one's postoperative condition, providing one is alive, then one is presumably equally indifferent to one's preoperative condition.) As a policy, it would entail that a large part of a health service's (scarce) resources would be committed to saving (or attempting to save) and subsequently maintaining the lives of people who had suffered life-threatening and untimely illnesses and accidents. Yet, it is unclear that such an allocation of resources would significantly improve (let alone maximize) the health of the population as a whole.

4. Whose Values?

It has been noted that different groups of respondents may be expected to generate different evaluations of health states (and thus different QALY matrices). The problem of whose values to accept is not simply a question of epistemology (which is to say, which values are objectively true?), but rather a political and moral question (which is to say, which groups are to be allowed to determine the allocation of health care resources?). The problem may be reformulated, to ask whether the values of certain groups should be excluded, because they are ill-informed or grounded in morally unacceptable prejudices.

Williams's standard rule suggests that a major advantage of QALYs is that they screen out a respondent's social prejudices (e.g., his or her sexism, racism, or class bias). The respondent is confronted by a series of health conditions that are typically described independently of the characteristics of the people in them. It may, however, be suggested, that more subtle and specifically health-related prejudices cannot be filtered out. For example, the difference between responses elicited from patients and healthy volunteers (e.g., in the development of the Rosser-Kind index), tends to corroborate the hypothesis that those who have not experienced a condition cannot accurately predict the impact that the condition will have upon their quality of life. Further, other factors, such as the stigma associated with physical disabilities and mental illness may influence evaluations. QALY scores for stigmatized conditions may then be artificially low. This in turn will affect resource allocation to those with, say, physical disabilities. While more resources might be made available to "cure" the physically disabled (i.e., by restoring full physical functioning), resource may be drawn away from those who are "incurable" (for the quality of life of, say, being confined to a wheel chair, will appear artificially low, and will therefore appear as an inefficient use of resources in a cost per QALY calculation).

Superficially, these considerations suggest that only the values of (current or past) patients are relevant. On the one hand, the values of doctors are potentially suspect, for the initial motivation of much quality of life research was to challenge the dominance of a biomedical view (and evaluation) of health care outcomes. On the other hand, the healthy appear to be ill-equipped to make the necessary imaginative leap to evaluate a wide range of health states. Their responses may reflect fear and prejudice. Yet, even if it is accepted that patients can accurately evaluate the effect that their own condition has on quality of life (and this itself may be disputed), it is not clear that they would have any advantage over the healthy in evaluating conditions they have not experienced.

Williams expresses a personal preference for a populist approach to quality of life measurement, where all people are consulted. (Appropriate statistical techniques for establishing the final results can also serve to exclude extreme and unrepresentative opinions.) Similarly, Menzel advocates surveying a representative sample of the whole population to which the QALY calculation will apply. Such democratic approaches still raise problems. First, it is unclear what redress the individual (or even subgroup) has whose valuations diverge markedly from those of the community as a whole. (Menzel, for example, appears to assume too readily that there will be some level of consensus in the community.) Second, merely to adopt the views of the population (be they representative of a broad consensus or not), entails an implicit moral and political relativism that may be unacceptable to certain commentators. It is at this point that quality of life research begins to broach fundamental questions about the nature of a democratic and accountable health care system.

5. The Maximization of QALYs

It has been argued by Crisp that moral problems arise due to the overwhelming emphasis that the QALY approach places upon the maximization of QALY gain. To aggregate fractions of QALYs overtime entails that a sufficiently long period of time spent at a very low quality of life is better than a sufficiently short life of good quality. An extremely long life as an oyster can be preferable to a short life as a (fully competent) human being. Crisp seeks to avoid this implication by suggesting that lives of a sufficiently low quality are simply incommensurable with good quality lives, which is to say that it is impossible to trade a period of good quality life for any number of years of low quality life. However, one could not then compare a medical unit that maintained the lives of patients at extremely low quality (with no prospect of recovery), with a unit that gave its patients good quality of life (even if the resultant QALY gain was the same). Bluntly, if a discontinuity is built into the QALY calculation, then funding of the unit that merely maintains its patients at a low quality of life could not be justified on cost per QALY grounds. (Crucially, this may highlight the point that QALYs presuppose that efficient use of scarce health care resources is an important factor in determining resource allocation. It need not be the only thing, as Crisp's criticism assumes, so alternative grounds may be available to justify the unit's funding.)

A number of important issues are raised by Crisp's analysis. First, it suggests that there is something problematic in the simple aggregation of years of life. The value of a day confined to bed is not a simple fraction of the value of 10 years confined to bed. Crisp attempts to articulate this problem by advocating a "global view," or what can also be described as a "biographical" view of life. If one compares a health condition representative of a good quality of life, and one representative of a poor quality, the difference in value will, in large part, rest upon the accumulative achievements that make the good-quality life worthwhile. Even a short life in good health will allow the person to develop a life plan, and thus a meaningful life. If one's health is too poor, then that opportunity is radically inhibited, however long one lives. A second point that may be derived from this is the suggestion that, unless this problem of time is dealt with, then the claim that QALYs are ratio scales will not be borne out. A year at a QALY score of 1.0 is not simply five times as good as a year at a QALY score of 0.2.

This second point suggests a reply to Crisp. It may be suggested that the discontinuity that Crisp seeks may already be present in many quality of life indicators. In the Rosser-Kind scale, it is present in the value "0," as the score of a health state equivalent to death. To maintain a person in a health state that scores worse than "0" is, indeed, on cost per QALY calculations unjustifiable. Crucially, it is the nonarbitrary nature of the zero point on a scale that gives it its property as a ratio scale. Thus, if the meaning of the zero, and more precisely, of a state equivalent to death, can be explicated, and made, for example, part of Menzel's QALY bargain, then a community could be made to confront and articulate certain moral intuitions as to when life is no longer worth preserving. In sum, consideration of the QALY here begins to broach questions about enthanasia, and when, or if, it is in the real interests of a person not to go on living. (A QALY matrix that valued no health state as equivalent to, or worse than, death, would in effect mark the respondents' rejection of euthanasia.)

IV. CONCLUSION

The extensive research on quality of life indicators, on the one hand within epidemiology, health economics, and psychometrics, and on the other in ethics, has stimulated debate on a number of key issues within health care. Perhaps most basically, there has been much research on professional and lay understandings of health and expectations of the outcomes of health care. This in turn leads to fundamental questions about the contributions that different groups should make in determining the priorities and structures of health care provision. (It is not accidental, for example, that the Index of Well-Being was an integral tool to the public consultation exercises concerning Medicaid conducted in Oregon in the late 1980s.)

In the fields of resource allocation and medical technology assessment it is easy to make exaggerated claims on behalf of QALYs. The realization of the potential that QALYs have for establishing priorities and the efficiency of health care interventions depends heavily upon the reliability, not merely of the QALY matrices used, but also of economic and epidemiological data. These data are frequently either unavailable, or are of questionable reliability. QALYs do not then provide a simple solution to complex problems. QALYs can be misused, and the ethical criticism of their misuse must be carefully separated from criticisms of their proper or intended use. Crucially, QALYs cannot be used as an algorithm at the expense of all other thought and reflection. In issues of resource allocation the QALY approach may best be understood as helping to clarify the problems (including moral dilemmas) that have to be faced, rather than resolving them. QALY calculations demand a clear-sighted confrontation with the problems of the scarcity of resources, and the consequences of different ways of dealing with that scarcity. In clinical practice quality of life indicators have great potential in giving patients a new and more articulate voice, precisely by institutionalizing measures of health that complement traditional physiological measures.

Also See the Following Articles

AGEISM • DO-NOT-RESUSCITATE DECISIONS • HEALTH CARE FINANCING • PALLIATIVE CARE • PATIENTS' RIGHTS • RESOURCE ALLOCATION

Bibliography

Aiken, W. (1982). The quality of life. *Applied Philosophy* 1, 26–36.
Bowling, A. (1991). *Measuring health: A review of quality of life measurement scales*. Milton Keynes: Open University Press.
Bowling, A. (1995). *Measuring disease: A review of disease-specific quality of life measurement scales*. Milton Keynes: Open University Press.
Brooks, R. G. (1995). *Health status measurement: A perspective on change*. London: Macmillan.
Crisp, R. (1989). Deciding who will die: QALYs and political theory. *Politics*, 9, pp. 31–35.
Glover, J. (1977). *Causing death and saving lives*. Harmondsworth: Penguin.
Gudex, C., & Kind, P. (1988). *The QALY toolkit*. Discussion Paper No. 28, Centre for Health Economics, University of York, York.
Harris, J. (1987). QALYfying the value of life. *Journal of Medical Ethics*, 13, pp. 117–123.
Menzel, P. T., (1990). *Strong medicine: The ethical rationing of health care*. New York: Oxford University Press.
Nussbaum, M., & Sen, A. (1993). *The Quality of Life*. Oxford: Clarendon Press.
Orley, J., & Kuyken, W. (1994). *Quality of life assessment: International perspectives*. Berlin and Heidelberg: Springer-Verlag.
Patrick, D. L., & Erickson J. (1993). Assessing health-related quality of life for clinical decision making. In Walker, S. R., and Rosser, R. M. (Eds.), *Quality of life: Assessment and application* (2nd ed.). London: Kluwer Academic.
Rosser, R. M., & Kind, P. (1978). A scale of valuation of states of illness. Is there a social consensus? *International Journal of Epidemiology*, 7, pp. 347–558.
Walker S. R., & Rosser, R. M. (1993). *Quality of life: Assessment and application* (2nd ed.). London: Kluwer Academic.
Williams, A. (1985). Economics of coronary bypass grafting. *BMJ* 291, 326–329.
Williams, A. (1988). Ethics and efficiency in the provision of health care. In Bell, J. M., and Mendus, S. (Eds.). *Philosophy and Medical Welfare*. Cambridge: Cambridge University Press.

RACISM

Anthony J. Skillen
University of Kent

GLOSSARY

cultures Patterns of values, feelings, norms and practices that are socially transmitted. Racism is a cultural variable, being a function of socially transmitted disvaluations, disregardings and degradations of individuals in virtue of their being categorized as being, or failing to be, of a certain race. Racist culture's primary impact is cultural: status allocation; but it has political causes and consequences in respect of power distribution and economic causes and consequences in respect of the distribution of wealth.

ethnicity An identification or categorization of self or other on a quasi-racial basis, where that race or sub-race is held to be saliently distinguished, not only by racial phenotype, but by cultural practices held to signify membership through being seen as more or less specific, proprietary, "essential" or "natural" to that putative race or sub-race. Proponents of ethnicity as a politically and conceptual replacement for the "outmoded and discredited" concept of race should consider the degree to which their preferred concept, unlike the other, imports cultural essentialism and associated norms and expectations into

the heart of human identity. Race need not matter, "ethnicity", by definition, must matter.

races These are best defined, not by differentiation of characteristics general in a population that bred over thousands of years in relative isolation. Rather, they are such populations: genetic macro-families. Like clouds, they are, albeit older, permeable individuals; the concept of race is not a "type" concept. It is therefore an open and to a degree indeterminate question how many races there have been, how different in characteristics they are, and how much intermingling and pooling there has been, is, and will be among races. Racial identification and characterization are but a limited component of human genetics, which is likely to find other genotypic bases of human phenotypic similarities and differences of greater importance. Use of the concept of race, in other words, carries with it no presumption of the salience or ranking of human characteristics explicable as racial. It is bad genetics to think otherwise.

racism The attribution of responsibility for salient and ranked capacities and dispositions to the racial sets to which people are held to belong. The racist deems individuals to be disqualified from membership or from equality in treatment or respect on the basis of attributed characteristics themselves attributed to racial inheritance. Hatred or contempt are the emotional dimension of such perceptions, which may be more or less institutionally embodied and more or less theorized. Racism is an ideology.

THE TERM RACISM covers a multitude of thoughts, words, and deeds that are difficult to analyze and harder to overcome. Indeed, the contests around issues of race and racism contribute to the difficulty of a consensus-meriting account. Thus, for example, some argue that the very notion of "race" is itself an ideological construction without basis in biological science. Others emphasize the separation of the scientific study of races from political practices of racism. Others still, in the cause of "antiracism," emphasize the biological discreteness of races in the context of celebrating the distinctiveness and achievements of, for example, African or Hispanic Americans. Again, while some regret "racism" on the part of Black people or others denigrated or maltreated as groups, many argue that, like sexism, racism is essentially a practice of the dominant and hence cannot be attributed to the subordinated. Given the diversity of racist thought and practice, some think it best to talk of "racisms" in the plural, whereas others believe that there is a sufficient conceptual core to make it important to retain the singular "racism". If racist practices are defined as those in which a person is discriminated against on a race-membership basis, then it seems, counterintuitively, to follow that affirmative action and positive discrimination are paradigms of racism.

I. CONCEPTIONS OF RACISM

A. Racism as Accusatory Epithet

It is natural to think of the term "racist" as condemnatory by definition, hence, that to describe a practice or reaction as "racist" is to accuse it. On such an understanding, it would be self-contradictory for someone to say that they were justified in their racism, and a tautology to say that one disapproved of racism. On that view, "racist" functions like "bigoted" or "biased". But in some quarters and at some periods of history, racism is, and has been, perfectly respectable; part of "obvious common sense". This would be impossible if racism were by the very meanings of words an object of disapproval. If we build condemnation in, and on the other hand rightly think that certain thoughts, such as "Arabs are congenitally untrustworthy," are in fact racist, we will think, not that such propositions are false, silly, and self-fulfillingly destructive, but that they, being racist, are unthinkable, hence unworthy to be argued against. By this means, many deny racists the possibility of being educated out of their illusions as distinct from being censored from expressing them. And thus the "anti-racist" will think it sufficient that a proposition is racist

to remove it from discourse rather than to contest it through discourse. Opponents of racism may be better placed to criticize it if they recognize the term as having, like "fascism," "genocide," "authoritarianism," "elitism," "sexism," or "fundamentalism," substantial content, rather than as entailing unacceptability or political incorrectness simply in virtue of the meaning of words.

B. Racism as Skin Discrimination

It is commonly thought that a racist practice, person, or feeling is one of discrimination against or for someone simply on the basis of the color of their skin or some other surface attribute. This is the preferred definition, for example of Antony Flew, a philosopher who has written frequently in this area. Flew writes:

> For the defining characteristics by which one race is to be distinguished from another—skin pigmentation, shape of skull, etc.—are strictly superficial and properly irrelevant to all, or almost all, questions of aptitude and employability. To accord decisive weight to differences in respect of any strictly surface and trifling physical characteristics, when you are making discriminatory decisions which matter to the individuals concerned, is as grotequely unfair as to disqualify competing candidates because they are bald, or blond, or red-headed.

Rightly, Flew castigates such racism. Practices that discriminate against people or people who despise or are repelled by people for such superficial reasons as that their skin or body shape is different from their own are as vicious as they are unreasonable: how is it relevant to a person's capacity to be one's fellow citizen, neighbor, colleague, or friend whether they are of a certain pigment or shape of eyelid? How, as Martin Luther King, Jr., put it, can the color of a man's skin rather than the content of his character be the determinant of the respect he is accorded?

But it needs to be asked whether there are many racists in this "strictly superficial" sense. For it is not the case that very many understand by a person's being a member of a race simply that their skin color or skull shape are such and such. Some "White" people can be so shaped, haired, and pigmented that, when they tan in the sun in summer, they can pass as "colored," while some "Black" people are sufficiently fair to pass as White. If "surface features" defined racial membership, it would be hard to make sense of your being mistaken for a person of a certain race. Nor does it allow for the possibility, which many have believed to be realized in, for example Europe, the Middle East, and East Asia, that two racially fairly distinct "peoples" could have more or less coinciding skin color, and so on. Surface attributes are "morphological" indices of racial membership. But races are generally understood in terms of broad genealogical lines of descent. In this respect, races, like families, clans, and tribes are more, or usually less bounded collective particulars, historical "individuals". Thus, not only did the great Black scholar W. E. B. Du Bois regularly talk, without redundancy of "race and color"; this phrase occurs regularly in the classic *Report of the National Advisory Commission on Civil Disorders*, still a superb guide to the politics of race in America. If someone saw a European for the first time and took them to be suffering from a horrible skin disease, this would not be a racist perception; the deviant newcomer is not even seen as of a different racial population.

C. Racism as Biological Derogation

In her classic *Race and Racism*, the anthropologist Ruth Benedict defined racism, a term she was among the first to popularize (against its near synonym, "racialism"), as "the dogma that one ethnic group is condemned by nature to congenital inferiority and another group to congenital superiority." On this account, the mark of racism in its crudest and possibly most common form is the regulating idea in the racist mind that inferior "blood" defines individuals, categorized as belonging to certain (supposed) races, as essentially and centrally distinct from and inferior to others,(usually "us"). People thus classified are held to lack the rational or moral capacities of the "model" race. The anti-Jewish racist, whether in Medieval or Nazi Germany, for example, thought of Jews, first as a distinct and peculiar-looking race, and secondly, as born, not perhaps with a lack of intellectual capacity, (although this was to be Voltaire's foolish opinion) but with a cunning cleverness and less than fully "human" moral responsiveness, attributable moreover, not merely to circumstance and culture, but to blood-line inheritance. If Jewish people are a paradigmatic object of racist hate, Black people are standard targets of racist contempt. (English Nazis proclaim that they don't hate Blacks, because they are like children, manipulated for purposes of world domination by the wicked Jews!)

Skin color, cranial features, or other morphological characteristics are not the racist's focal preoccupation. Rather they are, in Erving Goffman's terms, "stigmata," marks of imperfect identity, in this case congenitally

constituted. They are taken as signs of a specific "nature" or "essence," which is seen as responsible equally for determining superficial physical characteristics and for sundry incapacities and disqualifications, whether temperamental, physical, moral, cultural, or intellectual. Thus, the Swedish taxonomist Linnaeus (von Linne) adorned his human botany with the following information regarding "The African": "black, phlegmatic, relaxed in posture, black hair etc.... crafty, indolent, negligent, annoints himself with grease, governed by caprice...." Eight years earlier, in 1798, the *Encyclopaedia Britannica* entry on "Negroes" reads, in a vein that it was to maintain into the twentieth century: "...vices the most notorious" that were congenitally "the portion of this unhappy race."

II. CONCEPTIONS OF RACE

A. Races as Human Types

Rather than seeing all humans as fellows, "cousins under the skin," the outright racist is a sort of genetic sectarian, for whom often quite mythical racial origins are the fundamental or dominant differentiating criterion of human identity and rank, overwhelming the things that make up our common humanity. The outright racist finds it therefore difficult to conceive members of the race that is the object of his disdain as having a noble or sophisticated thought or of feeling love or remorse "the way you and I do." These shortfalls he or she attributes, not to cultural or nurturing defects but to natural or innate, hence immutable, inferiorities. Cultural "backwardness," "barbarism," "savagery" or other ascribed shortcomings, therefore, will be seen as symptoms of a "human type's" inherent deficiencies relative to the viewer's usually narcissistic model of humanity.

Racists of this breed think of the "lowest" member of the preferred racial group as worthy of consideration or respect before the "highest" member of the derogated race or supposed race. The member of a certain supposed racial set, then, will be perceived as fundamentally different by virtue of their "alien blood"; as not "one of us." Thus, outright racists, be they White Americans or "good" Japanese, will regard any person of African, or in the second case, Korean, stock as beneath the consideration appropriate to what they perceive as the fully endowed human specimen, as if races were kinds of people such that relationships blind to these stratified classification defied the natural and proper order of things. Such perceptions and the practices they inscribe, normally rationalized by the pseudoscientific notions of "types" and "species" outlined above, constitute such racism as in opposition to a humanist vision. The worst of the derogated race tends to supply the racist's paradigm of "them," contrasted in the racist mind with the noblest of "our" contributors to humanity. It is interesting to watch such racism competing in the same mind with vulgar sexism, according to which any male merits more respect than any female.

The racist outlook has been legitimated in Biblical fundamentalist terms by reference to the different punitive fates divinely ordained for the offspring of Noah's son Ham (*Genesis*,10:25). Other fundamentalist racist theories postulated "Preadamite" species separately created, hence not made quite in God's image, and this "polygenic" theory was popular among encyclopedists determined to avoid reference to biblical tales. The common idea, illustrated in the quotation above from Linnaeus, was that there were more or less pure lines exhibiting the distinct and stereotyped characteristics proper to each "type," with the associated horse breeder vocabulary of "perfect specimens," "pure stock," "miscegenation," and so on. Racism became more urgently orthodox in the nineteenth century, with the twin development of biology and anthropology, academic servants of empire and aggressive White supremacy. Charles Darwin, like his friend Herbert Spencer, whose "Social Darwinism" is often regarded as a distortion rather than an amplification of his friend's teachings, had long thought gloomily of human races as disposed by nature unequally to fight each other to the death: "The varieties of man seem to act on each other in the same way as different species of animals—the stronger always extirpating the weaker.' (*A Naturalist's Voyage*. London: J. Murray, 1888, p. 435) On such a view, not only are racially distinct populations a natural byproduct of human evolution and environmental adaptation, they are naturally active megatribal units of evolutionary struggle. Among nineteenth-century thinkers of a racist turn of mind—that is to say, orthodox thinkers— Darwinesque ideas of differential "fitness," exposed by the competitive "struggle for survival" in a Malthusian world of multiplying scarcity, supplanted the more obviously mythological–Biblical and static rationalizations of hierarchical racial discrimination. Thus the Scot Robert Knox wrote *The Races of Men* in 1850 and the Frenchman Joseph de Gobineau, with more virulent effect, wrote *Essay on the Inequality of the Human Races* in 1853. Spencer illustrates this deep current:

We know that there are warlike, peaceful, nomadic, maritime, hunting, commercial races— races that are independent or slavish, active or slothful—races that display great varieties of disposition; we know that many of these, if not all, have a common origin; and hence there can be no question that these varieties of disposition, which have a more or less evident relation to habits of life, have been gradually induced and established in successive generations and have become organic (*The Principles of Psychology*. London, Macmillan, 1855, p. 526–527).

Ernst Haeckel wrote in the early twentieth century of the relative proximity in qualities and worth of the "lower races" to the brute beasts: "The morphological differences between two generally recognized species— for example between sheep and goats—are much less important than those between a Hottentot and a man of the Teutonic race." These icily florid texts helped not so much to create, as to articulate, the concept of a competitive race war, conducted especially in Africa and later enacted by the Nazis. At a more insidious level, this took the form of eugenic programs of sterilization, race-hygiene immigration control, and grim warnings against interracial mating in the standard guides for young people contemplating the formation of conjugal unions. One such marriage manualist was the psychologist of "instinct," William McDougall, whose illustration of the importance of race was the thought experiment of swapping all English and French neonates. The consequence, he claimed, would be that English culture would shift to the point where its temper and institutions, including religion, would be Gallicized (*The Group Mind*. London: Longmans, 1920, p. 165).

It is possible to find such thinking among the old texts in any library reading room. But it is surely rash to imagine that there was not a parallel racism in popular culture. The colonial settler, the plantation or mine foreman, the soldier, the worker threatened by cheap imported labor, the father shocked by his daughter's betrayal of her heritage, do not await the corroborating voice of science. That is one reason why it is rash to think confidently of racism as a phenomenon peculiar to the "modern" age of science and world conquest.

B. Racism as Cultural Supremacism

Although it is a common bedfellow of racism, the attribution of cultural inferiority is not as such racist. The attributor might regard "barbarism" as a stage that, under benign and "enlightened" impact, at first coercively and then paternalistically imposed, will be transcended. The natives of Africa and India were for John Stuart Mill(*On Liberty*), like "children" because they had yet to develop. Virtually all post-Enlightenment humanist conceptions of "progress," "development," and "modernization," including those of Marx and John Dewey, have had such a graded conception of human cultures. This view may be objectionably Eurocentric, parochially blind to the peculiar evils of "modernity" and conducive to all sorts of barbaric interventions. It may be an ideological mask of racism. But, in itself, it lacks the specific differentia of racism, which entails a notion of unchangeable difference and inferiority incompatible with humanist universalism . This contrast is shown in Joseph Conrad's novel, *Heart of Darkness*, where the agent of Belgian empire, Kurtz, defaces his own manual of civilizing paternalism with the racist scribble, "Exterminate all the brutes!"

Because racism is a cultural phenomenon, a matter of acquired priorities in valuation and identification, it does not follow that race is a cultural phenomenon, any more than a cultural preference for dark-eyed girls would make being a dark-eyed girl a cultural fact. Racist cultural practices, through their often coercive constriction of mating practices, obviously affect the racial composition of the planet, but that does not make one's racial composition less of a biological consequence of culture. The notion of "ethnicity," with its reference both to cultural values and affinities and to "roots" and "homeland," tends to blur this nature/nurture distinction, sometimes with the consequence that both self-identifications and other identifications are such as to imply an essential racio-cultural oneness and distinctness, often the bogus basis of quasi-tribal conflict.

C. Inferiority and Otherness

Ruth Benedict's definition of racism is that it is a belief in biologically inherited general inferiorities and superiorities among racial groups. This belief or cluster of beliefs is held to justify hierarchically discriminatory practices—most glaringly, slavery or genocide.

But it might be argued that this is an inadequate model of racism, even as an individual cast of mind, on the grounds that racism does not necessarily entail such beliefs. But compare the difference between chauvinism and xenophobia: the chauvinist believes his nation to be supreme in virtue; the xenophobe need have no such assumptions. The former looks down on the inferior outsiders; the latter may just be "clannishly" threatened by them and want them excluded from his group. They are—"different from us," "alien"; we have "alienization without hierarchization". What a xenophobe is phobic toward will be contingent on what it is with which he or she "identifies": be it a linguistic, or some other dimension of culture or way of life. But where that strangeness is antipathetically felt in "racial" terms, it might be argued that we have racism: "we" don't want "them" here, where the "others" are taken as such by virtue of "something physical," which makes them inherently and irremovably alien.

The internal and external conditions of the constitution or formation of "groups" and the "identities" of their members are a major topic in the social sciences. The model presented above, however, may be felt to be capable of development in two quite opposite directions. On the one hand it could be urged that, given the contingency and indeed arbitrariness of this whole self–other categorization process, the important thing to examine is the variation of conditions that determine both the principle of division: when biological? when linguistic? when confessional?—and the variation in conditions that determine whether the differentiations are antagonistic and if so, in what ways. Historical materialists, especially Marxists, tend to argue that race consciousness, especially antagonistic and hierarchical racial identifications (racisms), are dependent on conditions of scarcity and competition or exploitation being represented and experienced in terms of racist ideologies. (A classic text in this vein is *Caste, Class and Race*, by Oliver Cromwell Cox, New York, Monthly Review Press, 1948.)

On the opposing hand, biological materialists, and now especially sociobiologists, have long claimed that the apparent arbitrariness of the situation depicted in the model is a function of its very "naturalness" and "instinctiveness": of course people feel affinity with those of their "own kind"; it is as natural, some seem to think, as the mutual recognition of animals of the same or different kinds. By this way of reckoning, inter-racial estrangement and animosity are "natural" and not in need of special explanation. Such "biological determinisms" are also found in analogous talk of "territoriality" as an "instinctive" "imperative" or of "aggression" as an irresistible component of the genetic makeup of human males. By that account, then, racist belief systems are "rationalizations" of something more primitive and nonrational. "Naturally" alien to "us," those of other races, then, may be "constructed" as humanly deficient that "we" might, in our own eyes, legitimately deal with them in ways that accord with "their nature" and the "needs" of our own "group": by extermination, enslavement, exclusion from or restriction of territorial access, market exchange toleration, assimilation or intermarriage. Such biologism forgets that the bases on which humans seem capable of constituting themselves as members of discrete and antagonistic "kinds"— "usses and thems"—are depressingly various. Were it, moreover, the case that racial selectivity and antagonism was part of our constitutional predisposition, it would no more justify nurturing such genetic parochialism than other pernicious tendencies we are blessed with. Meanwhile, as any observer of multiracial nurseries will confirm, children uncontaminated with the racist culture that they may emerge from or be destined to enter are "naturally" nonracial in their affiliations and conflicts.

The above discussion brings out a dimension of racism that might be missed were the focus to be entirely on issues of claims that members of such and such racially identified sets tended to fall above or below some mark in respect of valued and important human attributes. It is a familiar fact that, within any group, people tend to think of each other as differently gifted by "nature"—brother Bill is strong, cousin Leila is clever, nephew Moosa has a beautiful voice, and so on. Such distinctions, which we are often content to regard as inborn, are not incompatible with the sense of fellowship and common membership of communities. Yet the racial xenophobe will feel "one" with his or her talentless "kith and kin" and alien to his or her peer just because of their racial differentness.

So it is possible to abstract "alienization" from "derogation" as dimensions of racism. And it is possible to distinguish degrees of emphasis on the numerical distinctness of a group in virtue of its distinct "origins" (genealogy—"foreigners," "strangers," "outsiders," "natives") from emphasis on the qualitative (morphological and behavioral) differences attributed to them ("short," "stupid," "dirty," "lazy," and so on). But it is as rare to find racial clannishness and xenophobia unrationalized by racial clan chauvinism as it is to find statistically defended claims about race-group averages in the absence of a preoccupation with differentiated racial categories. It is reasonable to conclude that a typical point of practical classification into "groups" is exclusion or subordination of the "groups" so constituted, hence that racism always needs to be understood in the context of historical and practical situations of exclusion and hierarchy. Given that racism is so bound up with the very ideology of the "group identity" and "ethnicity" in terms of which exclusion and oppression are being practiced, and hence with the laying down of criteria of eligibility for differentiating practices, it may be wisest not so tightly to define racism as to ignore this

typical entanglement and at the same time to allow the relative salience of the "otherness" and "inferiority" strands to be examined concretely in diverse cases.

D. Racism, Categories, and Continua

Blond hair is a very different color from black hair, but few infer from this that blond- and blackhaired people constitute, as such, different types of people, (though there are those who think red hair is a temperamental symptom, or even that blondes have a special sexuality.) Contrasting skin color and other manifest features, even if they are racial, do not entail fundamental human differences. So even where it is possible to perceive polar contrasts, it does not follow that individuals thus contrasted are importantly different in important respects. But many people's hair and skin falls between extremes along various dimensions, forming statistically recordable continua. So it is with other characteristics. Some of these characteristics are important: ethical, temperamental, athletic, medical, artistic, practical, intellectual. There is no a priori reason why there might or might not be genetic and even racial explanations for some measure of differences in such characteristics. This is an issue requiring sense, humility, and knowledge: the philosopher who says that because human nature is one and because man's nature is to be rational, it follows that all important human differences must be a function of environment, is indulging in as much a priorism as the racist who says, stupidly, that because Blacks and Whites are different and Whites are intelligent, Blacks must be stupid. As we have seen, racism is marked by a global, stereotyping, prejudiced way of seeing and relating to human beings: "Your Negro is lazy in a quite different way from your Mexican; now take your Chinese. . . ." Racist thought and practice entails treating the individual as primarily a member of this or that deep-genetic lineage, his or her humanity qualified and limited by virtue of that lineage. David Hume, for example, lent his empiricist authority to racism among the intelligentsia with the casual observation in 1748 that Negroes were constitutionally incapable of culture, civilization, or intellectual activity:

In Jamaica, indeed, they talk of one Negroe as a man of parts and learning; but t'is likely he is admired for very slender accomplishments like a parrot, who speaks a few words plainly (Of National Characters. *Essays Literary Moral and Political.* London: Ward, Lock and Bowden, 1890. Footnote, pp. 123–124).

Hume here exhibits a pure form of racist vision: he does not say merely that Negroes are generally stupid and savage although there are some exceptions; even the "one" putative exception is by Hume deemed apparent only—a mere mimic of intelligent discourse. Such, in Thomas Kuhn's terms, is the racist "paradigm" that, having allocated people to their appropriate racial classes, it imposes an understanding on everything as expressive of the specific essential nature and potential of that type. Thus, for Hume, an intelligent Black man is as impossible as a domesticated tiger; other racists might think of specific and limited kinds of intelligence or virtue as predicable of different races. Less extreme racists will of course allow for exceptions, the depth of their racism being shown in their degree of concern to offer "special" explanations for the "exceptional" individual. For this reason Antony Flew's defense of the I.Q. "racial difference" school of Jensen, Eysenck, Shockley, Herrnstein, Murray, and others against the charge of racism on the grounds that, because they are concerned with "only the average characteristics of that set as a whole" (*A Future for Anti-Racism?*, U.K. Social Affairs Unit, 1992, p. 10) must be questioned. For much depends here on the degree and kind of "average" difference one is talking about, as well as on the context in which such supposed differences are adverted to. Flew claims that no inference about individuals follows from premises about group averages, but if such inferences are appropriately modified in probabilistic terms, they do follow. Whether the premises of such inferences are true is a different matter.

E. Race, I.Q., and Intelligence

While Alfred Binet was disposed to draw conclusions that endorsed his racist prejudices from his invention, the Intelligence Quotient Test, and was thus to talk of the less-than-fully human capacity of sundry lesser races for the abstract thought that supposedly flourished among the Nordics, the I.Q. test as such goes with a quantitative and statistical ranking; in the first instance of greater or lesser concern or aptitude to score well on these standard tests. Methodological questions abound about what these tests indicate beyond themselves (their "validity") and in particular whether, as Charles Spearman maintained, they indicate "general intelligence" ("g") or a more or less overlapping array of kinds of intelligence (L. L. Thurstone), let alone whether pen and paper tests test the range of valuable forms of intelligence. In America, it seems that "Blacks" score lower on average than "Caucasians" who are in turn currently outscored by "Jews" and "Asians."

Whereas Hume typified the racist notion that such categories or sets fall into discrete bundles of sorts of ability, these "bell curve" scores include many high-scoring Blacks and many low-scoring Whites distributed along a continuum.

Let us, optimistically, assume that it is possible to devise a range of tests that, with minimal bias, measure abilities important to the conduct of theoretical and practical affairs in a "modern" society. It does not seem to be reasonable to urge that, if such tests turn out to yield different mean scores for different racial sets (or genders, or social classes), it would follow of necessity that such tests were racist. On the other hand, especially if differential life chances were to be allocated on the strength of such tests, it would be a different matter whether their administration and use would, in context, be racist. Maybe the scores reflect socially and historically (environmentally) produced differences in ability, which do not show innate (hereditary) potential capacity. After all, American studies of formerly downgraded and underprivileged racial groups, European and Asian, have shown that their average I.Q. has risen in a generation by up to 15 points, a change wholly attributable to environmental factors. If social disadvantages explain lower scores, it is hardly fair further to privilege those with good scores. Rather, to the extent that individuals' abilities and performances have been adversely affected by unfairnesses in circumstances, particularly by such things as racism, it is arguably fair, other things being equal, to try to act "affirmatively" in relation to that individual in such a way that the realization of their capacities will not be prevented by those factors that have already hampered it. On the face of it, the practical issue itself becomes a live one on the strength of the validity of comparing and contrasting people's actual abilities and performances with their postulated potential; and this idea seems one that must be framed in terms of some notion of innate or natural gifts and limitations. That is why so much of the "I.Q. debate," whether in relation to class or race, is preoccupied with the "heredity/environment" issue. Basically, the hereditarian conservatives maintain that the race, class, and gender stratification evident in society tracks the largely innate capacities and dispositions of the sectors so stratified. When it is considered that quite seriously mentally handicapped people can be found in sheltered workshops doing tasks more varied and stimulating than are on offer to many so-called "unskilled workers," and when the foolishness commonly evident among society's elite members is also considered, the idea of such a harmony of capacity and achievement might well seem implausible. Surely if we do begin with a notion of "innate potential" we are soon led to question the level of people's actual existence. But that point does not address the issue of the ordering of roles: maybe we could all be much better at many things; that would still leave us less good than some other candidate for the place. Prescinding from issues of the difficulty, character, and content of socially available roles, and also from issues of the rewards attached to different roles, rank ordering in any sort of just meritocracy would seem to have some appropriate relation to relative capacity.

Antiracists cannot avoid confronting the specific arguments and evidence of those who stress that not only is intelligence largely accounted for by genetic factors, such genetic factors include race-affected variables. It is worth making some methodological points:

1. In most Western societies, as a result of racist attitudes to racial mixture, the vague term "black" is applied to anyone with "significant" morphological distinctness of skintone and with significant accreditedly Black ancestry. But any serious study of the genetic importance of race would need some criterion of "how black" or otherwise someone is. As, especially in the United States "blackness," despite the history of centuries-old mingling, tends socially to be an either-or attribution, associated with racist stereotypes, expectations, and practical treatment, any study that claimed to be of "inherited" racial differences but did not control for such variations in degree would be to that extent invalid. An environmentalist hypothesis would be that, unlike socially ascribed "blackness," degrees of biological blackness would not correlate with different capacity measures.

2. Despite the fact that African American girls have been recorded as attaining both higher I.Q. scores and higher school and professional levels than their male counterparts, it is difficult to find a substantial discussion of this fact in the literature. Unless the claim is that there is a greater relevant genetic difference between Black males and females than between White males and females, this discrepancy, readily explicable in social-psychological and functional terms, is an embarrassment to the defenders of major racial differences. Gender would also be relevant if, for example mixed-race offspring with White mothers scored significantly differently from those with the same racial-genetic mixture but with Black mothers. This difference would be environmentally explicable, in terms of parenting patterns and formative milieu.

3. More generally, the notion of hereditary-versus-environmental explanation needs to be considered carefully in the light of the obvious fact that at least for many characteristics, "genotype" requires specific and specifically staged environmental inputs in order for that genotypical variable to be activated; e.g., the relation of growth to infant calcium intake. The genes relevant to the phenotypical characteristic of height may be "fixed" but height is clearly affected by environment. Broadly, genes interact with each other as well as with their environment in the production of their effects. The near-fatal attack on interventionist programs on the grounds that, because the basis of intelligence is hereditary, the attainment levels of society's members are immutable, suggests callousness tinged with racism rather than the sadly wise denial of "our generous impulse" that is its guise. The idea that any normal Black person's genes render them incapable of literacy, numeracy, and the capacity to participate reflectively as fellow citizens, neighbors, workmates and life partners is as fatuous as the proposition that their natural lot is to live, when not menially employed, intermittently active in a life of crime and violence.

These doubts are affirmed on the basis of assumptions of a broadly empirical nature, that humans are overwhelmingly akin, regardless of our racial lineages. Suppose these assumptions proved false, and there turned out to be major and significant race-related differences along important value dimensions, then there would still be a difference between a racist way of responding to this and a response that is anti- or nonracist. For what the racist would take as a vindication of global exclusion and derogation, their opponents would take as part of the complex variation of social life, requiring greater rather than lesser societal concern and input in the concern that individual human beings fulfill themselves in the greatest freedom and mutual harmony.

F. Racism and Race

But what are races and is it possible to talk of races without entering the discourses of racism? Robert Miles, in his important text *Racism*, for example argues that, although there is racism there are no races: the whole concept is an ideological illusion exposed by such genetic scientists as Julian Huxley. But what is it to assert or deny that there are races or that an individual might belong to this or to that race? We might provisionally take it that the issue would be a biological and historical one: that whether you are or are not of a certain racial category is a matter of genetic descent.

As argued earlier, it seems mistaken to think that the concept of race refers only to individuals' corporeal attributes; it explains those attributes along temporal, causal paths on which thousands and thousands of begettings have occurred. The concept, moreover, seems to distinguish more or less temporarily remote, more or less isolated ancestral populations, (analogous to flocks) with more or less distinct characteristics. This is and should be vague. But it would mean that two ancestral populations that were similar in observable characteristics but had in fact had no significant mutual sexual contact would be two, albeit very similar, races, not one, although these distinct populations may be assumed to have themselves descended, with all humankind, from common ancestors, from whose territory they each strayed—provided they separately acquired the said similarities during the period of their mutual isolation. On such a view, it would be fallacious to infer from the fact that two people are of different races that this difference is important, let alone fundamental, to the question of their having different characteristics, let alone differences rankable in terms of hierarchies of value. The issue of such putative qualitative differences would remain open.

On this view, that the notion of race is a "biological descent" one, we can say of views of race that imply that racial identity is a matter of the male, or of the female, line or that a person is a member of a certain race if he or she has but a grandmother who is a member of that population, or that racial mixing produces either "degeneracy" or infertility, that such views involve false understandings of biology (as Aristotle believed that women provided only the "matter" in generation and the male seed the "form"). Otherwise, they are about something that is not just a matter of race, but of the social categorization of people: a broadly cultural or political matter. If the concept of race is one referring to biological descent, then it need be of no great interest or importance: a priori, racial membership might or not be a good predictor of anything very significant—in the absence of cultural norms and practices that make such differences make a difference.

Races, then like families or groups or flocks, are permeable "individuals," not "types." It might be said that the concept of "race" thus sketched is both woolly and at the same time fails to take due regard for the false rigidities of actually existing "race" discourse, which tends falsely to suggest an idea of "pure" membership, and that such membership types people along salient human dimensions. But this may not be an overwhelming objection to the concept of race as such: is it not a fact that some societies are more racially mixed and others more racially segregated than others? "Race" may be too vague for genetic scientists once they get

genomically serious; it may be that it is scientifically more productive to talk in terms of "populations" defined either by particular histories or by frequencies of genotypical (now "fingerprintable") or consequent phenotypical characteristics. But it is possible that the prevalence of racism is the best explanation for the preference for avoiding a contaminated but not illegitimate concept with a perhaps small but valid part to play in human biology. If geneticists drop "racial" terminology in favour of talk of "inbred populations," or "genogroups," is there reason to think that this will function other than as a confusing euphemism in those cases where the population is specified in terms that amount to racial ones?

More enlightenment and better communication from the scientific community, now preoccupied with its genetic and genome projects, may follow if the public is educated about the complexities, subtleties, and interactional richness of the human genome, especially in respect of the issues of heredity and environment. Now that genetics has advanced beyond simplistic species-essentialism it may be both unreasonable and impractical to leave public understanding of "race" at the mercy of vulgar racist cultures and their demagogic spokespeople. In the introductory words of Ruth Benedict's classic study, "to recognize race does not mean to recognize racism." (*Race and Racism*. London: Routledge, 1942, p. vii).

III. THE POLITICS OF RACE

A. Is Race a Political Concept?

In the above biological definition, it could be said that racists "racialize" politics, by basing or rationalizing politically and humanly important choices in terms of supposed race-set membership and the attributes stereotypically ascribed to such membership. But many contemporary writers, surveying the gruesome racist scene, argue that race is itself a political concept. For them, races are constituted politically and culturally by activities and processes of group identification and the powers, statuses, and images bound up with such identifications. Hence, it is not just a political matter that racial affiliations get tangled into power relations, or that race is politically more or less important in different social formations; the very idea of "racial affiliation" is deemed itself to be political.

Some writers, taking "morally salient" hierarchy among pseudoscientifically distinguished races to be part of the very meaning of biological race discourse, nonetheless want to claim "race identity" as a potentially valid dimension of "lived experience," a matter of "ethnic" self-identity ("Black (etc.) pride"). On the other hand while affirming that the concept of race is an inherently political one, David Theo Goldberg criticizes "racialialized" politics on the grounds that it "orders membership in and exclusions from, the body politic." (The Semantics of Race. *Ethnic and Racial Studies*, Vol. 15, No. 4, October 1992, p. 543). Goldberg instances anti-Semitism in Europe and "racial" formulations of nationality as counterexamples to biological definitions of race. He also (page 560) deems it conceivable that women could be called a "race," provided certain exclusions were practiced. But it might be argued in response that national affiliations have typically involved racial claims to distinctiveness in the biological descent–nature sense, just as linguistic divisions have been held often to track the genetic descent of "peoples." By removing the possibility of discussion of the extent, if at all, to which Jews are racially distinctive and by assimilating confessional and cultural anti-Judaism with anti-"Semitic" racism—or for that matter racist conceptions that may be held by some Jews in relation to Arabs, for example, Goldberg's constructionism appears to assimilate too much. The fact that the "fluidity" of Goldberg's definition is sufficient to allow gender divisions, in the absence of some very weird biology, to be potentially thought of as "racial" might be thought a *reductio ad absurdam*, because it empties the term "race" of any meaning and it specifically prevents discussion of the relations between sexism and racism.

Some take this conceptual politicization to the point of looking forward to Cypriots and Jews coming to think of themselves as "black" insofar as they become practically united by an awareness of common oppression and discrimination. These constructionist views, according to which to be a member of a race is a function of purely social "ethnic" ascription, are to be distinguished from Robert Miles' view that race is a biological concept just as phlogiston was a chemical concept, but that just as there is no phlogiston, so there are no races. For Miles, then, the idea (ideology) of human races is an illusion and mask, by which humans are "racialized" into hierarchical bunches, the better with clear conscience to exploit, exclude, or exterminate them as if they were quite different in kind from the populations favored by the dominant. Practically, this goes with Miles' opposition to political currents, such as those supported by the above-mentioned constructionists, which endorse self-identification and organization among "blacks" on a "racial" basis.

As indicated in the previous section, however, it might be urged that it is excessively exiguous to deny any objective reference to the concept of race, or to assume in advance the findings of genetics with respect to whether and to what extent racial differences are biologically significant. We can reject crude quasi-species models of race without rejecting the concept of race altogether, at least at this stage of genetic understanding. On the line of thinking proposed here, one does not have, on the specious grounds that the very notion of race contains notions of natural "separateness," "qualitative hierarchy," or "central explanatory role," to eschew that term or to insist on always writing about "race" with quotation-marks. That course is proposed by Kenan Malik in *The Meaning of Race*, but it is interesting that having foresworn the concept in general, he is content to talk about the differential physiological evolution of the Inuit and the Masai in terms that, saving the banned word, are racial.

B. Structural Racism

The definition of racism so far defended has been of an "ideology," a sense, more or less elaborated, of certain people, racially identified, as being less than fully human or less demanding the respect or concern of the preferred racial group. But much modern literature contests this definition as "subjective," "psychological," "relating to individual prejudice." In practice, it may be urged, such a conception places emphasis on the need for individuals to be "educated" out of racist prejudices and animosities. But this is to ignore the fundamental "racist" reality, which is "not prejudice but domination."

> Stokely Carmichael said:
> When...white terrorists bomb a black church and kill five black children, that is an act of individual racism.... But when in that same city, Birmingham, Alabama, not 5 but 500 babies die each year because of lack of proper food, shelter and medical facilities, and thousands more are destroyed and maimed physically, emotionally and intellectually because of conditions of poverty and discrimination in the black community, that is a function of institutionalized racism (Black Power. *The Dialectics of Liberation*. Cooper, D., et al., (Eds.). Penguin, 1968, pp. 151–152).

In analyzing the term "institutional racism" it is important to distinguish two claims: claims about institutional functions or goals and claims about the effects of institutional practices. The British Government-commissioned *Education for All: the Report of the Committee of Enquiry into the Education of Children from Ethnic Minority Groups*, "The Swann Report" (London, HMSO, 1985), for example, included as "racist" practices whose "consequences" are that Black people "have poorer jobs, health, housing and life-chances than do the white majority" (page 6). This is a definition in terms of effect. Carmichael's definition, however, is not in such terms. He wants to claim that certain situations of disadvantage are, as a matter of fact, to be explained as the effects of "institutionalized racism," where that term picks out practices whose goals are racist, in the sense of being informed by racial hostility, contempt, or inhuman blindness or indifference to the fate of members "alienized and derogated" into disadvantaged racial sets. (The White Australia Policy, for example, worked through an English dictation test whose "effects" were that non-Whites failed. That was their racist intention.) Practices, nonracist, in themselves, may have unjust but unintended consequences for members of racial sets; racism proper would be shown in the refusal to change such practices when these effects became clear to their practitioners. Defining racism in terms of the effects of practices, rather than of the character of practices, can lead to an ignoring of the constitutive as distinct from the consequential damage of racism: the object of racist contempt is a victim of that contempt and the humiliation and degradation it entails, as well as of the independently sufferable material disadvantages consequent on that contempt. And this brings us back to the "ideological" definition, with the reminder that, if social practices operate so that their operatives sufficiently internalize their goals, it is even more the case that ideologies, such as racism, live in and through the practical activities whose cultural meaning they define. Critics of the "psychological" "prejudice" paradigm represented by Gordon Allport's *The Nature of Prejudice* ignore the way in which Allport and others situated and explained patterns of "racial prejudice" socially, as ideological structures. What could be more socially inscribed, and at the same time more potent, than our prejudices and the vocabularies that voice them?

C. Racism as Power

Because racism is an often quite central feature of political life, and because racism matters because of the practical havoc it wreaks, there is an attraction in defining racism in terms of power, so that societies are conceived of as racist just to the extent that social power is a function of membership of racial sets. Hence, individuals are conceived as racist to the extent that they exercise power over others in accordance with their race-set membership. Thus, many writers advocate definitions that center on relationships of domination and subordination. On such a view, ideas or "prejudices" cannot be "racist" unless they are expressible in domination over others. Thus, for example, it is sometimes argued that Blacks and their actions cannot in Euro-American societies be racist, because Blacks are the dominated group. Such a view might have to deal with several questions:

1. Is it reasonable to deny the racism of the claims such as that the lack of melanin in white skin is an index of genetic frigidity by contrast with black "sun people"? More generally, is it reasonable to deny that, understandably, members of subjected racial sets might react to the stability of their oppression with "racist" attributions of moral inferiority to their perceived oppressors?

2. Is it not normal for members of racial sets jointly disadvantaged to think of their competitors for crumbs from the master's table in "racist" terms? One might think here of vocabulary of mutual denigration common in African American and Mexican-American relations in Denver, Colorado, or Los Angeles, California, or in the relations among people of Afro-Caribbean and Asian subcontinental background in the United Kingdom. Racist divide-and-rule stategies work best when the ruled accept the racist terms of division.

3. Have not anti-Jewish and anti-Asian sentiments have been stirred and expressed in "racist" terms among Blacks in the United States? Have not Louis Farrakhan and other Islamic fundamentalist ideologues in Britain and America, in the name of "dignity," rabble-roused in terms not much different from Hitler's "uplifting" appeal to the humiliated and impoverished masses of Germany in the 1930s? Why must we think one has to be pure if one is a victim? Would these ideas become "racist" only were they to gain ascendancy?

4. The "power" definition seems to go with the idea that subjected groups have no power at all. But even if it were accepted that racism required power as well as prejudice, it should be recognized that powers, if unequal, are diverse—when the bullied get the chance to bully, it is still, however understandable, bullying that they are able to enact.

5. What of the racism which, where the "system" is successful, is internalized by its victims as self-contempt

or hatred? Why is the Black man who thinks "I'm only a dumb nigger," not just as much a vehicle of racism as the woman who says "I'm just a typical silly girl" is a vehicle of sexism? Ideologies are liable to infect their victims as well as their beneficiaries.

6. Is not racism a matter as much of degradation as of powerlessness or deprivation of goods specifiable independently of the contempt and downgrading implicit in racism itself? By saying that racism is a matter of power, not of how people regard each other, is it not already being conceded that the racist and his or her target belong effectively to different communities of discourse?

Generally, antiracism is arguably hindered by accounts of race and of racism that ignore the specificity and multitude of dimensions of social differentiation, exploitation, exclusion, and oppression. Although often combined with racism, other dimensions of invidious distinction are to be distinguished from racism.

D. Affirmative Action

Thirty years ago, the National Advisory Commission on Civil Disorders, arguing that the social pathology of Black males was overwhelmingly a function of the postslavery identity of Black Americans as an underclass race, urged that the evils of racism could not be addressed without a transformation in the status, income, and power of Black Americans: "Thus, upgrading the employment of Negro men to make their occupational distribution identical with that of the labor force as a whole would have an immense impact...."

In 1996, however, just when statistics have begun to show major advancements in American Blacks' income, employment, and educational levels, and when crime, teenage disorder, and other indicies of social defeat and alienation have appeared to go into decline, the collateral injustices, resentments, and anomalies that mark any transitional social engineering appear to have produced crises and collapses of the policies and vision of the affirmative action program. In November 1996, Californians voted in favor of the following proposition:

> The state shall not discriminate against or grant preferential treatment to, any individual or group on the basis of race, sex, colour, ethnicity, or national origin in the operation of public employment, public education or public contracting.

Here is an irony: racism entails discriminating against people primarily on the basis of their membership in racial categories. Yet the California law's primary target is "antiracist" programs of affirmative action and reverse discrimination. The problem can perhaps be formulated thus: for purposes of social engineering, affirmative action programs have sought reasonably to shift the race profile of American society. Affirmative action thus works within the categories of race ascription and ethnic highlighting that is part of the very syndrome of racism against which it is contending. The issue becomes: have you got the right proportion of Blacks or other racial minorities in your institution? To achieve that goal, given the stubborn facts of entrenched White resistance and resentment, and of the underequipment that is part of racism's insidious cultural legacy, less well-qualified Blacks may have to be preferred to Whites. Hence, despite progress, there was reinforced, on all sides, a racialized perception: a perception of self-and-other in terms of racial categories. As Justice Harry Blackmun said in deciding against Allan Bakke's celebrated claim that affirmative action is unconstitutional, "to get beyond racism, we must first take account of race." Hence, also a move to "blackness" among minorities, ethnic or otherwise, able to see themselves collectively as a victimized and disadvantaged category with a claim for special or compensatory treatment. (See Robert Hughes (1993). *Culture of Complaint, The Fraying of America*, New York: Oxford University Press.)

In *Taking Rights Seriously*, Ronald Dworkin argues that because it is right that there be affirmative action to pay for the historical and structural harms done to Blacks, and because this entails that candidates otherwise better qualified might fail to secure desired positions, this cannot be a violation of the latter's rights. Hence, White complainants have no case. This seems a crude view. Arguably, better qualified candidates do have a legitimate grievance, even when overall, the right thing is done in overriding their claims. Similar things happen, for example, when property might for overridingly good reasons be compulsorily purchased from someone who is an innocent occupier and, hitherto, owner. No gain in clarity or social justice is gained by denying the validity of such grievances regarding the collateral injustice that rectification entails; rather such grievances need to be addressed in a fair-minded spirit. Here there may be an irreducible but not thereby undecidable conflict of entitlements. But affirmative action, as the term implies, is forward looking, both in relation to the individual and to the overall racial structure and culture of the society. A member of a disadvantaged group, it is assumed, has the capacity, despite barriers to their gaining relevant qualifications, to flourish in the more honored and nurturing environment. Moreover, through his or her success, individuals who belong to the same racially identified group will have their aspirations and horizons raised. This latter "role-model," barrier-overcoming effect may justify giving preferential treatment to an individual even though, for particular reasons, he or she has not personally suffered the disadvantages common to the racial set of which they are a member, hence has no personal claim in justice over a member of the privileged set who may personally have lacked those common privileges. But such utilitarian practices bring their disutilitarian backlashes with them, and it is arguable that affirmative action should, in general, be premised on individuals' rather than categories' disadvantages: is this person a victim of (inter alia) racism and of its corollary burdens and handicaps such that they are eligible for special consideration, relief, or assistance? In other words, for all its dubious motivation, the California proposition permits the antiracist institution legitimately to take account, among other barriers, of the damage wrought by racism or sexism or national chauvinism on the lives and attainments of their victims. This strategy does in principle enable racism to be fought in the name of the ideal of personal fulfillment and social justice, not of some amplified ideology of "racial identity." But such a fight will fail in the absence of struggle against racism itself.

Also See the Following Articles

AFFIRMATIVE ACTION • DISCRIMINATION, CONCEPT OF • ETHNOCULTURAL MINORITY GROUPS, STATUS AND TREATMENT OF • INTELLIGENCE TESTING • NATURE VERSUS NURTURE • POLITICAL CORRECTNESS • SEXISM

Bibliography

Back, L., & Solomos, J. (1996). *Racism and society*. London: Macmillan.
Blum, L. A. (1992) *Antiracism, multiculturalism and interracial community*. Boston: Office of Graduate Studies, University of Massachussetts.
Eysenck, H. J., & Kamin, L. (1981). *Intelligence: Battle for the mind*. London: Pan.
Flew, A. (1992). *A future for anti-racism?*. London: Social Affairs Unit.
Fraser, S. (Ed.) (1995). *The bell curve wars; Race, intelligence and the future of America*. New York: Basic Books.
Gould, S. J. (1981). *The mismeasurement of man*. New York: Norton.
Hewitt, R. (1996). *Routes of racism*. London: Trentham Books.
Jones, S. (1994). *The language of the genes*. Glasgow: Flamingo.
Hacker, A. (1995). *Two nations*. New York: Ballantine.
Hannaford, I. (1996). *Race: The history of an idea in the West*. Baltimore: Johns Hopkins University Press.
Hollinger, D. A., *Postethnic America*. New York: Basic Books.
Malik, K. (1996). *The meaning of race, history and culture in Western society*. London: Macmillan.
Miles, R. (1989). *Racism*. London: Routledge.
Pagliaro, E. H. (1973), *Racism in the eighteenth century: Studies in eighteenth-century culture*. Cleveland and London: Cape Western.
Thompson, L. A. (1989). *Romans and Blacks*. London: Routledge.
Zubaida, S. (Ed.). (1970). *Race and racialism*. London: Tavistock.

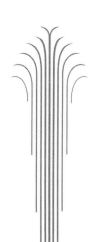

RAPE

Leslie Pickering Francis
University of Utah

GLOSSARY

rape (including date rape) Literally, nonconsensual sexual penetration (including by an acquaintance). Metaphorically, it is molestation, particularly in a form including sexual violence or sexual coercion.

THE DEFINITION, legal treatment, and moral assessment of rape have been highly contested historically. Rape has been viewed as an offense against the victim's legitimate mate, as an instrument of power, and as a crime of sex. More so than any other offense against the body, rape has been portrayed as a nonoffense, as desired by the victim, or as the victim's fault. For critics of gender oppression, rape is the symbol of male domination and female subordination in society.

I. POLITICAL AND SOCIAL HISTORY OF RAPE

Susan Brownmiller's *Against Our Will: Men, Women and Rape*, published in 1975, was a groundbreaking histori-

cal analysis arguing that rape should be viewed as a crime of power rather than a crime of sex. Brownmiller's account begins with early recorded law, that of Babylonian times, under which rape was essentially a crime of property damage; the victim was either the woman's father (who could no longer charge a bride price for a virgin daughter) or the victim's husband (whose property had been invaded). Under both Babylonian and Hebrew law, a married woman was considered a complicitor in her own rape, and so the line between rape and adultery was not clearly drawn; the husband had the legal right to rescue her from punishment, should he so choose, or to leave her to her fate. Female capture and the rape of the conquered were accepted and lawful practices. False accusations and the damage they caused the accused male, such as the accusation by Potiphar's wife that resulted in the imprisonment of Jacob, were also legendary.

In early English law, according to Brownmiller, the identification and criminalization of rape were tied to the acquisition of property. Although rape was punishable by death, with the rapist's land and possessions forfeit to the victim, she could save him by marriage, a practice evidently encouraged for purposes of land consolidation. This possibility existed even if the rapist was a nobleman and the victim a commoner but, Brownmiller observes, was not often exercised because of the unlikelihood that a nobleman would ever be convicted of such a rape. Brownmiller also comments that the crime of rape had by the twelfth century been extended to cover assaults against all women, rather than just virgins with property, but was seldom enforced.

Historically, rape has served as a powerful weapon of war. From the story of the Rape of the Sabine Women, supposedly associated with the founding of Rome, rape was a right of conquest. Brownmiller details how, from the Crusades to the English conquest of the Scottish clans in 1746, to the Vietnam War, rape was regarded at best as an expected but regrettable byproduct of war and at worst as a method of subjugating a conquered people. Rape has also been used as a reward granted to soldiers. Records of rape in the First and Second World Wars are especially extensive; Brownmiller contends, however, that rape has been less publicized than it ought to have been as an atrocity committed by the Nazis against Jewish women.

In American history, rape was a feature of the development of the frontier and of the institution of slavery. On the frontier, there are stories of White women captured and raped by Indians, of love relationships, and of women refusing to disclose Native American lovers for fear of retaliation. There are fewer stories of rapes by Whites against Native American women, a lacuna Brownmiller attributes to the general devaluation of Indian people. Slave women were the property— including the sexual property—of their masters. "Good breeders" were especially valuable, and their slave masters often fathered the children they bore. In *The Alchemy of Race and Rights*, for example, Patricia Williams traces her lineage to a great-great-grandmother-slave and a great-great-grandfather-White-lawyer. Slavery has left a legacy of violence against African-American women, and of ambiguity about the role of race in rape crimes.

The civil wars in Bosnia and Rwanda are contemporary reminders of the oppressive function of rape. Muslim women in Bosnia and Tutsi women in Rwanda were repeatedly raped during the "ethnic cleansings" in these societies. The evidence in Bosnia was that the rapes were in part intended to impregnate the women with children fathered by non-Muslims. Women in both societies now suffer the stigma of rape—or, even worse, illegitimacy—and are finding themselves social outcasts in their rebuilding societies. Despite its political nature and devastating consequences, such wartime rape continues to be viewed as "ill-treatment" rather than "torture" under international conventions, including the United Nations Convention against Torture and Other Cruel, Inhumane or Degrading Treatment or Punishment, and the European Convention for the Protection of Human Rights and Fundamental Freedoms. Victims of such wartime rape, even when the perpetrators are government officials or interrogators, are thus denied the protections given victims of torture. Aswad argues that at least those rapes perpetrated with government involvement, for political purposes, should be reclassified as torture under international law.

II. THE EPIDEMIOLOGY OF RAPE

Because the crime of rape is underreported, and there is controversy over the extent of this underreporting, actual rates of rape are difficult to ascertain. Estimates of rates in the United States range from lows of between 1 and 2% of women as victims over a lifetime, to highs of 40% or more. There is clear agreement in the empirical data that the United States has the highest rape rate of industrialized nations. Within the United States, rape rates vary significantly by state; higher incidence states such as Alaska report a rate five times that of lower incidence states such as Iowa. There is also clear agreement that rape rates have been rising worldwide; the FBI crime statistics in the United States, for example, show a 440% increase in reported rapes from 1960 to 1987.

Criminologists and social commentators have offered a number of explanations for the incidence of rape. Menachim Amir's innovative study in 1971, *Patterns of Forcible Rape*, sought to understand rape as a social phenomenon. Before Amir's study, rape had been largely viewed in psychiatric terms, as a crime of sexual repression and perversion. Amir's theoretical perspective was that rape should be analyzed in sociological rather than in individualistic psychological terms. Amir argued that the epidemiology of rape suggests that it is part of a subculture of violence, with higher rape rates in communities where there are higher crime rates generally and with a high percentage of offenders who have been charged with earlier offenses against the person.

Amir was one of a school of academic sociologists, led by Marvin Wolfgang, who approached the explanation of crime in terms of a subculture of violence. Building in some respects on this sociological approach, Susan Brownmiller argued from a feminist perspective that rape should be viewed as a crime of power, not a crime of sex. Brownmiller's book drew wide public attention for its thesis that rape is a manifestation of the social oppression of women, and for the linkages it drew between rape, the reaction to rape, and authoritarian social institutions. From

Amir's data, Brownmiller was particularly impressed by the observation that nearly half of all rapes are pair or group rapes, a statistic simply ignored by the individualistic psychological understandings of rape. Brownmiller's book was hailed for its sweeping analysis of how rape contributes to the subordination of women, from fairy tales to war. It also gained praise for her argument that women should fight back against the misunderstanding of rape in much of the criminal law of the day, and against the social forces that contribute to a culture of machismo.

Although its focus is legal reform rather than the sociological explanation of rape, Susan Estrich's *Real Rape* (1987) added to the discussion of the epidemiology of rape. Estrich argued that social institutions and the law took utterly different approaches to rapes in which the victim and the offender did not know each other, and rapes of acquaintances. Cases of stranger rape, particularly where violence was used, were identified as "real" rapes by police, prosecutors, and judges. Cases of "simple" rape, where one acquaintance pressed sex on another, were regarded as merely "technical" offenses, or perhaps not classified as offenses at all.

In the most recent extensive study of the epidemiology of rape, Baron and Straus presented a complex exploration of the interaction between demographic variables, gender equality, pornography, social disorganization, and support for violence, and the incidence of rape. They were interested in evaluating explanations of rape in terms of subcultures of violence in comparison to explanations in terms of gender oppression. They found direct support for the hypotheses that gender inequality contributes to rape, that pornography provides ideational support for rape, and that rape is a function of the level of social disorganization. They also found indirect support for the theory that cultural approval of violence is correlated with an increase in the rape rate. They attributed the correlation between the circulation of pornography and the rape rate to the underlying presence of a "macho" culture, rather than a cause/effect relationship between pornography and rape. They also found that urbanization, unemployment, and economic inequality are correlated with increased rape rates. Their conclusion is that "the fundamental causes of rape are to be found in sexism, economic inequality, and social disorganization...[s]ocial policy designed to reduce rape should focus on these underlying causes rather than on pornography" (p. 189). They thus regard both a subculture of violence and a culture of sexism as contributing factors to rape.

III. THE LEGAL HISTORY OF RAPE

Until recently, the law has defined the offense of rape in a quite restrictive manner. Both the definition of the offense and the rules of evidence have made indictments and convictions difficult to obtain. Significant legal reforms have been instituted in the United States, although their impact on conviction rates appears to have been modest at best. Changes in rape law in other English-speaking jurisdictions have been uneven, with Britain retaining the most stringent definition of the crime of rape.

A typical traditional definition of the crime of rape was a man obtaining "carnal knowledge, of a woman not his wife, by force or threat of force, against her will and without her consent." Several limits in this common law definition are particularly noteworthy. The definition only extends to heterosexual acts. It explicitly excludes marital rape. It requires acts of penetration. It requires force or threats of force by the attacker and nonconsent on the victim's side.

This definition gave rise to several evidentiary requirements. Proving the crime of rape required evidence that the sexual penetration was "against her will," in the language of Brownmiller's title. As frequently interpreted by courts, this has required showings of force on the part of the offender and active resistance on the part of the victim. Other evidentiary hurdles made convictions even more difficult to obtain. Because of concerns about fairness if a conviction could be obtained when the only evidence was the complainant's word against the defendant's, many jurisdictions required corroborating evidence for proof of rape. Jurisdictions also typically required that the complaint be "fresh"—that is, recent at the time it was made—not only because of the risk that evidence would dissipate but also because of suspicions about the veracity of a late-filed complaint. Finally, and most importantly for victims, evidence of past sexual history was regarded as relevant to the determination of whether a rape had occurred, and hence was regularly judged to be admissible. The victim, therefore, frequently seemed to be as much on trial as the defendant.

All of these limits have come under attack and have been modified in many American jurisdictions. The gendered language has been removed from rape statutes, allowing the possibility of prosecutions for same-sex rapes and rapes by women against men. Homosexual rape is, however, an infrequently reported offense, except when the victim is a young child, quite likely because of the marginalization and stigmatization of homosexuality generally. In Britain, rape is defined in terms of nonconsent, but the term is undefined and the practice appears to be to require a showing of force in most cases.

Another reform in the definition of rape has been the extension of the scope of the offense. The marital exception has been removed from many American statutes, although in many jurisdictions with significant limits. The historical justification for the exclusion, that wives were the property of their husbands, has long since given way to the view that the marriage relationship itself should be construed as general consent to sex. Jurisdictions working on this assumption, including many American states and Britain, have typically limited their repeal of the marital exemption to situations in which the marriage itself has been legally questioned, such as when the parties are legally separated or living apart under a court order.

In 1974, Michigan was the first American state to adopt comprehensive "modern" reforms of its rape statute. In addition to both the definitional and the evidentiary reforms discussed here, Michigan entirely restructured its rape statute to grade offenses of criminal sexual conduct. The grades range from lesser offenses of unwanted sexual conduct or sexual assault, to the more serious offenses of forcible intercourse. This restructuring, which has been a model for many jurisdictions, expands the scope of criminal conduct to sexual acts not including penetration, and to acts of coercion not including physical violence or overt resistance on the part of the victim.

As definitions of rape have changed, so have the rules of evidence. The requirements of resistance and corroboration have been abandoned as necessary to the proof of rape. The requirement of a fresh complaint has also been abolished, although it remains likely that victims who are slow to complain will be regarded with suspicion by law enforcement personnel and will find evidence difficult if not impossible to gather.

Perhaps most significantly for victims, "rape shield" laws are now in effect in most states and in the American federal courts. These laws ban the introduction of evidence of the victim's past sexual history as probative on the question of whether rape occurred. Victims thus need not fear that as a general rule they can expect to have their past sexual behavior paraded before the court. There are impressive limits to many rape shield laws, however. Past history evidence may be admissible to put the victim's credibility into question; for example, if she testifies about her prior behavior, her testimony may be impeached by past history evidence. Evidence of the victim's past history

with the defendant may also, in many jurisdictions with shield laws, be admissible to show that the present act of sex was consensual. A victim who has had a sexual relationship with the defendant and claims that a subsequent act was rape, therefore, may expect that evidence of this relationship will be admitted into court. This limitation is especially important in date rape cases, where the victim has had some prior interactions with the defendant. The assumption that prior consent is relevant to the determination of present consent will place the woman who is trying to end an unwanted relationship in a particularly difficult position if she alleges rape. In Britain, although a rape shield law is in place, defendants are allowed to petition the judge in the absence of the jury to admit past sexual history evidence when "it would be unfair to the defendant to refuse to allow the evidence to be adduced or the question to be asked."

In her extensive study, *Real Rape*, Susan Estrich both outlined these legal changes and argued that they had not made a great deal of difference in how courts actually handle rape cases. Police, prosecutors, juries, and judges, she contended, still see violent rape by a stranger—"real rape"—as different in kind from nonconsensual sex with an acquaintance—"simple rape." For example, Estrich noted that many courts still understand nonconsent in terms of whether there was force by the perpetrator or resistance by the victim. Estrich's work is a powerful traditional legal study of how prereform doctrines continue to function in the disposition of postreform cases. Estrich concluded by recommending the development of a separate category of offenses of sexual coercion to ensure that the legal condemnation of "simple rape" is manifest.

Empirical studies of rape in the criminal process bear out Estrich's contention that reform of rape law has had limited impact. Holmstrom and Burgess followed victims through police stations, hospitals, and courts, and argued that these institutions identify "real" victims based on cultural attitudes about how women ought to act. Victims of what are regarded as "real" rapes receive far more supportive treatment than victims who are taken to have brought what happened on themselves. Holmstrom and Burgess offered many suggestions for reform, including such simple ways of minimizing the impact of the courtroom experience on victims as giving them notice of when proceedings are to be continued.

Spohn and Horney studied the effects of reform legislation on the reporting and processing of rape in 6 jurisdictions over a 15-year period. They reported no clear patterns in the effects of the reform laws; the laws do not appear to have produced the increases in reporting and conviction rates that their proponents had hoped. One of the difficulties in analysis was the interaction between the rape reforms and the criminal justice systems in the jurisdictions studied; for example, whether or not the indictment process requires a grand jury, and how the prosecutor's office is organized, could be expected to confound the impact of rape law reform. Spohn and Horney did draw some limited conclusions, however. The Michigan reform does appear to have led to an increase in rape reporting rates, although not to an increase in conviction rates. General increases in reporting rates seem to have been linked to changes in social attitudes toward rape rather than to rape law reform per se. There does appear to have been some increase in indictment rates in some jurisdictions, although not in conviction rates. Prosecutors appear to continue to consider the availability of corroborating evidence in assessing the likelihood of conviction, and hence in judging whether or not to file charges. Finally, possibly because no rape shield statutes exclude evidence of prior sexual relationships between the victim and the alleged perpetrator, the benefits of legal reform, such as they are, appear to have been directed toward stranger rape rather than acquaintance rape cases.

In later studies, Spohn and Horney have attempted to assess whether reform of the rape statutes has brought more subtle changes in the treatment of rape in the criminal process. They argue based on data from Detroit that there have been changes in the cases reported to police, with more frequent reporting of simple or acquaintance rapes. They also found changes in the distribution of the rape cases bound over for trial, with an increase in the proportion of simple (nonaggravated) rape cases. They attribute these changes to an increased willingness of victims of simple rape to report and to press charges after the statutory reforms, and an increased willingness of prosecutors to file charges in cases of alleged simple rape. But despite the changes in the mix of cases brought into the legal system, Spohn and Horney find no changes in the ultimate disposition of rape cases. Conviction and sentencing determinations remain largely a function of whether aggravating factors such as the use of a weapon or injury to the victim were involved in the rape. From studies such as these, it seems apparent that social attitudes about the treatment of simple rape remain complex, and that the issue remains a fruitful area for philosophical investigation.

IV. PHILOSOPHICAL APPROACHES TO THE UNDERSTANDING OF RAPE

A. Liberal Theory

The protection of liberty is central to liberal theories about the nature and function of law. Following John Stuart Mill, liberals argue against the enforcement of morality on the ground that society's view of what is morally right does not justify the use of compulsion or control. Actions that wrong or harm individuals, but to which they consent—often called "victimless" crimes—are not appropriately criminalized on the liberal view. Thus, for a liberal, the dividing line between sex that should be criminalized and sex that should not be is the line between involuntariness and consent. Adultery, polygamy, sex between unmarried individuals, group sex, or homosexual sex should not be criminalized unless there is reason to believe one of the parties did not participate voluntarily. Sex that is judged to be immoral should not be condemned by the law on this basis alone. Rape law reform should abolish requirements irrelevant to the fact of consent, such as whether the victim resisted or the offender used force, but it should resist the tendency to criminalize sex that fails to meet idealized models of consent.

Liberal theory thus lays heavy emphasis on consent. There are notorious difficulties about what counts as consent, however. One obvious difficulty is determination of the capacity to consent. From Mill on, liberals have typically held that their views apply fully to adults only, and then only when the adults are in full possession of their faculties. The criminalization of sex when the "victim" is a minor or is incapacitated could thus be regarded as outside the ban on the legal enforcement of morality. Liberals may, however, hold more complex views about the ability of near-adults to consent; liberals who hold such views might not regard all sex with an underage victim as of a piece, but might urge criminalization of those cases in which coercion is highly likely, such as sex with young victims, or sex in which there is a significant age difference between the alleged offender and victim. Or they might support gradation of the seriousness of sex offenses based on the victim's underage status. Indeed, both liberals and feminists continue to debate the wisdom of paternalistic statutory rape laws generally, and of female-protective, gender-specific versions of these laws particularly.

Most difficult for liberals are cases in which consent is contested. Suppose, for example, that the victim gives apparent indications of consent—saying yes, expressing enjoyment of the event—but there are reasons for critique of whether the consent was genuine given the social context. Perhaps it is a fraternity party, where alcohol has been liberally and deliberately consumed, and the woman believes sex is part of the package, whether she really wants it or not. It is in their understanding of such circumstances that liberals part company from radical feminists such as Catharine MacKinnon. Liberals hold the view that as long as the woman was uncoerced and knowingly chose sex from a set of alternatives, her consent must be taken at face value. MacKinnon argues instead that attention should be directed to whether the circumstances were such that the woman could ask herself whether she "really wanted it" and the man was genuinely careful to ascertain her feelings.

Another issue for liberals in the treatment of rape is the protection of the rights of defendants. In defense of liberty, liberals hold that the burden should be on the state to prove guilt of the offender beyond a reasonable doubt. Due process protections for the accused are important to a system that minimizes the rate of unwarranted convictions. Such protections include the right to counsel, the right to confront accusers, and the right to insist that the state prove its case beyond a reasonable doubt. Insistence on these rights may make the system unpleasant for victims, who must testify, see their word put against the defendant's word, and undergo cross-examination aimed to undermine their credibility. The feminist criticism of this process—that the victim herself is wronged by being put on trial—speaks to a different issue than the liberal concern for rights of the accused: the need for changes in a social system, including a judicial system, that oppresses women.

Liberal theory does not ignore the plight of the victim, however. Many quite traditional questions of applied ethics arise over respect for the victim's autonomy. The victim is examined by law enforcement personnel (police and prosecutors) and by medical personnel, generally in a hospital emergency room, hopefully one where the staff is trained to deal with rape victims. Confidentiality is an initial concern. The victim may wish to ensure that what she tells the physician or lawyer be kept confidential. Yet she may not be consulted about the relevant limits on the conduct of either. The prosecutor is not her lawyer, but the lawyer for the state, and thus does not have a professional duty of confidentiality toward the victim. Although the physician may provide treatment, he or she may also see the function of the medical examination as retrieving and preserving evidence for the state. Especially when the victim is a minor, family members may press for information that the victim does not want to have shared: whether there was evidence of penetration, whether sperm was present, or whether the woman is virginal.

Another applied ethics issue concerning the victim is informed consent to health care. Rape victims may not be told what to expect from a medical examination, from antibiotic treatment to prevent infection, to a pelvic exam to inspect for injury or sperm, to treatment with the morning-after pill to prevent pregnancy. One study indicated, for example, that victims are typically not told that the morning-after pill functions as an abortifacient. Victims also may not be informed that they have a right to refuse treatment: medical personnel may coerce the victim to submit to an examination so that evidence may be gathered for the law enforcement team, or because they believe that treatment such as administration of an antibiotic is in the patient's interest. Such coercion may be particularly offensive to a victim who already feels that she has been violated by the rape itself.

Indeed, professionals dealing with rape victims exhibit clear problems of role confusion. The prosecutor represents the state, not the victim, yet the victim may not understand this situation and may be surprised that she is interrogated and not protected as would be a client. She may even be surprised to find out that this is "the state's" case, and may experience frustration at not being informed about what is going on during the proceedings. On the medical side, the health care personnel examining and treating her are her health care providers. But they may not act in this role, instead playing the role of investigators for the state; this deeply problematic role confusion may not be explained to the victim.

Another standard bioethics issue regarding the victim is access to health care. Victims may be expected to pay their own medical expenses, even when the examination is urged on them by law enforcement personnel. Victims who are uninsured or who have high deductibles in their insurance coverage may experience considerable hardship as a result. Although crime victim restitution statutes may help in some cases, they are likely not available in situations in which the decision is not to press charges in an alleged situation of simple rape. Thus, although liberal theory would reject the criminalization of immoral sex, and would urge protection of the rights of the accused, it also provides a good deal of scope for concern about treatment of the victim.

B. Radical Feminist Theory

Radical feminist theory is premised on the understanding of social relationships in terms of gender oppression. Radical feminists do not deny the importance of liberal reforms in improving the status of women, particularly efforts directed to protecting the rights of victims such as rape shield laws or, in the international context, the reunderstanding of rape as torture. Rather, they argue that the reformist program is far too limited. Reforms are premised on the protection of rights, of both victim and accused. To the extent that the evenhanded protection of rights presumes a level playing field, radical critics argue, it perpetuates gender domination in society. Far more sweeping reforms are needed instead.

Central to radical feminism is a reconceptualization of the basic structure of the offense of rape. Because women must live and survive in conditions of oppression, silence or passivity cannot be taken as consent. Instead, the law must insist upon the woman's active consent and on her having the space within which to give such consent. Along these lines, Lois Pineau has proposed a model of communicative sexuality, on which the sex is presumed to be undesired on the part of the woman unless she affirmatively communicates her desire for it. Stephen Schulhofer has argued that just as affirmative consent is required for medical treatment or the appropriation of property, and an ambiguous nonanswer will not do in these circumstances, so too affirmative consent should be required for sexual entry into a woman's body. These proposals regard liberal reforms that either expand the notion of force or change the standards of proof for nonconsent as perpetuating assumptions about the sexual role of a woman as passive and accepting, perhaps secretly and stereotypically desiring sex even if she does not say so. They urge the law instead to presume that the sex is unwanted unless it is the subject of explicit consent. They reject suggestions that women should be regarded as complicitor in their own rapes for behavior such as wearing seductive clothing, going to bars, or accepting rides, because of the burdens such judgments impose on women—burdens not imposed on men.

Antioch College, in its Sexual Offense Policy, has brought the radical program to reality. Antioch's policy prohibits all nonconsensual sex. It requires participants in sex to seek affirmative permission at every level. Responsibility is placed on the initiator to assure verbal consent from the other; and on the other to express unwillingness should there be a change of heart. At the first indication of unwillingness, sexual advances must stop, and there is to be no sexual pressure or harassment.

Because overcoming the sexual oppression of women takes center stage for radical feminist theory, treatment of the accused plays a lesser role. False negatives—in which a guilty perpetrator goes free—are far more damaging than false positives, in which a less-than-guilty instigator is convicted. Indeed, that conviction rates for rape are so low suggests that the stage is sloped precipitously against the protection of women. Instigators who are not prosecuted or who are acquitted, moreover, may well be complicitors in oppression even if they do not meet the exact legal standards for rape. This complicity might well characterize many date rapes, where the man presses himself threateningly upon the woman, and she responds passively or with what he takes to be ambiguous signals. To the extent that they reject rights-based analyses for their roots in liberal individualism, or for other reasons, radical feminists will also reject understanding of the situation of the victim or the accused in terms of rights.

Beyond the legal system, radical feminists direct their attention to the social causes of rape. The encouragement of attitudes of machismo and of female passivity are condemned. So are multiple forms of the exploitation of women, from prostitution to pornography. In their condemnation of the expression of sexualized violence against women in literature, art, and film, radical feminists are joined by conservative moralists.

Collective responsibility is another important issue for radical feminists. On the liberal view, the locus of blame is the offender. On the radical view, with institutionalized oppression of women at the forefront, there are questions both about the diminished responsibility of the offender and about the shared responsibilities of the larger community. May and Strikwerda argue that rape is "deeply embedded in a wider culture of male socialization" in Western societies. Those involved in the perpetuation of this acculturation—teachers, male leaders, even friends urging each other on—should take on responsibility for changing acculturation patterns. Although spreading responsibility beyond an individual perpetrator does not entail diminishing the responsibility of the perpetrator correspondingly—all may be fully responsible—deterministic social explanations of behavior may bring individual responsibility into question.

A final issue for some radical feminists is the intersection of gender, race, and class. Race is an important feature of the mythology of rape: the fear of Black men raping White women. Ironically, the demographics of rape could not be farther from the myth: the majority of rapes are committed by Black men against Black women. When a Black man is alleged to have raped a White woman, there is evidence that the rape is more likely to be perceived by police and prosecutors as "real," and sentences are likely to be higher. Conversely, when the victim of the rape is Black, the rape is less likely to be preceived as "real." Feminist critical race theorists face a dilemma: should they envision rape through the lens of race, the lens of gender, a combination ("race-plus"), or a newly transcendent mode of analysis? Kimberlè Crenshaw argues that gender-based analyses work to the benefit of White women and fail to challenge factors undermining the credibility of Black women; race-based analyses protect Black men whether their accusers are Black or White. To select either paradigm is to marginalize Black women.

Crenshaw suggests an understanding of the politics of "intersectionality": of how the situation of Black women is different, and how the twin factors of sexism and racism mutually reinforce oppression.

Also See the Following Articles

AUTONOMY • CONFIDENTIALITY, GENERAL ISSUES OF • FEMINIST JURISPRUDENCE • PORNOGRAPHY • PROSTITUTION • SEXISM • SEXUAL CONTENT IN FILMS AND TELEVISION • VICTIMLESS CRIMES

Bibliography

Andre-Clark, A. S. Note: Whither statutory rape laws: of *Michael M.*, The Fourteenth Amendment, and protecting women from sexual aggression. *Southern California Law Review*, 65: 1933–1992.

Amir, M. (1971). *Patterns in forcible rape*. Chicago: University of Chicago Press.

Aswad, E. M. (1996). Note: Torture by means of rape. *Georgetown Law Journal*, 84: 1913–1943.

Baron, L., & Straus, M. A. (1989). *Four theories of rape in American society*. New Haven: Yale University Press.

Brownmiller, S. (1975). *Against our will: Men, women and rape*. New York: Simon & Schuster.

Chappell, D., Geis, R., & Geis, G. (Eds.). (1977). *Forcible rape: The crime, the victim, and the offender*. New York: Columbia University Press.

Crenshaw, K. (1991). Mapping the margins: Intersectionality, identity politics, and violence against women of color. *Stanford Law Review*, 43: 1241–1299.

Dripps, D. A. (1992). Beyond rape: An essay on the difference between the presence of force and the absence of consent. *Columbia Law Review*, 92: 1780–1809.

Estrich, S. (1987). *Real rape*. Cambridge: Harvard University Press.

Fairstein, L. A. (1993). *Sexual violence: Our war against rape*. New York: William Morrow.

Holmstrom, L. L., & Burgess, A. W. (1983). *The victim of rape: Institutional reactions*. New Brunswick, NJ: Transaction Books.

MacKinnon, C. A. (1987). *Feminism unmodified: Discourses on life and law*. Cambridge: Harvard University Press.

May, L., & Strikwerda, E. (1994). Men in groups: Collective responsibility for rape. *Hypatia*, 9: 134–151.

Olsen, F. (1984). Statutory rape: A feminist critique of rights analysis. *Texas Law Review*, 63: 387–432.

Pineau, L. (1996). Date rape: feminist analysis. In L. Francis (Ed.), *Date rape: Feminism, philosophy, and the law*. University Park, PA: Penn State University Press.

Schulhofer, S. J. (1995). The feminist challenge in criminal law. *University of Pennsylvania Law Review*, 143: 2151–2208.

Spohn, C., & Horney, J. (1996). The impact of rape law reform on the processing of simple and aggravated rape cases. *The Journal of Criminal Law & Criminology*, 86: 861–884.

Spohn, C., & Horney, J. (1992). *Rape law reform*. New York: Plenum Press.

Temkin, J. (1987). *Rape in the legal process*. London: Sweet & Maxwell.

Williams, P. (1991). *The alchemy of race and rights*. Cambridge: Harvard University Press.

RELIGION AND ETHICS

Ian Markham
Liverpool Hope University College

GLOSSARY

anthropocentricism Making humans central in one's understanding of the significance of life.

apocalyptic Revelations about the end of the world.

caste The social hierarchy in Hinduism, with the priestly caste at the top, rulers second, and merchants third.

karma The moral law of cause and effect.

Mishnah A legal code based on the Torah: a complication of the oral teaching of the Jewish rabbis who lived from 30 B.C.E. to C.E. 219.

natural law Ethical requirements built into and discernable in the nature of things.

pietism A stress on individual salvation.

reductionist A complex notion used in a variety of ways. In this article the term describes all attempts to reduce the moral to a branch of biology, psychology, or sociology.

Samsara The interconnected nature of reality across time and space.

Sangha The Buddhist community, normally of monks.

secular Adjective applied to a society which is no longer affected by religious institutions or ideas.

Talmud A collection of rabbinic literature, comprising the Mishnah and the Gemara. A source of oral law.

telos Greek for the end. Used to describe "a purpose."

Torah When applied in its most precise form, the term describes the first five books of the Hebrew Bible.

RELIGION AND ETHICS are closely connected. All the major religious traditions share a sense that ethical decisions are matters of truth and discovery. Despite the complexity of each religion, there are certain themes that are central to most religions, including, for example, a commitment to love and the centrality of the family unit. For the purposes of applied ethics, the important areas of disagreement arise over the status of the individual and attitudes to wealth and war. This article will examine the relationship between religion and ethics in Hinduism, Buddhism, Judaism, Christianity, and Islam. Due to the limitation of space, many complexities within each tradition cannot be explored. At almost every point within this article, there are significant exceptions and differences.

I. ETHICAL METHODOLOGY IN RELIGION

A. The Character of Morality

Despite the considerable diversity of viewpoint between religions, there is agreement over one matter. Virtually all agree that morality is a matter of discovery and truth. In other words there are "moral facts" analogous to scientific ones, which transcend all individuals and human communities and are in some sense built into the structures of the universe. In the same sense that the existence of the moon is true for all people everywhere (regardless of their own perception), so Roman Catholics—to take one significant religious community—believe the moral command that "you should not take innocent life" is true for all people everywhere. Morality in a religious account is conceived as objective (transcending human communities) and absolute (when the moral truth is discovered it is true for everyone).

This contrasts strongly with certain contemporary trends in modernity that think of morality as a matter of culture and convention. This is a reductionist view of morality. Reductionist accounts of morality take several different forms. Richard Dawkins has pioneered an evolutionary view of morality, describing it as a selfish genetic propensity (see Dawkins, 1976). Others suggest a psychological account of morality; we inherit the morality suggested to us when young as we move from group to group. The pressure to conform to the group creates within us a psychological acceptance of the group morality. Those more influenced by Emile Durkheim tend to suggest that morality is a social mechanism that helps society work more effectively. If we were not moral, then our society would cohere less well (see Durkheim, 1915). The great strength of these accounts is that they focus on the mechanisms by which a moral sense develops within a person. Furthermore, they explain why moral codes vary so much: different cultures have formed different moral codes for different psychological and sociological factors. For example, Christians and Muslims disagree over polygamy. It could be argued that polygamy became necessary in an Islamic culture because a man taking a second wife became the best mechanism to provide for those widows created by war; it is not permitted in Christian cultures because alternative ways were found for providing for the war widow. This sociological need explains why the Muslim disagrees with the Christian over polygamy.

From the religious perspective the problem with these reductionist accounts is that the moral realm becomes less significant. If morality is simply a psycholog-

ical or social mechanism, then why should it be binding on me? If I am able to evade the psychological mechanism, then why should I be moral? The oldest question in the history of ethics is "why not be selfish?" These reductionist accounts only provide very limited and, often, highly pragmatic justifications. The second problem with reductionism is relativism. If different moralities are simply a result of different cultural factors, then what entitles one to judge a different culture? If we are unable to refer to anything that transcends these cultures, it is difficult to find a legitimate reason to condemn those cultures such as, for example, Nazi anti-Semitism. This leads to the third difficulty. The world discovered at Nuremberg that we cannot judge the Nazi culture unless we appeal to an external standard of morality. In short, justice depends on denying reductionism. The fourth difficulty is found in the writings of Immanuel Kant. He made much of the character of moral language. When one says "I really ought to go and help my friend," it sounds as if there is an external "ought" that is compelling one to take a course of action that conflicts with one's desires. This combination of factors (namely, the significance of morality, the danger of relativism, the transcendent nature of justice, and the character of moral discourse) is used by some apologists for religion as an argument for God. C. S. Lewis, a twentieth-century Christian writer, is a good, albeit popular, example of this (see C. S. Lewis, 1970).

So although there is considerable disagreement between the religions about the content of morality, there is agreement on the character of morality. At the very minimum, a religious worldview sees morality as transcending human communities, grounded, in some sense, within the structures of the universe, and binding on all people every where. Ronald Green, probably the most able contemporary writer on interfaith ethics, has gone a great deal further. He believes that most religions have a deep structure: this structure has three components. First, "a method of moral reasoning involving 'the moral point of view'; second, a set of beliefs affirming the reality of moral retribution; and third, a series of 'transmoral' beliefs that suspend moral judgement and retribution when this is needed to overcome moral paralysis and despair." (Green, 1988:3) It is especially interesting to note Green's emphasis on retribution, despite the fact that the modern Western mind can find it problematic. Ever since Kant, many believe that one is not being moral if one only does it for self-interest; morality should be disinterested. Don Cupitt, a contemporary philosopher of religion from Cambridge, England, has argued that a truly moral Christianity needs to disentangle itself from any sense of retribution, which will involve denying the objectivity of God (see Cupitt, 1988). To simply behave morally because one is fearful of hell sounds less adequate than to behave morally because one is persuaded of the intrinsic appropriateness of the moral obligation. Furthermore, many sociologists believe that hell has lost its power on the Western imagination. The majority of people in the West are not sufficiently sure of the reality of hell to deter them from bad behavior.

B. Religious Sources for Ethics

Having identified these shared assumptions about the nature of ethics, and some of the problems with them, it is now necessary to describe the different sources for ethics that are found within the different religious traditions. There are five sources that different strands of different religious traditions have recourse to when making ethical judgments.

The first is the sacred texts. All religions make "revelation" central. Keith Ward in his study, *Religion and Revelation,* has documented the ways in which revelation is central to religion (see Ward, 1994). The theistic traditions agree that knowledge of God depends on God revealing Godself to us. For many traditions, God is also the source of the moral order and has revealed his (or more rarely her) will in a scripture. In certain strands of Judaism, the Torah preexisted the creation and provided the blueprint for the order of creation. Although all Christians believe that in some sense the Bible is the "Word of God," reformed Christianity describe it as the sole source of authority. Some fundamentalist Christians describe the Bible as the infallible guide for human behavior. Similarly, Islam has a strong commitment to revelation as the source of morality. Islam cannot understand the Western separation of the sacred and the secular: the whole of the world and society is to be ordered according to the infallible word of God. The Eastern traditions make much of revelation. Certain schools of Hinduism talk about the Vedas as eternal, and the Laws of Manu provide clear guidance for the ordering of human society. Also, the Buddha talks about the Four Noble Truths as a discovery, which are now embodied in the texts that make up the scriptures of Buddhism.

The second source of moral guidance are the institutions and traditions of each religion. Often these are perceived as secondary (or supplementary) to the first source—the scriptures. In Christianity, those in the Roman Catholic tradition talk about the Church as the mechanism provided by God to interpret the scriptures for each new age. Pope John Paul II has made this a central theme of his pontiff. *Veritatis Splendor,* for example, cites as authority both the Bible and the tradition of past papal pronouncements and Church Councils. In Islam the hadith (traditions and stories about the prophet and his immediate followers) is extremely important in the formation of Islamic law. Generally, Judaism does not have institutional guidance, although an interesting exception is the Hasidism: a movement founded by the Baal Shem Tov in Volhynia and Podolia in the eighteenth century, from which the Lubavicher dynasty, which settled in America, developed. Certainly they give the chief Rabbi an authoritative teaching role for his followers. All Jews acknowledge to some degree the authority of the traditions that have developed in the Mishnah and the commentaries on the Mishnah known as the Talmud. These texts continue to provide opportunity for reinterpretation and reflection to new situations and new times. Some forms of Mahayana Buddhism do have an institutional authority and many strands of Buddhism make use of the history of monastic practice as an authoritative source for ethical insight.

The third source of moral guidance is human reason. Both Judaism and Islam have a fairly optimistic view of humanity. In both cases the gift of human reason, which distinguishes us from the animals, is a God-given resource that should assist us in arriving at the right moral judgment. Christianity complicates this picture with the doctrine of original sin. For Martin Luther, the fall was so severe that sin distorted the capacity of human reason to see the moral truth. We need to be saved from our sin and have our original righteousness restored through grace. However, the major religious traditions share a sense that although sin has deformed the capacity of humans to use their reason properly, it is still operational. Indeed, it is this idea that lies behind the Roman Catholic doctrine of natural law. Natural law assumes that all humans everywhere, without the explicit aid of Biblical revelation, are able to partially discern the moral truth. For this reason all people are without excuse.

This leads to our fourth source for moral knowledge, which is the natural order. Perhaps the best-known tradition that makes overt use of the natural world is the Roman Catholic one. Following Aristotle, St. Thomas Aquinas believed that God had built into the structures of his creation the natural law. The *telos* of each activity is the proper purpose for that activity. So, to take the best-known example, according to the Roman Catholic doctrine, the telos of the penis is procreation. Given this, it is an unnatural use of the penis to use it for masturbation or homosexuality. Furthermore, it is unnatural to prevent the penis from realising its natural end by using contraception. Equivalents to natural law are found in strands of other religious traditions. For example, the vitally important Hindu notion of dharma (right action) is grounded in the eternal law of the universe. Zaehner, a contemporary scholar on Hinduism, defines dharma as "the 'form' of things as they are and the power that keeps them as they are and not otherwise" (Zaehner, 1966:2). In Judaism there has been some debate as to the extent that Torah can been seen as revealing natural law. Philo was probably the first Jewish scholar to think in this way, and certainly the Noachite Laws (those laws required to be observed by the righteous Gentile) have been interpreted as a Rabbinic attempt to incorporate Natural law.

The fifth and final source for moral values is religious experience. There is, of course, a sense in which this source underpins all others as it is the human awareness of God that generates all religion; but for this awareness no religious ethics would exist. However, this source is identified separately because some traditions make direct awareness of God much more central to their ethical system. Some traditions talk about discovering what God wants for you through religious experience and prayer, which can sometimes run counter to the accepted ethic of an age. One of the most striking illustrations of this is the instruction given to Abraham to take his son Isaac and sacrifice him on a mountain described in the Hebrew Scriptures (Genesis 22). All three of the Abrahamic traditions are fascinated by this narrative. Kierkegaard, the Danish philosopher, thought the story illustrated the obligation of obedience and the willingness to become the "solitary individual" willing to transcend the conventional understanding of morality (see Kierkegaard, 1983).

Thus far we have seen that, despite all the diversity, there is a shared outlook on the ethical realm; all traditions agree that ethics are a matter of truth and discovery. We have also seen that each tradition uses the same type of resource to discover the truth; they all cite scripture, human reason, tradition, authoritative institutions, and religious experience.

II. SHARED ETHICAL INSIGHTS

Generalizations about religious traditions are very difficult. This is for two reasons: first, there are very few generalizations that are true for every adherent in a tradition; second, there are very few ideas within a tradition that are not found in a different religious tradition. Certain ideas within a strand of a tradition will have an equivalent in another one. For example, the small Christian group known as the Quakers share a commitment to nonviolence with the Jewish religious peace movement Oz Veshalom. (Oz Veshalom takes the principle of *pikuah nefesh*—the saving of life—as an important reason why land should be exchanged for peace. Perhaps one should add that, unlike the Quakers, not everyone in the movement is committed to pacifism, although many are sympathetic). Both the Quakers and the Jewish peace movement disagree with the majority in their own traditions. The point is this: it is not that all traditions disagree nor that all traditions agree but that some strands of each tradition agree with each other and therefore disagree with the strands of other religious traditions.

Once this is seen one should be hesitant about all attempts to create a global theology. John Hick (a Christian philosopher committed to the view that all religions are equally valid ways of being "saved" from sin) talks about a shared soteriological emphasis across the world religions (see Hick, 1989). The problem here is that this language is completely alien to the non-Christian traditions. Hans Küng has suggested that the world religions should converge around a global ethic (see Küng, 1991). In both cases, the complexity of the ethical traditions can be easily disregarded. The project makes it very easy to overlook the considerable diversity both within and across religious traditions.

Yet given that we must avoid certain simplistic identification of ethical equivalents across religious traditions, it is helpful to note that the orthodox traditions (i.e., the traditional ones) do share certain themes. I shall now identify four such themes.

A. A Commitment to Love, Compassion, and Justice

First, there is a shared commitment to love, compassion, and justice. Although these qualities are understood in different ways within different traditions, there is undoubtedly a sense in which these are universally recognized virtues. The Talmud sets out Rabbi Hillel's famous summary of the Jewish law: "What is hateful to you, do not to your neighbour: that is the whole Torah, while the rest is the commentary thereof; go and learn it." Jesus inherited this theme and summed up the law in the two commandments: "Hear O Israel: The Lord our God, the Lord is one; and you shall love the Lord your God with all your heart, and with all your soul, and with all your mind, and with all your strength"; and the second, "You shall love your neighbour as yourself" (Mark 12:29-31). When Mohammed was asked, "whose Islam is good?" he gave a similar reply. "One who feeds others and greets those whom he knows and those whom he does not know." In Hinduism one finds compassion is the third of the three Da's, which is the foundation of all Hindu ethical reflection.

It is often said that the world religions share this emphasis. We have already noted how Hans Küng has made compassion the basis of his global ethic. There are difficulties here. First, this shared theme of love runs parallel with other themes that are much more problematic. Most religious traditions have, at some stage or other, found no problem with loving your enemy to death (i.e., deciding that death is preferable for the enemy rather than the enemy continuing to propagate error). Second, in some traditions, the loving is conceived of more individually, while in others it takes a more corporate form. So the more pietistic forms of Christianity stress the importance of individual charity to those who need, while more Catholic forms tend to stress the social dimension.

This difference between pietism and a more social gospel that is found within Christianity is also reflected across the world religions. Conceptually, Islam does not separate out the individual from the group. One of the five pillars is almsgiving; it is a religious duty to provide for the servants of Allah and the poor. Generally, Islam is a social, community-orientated religion. While at the other end of the spectrum, certain strands of Buddhism can be highly individualistic. To imagine that one should try and change the world is one of those illusions that one should detach oneself from. This is a difference we shall return to.

B. The Centrality of the Family

The second theme that is found across the major traditions is the centrality of the family. The great creation myths often have the complementary nature of men and women at its heart. Genesis, for example, provides the foundation text for Judaism, Christianity, and Islam. Eve (representative women) was created to help Adam (representative man). Both are created in the image of God. Jesus in the Gospels describes the state of one man and one woman as God's intended vision for marriage. It is for this reason that Jesus describes divorce as wrong.

The Law of Manu in Hinduism stresses the importance of roles: children should obey their parents and wives should obey their husbands. This all links with the stress on the caste system—each person is great in their place. It is the order of family life that can provide an effective bulwark against the potential disorder of samsara. The Buddha also saw the importance of family

as the resource that enabled the rest of society to operate effectively.

Of course, there are numerous differences in detail. Divorce is permitted in some traditions and not in others. Polygamy is encouraged in some and discouraged in others. Attitudes to contraception vary considerably. Despite this disagreement, it remains true that the traditional family remains the ideal and basic form of human organization. It is also worth noting that there is also agreement on the patriarchal structure of the family. The New Testament writer of the epistle of Timothy (almost certainly not Paul) enjoins wives to obey their husbands. And the Laws of Manu clearly states that "In childhood a female must be subject to her father, in youth to her husband, when her lord is dead to her sons; a women must never be independent." Despite the proliferation of female deities in Hinduism, it remains just as patriarchal in practice as Christianity.

C. Significance of Ritual in Ethics

The third shared theme across the traditions stresses the centrality of ritual in forming the virtuous person. Although at the edges some traditions have an ideological objection to too much ritual, the majority make it the heart of religious practice. Ritual is the mechanism by which life becomes religious. Rituals mark the start and end of life; weddings and the birth of children are marked by religious rituals. Days, weeks, months, and years are all organized around a religious calendar that will involve certain rituals. Fasting on certain holy days is common to most religious traditions. The dietary laws of Judaism and Islam turn the act of eating into a religious activity. It is precisely because one cannot eat absolutely anything that one is reminded of one's obligations before God. Rituals provide the disciplines that protect the person from evil.

Some contemporary commentators believe that ritual is the key to the moral life. The Chief Rabbi of the United Hebrew Congregations of the British Commonwealth, Dr. Jonathan Sacks, has made this a central theme of his work. He writes, "Without holy times, there is no framework or architecture of time, merely the rush and press of random events. A civilisation needs its pauses, its intervals, its chapter-breaks if it is to be a civilisation at all" (Sacks, 1995:128). In short, families, communities, and nations all need those vital pauses that enable one to think about life in the bigger perspective.

It is the habitual nature of ritual that makes it so helpful in supporting morality. For Sacks, the social ecology of a culture will break down once everyone starts to think consciously about the appropriate course of action. Telling lies, stealing, and seducing someone who is married should be unthinkable acts. The life lived in the context of constant reminders of God—through prayer, observing dietary obligations, keeping Shabbat—will be a life that will exclude the very possibility of behaving in ways that are inappropriate. Because our God-consciousness is heightened, so our opportunities to misbehave will be reduced.

D. Medical Ethics

The fourth area of widespread ethical agreement is in the area of medical ethics. Most religious traditions stress the centrality and importance of the human person. The sanctity of human life is considered a virtual absolute. This is not to say that under no conditions may human life be taken; most religious traditions have very ambivalent attitudes to war or capital punishment. But human life is given a special status in ethical reflection.

For Roman Catholics, the sanctity of human life is a theme of *Evangelium Vitae* (The Gospel of Life). Pope John Paul II reiterates the teaching that human life begins at conception; and the deliberate killing of the unborn is murder. He talks about a "culture of death," one in which the unborn are disposed of because they are inconvenient, the elderly are under threat of euthanasia because of a growing anxiety about resources involved in keeping them alive, and even capital punishment, although permitted, is very problematic.

Although most religious traditions are sympathetic to these Roman Catholic positions, there is a little bit more flexibility. Most are opposed to abortion, although they do not necessarily talk about the sacredness of human life from conception. Judaism has always been clear that the viability of the fetus is important in determining its status. If the fetus is clearly able to survive outside the womb, then it would be murder. However, if that is not the case, then the situation is more complicated. Certainly if the mother's life is in danger, then abortion is permitted. Hassan Hathout in *Islamic Perspectives in Obstetrics and Gynaecology* takes a similar line. He writes, "All jurists of all sects unanimously agree that abortion after sixteen weeks is a grave and punishable sin. A small minority showed leniency before sixteen weeks, and a small minority showed leniency before seven weeks" (Hathout, 1986:69).

For Hinduism, the fetus is covered by the ideal of ahimsa (noninjury). You should reverence all life, including the young and unborn. Likewise, one of the five precepts in Buddhism is that one should not kill

and this is normally considered to extend to the unborn. The same principles also operate at the other end of life. Although death is not feared, it is not to be anticipated either. The gift like quality of human life (a gift from God) means that one should not refuse the gift before it is time to do so.

III. DIFFERING ETHICAL OUTLOOKS

Having briefly examined certain areas of agreement, it is now necessary to turn to those areas that provoke disagreement. It will not come as a surprise to discover that there are many such areas. However, for the purposes of this article, I shall examine four such areas.

A. The Significance of the Individual

In the early Buddhist texts one finds the Buddha depicted as a person who discovered the way and can show others how they must obtain the way for themselves. In this respect, at least, Therevada Buddhism is individualistic. Although it is good to be part of the Sangha (the community), it is not essential. It is possible to be lay and make significant progress to Enlightenment (see Gombrich, 1988:72-8). In this respect it resembles certain strands of protestantism, which stress the importance of individual salvation and how unnecessary intermediaries—in the form of priests—are.

Compare the central role being given to the individual with orthodox Judaism, one finds a completely different outlook. In the same way you cannot change your language, so you cannot change your Judaism. It is just part of you. A similar sense is found in Hinduism. With all the givens of birth—the family, occupation, and location—come all the givens of your previous karmic lives. Islam is similar. Being a Muslim in private is impossible: the five pillars embrace a social dimension. You cannot give alms to the poor unless you are part of the community.

Many historians of ideas have noted how the Protestant concept of individual salvation was important for the growth of modern western democracy. It is as an individual becomes important *qua* individual that the whole concept of each individual having their own and equal say in their government becomes intelligible. With individualism comes romantic love, the entitlement to marry whomever one pleases, and an abhorrence of arranged marriages. With individualism comes a sense that one is entitled to pursue one's own aspirations rather than surrender these aspirations for the sake of duty or the community. Perhaps one of the reasons why Buddhism is so attractive to the West is this powerful individualist message.

B. Attitudes to the Environment and Ecology

Lynn White in his seminal article published in 1967 argued that it was the anthropocentricism of Christianity that is largely responsible for the ecological crisis. He suggested that it was the doctrine that humans are created in the image of God that led to the privileged status of the human. If everything nonhuman is there for the use of humans, then there is no obligation to worry about exploitation and abuse of the environment.

It is true that humans have a higher status in Judaism, Christianity, and Islam. Every tradition gives the human a more significant role to some extent: for the main schools of Hinduism and Buddhism, the human is the only creature capable of cumulating more good or bad karma. However, many in the Green movement have found Buddhism especially, and to a lesser extent, Hinduism, an inspiration to their ecology. For both traditions tend to locate the human on a wider plane than the Judaeo-Christian tradition. Within the Judaeo-Christian tradition, the world started recently and apocalyptic expectations mean that the world is not expected to go on much longer. Each individual is a unique soul which has one life. While Hindus and Buddhists both work on a much bigger perspective: the world is ages old, possibly eternal, and it will continue for ages to come. Each individual has already lived many lives and, probably, has many more lives to come. With this outlook, the nonhuman world becomes much more important. It is not temporary, but instead religiously significant.

Whether in practice one's metaphysical assumptions about the world actually makes a difference in the way you treat it is a moot point. Granted, the Christian West has bigger and better tools that can reap more destruction, but environmentalists have to admit that damaging the environment is a global phenomena, which is not unique to Christians.

C. Attitudes toward Wealth

Once again, although religious people disagree about the appropriate attitude toward wealth, it is a disagreement found both within traditions and across traditions. Judaism embodies the tension. The Deuteronomist (the writer of the book of Deuteronomy) strongly implies that those who are faithful in observing the Torah can expect material prosperity: "I call heaven and earth to witness against you this day, that I have set before you life and death, blessing and curse; therefore choose life, that you and your descendants may live, loving the LORD your God, obeying his voice, and cleaving to him; for that means life to you and length of days, that you may dwell in the land ..." (Deuteronomy 30:19-20). Although the Deuteronomist was not directly thinking of wealth, one can see how it led to an affirmation of wealth as sign of God's providence. However, the eighth-century prophets of Israel found themselves denouncing the rich because they exploited the poor. One strand celebrates wealth as a sign of God's favor, the other condemns it as a sign of exploitation.

The same tension is found in Christianity. In the teaching of Jesus, the prophetic strand dominates. And with the early Church expecting the imminent end of the world, then possessions were shared within the community (see Acts 4:32). The monastic tradition retained the same radical emphasis and suspicion of wealth.

In Hinduism, wealth is more clearly a sign of karmic good fortune, although of course the way one now uses that fortune is the test for the current life. To be wealthy and completely indifferent to suffering would bring bad karma upon one.

The Buddhist attitude is harder to succinctly summarize. The fifth aspect of the eightfold path (right livelihood) stresses the need to work appropriately and in a way compatible with the best quality of life. E. F. Schumacher (author of *Small is Beautiful*) saw in Burma an ideal which is called "Buddhist economics." Schumacher argued that the West sees the ideal for industrialists is "output without employees" while for employees it is "income without employment." Instead, Schumacher argues, "the Buddhist point of view takes the function of work to be least threefold: to give a man the chance to utilise and develop his faculties; to enable him to overcome his egocentredness by joining with other people in a common task; and to bring forth the goods and services needed for a becoming existence" (Schumacher, 1975:51).

At the heart of this disagreement between and within the world faiths is whether wealth and work are distractions from the greater task of salvation or enlightenment. Much depends on one's general attitude to the world and to life. For those more affirming of the world, wealth can be a legitimate delight within it; for those suspicious of the world, withdrawal from the temptations of wealth can be important.

IV. ETHICS AND LIBERAL RELIGIOUS OUTLOOKS

One of the interesting features of current religious debates is the way in which modernity has created alliances across traditional hostilities. With the rise of liberalism and related qualities such as toleration and feminism, we have seen the emergence of different forms of each religious tradition. In short, the situation now is that conservatives in each religious tradition have a great deal more in common with conservatives in other traditions than the liberals in their own.

Toleration has been a particular problem. Historically, religious traditions have been forced to find ways of coexisting in the same city and country. However, they did so with suspicion and fear. For Christians and Muslims, the commitment to the truth of their own divine revelation entailed an opposition to all those in error. Given that one's eternal destiny depended on being a Christian, then one can understand the hostility to those who would lead others to damnation. Islam has an explicit obligation to make sure that the "People of the Bank" (Jews and Christians) are free to worship; however, despite this, the desire to ensure that the young are not misled did lead to significant restrictions.

For the Eastern traditions, the history is more complex. Given the diversity of view within Hinduism, it is difficult to see how anything could be considered unacceptable within it. Hinduism has an amazing capacity to embrace a different tradition within its own rich story; so Jesus can become yet another guru or even an incarnation of Vishnu. Nevertheless, because Hinduism is tied up very closely with the aspirations of the people of India, it has found certain religions at certain times very problematic. Buddhism, as it spread into China and Japan, shared the Hindu capacity to find ways of including certain indigenous practices into its belief system. However, Buddhists too had moments when they saw another tradition as threatening and found it difficult to tolerate.

Thus, toleration is problematic. Most religious traditions justify it pragmatically. Once in power, most traditions find it difficult to resist the temptation to censor to some degree its rivals. It is the liberals in most traditions who make the theological adjustments and welcome a complementary viewpoint as intrinsically worthwhile.

A similar story can be seen in respect to feminism. Again, all religious traditions have strands and arguments that are opposed to patriarchy. Almost all the founders of most religious traditions are affirming of women. Mohammed insisted that women can inherit property and he denounced female infanticide (a common practice then) in the strongest possible terms. Jesus was happy to teach women and had women followers. The Buddha permitted women to join monastic communities and discover the way to Enlightenment. In all these cases the founders of these traditions seem to be at odds with the overwhelming patriarchy of the religion they founded.

Once again, it is the liberals in most traditions that are finding ways of addressing the concerns of contemporary feminism. Reform Judaism disagrees sharply with Orthodoxy over this question. The movement for the ordination of women priests remains one of the most divisive issues in Christendom. Comparable movements can be found in most religious traditions.

The overwhelming impression of most scholars of religion is that these two issues (toleration and feminism) determine whether one is basically liberal (i.e., willing to adapt the tradition to a changing world) or conservative (inclined to see such change as a betrayal of the truth of the revelation). Not everyone would see this divide in these terms. The author of this article has argued elsewhere that toleration needs to be grounded in religion (see Markham, 1995). But it must be conceded, this is still a minority position.

V. RELIGION AND APPLIED ETHICS

In the concluding section of this article it is helpful to bring out some of the implications of the above discussion for applied ethics. Due to the limitations of space, two such areas will be examined. The first is business and the second is medicine.

A. Business

One's attitude to business is crucially determined by one's attitude to wealth. We have already seen how religious traditions divide over this issue: is it a blessing or a result of exploitation? However, it is no coincidence that many religious traditions are behind moves to encourage business ethics. Interestingly, many discussions of business ethics start by trying to justify being ethical in terms of it being good for business: it pays to be ethical, because the company is more likely to be respected and trusted and so on. Most religious believers would also want to add that it is intrinsically right to be honest and straight in one's dealings.

Because work is a human necessity, then, it is hardly surprising that most religious traditions encourage employment. For Judaism, Cohen writes, "The dignity of labour is upheld throughout the Talmudic literature. 'Great is work for it honours the workmen' (Ned 49b) is the keynote struck on this theme" (Cohen, 1949:192). However, the Talmud ensures that high ethical standards are expected of the employers and employees.

Christians inherited from Judaism this sense that work is important, despite the greater emphasis laid on the idea that work was part of God's punishment of Adam for sin. As with Judaism, the importance of justice and integrity has led to demanding expectations of employers and employees. Indeed, it this stress of justice that led much Roman Catholic social teaching to be suspicious of capitalism. It took a Polish Pope, deeply fearful of Communism, in his encyclical *Centesimus Annus* to unequivocally support the market as a better economic system than the alternatives. However, even here the Pope stresses the need to find mechanisms to enable the poor to share in the wealth of capitalism.

Islam has a positive attitude to business. After all, the prophet himself was undoubtedly involved in commercial activity. However, all commercial activities need to operate in a socially responsible way. For many years, Islamic political theorists saw Islam as the middle way between capitalism (an indifference to the suffering of the exploited) and communism (an inability to successfully create wealth). Since the demise of communism, it is no longer fashionable to talk in such terms, but it remains true that they feel unbridled capitalism is wrong.

One continuing problem for Islam is its opposition to usury. The problem arises because modern economies depend on those having money being able to lend it to make more and those needing money being able to borrow it from others. Many have examined the ways in which the oil-rich nations of the Middle East manage to combine this opposition to usury with the ways that investment opportunities are created and realized.

We have already noted how some talk about a Buddhism economics, one that celebrates work within an appropriate context of values and responsibility. It is interesting to see that on the business front, those strands of religion that affirm wealth creation and business agree that the important thing is to make sure business serves the whole community and not just the risk-takers.

B. Medical Discoveries

Perhaps the single most contentious area of applied ethics are all those surrounding medicine. On the whole contemporary religious reflection views medical tech-

nology with suspicion. This is hardly surprising, as religion likes to claim an expertise for God in the creating and developing of life. To discover that it is now possible to create clones of sheep or bring a sperm and ovum together to conceive life in a test tube seems very threatening.

Yet given this general suspicion it is interesting to discover significant exceptions. Hassan Hathout works carefully through the Qur'an and brings out the implications for reproduction. He writes, "Attempts to cure infertility are therefore not only permissible, but are even a duty so that a couple may contribute to the preservation of the race and supplying society with useful human elements to take their place in the future generation" (Hathout, 1986:127). This means in practice that artificial insemination by husband and *in-vitro* fertilization are acceptable, provided it is within marriage and involves no donor sperm, while surrogacy is not. Compare this fairly nuanced position with the blanket condemnation by Pope John Paul II in *Evangelium Vitae:* "This moral condemnation also regards procedures that exploit living human embryos and foetuses—sometimes specifically 'produced' for this purpose by *in vitro* fertilisation—either to be used as 'biological material' or as *providers of organs or tissue for transplants* in the treatment of certain diseases. The killing of innocent human creatures, even if carried out to help others, constitutes an absolutely unacceptable act." (Pope John Paul II, 1995:113f).

Generally, most religious traditions are unhappy about many of these medical technological developments. Religious people are unhappy with the possible implications of these developments. Are we slowly realizing Huxley's vision of a "brave new world"?

VI. CONCLUSIONS

Throughout this article the complex relations between religion and ethics have been stressed. The orthodox (i.e., traditional) form of each religious tradition shares the same methodology, and certain shared themes. Positively, one finds an emphasis upon love and the family; negatively, one finds a stress on patriarchy and intolerance. In the realm of applied ethics, one finds that religion has two effects: first, it tends to be conservative, so many technological developments are viewed as problematic; second, it is often very demanding, so in business it wants the highest ethical standards of behavior by employers and employees.

Perhaps the most significant contribution a religious ethic makes to contemporary debate is the challenge to an age dominated by relativist and secular assumptions. Given that the majority of people, both historically and today, are religious, this could prove to be a very significant difference.

Also See the Following Articles

BIOETHICS • BUSINESS ETHICS • THEORIES OF ETHICS, OVERVIEW

Bibliography

Carmody, D., & Carmody, J. *How to live well: ethics in the world religions*. Belmont: Wadsworth Publishing Co.

Cohen, A. (1949). *Everyman's Talmud*. New York: Schocken Books.

Cupitt, D. (1988). *A new Christian ethic*. London: SCM Press.

Dawkins, R. (1976). *The selfish gene*. (Oxford: Oxford University Press.

Durkheim, E. (1915). *The elementary forms of the religious life*. London: George Allen and Unwin.

Gombrich, R. (1988). *Theravada Buddhism*. London: Routledge.

Green, R. M. (1988). *Religion and moral reason*. Oxford: Oxford University Press.

Hathout, H. (1986). *Islamic perspectives in obstetrics and gynaecology*. Islamic Organizations for Medical Sciences.

Hick, J. (1989). *An interpretation of religion*. London: Macmillan Press.

Holm, J., & Bowker, J. (1994). *Making moral decisions*. London: Pinter Publishers.

Kung, H. (1991). *Global responsibility*. London: SCM Press.

Kierkegaard, S. (1983). *In fear and trembling. Repetition*. (H. V. Hong, Ed.). Princeton: Princeton University Press.

Lewis, C. S. (1970). *Mere Christianity*. London: Fontana.

Markham, I. (1996). *A world religions reader*. Oxford: Blackwell Publishing.

Markham, I. (Ed.). (1994). *Plurality and Christian ethics*. Cambridge: Cambridge University Press.

Pope John Paul II. (1991). *Centesimus Annus*. London: Catholic Truth Society.

Pope John Paul II. (1993). *Veritatis Splendor*. London: Catholic Truth Society.

Pope John Paul II. (1995). *Evangelium Vitae*. London: Catholic Truth Society.

Sacks, J. (1991). *The persistence of faith*. London: Weidenfeld and Nicolson.

Sacks, J. (1995). *Faith in the future*. London: Darton Longman and Todd.

Schumacher, E. F. (1975). *Small is beautiful*. New York: Harper and Row.

Ward, K. (1994). *Religion and revelation*. Oxford: Oxford University Press.

White, L. (1967, March 10). The historical roots of our ecologic crisis. *Science 155*, No. 3767.

Zaehner, R. C. (1966). *Hinduism*. Oxford: Oxford University Press.

RELIGION IN SCHOOLS

*Mairi Levitt and †Gaynor Pollard
*University of Central Lancashire †University College Chester

GLOSSARY

child-centered Describing education that begins with the child's own life experiences, taking account of moral and faith development theories.

confessional Instructing in one religious tradition with the aim of nurturing agreed upon beliefs, values, and practices.

ethos The values, attitudes, and relationships that shape the character of a school and are evident in daily practice and in the physical environment.

experiential Describing a classroom methodology that aims to recreate, as far as is possible the believer's experience in order to facilitate personal reflection and to develop an empathetic response.

implicit Describing an approach that aims to assist the child in a personal search for meaning in life and therefore focuses on experience and insight rather than information about religious phenomena.

multifaith religious education Education that allows the study of a variety of faith traditions, either discretely or thematically, using common areas and aiming to promote knowledge and understanding without necessarily suspending belief.

neoconfessional Describing an approach that takes into account the children's interests and stage of psychological/moral development in order to make religious education more relevant to them in content and methods, while still holding to the aim of inculcating one religious tradition.

phenomenological Describing an approach that aims to study the phenomenon of religion in an objective way in order to increase knowledge and understanding of religions, suspending commitment to any particular tradition. Also known as an explicit approach.

school worship Corporate worship for all pupils as a daily practice, either denominational, broadly Christian, or inclusive of a variety of faith positions.

secularization The separation of human experience into categories of secular and sacred, evident in industrial societies. It is assumed to be associated with modernization, where religious authority has become increasingly marginalized and fragmented.

spirituality The human desire to reach that which is outside the ordinary and everyday, and which may be located in a god.

voluntary schools Schools normally connected with religious foundations and reflecting their foundation in ethos, religious education, and worship.

RELIGIOUS EDUCATION (RE) IN SCHOOLS is one of the largest enterprises in applied ethics. The particular

TABLE I

Four Models of Religion in Schools

1. Religious education and worship excluded from schools
2. Religious teaching available as an option in some schools
3. Religious education as part of the curriculum
4. Religious education and worship as part of the curriculum

values it seeks to convey depend upon its social context; these might include the nurture of young Catholics or Muslims, helping young people in their personal search for meaning, or the development of empathy and tolerance in a multifaith society. In societies with competing ethical systems which define themselves in opposition to each other, the teaching of values through religious education is itself problematic and, as seen in the four models in Table I, has been tackled in different ways.

I. THE ETHOS OF SCHOOLS AS PURVEYORS OF CULTURAL TRUTHS AND VALUES

The place of religion in schools cannot be understood in isolation from the place of religion in the wider society. Despite the association of industrialization with secularization, the end of the 20th century has seen not only the persistence of varying degrees of religious expression but also the rise of religious fundamentalisms. In the face of this situation it is difficult to maintain the view that a purely secular education is possible. One of the tasks of the education system is to socialize the young into the values of society, and religion is a major vehicle by which those values are conveyed. Discussion of dominant values must take into account postmodernist influences, the collapse of grand narratives (religious or secular), and the fragmentation of value systems.

Within the school system religion will operate in a variety of value bases. Since religion is present in particular social conditions it is impossible to isolate some "pure" form of religion unconnected to the political, cultural, and economic spheres. Robinson Crusoe was alone on a desert island but the form of Christianity he took with him was a product of his previous life and influenced his actions in his new one. Religious attitudes may affect all curriculum subjects, where claims are made for truths or values. This has been particularly evident in some North American states, where believers in a Biblically based six-day creation

scheme have successfully opposed the teaching of evolutionary theories in science. In the United Kingdom, some Christian groups have successfully campaigned for the removal from local school libraries of children's literature that is based on witchcraft and have protested against the teaching of Halloween. However, religion in schools manifests itself primarily through school ethos and religious education. School ethos is produced by the attitudes of the school staff and parents toward the purposes of education. The dominant value base will produce the ethos of the school and will affect the whole of the child's education. Table II lists possible value bases.

Education systems are subject to the demands of industry and commerce for workers with particular skills and attitudes to meet future *economic* needs. Protestant Christianity has been associated with the origins of the work ethic, the duty to work within one's calling however humble. In a modern school system, schools with an ethos based on preparing children for the world of work will aim to instil appropriate values through a relevant curriculum with some input from industrial advisors, links with local employers, and work experience.

The selection of curriculum content will be dependent upon what is perceived to be of value to *cultural* heritage and development. In Western countries this is often derived from a Christian past, but may also include elements from minority traditions. Any subject matter which retains its link with the past is bound to include a substantial element of religious influence, since religious beliefs were the starting point for attempts to make sense of or to celebrate the world in past generations. Religions are manifest in particular cultural settings so it is, of course, difficult to separate out these elements. For religions that are in a minority the cultural basis will be particularly important as they

TABLE II

Possible Value Bases

Value base	Aims of the school system
Economic	To meet future economic needs
Cultural	To pass on a cultural tradition to the next generation
Nationalistic	To establish and develop a sense of nationhood
Individualistic	To develop individuals according to their potential, which may involve selection
Egalitarian	To facilitate social mixing and cooperative practices
Conformist	To produce good citizens with traditional values

seek to pass on cultural and religious traditions to the next generation. In Finland's senior secondary schools the course for the Lutheran majority states first that religion is studied as a global human phenomenon, whereas the course for the Greek Orthodox minority states its purpose as educating students to become active members of the church and Finnish society, taking into account the community nature of the Orthodox churches and parishes (National Board of Education, 1994. *Framework Curriculum for the Senior Secondary School*. Helsinki). In those countries which exclude religion from the school system, i.e., the USA and Albania, there are other vehicles for the transmission of cultural values which are beyond the scope of this article.

A *nationalistic* value base aims to establish and develop a sense of nationhood. Religion has been recognized as providing an element of social cement which will enable diverse communities and individuals to identify with the larger grouping of the nation state. This identification will often be at the expense of minority religions, who may find themselves excluded from national identity.

Individualistic values schools aim to develop individuals according to their potential, which may involve selection of pupils according to ability or interests. One element of personal potential is the capability for spiritual development. Although this need not be religious, it would certainly include religion. The United Nations Convention on the Rights of the Child 1989 Article 17 includes the right of all children to access to information and material from a diversity of national and international sources, especially those aimed at the promotion of his or her social, spiritual, and moral well-being and physical and mental health.

An *egalitarian* ethos emphasizes the equality of human beings, a basic tenet of major world religions. Religious traditions, although tending to support hierarchies and sometimes to provide institutional backing and authority for discrimination, have also provided a literature and tradition on how to accomplish cooperation. An aim for religious education taken from a 1989 syllabus used in all schools in one area of England could be called egalitarian: "... [to create in pupils] a capacity for tolerance and empathy, to enable them to live with people of different ways of life, without feeling threatened; to remove sources of racial, religious and social conflict" (Cornwall Education Committee, 1989. *Syllabus for Religious Education in Cornwall*. p. 7).

Religious education can therefore contribute to creating good citizens in this way; however, it has also been a vehicle for instilling *conformist* values through the identification of individuals with a particular religious tradition. This identification involves shared language, often derived from a sacred text, agreed ways of looking at the world, and a shared moral code.

> Never has there been a greater need for an assertion, an improvement and re-establishment of religious education in schools. There is considerable violence not only at football matches but in many other areas. One in three of the population is convicted of a criminal offence by the age of 28. Families are under great stress with the breakdown of one in three marriages. (UK Conservative member of parliament in 1988 debate on RE in schools. Levitt, 1996. p. 35.)

The assumption running through this comment is that morality can and should be taught through religion (and even that that is the *only* way it can be taught). Religious education is seen as acting in a straightforward, direct way to improve standards of behavior in society and ensure that children know the difference between right and wrong.

II. THE PRACTICE OF RELIGIOUS EDUCATION IN SCHOOLS

A. Confessional Religious Education

The practice in most European countries has been to provide confessional religious education either throughout the school system with clergy or approved lay people invited in to teach or in separate schools funded wholly or in part by the state. In the former communist countries, where religious education was forbidden in school, it is now being introduced, for example, in Hungary, Bulgaria, Georgia, and eastern Germany. The particular faith, or faiths, which are confessed will depend on the religious map of the country; thus Turkey provides Islamic education (compulsory since 1982) and the Republic of Ireland provides Roman Catholic or Protestant teaching. In most cases of confessional religious education the school takes on the role of a church, mosque, or synagogue and teaches a religion as true, in order to strengthen and develop the child's faith. The teacher's role is then to nurture the child in the faith. Whereas in other school subjects the emphasis may be on the teaching of skills and acquiring of knowledge in preparation for examinations, the success of religious teaching of this type would be measured by the way the child lives or her future life rather than by qualifications or knowledge. The following quotations, from different cultures and about 40 years apart, illustrate confessional aims for school RE.

> [An aim for primary RE in Greece is] the reinforcement of trust in the Christian religion and the strengthening of children's active participation in the religious life of our nation. (G. Tsakalis, 1993. *Br. J. Religious Education* 15(2), 29)

> To teach Christianity to our children is to inspire them with the vision of the glory of God in the face of Jesus Christ, and to send them out into the world willing to follow Him. ... (1951 RE syllabus from Cambridgeshire, England)

The teaching of confessional religious education defined in these ways depends upon a supply of teachers committed to the faith which is to be taught, or an availability of clergy or skilled lay people, and support from the school community as a whole. While voluntary schools could teach a religion as a living faith, with worship at its center, other schools do not have a religious foundation and cannot assume that all teachers will practice a religion themselves. Confessional RE may then become a series of "facts" about a religion which can be taught with more or less conviction.

B. Neoconfessional Religious Education

Modern versions of confessional RE take account of changes in educational theory and practice which put more emphasis on the needs and capacities of the child. The influence of research on children's religious development has particularly altered the approach with younger children where it was felt that too much had been taught too soon. Instead religion must be relevant to the child. With younger children it might be taught through cross-curricular themes, such as "light"; with older children it might begin with moral and social problems which they have encountered. Acts of religious worship may also be devised especially for the children in which they can take an active part.

Parallel developments in popular theology centered on John Robinson's *Honest to God*, published in 1963, which was based on his selection from the ideas of Bultmann, Bonhoeffer, and Tillich. He proclaimed that Christianity must show it is "relevant" to modern people and the image of God as "out there" must go, "for I want God to be as real for our modern secular, scientific world as he ever was for the ages of faith" (1963. *The Honest to God Debate.* p. 279. S.C.M. Press, London.).

Critics of confessional RE label the approach "indoc-

trination" rather than "education." The approach of teachers committed to religious nurture sits uneasily in the compulsory school system in modern societies which in other areas stress the need to treat children as autonomous individuals who should be presented with choices. There are also practical and ethical problems in maintaining confessional RE in societies which are multicultural and multifaith. Children might be divided for religious education according to their parents' faith or divided into separate schools. Parents may also be able to withdraw their children from the subject. However, whatever arrangements are made, those from different religions (or none) have to coexist.

The provision of religious worship in school is rare and depends upon the relationship between the state and religious communities. Daily worship is compulsory in *all* state schools only in Britain, where there is a parental right to withdraw children. Worship is an expression of personal faith and might be regarded as a natural extension of religious education in schools which have children from the same faith background. However, apart from some voluntary schools, almost all schools have children from a variety of religious traditions or none, making the organization of school worship a challenging task. The revised 1988 legislation which applies to England and Wales states that collective worship should be "mainly or wholly of a broadly Christian character," and the 1994 guidelines state that it "should be concerned with reverence or veneration paid to a divine being or power." Schools may apply for the requirement for mainly Christian worship to be lifted for the whole school or certain pupils, but only a small minority have done so. In practice school worship is an accepted part of education and enjoys high levels of parental support, even though only around 16% of the adult population attend a religious service at least two or three times a month, a lower proportion than that in the USA or Ireland. Among headteachers and religious leaders, including Christians, it is less popular. Headteachers are mainly concerned with the problems of organizing and leading worship on a daily basis, whereas Christian leaders have been concerned that state schools cannot be expected to provide worship with integrity, which might have a negative affect on pupils' attitude toward all religious worship.

C. Phenomenological Religious Education

This approach depends on a distinction being made between seeking to convert children to a faith and giving them knowledge and understanding of faith. A Church of England Commission on religious education clearly separated the task of the Church from that of the ordinary school: "To press for acceptance of a particular faith or belief system is the duty and privilege of the Churches and other similar religious bodies. It is certainly not the task of a teacher in a county school" (Durham Commission, 1970 *The Fourth R.* p. 103. National Society and S.P.C.K., London.).

Instead, children were to learn about religions in an objective and nonjudgmental way to promote knowledge and understanding. The approach was seen as suitable for a situation where, even if the children in a particular school were not from different faiths, people were more aware of alternatives to Christianity and less certain that they were all in error. A good teacher of religious education needs the qualities of a good teacher rather than a personal belief. Teachers are expected to "bracket out" their personal beliefs in order to engage with a variety of faiths without prejudice. The teacher will therefore need knowledge and understanding of those faiths and the same degree of professionalism as in any other subject. Teachers using this approach are often keen to encourage pupils to take the subject in public examinations and to dispel the view that religious education is only useful for those aiming for ordination or the life of a religious follower.

Ninian Smart's writing on the dimensions of religion (ritual, mythological, doctrinal, ethical, social, and experimental) was influential in the phenomenological approach, both in schools and in the development of religious studies courses in universities (Smart, 1971 *The Religious Experience of Mankind.* Fontana Press, Glasgow.). This encouraged the thematic teaching of religions and avoided an approach that began by comparing other religions with Christianity. Texts for schools used themes, such as sacred writings and festivals, to present multifaith and multicultural materials.

This approach has a number of problems, including the sheer amount of information that could be put in a syllabus, the dangers of trivializing or distorting complex beliefs and practices, and the practicality and desirability of maintaining an open, nonjudgmental approach. At its worst this approach can lead to a superficial overview of a wide range of beliefs from animism to Bah'ai, taught by teachers who have not had the benefit of any academic study of these beliefs. An objective approach could lead to the view that it did not matter what anyone believed, rather than inviting pupils to take religion seriously, and might inhibit commitment to and participation in the life of faith. A common criticism of multifaith RE came from the Chief Rabbi in Britain: "... a touch of Christianity; a dash of Judaism; a slice of Islam; and so on through a fruit cocktail of

world faiths. ... In trying to teach all faiths it is possible that we succeed in teaching none" (Chief Rabbi Jonathan Sacks House of Lords Debate. Quoted in Levitt, 1996. p. 37.).

Supporters of a phenomenological multifaith approach have argued that it is a way to allow all children to study religion without compromising their own particular beliefs. However, the open/nonconfessional approach is not acceptable to all religious groups. In Britain some Muslims and Christians argue that younger children are confused when ideas are introduced which clash with their own faith and that teachers lack knowledge to teach each faith properly. To comply with the law in England and Wales, religious education syllabi, other than those for voluntary aided schools, must "reflect the fact that the religious traditions in Great Britain are in the main Christian whilst taking account of the teaching and practices of the other principal religions as they are represented in Great Britain." (*Education Reform Act,* 1988. p. 2044. H.M.S.O., London.) Thus wholly Christian religious education has been illegal, except in voluntary aided and private schools, since 1988, but nevertheless Christianity is privileged in terms of allocated curriculum time.

D. Experiential Religious Education

Phenomenological religious education, when striving to be objective, could become a dry description of religions in which children learn the five pillars of Islam and the four noble truths of Buddhism as they might learn about events in history. However, exponents of the approach argue that as well as being descriptive and objective, it should also be experiential. In the same way as a history teacher may try to help children feel what it was like to live in a previous age by visiting a historic house or reading a contemporary account, religious education teachers help children to experience living religion and what it means to those who practice it. The ideal way to experience a faith different from one's own might be to live for a time in another faith community, to observe and talk to members, and to take part. In practice teachers use methods of other subject areas to bring the topics alive—videos, visits, poetry, and personal accounts. A member of the relevant faith community might visit the classroom, after the teacher has done preparatory work with the children, and help them to enact a Christian marriage service or a Passover meal. The approach encourages children to be receptive to religious or spiritual experiences.

For those concerned about the effects on children of studying faiths other than their own, the experiential approach holds more dangers than other multifaith approaches. Children do not only study other religions as an academic subject but meet their members and participate in their rituals. Opponents fear that children will be confused by those alien rituals, or even be led away from their own faith and culture.

III. THE EDUCATIONAL SYSTEM AS A MEANS OF NATIONAL SELF-DEFINITION

A. Religious Education and Identity Formation

Among the many expectations of the purposes of religious education, one of the most controversial is its role in the formation of identity. Many denominational schools are popular with parents for their perceived role of inducting children into a Christian culture, a moral worldview, and an agreed identity. In 1992 David Pascall, the chairman of the National Curriculum Council for England and Wales, made the statement that, although we should be ready to acknowledge the "new perspectives and insights introduced into British society by immigrants," he would align himself unequivocally with those who spoke up for the idea of a "dominant culture." (Quoted by Halstead "The Final Frontier." *Times Higher Educational Supplement.* Dec. 18, 1992.). The dominant culture for the UK meant "the Christian faith, the Graeco-Roman influence, the Liberal Enlightenment, romanticism and the development of modern humanism." Many reacted strongly to the idea of a "dominant" culture, with its negative overtones of power and superiority. More recently the debate was extended by Nicholas Tate, chairman of the Schools Curriculum and Assessment Authority, who called on schools to teach "the best that has been known and thought" (Reported in *Times Higher Educational Supplement* Feb. 16, 1996.) He outlined four themes:

1. Pupils should not be encouraged to choose their own culture from an array of possibilities, which would reinforce the current sense of rootlessness
2. The school curriculum should be a force for continuity "as a basis for a living, changing tradition, not to preserve some fossilized version of the past"
3. Our sense of culture must be anchored in its classical roots, in European civilization, and in Christianity
4. We should aim to develop in young people a

sense that some works of art, music, literature, or architecture are more valuable than others

It is clear that religion in schools can be used as a means of asserting cultural identity, against minority cultures. This perspective contrasts with much of the teaching of religious education in British schools, where the emphasis is placed on the importance of devleoping empathy and tolerance across a range of beliefs.

The question of identity formation in religious education is perhaps felt most urgently in those Eastern European countries who have recently emerged from communist regimes, where religion was not part of the work of the school. The developing market economies have found that there is no shortage of religious groups from the West who wish to share their faith and will work in schools. Two models that are possibilities for these countries to consider are those represented by the British and French systems. In Britain the emphasis is on local loyalties and identification with the individual school. This includes the articulation of values; the corporate identity of the school expressed, for example, in the wearing of uniforms and representing the school in sports teams; and ensuring that religions represented in the school are included in acts of corporate worship and the religious education curriculum. Although parents have the right to withdraw their children from religious education and school worship, this right is rarely exercised. In France the emphasis is on national identity, represented in the national curriculum by the notion of *tous les petits francais* (all the young people of France). In contrast to Britain, where religion is believed to be an important part of identity formation, the French state system is completely secular, with the exception of Alsace. Where religion does appear, it is confined to voluntary or interconfessional schools, and parents may withdraw their children from this provision.

The debate about the role of religious education in identity formation is linked to the development of the understanding of the person. In modernist thinking education is about the establishment of the stable, integrated, individual personality, which may include religious faith. In postmodernist thought the possibility of identifying individual identity is challenged, given a situation where the individual subject is bombarded with a huge range of competing ideas, and education becomes a matter of identifying the processes that are needed in order to navigate through this information and remain open to further possibilities. In terms of religious education this means that an emphasis is laid on skills rather than on nurture in a particular manifestation of faith.

B. Religion as a Ground of Divisiveness

Those countries which choose to exclude religion from state schools often do so on the grounds that study in religions may produce conflict, and that the religious foundation of a school might divide communities. This is a particularly important rationale in the USA, which has a strong commitment to religious freedom in a multiethnic and multireligious society. A country that has taken a different stance in Northern Ireland, with communities engaged in long-term religious and political conflict. Attempts to found joint Protestant–Catholic schools have been applauded on the grounds of community building and are regarded as initiatives for peace.

Despite the limited success of the Northern Ireland initiative there remains a feeling of urgency about the resolution of religious conflict within and between communities and countries. An increased awareness of religious plurality has made the process of working out various strategies to enable different groups to live together peacefully an ethical necessity. The Roman Catholic theologian Hans Kung has embarked upon a project to address the issue of world peace by attempting to work for peace between religious groups by means of education. His project involves collecting information and interpretations of world faiths and making them available to all. This rationale has been actively pursued in schools in the United Kingdom for some time. There are also indications that other European countries are regarding this work as central to their religious education. The philosophy underlying this political agenda means that religious education moves from a primarily confessional base to one that owes more to the sociology of religion. Personal religious views and privileged truths are subsumed to the task of attempting social harmony. The fact that religious education varies from country to country and from region to region more than any other academic subject indicates that it is dealing with issues that touch raw nerves. Multifaith religious education is an attempt to work with pluralism and difference rather than to combat a multiplicity of religious truths by nurture in one. Such education incorporates the skills of dialogue and conflict resolution, and promotes imaginative visions of peaceful societies. One of the difficulties it must overcome is the deeply felt beliefs of those who hold that the study of a religious tradition outside their own compromises their own faith and dilutes commitment. A central question remains as to whether religious freedom, so dearly prized in the West, includes the freedom to withhold education in a variety of traditions, and whether the best way of deal-

ing with the problem is to remove religion from schools altogether.

Another complication is the question of worship in state schools. In England and Wales, where daily worship is a legal requirement, there are those who believe that such an activity is an anachronism which allows Christianity a privileged position and alienates those of other faiths or none. Many children are required to be present at an activity which is outside their experience and commitment. To balance these objections, there is strong evidence that parents believe that the daily act of worship plays a role in the moral development of the child and, far from causing division, actually enables community values and solidarity to be expressed and celebrated.

IV. CONCLUSION

Despite predictions that the process of secularization would reduce the significance of religion into the 21st, there seems much evidence to the contrary. Nurturing children and young people in a religious faith and taking account of a spiritual dimension of life retain an important place in the minds of parents, and continue to press claims on school curricula. The desire to provide religious education in school and to retain the freedom to nurture in a religious faith in voluntary schools appears to have little to do with the worshipping habits of parents.

The issue of whether the state should provide a religious education is particularly urgent in those Eastern European countries recently emerging from a communist policital order. The former Soviet country of Georgia, among others, is already seeking curriculum guidance from religious educationalists in the United Kingdom in order to reestablish the subject on the curriculum.

A long as religious education is represented on the curriculum of schools it will remain a significant force for the delivery of moral education. Many children encounter their first formal ethical teaching in the context of religious frameworks, and continue to relate moral issues to the worldviews of religious systems, even when they have abandoned personal religious faith. No examination of ethical thinking can afford to ignore the influence of religion in school and its role in forming opinion on ethical issues.

Also See the Following Articles

ETHICS EDUCATION IN SCHOOLS • MORAL DEVELOPMENT • PLURALISM IN EDUCATION • RELIGION AND ETHICS

Bibliography

Cooling, T. (1994). *A Christian Vision for State Education.* S.P.C.K., London.

Francis, L., and William, K. (1995). *Teenage Religion and Values.* Gracewing, Leominster, England.

Grimmitt, M. (1987). *Religious Education and Human Development.* McCrimmon, Great Wakering, Essex.

Hammond, J. (1990). *New Methods in RE Teaching. An Experiential Approach.* Oliver & Boyd, Edinburgh.

Levitt, M. (1996). *Nice When They Are Young: Contemporary Christianity in Families and Schools.* Ashgate, England/Vermont.

Spinder, H. (Ed) (1992). *RE in Europe. A Guide to the Position of Religious Education in 15 European Countries,* 2nd ed. Inter-European Commission on Church and School, Münster, Germany.

Watson, B. (1993). *The Effective Teaching of Religious Education.* Longman, London.

REPRODUCTIVE TECHNOLOGIES, OVERVIEW

Lucy Frith
The University of Liverpool

I. The Arguments for Reproductive Technologies
II. The Arguments against Reproductive Technologies
III. Particular Ethical Problems
IV. Conclusion

GLOSSARY

artificial reproductive technology (ART) A generic term for techniques that artificially assist conception, such as IVF and GIFT.

clinical pregnancy The ultrasound evidence of a fetal heart beat.

donor insemination (DI) The insemination of a woman by donor sperm.

egg retrieval Successful egg collection procedure, used in the IVF procedure.

embryo A fertilized egg that is between two and eight weeks of development.

embryo transfer Transfer of embryos to the uterus from the petri dish (where fertilization has taken place).

gamete The male sperm or the female egg.

gamete intrafallopian transfer (GIFT) A process in which sperm and eggs are mixed together and transferred to one or both of the woman's fallopian tubes, where fertilization takes place.

Human Fertilization and Embryology Authority

(HFEA) A body set up in the United Kingdom by the Human Fertilization and Embryology Act 1990, to oversee and regulate new developments in ART.

in vitro fertilization (IVF) A process in which sperm and eggs are collected by egg retrieval and mixed in a petri dish, where fertilization takes place, and then the embryo(s) are placed in the uterus.

oocyte An unfertilized ovum.

ARTIFICIAL REPRODUCTIVE TECHNOLOGIES (ARTs) have given urgency to questions that have always perplexed humanity, such as the reasons for wanting children, the implications of infertility, what it means to be a parent, and the strength of the genetic bond between people. In 1978 scientific developments in embryology and embryo transfer culminated in the birth of the world's first baby born as a result of IVF in Britain. This event prompted extensive ethical debate over the acceptability of ART, with opinions ranging from whole-hearted support to condemnation. The issues raised fall into two categories: arguments for and against the use and development of ART and the ethical dilemmas created by specific aspects of ART. The discussion will focus on the Anglo-American debate over ART, recognizing that these debates have taken different forms in other countries.

I. THE ARGUMENTS FOR REPRODUCTIVE TECHNOLOGIES

A. Helping the Infertile

Artificial reproductive technologies are often portrayed as a response to the needs of the infertile (approximately 1 in 10 couples, although figures vary). Being unable to have a child can be a significant problem that affects an individual's most important choices about the type of life they wish to live. The frustration of this desire is thought to cause immense suffering, and medical science has responded by developing techniques designed to alleviate infertility. This poses the question as to why the infertile should be helped. On what basis should the infertile have their desire for a child met? There are three main justifications for the claim that the infertile should be helped.

1. Infertility Is a Disease

The first justification for helping the infertile is that infertility is the kind of condition that merits medical treatment. Robert Winston, a British fertility specialist, said, "Infertility is actually a terrible disease affecting our sexuality and well-being." This position appeals to a particular definition of what it means to be healthy. If health is defined as the optimal physical functioning of an organism then it could be argued that if infertility is caused by some form of physical malfunction then this should be treated. A wider definition of health could be employed to support the claim that infertility is a disease such as the World Health Organization's (WHO) definition, that health is a complete sense of well-being. It could be argued that infertility treatments are enabling the infertile to function as fully healthy individuals and should be part of health care provision. Conversely, it could be said that infertility cannot be characterized as a disease itself; rather, it is the effect of other conditions, such as fallopian tubal blockage. Infertility treatments do not "treat" infertility, they only ameliorate the effects of other conditions. Nevertheless, many established medical treatments fall into this category, for instance, diabetes is not treated but its unpleasant side-effects are managed, so this in itself does not constitute an argument against the merits of medical treatment for infertility.

2. The Desire for a Child

One of the problems with the WHO's definition of health is that it could include within the health remit anything that contributes to an individual's well-being (and this could mean that we are obliged to provide video recorders, racing bikes, or anything else that enables people to have a complete sense of well-being). Hence, it is necessary to have some mechanism for distinguishing between wants and, more importantly, needs. Leaving aside the problem of what might constitute a distinction between health and social needs (such as welfare benefits), those who are building a case for the importance of helping the infertile need to have an argument to support the claim that having a child is a need rather than a want.

The argument that is often used to support this claim is that humans have a biological imperative to reproduce. Professor Edwards, who was the doctor involved in the birth of the first IVF baby, considers that the genetic pressures to have children are the very foundation of our nature and that it is such pressures which lie at the heart of most couples' desire for children. By seeing the desire to have children as biologically based, proponents of this view argue that it is a desire that cannot be changed, because it is innate, or at the very least cannot be substantially altered. Thus, in order for people to live fulfilled lives they must have certain basic needs satisfied, and having children is one such need.

3. The Right to Reproduce

The final reason for helping the infertile builds on the previous argument and contends that the infertile have the same right to reproduce as the fertile do. This is an area of debate that has been changed radically by the scientific development of ARTs. The right to reproduce, free from interference is generally viewed as a basic human right. Enshrined in many declarations of human rights is the right of "men and women of full age.... to marry and found a family." (United Nations Declaration of Human Rights). Article 8 of the European Convention on Human Rights states: "everyone has the right to respect for his private and family life." The U.S. Supreme Court has on various occasions supported procreative liberty and has upheld the protection of those within marriage to found a family.

These articles and rulings are usually understood as stipulating what can be called a negative right, that is, a right not to have one's reproductive capacities interfered with against one's will. This negative right is a right to be free from unwarranted interference from the state (or anyone else seeking to impede a couple's reproductive capacities). Such articles were formulated with prohibitive policies in mind, such as enforced sterilizations or the prevention of interracial marriage.

The infertile, however, in order to exercise their freedom and therefore their right to reproduce need some assistance. This assistance should be forthcoming as a couple's interest in reproduction is, arguably, the same no matter how reproduction takes place. "The values and interests underlying a right of coital reproduction are the same, no matter how reproduction occurs. [Such values] strongly suggest a married couple's right to noncoital reproduction as well and, arguably, to have the assistance of donors and surrogates, as needed" ((1994). The Ethical Considerations of the New Reproductive Technologies. Report of the Ethics Committee of the American Fertility Society (ECAFS)). Accordingly, the infertile have to rely on some notion of positive rights that places an obligation on others to provide them with the means they need to reproduce. This raises the question of whether there is a link between the technical possibility of something (in this case a medical technique) and the right to have the resources made available to enable access to that technique.

John Robertson puts forward a rights-based argument to support the extended use of ARTs but not, however, any positive measures that would ensure equal access to such technologies. He begins by arguing that the concept of procreative liberty should be given primacy when making policy decisions in this area. Procreative liberty is the freedom to decide whether or not to reproduce. At first sight this appears to be a negative right not to have one's reproductive capacities interfered with. However, Robertson endorses subsidiary enabling rights to procreation, that is, someone has the right to something if it can be regarded as a prerequisite for procreation. For the infertile ART would be a necessary prerequisite to enable them to have children and hence they have a right to such treatment. This effectively turns a negative right (not to be interfered with) into a positive right (to have something made available to one). This enables the infertile to exercise their reproductive rights and could be said to redress the disparity between the infertile and the fertile.

B. Reproductive Choice

ARTs broaden the range of reproductive options that are available for both the infertile and, in certain circumstances, the fertile. Any extension of choice is frequently portrayed as desirable and this is just as true for reproductive choices. To extend the reproductive choice of the infertile can be viewed as a positive development. Having children is a desirable end for people to pursue and extending the availability of options to help them fulfill this end is correspondingly a desirable state of affairs. Here a distinction could be made between having children (which would include reproduction and bring-

ing up the children) and the right to reproduce, that could be fulfilled solely by allowing the infertile the means to reproduce, say, by donating their gametes. The infertile would wish to advance the claim that they should be able to have children and this includes, with ART, reproduction. In a letter to *The Lancet* Professor Edwards states, "It is impossible to put a price on the benefits to society of producing wanted children raised in a caring environment." Hence, ARTs are seen as mechanisms for extending people's reproductive choices and this is something that is beneficial both for the individual involved and society.

C. Genetic Screening

Another set of arguments in favor of ARTs are that such techniques can be used to screen for genetically inherited diseases and ensure that any child born is free from abnormality. Carl Wood, an Australian fertility specialist, stated, "It may be possible for the test-tube procedure to reduce the incidence of, or eliminate, certain defects from the population." Thus, ART could also be of use to those who are fertile but may carry some risk of transmitting a genetic disease. This justification for ART is based on a different set of arguments than those used to justify ART on the grounds of helping the infertile. There is the additional assumption that it is morally important to ensure that only perfectly healthy children or those free of a certain condition are born, on the grounds that we should avoid unnecessary suffering where we can.

Pre-implantation diagnosis is a technique that enables cells to be removed in vitro and tested to detect a genetic disorder. If the embryo is found to be defective then embryo transfer does not take place. This technique will have wider application in the future with the development of the human genome project, and this will make it possible to detect the genes for an increasing number of genetic disorders. ARTs thus enable genetic screening to take place at an earlier stage (before implantation) rather than when the pregnancy is already established, thereby avoiding the physical, emotional, and, some might argue, moral costs of terminating a pregnancy. If genetic screening is seen as desirable then it can be argued that it is preferable to carry it out as early as possible. It is also possible at this stage to determine the sex of the embryo. This can be useful when there is a danger of a sex-linked genetic disease and only embryos of the relevant gender are discarded rather than forgoing a pregnancy altogether.

D. Conclusion

Those who argue in favor of the use and development of ARTs claim that such techniques bring great benefit to the individuals involved, the infertile. Childlessness is seen as a great handicap and consequently treatment for infertility should be given a high priority. It can also be argued that ARTs are necessary to enable the infertile to exercise their fundamental human right to reproduce. Further, ARTs are heralded as providing benefits for society as a whole because these techniques can help prevent genetically inherited disease and advance scientific knowledge about the human reproductive system that could have, as yet, unforeseen benefits.

II. THE ARGUMENTS AGAINST REPRODUCTIVE TECHNOLOGIES

Some of the arguments against ART will be direct rejoinders to the above case for ART, and some of the arguments will raise different concerns.

A. Criticisms of the Case for Reproductive Technologies

1. Infertility Is Not a Disease

It has been argued that infertility is purely a social problem and one that does not need medical intervention. Couples could have counselling to come to terms with this inability, which is an inability to participate in social customs rather than any specific medical problem. Infertility is often seen as a problem for the couple, rather than the individual in the couple. This creates the problem of whether life-style choices, such as opting to form a relationship between the same sex and hence as a couple being unable to have children, can be seen as a case of genuine infertility when both individuals are perfectly able, physically, to produce children. More generally, infertility is a consequence of certain physical problems, such as blocked fallopian tubes. There is no specific condition of infertility itself that medicine can be called upon to cure. Hence, the problem of infertility is a response (to a situation) not a condition itself and such responses could be realigned. It is the effect of these physical problems that are detrimental in a society that purports to value children and the parental role, particularly for women. Thus, if medicine seeks a role in the treatment of infertility it could be said that this is medicalizing a problem that is predominantly social in origin. One of the difficulties with this view is that it is hard to distinguish clearly between social and medical problems as the two often have a complex and interactive relationship. The refutation of the claim that infertility is a disease rests heavily on the view one takes as to the importance of having children.

2. The Desire for Children Is Not Genetically Determined

Those who argue that ARTs provide a necessary and vital service for the infertile have often claimed that the desire for a child is biologically conditioned and is a central element for humans to flourish. In contrast to this the socially constructed nature of the desire for a child is advanced. Here it is the social pressure to reproduce that creates and determines the desire for a child. This view highlights the existence of pronatalism, an attitude or policy that encourages reproduction and promotes the role of parenthood. Pronatalism particularly affects women who are encouraged to become mothers. In a patriarchal society true femininity is often equated with childbearing, and motherhood is thereby regarded as a necessary aspect of womanhood.

Thus, having a child does not have to be a fundamental part of everyone's life. We can make individual choices over whether or not to have children and the importance reproduction will have in our lives. The way in which society pressures women to have children and the focus on genetic relationships can be said to be socially determined ways of constructing our reproductive relationships. It could be argued that we do not have to respond to such pressure to reproduce, and it is important to give women the freedom to have other life options that are equally valued and respected.

3. There Is No Positive Right to Reproduce

Robertson's claim that there should be subsidiary enabling rights to help the infertile reproduce, that there should be some form of positive right to reproduce, could clearly be problematic. Laura Purdy (a feminist philosopher) argues that Robertson adopts a position that blurs the distinction between negative and positive rights, "Robertson sees the right not to reproduce and the right to reproduce as two sides of the same coin. From this fact, he seems to infer that the strong right not to reproduce implies an equally strong right to reproduce and also that this strong right to reproduce provides as much support for assisted reproduction as for so-called natural reproduction." Embedded in this discussion of reproductive rights is the assumption, made by Robertson, that the issues raised by natural reproduction are similar to those raised by artificial reproduction. Christine Overall, a feminist critic of

ART, argues that the issues raised by the two different forms of reproduction are fundamentally different and correspondingly the right to use ART needs a different burden of proof, as ARTs might be harmful, from the right to be free from reproductive interference.

It can also be argued that Robertson's focus on procreative liberty could only be used to prevent legislation against ART, that would ensure the existence of access, rather than upholding any positive rights that could be used to actually enable access and hence make ART available to a greater number of couples.

It is not generally recognized that just because the means are available to achieve some end, people have a right to that means. There exist few positive rights to health care (and it might be objected that ARTs are not strictly health care measures) even of the life-saving nature. Hence, it is by no means clear that there is a good argument to support the claim that there should be a positive right to reproduce (that the infertile should have the means made available for them to reproduce) or what the practical (e.g., financial) implications of such a right would be.

4. Ethical Problems Raised by Genetic Screening

The claim that ART is of benefit to society because it can provide some sort of quality control over the type of children born is by no means accepted by all. Difficult ethical problems are raised, such as which genetic diseases should be identified by pre-implantation diagnosis and the extent to which it should be used.

The issue of genetic screening also has implications for recipients and donors of genetic material (eggs and sperm). The Human Fertilization and Embryology Authority (HFEA) has considered the potential problems raised by the increased use of screening for carrier status of genetic diseases. For instance, "People might not be willing to come forward as donors because they do not wish to be screened for genetic disorders" (HFEA, Annual Report, 1995). This could reduce the supply of gametes by curbing donations. This is a concern because gametes, particularly eggs, are already in short supply. There could also be the problem of those who do present themselves to become donors as they may find that they are carriers of some genetic disease creating, possibly, unforeseen devastating implications for them and their families.

B. The Feminist Position

It is important to be aware that feminists do not speak with one voice and not all feminists share the same views of ART. ARTs are important areas for feminist discussion as they directly effect the way some women reproduce and represent another medical involvement in women's lives.

1. Harm to Women

The central tenet of any feminist position is the concern for how ART will affect the individual woman and, at a general level, are these technologies harmful or beneficial to women as a group? One school of feminist thought represented by writers such as Gena Corea view ART as intrinsically harmful to women. ARTs are practices constructed by a patriarchal medical and technological establishment to further control and colonize women's bodies. It is emphasized that these technologies reinforce a biologically deterministic view of women that subordinates women's identity to their reproductive role, rather than seeing them as full human persons with a range of interests. It is the social context in which the technologies are developed that makes them inherently harmful to woman. Hence, ARTs are not benign techniques that could possibly be harmful to women; instead, they are deliberately constructed mechanisms of control.

This view has been criticized by supporters of other schools of feminist thought, such as Michelle Stanworth, who see ARTs as benign technologies, that could be used inappropriately but are not inherently harmful to women. The crucial issue for this school of thought is that ARTs are adequately controlled, so that regulatory structures ensure that women are protected from abuse and exploitation. This view stresses that ART should operate in an ethical framework, one that recognizes the potential harms to women (and seeks to minimize them) and ensures that women are adequately informed as to the possible risks and side effects of ARTs.

In order for ART to be carried out in an ethically acceptable way women must be fully informed as to the exact nature of the procedures and possible outcomes. One area that has been heavily criticized is the misrepresentation of the success rates of IVF. It is claimed that women are not given accurate information as to the likelihood of achieving a successful pregnancy and consequently have not given fully informed consent to the procedure.

The overall success rates for IVF treatment are still relatively low. Any couple receiving IVF will have had a history of infertility and will have been trying for some time to have a child. Once accepted on the IVF program there is no guarantee that a pregnancy will be achieved. In the United Kingdom, due to the HFEA, national information is available that gives an approximate indication of general success rates. In 1993 out of 21,823 treatment cycles, there were 3921 clinical pregnancies and 3089 live births. Per treatment cycle there is an 18% clinical pregnancy rate and a 14.2% live birth rate (HFEA, Annual Report, 1995).

Due to the low success rates it has been argued that IVF cannot be seen as a therapeutic procedure but rather as an area of research (see R. Rowland (1993). *Living Laboratories: Women & Reproductive Technology*. London: Cedar). This raises the question of whether it is ethically justified to offer IVF to women as a therapeutic procedure when they are more accurately taking part in a research project. In order to answer this question it is necessary to come to some decision over what is an acceptable success rate, i.e, when is a success rate so low that the technique should still be considered to be at the research stage? The success rate of IVF could be compared to natural conception rates (approximately 25%) and, arguably, in the light of this the rates are not so low.

It is important that women are given correct information about the success rates and possible risks of the procedure (such as hyperstimulation syndrome and long-term effects of the superovulatory drugs used). Then women will be able to make up their own minds as to whether they wish to undergo a painful and invasive procedure and the level of risk and discomfort they are prepared to accept. If fully informed consent is given then the woman's autonomy has been respected. If IVF is the only way a woman might be able to have a child she may be prepared to undergo the procedure even though the success rate is low, as any percentage of success with IVF is greater than the zero success rate of not having the procedure.

2. Reproductive Choice

While some feminists argue that the existence of ART extends women's procreative choices as women are free to choose another set of options, others argue that women do not freely choose to use these procedures but are responding to pressure that is exerted by society and particularly by partners. The overriding pressure, noted earlier, is an effect of the pronatalist context in which ART operates and the corresponding pressures on women to become mothers and provide genetically related offspring for partners. "The decision to use IVF is carried out within a strong pronatalist context,... These kind of ideologies, reinforced by economic structures, pressure women to 'choose' motherhood.... Though some choices are available within firmly delineated limits, we are encouraged to choose the socially acceptable alternative" (P. Spallone & D. Steinberg

(1987). *Made to Order: The myth of reproductive and genetic progress*. Oxford: Pergamon Press).

Whether or not one accepts these claims very much depends on which wider theories of individual and societal interaction are held. There are other ways that ART can operate as constraining factors on women's procreative choices. It has been claimed that the very existence of ART can constrain and influence choices. In an article describing his own experience of infertility treatments Paul Lauritzen says, "The problem here might reasonably be described as the tyranny of available technologies. This 'soft' form of coercion arises from the very existence of technologies of control.... once the technology of control exists, it is nearly impossible not to make use of it." Here what are presented as new options can quickly become seen as the standard of care that women are not really free to refuse. Barbara Rothman has summarized this point: "taking away the sense of inevitability" in relation to infertility and "substituting the 'choice' of giving up does not in any real sense increase such couple's choice and control." (in Arditti, R., & Kline, R. (Eds.). *Test-Tube Women*, Pandora Press). It is argued that to be childless due to infertility is no longer seen as an acceptable option unless women have tried to conceive by using ART. Even then, if conception does not take place the feeling of failure and the stress, strain and costly medical treatment can all take their toll.

C. Reproductive Technologies as Unnatural Practices

Another set of arguments against the fundamental principles of ART is the Roman Catholic view. ART is viewed as an unwarranted interference with nature and what is perceived as God's will. ART is a deviation from normal intercourse and, in separating the unitive and procreative aspects of sexual intercourse, they devalue the reproductive process. To introduce a third person into this process is seen as defiling the sanctity of marriage and the family. A second area of concern for religious groups is the treatment of the human embryo and this will be considered in a later section.

D. Conclusion

The arguments against ARTs vary. Some, such as certain feminist and religious views, object to the very principle of ART, albeit for very different reasons. Other views are concerned that ART should operate in a safe and well-regulated way so that those participating in the treatments will not be unduly harmed. Despite opposition IVF has now been recognized as a therapeutic technique and this is exemplified by countries such as Australia having Medicare benefits approved for IVF and GIFT by the Federal Budget in 1990. ARTs have been considered and regulated by various legislative bodies (notably the British Parliament in the 1990 Human Fertilization and Embryology Act). Hence, the fundamental principles that lie behind ART have been publically accepted and the debate over whether to have ART, in any form, has largely been superseded by debates concerning how to regulate ART and how to best ensure that progress in ART proceeds ethically and responsibly.

III. PARTICULAR ETHICAL PROBLEMS

Once ARTs become used as therapeutic techniques for alleviating infertility practical ethical problems arise.

A. The Treatment of Embryos

Embryo research is an integral part in the scientific development of IVF and related techniques and, in enabling embryos to be created outside the body, it has opened up a whole area of debate over the moral status of the embryo. The debates over the moral status of the embryo and the practical problems of research protocols, storage, disposal, and ownership of embryos will be examined. The focus of this section will be on the embryo up to the eighth week of development and will not be concerned with fetuses at a later stage of development to distinguish this consideration from the abortion debate and concerns over the changing status of the fetus as it develops.

1. The Moral Status of the Embryo

The issue is how should embryos be regarded in the moral sense; that is, some decision needs to be made about what kind of entity they are, so that embryos can be treated in the morally appropriate way. Here the question is one of determining whether the difference between an embryo and an adult is a *morally relevant* difference. At one end of the spectrum, there are those who would claim that as the embryo is a human being it should be accorded full moral status and therefore be treated with the same regard as any adult. This view is held by the Roman Catholic Church, which teaches that morally relevant life begins at conception; the embryo has a right to life that must be respected. At the other end of the spectrum,

there are those who would contend that only persons should be accorded moral status and it is this moral status upon which a right to life is based. A person is defined as a self-conscious, thinking, feeling being, and under this definition the embryo does not qualify as a person, it is simply a collection of cells and therefore it has no right to life.

Although there is a lack of consensus over what moral status one should give the embryo there has been a practical response to this problem by regulatory bodies. In the United Kingdom The Warnock Report (1984) (the result of a public committee of inquiry into ART) framed the question in terms of, "How is it right to treat the human embryo?" and concluded that, "the embryo of the human species should be afforded some protection in law." This is in effect taking the middle ground, not according the embryo with rights on a par with an adult, but not equating the embryo with a morally insignificant group of cells.

2. Embryo Research

Embryo research has caused considerable controversy. The issue of the acceptability of research on embryos is closely related to the conclusions reached about the moral status of the embryo. If the embryo is considered to have full moral status, on a par with an adult, then the same considerations that guide research on adults should pertain to the embryo, such as seeking consent from the subject and ensuring that the research only involves reasonable risks. However, the embryo cannot consent and this raises the problem of who should consent on behalf of the embryo. Further, embryo research often involves the destruction of the embryo and it could be argued that this is an unreasonable level of harm for a research subject to undergo.

If the embryo is considered to have no moral status then there will be less concern for the embryo's welfare and it is more likely that research will be permitted. However, just because the embryo is considered to have limited moral status, in comparison with an adult, it could be argued that this does not imply the embryo is morally insignificant. Embryo research might be permitted if it operates under strict guidelines. An analogy could be drawn here between embryo and animal research. Animal research is permitted but only in carefully supervised conditions and for significant medical benefit.

It is generally thought that embryo research should be subject to time limits (determined as days after fertilization) after which research on the embryo should not be permissable. One of the main practical ethical dilemmas in this area is where to draw such a suitable cut off point. In the United Kingdom this line has been drawn at 14 days from the day that the gametes were mixed and, therefore, an embryo cannot be used after the appearance of the primitive streak. This has been echoed in the United States by the 1994 *Report of the National Institutes of Health Human Embryo Research Panel.*

The appearance of the primitive streak (at 14 days) marks the point at which the embryo becomes morally significant, as it is argued that this is when the embryo has developed irreversible individuality, and reflects the view that the embryo becomes more morally important as it develops. There is a possible problem in determining when, precisely, in its developmental stages an embryo or indeed fetus gains moral status, as biological development is a gradual process and it is impossible to point to one stage where moral status is suddenly conferred. This 14-day cut-off point has attracted criticism on the grounds that it is an arbitrary point of demarcation. Warnock has responded to this by stating that, "the point was not however the exact number of days chosen, but the absolute necessity for there being a time limit set on the use of embryos." This illustrates that there is no firm consensus on when the embryo becomes morally significant but there is a necessity for practical guidelines.

A further dilemma is the source of the embryos for research. Research can utilize embryos created specifically for the purposes of research or spare embryos created during the process of IVF. One objection to creating embryos specifically for research is based on the argument that this reduces the embryo to a commodity, treating it as a mere product and thereby devaluing the procreative process. It could also be argued that if embryos are created specifically for research purposes then increasing numbers will be created to satisfy the demands of researchers. A separation principle could be invoked here (separating the process of creating embryos from their final use) that states that the creation of embryos should not be linked to any future research plans and only spare embryos should be used. A counter to this would be that if embryo research is acceptable, this is due to claiming that embryos have no moral status and if they have no moral status then the source of the embryos is irrelevant. This tension is summarized by John Harris; "I cannot but think that if it is right to use embryos for research then it is right to produce them for research. And if it is not right to use them for research, then they should not be so used even if they are not deliberately created for the purpose."

3. The Storage of Embryos

In a typical IVF cycle around six embryos will be created and good-practice guidelines in the United Kingdom stipulate that a maximum of three embryos should be transferred. The couple have a choice of either having these spare embryos destroyed, used for research, or frozen for future use. If the IVF attempt fails or if future egg retrieval is impossible (due to the woman's age for example) couples can use these stored embryos for further IVF treatments. There are a number of potential problems with the storage of embryos. How long should embryos be stored? Should there be a time limit or can they be stored indefinitely? Freezing embryos can create problems in the future if there are disputes over ownership of the embryos if the couple splits up or if one partner dies. Who should have the casting decision as to what to do with the embryos? This is a problem of deciding whether the embryo should be treated like an existing child or whether there are different concerns here, as the embryo only has the potential to become a child. One response might be to use a detailed consent form setting up the storage terms to preempt these problems but no consent form, however well worded, can anticipate every possible future circumstance.

B. The Donation of Gametes

Infertility treatments have used donor gametes to benefit patients whose own gametes are not viable. Factors such as abnormal sperm findings or a woman who has unhealthy oocytes but is otherwise able to carry a pregnancy can indicate the need for donated material. The donation of genetic material has created a large number of ethical dilemmas, such as who is to be considered the parent of the future child and the possible effect on the welfare of the future child.

1. Determining Who Is the Parent and What Are the Welfare Concerns of the Child

The use of donor gametes raises the troubling problem of who should be considered to be the parent of the future child. When the sperm donor gives his sperm he also gives up any future parental role and the donor's anonymity is guaranteed. In the United Kingdom it is the husband of the woman undergoing the infertility treatment who is considered to be the father of any resulting child. This provision also extends to couples who are not married. The principle of anonymity is also embraced by the Ethics Committee of the American Fertility Society (1994) as it is seen to be important to encourage men to donate and safeguard them from becoming unwittingly responsible for their genetic offspring.

Although the principle of anonymity is seen as important in gamete donation, there are circumstances where family members or close friends might want to donate gametes to help those they are close to. This could cause potential problems with the future relationship between the donor and the child. Donors may see themselves as the "real" parents, a belief encouraged by regular contact, and may believe they have a legitimate say in how the child is brought up.

The case of egg donation can raise complex problems. Traditionally one could always be certain who one's mother was; however, with egg donation a woman can become pregnant with a child to whom she is not genetically related. It is only through the technique of IVF that the gestational and genetic aspects of motherhood have been able to be separated. So which of these functions is to be held as the true indicator of motherhood? Is one more important than the other?

The ethical problems with all gamete donation are those of potential harm to the donors, the recipients of the gametes, and the future children. Gamete donation is not akin to other forms of donation made in a medical context, it is the giving of genetic material that will be used to create offspring that are genetically related to the donors. The issue here is one of the importance given to the genetic relationship. Donors may always be mindful of the fact they may have children they will never meet, that some part of their genetic inheritance exists that they are not aware of. This might be particularly pertinent for egg donors as women are only able to donate a limited number of eggs. The recipients of the donated material may feel that the child is not really theirs or the future child might not see one or both of their parents as their "real" parent.

Conversely, it might be the social relationships between parents and children that are the important defining factor and there would be no particular disbenefit in rearing children to whom you are not genetically related. Adoptions can be successful and many men rear children who are not genetically theirs (even if they are unaware of it). With egg donation as the Ethics Committee of the American Fertility Society note, the possibility of bonding between the surrogate gestational mother and the fetus in utero is an unresolved issue and this could be an important source of maternal bonding.

In the United Kingdom the mother of the child is deemed to be the pregnant woman and the gestational function determines the legal motherhood not the genetic relationship. However, there is more ambiguity in the United States for example, and the Ethics Committee of the American Fertility Society (1994) notes that, "the legal status of rearing rights and duties in offspring of donor oocytes has not been definitively established."

2. Payment of Donors

It is generally accepted that donors of gametes should not receive any payment over and above a minimal compensation for time and inconvenience. It is argued by the HFEA that altruistic donation is to be encouraged and that any payment could have the detrimental effect of encouraging inappropriate motivation (such as merely seeking financial benefit) on the part of the donors and causing possible pressure that potential donors might feel if there was excessive inducement. This could possibly exploit the less well off in society, as it is likely that they would be the ones to respond to financial inducement. This concern reflects the general problem of the ethical acceptability of paying people for their body parts (i.e., organs) or body products (i.e., blood). It could be argued that there are additional ethical problems in the case of selling gametes as the vendors are not only selling body products but they are also selling their genetic material. Conversely, one could argue, as Harris does that not allowing payment is compounding the problems of those who are less well off by depriving them of a source of income.

The issue of payment for donors is important due to the shortage of gametes, particularly oocytes, and ways of encouraging donation are frequently debated. To encourage women to donate eggs they are often given free treatment or free sterilization in exchange for their eggs. It could be argued that this is ethically on a par with providing payment, as such services could operate as an inducement to donate eggs and it is likely that those with limited financial resources would be the ones most susceptible to such inducements and hence more inclined to undergo such procedures.

C. Access to Reproductive Technologies

The possibility of infertility treatments has raised the issue of who should have access to such provision. Should ARTs be given to single women, nonheterosexual couples, postmenopausal women or women who are HIV positive? This is a concern over their suitability as parents. In the United Kingdom the HFEA does not lay down precise guidelines as to who should or should not receive infertility treatment, but states that treatment centers should have clear written procedures to follow for assessing the welfare of the potential child.

Hence, the welfare of the future child is held to be of paramount importance, but there is considerable disagreement over how such welfare is to be protected. However, it could be argued that if the main reason for ART is to alleviate the suffering of the infertile then the welfare of the child should not be of paramount concern.

1. The Welfare of the Child

To establish which individuals should receive infertility treatment on the basis of who will be a suitable parent is a difficult decision. It could be argued that this is not a medical question and medical practitioners are no more expert in deciding what makes a good parent than anyone else. This kind of decision is particularly vulnerable to the prejudices and preconceived ideas of individual practitioners. The Ethics Committee of the American Fertility Society (1994) broadly states that the best interests of the child are served when it is born and reared by a heterosexual couple in a stable marriage. However, they do note that there might be a role for other patterns of parenthood and do not recommend the legal prohibition of ART for nontraditional families. In the United States as in the United Kingdom, the matter is largely left to the treatment centers and individual practitioners to decide who is suitable to be a parent and therefore this could give scope for unwarranted discrimination.

2. Particular Cases

In the United Kingdom with regard to single women and lesbians, the HFEA Code of Practice states that attention should be paid to the child's need for a father and where the child has no legal father, "centres should consider particularly whether there is anyone else … willing and able to share responsibility for meeting those needs." This is a relatively progressive provision. Many countries (e.g., France) restrict access to married or stable heterosexual couples.

Another focus of concern has been the issue of whether postmenopausal women should receive infertility treatment. There have been various cases reported in the media, most notably a clinic in Italy that treated a 62-year-old woman, believed to be the oldest ART mother. The question is, is it ethically acceptable to give postmenopausal women infertility treatment?

In answering this question, one possible starting point is to consider the welfare of the child. Is it self-evidently harmful for a child to have parents who are older than the norm? The trend in the developed world seems to be that more women are delaying having children until their late 30s and early 40s. The normal age

to have children appears to be slowly rising. Accordingly, it seems to be almost impossible to determine what is the normal age for childbearing in a society where changing social circumstances and improvements in health can shift that point.

In considering the acceptability of treatment for older women it is a matter of degree. We might think that 60 is too old but 50 is just acceptable. This creates the problem of how we are to justify these two different limits. In response to this, there have been attempts made to determine a suitable cut-off point after which treatment should not be given.

There could be two cases that present themselves to infertility clinics. Those women who require egg donation (for IVF) and those women who can use their own eggs. The women who require egg donation may not necessarily be those in the "older" age bracket, they may have a high risk of transmitting a serious genetic disease or they may have undergone a premature menopause. However, if a woman is postmenopausal she will require egg donation in order to conceive. It is argued that this could be used as the cut-off point for those seeking ARTs. If the woman has reached the menopause then her fertile time is over (biologically) and this would provide an objective, testable cut-off point that was not subject to individual practitioners interpretation and judgment.

However, this seemingly straightforward solution masks two difficult problems. First, some women, albeit a very few, menopause prematurely, sometimes in their 20s. Would we want to say that a woman in this situation is not to receive treatment? The response to this might be that we mean the average age of menopause and not the menopause itself. But this throws the debate back to interpreting norms and deciding who should have treatment purely on the grounds of age. A woman of 40 who has reached menopause may think that it is too early to give up the thought of children, so how are we to distinguish between her and the 20-year-old when deciding who should get treatment if not by age?

Second, the current state of medical research maintains that it is the age of the oocytes that leads to age related declines in fecundity, not the age of the uterus. So, women over, say, 40, although they have not yet reached menopause, may wish to have donor eggs provided to minimize the risk of miscarriage. Thus, with the use of donor eggs the menopause ceases to be a biologically relevant cut-off point. Again, the decision comes back to making a judgment of whether to treat on the basis of an individual's age rather than a biologically determined cut-off point.

These issues frequently come to a head when applied in a practical context, that is, over how to allocate scarce resources such as donated oocytes. Only giving infertility treatment to those who can provide their own gametes is one way of restricting access and this can be extended to only allowing fertilization between partners (as is the policy in Sweden). Germany allows treatment only if the woman can provide her own gametes.

Any decision on how to promote the future welfare of the child is going to be a difficult and necessarily speculative one. It is often seen as unfair that the infertile have to prove that they will make good parents while the fertile have no such constraints. It is important to base decisions about who should be treated on genuine concerns for the welfare of the child (while recognizing this is very difficult to ascertain), not on prejudice nor on an unwarranted preference for so-called traditional family units.

IV. CONCLUSION

Reproductive technologies raise many disturbing and difficult ethical dilemmas both for the practitioners involved with the techniques and the general public. One of the difficulties in both regulating ART and considering the ethical implications is the speed with which new techniques and processes are developed. It is imperative that such developments only proceed after careful consideration as to the short- and long-term implications, both for those who use them and for society as a whole.

Also See the Following Articles

BIRTH-CONTROL TECHNOLOGY • EMBRYOLOGY, ETHICS OF • FETUS • GENETIC SCREENING • INFERTILITY • INFORMED CONSENT

Bibliography

Alpern, K. D. (Ed.). (1992). *The ethics of reproductive technology.* Oxford: Oxford University Press.

Basen, G., Eichler, M., & Lipman, A. (Eds.). (1993). *Misconceptions: The social construction of choice and the new reproductive technologies.* Quebec: Voyageur Publishing.

Boling, P. (Ed.). (1995). *Expecting trouble: Fetal abuse & new reproductive technologies.* Boulder: Westview Press.

Corea, G. (1988). *The mother machine.* London: The Women's Press.

Van Dyck, J. (1995). *Manufacturing babies and public consent: Debating the new reproductive technologies.* Basingstoke: Macmillian.

Evans, D. (Ed.). (1996). *Creating the child: The ethics, law & practice of assisted procreation.* The Hague: Martinas Nijhoff Publishers.

Evans, D. (Ed.). (1996). *Conceiving the embryo: Ethics, law & practice in human embryology.* The Hague: Martinas Nijhoff Publishers.

Harris, J. (1992). *Wonderwoman and Superman.* Oxford: Oxford University Press.

Overall, C. (1993). *Human reproduction: Principles, practices, policies.* Toronto: Oxford University Press.

Purdy, L. (1996). *Reproducing persons.* Ithaca, NY: Cornell University Press.

Robertson, J. (1994). *Children of choice.* Princeton: Princeton University Press.

Stanworth, M. (1987). *Reproductive technologies.* Oxford: Polity.

Warnock, M. (1985). *A question of life: The Warnock report.* Oxford: Basil Blackwell.

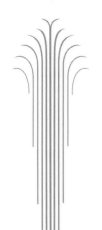

REPUTATION MANAGEMENT BY CORPORATIONS

Charles J. Fombrun
New York University

GLOSSARY

corporate identity The core, distinctive, and enduring characteristics of a company that are revealed in the actions and initiatives of its employees, and in the procedures, systems, and strategies that they enact.

corporate reputation A perceptual representation of a company's past actions and results that describes the firm's overall appeal to its key constituents.

organizational legitimacy The degree of alignment between a company's expressed values and those of the wider society in which the company operates.

COMPANIES own both tangible and intangible assets. Chief among a company's intangible assets is its reputation—the salient characteristics that observers ascribe to the company. Research suggests that a company's reputation is rooted in the perceptions of its employers, customers, investors, and other stakeholders. When surveyed, senior managers regularly point to a company's reputation as among the most important success

drivers and ponder how to induce and maintain favorable assessments of their companies by both employees and outsiders observers.

In fact, a company's reputation does not come simply from doing "good public relations" or from efforts merely to manipulate a company's external image. Rather, corporate reputations are built from the inside out: They reflect a company's culture, and derive from answers to such questions as: Who are we? What values do we support? What do we stand for? Insofar as a company's actions express the values held by the wider society in which the company operates, then its actions will be ascribed favorable regard, reputation, and hence *legitimacy*.

A company's reputation—and ultimately its legitimacy—therefore sit on the bedrock of its *corporate identity*—the core values that shape its actions, its communications, its culture, and its decisions. Reputation management is therefore a long-term effort that involves establishing close contact and rapport with stakeholders, and making those relationships a vital part of the strategic management of the company at all levels. In fact:

- A good reputation is a reflection of a company's values and beliefs, its "common core."
- A good reputation develops from systematic management of activities throughout a company that increase employee trust, pride, and commitment.
- A good reputation develops from a culture that mandates everyday excellence in all activities.

I. DIFFERENT VIEWS OF REPUTATION

There are many approaches to understanding corporate reputations. Two prevail: A view of reputation as an outcome of "principled" behavior; and a view of reputation as an expression of "enlightened self-interest."

A. Reputation as an Outcome of Principled Behavior

Many corporate observers propose that companies have fundamental social responsibilities to fulfill. As recognizable institutions with legal status of their own, companies and their managers are expected to act responsibly simply because that is "the right thing to do." Just as the Bible prescribes a code of conduct for Christians, the Koran for Muslims, the Torah for Jews, the Upanishads for Hindi, so does a principled approach seek to enumerate the rules by which to judge the actions of a company. From this perspective, reputation deservedly accrues to a company because it acts in morally defensible ways: It adheres closely to a code of conduct that defends basic *human rights* of all employees and consumers, for instance, as well as the *property rights* of shareholders, and the *political rights* of individual citizens. A principled approach to reputation management therefore tries to articulate the sacred and symmetrical duties and obligations that all companies must demonstrate if they are to be seen as "legitimate" by the communities and societies in which they operate—and thereby achieve favorable reputations.

The growing popularity of "corporate ethics statements," "business conduct guidelines," "ethics officers" reflects recognition by many leading companies that standards and rules can serve as guideposts for individual behavior, and thereby induce observers to ascribe "social responsibility" to companies, and so enhance their reputations. For instance, IBM's "Business Conduct Guidelines" is a 42-page document that prescribes specific standards to which the company claims to adhere in four areas: (1) the personal conduct of employees and the protection of IBM's assets; (2) obligations from conducting IBM's business with other people and organizations; (3) conflicts of interest affecting IBM that may arise outside the company; and (4) competition rules.

The aerospace giant Lockheed Martin is even more ambitious and explicit. As its publication entitled "Setting the Standard: Code of Ethics and Business Conduct" claims:

Lockheed Martin aims to 'set the standard' for ethical business conduct. We will achieve this through six virtues: Honesty, Integrity, Respect, Trust, Responsibility, and Citizenship.

Honesty: to be truthful in all our endeavors; to be honest and forthright with one another and with our customers, communities, suppliers, and shareholders.

Integrity: To say what we mean, to deliver what we promise, and to stand for what is right.

Respect: to treat one another with dignity and fairness, appreciating the diversity of our workforce and the uniqueness of each employee.

Trust: to build confidence through teamwork and open, candid communication.

Responsibility: to speak up—without fear of retribution—and report concerns in the workplace, including violations of laws, regulations and company policies, and seek clarification and guidance whenever there is doubt.

Citizenship: to obey all the laws of the United States and the other countries in which we do business and to do our part to make the communities in which we live better" (Lockheed Martin, "Setting the Standard," Internal Document, June 1996).

B. Reputation as a Result of Enlightened Self-Interest

One can also take an instrumental, teleological view of reputation management. Four key perspectives can be used to justify such a view. All four converge in regarding a company's reputation as a form of intangible wealth produced partly through relationships with customers, partly through relationships with other key constituents. Shareholder value and "reputational capital" are created because a good reputation builds *competitive advantage*: It acts like a barrier that impedes rivals; it provides a company with an enhanced license to operate; and it is a "protective shield" against sudden downturns and crises.

1. The Marketing View

Often "reputation" is used interchangeably with the term "brand." A brand describes a company's distinctiveness and attractiveness *to its customers*. A company builds "brand equity" by investing in customer-oriented programs that enhance loyalty, increase name awareness, and broaden product associations. The branding process usually focuses on products, but marketers also recognize how corporate brands (or reputational halos) generate brand share of preference with customers. By linking the corporate name closely with favorable attributes (e.g., quality, value, dependability, innovation, community-mindedness, good management, environmental concern) corporate branding builds a special relationship with target audiences, motivating them to some form of positive action.

2. The Accounting View

Like brands, reputations are a form of goodwill: They are *intangible assets* that provide real benefits but are difficult to quantify. To avoid misstatement, conservative accounting policies in the United States currently do not capitalize intangible assets in financial statements, and favor expensing all activities and programs related to brand shaping and reputation building. However, disparities in the accounting treatment of goodwill around the world, and concern over the misleading character of historical cost reporting in merger situations has led to growing interest in ways to incorporate brand values and reputational capital as assets into financial statements.

3. The Stakeholder View

Corporate reputations describe *perceptions* about a company held by internal and external constituents. Internal constituents include all of a company's employees, managers, and directors. External constituents encompass shareholders, customers, suppliers, host governments, and the media. Stakeholder views contend that a company's reputation describes the net assessment that constituents make of a company's ability to meet their expectations.

4. The Strategic View

Finally, reputations are a source of competitive advantage. In this view, companies build advantage in one of four ways: From developing a protected market position, from owning proprietary physical assets, from developing a unique corporate culture, or from earning a good reputation. Table 1 suggests how these sources of advantage derive from a company's ability to control

TABLE 1
Sources of Competitive Advantage

	Internal relations	External relations
Resources	*Physical assets*	*Market position*
Perceptions	*Corporate culture*	*Reputation*

either *economic* resources, or *perceptions, internally* and *externally*.

II. WHY COMPANIES ARE INVESTING IN REPUTATION MANAGEMENT

Historically, many large companies have tried to maintain a low public profile in the media and with the general public. Specific issues were addressed reactively, a strategy aimed largely at containing publicity and engaging relevant stakeholders ex post in rational debate. With few exceptions, this "introvert" approach was successful in limiting visibility and exposure. Today the introvert strategy is obsolete, and most companies try to benefit from active reputation management. On one hand, companies are increasingly vulnerable to reputational attack. The size, scope, and domain of their activities attracts attention from many traditionally disenfranchised stakeholders; many also operate in politically sensitive areas or with technologies that pose a significant environmental challenge. On the other hand, continued growth in a competitive market requires increased support from all stakeholders. Having a reputational edge can therefore help a company to achieve the greatest gains and meet with the least resistance.

- *Growing Vulnerability*: Media coverage of large global companies is on the rise. Their sheer size guarantees that there exists a very large group of stakeholders with vested interest in the nature and scope of their business. Increased visibility therefore appears inevitable, with or without highly publicized crises. More rapid communication also makes the diffusion of information and misinformation easy and inexpensive. *It magnifies a global company's vulnerability to stakeholder action, and increases the value of having a good reputation in the face of negative propaganda.*
- *Growth Objectives*: Most companies have ambitious growth objectives. Achieving them requires increased understanding and acceptance of their activities—being a welcome member of the world community. Many global companies operate in areas that are either politically sensitive or that pose significant environmental challenges. Under those difficult and competitive conditions, companies benefiting from a reputational edge will achieve the greatest gain and meet with the least resistance.

On the upside, companies can also benefit from systematic reputation management:

• *Competitive Advantage:* A good reputation acts like a barrier that impedes rivalry; it provides a company with an enhanced license to operate; and it raises a "protective shield" against downturns and crises. A strong reputation can therefore help a company outdistance rivals in existing businesses and outdo them in competing for new business.

• *Financial Benefits:* A change in reputation affects a company's share price because it induces shareholders to revise their estimates of the company's *future* cash flows. These estimates themselves derive from changed perceptions of the company by all stakeholders, particularly customers and employees. A company that is better-regarded should therefore enjoy higher market value and a lower cost of capital.

Recent research provides support for the instrumental benefits of good reputations, measured principally through surveys of executives describing how they regard companies. These studies suggest the following relationships:

• *Reputation and Profitability:* After controlling for other key factors, a study of *Fortune 500* companies showed that corporate reputation affected profitability in excess of the industry average.

• *Reputation and Market Value:* A study of 216 companies found that there was a relative premium on the stock market values of firms with stronger reputations for social responsibility, after controlling for financial performance.

• *Reputation and Analysts' Forecasts:* An analysis of 303 companies reported that one-year corporate earnings-per-share forecasts made by financial analysts were most heavily explained by standard performance indicators, but were also partly influenced by the nonfinancial component of the company's reputation.

• *Reputation and Cost of Capital:* A study of 10 portfolios of companies demonstrated that investors were willing to pay more for companies with higher reputation but comparable risk and return, thereby lowering the company's cost of capital.

• *Reputation and Competitive Advantage:* A study of 64 companies showed that intangible resources were a distinct source of sustainable competitive advantage that enhanced a company's profitability.

• *Reputation and Job Applicants:* A study of 200 business undergraduate students found that they were more attracted to jobs in high-reputation companies—those whose workplaces were referenced in various ooks describing the "100 Best Companies to Work For ..."

• *Direct Costs of Reputation Loss:* A study of 12 major corporate crises showed that they have significant impact on the market values of companies. Associated with each negative reputational event in a one-week window around the event with billion dollar losses that represented gross changes of 5% to 15% in the market values of those firms.

• *Reputation and Market-Value Added:* A study of the relationship between net market-value added (MVA) and *Fortune's* index of reputation in 1995 found that a company's reputation was positively associated with both MVA and profitability, and negatively associated with the company' cost of capital.

Together, these studies suggest that reputation management is about building "reputational capital"—analogous to a bank account in which a company seeks to maintain a positive balance by making frequent deposits and only occasional withdrawals. Whether from a principled approach or from a more instrumental view, reputation management therefore involves building, maintaining, and defending the reputational capital that a company accumulates from maintaining good relationships with all of its stakeholders. By implication, reputation management requires a close look at every facet of a company's business to ensure that the company is best at everything it does, in the hope of becoming a preferred employer, supplier, and investment.

III. PRINCIPLES OF REPUTATION MANAGEMENT

Ultimately, both the principled approach and the instrumental approach to reputation management converge. They suggest that a company builds a favorable reputation by creating consistent perceptions of credibility, trustworthiness, and responsibility with its four key constituencies: Customers, investors, employees, and local communities.

A. Credibility

As customers, we are concerned that companies be credible: We want a company's claims for its products to prove true. We demand that the products of companies we respect be of better quality and reliability than those of lesser known competitors—even if sold at the same price.

The effects of reputation on customers are arguably strongest in the service sector where judgments of quality are especially difficult to make. Lacking any objective measure of performance, service providers rely heavily on their reputations to attract clients, and must deliver the quality that they claim if they are to retain those clients.

Like other service-based businesses, individual lawyers, accountants, consultants, doctors, realtors, insurance agents, and investment agents survive largely by word of mouth advertising—personal referrals that convey reliability and credibility. That is why law firms, auditors, consulting firms, and investment banks struggle to build a reputation for scrupulous honesty and integrity. Once established, these service companies rely on their reputations to attract other corporate clients: In effect, client companies *rent* the reputations of their lawyers, accountants, bankers, and consultants as a way to signal their own credibility and integrity to key constituents.

As investors, we also expect companies to be credible. We ask that managers live up to the claims and commitments that they make in press releases, annual reports, and other communications. Having entrusted them with our hard-earned savings, we demand that they show good faith in their dealings with us: That they convey accurately the risks of their strategies, warn us of impending problems, and disclose material facts that might influence our assessment of their performance.

B. Trustworthiness

As employees, we ask that the companies we work for be *trustworthy*. While we demand that explicit contracts be honored, we also expect implicit contracts also be respected. We count on being treated fairly and honorably in job assignments, salary decisions, and in promotions. We ask of companies that they respect our fundamental rights as individuals and as citizens.

These expectations place tremendous pressure on companies to develop policies and programs that support the well-being of all their employees. Humane treatment involves, not only concerns for health and safety, but a growing regard for employees as *partners* in the work process. In many companies, employees are, in fact, part owners of the company through their pension funds or stock purchase plans. At a minimum, these employee-owners have earned the right to participate in the strategic decisions of the companies they work for. And they are demanding it.

Rapid developments in information technology are also opening up channels of communication and decision-making and enhance employee involvement. Pro-

gressive companies recognize the opportunity by creating programs that support employees' endeavors. The commitment to self-realization of all employees, including minorities, the handicapped, and other disenfranchised groups, represents a genuine commitment in better regarded companies. They work hard to establish trust with employees, whether those employees are unionized or not. By establishing trust with employees, those companies build reputation.

C. Responsibility

Finally, communities ask that companies recognize their *responsibility* to participate in the social and environmental fabric of their neighborhoods. After all, most employees live in the communities in which they work. They benefit from the local infrastructure. The popular concept of sustainability proposes that companies should at least put back as much as they take from their social and physical environments. Companies that ignore the well-being of their local communities therefore demonstrate a glaring disregard for its residents.

In the past decade, many companies have stepped in where government has failed: In education, in the inner city, in the environment. Leaders like U.S. Vice President Al Gore ask that companies incorporate so-called "externalities" into their strategic decisions—that they internalize the clean-up costs of industrial waste and of air, water, and land pollution. Beyond asking that companies pay economic penalties, however, one also hears in their demands a clear expectation that companies demonstrate *responsible citizenship* in the societies in which they operate. Much as populations of a prey can be wiped out by overconsuming predators, so is the human species threatened, they point out, by irresponsible companies who overconsume our natural and human resources. For them, citizenship means favoring *sustainable business*, activities that take out of society and the environment no more than they put back.

Company-supported volunteerism, community networking, environmentalism, employee participation, and workplace equity are practical means that many top companies like Xerox and Johnson & Johnson take to reduce employee alienation, to achieve social integration, to improve their reputations, and so to sustain their long-term viability. They go beyond simple philanthropy: Adopt-a-school programs, for instance, demonstrate the corporate sector's recognition that these activities are forms of *enlightened self-interest:* By supporting the local community, they help to upgrade the workforce, to minimize disruptions, and to increase a company's competitiveness.

IV. CONCLUSION

In sum, a reputation comes into being as internal and external observers struggle to make sense of a company's past and present actions. The reputation that we ascribe to the company aggregates many personal judgments about the company's credibility, reliability, responsibility, and trustworthiness. It also has the following characteristics:

- A reputation is a *derivative* feature of an industry that crystallizes a company's perceived ranking in a field of other rivals.
- A reputation is created from the *bottom-up* as each of us applies our own personal combination of economic and social, selfish and altruistic criteria in judging a company.
- A reputation is a snapshot that reconciles the multiple images of a company held by *all of its constituencies*. It signals the *overall attractiveness* of the company to employees, consumers, investors, and local communities.

In turn, companies try to improve their reputations by (a) building internal systems that shape strong corporate identities and (b) projecting their enduring characteristics to outside constituencies through resource allocations and corporate communications. Whether de factor or de jure, reputation management is likely to remain a central feature of the managerial landscape in the years to come.

Also See the Following Articles

CONSUMER RIGHTS • CORPORATE RESPONSIBILITY

Bibliography

Aaker, D. (1991). *Managing brand equity*. New York: The Free Press.

Conference on Corporate Reputation, Image, and Competitiveness. (1997, January). New York University, Stern School of Business.

Gregory, J. (Forthcoming). *Leveraging the corporate brand*. Chicago: NTC Business Books.

Fombrun, C. (1996). *Reputation: Realizing value from the corporate image*. Boston: HBS Press.

Rindova, V., & Fombrun, C. (Forthcoming). Constructing competitive advantage. *Strategic Management Journal*.

Wilson, R. (1983). Auditing: Perspectives from multiperson decision theory. *Accounting Review, 58*, 305–318.

RESEARCH ETHICS

Caroline Whitbeck
Case Western Reserve University

GLOSSARY

applied research Research that applies scientific knowledge to practical issues such as disease.

basic research Research that examines phenomena with the goal of obtaining scientific knowledge but not with a direct intention to make practical use of this knowledge.

cooking data An informal term for the unethical practice of presenting only data that fits one's hypothesis while intentionally discarding or omitting data that are in conflict with it.

fabrication In the context of research ethics, the act of inventing data or experiments that did not in fact take place.

falsification In the context of research ethics, the act of intentionally altering or misrepresenting data, experiments, or credentials.

plagiarism The intentional misrepresentation of the writing, ideas, or work of another as being one's own; for example, the extensive use of material written by another without attribution.

research misconduct In technical use in research ethics, improper research activity such as: fabrication, falsification, or plagiarism (see definitions above).

scientific fraud An intentional effort to represent as factual or true what one knows to be false; for example, the fabrication of experimental data.

RESEARCH aims to increase knowledge. Knowledge is recognized to have value in its own right, apart from the positive or negative ends that the knowledge enables people to pursue. Hypotheses, experiments, research reports, and other products of research are judged in terms of their knowledge, or "epistemic" value, as true, important, fundamental, fruitful, or significant for future research. Such epistemic evaluations are distinct from any evaluation of those products for their moral, pragmatic, aesthetic, or religious value. Arguably, some knowledge, such as knowledge of how to develop biological weapons ("germ warfare") or effective means of torture, is evil because its intended use is morally reprehensible. The moral evaluation of such knowledge as evil is independent of any epistemic evaluation, although both moral and epistemic evaluation influence decisions about what knowledge to pursue or preserve.

Ethical evaluation of research based on its aims and products, the so-called "end-use question," arises most often in applied as contrasted with basic research. Research is considered applied insofar as it addresses practical questions, such as the treatment of disease or the construction of power plants. Basic research examines phenomena without immediate reference to practical concerns. It pursues knowledge for its own sake. Basic research usually does influence subsequent applied research, however; that is the rationale for publicly funding basic research more generously than other areas of human accomplishment, such as the arts. The applied research that grows out of a basic research study is so varied and unpredictable that usually it is not possible to identify the basic research with any of those applications. The famous case of Arthur Galston, whose botany dissertation was used as a basis for making the military defoliant agent orange, illustrates how difficult it may be to foresee some applications of any research. (Basic research is sometimes called "pure research," but this term obscures the influence of the expectations and assumptions of researchers on the course of any research. No research, even basic research, is free of bias. Some biases, such as disciplinary bias—the influence on research of the assumptions and methods that characterize a particular field or discipline—cannot be eliminated.)

Research, once the occupation of leisured gentlemen, has grown greatly in the last 50 years. Research itself, the ethically significant problems that arise in it, and the norms and practices intended to govern the resolution of those problems are undergoing rapid evolution. This rate of change makes research ethics quite unlike other areas of professional ethics. To understand research ethics today, one must understand the causes and patterns of change within research, such as the unprecedented level of collaboration that risks a dissolution of accountability by researchers. The issues in research ethics are no longer simply whether researchers are honest in reporting their results and acknowledging their intellectual debts. The problems and issues are complex ones of the trustworthiness of the various parties in the enormous collaborative venture that research has become.

The subtle and complex questions of what research behavior is responsible and trustworthy have until recently received less attention than a narrow class of major malfeasance called "research misconduct." At least in the United States the attention to misconduct has focused on how misconduct is to be defined, and the discussion of that question has been complicated by a struggle between researchers and the government over how much discretion government agencies should have in deciding the grounds for research misconduct charges.

I. THE SCOPE OF RESEARCH ETHICS

Not all ethically objectionable behavior in a research setting counts as a violation of research ethics. For example, if an investigator takes home pieces of lab equipment for personal use, that would count as stealing, or at least as misappropriation of property, rather than as a violation of research ethics. Research ethics concerns only a subset of the professional responsibilities of researchers. In particular it does not include consideration of the ends to which new knowledge can or will be put. Therefore, although research directed to finding more effective biological weapons would be reprehensible, the ethical standards it would contravene would not be those of *research ethics.*

A positive characterization of research ethics requires a positive characterization of research responsibility. Responsibility for research results and fairness in crediting the research contributions of others are two general areas of this responsibility.

Laboratory safety is an area of professional responsibility for investigators but is not usually considered a part of research ethics. Laboratory work may present hazards to laboratory workers or to the general public. In the United States the health and safety of laboratory workers comes under the purview of the Occupational Safety and Health Administration (OSHA) rather than the government funding agencies concerned with research misconduct. (OSHA establishes and enforces health and safety standards and shares information about good practices for preventing occupational disease and injury to workers generally.) Risks to the public are covered by a variety of regulations and local statutes.

Environmental protection is another area of professional responsibility related to the responsibility for laboratory safety that usually is not counted as an area of research ethics. Improper disposal of hazardous substances, for example, is a crime, but like unsafe laboratory practices, it is not generally a ground for debarment from grant competition, and it tends not to be included in discussion of research ethics.

II. THE HISTORY OF DISCUSSION OF RESEARCH ETHICS IN THE UNITED STATES

The public and professional discussion of research ethics has significantly differed from areas of professional ethics such as health care ethics and engineering ethics in emphasizing wrongdoing, and more specifically a rather narrow class of serious wrongdoing called "research misconduct." Despite the wide use of negative examples in elucidating responsibility in other science-based professions, criteria for good practice rather than negligence and malfeasance are usually the central topic of discussion.

Admittedly, generalizations about standards for responsible research practice are complicated by the differences between disciplines or fields that influence the sorts of ethical problems or temptations that arise and the best way to address them. Among those disciplinary differences are different expectations about the approximate number of researchers needed to conduct a typical study, and so the length of the author list—which may number more than 100 in high-energy physics; social and political differences in the structure of research groups, such as differences in the role of lab heads in science as contrasted with their role in engineering laboratories; differences in expectations about the sharing of research materials; and differences in the training of graduate students because of the presence or absence of postdoctoral experience for researchers in a discipline.

For whatever reason, the subject of research misconduct has taken center stage in research ethics. Even though cases of so-called "scientific fraud"—that is, intentional deception aimed at inducing others to believe something that one knows to be false, or at least has no reason to think true—are rare among misconduct cases, fraud is the topic that has caught the popular imagination.

The most frequent charge of research misconduct is plagiarism, and when a charge of faking data is born out, it is usually found that perpetrators have tried to strengthen the case for a conclusion they believe to be true rather than commit fraud in the strict sense. The rarity of data faking is obscured by the absence of a historical perspective on research practice. For example, in their book *Betrayers of the Truth,* Broad and Wade include figures in the history of science who used methods that seem outlandish by current standards but were acceptable by their own.

The subject of research misconduct is not new among researchers. In 1830, the English mathematician and inventor Charles Babbage wrote an influential book on dishonesty in scientific research. In that work he defined several terms to describe research misconduct, including one that is still in use today: "cooking the data." To cook the data is to select only those data that fit one's hypothesis and to discard those that do not.

Despite Babbage's early work, the research community is now reinventing the language in which to discuss responsible research behavior and departures from it, partly because science has grown so rapidly in recent decades and research practice has changed. Data now come in many forms—no longer just as observations to be recorded in laboratory notebooks. The rules that apply to recording data in a notebook do not fit these new forms of data. The need for large-scale studies has produced collaboration among many individuals and often across institutions. These collaborations have created new occasions for error, confusion, and misrepresentation that have led to questionable findings or have eroded public confidence in the value of research. Furthermore, as science has become more specialized, collaboration among investigators with different expertise has become more common. Researchers usually have only a very general idea of the standards of research practice that apply to work in other disciplines.

From the 1950s to the early 1980s, during a period of unprecedented expansion of scientific research, the subject of research integrity received little attention within the research community. That a researcher would commit a major breach of trust seemed almost unthinkable. As historian Steven Shapin argues, researchers have long engaged in heated debates over facts and theories, but those debates have largely assumed that those engaged in the debate are honorable. The skepticism that is familiar to researchers as an established part of scientific review is directed toward exposing mistakes, but not wrongdoing. Researchers have been slow to accept the discovery that some of their number have behaved dishonorably.

In the United States the American Association for the Advancement of Science did form its Committee on Scientific Freedom and Responsibility in the 1970s, but the report that John Edsall wrote for this committee in 1975 stood virtually alone as a statement on research ethics. Although he and one or two others had been raising a variety of ethical issues since the 1950s, few others took up the subject. In contrast, many engineering societies and at least one scientific society, the American Chemical Society (ACS), had been actively discussing the professional responsibilities of engineering and industrial chemistry for a half century and more, and that discussion had become more public-spirited beginning in the 1950s.

In the United States recognition of the gross mishandling of misconduct cases in the 1980s led to government mandates of procedures for handling charges of serious wrongdoing and precipitated a public as well as a professional discussion of research ethics. The attention to malfeasance by researchers was much needed, but unfortunately, the discussion quickly became polarized. Some charged that research was riddled with "fraud," while others claimed that the charges of fraud in science were exaggerated and that the attention to research misconduct was part of a campaign to discredit science and drastically reduce public funding for it. The only point of general agreement was that institutions needed better ways to handle charges of wrongdoing. Furthermore, disputes about the latitude that the government should have in deciding what actions to investigate began masquerading as debates about the definition of the term "misconduct," further confusing the attempt to develop appropriate concepts for understanding research ethics. This polarized debate has only recently begun to give way to a more nuanced discussion of ethical standards for research practice.

Many U.S. institutions did establish or improve their guidelines for the conduct of research in the 1980s, but legalism so dominated the discussion of research conduct that ethical concerns were often distorted. Emphasis fell on legal and quasi-legal procedures for handling allegations of research misconduct. Subtler issues of trust and trustworthiness were largely ignored, and some otherwise sensible people forgot what they knew about ethics. For example, some people with a generally good command of English claimed that we do not have a definition of "plagiarism." Plagiarism has a clear definition; it is the representation of another's work or ideas as one's own. What is wanting is a specification of the evidentiary standards to be used in quasi-legal misconduct proceedings. Others treated fraud or research misconduct, the charges that warrant formal investigation, as the only ethical issues.

Misconduct occupied the center stage alone, so that even the relationship of instances of outright misconduct to other ethical aspects of a situation were often ignored. The most important was the tendency for instances of misconduct to occur in research environments where a host of other offenses, disputes, disappointments, and derelictions of duty—poor mentoring, harassment, disagreements about authorship and ownership of data, and failure to share data—have gone unresolved. Only recently have there been signs of a new period in which the vocabulary for research ethics has expanded to include consideration of all the factors that contribute to responsible research practice.

III. CURRENT DEFINITIONS OF MISCONDUCT

The term "research misconduct" is not applied to all breaches of research ethics. Some argue that intent to

mislead others is necessary for research misconduct. (Intent to deceive is one of the defining characteristics of fraud.) But negligence or recklessness has been the basis for uncontested judgments of misconduct by universities and by the National Science Foundation. For example, in one case a university investigator habitually took notes in which he failed to differentiate between his own prose and that of others and used the undifferentiated compilation in writing his grant proposals.

Largely for reasons of institutional jurisdiction, even serious abuse of research subjects is not generally classified as "research misconduct," although the treatment of human and animal research subjects is considered a part of research ethics. The current standards for the use of human subjects in research actually predate recent attention to research ethics. The World Medical Association (WMA) led the United States in the promulgation of the informed consent standard for such experimentation. The WMA's Helsinki declarations, first issued in 1962 and subsequently revised in 1964 and 1975, elaborated on the informed consent standard that the Nuremberg code set forth in 1946 in response to the discovery of the brutal human experiments carried out by the Nazis. Only in the 1970s did a series of U.S. court decisions and institutional reforms establish the standard of informed consent for all research facilities that receive U.S. government funds.

Because the abuse of experimental subjects was already regulated, it did not need to be included under new "misconduct" regulations established in the 1980s. Researchers have been debarred from grant competitions by government funding agencies for violation of standards for the treatment of research subjects, however, just as they have for what is considered research misconduct, so the exclusion of the abuse of research subjects from the categories of research misconduct amounts to very little. The exclusion simply illustrates that the term "research misconduct" is a *technical term* and not a synonym for wrongdoing in research.

In the United States definitions of misconduct proposed in the 1980s began by specifying three acts that exemplify or constitute research misconduct: fabrication—making up data or experiments or other significant information in proposing, conducting, or reporting research; falsification—changing or misrepresenting data or experiments or other significant information, such as the investigator's qualifications and credentials; and plagiarism.

The definition of "misconduct in science and engineering" that the National Science Foundation (NSF) uses is:

fabrication, falsification, plagiarism, or other serious deviation from accepted practices in proposing, carrying out, or reporting results from activities funded by NSF; or retaliation of any kind against a person who reported or provided information about suspected or alleged misconduct and who has not acted in bad faith.

Donald Buzzelli of the Office of the Inspector General at NSF argues that "falsification, fabrication and plagiarism" were intended as *examples* of "serious deviations from accepted practice," not the defining instances of such deviation, a point that the "other serious deviation" clause simply spells out. The NSF and the Department of Health and Human Services (HHS), which includes the National Institutes of Health (NIH), are the agencies that have the greatest regulatory oversight of research. Therefore, their definitions determine the conditions under which charges of wrongdoing are the concern of those agencies.

Fearful that a broad definition of what can be considered misconduct will give funding agencies the opportunity to interfere with the conduct of research, groups representing the interests of investigators, including the National Research Council (NRC), the research arm of the U.S. national academies (the National Academy of Sciences, the National Academy of Engineering, and the Institute of Medicine), have strenuously objected to the phrase "or other serious deviation from accepted practices in proposing, carrying out, or reporting results." The NRC convened a panel to look into ethical standards of research conduct, and it issued its report, *Responsible Science: Ensuring the Integrity of the Research Process,* in 1992. That report defines misconduct as "fabrication, falsification, and plagiarism in proposing, conducting, and reporting research."

The NRC panel classified as "other misconduct" much of what the NSF counts as "other serious deviation from accepted practices," that is, something that is clearly wrong but most of which is not the business of the government overseers to control. The panel did recognize, however, that some of what they call "other misconduct," in particular, retaliation against a whistleblower, is directly associated with research misconduct.

In their role as custodians of the public's money, funding agencies explicitly include all deception in proposing research in their definition of misconduct. They have considered lying in a grant proposal about something other than research results to be "other serious deviation from accepted practice." Presumably this is because "fabrication and falsification" are reserved for misrepresentation of data and experiments.

The actions that the NSF or HHS have counted as research misconduct under the controversial "other serious deviation" clause include cases of sabotage of experiments (as contrasted with general vandalism of a research site) and setting up a training program as a means for coercing sexual favors from trainees (as contrasted with sexual harassment in general), and gross misrepresentation of the numbers of minority students served by an educational program in a grant proposal (and thereby deceptively strengthening their proposal). It is hard to object to government funding agencies pursuing such malfeasance under *some* authorization, whatever it is called, but the cases do show marked variation.

In 1995 the Commission on Research Integrity, set up by the HHS, offered a new and much longer definition with examples. The drafters specifically avoided specifying the acts that count as research misconduct. Their definition discusses general criteria for judging some wrongdoing to be research misconduct. They say, in part:

> research misconduct is significant misbehavior that fails to respect the intellectual contributions or property of others, that intentionally impedes the progress of research or that risks corrupting the scientific record or compromising the integrity of scientific practices.

Both the report and this definition also have their critics, and the new definition is unlikely to be adopted. Definitions of misconduct are likely to move away from the simple "falsification, fabrication, and plagiarism" mold but to remain controversial for the immediate future.

IV. COMMON PROBLEMS AND TEMPTATIONS

Although research misconduct has received the greatest attention, many more common ethical problems call for response on a daily basis. Good intentions are not enough for responsible research conduct; one must also know how to respond well when other common factors constrain the options. In publishing, research investigators recognize the importance of informing readers about the data selection methods, but if research investigators publish in a journal that severely limits the space given to each article, completeness in disclosure may have to be traded off against completeness in the discussion of other elements of their research. Researchers must continually make decisions not only about what is true but about what is most important to disclose in their research. In these circumstances some are tempted to leave out information that might make their research look weak even if they would never simply discard data that did not fit their hypothesis. Deadlines for grant and paper submissions and research sponsors' demands only increase the pressure under which the decisions are made.

A. Ethics in Publication

Scientific publication raises many important problems of research ethics and exemplifies the need for developing explicit ethical norms for research practice. The evolution of these problems illustrates the factors that have transformed research practice in recent decades. For these reasons, scientific publication is an instructive place to begin the examination of specific problems and temptations common in research.

The marked increase in collaborative research and multiply authored publications in recent decades has complicated the assignment of research responsibility. With the presence of many authors, accountability may be endangered. The credit that goes with authorship must be matched by responsibility for the work. A practice that has grown with the number of authors and that has further contributed to the dissolution of responsibility is that of "gift authorship"—the inclusion as authors of persons who have not made significant contributions to the research. To counter both trends, the research community has widely accepted the standard that "[u]nless responsibility is apportioned explicitly in ... [a] paper, the authors whose names appear on a paper must be willing to share responsibility for all of it" (Committee on Science, Engineering and Public Policy of the National Academy of Sciences, National Academy of Engineering and Institute of Medicine, 1995, *On Being a Scientist* 2nd ed. Washington, DC: National Academy Press. The statement was also contained in the first (1989) edition of *On Being a Scientist,* which was substantially different in other respects). Although it is necessary to match credit with responsibility, actual specification of what each author has contributed to a paper may run afoul of a journal's willingness to expend the space to make such a statement, especially for research papers with 20 or more authors.

Realization of the need for clear norms and expectations for responsible behavior in publication has led some professional and scientific societies to make explicit rules and ethical expectations for authors, editors, and reviewers. More and more journals are making their requirements for format and ethical practice explicit.

The Council of Biology Editors has published an extensive discussion of the ethics of publication in medicine and biology, where the nature of research, especially large clinical studies, raises distinctive issues. The American Chemical Society, one of the most active organizations in the area of professional ethics, took the lead in devising a thoughtful, detailed set of guidelines, which has since become a model for some other professional societies, especially those in the physical sciences. Such statements are usually published at least once a year in the journals. The Ethical Guidelines to Publication of Chemical Research by the American Chemical Society are especially detailed and thoughtful.

Such rules and guidelines reveal the ethically significant problems and temptations that arise for authors, reviewers, and editors of technical publications and provide rules that show how honesty and fairness may be manifest in such problem situations. Journals do not all agree on the specifics, especially where these go beyond guidelines and become strict requirements. One journal may say that all authors have to sign a statement that they have seen and agree with the final version of a submitted manuscript. Another may require the submitting author to ensure that all the authors have seen the final version. Journals' opinions about the circumstances under which a reviewer of a manuscript may show a manuscript to another person also vary.

Consider, for example, the standards of professional responsibility required of reviewers for journals whose editors are professional editors rather than researchers. The majority of technical journals are edited by researchers who are able to independently assess the merit of most submitted manuscripts. Reviewers only make recommendations to these editors. The editors of some very prestigious journals are not themselves researchers, however. Journals whose editors are not researchers are much more dependent on reviewers' reports. Some of these journals only use one reviewer because of the number of submissions they receive. For these journals a reviewer has a heavier ethical burden to maintain the fairness of the review process than does one of several reviewers of a manuscript who makes recommendations to the investigator-editor.

Conflict of interest in the review of manuscripts and grant proposals is a major concern in research ethics where evidence of reviewers and editors taking unfair advantage of an author's unpublished work has mounted. At the same time, because reviewing is a service to the discipline, it is important to develop norms that do not place excessive burdens on reviewers. For example, a simple rule instructing reviewers to let nothing in a manuscript influence the reviewers' own work would fail to take account of the predicament of reviewers who gather from reviewing a manuscript that their own current line of research will be fruitless.

The familiar issue of properly crediting sources in acknowledgments and citations as well as in the author list and the responsibility of reviewers receives emphasis in guidelines and works on research responsibility, but apart from differences in the citation criteria used for research reports and for review articles, there are many judgments to be made about *how* to cite the relevant literature without consuming excessive journal space.

Although as noted above, the responsibility for laboratory safety is often not included under the heading of research ethics, some guidelines on ethical responsibility in the publication of research do remind authors to identify any unusual hazards that occur in the conduct of their research to protect those who may replicate or build on the work.

Guidelines that enjoin authors not to fragment their research reveal the temptation to do so to researchers who, with justification, feel they are evaluated primarily on the number of their publications. Indeed, especially in medical fields, some departments tell junior faculty that tenure requires a certain number of publications (and continued grant support). Exhortation to junior faculty is not enough to combat fragmentation of research, and some universities have changed their policies to reward quality rather than quantity by limiting the number of publications a faculty member can offer for evaluation at the time of promotion or tenure.

Reviewers and editors, as well as authors, have ethical responsibilities in the conduct of their work. The case of Vijay Soman is a particularly flagrant example of plagiarism by a reviewer and illustrates the institutional mishandling of misconduct cases.

The obligations for both editors and reviewers not to use information from an unpublished manuscript are emphasized in ethical guidelines. The obligation for editors may be more stringent: editors are admonished to pass on to another person the editorial responsibility for a manuscript that is closely related to their own past or present research. Reviewers are advised to be sensitive to the appearance of a conflict of interest in such cases, and if in doubt, to return the paper advising the editor of the bias or conflict of interest. Presumably it is difficult to get a knowledgeable review unless the reviewer is familiar with the area, and then the area is very likely to be one in which the reviewer works. The

assumption in these guidelines is that the editor is also a researcher rather than a professional editor. In that case, the editor may recognize and control the bias of a reviewer. However, no "second opinion" is available to compensate for editorial bias.

B. Ensuring Fairness in Competition

Publication is one area where the motives of competition may interfere with performing the professional tasks necessary to the flourishing of research. The more general problem for the research community as a whole is that of ensuring that the standards of fairness are met in an increasingly competitive research environment. Without a sound basis for trust, the extensive cooperation that undergirds research practice breaks down. In the 1950s and 1960s the world's research community was smaller and personal acquaintance gave researchers a certain confidence in one another. As the number of researchers has grown, personal acquaintance has become rarer and the need for cooperation between strangers has increased. At the same time, at least in the United States, where funding has not kept pace with the growth in the number of investigators, competitive pressures have become extreme in some fields.

Without concerted efforts to maintain and restore trust, the practice of sharing knowledge and materials has often broken down in competitive fields such as biology and medicine, where research has extensive commercial applications. In other fields, such as engineering, the expectations of commercial application are of much longer standing and the communication about what information researchers will or will not share tends to be quite straightforward. Fields in which research has had commercial applications for only a few decades report more devious strategies, such as alleging that requested research materials "were lost in the mail."

Some journals have sought to counter the trend by requiring that researchers publishing in them provide to other investigators any scarce materials required to replicate the published experiments. Increasingly, transfer agreements stipulating restrictions on the use the recipient investigators may make of the research materials accompanies transfer. Reliance on legalistic restrictions to delineate fair from unfair competition is coming to replace a more general trust and openness in communication.

C. Research Supervisors and Supervisees

The growth in research has produced a marked growth in the number of thesis students supervised by a single faculty member. In fields like chemistry and molecular biology a single faculty member may have 20 or more graduate students. In those fields, it is common to have postdoctoral researchers as well. Although postdocs, as they are called, may take on some of the supervision of graduate students, they are often in competition with those students. Postdocs are under pressure to establish their research reputations, and if they see a graduate student is working on an interesting question, they may be tempted to move in on that student's research. In such a potentially explosive environment students are expected to learn not only the latest research methods and findings but also the norms of research ethics.

In fields such as computer science and engineering, where there is also the potential for significant financial gain from one's research and some of the same potential conflicts of interest for university researchers working with industrial sponsorship, postdocs are rare and laboratories tend to be the working environment of multiple faculty members who share the cost of research equipment and who may provide a moral community less dependent on the character of a single individual. Perhaps for these reasons fewer complaints of serious malfeasance have been reported in "hot" engineering fields than in hot science fields. Mentoring of graduate students is under pressure in many disciplines, however.

In all fields ethical issues arise about the relationship between supervisors and supervisees because of the great importance of thesis supervisors for the development and early careers of research investigators. The power possessed by a research supervisor makes potential conflicts of interest very significant. Research supervisors inevitably have responsibility for the advancement of knowledge in their field and for the maintenance of standards for publication and funding within it. They have obligations to provide reports or products to research sponsors, they are responsible for the quality of those products and reports, they have an interest in their own career advancement, they have responsibilities to colleagues, and they may even have financial interests in, or consulting relationships with companies that make commercial application of their research. These interests and responsibilities may interfere with furthering their students' educational goals, but the situation does not lend itself to simple remedies of disclosure or divestiture of one of the potentially competing interests. Disclosure is superfluous and divestiture is not possible (although universities typically limit the amount of effort that faculty members can spend on

outside activities). Indeed, teaching students how to handle such competing responsibilities is arguably part of the mentoring responsibilities of a thesis supervisor. Some research universities have instituted rules, such as a rule against supervisors hiring their own thesis students to help with their consulting work. Such rules help to prevent situations in which supervisors' interests in retaining talented students is not further complicated by the demands of their consulting work. If students do feel that supervisors attend to their intellectual and professional development, they are more likely to appreciate the collaborative nature of the research enterprise and the importance of being trustworthy to maintain it.

V. SUPPORTS FOR ETHICAL BEHAVIOR

The need for new supports for ethical practice have produced proposals and practices for advising the perplexed and for supporting the conscientious complainant. Along with the mandated procedures for handling charges of misconduct mentioned above, many universities and research facilities have not only a research standards officer who handles such charges but also various sorts of neutrals who can be consulted confidentially for advice. Often the role of general ombudsman is not sufficient because the neutral advisor needs also to deeply understand research practice. A person with established research credentials who is also credible in the role of neutral is hard to find.

All fields have been included in the call for efforts to educate students about research ethics, and some U.S. federal agencies have mandated education in research ethics as part of any training programs they fund. The research ethics education that has been devised to answer such requirements at best covers only basic issues. Despite pioneering efforts by a few university departments, even university faculty members, including those who are quite scrupulous in their own behavior, are often inarticulate about the ethical norms they rely upon and are ignorant of their colleagues' views and practices. As a result, graduate students and trainees often are at a loss to explain the differences among the practices of faculty members or to differentiate acceptable variation from unacceptable violation of the norms. The larger need is for researchers to be reflective, articulate, and forthcoming with their colleagues and trainees about trustworthiness in research practice.

Also See the Following Articles

PLAGIARISM • PUBLISH-OR-PERISH SYNDROME • RESEARCH
ETHICS COMMITTEES • RESEARCH METHODS AND
POLICIES • SCIENTIFIC PUBLISHING

Bibliography

Alberts, B., & Shine, K. (1994, December 9). Scientists and the integrity of research. *Science,* **266,** 1660.

Broad, W. J., and Wade, N. *Betrayers of the truth.* New York: Simon and Schuster.

Buzzelli, D. E. (1994). NSF's definition of misconduct in science. *The Centennial Review* **38,** 273–296.

Djerassi, C. (1989). *Cantor's dilemma.* New York: Doubleday.

Djerassi, C. (1994). *The Bourbaki gambit.* Athens: The University of Georgia Press.

Kiang, N. (1995, October). How are scientific corrections made? *Science and Engineering Ethics,* **1,** 4, p. 347.

Macrina, F. L. (1995). *Dynamic issues in scientific integrity: Collaborative research.* Washington, DC: American Academy of Microbiology.

National Academy of Sciences Panel on Scientific Responsibility and the Conduct of Research. (1992). *Responsible science: Ensuring the integrity of the research process* (Volume I). Washington, DC: National Academy Press.

Pfeifer, M. P., & Snodgrass, G. L. (1990). The continued use of retracted, invalid scientific literature. *Journal of the American Medical Association* **263,** **10,** 1420–1423.

Shapin, S. (1994). *The social history of truth.* Chicago: University of Chicago Press.

Shrader-Frechette, K. (1994). *Ethics of scientific research.* Lanham, MD: Rowman & Littlefield Publishers.

Whitbeck, C. (1997). *Ethics in the works: Understanding ethical problems in engineering practice and research.* New York: Cambridge University Press.

Woolf, P. (1994). Integrity and accountability in research. In D. H. Gustin & K. Keniston (Eds.), *The fragile contract: University science and the federal government.* Cambridge, MA: MIT Press.

RESEARCH ETHICS COMMITTEES

Claire Foster
Centre of Medical Law and Ethics, King's College

GLOSSARY

equipoise Also known as the "uncertainty principle." The researcher in equipoise is in a state of not knowing whether a new treatment is better or worse than a standard treatment, such that it would medically be acceptable to randomize patients into groups receiving either the new or the standard treatment.

nontherapeutic research Research that does not involve any therapeutic intention for the research subjects, who are often though not always healthy volunteers.

phases of drug trials All new medicines have to be tested rigorously before they receive a license for marketing. There are four phases of drug trials: phase one in healthy volunteers, phase two in a few patients, phase three in a considerable number of patients, phase four postmarketing studies to extend knowledge and application of medicine.

placebo A dummy treatment, often disguised to look like the treatment to which it is being compared.

randomization: Random allocation of treatments in a research project to avoid bias.

therapeutic research Research that is undertaken in the context of treatment. The research subjects are therefore patients.

RESEARCH ETHICS COMMITTEES are groups of people drawn from the medical, nursing, and paramedical professions, and lay people, who have the responsibility of ensuring that healthcare research projects involving human subjects are ethically acceptable. These committees meet on a regular basis and look at all proposals for research on humans that is to be conducted within a certain geographical boundary. In most countries that conduct research on humans it is required by custom or by law that a researcher always seeks the approval of his local research ethics committee before commencing his research. The research ethics committees' criteria for ethical acceptability are that the research itself is sound, and reasonable, and that it asks a good question that will ultimately be of benefit; that the research subjects will come to no harm from participating in the research; and that the research subjects' dignity as humans will be respected in all possible ways: most importantly, that their consent will be sought before enrolling them in the research.

I. THE HISTORY OF RESEARCH ETHICS COMMITTEES

Although research has always taken place in the medical world in more or less controlled ways, concern with the distinctly ethical aspects of its conduct has only really appeared since the Second World War. There were some well-documented atrocities committed by doctors during the Nazi regime in the name of research, the grisly details of which can be read in accounts of the Nuremberg Trials. Following this a code of practice for human experimentation, known as the Nuremberg Code, was drawn up, the first principle of which begins: "The voluntary consent of the human subject is absolutely essential."

There is no clear indication that the Nuremberg Code was widely used in the decades following the war, although the absence of documentation does not itself constitute proof that researching doctors were ignorant of it. More widely known and used was the Declaration of Helsinki of the World Medical Association, which was first drawn up in 1964. There was certain resentment at the drawing up of guidelines, which were widely regarded as restricting of the work of doctors. In Britain in 1963 Sir Austin Bradford-Hill asserted:

> In my own experience of collaboration with doctors the problem calls for close and careful consideration in the *specific circumstances of each proposed trial* (Bradford-Hill's italics). No doubt, of course, one can enunciate some very broad principles of ethical behaviour, principles which are an intrinsic part of the doctor's training. But I do not myself believe that it is possible to go very much beyond that, that one can harness the broad principles to precise rules of action that are applicable in all circumstances. (Marc Daniels Lecture, April 20, 1963.)

It was inherent in the professional ethos that those who practiced medicine would behave impeccably. The tradition of Hippocrates, if not the actual swearing of any oath, was still alive, and doctors resented more restrictions on their freedom.

However, this was not to prove to be enough. Both within the medical profession and the lay public, concerns were rising at the license with which doctors seemed to be using their trusting patients as means to their own research ends—without telling them.

Significant change came in the United Kingdom when Dr. Desmond Laurence, a Fellow of the Royal College of Physicians, wrote an open letter to its President, Sir Max Rosenheim. In it he stated:

> The new Surgeon-General of the United States Public Health Service, Dr. William H. Stewart, has published a statement on the responsibility of institutions for work done inside them: "We are assuming, essentially, that the medical school, hospital, or other research institution—by accepting the administration of public funds—accepts also a share of the public responsibility for their use. We are asking that the institution assure us that research proposals related to the use of human subjects are being systematically subjected to independent review, and we are urging that qualified individuals from outside the scientific area be involved in this review." (Quoted in the Report of the Committee on the Supervision of the Ethics of Clinical Investigations in Institutions, July 1967.)

Dr. Laurence went on to suggest that a similar mechanism be established in the United Kingdom, whereby an independent group of doctors should take a detached view of any research proposal by their colleagues and decide whether it was ethical or not. The Ministry of Health took up the call and in 1968 sent a letter to hospital boards of governors and other relevant bodies asking that the enclosed guidance from the Royal College of Physicians be followed. And so in the United States by means of federal law, and in the United Kingdom by means of request from the government, research ethics committees were born.

It has been the mark of research ethics committees that their establishment and development has been evolutionary rather than fixed from the start. The main reason for this is that they, unsurprisingly, reflect the ethical views of the societies in which they exist. Over the last 30 years our views of what constitutes ethical behavior have changed. From considering that ethics consists of doing what is right by one's own standards of behavior, we have moved to determining our behavior by reference to the rights of others. So, for example, in the context of medical research on humans, a researcher might once have been happy to go by his own judgment as to when he might justifiably conduct research on his patients without telling them, as indicated by Sir Austin Bradford-Hill in the same lecture quoted above:

If the patient cannot really grasp the whole situation, or without upsetting his faith in your [the doctor's] judgment cannot be made to grasp it, then in my opinion the ethical decision still lies with the doctor, whether or not it is proper to exhibit, or withhold, a treatment.

Now, however, a doctor would regard it as essential to consult his patient's wishes first. So, reflecting this, the early research ethics committees, which as far as we know consisted only of doctors, would consider the relevant ethical questions to be whether or not the research is well designed and answers an important question, and whether the research subjects would be harmed as a result of being in the research. One research ethics committee had its applications and minutes of its meetings looked at by some researchers over the decade of the 1970s to see what were the committee's major ethical concerns. They were found in 1971 to be the number of subjects in the study sample, in 1975 to be risk to research subjects, and in 1979 to be risk to research subjects. Now there is no research ethics committee that would not regard seeking consent from research subjects before enrolling them in research as paramount. Most research ethics committees would claim that the aspect of the research on which they spend the most time is the information that is to be provided to potential research subjects before they decide whether to participate in the research.

It would be fair to suggest that the continual reminders to researching doctors that they should seek consent before enrolling subjects into their research projects has played its part in changing the view of patients as passive recipients of medical care to that of persons whose consent must be obtained before anything happens to them in the medical context. It should be pointed out that the imperative to seek consent in the context of research is given added emphasis because of the effect on the doctor–patient relationship that the research aspect of the treatment has. The relationship between a doctor and a patient is based upon the assumption that the doctor is going to do the very best for his patient, and that his decisions will be geared toward that end. In therapeutic research the relationship is changed, for the doctor is not only seeking the good of his patient, he is also seeking to discover generalizable knowledge as a result of their interaction. Unless the patient is explicitly told that he will be used as a means to the doctor's, or the wider public's, ends, he will not make that assumption. It is incumbent upon the doctor, therefore, to let his patients know if such an element is to be introduced into their relationship.

In nontherapeutic research the issue is clearer, the absence of consent seeking more obviously errant.

II. MEMBERSHIP AND CONSTITUTION OF RESEARCH ETHICS COMMITTEES

Research ethics committees customarily have 8 to 12 members. The membership consists of medical and nursing professionals, and lay people. The medical members usually include those who themselves conduct research, both in hospital and in general practice settings. The nurse members should include those who are in active practice with patients, on the grounds that this puts them in a good position to know what any research project would be like for the research subjects. The lay members have only one qualification in common, and that is that they have no relationship with the health service. Preferably they know nothing at all about medicine or research. This ignorance places them in a good position to judge the research projects they see from the perspective of the general public, whence research subjects will come. Lay members can tell better than the healthcare professionals whether the information to be given to patients would be comprehendible or not. Hence, the total membership of a research ethics committee should make it capable of assessing the scientific validity of a research project, knowing what it involves the research subjects in, and being assured that informed and voluntary consent will be sought. All the members need to be capable of analyzing the moral issues at stake, however, and here it seems necessary to provide training for members so that they can carry out this function satisfactorily. As far as ethical analysis goes, all the members of the committee are lay, unless one of the nonmedical members happens to be a moral philosopher, and some committees have included such professional thinkers among their members. However, one of the important reasons for having committees, rather than individuals, to make decisions about a research project's ethical acceptability is that all participate in and share the responsibility for, the decision as a whole. It matters that all members are happy with the scientific validity, all are happy about what research subjects are being asked to do, and all accept the viability of the proposed consent procedure, even if individual members are not expert to make these judgments on their own. The scientific members therefore need to be able to explain to the nonscientific members the justification for a research project; the nurses who can empathize with the research subjects likewise need to share their understanding with other members. If a moral philosopher is a member then his understanding of the moral issues needs to be shared too.

Researchers who wish to have their proposed research considered by a research ethics committee will complete an application form that asks the questions the committee regards as pertinent to ethical review (see below). Committee members receive the completed application forms before the meeting at which they are to be discussed, so that they can read them and consider them first. The committee will meet usually once a month and discuss each of the research projects in turn, either by interviewing the individual researchers or by referring to the paperwork alone. The discussion needs to be frank and full, so that the issues that matter are covered adequately. Interests are expected to be declared: this can sometimes be a subtle matter, for example, if one has strong views about abortion and a given research project involves using material from aborted fetuses, it is questionable whether one has interests that need to be declared or not.

Decisions are usually reached by means of consensus. At its best, this means that the committee members are all satisfied with the decision and share it. If some members are stronger or louder than others it may mean that certain quieter members' views are not given adequate airing and the consensus is only an appearance. Some committees vote as standard practice, others only when there is significant disagreement and a decision has to be reached. Importantly, the majority that a research ethics committee accepts needs to be one that includes the different kinds of members: a decision that only the lay members agreed with would be skewed, as it would be if it were only the doctors who agreed with it.

Research ethics committees, although existing to ensure that research subjects are properly cared for, usually have no direct contact with the research subjects. Their point of contact is the researcher, who ultimately bears moral responsibility for the research subjects he is using. This is important to realize: the research ethics committee's role is essentially advisory, and the members of the committee, although they have a duty to fulfill their function of deciding upon the ethical acceptability of research to the very best of their ability, cannot bear the direct moral responsibility of the research and the consequences that flow from it. This must lie primarily with the researcher who actually carries out the work, and secondarily with the sponsor of the research. There is indirect responsibility, of course, and if a research subject, injured as a result of being in a trial, decided to sue on a "catch-all" basis, members of re-

search ethics committees could well be individually liable in such an action.

Inevitably the relationship of the research ethics committee with the researcher is somewhat confrontational. This is because, for the researcher, the committee is just one more hurdle he has to scramble through before he can commence his research. Ethical clearance is one of the last hurdles, and he might have spent months trying to put together his proposal before it comes before the committee. If the committee chooses to regard the research as unethical for one reason or another he could find himself in the position of having wasted a considerable amount of time. If the committee wishes him to introduce changes to make his research more ethical he would be less distraught, perhaps, but most researchers would be disgruntled, not least because it is not in most people's nature to be deliberately unethical; hence, if the committee implies that one is being unethical this is something of an insult. The system of ethical review rather asks for such a relationship, however. A more educational approach taken by committees, one that perhaps started earlier on in the development of a research project, would undoubtedly lead to more fruitful work being done and would circumvent the current difficulties.

III. THE FUNCTION OF RESEARCH ETHICS COMMITTEES

The question of what makes a research project ethical is one that research ethics committees have considered over a period of about 30 years within their committees, as they looked at the research projects on which they had to give their views. Not being guided by laws (at any rate in the U.K.) about what was or what was not acceptable in human research, it was pretty much up to research ethics committees to fashion for themselves the ethical principles that were to govern research. In a way this was a haphazard approach: the government might have advised committees with more certainty about what they were to insist upon in the standards of research. However, it had some advantages. It meant that committees could adopt a flexible and responsive attitude toward the research proposals they looked at. They could make decisions based upon the particular set of circumstances in which each proposal rested, and each decision would be tailor made for that proposal. The situation of each proposal informed the committee about whether something was absolutely wrong or not, rather than an externally imposed system. For example, sometimes research involving invasive techniques on children would be appropriate, sometimes not. A research ethics committee that was merely imposing external rules as a regulating body would have no flexibility in such situations: as it was, they could decide for themselves what was best.

To a certain extent this is still true in the United Kingdom, although there are more rules for research ethics committees to take into account. There are also cases in law that have set common law precedents, which committees need to follow. One such example is the Gillick case, in which a judge ruled that if a child was competent to understand his treatment and its consequences, then that child's consent overrode that of his parents. It was his competence to consent rather than his age that was the deciding factor. The doctor was the one to decide on the competence of the child. So in a research project involving children research ethics committees would need to make sure that the researcher was aware that if his research subjects were competent to understand the research then their consent was to be sought and it was to take precedence over the consent of their parents.

The flexibility of approach does not mean that there is no need for systematic analysis of the moral issues at stake in any given research project. A framework can be adopted to help a committee to be sure that it has conducted a sound and reasonable ethical analysis. The following framework is based upon a theoretical moral philosophical approach that identifies three ways of thinking about morality. They are:

i. Goal-based morality, in which the moral agent asks if the outcome of his action is good. The outcome of the action is the important factor in deciding about the moral worthiness of the action itself.

ii. Duty-based morality, in which the moral agent considers his proposed action in the light of his moral principles. These will be such as the Ten Commandments or their equivalent. If his action does not accord with these principles, for example if it involves lying or stealing, then he will not regard his action as right. Notice that this is more of a negative comment on an action—this action is not acceptable—than a positive comment such as the goal-based moralist might make, for whom some actions will be morally obligatory because the outcome is positively good, rather than simply "not bad."

iii. Rights-based morality: the moral agent, rather than considering whether his actions will violate any of his own moral principles, asks whether those most affected by his action want it to happen. Here the emphasis of the decision moves from the agent of the action to its recipients.

These three approaches to a greater or lesser extent mirror some of the thinking processes we go through before undertaking actions. Some of us will favor the goal-based approach, others the duty-based and still others the rights-based. Importantly, a member of a research ethics committee needs to take all three seriously when considering research proposals, in the following way. The three approaches are loosely echoed in three sets of questions which need to be asked of each research project for it to be properly reviewed. These are:

i. (Goal-based) Scientific value and validity: Is the research important? Will the study answer the question being asked? Here the research ethics committee considers the question the research is asking. The research is judged on its hoped-for outcome. It needs to be justified on a goal-based analysis first, because if the research is invalid scientifically there is no point going on to consider matters related to the welfare of research subjects: the research will already be regarded as unethical.

ii. (Duty-based) Welfare of the research subject: What will participating in the research involve? Are the risks to which the research subject will be exposed justifiable and acceptable? On a duty-based approach, the question of whether it is right to do certain things to people in the name of research is considered. Even if the research is highly desirable with regard to its expected outcome, for example, if it is seeking a much-needed remedy for a disease, it may involve exposing the research subjects to risks that are too great to be acceptable on a duty-based consideration. Here the research ethics committee is at its most paternalistic. This is important: it is not sufficient that the committee should ensure that the research is good scientifically and that the research subjects' consent will be sought. A view needs to be taken on whether research subjects should be asked in the first place, and this requires a duty-based approach.

iii. (Rights-based) Humanity of the research subject. Will consent be sought? Will confidentiality be respected? The committee, having assured itself that the research itself is worth doing and that the risks to which subjects will be exposed are acceptable in the circumstances, must now ensure that no subject is used merely as a means to the researcher's end. Subjects must agree to be used, and this means they must give voluntary and informed consent to participating in the research.

Moreover, their confidence must be respected: it will make no difference to the outcome of the research if pictures of research subjects are spread over the pages of the *British Medical Journal,* because it will not affect the outcome of the research, nor will it be harmful to them physically, but their dignity will not be respected. Essentially these rights-based questions ask the researcher to consider the research subjects as human beings, and not merely as means to his ends.

Each of these areas of consideration can be expanded to include more detailed questions: the scientific validity can only be judged against specific information such as the sample size of the research, and the size of difference that is being looked for. The welfare of the research subjects is only going to be judged properly if all their circumstances are considered: are they patients, for example, or healthy volunteers? Is the research therapeutic or nontherapeutic? How many extra tests and other procedures will they have to undergo? Respecting the humanity of the research subjects depends upon the standard of information they will be given. Is it comprehendable? Is it being given in circumstances conducive to a reasonable response? Will subjects be given time to consider their decision?

Importantly, some research projects cannot honour one or more of the three sets of moral obligations.

i. Usually research projects satisfy the goal-based requirement of being necessary and important. However there are some projects that cannot offer assurance to begin with that they will produce answers that will be of any use to health care. Some projects seek knowledge for its own sake, not yet attached to any achievable clinical goal. Some projects are conducted by students, who need to learn how to conduct research and are perhaps only repeating a previous study for the purposes of their own education. In each of these cases the research ethics committee is going to need to be flexible and make a fresh decision depending on circumstances. Here we can appreciate the fluidity of the system, properly used. If there were a hard and fast rule that only research which could demonstrate a priori that it was going to be of use to future patients could be approved by a research ethics committee then much research which has ended up being invaluable would never have taken place.

ii. The duty-based requirement of ensuring that research subjects are not harmed by taking part in research, on a strict interpretation, is never fulfilled if the research is nontherapeutic. Nontherapeutic research is so called because it has no element of treatment in it

for the research subjects. One example of such research is phase one trials of drugs, when completely new drugs are given to healthy young men in order to observe the drugs' pharmacokinetics, their safety and their tolerance, but not their therapeutic advantages. Another example would be questionnaire-type surveys, or surveys of medical records, for epidemiological purposes. In these cases there is no intention to benefit the research subject, but only to use them as a means to obtain knowledge for the sake of others. A strict interpretation of the duty-based requirement to do no harm would point to the fact that even the very small risk that one might expect research subjects to be exposed to in a nontherapeutic research project is balanced by no benefit to those research subjects and therefore the duty-based requirement is not fulfilled. In therapeutic research, in which research is conducted within the context of treatment, the duty-based requirement is fulfilled if there is equipoise. By this is meant that for the researcher there is a balance of opinion about the efficacy of the new treatment as against what the research subject as a patient would receive as standard treatment, had he not been in the trial. In fact, in most therapeutic research the treatment being studied is compared to the standard treatment, in order to discover whether there is any therapeutic advantage in the new treatment. Patients enrolled into the trial will be randomly allocated to the standard or the new treatment to avoid bias. Often the researcher and the research subjects will not know even while the trial is going on which treatment they are receiving, if it is possible to make the two treatments look identical. This is acceptable if the researcher is in equipoise, because for him it will be acceptable to his duty of care as a doctor to give either treatment to his patients in the trial. New treatments may be compared to placebo; this is acceptable on a duty-based approach if the standard treatment is currently no treatment. What would not be acceptable in therapeutic research would be to give patients in the trial an inferior drug, or placebo, when a standard treatment exists. It is sometimes the case that the goal-based requirement of doing good research pulls against the duty-based requirement not to do harm. This might be said to be so in nontherapeutic research when the goal-based requirement to discover new treatments demands that individuals take risks in order to help others. Researchers may argue that they have to compare their new treatment against placebo, even if a standard treatment exists, because they need to show that their treatment is better than nothing, rather than the "best yet."

iii. The rights-based approach fails to be fulfilled when for one reason or another consent is not sought from people before they are entered into a trial. This would be unacceptable in cases where research subjects are capable of giving consent, but in some cases they are not, for example, if they are young children, or if they are mentally incapacitated, or if they are unconscious. Research is still needed on such groups of people. More contentiously, there may be goal-based requirements that demand that consent is not sought. Some research involves deception that, unlike randomization, cannot be consented to first. An example of this was a research project in which some subjects were given counseling after surgery and others were not. Their consent was not sought for this because it would have affected the results of the research and made them unreliable—a goal-based requirement. Sometimes the duty-based requirement pulls against the rights-based approach, in cases where the researcher feels it would be distressing to ask for research subjects' consent to take part in research, but the research itself is necessary and therapeutic, offering the opportunity for new treatments both to the research subjects as well as to future patients. The most difficult research project of all is the one that can fulfill only the goal-based requirement of offering a desirable outcome. If it is nontherapeutic, and the research subjects are, say, babies, and cannot consent, then neither of the other two sets of criteria can be met. The research ethics committee will have to come to a decision as to whether, in any given case, this is acceptable or not. Very occasionally it may be.

It should be clear from the above that the task of the research ethics committee is a delicate one, in which a fine balance between sometimes competing moral claims has to be found. It is important to appreciate this task, and to understand the need for flexible but rigorous thinking on the part of committee members. It is difficult to imagine hard and fast rules that would adequately govern the decisions of committees. Rather, one hopes to see good training in moral decision-making so that the decisions that research ethics committees come to are founded on sound and reasonable processes.

IV. THE STRENGTHS AND WEAKNESSES OF RESEARCH ETHICS COMMITTEES

Surveys of research ethics committees in the 1990s indicate that their standards of practice are high. Over the 30 years in which these committees have been used

as the principal method by which we ensure that the research that is conducted on human subjects is done ethically, their practices have refined until they are really very good. Any researcher applying to a research ethics committee will find his work carefully examined and the ethical issues thoroughly thought through. However, these high standards are internal to each committee, because each works independently. Each has a different application form and different policies that have been developed within committees rather than between them. The differences between committees can be seen in numerous little ways, such as the way in which different committees deal with the same information sheet to research subjects, asking for various and often mutually contradictory changes. For example, some research ethics committees insist that the research subjects are told if the researcher is being paid to do the research. Others insist that they are not told. Another example is of some committees insisting that information about compensation for injury is included, others insist that it should not be. There are endless disagreements about how much information should be given about side effects and risks of drugs to be administered during the trial, or of procedures research subjects will have to undergo.

This sort of disagreement is not evident in single-center research projects. The researcher will go to one research ethics committee and abide by its conditions and, apart from differences between the view of the researcher and of the committee (see below), there is no conflict.

However, there are increasing numbers of large-scale multicenter trials going on, not only nationally but also internationally. In many countries there are only local research ethics committees, not (yet) national committees. The local committees are geographically based within health districts and so are responsible for local populations. Hence, if a project spans more than one district the researcher must seek approval from all the research ethics committees whose districts are involved. This may mean going to just a handful of committees, but it may mean going to every committee in the country if the project is, for example, a national epidemiological project.

Even if the researcher has to seek approval from only a handful of research ethics committees he may very well receive different advice from each. Researchers are disturbed by these differences of opinion because the issues that are under debate are about the *ethical* acceptability of their research. Doctors and nurses conducting research are in professions that are bound by ethical codes. They will be concerned if there is some doubt as to the ethics of their proposed work. Naturally enough, they will want to be satisfied that their research is ethical. Different views from different committees will only cause confusion.

Is there any reason to be concerned about such confusion? If research ethics committees are only considering the ethics of a research project, and their conclusions differ, does that mean that some research is genuinely unethical, or that conclusions about ethical questions are by their very nature going to differ? If they do differ by their very nature, and research ethics committees are by and large demonstrably competent, does it make sense for a multicenter researcher to go to more than one committee? If it is the case that research ethics committees will come to different conclusions not by virtue of the incompetence of some of them but because it is in the nature of these sorts of decisions that differences will be seen, then the matter is simply resolved by creating a system whereby multicenter research need be seen by no more than one committee. The balances that need to be struck between moral claims that we saw in the previous section would suggest that we are always going to see differences between the decisions of different committees. Hence, the problem is easily solved at the practical level.

Another difficulty with the system is that of its confrontational nature, as we described when we looked at the nature of the relationship of committees with applicant researchers. Would a more educational approach be more intelligent? That is, the ethical issues should be addressed much earlier on in the process of developing a research protocol, and not at the end by a sometimes hostile board of advisors—or so it can seem to the researcher. If we regard a less confrontational, more educational approach to be more appropriate to the intended goal, the question then arises as to whether research ethics committees are the right bodies to be fulfilling that role. One can imagine that researchers might seek ethical advice earlier on in the development of their research ideas. However, we have seen that not all research can fulfill all moral requirements but that it might sometimes be acceptable, the important point being that no hard and fast rule can be made for all circumstances. In such cases it seems that the decision as to whether a particular project is ethical or not has to be made as a single, discrete event, taking all the circumstances into account and looking at them all at once. In most cases these circumstances will not be clear until the proposal is in its final form. It is not clear in such cases that we could invent a better system than the one we already have, providing research ethics committee members are sensitive enough, and thorough enough, to do their work in a sound and reasonable way.

Also See the Following Articles

HUMAN RESEARCH SUBJECTS, SELECTION OF • PLACEBO TREATMENT • RESEARCH ETHICS • SCIENCE AND ENGINEERING ETHICS, OVERVIEW

Bibliography

Botros, S., & Gilbert, F. C. (1993). The moral responsibilities of research ethics committees. In *Dispatches* 3, 3.

Evans, D., & Evans, M. (1996). *A decent proposal.* Chichester: Wiley and Sons.

Foster, C. (1994). Whither local research ethics committees? In *Dispatches* 5, 1.

Foster, C. (1995, July/August). Why do local research ethics committees disagree with each other? In *Journal of the Royal College of Physicians,* 29, 4.

Foster, C. (Ed.). (1996). *Manual for research ethics committees* (4th ed.). London: King's College.

RESEARCH METHODS AND POLICIES

Charles Weijer
University of Toronto

I. Research Methods
II. Research Policies

GLOSSARY

bias Systematic error in a research study predisposing results towards mismeasure or false conclusions.

clinical equipoise A state of genuine uncertainty in the community of expert practitioners as to the preferred treatment for a given medical condition; an ethical precondition for human experimentation (see Freedman, 1987a).

control treatment The medical intervention to which the experimental treatment of interest is compared; the best (or most prevalent) standard treatment for the medical condition or, if *no standard treatment exists,* placebo.

experimental treatment The medical, surgical, or psychosocial intervention of interest in a research study.

placebo A chemically inert substance given in the guise of medication (or other sham treatment) and usually designed to have the same appearance (e.g., color) and route of delivery (e.g., pill, capsule, injection) as the experimental treatment.

randomization The allocation of research subjects to differing treatments within a study by a chance or probabilistic mechanism.

RESEARCH is defined by the *New Shorter Oxford English Dictionary* as "a search or investigation undertaken to discover facts and reach new conclusions by the critical study of a subject or by a course of scientific inquiry." This article will focus on biomedical research that involves human subjects. Important benefits accrue to society from such research: psychologists and other behavioral researchers shed light on the complexities of the mind, medical researchers elucidate the causes of human disease and evaluate the safety and efficacy of novel treatments, and geneticists decode the very blueprint of the human organism. But as important as such information is, it cannot be obtained legitimately at any cost. As we shall see, many examples of unethical research exist—research that has treated scientific method or research subjects (or both) with utter disregard. Research involving human subjects must be carefully regulated by ethical principle and governmental policy to ensure that the highest scientific and ethical standards are maintained.

The purpose of this article is threefold. First, to familiarize the reader with important types of research involving human subjects. Basic information on the scope of research methods and specific information on methods that have attracted the most attention from ethicists and policy makers will be provided. Second, the article will lay out a framework for ethical and regulatory issues in human subjects research. Widely accepted principles for the ethical conduct of research will be discussed, as will recent suggestions for additional standards. Third, the essay will point out areas of current controversy and interest in the rapidly expanding field of research ethics.

I. RESEARCH METHODS

A. The Purpose and Scope of Empirical Research

1. Defining Research

Deciding what counts as research in medicine can, at times, be a difficult matter. The question has important normative ramifications. Interventions—drug treatment, radiation therapy, surgery, behavioral interventions—considered standard medical practice are governed by the norms of the physician–patient relationship. As such, these interventions are only subject to review after the fact, be it by hospital committees, professional organizations, or the courts. If interventions are considered research, different standards apply. Research must conform to guidelines and regulations set out in a variety of policies. Such policies typically require that research be reviewed in advance by research ethics committees (RECs in the United Kingdom; IRBs, Institutional Review Boards, in the United States; and REBs, Research Ethics Boards, in Canada) and lay out standards for, inter alia, scientific validity and value, an acceptable balance of potential benefits and harms, and informed consent.

Research might be identified as separate from medical practice on the basis of any one of a variety of characteristics, including design, intent, and the use of novel drugs or procedures. Perhaps the most widely promulgated definition is that found within the Common Federal Rule—unified regulations for the conduct of human subjects research adopted by 16 U.S. government departments and agencies. The Common Federal Rule defines research as "a systematic investigation, including research development, testing and evaluation, designed to develop or contribute to generalizable knowledge." (Federal Policy for the Protection of Human Subjects; Notices and Rules. (1991). *Federal Register* 56, 28001–28032.) The key distinguishing feature of research, according to the definition, is the *intention* to produce widely applicable knowledge; accordingly, untested ("nonvalidated") treatment given to individual patients and quality assurance studies within individual institutions may not be classified as research. The U.S. Food and Drug Administration (FDA), on the other hand, defines research differently: research involves use of novel drugs or procedures. Hence, the use of an untested treatment for the treatment of an individual patient may be considered research under FDA regulations.

The distinction between research and medical practice is further muddied by the fact that research studies often contain a mixture of standard and experimental interventions. Rather than attempting to classify an *entire protocol* as medical practice or research, Freedman and colleagues have argued for an *intrastudy* demarcation of research and therapeutic interventions (Freedman, Fuks, Weijer, 1992). Two levels of demarcation are involved in the process described. First, elements of a study protocol that represent standard medical practice are distinguished from research interventions; as explained above, different norms govern standard practice and research. Second, research interventions themselves are then divided further: research interventions that carry therapeutic intent must be considered separately from interventions without therapeutic intent (discussed further in section on "beneficence").

2. Scope of Research Questions

The scope of questions in medical research is very broad indeed. A surgeon may wonder if a new surgical technique is promising; a psychologist may attempt to determine the psychological consequences of a subject's decision to enter a research study; an epidemiologist may ask, "Is a particular disease associated with exposure to an environmental factor?"; a pharmaceutical company may try to prove that a new drug is both safe and efficacious for the treatment of one type of disease; and a geneticist may inquire, "What is the gene (or genes) that causes (or predisposes to) a given disease?" Each of these research questions in turn implies a differing methodological approach.

B. Important Research Methodologies

A wide variety of research methods exist in biomedicine: case series, observational study, case-control study, clinical trials (including randomized controlled trials), and genetic studies are but a few of the most important types. The critical determinant of research design is the study question itself; a precisely formulated question entails a particular research methodology. Other practical factors, of course, influence choice of design, including the availability of research subjects, cost, and ethics.

1. Case Series

Case series reports, until not too long ago, formed the basis of much of medical practice. A case series is essentially a record of clinical practice in which the clinician's experience with one or more similar patients is reported. Case series can be used to provide information on how to apply a new medical intervention, demonstrate its feasibility, and identify complications or other barriers to its implementation. The surgeon with a new operative technique, for example, may elect to examine systematically the intervention on a series of patients to obtain just this sort of information. The case series is an inexpensive study method, but further research using other designs is needed to provide reliable evidence of efficacy. Case series may mislead when the reporting of cases is incomplete (e.g., only successes are reported), or, more subtly, if clinicians—intentionally or unintentionally—select preferentially certain types of patients for inclusion in the study, for example, patients with the best prognosis.

2. Observational Study

Observational studies are a large class of study designs in which data is collected from research subjects who are nonrandomly assigned to treatments or outcomes. Observational studies are typically classified as either prospective or retrospective (retrospective designs will be discussed in the next section). In a prospective study, often called a cohort study, research subjects are nonrandomly assigned or assign themselves to treatments and data is collected on outcomes of interest. Cohort studies can provide useful information on cause-and-effect relationships and data on the safety and efficacy of medical interventions, particularly when a randomized controlled trial is not feasible. For example, the psychologist interested in consequences of research participation may choose to follow a cohort of subjects who have decided to participate in a research study or not. A major problem with cohort studies involves the comparability of the study groups arising from subject (e.g., healthier and more hopeful subjects may select research participation making it appear that participation itself has a tonic effect) or treatment-related factors (e.g., only healthier and more hopeful subjects are eligible for or offered research participation, again, predisposing one to false conclusions). While design and analytic techniques exist to control for known factors, important but unknown factors cannot be controlled for in such studies.

3. Case-Control Study

Case-control studies are a well-known example of a retrospective observational study. In case-control designs, subjects are chosen on the basis of having an outcome of interest or not, that is, they are either a "case" or a "control." The two groups are then compared for exposure to antecedent factors. Case-control studies can provide important clues to cause-and-effect relationships and are most useful in studying infrequent events or circumstances in which other designs would be unethical. For example, the epidemiologist wishing to investigate environmental factors associated with a particular disease may compare persons with the disease and carefully matched controls for their exposure to environmental factors. Case-control studies are not without their challenges, however: evidence of cause-and-effect is not as strong as in prospective studies and study results may be biased by factors such as recall.

4. Clinical Trials

Clinical trials are a collection of study designs specifically conceived for the rigorous evaluation of the safety and efficacy of new medical treatments. New treatments, particularly new drugs, pass through a fairly standard progression of study types. For example, a pharmaceutical company with a promising new drug will generally first test the drug in animals for safety and, if animal models of the disease of interest exist, efficacy as well. Human testing begins with the *phase I clinical trial* in which safety and pharmacodynamics (the way the human body breaks down the drug) is assessed in a small group of subjects, often healthy volunteers. In the *phase II clinical trial* the efficacy of the drug in treating the disease of interest is tested in a small group of patients. If the new drug shows promise based on one or more phase II studies, a *phase III clinical trial,* usually a randomized controlled trial (RCT), will be carried out.

In a RCT, the new treatment is compared with standard treatment for the disease (or placebo, if no standard treatment exists) by randomizing subjects to treatment and following them until some outcome occurs (or for a fixed period of time). Major advantages are conferred on RCTs by randomization: systematic biases that arise when physicians or subjects choose the treatment are protected against, unknown biasing factors are randomly distributed, and this, in turn, enables such factors to be rigorously allowed for by statistical methods. For all their advantages, RCTs may be difficult to conduct if the treatments to be compared are very different (subjects will be reluctant to enroll), or if the outcome of interest is infrequent (the trial must be large and therefore costly).

5. Genetics Research

Genetics research has undergone a revolution in the last two decades. Technological advances in molecular genetics, methodological advances in genetic epidemiology, and increased public funding have led to an explosion in knowledge about the relationship between the structure of human genes and disease. How might a genetics researcher attempt to uncover the genetic basis of a particular disease? Often the starting point is a family or collection of families in which the disease is unexpectedly prevalent. By constructing a pedigree—a family tree that includes information on whether individual family members have the disease—geneticists gain clues to the mode of inheritance of the disease. If blood samples are taken from family members, the inheritance of the disease trait can be matched to DNA sequences whose location is known, thereby providing information on the location of the disease gene or genes. The next stage typically involves actually determining the chemical makeup (sequence) of segments of DNA in which the disease gene is likely to reside.

The geneticist's job is not over once the gene has been identified. Additional questions include: What is the mechanism by which the gene causes the disease? How can this information be used to treat the disease? If no good alternatives exist, can the disease be treated by replacing the "defective" gene (gene therapy)?

II. RESEARCH POLICIES

A. Historical Background

1. Unethical Research

Perhaps the best known example of unethical research is the heinous human experimentation carried out in Nazi Germany during World War II. German physicians and scientists subjected Jews, Russians, Gypsies, political prisoners, homosexuals, and others to a wide range of research. Overall, the experiments were characterized by disregard for the welfare of research subjects, poor or no informed consent, and shoddy scientific design (Caplan, A. L. (1992). *When medicine went mad: Bioethics and the holocaust.* Totawa, N.J.: Humana Press). The efforts of the Nazi state to eliminate non-Aryan people (policy of "racial hygiene") led to experiments examining sterilization techniques and methods of mass murder. Other research studies motivated by the exigencies of war, for example, the hypothermia experiments at Dachau, were sparked by high losses of Axis aviators shot down in the North Sea (Berger, R. L. (1990). Nazi science—the Dachau hypothermia experiments. *New England Journal of Medicine* 322, 1435–1440). In the Dachau experiments, research subjects were immersed in tanks of ice water and either observed

until death or a variety of revival techniques were tested. Approximately 25% of the research subjects died as a direct result of their participation in the hypothermia experiments.

The Tuskegee syphilis experiment remains one of the most widely known examples of unethical research in the United States. (Jones, J. H. (1993). *Bad blood: The Tuskegee syphilis experiment.* New York: Free Press). Perhaps the longest running research project funded by the U.S. Public Health Service (1932–1972), the Tuskegee syphilis study examined the course of untreated syphilis in 400 African American men in Alabama. When penicillin, a safe and highly effective treatment for the disease, became available after World War II, it was withheld from study subjects. Furthermore, the men in the study were lied to and told that invasive tests, such as spinal taps (withdrawing fluid surrounding the spinal cord with a needle), done solely for research, were "treatments." It is estimated that 20% of the study participants died prematurely.

Unethical behavior in research studies, sadly enough, continues into this decade. According to a 1993 report from the U.S. Office for Research Integrity (ORI), Dr. Roger Poisson, a well-respected surgeon and cancer researcher at St. Luc Hospital in Montreal, Canada, falsified data on 99 of 1511 women with breast cancer entered in clinical trials of the National Surgical Adjuvant Breast and Bowel Project. (Angell, M., & Kassirer, J. P. (1994). Setting the record straight in the breast-cancer trials. *New England Journal of Medicine* 330, 1448–1449.) In the majority of cases, the data falsification involved information relevant to criteria for clinical trial eligibility—a checklist of requirements that prospective subjects must fulfill. In other cases, informed consent was not obtained properly from research subjects or serious medical contraindications to the use of one of the study treatments were ignored. During the 13-year period (1977–1990) that the fraud went undetected, Dr. Poisson received approximately $1 million in research funding from the U.S. National Cancer Institute and was a co-author on a number of articles in the prestigious *New England Journal of Medicine.* As a result of the ORI investigation, Dr. Poisson was barred from receiving grants or contracts from the U.S. government for an 8-year period.

2. Policy Development

Many policy initiatives, national and international, were begun as a direct response to the revelation of improprieties in the conduct of research. For example, the *Nuremberg Code* (1947), an important early statement in which 10 principles for research are laid out, arose out of the tribunal that prosecuted German war criminals after the war. Another important early statement is the United Nation's *International Covenant on Civil and Political Rights* (1958), in which the individual right not be experimented upon without informed consent is codified. The World Medical Association's *Declaration of Helsinki* (1964, revised 1975, 1983, 1989) remains one of the most influential international statements governing the conduct of research. Article II.3 of the *Declaration* makes explicit the important requirement that the medical care of the research subject ought not be disadvantaged by study participation.

Perhaps the most important recent international document is the *International Ethical Guidelines for Biomedical Research Involving Human Subjects* (1993) by the Council for International Organizations of Medical Sciences (CIOMS). The CIOMS document lays out 15 guidelines for the conduct of research covering a wide range of subjects. The document is of particular relevance for first-world researchers proposing to conduct studies in underdeveloped countries. Article 8 requires that such research is only allowable if (1) the study could not be conducted in the developed country, (2) the research is responsive to the needs of the community being studied, (3) informed consent is obtained, and (4) the study is reviewed by an ethical review committee that includes persons with appropriate anthropological expertise. Epidemiological research raises some discrete ethical concerns and these are dealt with in another CIOMS document, *International Guidelines for Ethical Review of Epidemiological Studies* (1991).

In addition to international requirements, the conduct (and review) of research is governed by national guidelines (or regulations) in many countries, including the United States, England, Ireland, Australia, New Zealand, and Canada (see McNeill, 1993, pp. 53–84). In the United States, the review of research proposals for ethical acceptability began in 1966 with a directive from Surgeon General Stewart requiring that all U.S. Public Health Service research be reviewed by local committees. Following the revelation of ethical improprieties in the Tuskegee syphilis study, the Department of Health, Education and Welfare (now the Department of Health and Human Services) issued the first regulations governing the conduct of research in 1974. In the same year, a national commission, the National Commission for the Protection of Subjects of Biomedical and Behavioral Research (hereafter, the "National Commission"), was created to study ethical issues in the conduct of human experimentation. The final report of the National Commission, entitled the *Belmont Report*—discussed in the next section—was issued in

1979. The conduct of research ethics review was subsequently scrutinized by another body, the President's Commission for the Study of Ethical Problems in Medicine and Biomedical and Behavioral Research (1980–1983). Revisions to the Department of Health and Human Services regulations governing human subjects research were made in 1983 and in 1991.

B. The *Belmont Report*: An Ethical Framework for Research

In the *Belmont Report*, the members of the National Commission formulate an ethical framework for research involving human subjects composed of three ethical principles: respect for persons, beneficence, and justice. The principles were chosen because of their general acceptance in our cultural tradition and their particular relevance to research. Recognizing that rules governing the conduct of research would at times come into conflict, the members of the National Commission sought to "provide an analytical framework that will guide the resolution of ethical problems arising from research involving human subjects." What are the three principles and how do they guide the conduct of human subjects research?

1. Respect for Persons

The principle of respect for persons holds that the choices of autonomous individuals ought to be respected (unless those choices will harm others). An autonomous individual is one who is "capable of deliberation about personal goals and of acting under the direction of such deliberation." The principle furthermore requires that persons who are not capable of such deliberation and action, that is, those who are not autonomous, are entitled to protection. Various groups are "at risk" of not being capable of autonomous choice, including persons at the extremes of life and those with mental illness.

The principle of respect for persons forms the ethical basis for the requirement of informed consent for research participation. Three essential components of informed consent have been described: voluntariness, information, and comprehension. Consent to research participation should be freely given. Clearly problematic cases involve individuals whose consent has been coerced or who have been offered undue inducement (e.g., large sums of money, or exaggerated claims of potential benefit); uncertainty surrounds cases involving individuals, such as prisoners, who may, by virtue of their circumstances, be less capable of exercising free choice. Information requirements for informed consent are typically laid out in individual guidelines. The Common Federal Rule (cited above), for example, requires that potential research subjects be informed, *inter alia,* of (1) the fact that the study involves research, the purpose of the research, the duration of participation, and the procedures involved, (2) risks and discomforts, (3) potential benefits, (4) alternative procedures or treatments, (5) how confidentiality will be maintained, (6) whether compensation or medical treatment is available in the event of injury, (7) who to contact with questions or in the event of injury, and (8) the right to withdraw from the study without penalty. Finally, reasonable steps ought to be taken to ensure that the information was understood by the subject.

2. Beneficence

The principle of beneficence recognizes that there is a general obligation to protect individuals from harm and to ensure their welfare. The principle is operationalized in terms of two complementary rules: "(1) do not harm and (2) maximize possible benefits and minimize possible harms." In the context of research, the principle underpins the requirement that research present participants with a favorable balance of potential benefits and risks.

But how does one "balance" risks and potential benefits? As mentioned above, Freedman and colleagues have argued that a systematic approach for the analysis of research risk requires that therapeutic and nontherapeutic risks be considered separately (Freedman, Fuks, Weijer, 1992). Therapeutic risks, that is, the risks associated with procedures administered with therapeutic intent, must pass the test of clinical equipoise. In other words, there must exist a state of genuine uncertainty among expert practitioners as to the preferred treatment for the condition in question (Freedman, 1987a). For a nonvalidated treatment to be in equipoise, its anticipated therapeutic index, including its risk benefit ratio, must be thought to be equivalent to those of standard treatments in clinical practice.

By definition, nontherapeutic procedures present risk to subjects without the prospect for direct benefit and hence a difference calculus must be applied to them. The calculus involves two components. First, nontherapeutic research risks must be minimized. If a less-risky procedure can be used to gain equivalent information, it must be used. Second, nontherapeutic research risks must be balanced by the knowledge that can reasonably be expected to be gained from the study. Thus, nontherapeutic research risk is justified not by

a favorable balance of benefits and harms, but rather by a favorable balance of knowledge and harms.

3. Justice

Justice demands that the risks and potential benefits of research be distributed equitably. Historically, concern has centered around the inappropriate inclusion of vulnerable individuals in research. In the 1980s, with the advent of HIV/AIDS, individuals began to demand access to potentially life-saving treatments within clinical trials. As a result, it is now recognized that research protocols ought not exclude without good reason individuals who may benefit from study participation.

In the 1990s, a new justice-related issue has come to the fore: the applicability of the results of research. Certain groups, including women and members of minority groups, have routinely been excluded from certain categories of research study. For example, women in their reproductive years were routinely excluded from early-stage drug studies and women of all ages were often barred from studies of new cardiovascular treatments. The systematic exclusion of these groups has led to a lack of knowledge regarding best treatment for a number of medical conditions. In an attempt to remedy this situation, the U.S. National Institutes of Health (NIH) issued the *NIH Guidelines on the Inclusion of Women and Minorities as Subjects in Clinical Research* (1994). These guidelines require that women and minorities be adequately represented in all NIH-funded research. Furthermore, when there is good reason to believe that treatment differences may exist based on gender or race, studies must be large enough to examine such differences.

C. New Principles

Although the principles articulated in the *Belmont Report* were intended to be comprehensive, some have suggested that additional principles are needed to guide the conduct of research. Three additional principles are discussed here: validity and value, honesty and accuracy, and respect for communities.

1. Validity and Value

Research studies must be soundly designed (valid) and pose important research questions (valuable). But whereas scientific validity is an absolute prerequisite to ethical acceptability, the value of an experiment is only a relative requirement (Freedman, 1987b). A valid study design is one that has the potential to accurately and reliably answer the study question (hypothesis). An invalid design does not and, therefore, human subjects are placed at risk unnecessarily and limited financial resources are squandered. For these reasons, an invalid study is never ethical. Evaluating the validity of a study calls for expertise in scientific methodology.

A study may, however, be scientifically valid but without value, that is, the research question asked is not important. The value of a study reflects the importance of the study hypothesis, in other words, it asks, How significant—to science, medicine, and society—is the knowledge likely to result from the study? In the section on "beneficence" we noted that nontherapeutic research risks were justified by the importance of the knowledge likely to be gained from a study. Turning this claim around, the degree of "value" required by a study depends on the amount of risk presented to research subjects. Even if the risk presented to subjects is small, trivial research questions are unlikely to be acceptable. As the degree of risk increases in a study, so too must the importance of the study question to society. The evaluation of value requires a broader range of representation than the evaluation of validity: certainly experts from the field in question are needed to judge the importance to science, but others, including community representatives, are required to weigh the importance to society at large.

2. Honesty and Accuracy

The breast cancer research fraud involving Dr. Roger Poisson highlights all too well the fact that ethical issues in research go beyond the study proposal itself. The research study must actually be conducted in accordance with the approved study protocol. Critical areas of conduct include: weighing the impact of new information, from the study and without, on the balance of benefits and harms within the study; obtaining informed consent from research subjects properly, that is, ensuring that subjects are informed and that they understand the consent information; warranting that study procedures as laid out in the protocol are adhered to; and, guaranteeing that data are collected in an accurate and timely fashion. Research ethics committees have an obligation to periodically monitor the conduct of research to ensure that investigators comply with these requirements (Weijer, et al., 1995).

Ethical concerns in research even extend beyond the completion of subject participation in the study. In order for the study results to impact optimally upon clinical practice, they must be reported in a timely and accurate fashion. For example, the Declaration of Helsinki requires that "[i]n the publication of his or her results, the physician is obliged to preserve the accuracy of the results." Researchers must ensure that study methods are reported completely. Procedures for the selection of research subjects must be fully disclosed for two reasons: to allow other researchers to replicate the study, and to allow clinicians reading the study to determine if the results of the study are applicable to patients in their practice. Investigators must carefully and comprehensively discuss all statistical tests employed in the data analysis; reporting only "positive" tests misleads the reader. Finally, study conclusions must not make exaggerated claims about the strength of evidence that the study presents or the scope of the patient population to which it applies.

3. Respect for Communities

The framework for the ethics of research as we have discussed it has focused largely on individual research subjects (and groups insofar as they might be wrongfully included in, or excluded from or underrepresented in research). When research involves other communities, particularly isolated or remote communities, new issues arise. Autonomous communities have their own politics, beliefs, and values, and research may disrupt any of these elements. In a community that undertakes decisions through a collective process, the mere act of seeking individual informed consent may harm the political structure. Providing information on disease prevention or treatment may impact negatively on beliefs regarding disease causation and traditional healing. Communities that believe in natural harmony may be offended by plans to take tissue samples from research subjects. If research is to avoid these harms, it seems we need a new principle, "respect for communities" (McCarthy, C. R. (1993). A North American perspective. In Bankowski, Z., & Levine, R. J., *Ethics and research on human subjects: International guidelines*. Geneva: Council for International Organizations of Medical Sciences, 208–211).

How should researchers show "respect for communities?" When conducting research that involves isolated communities, investigators should endeavor to protect the community from harm. While work remains to be done on operationalizing this principle, some rules seem fairly well established (e.g., Australia National Health and Medical Research Council. (1991). *Guidelines on ethical matters in Aboriginal and Torres Strait Islander health research*. Canberra: NHMRC: Publication No. E13.) First, researchers ought to acquire a reasonable amount of knowledge about the customs and traditions of a community before approaching it for research participation (the involvement of an anthropologist may be key). Second, before individuals are approached for study participation, permission to conduct the research ought to be obtained from the appropriate authorities in the community. Third, ideally, research projects should be responsive to local needs; when projects do not provide such direct benefits to communities, it may be appropriate to provide other culturally appropriate benefits to the community (e.g., needed equipment, health care). Fourth and finally, research studies ought to provide community members with an opportunity to participate in the design, conduct, analysis, and reporting of the research.

D. New Challenges

As far as the ethics and regulation of research has come over the last decades, important challenges remain. Genetics research poses a difficult set of questions for ethics and policy. (Glass, K., Weijer, C., Palmour, R., Shapiro, S., Lemmens, T., Lebacqz, K. (1996). Structuring the review of human genetic protocols: gene localization and identification studies. *IRB: A Review of Human Subjects Research* 18(4), 1–9.) As we indicated above, the current ethical framework focuses on the isolated research subject, but genetics studies often involve *related* individuals. How can the current framework acknowledge the morally relevant differences that occur when dealing with related research subjects? Also, genetic studies often seem to pose risks to individuals other than the research subject. For example, genetic studies often collect information on the health status of the research participant's family members and study results may provide information of the genetic risk of those same family members.

The involvement of patient communities in research poses another set of challenges for research ethics. A number of patient communities, including persons with HIV/AIDS and women with breast cancer, have demanded, and are beginning to receive, a role in the planning of research (Weijer C. (1995). Our bodies, or science. *The Sciences* 35(3), 41–45). Clearly, a number of aspects of the actual design of studies seem to call for community input: How much benefit is important? What study procedures are acceptable? But how can input from community members be incorporated while preserving the highest scientific standards? Clearly, further work and reflection is needed in both of the above areas.

Also See the Following Articles

GENETIC RESEARCH • HUMAN RESEARCH SUBJECTS, SELECTION OF • INFORMED CONSENT • PLACEBO TREATMENT

Bibliography

Council for International Organizations of Medical Sciences (CIOMS) (1993). *International Ethical Guidelines for Biomedical Research Involving Research Subjects.* Geneva: CIOMS.

Freedman, B. (1987a). Equipoise and the ethics of clinical research. *New England Journal of Medicine* 317, 141–145.

Freedman, B. (1987b). Scientific value and validity as ethical requirements for research: a proposed explication. *IRB: A Review of Human Subjects Research* 17(6), 7–10.

Freedman, B., Fuks, A., & Weijer, C. (1992). Demarcating research and treatment: a systematic approach for the analysis of the ethics of research. *Clinical Research* 40, 653–660.

Levine, R. J. (1988). *Ethics and Regulation of Clinical Research.* (2nd ed.). New Haven: Yale University Press.

Mastroianni, A. C., Faden, R., & Federman, D. (1994). *Women and Health Research: Ethical and Legal Issues of Including Women in Clinical Studies* (Vol. 1). Washington, D.C.: National Academy Press.

McNeill, P. M. (1993). *The Ethics and Politics of Human Experimentation.* New York: Cambridge University Press.

Office for the Protection from Research Risks. (1993). *Protecting Human Research Subjects: Institutional Review Board Guidebook.* Washington, DC: U.S. Government Printing Office.

Shapiro, S., & Louis, T. (Eds.). (1983). *Clinical Trials: Issues and Approaches.* New York: Marcel Dekker, Inc.

U.S. Advisory Committee on Human Radiation Experiments. (1996). *Final report of the Advisory Committee on Human Radiation Experiments.* New York: Oxford University Press.

Weijer, C., Shapiro, S., Fuks, S., Glass, K. C., & Skrutkowska, M. (1995). Monitoring clinical research: an obligation unfulfilled. *Canadian Medical Association Journal* 152, 1973–1980.

RESOURCE ALLOCATION

Darren Shickle
University of Sheffield

GLOSSARY

gross national product (GNP) and gross domestic product (GDP) Economists' terms for the value of all final goods and services produced by a national economy.

HEALTH CARE RESOURCES are increasingly scarce as the average age of the population increases, expectations of health rise, and new medical techniques are developed, despite significant increases in spending in most countries. Prioritization for health care is receiving increasing political, media, and public attention within most societies. There has always been rationing of health care, with some people having to wait or go without, usually because of an inability to pay. However, the nature of the prioritization debate has meant that the resource allocation decision-making process is now being made overt and explicit. The ethical basis of these decisions is also being questioned. Despite the

financial realities, there are some who use ethics to argue against any form of rationing. It is, however, more productive to use ethics to guide the prioritization process.

I. SCARCE HEALTH CARE RESOURCES: AN INTERNATIONAL PROBLEM

A. United Kingdom

1. Relative Increase in Health Care Budget

In 1973, £3.364 billion was spent on all forms of health care in the United Kingdom (equivalent to £60 per person). By 1993, U.K. expenditure on health care had increased to £43.313 billion (£745 per person). When inflation is taken into account, £207 was spent in 1993 on health care for every £100 that was spent in 1973.

2. Health Care Inflation

The rate of health care inflation tends to be higher than that for the general retail index. There will be examples of new technology saving money, for example, by reducing the length of hospital stays. However, on the whole the new technology is usually more expensive. The new technologies also mean that treatment can be provided for diseases where in the past little could be offered. While this is to be welcomed, it means that the increased range of services that could be provided by the health care system further increases the demands for resources.

3. Demographic Changes

Improvements in health care and general living standards have meant that the U.K. population is healthier and living longer. One of the consequences of this success is that health care systems are having to care for an increasing elderly population. In 1948, 1.7 million people in the United Kingdom were over 75 years of age, with 200,000 of these people over the age of 85. By 1994, the number over the age of 75 had increased by a factor of 2.4 (to 4.1 million) while the number over 85 had increased by a factor of 5 (to 1 million). Older people tend to require more health care (Fig. 1), so further increasing the demands on scarce resources (Fig. 2).

Society's expectation of health has changed with time. Not only does the population expect to live longer, they are also less tolerant of minor physical abnormalities and impairments.

Thus despite expansion in budgets (even after allowing for inflation), health care resources are perceived as becoming increasingly scarce. The 1990 NHS and Community Care Act was an attempt by the U.K. Government to deal with this growing tension, by introducing an internal market in health care. Health authorities became purchasers of health care, assessing the health status and needs of the population for which they are responsible (while they always had this role, the Act made this more explicit). The providers of health care, hospitals and community services, were allowed more managerial freedoms to develop services as they deemed appropriate. The quantity, quality, and cost of services is negotiated and specified via a contract. General practitioners could also choose to control a fund of money to directly purchase some care on behalf of some of their patients. The government has also encouraged delivery of services based on evidence of effectiveness and the opinions of the public. Political and geographical realities has meant however, that market forces have been largely restrained.

B. United States of America

When President Bill Clinton took office in 1993 he was determined to tackle two related crises in health care: the number of Americans without health insurance and spiraling health care costs. It was estimated that 37 million Americans had no insurance and that another 22 million had inadequate coverage. In 1993, health care consumed 14% of the gross national product, and it was projected to rise to 19%. There was a danger that spiraling health costs would bankrupt the government and cripple American businesses, which largely bare

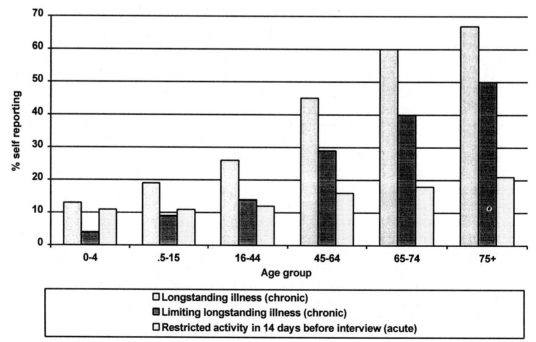

FIGURE 1   Acute and Chronic Morbidity in U.K. within Different Age Groups (1993). Source: Office of Population Censuses and Surveys (1995). *General Household Survey 1993. Series GHS No. 24.* London: HMSO.

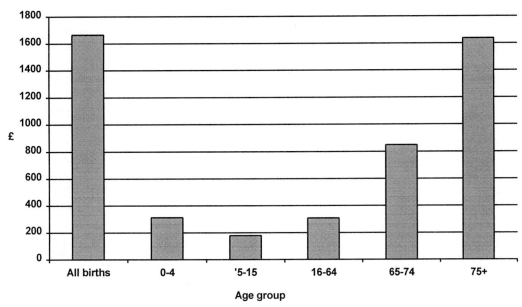

FIGURE 2   Estimated Per-head NHS Spending in U.K. by Age Group (1993/94). Source: Office of Health Economics (1995).

the costs of health insurance. The First Lady, Hillary Rodham Clinton, was appointed to lead a task force to produce a plan to tackle these problems. The subsequent proposals failed in Congress.

The recognition within the United States that health care resources are scarce and that rationing is necessary is not new. In 1932, the Committee on the Costs of Medical Care recognized that many Americans did not receive health care that was adequate either in quantity or quality, and the costs of service were not equitably distributed. They believed that the result was a significant amount of preventable physical pain and mental anguish, needless deaths, economic inefficiency, and social worth. The Committee therefore argued that regional and comprehensive health planning were needed to control health care costs and to achieve an equitable distribution of health care.

In March 1983, The President's Commission for the Study of Ethical Problems in Medicine and Biomedical and Behavioural Research produced a report on "Securing Access to Health Care: The Ethical Implications of Difference in the Availability of Health Services." In a letter submitting the report the Commission chairman commented that:

in examining the special nature of health care, we discern in our country's traditional commitment to fairness an ethical obligation on the part of society to ensure that all Americans have access to an adequate level of care without the imposition

of excessive burdens. This obligation does not require that everyone receive all health care that he or she may want or even that conceivably be of benefit. Instead, it is a moral responsibility to see that adequate care is accessible, a commitment that recognizes the competing claims on available resources of other worthwhile social goals.

The most often quoted example of health care prioritization occurred in Oregon. In 1991, the Oregon state government petitioned the U.S. federal government for permission to alter the way in which the state used federally allocated funds. The Oregon state program was premised on two basic assumptions:

• all uninsured poor people should have publicly funded health care coverage;
• coverage for this population can be made affordable to the taxpayers through explicit prioritization and the delivery of covered services through managed care systems.

A state law was passed to expand the state Medicaid program to cover all residents with incomes below the federal poverty level. However, the covered services to which the Medicaid-eligible population was entitled would change. A prioritized list was devised containing health conditions and their treatments. The list was limited to primary and acute services and excluded long-term care. The condition-treatment pairs were ordered following extensive public consultation. The state legislature was provided with the costed prioritized list. Starting at the top of the list, it determined what could be funded from available resources along with an acceptable "basic" package. Those services on the list below the line would not be provided.

The Oregon Plan was eventually granted the federal wavers in March 1993, and went into effect in February 1994, making an additional 115,000 Oregon citizens eligible for Medicaid coverage. The early experience suggests that the system has been successful in reducing health care usage in the state.

C. New Zealand

A new government came into power in New Zealand in 1990, having promised to reduce public debt while not increasing taxes. To meet these commitments it was necessary to reduce public spending, including that on health care. This economic policy was associated with an increasingly widely held promarket ideology and belief that the public health system was failing. A task force set up to make recommendations rejected a radical change from a tax funded system to one based on private insurance. The 14 Area Health Boards were abolished in July 1993 in favor of four publicly funded Regional Health Authorities. The document that laid out the reforms stated that:

> in the past, rationing has been done informally and often without public scrutiny or control. Defining a set of 'core health services' more explicitly will help ensure that the services the public believe to be the most important will be provided. It will also acknowledge more honestly that there are limits to the health services we can afford.

The statement of core services was meant to act both as a guarantee of a minimum entitlement that the individual could expect, as well as a way of capping the risk to the state of spiraling health care costs. The individual was expected to take additional insurance to cover those services outside the core. The Department of Health invited a public debate on how the core services should be defined. There was discussion as to whether the core would specify those services that would be provided or those that would not. In practice, the process proved to be too problematic. Instead, the National Advisory Committee on Core Health Services abandoned the concept of a definitive list in favor of a "qualified list" that sets out clinical circumstances in which a given treatment is deemed appropriate. The Committee recommended that the core contain all services historically provided but with treatment protocols controlling their use, determined by "when they provide a benefit, when they are cost-effective, when they are a fair and wise use of available resources, and when they are in accord with the values of communities."

D. The Netherlands

In 1990 the Netherlands Government Committee on Choices in Health Care was asked "to examine how to put limits on new medical technologies and how to deal with problems caused by scarcity of care, rationing of care and the necessity of selection of patients for care." In laying out the tasks for the Committee the State Secretary for Welfare, Health, and Cultural Affairs posed three questions: Why must we choose? What kind of choices do we have? and How should we make the choices? The Committee was expected to propose strategies to improve choices at different levels of health care: national (macro), institutional (meso), and individual caregiver (micro).

The Committee expressed a clear opinion that "choices in health care are unavoidable and necessary." A community-orientated approach was preferred in which individual rights and professional autonomy were limited in the interests of equity and solidarity in health care. The Committee advised that the basic package of the mandatory health insurance should contain only care that meets the following four criteria: the care must be necessary, effective, efficient, and cannot be left to the individual's responsibility. The Committee applied its criteria to different types of health services and, as in New Zealand, it was concluded that it was not feasible to exclude complete services and treatments from the basic health care package because effectiveness of care has to be assessed in relation to characteristics of each case. The importance of health professionals in determining whether treatment will be effective meant that the Committee concluded that physicians have the primary role in ensuring that health care was appropriate. However, health professionals should be "accountable for the quality of their actions, and for the financial implications there of." Treatment choices would have to be made in the context of standards and guidelines drawn up by professional organizations although the Committee recommended that the government encourage extensive public discussion on choices in health care.

II. ARGUMENTS AGAINST PRIORITIZATION

Rationing is becoming increasingly explicit, although prioritization of health care is not new. For example, there may be waiting lists for a particular treatment, or a service may not be available at all. The overt nature of prioritization is to be welcomed, because it allows those who are denied treatment to understand why their demands have been rejected, and if necessary to challenge the decision, or even to campaign for alterations in the prioritization mechanism. Although most Western countries have deemed it necessary to take some action to deal with the problem of scarce health care resources, three fundamental arguments have been proposed against the need to ration of health care:

A. The myth of infinite demand: an increase in health care spending, especially targeted towards those in "real" need, could satisfy all demands for health care, and hence make prioritization unnecessary. There is another variant on this argument that suggests that additional spending on preventive measures in the present would reduce future morbidity, thus releasing resources to treat any remaining unmet need.
B. Health care is a right: if there is a right to health care, then obligations to provide health services should be met in preference to demands for services for which no such right exists.
C. Incommensurability: even if it is accepted that resources are scarce, then it is not possible to prioritize because it is not possible to place a value on life or its quality; thus, comparisons cannot be made.

A. Never Enough or the Myth of Infinite Demand

When the NHS was first established in the United Kingdom in 1948, it was thought that there would be an initial increase in demand for health care, as people with unmet needs who could not previously afford treatment came forward for treatment. However, after the backlog was dealt with, it was expected that the population would be healthier, and so the resources required to fund the NHS could be reduced. In practice, demand has increased year-on-year. It is widely considered that demand for health care will be "infinite," with increased funding never being enough. However, there are those who still argue that rationing is not inevitable:

. . . is demand for health care infinite? After all, many diseases have been eradicated completely, at least in the Western world, and we all have a finite number of limbs and organs to be replaced, removed, or remodelled. Are we really sitting on a complex mass of health problems just waiting to explode as soon as we know that they can be treated? And just because medical science is increasingly capable of prolonging life, will patients necessarily welcome more medical intervention and perhaps more discomfort at the expense of greater quality of life? . . . Are we sure that demands could not be met completely with a relatively modest increase in resources. If demand were to be met in full, and care was available— unrationed and as soon as it was needed—we could avoid costly and unnecessary problems associated with waiting for treatment (Hancock, C. (1993). Getting a quart out of a pint pot. In: Anon. (Ed.). Rationing in action. London: BMJ Publishing Group).

In a U.K. survey on attitudes to health care rationing among the public, doctors, and NHS managers, 51% of the public advocated "unlimited funding and said that the extra money should come from higher income tax and national insurance contributions and lower defense spending." A significant minority of doctors (17%) also believed that funding should be unlimited, although virtually all of the managers said that NHS spending should be restricted within budgets, even if that meant that some treatments would have higher priority than others. When asked where the extra money should come from, both the public and doctors said that income tax and national insurance should be increased and spending on defense reduced.

A survey conducted in the United Kingdom asked members of the public how they would wish to see available resources allocated to the various areas of public spending. The public's preferences were not dissimilar to the proportion actually spent on each, although, not surprisingly, they appeared to wish to spend more on health care and less on defense than was actually being spent. If these preferences had been translated into actual budget allocation, it would have meant an additional £5 billion available for health care (a 25% increase in the actual budget). It should be noted however that despite various opinion surveys regularly indicate that the public would be willing to pay increased taxes towards the NHS, they have not demonstrated this at the ballot box (although general elections are fought on many issues other than health).

Arguments in favor of spending more on health care are particularly common in the United Kingdom, because of the relatively low percentage of public spending allocated to the National Health Service. For example, Doyal rejected arguments in favor of an infinite demand and suggested that:

> if Britain spent roughly the same percentage of gross national product as many other countries in the European Union on the satisfaction of objective need for health care, a much higher percentage of disability than at present could be reduced or eliminated. There can be no stronger argument for increasing spending on health care than this.

In 1992, the United Kingdom spent 7.1% of its gross domestic product on health care (public and private expenditure). Most other European and OECD member countries spend considerably more on health care (Fig. 3). For example, the average percentage of GDP spent by countries in the European Union in 1992 was 8.3%, with an average of 9.9% being spent across all OECD countries.

The proportion of GDP spent on health care within the United Kingdom has actually been rising although the percentage increase in GDP spending on health care within other OECD countries has been even greater (Fig. 4). However, there are opportunity costs consequent from spending more on health. Because money can only be spent once, the increase in health care spending has been associated with a decrease in other areas (Fig. 5).

Doyal pointed out that the health care system was not as efficient as it could be, and hence implied that such cost improvements should be made before resorting to rationing. He also argued that the rate in growth necessary to care for a more elderly population could "be reduced by more accurate needs assessment; by more effective prevention through integrated primary, secondary, and community care; and by general acceptance of consistent guidelines which would rule

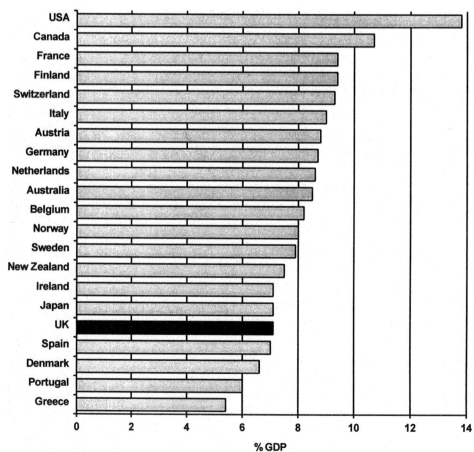

FIGURE 3 Total Health Expenditure as Percent of GDP, 1992. Source: Office of Health Economics (1995).

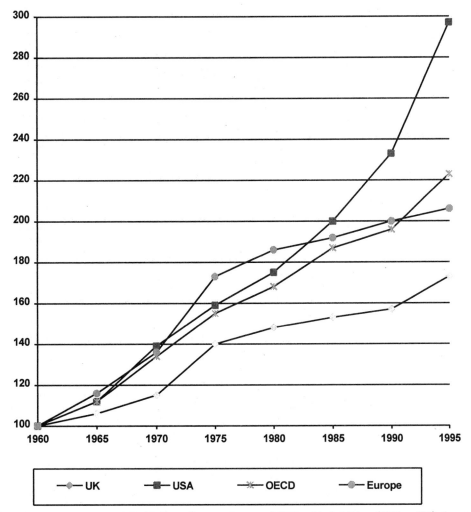

FIGURE 4 Relative Increase in Total Health Expenditure as Percent of GDP at Market Prices (1960 = 100). Source: Office of Health Economics (1995).

out the provision of futile and often very expensive life saving treatment."

While such measures may well result in a more effective and efficient use of resources, they do require disinvestment and the refocusing of resources. Doyal's argument is therefore supportive of the need for rationing.

However, there is a more fundamental response to those who argue that more should be spent on health care, because diverting money to health care from other areas of public spending may actually harm the public health. In a discussion of the proportion of societal resources that should be allocated to health care as opposed to "other social goods such as education, defense, the elimination of poverty, and the improvement of the environment," Childress quoted Flew's argument

that "morally, so long as hospitals are needed, hospitals must always have priority over amusement parks." The grounds for this argument are that pain is not symmetrical with pleasure and that the more fundamental duty is to alleviate pain. In response, Childress felt that:

it is not evident (a) that hospitals are primarily to alleviate pain, and (b) that they should always take priority over all other social goods that do not contribute to the aim of hospitals, whether it is the alleviation of pain or some other goal. Health may be a condition for many values for individuals and the community, but it does not have finality or ultimacy. It is not true that when it comes to health, no amount is too much."

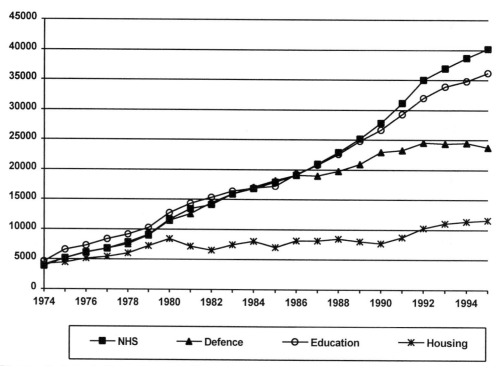

FIGURE 5   Trend in Budget for Various Sectors of Public Spending in U.K. (1974–1995). Source: Office of Health Economics (1995).

While more could be spent on health care, a patient who does not receive health care may not be able to claim that it is unjust that resources are spent elsewhere, for example, to give someone else a better standard of education.

Can one complain of injustice if society puts more money into space programs or defense than health care? "Wrong" priorities may not be unjust unless there are certain basic needs or rights that must be satisfied for justice to be realized.

Indeed, it may well be that the health of society can be better served by investing in other sectors of public spending other than medical care. Carlson argued that there were five major influences on health, which he ranked in order of importance as: environment, lifestyle, society, genetics, and medical care (Carlson, R. J. (1981). Alternative Legislative Strategies for Licensure; Licensure and Health. In: Childress, J. F. *Priorities in Biomedical Ethics*. Philadelphia: The Westminster Press). He considered medical care to be the least important determinant of health, giving it a weighting of approximately 6%. Thus, if one wishes to improve the public health, increasing medical care is probably not the most effective strategy.

Harris also recognized the dangers of investing in health care without considering the consequences:

Those who place an infinite value on human life will have many problems to resolve. They would have to believe that they must go on saving lives even if the consequences of so doing were ruinous for many other important aspects of life. And of course, if such things as housing, sanitation, and other areas of social welfare are to be neglected so that resources may be directed to more immediate life-saving measures, there will be a delayed feedback effect and the lack of these services will begin to cost lives.

However, Childress felt that:

As long as medical care is perceived as important to health or at least increases our sense of security, perhaps we ought to promote equal access to it. Despite the apparent oddity of arguing for equal access to what is ineffective, the principle of equality may indicate that such a policy is morally defensible and even mandatory.

While medical care may be perceived as important, what of the argument that access to it is a right?

B. Is There a Right to Health Care?

Doyal believes that health is a basic human need because:

> Physical and mental health are necessary conditions ... for optimally successful social participation. Without such participation, people have no chance to flourish.

This definition is consistent with a sociological definition of health whereby health is a means of developing a social role. Physical and mental illness impairs the ability to interact with others and hence "to learn who we are and what we can do as people through our interaction with others." According to Doyal, therefore, ill health threatens both short- and long-term well-being. He further argues that there is an obligation to help others to flourish, and that ill health impairs the ability to discharge this duty. If it is argued that the individual "ought" to help others, then it is necessary that the individual "can" do it. For these reasons Doyal argues that "appropriate health care" is also a basic human right, because:

> it logically follows that if we wish to impute moral duties to others then we have no option but to accept that they have the right to appropriate health care to enable them to do their best to be good citizens.

The "ought-implies-can" argument can be applied in other ways. Can it be said that society "ought" to meet demands made under a right to appropriate health care, if it "cannot" afford to provide the necessary services?

Doyal argued that there should be evidence that patients "are obviously disabled by their unmet needs" and that the proposed treatments are likely to be effective. He believed that the fact that "a patient wants, or a clinician prefers to provide treatments of a certain kind are of no moral consequence in themselves." He thereby suggested that there is only a right to "appropriate" and "effective" health care.

In the context of health care provision within the United Kingdom, individuals do not have an automatic right to the health care that they desire. Even within the Beveridge Report all that was promised were "equal opportunities in securing the medical care needed." With only limited resources available to be spent on health care, if one patient's treatment consumes large amounts of money, then others will have to go without. What they should expect is that their health needs are given equal consideration to someone with a similar health problem. This is the "principle of equal consideration of interests":

> The essence of the principle of equal consideration of interests is that we give equal weight in our moral deliberations to the like interests of all those affected by our actions. This means that if only X and Y would be affected by a possible act, and if X stands to lose more than Y stands to gain, it is better not to do the act. We cannot, if we accept the principle of equal consideration of interests, say that doing the act is better despite the facts described, because we are more concerned about Y than we are about X. What the principle really amounts to is this: an interest is an interest, whoever's interest it may be (Singer, P. (1993). *Practical Ethics*, p. 21. Cambridge: Cambridge University Press).

Thus, if both X and Y are in pain, and the relief of pain is considered to be morally desirable, then the principle dictates that we should try to relieve pain, whoever is suffering it. However, if X's pain is worse than Y's then the principle would give more weight to relief of X's pain. Singer suggested that if the degrees of pain were equal then other factors could be considered, especially if others are affected. Thus, in the event of an earthquake, Singer might give priority to the relief of a doctor's pain in order that he/she could help relieve the pain of others. However, the principle remains intact, as Singer points out that "the doctor's pain itself counts only once, and with no added weighting." Thus, just as with a pair of scales, the choice of action depends on who has the more pain, or if several interests combine to outweigh a smaller number of interests. Utilitarianism incorporates "justice," not only because it maximizes benefits to society, but when weighing the consequences of an action for individuals "each counts as one and no-one for more than one."

Equal consideration of interests does not mean equality of treatment. Singer described two victims of an earthquake, one experiencing severe pain due to a crushed leg, while the other had only slight pain as a result of a gashed thigh. If there were only two "doses" of morphine available, how should they be distributed? Equal treatment would suggest that each person should have one "dose" each. This would result in a pain-free state for the person with a gashed leg, while the more severely injured person would probably still be in pain. Thus, the inequality of pain suffered between the two remains. One solution to this would be to give a "double dose" to the patient with a crushed leg. By giving the second dose of morphine to the patient with the crushed leg it is possible that the combined total of pain suffered by these two individuals, may be reduced by a greater amount than by the equal distribution of morphine. As a consequence the inequality in pain suffered is reduced. Thus equal consideration of interests may result in an inegalitarian but equitable decision, that is, to give all the morphine to one, and none to the other.

C. Incommensurability: "You Can't Put a Value on Life"

It is possible to accept that health care resources are finite and insufficient to meet all demands for health care and yet reject any attempt at prioritization. A number of arguments have been proposed to support the belief that life is an incommensurable value, and hence it is not possible to trade the life of a patient who potentially could be saved, for any other life or any other outcome associated with utility. For example, as Williams argues:

> In cases of planning, conservation, welfare, and social decisions of all kinds, a set of values which are, at least notionally, quantified in terms of resources, are confronted by values which are not quantifiable in terms of resources: such as the value of preserving an ancient part of a town, or of contriving dignity as well as comfort for patients in a geriatric unit.

Griffin has rejected Williams' arguments:

> "... that some values lend themselves to quantification in terms of resources and others do not shows nothing.... If we are able to enhance the dignity of some geriatric patients by giving them greater privacy or enhance their comfort by giving them better heating, how should we decide which to do? ... If Williams' point is that these two values cannot be got on the same scale, then he is wrong. The patients, when informed, can rank them—and in the strong sense.

Harris argues that a person who knows for certain that they only have a short time to live can place a value on their remaining time equal to that of a person who has a much longer life expectancy, "precisely because it is all the time left." Thus, if two patients both say that they value their life highly, no matter how the quality of their lives or their probable life expectancy is judged by a neutral party, then Harris' argument would support an equal right to treatment.

> All of us who wish to go on living have something that each of us values equally although for each it is different in character, for some a much richer prize than for others, and we know of us its true extent ... Whether we are 17 or 70, in perfect health or suffering from a terminal disease we each have the rest of our lives to lead. So long as we each fervently wish to live out the rest of our lives, however long that turns out to be, then if we do not deserve to die, we each suffer the same injustice if our wishes are deliberately frustrated and we are cut off prematurely.

The only way to resolve the dilemma of allocating limited resources that are insufficient to meet the needs of all patients would therefore be the adoption of a lottery, with random allocation of treatment. Arguments for a lottery are largely based on the only-judge principle. In his essay "On Liberty" Mill stated this principle as "no one but the person himself can judge." A third party, when trying to judge best interests, can only predict what they would do if they were in the same circumstances. However, such judgments can only be guesses, and there are no right answers other than the answer that the subject ultimately delivers. The principle is based on the "privileged-access" argument:

> Each of us ... has privileged access to his own mental states, conspicuously among them thoughts, feelings and emotions. Much though others may empathize with me—imagining themselves in my place, feeling pain in my pain and taking pleasure in my pleasure—they are in the final analysis only feeling feelings like mine. They cannot experience my feelings without putting themselves in my place quite literally, occupying my body and my mind as well (Goodin, R. E. (1995). *Utilitarianism as a public philosophy*. Cambridge: Cambridge University Press).

A patient may say that it is in their interests to have a particular treatment, but many others may also say that it is in their interests to have access to the scarce resources.

> Statements of interests entail *claims*, not just demand. To say "I want x" is a demand. We do not need to know why, only that you want x, to

comprehend fully the nature of the predisposition and (if we are in the business of want-satisfaction) to act upon it.

However, the business of health care is need satisfaction. Goodin believed that to say "it is in my interests that I should have x" is "to say something about the reasonableness of a want." Thus, some judgment has to be made of the reasonableness of these various claims, even if it is only to allow access to a lottery. Goodin pointed out that "in order to serve as social guides, statements about interests must be interpersonally intelligible." It is necessary to come to some understanding as to why an individual thinks it is in their interests to be treated. However, to come to this understanding it is necessary to "mirror" the patient's mental processes. The privileged-access argument, if accepted, would make this impossible. The privileged-access argument and the only-judge principle are therefore fundamentally different because people can have privileged access to their mental states without being the sole judges of interests.

Usually (not always) an individual is probably (but not necessarily) the best judge of their interests but they are certainly not the only judge. There are certainly grounds for challenging the status of the individual as best judge if their mental capacities are impaired by illness, either directly or indirectly.

Although Harris' arguments tend to reject any criteria for prioritization (other than when there has been "a fair innings"), he recognized that there was no moral duty on a doctor to save life if, for example:

• There is something of comparable (or greater) moral importance the doctor must do and he/she cannot do both;
• It would be better for the patient if the doctor did not attempt to save them or some other good will be achieved by their death or by refraining from saving them for which end the sacrificing of life would be justified;
• The patient would be better off dead.

By virtue of these exemptions, Harris is himself conceding that others are able to make judgments on "best interests." Also, the fact that Harris can conceive that there could be something of "comparable or greater moral importance" than saving a life, suggests that it is not an incommensurable value. Harris' exemption for nonintervention when "the patient would be better off dead" is also contradictory. Harris may have only intended this exemption to come into operation when

the patient was unconscious, or otherwise unable to say to what extent they value their life. However, without this caveat, it suggests that there are circumstances when a third party can judge the quality of life of a patient, and use this opinion (no matter how subjective it may be) to decide whether some other patient would benefit more from a scarce treatment.

Griffin also quoted an example where quantity and quality of life may be compared:

The French government knows that each year several drivers lose their lives because of the beautiful roadside avenues of trees, yet they do not cut them down. Even aesthetic pleasure is allowed to outrank a certain number of human lives.

Economists have used this approach to place various estimates on human life by examining the cost of various public policies where life is at stake. For example, there may be alternative strengths of barriers that could be placed in the central reservation of motorways to prevent traffic involved in an accident from crossing from one carriageway to the other. The stronger barrier costs more (say £1 million more for a stretch of motorway) but it would save more lives (for argument, 10 lives until it has to be replaced). If the motorway planners decide to use the weaker barrier, they are implying that 10 lives are worth less than £1 million, or else they would prefer the utility that could be obtained in using the £1 million for some other purpose. On this calculation, a life is worth less than £100,000. While such calculations may be crude, it demonstrates that some value can be attached to a life. It may not be an accurate value, but it is at least commensurable.

It might be thought that there is something wrong in using money as the common measure for conflicting values:

[It is not] an accidental feature of the utilitarian outlook that the presumption is in favour of the monetarily quantifiable ... It is not an accident, because (for one thing) utilitarianism is unsurprisingly the value system for society in which economic values are supreme...

Williams is confusing the use of money as a common measure, with a supreme value. Money is valued because it enables other commodities or services to be purchased from which an individual may derive utility. Money acts as a means rather than an end. There may be misers who apparently love money for its own sake.

However, even those prone to avarice may value the security or potential utility that their savings provide.

III. DISTRIBUTIVE JUSTICE: EQUALITY OR EQUITY?

If the arguments against rationing are rejected, how should the scarce resources be distributed justly? The Greek word for justice was the same as that for equality. Aristotle wanted to make a clear distinction between equality and equity. He rejected claims that justice meant equal shares for all. Aristotle distinguished between justice in the widest sense of overall goodness or "complete virtue" and its use in the narrow sense of equality of treatment. For example in *Politics*, he describes the nature of distributive justice as follows:

> Justice is considered to mean equality. It does mean equality—but equality for those who are equal, and not for all. Again, inequality is considered to be just; and indeed it is—but only for those who are unequal, and not for all ... A just distribution is one in which there is a proportion between the things distributed and those to whom they are distributed.

Aristotle also discussed distributive justice in *The Nicomachean Ethics*:

> ... if they are not equal, they will not have what is equal, but this is the origin of quarrels and complaints—when either equals have and are awarded unequal shares, or unequals equal shares. Further, this is plain from the fact that awards should be 'according to merit'; for all men agree that what is just in distribution must be according to merit in some sense, though they do not all specify the same sort of merit....

The principle of justice that is usually attributed to Aristotle is that "equals should be treated equally and unequals should be treated unequally in proportion to the relevant inequalities."

However, as Gillon has pointed out:

> The reason that Aristotle's formal principle remains so widely accepted is, of course, that it has little substantive content. It requires an equality of consideration ...; fairness in the sense that conflicts are to be settled by mutually agreed principles of justice ...; and impartiality in the sense that inequalities of treatment cannot be arbitrary ... but must be justified on the basis of, and in proportion to, relevant inequalities ...

Justice remains an "essentially contested concept," if just prioritization is to be performed, agreement is required on which "inequalities" are "relevant." The various options were described by Raanan Gillon's 8-year-old daughter when she was asked how to decide which of three dying patients should have access to the only available lifesaving machine:

> "Well," she told me, sparing a minute or two from her television programme, "you could give it to the youngest because she'd live longer (welfare maximisation), or you could give it to the illest because she needs it most (medical need), or you could give it to the kindest because kind people deserve to be treated nicely (merit). No, you couldn't give it to the one you liked best (partiality), that wouldn't be fair." Nor, she decided, would "eenie meenie minee mo" (lottery) be fair because the one who needed it most, or the youngest, or the kindest might not get it. Nor did she (much to my surprise) think that the Queen should get it in preference to the poor man (social worth)—"because she's got so much already and the poor man hasn't." Of all the methods, her preferred one was to choose the illest because he needed it most—but not surprisingly, she could not say why that was a better option than the others.

For prioritization criteria to be morally acceptable, the rational that underpins them needs to be ethically explicit. Despite the limited scope of the public surveys conducted so far, a number of themes have emerged:

- a willingness to pay for experimental, "high-tech" life-saving treatments rather than more cost-effective treatments that will improve quality of life, which are more likely to maximize utility from the scarce resources available;
- preference for treating the young rather than the old;
- a willingness to discriminate against those patients who were partially responsible for their illness due to choice of "unhealthy" lifestyle (e.g., smoking cigarettes, drinking excess alcohol);
- preference for treating patients with dependents

(e.g., spouse, children) rather than those who have none.

IV. UTILITARIAN SELECTION: MAKING BEST USE OF SCARCE RESOURCES

Childress criticized "utilitarian selection" because he believed that it fails to recognize that "rational people may have very good reasons for choosing impersonal mechanisms of allocation; these mechanisms may express and realize their principles and values better than any other method." Childress also suggested that utilitarian selection would be unworkable because of the "absence of clear and acceptable criteria of social worth in a pluralistic society. Because of the variety of criteria, different communities often make different judgements."

Instead Childress supported the use of queuing or random selection by a lottery because he believed that it expressed principles and values that were particularly important to society, that is, equality of opportunity and personal dignity. He also believed that this approach supported trust between health care professionals and their patients, which would be difficult to maintain if patients are subjected to comparative assessments or are treated as "means to some social end."

Indeed, Glover also recognized the difficulties of comparing a mother with a doctor, both of whom may attract our sympathies. This argument only supports what is self-evident, that is, that making choices within health care resource allocation is difficult. It does not deny that people may have preferences, only that there may not be a consensus as to what these may be. Further, this should not mean that no efforts should be made to see whether a majority, or at least a significant minority, of the population share the same preference.

Dickenson argued that health care allocation based on market principles was neither objective nor fair. She believed that "allocation by the egalitarian principle of randomisation best meets the deontological criterion of respect for persons. She criticized the "fallibility of the utilitarian calculus in life-and-death matters.... Although lotteries are not rational in their operations, they are profoundly just" (Dickenson, D. (1995). Is Efficiency Ethical? Resource Issues in Health Care. In: Almond, B. (Ed.), Introducing Applied Ethics. Oxford: Blackwell).

However, as pointed out by Chadwick:

If a priority setting policy maximises less utility than it can then fewer people are being helped than could be helped, and surely this is unjust—those who lose out under such an arrangement might understandably see it as unjust" (Chadwick, R. (1993). Justice in priority setting. In: Anon. (Ed.), Rationing in Action. London: BMJ Publishing Group).

Basson contended that "random selection has no place in scarce medical resource allocation except when our primitive techniques for social value rating fail to distinguish among candidates in any way" (Basson, M. D. (1979, September). Choosing Among Candidates for Scarce Medical Resources. *Journal of Medicine and Philosophy*, 331.). Likewise Fletcher suggested that the refusal to be rational "is a deliberate dehumanization, reducing us to the level of things and blind chance." (Fletcher, J. (1981). The Greatest Good of the Greatest Number: A New Frontier in the Morality of Medical Care. Sanger Lecture No. 7. Richmond, VA.: Medical College of Virginia, Virginia Commonwealth University. Quoted in Childress, J. F. *Priorities in Biomedical Ethics*. Philadelphia: The Westminster Press).

Bibliography

Anon. (Ed.) (1993). *Rationing in action.* London: BMJ Publishing Group.

Callahan, D. (1987). *Setting limits: Medical goals in an aging society.* Washington DC: Georgetown University Press.

Childress, J. F. (1981). *Priorities in biomedical ethics.* Philadelphia: The Westminster Press.

Daniels, N. (1985). *Just health care.* Cambridge: Cambridge University Press.

Doyal, L. (1995). Needs, rights, and equity: moral quality in health-care rationing. *Quality in Health Care* 4, 273–283.

Gillon, R. (1986). *Philosophical medical ethics.* Chichester: John Wiley & Sons.

Griffin, J. (1988). *Well-being: Its meaning, measurement and moral importance.* Oxford: Claredon Press.

Harris, J. (1989). *The value of life.* London: Routledge.

Maxwell, R. J. (Ed.). (1995). Rationing health care. *British Medical Bulletin,* 51, (4), 761–962.

Netherlands Government Committee on Choices in Health Care (Chairman Dunning, A. J.). (1992). *Choices in health care.* Rijswijk, Netherlands: Ministry of Welfare, Health and Cultural Affairs.

Office of Health Economics. (1995). *Compendium of health statistics.* London: Office of Health Statistics.

U.S. Congress, Office of Technology Assessment. (1992). *Evaluation of the Oregon Medicaid proposal.* OTA-H-531. Washington DC: U.S. Congress.

Williams, B. (1972). *Morality: An introduction to ethics.* Cambridge: Cambridge University Press.

RIGHTS THEORY

William Cooney
Briar Cliff College

I. Rights, Codes, and Declarations: A Brief History
II. Distinctions within Rights Theory
III. Rights Theory and Moral Traditions
IV. Recent Rights Issues

GLOSSARY

acquired right A right that is acquired by an individual or group upon the meeting of some agreed to condition(s)—for example, contractual rights which are acquired when two parties enter into an arrangement.

correlativity thesis The notion that for every right of an individual or group, there exists a corresponding duty on the part of others to respect that right.

doctrine of forfeiture The view that the right(s) of an individual or group can be lost or forfeited due to some infraction.

human right A right that pertains to an individual simply by virtue of the fact that he or she is a human being—for example, the right to life and freedom.

imprescriptible right A right that is considered inalienable or absolute.

incommensurability thesis The view that the basic human goods (life, health, knowledge, friendship, etc.) are incomparable in the sense that they cannot be weighed or measured against each other.

lex talionis A Latin term referring to the right of just retaliation by injured parties.

THE RIGHT TO LIVE, the right to die, the right to freedom, the right to be treated equally, the right to know, the right to choose, the right to vote, the right to own property, the right to health care, the right to employment, the right to participate, the right to compensation, the right to a fair and speedy trial, the right to be informed, the right to free speech and thought, the right to self-defense, the right to education, the right to peaceful assembly, the right to privacy, the right to free exercise of religion—these claims, and many more, give indication that we seem to live in a world filled with rights.

But what does it all mean? Does the simple claim to a right automatically grant the entitlement? Certainly not, since many rights go unreceived and not all nations and constitutions recognize the entire list of rights just given. And do all rights have equal status? If so, how can one resolve conflicts between competing rights? One's right to self-defense, for example, may compete with another's right to life. What exactly does it mean to have a right to something? And what in particular are the corresponding duties related to such rights? It seems that rights and duties are something like reverse sides of the same coin, since having a right to something can have little meaning if we do not also recognize a corresponding duty to respect that right. But not all philosophers agree concerning precisely how duties are related to rights.

Rights theory is that field of study which aims at addressing these and many other issues concerning rights and duties. It is a discipline which involves the interplay of ethical, philosophical, economic, political, legal, and theological ideas, having a long and disparate heritage. We shall begin with a brief history of ideas concerning rights, go on to look at the various distinctions found in rights theory, and then examine rights as they are found within the main moral traditions. Finally, we will take a brief look at some recent rights issues.

I. RIGHTS, CODES, AND DECLARATIONS: A BRIEF HISTORY

Most philosphers trace the notion of rights back to the conceptions of natural law found in the ancient Greek and Roman traditions. The Greeks distinguished between nature (*physis*) and laws of custom or convention (*nomos*). Heraclitus (ca. 500 B.C.) and the stoics (beginning around the 4th century B.C.), in particular, maintained a view of the universe penetrated with *logos* (the general principle, law, or rule of nature), which could be known by pure reason alone. Socrates (469–399 B.C.), Plato (428–348 B.C.), and Aristotle (384–322 B.C.) also went beyond mere conventionalism or custom to give an account of morality grounded in human nature itself. This view was later echoed by the Roman jurist Cicero (106–43 B.C.) who wrote that "there is in fact a true law— namely, right reason—which is in accordance with nature, applies to all men, and is unchangeable and eternal. By its commands this law summons men to the performance of their duties" (*The Republic*, III, 22).

However, we ignore history if we do not go further back in time, long before the Greeks and Romans, to other cultures who had quite sophisticated principles and codes concerning rights. Most historians and anthropologists theorize that among primitive peoples there existed the original right of *lex talionis* (a term coined by Cicero), or the right of retaliation or revenge. This, it is argued, evolved into a series of laws, rules, and codes covering punishment, exchange for damages to the injured party, property rights, and the like. It is believed that the power to enforce such laws originally existed as a right of the individual, but was later transferred to the community or state, so that by the time of Hammurabi (ca. 18th century B.C.), for instance, we see a king committed to the duty "to cause justice to prevail . . . [and] to prevent the strong from oppressing the weak" (*The Code of Hammurabi*, prologue). The *Code of Hammurabi*, unearthed in Susa, Iraq, in 1902, provides a very detailed record on such matters. It lists

some 285 laws under the categories of personal property, real estate, business and trade, the family, injuries, and labor. Even before the Babylonian record, as archeological and historical evidence gives indication, the mingling groups of people of the Nile, as early as 4000–3000 B.C., had already forged a style of governance and a system of rules. By the time of the Fifth Dynasty (ca. 2700 B.C.), Egyptian society had developed intricate laws and sophisticated codes concerning such matters as proper social behavior, sexual morality, and estate or property rights. In the Middle East (ca. 13th century B.C.) the Mosaic laws were being crafted to cover almost every aspect of human activity. A tradition of law and codes was also developed in India among the Brahmin or priestly class (ca. 800 B.C.), culminating in the *Code of Manu* (ca. 200 B.C.), which provided rules and duties (*dharma*) under a caste system. In China, too, the various rules and duties were handed down in the classic book of divination, the *I Ching* (ca. 1000 B.C.), and later in the works of both the Taoists (ca. 600 B.C.), who provided an Asian version of natural law seen in the concept of *tao* (the way or path of the universe), and the Confucian texts (ca. 500 B.C.), which focused on the principle of *li* or right conduct. These Asian texts and principles contributed to the ethical codes later developed in Japan (ca. 3rd century) and led to such developments as the Bushido Code (ca. 1650), emphasizing loyalty, honor, courage, and proper behavior.

In the West, the Greek and Roman traditions were continued and modified throughout the period of the Middle Ages by thinkers such as Augustine (354–430) and Thomas Aquinas (1225–1274) who combined the notion of natural law with the view of nature as the product of God's divine, creative act, thus giving rise to their concept of eternal law. The next important period comes in 17th century England with the rise of social contract and natural rights theories as proposed by such thinkers as Thomas Hobbes (1588–1679) and John Locke (1632–1704). Their writings, along with those of the French thinker Jean Jacques Rousseau (1712–1778), had a profound influence on the views of Thomas Jefferson (1734–1826) and inevitably made their way into the famous notion of "inalienable rights" as found in the American Declaration of Independence (1776). In France, the Declaration of the Rights of Man and of Citizens appeared in 1789. And the Bill of Rights was added in the form of amendments of the U.S. Constitution in 1791.

During the 18th and 19th centuries in England, the notion of natural or human rights came under attack by thinkers such as Edmund Burke (1729–1797), who considered ideas like human equality to be "monstrous fictions"; David Hume (1711–1776), who believed them to be based on an unreal metaphysics; and Jeremy Bentham (1748–1832), who feared that they would be seen as unlimited entitlements and therefore endanger the greater social good. Thomas Paine's *Rights of Man,* written in 1791 as a reply to Burke's ideas, was suppressed in England, and a general period of disfavor followed concerning the philosophy of individual rights. In 19th century America, however, human rights issues were at the forefront during the debate about slavery which prompted the Civil War and ultimately led to the Emancipation Proclamation (1863) and the 13th amendment to the Constitution which banned slavery (1865). The great World Wars of the 20th century, and the Nazi atrocities in particular, had the effect of drawing greater attention to human rights. During the Nuremberg trials of 1945 implicit agreements with respect to the right to life and freedom from torture were forged. Clear norms were ultimately established covering a broader range of rights in the Universal Declaration of Human Rights adopted by the General Assembly of the United Nations in 1948. The issue of civil rights, especially for people of color, emerged as a central debate in America, leading to the Civil Rights Act of 1964, and, in the next decades, included a focus on equal rights for women. More recently we have seen international agreements reached between nations such as the Helsinki Accords (1975) which have created widespread expectations about the protection of human rights around the world. Concerning these accords, there were also follow-up meetings in Vienna (1986–1989) and in Copenhagen (1990) which reaffirmed the commitment to such protections. Regarding the issue of women's rights, of note is the 1995 Conference on Women in Beijing. We have also seen the rise of nongovernmental, watchdog organizations such as Amnesty International (having 500,000 members in more than 150 countries) which are concerned with protecting the increasingly endangered human rights, especially in the Third World. Most recently we have even seen the discussion about rights extended into the consideration of rights for nonhumans as well, e.g., environmental rights and animal rights in particular.

II. DISTINCTIONS WITHIN RIGHTS THEORY

A. The Order and Ranking of Rights

In order to assist the organization and understanding of rights, theorists have provided many distinctions.

The French jurist Karel Vasak, for example, has focused on an evolutionary model distinguishing rights according to a scheme based on the battle cry of the French Revolution: *liberté*, the civil and political rights developed in the 17th–18th centuries; *egalité*, the economic, social, and cultural rights which evolved during the 19th century; and *fraternité*, the rights of solidarity between nations emerging in our current global community (1977. *UNESCO Courier,* Nov.).

Other distinctions are more common. For example, many theorists distinguish between natural or human rights, which an individual has by virtue of the fact that he is a human being, and acquired rights, which pertain to specific arrangements, such as acquiring through payment the right to live in a particular dwelling, or in attaining the right to drive an automobile when one reaches a certain age and acquires the requisite skills and license.

It is also usual for theorists to provide a hierarchical arrangement to address the intuition that some rights seem more basic, primary, or fundamental than others. The right to life certainly is more weighty than other rights, such as the right to drive an automobile. This distinction is also used to help adjudicate between competing or conflicting rights. We can outline these differences by distinguishing between foundational and implied rights.

Foundational rights (some call them basic or primary) are those that are normally called human, moral, or natural rights. They are the kinds of rights claimed to be "inalienable" by the Declaration of Independence: "We hold these truths to be self-evident, that all men are created equal, that they are endowed by their Creator with certain inalienable Rights, that among these are Life, Liberty and the pursuit of Happiness." This statement reflects two important features typically held to be inherent in foundational rights: they are an essential part of who we are as human beings—therefore we must not be separated from them (they are "inalienable")—and they are known by intuition ("self-evident") rather than by demonstration or deduction.

It appears a dictate of logic that chief among foundational rights is the right to life, for it seems an important condition for the reception of all other rights. But it is certainly not a necessary condition, since justice requires us to recognize the right against the disrespectful and indecent treatment of corpses as well. It is also clear that the list of foundational rights offered by theorists is rather short, including those such as life, liberty, privacy, and few others (some, for instance, include the right to property).

Implied rights (some call these derivative or secondary) are those which can be implied by, or derive their existence from, foundational rights. An implied right like the right to health care, for example, can be derived from the right to life. Implied rights are not only founded upon foundational rights, but can often provide some instrumental value and additional meaning to them. The implied right to work certainly enhances the value and quality of one's foundational right to life.

Implied rights can be divided into at least three categories: legal, constitutional, and contractual rights. The various laws and documents which are adopted by a particular state or nation will provide the conditions for legal and constitutional rights. Just laws and constitutions will recognize the foundational rights such as life and liberty. Contractual rights are those which obtain when two or more parties enter into an agreement. These are conditioned upon at least four elements: freedom, so that the contract is not forced or coerced; knowledge, concerning the precise nature and elements of the agreement; nonmisrepresentation, as a protection against fraud; and nonillegality, so that no legitimacy is given to the commission of illegal acts.

Though the distinction between foundational and implied rights provides a useful recognition of the intuitive difference between rights, its second use—as a way to help adjudicate between competing rights—is less cut and dry. That is, it is not always clear exactly how to accomplish such a task. Do foundational rights always outrank implied rights? And what do we do in a case where two foundational rights are in competition? This can be especially difficult for those theories which maintain the "incommensurability thesis," which argues that the basic human goods (life, health, knowledge, friendship, etc.) cannot be measured against one another since there is no common unit applicable.

B. Negative and Positive Rights

Another important distinction within rights theory involves the precise relationship between rights and duties. The "corelativity thesis" claims that rights and duties are correlative and complementary. This implies that all rights require a corresponding duty, such as the duty of others to respect that right. The correlativity thesis can lead to some misunderstandings, however. It seems to hold whenever we are considering the rights of one person or group, and the corresponding duty on the part of others to respect those rights. But the thesis does not always apply when we are considering the rights and duties of the same individual or group. There appear to be many rights, in this regard, which do not have corresponding duties. Having a right to pursue a lawsuit, for instance, does not imply the duty to do so. Having a right to x, therefore does not always imply a correlative duty to bring x about—nor does life afford enough time or opportunities to fulfill the majority of our rights. But do all duties imply correlative rights? There seem to be fewer exceptions here, but some can be noted. For example, one can feel a moral duty to help or come to the aid of another, even if it is not also felt that the other has an actual right to that aid, perhaps due to some misconduct leading to the forfeiture of that right. Also, many accept the duty to treat animals with kindness without actually granting animals rights. An absolutist rendering of the correlativity thesis, therefore, seems unacceptable.

What then is the proper relationship between rights and duties? The answer to this turns on another and more fundamental question: What is our basic moral duty to ourselves and others? Some answer that the primary duty is the affirmative "To do good," while others provide a negative principle such as "Not to do harm" or "Not to interfere with others." This difference has given rise to the distinction between negative and positive rights.

Negative rights theory holds that the overriding moral principle is noninterference. The chief duty of a citizen, it contends, is to refrain from harming the interests of others. Such a view is held by leading libertarian philosphers, for example, who hold that the primary duty of government is to prevent infringements on our liberty or freedom. This theory raises serious questions concerning not only governmental responsibilities, but individual ones as well. When the negative rights theorist grants such rights as the right to employment, for example, that is usually construed to mean the right to pursue a job without barriers like discrimination. But if the pursuit fails, the negative rights theorist does not recognize any positive duty to come to the aid of the individual, such as in affirmative action programs, which would be adamantly opposed. The negative rights theorist may be willing to provide further help and support, but he would do so only as an act of kindness or charity, not out of moral duty. This position is maintained toward such issues as welfare, health care, and other social concerns.

The negative rights position is closely tied to the view of egoism, which holds that the primary motivation behind all human behavior is self-interest. The principle of noninterference, it is claimed, is best suited to uphold a climate of self-interest for all citizens within society. And the theory of politics it typically supports is that of laissez-faire. This hands-off style of government follows the motto, "that government which governs least, governs best," and provides, it is argued, less danger of governmental infringement on rights.

The positive rights theorist, on the other hand, contends that the basic moral duty toward others includes affirmative obligations. Rights are seen as requiring some positive response, i.e., some act of commission, and not simply the acts of omission supplied by the principle of noninterference. In considering the right to employment, then, the positive rights theorist has in mind more than simply the refraining of all unjust impediments and obstacles such as discrimination. Affirmative action programs could be supported in terms of compensatory justice.

Positive rights theory is linked to the view of altruism, which contends that human beings are not merely self-interested, but social beings capable of acts of compassion toward others. In terms of politics, the positive rights view would require a more involved, active type of governance.

Any absolutist rendering of negative or positive rights would seem to encounter several difficulties. If one holds that all rights are purely and simply negative, he is faced with an apparent inconsistency. A negative right not to be interfered with, for instance, would certainly require some positive duties of enforcement and contribution within society—a police force, a military, etc. And most ethicists would agree that some positive duties seem called for, at least in cases where there is a great danger to another, and no or little risk in coming to his aid. For example, if a traveler encounters a victim of an automobile accident, he may be tempted to pass on by, resorting to the principle of noninterference. But most would argue that morality requires some positive response here, even if only the minimal act of calling the police. And if, on the other hand, one holds to an absolute positive rights view, he may be fairly charged with impracticality. If citizens and society as a whole are morally bound to aid the rights of others, how will this be managed? A child may be in dire need of a kidney transplant, for example, but there is no health insurance to cover the cost. His right to life seems seriously challenged, and under a positive rights framework we must come to his aid. But can states simply assume such a burden for him and for all? Are there enough resources in the world to cover all such positive responses?

III. RIGHTS THEORY AND MORAL TRADITIONS

A variety of approaches on rights and duties can be traced through the major moral traditions. In the following we shall briefly examine the views of natural law, natural rights and social contract theories, Kantian ethics, utilitarianism, and justice theories.

A. Natural Law

The theory of natural law has its roots in ancient stoicism, Aristotle, and Roman law. The Judeo-Christian tradition, as we have already noted, joined to this the concept of nature as designed by God. Today, therefore, natural law ethics is closely tied to various religious traditions such as Roman Catholicism, though not exclusively so. In its most general form this theory holds that right conduct is that which follows nature rather than convention or custom. This tradition has been greatly influenced by the teleological view of nature as presented by Aristotle and Aquinas, and therefore holds that all things in nature, including human beings, are designed toward specific goals or ends (*telos*, in Greek). Ethics, then, is concerned with the promotion of this natural, developmental process.

A natural law view on rights, by consequence, begins with the requirement that rights be compliant with these goals. One can see, for instance, the application of natural law to those rights issues concerning acts like abortion and euthanasia. Typically natural law will oppose any supported right to abortion, arguing that such an act would directly interfere with the natural developmental process of life itself. A right to euthanasia, too, is often opposed on the grounds that it interferes with the natural process of death.

Natural law will not support the spirit of defiant individualism, which argues that individuals always have a right to decide matters over their own lives and bodies. It holds that human beings derive their existence and value from God's design in the first place, and any rights granted must be those respectful of the teleology God has designed into nature.

This theory does not limit rights to the negative variety. It sees humans as social creatures having positive rights and duties toward one another—one need only consider the teachings of Jesus (as offered in the parable of the Good Samaritan, for example) to understand this. But a positive rights view seems also to be implicit in the teleological approach offered by Aristotle: "Every art and every inquiry and similarly every action and pursuit, is thought to aim at some good; and for this the good has rightly been declared to be that at which all things aim" (*Nichomachean Ethics,* book I, chap. 1). The end of ethical action is, therefore, a positive good and not simply the avoidance of evil. This is also made clear by Aquinas, who teaches that "every agent intends to attain good" as well as to "avoid evil" (*Summa Theologica,* I–II, 20, 4c).

B. Natural Rights and Social Contract Theories

As we have seen, natural rights and social contract traditions have their beginnings in the work of such philosophers as Thomas Hobbes, John Locke, and Jean Jacques Rousseau. We have also noted the direct influence on Thomas Jefferson, and, consequently, many American ideas, particularly about individual liberty and a laissez-faire form of government, can be traced to these traditions.

While these theorists do refer to the principle of natural law, they nevertheless provide a clean break from the natural law tradition. Natural law theorists, for instance, had assumed that humans have an altruistic, social nature. This implied that society was in fact the natural state for the human being. Natural rights and social contract theorists rely, contrarily, on egoism or the principle of self-interest (although Rousseau made an important distinction between selfishness and self-love, contending that selfishness and competition arise more out of society than out of human nature). Society has arisen, accordingly, as a compromise or contract between citizens in order to help ensure the long-term self-interest of all, and to protect natural, human rights. This view is clearly reflected in the position taken in the American Declaration of Independent: "That to secure these rights. Governments are instituted among Men, deriving their just powers from the consent of the governed. ..." The state of nature (i.e., before governments existed) provides a very unmanageable environment. Hobbes argued that in such a state life would be "solitary, poor, nasty, brutish, and short ..." (*Leviathan,* chap. 13). And Locke agreed, saying that the state of nature would be "very uncertain and constantly exposed to the invasion of others," and that government comes to exist and the citizen consents to it "only with an intention ... to preserve himself, his liberty and property ..." (*Second Treatise on Government,* chap. IX, sec. 123 and 131).

Hobbes seems to have limited the term "natural right" primarily to the right of self-preservation. Locke widened its use, focusing on rights to personal freedoms and, more than anyone else, on the right of private property—a right which must have been attractive to the growing middle classes, and in this regard some rightly refer to him as one of the forefathers of modern capitalism.

Unlike the natural law tradition which places priority on the teleology of nature as designed by God, these theorists gave primacy to individual entitlements. One can see a modern application in the issues of abortion and euthanasia, where personal rights have become paramount, at least in the legal and constitutional aspects of the debate. In this respect the U.S. Supreme Court ruling which legalized abortion (*Roe v. Wade,* 1973) can be seen as representative of the natural rights view. There the issue was not the natural process underway in fetal development, but whether or not there was a personal right to abort. The ruling used the Constitutional right to privacy (4th amendment) interpreted broadly enough to include a woman's right to choose to terminate a pregnancy. And while there has not yet been a clear ruling on the euthanasia issue, in the Supreme Court decision of 1990 involving the case of Nancy Cruzan, the focus was on a state's right to demand "clear and convincing evidence" of the personal wishes of the injured party, thus echoing, again, the natural rights perspective.

Natural rights and social contract theories generally provide only a negative rights view, highlighting the principles of noninterference and self-interest.

C. Kantian Ethics

As developed by Immanuel Kant (1724–1804), Kantian ethics argues that moral behavior is guided by the categorical imperative, which has several formulations. The first two formulations, "act only according to the maxim by which you can at the same time will that it should become a universal law," and "act as though the maxim of your action were by your will to become a universal law of nature" (*Foundations of the Metaphysics of Morals,* 422), require us to act according to the dictates of universality and reversibility. The maxim, or reason behind our action, should be one that we could wish to be practiced universally by others (universality), and one which we could reasonably wish to be on the receiving end of (reversibility). This would clearly support a right against discriminatory treatment, for example, since one could not reasonably wish that discrimination be practiced universally, and especially not toward onself.

The third formulation, "act in such a way that you always treat humanity, whether in your own person or in the person of any other, never simply as a means, but always at the same time as an end" (*Foundations*, 429), calls attention to the fact that ethics goes beyond abstract principles and deals directly with the dignity of human persons. It also goes beyond the natural rights tradition in emphasizing that ethics includes duties toward self, and not simply duties toward others.

While Kant focused his attention more on duty, saying that "the first proposition of morality is that to have moral worth an action must be done from duty" (*Foundations,* 400), Kantian and neo-Kantian ethics would certainly include those rights consistent with the categorical imperative. Concerning rights to abortion and euthanasia, for example, one would have to consider the maxim behind the desired act and subject it to the principles of universality, reversibility, and the dignity of persons. Desiring an abortion based simply on the sex of the child, for example, would not satisfy such principles and would clearly be rejected by this tradition. However, a right to a "therapeutic" abortion (e.g., where the life of the mother is threatened and the fetus will die in any case) could be supported. Obviously the dignity of persons criterion requires one to consider also the status of the fetus: is it a full-fledged person? And a right to euthanasia based on economic hardship (since the medical technology needed for sustaining life is costly) will be less legitimate in this tradition than in those grounded in respect for the patient's wishes to die with dignity.

Kantian ethics is often cited as an example of positive rights theory. It is clear that Kant himself, especially in his emphasis on moral duty, would reject any exclusive negative rights view.

D. Utilitarianism

Utilitarianism, as developed by Jeremy Bentham and John Stuart Mill (1806–1873), is guided, as Mill states it, by the criterion of "Utility, or the Greatest Happiness Principle [which] holds that actions are right in proportion as they tend to promote happiness, wrong as they tend to produce the reverse of happiness." (*Utilitarianism*, chap. II). The happiness desired as the outcome of behavior is "not the agent's own happiness, but the greatest amount of happiness altogether …" (chap. II).

Even though he staunchly defended liberty, Mill nevertheless argued that rights are founded on utility, so that under utilitarianism the individual must be willing to sacrifice personal interests for the collective good. As we have already briefly noted, Bentham attacked the notion of natural rights very directly. In his *Anarchical Fallacies*, Bentham leveled an attack on the French Dec-

laration and the notion of natural rights in general. Therein he argues that "there are no such things as natural rights—no such things as rights anterior to the establishment of government …" (*Anarchical Fallacies*, art. II, sentence 1). Here Bentham is rejecting the social contract notion which claims that governments arise out of, and get their power from, the protection of natural rights which human beings have simply by virtue of their humanity. "The origination of governments from a contract," he states, "is a pure fiction, or in other words, a falsehood," and "contracts come from government, not government from contracts." (*Fallacies*, art. II). So it is clear that Bentham's critique is based in his rejection of certain assumptions held by the natural rights/social contract theorists, leading him to the famous conclusion that "natural rights is simple nonsense: natural and imprescriptible rights, rhetorical nonsense,—nonsense upon stilts" (*Fallacies*, art. II).

But Bentham was also convinced that the natural rights/social contract tradition held to the view of "unbounded" rights. "Observe the extent of these pretended rights," he says, "each of them belonging to every man, and all of them without bounds" (*Fallacies*, sentence 2). Clearly Bentham's concern was that unlimited rights could present a threat to the greatest happiness overall. However, this concern seems unsupported by Locke's version of rights, since he recognized that "though this be a state of liberty, yet it is not a state of license …" (*Second Treatise*, chap. II. sec. 6). Natural rights are limited or bounded by Locke in that "no one ought to harm another in his life, health, liberty, or possessions" (chap. II, sec. 6). And the right to private property, as the fruit of labor, is also bounded. Locke responds directly to those who object to a right to property based on the view that

> anyone may engross as much as he will. To which I answer, Not so. The same law of nature that does by this means give us property, does so bound that property too. "God has given us all things richly" (1 Tim. vi. 17), is the voice of reason confirmed by inspiration. But how far has He given it us? To enjoy. As much as anyone can make use of to any advantage of life before it spoils, so much may his labor fix a property in: whatever is beyond this, is more than his share, and belongs to others. Nothing was made by God for man to spoil or destroy. (chap. V, sec. 30)

Even one's right to life is bounded by what some call Locke's doctrine of forfeiture (chap. XV, sec. 172), wherein he recognizes that the murderer has "declared war against all mankind, and therefore may be destroyed ..." (Chap. II. sec. 11).

The utilitarian objection to natural rights is nonetheless firmly embedded. Any rights granted will only be those consistent with the happiness principle. Concerning rights to abortion, euthanasia, and the like, the chief question will not be what the law of nature dictates—not whether there is a firm right to these actions, nor whether the maxim of such acts satisfy the principles of universality and the like (utilitarianism is concerned with consequences, not motives). The one and only question is, will the permission of such acts lead to the overall greater happiness? The utilitarian will not be concerned with whether what is required is a negative or positive rights view. Either can be supported, so long as it serves utility.

E. Justice Theories

Justice theorists focus primarily on three areas: retributive justice, which considers appropriate penalty or punishment for wrongful acts; compensatory justice, which is concerned that injured parties be redressed or remunerated; and distributive justice, which concentrates on the most just way to distribute benefits and burdens within a society. In each of these areas justice theories contain the assumption of rights—the right to retribution, the right to compensation, and the right to a just distribution of benefits and burdens. How precisely these rights are worked out depends on which justice theory we consult. The more pervasive and complex questions are raised in distributive justice, for it asks the more basic, philosophical question first raised and addressed by Plato in his *Republic*, namely, "what is the most just kind of society?" In answering such a question theorists become entangled not only in ethics, but in legal, social, economic, and political philosophy as well. And there have been many famous answers offered throughout history: egalitarianism, which places the emphasis on exactly equal shares of society's benefits and burdens; capitalism, which distributes these according to the criterion of individual achievement and contribution within a free market; and socialism and communism, which select needs and abilities as the guide, based on the famous remark from Karl Marx (1818–1883), "From each according to his ability, to each according to his need" (*Critique of the Gotha Program*). In more recent times two contemporary American justice theorists, Robert Nozick and John Rawls, have provided opposing views which, interestingly enough, claim to be based on Kantian ethics, at least in part.

Nozick is a leading libertarian (a position held also by economic theorists such as F. A. Hayek and Milton Friedman). Libertarianism is the view that the primary right of individuals is the negative right to be free from constraints, coercion, or other forms of interference from others (see Nozick's 1974 book *Anarchy, State, and Utopia*, p. ix. New York: Basic Books, Inc.). Nozick contends that this right against constraints is grounded in "the underlying Kantian principle that individuals are ends and not merely means; they may not be sacrificed or used for achieving of other ends without their consent" (*Anarchy*, p. ix). And this right takes precedence, according to Nozick, over all other rights. The distribution of benefits and burdens, therefore, and all the rights pertaining to that distribution, must be grounded in the basic right of freedom from interference, which, in turn, implies the basic, negative rights of life, liberty, and property.

Critics charge that Nozick has highlighted the right to freedom at the expense or sacrifice of other rights. Fairness seems to require, for example, a right to basic goods in a society (education, housing, health care), and this may require governments to impose, through taxation, a certain form of distribution of benefits that the libertarian is not willing to freely choose. Nozick would certainly oppose such impositions from society, since what he proposes is a minimalist, laissez-faire governance. There is no place in this theory for any positive rights (with the exception of some which pertain to contractual agreements), and it is difficult, therefore, to see how this can be made fully consistent with Kantian principles.

John Rawls, a leading contractarian philosopher, has provided a position which sees fairness as the primary condition of justice. Contractarianism, as Rawls develops it (*A Theory of Justice*, 1971. Cambridge: Harvard University Press.), combines the social contract view (or what he calls the "original position") as expressed by Locke and Rousseau, with some principles from Kant. In particular Rawls proposes the "veil of ignorance," which, like Kant's categorical imperative, ensures universality and reversibility. Under the "veil" (a notion which harkens back to the phrase "justice is blind"), citizens entering into the hypothetical contract which forms society will not know what their station in life is—i.e., whether they are rich or poor, black or white, male or female, etc. Rawls goes on to argue that those willing to adopt the original position and the veil of ignorance would provide two principles of justice. The first of these states that "each person is to have an equal right to the most extensive total system of equal basic liberties compatible with a similar system of liberty for all" (*Justice*, p. 62). The second principle holds that "social and economic inequalities are to be arranged so that they are both: (a) to the greatest benefit of the least advantaged ..., and (b) attached to offices and positions open to all under conditions of fair equality of opportunity" (*Justice*, p. 62). In asserting such principles, Rawls provides for a rights theory which certainly goes beyond mere negative or "freedom from" rights. A just society, as he envisions it, has the positive duty to ensure fairness and equality, and where there is inequality, as his second principle maintains, society has the positive obligation of ensuring that the "least advantaged" members are protected from exploitation—a principle which does seem consistent with Kant's admonition not to treat people as mere means to selfish ends.

Nozick directly opposes Rawl's two principles because he believes that they restrict individual freedoms without consent. And, as we have already seen, libertarianism would object strongly to any positive duty on the part of society to provide structures which protect the least fortunate. This would open the door, it is argued, to too much government interference and control, and, ultimately, a loss of individual freedoms.

V. RECENT RIGHTS ISSUES

As our society advances, so too do the concerns about rights. With the rise of sophisticated computer technologies, for example, come difficult questions concerning a variety of rights—e.g., how the right to privacy can be safeguarded in a world where electronic information about individuals can be accessed and even bought and sold by companies anywhere in the world who are interested in learning about purchasing patterns and the like. There are also some very pending rights questions attached to the burgeoning World Wide Web. How will information be managed and controlled? How will we protect copyrighted materials? How can we protect consumer's rights against the seemingly endless opportunities for coercive and manipulative commerce? Shall we allow any and all information free and equal access to the Internet? What about the activities of so-called "hate groups" who already have up and running homepages spreading violent, anti-Semitic, racist, and sexist messages around the world? How shall we limit the flow of pornographic materials, long the subject of rights groups interested in protecting women and children from the harmful influences of that industry? These and many other questions are being addressed around the world. In the U.S., for instance, Congress passed a Telecommunications Bill (1996) meant to tackle some of these issues. But there are many who are skeptical about its success. The Communications Decency Act, one portion of the Bill meant to handle pornographic materials, was banned by a panel of federal judges who found it unconstitutional. The U.S. Supreme Court has agreed with their decision.

Various developments in medical technology, too, raise serious questions about rights. Is there a right, for example, to the use of fetal tissue? There appear to be a variety of promising uses in the areas of diabetes, Alzheimer's, Parkinson's, and other diseases. And with the advances in areas such as *in vitro* fertilization (test tube conception), too, come serious questions concerning reproductive rights. Also, as more information is learned concerning genetic technology, especially as a result of the Genome project and other efforts to map human genes, rights issues will continue to emerge; shall we become eugenicists and design our offspring with certain characteristics we deem valuable? Will there someday be a right to offspring with certain body types, hair color, IQs, etc.? And as the technologies of life advance, what about the technologies of death? There are already some major shifts of perspective regarding, for example, a right to physician-assisted suicide. Recently in the United States some state Supreme Courts have found bans on such practices to be unconstitutional.

And in the area of economic growth technologies, too, there arise possible threats to the environment. This has given rise to the whole area of environmental rights. Among the very important rights concerns are duties to future generations, duties to the natural environment itself (e.g., protection of the world's rainforests and endangered species), and concerns related to the effects of overpopulation.

As a result of considering to what extent species must be protected, some have been led to the assertion of animal rights. Should rights be extended to nonhuman animals? If not, why is it that only human beings are deserving of rights and protections? Peter Singer, the Australian philosopher widely considered the father of the animal rights movement because of his groundbreaking book *Animal Liberation* (1975; second edition in 1990), offers the argument of "speciesism." If we do not extend rights to animals, he contends, we are on the same level as the racist who does not accord rights to nonwhites and the sexist who restricts full rights to men only. Speciesism, he argues, is no more tolerable, no more rational, no more justifiable than racism and sexism.

As we move into the 21st century, rights theorists can contemplate an evermore widening field of study. What does it mean to have a right to something? Who or what can be said to be entitled to a right? And what are the corresponding duties related to these rights?

Bibliography

Brownlie, I. (Ed.) (1992) *Basic Documents on Human Rights,* 3rd. ed. Clarendon Press, Oxford.

Cranston, M. (1973). *What Are Human Rights?* Taplinger, New Jersey.

Dworking, R. (1977). *Taking Rights Seriously.* Harvard University Press, Cambridge.

Gewirth, A. (1982). *Human Rights.* University of Chicago Press, Chicago.

Machan, T. (1989). *Individual Rights.* Open Court Press, LaSalle, IL.

Maritain, J. (1943). *The Rights of Man and Natural Law.* Trans. D. C. Anson. Scribner's, New York.

Melden, A. I. (Ed.) (1970). *Human Rights.* Wadsworth, Belmont, CA.

Nickel, J. (1987). *Making Sense of Human Rights.* Univ. of California Press, Los Angeles.

Waldron, J. (Ed.) (1984). *Theories of Rights.* Oxford Univ. Press, Oxford.

Winston, M. E. (Ed.) (1989). *The Philosophy of Human Rights.* Wadsworth, Belmonth, CA.

ISBN 0-12-227068-1

90038